Czech (& Central European)
Yearbook of Arbitration®

Czech (& Central European) Yearbook of Arbitration®

Volume V

2015

Interaction of Arbitration and Courts

Editors

Alexander J. Bělohlávek
Professor
at the VŠB TU
in Ostrava
Czech Republic

Naděžda Rozehnalová
Professor
at the Masaryk University
in Brno
Czech Republic

JURIS

Questions About This Publication

For assistance with shipments, billing or other customer service matters,
please call our Customer Services Department at:
1-631-350-2100

To obtain a copy of this book, call our Sales Department:
1-631-351-5430
Fax: 1-631-673-9117

Toll Free Order Line:
1-800-887-4064 (United States & Canada)
See our web page about this book:
www.arbitrationlaw.com

Printed in the United States of America.
ISBN 978-1-937518-71-4
ISSN 2157-9490

JurisNet, LLC
71 New Street
Huntington, New York 11743 U.S.A.
www.arbitrationlaw.com

The title *Czech (& Central European) Yearbook of Arbitration*® as well as
the logo appearing on the cover are protected by EU trademark law.

Typeset in the U.S.A. by Juris Publishing, Inc.

We regret to announce the death of our most reputable colleague Prof. Pierre Laive from Switzerland. We are thankful for his efforts invested in our common project. His personality and wisdom will be deeply missed by the whole editorial team.

Address for correspondence & manuscripts
Czech (& Central European) Yearbook of Arbitration®
Jana Zajíce 32, Praha 7, 170 00, Czech Republic
www.czechyearbook.org

Editorial support:
František Halfar, Jan Halfar, Lenka Němečková, Karel Nohava

Impressum

Institutions Participating in the CYArb® Project

Academic Institutions

University of West Bohemia in Pilsen, Czech Republic
Faculty of Law, Department of International Law &
Department of Constitutional Law
Západočeská univerzita v Plzni, Právnická fakulta.
Katedra mezinárodního práva & Katedra ústavního práva

Masaryk University (Brno, Czech Republic),
Faculty of Law, Department of International and European Law
Masarykova univerzita v Brně, Právnická fakulta,
Katedra mezinárodního a evropského práva

Pavol Jozef Šafárik University in Košice, Slovak Republic
Faculty of Law, Department of Commercial Law and Business Law
Právnická fakulta UPJŠ, Košice, Slovensko. Katedra obchodného a
hospodárskeho práva

VŠB – TU Ostrava, Czech Republic
Faculty of Economics, Department of Law
VŠB – TU Ostrava, Ekonomická fakulta, Katedra práva

**Institute of State and Law of the Academy of Sciences of the Czech
Republic, v.v.i.**
Ústav státu a práva Akademie věd ČR, v.v.i.

Non-academic Institutions Participating in the CYArb® Project

International Arbitral Centre
of the Austrian Federal Economic Chamber
Wiener Internationaler Schiedsgericht (VIAC), Vienna

Court of International Commercial Arbitration Attached
to the Chamber of Commerce and Industry of Romania
Curtea de Arbitraj Comercial Internaţional de pe lângă Camera
de Comerţ şi Industrie a României, Bucharest

Arbitration Court Attached to the Hungarian Chamber
of Commerce and Industry
A Magyar Kereskedelmi és Iparkamara mellett szervezett
Választottbíróság, Budapest

Arbitration Court Attached to the Economic Chamber
of the Czech Republic and Agricultural Chamber of the Czech Republic
Rozhodčí soud při Hospodářské komoře České republiky
a Agrární komoře České republiky, Prague

Arbitration Court Attached to the Czech-Moravian Commodity
Exchange Kladno
Rozhodčí soud při Českomoravské komoditní burze Kladno
(Czech Republic)

ICC National Committee Czech Republic
ICC Národní výbor Česká republika

The Court of Arbitration at the Polish Chamber of Commerce in Warsaw
Sąd Arbitrażowy przy Krajowej Izbie Gospodarczej w Warszawie

Slovak Academy of Sciences, Institute of State and Law, Slovak Republic
Slovenská akadémia vied, Ústav štátu a práva. Bratislava, Slovensko

| | |

Proofreading and translation support provided by: Agentura SPĚVÁČEK, s.r.o., Prague, Czech Republic, and Pamela Lewis, USA.

Contents

CASE LAW

Czech (& Central European) Yearbook of Arbitration

BIBLIOGRAPHY, CURRENT EVENTS, CYIL & CYArb® PRESENTATIONS, IMPORTANT WEB SITES

Alexander J. Bělohlávek

All contributions in this book are subject to academic review.

List of Abbreviations

AAA	American Arbitration Association
AC	Arbitration Court at the Economic Chamber of the Czech Republic and Agricultural Chamber of the Czech Republic
ACICA	Australian Centre for International Commercial Arbitration.
ADR	Alternative Dispute Resolution
ArbAct	Act of the Czech Republic No. 216/1994 Coll., on Arbitration and the Enforcement of Arbitral Awards, as amended
CC	Act of the Czech Republic No. 89/2012 Coll., the Civil Code
CCP	Act of the Czech Republic No. 99/1963 Coll., the Code of Civil Procedure, as amended
Charter	Resolution of the Presidium of the Czech National Council No. 2/1993 Coll., on the promulgation of the Charter of Fundamental Rights and Freedoms as part of the constitutional order of the Czech Republic, as amended
CIArb	Chartered Institute of Arbitrators
CIETAC	China International Economic and Trade Arbitration Commission
CivC	Act of the Czech Republic No. 40/1964 Coll., the Civil Code, as amended
CJA	Act of the Czech Republic No. 6/2002 Coll., on Courts and Judges, as amended
CJEU	Court of Justice of the European Union

ComC	Act of the Czech Republic No. 513/1991 Coll., the Commercial Code, in effect until December 31, 2013
ConCourt	Constitutional Court of the Czech Republic
CPR	Conflict Prevention and Resolution
CR	Czech Republic
EBH	Equal Treatment Authority
ECHR	European Court of Human Rights
EU	European Union
European Convention (1961)	European Convention on International Commercial Arbitration, done in Geneva on 21 April 1961
ExecC	Act of the Czech Republic No. 120/2001 Coll., on Execution Agents and Execution, as amended
Geneva Protocol (1923)	Protocol on Arbitration Clauses, Geneva, 24 September 1923.
IBA	International Bar Association
ICC Guide (2014)	Effective Management of Arbitration. A Guide for In-House Counsel and Other Party Representatives
ICC Rules	Rules of Arbitration of the ICC International Court of Arbitration
ICC	International Chamber of Commerce (often used in terms International Court of Arbitration attached to the International Chamber of Commerce)
ICJ	International Court of Justice
ICSID	International Center for Settlement of Investment Disputes
IJB	International Judicial Bodies
InsAct	Act of the Czech Republic No. 182/2006 Coll., the Insolvency Act, as amended
LCIA Rules	LCIA Arbitration Rules – The London Court of International Arbitration (see also 'LCIA')
LCIA	London Court of International Arbitration (see also 'LCIA Rules')
MDC	Multi-door courthouses
NAFTA	North American Free Trade Agreement
New York Convention (1958)	New York Convention on the Recognition and Enforcement of Foreign Arbitral Awards (1958)
Panama Convention	Inter-American Convention
PCA	Permanent Court of Arbitration
PCIJ	Permanent Court of International Justice
Polish Lewiatan Rules	Rules of the Court of Arbitration at PKPP Lewiatan
SC	Supreme Court of the Czech Republic

SCC Rules	SCC Institute Arbitration Rules. Arbitration Rules of the Arbitration Institute of the Stockholm Chamber of Commerce (see also *SCC*)
SCC	Stockholm Chamber of Commerce. In this book in the sense of the Arbitration Institute of the Stockholm Chamber of Commerce (see also 'SCC Rules')
TFEU	Treaty on the Functioning of the European Union
UML	UNCITRAL Model Law on International Arbitration[1]
UNCITRAL Rules 1976	UNCITRAL Arbitration Rules within the meaning of the UN General Assembly resolution 31/98 of 15 December 1976[2]
UNCITRAL Rules 2010	UNCITRAL Arbitration Rules within the meaning of the UN General Assembly resolution 31/98 of 15 December 1976,[3] as amended in 2010 by the UN General Assembly resolution 65/22[4]
UNCITRAL Rules	UNCITRAL Arbitration Rules; either the UNCITRAL Rules 1976 or the UNCITRAL Rules 2010 or generally the standard of these rules, depending on the context. If in doubt, it is necessary to apply the last version, i.e. the UNCITRAL Rules 2010.
UNCITRAL	United Nations Commission on International Trade Law[5]
VIAC	Vienna International Arbitration Centre
Vienna Rules	Vienna Arbitration Rules

---

[1]   The template was approved on 21 June 1985 as UN Document A/40/17, Annex I, within the framework of the unification program of the UN Commission on International Trade Law (UNCITRAL).

[2]   Available online in English at: http://www.uncitral.org/pdf/english/texts/arbitration/ arb-rules/arb-rules.pdf (accessed on 5 May 2014). Also available in other UN languages.

[3]   Available online in English at: http://www.uncitral.org/pdf/english/texts/arbitration/ arb-rules/arb-rules.pdf (accessed on 5 May 2014). Also available in other UN languages.

[4]   Full text of the UNCITRAL Rules 2010 is available online in English at: http://www.uncitral.org/pdf/english/texts/arbitration/arb-rules-revised/arb-rules-revised-2010-e.pdf (accessed on 5 May 2014).

[5]   See www.uncitral.org.

Articles

Czech (& Central European) Yearbook of Arbitration

Aslan Abashidze | Anait Smbatyan

Theoretical Considerations of the Interaction of International Arbitrations and Courts in International Law

Key words:
arbitration | court | interaction | international law | jurisprudence | citation

Aslan Abashidze, Doctor of Law, Professor, Head of the Department of International Law, Peoples' Friendship University of Russia (PFUR), Member of the UN Committee on Economic, Social and Cultural Rights, Head of Commission on International Law, United Nations Association of Russia; author of over 400 publications including monographs and textbooks on international law of human rights, international humanitarian law, law of external relations, peaceful resolution of international disputes, international environmental law, international law of the sea, international criminal law, and international space law.
e-mail: aslan.abashidze@gmail.com

Abstract | *The proliferation of international courts and tribunals has been one of the most evident trends in international law development and has had a pronounced effect on the evolution of international justice since the last quarter of the 20th century. International courts and arbitration tribunals interact by means of mutual reliance on legal positions formulated earlier resulting in the emergence of a foundation of the system of international courts and arbitration tribunals – their common jurisprudence. The highest authority on issues of general international law is ascribed to the decisions of the Permanent Court of International Justice and the International Court of Justice. This trend is most convincingly manifested in international investment arbitration awards.*

Anait Smbatyan, PhD in Law, Head of Trade Law and Foreign-Economic Activity Department, the Diplomatic Academy of the Ministry of Foreign Affairs of the Russian Federation, author of over 50 publications on international trade law and international justice.
e-mail: anait_smbatyan@mail.ru

| | |

I. Evolution and Development of International Courts and Arbitrations

1.01. Until 1922 international inter-state disputes were resolved solely by *ad hoc* tribunals. The first attempts at establishing permanent international judicial bodies (IJB) were made during the Hague Peace Conferences but they were not successful. Despite the fact that the Permanent Court of Arbitration (PCA) was established in 1899 the name of this body was misleading: the work of the PCA was similar to *ad hoc* proceedings. A significant breakthrough in the movement towards establishing of a permanent IJB was made in February 1920, when the League of Nations Council formed a special commission of 10 competent lawyers who started working on the draft Statute of the Permanent Court of International Justice (PCIJ). The PCIJ Statute became effective on September 2, 1921. The first PCIJ ruling was made in 1922.

1.02. The historical importance of the PCIJ rested, in the first place, on the fact that it became the first ever permanent IJB. Second, the PCIJ had universal jurisdiction. Third, owing to the activities of the PCIJ for the first time in history of international law decisions of an IJB stretched beyond the settlement of specific disputes. In making its decisions and advisory opinions the PCIJ followed the principle of consistency which enhanced predictability in dispute resolution. Fourth, the PCIJ managed to strike a balance between consistency in dispute resolution and the development of international law. Fifth, it may be safely stated that with the setting up of the PCIJ, international law acquired all characteristics of an established mature system of law. The Russian professor Ruben Kalamkaryan writes that 'with the establishing of the Permanent Court of International Justice the world order based on the *Rule of Law* obtained the outlines of a realistically achievable result.'[1] It is also important to note that the PCIJ Statute, including all later amendments and additions, was drafted by a group of renowned international law practitioners of their time, including some authors of fundamental works on international law such as the Italian international lawyer Dionissio Anzilotti. Despite the fact that many innovative proposals were not included in the final draft of the Statute, it was nonetheless a reflection of the best achievements in legal thought of the first quarter of the 20th century. The establishment of the PCIJ

---

[1] Ruben Kalamkaryan, *International Court of Justice as Administrative and Judicial Body of International Community for the Resolution of International Disputes*, (2) INTERNATIONAL LAW AND INTERNATIONAL ORGANIZATIONS 96 (2011). Footnote omitted.

was also one of the best documented processes in the history of IJBs. It detailed verbatim records and reports of the negotiation process on drafting the PCIJ Statute. Further documents regulating its activities are available on the official web site of the International Court of Justice.

1.03. The Permanent Court of International Justice remained active until February of 1940, and existed formally until 31 January 1946. At that time, its judges submitted their resignations to the UN General Secretary in connection with the establishment of the International Court of Justice (ICJ) as one of the six principal United Nations' bodies and at the time as its principal judicial body. At its final session in October of 1945 the PCIJ made a decision to transfer its archives and property to the ICJ, and on 5 February 1946 the General Assembly and the UN Security Council elected the first judges. In April of 1946 the PCIJ was officially dismissed, and at its first session the ICJ elected as its President the last PCIJ President – Judge Jose Gustavo Guerrero. With the exception of some minor, mostly technical amendments the International Court of Justice Statute was identical to the Statute of the PCIJ.

II. The Rise of International Law and the Proliferation of International Courts and Tribunals

1.04. Within the historical context of the development of international relations, the second half of the 20th century, and particularly its last quarter, saw an unprecedented rise of international law authority. Russian professor Igor Lukashuk has said that after WWII the 'victory of the anti-Hitler coalition marked the beginning of the golden age of international law'.[2] During that period a lot was done in the area of international law codification, particularly the signing of some of the most important and fundamental multilateral agreements. The Active growth of international cooperation and in some spheres its high rise, contributed to the expansion of the regulatory effect of international law in new areas of political, economic, social, cultural, business and other spheres of life. Numerous issues which had traditionally been considered a prerogative of municipal public law began to be viewed predominantly using an approach derived from international law. As a

---

[2] Igor Lukashuk, *Victory in World War II and the Development of International Law*, (4) INTERNATIONAL PUBLIC AND PRIVATE LAW 3 (2005). See also: Oleg Khlestov, *Forecast for International Law Development in the 21ˢᵗ century*, (2) MOSCOW INTERNATIONAL LAW JOURNAL 26, 28 (2001); Igor Lukashuk, *Globalization and law*, (12) STATE AND LAW 112 2005.

result of the successful and fast growing practice of dispute settlement in various areas, was a dramatic increase of the body of norms utilized in such settlement, mostly in form of treaties as a source of international law. At the same time, in addition to a new content the latter also acquired a new, significantly higher status. The sphere of influence of international law extended even to private individuals, which in the beginning of the 20th century would have seemed quite unthinkable. Simultaneously with the international development and strengthening of its international law's authority as the regulator in international relations some institutional changes also took place: the number of international organizations with competence in regulation of international relations in various spheres of international law grew rapidly.

1.05. One of the marked trends in international law over the last quarter of the 20th century and into the beginning of the 21st century with a pronounced effect on the evolution of international justice was a notable increase in the number of international courts and arbitration tribunals. During that period, many IJB's were established. The following is a partial list of institutions founded during that time: the Court of Justice of the European Union,[3] European Court of Human Rights,[4] International Criminal Court,[5] African Court on Human and People's Rights,[6] International Tribunal for the Law of the Sea,[7] WTO Dispute Settlement Body,[8] Court of the Eurasian Economic Community,[9] Economic Court of the Commonwealth of Independent States,[10] Court of Justice of the European Free Trade Association,[11]

---

[3] The CJEU operates on the basis of the Single European Act of 1986, the Treaty of Nice 2001, and the Treaty of Lisbon 2007.

[4] Established on the basis of Convention for the Protection of Human Rights and Fundamental Freedoms of 1950, and came into effect on 3 September 1953.

[5] The Rome Statute of 17 July 1998, became effective on 1 July 2002.

[6] The Protocol to the African Charter on Human and Peoples' Rights on the Establishment of an African Court of Human and Peoples' Rights, opened for signature 8 June 1998, available at: http://www.achpr.org/instruments/court-establishment/ (accessed on 22 March 2014).

[7] The United Nations Convention on the Law of the Sea of 10 December 1982.

[8] Established in accordance with the Dispute Settlement Understanding. Annex 2 to the Marrakesh Accords signed in April 1994 and effective from 1 January 1995.

[9] The Court of the Eurasian Economic Community Statute of 5 July, 2010.

[10] Agreement of the Status of the Economic Court of the Commonwealth of Independent States of 6 July 1992.

[11] Agreement between the EFTA States on the Establishment of a Surveillance Authority and a Court of Justice (ESA/Court Agreement) with Protocols, 2 May, 1992 .

arbitration mechanism of NAFTA,[12] arbitration mechanism of MERCOSUR,[13] International Center for Settlement of Investment Disputes,[14] Court of Justice of the Andean Community,[15] International Criminal Tribunal for Former Yugoslavia,[16] International Criminal Court for Rwanda,[17] Special Court for Sierra-Leone,[18] Special Tribunal for Lebanon[19] and many other IJBs, including ones which are not yet active.[20] Alongside the permanent IJBs *ad hoc* tribunals have also been set up. Professor Lyudmila Anufrieva noted that 'the 20th century, though mostly its latest period, may be associated in the history of modern international law with the emergence and evolution of international courts...'[21] According to the French researcher Alain Pellet 'the international society is no longer a society without a judge (as it used to be)'.[22]

1.06. The pronouncements of the ICJ President Gilbert Guillaume attracted significant public attention in connection with the growing number of IJBs. The Judge warned the IJB to be cautious in stating their case-law. Such law, the judge argued, should be consonant with the practice of

---

[12] The North American Free Trade Agreement (NAFTA) was signed on December 17, 1992 and came into force on January 1, 1994.

[13] The Treaty Establishing a Common Market between the Argentine Republic, the Federal Republic of Brazil, the Republic of Paraguay and the Eastern Republic of Uruguay. (Treaty of Asuncion) signed on March 26, 1991 and came into force on 29 November 1991.

[14] Established under the Convention on the Settlement of Investment Disputes between States and Nationals of Other States (the ICSID or the Washington Convention) of 18 March 1965.

[15] Protocol Amending the Treaty Creating the Court of Justice of the Cartagena (May 28, 1996).

[16] See UN Document S/ Res/ 827 (1993), 25 May 1993 r.

[17] See Document UN S/ Res/ 955 (1994), 8 May 1994.

[18] Established on the basis of the Agreement between UN and the Government of Sierra Leone on establishing the Special Court for Sierra Leone following Resolution 1315(2000) of the UN Security Council of 14.08.2000. See: Document UN S/2002/246, 8 March 2002.

[19] Established on the basis of Agreement between the UN and the Lebanese Republic on establishing the Special Tribunal for Lebanon following Resolution 1664(2006) of the UN Security Council of 29.03.2006. See Document UN S/ Res/ 1757 (2007), 30 May 2007.

[20] According to the research team 'Project on International Courts and Tribunals' data at present there are about 125 IJBs, available at: http://www.pict-pcti.org/publications/synoptic_chart/synoptic_chart2.pdf (accessed on 22 March 22 2014).

[21] Lyudmila Anufrieva, *International Justice: Regional Judicial Institutions in Eurasian Integration*, (9) EURASIAN LAW JOURNAL 15 (2013).

[22] Alain Pellet, *Shaping the Future in International Law: The Role of the World Court in Law-Making, in LOOKING TO THE FUTURE – ESSAYS ON INTERNATIONAL LAW IN HONOR OF W. MICHAEL REISMAN*, Leiden: Nijhoff 1082 (2010).

the International Court of Justice as the principal judicial body of the United Nations. According to the Judge, the jurisdiction of the ICIJ was *ipso facto* compulsory in all legal disputes in accordance with Article 36 of the Statute. Moreover, it would have been quite deplorable if different courts assumed conflicting positions on specific problems.[23] In his other address to the UN General Assembly Judge Guillaume voiced his concern that inconsistency in dispute resolution by various IJBs might threaten the integrity of international law:

> Proliferation of international courts gives rise to a serious risk of conflicting jurisprudence, as the same rule of law might be given different interpretations in different cases. This is a particularly acute risk, as we are dealing with specialized courts that are inclined to favour their own disciplines... Judges themselves must realize the danger of fragmentation in the law, and even conflicts of case-law, born of the proliferation of courts. A dialogue among judicial bodies is crucial.[24]

1.07.   The statements of Judge Guillaume, concordant with the concerns expressed earlier by Stephen Schwebel, another President of the Court,[25] triggered academic discussions on the issue of the effect of IJB proliferation on the integrity and systemic nature of international law, and what measures should be taken in order to prevent possible negative effects caused by the lack of IJB hierarchy. It seemed that the problem was not the fact of IJB proliferation per se, but the non-systematic character of this process and the lack of any formal ties between the newly created IJBs. In this "connection the issue of correlation of decisions made by various international courts and tribunals came to the foreground.

III.   Correlation of International Courts and Tribunal Decisions and Their Importance

1.08.   As is known in international law, there is no statutory recognized hierarchy of sources. The only exception is Article 38 of the International Court of Justice Statute which repeats the wording of Article 35 of the PCIJ Statute.

---

[23]   Gilbert Guillaume, *The Future of International Judicial Institutions*, 44 INTERNATIONAL AND COMPARATIVE LAW QUARTERLY 862 (October 1995).

[24]   Statement of the President of International Court of Justice to the United Nations General Assembly of 26 October 2000, available at: http://www.icj-cij.org/court/index.php?pr=84&pt=3&p1=1&p2=3&p3=1 (accessed on 25 March 2014).

[25]   ICJ Press Communique 99/46 of 26 October 1999.

1.09.   Article 38 of the International Court of Justice Statute provides that in deciding such disputes as are submitted to it, the Court shall be guided by:

a) international conventions, whether general or particular, establishing rules expressly recognized by the contesting states;

b) international custom, as evidence of a general practice accepted as law;

c) the general principles of law recognized by civilized nations;

d) subject to the provisions of Article 59, judicial decisions and the teachings of the most highly qualified publicists of the various nations, as subsidiary means for the determination of rules of law.

1.10.   It is interesting to note that Article 59 of the International Court of Justice Statute providing that the 'decision of the Court has no binding force except between the parties and in respect of that particular case', was not initially present in the PCIJ Statute, nor was there any reference to it in Article 35. Article 57bis was added to the PCIJ Statute later. However this did not predetermine the influence of PCIJ rulings, or later the rulings of the International Court of Justice, nor the decisions of other IJBs in the subsequent practice of international dispute settlement or the development of the international law. This fact was restated by Judge Robert Yewdall Jennings:

> The Court begins its discussion of Article 59 by citing the observation of the Permanent Court of International Justice *(Series A, No. 13,* p. 21) that "the object of Article 59 is simply to prevent legal principles accepted by the Court in a particular case from being binding also upon other States or in other disputes" (see paragraph 42 of the Judgment). This is no more than to Say that the principles of decision of a judgment are not binding in the sense that they might be in some common law systems through a more or less rigid system of binding precedents. But the slightest acquaintance with the jurisprudence of this Court shows that Article 59 does by no manner of means exclude the force of persuasive precedent. So the idea that Article 59 is protective of third States' interests in this sense at least is illusory.[26]

1.11.   Despite the fact that the list of sources set forth in Article 38 of the Statute *de jure* applies only to the International Court, the wording of this article, apparently for the lack of any other, is recognized by IJBs

---

[26]   Continental Shelf (Libyan Arab Jamahiriya/Malta), ICJ Reports 1984. P. 157. Para. 27. Sir R. Jennings, dissenting opinion.

and the international community as an authoritative statement of the legal force of various sources of international law.[27]

1.12. Article 38 of the Statute recognized the doctrinal approach to sources of law prevailing both in the theory and practice of international law at the time of drafting of the PCIJ Statute. The inapplicability of the principle stating that previous court decisions shall be binding for future disputes reflected the historical evolution of this issue. This is fair enough. Prior to the PCIJ, all IJBs were established exclusively as *ad hoc* tribunals for the resolution of specific disputes. During that period international disputes involved, as a rule, the interests of only two states. The *ad hoc* tribunals' awards could be binding only for the parties in the dispute. That was exactly why the concept of the bilateral nature of international disputes and hence the decisions made as a result of the examination of cases was assumed by the PCIJ Statute, and later by the International Court of Justice Statute.

1.13. The practice of the international judiciary gives evidence that international courts and tribunals perceive earlier decisions not only as a 'subsidiary means for the determination of rules of law', as it is stated in Article 38 of the International Court of Justice Statute. In fact every conclusion on the merits of the case is supported with arguments based on the earlier formulated legal position. This trend is most convincingly manifested in international arbitration awards.

IV. The Citation of Decisions and the Reliance on Prior Legal Positions

1.14. The parties submitting their complaints to international courts and arbitration tribunals proceed from the expectations formed under the influence of previous international jurisprudence with regard to similar dispute resolutions. The arguments of the parties include numerous references to legal positions formulated by various IJBs. Moreover, every conclusion is supported with such references.

1.15. International judges and arbiters also pay significant attention to their legal positions. Practically none of their decisions is free from references to previous jurisprudence. The volume of citations is not limited in any way and may be quite significant. The experience of other judges enhances the arguments, helps to disclose new aspects of law, and allows the judges to investigate new ideas and approaches. Citation of each other's conclusions helps to mitigate the negative

---

[27] See for example: Prosecutor v Zdravko Mucic aka "Pavo", Hazim Delic, Esad Landzo aka "Zenga", Zejnil Delalic. IT-96-21-T. Judgment of 16 November 1998. Para. 414.

consequences of the fragmentation of international law, and contributes to the strengthening of international legal order. This is particularly important given the diversification of international law and the specialization of separate legal orders including regional orders. This trend is most vividly manifested in the interaction between international courts and arbitration tribunals. A good example can be seen in the interaction between international investment arbitration tribunals established under the Convention on the Settlement of Investment Disputes between State and Nationals of Other States and the International Court of Justice.

1.16. The rulings of the International Court of Justice *de jure* are not superior to the decisions of any other IJB. At the same time the legal positions of the Court, particularly the ones formulated with regard to the general issues of international law enjoy a widely recognized authority. Specialized IJBs, as a rule, take them into account, and less frequently they are declined with a well reasoned argumentation. There seems, however to have been no precedents in judicial practice when the opinion of the Court was ignored. As was mentioned by Professor Galina Shinkaretskaya 'the very reputation of the lawyers representing the International Court of Justice, and the robustness of its argumentation earned the works of the ICJ a general recognition in the international community as the most authoritative summary of the norms of international law'.[28] Because of its unique position the International Court of Justice *a priori* enjoys intellectual leadership.

1.17. There is a strong trend to base international investment tribunals' awards on legal positions of the International Court of Justice and the Permanent Court of International Justice. For instance, in *Saluka Investment BV* v *The Czech Republic* the Arbitration utilized existing precedent in coming to the following conclusion:

> The term 'measures' covers any action or omission of the Czech Republic. As the ICJ has stated in the *Fisheries Jurisdiction Case (Spain v Canada)* [i]n its ordinary sense the word is wide enough to cover any act, step or proceeding, and imposes no particular limit on their material content or on the aim pursued thereby.[29]

1.18. In *ADC Affiliate Limited and ADC & ADMC Management Limited* v *The Republic of Hungary* one of the main issues was a question about

---

[28] Galina Shinkaretskaya, *International Law and Peaceful Settlement*, (3) INTERNATIONAL LAW AND INTERNATIONAL ORGANIZATIONS 144 (2011).

[29] *Saluka Investment BV* (The Netherlands) v *The Czech Republic*. Partial Award of 17 March 2006. Para. 459.

the applicability of the standard of compensation for acts by States unlawful under international law. The claimants argued that the respondent's deprivation of its investments was a breach of the bilateral investment treaty and as an internationally wrongful act was subject to the customary international law standard as set out in *Chorzow Factory*.[30] The Respondent contended that the BIT standard was a *lex specialis* which came in lieu of the customary international law standard. The Arbitration set out its position as following:

> The customary international law standard for the assessment of damages resulting from an unlawful act is set out in the decision of the PCIJ in the *Chorzów Factory* case had subsequently been affirmed and applied in a number of international arbitrations relating to the expropriation of foreign owned property.

1.19.   In confirmation of its statement the tribunal provided a focused and very convincing reference to a series of decisions made by the International Court.[31]

1.20.   In the award *Lance Paul Larsen v the Hawaiian Kingdom*, the Arbitrators considered the principle formulated by the International Court of Justice in the *Monetary Gold* case,[32] according to which an IJB cannot decide a dispute between the parties submitted to it if the matter of dispute constitutes the rights or obligations of a state which is not a party to a given judicial proceeding.[33] Arbitrators relied on the following judgments of the PCIJ and the ICJ: Military *Activities in and against Nicaragua*,[34] *Land, Island and Maritime Frontier Dispute*,[35] *Phosphate Lands in Nauru*,[36] and *East Timor*.[37] As was correctly stated

---

[30]   *Chorzow Factory (Claim for Indemnity) (Merits), Germany v Poland*, P.C.I.J. Series A., No. 17 (1928).

[31]   *ADC Affiliate Limited and ADC & ADMC Management Limited v The Republic of Hungary.* ICSID Case No. ARB/03/16. Award of the Tribunal. Para. 493. Investment Arbitration makes reference to the legal views of the International Court of Justice in a wide range of other cases. See for example: *National Grid plc v The Argentine Republic.* Decision on Jurisdiction. June 20, 2006. Para. 70; *Siemens A.G. v The Argentine Republic.* ICSID Case No. ARB/02/8. Decision on jurisdiction. 2 August 2005, para. 97.

[32]   Monetary Gold. ICJ Reports 1954.

[33]   Lance Paul Larsen v the Hawaiian Kingdom. Permanent Court of Arbitration. Award of 5 February 2001. P. 14–15.

[34]   Military Activities in and against Nicaragua, ICJ Reports 1984. P. 431. Para. 88.

[35]   Land, Island and Maritime Frontier Dispute (El Salvador/Honduras), ICJ Reports 1990. P. 116. Para. 56.

[36]   Phosphate Lands in Nauru, ICJ Reports 1992. P. 240 at 258–62. Paras. 48–55.

[37]   East Timor, ICJ Reports 1995. P. 90 at 102–105. Paras. 28–35.

by the Arbitration, notwithstanding the fact that the Court came to different conclusions in these cases, every time it applied the *Monetary Gold* case which stated as follows:

> To adjudicate upon the international responsibility of a State without its consent would run counter to a well-established principle of international law embodied in the Court's Statute, namely, that the Court can only exercise jurisdiction over a State with its consent. The determinative will be the fact that its legal interests would not only be affected by a decision, but would form the very subject-matter of the decision.[38]

1.21. Arbitration even deemed it necessary to provide a conceptual definition of its attitude towards the legal opinions of the principal judicial body of the international community. 'Although there is no doctrine of binding precedent in international law, it is only in the most compelling circumstances that a tribunal charged with the application of international law and governed by that law should depart from a principle laid down in a long line of decisions of the International Court of Justice'.[39]

1.22. The case concerning *Auditing of Accounts between the Kingdom of the Netherlands and the French Republic*,[40] contains a comprehensive, in-depth analysis of decisions involving the issue of international treaty interpretation. The tribunal analyzed a wide range of decisions made by different IJBs. For instance, the fact that Articles 31–32 of the Vienna Convention on the Law of Treaties represented the codification of customary international law in this sphere was substantiated through references to the ICJ decisions in *Territorial Dispute (Libyan Arab Jamahiriya/Chad)*,[41] *Maritime Delimitation and Territorial Questions between Qatar and Bahrain*,[42] *Oil Platforms (Islamic Republic of Iran v United States of America)*,[43] *Kasikili/Sedudu Island (Botswana/*

---

[38] Monetary Gold. ICJ Reports 1954. P. 32.

[39] Lance Paul Larsen v the Hawaiian Kingdom. Permanent Court of Arbitration. Award of 5 February 2001. Para. 11.21.

[40] Case Concerning the Auditing of Accounts between the Kingdom of the Netherlands and the French Republic Pursuant to the Additional Protocol of 25 September 1991 to the Convention on the Protection of the Rhine against Pollution by Chlorides of 3 December 1976. Arbitral award of 12 March 2004.

[41] Territorial Dispute (Libyan Arab Jamahiriya/Chad), I.C.J. Reports 1994. P. 21. Para. 41.

[42] Maritime Delimitation and Territorial Questions between Qatar and Bahrain (*Qatar v Bahrain*), Jurisdiction and Admissibility, I.C.J. Reports 1995, p. 18. Para. 33; I.C.J. Reports 1996 (II). Para. 23.

[43] Islamic Republic of Iran v United States of America (Preliminary Objections),33; I.C.J. Reports 1996 (II). P. 812. Para. 23.

Namibia),[44] *Sovereignty over Pulau Litigan and Pulau Sipadan (Indonesia/Malaysia),*[45]and *LaGrand (Germany v United States of America).*[46] A conclusion that Article 32 of the Vienna Convention does not restrict the use of supplementary means of interpretation to cases in which the result of the application of the provisions of Article 31 would be ambiguous, obscure or manifestly absurd or unreasonable was supported by a detailed review of conclusions made by different IJBs on the issue of reference to the preparatory works.[47] The Tribunal reviewed arguments and evidence contained not only in the ICJ decisions, but also in arbitration tribunals' awards. In particular they drew on the awards of the Franco-American Arbitral Tribunal in a case concerning the *Air Services Agreement of 27 March 1946 between the United States of America and France,*[48] and of the Franco-Mexican Claims Commission in the case concerning *Georges Pinson (France) v United Mexican States.*[49] The tribunal also deemed it necessary to analyze the conclusions reached by various IJBs with regard to rejecting interpretations which could lead to 'absurd',[50] 'unreasonable'[51] or 'not reasonable'[52] results, and later emphasized its findings with legal opinions made by the PCIJ and the ICJ.[53]

---

[44] Kasikili/Sedudu Island (Botswana/Namibia), I.C.J. Reports 1999. P. 1059. Para. 18.

[45] Sovereignty over Pulau Litigan and Pulau Sipadan (Indonesia/Malaysia), Judgment of 17 December 2002. Para. 37.

[46] LaGrand (*Germany v United States of America*), I.C.J. Reports 2001. P. 501. Para. 99.

[47] Case Concerning the Auditing of Accounts between the Kingdom of the Netherlands and the French Republic Pursuant to the Additional Protocol of 25 September 1991 to the Convention on the Protection of the Rhine against Pollution by Chlorides of 3 December 1976. Arbitral award of 12 March 2004. Paras. 70–72.

[48] Air Services Agreement of 27 March 1946 between the United States of America and France (Award of 9 December 1978).

[49] *Georges Pinson* (France) v *United Mexican States* (Decision No. 1 of 19 October 1928, Reports of International Arbitral Awards. Vol. V. P. 422. Para. 50).

[50] *Georges Pinson* (France) v *United Mexican States* (Decision No. 1 of 19 October 1928, Reports of International Arbitral Awards. Vol. V. P. 425. Para).

[51] *John W. Browne* (United States) v *Panama* (Decision of 26 June 1933, Reports of International Arbitral Awards, Vol. VI. P. 334).

[52] Naomi Russell, in her own right and as *Administratrix and Guardian* (USA) v *United Mexican States*, Decision No. 5 of 24 October 1931, Reports of International Arbitral Awards. Vol. V. P. 820. Para.

[53] Case Concerning the Auditing of Accounts between the Kingdom of the Netherlands and the French Republic Pursuant to the Additional Protocol of 25 September 1991 to the Convention on the Protection of the Rhine against Pollution by Chlorides of 3 December 1976. Arbitral award of 12 March 2004.

1.23. A *rebuttable presumption* has formed within international law that conclusions made by the International Court of Justice on issues of general international law are well-substantiated and creditable. According Judge Georges Abi-Saab

> the ICJ has to play this central role and act as a higher court in a legal order that does not provide for formal hierarchy (except within the UN institutional system, where the ICJ is the principal judicial organ), a part that must then be earned as a *primus inter pares*, followed not out of legal compulsion, but through recognition of and deference to its intrinsic authority and the quality of its legal reasoning and findings.[54]

1.24. Such an important mission cannot be fulfilled if the Court claims a formal legal superiority over all other IJBs. The authority of the Court, the influence exerted by its decisions on the practice of international dispute resolution, the expectations and behaviour of various actors, as well as the evolution of international law must rest exclusively on robust substantiation, and the conclusiveness of legal positions formulated therein. Unfortunately the possibilities for the wide application of law provisions of the International Court of Justice in the practice of other IJBs are limited for both objective and subjective reasons. On the one hand, because of the relatively low load of cases and the historically developed 'specialization' on a selected category of disputes the International Court of Justice cannot make pronouncements on a wider range of issues which are submitted for consideration to other IJBs. On the other hand, the Court uses far from all of its available opportunities to express its opinion. As a rule, the most significant restriction is the excessively conservative approach of the Court apparently resulting from the burden of political responsibility.

1.25. Throughout its history the International Court of Justice has tried to avoid making references to the judicial practice of other IJBs. The reason for that could be that, because of the close attention drawn to the principal judiciary body of the international community, any reference to a decision made by another IJB, or more importantly, reliance on its legal position requires strong argumentation in order for the Court to avoid the appearance of bias.

---

[54] Georges Abi-Saab, *Fragmentation or Unification: Some Concluding Remarks*, 31 INTERNATIONAL LAW AND POLITICS 930 (1999). Footnotes omitted, available at: http://www.pict-pcti.org/publications/synoptic_chart/synoptic_chart2.pdf (accessed on 22 March 2014).

1.26. In several cases, the arbiters of international investment arbitrations recognized that any earlier decisions are not binding for further disputes. Nonetheless, they added that they believed it advisable and/or recommended to take into account the conclusions made.[55] One of the interesting examples, and quite significant from the point of view of arbitration awards analysis, was an ICSID decision in *AES Corporation v The Argentine Republic*. In that case the plaintiff tried to convince the arbiters that in the given case the defendant's objections were also of a 'purely theoretical, if not futile, nature' while referring to the fact that the arguments provided by Argentina against ICSID jurisdiction were dismissed in five previous proceedings. In response to this, Argentina explained that

> the reading of some awards may lead to believe that the tribunal has forgotten that it is acting in a sphere ruled by a *lex specialis* where generalizations are not usually wrong, but, what is worst, are illegitimate. Repeating decisions taken in other cases, without making the factual and legal distinctions, may constitute an excess of power and may affect the integrity of the international system for the protection' of investments.

1.27. The tribunal having carefully studied its jurisprudence in similar cases had, in fact, admitted that ICSID jurisprudence was developing in the direction of *jurisprudence constante*.

V. The Shaping of the System of International Judicial Bodies

1.28. The lack of any IJB hierarchy and the fact that they do not represent an interdependent plurality raises a question of the very existence of the IJB's system in principle, as well as how the links between its structural elements – international courts and arbitration tribunals – are organized.

1.29. The most common graphic representation of a system is traditionally understood as a vertical structure or a pyramid. These notions have been borrowed from the intrastate judicial systems and are based on

---

[55] *Liberian Eastern Timber Corporation* (LETCO) v *Republic of Liberia*. ICSID Case No. ARB/83/2, Award 31 March 1986. P. 352; *Marvin Feldman* v *Mexico*. Case No. ARB(AF)/99/1. Award 16 December 2002. P. 107; *EnCana Corporation* v *Ecuador*. London Court of International Arbitration. Award of 3 February 2006. Para. 189; *El Paso* v *Argentina*, Decision on Jurisdiction. June 20, 2006. Para. 39; *Jan del Nul and Dredging International* v *Egypt*, Decision on Jurisdiction, 16 June 2006. Paras. 63–64; *Grand River Enterprises Six Nations Ltd.* v *United States*. NAFTA/UNCITRAL Arbitration. Decision on Jurisdiction, 20 July 2006. Para. 36; *World Duty Free Company* v *Kenya*. ICSID Case No. ARB/00/7. Award 4 October 2006. Para. 16.

the traditional, stereotyped perception of the understanding that only hierarchical systems are capable of operating efficiently. This arrangement requires a rigid organization of procedures for the interaction between the parts constituting an organic whole. The national legal acts, as a rule, provide for the strict hierarchy of judiciary bodies with clearly defined legal relations of subordination between them.

1.30. No IJB's system that could meet this description has ever existed. At the same time, despite the fact that IJBs are independent and are not subordinate either to each other, or to any single central authority, this does not imply a lack of a system. In this case the concept of independence does not exclude, but rather predefines the specifics of the system's evolution. Schematically the IJB's system is a horizontal, peer-to-peer system, the development of which is driven by the activities of its constituent elements – IJBs – without any external regulation. The horizontal IJB's system is a self-organizing structure. The IJB's system may only function provided that each of the IJBs maintains its full and ample independence. Such independence is the *sine qua non* condition of the very existence of the IJB's system, and, in fact, also of the relevance and authority of international justice as such. The process of the IJB evolution is objective in nature.

1.31. The horizontal organization of the IJB's system may raise concerns about potential conflict of jurisdiction between international courts and arbitration tribunals. Analysis of international dispute resolution demonstrates that it is premature to discuss any conflict of jurisdictions as a systemic phenomenon. According to Russian international law scholars the problem of 'forum shopping' should be treated as a 'natural and normal consequence of proliferation of the permanent judiciary bodies with overlapping competences'.[56] Moreover, in reality conflicts of jurisdiction between the permanent courts and *ad hoc* arbitration tribunals do not arise, owing to the fact that the latter's jurisdiction is restricted to deciding specific disputes and never overlaps with the jurisdiction of permanent international courts.

1.32. The study of the practice of various IJBs demonstrates that judges do take into account how legal positions they have formulated correlate with earlier decisions on similar issues, and what effect they could have on the practice of international dispute resolution. It may be presumed that this is not dictated by the awareness (or intuition) of the need to

---

[56] ASLAN ABASHIDZE, ALEXANDER SOLNTSEV, KONSTANTIN AGAICHENKO, PEACEFUL RESOLUTION OF INTERNATIONAL DISPUTES: CONTEMPORARY PROBLEMS. People's Friendship University of Russia 299 (2011).

strengthen the IJB's system which is obviously in all of their interests. In situations when these factors are ignored it is frequently the result of individual judges with strong ambitions, the strong protection of one's own qualification or competence, or ignorance of the practice of other IJBs. According to the Russian professor, Marina Nemytina 'the *evolution of judicial practice in order to uphold its uniformity and sustainability is an objectively inherent function of a judiciary system'.*[57] There are all reasons to believe that the systemic, system preservation functions are a 'genetic' feature of all IJBs. Judge Georges Abi-Saab believes that

> the consciousness of the need for a common framework, and the requirements of such a framework, together with the adoption of judicial policies supportive of them, would serve as a self-fulfilling prophecy. Thus, from the exploded constellation of proliferating judicial organs, each endeavouring to fulfil all the components of the judicial function as best as it can and *faute de mieux,* a tendency would form towards the coalescence of judicial activity in a manner conducive to the emergence and hardening of an international judicial system.[58]

1.33.   Professor Cesare Romano was even more emphatic in his statement: '[The] International judiciary system is emerging *de facto* in the minds and by means of actions of men and (several) women vested with the status of international judges'.[59] The interaction between international courts and arbitrations occurs mainly through citations and a reliance on legal positions formulated by them, resulting in the formation of the foundation of the system of international judicial bodies – their common jurisprudence.

| | |

---

[57]   MARINA *NEMYTINA, RUSSIAN LAW AS INTEGRATION ENVIRONMENT,* Nauchnaya kniga 151 (2008).

[58]   Georges Abi-Saab, *Fragmentation or Unification: Some Concluding Remarks,* (31) NEW YORK UNIVERSITY JOURNAL OF INTERNATIONAL LAW AND POLICY 929 (1999).

[59]   Cesare Romano, *The Dark Side of the Moon: Fragmentation of Institutions Applying International Legal Rules,* 5(2) PUENTE @ EUROPA 56 (2007). Footnote omitted.

Czech (& Central European) Yearbook of Arbitration

Summaries

FRA [*Considérations théoriques sur les interactions dans le droit international entre les procédures d'arbitrage international et les tribunaux*]
Le renforcement du rôle des tribunaux et des forums internationaux est une des tendances les plus manifestes de l'essor du droit international et a des répercussions importantes sur le développement de la justice internationale depuis le dernier quart du XXe siècle. L'interaction des tribunaux internationaux avec les cours internationales d'arbitrage est notable : elles se réfèrent réciproquement les unes aux points de vue formulés dans le passé par les autres. La nécessité de créer une plate-forme pour cet échange de points de vue - exprimés avant tout dans leur jurisprudence - apparaît de plus en plus cruciale. On est en devoir de considérer la Cour internationale de justice et son ancêtre, la Cour permanente de justice internationale, comme les plus hautes autorités auxquelles se référer pour les questions de droit international général. Les décisions d'arbitrage rendues dans les litiges en matière d'investissement sont celles qui témoignent le plus de cette tendance.

CZE [*Teoretické úvahy o interakci mezinárodního rozhodčího řízení a soudů v mezinárodním právu*]
Posilování úlohy mezinárodních soudů a fór je jedním ze zcela zjevných trendů ve vývoji mezinárodního práva a má výrazný vliv na rozvoj mezinárodní spravedlnosti od poslední čtvrtiny 20. století. Vzájemná interakce mezi mezinárodními soudy a rozhodčími soudy je poznamenána tím, že se vzájemně odvolávají na názory jimi dříve formulované. Stále více se tak projevuje nutnost vytvoření platformy pro tuto názorovou výměnu vyjadřovanou především v jejich judikatuře. Za nejvyšší autority v otázkách obecného mezinárodního práva je nutné považovat dřívější Stálý soud mezinárodní spravedlnosti a Mezinárodní soudní dvůr. O tomto trendu nejvíce svědčí rozhodčí nálezy vydávané v investičních sporech.

| | |

POL [*Komentarz teoretyczny odnośnie interakcji między międzynarodowym postępowaniem arbitrażowym i sądami w prawie międzynarodowym*]
Interakcja między sądami międzynarodowymi i sądami arbitrażowymi odbywa się przede wszystkim w zakresie wzajemnego cytowania i odwoływania się do opinii prawnych, wydawanych przez nie w orzecznictwie. Zmiany w tej kwestii świadczą o konieczności stworzenia systemu międzynarodowych organów sądowniczych, które stworzyłyby

dla tej interakcji wspólną platformę. System międzynarodowych organów sądowniczych stanowi platformę o charakterze horyzontalnym, a jego rozwój jest w swej istocie obiektywny.

DEU [*Theoretische Erwägungen zum Wechselspiel zwischen internationalen Schiedsverfahren und den Gerichten im Völkerrecht*]
Internationale Gerichte und Schiedsgerichte interagieren v. a. insofern, als sie sich gegenseitig zitieren und sich auf die Rechtsauffassungen berufen, die die jeweils andere Seite in ihrer Rechtsprechung zum Ausdruck gebracht hat. Die Entwicklung in diesem Bereich zeigt, dass die Schaffung eines Systems internationaler gerichtlicher Stellen vonnöten ist, welches eine gemeinsame Plattform für dieses Wechselspiel schaffen würde. Dieses System internationaler gerichtlicher Stellen ist ihrem Charakter nach eine horizontale Plattform, deren Entwicklung wesensmäßig objektiv ist.

RUS [*Теоретические размышления о взаимодействии международного арбитража и судов в международном праве*]
Взаимодействие между международными судами и арбитражными судами реализуется, в основном, посредством взаимного цитирования и ссылок на правовые заключения, содержащиеся в документах судебной практики. Развитие в этой области показывает необходимость создания системы международных судебных органов, способных для такого взаимодействия создать единую платформу. Система международных судебных органов является платформой горизонтального характера, и развитие этой системы по своей сути является объективным.

ESP [*Consideraciones teóricas acerca de la interacción entre el procedimiento de arbitraje internacional y los tribunales de derecho internacional*]
La interacción entre los tribunales internacionales y los tribunales de arbitraje tiene lugar principalmente por el hecho de que los tribunales se citan mutuamente y apelan a las opiniones legales expresadas por los mismos en la jurisprudencia. El desarrollo de esta cuestión muestra la necesidad de establecer un sistema de órganos judiciales internacionales que creen una plataforma común para esta interacción. El sistema de órganos judiciales internacionales es una plataforma horizontal y su desarrollo es por naturaleza objetivo.

| | |

Alexander J. Bělohlávek

Seat of Arbitration and Supporting and Supervising Function of Courts

Key words:
seat of arbitration | place of arbitration | supporting and supervising function of courts | place of hearing | choice of seat of arbitration | recognition of arbitral award | enforcement of arbitral award | internationalization of a domestic dispute | arbitrability | autonomy of the parties | place when the arbitral award has been signed | lex fori | lex arbitri | lex loci arbitri

Abstract | The seat of arbitration has essential practical importance in arbitration, and it directly determines a number of issues: arbitrability, determination of governing law, whether substantive, or (mainly) procedural, and annulment of the arbitral award or its recognition and enforcement etc. Pursuant to author´s opinion the seat of arbitration is the main factor determining arbitration, while denationalization of arbitration seems to be a myth widely remote from international reality. The seat of arbitration need not be the place in which the individual procedural acts are conducted. From the seat of arbitration has to be distinguished also the place, where the arbitral award has been rendered and/or signed. Consequently, the place where the arbitral award is made usually determines whether the award is a domestic or a foreign award. The seat of arbitration can exceptionally be changed in course of arbitration, but not after an arbitral award has been rendered. International arbitration is usually subject to a two-tier control exercised by courts. The first control is exercised by the state of the seat of arbitration, and the second control is exercised by the state in which the parties seek recognition and enforcement. Consequently, if the parties internationalize their dispute (both parties from the same country agree on a seat of arbitration in a different country) and the arbitral award is rendered abroad (foreign arbitral award vis-à-vis the country of parties' origin/domicile), the award has no effects in the country of parties´ origin/domicile until its recognition.

Alexander J. Bělohlávek, Univ. Professor, Prof. zw., Dr.iur., Mgr., Dipl. Ing. oec/MB, Dr.h.c. Lawyer admitted and practising in Prague/CZE (Branch N.J./US), Senior Partner of the Law Offices Bělohlávek, Dept. of Law, Faculty of Economics, Ostrava, CZE, Faculty of Law and Administration WSM Warsaw, POL, Dept. of Int. and European Law, Faculty of Law, Masaryk University, Brno, CZE (visiting), Chairman of the Commission on Arbitration ICC National Committee CZE, Member of the ICC International Court of Arbitration, Arbitrator in Prague, Vienna, Kiev etc. Member of ASA, DIS, Austrian Arb. Association. The President of the WJA – the World Jurist Association, Washington D.C./USA. e-mail: office@ablegal.cz

| | |

I. Definition of the 'Seat of Arbitration'

2.01. The institution of the place where arbitration is held (abbreviated as the seat of arbitration or the place of arbitration) used to be often unduly dismissed by the parties in the process of negotiating their arbitration agreements.[1] In recent years, however, an agreement on the seat of arbitration has become a *regular component* of arbitration agreements, at least in international disputes. In any case, the seat of arbitration has a major practical importance in arbitration, and it directly influences a number of issues: arbitrability; determination of governing law, whether substantive or procedural; and annulment of the arbitral award or its recognition and enforcement. The seat of arbitration, of course, need not necessarily be the place in which the individual procedural acts are conducted, especially the place where *hearings* are held; quite the contrary, it is principally possible for the case to be fully resolved without the arbitrators and/or the parties actually visiting the seat of arbitration which was chosen by the parties or otherwise determined.[2]

2.02. This article does not distinguish between the forum,[3] the place of arbitration, or the seat of arbitration. All said expressions denote, at least according to the domestic approach, the place/seat of arbitration in the legal sense (the legal domicile of the particular arbitration, or *seat of arbitration*[4]), i.e. the factor determining the connection of

---

[1]   Unless stipulated otherwise, the words arbitration clause and arbitration agreement used in this article are interchangeable.

[2]   GARY B. BORN, INTERNATIONAL COMMERCIAL ARBITRATION, Kluwer Law International 1249 (2009).

[3]   Many authors refusing to use the term „forum' in connection with arbitration and they argue that the term „forum' is connected to courts (state courts) only. In the opposite the author of this article is of the opinion that arbitrators and arbitration courts (arbitration tribunals) serve to meet the same tasks as courts (state courts) and therefore the term „forum' may also be used for arbitration.

[4]   *Redfern* and *Hunter* distinguish the *'seat of arbitration'* and the *'place of arbitration'*. *'Seat of arbitration'* is supposed to designate the place of the proceedings, whereas *'place of arbitration'* means the place of hearings (the place where the arbitral proceedings actually take place). They do admit, however, that both terms are often used interchangeably in practice (ALAN REDFERN; MARTIN HUNTER; NIGEL BLACKABY; CONSTANTINE PARTASIDES, LAW AND PRACTICE OF INTERNATIONAL COMMERCIAL ARBITRATION, London: Sweet & Maxwell 270 (2004)). Similarly, *Gary Born* also primarily employs the term *'seat of arbitration'* and adds that the phrase *'place of arbitration'* is also used in practice (GARY B. BORN, *supra* note 2, at 1246). However, domestic terminology of many countries, as for instance in the most countries of continental civil law jurisdictions, mostly refers to the legal domicile of particular proceedings as the *'place of arbitration'*, sometimes – in

arbitration to a specific legal system in the international arena.[5] As mentioned above the seat of arbitration **must be distinguished from the place of hearings** (usually referred to as the *'venue'* or *'place of hearing'*), i.e. the place where the arbitral proceedings actually take place (for instance, the place where oral hearings are held, the place where a witness is interrogated, etc.). In this connection, some authors refer to the **place of arbitration in the geographical sense.**[6, 7]

II. Meaning of the Seat of Arbitration

II.1. Importance of the Seat of Arbitration

2.03.   The assessment of the seat of arbitration highlights one of the typical features of arbitration, namely the great autonomy of the parties; it also demonstrates the weakening of the connection between the seat of arbitration and the arbitration process itself, in the case of international arbitration. The reason is that litigation is governed by the principle

---

conjunction with international sources – also *'seat of arbitration'*; both expressions are treated as synonyms designating the legal localization of a particular dispute in a particular place, with the corresponding connections to the applicable law. 'Seat of arbitration' is probably more precise. However, considering the domestic terminological usages, it is certainly not a mistake to use both expressions, i.e. *'seat of arbitration'* and *'place of arbitration'*, as synonyms. Nevertheless, a comparison with international sources always requires that we identify the meaning of the particular term used.

[5]   Naděžda Rozehnalová, *Určení fóra a jeho význam pro spory s mezinárodním prvkem – I. část* (*Determination of the Forum and Its Importance for Disputes with an International Dimension – Part I*), (4) BULLETIN ADVOKACIE 16 (2005).

[6]   NADĚŽDA ROZEHNALOVÁ, ROZHODČÍ ŘÍZENÍ V MEZINÁRODNÍM A VNITROSTÁTNÍM STYKU (*Arbitration in International and National Transactions*), Praha (Prague / Czech Republic): ASPI (currently Wolters Kluwer) 209 (2008).
Just for example the terminology used in Section 17 of the Czech Act on Arbitration (Act No 216/1994 Coll., as amended) somewhat inaccurate or at least misleading when it refers to the *place where proceedings are held*. However, it cannot be interpreted as the place where hearings are held (i.e. location of the procedure) but as the legal domicile of the dispute, as the distinction is elaborated on below. As we shall see below, these two concepts must be principally distinguished as entirely different institutions. Unfortunately, legal practitioners are not always diligent in differentiating between the two phrases. The most national laws and rules on arbitration however do correctly use either 'place of arbitration', or seat of arbitration.

[7]   For more details regarding the connection between the seat of arbitration and the place of hearings (place where evidence is examined), see Phillip Capper, *When is the 'Venue' of an Arbitration its 'Seat'?*, 2009, available at: http://kluwerarbitrationblog.com/blog/2009/11/25/when-is-the-%E2%80%98venue%E2%80%99-of-an-arbitration-its-%E2%80%98seat%E2%80%99/ (accessed on 15 April 2014).

that the court always applies its own procedural rules (the principle of *lex fori*), which is a traditional and generally recognized principle that applies in most jurisdictions without any reservations.[8]

2.04. Consequently, there are no conflicts as such in the case of procedural rules applicable to court proceedings. This branch of law is controlled by the principle of territoriality, and the courts' procedural rules have a clearly territorial nature; in other words, litigation excludes the possibility of conflicts with the procedural rules of other countries. The state adopts its own procedural rules in order to regulate the procedure applied by courts, other state authorities, parties, and other participants to the proceedings conducted in the territory of the state. This activity is exclusively limited to the territory of the given state. When declaring a connection to the territory of states, i.e. especially when determining the jurisdiction (international jurisdiction) of courts, the state should take account of the connection between the situation (the factual and legal findings and circumstances of applying a particular law) and the territory of the state (personal or territorial). Assuming jurisdiction over situations which have no [special] connection to a particular territory could be perceived as interference with the internal affairs of another state,[9] i.e. a violation of sovereignty.

2.05. However, arbitration is different, because arbitrators (arbitral tribunals) cannot be considered state authorities,[10] despite the fact that their

---

[8] ZDENĚK KUČERA, MEZINÁRODNÍ PRÁVO SOUKROMÉ (*Private International Law*), Brno: Doplněk 376 (2004).

[9] Naděžda Rozehnalová, *supra* note 5, at 17.

[10] For more details concerning the nature of arbitration, see: Alexander Bělohlávek; Tereza Profeldová, *Arbitration in the Case Law of the Constitutional Court of the Czech Republic with Regard to the Nature and Purpose of Arbitration, in* THE RELATIONSHIP BETWEEN CONSTITUTIONAL VALUES, HUMAN RIGHTS AND ARBITRATION: CYARB – CZECH (& CENTRAL EUROPEAN) YEARBOOK OF ARBITRATION, New York: Juris 350–355 (Alexander Bělohlávek ed., 2011); GARY B. BORN, *supra* note 2, at 184; Přemysl Hochman, *K právní povaze rozhodčích nálezů: Ústavní soud není příslušný k projednání návrhu na jejich zrušení* (*Concerning the Legal Nature of Arbitral Awards: The Constitutional Court Does Not Have Jurisdiction to Hear a Motion to Annul an Arbitral Award*), (11–12) BULLETIN ADVOKACIE 111 (2002); Miluše Hrnčíříková, *Platnost rozhodčí smlouvy aneb jaký vliv může mít určení povahy rozhodčí smlouvy na praxi* (*Validity of the Arbitration Agreement a.k.a. Influence of the Determination of the Nature of the Arbitration Agreement in Practice*), (8) PRÁVNÍ FÓRUM, 373 (2011); JULIAN D M LEW; LOUKAS A MISTELIS; STEFAN KRÖLL, COMPARATIVE INTERNATIONAL COMMERCIAL ARBITRATION, Kluwer Law International 71–97 (2003); PŘEMYSL RABAN, ALTERNATIVNÍ ŘEŠENÍ SPORŮ, ARBITRÁŽ A ROZHODCI V ČESKÉ A SLOVENSKÉ REPUBLICE A V ZAHRANIČÍ (*Alternative Dispute Resolution, Arbitration and Arbitrators in the Czech and Slovak Republics and Abroad*), Praha (Prague/Czech

duties are similar to the duties of the courts and that they could frequently be defined as 'different authorities'; moreover, the parties to arbitration are principally endowed with a high degree of autonomy. Hence, the choice of the seat of arbitration is usually at the discretion of the parties themselves (for details regarding the choice of the seat of arbitration, see below). The seat of arbitration then influences and determines other issues relating to arbitration, and the importance of the seat can differ depending on the classification of arbitration in a given country. Some authors argue that the importance of the seat of arbitration has been on the decline, because the individual national laws regulating international arbitration are subject to mutual harmonization, which is significantly facilitated by the New York Convention (1958).[11]

2.06. International arbitration is usually specific for the application of two or more legal systems, each of which regulates a different category of issues. Consequently, international arbitration is typical for the comprehensive interaction of multiple legal systems. It is possible to encounter as many as five different legal systems which determine the status of a particular arbitration and which can differ in the individual proceedings:[12, 13] (i) the law applicable to the capacity of the parties to enter into an arbitration agreement and the law applicable to the arbitrability of the dispute; (ii) the law governing the arbitration

Republic): C. H. Beck 129 (2004); NADĚŽDA ROZEHNALOVÁ, *supra* note 6, at 52; KVĚTOSLAV RŮŽIČKA, ROZHODČÍ ŘÍZENÍ PŘED ROZHODČÍM SOUDEM PŘI HOSPODÁŘSKÉ KOMOŘE ČESKÉ REPUBLIKY A AGRÁRNÍ KOMOŘE ČESKÉ REPUBLIKY (*Arbitration in the Arbitration Court at the Economic Chamber of the Czech Republic and Agricultural Chamber of the Czech Republic*), Plzeň: Aleš Čeněk 20 (2003).

[11] Gabrielle Kaufmann-Kohler, *Identifying and Applying the Law Governing the Arbitration Procedure – The Role of the Law of the Place of Arbitration, in* IMPROVING THE EFFICIENCY OF ARBITRATION AGREEMENTS AND AWARDS: 40 YEARS OF APPLICATION OF THE NEW YORK CONVENTION. ICCA Congress Series, The Hague: Kluwer Law International 336 (A. J van den Berg ed., 1999).

[12] Adopted from ALAN REDFERN; MARTIN HUNTER; NIGEL BLACKABY; CONSTANTINE PARTASIDES, *supra* note 4, at 77–78.

[13] This classification can differ from one author to another. See, for instance: Monika Pauknerová, *Rozhodčí řízení ve vztahu k zahraničí – otázky rozhodného práva* (*Arbitration in Relation to Foreign Countries – Issues of Applicable Law*) (12) Právní rozhledy 587 (2003); JEAN-FRANÇOIS POUDRET; SEBASTIAN BASSON; STEPHEN BERTI; ANNETTE PONTI, COMPARATIVE LAW OF INTERNATIONAL ARBITRATION, London: Sweet & Maxwell 84 (2007); ANDREW TWEEDDALE; KEREN TWEEDDALE, ARBITRATION OF COMMERCIAL DISPUTES: INTERNATIONAL AND ENGLISH LAW AND PRACTICE, Oxford: Oxford University Press 215–253 (2005).

Czech (& Central European) Yearbook of Arbitration

agreement; (iii) the law governing the arbitral proceedings (*lex arbitri*); (iv) applicable substantive law (the law applicable to the merits of the dispute); (v) the law applicable to the recognition and enforcement of the arbitral award (if a party seeks recognition and enforcement in multiple countries, the number of the applicable legal systems can be higher).

2.07. All of the above-mentioned issues may be governed by one and the same law. At the same time, however, each of the above-mentioned issues may be governed by a different legal system, and all will have to be considered in one and the same proceedings. The importance of the seat of arbitration for the determination of the law applicable to the individual issues often depends on the theory which the state employs to classify arbitration in general, as well as on the theory which the state employs to determine the importance of the seat of arbitration.

II.2. Localization Theory (the *Seat Theory*)

2.08. The traditional approach mandates the existence (determination) of the seat of arbitration, which then connects arbitration to the legal system of a given state. This approach is called the localization approach, and it identifies the law of the seat of arbitration (*lex loci arbitri*) with the law governing the arbitration (*lex arbitri*). In other words, this approach stipulates that the law of the seat of arbitration shall govern the arbitration, whether chosen by the parties or determined by the arbitrators or the court.

2.09. This traditional and generally accepted concept also influenced the Geneva Protocol 1923[14] and the New York Convention (1958) The Geneva Protocol 1923 stipulates that the arbitral procedure shall be governed by the will of the parties and by the law of the country in whose territory the arbitration takes place. In this case, the dualism of the will of the parties and the law of the seat of arbitration as the *lex arbitri* is expressed in very clear terms. The New York Convention (1958) employs the criteria of the '*country where the arbitration took place*'[15] and the '*country in which the award was made*'.[16] It thereby establishes a clear territorial connection between the seat of arbitration and the *lex arbitri*.

2.10. This trend is also confirmed by the UNCITRAL Model Law (UML). As concerns contemporary arbitration laws, the strongest connection

---

[14] The Geneva Protocol 1923 was replaced with the New York Convention (1958) based on its Article VII(2) (of the New York Convention (1958)).

[15] Article V(1)(d) of the New York Convention (1958).

[16] Article V(1)(a) of the New York Convention (1958).

between the seat of arbitration and the *lex arbitri* can be found in the Swiss and English *lex arbitri*. This concept has also been relatively meticulously adhered to by Czech law in the Act on Arbitration. The Swiss IPRG [Switzerland][17] stipulates that the Act shall apply only if the *seat of the arbitral tribunal* is in Switzerland and if at least one of the parties did not have their seat (registered office) or residence in the territory of Switzerland at the conclusion of the arbitration agreement. The law applicable in England[18] stipulates that certain parts of the Arbitration Act shall apply only if the seat of arbitration is in the territory of England, Wales, or Northern Ireland, whereas other provisions shall also apply if the seat of arbitration is not located in the territory of England, Wales, or Northern Ireland, or if the seat of arbitration has not been determined at all.[19]

2.11. The above-said indicates that the seat of arbitration is not only a question of geography; it also represents a territorial connection between arbitration and the law of the place where the arbitration is formally (legally) localized. Moreover it also determines the arbitrability of the dispute as well as the jurisdiction of courts (state courts) to execute their supporting and controlling role over all and any arbitrations seated in the place (seat) of arbitration. Consequently, the seat of arbitration ought to be the focal point of arbitration; at the same time, it is not required that the entire proceeding be held in that place. On the contrary, a good deal of arbitration is particular for the fact that the place (seat of arbitration) is rather imaginary from a geographical perspective. The hearings are held in a different country, sometimes even in the territory of more than one state. Nevertheless, the parties and the arbitrators ought to consider the suitability of the solution according to which the arbitral proceedings are at least partially held in the chosen seat of arbitration; in other words, wherever possible, at least some of the hearings ought to be held in the seat of arbitration. Otherwise the seat of arbitration is purely fictitious – it was chosen by the parties (or the arbitrators, as the case may be) but was not actually used, because all hearings, interrogations of witnesses, etc. were held

---

[17] Article 176(1) of the IPRG (Switzerland). An approximate translation to Czech was also published in: ALEXANDER BĚLOHLÁVEK, ROZHODČÍ ŘÍZENÍ, ORDRE PUBLIC A TRESTNÍ PRÁVO: INTERAKCE MEZINÁRODNÍHO A TUZEMSKÉHO PRÁVA SOUKROMÉHO A VEŘEJNÉHO (*Arbitration, Ordre Public and Criminal Law: Interaction between International and Domestic Private and Public Law*), Praha (Prague/Czech Republic): C. H. Beck (2008), Part II – The laws of selected states.

[18] Act on Arbitration 1996, England and Wales. An approximate translation to Czech was also published in: ALEXANDER BĚLOHLÁVEK, *supra* note 17.

[19] ANDREW TWEEDDALE; KEREN TWEEDDALE, *supra* note 13, at 714–715.

elsewhere. In such case, the parties may run the risk that the courts in the seat of arbitration will refuse their jurisdiction due to the missing link connecting the arbitration to the seat of arbitration.[20]

2.12. According to the localization theory, the law of the seat of arbitration (*lex loci arbitri*) also becomes the *lex arbitri* and usually determines the following issues which are classified under the *lex arbitri* (apart from other areas, which could also be covered by the *lex arbitri*):[21] (•) the formal validity of the arbitration agreement; (•) the arbitrability of the dispute; (•) the composition of the arbitral tribunal; (•) fundamental procedural guarantees; (•) the auxiliary and supervisory roles of the courts; (•) the judicial review of arbitral awards.

2.13. However, the precise scope of the particular *lex arbitri* may differ from one jurisdiction to another, because the states determine what issues relating to arbitration conducted in their territory will be regulated and how. Indeed, this confirms that a purely contractual perception of arbitration (the contractual theory of arbitration) will hardly stand the test of the modern concept of arbitration. Besides, the scope of the *lex arbitri* may be different for domestic arbitration and for international arbitration – international arbitration lays stronger emphasis on the autonomy of the parties; consequently, the *lex arbitri* relating to international arbitration is usually less voluminous[22] – see the *lex arbitri* of Switzerland or France.[23]

II.3. Delocalization Theory[24]

2.14. This theory argues that international arbitration would be substantially simpler if it could rely on a universal *lex arbitri* which would not differ with the seat of arbitration. Neither the arbitrators nor the parties

---

[20] For more details, see the decision in *Titan v Alcatel* quoted elsewhere in this chapter.

[21] According to JEAN-FRANÇOIS POUDRET; SEBASTIAN BASSON; STEPHEN BERTI; ANNETTE PONTI, *supra* note 13, at 83.

[22] Alexander Bělohlávek, *Procesní předpisy a rozhodčí řízení* (*Procedural Laws and Arbitration*) (12) PRÁVNÍ FÓRUM 431 (2007).

[23] ALAN REDFERN; MARTIN HUNTER; NIGEL BLACKABY; CONSTANTINE PARTASIDES, *supra* note 4, at 80.

[24] For more details, see: GARY B. BORN, *supra* note 2, at 1299; FRASER DAVIDSON, ARBITRATION, Edinburgh : W. Green 300 (2000); Dejan Janicikevic, *Delocalization in international commercial arbitration*, in 3(1) FACTA UNIVERSITATIS (Series Law and Politics) 63–71 (2005), available online at the website of the University of Niš at: http://facta.junis.ni.ac.rs/lap/lap2005/lap2005-07.pdf (accessed on 26 September 2014); JEAN-FRANÇOIS POUDRET; SEBASTIAN BASSON; STEPHEN BERTI; ANNETTE PONTI, *supra* note 13, at 91; ALAN REDFERN; MARTIN HUNTER; NIGEL BLACKABY; CONSTANTINE PARTASIDES, *supra* note 4, at 91–92.

would have to analyze the peculiarities of the individual *leges arbitri*. Consequently, delocalization endeavors to separate international arbitration from the law of the state in whose territory the arbitral proceedings are conducted. The contemporary system of state control over arbitration is twofold—first, at the level of the *lex arbitri*, then at the level of the state in which the party seeks recognition and enforcement of the award. The delocalization of arbitration would have the result of eliminating the former system of control; in other words, the only system of supervision would apply to the petition for recognition and enforcement of the award – international arbitration would be *supranational* (*transnational*, cross-border, or *floating*).

2.15. Delocalization of arbitration is based on the autonomy of the parties; according to this theory, arbitration rests (principally) exclusively on the agreement of the parties. The presumption is that: (i) international commercial arbitration is subject to sufficient self-regulation, whether under the rules adopted by the parties themselves or under the rules adopted by the arbitrators and (ii) the only control should apply at the stage of recognition and enforcement of the arbitral award.

2.16. The problem is, however, that even though most arbitration is completed without any reference to the *lex arbitri*, the *lex arbitri* still exists and might have to be applied, especially in those situations which require the exercise of state power, i.e. typically freezing of property, temporary seizure of goods, etc. The arbitrators usually lack the jurisdiction to perform such acts and are forced to ask the courts for assistance – and it is the *lex arbitri* which regulates the role of the courts in arbitration. Besides, the *lex arbitri* usually determines the nature of the award in the territorial sense (the domicile of the arbitral award, the so-called *nationality* of the arbitral award), i.e. whether it is a Czech, Austrian, or Italian arbitral award. Thanks to its 'domicile', the arbitral award may subsequently profit from the international treaties binding on the state of origin of the award.

2.17. At present, the delocalization of arbitration is possible only if allowed by the *lex arbitri*. An exception to the rule is arbitration pursuant to the ICSID Rules which is completely based on international law. A country which opted for a very high degree of delocalization was Belgium. The Act of 27 March 1985 supplemented Article 1717 of the Belgian Code of Court Procedure, which stipulated that the losing party does not have the right to challenge an award rendered in international arbitration if at least one of the parties had its seat/registered office in, or any other connection with, a country different from Belgium. Nonetheless, this provision was subsequently repealed, because it deterred, rather than attracted, the parties with respect to their choice of Belgium as the seat of arbitration. The example of Belgium clearly illustrates that the ideas of the denationalization of arbitration are somewhat *chimerical,* especially because states desire to preserve a certain degree of control over arbitration; it also demonstrates the fact that the denationalization of arbitration generally does not even correspond to the actual interest of the parties. The reason often inheres in the greater security guaranteed in localized proceedings. Consequently, the denationalization of arbitration has never been fully implemented, and it appears that it has become a very marginal issue. Nevertheless, it is still possible to witness attempts to realize this theory in practice, and some authors and academics still openly support the idea.

III. Seat of Arbitration; Place of Hearings; Place Where the Arbitral Award Is Made and Signed; Classification of an Arbitral Award

III.1. Distinguishing the Seat of Arbitration from the Place of Hearings

2.18. The seat of arbitration need not coincide with the place where evidence is examined. The parties have the right to agree on the procedure, i.e. the procedure of taking evidence and the place where evidence will be examined, although such detailed agreement among the parties is rather exceptional, and if it were already incorporated in the arbitration, this could often be rather impractical. It is usually suitable to leave the issue of the place where evidence will be examined at the discretion of the arbitrators who, in the absence of agreement of the parties, are not only entitled to decide on the conduct of the proceedings, including the procedure of taking evidence, but are also obliged to conduct the proceedings without unnecessary formalities while giving all parties an equal opportunity to exercise their rights when trying to establish the facts of the case necessary for a decision.

2.19. Naturally, the examination of evidence might occur in several places during one and the same proceedings. As opposed to the place where evidence is examined and/or the place where hearings are held, the seat of arbitration is the place which ought to unify the entire proceedings. As repeatedly emphasized in this article, the place of hearings (including the place where evidence is examined) has no principal legal relevance; it is a purely organizational issue, unless it would *de facto* deprive any of the parties of the right to plead their case.

2.20. It is possible that despite the absence of agreement among the parties, the arbitrators will not decide where the seat of arbitration is located.

In such case, it is necessary to assess the seat of arbitration according to the particular circumstances of the case – it will usually be the same as the seat of the chairman of the arbitral panel or the place where most hearings were held (in such case, the seat of arbitration would merge with the place of hearings), unless it is obvious that it ought to be a place unrelated to the arbitrators, the parties, and the dispute (i.e. hearings will not be held in the seat/registered office or residence of any of the arbitrators, but in premises rented only for the hearings. It is by no means exceptional, especially in international disputes, that the arbitrators rent rooms in a suitable facility for the purpose of holding hearings, for instance, in a hotel, in commercial and administrative centers,[25] etc.). After all, even the explicit rule incorporated in Article 20 of the UML is based on a strict differentiation between the seat of arbitration and the place for consultations among members of the tribunal (panel), for hearing witnesses, parties or experts, or for the inspection of goods, other property, or documents. As repeatedly emphasized, the seat of arbitration is very important. On the other hand, it is not possible to hold the parties liable for the inactivity of arbitrators who fail to determine the seat of arbitration or do not determine it with sufficient precision.

III.2. Place Where the Arbitral Award Is Made

2.21. Apart from the above-mentioned issues, the seat of arbitration also influences the place where the arbitral award is made. The reason is that the seat of arbitration is also usually considered to be the place where the award is made. Most legal systems stipulate (or at least factually assume) the presumption that the determination of the place where the arbitral award is made is not legally contingent on the place where the terms of the arbitral award were debated or where the arbitral award was signed – unless the parties agree otherwise.[26] The same presumption is also incorporated in the rules adopted by certain permanent arbitral institutions.[27]

2.22. Consequently, the place where the arbitral award is made usually determines whether the award is a domestic or a foreign award.

---

[25] Such procedure is common in major international arbitration; it is also common in proceedings conducted by the International Court of Arbitration at the International Chamber of Commerce in Paris (ICA).

[26] See also: Frederick Alexander Mann, *Where is an Award „made'?* 1(1) ARBITRATION INTERNATIONAL 107–108 (1985); JEAN-FRANÇOIS POUDRET; SEBASTIAN BASSON; STEPHEN BERTI; ANNETTE PONTI, *supra* note 13, at 103–104.

[27] JULIAN D M LEW; LOUKAS A MISTELIS; STEFAN KRÖLL, *supra* note 10, at 646.

However, if the parties agree on a particular seat of arbitration (or at least the state where the seat of arbitration will be located), the place where the arbitral award is made must be identical to the seat of arbitration, or it must, at least, be located in the territory of the same state. The reason is that, if the parties explicitly choose the seat of arbitration, their agreement can have a real basis in the expectations of the parties regarding the potential future enforcement of the arbitral award in a particular state. Such enforcement includes the possibility of applying applicable international treaties, whether bilateral[28] or multilateral, or the existence of reciprocity in the enforcement of arbitral awards in relations between the state where the award was made and the state of enforcement, etc.

III.3. Place Where the Arbitral Award Is Signed

2.23. The place where the award (or the resolution terminating the proceedings) is made must not be confused with the place where the decision is signed. In this connection, we can refer to the relatively unequivocal Slovak law. This law stipulates that, if the seat of arbitration was in Slovakia and the parties did not agree otherwise, the decision is considered made in that seat of arbitration in Slovakia (i.e. in the seat of arbitration), irrespective of the place where it was signed, the place from which it was dispatched, or the place where it was delivered to. The same interpretation can be, and commonly is, also applied for instance in the Czech Republic, even though the Czech Act on Arbitration lacks any explicit rules of this sort. Moreover, the above-quoted rules in the Slovak Act on Arbitration provide a relatively solid basis for the potential future introduction of online arbitration[29] which, according to the information available, has not yet been applied in Slovakia. The reason is that the issue of the place where the award was made is considered one of the most important and most controversial with respect to the electronic case management of disputes in arbitration.[30]

---

[28] NADEZDA ROZEHNALOVA, MEZINARODNI PRAVO OBCHODNI, II. díl – Řešení sporů (*International Commercial Law*, Part II – Resolution of Disputes), Brno (Czech Republic): Masaryk University 176 (1999).

[29] Online arbitration is not contrary to domestic arbitration laws either; it must only be considered a specific agreement on the conduct of the proceedings in terms of Section 19(1) of the Czech Act on Arbitration.

[30] See also M. H. M. Schnellekens, *Online Arbitration and E-commerce*, 9(2) ELECTRONIC COMMUNICATION LAW REVIEW 113–125 (2002).

2.24. However, there is also an alternative opinion which argues that the arbitral award is made in the place where it was signed. Such a decision was rendered by an English court in *Hiscox* v. *Outhwaite*,[31] in which the arbitration was held in London but the award was signed in Paris. This approach, however, was abandoned in England in 1996 in consequence of the Arbitration Act 1996 (England and Wales). Nonetheless, it is not possible to rule out the possibility that the seat of arbitration would in certain countries and in a particular situation be purely fictitious,[32] and in such case the place where the arbitral award was signed would prevail over the determination of the place where the award was made according to the seat of arbitration.

IV. Determination (Choice) of the Seat of Arbitration in International Arbitration

IV.1. Autonomy of the Parties in Determining the Seat of Arbitration

2.25. The seat of arbitration is more important in international arbitration than in domestic (national) proceedings. International arbitration generally adheres to the principle stipulating that the parties may themselves choose the seat of arbitration; and they should indeed avail themselves of this opportunity, especially in *ad hoc* arbitration. Otherwise they run the risk that the seat of arbitration will be determined contrary to their expectations, which might result in unexpected situations, for instance, as concerns the application of procedural rules, problems with recognition and enforcement, etc. The seat of arbitration may be chosen any time before the commencement of the arbitral proceedings, i.e. both in the arbitration clause itself and at any moment after the dispute arises. There are opinions, advocated in certain countries, that the choice can actually also be made retroactively, after the arbitral award is made.[33] However, the author believes the parties cannot agree on the seat of arbitration after the arbitral award was rendered, like they cannot change mutually arbitration agreement after the termination of the proceedings. The reason is that the autonomy of the parties with respect to a particular

---

[31]   Decision in *Hiscox* v *Outhwaite*, published in (neutral citation): (1992) A. C. 562.

[32]   For more details, see the decision in *Titan* v *Alcatel* quoted elsewhere in this article.

[33]   Decision of the OLG Düsseldorf (DEU), Case No. 6 Sch 02/99 of 23 March 2000, published in the CLOUT Database under the Ref. No. 374 and available at: http://www.uncitral.org/clout/showDocument.do?documentUid=1598 (accessed 15 April 2014).

dispute ends on or before the day the arbitral award becomes final and conclusive, and it is principally impossible to change the legal domicile of the proceedings after the arbitral award was rendered. Due to the qualities of the arbitral award and with respect to the nature of the arbitral award as an authoritative decision of an *independent authority* (different than a public authority),[34] it is not possible to change the circumstances which could, principally, have a major influence on the procedural requirements, incl. such essential issues like arbitrability, or jurisdiction and competence of courts executing supporting and controlling power over arbitration.

2.26.   The parties' choice of the seat of arbitration may be either explicit or implied. For instance, an implied choice would be if the parties chose a permanent arbitral institution and thereby either directly determined the seat of arbitration or at least selected the applicable arbitration rules, which, in most cases, contain provisions regulating the mechanisms for the determination of the seat of arbitration. Most rules adopted by permanent arbitral institutions presume that the seat of arbitration coincides, in the absence of choice by the parties, with the seat of the permanent arbitral institution. These rules, however, mostly allow the autonomy of the parties as concerns a seat of arbitration different from the seat of the permanent arbitral institution.[35] *Ad hoc* arbitration naturally allows only a direct choice of the seat of arbitration. In the absence of the parties' agreement on the seat of arbitration and in the absence of any rule for the determination thereof, the presumption is that the seat of arbitration will be determined by the arbitrators. This should naturally occur at an early stage of the proceedings, at best before the arbitrator(s) commence discussing the case, so the arbitrators and the parties have a clear idea of the laws and

---

[34]   Cf. Judgment of the Czech Constitutional Court Case No. I ÚS 3227/07 of 8 March 2011.

[35]   See for example: Article 18 of the ICC Rules (2012 version); Article 16 of the LCIA Rules; Article 20 of the SCC Rules; Article 19 of the ACICA Arbitration Rules (Australian Centre for International Commercial Arbitration); available at: http://acica.org.au/acica-services/acica-arbitration-rules (accessed on 26 September 2014); Article 7 of the CIETAC Arbitration Rules (China International Economic and Trade Arbitration Commission); available at: http://www.cietac.org/index.cms (accessed on 26 September 2014); Article 13 of the AAA Arbitration Rules; available at: http://www.adr.org/aaa/faces/rules/searchrules/rulesdetail?doc=ADRSTG_002008&_afrLoop=2606091966732848&_afrWindowMode=0&_afrWindowId=pathckil3_34#%40%3F_afrWindowId%3Dpathckil3_34%26_afrLoop%3D2606091966732848%26doc%3DADRSTG_002008%26_afrWindowMode%3D0%26_adf.ctrl-state%3Dpathckil3_86 (accessed on 26 September 2014); Article 14 of the UML.

rules governing arbitrability, the validity of the arbitration agreement, and appropriate procedure. Such determination is indispensable, especially if the arbitrators are called upon to resolve a jurisdictional challenge or otherwise consider the fulfillment of procedural requirements.

2.27. As concerns the choice of a particular place as the seat of arbitration, it is desirable to take into account several factors.[36] First of all, the parties may be interested, primarily in international disputes, in the choice of a neutral place as a manifestation of their effort to guarantee equal standing to both parties; if the chosen seat of arbitration is located in the state where one of the parties has its seat/registered office or residence, it very often (although not always) constitutes an advantage for the party. Nevertheless, the parties may principally agree on a seat of arbitration located in the state where one of the parties has its seat/registered office, and this agreement is, naturally, valid. On the other hand, arbitrators in *ad hoc* proceedings dealing with international disputes usually try to choose a neutral place in order to avoid any *à priori* doubts regarding their equal treatment of the parties. At the same time, however, the choice of the seat of arbitration should guarantee that the place will be accessible to both parties and to the arbitrator(s) within a reasonable period of time and without any excessive travel expenses. The choice of the seat of arbitration should also reflect other expediency criteria, potential legal obstacles hindering access to the seat of arbitration for any of the parties (such as potential visa requirements which could apply to the parties or their legal counsel, the arbitrator(s), or potential witnesses), etc. The costs in a particular country may also be a major consideration, although this may usually be overcome by transferring the actual hearing of the dispute to a country different from the state of the [legal] domicile of the proceedings (place/seat of arbitration).

2.28. The parties should also take into account other economic factors, such as the possibility of transferring the required finances from/to the seat of arbitration, the availability of local professionals – lawyers or other advisors, experts, etc. (including the possibility of the parties to afford their services). There are also other practical considerations, such as the availability of premises suitable for hearings, accommodations for the parties and arbitrators, good communication infrastructure, as well as the availability of clerks, interpreters, and other administrative personnel.

---

[36] ALAN REDFERN; MARTIN HUNTER; NIGEL BLACKABY; CONSTANTINE PARTASIDES, *supra* note 4, at 270. Regarding the factors which the parties ought to take into account when choosing the seat of arbitration, see also GARY B. BORN, *supra* note 2, at 1680.

2.29. However, the parties should primarily consider the law of the seat of arbitration (local laws on arbitration – *lex arbitri*), because, as analyzed below, the *lex arbitri* in the seat of arbitration influences a number of issues relating to the arbitration agreement, procedure, etc. The laws of the individual states exhibit major differences as concerns their approach to arbitration, and it cannot be denied that the discretion reserved for arbitration in individual jurisdictions can vary significantly from one state to another. Naturally, it is more advantageous for the parties to choose their seat of arbitration in an arbitration-friendly state – otherwise they would have to deal with less favorable conditions regarding their autonomy and other obstacles. A less usual seat of arbitration[37] or a seat of arbitration with which the parties have no experience yet, merits an analysis of the local legal environment prior to the actual choice of that particular place. The parties will thereby prevent certain negative consequences with respect to a number of issues, for instance, the potential invalidity of the arbitration agreement. Such an analysis is also advisable if the parties come from a legal environment different from the legal environment in the seat of arbitration (for instance, the parties come from a country with the continental legal culture but consider choosing the seat of arbitration in a *common law* country or in a country with the Dutch-French system, etc.).

---

[37] Regarding the statistics of the frequency with which the individual seats of arbitration are chosen by the parties, see also: GARY B. BORN, *supra* note 2, at 1687; MICHAEL BÜHLER; THOMAS H WEBSTER, HANDBOOK OF ICC ARBITRATION. COMMENTARY, PRECEDENTS, MATERIALS, London: Sweet & Maxwell 189 (2005). It is necessary to point out, though, that the statistics are rather misleading. For example, the most frequented seats of arbitration in international disputes are allegedly France, Switzerland, and England. However, the data referring to France and England are misleading, because the number of disputes domiciled in France is influenced by the seat of the ICC Court and France often becomes the seat of arbitration for disputes in which the parties do not agree otherwise. The number of disputes in England is especially influenced by the fact that many banking and insurance corporations are established there. On the other hand, legal practitioners (together with the author) have principal objections to England being a suitable seat of arbitration – both due to the large number of interventions by courts and due to the extreme costs of resolving disputes in England; last but not least, English courts have recently adopted a number of surprising, almost extreme decisions which have confounded lawyers all over the world. It is also necessary to remember that the published statistics are to a great extent subjectively influenced by the country from which the persons who publish and / or interpret these statistical data come from, as they naturally tend to favor their own domicile.

2.30. The enforceability of the award is also very important in practice – an unenforceable award is basically useless. Consequently, it is advisable to choose, as the seat of arbitration, one of the states bound by the New York Convention (1958)

2.31. In the absence of choice by the parties, the seat of arbitration will be chosen by the arbitrators / arbitral tribunal.[38]

IV.2. Legitimate Interest of the Parties in Determining the Seat of Arbitration

2.32. The parties' agreement may also define the seat of arbitration in negative terms. Although the negative definition cannot be considered an agreement on a particular place, it can serve as a guideline for the arbitrator(s) in assessing the legitimate interests of the parties, and it must be presumed that the negative definition was usually motivated by the parties' concerns over the possibility to assert their rights in the proceedings to the fullest extent. In the absence of the parties' agreement, the seat of arbitration shall be – as mentioned above – determined by the arbitrators, who ought to take into account the legitimate interests of the parties. The legitimate interests must always be assessed depending on the actual situation. If the arbitrators determined the seat of arbitration in a state which would be inaccessible for the parties or their counsel (for instance, they would not be granted an entry visa), such determination would constitute a denial of the possibility to assert the party's rights and to participate in the proceedings or to present the party's arguments regarding the request for arbitration (statement of claim) and the proceedings as such; this would constitute grounds for annulment of the arbitral award by a court under many domestic laws on arbitration as well as grounds for refusing the recognition and enforcement of a foreign arbitral award under the terms of Article V(1)(b) of the New York Convention (1958) or under the terms of Article IX of the European Convention on International Commercial Arbitration (Geneva, 1961). However, these administrative obstacles can be eliminated by transferring the hearing of the dispute to a place different from the seat of arbitration; the place of hearings does not principally influence the procedural status of the particular arbitration.

2.33. Nonetheless, the legitimate interests of the parties must also be considered from the perspective of their desire to minimize the costs of proceedings, i.e. increase the economic efficiency of the proceedings.

---

[38] See also JULIAN D M LEW; LOUKAS A MISTELIS; STEFAN KRÖLL, *supra* note 10, at 646.

Czech (& Central European) Yearbook of Arbitration

Indeed, the arbitrators should keep this concern in mind throughout the entire proceedings; the determination of the seat of arbitration can be considered a factor which usually substantially influences the economic efficiency and the costs of the proceedings. The seat of arbitration determined by the arbitrators ought to have, wherever possible, a definite fixed and significant connection to the dispute, whether to the parties, the arbitrators, the subject matter of the dispute, or the expected course of the proceedings, including the taking of evidence. The general rule says that the stronger the international dimension, the bigger the margin of discretion afforded to the arbitrators in determining the seat of arbitration. Sometimes, however, it is desirable for the dispute to be handled in a neutral place – this interest may actually prevail over other interests, some of which are mentioned above. Such an interest is, indeed, nothing unusual in international disputes; it is even possible to say that it is a rule. In such cases, the usual preferred choice is a place which could be considered halfway between the parties, which neither of the parties could consider discriminatory.

IV.3. Changing the Seat of Arbitration

2.34. One may also ask whether the seat of arbitration could be changed in the course of the proceedings. Domestic (national) laws and rules on arbitration do not exclude this possibility; consequently, it must be allowed. In any case, if the parties enter into a new agreement regarding the seat of arbitration in the course of the proceedings, it is legitimate to require that the agreement be contingent on the consent of the arbitrators. Nevertheless, such situations occur only very rarely.[39]

2.35. International practice has documented only a few cases of this sort in the history of disputes handled and resolved by the ICC Court. For

---

[39] For instance the Czech Republic has a very reach arbitration practice, as at least 1/5 to ¼ of all property disputes in the Czech Republic will be decided by using arbitration (approx. 120 to 150 Thousands of arbitral awards will be rendered in the Czech Republic per year). Author discovered just a single case from the Czech arbitration practice in which the seat of arbitration changed during the proceedings, but not upon agreement of the parties. The seat of arbitration was changed by arbitrator´s decision and this decision was justified by the fact that the party demanding observance of the parties' agreement on the seat of arbitration failed to pay the corresponding advance payment on the increased costs of arbitration incurred in connection with such seat of arbitration. A decision on changing the seat of arbitration in the course of a dispute handled by the Arbitration court attached to the Economic Chamber of the Czech Republic and Agrarian Chamber of the Czech Republic under Case No. 96/11.

example, the available sources mention a case in which the seat of arbitration, chosen in a dispute between parties from the Far East, was Bangkok, Thailand. It transpired during the proceedings that that place was unsuitable as the seat of arbitration for hearing and resolving the dispute, due to the lack of any local law relating to arbitration and due to the fact that at that time, Thailand was not yet bound by the New York Convention (1958) The parties therefore agreed on, and the arbitrators and the above-mentioned arbitral tribunal approved of, a change, and the proceedings were thereafter conducted in Kuala Lumpur, Malaysia.[40] In another documented case, the arbitrators refused the seat of arbitration agreed by the parties in a country substantially unstable from political and security perspectives; the parties, however, refused any change. The seat of arbitration was not changed, but the situation was accepted as grounds justifying the resignation of the chairman of the tribunal.

2.36. Even though these cases are rather exceptional, the practice of international arbitration has documented several of them. The generally accepted rule is, however, that changing the seat of arbitration in the course of the proceedings requires a general consensus, i.e. the consent of the arbitrators and parties alike.[41] Otherwise, there have to be exceptional reasons in order to justify a change in the seat of arbitration during the course of the proceedings, either based on the arbitrators' decision if the parties do not agree, or, conversely, based on an agreement by the parties without the arbitrators' consent; the latter alternative may be pursued providing the proceedings are institutionalized arbitral proceedings and the change is at least approved by the arbitral tribunal as such. A similar procedure could probably be applied to domestic arbitration, in which, however, changing the seat of arbitration is not usually connected with such consequences (primarily legal consequences) as in international arbitration. If the seat of arbitration is changed to be outside the territory of the state, it is necessary to make sure that the local law in the country of the new seat of arbitration will allow the recognition of all procedural steps which have so far been adopted in the proceedings. It is necessary to point out, once again, that the whole process is controlled not only by the agreement of the parties and the potential decisions of the arbitrators but also by the law valid and applicable in the seat of arbitration.

---

[40] Sigvard Jarvin, *The place of arbitration*, 7(2) ICC BULLETIN 58 (1996).

[41] In the case of proceedings at the ICC Court – after the signing/approval of the *Terms of Reference*.

V. Seat of Arbitration and Annulment of the Arbitral Award by the Court

V.1. Fundamental Rule – Jurisdiction of the Courts in the Seat of Arbitration

2.37. If a party intends to challenge an arbitral award in court, the party must do so with the competent court. The general rule is that jurisdiction (international jurisdiction) is vested in the court of the state in whose territory the seat of arbitration was located.[42] Consequently, if the arbitration was conducted in Switzerland (the seat of arbitration was in Switzerland), the competent court is the Federal Supreme Court; the competent court in France would be the Court of Appeals in Paris, etc.

2.38. Indeed, the principle requiring a connection to jurisdiction (international jurisdiction), which is generally tied to the existence of territorial jurisdiction, also served as the basis for example for Section 43 of the Czech Act on Arbitration.[43]/[44] In other words, Czech law is based on the principal importance of the seat of arbitration. However, the same rule also applies in Austria,[45] which is very close to the Czech concept of arbitration, as well as in many other countries; it is possible to consider such approach as prevalent.

---

[42] JULIAN D M LEW; LOUKAS A MISTELIS; STEFAN KRÖLL, *supra* note 10, at 667.

[43] Section 43 of the Czech Act on Arbitration reads as follows: „The proceedings under this Act shall be conducted by the court with territorial jurisdiction in the district where the arbitration was or has been held, if such place is in the Czech Republic. Otherwise, the proceedings shall be conducted by the court which would have territorial jurisdiction in the absence of an arbitration agreement. The proceedings pursuant to Section 9 and Section 12(2) shall be conducted by the court which has territorial jurisdiction over the place where the registered office or the residence of the claimant or the respondent is located, if the territorial jurisdiction of the court in the Czech Republic cannot be determined.'

[44] Cf. also NADĚŽDA ROZEHNALOVÁ, *supra* note 6, at 297. The author of this article shares the opinion advocated by N. Rozehnalová.

[45] Austrian courts have international jurisdiction if the seat of arbitration (*Sitz des Schiedsgerichts*, i.e. the terminological equivalent of the '*seat of arbitration*' – regarding this terminological issue, see above) is located in Austria (see Section 577 of the Austrian Code of Civil Procedure (ZPO) in conjunction with Section 611 of the Austrian Code of Civil Procedure (ZPO)'. Cf. also FRANZ T SCHWARZ; CHRISTIAN W KONRAD, THE VIENNA RULES. A COMMENTARY ON INTERNATIONAL ARBITRATION IN AUSTRIA, Alphen Aan Den Rijn: Kluwer Law International 663 (2009). If the seat of arbitration is not in Austria, or if it is not determined, the Austrian courts may only decide whether the arbitral award exists or not (see Section 612 of the Austrian Code of Civil Procedure (ZPO) in conjunction with Section 577(2) of the Austrian Code of Civil Procedure (ZPO)).

V.2. Exception – Jurisdiction of the Courts of the State under the Law of Which the Arbitral Award Was Made

2.39.   However, there is one exception to the above-mentioned rule which makes the jurisdiction (international jurisdiction) over the proceedings on annulment of an arbitral award dependent on the seat of arbitration, although it is considered, by some authors, a rather hypothetical exception.[46] The autonomy of the parties allows them to agree on the rules applicable to the proceedings, and they may actually choose the procedural rules of a country different from the state of the seat of arbitration. Such procedure is usually not very useful, because it *adds* yet another legal system, which complicates the situation and could give rise to problems in case of a conflict between the law of the seat of arbitration (*lex loci arbitri*) and the law chosen to apply to the procedure; nevertheless, this option is principally permissible.[47] This possibility is actually also envisaged by Article V(1)(e) of the New York Convention (1958) which stipulates that *'the award has not yet become binding on the parties, or has been set aside or suspended by a competent authority of the country in which, or under the law of which, that award was made'*[48] (bold added by the author for emphasis).

2.40.   This means that it is possible to stipulate that the annulment of an arbitral award will be subject to the jurisdiction of a court in the state under the law of which the award was made. However, this possibility has probably never been used in practice.[49] *Tweeddale* and *Tweeddale*[50]

---

[46]   ALAN REDFERN; MARTIN HUNTER; NIGEL BLACKABY; CONSTANTINE PARTASIDES, *supra* note 4, at 428.

[47]   See also: II KLAUS PETER BERGER, PRIVATE DISPUTE RESOLUTION IN INTERNATIONAL BUSINESS. NEGOTIATION, MEDIATION, ARBITRATION, Den Hague: Kluwer Law International 325 (2006); PHILIPPE FOUCHARD; EMMANUEL GAILLARD; BERTHOLD GOLDMAN; JOHN SAVAGE, FOUCHARD, GAILLARD, GOLDMAN ON INTERNATIONAL COMMERCIAL ARBITRATION, Den Hague: Kluwer Law International 634 (1999); Gabrielle Kaufmann-Kohler, *supra* note 11, at 336; ALAN REDFERN; MARTIN HUNTER; NIGEL BLACKABY; CONSTANTINE PARTASIDES, *supra* note 4, at 272.

[48]   In: *International Electric Corp.* v *Bridas Sociedad Anonima Petrolera, Industrial Y Commercial*, published in (*neutral citation*): 745 F. supp 172, 178 (S.D. N.Y. 1990), the U.S. District Court for the Southern District of New York concluded that the words '*under the law of which*' meant reference to the procedural rules governing arbitration, not substantive rules. The seat of arbitration was in Mexico, and the governing procedural law was Mexican law. Consequently, only Mexican courts have the jurisdiction to annul an award rendered in these arbitral proceedings.

[49]   ALAN REDFERN; MARTIN HUNTER; NIGEL BLACKABY; CONSTANTINE PARTASIDES, *supra* note 4, at 429.

[50]   ANDREW TWEEDDALE; KEREN TWEEDDALE, *supra* note 13, at 372

argue that the New York Convention (1958) does not clearly indicate which law is meant by the words 'the law of the country under the law of which it was made' – they maintain that this could apply both to the law governing the arbitration agreement and to the procedural law chosen by the parties.

2.41. As concerns the procedural law chosen by the parties, *Tweeddale* and *Tweeddale,* together with *Redfern* and *Hunter*, maintain that the parties may choose procedural rules different from the laws of the seat of arbitration. In such case, the party may challenge an award rendered in such proceedings both in the seat of arbitration and in the country the law of which the parties had chosen as the procedural law, providing both legal systems allow such a solution.

2.42. As concerns the latter possibility, i.e. the law applicable to the arbitration agreement, this option was tentatively mentioned in *Hitachi Ltd et Mitsui & Co Deutschland v Rupali Polyester*;[51] in said case, the Pakistani Supreme Court concluded that the clause regarding the choice of applicable law also determined the law governing the arbitration agreement. In said case, the parties had chosen Pakistani law, and the court therefore held that Pakistani courts had the jurisdiction to annul the arbitral award and that their jurisdiction could run parallel with the jurisdiction of the state in whose territory the award was made.

2.43. Moreover, *Tweeddale* and *Tweeddale* add that the courts in certain countries also have regard to the type of the award, i.e. whether it is a domestic or a foreign arbitral award. They name France[52] and Sweden as examples.[53]

---

[51] Decision in *Hitachi Ltd and Mitsui & Co Deutschland v Rupali Polyester*, published in: XXV Yearbook of Commercial Arbitration, 2000, Vol. 25, p. 46.

[52] As concerns France, it should be noted that French courts have only a limited possibility of review, unless the arbitration has another connection to France. If there is no such other connection, the courts may accept only partial jurisdiction, or even refuse their jurisdiction entirely. In: *SA Compagnie Commerciale André v SA Tradigrain France* (published in: REV. ARB. 773 (2001)), the Court of Appeals in Paris (*Cour d'appel de Paris*) ruled that the international or, conversely, domestic nature of arbitration has a direct influence on the possibility to challenge an arbitral award.

[53] We can also refer to the Swedish decision in *Alcatel* (decision of the Svea Court of Appeal of 2005 in *The Titan Corporation v Alcatel CITISA*, published in: Yearbook of Commercial Arbitration 2005), in which the parties chose Stockholm as the seat of arbitration, despite the fact that neither of the parties or the dispute itself had any connection to Sweden. The arbitrator came from Great Britain, and hearings were held in Paris and in London. The Swedish court concluded that it lacked jurisdiction to annul the

2.44. The courts are empowered to set aside usually such awards only, which have been rendered within the territory of their jurisdiction. Nevertheless, it is possible to imagine a situation which would authorize the court of the seat/residence of both parties (especially if it were one and the same country) to exceptionally accept jurisdiction over the proceedings on annulment of an arbitral award which was not made in the country where the court is located. This could exceptionally occur if the validity of the method of determining the seat of arbitration were challenged and if it were presumed that the agreed/determined seat of arbitration in which the arbitral award was made prevented any of the parties from exercising his or her rights to such extent that the party was effectively deprived of the possibility to plead his or her case before the arbitrators. Even this scenario, however, is rather theoretical, because annulment of an arbitral award must principally be sought in the place where the arbitral award was made (or in the seat of arbitration, as the case may be). However, such a possibility could occur, in the model situation described above, if one of the parties would be a consumer and the consumer sought annulment of the arbitral award (pursuant to applicable rules on jurisdiction in consumer matters). It is necessary to point out that in these cases an agreement on a seat of arbitration inaccessible to the consumer or obstructing the exercise of his or her rights constitutes one of the possible reasons for classifying the arbitration clause as an abusive term.[54] The court of the state in which both parties have their seat/registered office/residence, but in which the arbitration was not held based on their agreement, has the right to express its *reservations* with respect to the arbitral award in the proceedings on recognition/enforcement, if these *reservations* constitute circumstances which justify the refusal of recognition/enforcement of the arbitral award. The enforcement of a *foreign* arbitral award allows consideration of the fact that the *seat* of arbitration abroad did not provide to one of the parties the possibility to plead his or her case. After all, the agreement on the seat of arbitration outside the [same] domicile of the parties can also be influenced by considerations regarding potential future enforcement proceedings in a different country, although these intentions would not otherwise, with respect to a particular dispute, constitute any special international (foreign)

---

arbitral award, because the connection with Sweden was so weak that Stockholm could not be considered the seat of arbitration.

[54] For more details concerning these issues, see also ALEXANDER BĚLOHLÁVEK, OCHRANA SPOTŘEBITELŮ V ROZHODČÍM ŘÍZENÍ (*Consumer Arbitration*), Prague: C. H. Beck (2012).

dimension from the perspective of procedural or substantive law. In the situation described in the preceding sentence, however, the state of the seat/residence of the parties has no interest whatsoever in interfering with the arbitral award, the arbitration, and, ultimately, the autonomy of the parties.

VI. Internationalization of a Domestic Dispute and Enforcement of an Arbitral Award

2.45. Internationalization of a domestic dispute concerns situations, when a dispute does not report any international dimension, however the parties agree on the seat of arbitration abroad. As concerns the potential limitations applicable to the choice of the seat of arbitration, the parties ought to consider where they will use the award, i.e. in which country they will seek recognition and enforcement. The overwhelming majority of recognitions and enforcements are governed by the New York Convention (1958), which defines the grounds for a refusal to recognize and enforce an arbitral award in Article V New York Convention (1958); the list is exhaustive, i.e. no other reasons may be included under said Article.

2.46. As mentioned above, international arbitration is usually subject to a two-tier control exercised by the state. The first control is exercised by the state of the seat of arbitration, and the second control is exercised by the state in which the parties seek recognition and enforcement. Consequently, if the parties internationalize their dispute and the arbitral award is rendered abroad (foreign arbitral award vis-à-vis the country of parties' origin/domicile), the award has no effects in the country of parties´ origin/domicile until recognition. A court of the parties´ origin may therefore refuse the arbitral award pursuant to Article V of the New York Convention (1958). The grounds for refusal are as follows:[55] (i) the parties to the arbitration agreement were under incapacity to act; (ii) the arbitration agreement is not valid under the law to which the parties have subjected it or under the law of the country where the award was made; (iii) the party against whom the award is invoked was not given proper notice of the appointment of the

---

[55] For more details regarding the individual grounds, see also: II KLAUS PETER BERGER, *supra* note 47, at 591; GARY B. BORN, *supra* note 2, at 2701; JULIAN D M LEW; LOUKAS A MISTELIS; STEFAN KRÖLL, *supra* note 10, at 687; JEAN-FRANÇOIS POUDRET; SEBASTIAN BASSON; STEPHEN BERTI; ANNETTE PONTI, *supra* note 13, at 849; ALAN REDFERN; MARTIN HUNTER; NIGEL BLACKABY; CONSTANTINE PARTASIDES, *supra* note 4, at 430; ANDREW TWEEDDALE; KEREN TWEEDDALE, *supra* note 13, at 407

arbitrator or of the arbitration proceedings or was otherwise unable to present his case; (iv) the award deals with a difference not falling within the terms of the arbitration agreement, or it contains decisions on matters beyond the scope of the arbitration clause; (v) the composition of the arbitral authority was not in accordance with the agreement of the parties or in accordance with the law of the country where the arbitration took place; (vi) the award has not yet become binding on the parties or has been set aside or suspended by a competent authority of the country in which, or under the law of which, that award was made. The decision-making authority (court) may have regard to these grounds for refusing recognition and enforcement only if they were invoked by the party against whom the award is invoked. But the New York Convention (1958) contains two more reasons which the decision-making authority may take into account of its own motion (*ex officio*), namely (i) the subject matter of the difference is not capable of settlement by arbitration under the law of the country where recognition and enforcement is sought; (ii) the recognition or enforcement of the award would be contrary to the public policy of the country where recognition and enforcement is sought.

2.47. Consequently, the court of parties´ origin could, if petitioned to recognize and enforce an arbitral award issued in potentially *artificially*[56] internationalized proceedings, avail itself of at least two reasons justifying the refusal of recognition and enforcement of the award – lack of arbitrability and public policy exception. In that connection, the public policy exception includes fundamental values on the observance of which the state insists without any qualifications, such as violation of the impartiality of the arbitrator, violation of basic procedural principles, e.g. equality of the parties, etc.[57] The court of parties´ origin would therefore have at its disposal an instrument for protecting its fundamental values and preventing the parties from circumventing these values by *artificial internationalization*. This is why the author believes that there is no reason to limit the parties' choice in this regard. The reason is that a foreign arbitral award has no effects in the country of parties´ origin until it is recognized.

| | |

---

[56] This word could be considered inappropriate if we realize that the seat of arbitration is principally influenced by the expression of the parties' private-law autonomy.

[57] For more details, see NADĚŽDA ROZEHNALOVÁ, *supra* note 6, at 333

Summaries

FRA [*Le siège de l'arbitrage et les fonctions d'aide et de contrôle des tribunaux*]

Le siège - le lieu - de l'arbitrage est d'une importance pratique essentielle pour l'arbitrage et a un impact direct sur un grand nombre de questions: l'arbitrabilité, la détermination du droit applicable comme droit matériel mais surtout comme droit procédural, ainsi que les possibilités d'annulation de la sentence arbitrale ou de sa reconnaissance et de son exécution, ... De notre point de vue, le siège de l'arbitrage est un élément fondamental de l'arbitrage, car la dénationalisation de l'arbitrage est un mythe totalement coupé des réalités internationales. Le siège de l'arbitrage n'est pas nécessairement le lieu auquel sont effectués les actes de procédure. Il est nécessaire de distinguer le siège de l'arbitrage du lieu où la sentence arbitrale a été rendue et/ou signée. La logique veut que le lieu où la sentence arbitrale a été rendue détermine généralement s'il s'agit d'une sentence étrangère ou nationale. On peut exceptionnellement modifier le siège de l'arbitrage en cours de procédure; on ne peut le faire en revanche, une fois la sentence arbitrale rendue. L'arbitrage international est généralement soumis à un contrôle judiciaire à deux niveaux. Un premier contrôle est exercé par l'État du siège de l'arbitrage, un second contrôle par l'État dans lequel sont demandées par les parties la reconnaissance et l'exécution de la sentence arbitrale. Par conséquent, lorsque les parties internationalisent leur litige (des parties ayant leur siège dans un même État conviennent d'un siège / lieu d'arbitrage dans un autre État) et que la sentence arbitrale est rendue à l'étranger (c'est une sentence étrangère par rapport à l'État d'origine/de résidence des parties), cette sentence n'a des effets dans l'État du siège/de résidence des parties que si elle y est reconnue.

CZE [*Sídlo rozhodčího řízení a pomocná a kontrolní funkce soudů*]

Sídlo (místo) rozhodčího řízení má pro rozhodčí řízení zásadní praktický význam a přímo ovlivňuje řadu otázek: arbitrabilitu, určení rozhodného práva jak hmotného tak především procesního, jakož i možnosti zrušení rozhodčího nálezu nebo jeho uznání a výkon apod. Podle názoru autora je sídlo (místo) rozhodčího řízení hlavním faktorem ovlivňujícím rozhodčí řízení, neboť denacionalizace rozhodčího řízení je mýtem naprosto odtrženým od mezinárodní reality. Sídlo (místo) rozhodčího řízení nemusí být místem, v němž jsou činěny konkrétní procesní úkony. Od místa rozhodčího řízení je nutno odlišovat místo, kde byl rozhodčí nález vydán a/nebo podepsán. Logicky platí, že místo, kde byl rozhodčí nález vydán, obvykle určuje, zda jde o nález tuzemský nebo zahraniční. Sídlo (místo) rozhodčího řízení lze výjimečně změnit v průběhu rozhodčího řízení; toto však není možné po vydání rozhodčího nálezu. Mezinárodní rozhodčí řízení je obvykle podrobeno dvoustupňové soudní kontrole. První kontrolu vykonávají státy sídla (místa) rozhodčího řízení, druhou kontrolu vykonávají státy, v nichž strany požadují uznání a výkon. V důsledku toho platí, že pokud strany internacionalizují svůj spor (strany se sídlem ve stejném státě se dohodnou na sídle/místě rozhodčího řízení v jiném státě) a rozhodčí nález je vydán v zahraničí (jde o zahraniční rozhodčí nález ve vztahu ke státu původu/domicilu stran), má takový rozhodčí nález účinky ve státě sídla/domicilu stran pouze je-li v tomto státě uznán.

| | |

POL   [*Siedziba postępowania arbitrażowego oraz pomocnicza i kontrolna funkcja sądów*]

Siedziba (miejsce) postępowania arbitrażowego ma zasadnicze praktyczne znaczenie dla postępowania arbitrażowego i bezpośrednio wpływa na szereg kwestii: arbitralność, określenie prawa właściwego materialnego, a przede wszystkim procesowego, a także możliwość uchylenia orzeczenia arbitrażowego lub jego uznania i wykonania, itp. Zdaniem autora, siedziba (miejsce) postępowania arbitrażowego to główny czynnik wpływający na postępowanie arbitrażowe, bowiem denacjonalizacja postępowania arbitrażowego to mit całkowicie oderwany od międzynarodowej rzeczywistości. Siedziba (miejsce) postępowania arbitrażowego wpływa również na kompetencje sądów pełniących funkcję wspierającą i kontrolną w odniesieniu do postępowania arbitrażowego.

DEU   [*Der Sitz des Schiedsverfahrens und die Hilfs- und Kontrollfunktion der Gerichte*]

Der Sitz (Verfahrensort) des Schiedsverfahrens hat für das Verfahren ganz grundlegende praktische Bedeutung und wirkt sich unmittelbar auf eine Reihe von Fragen aus: Arbitrabilität, Bestimmung des (materiellen wie v. a. prozessualen) Schiedsrechts, aber auch die Möglichkeiten für eine Aufhebung des Schiedsspruchs oder umgekehrt seine Anerkennung und Vollstreckung usw. Nach Auffassung des Autors handelt es sich beim Sitz (Verfahrensort) des Schiedsverfahrens um den für das Schiedsverfahren bestimmenden Hauptfaktor, denn die Denationalisierung des Schiedsverfahrens ist für ihn ein völlig von der internationalen Realität losgelöster Mythos. Der Sitz (Verfahrensort) des Schiedsverfahrens hat außerdem Auswirkungen auf die Zuständigkeit der Gerichte, die eine unterstützende und prüfende Funktion gegenüber dem Schiedsverfahren ausüben.

RUS [*Местонахождение арбитража, а также вспомогательные и контрольные функции судов*]

Для арбитража местонахождение (место) арбитража имеет важное практическое значение и напрямую затрагивает ряд вопросов: арбитрабельность, определение применимого права как вещного, так, прежде всего, процессуального, а также возможность отмены или признания и приведения в исполнение арбитражного решения и т. д. По мнению автора, местонахождение (место) арбитража является основным фактором, влияющим на арбитраж, т. к. денационализация арбитража представляет собой миф, который полностью оторван от международной действительности. Местонахождение (место) арбитража также влияет на юрисдикцию судов, осуществляющих вспомогательные и контрольные функции в отношении арбитража.

ESP [*Sede del arbitraje y la función auxiliar y de control de los tribunales*]

La sede (lugar) del arbitraje tiene una importancia práctica crucial y afecta directamente a toda una serie de preguntas: arbitrabilidad, determinación de la ley aplicable sustantiva y, especialmente, procesal, así como la opción de cancelación del laudo arbitral o su reconocimiento y ejecución, etc. En opinión del autor, la sede (lugar) del arbitraje es el principal factor que afecta al procedimiento de arbitraje, puesto que la denacionalización del arbitraje es un mito totalmente desviado de la realidad internacional. La sede (lugar) del arbitraje también afecta a la jurisdicción de los tribunales que ejercen las funciones de apoyo y control en relación con el arbitraje.

| | |

Filip Čeladník

The English Approach to Challenges at the Seat: Should Courts Stay Away from the Challenges on the Merits as the Model Law Provides?

Key words:
arbitration | appeal on a point of law | substantive appeal | appeal on a question of law | Section 69 of Arbitration Act 1996

Abstract | *In England, a party to an arbitral proceeding may appeal to an English court on a question of law arising out of an award made in the proceeding. The right to appeal is subject to many restrictions; still it is one of the most important features differentiating English arbitrations from arbitrations conducted in other countries under the regime of the UNCITRAL Model Law. For decades, academics and professionals have been arguing whether the appeal on a question of law should be abolished, bringing various pro and con reasons. This article gives an account of why the substantive appeal should not be abolished by discussing the most important assertions. It starts by emphasising the theoretical aspects of arbitration, such as finality, speed, cost savings and party autonomy, and concluding by considering the practical impact upon England and English law and comparison with countries that adopted the UNCITRAL Model Law.*

Mgr. Filip Čeladník LL.M. is a member of the Law Society of England and Wales and the Czech Bar Association, practising both in London and Prague. He graduated from King's College London with Merits and is completing an LLM at Melbourne Law School in Australia and a PhD at Charles University in Prague. Further information is available at www.celadnik.com. e-mail: filip@celadnik.com

| | |

I. Introduction

3.01. Appeal of an arbitral award on a point of law exteriorizes the tension between legality and finality and divides the world of arbitration. In England, a guarantee of the correct application of the law vested in Section 69 of Arbitration Act 1996 (the Act) stands above the immanent features of arbitration and provides parties to a dispute with a right to challenge an arbitration award in the English courts on the merits of English law. By contrast, legal systems following the UNCITRAL Model Law on International Commercial Arbitration (the Model Law) differ considerably in the idea of court intervention through the challenges on the merits. The English approach clearly exceeds the grounds for appealing entirely on the basis of public policy or defects in jurisdiction, arbitrability or the arbitration process. However, arguments against appeal on a point of law prioritising the peculiar elements of arbitration are purely theoretical in nature and have but little practical significance when compared with the aspect of correct application of the law. Consequently, one of the most significant current discussions in the legal field of arbitration is whether the English approach to challenges at the seat on the merits should be abandoned. In order to answer the question, this paper first lays out a brief overview of the recent history and the current legal background of the English substantive appeal. What follows then presents arguments that the substantive appeal should prevail and also attempts to rebut the principal contentions to the contrary.

II. Historical Background

3.02. Since the infancy of English Arbitration Law more than sixty years ago, the English judges have had wider latitude to intervene in arbitration awards than their civil law colleagues. However, due to the excessive abuse of challenges on the 'error on the face of the award'[1] provided by the Arbitration Act 1950, and the modern theory of speed and finality in arbitration process, the need for a reduced role of the courts arose. Even though the 'special case' procedure under the regime of the Arbitration Act 1950 was abolished by the contiguous Arbitration Act 1979, the idea of limited court supervision over the application of law persisted. Lord Diplock in the *Nema* case acknowledged that the parties should be left to accept, for better or for worse, the decision of the tribunal that had

---

[1] Taner Dedezade, *Are you in? Or are you out? An Analysis of Section 69 of the English Arbitration Act 1996: Appeal on a Question of Law*, (2) INTERNATIONAL ARBITRATION LAW REVIEW 56–67 (2006).

chosen to decide the matter in the first instance.[2] In the *Antaios* case, the same judge emphasised the intentions of the Parliament to promote speedy finality in arbitral awards rather than insistence upon 'meticulous semantic and syntactical analysis of the words in which the business men happen to have chosen to express the bargain made between them, the meaning of which is technically, though hardly commonsensically, classified in English jurisprudence as a pure question of law'.[3] As a result of these and several other adverse decisions, along with adoption of the 1985 Model Law which contained no such thing as the substantive appeal, the Department Advisory Committee led by Lord Saville produced the 1995 Arbitration Bill which later formed the basis of the Act.

III. Basis of the Substantive Appeal

3.03.   Despite the Act being considerably influenced by the international concepts of arbitration and by the Model Law, the right to challenge arbitration awards on the merits has prevailed. It appears clear that the foreign impact affected principally the overall policy and the new foundations seeing that the English judicial authorities, being the source of law, were replaced by the statue. Nonetheless, the voices of the abolitionists were not unheeded completely and severe restrictions were established to limit the challenges on the merits to exceptional circumstances only. This aim was intended to be reached by imposing a number of procedural requirements stipulated in Subsection 3 which must be satisfied to obtain permission to appeal.

3.04.   These conditions comprise a requirement that the point of law must substantially affect the right of one or more parties. The court must also be satisfied that the point of law was the one which the tribunal was asked to determine.[4] Of particular importance is the prerequisite that the courts shall refuse any attempts to disguise questions of facts as one of law, a criterion recently ruled on in *Surefire Systems Ltd* v *Guardian*.[5] In this regard, even a total absence of any basis for a finding of fact cannot give rise to a question of law for the purpose of Section 69.[6] Moreover, Judge Hegarty QC in *Mary Harvey* v *Motor Insurer's Bureau* clarified that a question of law may arise if the conclusion

---

[2]   *Pioneer Shipping Ltd* v *BTP Tioxide Ltd* [1982] AC 724.

[3]   *Antaios Cia Naviera SA* v *Salen Rederierna AB* [1983] 3 All ER 777, CA, [1984] 3 All ER 299, HL.

[4]   *Mary Harvey* v *Motor Insurer's Bureau* QBD (Merc) (Manchester), Claim No: 0MA40077, 21 December 2011.

[5]   *Surefire Systems Ltd* v *Guardian ECL Ltd* [2005] BLR 534.

[6]   *Georgas SA* v *Trammo Gas Limited (The Baleares)* [1993] 1 Ll Rep 215 at 228.

reached on the basis of the facts found by the tribunal was 'outside the range which could properly have been arrived at by a tribunal which had properly directed itself as to the applicable law'.[7] To put it simply, the error must arise from a misapprehension or misapplication of the law.

3.05. In addition, leave to appeal shall be given only to an obviously wrongful application of the law or when the point of law is one of general public importance and open to serious doubt. Finally, there is a new requirement that the courts consider whether their intervention is appropriate and justified, in regards to the issues raised on the application for permission to appeal and the circumstances in which the arbitration was set up.[8] Application of this provision in practise can be illustrated in the case *Keydon Estates Ltd* v *Western Power Distribution (South Wales) Ltd* where it was said that the parties' choice of an experienced arbitrator in the relevant field of landlord and tenant was a strong reason why the parties should be left with the arbitrator's decision.[9] However, regardless of these restrictions and limitations, the consequence of which is that only a small portion of applications for appeal are granted permission, the right of appeal on a point of law remains subject to criticism.

IV. Should the Right of Appeal on a Point of Law Be Abolished?

3.06. A considerable amount of literature has been published addressing this question. In essence, the arguments for abolishing the substantive appeal can be divided into two categories. First, it is argued that parties to arbitration agreements opted for arbitration to resolve their disputes for the reasons that arbitral awards offer a final end to the dispute and that the arbitration process provides advantages of speed, cost savings and party autonomy.[10] Second, it is argued that the Model Law does not contain such a provision, and that many other countries have adopted the Model Law.[11] The remainder of this paper deals with each of these arguments separately.

---

[7] *Mary Harvey* v *Motor Insurers' Bureau* (QBD (Merc) (Manchester), Claim No: 0MA40077, 21 December 2011).

[8] *India Steamship Co Ltd* v *Arab Potash Co Ltd*, unreported, Colman J, 12 December 1997.

[9] *Keydon Estates Ltd* v *Western Power Distribution (South Wales) Ltd* [2004] EWHC 996 (Ch.).

[10] William H. Knull; Noah D. Rubins, *Betting the Farm on International Arbitration: Is it Time to Offer and Appeal Option?*, 11(4) THE AMERICAN REVIEW OF INTERNATIONAL ARBITRATION 531–576 (2000).

[11] Taner Dedezade, *supra* note 1, at 56–67.

IV.1. Does Appeal on a Point of Law Contradict the Basic Features of Arbitration?

3.07. The protagonists of the approach adopted by the Model Law criticise that the possibility to appeal on a point of law contradicts the very basic elements of arbitration. It is firmly established in the doctrine of arbitration that many parties select arbitration to resolve their disputes because an arbitration award offers an effective and early end to the dispute. Indeed, finality, in the sense of the lack of appeal on merits, along with corresponding advantages of speed and cost savings, are being pinpointed to be the salient features of arbitration. The right to challenge an award on a point of law is then logically accounted to be incompatible with the nature and function of arbitration as it frustrates the result of the process reached on the basis of these elements. This view is supported by Hew Dundas who writes that Section 69 of the Act conflicts with the principle of party autonomy and increases the costs of commerce.[12] Whilst such proclamations, finding their bases purely in theoretical dimension, appear to aim for the stars, the practical reality of arbitration is very much chained to the ground.

IV.1.1. Finality

3.08. To begin with the most highlighted aspect of an arbitration award, finality, means getting involved in the 'never ending war between two irreconcilable principles, the high principle which demands justice through the heavens fall, and the low principle, which demands that there should be end to litigation'.[13] Whilst the idea of arbitration to resolve a dispute early is undoubtedly attractive to parties, finality can be a universally positive quality in dispute resolution only if arbitrators never made mistake.[14] However, arbitrators make mistakes, as Stephen Younger also maintain.[15] When the mistakes fall within a foreseeable range, parties are generally willing to accept the risk but gross misinterpretation of a contract or granting hugely disproportionate remedies is less acceptable.

---

[12] Hew R. Dundas, *Appeals on question of law: section 69 revitalised*, 69 ARBITRATION 172 (2004).

[13] FRANCIS RUSSELL; ANTHONY WALTON; MARY VITORIA, RUSSELL ON THE LAW OF ARBITRATION. Indiana University (1982).

[14] William H. Knull, Noah D. Rubins, *supra* note 10, at 531–576.

[15] Stephen P. Younger, *Agreements to Expand the Scope of Judicial Review of Arbitration Awards*, 63(1) ALBANY LAW REVIEW 241 (1999).

3.09. This proposition has been addressed by several studies each of them reaching the same conclusion. Professors Hayford and Peeples as early as 1995 identified that litigation experts in commercial disputes are aware that the absence of a mechanism to correct erroneous results is unacceptable in high stakes disputes. This opinion was shortly after supported by research undertaken by Bühring-Uhle which revealed that the business community is awaking from the gold-leaf notion about arbitration as one-third of the fifty American and European lawyers and arbitration commentators had believed that the absence of appeal is not an advantage to arbitration. In the same year, Thomas Klitgaard expressed that speed and finality are virtues, but only if you win. They are not virtues if a fundamental mistake has been made. Parties not electing for correcting mechanism are assuming the risk of an unpredictable or fundamental erroneous decisions. There are similarities between the attitudes expressed by Bühring-Uhle and those described by Ringer & Seidel according to which business people and their lawyers view arbitration awards as essentially unreviewable and so they became wary of arbitration.[16] Subsequently, a study by Lipsky & Seeber was released ascertaining that 54.3 per cent of the 606 lawyers from Americas largest corporations would refuse to choose arbitration for the reason that the arbitration awards are difficult to challenge.[17] It can be expected that even more studies have been carried out in recent years. The conclusion to be reached from the aforesaid analysis is that the aspect of finality deteriorates the apprehension of arbitration in the commercial world.

3.10. It is certainly true that a final resolution would have been an advantage but only if arbitrators had never been wrong. This is unquestionably a state of affairs which cannot be achieved for the following reasons. In the first place, the international cases are increasingly complex and often involve legal principles and rules from multiple jurisdictions. The probability of being at fault then logically constantly rises. Persuasively in this respect Knull & Rubins argues that possible consumers will rather choose not to arbitrate because their transactions are too large to bear the risk of error without adequate means to correct those mistakes.[18] In the second place, arbitrators, unlike judges, are sometimes not even legally educated. Especially recently arbitration has gone through an extraordinary expansion and been attracting the

---

[16] James M. Ringer, Martin L. Seidel, *Judicial Review Clauses in Transnational Arbitration Agreements*, INSIDE LITIGATION 6 (1998).

[17] William H. Knull, Noah D. Rubins, *supra* note 10, at 531–576.

[18] Ibid.

attention of many speculators from diversified backgrounds and different professional origins. It can hardly be expected that laypersons possess a profound legal knowledge which is necessary for resolution of a complex legal issue involving foreign elements. On a side note, it can be expected that especially lay arbitrators will be more leashed and conduct the proceeding more punctually knowing their actions are easily challengeable.[19]

3.11. In the third place, scholars often accent the feature of the possibility to appoint an arbitrator of specialized knowledge or experience in a particular sphere who will be capable of resolving technical disputes. However, whilst such an arbitrator may understand the technical aspects of a dispute they will probably not be for this very reason a distinguished legal scholar. Finch went even further in asserting that it is in fact contrary to the principle of arbitration to refer questions for decision to those who are not experts in the field.[20] For example, the panels of arbitrators in maritime disputes often consisted of experts in the maritime sphere because of their commercial and technical skills and knowledge. However, tricky questions of law, often arising after the arbitration process has been commenced, are therefore not determined by legal experts. Consequently, the fact that the legal questions are determined by non-legal experts undermines one of the core purposes of arbitration to resolve the dispute by experts. Lord Justice Scrutton as early as in 1922 observed that where there are persons untrained in law, and especially when persons untrained in law are allowed to be addressed on legal points, there is a probability of them going wrong.

3.12. The disillusion with arbitration due to the absence of protection against arbitral error is coupled with an exposure to the unpredictability of arbitral awards. The business community is becoming aware that without the right to challenge awards, the results of arbitration are highly unpredictable as the losing party may end up with results which could have been hardly predictable. Hochman makes a valid point when saying that due to a lack of confidence that the decision will be objective, predictable and correct many contracting parties rather avoid arbitration.[21] Again, the unpredictability of an arbitration award may be acceptable in cases of minor importance but when the amount in

---

[19] John Lurie, *Court Intervention in Arbitration: Support or Interference?*, 76 ARB.: THE INT'L J. OF ARB., MEDIATION & DISP. MGMT. 447 (2010).

[20] Robert Finch, *London: Still the cornerstone of international commerical arbitration and commercial law?* ARBITRATION (2004).

[21] Stephen A. Hochman, *Judicial Review to Correct Arbitral Error: An Option to Consider*, 13 OHIO S. J. ON DISP. RESOL. 104 (1997).

dispute is large, the absence of any option to challenge the award on merits is from the commercial point of view intolerable. In particular, international arbitrations involve exceptionally large sums of money, and the disputed amounts in international arbitrations have been increasing substantially in recent years.[22] Therefore, there is undoubtedly some truth in the Ringer's idea that finality is a liability, rather than an asset, which discourages contracting parties from selecting arbitration.[23] Consequently, finality is the secondary advantage in highly-valued international arbitrations, if it can be considered as an advantage at all, as it causes an undesirable risk.

3.13. Another significant flaw in the theory of finality, again arising from ignoring the arbitration practise, is that the absence of a meaningful review court proceeding does little to guarantee that the arbitral award brings the dispute to the end. Prior to enforcing the arbitral awards, the courts at the place of enforcement must recognize the arbitration award. Article V of the New York Convention on the Recognition and Enforcement of Foreign Arbitral Awards provides bases upon which the awards can be challenged, in consequence of which, as Knull & Rubins speculates, the delivering an arbitration award may be the first step in a chain of court litigations in a variety of different jurisdictions where the losing party has substantial assets.[24] Moreover, a party grieving about the result often challenges the award in national courts by disguising the request for judicial review of the merits and by appealing on the basis of deficiencies in the arbitration procedure. Most often, the party complains about not being able to present its case, or that the award deals with a dispute not contemplated by or not falling within the terms of the submission to arbitration or contains decision on matters beyond the scope of the submission to arbitration. In other words, the losing party often exploits most of the offered ground for appealing just to increase its chances to revert an erroneous arbitral award. The winning party is thus dragged into court proceedings anyway.

IV.1.2. Speed

3.14. The prime theoretical purpose of arbitration was to offer a quicker means of a dispute resolution by avoiding national court proceedings. Logically, the scheme of resolving disputes in private proceedings held in front of arbitration tribunals with a possibility of onward challenges

---

[22] Julian D M Lew, *Interest on Money Awards in International Arbitration, in* MAKING COMMERCIAL LAW 543 (Ross Cranston ed., 1997).

[23] James M. Ringer, Martin L. Seidel, *supra* note 16, at 6.

[24] William H. Knull; Noah D. Rubins, *supra* note 10, at 531–576.

in national courts on merits incites the losing party to drag out the dispute and defer final resolution. However, the notion of speed fails to take into account that parties to a dispute certainly did not intend to speed up the proceeding at the expense of rightness and justness. It is submitted that the only legitimate arbitration award may be the one which was rendered upon fair application of the law. In this respect, the aspect of speed must be perceived as a pursuit of avoiding lengthy proceedings while sustaining legitimate resolution of the dispute. There can be no doubt, as Hill points out, that the object of arbitration is to obtain a fair resolution of disputes by an impartial tribunal without unnecessary delay.[25] Indeed, speed cannot be regarded as an utmost goal of arbitration. Rather, there must be an appropriate balance between resolving a dispute without an unnecessary waste of time on one side, which can be achieved by submitting the dispute to an arbitration tribunal instead to a national court, and achieving a rightful and legally correct arbitral award on the other side, which can be ensured by pertinent judicial scrutiny. In this regard, whilst the feasibility to appeal certainly does not prevent arbitrators from unintentionally misapplying law, they can be sure that if they deliberately wrongfully apply the law, the court will in all likelihood strikes down the award. Accordingly, the theoretical concept of speed ignores the actual demand of parties to reach a fair arbitration award.

IV.1.3. Money Savings

3.15. The objective of speed is closely related to the notion of a 'cheap' arbitration process. However, the aim of money savings is absolutely negligible in resolution of large-stakes disputes arising out of international transactions when compared with the possibility of significant errors in law. In fact, the question is whether we can even talk about cost savings as it has been generally accepted that international arbitration is a more expensive process than court proceedings. The costs of international arbitration are often incurred by substantial fees charged by the arbitrators and the arbitration institutions, travel costs of parties and arbitrators, logical expenses of renting hearing rooms, lodging, etc.[26] The higher cost is nevertheless justified by more effective enforcement of the arbitration awards. From

---

[25] Jonathan Hill, *Onward Appeals under the Arbitration Act 1996*, 31(2) CIVIL JUSTICE QUARTERLY (2012).

[26] GARY B. BORN, INTERNATIONAL COMMERCIAL ARBITRATION, Kluwer Law International (2009).

the appellate point of view, it would be highly contra-productive to pursue more expensive proceedings and not be protected against errors in the application of the law by the arbitrators.

IV.1.4. Party Autonomy

3.16. Finally, arbitration scholars often complain that appeal on a point of law contradicts the principle of party autonomy to craft the procedure according to needs, and hampers the use of intended specialized arbitration rules.[27] Criticism of it would have cogency only if the parties had not been able to avoid the possible appeal on points of law, and therefore had to face an inevitable and obligatory consecutive proceeding in front of a court. However, Section 69(1) expressly vests parties to an arbitration agreement with a right to exclude the appeal on a point of law by way of an agreement. Parties are free to decide whether they can afford the risk of an erroneous arbitration award and so not elect the option of judicial review or, if it be to the contrary, they have the full autonomy to keep the appellate procedure. In this regard, it must be clear from the agreement to arbitrate that the parties intended to exclude the appellate procedure. A mere provision that a tribunal should have absolute discretion and that any decision should be final and binding does not exclude the right to appeal to a court.[28] Alternatively, it has already been firmly established that where parties agree to arbitration, for example under the ICC Rules, Article 24 which provides that 'by submitting the dispute to arbitration, the parties shall be deemed to have undertaken to have waived their right to any form of appeal insofar as such waiver can validly be made'[29], or under the LCIA Rules they have 'otherwise agreed' for the purpose of Section 69.[30] In fact, this provision itself maximizes the principle of party autonomy by enabling parties to either accept the appeal or to exclude it.

3.17. More importantly, the antagonists fail to appreciate that even if there are many parties who may voluntarily opt for arbitration there are also those who are forced to arbitrate for clear absence of any acceptable alternative to domestic court proceedings. As Hunter strongly argues, the preference for arbitration has nothing to do with the advantages of speed and money savings but having no alternative than to litigate in

---

[27] Elizabeth Gloster, *Attempts to Thwart the Arbitration Process: Current Examples of How the Court Makes Parties Stick to Their Agreement to Arbitrate*, 73 ARBITRATION 407 (2007).

[28] *Al Hadha Trading Co v Tradigrain SA and ORS* [2002] 2 Lloyd's Rep. 512.

[29] *Sanghi Polyesters Ltd v The International Investor (KCFC)* [2000] 1 Lloyd's Rep. 480.

[30] Ibid.

the other party's home country.[31] These courts are often perceived to be unreliable for potential local bias, unknown system of law, unpredictable juries and the government interventions.[32] Parties having no choice but to arbitrate surely embrace safeguards against errors of arbitrators. This, combined with the above discussed fear of wrongful and unpredictable arbitration awards, has led parties in some cases to contracts not governed by English law to expressly agree to heighten the judicial review of arbitration awards.[33] Such agreements often provide an option of judicial scrutiny over errors of law, errors of fact, or both.[34] Clearly, a provision that parties may challenge the rendered arbitral awards on the merits goes too far beyond the theoretical standard terms in arbitration agreements.

3.18.   This gives rise to an interesting question of to what extent parties are entitled to exercise their autonomy. More precisely, whether tailoring the arbitral procedure to the extent that parties to arbitration agreements expand the scope of judicial review of arbitral awards *ultra vires*, beyond the competence of courts as provided by the legislation or the case law, is an exercise of the party autonomy. Originally, party autonomy meant entitlement to agree upon the substantive laws and procedures applicable to arbitrations; typically to dispense with technical formalities and procedures of national court proceedings, existence and scope of discovery or disclosure, the modes for presentation of fact and expert evidence, and other factors.[35] However, it is a diametrically different matter whether parties are allowed to extend the competence of courts to perform a revision of the merits even though this option is not anchored in the relevant legal source. In the United States, where most of these expanded arbitration agreements are being concluded, the courts are divided. The first group upholds the parties' intentions as much as possible.[36] The second group maintains that parties are not allowed to determine how courts shall

---

[31]   Martin Hunter, *International Commercial Dispute Resolution: The Challenge of the Twenty-first Century,* 16(4) ARBITRATION INTERNATIONAL 382 (2000).

[32]   See eg F. Celadnik, *Is China Friendly in Enforcing Arbitration Awards? A Critical Analysis of Certain Aspects of Enforcement of Arbitral Awards in China in View of International Standards,* available at: http://ssrn.com/abstract=2161351 or http://dx.doi.org/10.2139/ssrn.2161351 (accessed on 1 May 2013).

[33]   Leanne Montgomery, *Expanded Judicial Review of Commercial Arbitration Awards: Bargaining for the Best of Both Worlds,*68 UNIVERSITY OF CINCINNATI LAW REVIEW 530 (2000).

[34]   *LaPine Tech. Corp.* v *Kyocera Corporation,* 130 F.3d 884 (9th Cir. l997).

[35]   GARY B. BORN, *supra* note 26.

[36]   *Gateway Techs, Inc.* v *MCI Telecomm. Corp,* 64 F.3d 993 (5th Cir. 1995).

review arbitration awards.[37] For the time being, it remains ambiguous in the United States whether parties' autonomy enables tailoring the review of arbitration on the merits.

3.19. Europe in regards to this question is a fairly predictable forum. In France, The Paris Court of Appeal in *Societe Binate Maghreb v Soc Screg Routes*[38] held that the New York Convention and the Civil Code absolutely limit the parties' freedom to contract in the area of judicial review. In Switzerland, Article 192 of Swiss Law on Private International Law suggests that the expansion of such a ground for appeal would be impossible.[39] One may indeed argue that parties to an agreement still have a choice to create the arbitration appeal procedure. However, such an *ad hoc* appeal would still be conducted in the regime of arbitration wherewith all the above mentioned disadvantages are connected. Finally, in England, Section 69 of the Act grants parties with an absolute freedom to decide whether courts shall have competence over challenges on the merits. This implies that parties to a contract governed by English law have even wider autonomy as they may decide whether they want to retain the substantive appeal or to exclude it, a choice which is not given to the discretion of the parties in the Model Law countries.

IV.2. Should Section 69 of the Act Be Standardized in Accordance with the Model Law?

3.20. When the UNCITRAL produced the Model Law, many hoped and called for England to adopt it entirely. One of the main reasons was to abolish the right of appeal on a question of law deeply grounded in English law but being far from the grounds for appeal provided by the Model Law. Even though the Department Advisory Committee, whose principal object was to consider whether or not England should adopt the Model Law, decided not to embrace the approach of the Model Law and it proposed considerable restrictions of the substantive appeal. The result was a narrowed appeal on merits influenced by the general modern trend of limited courts' intervention. Lord Saville therein observed that appeal from an arbitration award has been very severally limited.

3.21. Regardless of Section 69 being framed in a way that entirely respects parties' decision to derogate the courts' power and reduce the extent of intervention in the arbitral process, it has retained the historical oddity of English law allowing appeal on a point of law. One has to appreciate

---

[37] 254 F.3 934 (10th Cir. 2001).

[38] *Societe Binate Maghreb v Soc Screg Routes* (1990 Rev. Arb. 863).

[39] William H. Knull, Noah D. Rubins, *supra* note 10, at 531-576.

that because of this particular aspect, English law has gained its world respect and demand. Veeder in this regard enthusiastically argue that due to this English oddity English Commercial law has been the most useful and popular system of law in the world trade.[40] The genuine significance of this oddity nonetheless rests in a much deeper layer than just allowing parties to challenge arbitral awards on their merits.

3.22.   In particular, this feature enabled intertwining private commercial arbitration and the English courts. Whilst the critics remonstrate that it is this specific attribute which enabled the courts' intervention into the party autonomy, its true outcomes lie in something else. The appeal on a point of law created, in the words of Veeder, the 'symbiotic link between commercial arbitration, the development of English law and the English Commercial Court'.[41] So, even if we accept that the courts tamper with the purely consensual system of arbitration which is, as discussed above, an entirely academic outlook ignoring the legal practise, the result was a development of English law. Accurately Veeder quotes Lord Diplock according to whom there must always be some kind of appeal on the merits available to the parties in English law, if this be a term of their agreement, which gives a degree of certainty to English law ultimately substantially contributing to the development of English Commercial Law.

3.23.   A positive correlation can be found between the aforesaid suspicious attitude of practitioners towards the lack of the substantial appeal and the English judges. The latter has always insisted on correct application of English law and progression of the commercial law system, irrespective of the consequences. Lord Justice Dyson illustratively emphasised that the more generous is the scope for challenging decisions by appeal or review, the greater is the challenge of eliminating error, but often at a heavy price. It is supported that there has been a long tradition in England that judges have always been prioritizing justice. Lord Artkin in *Ras Behari Lal v The King-Emperor* confirmed that 'finality is a good thing but justice is better'.[42] However, it bears emphasis, since the point is often misunderstood when speaking about justice in the context of arbitration. The antagonists fail to understand that the doctrine of appeal on a point of law does not pursue justice as some kind of a theoretical fabrication of the legal philosophy but an objective of the arbitration procedure itself. Evans J. in this regard

---

[40]   V. Veeder in COMMERCIAL LAW PERSPECTIVES AND PRACTICE, London: Butterworths (Mistelis ed, 2006).

[41]   Ibid.

[42]   *Ras Behari Lal* v *The King-Emperor* (1993) 50 T.L.R. 1.

argued in *Indian Oil Corp Ltd v Coastal (Bermuda) Ltd* that justice and fairness are not abstract concepts and the notion of justice has to be applied in the context of two contentious parties resolving their dispute by means of arbitration.[43]

3.24. This is to be interpreted that the courts should always bear in mind that two parties have agreed that their dispute should be resolved by an arbitral tribunal when considering whether granting permission to appeal will lead to justice. There is no doubt that this attitude is grounded in the courts' discretion to refrain from intervening even if other criteria for granting the permission to appeal are satisfied. Moreover, it must be stressed that injustice can suffer not only the losing party, as a result of the misapplication of the law, but also the wining party because of the permission to appeal. It was said in *HOK Sport Ltd v Aintree Racecourse Ltd* that the responding party may show that it would suffer substantial injustice if the leave to appeal is granted.[44] Therefore, the courts shall always consider justice in the circumstances of each individual case and in relation to each of the competing parties.

3.25. Turning back to the interaction of the commercial arbitration and the English courts, it is submitted that the common law system is unique and superior in the international commercial context because of the practise of the English judges. It has always been a contribution of the English judges that by creating new rules for situations not previously addressed, and so tailoring the law to practical needs, English law has become so flexible. The English judges have been capable to constantly shape the law to business needs because an immense number of cases had been brought every year before them. This subsequently resulted in English law being the leading legal system in the world.

3.26. Deep permeation of English Commercial Law and arbitration has therefore enabled a constant development of the law by direct involvement of the English judges in modern cases throughout the appellate procedure. However, Esposito warns that due to the general trend in international dispute resolution to arbitrate rather than litigate, the flow of cases to be decided by the English courts has diminished considerably.[45] Accordingly, Dundas doubts how English law will ever continue to develop considering how few arbitrated

---

[43] *Indian Oil Corp Ltd v Coastal (Bermuda) Ltd* ([1990] 2 Lloyd's Rep. 407 at 414, col. 2, at 415, col. 1.

[44] *HOK Sport Ltd v Aintree Racecourse Ltd* [2003] BLR 155.

[45] P. Esposito, *The development of commercial law through case law: Is section 69 of the English Arbitration Act 1996 stifling progress?* 74(4) ARBITRATION (2008).

disputes reach the courts.[46] This issue is particularly problematic in ship chartering and reinsurance where standard form contracts and clauses are widely used but the arbitral awards are kept in private. Existing problematic provisions are therefore not corrected and continue to cause complicated situations which may eventually lead to substantial repetitive financial losses. If the limitations on appeal on a point of law are not unstrung, it will constrain English law in the long terms. In a couple of decades, English law will no longer be attractive because of the absence of modern decisions. Consequently, it will contribute to English law if the English judges are enabled to deal with commercial cases referred to them by way of the substantive appeal. This will facilitate the constant evolution of English law and its worldwide reputation.

3.27. Moreover, English law has always encouraged predictability through the system of precedents. As discussed above, the lack of predictability dissuades businesses from arbitration. There can be no doubt that arbitrariness is not the same as arbitration. Prospects of the correct and predictable application of the law and the protective instrument of English eminent judges are qualities which parties seek when opting for English law. It is exactly the certainty and comprehensiveness of English law that Lord Diplock calls the courts to preserve in the light of changes in technology and commercial practice adopted in various trades. The courts certainly do not intend to be detrimental to the parties. The courts aspire for the arbitral awards to be the results of fair, impartial, predictable and integral arbitral processes. These are characteristics which undoubtedly also the parties expect the processes should have. Therefore, an option of the courts' supervisory role over the application of the law obviously increases the predictability of the arbitral awards. This will eventually increase certainty about the arbitration process and so maintain the popularity of arbitration in the world commercial community.

3.28. It is no wonder that many voices call for an increase in the number of appeals from arbitrations to the courts. Finch must surely be correct that the idea of limited intervention not only induces the aforesaid inhibited development of English law but also ignores the growing complexity of disputes.[47] Arbitration is undoubtedly no longer a simple process. Especially maritime arbitrations often involve highly complex contracts, difficult technical issues of marine engineering, work practises, various international codes and legal questions. Whilst there

---

[46] H. R. Dundas, *supra* note 12, at 172.

[47] Robert Finch, *supra* note 20.

are certainly arbitrators who are experts of commercial and technical aspects of maritime arbitration, few of them, as discussed above, are also experienced lawyers. Therefore, it is desirable to get the exceptionally knowledgeable and skilful English judges involved so they may, as the final instance, resolve legal issues upon consideration of the facts as founded in the arbitration proceedings.

3.29. Furthermore, the current practise indicates that the decline in the number of appeals deteriorates the position of London as a centre for international dispute resolution. 'London arbitration' is a term which represents a various range of disputes. It includes not only domestic and international arbitrations governed by English law but also specialized maritime and newly setup aviation and aerospace arbitrations. London is also often the seat of foreign arbitrations, involving either foreign law or foreign parties opting for English law to govern their arbitration process. Parties often opt for London arbitration because the substantive appeal is not offered by any other legal system. Therefore, imposing restrictions on the challenges on the merits could be a major factor, if not the only one, causing the drain of arbitrations seated in London.

3.30. This finding has important implications for revision of Section 69 in order to offer an appropriate appellate procedure. Finch in this regard suggests setting out more rigid conditions for appeal in order to evade the subjective approach of individual judges.[48] However, it seems that Finch fails to fully acknowledge that introducing new conditions will barely encourage parties to choose the London arbitration. It is submitted that the procedural requirements of Subsection 3 imposed upon the applicants are already stringent, extensive and profound. Because of that, only a small number of appeals are substantively judicially reviewed. The *ratio legis* of these limitations seems to be to allow revision only of the most serious and questionable awards. Therefore, judges have become even more reluctant to intervene than they were under the regime of the 1979 Act. These outcomes are rather disappointing.

3.31. A more reasonable approach to tackle the issue of London arbitration regress could be adopting exactly the opposite course of action. It is submitted that the limitations for appeal on a point of law should be eradicated. Parties to the arbitration agreements should be given a wider contractual freedom to determine whether, to what extend and under what conditions the arbitral awards shall be subject to the courts' supervision. The arbitration is, after all, a creation of a contract. In

[48] Ibid.

default of an agreement either excluding the court's authority or setting up the boundaries of revision, the merits of the arbitral award would be subject to a full judicial review. One important remark emerging from this proposal is that the courts would relinquish the authority to consider whether the permission to appeal is to be granted. Consequently, considerably more cases would pass through the first strainer and be heard and adjudicated. Surely this proposal is an intriguing one and will undoubtedly lead to an even more ferocious debate. Nevertheless, one has to remember that the parties would still have the capacity to dispose of the option to challenge the arbitral award if they intended to do so. By no stretch of the imagination can it be concluded that this proposed alternative would offer the parties the utmost autonomy to tailor the arbitration in accordance with their absolute needs. Such an option is not even remotely anchored in the Model Law.

V. Conclusion

3.32. A number of caveats need to be noted regarding the present study. One of the limitations lies in leaving aside the question of whether the substantive appeal tampers with the principal of confidentiality. This paper was also unable to analyse the ICSID international arbitration institution that provides perhaps the best known rules for recourse against arbitral awards. The study also did not evaluate the use of a clause module in an arbitration agreement that would establish standards of an arbitral appellate review. These areas have thrown up many questions in need of further investigation.

3.33. Returning to the questions posed throughout this study, it is now possible to conclude that the right of appeal on a point of law should not be abolished. This paper has primarily given an account of why the substantive appeal does not contradict the salient features of arbitration. In brevity, multiple analyses revealed that the business community had conceived the lack of appeal to be a disadvantage rather an advantage as the absence of a correction mechanism is unacceptable in high stakes disputes. It was also shown that finality would have been a positive feature should the arbitrators never been wrong, which is not achievable due to the increase of complexity in international arbitrations and the lack of legal education of arbitrators. Moreover, finality is also unacceptable because it exposes the parties to the unpredictable results, and it does not guarantee the end of contentions in legal practise. This essay then argued that speed of an arbitration proceeding must be perceived as a feature which enables reaching a fair resolution without undue delay, and that the corresponding feature of money savings is negligible in high stakes disputes. An important finding was also that parties to a dispute governed by English law have even a wider party autonomy than what parties have under the Model Law as they have the right to decide whether the courts shall have competence over the challenges on the merits or not.

3.34.   The second major outcome of this paper was that Section 69 should not be standardized in accordance with the Model Law. It was identified that the substantive appeal enabled English law to gain its world respect and demand by intertwining private commercial arbitration and the English courts. The English judges who always prioritized justice then provided for constant development of the law by tailoring the law to practical needs through the cases brought before them. The obvious conclusion to emerge from this study is that imposing procedural requirements on permission to appeal causes considerable obstructions for the cases to be adjudicated, in consequence of which English law will suffer in the long term perspective by a lack of rules addressing modern legal issues. The resulting need of unstringing the appellate procedure that has been identified at the end of this paper thus serves as a base for future studies. These should be done to investigate whether the unrestricted right of appeal on a point of law would ultimately support the continuous development of English law and elevate the iconic London arbitration.

3.35.   A number of caveats need to be noted regarding the present study. One of the limitations lies in leaving aside the question of whether the substantive appeal tampers with the principal of confidentiality. This paper was also unable to analyse the ICSID international arbitration institution that provides perhaps the best known rules for recourse against arbitral awards. The study also did not evaluate the use of a clause module in an arbitration agreement that would establish standards of an arbitral appellate review. These areas have thrown up many questions in need of further investigation.

|||

Summaries

FRA [*L'approche anglaise du recours devant des tribunaux dans des procédures d'arbitrage : les tribunaux ne devraient-ils pas abandonner l'examen de fond, conformément à la loi type de la CNUDCI sur l'arbitrage commercial ?*]
En Angleterre, tout participant à une procédure d'arbitrage peut faire appel devant un tribunal anglais relativement à des questions juridiques liées à la décision d'arbitrage. Bien que ce droit de recours soit substantiellement limité, il constitue une des caractéristiques principales différenciant une procédure d'arbitrage en Angleterre d'une procédure d'arbitrage dans un autre pays soumis au régime de la loi type de la CNUDCI. Cela fait déjà des décennies que les juristes en décousent pour savoir si ce type de recours relatif à des questions juridiques liées à la décision d'arbitrage devrait être supprimé ou non, avançant des arguments contradictoires. Le présent article se penche sur les principales argumentations et justifie pourquoi l'examen de fond des décisions d'arbitrage ne devrait pas être supprimé. L'accent est d'abord mis sur les aspects théoriques de la procédure d'arbitrage, comme par exemple sa finitude, sa rapidité, les économies de frais réalisées et la liberté contractuelle des parties. Les répercussions concrètes sur le droit anglais et sur l'Angleterre, ainsi qu'une comparaison avec les pays ayant adopté la loi type de la CNUDCI, font ensuite l'objet d'une analyse.

CZE [*Anglický přístup k odvoláním v místě sudiště: Neměly by se soudy vzdát v souladu se Vzorovým zákonem meritoriního přezkumu?*]
Účastník rozhodčího řízení v Anglii se může odvolat k anglickému soudu ohledně právní otázky související s rozhodčím nálezem. Přestože je toto odvolací právo podstatně omezeno, stále se jedná o jeden z nejvýznamnějších rysů, které rozlišuje rozhodčí řízení konané v Anglii od rozhodčích řízeních v jiných státech vedených v režimu Vzorového zákona UNCITRAL. Akademici a praktici se již desetiletí přou o to, zda by mělo být odvolání ohledně právní otázky zrušeno, argumentujíce přitom rozličnými důvody pro a proti. Tento článek se zabývá nejdůležitějšími tvrzeními a odůvodňuje, proč by neměl být hmotněprávní přezkum rozhodčích nálezů zrušen. Takto nejdříve zdůrazňuje teoretické aspekty rozhodčího řízení, jako například konečnost, rychlost, úsporu nákladů a smluvní volnost stran a závěrem se zabývá praktickými dopady na Anglii a anglické právo, jakož i komparací se zeměmi, které přijali Vzorový zákon UNCITRAL.

| | |

POL *[Angielskie podejście od odwołań w miejscu siedziby sądu: czy zgodnie z ustawą modelową sądy nie powinny odstąpić od badania spraw ad meritum?]*

Angielskie prawo postępowania arbitrażowego przewiduje unikalną możliwość wniesienia odwołania do sądu w odniesieniu do zapytania prawnego. Prawo to było przedmiotem szerokiej dyskusji i krytyki. Niniejszy artykuł przedstawia powody, dla których badanie materialno-prawne orzeczenia arbitrażowego powinno zostać zachowane oraz omawia najistotniejsze argumenty przeciwne.

DEU *[Der englische Ansatz zur Berufung am Schiedsort: Sollten die Gerichte nicht im Einklang mit dem Mustergesetz auf die meritorische Prüfung verzichten?]*

Das englische Schiedsverfahrensrecht eröffnet die in dieser Form einzigartige Möglichkeit, hinsichtlich unklarer rechtlicher Fragen die Gerichte anzurufen. Dieses Recht ist Gegenstand breiter Diskussionen und Kritik gewesen. Der vorliegende Beitrag präsentiert Gründe dafür, warum die materiellrechtliche Prüfung von Schiedssprüchen aufrecht erhalten werden sollte, diskutiert aber zugleich auch die wichtigsten Gegenargumente.

RUS *[Английский подход к обжалованиям по месту судебного процесса: Не следовало бы судам в соответствии с Типовым законом отказаться от территориального пересмотра?]*

Английское законодательство арбитража предлагает уникальную возможность обратиться в суд по правовым вопросам. Это право было предметом широкого обсуждения и критики. В данной статье представлены доводы в пользу сохранения пересмотра арбитражного решения с учетом материального права, а также в ней обсуждаются самые противоречивые аргументы.

ESP *[El enfoque inglés ante las apelaciones en la sede de jurisdicción: ¿No deberían los tribunales renunciar a la revisión meritoria según la ley modelo?]*

La ley inglesa del arbitraje ofrece una oportunidad única para apelar al tribunal sobre cuestiones jurídicas. Es una ley que ha sido objeto de amplia discusión y crítica. El artículo explica la razón por qué debe conservarse una revisión sustantiva del laudo arbitral, a la vez que analiza los argumentos contradictorios más significativos.

| | |

Michael Dunmore

Enforcement of Arbitral Awards: The Role of Courts at the Seat

Key words:
award | challenge | comity | domestic public policy | double exequatur | enforcement | European Convention | forum | Geneva Convention | international public policy | issue estoppel | judicial review | jurisdiction | local standard annulment | Model Law | national courts | New York Convention | Panama Convention | public policy | res judicata | seat | Set aside | supervisory court | territoriality | transnational legal autonomy

Abstract | When the New York Convention was drafted, one of its fundamental aims was to provide for a uniform system of enforcement of arbitral awards. One noteworthy feature of the New York Convention is that it has done away with the double exequatur requirement that was an element of the Geneva Convention for the Execution of Foreign Arbitral Awards 1927. However when an award is enforced, both the courts at the seat and those at the place of enforcement still have distinct roles to play. When an award is challenged, the proper forum to do so is at the court at the seat. These decisions should be given comity by foreign courts. However, this does not always hold true, largely due to subtle differences in laws in various jurisdictions, namely what is considered against public policy. This article will look at whether there is a diminished importance of courts at the seat of an arbitration and the role of courts at the seat in the enforcement of awards.

Michael Dunmore is an associate in the Dispute Resolution group at Baker & McKenzie (Gaikokuho Joint Enterprise) in Tokyo. His practice focuses on international arbitration. He completed his LL.M. in International Commercial Arbitration Law at Stockholm University, as well as his LL.B. at the University of Sydney; Master of Criminology at the University of Sydney and B.A.(H) at the University of Windsor. Mr. Dunmore is a dual qualified solicitor admitted to practice in England and Wales and

| | |

*   The author would like to thank Suganthy David and Oliver Cojo for their very helpful comments on draft versions of this article and editorial assistance.

I. Introduction

4.01. One of the most fundamental aspects of the New York Convention[1] is that a court at the seat does not need to confirm an award in order for it to be enforceable in a subsequent jurisdiction unless there is an application to set aside an award[2] or the review of an award is required. When an application to set aside an award is rejected, that decision is in theory considered res judicata, and in effect is a confirmation of the validity of that award. The court at the seat has primary supervisory jurisdiction of an award and the enforcement court is considered the secondary jurisdiction.[3] In the majority of cases comity is afforded to the decisions of the courts at the seat, as this is the proper forum to determine applications to set aside awards and hence their review.

in New South Wales, Australia. He has worked at numerous arbitration centres across Asia and in the international arbitration practice group of an international law firm in London. He has published various articles on international commercial arbitration. e-mail: michael.dunmore@bakermckenzie.com

4.02. There are, however, instances where proceedings are taken to resist the enforcement of arbitral awards despite similar or precursor proceedings have already been taken at the seat. In the majority of these instances, comity is afforded to the decision of the initial setting aside proceeding at the seat. However there exist a small number of cases where decisions made at the seat are not afforded comity in a subsequent jurisdiction where enforcement is sought. This largely occurs due to unique laws of the jurisdiction of the seat or some unsavoury conduct. The examination of the topic will be done though lenses of various theoretic approaches in an attempt to highlight the proper role of the courts.

I.1. Historical Underpinnings

4.03. For the purpose of this article, the historical scope of the enforcement of awards should be limited to the Geneva Convention. For enforcement proceedings to take place under the Geneva Convention,

---

[1]   *Convention on the Recognition and Enforcement of Foreign Arbitral Awards* ('*New York Convention*') (1958).

[2]   SIMON GREENBERG; CHRISTOPHER KEE; J ROMESH WEERAMANTRY, INTERNATIONAL COMMERCIAL ARBITRATION: AN ASIA PACIFIC PERSPECTIVE, Cambridge; New York: Cambridge University Press 415 (2010). (The authors state that majority of jurisdictions in the Asia-Pacific region and the Model Law uses the term 'setting aside'. The term 'vacated' is used in the United States.)

[3]   Albert Jan van den Berg, '*Should the Setting Aside of the Arbitral Award Be Abolished?*' 29(2) ICSID REVIEW 1 at 286 (2014).

awards were subject to the 'double exequatur' requirement. This required a leave of enforcement from the courts of both the country of origin and the country where enforcement was sought. This requirement does not exist under the New York Convention.[4] Rather, through the approach of the New York Convention, courts of the seat have the exclusive role to determine the setting aside of awards, which professor van den Berg highlights as the underlying premise of Article V(1)(e) of the New York Convention.[5]

I.2. Basic Requirements of the NYC for an Award to Be Valid

4.04. In order for an award to be valid, there must be a valid arbitration clause or agreement that refers a dispute to arbitration. For an arbitration clause to be valid, it must be in writing and signed by the parties or contained in an exchange of letters between the parties.[6] For an award to be enforceable under the New York Convention, it must meet a number of basic criteria. This includes an award being final, a submission of the original copy of the award (or certified copy thereof) as well as the original agreement in writing that has led to the dispute (or certified thereof). Lastly, a translation of that award if needed.

4.05. An award may be set aside or enforcement resisted under the New York Convention if one of the enumerated grounds for setting aside included in Article V are successfully argued.

I.3. Procedures under Other Conventions for Validity

4.06. In addition to the New York Convention, there are various other conventions through which recognition and enforcement of awards may be sought. All of them have similar mechanisms and wording to the New York Convention. The Inter-American Convention (Panama Convention) contains the same setting aside proceedings as the New York Convention. The European Convention[7] and Panama Convention[8]

---

[4]   ALBERT JAN VAN DEN BERG, THE NEW YORK ARBITRATION CONVENTION OF 1958, Deventer; Boston: Kluwer Law and Taxation 7 (1981).

[5]   Albert Jan van den Berg, *supra* note 3, at 266.

[6]   Article II(2).

[7]   European Convention on International Commercial Arbitration ('European Convention'), 484 U.N.T.S. 349 (1961), Article IX.

[8]   Inter-American Convention on International Commercial Arbitration ('Panama Convention') (1975), Article 5.

contain comparable provisions that follow the same grounds as Article V of the New York Convention.

4.07. Born highlights that in terms of recognition and enforcement of awards the European Convention goes further than the New York Convention. The European Convention specifically highlights that the setting aside of an award is not a basis to subsequently deny recognition if that decision falls under a list of enumerated grounds, including substantive review of the merits of the tribunal's decision or local public policy, as a jurisdiction may rightfully adopt whatever public policy it chooses.[9] This is highlighted in Article IX, which specifically addresses the issue of public policy and clarifies what the outcome should be in case a jurisdiction is party to both the New York Convention and the European Convention. Furthermore, under the European Convention just as the New York Convention, the setting aside of an award is not a basis for non-recognition if the decision rests on these grounds.[10]

4.08. National law provides a further basis for the enforcement of awards that have been set aside in a foreign country. In this respect, although a jurisdiction may be a signatory to the New York Convention or other Conventions, every jurisdiction is at liberty to enact their own laws that may contain unique characteristics that will allow for recognition of awards where other jurisdictions will not. Although, most national arbitration legislation reflects the grounds of the New York Convention, the grounds for setting aside awards are defined in national legislation and there is no requirement under the New York Convention to limit the grounds. As a result, the grounds under various national laws regarding setting aside can be considerably expansive or narrow.[11] For example, France has been considered a jurisdiction that has taken a liberal approach to the enforcement of awards, following a transnational approach to enforcement. This liberal approach is attributed to the fact that setting aside grounds under French law are narrower than under the Model Law.[12]

4.09. This article will further discuss these cases, in particular when an award is set aside at the seat and subsequently enforced. Those cases where this has occurred are noteworthy as this highlights instances where courts have not afforded comity to judgments of foreign courts at the

---

[9] GARY B. BORN, INTERNATIONAL COMMERCIAL ARBITRATION LAW, Alphen aan den Rijn: Wolters Kluwer Law & Business 3623 (2nd ed., 2014).

[10] Ibid, at 3623.

[11] Ibid, at 3164.

[12] Ibid, at 3361.

seat. In other words, these judgments highlight an approach that affords a diminished importance to the courts at the seat.

I.4. Theoretical Underpinnings

4.10. There are three main theories that underpin this topic. This article does not intend to go into great depth into these theories but rather introduce them so the readers may link and distinguish particular theories to decisions and practices.

4.11. The first theory is territoriality. The crux of this theory is that an award gains its power from the laws of where the arbitration is seated. Hence, the courts at where enforcement is sought are secondary to those at the seat.[13] Second is transnational legal autonomy (also termed Delocalized approach). Following this theory, an award gains its power from various sources, such as the agreement of the parties, the seat and the arbitrators. Under this second approach, no source alone is crucial to an award, as rather the award is delocalized.[14] Third is the local standards annulments approach, which is slightly different from the previous two theories. The local standard annulments approach focuses on the setting aside of awards based on local standards rather than international standards.[15] These grounds for setting aside may not be the same in other jurisdictions and, as a result, may not be given comity by foreign courts. This third approach is clearly present throughout this article and is used to attempt to demonstrate how comity is not given in some instances.

II. The Need for Confirmation

4.12. An argument can be made that there is a general degree of uniformity in international commercial arbitration. This uniformity exists not only in legislation, but in how awards are dealt with by various courts in states that are signatories to the New York Convention. However, there

---

[13] For a more in depth analysis of territoriality *See* Albert Jan van den Berg, *Enforcement of Annulled Awards*, 9(2) ICC INTERNATIONAL COURT OF ARBITRATION BULLETIN 15, 15 (1998); Nadia Darwazeh, *Article V (1) (e)*, *in* RECOGNITION AND ENFORCEMENT OF FOREIGN ARBITRAL AWARDS: A GLOBAL COMMENTARY ON THE NEW YORK CONVENTION 331–332 (Kronk et al. eds., 2010) at 301–344, 325.

[14] For a more in depth analysis of transnational legal autonomy *See* Emmanuel Gaillard, Legal Theory of International Arbitration, Leiden; Boston, Mass.: Martinus Nijhoff Publishers 33 (2010); Nadia Darwazeh, *supra* note 13, at 331.

[15] For more in depth analysis of Local Standards Annulment *See* Jan Paulsson, *Enforcing Arbitral Awards Notwithstanding a Local Standard Annulment (LSA)*, 9(1) ICC INTERNATIONAL COURT OF ARBITRATION BULLETIN 14 (1998).

exists no requirement under the New York Convention that only those grounds enumerated in Article V be followed. In some jurisdictions there are additional grounds to those included in the New York Convention, as will be examined later in this article; some courts substantively review awards while others do not. The New York Convention includes the grounds for exception to recognition and enforcement, but does not provide for the grounds to review or set-aside awards. These are left to domestic legislation.[16] Furthermore, concepts such as public policy are not interpreted equally internationally. As a result, a challenge to set aside an award in one jurisdiction may not be given comity in a subsequent jurisdiction where enforcement is sought. With this divergence of approaches by national courts one questions the need for confirmation.

4.13.   Professor van den Berg has investigated whether the setting aside of awards should be abolished. He goes through a very thorough and thoughtful analysis. One issue at the crux of his inquiry is the potential for double control through having judicial review at the seat and at the enforcement court. This is an issue that will be examined significantly throughout this article.

III. Proper Forum for a Challenge

4.14.   Once an award is rendered, if a losing party wishes to challenge that award, the proper forum to do so is at the seat, regardless if that award is going to be enforced at the seat or elsewhere. After the challenge at the seat (whether successful or not), there still exists the potential for enforcement proceedings and hence further efforts to resist enforcement may be necessary. However, efforts to resist enforcement should be distinguished from an application to set aside an award. The New York Convention limits the forum to make an application to set aside an award to the place where the award was made or under the law of which the award was made.[17] Nonetheless, considerable applications are made to refuse enforcement after an unsuccessful attempt to set aside awards is made, especially on public policy grounds.[18]

---

[16]   Linda Silberman; Maxi Scherer, *Forum Shopping and the Approach to Set-Asides, in* FORUM SHOPPING IN THE INTERNATIONAL COMMERCIAL ARBITRATION CONTEXT 314 (Ferrari ed., 2013).

[17]   GARY B. BORN, *supra* note 9, at 3163.

[18]   *A. v R.* [2009] 3 HKLRD 389 at 24.

III.1. Importance of the Seat

4.15.   The courts at the seat are the proper and only forum for the setting aside of an award. In *A. v R.*,[19] a Respondent whom did not make an application to set aside an award at the seat in Denmark made an application to resist enforcement of an award in Hong Kong. The Hong Kong Court stated that the Respondent should have first brought that challenge in the Denmark courts. As it had not done so, the Respondent waived its right to object at the enforcement stage. In a case decided by the Swedish Supreme Court.[20] The arbitration took place in Russia, under the law of which service can validly be effected if sent to the last known address of a party. A Respondent successfully resisted enforcement of an award despite the Respondent not first attempting to have the award set aside at the seat. In this instance the Respondent was successful in setting aside the award as it demonstrated it did not have knowledge that the arbitration had taken place until enforcement was attempted. In this case, the Respondent showed that it had moved before the arbitration took place thus all documents relating to the arbitration were not sent to its new address and as a result it did not have knowledge of the arbitration until enforcement. As a result, the Respondent successfully challenged the award under Article V(1)(b) of the New York Convention.

4.16.   A final case on the proper forum to challenge an award being the seat is *Karaha Bodas*, where an Indonesian court purported to set aside an award that was not seated in Indonesia. This decision was not given comity, as Indonesia was clearly not the appropriate forum to bring a setting aside proceeding.[21] These cases highlight that, absent exceptional circumstances, the proper forum to challenge an award is at the court of the seat of the arbitration.

III.2. Court Review of Awards

4.17.   In addition to being the proper forum for setting aside proceedings, courts at the seat are the proper and only forum for the review of awards. There exists a great deal of variation as to the degree of review conducted by courts, which may or may not be afforded comity by enforcement courts. In this regard, Born highlights a number of

---

[19]   Ibid.

[20]   Judgment of the Supreme Court of Sweden, 16 April 2010, Case No. Ö 13-09/NJA 2010 s. 219.

[21]   *Karaha Bodas Company, LLC v Perusahaan Pertambangan Minyak Dan Gas Bumi Negara and PT Pln (Perseo)*, 364 F3d 274, 308–10 (5th Cir 2004).

jurisdictions that can be considered to take an expansive review. These include United States, England, Singapore, China and Brazil.[22] The outcome of an expansive review process may run the risk of being denied enforcement, as it can be said that there is a trend away from the judicial review of the merits of awards. Nonetheless, this remains to be the proper function of the courts at the seat, where this function exists. Born highlights that a number of jurisdictions set aside international awards on the basis of judicial review of the merits of the awards.[23] However, this is clearly an unfavourable approach to take, as any review conducted should only be at the seat, as the court at the seat is the supervisory court of arbitrations in that jurisdiction.

4.18. One example of a jurisdiction that uses a more expansive review is Egypt, which added to the grounds for setting aside, the ground that 'the arbitral award failed to apply the law agreed upon by the parties to govern the subject matter in dispute.'[24] A further example illustrating this point is in *Yusuf Ahmed Alganim*, where the US Court of appeals highlighted that the grounds for setting aside awards are included in Chapter 1 of the Federal Arbitration Act, while enforcement is governed by Article V of the NYC.[25] The standard of review of awards in the US is 'manifest disregard of law'. In other words, where an arbitrator ignores the controlling rules of the law.[26] A final example of an approach taken on review is the English Arbitration Act, which includes a unique characteristic in terms of court review. This is found under Section 69 which provides that judicial review may be excluded if parties choose institutional rules or enter an agreement that excludes court review.[27]

4.19. The Review of awards is a particularly interesting feature of the role of the seat, as there is a degree of differentiation of scope of review between courts in various jurisdictions to no review by the courts in others. Despite the variation of the scope of review, it is the proper function of the courts at the seat and not of the enforcement court. To

---

[22] GARY B. BORN, *supra* note 9, at 3339.

[23] Ibid, at 3340 *Citing* England, Ireland, China, Singapore, Abu Dhabi, Libya, Saudi Arabia, Argentina, Egypt and the United States.

[24] Albert Jan van den Berg, *supra* note 3, at 6 *Citing* Law No 27 Concerning Arbitration in Civil and Commercial Matters 1994 (Egypt) art 52(1)(d).

[25] *Yusuf Ahmed Alghanim & Sons WLL v Toys 'R' Us, Inc; Tru (HK) Ltd*, 126 F3d 15 (2nd Cir 1997).

[26] GARY B. BORN, *supra* note 9, at 3329.

[27] Ibid, at 3372 *Citing Lesotho Highlands Dev Auth.* v *Impregilo SpA* [2006] 1 A.C. 221 (House of Lords); *Al Hadha Trading Co.* v *Tradigrain SA* [2002] 2 Lloyd's Rep. 512 (QB) (English High Ct.).

allow for review of an award at the enforcement court that is not the seat would undermine the New York Convention.[28]

IV. The Effect of Decisions of the Courts at the Seat on Enforcement Courts

4.20. One of the intents of the drafters of the New York Convention was to provide a simplified procedure for enforcement of awards, which as noted above removed the double exequatur requirement that existed in the Geneva Convention. However the seamless enforcement of awards determined in one jurisdiction and enforced in another still relies on the harmonization of domestic laws in each jurisdiction.

IV.1. The Effects of *Res Judicata* and Comity

4.21. Comity is a fundamental feature in the harmonization of international arbitration legislation and a function sought after by the New York Convention. Not all jurisdictions will give comity and res judicata effect to decisions by courts at the seat. This largely results from how jurisdictions perceive awards, whether this is from the territorial or delocalized approach or stepping back a jurisdiction can be perceived as following a local standards approach. Despite the differences in theoretical approaches, comity is alive in the arena of international arbitration. In *Minmetals Germany*,[29] it was stated that only in exceptional circumstances a court should not afford comity to the courts at the seat. This is, the correct approach to take.

4.22. *Minmetals Germany* has been adopted in a recent Australian case. In the case *Gujarat NRE Coke Ltd*,[30] an unsuccessful application was made in London, the seat of the arbitration, to set aside an award. At the enforcement stage, an Australian court held that issue estoppel precluded the Respondent to use the same arguments to resist enforcement that it had used in the setting aside proceeding. In doing so the court stated,

4.23. even if there were no issue estoppel or res judicata, it would generally be inappropriate for this court, being the enforcement court of a Convention country, to reach a

---

[28] *Gulf Petro Trading Company Inc (US), Petrec International Inc (USA) and others* v *Nigerian National Petroleum Corporation (Nigeria), Bola Ajibola (Nigeria) Jackson Gaiusobaseki and others*, F3d 2008 WL 62546 (5th Cir 2008).

[29] *GmBH* v *Ferco Steel Ltd* [1999] 1 All ER (Comm) 315 at 331.

[30] *Gujarat NRE Coke Limited* v *Coeclerici Asia (Pte) Ltd* [2013] FCAFC 109, 30 September 2013, unreported.

different conclusion on the same question as that reached by the court of the seat of the arbitration. It would be a rare case where such an outcome would be considered appropriate.[31]

4.24. On appeal, the judgment was correctly reaffirmed. In doing so, the Court of Appeal focused on the narrow scope where an enforcing court may diverge from those at the seat, such as the supervising court being corrupt.[32] When rending its judgment, the court did not weigh into issue estoppel but highlighted that an enforcement court should afford comity to the courts of other convention signatories.

4.25. Despite these recent developments highlighting comity being afforded to the judgments of courts at the seat, one must take note that a court is not bound to afford comity to a court's decision from another signatory to the New York Convention. Article V(1)(e) provides that enforcement may be refused, not must. This is additionally the case in regards to Article 2(a) of the Geneva Convention.

4.26. Within the same sphere as comity is issue estoppel, which was analysed in *Yukos*. Here, the Court of Appeal held that issue estoppel did not preclude the English court from revisiting the determination of a Dutch court's decision.[33] Although this is not the court of the seat, which is the topic of this article, this issue should be briefly touched on, as issue estoppel is closely aligned to comity. More recently, the Queen's Bench commercial court in *Diag Human SE*[34] held for the first time in England that issue estoppel prevented the enforcement of an arbitral award. This judgment has been criticized by Professor van den Berg, namely because issue estoppel is not a ground to deny enforcement under the New York Convention.[35] Nonetheless, this is an interesting case from the perspective of when an enforcing court will afford comity to judgments of foreign courts. The court itself stated,

4.27. a decision in a foreign court refusing to enforce an award under the New York Convention on public policy grounds of that state will not ordinarily give rise to an issue estoppel in England.[36]

---

[31] Albert Monichino; Alex Fawke, *Enforcement of Foreign Arbitral Awards, Issue Estoppel and Comity: Developments in Australia*, (1) ASIAN DISPUTE REVIEW 10 (2014) *Citing Gujarat NRE Coke Ltd* v *Coeclerici Asia (Pte) Ltd* [2013] FCAFC 109, 30 September 2013, unreported.

[32] Ibid, at 11.

[33] *Yukos Capital SARL* v *OJSC Rosneft Oil Co* [2012] EWCA Civ 855.

[34] *Diag Human SE* v *Czech Republic* [2014] EWHC 1639 (Comm).

[35] Sebastian Perry and Richard Wolley, 'Issue estoppel halts enforcement in London', available at:http://globalarbitrationreview.com/news/article/32682/issue-estoppel-halts-enforcement-bid-london/ (accessed on 29 May 2014).

[36] *Diag Human SE* v *Czech Republic* [2014] EWHC 1639 (Comm) at para 58.

4.28. In an earlier case, the English High Court dealt with issue estoppel in *Chantiers de l'Atlantique SA v Gaztransport & Technigaz SAS*[37] in regards to making an argument to set aside the award. Before the proceedings in England, a French court dismissed the argument that the award was valid in setting aside proceedings. After making the same arguments before the High Court, the English court held in obiter that the argument was barred on the basis of issue estoppel.[38] Likewise the Paris Court of Appeal dismissed a claim to set aside an award where the arguments made to deny enforcement were previously made in an unsuccessful attempt to set aside the award.[39] From these cases it is clear that both estoppel and comity have a considerable effect in regards to enforcement proceedings when an award is first challenged.

IV.2. Diverging Courts of Enforcement

4.29. Born highlights that nothing under the New York Convention prevents an award that was set aside at the seat to be subsequently enforced.[40] There have been a handful of cases that support this. This article will not delve into the facts behind all of these cases, but rather highlight a number of instances where decisions made by courts at the seat are not followed by foreign courts. These cases are of importance as they demonstrate the lack of harmonization and comity given to courts at the seat.

4.30. *Hilmarton*[41] and *PT Putrabeli*[42] were the first cases were this occurred. These cases were decided in France where courts take a delocalized approach to arbitration. French courts disregard comity when an award is set-aside.[43] Taking this purely delocalized approach, from the perspective of the courts at the seat, there is nothing that can be done nor should there be to affect how an enforcing court will treat an award if taking a purely delocalized approach to enforcement.

---

[37] [2011] EWHC 3383 (Comm).

[38] Maxi Scherer, *Effects of Judgments Relating to International Arbitral Awards: Is the 'Judgment Route' the Wrong Road?*, 4(3) JOURNAL OF INTERNATIONAL DISPUTE SETTLEMENT 587, 592(2013) Citing *Chantiers de l'Atlantique SA v Gaztransport & Technigaz SAS* [2011] EWHC 3383 (Comm) at [313]–[318].

[39] *Maksimov v Novolipetsk Mettallurguicheski Kombinat* (NLMK) Paris, April 1 2014, No 12/15479.

[40] Gary B. Born, *supra* note 9, at 3623.

[41] *Hilmarton Ltd. v Omnium de Traitement et de Valorisation Cour de Cassation* [Cass. 1e civ.] Mar. 23, 1994, Revue de l'Arbitrage 327 (1994).

[42] *PT Putrabeli v Rena Holding, Ltd.*, Cour de Cassation [Cass. 1e civ.] June 29, 2007, Revue de l'Arbitrage 507 (2007); XXXII Yearbook Commercial Arbitration 299 (2007).

[43] Linda Silberman and Maxi Scherer, *supra* note 16, at 318.

4.31. A further look at the relationship of an enforcing court to the court at the seat is *Corporación Mexicana* [44] where an award that was set aside by Mexican courts was subsequently enforced in the Southern District of New York. The setting aside occurred based on the application of a retrospective law. This case stands for the proposition that if a court at the seat determines an issue in violation of international public policy it can be expected that the award will not be afforded comity elsewhere. Had a retrospective law not been applied to set aside an award, a diverging opinion by the enforcement would not have been rendered. Applying a retrospective law can be considered against international public policy and it can be considered that the Mexican court's decision should not be afforded comity as a result.

IV.3. Setting Aside on Public Policy Grounds

4.32. There are two types of public policy: international public policy and domestic public policy. A violation of international public policy includes various acts such as bribery, corruption or a violation of due process. International public policy has been defined generally as acts that 'violate the most basic notions of morality and justice.'[45] When this occurs, such as in *Corporación Mexicana*, where a retrospective law was applied to set aside an award, it can be understood an enforcement court will not afford comity to such a judgment. The second type of public policy is domestic public policy, which includes violations of unique laws to a jurisdiction. This for example can include Qatar law where an award must be rendered in the name of his Holiness the emir of Qatar in order to be enforceable.[46]

4.33. It is the proper role of the courts at the seat to set aside an award on both grounds and it is proper for a jurisdiction to determine what is against its own laws. However, when a unique public law is applied to set aside an award, the award may validly be enforced in a subsequent jurisdiction. One such instance of this occurring is *Maximov v. Novolipetsky Steel Mill*. In this case, the Moscow Arbitrazh Court at the seat set aside the award for being not arbitrable as corporate disputes in

---

[44] *Corporación Mexicana de Mantenimiento Integral, S. De R.L de C.V (COMMISA)* v *Pemex-Exploración y Producción, No. 10 Civ. 206 (AKH)*, 2013 WL 4517225, (S.D.N.Y. Aug. 27, 2013).

[45] *Parsons & Whittemore Overseas Co., Inc.* v *Société Générale de l'Industrie du Papier RAKTA and Bank of America* 508 F. 2d 969 (2nd Cir., 1974). at 251; *Hebei Import & Export Corp.* v *Polytek Engineering Co. Ltd.* (1999) 2 HKCFAR 111 at 118.

[46] *Abnaa El Khalaf Company et al.* v *Sayed Aga Jawwed Raza*, Court of Cassation of Qatar, 12 June 2012.

Russia are not arbitrable under Russian law. However after being set aside, the award was successfully enforced in France.[47] Despite the uniqueness of a law, as highlighted in *A. v. R.*, the proper forum for a challenge is the seat of the arbitration. This is regardless of the perceptions of the courts at the seat by a challenging party. Despite any unique public policy that will result in the award being set aside. If a party does not raise a challenge in the appropriate forum, it may be estopped from doing so at a later stage.[48] If there is a unique public policy, it can be expected that forum shopping will occur after a setting aside and the award will be enforced in a jurisdiction other than the seat.

4.34. Article V(1)(e) of the New York Convention poses an issue that various jurisdictions may have their own expanded definition and scope of what is against public policy, which is referred to above as domestic public policy. This creates the potential problem that an award will be set aside based on a unique law of a jurisdiction and then subsequently enforced in a second jurisdiction, which clearly goes against comity and downplays the importance of the courts at the seat. This local standards annulment approach can be seen as diminishing the role of the courts at the seat. However, it can be rightly stated that if the law at the seat differs from that of the enforcement courts, no issue preclusion should be given.[49]

V. The Way Forward for Courts at the Seat

4.35. In order to achieve uniformity and enforceability in arbitral awards, there is a need to have uniform enumerated grounds for the setting aside and review of awards by courts at the seat. This implementation would follow in line with the enumerated grounds for the recognition and enforcement of arbitral awards in the New York Convention. This exists to an extent with the Model Law. Of course, not every jurisdiction has adopted the Model Law and some have adopted variations of it. Following this, adopting the Model Law is a potential solution to uniformity and to having a court at the seat's decision being given comity by enforcing courts. A second approach to take for a court's decision to be given comity is to follow international practices in domestic legislation and international public policy. However in regards to the second suggestion, there will be countries that will play lip service to international practices but they won't adopt it, purely for sovereignty purposes. Nonetheless, adopting these two suggestions

---

[47] *Maximov* v *Novolipetsky Steel Mill*, Tribunal de Grande Instance de Paris, May 16, 2012.

[48] *A. v R.* [2009] 3 HKLRD 389 at para 65.

[49] Maxi Scherer, *supra* note 38, at 594.

would lead to greater comity being afforded between courts and consistency in decisions internationally.

V.1. Judicial Approaches to Confirmation

4.36.   At one end of the spectrum of this argument is that comity should be afforded to all judgments of the courts at the seat. At the other end, an enforcing court should conduct its own review of an award. Though the latter approach is clearly not preferable, as this is not the best court to determine issues of national legislation of another jurisdiction. From this, the most appropriate approach to take is that of a local standards annulment approach in both determining challenges to awards and in the recognition and enforcement of awards.

4.37.   Taking the approach from the decision in *Gujarat* mentioned above, a court should only diverge from the decision of the courts at the seat in limited circumstances. The most extreme of these situations where comity will not be afforded to a decision is where corruption has occurred.[50] This principle of course draws further discussion of *Dallah*,[51] where the enforcement proceedings in England occurred prior to the setting aside proceedings in France.[52] Van den Berg highlights that had this been the inverse, there is a strong presumption that courts in England may have afforded comity to decision of the French court.[53] As a result, the award which was not set aside in France on the same grounds could have been enforced based on comity had the French court decided the matter before enforcement was sought in England. This would have been the opposite conclusion that was in fact reached by the English courts.

4.38.   Following a local standard annulments approach, comity should not be given to an award that is against the laws of the jurisdiction of enforcement. This narrow scope to deny comity to a judgment is supported by both the 'may' included in the New York Convention and in case law. This applies to either a successful or unsuccessful challenge decision.[54]

---

[50]   Albert Monichino, Alex Fawke *Supra* note 31, at 13 *Citing Yukos Capital SARL v OJSC Rosneft Oil Co* [2012] EWCA Civ 855.

[51]   *Real Estate and Tourism Holding Co v The Ministry of Religious Affairs, Government of Pakistan* [2010] UKSC 46.

[52]   *Gouvernement du Pakistan—Ministère des affaires religieuses v Société Dallah Real Estate and Tourism Holding Company*, Cour d'appel de Paris, Case nos 09/28533, 09/28535 and 09/28541 (17 February 2011).

[53]   Albert Jan van den Berg, *supra* note 3, at 270.

[54]   *See supra* note 20: Judgment of the Supreme Court of Sweden, 16 April 2010, Case No. Ö 13-09/NJA 2010 s. 219 (where enforcement was successfully resisted); *See Supra* note 44:

VI. Conclusion

4.39. At the commencement of this article, it was highlighted that one of the intents of the New York Convention was to remove the double exequatur requirement for leave to be given. However one may argue that with challenge proceedings, court review in addition to separate enforcement proceedings, double exequatur in an alternative form exists. This can be exemplified by a statement made by the court in *Diag Human SE* while discussing various degrees of review of awards stated proceedings in multiple forums could result in, 'the potential danger of reintroducing the abandoned "double exequatur" (or at least a modified form of it) by the back door which should be avoided'.[55] This statement holds considerable weight. As mentioned earlier there is in fact a varying degree of review and decisions on setting aside applications, which potential could lead to an enforcing court second guessing the decision of the courts at the seat. Furthermore, there is some investigation of awards conducted at the enforcement stage by courts. Nonetheless, it is the court at the seat that is the proper forum to conduct such review as this is the court of 'primary jurisdiction' and is the supervisory court, whereas the court where enforcement is sought is the 'secondary jurisdiction'.[56]

4.40. In terms of distinguishing between courts of primary and secondary jurisdiction, taking a delocalized perspective, the place where enforcement is sought is the most important forum. From this approach, courts at the seat have a diminished importance in regards to enforcement. This can be reconciled by the fact that if an award is set aside on a ground at the seat that is unique to that particular jurisdiction, many courts will not afford comity to the judgment in case it violates the laws of the enforcing jurisdiction or international public policy. However these instances are rare. In most cases, the decisions by the courts at the seat are afforded comity by enforcing courts.

4.41. Despite the importance in terms of where enforcement is achieved, 'the courts in the country of origin should have the last word is the

---

Corporación Mexicana de Mantenimiento Integral, S. De R.L de C.V (COMMISA) v Pemex-Exploración y Producción, No. 10 Civ. 206 (AKH), 2013 WL 4517225, (S.D.N.Y. Aug. 27, 2013); *Bechtel v the Department of Civil Aviation of the Government of Dubai*, UAE Petition No 503/2003 (Judgment of May 15, 2004); *Ministry of Defense of the Republic of Egypt v Chromalloy Aeroservices Inc.*, Judgment of December 5, 1995, in XIX Y.B. Comm. Arb. 265 (Cairo Court of Appeal) (1999). (where enforcement was granted after an award was set aside at the seat).

[55] *Diag Human SE v Czech Republic* [2014] EWHC 1639 (Comm) at para 19.

[56] Albert Jan van den Berg, *supra* note 3, at 286.

| 83

prevailing view in practice'.[57] It is the proper role of the court at the seat to decide cases according to the law of the seat. It is also the proper role to do so within the norms of international public policy. When cases are decided outside of this scope, there is a risk that a judgment will not be afforded comity. When the judgment of a court at the seat is denied comity, a jurisdiction may run the risk of being perceived as an outlying or corrupt jurisdiction and disturbs certainty and consistency which undeniably no jurisdiction desires to have.

| | |

Summaries

FRA   [*L'exécution des sentences arbitrales : le rôle des tribunaux dans le pays où la sentence a été rendue*]

Un des principaux buts de la Convention de New York était d'établir un système unifié pour l'exécution des sentences arbitrales. Elle formulait le principe fondamental de l'élimination de la double exequatur – principe sur lequel reposait déjà la Convention de Genève (1927). En tous les cas, les tribunaux remplissent des fonctions différentes dans l'exécution des sentences arbitrales, qu'ils soient situés dans le pays où la sentence est rendue ou dans le pays où l'on cherche à faire exécuter la sentence. En règle générale, leurs décisions sont reconnues par les tribunaux d'un autre pays, mais ce n'est pas toujours le cas, pour des raisons tenant aux différences entre les droits des États. Les différences de conception de l'ordre public en donnent un exemple. Le présent article analyse le rôle des tribunaux dans le pays où la sentence est rendue en relation avec l'exécution de cette sentence, et se penche sur la question de l'éventuelle diminution des compétences des tribunaux dans le pays où la sentence est rendue.

CZE   [*Výkon rozhodčích nálezů: úloha soudů v místě sídla rozhodčího řízení*]

Jedním z hlavních cílů při koncipování Newyorské úmluvy bylo vytvořit jednotný systém pro výkon rozhodčích nálezů. Důležitým principem vyjádřeným v Newyorské úmluvě je odstranění duplicitního uznávání (exequatur) řízení jako požadavku, na němž spočívala ještě Ženevská úmluva (1927). Nicméně při výkonu rozhodčích nálezů plní soudy v místě sídla řízení a soudy v místě výkonu odlišné funkce. Obecně platí, že jejich rozhodnutí jsou akceptována soudy v jiném státě. Vždy tomu

57   Ibid, at 286.

tak ovšem není, a to z důvodů spočívajících v rozdílech mezi právními řády jednotlivých států. Příkladem jsou třeba odlišnosti v pojetí veřejného pořádku. Tento článek zkoumá úlohu soudů v místě sídla rozhodčího řízení ve vztahu k výkonu rozhodčích nálezu a zabývá se otázkou, zda dochází k případnému snižování významu pravomocí soudů v místě sídla řízení.

| | |

POL   *[**Wykonywanie orzeczeń arbitrażowych: rola sądów w miejscu siedziby postępowania arbitrażowego**]*
Orzekanie i działalność sądów w miejscu siedziby postępowania arbitrażowego jest istotna również w świetle wykonywania orzeczeń arbitrażowych. W miejscu siedziby postępowania arbitrażowego rola ta polega na postępowaniu odwoławczym przeciwko arbitrom i postępowaniu w sprawie rewizji lub uchylenia orzeczenia arbitrażowego. Generalnie orzeczenia sądów w miejscu siedziby postępowania są akceptowane przez sądy zagraniczne. Jednak nie dzieje się tak zawsze. Niniejszy artykuł bada rolę sądów w miejscu siedziby postępowania arbitrażowego w świetle wykonywania orzeczeń arbitrażowych oraz zajmuje się kwestią, czy dochodzi do ewentualnego obniżania znaczenia uprawnień tychże sądów w miejscu siedziby postępowania.

DEU   [**Die Vollstreckung von Schiedssprüchen: Aufgabe der Gerichte am Sitz des Schiedsverfahrens**]
Die Entscheidungs- und sonstige Praxis der Gerichte am Sitz eines Schiedsverfahrens ist unter anderem auch im Zusammenhang mit der Vollstreckung der Schiedssprüche von Bedeutung. Am Sitz des Schiedsverfahrens besteht diese Rolle darin, Verfahren wg. Einreden gegen einzelne Schiedsrichter sowie Verfahren wg. einer etwaigen Revision oder Aufhebung von Schiedssprüchen zu führen. Allgemein ist es eher so, dass die Entscheidungen von Gerichten am Schiedsort von den ausländischen Gerichten anerkannt werden - keinesfalls gilt dies aber ohne Ausnahme. Der vorliegende Beitrag untersucht die Aufgabe der Gerichte am Sitz des Schiedsverfahrens hinsichtlich der Vollstreckung von Schiedssprüchen und befasst sich mit der Frage, ob die Bedeutung der Zuständigkeit dieser Gerichte am Schiedsort womöglich geschmälert wird.

RUS   *[**Приведение в исполнение арбитражных решений: роль судов в месте нахождения арбитража**]*
Процесс принятия решения и деятельность судов в месте нахождения арбитража также важны в связи с приведением в

Czech (& Central European) Yearbook of Arbitration

исполнение арбитражных решений. В месте нахождения арбитража эта роль заключается в разбирательствах относительно возражений против арбитров, а также относительно любого пересмотра или отмены арбитражного решения. Считается, что решения судов в месте нахождения арбитража признаются иностранными судами. Это, однако, не всегда бывает так. В данной статье исследуется роль судов в месте нахождения арбитража в связи с приведением в исполнение арбитражных решений и рассматривается вопрос, уменьшается ли значимость компетенций таких судов в месте нахождения разбирательства.

ESP [*Ejecución de laudos arbitrales: el papel de los tribunales en el lugar de la sede del arbitraje*]
La toma de decisiones y la actividad de los tribunales en el lugar de la sede del arbitraje son significativas en relación con la ejecución del laudo arbitral. En el lugar de la sede del arbitraje esta función consiste en procedimientos sobre las objeciones de los árbitros, así como en procedimientos sobre una posible revisión o anulación del laudo arbitral. En general, las decisiones de los tribunales en el lugar de la sede del arbitraje son aceptadas más bien por tribunales extranjeros. Sin embargo, no siempre ocurre así. Este artículo examina el papel de los tribunales en el lugar de la sede del arbitraje en relación con la ejecución del laudo arbitral y aborda la cuestión de si se reduce la importancia de las competencias de los tribunales en el lugar de la sede del proceso.

| | |

Cristina Ioana Florescu

Excessive Judicialization– an Obstacle to Efficiency in Arbitration

Key words:
arbitration | efficiency | guerilla tactics | arbitrators | counsels | parties | time and cost control | guidelines | sanctions

Abstract | As in global trade and investments, international arbitration has increasingly become the main method of solving international disputes. This paper focuses on finding some solutions to achieving efficiency in arbitration, including the downsizing of rigidity and reducing the trend toward judicialization of arbitration and getting it back to its founding principles.

A number of proposals and sanctions are identified to allow a faster and more cost-effective procedures and to save efficiency in arbitration. Besides the users and their counsels, the arbitrators and arbitral institutions are actually involved, play a role and are called to contribute to positively, constructively, flexibly solve this issue. By avoiding common mistakes and open discussion among all the participants in the arbitration process, cost and time efficiency can be achieved.

Many new developments, ideas and trends are set to appear in the near future as the issue of efficiency is more broadly debated, analyzed by doctrine, tested by the practitioners and commented on at conferences.

Dr. Cristina Florescu is a lecturer at the Faculty of Law and Public Administration, Spiru Haret University, Bucharest, Romania and a lawyer with her own commercial and arbitration law practice (Bucharest Bar). She is also an arbitrator at the International Court of Commercial Arbitration (Chamber of Commerce and Industry of Romania), Bucharest and at the Vienna International Arbitration Centre (VIAC). She participates regularly as an international arbitrator (member of the jury) to W.C. Vis Moot, Vienna and FDI Moot. A PhD graduate, with a doctoral thesis in the field of commercial arbitration published in Romania, she is a participant and speaker at numerous scientific sessions and seminars/webinars, international and domestic conferences in arbitration and commercial law fields.

| | |

I. Introduction – Arbitration's Advantages in the Light of Efficiency

She has publications in several specialized journals, reviews, collections of essays, books, courses in commercial law, mediation and arbitration field.
e-mail:
crisflorescu@gmail.com

5.01. During the current uncertain and difficult economic times, many people have experienced severe financial difficulties and all arbitration users and providers have become more conscious that arbitration has become a lengthy and costly process. Arbitration used to be exercised as an alternative to court proceedings which were perceived as inadequate, inefficient, long, expensive, too formalistic, routine and rigid for the settlement of international businesses.

5.02. There are several advantages of arbitration compared to litigation. The parties' can avoid submitting to the jurisdiction of the national courts of one party. They can benefit from the efficiency of arbitration. They can tailor the proceedings according to the particular needs of their case. Finally, they can obtain a final, binding and globally enforceable award.[1] The neutrality, flexibility, and enforceability of arbitration, not to mention the parties' opportunity to choose the arbitrators deciding the dispute are the advantages which tip the balance for arbitration.[2]

5.03. Another decisive benefit is the constitution of the arbitral tribunal, as the selected arbitrators are usually professionals in specific types of contracts, with extensive experience in domestic/international commercial contracts and conduct of the proceedings. This opportunity for the parties to nominate their arbitrators to decide the dispute is based on the widely accepted principle of party autonomy in arbitration, subject of course to certain constraints compelled by applicable law and the rules of the arbitration. The arbitrators' choice is a delicate task, yet it is a vital, even primary step for the future conduct and finality of the process.

5.04. The arbitral tribunal plays an essential role in the effective conduct of all the procedural stages of the proceedings and the determination of the merits of the case, as the case lies under the tribunal's care and control. As distinguished authors have said,[3] the ability to appoint the

---

[1] Michael MacIlwrath; Roland Schroeder, *The View from an International Arbitration Customer: In Dire Need of Early Resolution*, 74(1) ARB 3, 4 (2008).

[2] Irene Welser, *Efficiency – Today's Challenge in Arbitration Proceedings*, in AUSTRIAN YEARBOOK ON INTERNATIONAL ARBITRATION, Vienna: C.H. Beck 151 (Klausegger, Klein, Kremslehner, Petsche, Pikowitz, Power, Welser, Zeiler eds., 2014).

[3] R. Doak Bishop; Lucy Reed, *Practical Guidelines for Interviewing, Selecting and Challenging Party-Appointed Arbitrators*, 14(4) ARB INT'L 395, 429 (1998).

decision makers constitutes a defining aspect of the arbitral system. It also provides a powerful tool if it is wisely exploited by a party. Other specialists[4] have considered the arbitral tribunal's role in the arbitration process to be more of an effective anti-abuse mechanism, provided that arbitrators give proof of their experience, capability and case management skills. The arbitral tribunal can eventually be the most recommendable and efficient tool to counterbalancing the guerilla tactics[5] the parties and their counsel might use in order to protect and preserve the arbitration process from deriving from its initial intention and advantages.

5.05. Confidentiality is also an advantage. This is because, unlike national court proceedings, arbitration is private and takes place away from the public eye. Persons not involved in the proceedings are allowed to participate in the arbitration only with the express approval of the arbitral tribunal and the parties.

5.06. Arbitration can be institutional or ad-hoc. The difference is that in ad-hoc arbitration parties and the nominated arbitrators have total control of the arbitration and therefore may avoid the institutional costs. However, it is an extra burden for them to take care of all the administrative and procedural matters which are otherwise regulated by institutional rules, which make the process easier and sometimes even less expensive and time consuming. That it is the reason why the most used form of arbitration is the institutional one. Along with the administrative costs being insured, the institution already has the mechanism set in place to settle all the problems that can be encountered in arbitration proceedings, according to the rules of the respective institution selected.

5.07. Therefore, there is a sensitive discussion involved in the selection of the preferred arbitral institution, weighing the international power, the administering experience of the institution in handling a large number of cases, and the possession of a modern set of rules, balanced with affordable arbitration costs and fees scale, and an attractive list of qualified arbitrators.

---

[4]   William W Park, *Arbitration's Discontents: Of Elephants and Pornography*, 17(3) ARB INT'L 263, 271, 272 (2001).

[5]   Günther J. Horvath, *Guerilla Tactics in Arbitration, an Ethical Battle: Is There Need for a Universal Code of Ethics?*, *in* AUSTRIAN YEARBOOK ON INTERNATIONAL ARBITRATION, Vienna: C.H. Beck 297, 313 (Klausegger, Klein, Kremslehner, Petsche, Pikowitz, Power, Welser, Zeiler eds., 2011).

5.08. Although the main mission is to promote its use as much as possible, it is also fair to mention some disadvantages of arbitration.[6] One of the most prominent disadvantages relates to the powers of arbitral tribunals. Unlike national courts, the arbitrators cannot directly enforce their own orders and awards, and they have more limited powers than judges. In multi-party arbitration the non-signatory issue is very delicate, as extending the arbitration agreement to third parties is a difficult and risky decision which can be challenged. There are also other aspects such as the number of the arbitral tribunal members. Often this is numbered at three, but this could lead to supplementary costs and time, and split decisions in the course of reaching a unanimous award. The most unpleasant tendency is that arbitration becomes more expensive than national court proceedings and is attacked too often by all kinds of guerrilla tactics.[7]

5.09. Undoubtedly, workable solutions[8] are necessary to enable escalating value and the settlement of complex disputes in a much shorter time frame, all while reducing arbitration costs. One of these solutions could be the reshaping of the proceedings and the imposition of the modern trends of flexibility, versatility, and polyvalence of the common modern disputes in arbitration. This is a solution found mainly by arbitration service providers, who have drafted guidelines and protocols to cover several issues related to inefficiency that have appeared in practice. But the implementer of those possible solutions in the realm of arbitration is the arbitral tribunal itself. They have the honour and the burden to build confidence in an efficient process that needs to be established for arbitration to run forward smoothly, for its support, future elevation and promotion.

---

[6] CRISTINA FLORESCU, ARBITRAJUL COMERCIAL. CONVENTIA ARBITRALĂ SI TRIBUNALUL ARBITRAL, Bucureşti: Universul Juridic 91 (2011). See also JACOB GRIERSON; ANNET VAN HOOFT; CORINNE NGUYEN, ARBITRATING UNDER THE 2012 ICC RULES, The Hague: Wolters Kluwer 28 (2012).

[7] See a book especially dedicated to this topic: GUERILLA TACTICS IN INTERNATIONAL ARBITRATION, The Hague: Kluwer Law International (Günther J Horvath; Stephan Wilske eds., 2013).

[8] R. Wayne Thorpe, *Case Management and Cost Control for Commercial Arbitration* (2012), available at: http://www.jamsadr.com/files/Uploads/Documents/Articles/Thorpe-Case-Management-ABA-2012-06.pdf (accessed on 25 June 2014).

II. Excessive Judicialization – hindering Efficiency in Arbitration

5.10. To find solutions to the issue of better case-management in arbitration, one should identify the cause of the problem, and this is that arbitration has become too much like litigation, i.e. there has been a 'judicialization' of international arbitration. This concern is in line with the general complaint that international arbitration already suffers from judicialization and the loss of distinct arbitration characteristics as a result of the adoption of court-like features.[9]

5.11. The most important differences between arbitration and litigation – and from which the fundamental value of arbitration emerges – are the ability of users to tailor processes to better serve their particular needs[10] in a friendly and courteous environment, with judges appointed by the parties. A number of conflicts emerge frequently in discussions.[11] These include pathological clauses in agreements, the selection or challenges of arbitrators, procedural timetables and time-limits for the submissions that are to be made as well as their number and length, the possible bifurcation of the proceedings with lengthy discussions on jurisdiction, and the behaviour of counsels that import trial practices into arbitration.[12] Such obstructions that banish efficiency have been described in numerous papers, books, conferences or seminars for many years now and I do not intend to present extensive insights here on the formation of each of these issues, or on how they appear and what effect each of them triggers in the proceedings. Rather, I want to to try to focus on possible solutions for improving arbitration, and who can apply those solutions.

---

[9] See a paper that is a contemporary debate on efficiency: Alan Redfern, *Stemming the Tide of Judicialisation of International Arbitration*, 2 WAMR (WORLD ARBITRATION AND MEDIATION REVIEW) 21, 37 (2008).

[10] T. J. Stipanowich, *Arbitration: The "New Litigation"*, 1 U ILL L REV (UNIVERSITY OF ILLINOIS LAW REVIEW) 1–59 (2010).

[11] Mads Bryde Andersen; Anders Ryssdal; Stefan Lindskog, *Achieving Efficiency in International Arbitration: Some Strategic Suggestions for Arbitral Tribunals in ICC Proceedings*, 22 (2) ICC BULL 5, 7 (2011).

[12] These include discovery, motion practice, delaying the procedure, strategic or tactical reasons, interposing constant objections, harassing witnesses, redundant testimony, the production of a large volume of documentary evidence confusing and burdening the case, lengthy and costly expert evidence, multi-day hearings, and a lot of other guerilla tactics, as described in the book dedicated to this topic. See GUERILLA TACTICS IN INTERNATIONAL ARBITRATION, *supra* note 7.

5.12. Recently, two in-house attorneys for one of the world's leading companies suggested that arbitration is more about due process:

> The overriding objectives [of businesses in choosing an appropriate forum for resolving disputes] . . . are fairness, efficiency (including speed and cost) and certainty in the enforcement of contractual rights and protections. These are complementary objectives, and to focus on one at the expense of the others leads to a result inconsistent with the expectations of the business world and denies basic commercial needs. Too often the practice of . . . arbitration has done just that, by focusing on perceived concepts of due process to the detriment of efficiency, resolution and certainty.[13]

5.13. This is because the arbitrators' duties are to render awards that are final and enforceable, without reasons for annulment or non-recognition by any authority called to review the award. By trying to weigh the arbitrators' duty of due process with insuring efficiency, accuracy and fairness, the arbitral tribunals have been unable to overcome the issue of award enforcement.[14] Arbitrators are afraid of this consequence and therefore they have become less operative in considering all the parties' adequate opportunity to be heard.

5.14. As a result, enhancing efficiency could reduce fairness and accuracy[15] and arbitrators are obliged to respect their duties and avoid liability for excess of authority. Therefore, it is not an easy task to improve the proficiency of proceedings and assure a time and cost efficient management of the case.

III. The Arbitrators' Responsibility in Achieving Efficiency

5.15. The responsibility of arbitrators in achieving efficiency is a very broad subject, tackled and analyzed by several specialists in arbitration, and cannot be exhaustively covered here. All the service providers' rules, proposals and guidelines are indeed a solution to the excessive judicialization brought into arbitration by the guerilla tactics imported from litigation. However the arbitral tribunal is the group called on to

---

[13] Michael MacIlwrath; Roland Schroeder, *supra* note 1, at 3, 10.

[14] William W. Park, *Two Faces of Progress: Fairness and Flexibility in Arbitral Procedure,* 23 ARB INT'L 499 (2007).

[15] William W. Park, *The Four Musketeers of Arbitral Duty: Neither One-For-All nor All-For-One, in* IS ARBITRATION ONLY AS GOOD AS THE ARBITRATOR?, STATUS, POWERS AND ROLE OF THE ARBITRATOR, Paris: ICC Institute of World Business Law, 8 (1) ICC Dossiers 25, 29 (Y. Derain, L. Levy eds., 2011).

implement them, as well as to conduct, organize and police the proceedings.

5.16.   As mentioned above, the arbitral tribunal is the ultimate solution to limit the guerilla tactics used by the parties and their counsels and to counterbalance them with strategic, correct, concrete and feasible procedural measures, as well as to insure the smooth forward motion of the process in an efficient manner and, moreover, to protect the award from due process challenges.

III.1. Possible Methods for Countering Guerilla Tactics

5.17.   An arbitral tribunal has some possible solutions to excessive judicialization. The first is to anticipate and prevent guerilla tactics when they appear from the start, and better still to prevent them even before they start. If not, these abusive tactics can be stopped or sanctioned by different measures, depending on the stage of the arbitration proceedings.

5.18.   But this will depend on the severity of the encountered tactics and must also be considered in accordance with the specificity of the case. For example, if the counsels come from a background in common law where lively advocacy is the norm,[16] this cannot be sanctioned as guerilla tactics, and there must be discussion as to what extent such an advocacy can be accepted and what limits must be imposed. Counsels employ various strategies and tactics within the limits of the law during arbitral or court proceedings that they consider suitable to obtain the best result for their client. The ability of the counsel to design the strategy, enforce it and obtain their best result is positive and has nothing to do with guerilla tactics.[17]

5.19.   It has been wisely said[18] that client conduct and body language can be observed in a hearing and be recognized early as clues for possible troubles to come, based on the legal tradition, basic style, or personally or strategically malicious intent.

5.20.   Early action must be taken and gently calibrated to the severity of the tactics used. Usually, a clear, firm and polite warning should suffice, but sometimes the counsel continues to remain aggressive or to use more subtle approaches that confirm their determination to continue the abusive maneuvers for which they were admonished. Then stronger

---

[16] Lucy Reed, *Sanctions Available for Arbitrators to Curtail Guerilla Tactics, in* GUERILLA TACTICS IN INTERNATIONAL ARBITRATION, *supra* note 7, at 93, 96.

[17]   Despina Fruth Oprişan, *Facing the Reality of Guerilla Tactics in Romania*, 7(2) TDM 3, 5 (2010).

[18]   Lucy Reed, *supra* note 16, at 96.

measures are required. Indeed, the discipline of the counsel and the methods they adopt are sensitive matters and if the counsel does not respond to the polite warnings, then graduated discipline[19] should be imposed. This can include everything from a recess with a private discussion to more powerful tools, such as cost sanctions to parties or the counsel or even the exclusion of counsel from the proceedings.

5.21. One option to prevent and stop such chaos and disobedience would be a reference and inclusion of a code of conduct in a procedural order. This is advisable and effective, subject to appropriate customization to the behaviour. It is also important for the consequences[20] of not respecting the individualized rules of conduct to be mentioned, as uniformity is difficult to achieve and not even desirable.

5.22. Another choice could be an interim measure for security for costs, to cover the supplementary time and costs produced as damage to the other party by not respecting arbitral discipline.

5.23. Another approach is a more formal sanction, penalizing improper conduct when allocating costs[21] in the last instance. This sends a strong alarm that inefficiency is punished and the tribunal is prepared to be proactive and also focus on the parties and counsels' conduct.[22] For this formal sanction, the authority of the tribunal to proceed with it is a delicate subject. This issue is covered under modern rules, such as in 2012 ICC Arbitration Rules Art. 37 (5),[23] but some arbitrators may be reluctant to use this approach as long as no formal authority is explicitly given by the applicable rules or law, as this might jeopardize the award's finality.

5.24. The will of the parties could also be characterized as a limit for the arbitrators' role and procedural powers. An arbitrator in exercising their mission and functions should be aware of the extent of such procedural powers. On the other hand, an arbitrator enjoys a measure of autonomy in this exercise and therefore is compelled to support a proactive and autonomous role, subject to the rules governing arbitration. This freedom assures the legal framework of the arbitration

---

[19] Ibid, at 99.

[20] Ibid, at 98.

[21] White and Case, Queen Mary University Of London School of International Arbitration, *2012 International Arbitration Survey: Current and Preferred Practices in the Arbitral Process*, 41.

[22] Andrew Clarke, *International Arbitration: Current Corporate Concerns*, 20(2) ICC BULL 41, 49 (2009).

[23] Recently adopted (5 June 2014) Romanian Arbitration Rules have the same idea newly incorporated in Art. 43 (3), which complements arbitration law Art. 573 (3) (New Civil Procedure Code in force from 15 February 2013).

process and the whole conduct of arbitration, as the parties' impact on the efficiency and cost-effectiveness is made mostly in the preliminary choices and their flexibility.

5.25. Another method to discourage counsel's guerilla tactics is an explicit criticism of their conduct expressed in the final award, as this officially affects their reputation and future nomination to such a position. The public perception of such behaviour is negative since so many debates of undertaking efficiency are carried on globally.

5.26. Along the same line, this could also be done during the proceedings, but before reaching the final award. If the counsel's behaviour becomes unbearable and contradicts with the hearing police,[24] as an extreme measure, the tribunal has the general authority to exclude counsel from the arbitration[25] and to impose a fine accordingly.[26]

5.27. State courts have the option to dismiss a part of the case, some parts or the entire case for abusive tactics. Arbitrators may apply similar sanction by issuing a preliminary judgment[27] in specific circumstances, in the most drastic cases.[28] The offending party also risks an adverse inference (used in civil and criminal cases in court), meaning the tribunal is permitted to draw a negative conclusion from the guerilla tactic used and so to sanction the party that takes advantage of it.

---

[24] As in civil courts, there are countries where the judge has this power to exclude participants from the hearing as a coercive measure.

[25] In practice, to protect the integrity of the proceedings, the tribunals have decided that such exclusion is permissible due to inherent powers to do so. See a recent ICSID decision from May 2008, *Hrvatska Elektroprivreda d.d* v *Republic of Slovenia*, ICSID Case no. ARB/05/24. The impact of this case was seen in *Rompetrol Group N.V. v Romania*, ICSID Case no. ARB/06/3 in the decision in 2010, holding that this *Hrvatska* decision can be considered as an ad-hoc decision for late disclosure. Anyhow, even if is not commercial but investment arbitration jurisprudence, the concept of inherent authority of the arbitral tribunal derives from the same contractual principles.

[26] See Bernard F. Meyer; Martina Wirz, *Experiences Form the Civil Law System, in* GUERILLA TACTICS IN INTERNATIONAL ARBITRATION, *supra* note 7, Chapter 3, 134, 138-139.

[27] *Libananco Holdings Co. Limited* v *Republic of Turkey*, ICSID Case no. ARB/06/8, Decision on Preliminary Issues, June 2008, para. 72, 78.

[28] Günther J Horvath; Stephan Wilske, Jeff C. Jeng, *Lessons to Be Learned for International Arbitration, in* GUERILLA TACTICS IN INTERNATIONAL ARBITRATION, *supra* note 7, Chapter 3, 278, 288.

III.2. Interaction of the Arbitrators with the Court in Countering Guerilla Tactics

5.28.   Special attention should be paid to the idea of a tribunal seeking assistance from the state court, as it is globally recognized that parties use arbitration precisely to avoid their intervention into the arbitration process.

5.29.   Even if obvious guerilla tactics are taking place, tribunals usually preclude initiating court assistance on their own or as a response to a formal party request.[29] In doing so, the arbitrators respect their mission of taking the initiative of conducting the proceedings with professionalism and experience, without any outside support of other judges and courts. This also affirms their confidence and the potential of managing the case by themselves even in hard times, saving their reputation.

5.30.   The solution is that the tribunal addresses the issue with a procedural order and later in its award if necessary, using fair, reasoned and clear wording. The tribunal should prove that it is proactive, not biased, facing against all odds and living up to the parties' expectations and the powers granted to it. Otherwise the parties would have chosen litigation in the first place.[30]

5.31.   The tribunal's right and duty is to not tolerate any observed guerilla tactics, to establish the facts of the case and to render an enforceable award without violation of international or transnational public order. Even in the case of breaching of public order or some other illegality,[31] the tribunal must ensure the autonomy and sanctity of the arbitral process. They must find appropriate tools to counter extreme guerilla tactics without undermining the award's enforceability and without the intervention of courts.

5.32.   It has been well stated[32] that the relationship between arbitration and the courts is based on a paradox.[33] The more high-level developed and

---

[29]   Richard H. Kreindler, *The Role of State Courts in Assisting Arbitral Tribunals Confronted with Guerilla Tactics, in* GUERILLA TACTICS IN INTERNATIONAL ARBITRATION, *supra* note 7, Chapter 2, 102, 103.

[30]   Ibid, at 104.

[31]   Richard H. Kreindler, *Aspects of Illegality in the Formation and Performance of Contracts, in* INTERNATIONAL COMMERCIAL ARBITRATION: IMPORTANT CONTEMPORARY QUESTIONS, The Hague: Kluwer Law International 212, 262 (A. J. van den Berg ed., 2003).

[32]   Richard H. Kreindler, *supra* note 29, at 105.

[33]   It is not quite an incongruity; the explanation is that it is based on respecting the fundamental party autonomy principle of arbitration. Parties elected for arbitration all the

experienced[34] the arbitration seat, the less likely the courts would intervene or assist the arbitral tribunal.

5.33. There are no arbitration laws, rules or guidelines, listing situations in which parties or arbitral tribunals should refer to courts' assistance or interventions. There are situations related to ad-hoc arbitrations where the court's intervention may be needed more. However, usually the court's intervention is more connected to interim measures, the taking of evidence, setting aside awards or their recognition and enforcement. It is usually less related to the appointment of the arbitrators, the investigation on the issue of illegality (associated with guerilla tactics) or insolvency or other violation of the viability and functionality of arbitration.[35]

III.3. Less Sanctions, More Effective Communication and Respect of Inherent Arbitration Features

5.34. Nevertheless, as one may observe, some of the sanctions proposed and already used by arbitral tribunals derive from the courts' territory. Hence, litigation-inspired sanctions in fighting court-like guerilla tactics mean using similar weapons. This might appear a suitable, practical and realistic solution. At the same time, this means to reply to a war by starting another one, meeting injustice with injustice instead of justice. This seems counterproductive and the message transmitted is not an invitation to settlement, or to a positive, polite and elegant reaction, as arbitration should be.

5.35. We must not forget that arbitration is a private dispute resolution, where civility, decency and courtesy should prevail at any time. Besides securing efficiency, the arbitrators' mission is primarily setting the frame for a process conducted with good manners and consideration, in a less rigid and formalistic way. The solution is not for arbitrators to sharpen their weapons but their vigilance. They should not look for counter measures, but strive to set an example of effective conduct for all the participants from the beginning. The example has to start from the behaviour inside the tribunal, among the members. This is the primary responsibility of the tribunal's president, from whom the cohesive strength emanates.

---

way, so the intervention of the court should also be an exception, and reduced to a minimum, used only when there is no other way out.

[34] This is explained by the degree of the experience hosting international arbitrations and entertaining actions to set aside international arbitration awards developed in the respective place.

[35] Richard H. Kreindler, *supra* note 29, at 107.

5.36. Nevertheless, the co-arbitrators also have to balance and apply a basic standard for acceptable behaviour as they usually together nominate the president of their tribunal. Furthermore, all have to work together in a friendly environment, which should invite stylishness, professionalism, and a minimal level of manners and conduct. The tribunal is to be keenly attentive to the compliance of this standard by all participants to the process, in a fair and principled manner. They should instruct participants in all of the tribunal's expectations for the proceedings efficiently, in due time and in the most convenient and appropriate way.

5.37. There is no general tool or recipe available for arbitrators to apply in each and every case. A one-size-fits-all solution is not possible, as every dispute has its particularities, different legal background and distinct culture, with different expectations and interests, in an international environment. The members of the arbitral tribunal have the duty to reasonably balance the opposed views, as well as to ensure necessary communication among themselves to make the best and easiest choices. This will lead them to achieve the desired efficiency, in keeping with the goals and advantages of arbitration.

5.38. The conclusion is that the aspiration towards efficiency in arbitration involves balancing fairness and accuracy with reducing any possible delay and/or undue cost.[36]

IV. The Parties and Their Counsels' Position in Excessive Judicialization

5.39. Besides the role of arbitrators succinctly described above, the responsibility for this unpardonable evolution of arbitration's judicialization rests with the parties themselves and their counsel.[37] They are primarily responsible, because in practical circumstances they are the ones who bring the litigation-like style to arbitration.

5.40. One should not forget that the arbitration' users are not always sufficiently equipped to face a costly process and third party funding is a new concept to be considered for a party to be able to afford

---

[36] Lucy Reed, *More on Corporate Criticism of International Arbitration*, available at: http://kluwerarbitrationblog.com/blog/2010/07/16/more-on-corporate-criticism-of-international-arbitration/ (accessed on 25 June 2014); see also White & Case LLP and School of International Arbitration, Queen Mary, University of London, *International Arbitration Survey: Choices in International Arbitration* (2010).

[37] Frederic Gillion, *Impact of the New ICC Rules (2012) on the Management of Construction Arbitration Cases* available at: http://www.fenwickelliott.com/files/fred_gillion_-_eic_june_article.pdf (accessed 25 June 2014).

arbitration. Therefore, the parties' counsels should take this idea into account when it is the case and act accordingly to save arbitration costs.

5.41. The parties themselves complain about lost efficiency in arbitration and at the same time they employ counsels whom they instruct to use all the necessary means to win at all cost. There is a contradiction here, as they infringe a general principle of law: no party can invoke its own dishonesty in its defence.[38] Also it is an inevitable divergence between the parties' wish of a speedy and efficient arbitration, and the principle of the parties' right to be heard in the procedure. This is often invoked by the parties as soon as they need an argument to harass the smooth flow of the process according to a certain interest.

5.42. Ideally, arbitration should flow smoothly forward without special difficulties, given the parties' common interest to settle their dispute in a timely and cost efficient manner.[39] But this paradigm changes in the real world, where the parties' already antagonistic standpoints are exacerbated by counsels' practice and the big interests that haunt high profile, complex arbitration cases, sometimes involving multiple contracts and parties.

5.43. In these cases, the parties advised by their counsels' fight strongly for every step, opposing the other party with abusive strategies and dilatory tactics that disturb the proficiency and efficiency sought in arbitration. Thus the arbitrators are forced to take a position against the parties' actions and set forth a clear procedural timetable where all the disputable aspects can be strictly regulated. This leaves them no room for any further possible conflict that might generate further wastes of time and money.

5.44. Nevertheless, to save time and costs, the parties must decide on their priorities and balance all their needs together with their counsels. If they request efficiency then they will have to agree on cutting the costs and reducing the time by reducing all the tactics and the dilatory maneuvers usually used, which place high demands on the development of the proceedings.

5.45. Such abusive strategies may include proposing new claims, producing excessive documentation, putting forward endless evidence requirements, challenging the arbitrators' impartiality and independence, complicating the proceedings by proposing extended time-limits, an unreasonable number of submissions, a cumbersome document production process or an excessive and unnecessary number

---

[38] *Nemo auditur propriam turpitudinem allegans.*

[39] Mads Bryde Andersen; Anders Ryssdal; Stefan Lindskog, *supra* note 11, at 6.

of witnesses and experts to be heard during a long evidentiary hearing. The main idea is that to make arbitration faster and cheaper, and to achieve this it may be necessary to forego certain steps, such as additional rounds of briefs, excessive document production, longer hearings, more experts, and the like.[40]

5.46. But more important is to draft a good arbitration clause from the beginning. It is important to ensure that the specific business needs of the parties are met effectively and the clause will not contain too many elements or words that could trigger pathology. The clause should be simple but not too simplistic, as suggested by Frédéric Eisemann.[41] A pathological clause can add mounting procedural costs and time[42] and could induce fatal effects.[43] Therefore the standard clause is preferable, and its tailoring is required only in special cases when this is indeed indispensable. Such changes are to be made only after consulting specialists with necessary expertise, and not risking to conclude midnight clauses very difficult to be saved afterwards. The discussions on jurisdictional matters can take years and can also involve state courts.

5.47. The parties chose arbitration to exclude the state courts' intervention. Therefore the litigation-like practice of counsel behaviour should be excluded and all the features similar to litigation should be reduced to a minimum in arbitration. Otherwise parties have sought efficiency in vain, since importing litigation-like guerilla tactics is an inefficient manner in which to solve issues in arbitration, as long as the parties specifically chose to exclude litigation and its features by resorting to arbitration. The parties and their counsels should be aware that counsel's conduct in front of the arbitral tribunal should be different from the one in front of the state courts.

---

[40] *Debevoise & Plimpton LLP Protocol to Promote Efficiency in International Arbitration (2010)*, available at: http://www.debevoise.com/files/News/2cd13af2-2530-40de-808a-a903f5813bad/Presentation/NewsAttachment/79302949-69b6-49eb-9a75-a9ebf1675572/DebevoiseProtocolToPromoteEfficiencyinInternationalArbitration.pdf (accessed on 25 June 2014)

[41] Frédéric Eisemann, La clause d'arbitrage pathologique, in COMMERCIAL ARBITRATION ESSAYS IN MEMORIAM EUGENIO MINOLI 129, 130 (U.T.E.T., 1974).

[42] *Insigma Technology Co. Ltd. v Alstom Technology Ltd., where the clause provided for ICC Rules administered under SIAC institution, a case that made history and led to the changing of 2012 ICC Rules to the Art. 1(2) and 6 (2), which states that ICC is the only institution that administers ICC Rules and ICC Rules once mentioned in a clause triggered automatically ICC as the administering body.*

[43] Several years after the award is granted, the winning party may encounter the situation when enforcing the award of not finding sufficient assets to be satisfied according to the sum awarded.

5.48. One implication of this is that parties and counsels should not be perceived as one. The counsels represent the parties and they can negatively affect the efficiency of the proceedings by adopting tactics that are not expressly advised or known by the parties, but which counsels consider helpful for their cause. In such a case, the counsels should bear the burden of being sanctioned for pursuing such tactics and this may trigger a breach of professional or ethical obligations. But sometimes, the parties themselves request the exercise of such abusive strategies and here one finds a clear distinction, the parties cannot be penalized except for criminal law issues.

5.49. It almost impossible to reconcile all three concepts: time efficiency, cost saving and quality of the award. As parties are calling for all three, international practice often results in long and costly proceedings, qualified as inefficient. The parties should understand that good quality arbitration implies both the accuracy of the award and a high quality of the proceedings.

5.50. One scholar[44] makes ten interesting proposals in this respect:

- a limit of 100 pages maximum for parties' submissions;
- oral pleadings at a terms of reference meeting and subsequent recommendations by the arbitral tribunal;
- the proposal and encouragement of settlement agreement offers from the parties;
- no written witness statements;
- interrogation by arbitrators;
- absolutely no document production;
- directives by tribunal as to material issues;
- comprehensive opening statements and discussion on the merits;
- the parties' assistance in writing the final award;
- explicit cost sanction for inefficient handling of proceedings; and
- financial incentive for the arbitral tribunal to render the award quickly.

5.51. Although all the proposals for increasing efficiency are supported by very durable arguments, some of them are already used in practice if not all the time, while others are not so easy to implement and have been used less or not at all. I doubt the willingness of the arbitrators and the parties to introduce them all. Even if all these proposals deserve consideration it is preferable that all the arbitration participants be encouraged to cooperate in reaching efficiency.

---

[44] Jörg Risse, *Ten Drastic Proposals for Saving Time and Costs in Arbitral Proceedings*, 29(3) ARB INT'L 453-466 (2013).

V. Recent Developments in Soft Law regarding Arbitration Case Management Practices

5.52. During the last decade it is notable that the arbitration community has increased efforts to insure efficiency in arbitration. They have done so by issuing or improving guidelines, standards, codes of best practices and by adopting new arbitration rules that address specific tools for an efficient case-management. This so-called 'soft law' creates intra-practitioner directives aimed at enhancing procedural uniformity among arbitrators and counsels from different judicial traditions.[45]

5.53. Several arbitral institutions have provided new rules and a lot of them are struggling to improve and implement guidelines, best practices and protocols. These are not intended to be exhaustive but only soft law, to encourage the revision and the development of efficiency in arbitration. It is a hot topic these days and a number of conferences, seminars and workshops all over the world are debating the ideas put forward in these guidelines and rules of arbitration. The main arbitral service providers have recently revised their rules. These include UNCITRAL Arbitration Rules 2010; ICC, SCC, CIETAC, PCA, Swiss Rules – 2012; VIAC, SIAC, CEPANI, CPR – 2013; LCIA, CACIR – 2014. This progress is continuing as the subject of effectiveness in arbitration is treated in more depth, in all the stages of the process.

V.1. The Evolution of the ICC Commission on Arbitration and the ADR Proposals on Efficiency

V.1.1. Emergency Arbitrator

5.54. As described above, the International Chamber of Commerce Rules of Arbitration (ICC Rules) and the Swiss Rules of International Arbitration (Swiss Rules) have recently been revised. Several provisions were considered that aimed to reduce time and cost. Both the revised ICC Rules and the Swiss Rules have followed the example of The Arbitration Institute of the Stockholm Chamber of Commerce (SCC) and have incorporated a provision for the appointment of an emergency arbitrator: 'This is intended to reduce the involvement of the state courts where parties wish to apply for urgent interim measures prior to the constitution of the arbitral tribunal'.[46]

---

[45] William W. Park, *supra* note 14, at 25.

[46] Claire Davies, *More Efficient and Cost-Effective Arbitration: Changes Made to the ICC and Swiss Rules in 2012*, 22 October 2012, available at: http://www.bristows.com/articles/more-efficient-and-cost-effective-arbitration-changes-made-to-the-icc-and-swiss-rules-in-2012 (accessed on 25 June 2014).

5.55. When appropriate, the parties can use this effective tool in institutional arbitration before the constitution of the arbitral tribunal. This tool has more recently been offered by a few main arbitration providers, such as ICC, SCC, SIAC, LCIA, ICDR and a few others. This is an attempt to improve the functioning and practical benefits of arbitral rules. These institutions have started developing expedited or emergency procedures to assist parties in situations where a party seeks relief. This applies in such cases where the party truly cannot wait for the constitution of an arbitral tribunal and they need urgent interim relief before an arbitral tribunal has been formed. Prior to the development of these procedures parties would normally have to apply to national courts for emergency relief or await the constitution of the tribunal.[47]

5.56. Such procedures do offer a practical solution to a temporal problem and moreover such decisions may lead the parties to settlement.

V.1.2. The ICC Guidelines Related to Efficiency

5.57. In 2007, the ICC Commission on Arbitration issued guidelines entitled 'Techniques for Controlling Time and Costs in Arbitration' [Techniques, (2007)]. These developed and followed on the guidelines issued in March 2003 entitled 'Guidelines for Arbitrating Small Claims under ICC Rules of Arbitration'.[48] The latest guide in this domain, launched on 6 June 2014, is entitled 'Effective Management of Arbitration. A Guide for In-House Counsel and Other Party Representatives' (2014 ICC Guide) which is intended to assist the arbitration participants by providing an extensive toolkit for making the best decision when it comes to efficiency. Indeed, the 2014 ICC Guide takes into consideration a lot of possible practical aspects that are flexible in arbitration. These can be tailored by the parties to their needs and in accordance with the value and the complexity of the case.[49]

5.58. Usually, the institutional rules do not provide in-depth issues and solutions for every aspect of how proceedings are to be conducted.

---

[47] Raja Bose; Ian Meredith, Emergency Arbitration Procedures: A Comparative Analysis, in 5 INTERNATIONAL ARBITRATION LAW REVIEW (2012), available at: http://www.klgates.com/files/Publication/33e561cb-b459-47f5-bab1-856c51d8459b/Presentation/Publication Attachment/f5e1a648-049e-4f63-afcf-f8d4dc91bae2/Emergency-Arbitration-Procedures_A-Comparative-Analysis.pdf (accessed on 25 June 2014).

[48] In fact, in the Introduction it is stated that the suggestions made in the guidelines can be used by any party who seeks to reduce cost and time for arbitration, even in 'large claims'.

[49] See also the mentioning of this Guide by Christopher Newmark, *Controlling Time and Costs in Arbitration, in* THE LEADING ARBITRATORS' GUIDE TO INTERNATIONAL ARBITRATION, New York: Juris Publishing Inc. 491 (L.W. Newman, R.D. Hill eds., 2014).

However, it is not recommendable for guidelines to be precisely regulated to fit all disputes, since the flexibility of procedural matters is the feature most welcomed and appreciated in international arbitration. But it is important to be well advised of all the possible aspects that might intervene in arbitration proceedings before they start. Most of all it is important to anticipate and prevent any dilatory or guerilla tactics. If this is not working properly in due time, it is important to know how to stop and even sanction them later, as well as to calibrate the proceedings and find a clear and concrete way to address any problem along the process.

5.59.   To address this concern, the 2014 ICC Guide brings forth several different procedural options available to parties to promote effective case management. These can be deployed at the beginning of arbitration and throughout the proceedings. The 2014 ICC Guide encourages parties and their counsel to approach case management from a cost/risk/benefit overview. Certainly, all the advice and proposals invite participants to bear in mind the value, complexity, actual needs, chosen rules, applicable law and panel of arbitrators. This will allow them to best tailor all possible aspects from the outset of the dispute in the most convenient manner to ensure a smooth exercise of the process. Even if the 2014 ICC Guide was merely elaborating on the 2012 ICC Rules of Arbitration, it can be applied to arbitrations conducted under any rules, and in large and small cases alike, because it leaves room for a lot of flexibility over the myriad of aspects presented.

5.60.   The ICC Guide is composed of three main parts: First, a discussion of settlement considerations; second, a discussion of the case management conference; and third, a series of eleven topic sheets dealing with a specific stage or procedural issue in the arbitration process. Non-programmatic

5.61.   The topic sheets are definitely the most innovative part of this Guide, as they address the aspects in a non-programmatic manner. By not providing firm and rigid, or routine and quick answers, they instead offer a useful durable methodology for strategic decision-making. These topic sheets propose some thoughts on the covered topics in a descriptive manner. They begin by presenting the issue in discussion, the specific provisions and soft law, if any, the impact and the consequence on efficiency. This is followed by a main idea/ question related to the issue to which options are presented by variants from a minimum to a maximum range of possible solutions. After the presentation of the pros and cons related to time and cost-efficiency in general – the cost/ benefit/ risk analysis is put forward with questions to ask and other possible points to consider, enabling readers to decide on the most appropriate solution to respective topic.

5.62. The topic sheets manage the specific steps used in the international arbitration process and each of them deals with the cost/risk/ benefit decisions to be ascertained. This is presented even for cases when such a step would not be absolutely necessary, but it is advisable to be at least analyzed as a possibility. The following eleven topics are covered:

- Requests for arbitration;
- Answer and counterclaims;
- Multi-party arbitration;
- Early determination of issues;
- Rounds of written submissions;
- Document production;
- Need for fact witnesses;
- Fact witness statements;
- Expert witnesses;
- Hearing on the merits;
- Post-hearing briefs.

5.63. The Guide does not intend to be regulatory or to provide ultimate or perfect answers to these issues. Rather, it is designed to propose some questions and possible answers to the most frequent procedural issues that in-house counsel and other party representatives may come across in arbitration. Therefore, the 2014 ICC Guide contains conscious and judicious suggestions to the management case of an arbitration, with a particular view to the smooth running of the proceedings. The goal is to insure the overall time and costs of the process are kept to a minimum, in balance with the value and complexity of the case.

V.1.3. The 2012 ICC Rules on Arbitration

5.64. Acting in response to the critique of inefficiency in arbitration, several arbitral institutions have recently embarked on the task of revising their arbitration rules, with the primary aim of making the arbitration process more efficient.[50]

---

[50] JACOB GRIERSON; ANNET VAN HOOFT; CORINNE NGUYEN, *supra* note 6, at 12; Claire Davies, *supra* note 46; David Earnest; Raul Gallardo; Garðar Víðir Gunnarsson; Tobiasz Kaczor, *Four Ways to Sharpen the Sword of Efficiency in International Arbitration*, YOUNG ICCA GROUP PAPER (2013) available at: http://www.arbitration-icca.org/media/0/ 13630881906410/four_ways_to_sharpen_the_sword_of_efficiency_yicca_group_paper.pdf (accessed on 25 June 2014).

5.65. The 2012 ICC Rules made suggestions based in two principles. The first is that the parties should work together with the arbitral tribunal and 'make a conscious and deliberate choice', regarding all the necessary specific procedures for the respective case, as early as possible. The second is the proactive cooperation between all the participants in arbitration in order to better manage the procedure from the outset of the case.[51] Starting from these principles, the 'Techniques for Controlling Time and Costs in Arbitration' made some proposals which were subsequently followed by the adoption of new 2012 ICC Rules. According to the new rules, the Techniques were redrafted in a second edition in 2012. All the provisions of the 2012 ICC Rules culminate with Appendices IV and V, with the former dedicated to Case Management Techniques and the latter which delineates the rules for an Emergency Arbitrator. Both of these annexes were created to meet the request of efficiency in arbitration.

5.66. The 2012 ICC Rules proposals differ from the previous set of rules (1998 ICC Rules),[52] and are located in Article 22 (Conduct of Arbitration), Article 24 (Case Management Conference and Procedural Timetable), Article 27 (Closing of the Proceedings and Date for Submission of Draft Awards), as well as the new emergency arbitrator provisions (Article 29 and Appendix V).

5.67. Article 22 (1) of the 2012 ICC Rules requires that the arbitral tribunal and the parties 'make every effort to conduct the arbitration in an expeditious and cost effective manner having regard to the complexity and value of the dispute'.

5.68. It is important to note that even these rules emphatically state that the arbitrators must be involved in good management, not just the parties, as the parties' freedom of choice is the cornerstone of arbitration.

5.69. All the participants have to take the complexity of the case into account. This means that high profile arbitrations should be given more reflection, as they involve large monetary amounts, state parties and/or a special arbitral tribunal in the dispute. In what follows I have outlined a few ideas on these three relevant issues when high profile cases are debated.

5.70. Regarding large monetary amounts, the advance on costs, provisional advance and fee of the arbitrators are involved in high complexity cases. In such cases, all these costs and fees are above average and distinctive consideration should be paid. As has often been seen, these large monetary amounts need special handling from the Secretariat and the arbitrators.

---

[51] Techniques, (2007).

[52] Frederic Gillion,, *supra* note 37.

5.71.   Also such cases might involve the request for the production of documents, but their relevance to the case is measured. Overly substantive briefs may appear when parties repeat themselves and page limits are required, though this is more common in post hearing submissions.

5.72.   Another issue could be the significant numbers of fact witnesses or experts the parties might request, but the arbitral tribunal should establish if they are indeed necessary and if they should be really brought to the hearings.

5.73.   Other aspects that often intervene are related to bifurcation, parallel proceedings, anti-suit injunctions (conservatory and provisional measures) and arbitrators' challenges. All of these can be covered by a suitable drafting of the first procedural order.

5.74.   Regarding the issue of the state parties, the arbitrators' appointment process is carefully examined and their neutrality is discussed. The number of arbitrators will be three. Any suspicious political pressure on arbitrators or witnesses, especially when dictatorial states are implicated, should be scrutinized and thus more people in the ICC Secretariat will be dealing with the award in this scrutiny process.

5.75.   As concerns the arbitral tribunal, in high profile cases it might be possible for administrative secretaries be appointed for each arbitrator. It is important that arbitrators should be free of conflict of interests of any type, especially those related to state parties. The arbitrators' availability is another important issue, as the more complex case will necessitate more efforts, time and dedication.

5.76.   Some high profile cases involve multiple parties and/or multiple contracts class actions or technically complex issues The publicity of a case if it has a high profile and or is complex involving high monetary value or renowned parties or state parties is also a significant factor, as confidentiality of the proceedings is not always guaranteed. That of the deliberations is, at least in theory.

5.77.   Also the case management conference and case management techniques are to be tailored proportionally to the large monetary amounts at stake. Appendix IV of the 2012 ICC Rules stipulates that in cases of a low value, the cost and time are to be tailored to the amount in dispute, as a low monetary amount does not justify a special and complicated procedure with lots of rules for conduct. Sometimes it might even be sufficient for a paper submission without an oral hearing or other supplementary discovery, witnesses, experts or other measures. But this is not a rule; exceptions appear all the time when low profile cases need a lot of arbitral tribunal attention, oral hearing, provisional measures, expert and witness involvement and so on. Thus, the way arbitration is conducted depends on the particular factual and legal circumstances of the case.

5.78. The case management conference is a good starting point to ensure effective case management in any arbitration. This could be related to the Terms of Reference and, in general, is important for the parties and arbitral tribunal, as it sets the frame of the first procedural order and the procedural timetable. Paragraph 1 in conjunction with paragraph 4 in Article 24 of the 2012 ICC Rules propose that when drawing up the Terms of reference or as soon as possible thereafter, the arbitral tribunal shall convene a case management conference which may be conducted through a live meeting[53] to consult the parties on procedural measures which may be adopted pursuant to Article 22 (2). This is a key innovation issue of the 2012 ICC Rules and it is important that even the institutional rules promote a mutual agreement between the parties and the arbitral tribunal. This is a primary way that efficiency in arbitration can be achieved. Some of the possible measures mentioned in this article could be the ones that are found in the techniques described in Appendix IV to the 2012 ICC Rules.

5.79. The first procedural order is important for a good start, as it may be regarded as a procedure roadmap. It provides a framework for the parties' representatives to consult together on procedural measures that may be adopted pursuant to Article 22 (2). Article 24 (4) authorizes the arbitral tribunal to request the attendance at this order in person or through a representative. However, it is recommended that these persons have enough authority to take the necessary procedural decisions and would therefore have a real effect on cutting time and costs.

5.80. Another newly released aspect of Article 27 is that the parties should be better informed of the date by which the arbitral tribunal is expecting to issue its draft. The Rules request the arbitral tribunal inform the parties as soon as possible after the last hearing or the last authorized submissions, not just the Secretariat as was previously the case. These are improvements related to the issue of time. The issues at stake are the closing of the proceedings and the date for submission of the draft award to the Secretariat for the scrutiny process.

5.81. Correlated with decisions on the costs of the arbitration, the arbitral tribunal is encouraged to consider all relevant circumstances to establish these costs, especially a reward for the parties' efforts to insure the proficiency of the proceedings. Article 37 (5) stipulates that these costs should be awarded to the extent that each party contributes to the development of an efficient and cost effective case management.

---

[53] This means a meeting in person, by video conference, telephone or similar means of communication.

5.82. Finally, Appendix IV is a very useful tool to assist the arbitral tribunal's efforts in performing a more active role. This is a very delicate task, best done by balancing all of the incumbent requirements and duties, and reconciling speed with justice.

5.83. The list of the indicated suggestions made by the institution contains the following case management techniques that should be used by the parties together with their tribunal in seeking efficiency: bifurcation, rendering partial awards, identifying issues that can be resolved by agreement between the parties, identifying issues to be decided solely on the basis of documents, techniques related to the production of documentary evidence, limiting the length and scope of written submissions, limiting the length and scope of written and oral witness/expert evidence, the use of IT enabling online communication among the parties, organizing a pre-hearing conference, and informing the parties on the amicable settlement facilities. In the conclusion of this Appendix, the 2007 'Techniques for Controlling Time and Costs in Arbitration' guidelines are mentioned for complementing these suggestions and to promote the finding of appropriate solutions.

5.84. All of these norms are not really new, as in practice tribunals have already sought to implement them and they have tried even to sanction in costs dilatory or bad faith acts or parties' failure to respect their part of obligations.

V.2. Other Guidelines and Protocols Related to Efficiency

5.85. Not surprisingly, many specialists, scholars, practitioners, counsels and arbitrators are preoccupied with efficiency in arbitration, and one can find several other proposed guidelines, protocols and principles concerning this issue. One of these is entitled 'The College of Commercial Arbitrators Protocols for Expeditious, Cost-Effective Commercial Arbitration: Key Action Steps for Business Users, Counsel, Arbitrators and Arbitration Provider Institutions'. This document was generated following a summit in 2009 to which users (mainly in-house counsel), outside counsel, arbitrators and providers were invited. The exchange of ideas on concerns about current arbitration practice in business to business disputes focused heavily on issues related to cost and delay, and was materialized in these CCA Protocols in the fall of 2010. The document addresses the concerns presented at the Summit and proposes nearly 50 'protocols' for use by all arbitration specialists. It is intended to improve the quality and effectiveness of arbitration among the participants to proceedings.

5.86. Another recent guideline which impacts the present topic is the 2013 IBA Guidelines on Representation in International Arbitration. This document includes several principles for a uniform code of standards in international arbitration. Even if the tribunals and the courts of the seat are called to apply such standards, the introduction of these guidelines can be a useful tool for tribunals and counsel to emphasize to parties that there is a standard of behaviour expected in an arbitration. However, the guidelines apply only at the discretion of the parties and do not grant tribunals the enforcement powers reserved for Bars or other professional bodies. Currently, tribunals can only regulate the conduct of parties through the allocation of costs.[54]

5.87. There are organizations that promote private dispute resolution and serve as a primary multinational resource for management and resolution of business related disputes. For example, the International Bar Association (IBA) promotes rules, guides and other materials to assist and support the legal community. They also address other areas such as standards, principles and ethics related to the present topic, and have published other well known practice rules and guidelines especially issued in the field of arbitration which are widely appreciated and broadly applied. These are the IBA Rules on Taking of Evidence in International Arbitrations (2010), Guidelines for Drafting International arbitration Clauses (2010), Guidelines on Conflicts of Interest in International Arbitration (2004).

5.88. Additionally, the International Institute for Conflict Prevention and Resolution (CPR) is actively involved in this field, organizing committees on various subjects and elaborating guidelines and protocols for developing procedures to be adopted. These include the CPR Protocol on Disclosure of Documents and Presentation of Witnesses in Commercial Arbitration (2009), Guidelines on Early Disposition of Issues in Arbitration (2011), Guidelines for Arbitrators Conducting Complex Arbitrations (2012).

5.89. Another framework is the Chartered Institute of Arbitrators (CIArb) Protocol for Use of Party-Appointed Expert Witnesses in International Arbitration (2007) and their Practice Guideline: The Interviewing of Prospective Arbitrators (2008), both of which are valuable tools on the analyzed topics.

5.90. Finally, there are other relevant soft law tools which deal with this subject and the best practices in the advocacy field. These include the

---

[54] International Arbitration, Roundtable, Litigation & Dispute Resolution, FINANCIER WORLDWIDE MAGAZINE (2014), available at: http://www.financierworldwide.com/roundtable-international-arbitration-jun-2014 (accessed on 25 June 2014).

IBA General Principles of the Legal Profession (2006), The Hague Principles on Ethical Standards for Counsel Appearing before International Courts and Tribunals, Turin Principles of Professional Conduct for Legal Profession (UIA 2002), New York Rules of Professional Conduct and others.

VI. Conclusions

5.91.   The cost of complex, high-profile arbitration has always raised the standards and the increased role of the counsels in the process is not contributing to the economic well-being of those arbitration costs. In the near future, it will hardly be possible for arbitration to be perceived as inexpensive.

5.92.   The parties together with their counsels must decide on their priorities and balance all their needs. If they desire efficiency then they will have to agree on cutting costs and saving time by lowering the high demands on the developments of the proceedings, as well as reducing the use of all abusive tactics and dilatory maneuvers. The list of proposals in this paper is not a comprehensive one – this being not even possible – as long as in real life new tactics and abusive maneuvers will be created and used in practice by the parties and their counsels in pursuing of the win at all costs and risks.

5.93.   Nevertheless, one should not forget that the conduct of every arbitration is unique and depends on the particular factual and legal circumstances of that case. Following a strict arbitration recipe in every case is not possible or advisable. All of the guidelines and protocols mentioned here should be treated as nothing more than a procedural roadmap for participants in arbitration to become accustomed to the specificity of every case. We are looking forward to seeing new proposals afterwards, maybe regulated as soft law (as the new 2014 ICC Guide), as long as they promote real efficiency.

5.94.   The goal of arbitration is to secure a proper, balanced, due process and efficient settlement of the parties' dispute by reputable, experienced and specialized arbitrators. Therefore, in arbitration confidence is a significant liaison. The procedural environment has to generate fewer rules. It should be less judicialized and more focused on party autonomy in shaping the procedure according to the specificity of every case. If the participants understand how to proficiently communicate, good results will lead to less time and cost complaints and arbitration will not be charged with accusations of inefficiency.

|||

Summaries

FRA   [*Une judicalisation excessive, un obstacle à l'efficacité de l'arbitrage*]

L'arbitrage international est devenu le principal moyen de résolution des litiges internationaux, dans le domaine des investissements internationaux comme dans celui des échanges commerciaux internationaux, dans notre monde globalisé. Le présent article analyse quelques procédés cherchant à améliorer l'efficacité de l'arbitrage, en particulier l'allégement de son formalisme et l'atténuation des tendances constituant à « justicialiser » l'arbitrage, qui vont à contre-courant des principes fondamentaux de l'arbitrage.

Il a été possible d'identifier dans le passé un certain nombre de sanctions possibles permettant une accélération et une plus grande efficacité (en termes de coût) de la procédure et donc de garantir l'efficacité de l'arbitrage en tant que tel. En dehors de ceux qui ont recours à l'arbitrage (les parties de la procédure d'arbitrage) et de leurs représentants légaux, les juges arbitres et les cours permanentes d'arbitrage – jouant ainsi un rôle de premier plan dans ce processus – appellent de leurs vœux une résolution plus constructive et plus transparente des litiges, et y engagent aujourd'hui leurs efforts. Nous affirmons ici qu'il est possible d'aboutir à une plus grande efficacité en termes de coûts et de temps, sans que la communication entre les acteurs de la procédure en soit affectée.

Ces derniers temps, on a enregistré des évolutions considérables – ainsi qu'un grand nombre de propositions et de tendances – allant dans ce sens, et il est fort probable que cette problématique soit de plus en plus discutée et analysée à la lueur des différentes doctrines juridiques – et trouve des applications concrètes dans la pratique –, comme elle devrait être de plus en plus souvent un sujet de débat dans bien des conférences.

CZE   [*Excesivní judicializace, překážka pro efektivní rozhodčí řízení*]

Stejně jako v globalizovaném obchodním styku a v oblasti mezinárodních investic, se mezinárodní rozhodčí řízení stalo hlavním způsobem řešení mezinárodních sporů. Tento příspěvek se zabývá analýzou některých postupů, jak dosáhnout efektivního rozhodčího řízení, včetně zmenšování jeho formálnosti a redukce trendů, které představují judicializaci rozhodčího řízení a které tak jdou proti jeho základním principům.

V průběhu času bylo možno identifikovat řadu možných sankcí, které umožní rychlejší a efektivnější (co do nákladů) řízení a tedy garantovat efektivnost rozhodčího řízení jako takového. Vedle těch, kteří využívají rozhodčího řízení (stran rozhodčího řízení) a jejich právních zástupců, se o to momentálně snaží rozhodci a stálé rozhodčí soudy, kteří tak hrají významnou roli v tomto procesu a volají po tom, aby bylo možno rozhodovat spory konstruktivně a pružně. Autorka tvrdí, že lze dosáhnout časové a nákladové efektivity, aniž by docházelo k nedorozuměním mezi subjekty zúčastněnými na řízení.

V poslední době lze v tomto procesu zaznamenat značný vývoj, stejně jako mnoho návrhů a trendů a lze se domnívat, že tato problematika bude stále více diskutována a rozebírána podle jednotlivých právních doktrín a prověřována praktiky, stejně jako bude předmětem diskusí na řadě konferencí.

| | |

POL [*Nadmierna judycjalizacja, przeszkoda dla efektywności postępowania arbitrażowego*]

W postępowaniu arbitrażowym zaleca się, aby wszystkie uczestniczące w nim podmioty przygotowały się celem efektywnego przebiegu postępowania, który należy zakładać już od samego początku sporu. Niniejszy artykuł omawia pewne rozwiązania zmierzające do prowadzenia efektywnego postępowania arbitrażowego, w tym złagodzenie i ograniczenie trendów, będących przejawem judycjalizacji postępowania arbitrażowego wbrew podstawowym zasadom postępowania arbitrażowego.

DEU [*Übermäßige Judizialisierung, ein Hindernis für effektive Schiedsverfahren*]

Im Schiedsverfahren kann die Empfehlung für alle Beteiligten nur lauten, sich auf einen effektiven Verfahrensverlauf vorzubereiten und diesen bereits von Streitbeginn an vorauszusetzen. Der vorliegende Beitrag befasst sich mit einigen Lösungen, die auf ein effektives Schiedsverfahren abzielen und die u. a. vorsehen, bestimmte Trends zu mäßigen bzw. abzubauen, welche eine fortschreitende Judizialisierung des Schiedsverfahrens verkörpern und von daher gegen die grundlegenden Prinzipien des Schiedsverfahrens gerichtet sind.

RUS [*Чрезмерная юридикализация, препятствие для эффективного арбитража*]

В арбитраже можно порекомендовать, чтобы все участвующие субъекты подготовились к эффективному ходу процесса, и ожидать такой ход процесса с самого начала спора. В данной статье рассматриваются некоторые решения в целях достижения эффективного арбитража, в том числе смягчение и ограничение тенденций, которые представляют юридикализацию арбитражного разбирательства, и которые направлены против основных принципов арбитража.

ESP   **[*Judicialización excesiva, obstáculo para un arbitraje eficaz*]**
En el procedimiento de arbitraje es recomendable que todas las partes interesadas se preparen para un desarrollo efectivo del procedimiento y lo asuman desde el mismo comienzo de la controversia. Este trabajo aborda algunas de las soluciones para lograr un procedimiento de arbitraje eficiente, incluyendo la mitigación y reducción de las tendencias que representan la judicialización del arbitraje y que van en contra de los principios básicos del arbitraje.

||||

Jiří Grygar

The Interaction of Arbitration and Mediation in Relation to Justice

Key words:
justice | arbitration |
mediation | constitutional
limits | the right to due
process

Abstract | *This article points to the line of historical development from 1989 to the present, and examines how economic processes in the Czech Republic led to the rapid development of arbitration. Subsequent regulation of the activities of the so-called arbitration centres and of the content of arbitration clauses by case law and consequently also to legislative changes are also examined here. I also describe the response of the courts against abusive practices in consumer disputes as a result of prior opinions of the judiciary to the negative phenomena in the context of arbitration. Subsequently the paper deals with mediation and other alternative dispute resolution methods, and its implementation, as well as its weaknesses in relation to proceedings before the courts. This article also responds to the implications of the re-codification of civil law in the Czech Republic, effective from 2014, and the new regulation of the proceedings before the arbitration commission of the association, newly incorporated in the Arbitration Act. It summarizes the interaction of these methods in relation to economic reasons, draws conclusions regarding the court's actions and assesses the need for legislative changes.*

JUDr. Jiří Grygar, Ph.D. (36), is a judge of the District Court of Prague – East (7 years), civil section, specializing in international and EU law. Previously he worked at the Law Faculty of Palacký University in Olomouc and also lectured at the Judicial Academy in Kroměříž (theory of law). In 2006-2008, he served as a legislative advisor to the Minister of Justice. He co-authored the amendments to the civil procedural law and authored or co-authored books on the theory of law and the philosophy of law, protection of fundamental rights in the EU, comments on the Mediation Act, the Private International Law Act and other books and publications in legal journals.
e-mail:
GrygarJiri@seznam.cz

||||

I. Introduction

6.01. The development of democratization and the economic in the Czech Republic after 1989 is reflected in the legal environment. It is possible to clearly document the interaction of traditional institutes of European legal systems – arbitration and mediation – both with each other and in relation to justice. This condition can be called osmosis in a certain sense, and can be described as a manifestation of socio-economic and legal interpenetration in post-communist democracy.

II. Historical Factors Impacting Arbitration and Justice in the Czech Republic

6.02. Under socialism it was essentially determined that for working people, everything should be as cheap or preferably free. To some extent this was reflected in the legal sector in the provision of legal services and public services of the courts, especially when the level of court fees was set very low in order to optimize access to justice. This situation, which was maintained for several generations, necessarily led to the fact that people were not motivated to seek non judicial solutions and alternative ways of resolving disputes. This indeed corresponds to the power theory approach of the communist state to the citizen. This led to distortion of the rational approach to dispute resolution – that it is normal to conclude an agreement and not to pursue a court case.

III. Democratic Changes

6.03. Since 1989 and the advent of a democratic regime many legal professions were commercialized. In particular, commercialization occurred within the fields of advocacy,[1] notaries[2] (although they still are to some extent delegated powers of the state, as in matters of inheritance) and also the newly introduced institute of the 'court executors'[3] (when the correct designation, given their activities should rather be 'private bailiffs'). Two factors led to an increase in the number of disputes. Primarily, the flowering of entrepreneurship increased disputes, especially in areas which had an impact on a large number of low-income and middle-class people, such as insurance, the provision of banking services and other consumer affairs businesses. Additionally,

---

[1] The Act no. 128/1990 Coll., Advocacy Act; subsequently replaced by Act no. 85/1996 Coll., Advocacy Act.

[2] The Act no. 358/1992 Coll., Notary Act.

[3] The Act no. 120/2001 Coll., Act on Court Executors and Enforcement (Enforcement Order Act).

the increased mobility of the population and reduced state control over this mobility started to increase the number of disputes. The free political situation has spurred a growth of bad payment debts among the young generation. A typical dispute has become a dispute about the payment of a sum of money, usually in small amounts, typically a few thousand Czech crowns, , due to insurance or credit to purchase such things as household equipment or electrical devices. There is also an increase in 'experiential debts', the debts used to finance a vacation or any other kind of personal consumption, which would otherwise have been unattainable due to their financial situation. This has led to the gradual increase in indebtedness of Czech households (1.15 trillion Czech crowns in 2013;[4] 1$ = approx. CZK 20; 1 € = approx. CZK 27.5).

IV. The Reasons for the Onset of Arbitration

6.04.   Czech justice was not prepared for the enormous increase in disputes which arose as a result of the foregoing conditions. This was the case in multiple arenas. In the field of legislation there was an incorrect setting of procedural rules. Additionally, there were personnel issues, as the period saw a massive exodus of experienced judges to the commercial sector in the 1990s, driven by higher revenue in the advocacy. As well as weak administrative staffing of the administrative personnel. Finally, there were material and economic problems, as the salaries of judges at that time were quite low as were the salaries of the administrative personnel –a problem that persists to the present day.[5] There was a backlog in courts and this led to the prolongation of the proceedings. Creditors (especially large companies) therefore looked for other ways to resolve such disputes. Their choice fell logically to arbitration. It should be noted that arbitration was in the Czech legal framework in earlier times, but was reserved for international trade.[6] The situation changed with the adoption in 1994 of a new law on arbitration[7], which was quite modern for that time. One weakness of this law, as discussed below, was the introduction of a limit that permanent arbitration courts may be established by a special law act or under a specific law

---

[4]   Cf. the report of Czech National Bank, available at: http://www.cnb.cz/miranda2/export/sites/www.cnb.cz/cs/financni_stabilita/zpravy_fs/fs_2011-2012/fs_2011-2012_realna_ekonomika.pdf (accessed on 13 November 2014).

[5]   Available at: http://www.novinky.cz/domaci/211228-demonstrovat-budou-i-urednici-ze-soudu-a-zastupitelstvi.html (accessed on 13 November 2014).

[6]   The Act no. 98/1963 Coll., Act on arbitration in international trade and the enforcement of arbitration awards.

[7]   The Act no. 216/1994 Coll., Act on arbitration and the enforcement of arbitration awards.

act[8] and that otherwise the arbitration performance is *ad hoc*. It was therefore not possible to effectively constitute arbitration bodies organized on a commercial basis and provide to the arbitrators the necessary administrative background, as well as to standardize their procedural practices. As an alternative example, progressive regulation in the Slovak Republic made such a procedure possible.[9]

V. Claim Management by Formation of Large Packets of Claims

6.05. The motive of major creditors in dealing with large packets of claims was naturally to appease its growing portfolio. Czech tax regulations did not and do not allow effective tax depreciation even in apparently uncollectible debts. The creditor is forced to have its claim submitted to court or to arbitration, if the arbitration clause was agreed upon and then apply for the enforcement of the so-obtained title. Write-offs took place only after it was found that the enforcement was irrelevant. As a consequence of this, large companies have begun to enter into contracts for the assignment of their claims, usually with newly established companies, founded just for such a purpose. Large packets of claims against individual debtors are forwarded to these companies. This effectively rids the creditor of the burden of debt collection on its own behalf and on its account, even at the cost of some financial losses as the result of the packets of the claims being forwarded at a lower price than their nominal value. With a referral for a price much lower than the nominal value[10], such activity was very profitable, even taking into account the fact that many subsequently obtained enforcement orders cannot be executed because the debtor has no assets, or because the debtor's residence is unknown. The reason for the generation of profit was the pathological status, when profit was achieved not by the collection of debt itself and its accessories, but by the refunds of costs whether in court proceedings or arbitration. This situation arose in relation to justice due to an incorrectly set level (flat rates) for advocates' fees[11] and in relation to arbitration in the absence of clear legislation on recoverable costs in arbitration.

---

[8]   § 13 of the Act no. 216/1994 Coll., on arbitration and the enforcement of arbitration awards.

[9]   § 12 of the Act no. 244/2002 Coll., on arbitration.

[10]   At approx. 1/3 nominal value; there are no statistical data in this area and I use a personal estimate based on practical experience.

[11]   Decree no. 484/2000 Coll., on establishing a flat rate of remuneration for the representation of a party by an advocate or notary public in the decision on costs in civil

VI. The Heyday of Debt Default

6.06. The original creditor or a new creditor under a contract of assignment of receivables (claims forwarding) is motivated to act as quickly to obtain an enforceable title (a court judgment or arbitral award), so that it could be executed, because the level of voluntary compliance by the debtors after the judgment or an arbitral award is small. The Czech Republic has approximately 10 million inhabitants. In the last few years, approximately 750,000 to 1,000,000 enforcement orders were ordered each year; a ratio of 1:10 to the population.[12] Such a situation is clearly pathological and indicates the state of society and economy of the country more than other socio-economic indicators. Unfortunately, there is no available evidence of the number of enforcement orders conducted on the basis of arbitration awards. The Ministry of Justice reported an estimate of approximately 70,000 per annum, but such a low number is clearly not correct.

VII. Negative Phenomena in Arbitration

6.07. On a massive scale, creditors began to use arbitration and in virtually all consumer contracts an arbitration clause was inserted, usually within the general terms and conditions. Given the above specifics about the possibility of the establishment of permanent arbitration courts, the permanent arbitration courts were unused and arbitrators were appointed ad hoc. In this context so-called *arbitration centres* were established either as a company or as an association. In effect they were a service organization for the group of ad hoc arbitrators, which they brought together. Also, even in the the the case where the arbitration clause called for an ad hoc dispute arbitrator with no ties on any arbitration centre, doubts often appeared about their independence. For example a company with a multi-million dollar turnover appointed a person without a university education, living in a small village on the outskirts of the Czech Republic, as an ad hoc arbitrator.

6.08. The establishment of arbitration centres and their activities represented a gray area in relation to the applicable legislation. That in itself probably would not constitute a negative phenomenon, but

---

proceedings and on amending Decree of the Ministry of Justice no. 177/1996 Coll., on advocates' fees and compensation for lawyers providing legal services (advocates tariff). This decree was annulled by the Constitutional Court on 07.05.2013.

[12] See the statistical data of the Czech Ministry of Justice, available at: http://cslav. justice.cz/InfoData/prehledy-agend.html;jsessionid=c36ffe3512db90674a7b4773510e (accessed on 13 November 2014).

subsequently from the scale of their 'production' and content of arbitration awards it started to be obvious that often the principles of due process are not fully respected and that the arbitrator is seeking to satisfy the creditor rather than seeking a fair decision in the case. The weakness of arbitration clauses drawn in relation to the arbitration centres was that they usually did not designate a specific person as ad hoc arbitrator, but contained a clause that the arbitrator should be appointed by the arbitration centre from the list of arbitrators associated with this arbitration centre. However, there was such a mass 'production' of arbitration awards which subsequently spilled over to the courts, together with applications on their enforcement, which led to a boom of enforcement orders. Approximately 250,000–300,000 enforcement orders were carried out by the courts, and approximately 500,000–750,000 enforcement orders were carried out by the 'private' bailiffs on behalf of the courts.[13] Here it should be noted that enforcement orders based on arbitration awards, were ordered by the courts without major reservations. At the same time it is necessary to say that such an inherently formalistic approach was subsequently approved by the higher courts.[14]

VIII. Response of Justice to the Negative Phenomena in Arbitration

6.09. The response of justice to such situation was due to a certain inertia of justice gradually changing. Over time credence began to be given to originally isolated opinions that in the business of claims, by its nature based not on the debt itself but on a different economic reason, the conduct of proceedings for the costs of the proceeding, should be resolutely stopped. From a social point of view such practices were reasonably perceived as impoverishment of the poor. The courts of first instance, therefore, gradually began to reject proposals for a writ of enforcement with reference to the regulation of consumer protection law in accordance with European Union law. Subsequently, this judicature course was supported by higher courts, including the Supreme Court and the Constitutional Court.

---

[13] See the statistical data of the Czech Ministry of Justice, available at: http://cslav. justice.cz/InfoData/prehledy-agend.html;jsessionid=c36ffe3512db90674a7b4773510e (accessed on 13 November 2014).

[14] Cf. for example the Decision of the Supreme Court of 30.10.2008 no. 20 Cdo 2857/2006; of 31.8.2010 no. 20 Cdo 3284/2008.

6.10. The Constitutional Court stated[15] that the right to a lawful judge (the right to due process) can also be reasonably applied to arbitration proceedings because arbitration is something of a departure from traditional judicial proceedings. This is because there are only very limited possibilities of judicial review and that unless the decision was made by an ad hoc arbitrator, the choice of which was carried out according to transparent rules, the result of this decision can not be acceptable. Subsequently, the Constitutional Court stated[16] that it is possible to question (a lack of) the powers of the arbitrator in the enforcement proceedings.

6.11. The Supreme Court also rejected its previous judicature line[17] and concluded that unless the arbitral award was not delivered by an arbitrator whose selection was carried out according to transparent rules[18], the result of the decision could not be acceptable. Such an is award is not eligible as enforceable title under which an enforcement order could be issued, because the arbitrator designated on an absolutely invalid arbitration clause had no jurisdiction to issue an arbitration award under the Arbitration Act. If the enforcement has already been ordered, and if the court additionally finds lack of jurisdiction of the authority which issued the enforceable title, it is necessary to stop the enforcement at any stage for its inadmissibility, even if the debtor did not object to the absence of an arbitration agreement.[19]

IX. Legislative Changes in Arbitration

6.12. The change in the case law established legislative changes which introduced a restrictive amendment of the Arbitration Act in relation to disputes in consumer contracts.[20] The obligation was introduced for the negotiation of a separate arbitration clause from the main contract, and an increased duty to instruct consumers about the consequences of their arbitration clauses. This amendment also saw the introduction of specialization of the arbitrators in consumer disputes and the

---

[15]   Decision of the Constitutional Court of 3.4.2012, no. IV. ÚS 2735/11.

[16]   Decision of the Constitutional Court of 27.9.2012, no III. ÚS 1624/12.

[17]   Cf. the Decision of the Supreme Court of 30. 10. 2008, no. 20 Cdo 2857/2006; of 31. 8. 2010, no. 20 Cdo 3284/2008.

[18]   Such as if the arbitrator was designated by a legal entity that is not a permanent arbitration court established by law.

[19]   Cf. the Decision of the Supreme Court of 28. 7. 2011 no. 31 Cdo 958/2012 or no. 20 Cdo 2227/2011.

[20]   The Act no. 19/2012 Coll.

introduction of registration of such specialized arbitrators in a registry maintained by the Ministry of Justice, as well as increased demands for their education (the obligation of higher education including a master's degree). It can be argued that to achieve the necessary changes, the above-described changes in the Czech judiciary probably would be sufficient. The adoption of legislative changes was motivated not by the need for real change, but by a populist effort, because after the case law was changed, it became a popular topic in the media, and therefore a politically interesting topic.

X. Reaction of Creditors to Changes in Arbitration

6.13. As a result of these changes thousands of enforcement proceedings conducted on the basis of arbitral awards were stopped, because they lost their character of an enforceable title. This was followed by the movement of the mass of cases from resolution in arbitration to the courts. It must be said that a considerable part of disputes at the time of the arbitration boom continued to be administered in proceedings before the courts. In any case, it became apparent that the characteristics of the Czech population described in the introduction in its approach to judicial procedures usually took the form of procedural passivity or absconding with the short-sighted aim of lengthening the trial. The latter occurred often without the knowledge of how it increases costs, which would later be applied. However, due to procedural passivity of most of the defendants, decisions in these cases were and still are made without a hearing, though this was only if it was not possible to deal with it in the first phase by way of the payment order. The decision making is therefore based on the documentary evidence by using a legal fiction of a consent of the parties that they agree with the decision in the case without a hearing, because they previously did not respond to a court's question whether they do agree with such procedure.[21] Such things are approximately 1/4 to 1/3 of cases before the judges of first instance.[22] Usually this is popularly known as a petty dispute or minor claims or small claims (a sum of money up to CZK 10,000, which is approx. USD 500). Such cases are not appealable[23] and the only possible remedy is the constitutional complaint.

---

[21] According to § 115a in conjunction with § 101 point 4 of Act no. 99/1963 Coll., Civil Procedure Code.

[22] There are no statistical data in this area and I use a personal estimate based on practical experience.

[23] § 202 point 2 of Act no. 99/1963 Coll., Civil Procedure Code.

XI. Related Negative Phenomena

6.14. There was a gradual increase in court fees, with the legislators goal being to moderate the number of small claims cases before the courts. However, the court fees are still relatively low compared to neighbouring countries.[24] Therefore, in this direction no significant effects on the number of pending cases occurred. We can point to a large number of cases pending before the Czech courts in comparison with other European countries,[25] where even in comparable large states the amount of such cases is lower than in the Czech Republic by tens of percent. As already indicated above, in matters of small claims of consumer disputes the main economic reason of the claimant was often the costs of the proceeding rather than the debt itself and its accessories. This is true even under the condition that the claimant will subsequently manage to recover such costs from the debtor. Additionally, many of the obtained enforcement titles can not be executed either because the debtor has no assets or the debtor's residence is unknown. Even so such activity was very profitable, due to an incorrectly set level of advocates' fees (which are part of the cista for the creditor) which have been drafted as a flat rate for the entire proceeding (i.e. as a percentage of the subject of the dispute).[26]

XII. Response of the Courts

6.15. Courts of the first instance responded again (with a certain delay) and in cases where the amount of the costs often exceeded the value of the defendant's debt and its accessories several times, they began to reduce those costs to the level of the value of the amount claimed.

6.16. This approach was subsequently confirmed in the decision of the Constitutional Court. The court stated[27] that this approach cannot be described as arbitrary or disproportionate, if the lower court concluded from the specific facts that the claimants costs based on legal representation by an advocate were not necessary for effective exercise

---

[24] Compare the Czech Act no. 549/1991 Coll., on court fees, and the German law on court fees – 'Gerichtskostengesetz' (18 June 1878, RGBl. S. 141) and 'Gesetz über Gerichtskosten in Familiensachen' (17 December 2008; BGBl. I S. 2586, 2666) or Austrian 'Gerichtsgebührengesetz' (27 November 1984, BGBl. Nr. 501/1984).

[25] Compare the statistics of the European Commission for the Efficiency of Justice, available at: http://www.coe.int/T/dghl/cooperation/cepej/default_en.asp (accessed on 13 November 2014).

[26] Decree no. 484/2000 Coll.

[27] Decision of the Constitutional Court of 27.12.2011 no. IV. ÚS 2777/2011.

of their rights (i.e. if the court awarded the claimant to recoverable costs of only a court fee). Further, they noted that this was the case if the court gave sufficient reasons for its decision in accordance with the requirements of due process, which can be applied to decisions on costs. The Constitutional Court also concluded that the applicant's right to legal assistance could not be violated while they were before the court of first instance represented by an advocate.

6.17. Approximately three months afterwards the Constitutional Court concluded[28] that it seems fair to determine the amount of remuneration for representation by an advocate as equivalent to the principal amount claimed in small claims cases (the proceedings of which the judgment of the first-instance court is not appealable). These were made as 'forms' claims, taking into consideration the proceedings, the parties, the specifics of the case and fluency of the proceedings before the courts of first instance. Drafting of a form application represents an administrative act rather than performance of an act of legal services. The defendant is a consumer and it is a legal relationship in which the debtor is *de facto* excluded from the possibility to negotiate a commitment with other content. At the same time, it is not important whether the right for pecuniary interest is recovered by the original creditor or his legal successor. The Constitutional Court stated that it considered that the costs should compensate for reasonable expenses of the winning party in the enforcement or protection of their rights, but in these cases the costs in the connection with the representation by an advocate in all the circumstances is lower than their pay as a flat rate laid down by law (Decree of the Ministry of Justice no. 484/2000 Coll., or decree no. 177/1996 Coll., *'Attorney Tariff'*). If a claimant was entirely successful in the dispute, usually they have the right to recover costs. This does not mean that the court decides on their compensation 'mechanically'. Rather, it must consider whether other relevant circumstances exist that have a substantial effect on the granting or withholding of compensation of the costs which were purposefully expended and what possible ways will be used to determine them. Furthermore, if ordinary courts choose an exceptional procedure for which they have legal support when deciding on costs, in which the compensation is still based on the principle of success in the case, and the use of legal exemption is also supported by arguments, then they can not be reproached for insufficient protection of the rights and freedoms guaranteed by constitutional order. The Constitutional Court pointed out that they had to unify the jurisprudence of the ordinary

---

[28] Decision of the Constitutional Court of 29.3.2012 no. I. ÚS 3923/2011.

courts in the form of a judgment in the so-called small claims matters, because there is no other authority which could then make a judgment of a binding manner. Since the consumer is effectively excluded from the opportunity to negotiate terms of other content, then it is fair that remuneration for the advocate representing the claimant should be determined so that it does not exceed one times of the claimed principal. This is with specific regard to the need to respect the principle of proportionality between the amount of expended costs and the amount of compensation cost.

6.18.   Similarly, in its judgment I. ÚS 988/12 of 25 7th 2012, the Constitutional Court commented on the rule according to which the successful party can only obtain compensation of reasonably expended costs. The court ruled that this party shall be subject to any costs, including the costs associated with the representing advocate (to pay for representation, cash expenses and for the value added tax). The Constitutional Court stated that for reasonably incurred costs, the only costs which can be considered are those which the procedural party necessarily had to spend, in order to properly defend its violated or threatened subjective law in court. Costs associated with the representation of an attorney will usually conform to this definition. The Constitutional Court stated that this rule can not be absolute, or of an unconditional nature. There can also be situations where the costs associated with the representation of an attorney can not be regarded as necessary for the proper enforcement or protection of rights in court. That is especially the case of any misuse of the right to representation by an attorney.

XIII.   Subsequent Legislative Changes

6.19.   In force from 1 March 2012, in the period between the two decisions of the Constitutional Court, the decree was amended laying down an advocate's flat rate sum for the representation of a client in court[29] (Decree no. 484/2000 Coll.). This also set a more gradual decrease and spacing in commissions in cases where the subject-matter does not exceed CZK 10,000 (small claims).

---

[29]   Decree no. 64/2012 Coll., on amending Decree of the Ministry of Justice no. 484/2000 Coll., on establishing a flat rate remuneration for the representation of a party by an advocate or notary public in the decisions on costs in civil proceedings and amending Decree Ministry of Justice no. 177/1996 Coll., on remuneration and compensation of advocates for the provision of legal services (advocates tariff), as subsequently amended.

XIV. Further Reaction of the Constitutional Court

6.20. Less than two weeks after the above mentioned judgment, the Constitutional Court derogated the decree which regulated the flat rate (lump-sum) remuneration of advocates, for reasons of unconstitutionality.[30] The Constitutional Court stated that the determination of flat rates for advocates completely ignored the factual complexity of the dispute, the number of operations conducted in the matter, the time and effectiveness of law enforcement or defence of a claim. They further stated that the reported costs would regularly be in gross disproportion to the value of the dispute. This leads to a sanctioning of unsuccessful parties and the amount of costs being inconsistent with the principle of proportionality of sanctions. This is de facto imposition of sanctions without law.

XV. Reservations to the Decisions of the Constitutional Court

6.21. It is possible to have some reservations about the arguments of the Constitutional Court. Firstly, the Constitutional Court examined one decree twice in a short time interval, and the derogation occurred in the latter case without anything changing in the interim. Second, in its annulling decision the Constitutional Court did not provide the legislature any new clear regulation and did not set the borders of such regulation. The derogation of flat rates costs legislation started the application of a historically older prescription, namely defining an advocate's fee for each individual act of legal aid.[31] But the reason for this was that in 2000 the flat rate regulation was adopted because advocates were motivated to stretch the length of the proceedings in order to obtain a higher remuneration for performing more legal assistance. In other words, it began to be applied to other legislation, but the amount of advocates' remuneration remained comparable to the prior situation.

XVI. Subsequent Legislative Changes

6.22. The logical step followed by the legislature was that the amendment[32] of advocates' tariffs decreased the amount of remuneration for the

---

[30] The plenary judgment of the Constitutional Court of **17. 4. 2013** no. **Pl.ÚS 25/12.**

[31] Decree Ministry of Justice no. 177/1996 Coll., on remuneration and compensation of advocates for the provision of legal services (advocates tariff).

[32] Decree of 26 June 2014, no. 120/2014 Coll., on amending Decree of the Ministry of Justice no. 177/1996 Coll., on remuneration and compensation of advocates for the provision of legal services (advocates tariff).

individual acts of legal assistance and also limited their amount. However, it must be noted that the size of reduction is questionable. The new fees obviously do not match the average prices of legal services of the advocates. The question is – are they set below the level of economic efficiency in the relation to real costs or not? From the explanatory report to the new regulation it is evident that this aspect of the matter was not considered at all and that the level of remuneration was fixed at the sole discretion of the legislature. This would obviously fail the constitutional test of proportionality.

XVII. Mediation

6.23.   Mediation as well as arbitration is one of the classic institutions of dispute resolution. Just as arbitration functioned in the Czech legal order during the socialist era, so mediation as an institution began to appear during the 1990s.[33] With the arrival of freedom of enterprise, people who performed mediation, performed it as a business with a trade license under the Trade Act. In that time legislative regulation of mediation was completely missing. Although it was originally a feature developed for the Anglo-Saxon legal system, mediation creates untapped positive potential for a continental system of law. In pursuit of more effective dispute settlement and reduction of the burden on the courts, the Czech Ministry of Justice reforming of civil and procedural law included a requirement for the inclusion of mediation into the civil trial. However, a major obstacle in the Czech Republic was a lack of finances. There was indeed the political will to integrate mediation into the Czech legal order, but there were not necessary financial resources available. Therefore, a minimalistic regulation was prepared.[34] This was essentially based on the idea that the court suspends its judicial proceedings for the purpose of mediation or other similar proceedings, provided that the parties agree and if the financing of such extrajudicial proceedings will be secured from the state budget or private sources, but always in the relation to the specific case. It was based on the assumption that either party to the dispute, or at least some of them, or some other entity (i.e. NGO´s) would be willing to finance the mediation procedure. After the adoption of this amendment (Act No. 295/2008 Coll.) the process continued to define the thesis of a

---

[33]   For example, the Association of Mediators of the Czech Republic was founded later, in 2000.

[34]   In the interest of full disclosure, I participated in the conception and creation of this regulation.

comprehensive treatment system of mediation, whose final version is the Mediation Act (Act. No. 202/2012 Coll. – Mediation Act).[35]

XVIII. The Mediation Act

6.24.   One of the main reasons for the adoption of the Mediation Act, in addition to modernizing Czech procedural law was the Czech Republic's obligation to transpose the European Parliament and Council Directive No. 2008/52/EC of 21 May 2008 on certain aspects of mediation in civil and commercial matters, into the national legal order. This directive applies to a relatively narrow range of cases with an international element. At the time of adoption of the Directive, some states already had a long-term and well-functioning system of mediation at their national level. These states have therefore taken a minimalistic approach to the transformation of the Directive or implemented it outside their national regulation of mediation as a self standing act. The obvious reason was that they did not want a small European legislation to impact their well-functioning system, which in practice turns out to be a much larger number of cases when compared to the national number of conflicts and disputes with an international element. An example can be seen in Austria.[36] Unfortunately, in the Czech Republic this rational approach has not been accepted and the Mediation Act contains provisions on mediation for all types of litigation, regardless of the existence of a cross-border element. Likewise, as mentioned above, the same applies in the relation to the possibilities of access to the position of a mediator by the Mediation Act. This is a critical evaluation of the excessive approach to regulate the conditions of the legitimation of the arbitrator.

XIX. Expectations and Facts Relating to the Mediation Act

6.25.   Discussion of the draft law on mediation aroused great emotions and surprisingly took hold as a big topic. Given that the remuneration of mediators in practice is close to the remuneration of advocates, and that a flat rate fee is paid at the first meeting with a mediator from the state budget, and the number of things that can be solved through mediation, this created an atmosphere of a mediation boom with a visions of potential profits. An experienced mediator can really

---

[35]   The Act no. 202/2012 Coll., on Mediation and amending certain Acts (Mediation Act).

[36]   Zivilrechts-Mediations-Gesetz (BGBl. I Nr. 29/2003) and 'Mediationsgesetz' (EU-MediatG) (BGBl. I Nr. 21/2011).

contribute to resolve disputes and straighten relations between parties better than (or at least in different way from) the authoritative decision of the court or arbitrator. Unlike in mediation the parties in court deliberately withhold their potentially dangerous information and not unlike a mediator do not separately negotiate with parties (*caucus*) out of respect for the principle of equality of arms. The explanatory report to the Mediation Act pointed to a very high success rate of resolving conflict cases, up to 75% according to world statistics.[37]

6.26.   Several main reasons were given for this effectiveness. First, mediation attempts to enable all persons an alternative solution to their conflicts by rapid and cultivated alternative dispute resolution. Secondly, it lightens the burden of the courts, by providing the opportunity to avoid court litigation and to solve conflict without long waiting periods, and without unnecessary financial cista. Thirdly, it lightens the long-term mental load on the parties. Finally, it protects the interests of children in mediation in matters with an impact on family. However, the main weakness of these considerations is the lack of motivation of creditors, whether for economic reasons or simply from their position. Regarding the economic motivation, the mediation must be significantly cheaper than court proceedings or arbitration. Failing that, it must bring other benefits that balance higher costs. Such benefits would include speed and the conservation of a long-term positive relationship between the parties with the possibility of continued cooperation. Thus, these are the same arguments for which the parties are turning to arbitration rather than the courts. However, in practice the price of services of a mediator ranges at a similar level as the services of advocates and therefore in this sense lacks a motivating factor. The same is true concerning the price of the mediation and court fees, which in the Czech Republic are not high. The creditor is also not motivated to any form of settlement, if they are aware that their claim is provable in court and if at the same time they have no economic interest in any other future contracts with the debtor. The mediation agreement, unlike the arbitration award is not an enforceable title according to Mediation Act. Also, the Mediation Act does not allow the court to order the parties to mediate. It only allows the ordering of the participants to attend mediation for a maximum of 3 hours, during which time the mediator has a chance to convince them to conclude a contract of mediation. This contract would include the way in which remuneration would be determined and on which of the participants it

---

[37]   See information on the symposium on Mediation in the public sphere, New Ways of Solving Conflicts and Participation in the EUREGIO, Osnabrück, January 2007.

would apply. It is therefore an economically and practically unfortunate solution. All these factors have resulted in alternative dispute resolution forms from court proceeding towards mediation being exceptional, especially with regard to disputes between an entrepreneur as a creditor and a consumer as a debtor.

XX. Other Methods of ADR

6.27.   The above mentioned conclusions regarding mediation apply *mutatis mutandis* to any other methods of alternative dispute resolution. Due to the current European Union legislation it will primarily involve the Regulation on consumer ODR,[38] which will come into effect from 9 January 2016. This is basically the introduction of 'electronic marketplace' methods of alternative dispute resolution and their subsequent electronic realization. Additional legislation includes the Directive on consumer ADR,[39] for which the transposition deadline ends 9 July 2015.

XXI. Re-codification of Civil Law

6.28.   On 1 January 2014, the new Civil Code entered into force,[40] as well as other legislation related to its adoption. Regulation of mediation was not affected by these changes. However, the same is not true for arbitration. The new Civil Code restores the institute of 'association' as a fundamental legal form of voluntary association in a specific common goal. The Civil Code in the regulation of the association and its organs regulated the institute of arbitration commission (in § 265 to § 267). This provides that the arbitration commission decides disputed matters within the association self-government to the extent determined by statutes of the association. Unless the statutes set otherwise, the arbitration commission shall decide disputes between the member and the association concerning the payment of membership fees and it shall review the decision to expel a member of the association. The provision

---

[38]   REGULATION (EU) No. 524/2013 OF THE EUROPEAN PARLIAMENT AND OF THE COUNCIL of 21 May 2013 on online dispute resolution for consumer disputes and amending Regulation (EC) No. 2006/2004 and Directive 2009/22/EC (Regulation on consumer ODR).

[39]   DIRECTIVE 2013/11/EU OF THE EUROPEAN PARLIAMENT AND OF THE COUNCIL of 21 May 2013 on alternative dispute resolution for consumer disputes and amending Regulation (EC) No. 2006/2004 and Directive 2009/22/EC (Directive on consumer ADR).

[40]   The Act no. 89/2012 Coll., The Civil Code.

of § 267 of the Civil Code states only that the proceedings before the arbitration commission will be regulated by a separate law. For any of the above mentioned provisions of the Civil Code, it is not apparent that the arbitration commission of the association should have the courts discretion in the extent of its competence, or that it could issue enforceable decisions. The procedural regulation of the proceedings before the arbitration commission of the association was not performed by a separate law, as originally intended, but was incorporated into the Arbitration Act (§ § 40e to 40k). However in my opinion that is wrong, as it goes beyond the frame of self-government and harms the institution of arbitration.

XXII. Regulation of the Proceedings before the Arbitration Commission of the Association

6.29.   The legislature, impermissibly mixes the term '*the proceedings before the arbitration commission of the association*' (meaning the process in the implementation of autonomous self-government) with the term '*arbitration*' within the meaning of the voluntary exclusion of jurisdiction of the court in the purpose of the delegation of decision-making powers on the arbitral tribunal with the purpose of issuing an authoritative and enforceable decision. Even if that were so, it would be an inadmissible procedure, because it is important to realize that in classical arbitration, the exclusion of the case at issue (if is arbitrable) from the decision-making powers of the court occurs, on the basis of the free decision of the parties, through a negotiated arbitration clause. The arbitration commission of the association's decision-making power could then be inferred from the fact that every member of the association gave such consent by implication (i.e. a similar effect as concluded by the arbitration clause) with his entry into the association. Even this, however, cannot be the case, because the statutes are a special type of contract, which may not always have unconditional approval of all members of the association (which the explanatory report also states). Therefore one cannot automatically infer that a member of the association thus expressed their agreement with the delegation of decision-making powers of the court to the arbitration commission of the association. How the legislature concluded the competence of the authority of the association to issue enforceable decisions is unclear. I am therefore convinced that the regulation of proceedings before the arbitration commission of the association is the withdrawal of the right to a lawful judge (due process of law).

6.30. According to § 40f point 1 of the Arbitration Act, the proceeding before the commission is initiated on the date the application is received at the address specified in the statutes of the association. If no such address is listed in the statutes, the application shall be addressed to the Commission of the seat of the association. From the cited provision, it is not clear who the addressee should be. Whether the association or commission, respectively, the effects of the initiation of proceedings occur simply by delivery to the address of the association and not by the fact that the application really entered the dispositional sphere of the commission.

6.31. According to paragraph 40f point 2 of the Arbitration Act, the statutes and internal regulations in the statutes expressly marked or written by agreement of the parties notwithstanding the Arbitration Act (i.e. differently from the regulation of § 19) can modify the procedure, regulating the Commission's proceedings. It should be noted that § 19, which sets out the procedure of an arbitration trial, is the legal minimum for a right to due process in arbitration. If the arbitration commission of the association can exclude this possibility, then logically such a requirement cannot be met and it means nothing else than hacking the systematics of arbitration.

6.32. According to § 40j point 1 of the Arbitration Act the court can, on the application of a party, cancel an arbitration award issued by the commission if the commission decided the dispute was in clear breach of good manners or public order. Thus, the cited provision has extended the grounds for annulment of an arbitration award compared to the list contained in § 31. Firstly, as regards the form, it must be pointed out that the reason for cancellation for breach of good manners should be that such a defect is manifested in the decision of the commission itself (in the arbitration award) and not in its previous process, as set out in the cited provision. Apparently, it is just an incorrect wording by the legislature, which was apparently referring to the decision itself and not the action of the commission. Second, in terms of content, the conflict with good manners or public order are universal corrective in the entire field of civil law, respectively, they are accepted by the entire legal system. I believe, therefore, that the provision constitutes senseless and unnecessary 'legislative wadding' that did not have to be subject to explicit legal regulation.

XXIII. Summary

6.33. From the facts described above, it is clear that the Czech courts adequately respond to the excesses in the business scene and their manifestations in both arbitration and justice itself. The legislature is trying to copy these judiciary lines, with varying degrees of success, in some cases without significant practical needs, when controversial issues have already been resolved by the case law of the judiciary. The exact opposite can be found in the work of the legislature, with occasional expressions that in order to achieve the objectives address the symptoms, not the causes, of the negative state. In relation to business with the claims concerning consumer contracts there would be a rational solution to take measures to limit forwarding of (often) unenforceable debts, for example by improving access of companies for tax write-off of such debts, or to allow courts in the event of the application of such claims to review the limitation period *ex officio*. There are often suits brought with long barred claims with the hope that the debtor will be passive and will not raise an objection of limitation, often from ignorance, if not represented by a lawyer. As a result of the current situation, in my opinion, there is an unnecessary negative perception of the advocates, judges, as well as justice, within the whole society.

XXIV. Conclusion

6.34. Judiciary, arbitration and mediation, as well as other methods of alternative dispute resolution, form a natural and relatively conflict-free interaction. Any excesses the judiciary can effectively deal with. Legislative activity, however, leads to an artificial blending of these institutions, often at an exorbitant price, which is the disruption of the internal structure of the respective institution. It is also clear that the primary reasons for the interaction are based on the economic reality of society and find their projection in the institution of arbitration, mediation or other alternative dispute resolution methods. It is hardly possible to talk about their mutual rivalry, or of any rivalry with justice, but only about their 'attractiveness' in terms of the efficiency of debt recovery, especially in the eyes of creditors, as the initiators of proceedings.

| | |

Summaries

DEU *[Das Wechselspiel von Schiedsverfahren und Mediation in Bezug auf die Justiz]*
Unter Verweis auf die historische Entwicklungslinie vom Jahr 1989 bis zur Gegenwart beschreibt der Artikel die stürmische, von wirtschaftlichen Gründen getragene Entwicklung der Schiedsgerichtsbarkeit in der Tschechischen Republik, gefolgt von der Regulierung der Streitschlichtungstätigkeit an den sog. Schiedszentren und des Inhalts von Schiedsklauseln durch die Rechtsprechung der Gerichte und späterhin durch gesetzgeberische Änderungen. Beschrieben wird außerdem das Vorgehen der Gerichte gegen missbräuchliche Praktiken in Verbraucherstreitigkeiten, die sich in Bezug auf die Justiz in Folge des früheren Herantretens der Gerichtsbarkeit an negative Erscheinungen im Rahmen der Schiedsgerichtsbarkeit etabliert hatten. Schließlich befasst sich der Beitrag auch mit dem Problemkreis Mediation (und den übrigen Methoden der alternativen Streitbeilegung) und deren unabhängig vom Schiedswesen stattfindender Betrieb sowie deren Schwachstellen im Verhältnis zu Verfahren vor den Gerichten. Der Artikel reagiert außerdem auf die Folgen der grundlegenden Neugestaltung des Zivilrechts in der Tschechischen Republik, die zu Jahresbeginn 2014 in Kraft getreten ist, sowie auf die neue Regelung von Verfahren vor der Schiedskommission von Vereinen, die ins Schiedsverfahrensgesetz mit aufgenommen wurde. Er fasst das Wechselspiel zwischen den genannten Methoden in Anknüpfung an die dahinter stehenden wirtschaftlichen Gründe zusammen, zieht Schlüsse bezüglich der Vorgehensweise der Gerichte und bewertet den Bedarf an gesetzgeberischen Änderungen.

CZE *[Vzájemná interakce arbitráže a mediace ve vztahu k justici]*
Příspěvek popisuje s poukazem na linii historického vývoje od roku 1989 do současnosti, jak z ekonomických důvodů došlo v České republice k bouřlivému rozvoji arbitráže a následné regulaci činnosti tzv. arbitrážních center a obsahu rozhodčích doložek prostřednictvím judikatury soudů a následně též legislativními změnami. Dále popisuje postup soudů proti zneužívajícím praktikám ve spotřebitelských sporech, které se ve vztahu k justici etablovaly v důsledku předchozího postupu justice vůči negativním jevům v rámci arbitráže. Následně se zabývá problematikou mediace, jakož i ostatních metod alternativního řešení sporů, a její realizace nezávisle na arbitráži, jakož i jejím slabinám ve vztahu k řízením před soudy. Reaguje také na důsledky rekodifikace civilního práva v České republice, účinné od roku 2014, a na novou úpravu řízení před rozhodčí komisí spolku, začleněnou do zákona o

rozhodčím řízení. Shrnuje vzájemnou interakci uvedených metod v návaznosti na ekonomické důvody, činí závěry ohledně postupu soudů a hodnotí potřebu legislativních změn.

| | |

POL [*Wzajemna interakcja między arbitrażem i mediacjami w stosunku do sądownictwa*]

Niniejszy artykuł analizuje w perspektywie historycznej (od 1989 roku) rozwój arbitrażu w Czechach, negatywne zjawiska w arbitrażu, późniejszą regulację w zakresie tzw. centrów arbitrażu oraz treści klauzul arbitrażowych wskutek praktyki orzeczniczej sądów i w efekcie zmian legislacyjnych. Opisuje problematykę mediacji oraz pozostałych metod alternatywnego rozstrzygania sporów, nowe regulacje dotyczące postępowania przed komisją arbitrażową stowarzyszenia i wzajemne interakcje między wspomnianymi metodami.

FRA [*Les interactions de l'arbitrage et de la médiation dans leurs relations avec la justice*]

Le présent article retrace l'histoire de l'arbitrage en République tchèque (depuis 1989), ses aspects négatifs, la régulation consécutive desdits centres d'arbitrage et le contenu des clauses compromissoires à travers la jurisprudence des tribunaux et les modifications législatives qui ont suivi. Nous examinerons ici la problématique de la médiation comme celle des autres méthodes de résolution alternative des litiges, ainsi que la nouvelle réglementation adoptée pour les procédures menées devant la commission arbitrage d'une confédération, et les interactions entre les méthodes décrites.

RUS [*Взаимодействие арбитража и медиации по отношению к юстиции*]

В статье описывается историческое развитие (с 1989 г.) арбитража в Чешской Республике, негативные явления в арбитраже, последующее регулирование т. н. арбитражных центров и содержания арбитражных оговорок документами судебной практики судов и последующими изменениями в законодательстве. Рассматривается проблематика медиации, а также прочих методов альтернативного урегулирования споров, новое регулирование разбирательства в арбитражной комиссии ассоциации и взаимодействие указанных методов.

Czech (& Central European) Yearbook of Arbitration

ESP   [*Interacción mutua entre el arbitraje y la mediación en relación con la justicia*]

El artículo describe el desarrollo histórico del arbitraje (desde 1989) en la República Checa, los fenómenos negativos del arbitraje, la regulación posterior de los llamados centros de arbitraje y el contenido de la jurisprudencia de las cláusulas de arbitraje de los tribunales y los subsecuentes cambios legislativos. Aborda la problemática de la mediación y otros métodos de resolución alternativa de controversias, la nueva forma de los procedimientos ante la comisión de arbitraje del gremio y la interacción mutua de los métodos anteriores.

|||

Czech (& Central European) Yearbook of Arbitration

Andrzej Kubas | Agnieszka Trzaska

Two Examples of Interaction between State Courts and Arbitration: Ruling on the Competence of an Arbitral Tribunal to Adjudicate and Injunctive Relief in Arbitral Proceedings

Key words:
Arbitrability | arbitral
tribunal | arbitration |
arbitration law | interim
measures | interim relief |
jurisdiction | jurisdiction
provisions | litigation |
model law | national
courts | New York
Convention | preliminary
rulings | state courts |
UNCITRAL Model Law

Abstract | *Although international arbitration has achieved a substantial level of independence from state courts, the role of such courts is still important for effectiveness of arbitral proceedings. Interactions between state courts and arbitral tribunals may be particularly intensive in those areas in which tribunals and state courts have parallel or concurrent competence in the course of arbitration. State courts play an important part in the examination of the jurisdiction of the arbitral tribunal in a given case. Such an examination may take place before initiation of arbitration if the other party raises a charge of arbitration agreement in separate proceedings, or during arbitration itself when the state courts can control the decision of the arbitral tribunal on its jurisdiction. The state court's decision that arbitration is the proper forum for hearing parties' dispute is binding both on the arbitral tribunal and the parties themselves. It is also binding on the state courts in post-arbitration proceedings as far as these may concern the circumstances which the court examined when it referred the parties to arbitration. Various interactions between state courts and arbitral tribunal may take place in the course of deciding on temporary relief (formally known as the securing of claims).*

Prof. Andrzej Kubas
is an attorney at law
and partner at the
Polish law firm Kubas
Kos Gałkowski –
Adwokaci and a
professor at
Jagiellonian University.
He is the author of
various publications in
the field of arbitration,
court proceedings, civil
and commercial law,
insurance law and
reinsurance. He is an
expert in the scope of
civil and commercial
law as well as cross-
border court and
arbitration
proceedings. He
supervises the KKG's
litigation and
arbitration proceedings
team. Prof. Kubas is
also an arbiter of the
Court of Arbitration at
the Polish Chamber of
Commerce. Email:
andrzej.kubas@kkg.pl

Agnieszka Trzaska is
an attorney at law at
the Polish law firm of

| | |

I. Introductory Remarks

7.01. Admittedly, the system of arbitration maintains far reaching independence from the state courts, yet this independence is not absolute and for systemic and pragmatic reasons it must have its limits. These limits can be set by the nature of the case, as not all cases are arbitrable after all,[1] but also, as examples in literature aptly indicate, the inadmissibility of engagement by the arbitral tribunal in any 'acts that would require the state system of coercion to be used'.[2] Hence, if a party to arbitration proceedings does not of its free will enforce an award issued in relation thereto, the winning party may enforce the award solely via institutions of the state administration of justice in the country of enforcement. Especially in international arbitration, voluntary submission to an arbitral award should be a key principle and in practice this is frequently the case. However, it seems that the 'force' of the arbitral tribunal's authority as well as legal awareness

Kubas Kos Gałkowski – Adwokaci. She has experience in international commercial arbitration and economic matters, including disputes between company shareholders. Ms. Trzaska has extensive experience in the preparation of opinions in the scope of civil law and commercial law. She has participated in projects related to bankruptcy proceedings and she has also worked on the team ensuring the provision of comprehensive legal services for one of the leading banks in Poland. Email: agnieszka.trzaska @kkg.pl

---

[1]   In the jurisprudence of international arbitration it is stated that certain types of disputes cannot be arbitrated – the so called non-arbitrability doctrines. See Article II.1. of the below defined NYC and Articles V.2. and Articles 24.2.b and 36.1.b.i of the UNCITRAL Model Law. Legislation of particular countries differ as to specific solutions in that regard, excluding certain types of cases from arbitral jurisdiction, generally speaking for policy reasons. In particular, this refers to cases concerning such areas in which the parties' autonomy is subject to material limitations. In most cases the following types of case are subject to exclusive state courts' jurisdiction and cannot be referred to arbitration by the will of the parties: insolvency cases, labor disputes, consumer cases, industrial property cases as to granting of such protection – see GARY B. BORN, INTERNATIONAL ARBITRATION: LAW AND PRACTICE, Alphen aan de Rjin: Kluwer Law International 82-85 (2012). Also ALAN REDFERN, MARTIN HUNTER, NIGEL BLACKABY, CONSTANTINE PARTASIDES, LAW AND PRACTICE OF INTERNATIONAL COMMERCIAL ARBITRATION, London: Sweet & Maxwell 163–172, paras. 3.12–3.34 (2004). See also Article 2059 of the French Civil Code of Procedure, Article 1030 of the German Code of Civil Procedure (ZPO), Article 177 (1) of the Swiss Federal Statue on Private International Law.

[2]   Tadeusz Ereciński, Arbitraż a sądownictwo państwowe (*Arbitration and state court system*), 2 PRZEGLĄD USTAWODAWSTWA GOSPODARCZEGO (REVIEW OF ECONOMIC LEGISLATION) PUG 2 et seg. (1995). TADEUSZ ERECIŃSKI; KAROL WEITZ, SĄD ARBITRAŻOWY, (COURT OF ARBITRATION), Warszawa: Lexis Nexis 53–54 (2008) and literature therein presented.

and the integrity of parties are not always enough to cause this. This is because of the substantial threat, existing in all contemporary legal systems, of a forced enforcement of an arbitral award through institutions of the state (in particular due to the universal nature of the New York Convention of 1958[3]) and *imperium* only they are entitled to. Within recent years there has been a visible tendency in arbitral jurisdiction, to loosen the limitations on the freedom of arbitral jurisdiction imposed by the interference of state courts, especially in international arbitration. In all European legal systems, it would be an exaggeration to say that the competences of the arbitral and state judiciary collide, but they certainly come into contact in several substantial areas. Specifically, these include: *ad hoc* establishment of an arbitral tribunal, settlement of doubts regarding the competence of the arbitral tribunal, securing of claims pursued in arbitration, cooperation in some procedural action, particularly hearing of evidence, and finally recognition and/or ascertainment of enforceability of arbitral awards issued by both domestic and foreign arbitral tribunals. The present paper draws attention to two of the above mentioned 'points of contact' between the state courts and arbitration, namely: ruling on the competence of arbitral tribunals and the securing of claims pursued before them.[4]

---

[3] Convention on the Recognition and Enforcement of Foreign Arbitral Awards (the NYC) (New York, 1958) (adopted 10 June 1958, entered into force 7 June 1959, 4739 UNTC (, ratified by 152 states, see: http://www.uncitral.org/uncitral/en/uncitral_texts/arbitration/NYConvention_status.html (accessed on 22 September 2014).

[4] These issues have been discussed for some time in both Polish and European jurisprudence. For example: Tadeusz Ereciński, , *supra* note 2, at 2 and subsequent; TADEUSZ ERECIŃSKI; KAROL WEITZ, *supra* note 2, at 53–61. Sławomir Cieślak, *Stosunek postępowania arbitrażowego do innych rodzajów postępowania cywilnego* (*Relation of arbitration to other types of civil proceedings*), 4(16) KWARTALNIK ADR ARBITRAŻ I MEDIACJI (*ADR Arbitration and Mediation Quarterly*) 15, 25–27 (2011). Włodzimierz Głodowski, *Zabezpieczenie roszczeń dochodzony przed sądem polubowny* (*Securing of claims pursued in arbitration*), Materiały pokonferencyjne 'Perspektywy rozwoju sądownictwa arbitrażowego', Katowice, 20.–21.11.2008, (Post-conference materials form conference 'Perspectives of arbitration', Katowice, 20-21.11.2008). Michał Kocur, *Zabezpieczenie roszczeń dochodzonych przed sądem polubownym* (*Securing of claims pursued in arbitration*), 15 MONITOR PRAWNICZY (*Legal Monitor*) 794 and subsequent (2005); Adam Górski, *Postępowanie zabezpieczające przed sądem polubownym w świetle nowelizacji KPC z 28.7.2005 r.* (*Securing of claims in arbitration under the amendment of CCP of 28.7.2005*), 18 MONITOR PRAWNICZY (*Legal Monitor*), 971 and subsequent (2006); Andrzej W. Wiśniewski, *Charakter prawny instytucji arbitrażu w świetle nowelizacji polskiego prawa arbitrażowego* (*Legal nature of arbitration under the amendment of Polish*

II. Examining the Competence of Arbitral Tribunals

II.1. Examining the Arbitral Tribunal's Competence Prior to Commencement of Arbitral Proceedings

7.02. The state court can settle issues related to the competence of an arbitral tribunal in a specific case, even before formal commencement of the arbitral proceedings themselves. This occurs when the defendant raises the charge of a binding arbitration agreement prior to engaging in a dispute on the merits of the case, but after an action before a state court was brought. Such an approach, favourable for arbitration, is 'guaranteed' by the provision of Article 2 of the NYC, which stipulates as follows: *'The court of a Contracting State,* when seized of an action in a matter in respect of which the parties have made an agreement within the meaning of this article, shall, *at the request of one of the parties, refer the parties to arbitration, unless it finds that the said agreement is null and void, inoperative or incapable of being performed.'* (emphasis by the authors) and Article 8 of the UNCITRAL Model Law, i.e. domestic legislation of countries that implemented this Model Law.[5]

7.03. The charge that parties are bound by an arbitration agreement should be raised by a party when it engages in its first procedural act in the case, before engaging the merits of the case.[6] Usually, such first procedural act is an answer to the statement of claims, which also includes the other charges and statements on the merits of the case,

---

arbitration law), 2 KWARTALNIK ADR ARBITRAŻ I MEDIACJI (*ADR Arbitration and Mediation Quarterly*) 73 and subsequent (2008); Grzegorz Żmij, *Środki tymczasowe i zabezpieczające w międzynarodowym arbitrażu handlowym* (*Temporary and securing reliefs in international commercial arbitration*), in ROZPRAWY PRAWNICZE. KSIĘGA PAMIĄTKOWA PROFESORA MAKSYMILIANA PAZDANA (*Legal Dissertations. Commemorative Book of Professor Maksymilian Pazdan*), Kraków: Zakamycze 557 and therein invoked literature (2008) in particular: Alexander J. Bělohlávek, *Arbitration from Perspective of Right to Legal Protection and Right to Court Prodeeding* (*the Right to Have One's Case Dealt with by a Court*): *Significance of Autonomy and Scope of Right to Fair Trail,* in CZECH & CENTRAL EUROPEAN YEARBOOK OF ARBITRATION 50 (Alexander J. Bělohlávek; Naděžda Rozehnalová (eds.), 2011). ALAN REDFERN, MARTIN HUNTER, NIGEL BLACKABY, CONSTANTINE PARTASIDES, *supra* note 1, at 388–415.

[5] See Section 1032 of the German ZPO, Sec. 9-11 of the English Arbitration Act of 1996, Article 1165 of the Polish Code of Civil Procedure.

[6] See Article VI Section 1 of the European Convention on International Commercial Arbitration, Geneva (adopted 21 April 1961, entered into force 7 January 1964) 7041 UNTC, currently 31 states are parties to this convention: https://treaties.un.org/pages/ViewDetails.aspx?src=TREATY&mtdsg_no=XXII-2&chapter=22&lang=en#3 (accessed on 22 September 2014), ('Geneva Convention of 1961').

raised as potential statements and charges in the event that the charge of lack of the state court's competence is not allowed. However, this formal charge should be formulated and included in the pleading (an answer to the statement of claims) in the first order, in those legal systems that qualify such a charge as a procedural one. If the court finds the charge justified, it will refer parties to arbitration. The provisions of NYC and those of the UNCITRAL Model Law do not specify the form of such a decision, and therefore the procedural law of a particular state will regulate this issue. In the case of Polish courts, the statement of claims is rejected without examining the merits of the case.[7] When rejecting the statement of claims, the state court does not remit the case to the arbitration tribunal, even when it is a permanent court of arbitration that has jurisdiction. In such a situation, the claimant decides whether to lodge a new statement of claims before an arbitration tribunal after a failed attempt to pursue claims before a state court, or whether it will cease pursuing its claims at all.

7.04.   Both the mentioned domestic and international regulations provide that the state court examining the charge of arbitration agreement is competent to assess the validity, effectiveness and enforceability of the arbitration agreement.

7.05.   In turn, the French law on arbitration (Article 1448 of the French CCP[8]) has adopted a different formula. If the charge of a binding arbitration agreement is raised, it recognises, *prima facie*, the competence of the court of arbitration. In such a case, the French court refers parties to arbitration unless '(...) the agreement is obviously invalid or obviously inapplicable in the given case'. If the arbitral tribunal has already been established, then the French court will not even examine an obvious invalidity or unenforceability of the arbitration agreement. Rather, it will simply refer parties to arbitration where they shall exercise their right to raise appropriate charges. Such a regulation 'guarantees' that the arbitral tribunal has priority, before the state court, in deciding on its own competence to hear the dispute. In the jurisprudence of international arbitration it is also emphasized that

---

[7]   See: Article 1195 (1) of the Polish CCP. Similarly Section 1032 of German ZPO. The English Court will stay the proceedings - see Section 9-11 English Arbitration Act of 1996.

[8]   See: GARY B. BORN, *supra* note 1, at 52. The full text of the Article 1448(1) of the French Code of Civil Procedure provides as follows: 'When a dispute subject to an arbitration agreement is brought before a court, such court shall decline jurisdiction, except if an arbitral tribunal has not yet been seized of the dispute and if the arbitration agreement is manifestly void or manifestly not applicable. A court may not decline jurisdiction on its own motion. Any stipulation contrary to the present article shall be deemed not written'.

the arbitral tribunal should be the first to decide on its own jurisdiction. Thus '(…) if there is any plausible argument that a valid arbitration agreement exists, the arbitrators should be permitted initially to resolve the jurisdictional issues (subject to subsequent judicial review); only if it is clear that there is now a valid arbitration agreement, may a claim be litigated.'[9] The right of an arbitral tribunal to resolve the matter of its own jurisdiction over the dispute when the arbitration has already been initiated is also stipulated in Article VI Section 3 of the Geneva Convention of 1961:

> Where either party to an arbitration agreement has initiated arbitration proceedings before any resort is had to a court, courts of Contracting States subsequently asked to deal with the same subject-matter between the same parties or with the question whether the arbitration agreement was non-existent or null and void or had lapsed, shall stay their ruling on the arbitrator's jurisdiction until the arbitral award is made, unless they have good and substantial reasons to the contrary.

7.06.   The state court in course of examination of the charge of the arbitration agreement assesses the existence, validity, and enforceability of such an agreement (such is the case in Poland and other countries that adopted the solution from Article 8 of the UNICITRAL Model Law). In such cases, it should be assumed that if the state court's decision allowing the charge of the arbitration agreement (in other words: decision referring parties to arbitration)[10] becomes valid and final, then in the subsequent arbitration proceedings, parties may no longer question the arbitral tribunal's jurisdiction. The latter, as well as the parties, are bound by the state court's ruling 'in favour' of arbitration. Exceptions to this include if new previously unknown facts or evidence indicating that the arbitration agreement is invalid, ineffective, unenforceable, or lost its force are revealed after the state court's decision had been issued. Jurisdiction can also be questioned if the claims raised in arbitration go beyond the limits of the clause or the new claims are not arbitrable. In such a situation, the party questioning the jurisdiction of the arbitral tribunal may raise this charge again in the arbitral proceedings, observing the requirements for it to be raised in an appropriate time.

7.07.   An original solution – as far as the assessment of the jurisdiction of an arbitral tribunal by a state court is concerned – is contained in German Code of Civil Procedure, which stipulates that a party may file a

---

[9]   GARY B. BORN, *supra* note 1, at 54.

[10]   In Poland this is referred to as the decision on rejection of the statement of claims.

petition with the court for determination of admissibility or inadmissibility of arbitration in a given case.[11]

II.2. Examining the Competence of the Arbitral Tribunal in the Course of the Arbitral Proceedings

II.2.1. The Principle of Competence – Competence

7.08.   In accordance with the *competence-competence* principle, commonly recognised both in legislation and in arbitration practice[12] as well as the rules of leading arbitration institutions,[13] the assessment of whether a specific dispute arising between parties is to be resolved in arbitration[14] should be made by the arbitral tribunal which is competent to consider and rule on its own jurisdiction.

7.09.   It is doubtful whether the arbitral tribunal may rule on its non-competence *ex officio* (on its own motion) or only to a raised charge. From granting a general competence to the arbitral tribunal to rule on its own jurisdiction, one might reason that it is also entitled to examine this issue *ex officio*. Yet we are of the opinion that it should be adopted as a principle that the arbitral tribunal assesses its jurisdiction only when a party raises a suitable charge.[15] The failure to raise the charge of the lack of an arbitral tribunal's jurisdiction within the prescribed time

---

[11]   Section 1032 (3) of the German ZPO states that until the arbitral tribunal has been formed, a petition may be filed with the courts to have the courts determine the admissibility or inadmissibility of arbitration proceedings.

[12]   See: Article 16 (1) of the UNCITRAL Model Law, Section 1040 (1) of the German ZPO, Article 592 (1) of the Austrian of the ZPO, Section 30 (1) of the English Arbitration Act of 1996, Article 1465 of the French CCP, Article 1180 § 1 of the Polish CCP.

[13]   See: Article 23 (1) of the UNICITRAL Arbitration Rules, as revised in 2010 (UNICITRAL Rules), Article 24.2 sentence 1 of the Vienna Arbitration Rules (in force from 1 July 2013) (Vienna Rules), Article 23.1 of the new LCIA Arbitration Rules (effective from 1 October 2014) (LCIA Rules), Article 6 of The ICC Arbitration Rules (in force from 1 January 2012) (ICC Rules). § 27.1 of the Rules of the Court of Arbitration at PKPP Lewiatan (enforced from 1 march 2012) (Polish Lewiatan Rules).

[14]   This assessment in principle comes down to examining whether the parties concluded a valid arbitration agreement that is effective and enforceable, and whether the dispute submitted for adjudication is included in the subjective and objective scope of the arbitration covenant, as well as whether the very dispute submitted by parties is arbitrable, i.e. whether it may be subject to the tribunal's cognizance at all.

[15]   Thus in Polish doctrine Tadeusz Ereciński [in]: Tadeusz Ereciński, Karol Weitz, *supra* note 2, whereby the author indicates that examination of the so-called arbitrability of the dispute submitted to its adjudication should be an exception from this rule. Sławomir Cieślak, *supra* note 4, at 15, 19.

limit results in the expiration of the party's right to question this jurisdiction in the further course of proceedings before this court. Allowing the arbitral tribunal to rule *ex officio* would practically render the regulation limiting a possibility of raising such a charge by a party pointless. A regulation to the contrary would mean that in such an event, at any status of the case, a party would be able to 'indicate' to the arbitral tribunal a need to examine the issue of its competence *ex officio*, which would render any statutory limitations and requirements in terms of questioning the tribunal's jurisdiction merely illusory. However, this does not pertain to examination of the tribunal's competence from the point of view of the arbitrability of the case. Nevertheless, in certain cases, it seems justified to grant the arbitral tribunal the right to issue a negative decision regarding its own jurisdiction for reasons other than the non-arbitrability of the case. It may happen that the charge of the lack of jurisdiction of the arbitral tribunal is not raised effectively, yet the lack of such jurisdiction is beyond the tribunal's doubts and this lack of jurisdiction follows from reasons which may neither be repaired in the course of the proceedings nor upon their conclusion. In our opinion, the arbitral tribunal may rule on its non-competence *ex officio* in such a case. The postulate for the arbitral tribunal's right to examine its jurisdiction *ex officio* is substantiated particularly in cases when lack of such jurisdiction is connected with the lack of arbitrability of the dispute. Such a defect may lead to a refusal of recognition or ascertainment of enforceability of the award issued in the case and, in principle, regardless of whether such a charge is raised in the recognition proceedings or not. (See: Article 5. 2.A of the NYC). Obviously, such a stance requires the arbitral tribunal to 'examine' the law of the state where the award is to be recognised or enforced. It may be an onerous task at times, especially when the legal system to be analysed is based on different principles, different values, and it operates in a different social and civilizational context. Nevertheless, the tribunal has to be able to meet this challenge. It would be entirely irrational to expose a party to the risk of engaging and conducting a sometimes extremely time-consuming and costly arbitral proceeding when it is known from the very start that it will not lead to the result intended by the parties, namely the issuance of a ruling that will be effective or that can be enforced if the losing party does not surrender of its own free will. Occasionally there are 'transgressions' of other types which can impact the tribunal's jurisdiction or lack thereof. These include when the arbitration clause does not extend to the case at hand, or it is invalid in light of the documents submitted on file. For example when an arbitration covenant is concluded by a person not authorised to represent the legal person, or an attorney acts without the power of attorney or transgressing the scope of such a power of attorney or when there is a failure to remedy such a defect in the manner required by the statute. In such cases, it is necessary to assume that without a charge raised by the party, the tribunal is not authorised to issue a decision *ex officio*. It is so since these defects, although extremely grave, may still be convalidated by parties in the course of the arbitral proceedings.

7.10.   As regards the issue of the charge of non-competence or transgressing the scope of the arbitration agreement raised by a party, the arbitral tribunal may decide by issuing a separate ruling regarding its jurisdiction. However, it may also adopt a stance thereto only in the award settling the case as to its merits, with the manner of settling these issues remaining at the arbitral tribunal's discretion in principle[16] Obvious practical issues seem to favour the issuance of a separate decision, especially because the tribunal convinced of the legitimacy of its ruling does not have to stay the arbitral proceedings when the party dissatisfied with the court of arbitration's decision dismissing the charge of its non-competence petitions a state court for resolution. German arbitral regulation (Article 1040.3. of the German ZPO and Section 592.1. of the Austrian ZPO) indicates that dismissing such charges by the tribunal in a separate ruling should be a principle. The same process dominates in proceedings before Polish permanent courts of arbitration. In turn, the regulation of the English Arbitration Act of 1996 assumes that the parties' agreement on the preferred form of settlement shall be decisive in this extent.

7.11.   When the arbitral tribunal hears the charge raised and dismisses it, finding itself competent in the case, and this ruling is issued as a separate decision, national legislations furnish the parties with the possibility to challenge such a decision on jurisdiction before a state court. Obviously, in hearing the appeal, the state court is not bound by factual findings or the legal assessment made by the court of arbitration for the needs of examination of the jurisdiction in the case. The court performs its own assessment in this scope. In finding that the arbitral proceedings in the case are inadmissible and contrary to the assessment expressed by the arbitral tribunal, it is assumed that the state court

---

[16]   See: Article 16 of the Model Law, Section 31.4 of the English Arbitration Act of 1996, Article 1465 of the French CCP , Article 186.3 of the Swiss Federal Statute on Private International Law, Article 23.3 of the UNCITRAL Rules, Article 6(3) of the ICC Arbitration Rules, Article 23.4 of LCIA Arbitration Rules, Article 24.2 of the Vienna Rules, .Sec. 27.4 of the Polish Lewiatan Rules.

ought to set the challenged decision of the tribunal aside and ascertain its non-competence. A final ruling of the state court is binding for the arbitral tribunal, which in such a situation should terminate the ongoing proceedings without issuing a decision as to the merits of the case. Yet, if it continued to proceed despite that and issued an award, then such an arbitral award would be subject to setting aside in the frames of the complaint proceedings or it would be refused recognition or enforcement. In the above-mentioned post-arbitration proceedings, the state court would be bound by an earlier ruling of the state court on the lack of the tribunal's jurisdiction in the case.[17] Sometimes it is claimed that such a verdict would be simply invalid.

7.12. In case the arbitral tribunal negatively settles the issue of its own jurisdiction in the dispute, such a ruling usually tends to be final and is not subject to verification by the state court.[18]

7.13. As already mentioned above, the arbitral tribunal in principle rules on its competence by means of a separate preliminary ruling only when an adequate charge is raised by the defendant. If it does not raise the charge of non-competence (lack of jurisdiction) in the arbitration proceedings, it is doubtful whether the party may effectively challenge the award issued by this court, basing the complaint for the setting aside of the arbitral award lodged with the state court on the charge of the lack of the arbitration agreement or its non-validity, non-effectiveness or lack of binding force according to the law applicable thereto.[19] In our opinion, the party that did not raise such a charge before the arbitral tribunal within the prescribed time limit or did not raise it at all does not lose the right to raise it in the motion for setting aside of the arbitral award.[20] Yet, when hearing the motion for setting aside, the state court may arrive at a conclusion that the defects of the arbitration agreement were cured by the defendant's passive conduct in the course of the arbitral proceedings. The Defendant's conduct during

---

[17] On the grounds of the Polish CCP – Article 356.1 of the CCP in conjunction with Article 1180. 3. sentence 2. Of the CCP, Article 1207.2, Article 13.2 of the CCP.

[18] Such a solution is provided in Article 16 of the Model Law, provisions of the Polish CCP drawing thereon–see: Article 1180.3 of the CCP, Article 1205 of the CCP.

[19] See Article V.2. of the Geneva Convention of 1961. .

[20] For an opposite view see Tadeusz Ereciński, Karol Weitz, *supra* note 2, at 246 and subsequent, who stated that the lack of raising a charge on an arbitration agreement before the state court causes its preclusion and in result bars a party from invoking this charge in a motion for setting aside of an arbitral award as well as in the proceedings for recognition or enforcement of an arbitral award. According to Tadeusz Ereciński and Karol Weitz, whose view we share in that regard, a lack of effective raising of a charge on an arbitration agreement does not cause its expiration.

the arbitration proceedings may be treated as a tacit acceptance of the arbitral tribunal's jurisdiction. However, this is not the case if the arbitration award dismissing the charge of non-competence is subject to the state court's control as a result of a suitable motion lodged by a party. If this occurs and the state court accepts it by virtue of the valid decision, then in our opinion, referring once again in the motion to this charge is ineffective, based on the same circumstances. The same applies to the proceedings for the recognition or ascertainment of the enforceability of an arbitral award in which such an award is subject to the control of the state court within the limits prescribed in procedural statute or international agreements. However, if the defects of the arbitration agreement removable by parties' will are not cured (removed or repaired), until the moment the state court rules on the legitimacy of the complaint or on the recognition or ascertainment of enforceability of the arbitral award, then in our opinion, the state court will set such an award aside or refuse to ascertain its enforceability regardless of whether or not a party raised such a charge in the course of the arbitral proceedings. The fundamental principle of arbitral proceedings provides that the arbitral tribunal may act only in arbitrable cases and only on the grounds and within the limits of the arbitration agreement binding the parties. State courts, therefore, may not accept these arbitral awards which violate this fundamental constitutional principle.

II.3. Examining the Competence of the Court of Arbitration by the State Court in the Incidental Proceedings

7.14.   The issue discussed in this paper – i.e. the matter of examining the arbitral tribunal's competence in a given case by the state court – is connected to another issue. There arises a question whether the state court has the authority to perform such an assessment only in the scope of proceedings designed specifically for this purpose on the examination of the charge of the lack of jurisdiction as a result of challenge of the tribunal's decision on its jurisdiction. Or perhaps such authority exists also in the scope of other incidental proceedings in the course of the arbitral process.[21]

---

[21]   Obviously, we are going to omit in this paper post-arbitration proceedings where the lack of tribunal's jurisdiction or a dispute's non-arbitrable nature constitute prerequisites for the setting aside or refusal of the recognition/ascertainment of enforceability of the arbitral award.

II.3.1. Procedures related to the establishment of the tribunal's composition

7.15. In considering the chronology of state court's potential interventions in arbitral proceedings, a question arises at the outset whether the state court has the authority to refuse to perform such an appointment, in the scope of the procedure for the appointment of a super-arbitrator, and thereby indicating that arbitration is not competent in the dispute.[22] We are of the opinion that it does not. The mere lack of a valid, effective, and enforceable arbitration agreement on the date of commencement of the proceedings may be repaired by the parties concurrently submitting the dispute for adjudication by the court of arbitration. The state court depriving them of such a possibility would be contradictory to the principle of parties' autonomy. Some legislation,[23] nevertheless, allow for such an assessment and such a settlement already at this initial stage of the state court's intervention.

7.16. A different situation is when the non-competence of the arbitral tribunal in a given case does not follow from transgressions related to the arbitration agreement itself, but from an irremovable lack of the dispute's arbitrability (i.e. inadmissibility for a given type of case to be heard by a court of arbitration). In such a situation, the state court refuses to appoint an arbitrator or presiding arbitrator, *ipso facto* depriving the arbitral tribunal of the possibility to decide on its own jurisdiction. The issue of arbitrability is regulated by mandatory provisions. The state court may not evade from applying them as a prerequisite of its own decision meant to provide an opportunity to conduct the case in the proceedings, which would be *ab initio* affected by a defect impossible to cure.

---

[22] Article 179.3 of Swiss IPRG which stipulates that in proceedings for selection of an arbitrator, the state court examines the existence and validity of the arbitration agreement. Refusal of undertaking of action due to invalid or non-binding agreement can happen only if those deficiencies are evident. An opposite view (see literature cited by the Tadeusz Ereciński, Karol Weitz, *supra* note 2, at 188 in note 123) prevails under German and Anglo-American laws.

[23] See Article 1455 of the French CCP, which provides: 'If an arbitration agreement is manifestly void or manifestly not applicable, the judge acting in support of the arbitration shall declare that no appointment need be made. An order in this scope can be challenged.'

II.3.2. Examining competence in the frames of legal assistance

7.17. Due to the 'private' nature of arbitration and the inability to use coercion, a majority of national legislation[24] provide for a possibility within arbitral proceedings to turn to the state court for assistance in performing specific acts related to arbitral proceedings, in particular connected to evidentiary proceedings. The question raises whether the state court may refuse to perform a specific act (the performance of which was sought by the arbitral tribunal or, on the grounds of such tribunal's authorisation, one of parties to arbitral proceedings) on the basis of the lack of tribunal's jurisdiction in the dispute for whose needs such an act is to be performed. It is a controversial issue.[25] In our opinion, such a refusal is substantiated only on the grounds of the cases of non-arbitrability. Additionally, this is true exclusively when this issue was not previously verified by the state court in the context of the state court's examination of whether the arbitral tribunal has jurisdiction. The state court may not co-operate with actions contradicting the law (as a rule stemming from the principle of the rule of law). Allowing the state court for arbitration proceedings in a case concerning matter which cannot be resolved in arbitration would be such an action contradicting the law, in the case at hand, with provisions firmly setting the inviolable limits of the autonomy of will of the parties.

7.18. However, it is indicated that examination by the state court of competence of the arbitral tribunal in a given case within the framework of incidental proceedings is not binding for the arbitral tribunal. This is unlike the verification of correctness of the arbitral tribunal's ruling dismissing the charge of its alleged lack of jurisdiction.

---

[24] Article 27 UNCITRAL Model Law provides that the arbitral tribunal or a party with the approval of the arbitral tribunal may request from a competent court of this State assistance in taking evidence. The court may execute the request within its competence and according to its rules on taking evidence, Sections 42–45 *Powers of court in relation to arbitral proceeding* English Arbitration Act of 1996. Article 1192 of the Polish CCP. Section 1050 of the German ZPO. Articiel 184.2 of the Swiss IPRG.

[25] Karol Weitz, *Przesłanki i zakres pomocy sądu państwowego dla sądu polubownego w postępowaniu dowodowym* (art. 1192 KPC) (*Preconditions and scope of legal aid of the state court in arbitration in evidentiary proceedings* (Article 1192 KPC)), 2 KWARTALNIK ADR ARBITRAŻ I MEDIACJI (*ADR Arbitration and Mediation Quarterly*) 9 (2009).

III. State of Litispendence between a Court of Arbitration and a State Court

7.19. The issue discussed in this paper is also connected to the matter of a mutual relation between proceedings before the state court and an arbitral tribunal if the claimant lodged the statement of claims in the same case with both courts (state and arbitration), taking advantage of the possibilities provided by procedural legislation.

7.20. Hence, is it possible to speak of the litispendence of the case in such a situation if the same claim between the same parties is subject to proceedings pending before both the state court and arbitral tribunal? If, in the proceedings before the state court, the charge of a binding arbitration clause is raised at an appropriate time, then the state court's final decision on the legitimacy of this charge ultimately settles the existence or non-existence of the tribunal's jurisdiction in the case, in a manner binding both for the arbitral tribunal and parties to the dispute. Such a charge not being effectively raised before the state court most frequently results from failing to comply with the preclusion time limit for raising the charge. If this occurs, then the state court's competence, only provisional at the moment of initiation of the action, also becomes definitive and in the same proceedings may not be questioned by either party. However, a doubt then arises as to whether the state court's competence, resulting from party's forbearance (concealment) of the effects of the binding arbitration agreement, has the same binding force for the arbitral tribunal as the state court's decision on the formally correct charge raised by a party. If a party raises the charge of non-competence of the arbitral tribunal in the same case pending before the arbitral tribunal, then the said court shall rule on its own competence. In this situation, litispendence of the case before the state court is not an obstacle for the court of arbitration to recognise itself as competent to hear the case and to conduct arbitral proceedings. The party whose charge of non-competence of the arbitral tribunal was not allowed by the tribunal may petition the state court to verify this stance within the framework of special appeal proceedings. The judgement issued by the state court will therefore be binding both for parties and the arbitral tribunal. However, what happens when the ruling of the arbitral tribunal confirming its 'parallel' competence is not challenged and becomes final and valid? Does it mean that it will be possible or necessary for two proceedings to be pending before two different courts using different rules of procedure and adjudication and a possibility to issue two radically different rulings? Neither national statutes nor the model law regulate the manner for solving this 'competition' of proceedings. We are of the opinion that in such a situation, the arbitral tribunal should suspend the arbitral proceedings until the final conclusion of the proceedings before the state court. The verdict issued by the court of arbitration and colliding with the ruling issued by the state court would stand slim chances for recognition or ascertainment of enforceability in recognition proceedings. A state where two conflicting court rulings issued in the same case with the same 'binding force' function in so-called 'legal transactions' would undoubtedly stand in contradiction with the fundamental principles of public policy.[26]

IV. Securing of Claims Pursued in Arbitration

7.21.   As indicated at the beginning of this paper, one of the spheres in which arbitration 'competes' with state courts is in making decisions on temporary relief for claims pursued in arbitration. This is formally referred to as the securing of claims, also called interim or relief measures. All court proceedings before both state and arbitration courts aim at granting the entitled party real legal protection. Among other measures, an indispensable condition of such protection comes from the possibility of real and effective enforcement of court rulings in compliance with their contents. Securing claims pursued before both state and arbitration courts constitutes the most important and efficient legal instrument ensuring enforceability and effectiveness of judgements to be issued, in most cases. The granting of relief may be pronounced by both state and arbitration courts. Such a parallel model of competence is adopted in Article 9 of the UNCITRAL Model Law and is prevailing in arbitration laws of some specific counties and also accepted by most rules of permanent courts of arbitration. During recent years the competences of arbitral tribunals were expanded. This is evidenced by amendments to Article 17 of the Model Law and expansion of the particular rules of permanent courts of arbitration. Only a few legal systems forbid arbitral tribunals deciding on such matters.

7.22.   A parallel jurisdiction of state and arbitration courts in the scope of granting relief breeds a question whether a party may file a motion for such measures simultaneously with the state court and the arbitral tribunal before which the case is pending. The parallel competence of both courts in the scope of relief settles the query affirmatively *prima facie*. If so, then it is necessary to pose another question, namely: are

---

[26]   The public policy clause, see: Article VI.3 of the Geneva Convention or 1961.

the proceedings to both motions for relief to be prosecuted independently of each other? Following on this question, can judgements to be issued in them be issued without taking into account the 'competitive' proceedings related to the same 'incidental' issue as well as the outcome of such proceedings in the form of the judgement related to an analogical motion? It is obvious that in light of the applicable rules (e.g. of permanent courts of arbitration or national arbitration legislation) it will be the arbitral tribunal which will enjoy a broader 'freedom' in making the decision as to whether and in what form to grant temporary relief. Conversely, the state court will apply its own procedural rules which in most cases prescribe preconditions for interim measures and their allowable forms.

7.23. Which court's competence should take precedence on the matter? Of course, the above issue does not arise if the applicable rules prohibit (at least for the time being) a party from freely turning for temporary relief to the state court as is the case with some rules of permanent courts of arbitration.[27]

7.24. In such situation – the arbitral tribunal should consider the possibility of staying the arbitral proceedings. This is true particularly in situations in which the outcome of other court or administrative proceedings is of significance as a binding prejudicial decision or at least a decision settling an issue important for the final arbitral award. The fact that the court of arbitration is not generally bound by provisions on proceedings before state courts has an important effect. Even though the procedural acts do not contain the mentioned normative rules, the court of arbitration may independently issue a decision on the suspension of the proceedings following a consideration of advisability

---

[27]   See Article 28.2. of the ICC Rules: 'Before the file is transmitted to the arbitral tribunal, and in appropriate circumstances even thereafter, the parties may apply to any competent judicial authority for interim or conservatory measures. The application of a party to a judicial authority for such measures or for the implementation of any such measures ordered by an arbitral tribunal shall not be deemed to be an infringement or a waiver of the arbitration agreement and shall not affect the relevant powers reserved to the arbitral tribunal', and Article 25.3. of the LCIA Rules: 'The power of the Arbitral Tribunal under Article 25.1 shall not prejudice any party's right to apply to a state court or other legal authority for interim or conservatory measures to similar effect: (i) before the formation of the Arbitral Tribunal; and (ii) after the formation of the Arbitral Tribunal, in exceptional cases and with the Arbitral Tribunal's authorization, until the final award. After the Commencement Date, any application and any order for such measures before the formation of the Arbitral Tribunal shall be communicated promptly in writing by the applicant party to the Registrar; after its formation, also to the Arbitral Tribunal; and in both cases also to all other parties'.

(including in particular the so-called procedural economy). This is because the definition of the manner of proceeding within a scope not regulated by the parties to the arbitration covenant falls within this court's exclusive competence.

7.25.   Full formally independence of securing proceedings pending before and adjudicated in both courts has the result that the decision of the arbitral tribunal may differ from that of the state court regarding the same issue, at least theoretically. It is not that bad if the arbitral tribunal dismisses the motion and the state court allows it. In that eventuality, only the state court's decision will be enforced. In a situation to the contrary where the state court dismisses the motion and the arbitral tribunal allowed it, the situation is already different. In this situation, the arbitral tribunal's decision granting the securing of claims must be either recognised or ascertained as enforceable by the state court. Admittedly, the state court's previous decision, negative for the applicant, has no formal binding force for the arbitral tribunal. In consequence of this, the state court may not refuse the recognition or ascertainment of enforceability of arbitral decision in scope of temporary relief merely on this basis. However, it is difficult not to agree with the view that the state and arbitration courts' radically different assessment of the same pre-requisite for relief[28] constitutes an undesirable anomaly.

7.26.   For the applicant, the sense of such a 'parallel' proceeding on the issue of relief consists of the fact that out of two potential decisions, the applicant shall be able to choose to enforce the most advantageous one, stipulating a wider range and a more effective manner of relief. If the decision of the arbitral tribunal on the granting of the relief precedes the state court's decision, the latter may refuse the granting of the relief due to the lack of the 'legal interest in the relief' if it finds that the relief granted by the arbitral tribunal sufficiently protects applicant's interests.

7.27.   From the short comments above it follows that, in the opinion of the authors of the present study, the present regulation assuming the independent parallel competence of state courts and arbitral tribunals as regards the issue of securing of claims pursued in the arbitration is not the best of solutions. We are of the opinion that the exclusive nature of the arbitral tribunal's competence after initiating the proceedings before them should extend to all the issues related to a given case, including the securing of the claim pursued.

---

[28]   Which is usually the applicant's making the pursued claim plausible.

V. Summary

7.28. In spite of the arbitration's independence from the system of state courts there are numerous situations in which these two come into interaction. State courts play particularly important role in examination of jurisdiction of arbitral tribunal in a given case, *i.e.* in examining whether the parties concluded a valid arbitration agreement that is effective and enforceable, and whether the dispute submitted for adjudication is included in the subjective and objective scope of the arbitration agreement. They also examine whether the dispute submitted by the parties to arbitration is arbitrable, *i.e.* whether it may be subject to arbitration at all. Such examination can take place before the initiation of arbitral proceedings – if one of the parties starts proceedings before a state court despite the fact that there is an arbitration agreement and the other party raises in an appropriate time the charge of existing arbitration agreement. The decision of the state court in favor of arbitration will be binding to the state courts and the parties. In particular, the jurisdiction of the arbitral tribunal is examined by the state court in course of the proceedings 'in the second place', *i.e.* after the arbitral tribunal itself made a decision on its jurisdiction and issued a separate decision which was challenged by one of the parties. Such model of resolving those issues is the most preferable one and a decision on the jurisdiction should be pursued at the earliest stage of proceedings. Obviously, the matters connected with the lack of jurisdiction of arbitral tribunal may be subject to a charge in the proceedings for setting aside of an arbitral award as well as they may be precondition for refusal of recognition or enforcement of the arbitral award, however those issues were omitted in the present paper because one cannot speak of interactions between state courts and arbitral tribunals when the arbitration already ended. Issues related to the examination of jurisdiction of arbitral tribunals in the dispute may also appear within incidental proceedings before state courts which are pending in connection with arbitration. This refers to substitute proceedings for appointment of arbitrator by state court or in proceedings for legal aid exercised by state court at the motion of arbitral tribunal – in both cases it should be assumed that the examination of arbitral jurisdiction may only concern the matter of arbitrability. Even if the arbitration agreement itself contains certain defects parties should not be deprived of possibility of curing them in further course of arbitration. In terms of principle 'parallel' powers of state courts and arbitral tribunals as to examination of arbitral jurisdiction in a case (meaning – as to the validity, effectiveness and enforceability of the arbitration agreement) should be assessed as a proper solution. The case is different with parallel competences of both courts as far as securing of claims (temporary relief) pursued in arbitration is concerned – in such instance it seems that it would be preferable to equip the arbitral tribunals with exclusive jurisdiction on that matter, which is the solution adopted in some of new revised rules of permanent courts of arbitration.

| | |

Summaries

DEU [*Zwei Beispiele der Interaktion zwischen der staatlichen und schiedsrichterlichen Gerichtsbarkeit: Entscheidung über die Zuständigkeit des Schiedsgerichts und sichernde gerichtliche Maßnahmen im Schiedsverfahren*]

Obwohl die internationale Schiedsgerichtsbarkeit schon ein bedeutendes Niveau der Unabhängigkeit von den nationalen Gerichten erreicht hat, bleibt die Rolle dieser Gerichte für die Effektivität dieses Verfahrens weiterhin erheblich. Die Interaktionen zwischen der nationalen Gerichten und der Schiedsgerichten können auf den Ebenen besonders intensiv sein, wo die nationalen Gerichte und Schiedsgerichte während des Schiedsverfahrens parallele/konkurrierende Kompetenzen besitzen. Nationale Gerichte spielen eine wesentliche Rolle bei der Prüfung der Gerichtszuständigkeit in der konkreten Angelegenheit. Diese Prüfung kann vor der Einleitung des Verfahrens erfolgen (wenn die andere Partei eine Schiedsgerichtseinrede erhebt) oder während des Schiedsverfahrens als die nationalen Gerichte die diesbezügliche Schiedsgerichtsentscheidung kontrollieren. Die Anerkennung des Schiedsgerichts als des zuständigen forum durch das nationale Gericht bleibt verbindlich sowohl für das Schiedsgericht und für die Parteien, als auch für die nationalen Gerichte dieses Staates im Gange der Verfahren nach dem Schiedsverfahren (bezüglich des Tatbestandes, den das nationale Gericht erwogen hat, als es die Parteien zum Schiedsverfahren verwiesen hat). Verschiedene Interaktionen zwischen der nationalen Gerichten und Schiedsgerichten können auch bei Entscheidung über die vorbeugenden und einstweiligen Maßnahmen entstehen.

CZE [*Dva příklady interakce mezi státními soudy a rozhodčím řízením: rozhodování o pravomoci rozhodčího soudu k rozhodnutí ve věci samé a předběžný petit v rozhodčím řízení*]

Ačkoliv je mezinárodní rozhodčí řízení zásadně nezávislé na státních soudech, je úloha těchto soudů významná pro efektivitu rozhodčího řízení. Interakce mezi státními soudy a rozhodčími soudy může být v některých případech intenzivní v takových oblastech, kde jsou rozhodčí soudy a státní soudy nadány paralelními nebo konkurujícími pravomocemi v průběhu rozhodčího řízení. Státní soudy hrají významnou úlohu při zkoumání pravomoci rozhodčích soudů v konkrétní věci. Takové zkoumání může probíhat před zahájením rozhodčího řízení, pokud strana uplatní námitky proti rozhodčí smlouvě v samostatném řízení, nebo v průběhu samotného rozhodčího řízení, pokud jsou státní soudy oprávněny kontrolovat rozhodnutí rozhodčího soudu o jeho pravomoci. Rozhodnutí státních soudů o tom, že rozhodčí řízení je řádným fórem pro slyšení ve věci sporu mezi stranami, je závazné jak pro rozhodčí soudy tak pro strany samotné. Takové rozhodnutí je rovněž závazné pro státní soudy v postrozhodčím řízení, když tato rozhodnutí se mohou týkat okolností, kterými se soudy zabývají na návrh stran rozhodčího řízení. K různým druhům interakce mezi soudy a rozhodčími soudy může docházet v průběhu rozhodování o předběžných petitech (označované též jako zajišťovací návrhy).

| | |

POL [*Dwa przykłady interakcji sądownictwa państwowego i arbitrażowego: rozstrzyganie o właściwości trybunału arbitrażowego w sprawie i zabezpieczenie roszczeń dochodzonych w arbitrażu*]
W artykule poruszono kilka praktycznie istotnych kwestii występujących na gruncie dwóch „punktów stycznych" sądownictwa powszechnego i arbitrażowego, a to: orzekania o właściwości sądów polubownych oraz zabezpieczenia roszczeń przed nim dochodzonych, czyli tych dziedzin, w których kompetencje sądów arbitrażowych i państwowych mogą występować równolegle, konkurencyjnie wobec siebie.

FRA [*Deux exemples de l'interaction entre des tribunaux nationaux et des tribunaux arbitraux: une décision sur la compétence d'un tribal arbitral de juger et d'appliquer des mesures conservstoires dans la procédure arbitrale*]
Cet article aborde des questions importantes dans la pratique, se produisant sur la base de deux 'points de connexion' d'une juridiction de droit commun et arbitrale, c'est-à-dire: le jugement sur la compétence des tribunaux arbitraux et sur des mesures conservatoires relatives aux prétentions revendiquées devant ces tribunaux – alors des domains dans lesquels des compétences des tribunaux arbitraux et nationaux peuvent se produire parallèlement, compétitivement les uns contre les autres.

RUS [*Два примера взаимодействия между государственными и арбитражными судами: принятие решения относительно компетенции арбитражного суда на рассмотрение по существу и предварительное решение в арбитраже*]

В данной статье рассматриваются несколько важных практических вопросов, связанных с двумя «связывающими звеньями» между арбитражем и государственными судами. Речь идет о решении относительно компетенции арбитражного суда, а также заявлениях об обеспечении иска (решение о предварительных мерах) в отношении арбитражного разбирательства. В этих двух областях компетенции арбитражных судов и государственных судов могут конкурировать друг с другом.

ESP [*Dos ejemplos de interacción entre el procedimiento civil y arbitral: toma de decisiones sobre la jurisdicción del tribunal de arbitraje ante la decisión en los méritos del caso y la propuesta preliminar en procedimientos de arbitraje*]

Este artículo aborda varias cuestiones prácticas e importantes relativas a los dos "vínculos" entre el procedimiento arbitral y los tribunales nacionales. En concreto versa sobre las decisiones relativas a la competencia del tribunal arbitral y a las propuestas de garantía (decisiones sobre medidas provisionales) en relación con el procedimiento arbitral. En estas dos áreas, los tribunales de arbitraje y los nacionales pueden competir entre sí.

| | |

Petre Lazaroiu | Marieta Safta

Interaction of Arbitration and Constitutional Courts

Key words:
commercial arbitration
court | constitutional
court | constitutional
review | effects of
decisions of the
Constitutional Court

Abstract | *This study intends to analyse the interaction between constitutional courts and commercial arbitration courts in the European context, with particular reference to the current situation and regulations in Romania. The analysis has as main coordinates the applicable regulatory developments and the constitutional review carried out upon notification by commercial arbitration courts, highlighting the jurisprudential benchmarks. The commercial arbitration courts have the possibility to notify the Constitutional Court for settlement of exceptions of unconstitutionality of laws and ordinances in cases brought before them. This was introduced during the 2003 revision of the Constitution of Romania. Thus, before that time we could only talk about how commercial arbitration courts were enshrined in the case-law of the Romanian Constitutional Court. After 2003, the analysis concerned the notifications addressed to the Constitutional Court by commercial arbitration courts, including international courts, as well as the procedural and substantive questions raised in those notifications. We refer specifically to the notification of the Constitutional Court by the International Court of Arbitration of the International Chamber of Commerce in Paris, France and the resolutions thereof. The study is intended also as an invitation to reflect and debate on the solutions identified, and on the effects they produce.*

Petre Lazaroiu – currently holds the office of Judge of the Constitutional Court of Romania, an office he was appointed to in 2008. He is also Lecturer at the 'Dimitrie Cantemir' Christian University of Bucharest, where he is Coordinator of the Financial and Fiscal Law Course and the Banking and Financial Law Course.
e-mail: petre.lazaroiu@ccr.ro

Marieta Safta – is currently the First Assistant Magistrate of the Constitutional Court of Romania, an institution where she has been employed since 2003. Marieta Safta is also Lecturer within the 'Titu Maiorescu' University of Bucharest, where she is Coordinator of the Constitutional Law Course and the Political Institutions Course.
e-mail: marietasafta @yahoo.com

| | |

I. General Considerations – Constitutional Courts, Role and Responsibilities

8.01.   The constitutional courts are those courts that are principally engaged in constitutional review, checking the conformity of laws and other normative acts with the Basic Law. The last decades have been characterised by a convergence, at the global level, towards the idea of constitutional supremacy, institutionally guaranteed by constitutional review exercised by courts or bodies established for this purpose.[1] The extension of constitutional review was accompanied by an increase in complexity and in the instruments available to constitutional courts, as well as by the regulation of new areas of competence, subsumed to the broader concept of constitutional justice, which includes constitutional review, but it not restricted to it.[2]

8.02.   Current 'models' of constitutional review with the widest expansion include the European or the Kelsenian model. This is a review exercised by a single, special and specialised body of constitutional jurisdiction. There is also the American model, which consists of constitutional review exercised within the powers vested in the courts. There are intermediary variants, as well as specific particularities within different countries in terms of organisation, powers of this type of court and effects of the decisions it pronounces.

8.03.   In Romania, constitutional review exercised by the judicial power was initially enshrined in the 1932 Constitution,[3] and confirmed in the 1938 Constitution. After World War II, constitutional review of laws was eliminated (in the Constitutions of 1948 and 1952 respectively). The 1965 Constitution provided that 'the Grand National Assembly shall exercise general review on the application of the Constitution and it alone shall decide on the constitutionality of laws' but actually no such review existed. After the fall of the Communist regime, the 1991 Constitution enshrined the European model of constitutional review, and it established the Constitutional Court as an authority independent

---

[1]   Tom Ginsburg; Mila Versteeg, *Why Do Countries Adopt Constitutional Review?*, available at: http://www.utexas.edu/law/wp/wp-content/uploads/centers/clbe/versteeg_why_do_countries_adopt.pdf (accessed on 6 October 2014).

[2]   ION DELEANU, INSTITUȚII ȘI PROCEDURI CONSTITUȚIONALE – ÎN DREPTUL ROMÂN ȘI ÎN DREPTUL COMPARAT (*Constitutional institutions and procedures – in Romanian law and comparative law*), Bucharest: C.H.Beck Publishing House 828-832 (2006).

[3]   According to Article 103 of the 1923 Constitution of Romania, 'Solely the Court of Cassation, in Joint Sections, is entitled to rule on the constitutionality of laws and to declare inapplicable those laws that are contrary to the Constitution. The adjudication on constitutionality shall be limited to the case pending before the court.'

of any other public authority, whose role was to ensure the supremacy of the Constitution.

8.04. Regardless of their organisation, operation and powers, the role of constitutional courts is subsumed to the requirement of ensuring the supremacy of the Constitution. It determines a system of complex relations with public authorities that are representative or have a fundamental role in the State. In this framework, they also have a fundamental role to play with commercial arbitration courts.

II. Relationship between Constitutional Courts and Ordinary Courts/Commercial Arbitration Courts

8.05. As regards the relationship between Constitutional Courts and Ordinary Courts/Commercial Arbitration Courts, the way it is configured differs depending on the specific regulation of the role and powers of constitutional courts in various legal systems. It is especially significant that ordinary courts or commercial arbitration courts have the possibility to notify the constitutional courts in order to exercise the constitutional review of legal provisions applicable to the dispute subject of the arbitration, as well as the effects of decisions delivered by them on the activity of the commercial arbitration courts.

8.06. Thus, we note that even where special legislation specifically and distinctly provides the possibility of notification of the constitutional court by the commercial arbitration courts,[4] there are no distinctions in terms of effects of decisions delivered by the constitutional courts. On these effects, it is worth mentioning that within the American model of constitutional review, the decision of the Supreme Court is binding for all hierarchically subordinated courts, as well as for the Court itself. At the same time, the lower level courts are generally focused on aligning their own case-law with the case-law of the Supreme Court in order to avoid the admission of appeals filed against their own judgements Within the European model of constitutional review of laws, the decision ascertaining the unconstitutionality is binding both on the court that notified the Constitutional Court and on all other courts (In some cases, the legal text which was found unconstitutional continues to exist in legal order and must be applied in any situation except the dispute where the preliminary question was raised, even if that provision was declared unconstitutional. But, in a different dispute the court that would have to deal with a question of identical subject

---

[4] Article 146 d) of the Constitution of Romania, Article 125 of the Constitution of the Russian Federation.

matter no longer has an obligation to notify the Court. In this case, the ordinary court will apply the solution pronounced by the Court, which is binding. When we talk about the binding nature of the decision, we mean both the reasoning part and the operative part. If the Constitutional Court finds that the impugned rule is unconstitutional and it invalidates it – the ordinary court, and where applicable, the commercial arbitration court, must apply the respective provision in accordance with the Constitution and with the decision of the Constitutional Court, given the binding nature of such a decision. The decision of the Constitutional Court constitutes grounds for review of the judgement delivered if it has not yet been executed. Following the finding of unconstitutionality, the respective decision is a new fact that was not taken into account upon initial settlement of the case. This allows the initiation of the procedure of review of the judgement delivered by the ordinary court against the person who filed the individual request. Based on this review the Constitutional Court pronounces the decision of unconstitutionality and thus invalidates the respective rule. The decision of the Constitutional Court also constitutes grounds for review of judgements of ordinary courts against those persons who were entitled to notify the Constitutional Court on the day when the Constitutional Court delivered its decision on the constitutionality of the statutory provision.[5]

III. Relationship between the Constitutional Court of Romania and the Commercial Arbitration Courts

III.1. Constitutional Framework

8.07. Pursuant to Article 146 d) first sentence of the Constitution of Romania, the Constitutional Court 'rules upon exceptions of unconstitutionality of laws and ordinances which are raised before courts of law or courts of commercial arbitration'. The possibility of courts of commercial arbitration to notify the Constitutional Court with an exception of unconstitutionality was introduced during the 2003 revision of the Constitution. This change reflected the will of the

---

[5] Information extracted from the General Report of the XVth Congress of the Conference of European Constitutional Courts, held in Bucharest on 23-25 May 2011 and published in Constitutional Justice-Functions and Relationship with the Other Public Authorities, Official Gazette, Bucharest 2011, Part III Enforcement of the Constitutional Court decisions, available at: http://193.226.121.81/congres/ROMANIA%20eng.pdf (accessed on 9 October 2014).

derived constituent legislature to enlarge the scope of subjects who can notify the Constitutional Court in order to exercise constitutional review.

8.08.   Similarly, Article 125 of the Constitution of the Russian Federation specifically lists commercial arbitration courts amongst the subjects that can notify the Constitutional Court. However, constitutions often make no distinction between the courts that can notify the Constitutional Court in order to exercise constitutional review, and use words such as: 'any court',[6] 'court',[7] 'any natural or legal person',[8] 'jurisdictional authority'.[9] Given the lack of distinction at the constitutional level, it is necessary to analyse the infraconstitutional legislation, respectively the regulation and classification of commercial arbitration courts at the infraconstitutional level.

8.09.   Concerning the effects of the decisions of the Constitutional Court in relation to the commercial arbitration courts, the Constitution of Romania establishes in Article 147 (4) that 'decisions of the Constitutional Court shall be published in the Official Gazette of Romania. As from their publication, decisions shall be generally binding and take effect only for the future.' The text does not distinguish according to the type of decisions or according to authorities / subjects to whom it is addressed. This means that commercial arbitration courts are required to abide by all decisions of the Constitutional Court and see to their application in cases that are referred to them.

III.2.   Legal Framework

8.10.   In Romania, the relevant constitutional provisions are completed by the provisions of Law no.47/1992 on the organisation and functioning of the Constitutional Court,[10] as well as by the provisions of the Code of Civil Procedure.

8.11.   Referring to the settlement of the exception of unconstitutionality raised before courts of law or courts of commercial arbitration, Article 29 of Law no. 47/1992 resumes, under paragraph (1), the provisions of Article 146 d) of the Constitution of Romania. Paragraph (4) of the

---

6   Article 142 of the Constitution of Belgium, Article 193 of the Constitution of Poland.

7   Article 100 of the Constitution of Germany, Article 35 of the Constitution of Spain, Article 17 of the Constitution of Latvia, Article 101 of the Constitution of Armenia, Article 150 of the Constitution of the Republic of Montenegro.

8   Article 38 of the Constitution of Croatia.

9   Article 23 of the Constitution of Italy.

10   Republished in the Official Gazette of Romania, Part I, no.807 of 3 December 2010. | 163

same article states that 'The case shall be referred to the Constitutional Court by the court before which the exception of unconstitutionality was raised [...]'. It uses the generic word 'court' both for courts of law and for courts of commercial arbitration. Further, the procedure of notification and settlement of the exception of unconstitutionality is identical for all mentioned courts. Likewise, there is no differentiation in terms of effects of decisions delivered by the Constitutional Court.

8.12. The Code of Civil Procedure[11] regulates arbitration in Book IV – About arbitration (Articles 541-621), namely:
Title I-General Provisions
Title II – Arbitration agreement
Title III – The arbitration tribunal
Title IV-Arbitration procedure
Title V – Cancellation of the arbitration decision
Title VI – Enforcement of the arbitration decision
Title VII – Institutionalized arbitration

8.13. Article 541 1) of the Code of Civil Procedure defines arbitration as 'an alternative jurisdiction with a private character.' Pursuant to paragraph 2 of the same article:

in the administration of this jurisdiction, the disputing parties and the competent arbitration tribunal may establish rules of procedure derogating from general law, provided that those rules do not conflict with public policy and with the binding provisions of the law.

III.3. Jurisprudential Benchmarks

III.3.1. Notification of the Constitutional Court by Romanian courts of commercial arbitration

8.14. Having analysed the cases where the Constitutional Court was notified by Romanian courts of commercial arbitrations, we find it interesting that in the vast majority of cases the statutory texts subject to constitutional review refer precisely to the rules on commercial arbitration (i.e. the provisions of Articles 340-368, respectively Book IV 'About arbitration' of the old Code of Civil Procedure). It is reasonable to question the issue of the legal nature of arbitration and of commercial arbitration courts.

---

[11] Law no.134/2000 on the Code of Civil Procedure, republished in the Official Gazette of Romania, Part I, no.545 of 3 August 2012.

8.15. The main challenges brought before the Constitutional Court were aimed at the fact that the provisions of the Code of Civil Procedure

allow arbitration tribunals to administrate justice, although they are not courts of law and they are not established by law, [but] only by the agreement of the parties, and the arbitration decision is not subject to judicial review on all aspects of the case.' Thus, it was argued that the legal provisions challenged for unconstitutionality are 'setting up a parallel justice' and 'the court of law does not exercise a full jurisdiction review over cases decided by arbitration tribunals. It is thus prevented free access to justice, enshrined by Article 21 of the Constitution, text that sanctions any filters against the access to courts.[12]

8.16. Similarly, it was claimed that

the impugned legal texts refer to an exceptional court, prohibited by the Constitution, composed of persons who are not independent judges, who are not subject to law, but resolve a dispute which falls within the exclusive jurisdiction of the courts, according to Law no. 304/2004 regarding the judicial organisation.[13]

8.17. Rejecting as unfounded the raised exceptions of unconstitutionality, the Court held that arbitration is an exception to the principle that justice is meted out by courts and represents 'that effective legal mechanism designed to ensure a fair, confidential, more rapid and less formal trial, resulting in decisions that can lead to forced execution'.

8.18. Making a differentiation in this respect between courts of law and courts of commercial arbitration, the Court held that the latter

are not courts in the sense of Article 126 and Article 73 (3) of the Constitution, but jurisdictions expressly mentioned in the Basic Law under Article 146 d), and their establishment is not conditional on the adoption of an organic law. Disputes settled by commercial arbitration courts result in decisions that can be subjected to judicial review under the terms of Article 364 of the Code of Civil Procedure.[14]

---

[12] Challenges mentioned in Decision no. 533 of 31 May 2007 on the exception of unconstitutionality of Article 364 of the Code of Civil Procedure, published in the Official Gazette of Romania, Part I, no. 416 of 21 June 2007.

[13] Challenges mentioned in Decision no. 8 of 9 January 2007, on the exception of unconstitutionality of the provisions of Articles 340-368 of the Code of Civil Procedure.

[14] Decision no. 1121 of 10 September 2009, published in the Official Gazette of Romania, Part I, no. 727 of 27 October 2009.

8.19. Arbitration is organised and conducted in accordance with the arbitration agreement between the parties, in compliance with the principle of free will, provided that public order, morality, and the binding provisions of the law are respected, as stipulated in the provisions of Article 341 of the Code of civil Procedure. Therefore, the parties may establish the rules for determining the arbitration tribunal, the rules on the appointment, revocation and replacement of arbitrators, the time and place of arbitration, the procedural rules that the arbitration tribunal must follow in settling the dispute and, in general, any other rules for the good conduct of arbitration. All of these characteristics are settled using the arbitration agreement or by an addendum subsequently signed. If the parties have not agreed on such rules, the arbitration tribunal shall be able to regulate the procedure to be followed.

8.20. Concerning the alleged violation of the constitutional provisions that stipulate that justice shall be meted out only by the courts of law, the Court found that

the commercial arbitration courts do not meet the characteristic features of extraordinary courts, as the procedure they follow does neither infringe nor restrict the procedural rights of the parties set forth in the Code of Civil Procedure or other rights and freedoms thereof.

8.21. The Court also held that 'the Constitution itself, in Article 146 d), recognizes the existence of commercial arbitration courts, stating that exceptions of unconstitutionality can be raised also before these courts, besides the courts of law.'[15]

8.22. Regarding the alleged violation of Article 21 of the Constitution on free access to justice, the Court found that

before the arbitration court the case is considered under all aspects raised by the parties, and free access to justice is in no way hampered since there is an opportunity to promote action for annulment which constitutes a judicial remedy (and therefore a method of access to justice) required by law.[16]

---

[15] For the qualification of commercial arbitration courts as courts for the purposes of art.267 of the Treaty on European Union, See *Ascendi* Case – C-377/13.

[16] Decision no. 533 of 31 May 2007 on the exception of unconstitutionality of the provisions of Article 364 of the Code of Civil Procedure, published in the Official Gazette of Romania, Part I, no. 416 of 21 June 2007; Decision no. 181 of 6 March 2007, on the exception of unconstitutionality of the provisions of Article 360 of the Code of Civil Procedure, published in the Official Gazette of Romania, Part I, no. 291 of 3 May 2007; Decision no. 395 of 9 May 2006 on the exception of unconstitutionality of the provisions of Article 340, Article 340¹, Article 341, Article 342 and Article 359⁶ of the Code of Civil

8.23. Another challenge brought before the Constitutional Court, raised *ex officio* by a commercial arbitration court, was that the provisions of Article 340 of the old Code of Civil Procedure infringe free access to justice and the right to a fair trial because they prevent legal persons of public law from using the arbitration procedure. In reply to these challenges, the Constitutional Court held that

> the provisions of the Code of Civil Procedure do neither specifically mention nor prohibit the State and the administrative-territorial units to use the arbitration procedure, so it cannot be accepted that the impugned statutory provisions contravene in any way the provisions of the Constitution.

8.24. The rule invoked by the author of the exception was, in fact, established by the Rules of Arbitration Procedure of the Commercial Arbitration Court attached to the Cluj Chamber of Commerce and Industry, an act that could not constitute the subject matter of the constitutional review, which can only refer to laws and ordinances. For these reasons, the Constitutional Court rejected the exception of unconstitutionality as inadmissible.[17]

8.25. It is therefore noted that, judicially, the Constitutional Court has made a number of clarifications on the nature and characteristic features of commercial arbitration, from the perspective of constitutional texts of reference.

8.26. Similar clarifications are also made in the case-law of other Constitutional Courts, such as to establish the role and status of commercial arbitration courts, respectively of arbitrators. For example, the Constitutional Court of the Czech Republic, modifying its case-law on the subject, described arbitration as an alternative with integral value to proceedings before a court. The Court noted explicitly that

---

Procedure, as well as Article 13 (3) and (6) of Decree-Law no.139/1990 on the Chambers of Commerce and Industry in Romania; Decision no.1277 of 8 October 2009 on the exception of unconstitutionality of the provisions of Article 4 i) of the Law no. 335 / 2007 on the Chambers of Commerce of Romania, published in the Official Gazette no775 of 12 November 200; Decision no. 263 of 16 March 2010 on the exception of unconstitutionality of Article 343[1] (1) and Article 343[3] of the Code of Civil Procedure, published in the Official Gazette of Romania, Part I, no. 295 of 6 May 2010; Decision no. 1027 of 14 September 2010 on the exception of unconstitutionality of the provisions of Article 353[1] of the Code of Civil Procedure, published in the Official Gazette of Romania, Part I, no. 739 of 5 November 2010.

[17] Decision no. 331 of 10 April 2012 on the exception of unconstitutionality of Article 340 of the Code of Civil Procedure, published in the Official Gazette of Romania, Part I, no. 384 of 7 June 2012.

arbitrators are an 'authority' that finds and must find the applicable law. Previously, the Court had established that arbitrators are persons with private-law status, to whom, through procedural agreement, the parties in conflict transfer the power to debate and decide on their dispute. If the arbitrator and the permanent court of arbitration are not bodies of public power, their decision or any other measure, then they cannot constitute the subject matter of a constitutional complaint. As held in the specialised literature, the current orientation and position represents a qualitative improvement in the case-law of this Court in relation to the 2002 case-law.[18]

III.3.2. Notification of the Constitutional Court by foreign courts of commercial arbitration

Procedural framework

8.27.   A situation which has raised more complex questions was referred to the Constitutional Court of Romania by a foreign arbitration court, the International Court of Arbitration of the International Chamber of Commerce in Paris.

8.28.   By Decision no. 123 of 5 March 2013, published in Official Gazette of Romania, Part I, no. 214 of 16 April 2013, issued on that occasion, the Court analysed the conditions of admissibility laid down by Article 29 (1) Law no. 47/1992 on the organisation and functioning of the Constitutional Court. The Court specifically examined the notification of the Constitutional Court by 'a court of law or a court of commercial arbitration'. The normative acts that constitute the subject matter the exception must be 'in force'. The impugned provisions must be 'related to the settlement of the case', as well as with the substantive aspects of the case. In particular, there must be compliance by the impugned statutory texts with the constitutional provisions governing the right to property. The exception of unconstitutionality concerned a series of emergency ordinances and laws approving them These ordinances and laws concerned a right granted to employees, board members and pensioners, whose last function was that exerted in the privatized companies ('employees with the right of preference'), to purchase shares at the price paid by the strategic investor.[19]

---

[18]   For a general presentation of relevant cases, see ALEXANDER J BĚLOHLÁVEK, PROTECȚIA CONSUMATORILOR ÎN PROCEDURA DE ARBITRAJ (*Consumer protection in the arbitration procedure*), Bucharest: C.H.Beck Publishing House 261 (2012).

[19]   Government Emergency Ordinance no.143/2007 amending Article 6 (2) and (4) of Government Emergency Ordinance no.114/2005 on measures for the conduct and

8.29.   In relation to all these admissibility conditions, it is the notification of the Court by 'a court of law or a court of commercial arbitration' that is relevant for this study. The other causes of inadmissibility are relevant only because they bring into discussion the effects of the decisions of the Constitutional Court, including the fact that such a decision establishes the constitutional and legal framework of analysis for the sole arbitrator.

---

completion of the privatization of subsidiary companies of electricity distribution and supply 'Electrica Moldova' – S.A. and 'Electrica Oltenia' – S.A., published in the Official Gazette of Romania, Part I, no 880 of 21 December 2007; Law no.147/2008 for approval of Government Emergency Ordinance no.143/2007 amending Article 6 (2) and (4) of Government Emergency Ordinance no.114/2005 on measures for the conduct and completion of the privatization of subsidiary companies of electricity distribution and supply 'Electrica Moldova' – S.A. and 'Electrica Oltenia' – S.A., published in the Official Gazette of Romania, Part I, no. 553 of 15 July 2008; Government Emergency Ordinance no.116/2008 amending Article 6 (2) and (4) of Government Emergency Ordinance no.114/2005 on measures for the conduct and completion of the privatization of subsidiary companies of electricity distribution and supply 'Electrica Moldova' – S.A. and 'Electrica Oltenia' – S.A., published in the Official Gazette of Romania, Part I, no. 673 of 30 September 2008; Law no.166/2009 for approval of Government Emergency Ordinance no. 116/2008 amending Article 6 (2) and (4) of Government Emergency Ordinance no. 114/2005 on measures for the conduct and completion of the privatization of subsidiary companies of electricity distribution and supply 'Electrica Moldova' – S.A. and 'Electrica Oltenia' – S.A., published in the Official Gazette of Romania, Part I, no. 331 of 19 May 2009; Government Emergency Ordinance no. 126/2010 amending Article 6 (2) and (4) of Government Emergency Ordinance no.114/2005 on measures for the conduct and completion of the privatization of subsidiary companies of electricity distribution and supply 'Electrica Moldova' – S.A. and 'Electrica Oltenia' – S.A., published in the Official Gazette of Romania, Part I, no 888 of 30 December 2010; Law no. 79/2011 for approval of Government Emergency Ordinance no. 126/2010 amending Article 6 (2) and (4) of Government Emergency Ordinance no. 114/2005 on measures for the conduct and completion of the privatization of subsidiary companies of electricity distribution and supply 'Electrica Moldova' – S.A. and 'Electrica Oltenia' – S.A., published in the Official Gazette of Romania, Part I, no. 431 of 14 June 2011; Government Emergency Ordinance no. 116/2011 approving some measures on the sale of stakes held by the Trading Company for Distribution and Supply of Electricity 'Electrica' – S.A. and amending Government Ordinance no.31/2004 on measures for privatization of the Trading Company of Gas Distribution 'Distrigaz Sud' – S.A. Bucharest and of the Trading Company of Gas Distribution 'Distrigaz Nord' – S.A. Târgu Mureş, as well as of the subsidiary companies for distribution and supply of electricity, published in the Official Gazette of Romania, Part I, no. 931 of 29 December 2011; Article 3 of Government Emergency Ordinance no. 120/2011 on the extension of time limits, published in the Official Gazette of Romania, Part I, no. 926 of 28 December 2011.

Admissibility of the notification of the Constitutional Court of Romania by a foreign arbitration court

8.30. As mentioned above, the court of commercial arbitration which notified the Constitutional Court in the present case is the International Court of Arbitration of the International Chamber of Commerce in Paris. The author of the exception and the sole arbitrator took the view that this is 'a court of commercial arbitration' according to Romanian law, while the defendant has held that it does not fall within the constitutional text of reference.

8.31. On these claims, the Court found that according to the logical interpretation of the provisions of Article 146 d) of the Constitution and of Article 29 of Law no. 47/1992 on the organisation and functioning of the Constitutional, texts governing the competence of the Constitutional Court of Romania to settle 'exceptions of unconstitutionality of laws and ordinances raised before courts of law and courts of commercial arbitration.' This leads to the conclusion that the legislature did not make any distinction between commercial arbitration courts in relation to the place where they operate. Under the principle 'where the law does not distinguish, neither should we distinguish *(ubi lex non distinguit nec nos distinguere debemus)*' such a distinction is not permitted and therefore the Constitutional Court of Romania was legally notified, even if the notification came from a court of commercial arbitration established in France. This argument is supported by the systematic and teleological interpretation of the relevant legal provisions retained in the considerations that underpinned the decision of the Constitutional Court.

8.32. Thus, the systematic interpretation of the Constitution reveals that the constituent legislature expressly referred to the national courts system [covered by the same texts – Article 146 d) of the Constitution and Article 29 of Law no. 47/1992], through the reference made in Article 126 of the Constitution to the High Court of Cassation and Justice and its role in the uniform interpretation and application of the law by the courts. As concerns commercial arbitration courts there is no such a reference, clarification or explanation, and the constituent legislature's approach is manifestly wider. This approach can be justified by the specificity of the commercial arbitration court against the ordinary court, given the contractual, jurisdictional and mixed legal nature of arbitration.

8.33. Addressing the same legal texts from a teleological perspective, the Court found that the objective pursued by the legislature in the constitutional revision of 2003 by introducing the commercial arbitration courts within bodies before which the exception of unconstitutionality can be raised, was to ensure the widest possible access to constitutional justice. This vision of the courts that may notify the constitutional Court is in line with the interpretation that the European Court of Human Rights gave in its case-law to the concept of 'tribunal' provided by Article 6 of the Convention for the Protection of Human Rights and Fundamental Freedoms. As it stated, it

> is not necessarily to be understood as signifying a court of law of the classic kind, integrated within the standard judicial machinery of the country [...]; thus, it may comprise a body set up to determine a limited number of specific issues, provided always that it offers the appropriate guarantees.[20]

8.34. However, if an exception of unconstitutionality concerning Romanian law, in relation to the Constitution of Romania, is raised before a commercial arbitration court, regardless of its location, a refusal by the Constitutional Court to settle such an exception would come against the will of the constituent legislature. In particular, the exception would be in breach of Article 21 – *Free access to justice*, Article 142 (1) on the role of the Constitutional Court as guarantor for the supremacy of the Constitution and Article 1 (5) which states that 'Observance of the Constitution, of its supremacy, and the laws shall be obligatory in Romania.'

8.35. The Court noted, however, that any interpretation limiting the scope of commercial arbitration courts and their circumstantiation only to commercial arbitration courts located in the territory of Romania cannot be accredited as a procedural condition for exercising the right of free access to constitutional justice. This is because the choice of the place of arbitration outside Romania cannot be interpreted as a waiver of the fundamental right of free access to justice. Such an interpretation would amount to a genuine sanction applied to the parties to the arbitration agreement for their option to submit settlement of disputes (arising out of a contract signed in Romania and governed by the Romanian law) to the jurisdiction of a court of arbitration located in another country. This is so even though the Romanian law (Article 369[1] of the Code of Civil Procedure in effect at the conclusion of the privatization contract) expressly provides such option, without any restrictions. On the other hand, the commercial arbitration court, in such a case, would find itself obliged to apply an allegedly unconstitutional law, without any procedural possibility to verify or to rule on the challenges of unconstitutionality. This is because the only competent court that can carry out the constitutional review of the law

---

[20] Judgement in *Campbell and Fell* v *the United Kingdom*, 28 June 1984, paragraph 76 and judgement in *Lithgow and Others v. the United Kingdom* of 8 July 1986, paragraph 201.

in relation to the Constitution of Romania is the Constitutional Court of Romania.

8.36. There are requirements established by law i.e. the procedural requirements that must be met so that the holder could reclaim his subjective right. However, even if they represent restrictions on the free access to justice, they have a solid and indisputable justification given the aim pursued. This consists of the restriction of the abusive use of the respective right, but they must be sufficiently reasonable as to not lead to an excessive restriction on the exercise of the respective right, likely to question its very existence. Moreover, the interpretation of such requirements must not lead to a restriction on the exercise of rights beyond the aim pursued in adopting them. The addition of another condition, which would restrict the scope of bodies before whom the exception of unconstitutionality can be raised, even though this is already limited by the constituent legislature to courts of law and courts of commercial arbitration would result in an excessive restriction on the access to justice. This would be both in terms of access to constitutional justice and in terms of access to a court of commercial arbitration. The possibility of the parties to freely express an option on the place of arbitration would be limited by the restriction to raise exceptions of unconstitutionality before some of these courts.

8.37. For these reasons, the Court ascertained the compliance with the condition of notification of the Constitutional Court by 'a commercial arbitration court' provided by Article 146 d) of the Constitution and Article 29 (1) of Law no. 47/1992. Thus, the Constitutional Court considered that it had been legally referred to and competent to rule on an exception of unconstitutionality raised on normative acts belonging to the Romanian law system, and challenged by Romanian legal entities, before courts of arbitration that are not located in Romania.

Effects of the decision of the Constitutional Court in relation to the foreign Arbitration Court and the establishment of the constitutional and legal framework of analysis for the sole arbitrator

8.38. The case at issue, which put a novel legal problem before the Constitutional Court was unique both for the doctrine and for the practice of law in Romania. It also called into question the effects of the decisions of the Constitutional Court.

8.39. With respect to these effects, the Court held that, when determining the place of arbitration in another country, the arbitration agreement does not encroach in any way on the substantive law governing the legal relationship between the parties. Thus, even if the place of arbitration is Paris, the law applicable to the legal relationship between the parties to dispute is Romanian law, as it clearly results from the terms of the privatization agreement concluded in the case at issue. In case of institutional arbitration, the option for a court of arbitration determines the setting of the applicable procedural rules. With reference to the place of arbitration, it also determines the classification of the decision delivered as national or foreign. Regardless of the rules of procedure, the existence of 'interference' by the Constitutional Court of Romania in the administration of justice in another country (in this case, France) cannot be claimed, as long as this Court's jurisdiction is exclusive, special and specialised. It is distinct from that of the French courts of general jurisdiction, which are not competent to exercise the review of constitutionality of Romanian laws.

8.40. In terms of the carried out constitutional review, the Constitutional Court further analysed the compliance with the admissibility conditions. This concerned whether or not the normative acts that constitute the subject matter of the exception are 'in force', and whether or not they are 'related to the settlement of the case'.

8.41. The Court in its Decision no. 766 of 15 June 2011, published in Official Gazette of Romania, Part I, no. 549 of 3 August 2011, emphasized the interpretation of the phrase 'in force' within Article 29 of Law no. 47/1992. It held that texts that restrict the application of constitutional review only to laws and ordinances in force, and that this review concerns 'the provisions applicable in the case, even if they are no longer in force', but whose legal effects continue also after they come out of force. Such an approach was justified by the fact that although repealed, 'the civil law can be applied after its expiry, in certain circumstances, according to the principle *tempus regit actum*'. As a result, the Court held that

> the phrase 'in force' in the wording of Article 29(1) and Article 31(1) of Law no. 47/1992 on the organisation and functioning of the Constitutional Court, republished, was constitutional insofar as interpreted in the sense that laws or ordinances or provisions of laws or ordinances whose legal effects continue to occur although they are no longer in force can also be subjected to constitutional review.

8.42. The Court further noted that some of the impugned normative acts had exhausted their legal effects before the date on which the applicant has exercised its option to purchase the shares in question. Thus, these normative acts are not laws or ordinances 'in force' in the sense of this phrase, as established by Decision no. 766/2011 of the Constitutional Court, as they cannot continue to produce legal effects on acts and deeds (e.g. the option to purchase) signed or occurred after the date when the legal effects of the normative acts were exhausted by expiry as of right of the terms established therein. Therefore, the exception of unconstitutionality raised on those normative acts[21] was rejected as inadmissible because they are no longer 'in force' in the sense of Article 29 (1) of Law no.47/1992, in the interpretation given to this legal text by Decision no.766 of 15 June 2011 of the Constitutional Court.

8.43.   Concerning the requirement that the impugned acts be 'related to the settlement of the case', the Court held that, from amongst the normative acts identified as being 'in force' in the sense of Article 29 of Law no.47/1992, only the acts issued after the date of exercise of the option to purchase the shares in question by the applicant are related to the settlement of the case. The Court held that even if formulated very broadly, the challenge of the author of the exception concerns the normative acts that successively amended the time limit set by law for the exercise of employees' right of option. It did not affect the text that governs this time limit, adopted before the time when the applicant exercised the option to purchase the shares and in relation to which the statement of grounds shows that an option to purchase was exercised.

8.44.   Regarding the impugned provisions, the Court found that they do not violate the provisions of the Constitution or those of Protocol No. 1 to the Convention for the Protection of Human Rights and Fundamental Freedoms, which enshrine the right to property, or the constitutional provisions relating to the prohibition of discrimination.

8.45.   The decision of the Constitutional Court is final and generally binding, under the terms of Article 147 (4) of the Constitution, cited above. Upon applying Romanian law to the case at issue, the sole arbitrator must respect the decision of the Court in terms of constitutionality thereof. From this perspective, the decision of the Constitutional Court represents a 'common body' with the provisions applicable to the dispute, insofar as issues of constitutionality thereof are at stake. Given the equally binding nature of the operative and of the reasoning aspects of the decision of the Court, we consider that the binding nature refers both to the review on compliance with the Constitution and to the review on compliance with the Convention exercised by the Constitutional Court. The sole arbitrator may apply the provisions of the Convention for the Protection of Human Rights and Fundamental Freedoms and those of the Protocols to the Convention, but only on matters that were not examined by the Constitutional Court and on which it did not adjudicate by this decision.

---

[21]   Government Emergency Ordinance no.143/2007, Law no.147/2008 on the approval of Government Emergency Ordinance no.143/2007 and Government Emergency Ordinance no.116/2008.

IV. Conclusions

8.46. The examination of the case-law, as well as the elements of comparative law, envisaged above, reveal that the relationship between commercial arbitration courts and the constitutional courts continues to raise legal issues of great complexity. This is especially true when external elements are also involved. These elements determine controversies concerning the admissibility of the notification to a Constitutional Court.

8.47. Likewise, we note a hesitant behaviour of the parties, and specifically of the commercial arbitration courts to raise exceptions of unconstitutionality in arbitration cases. The main issues brought to the Constitutional Court of Romania, as indicated, are those concerning the nature and role of commercial arbitration, and not the substantive issues relating to the constitutionality of the regulations applicable to the legal relationship between the parties. Even in these circumstances, we can note the contribution of the constitutional court in defining and, from this perspective, strengthening the role of commercial arbitration courts.

|||

Summaries

FRA   [*Interactions entre les procédures d'arbitrage et les cours constitutionnelles*]

L'objectif du présent article est d'analyser les interactions entre les cours constitutionnelles et les cours d'arbitrage dans la résolution de litiges commerciaux dans un contexte européen, tout en examinant par ailleurs la situation actuelle et la réglementation en Roumanie. Nous nous pencherons sur les développements d'une réglementation applicable et sur l'examen constitutionnel effectué sur proposition des cours d'arbitrage dans les litiges commerciaux, tout en soulignant les éléments essentiels sur lesquels s'appuie le droit dans ce domaine. Les cours d'arbitrage amenées à résoudre des litiges commerciaux ont la possibilité d'initier une procédure auprès de la Cour constitutionnelle, afin de juger d'une possible inconstitutionnalité des lois et des réglementations dans des affaires dont elles ont la charge. Cela a conduit à une modification de la constitution roumaine en 2003. Il était auparavant uniquement possible de débattre de l'application d'une jurisprudence constitutionnelle par les cours d'arbitrage. Nous étudierons ici la pratique des recours des cours arbitrales devant la Cour constitutionnelle depuis 2003, y compris dans les cas où la cour d'arbitrage intervient dans un arbitrage international et se préoccupe autant de la problématique de la procédure que de celle du droit matériel, tel que cela apparaît dans les questions soumises à la Cour constitutionnelle. Nous nous pencherons également sur les cas où la procédure a été initiée auprès de la Cour constitutionnelle dans des affaires examinées par la Cour internationale d'arbitrage de Paris (CCI), et nous examinerons les décisions rendues dans ces cas précis. Le présent article est ainsi conçu comme une invitation au débat et comme une esquisse des effets d'une conception constitutionnelle.

CZE   *[Interakce rozhodčího řízení a ústavních soudů]*
Cílem tohoto příspěvku je rozbor vzájemného působení mezi ústavními soudy a rozhodčími soudy rozhodujícími spory v obchodních věcech v evropském kontextu, přičemž autoři přihlížejí i k současné situaci a úpravě v Rumunsku. Tento rozbor se zabývá vývojem použitelné úpravy a ústavním přezkumem realizovaným na návrh rozhodčích soudů v obchodních věcech, přičemž zdůrazňuje základní body, o něž se opírá právní věda v této oblasti. Rozhodčí soudy rozhodující v obchodních věcech mají možnost iniciovat řízení u Ústavního soudu za účelem rozhodnutí o možné neústavnosti zákonů a nařízení ve věcech, o nichž se před rozhodčím soudem vede spor. Tuto možnost připustila změna rumunské ústavy z roku 2003. Před touto změnou bylo možno diskutovat pouze o aplikaci ústavněprávní judikatury rozhodčími soudy. Příspěvek rozebírá praxi návrhů podávaných rozhodčími soudy k Ústavnímu soudu po roce 2003, a to včetně těch případů, kdy rozhodčí soud jedná v mezinárodní věci, a zabývá se jak problematikou procesní, tak hmotněprávní jak tato zaznívá v odpovídajících návrzích. Autoři se zabývají též případy, kdy řízení u Ústavního soudu bylo iniciováno ve věcech projednávaných Mezinárodním rozhodčím soudem ICC v Paříži (Francie) a rozhodnutími v těchto věcech. Příspěvek je proto koncipován jako podnět k diskusi na toto téma a jako nástin účinků dané ústavní koncepce.

|||

POL   *[Interakcja między postępowaniem arbitrażowym i sądami konstytucyjnymi]*
Niniejszy artykuł ma na celu analizę wzajemnego oddziaływania między sądami konstytucyjnymi a sądami arbitrażowymi, rozstrzygającymi spory w sprawach handlowych w kontekście europejskim, przy czym autorzy uwzględniają również aktualną sytuację i regulacje prawne w Rumunii. Niniejsza analiza obejmuje rozwój

właściwych regulacji prawnych oraz badanie spraw przez sądy konstytucyjnie na wniosek sądów arbitrażowych w sprawach handlowych, jednocześnie podkreślając podstawowe punkty, na których opiera się nauka prawa w tym zakresie.

DEU [***Wechselspiel von Schiedsverfahren und Verfassungsgerichten***]
Dieser Beitrag möchte die Wechselwirkung zwischen den Verfassungsgerichten und der Schiedsgerichtbarkeit in Handelssachen im europäischen Kontext analysieren, wobei die Autoren auch auf die aktuelle Situation und Rechtslage in Rumänien eingehen. Die Analyse befasst sich mit der Entwicklung des anzuwendenden Rechts und der (von den Schiedsgerichten selbst erbetenen) verfassungsrechtlichen Überprüfung von Fragen in Handelssachen; dabei hebt sie die Eckpfeiler hervor, auf die sich die Rechtswissenschaft in diesem Bereich stützt.

RUS [***Взаимодействие арбитражных и конституционных судов***]
Целью данной статьи является анализ взаимодействия между конституционными судами и арбитражными судами, рассматривающими и разрешающими споры в торговых делах в европейском контексте, причем авторы также принимают во внимание существующую ситуацию и регулирование в Румынии. Этот анализ рассматривает развитие применимого регулирования и пересмотр в конституционном суде, выполняемый по предложению арбитражных судов в торговых делах, причем выделяет основные пункты, на которые опирается юриспруденция в этой области.

ESP [*Interacción entre el arbitraje y el proceso constitucional*]
El objetivo de este trabajo es el análisis de la interacción entre el Tribunal Constitucional y los tribunales de arbitraje que resuelven controversias en materia comercial en el contexto europeo, tomando en cuenta la situación actual y la regulación en Rumanía. Este análisis se centra en el desarrollo de la regulación aplicable y en la revisión constitucional realizada sobre la propuesta de los tribunales de arbitraje en materia comercial, subrayando los puntos fundamentales en los que descansa la ciencia jurídica en este área.

| | |

Corinna Potocnik | Harald Sippel | Johannes Willheim

Can Arbitral Tribunals Seek the Support of National Courts to Obtain a Preliminary Ruling by the CJEU in Matters Involving EU Competition?

Key words:
Arbitration | Arbitral tribunal | Arbitral award | Arbitrability | EU Competition Law | European Court of Justice/CJEU | Interim measure | Lex arbitri | Preliminary Ruling | Setting Aside

Abstract | *Arbitral tribunals are not allowed to refer to the CJEU for a preliminary ruling, but need the support of state courts in doing so. In most jurisdictions of the EU Member States, arbitral tribunals are rather limited in seeking such support. This may lead to difficulties as arbitral tribunals are nonetheless bound to (correctly) apply EU law and EU competition law in particular, a field of law which often arises in international arbitration. This is problematic as EU competition law, an essential feature of the internal market, requires that the EU Commission and state courts cooperate so that the uniform application of EU competition law is guaranteed. However, within the EU, only six Member States provide for an implicit possibility of asking state courts for assistance in referring to the CJEU, while none of the other Member States except Denmark provide for general court assistance to arbitral tribunals; Denmark expressly permits arbitral tribunals to request the competent state court to refer to the CJEU for a preliminary ruling. In light of the ever-growing importance of arbitration as means of dispute resolution, it must be asked why only a single EU Member State ensures the uniform application of EU competition law during arbitral proceedings.*

Mag. Corinna Potocnik is an Associate with Willheim Müller Attorneys at Law in Vienna and specializes in EU competition law and international arbitration. Before joining Willheim Müller in 2012, she worked at an Austrian boutique law firm specialized in international arbitration as well as at the Permanent Mission of Austria to the United Nations in Vienna. Corinna Potocnik graduated from the University of Vienna with a focus on International Law.
e-mail:
c.potocnik@wmlaw.at

Dr. Harald Sippel, MBA FCIArb is an Associate with Willheim Müller Attorneys at Law in Vienna. His practice focuses on complex international disputes.

| | |

I. Introduction

9.01. As recently as October 2014, media reported on a landmark case: In setting aside proceedings, the French *Cour d'Appel de Paris* asked the Court of Justice of the European Union (CJEU) for a preliminary ruling to clarify an issue of EU competition law before it would decide whether to annul a series of ICC awards.[1] As far as can be seen, this was the first time a French court has made such a request to the CJEU in the context of setting aside proceedings. The *Cour d'Appel de Paris* essentially asked the CJEU for an interpretation of Art 101 TFEU, a core provision of EU competition law.

9.02. However, this leaves the question of why the arbitral tribunal itself did not refer the question to the CJEU, but only the competent court in the setting aside proceedings finally asked for interpretation of EU law. The answer is simple: arbitral tribunals are – pursuant to the case law of the CJEU – still not allowed to refer to the CJEU for a preliminary ruling. Despite the fact that arbitration has become a very important mechanism of dispute resolution in recent years, arbitral tribunals still need the help of national courts for such referrals.

9.03. This paper shall give an overview of the possibilities for arbitral tribunals to nonetheless receive a preliminary ruling on EU competition law issues from the CJEU and show the difficulties arbitral tribunals face in most jurisdictions of EU Member States in doing so. This paper has moreover to be seen in the special context of EU competition law as the set of rules of law on which the CJEU is asked for a preliminary ruling.

Mr. Sippel has acted as counsel, secretary to the tribunal and arbitrator (party-appointed arbitrator, sole arbitrator and presiding arbitrator) in *ad hoc* arbitrations and before major arbitral institutions (*inter alia* ICC, LCIA, and VIAC).
e-mail:
h.sippel@wmlaw.at

Dr. Johannes Willheim, M.B.L.-HSG, LL.M. (Chicago) is a founding partner of Willheim Müller Attorneys at Law. Johannes Willheim was trained internationally in corporate and commercial law, with a strong focus on EU and US antitrust law and economics. He has served as party representative as well as arbitrator in international arbitration proceedings. Mr. Willheim has acted as party representative in numerous arbitrations whose outcome depended on EU competition law. He regularly teaches international dispute resolution courses and seminars.
e-mail:
j.willheim@wmlaw.at

---

[1]   For more details on the case *see* e.g. Global Arbitration Review, *Yong,* Paris court turns to CJEU in set-aside case; available at: http://www.eplawpatentblog.com/2014/October/ 2014-09-23_CA_Paris_Genentech_c_Hoechst_RG_12-21810_Translation.pdf; http://www. brevet-invention-philippeschmittleblog.eu/contrat-technique-contractuelle/question-prejudicielle-cour-paris-recours-entence-arbitrale-clause-licence/; http://www.eplawpatentblog.com/eplaw/ 2014/10/fr-genentech-v-hoechst-and-sanofi-aventis-deutschland-referral-cjeu.html (accessed on 7 November 2014).

II. Preliminary Rulings

9.04. Art 267 of the Treaty on the Functioning of the European Union (TFEU) provides for a preliminary ruling by the CJEU regarding the interpretation of EU law. A question referred to the CJEU must be relevant to a specific case (thus no hypothetical questions are allowed). Moreover, no interpretation of national law can be sought from the CJEU. It is the national courts that must then assess whether a referral to the CJEU is necessary in order to decide the specific case. The CJEU will not, however, decide on the underlying dispute, but only give an interpretation on the EU law in question. The purpose of Article 267, which plays an important role in the development of legal concepts under EU law, is to ensure the uniform interpretation and application of EU law within the EU Member States.

9.05. Pursuant to Art 267 TFEU *'any court or tribunal of a Member State'* may bring a matter before the CJEU for a preliminary ruling. In its well-known decisions *Nordsee*[2] and *Denuit and Cordenier*,[3] the CJEU expressly held that this notion does not include arbitral tribunals, as *'the parties are under no obligation, in law or in fact, to refer their disputes to arbitration and the public authorities of the Member State concerned are not involved in the decision to opt for arbitration nor required to intervene of their own accord in the proceedings before the arbitrator.'*[4] Consequently, arbitral tribunals are not allowed to refer directly to the CJEU for a preliminary ruling, but need the assistance of state courts that qualify as court or tribunal within the meaning of Art 267 TFEU.

9.06. The *Nordsee* decision was issued in 1982 – 32 years ago. Although it is fair to say that, since then, arbitration has emerged as one of the most common and effective means for dispute resolution,[5] the CJEU has – until now – not taken the opportunity to reconsider its very strict position regarding arbitral tribunals seeking preliminary rulings from the CJEU.

---

[2]   C-102/81, *Nordsee v Reederei Mond*, [1982] ECR 1095, para. 13, confirmed in C-125/04, *Denuit and Cordenier*, [2005] ECR 923 and C-126/97, *Eco Swiss*, [1999] ECR 3055.

[3]   C-125/04, *Denuit and Cordenier*, [2005] ECR 923.

[4]   Ibid, para. 13

[5]   Siegfried H. Elsing, *Chapter I: Issues Specific to Arbitration in Europe, References by Arbitral Tribunals to the European Court of Justice for Preliminary Rulings, in* AUSTRIAN YEARBOOK ON INTERNATIONAL ARBITRATION 45–59 (Christian Klausegger; Peter Klein et al. (eds), 2013).

III. Arbitral Tribunals and the Application of EU Competition Law

III.1. The Arbitral Tribunal's Competence to Decide on EU Competition Law

9.07. At a first glance, it is not self-evident that an arbitral tribunal is competent to decide on EU competition law at all. The major counter-argument with regard to the arbitrability of EU competition law is the claim that EU competition law and the maintenance of effective competition is a matter of public interest that should be adjudicated upon only by publicly responsible institutions; the purpose of competition law is to protect competition itself rather than competitors.[6] Competition law issues should thus not be referred to an institution that – mostly confidentially – decides upon commercial interests of private parties (e.g., an arbitral tribunal).

9.08. However, there is large consensus on the arbitrability of (EU) competition law among courts in the EU[7] and at least since the CJEU's decision *Eco Swiss*, there can be no doubt on the arbitrability of EU competition law: although the CJEU has never explicitly dealt with the question of whether or not the EU competition rules would be arbitrable, the CJEU's decision in *Eco Swiss 'would be meaningless if arbitrators are excluded in principle from ruling upon and enforcing competition law.'*[8] Arbitral tribunals are even <u>bound to apply provisions of EU law including EU competition law</u>. This can also be derived from the *Eco Swiss* decision, where the CJEU clearly stated that an arbitral award risks being set aside if the arbitral tribunal does not comply with EU competition law.

9.09. In conclusion of the above, this results in the absurd consequence that arbitral tribunals must (correctly) apply EU competition law but may not refer to the CJEU for a preliminary ruling. Unlike national courts, arbitral tribunals can thus not ask for guidance and interpretation of rules of law that they are obliged to apply.

---

[6] Jean-Claude Najar, *Chapter 4: Arbitrating Competition Law: The User's Perspective, in* EU AND US ANTITRUST ARBITRATION: A HANDBOOK FOR PRACTITIONERS 119–154 (Gordon Blanke; Phillip Louis Landolt (eds), 2011).

[7] To take the example of Austria: *see* e.g. decision of the Austrian Supreme Court of 23/02/1998, 3Ob115/95; for further examples *see* Gordon Blanke, *Chapter I: The Arbitration Agreement and Arbitrability – EC Competition Law Claims in International Arbitration, in AUSTRIAN ARBITRATION YEARBOOK* 3–92 with further references (Christian Klausegger; Peter Klein et al. (eds), 2009).

[8] MICHAEL J MUSTILL; STEWART C BOYD, THE LAW AND PRACTICE OF COMMERCIAL ARBITRATION IN ENGLAND 117 (1989).

9.10. In this context, the provisions laid down in Art101 and 102 TFEU, which, in brief, prohibit anti-competitive agreements and the abuse of a dominant market position, are especially relevant.[9] Competition law issues will mostly arise from an *'ordinary contractual dispute submitted to arbitration,'*[10] whereas most of the time competition law issues are not presented as principal claims but raised as a defence by opposing parties.[11] Less often, but not unheard of, are claimants submitting an action for abuse of a dominant position.[12]

III.2 An Infringement of EU Competition Law Is a Ground to Set Aside an Arbitral Award

9.11. In general, there is no possibility of appeal against a decision of an arbitral tribunal. However, it is possible to refer to a state court to seek the annulment of such an award. Such annulment is generally limited to very specific and narrow grounds for setting aside, meaning some egregious errors must have occurred during the arbitral proceedings or in the arbitral award itself that must be corrected.

9.12. A ground to set aside an arbitral award that can be found in most jurisdictions is the protection of the national *ordre public* (or public policy). Arbitral awards may thus be annulled by the state court in case they violate public policy. The CJEU as well as a significant number of national courts in EU Member States[13] have recognised that EU competition law is part of each Member State's *ordre public*. The CJEU clearly stated that: *'where its domestic rules of procedure require a national court to grant an application for annulment of an arbitration award where such an application is founded on failure to observe national rules of public policy, it must also grant such an application where it is founded on failure to comply with the prohibition laid down in Article 85(1) of the Treaty* [now Art 101 TFEU].*'*[14] Consequently, an award rendered in any EU Member State that is in contradiction with EU competition law or that failed to adequately consider EU competition law is at risk of being annulled by the relevant Member State's national courts.

---

[9] This article will not go into more details with regards to the specific EU competition law rules and does not claim to provide a complete list.

[10] Gordon Blanke, *supra* note 7, at 3–92.

[11] Ibid, at 3–92.

[12] Ibid.

[13] For Austria *see* e.g. decision of the Austrian Supreme Court of 23/02/1998, 3Ob115/95.

[14] C-126/97, *Eco Swiss*, [1999] ECR 3055, para. 37.

III.3. Necessity of Uniform Application of EU Competition Law

9.13. There are several rules on special cooperation between national and EU institutions regarding the application of EU competition law in order to ensure a uniform application of EU law in general and EU competition law in particular.[15] The CJEU states that '[c]*onsistency in the application of the competition rules also requires that arrangements be established for cooperation between the courts of the Member States and the Commission.*'[16] In this sense, Art 15(2) of Regulation 1/2003[17] requires all Member States to forward to the European Commission a copy of any written judgment by a national court deciding on the application of Art 101 or Art 102 TFEU. This measure is intended to guarantee the uniform application of EU competition law within the EU Member States. Already this unique duty imposed on the EU Member States can leave no doubt on the special role EU competition law plays within the body of EU law.

9.14. Moreover, the Member States' courts may not take decisions running counter to the decisions adopted by the European Commission;[18] they may request the European Commission to transmit to them information or its opinion on questions concerning the application of EU competition rules.[19] Even more, the European Commission itself may – acting on its own initiative – submit written observations to courts of Member States where the coherent application of EU competition law rules so requires.[20] These provisions show clearly that EU competition law and, above all, its uniform application plays a central role.

9.15. Pursuant to Art 3(g) of the EC Treaty, EU competition law constitutes a 'fundamental provision which is essential for the accomplishment of the tasks entrusted to the Community and, in particular, for the functioning of the internal market.'[21] This fundamental statement, as well as the fact that any agreement infringing EU competition law is automatically null and void, can leave no doubt on the particularly important position EU competition law has within the system of EU

---

[15] Council Regulation (EC) No 1/2003 of 16 December 2002 on the implementation of the rules on competition laid down in Articles 81 and 82 of the Treaty, recital 22.

[16] Ibid, recital 21.

[17] Ibid.

[18] Ibid, Article 16.

[19] Ibid, Article 15 (1).

[20] Ibid, Article 15 (3).

[21] C-126/97, *Eco Swiss*, [1999] ECR 3055.

law. Moreover, the CJEU has expressly held that EU competition law must be 'automatically applied by national courts.'[22]

9.16. These provisions are completed by Art 267 EC Treaty stating that it '*is essential for the preservation of the Community character of the law established by the Treaty and has the object of ensuring that in all circumstances this law is the same in all States of the Community.*'

9.17. The above referred examples can leave no doubt on the special role EU competition law has within the Community and how strict the CJEU as well as the European Commission are regarding the uniform application of EU competition law.

9.18. As a summary and first conclusion of the above, it is fair to say that EU competition law rules play a central role for the functioning of the internal market and that the CJEU as well as the European Commission have set up several mechanisms to ensure uniform application of EU competition law among the EU Member States.

9.19. The obligation to uniformly apply EU competition law also applies to arbitral tribunals, who risk their award being set aside in case they do not (correctly) apply EU competition law. Above all, while 'courts and tribunals of Member States' (within the meaning of TFEU Art 267) may refer to the CJEU for a preliminary ruling and thus interpretation of EU competition law rules, arbitral tribunals, on whom the obligation to uniformly apply EU competition law also applies and who risk their award being set aside in case they do not (correctly) apply EU competition law, are not allowed to refer to the CJEU for a preliminary ruling.

9.20. Taking into consideration that the CJEU has not yet reconsidered its 32-year old *Nordsee* decision,[23] it seems obvious that it should be very easy for arbitral tribunals with the seat of arbitration in one of the 28 EU Member States to seek the support of national courts to obtain a preliminary ruling by the CJEU. Or... is it?

IV. The Support Arbitral Tribunals Can Seek of National Courts in Obtaining a Preliminary Ruling by the CJEU in Matters Involving EU Competition Law

9.21. The question of whether or not and if so, to what extent, an arbitral tribunal may seek support of national courts in obtaining a preliminary ruling by the CJEU in matters involving competition law – or, for the

---

[22] C- 295/04, *Manfredi* [2006] ECR 6619, para. 31.

[23] *Supra*, Section I.

sake of argument, in any matter involving EU law insofar as a preliminary ruling by the CJEU would be permissible[24] – depends on what *lex arbitri* is applicable to the arbitration.[25]

9.22. Depending on the *lex arbitri*, it is possible to identify four different approaches taken by the Member States, namely

   (i)   Member States that, in their arbitration acts,[26] do not provide for general court assistance[27] to arbitral tribunals;

   (ii) Member States that, in their arbitration acts, provide for an arbitral tribunal's possibility to seek enforcement of interim or provisional measures from state courts;

   (iii) Member States that have introduced, in their arbitration acts, the possibility for arbitral tribunals to seek assistance from national courts in those instances the arbitral tribunal itself does not have the competence to conduct the judicial act it wishes to conduct; and

   (iv) Member States that, in their arbitration acts, explicitly provide for an arbitral tribunal's possibility to request the competent state court to request the CJEU to give a preliminary ruling according to Art 267 TFEU.

IV.1 Member States that, in Their Arbitration Acts, Do Not Provide for General Court Assistance to Arbitral Tribunals

9.23. The term 'general court assistance' begs further clarification. What the authors intend to express with the term is explained easily be way of example. The Austrian Arbitration Act provides, in sec. 602 entitled 'Judicial Assistance', the following:

9.24. *'The arbitral tribunal, arbitrators who have been authorised accordingly by the arbitral tribunal, or a party with the approval of the arbitral*

---

[24] *Supra*, Section II.

[25] It is widely understood that this is the law of the place of arbitration. However, simply accepting this as a fact would be imprudent – *see*, for instance *Dharmananda*, The Unconscious Choice - Reflections on Determining the Lex Arbitri, Journal of International Arbitration, Volume 19 Issue 2 (2002).

[26] The term 'arbitration act', as used hereunder, is to be understood as the statutory rules of civil procedure governing the arbitration at the place of arbitration, regardless of whether such rules are contained in a distinct bill or contained as distinct section within the general rules of civil procedure (as would, to name but a few, be the case in Austria, France and Germany).

[27] The term general court assistance will be explained below, see Section IV.1.

> *tribunal, may request from the court to conduct judicial acts for which the arbitral tribunal has no authority.'*[28] (emphasis added)

9.25. 'General court assistance' as used in this paper thus refers to judicial acts over which the arbitral tribunal has no authority. It is through this type of act that an arbitral tribunal, as will be explained below,[29] may generally request assistance from the court (and, as such, may seek the support of a national court in obtaining a preliminary ruling).

9.26. EU Member States not offering the possibility of 'general court assistance' include the following countries: Belgium, Bulgaria, Croatia, Cyprus, Finland, Greece, Hungary, Ireland, Italy, Latvia, Lithuania, Luxembourg, Malta, the Netherlands, Portugal, Spain and Sweden.[30]

IV.2 Member States that, in Their Arbitration Acts, Provide for an Arbitral Tribunal's Possibility to Seek Enforcement of Interim or Provisional Measures from State Courts

9.27. At first sight, it may surprise what role interim measures in can play in obtaining a preliminary ruling from the CJEU under Art 267 TFEU. Some scholars, most notably *Assimakis Komninos*, who is among the most highly regarded scholars on this topic, is of the opinion that it is possible to – indirectly – obtain a preliminary ruling from the CJEU as per Art 267 by means of provisional measures:

> Recourse to state courts of the seat of arbitration might also be call for in obtaining provisional and conservatory measures. Although the modern trend is that arbitral tribunals can grant provisional measures themselves, there are still jurisdictions where this is not possible. Then there are those measures which are inherently connected with the state power of coercion, such as attachment, that again may have to be granted by state courts only.
> Provisional measures might be necessary to be taken in a foreign jurisdiction, different from the one of the seat of

---

[28] For an English version of the Austrian Arbitration Act, see AUSTRIAN ARBITRATION ACT SEC 577-618 Austrian Code of Civil Procedure, available at: http://www.viac.eu/en/materials/83-recht/gesetze/200-zpo-as-amended-2013 (accessed on 7 November 2014).

[29] *Infra*, Section IV.3.

[30] For better readability, the authors decided not to provide links to every single Arbitration Act relevant within the EU. As a general rule, insofar as the language reader has the required language skills, all arbitration acts of the 28 EU Member States can be found online.

arbitration. This transnational element is very likely to exist in a dispute involving EC antitrust issues. Such measures can only be ordered by the state courts of that jurisdiction, on the condition that they are allowed by their procedural law to offer such assistance. Such an exceptional possibility exists under the 1968 Brussels Convention on the Recognition and Enforcement of Judgments, which applies also to provisional and protective measures, even in case of arbitral proceedings that have been or may be commenced in another signatory country.[31]

9.28. If case one ascribes to *Komninos'* view, arbitral tribunals could thus seek assistance from state courts in obtaining a preliminary ruling from the CJEU as per Art 267 also by means of provisional measures. The EU Member States which, according to their relevant Arbitration Acts, provide for the possibility of seeking interim measures are France, Romania, Slovakia and the United Kingdom.[32]

IV.3 Member States that Have Introduced, in Their Arbitration Acts, the Possibility for Arbitral Tribunals to Seek Assistance from National Courts in Those Instances the Arbitral Tribunal Itself Does Not Have the Competence to Conduct the Judicial Act It Wishes to Conduct

9.29. Contra to those states which do not provide for the possibility of seeking court assistance for judicial acts over which the arbitral tribunal has no authority,[33] there are several EU Member States which expressly allow arbitral tribunals bound by the Arbitration Act of that country as *lex arbitri* to seek the assistance of the state's courts. The Austrian example has already been highlighted above.

9.30. Another EU Member State offering arbitral tribunals the possibility of seeking assistance from national courts when it does not have the competence to conduct the judicial act it wishes to conduct itself is Germany. As such, sec. 1050 of the German Arbitration Act reads as follows:

---

[31] Assimakis P. Komninos, *Assistance to Arbitral Tribunals in the Application of EC Competition Law, in* EUROPEAN COMPETITION LAW ANNUAL 2001: EFFECTIVE PRIVATE ENFORCEMENT OF EC COMPETITION LAW 365 (Claus-Dieter Ehlermann, Isabela Atanasiu (eds), 2003).

[32] Those jurisdictions which were listed in Sections IV.3 and IV.4 were left out in this enumeration.

[33] *Supra*, Section IV.I.

> The arbitral tribunal or, with the consent of the arbitral tribunal, a party may file a petition that the court provide support by taking evidence or **by taking any other actions reserved for judges that the arbitral tribunal is not authorised to take**. The court shall deal with the petition, unless it deems it to be inadmissible, in accordance with its procedural rules as applying to the taking of evidence or any other actions reserved for judges. The arbitral judges are entitled to attend the court hearing at which evidence is taken and to ask questions. (emphasis added)

9.31.   Besides Austria and Germany, among the EU Member States also the Czech Republic, Estonia, Poland and Slovenia enable arbitral tribunals to seek assistance from national courts in those instances the arbitral tribunal itself does not have the competence to conduct the judicial act it wishes to conduct.

9.32.   It is, therefore, accepted that when a question pertaining to the interpretation of EU competition law arises, an arbitral tribunal with its seat of arbitration in one of these countries would generally have the possibility of requesting a state court to refer this question to the CJEU.[34]

IV.4   Member States that, in Their Arbitration Acts, Explicitly Provide for an Arbitral Tribunal's Possibility to Request the Competent State Court to Request the CJEU to Give a Preliminary Ruling According to Art 267 TFEU

9.33.   So far, 27 jurisdictions have been 'covered', with only one outstanding: Denmark. Denmark stands out as the sole example where it is possible for arbitral tribunals to request the national courts to request a preliminary ruling from the CJEU in accordance with Art 267 TFEU.

9.34.   This is provided for in sec. 27(2) of the Danish Arbitration Act, which reads as follows:

> If the arbitral tribunal considers that a decision on a question of European Union law is necessary to enable it to make an award, the arbitral tribunal **may request the courts to request the Court of Justice of the European Communities to give a ruling thereon**. (emphasis added)

9.35.   As such – and thereby accounting for the fact that arbitral tribunals may not refer a question of EU (competition) law to the CJEU directly – the Danish Arbitration Act expressly grants arbitral tribunals with

---

[34]   For Austria and Germany, see Assimakis P. Komninos, *supra* note 31, at 374 *et seq.*

the place of arbitration in Denmark the possibility of seeking the national courts' assistance.

V. Conclusion

9.36.   The famous quote from *Hamlet*, '*Something is rotten in the state of Denmark*', insofar as regards an arbitral tribunal's possibility to seek assistance of national courts in obtaining a preliminary ruling from the CJEU according to Art 267 TFEU, could well be changed to '*Something is rotten in all EU Member States except for Denmark.*'

9.37.   The necessity of the uniform interpretation and application of EU (competition) law could not be stressed more; in fact, it is one of the key elements of EU law and indispensable for the functioning of the internal market! Therefore, when considering that arbitration is, internationally, the most important means of resolving disputes[35] and that arbitral awards, by means of the New York Conventional on the Recognition and Enforcement of Foreign Arbitral Awards (and, in Europe, in particular, the European Convention of 1961), are enforceable, it is simply unacceptable that a full 17 countries do not provide for any possibility at all for arbitral tribunals to refer a question of EU (competition) law to the CJEU, not even by relying on a state court's assistance.

9.38.   The authors of this paper highly doubt the possibility of obtaining a preliminary ruling by the CJEU by means of interim measures, as suggested by *Komninos*: firstly, such request by a state court would run counter to the very means of an interim measure, which is generally understood to be an order issued to preserve evidence or to protect assets **in case of urgency**.[36] (emphasis added) Taking into consideration that the *Cour d'Appel de Paris* expects that a decision by the CJEU is not to be rendered within the two next years,[37] such interim measure would probably set the world record for the time elapsed between the application for an interim measure and the decision thereon. The authors, therefore, take the view that such option is of a rather theoretical nature only.

---

[35]   GARY B. BORN, INTERNATIONAL COMMERCIAL ARBITRATION, Alphen aan den Rijn: Wolters Kluwer law & business 93 (2nd ed., 2014).

[36]   The definition of interim measures differs widely even among the 28 EU Member States. For a general description of interim measures, see European Judicial Network, Interim and precautionary measures – General Information, available at: http://ec.europa. eu/civiljustice/interim_measures/interim_measures_gen_en.htm (accessed on 26 October 2014).

[37]   Global Arbitration Review, *Yong*, Paris court turns to CJEU in set-aside case.

9.39. Besides that, this paper explicitly deals with the possibility of seeking assistance by an arbitral tribunal. Therefore, *Komninos'* suggested – theoretical – option would have to be further limited to only those instances where an arbitral tribunal seeks the court's assistance in enforcing interim measures (as can only one of the parties can request interim measures be ordered directly by state courts, thus only leaving the requests of enforcement to state courts).

9.40. In summary, the authors do not think that interim measures are a viable option for an arbitral tribunal seeking state court assistance in obtaining a preliminary ruling by the CJEU as per Art 267 TFEU.

9.41. Thus, only six countries provide the implicit possibility of requesting state court assistance in order to be able to refer a case to the CJEU, while only Denmark expressly provides for such possibility.

9.42. In light of the fact that arbitration has become an important means of dispute resolution, it must be doubted whether the CJEU's reluctance to allow arbitral tribunals to refer to the CJEU for preliminary ruling as well as the limited possibilities within the EU Member States to ask for the state court's assistance in referring to the CJEU should not be subject to revision. In particular, as the CJEU and the EU Commission promote the importance of a uniform application of EU law, it cannot be accepted that arbitral tribunals may not easily refer to the CJEU.

9.43. Member States that do not provide a possibility for arbitral tribunals to request state courts to refer their case to the CJEU for a preliminary ruling, thus mutually accept that an arbitral award which is not compliant with EU competition law can only be corrected in setting aside proceedings before a state court. This implies that any party seeking annulment of an arbitral award due to the fact that the arbitrators did not (correctly) apply EU competition law will have to initiate setting aside proceedings before a national court. If the national court – with or without seeking a preliminary ruling – decides to annul the award, the parties will face the situation where they will have to initiate new arbitration proceedings in order to finally resolve their dispute. The possibility of seeking a preliminary ruling by the CJEU during arbitral proceedings via state courts can thus save the parties a lot of time and money.

| | |

Summaries

DEU [*Können Schiedsgerichte die Hilfe staatlicher Gerichte in Anspruch nehmen, um eine Vorabentscheidung des EuGH in Fällen, die EU Kartellrecht betreffen, zu erhalten?*]

Schiedsgerichten ist es nach wie vor nicht erlaubt, sich direkt an den EuGH im Zuge eines Vorabentscheidungsverfahrens zu wenden. Vielmehr benötigen sie dazu die Unterstützung staatlicher Gerichte, die in den einzelnen Mitgliedstaaten der EU jedoch sehr limitiert ist. Dies ist insbesondere deshalb problematisch, weil Schiedsgerichte nichts desto trotz verpflichtet sind, EU Kartellrecht (korrekt) anzuwenden, sich aber nicht selbst an den EuGH zur Interpretation von EU Recht wenden können. Im Zusammenhang mit EU Kartellrecht gibt es darüber hinaus strenge Vorgaben für eine enge Zusammenarbeit der EU Kommission und der Gerichte, um die einheitliche Anwendung von EU Kartellrecht zu gewährleisten, was als unabdingbar für das Funktionieren des Binnenmarktes angesehen wird. Innerhalb der EU gibt es dennoch nur sechs Mitgliedstaaten, die eine indirekte Möglichkeit für Schiedsgerichte vorsehen, staatliche Gerichte um Unterstützung zur Einleitung eines Vorabentscheidungsverfahrens vor dem EuGH einzuleiten. Alle anderen Mitgliedstaaten sehen keine generelle Möglichkeit für Schiedsgerichte vor, staatliche Gerichte um Unterstützung zu ersuchen. Die einzige positive Ausnahme in diesem Zusammenhang ist Dänemark, wo Schiedsgerichte die zuständigen staatlichen Gerichte explizit um die Einleitung eines Vorabentscheidungsverfahrens anrufen können. Vor dem Hintergrund der wachsenden Wichtigkeit von Schiedsverfahren als Streitbeilegungsmechanismus bleibt es zu wünschen, dass in Zukunft noch mehrere Mitgliedstaaten dem positiven Beispiel Dänemarks folgen werden.

CZE [*Může rozhodčí soud žádat o podporu národní soudy za účelem získání vyjádření SD EU k předběžné otázce ve věcech soutěžního práva EU?*]

Rozhodčí senáty se nemohou obracet na SD EU s předběžnou otázkou, nýbrž potřebují v takovém případě podporu státních soudů. Ve většině právních řádů členských států EU jsou však rozhodčí soudy omezeny v souvislosti s takovými žádostmi. To může představovat komplikace obzvláště proto, že rozhodčí soudy jsou povinny (správně) aplikovat právo EU a zejména soutěžní právo EU, tedy oblast práva, kterého se často dotýkají spory projednávané v mezinárodním rozhodčím řízení. To přirozeně představuje problém, neboť soutěžní právo EU, které je esenciálním nástrojem vnitřního trhu, vyžaduje, aby Komise EU a státní soudy spolupracovaly a zajistily tak jednotnou aplikaci soutěžního práva EU. Pouze šest členských států EU však implicitně poskytuje možnost požádat státní soudy o pomoc při předávání žádostí SD EU; jediné Dánsko výslovně umožňuje rozhodčím soudům obracet se na příslušné státní soudy se žádostí o předání žádosti o vyjádření k předběžné otázce SD EU. Ve světle stále rostoucí důležitosti rozhodčího řízení jako prostředku pro rozhodování sporů je nutno položit si otázku, proč pouze jediný členský stát EU garantuje jednotnou aplikaci soutěžního práva EU v rozhodčím řízení.

| | |

POL [*Czy sąd arbitrażowy może wystąpić o pomoc do sądów krajowych w celu uzyskania opinii ETS UE odnośnie pytania prejudycjalnego w sprawach dotyczących prawa konkurencji UE?*]

Zdaniem ETS UE sądy arbitrażowe mają obowiązek (słuszny) stosowania prawa konkurencji UE, jednak nadal nie mogą zwracać się do ETS UE z zapytaniem prejudycjalnym. Żadne z państw członkowskich UE nie umożliwia sądom powszechnym wspierania sądów arbitrażowych w tym zakresie. Jedynie w Danii jednoznacznie umożliwiono sądom arbitrażowym zwracanie się do właściwych sądów krajowych celem przekazania do ETS UE wniosku o opinię na temat zapytania prejudycjalnego.

FRA [*Les Tribunaux d'Arbitrage ont-ils recours à une assistance des tribunaux étatiques pour lancer une procédure préjudicielle devant la CJUE concernant le droit européen de concurrence?*]

Malgré leur responsabilité d'appliquer le droit européen de concurrence correctement, les tribunaux d'arbitrage n'ont pas le droit de lancer une procédure préjudicielle devant la CJUE, mais ont besoin des tribunaux étatiques pour recevoir une interprétation de la part de la CJUE. Parmi les états membres de l'UE, uniquement le Danemark connaît une règle générale selon laquelle, les tribunaux d'arbitrage peuvent explicitement demander aux tribunaux étatiques de lancer une procédure préjudicielle devant la CJUE.

RUS [*Может ли арбитражный суд обратиться за поддержкой в национальные суды в целях получения мнения Суда Европейского Союза по предварительному вопросу из области конкурентного права ЕС?*]

По мнению Суда Европейского Союза, арбитражные суды обязаны (правильно) применять закон ЕС о конкуренции, но все еще не могут обращаться в Суд Европейского Союза с предварительным вопросом. Ни одно из государств-членов Европейского Союза не позволяет судам общей юрисдикции оказывать поддержку арбитражным судам в этом отношении. Только Дания явно позволяет арбитражным судам обращаться в соответствующие государственные суды в связи с направлением запроса в Суд Европейского Союза для получения мнения последнего по предварительному вопросу.

ESP   [*¿Podrá un tribunal arbitral solicitar apoyo a los tribunales nacionales con el fin de obtener una opinión del Tribunal de Justicia de la UE sobre la cuestión de previo pronunciamiento en materia de legislación de competencia comunitaria?*]
Según el Tribunal de Justicia de la UE, los tribunales de arbitraje deben aplicar (correctamente) la legislación de competencia comunitaria, sin bien aún no pueden dirigirse al Tribunal de Justicia de la UE con una cuestión de previo pronunciamiento. Ninguno de los Estados miembros de la UE permite a los tribunales generales apoyar a los tribunales de arbitraje en este sentido. Solamente Dinamarca permite explícitamente a los tribunales de arbitraje dirigirse a los tribunales nacionales competentes con la solicitud de pronunciación sobre una cuestión de previo pronunciamiento del Tribunal de Justicia de la UE.

| | |

Czech (& Central European) Yearbook of Arbitration

Alexander Sergeev |

Tatiana Tereshchenko

The Interaction of Arbitration and State Courts: A Growing Confrontation or a Peaceful Coexistence?

Key words:
Jurisdiction | autonomy |
state courts | arbitration |
court interaction |
UNCITRAL Model Law

Abstract | *In this article the question of the interaction between arbitration and state courts is considered in a bilateral aspect. We consider whether the state recognizes the jurisdictional nature of arbitration, on the one hand, and whether the forms of interaction between arbitration and state courts do correspond to the essence of arbitration, on the other hand. During the analysis the conclusion is demonstrated that the contract or non-jurisdictional theory of the legal nature of arbitration as simply a pre-trial settlement instrument should be left in the past. Arbitration proceedings are accepted worldwide as an alternative form of dispute resolution. In this regard such a common concept that 'justice is carried out only by the court' does not itself deny the jurisdiction of the arbitral tribunals. It is necessary to clearly distinguish such concepts as the state protection of rights and judicial protection, with the latter as a subspecies of the former. To give justice the sense that it forms a departure or the function of the state government only is not entirely consistent with the constitutional principle of the rule of law. Among the generally accepted legal ways of resolving civil disputes in modern society, arbitration means the existence of a dispositive or discretionary basis for civil substantial and procedural relations, arising from the contractual freedom along with the autonomy of the will of the participants in commercial and other economic*

Alexander P. Sergeev,
Doctor of Law,
professor of the Civil
Law Department at the
Law Faculty of St.
Petersburg State
Economical University,
counsel with DLA
Piper, Russian
Government Prize
laureate, President of
Arbitration Court
'IUS', arbitrator of
Arbitration Court of St.
Petersburg CIC, expert
in international
disputes on Corporate,
Contract, Intellectual
Property Law, author
and co-editor of more
than 100 articles, works
in Russian /English.
e-mail:
apsergeev2004@mail.ru.

**Tatiana A.
Tereshchenko,** Ph.D.
in Law, associate
professor of the Civil
Law Department at the
Law Faculty of St.
Petersburg State
Economical University,

activities. Because of this the character of interaction with the state courts is the result of a consensus, in which the state court provides the necessary support which ensures the enforceability of arbitral awards, and its controlling capabilities over arbitration proceedings are severely restricted by law. Such a general approach is confirmed through an examination of various issues related to the organization and conduct of arbitration (in particular, appointment, challenge and termination of the mandate of an arbitrator, the jurisdiction of the arbitral tribunal and the setting aside of the arbitral award), as well as through an examination of issues related to ensuring effective implementation of disputable interests of the parties. In particular, court assistance in taking evidence, the compatibility of court-ordered interim measures with the arbitration agreement, the recognition and enforcement of interim measures, and the recognition and enforcement of arbitral awards are all significant issues.

advocate of Law Firm 'Prime Advice Saint-Petersburg', FCIArb, arbitrator of Arbitration Court 'IUS', expert in international disputes on Corporate, Contract, Intellectual Property Law, author of more than 35 articles, works in Russian/English.
e-mail:
t.tereshchenko@ hlbprime.com, t_t.06@mail.ru.

| | |

I. Introduction

10.01. The interaction of arbitration[1] and state courts is a controversial and multidimensional issue. We do not attempt to consider all possible nuances of such an interaction in the present article. But it is possible to gain a more meaningful understanding of the issue from the point of such a general assumption so that one can say the nature of the interaction between arbitration and state courts and the assessment of its adequacy and sufficiency depends from the position arbitration takes in the justice system.

10.02. To make up position for this point, should we consider the interaction of arbitration and state courts to be a growing confrontation or peaceful

---

[1] In Russia the term 'arbitral tribunal' refers to commercial state courts, though in other countries and in international practice it is equivalent to the term 'arbitration'. Taking into account such different terminology traditions and trying to avoid any confusion, the terms 'arbitration', 'arbitration courts', 'arbitral tribunals' and their derivatives are used as synonyms in the present article. This does not differentiate between international and intra-national, institutional and ad hoc institutions (if not said otherwise), but simply stands opposed in meaning to the classical 'state courts '. Additionally, the term 'court' is used when speaking about different types of jurisdiction in a more general sense.

coexistence? More generally, does the international community of states recognize the autonomous jurisdictional nature of arbitration proceedings? The answer to these questions implies a set of circumstances which have to be taken into account. In particular, if the international community does recognize arbitration, does it trust it and to which extent? If it does trust it, should any support and supervision by the judicial authorities on behalf of the state be excluded? If support and supervision are needed, what are the boundaries? Finally, do different fields of interaction between arbitration and state courts exist now, and do they correspond to the nature of the arbitration?

II. Arbitration as an Alternative Form of Jurisdictional Dispute Resolution

10.03. The development of legal regulation, intra-national and international law enforcement practice in the 20th century led to the final discussion about grounds for existence of justice, based on the law itself, along with the state monopoly for judicial power execution, and its separation from each other. Though the history of arbitration and relevant legislation is outside the scope of this article,[2] analysis of it allows us to formulate the following conceptual points about the place of arbitration in the justice administration system.

10.04. The effective recognition and realization of rights proclaimed by the Universal Declaration of Human Rights[3] are impossible without the guarantee of the right to a fair trial. Free access to justice is recognized by the international community as a fundamental principle. In the case of disputes regarding civil rights and obligations, all people are entitled to a fair and public hearing within a reasonable time by an independent and impartial court, established by law, provided that all are equal before the court. These principles are enshrined in Article 6 (1) of the Convention for the Protection of Human Rights and Fundamental Freedoms[4] (the Convention on Human Rights), and in Article 14 (1) of the International Covenant on Civil and Political Rights.[5]

10.05. The European Court of Human Rights (ECHR) has acknowledged that the term 'court' in Article 6 (1) of the Convention on Human Rights should not to be understood as the jurisdiction of the classical type

---

[2] For the history of arbitration information see: Derek Roebuck, *Sources for the History of Arbitration*, 14 Arbitration International 237-343 (no. 3, 1998). JX1.A73.

[3] Adopted 10 December 1948 UNGA Res 217 A (III).

[4] Adopted 4 November 1950, entered into force 3 September 1953, CETS No.: 005.

[5] Adopted 16 December 1966, entered into force 23 March 1976, 999 UNITS 171.

only, integrated into the overall judicial system of the certain state. Because of this, Article 6 (1) of the Convention on Human Rights does not preclude the establishment of arbitration to resolve certain disputes, provided that they comply with the necessary guarantees[6].

10.06. This conclusion, made by the ECHR, is absolutely fair. No state holds a kind of exclusive privilege to exercise justice. The latter power has its basis not with the sovereignty of the state and its public source, but rather emanates from the law itself. Therefore, justice can be carried out not only through the institutions of statehood, but also apart from them.

10.07. Accordingly, jurisdiction[7] as a set of the statutory powers based on law is much wider in its content. It has a public nature in the state judicial system as well as non-state character in social institutions like arbitration. Participants of a civil relationship may take part in the administration of justice in the most general meaning of the term. This is not similar to the state judiciary branch. By virtue of the 'separation of powers' principle only legislative and executive authorities are prohibited from executing justice.

10.08. In this sense, such a common regulation as justice is carried out only by the court (i.e. with a narrow usage of term 'court') does not deny the jurisdiction of arbitral tribunals in particular and of the non-governmental institutions in general. It is necessary to clearly distinguish such concepts as the state protection of rights, on one hand, and judicial protection as its subspecies, on the other hand. If this was not true, one would assume that a state totally absorbs justice. However, such an assumption would lead to the conclusion that allocation of judicial protection in the rights protection mechanism (including legislation) would violate the principle of legal economy because of its redundancy. To give justice the sense that it forms a departure or the exclusive function of the state government only, is not entirely consistent with the constitutional principle of the rule of law.

10.09. In addition, everyone has the right to apply to international bodies for the protection of human rights and freedoms, including supranational

---

[6] For more details see: *Campbell & Fell* v *United Kingdom*, No. 7819/77, 7878/77, 28 June 1984; *Lithgov et al.* v *United Kingdom*, No. 9006/80, 9262/81, 9263/81, 9265/81, 9266/81, 9313/81, 9405/81, 8 June 1986; *Transado-Transportes Fluviais Do Sado, S.A.* v *Portugal*, No. 35943/02, 16 December 2003; *Regent Company* v *Ukraine*, No. 773/03, 3 April 2008; available at: http://www.echr.coe.int/Pages/home.aspx?p=caselaw&c= (accessed on 24 October 2014).

[7] From the Latin term 'jurisdictio' meaning proceedings. It is formed from word 'jus' - the right and 'dico' - to speak.

courts, which are not in the judicial system of a particular state (the ECHR for example[8]). This further indicates the absence of an indissoluble link between the national state and justice. Everyone is given the guarantee of the judiciary for the protection of rights and freedoms and the opportunity to defend those rights and freedoms by any means not prohibited by law.

10.10. Besides, the very fact of the creation of the arbitration institutions can be considered a kind of reflection of the independent jurisdictional nature of arbitration. In particular, currently permanent arbitration institutions can be established by any legal entity, especially by different chambers of commerce, stock exchanges and public commercial associations, except for public authorities and local governments. Examples include the ICC International Court of Arbitration,[9] the LCIA,[10] the Arbitration Court of Russian Arbitration Association,[11] the Arbitration Court of OSJC Gazprom,[12] etc.

10.11. Usually state courts have no role in the creation of arbitration institutions. At best, they can be notified about the formation of permanent arbitration courts. When this occurs, hard copies of documents, proving the formation of the arbitral tribunal, are sent to the competent state court. Such documents will generally include information about the decision to create the arbitration institution, its rules and charter, and the list of arbitrators. State courts are not generally informed about the creation of ad hoc arbitration courts. However, after the close of certain ad hoc arbitral proceedings, case materials together with the decision of the arbitral tribunal may be sent for archiving with the competent state court in compliance with the rules of substantive and territorial jurisdiction.

10.12. Thus, the current procedure for the creation of arbitration institutions is extremely simplified and uncontrolled by state courts or any public authorities. Arbitration courts appear without any kind of permission from a third party, statutes/rules of arbitration courts are not subject to state registration and arbitrators are not subject to any qualification requirements in a formal sense.[13]

---

[8]   For more details see: http://www.echr.coe.int/Documents/Court_in_brief_ENG.pdf (accessed on 24 October 2014).

[9]   See: http://www.iccwbo.org/about-icc/organization/dispute-resolution-services/icc-international-court-of-arbitration/ (accessed on 24 October 2014).

[10]   See: http://www.lcia.org/ (accessed on 24 October 2014).

[11]   See: http://www.arbitrations.ru/ (accessed on 24 October 2014).

[12]   See: http://www.gazprom.ru/about/arbitral/ (accessed on 24 October 2014).

[13]   For examples of such criticism, see the comments on the Russian Draft Law On Arbitration Courts (Arbitration Draft Law), available at: http://www.arbitrations.ru/press-

10.13. However, to show that any aspect of the issue still could be disputable and subject to revision, its worth to pay attention to contemporary legal reforms. For example, among different suggestions about legislative changes in Russia to the arbitration sphere, there is one based on idea that permanent arbitral institutions should be created only through the registration or licensing system. There are plans for the Ministry of Justice to authorize a permit for the creation of arbitration courts, based on a special decision issued by the so- called Interdepartmental Expert Council. This council consists of representatives from the federal authorities, the Chamber of Commerce, the Federal Chamber of Lawyers of the Russian Federation and the Supreme Court, and the legal representatives of the business community. Proponents of this hypothetical change argue that the current uncontrolled creation of arbitration courts creates conditions for numerous abuses in this sphere. One particular practice is the creation of so-called 'pocket' arbitrations or situations, when with the help of solutions of unknown arbitration courts a semblance of legality is given to illegal actions. However, the proposed legislative solution was severely criticized by the arbitration community, as it was perceived as a return to the command system and emerging from a desire to put the arbitration courts under the control of the state bureaucracy. In our view, such a negative reaction is reasonable, especially when the reasons for registration system are taken into account. It is obvious that abuses in a limited sphere should not be enough to create a distrust of arbitration as a jurisdictional social institute with public functions. However, some control by the state over the establishment of arbitration is needed, if only to take into account the public consequences of arbitration dispute resolution. After all, the state should not only be interested in arbitration courts carrying out their functions at the appropriate level. It also should do everything to facilitate this. Still, any measures should be in compliance with the jurisdictional and autonomous nature of arbitration.

10.14. Furthermore, dispositive provisions define the fundamental ground for civil legal relationships, based on the equality of participants, freedom of contract, the inadmissibility of voluntary interference in private affairs, and free establishment of the rights and obligations under the contract. Such dispositive provisions are applied to procedural relationships as well.[14] In civil proceedings dispositive basis means that

---

centr/news/kommentarii-raa-po-proektu-zakonov-o-treteyskikh-sudakh/ (accessed on 24 October 2014).

[14] For more details see: Decisions of the Constitutional Court of the Russian Federation No. 4-P, 14 February 2002, No. 1-P, 23 January 2007, No. 2-P, 5 February 2007, available at: http://www.ksrf.ru/en/Info/Publications/Pages/default.aspx (accessed on 24 October 2014).

the procedural relationships arise, change and terminate mainly on the initiative of the participants in the dispute. They have the ability to dispose of the procedural rights and controversial substantive law with the help of a court. This rule is also true for procedural matters arising in connection with arbitration proceedings, because the basis of these procedural relations is an agreement, under which the parties trust the protection of their civil rights to the arbitral tribunal, chosen by them, and agree to abide by its decisions.

10.15. In other words, among the legal generally accepted ways of resolving civil disputes, there are methods determined by the dispositive (discretionary) basis of civil substantial and procedural relations, and arising from the contractual freedom along with the autonomy of the will of the participants in commercial and other economic activities. An appeal to arbitral tribunals relates to such a method.

10.16. The choice of the form of rights' protection depends on the parties' discretion. When they wish to submit the dispute to arbitration according to their voluntary agreement, its competence becomes exceptional, as compared with state justice, and can be annulled only with the termination of the arbitration clause, agreed by the parties, or by the presence of other objective reasons[15] such as non-arbitrability of the dispute, the invalidity of the arbitration agreement, etc.

10.17. The procedure for the arbitration dispute resolution arises from civil law relationships, and includes the recognition of finality of arbitration decisions by the parties. Such a procedure is not contrary to the guarantee of the right of judicial protection. The completeness, timeliness and effectiveness of such a protection are provided by the possibility of appealing to the state court as prescribed by legislation. In particular, protection can be achieved by submitting an application for annulment of the arbitral award or for recognition and enforcement by issuance of a writ of execution to enforce the arbitral award.[16]

10.18. A similar approach is fully supported by the ECHR. The application of the relevant provisions of Article 6 (1) of the Convention on Human Rights comes from the fact that the parties in civil relations may conclude an agreement, including in the form of an arbitration clause in a contract, without the consideration of the case by the state court.

---

[15] For more details see: Decision of the Constitutional Court of the Russian Federation No. 123-O, 21 June 2000; available at: http://www.ksrf.ru/en/Info/Publications/Pages/default.aspx (accessed on 24 October 2014).

[16] For more details see: Decisions of the Constitutional Court of the Russian Federation No. 377-O, 4 June 2007; No. 754-O-O, 1 June 2010, available at: http://www.ksrf.ru/en/Info/Publications/Pages/default.aspx (accessed on 24 October 2014).

They can instead resolve the dispute through arbitration. Such a waiver of hearing by the state court does not violate the Convention on Human Rights, provided that it is performed without coercion.[17]

10.19. This confirms the legitimacy of referring civil disputes to resolution by arbitration courts, acting as civil social institutions, and endowed with important public functions.[18] This is based on the principle of the autonomy of the right to contract freedom. Public interest is provided by legal regulations, establishing procedures for the arbitration proceedings. This presupposes the existence of guarantees of fairness and impartiality inherent in any litigation in conjunction with Article 6 (1) of the Convention on Human Rights. Thus, the right to arbitrate a dispute should not be exercised by any reduction of guarantees' level, already achieved. It means the impossibility to exclude existing legal regulation, created to ensure the stability and dynamism of civil turnover and the predictability in the use of procedural opportunities for its participants.

10.20. The formation and operation of the arbitration courts, general principles for determining the categories of disputes that may be considered by the arbitral tribunals, provided by the parties to the dispute, a form of state control over the arbitration proceedings and the rights of the parties and other interested persons to challenge the results of the proceedings conducted by the arbitral tribunal, are established by law.[19]

10.21. Accordingly, the arbitral tribunals shall decide disputes in accordance with applicable substantive and procedural law, as well as with business

---

[17] For more details see: ECHR, Deweer v. Belgium, European Court of Human Rights, No. 6903/75, 27 February 1980, available at: http://www.echr.coe.int/Pages/home.aspx?p= caselaw&c= (accessed on 24 October 2014).

[18] For more details see: Decision of the Constitutional Court of the Russian Federation No. 10-P, 26 May 2011, available at: http://www.ksrf.ru/en/Info/Publications/Pages/ default.aspx (accessed on 24 October 2014).
This Decision is a good example of how high judicial authorities continue to dispute the discretionary power of arbitration courts. Hopefully, such attempts will be denied.

[19] It is hard to assess the impact of the Model law on International Commercial Arbitration as adopted by the United Nations Commission on International Trade Law on 21 June 1985, with amendments on 7 July 2006 (available at: http://www.uncitral.org/ uncitral/en/uncitral_texts/arbitration/1985Model_arbitration_status.html (accessed on 24 October 2014) (UNCITRAL Model law). It led to a significant impact on the development of arbitration because of its implementation in great quantity of countries. It covers all stages of the arbitral process including the arbitration agreement, the composition and jurisdiction of the arbitral tribunal and the extent of court intervention through to the recognition and enforcement of the arbitral award.

practices. Arbitration proceedings are based on the principles of legality, privacy, independence and the impartiality of arbitrators, as well as the possibility of the arbiters removal should they fall short of these principles. Likewise, the optionality, adversariality and equality of the parties are equally foundational.

10.22. Arbitral awards shall be binding and executed voluntarily as an effect of transferring the dispute to arbitration. The execution of the arbitral tribunal decision is the obligation of the parties who have signed the arbitration agreement. It shall be performed voluntarily and according to the terms set out in the decision. Thus, the voluntary execution of the arbitral award is the proper execution of the corresponding civil contract, by virtue of which the parties have recognized the competence of the arbitral tribunal chosen by them and the finality of its dispute resolution.

10.23. Moreover, arbitral awards involve a number of publicly significant effects similar to those of state courts decisions. For example, the award of the arbitral tribunal constitutes the grounds for termination of litigation proceedings between the same parties on the same subject and on the same grounds unless the arbitral award is cancelled or declared unenforceable.

10.24. In contrast with state court decisions, arbitral awards become enforceable only after passing the special procedure. Notwithstanding the autonomous judicial power of arbitration described above, that explains, why arbitral awards can be challenged by filing an application for annulment before the competent state court, as well as reviewed in a limited fashion in the case of application for the enforcement of decisions. In other words, if the decision of the arbitral tribunal has not been executed voluntarily, it is enforceable according to the rules of enforcement proceedings, applicable at the time of execution of the arbitral award on the basis of a writ of execution issued by the competent state court to enforce the arbitral award. Such procedures involve checking for the proper formation and conduct of the arbitration, based on the law requirements that apply for the purposes of enforcement.

10.25. Reasons for annulment of an arbitral award or recognition and enforcement of it are specified only by federal laws and international treaties. Usually such grounds refer to fundamental aspects of justice including the procedure of establishment of the arbitration, the possibility of considering the dispute as subject to arbitration proceedings, or the violation of public order.

10.26. Furthermore, when the arbitral tribunal has rendered its decision with respect to the rights and responsibilities of persons who did not participate in the arbitration and did not give permission for it, such persons can protect their rights. They do so using the same legal means that guaranteed protection against irregularities in litigation conducted by a state court, including the right to bring a separate action in a competent state court, as well as the right to challenge the decision of the arbitral tribunal in the dispute, going beyond legal conflict, subject to arbitration, in accordance with the proceeding, provided by the procedural legislation.

10.27. The rights of interested persons, including those not involved in the case, to appeal to the state court for protection of their rights violated by an unjust judgment, is part of the mechanism of judicial control, conducted by the state through its court system. The grounds for such control lie in the legal state obligation to create and maintain an effective system of protection of constitutional rights and freedoms through justice. This is an essential element of the normative content of the right to judicial protection, which is universally recognized. But, it is important to note that the need for such indirect control from state authorities does not exhaust the nature of arbitration. It is a social judicial institution with public features, predetermined by its value and functions.[20]

III. Key Aspects of the Interaction between Arbitration and State Courts

10.28. It is worth classifying all spheres of potential state court involvement as usually carried out in international practice, according to main needs of parties to disputes that may arise:[21]

A. Issues related to the organization and conduct of arbitration (**'procedural needs'**). These include the appointment of arbitrators, as well as the procedures for challenging and terminating their mandate, the jurisdiction of the arbitral tribunal and setting aside of the arbitral award;

B. Issues related to ensuring effective implementation of the disputable interests of the parties (**substantial needs**). These include any court assistance in taking evidence, the compatibility of court-ordered interim measures with the arbitration agreement, the recognition and enforcement of interim measures, and the recognition and enforcement of arbitral awards.

---

[20] All the features of arbitration described here are reflected in the many rules of arbitration centers known worldwide (such as the LCIA and the like).

[21] Additionally, it comes from the spirit of the UNCITRAL Model law.

10.29. Some of the key points raised by these issues[22] are analyzed in the following sections:[23]

A.1. The appointment of arbitrators, and the challenge and termination of their mandate

10.30. The will of the parties, set in the agreement to arbitrate, is given the prior role in the composition procedure. In case of absence of such provisions, rules based on the general assumption of equality of rights, should come into effect. Usually this means such formation of the arbitral body, which would balance the interests of the parties to legal conflict. In particular, the right to appoint an arbitrator is transferred to competent authority (represented by administrative body of the arbitration institution itself, state court, etc.) in case of absence the consensus between parties to dispute /arbitrators already appointed by each party in regard of the sole / third arbitrator respectively. Act of appointment in such a manner is secured by different means, from demands of

---

[22] The interaction between arbitration and state courts includes more aspects and forms than we have described here. Taking into account the objectives and scope of this article, we restrict ourselves to the general characteristics of the respective areas of interaction between arbitration and state courts. For more details about the interaction between arbitration and state courts see, for example: JULIAN D M LEW, LOUKAS A MISTELIS, STEFAN M KROLL, COMPARATIVE INTERNATIONAL COMMERCIAL ARBITRATION, Kluwer Law International 355–375 (2003); B.P. KARABELNIKOV, INTERNATIONAL COMMERCIAL ARBITRATION: TEXTBOOK.MOSCOW, Infotropic media 39–65 (2012).

[23] As far as UNCITRAL Model law was designed to assist states in reforming and modernizing their laws on arbitral procedure so as to take into account the particular features and needs of international commercial arbitration, it reflects worldwide consensus on key aspects of international arbitration practice having been accepted by states of all regions and the different legal or economic systems of the world. Legislation based on the UNCITRAL Model Law has been enacted in following countries: Australia, Austria, Azerbaijan, Armenia, Bahrain, Bangladesh, Belarus, Bermuda, Bulgaria, Brunei Darussalam, Hungary, Venezuela, Guatemala, Germany, Honduras, Georgia, Greece, Denmark, Dominican Republic, Egypt, Zambia, Zimbabwe, India, Jordan, Iran, Ireland, Cambodia, Canada, Kenya, special administrative district of Hong Kong and Macao in China, Costa Rica, Lithuania, Madagascar, Mauritius, the former Yugoslav Republic of Macedonia, Malaysia, Malta, Mexico, Nicaragua, Nigeria, new Zealand, Norway, Oman, Paraguay, Peru, Poland, Republic of Korea, Russian Federation, Rwanda, Serbia, Singapore, Slovenia; in the United States - Illinois, California, Connecticut, Louisiana, Oregon, Texas, Florida; Thailand, Tunisia, Turkey, Uganda, Ukraine, the Philippines, Croatia, Chile, Scotland, Sri Lanka, Estonia, Japan. Because of this, key aspects of interaction between arbitration and state courts are illustrated in present article, based on the provisions of the UNCITRAL Model law.

independence and impartiality of the candidates to be appointed as an arbitrator to finality of the decision subject to no appeal.[24]

10.31. Comprehensive guarantee of dispute resolution, done voluntary in impartial and independent manner, could not be complete without special declaration. By means of latter persons nominated as arbitrators are invited to make a kind of self-check by disclosing any circumstances given rise to justifiable doubts in their impartiality or independence to perform respective duties properly.[25]

10.32. Besides, there is a challenge procedure in respect of any arbitrator. Due to agreement and/or applicable rules, any party within reasonable term has the right to proceed with the statement based on the grounds that certain arbitrator is lacking that or this necessary arbitral qualifications. The only limitation. Only limitation is the absence of knowledge of that kind during the procedure of arbitrator' nomination. The issue of challenge should be decided by arbitral tribunal (unless the arbitrator withdraws voluntary) or even by competent authority if the party unsuccessful with the challenge would brought such a request. To balance possible dilatory tactics, the arbitral tribunal has the power to proceed with the case and even to make award, while the challenge is pending.[26]

10.33. Interested party can also ask the competent authority to decide on the termination of the mandate without right to appeal, in case the arbitrator de jure or de facto is not able to execute his/her mandate.[27]

10.34. Thus, the general approach on the formation of the arbitral tribunal has its basis in the freedom and dispositive autonomy of the parties, subject to the fundamental requirements of fairness and justice. Consequently, a state court may give some support to the process, but only if procedure has somehow failed, and only when it is authorized to do so.

10.35. To conclude, currently the state courts have authority in the formation of the arbitral tribunal or the challenging procedure, if otherwise not provided by law.[28] However, violation of the procedure in the formation

---

[24] Article 11 of UNCITRAL Model Law.

[25] Article 12 of UNCITRAL Model Law.

[26] Article 13 of UNCITRAL Model Law.

[27] Article 14 of UNCITRAL Model Law.

[28] For example, Russian legislation does not entitle state courts to certain powers in the formation or challenging procedure. The Draft Arbitration Law does not provide the state court with any authority at the stage of formation of the arbitration courts or nomination of the arbitrators. However, on the question of challenging the appointment procedure it proposes to give the party, the right to apply for arbitrator' disqualification before the competent state court, whose decision is not appealable. This can occur when the party is dissatisfied with the decision of the arbitral tribunal or of another competent body of the

of the arbitral tribunal or of the appointment of arbitrators may serve as the basis for refusal and the contesting of the enforcement of the arbitral award at the competent state court.

A.2. Jurisdiction of the arbitral tribunal

10.36. The arbitral tribunal is authorized to rule on its own competence (from foundation to mandate' extent), based on two general provisions. 'Kompetenz-Kompetenz' principle gives the arbitral tribunal the power to rule independently on its jurisdiction. Moreover, 'Separability' principle allows to treat arbitration clause separately from the other contract' terms.

10.37. A jurisdiction plea should be placed before the arbitral tribunal within reasonable term (for example, before the submission of the defense statement, if authority of the tribunal is disputable itself, or shortly after the justified doubt in regard of scope of arbitral powers) or even later, if the delay is grounded. The tribunal is free to decide the jurisdiction issue either as a preliminary question or in an award on the merits.

10.38. But the competence of the arbitral tribunal to rule on its own jurisdiction is subject to court control also. Court can take immediate control to avoid a waste of time and money, when the jurisdiction issue is considered like preliminary question. The risk and effect of dilatory tactics is safeguarded by the short time-period for resorting to the court (usually 30 days) and the discretion of the arbitral tribunal to continue the proceedings despite the pending plea before the state court.[29] If the arbitral tribunal decides to combine its decision on jurisdiction with an award on the merits, judicial review on the question is available during enforcement proceedings.

A.3. Setting aside of the arbitral award

10.39. As a general rule the decision of the arbitral tribunal is final and can not be appealed to the state court on the merits. However, as an exception, it may be challenged in the state court in the cases expressly provided by law, and only when the parties did not exclude such a possibility in their agreement.

10.40. This is why the setting aside procedure is usually treated as the exclusive recourse against an arbitral award, when a party may actively 'attack' the award.

---

arbitration. Given that such a right can be excluded by the party's agreement, this legislative proposal seems to be quite reasonable in facilitating conditions for a fair trial.

[29] See Article 16 of UNCITRAL Model Law.

10.41. The set aside procedure before the state court must be initiated in due time (commonly, within 3 months from the receipt of the award by the party) and place (usually where the arbitral award was rendered) An application must furnish proof of such serious grounds, like incapacity of the party; invalidity of the agreement to arbitrate, absence of proper notice within appointment procedure or other objective inability for party to present the case, any kind of matters not submitted to arbitration or going beyond the power of the arbitral tribunal, violation of the tribunal' composition procedure. Additionally, by its initiative the state court may set aside arbitral award, in case the dispute matter is not capable within the applicable law or contradicts the state public policy. The arbitral tribunal has the opportunity to resume arbitral procedure or by other means to eliminate the setting aside grounds, if the state court found such help appropriate and was requested by party to do so.[30]

10.42. Most of the grounds on which an arbitral award may be set aside are fairly specific and mostly limited to gross procedural violations committed in the course of the arbitration proceedings, except such grounds as non-arbitrability of the dispute or contradiction with fundamental principles of public policy. Since the fundamental principles of public policy are not specifically defined, this allows a considerable degree of judicial discretion. However, it is obvious that this can't be used as a tool for reconsidering the findings of the arbitral tribunal because of erroneous assessment of the parties' evidence or the erroneous application of the law.

10.43. In the case of cancellation of the arbitral award by a competent state court, any party may, in accordance with the arbitration agreement, revert to an arbitral tribunal. However, if the decision of the arbitral tribunal was cancelled in whole or in part due to the invalidity of the arbitration agreement, or because the decision was made in a dispute not contemplated by the arbitration agreement or not falling within the terms, or contains material on matters not covered by the arbitration agreement, the corresponding dispute cannot be subject to arbitration at all.

10.44. Furthermore, such a 'recourse' does not preclude a party from seeking court control by way of defence in enforcement proceedings, notwithstanding that grounds for setting aside an award generally are parallel to the grounds for refusing recognition and enforcement of the award (see below).

[30] See, Article 34 of UNCITRAL Model Law.

B.1. Assistance in taking evidence

10.45. During arbitration proceedings parties must often present evidence held by another party or a third person.

10.46. If it considers the evidence insufficient, the arbitral tribunal may invite the parties to submit additional evidence. If such evidence, available to the other party, is not provided, the arbitral tribunal, when making an award, can interpret this behaviour as unfair and consider it against the certain party. Thus, currently arbitration courts have no definite power to enforce rulings about evidence.

10.47. That explains the possibility to apply directly to the competent state court with a request for assistance in obtaining evidence (it can be done by the arbitral tribunal itself or, what is much more common, by one of the parties with the arbitral tribunal' approval). .In turn, the state court has no obligation to execute such a request within its competence and applicable rules on taking evidence, but may decide so.[31]

B.2. The compatibility of court-ordered interim measures with the arbitration agreement, and the recognition and enforcement of interim measures

10.48. Interim measures could be granted by the arbitral tribunal together with preliminary measures (to maintain status quo, to preserve assets or evidence, etc). But the arbitral tribunal has no such duty, but may do so, if it is requested at least by one of the party and not agreed otherwise. However, such ruling of the arbitral tribunal is lacking binding force and assumed to be executed by the disputing parties voluntarily. In other words, the procedural acts of the arbitration court for interim measures are binding for the parties, but are not recognized and enforceable by the state courts without some special procedure. That is why parties are entitled to proceed with the interim measure claims (as well as with the claims for preliminary orders[32]) directly before a competent court, in order to impose coercive measures to secure the claim, which would then be binding and enforceable.[33]

---

[31] See, for example, Article 27 of UNCITRAL Model Law. In Russia there is currently little evident interaction between arbitration and state courts on the issue of obtaining and securing evidence. To eliminate this gap the Draft law has language to entitle the arbitral tribunal itself or another party with the consent of the arbitral tribunal to request a competent state court for assistance in obtaining evidence in the manner prescribed by procedural legislation for litigation.

[32] Preliminary orders provide a means for preserving the status quo until the arbitral tribunal issues an interim measure adopting or modifying the preliminary order.

[33] See, for example, Article 17, 17A.17 B of UNCITRAL Model Law

10.49. Usually the application of interim measures should be submitted to the competent state court in the place of arbitration or to the location of the property in respect of which provisional measures can be taken, attached with a copy arbitration agreement and the statement of claim, duly certified (by the chairman of the arbitral tribunal or by a notary in case of ad hoc arbitration).

10.50. The competent state court should take into account not only litigation rules of certain kind, but to consider the specificity of international arbitration.[34] For example, there is an applicant' duty to prove the impossibility of the arbitral award' execution without imposition of interim measures, as well as the type and quantity of them proportionally justified. The state court shall determine the security claim or deny it. The regime for the recognition and enforcement of interim measures is generally the same as the framework for the recognition and enforcement of arbitral awards.

10.51. In case of granting the security measures, a writ of execution should be issued to make them enforceable.

10.52. In other words, the procedural acts of the arbitration court for interim measures are binding for the parties, but are not recognized and enforceable by the state courts absent some special procedure. This is why parties are entitled to proceed with the interim measures claims directly before a competent court.

B.3. The recognition and enforcement of arbitral awards

10.53. The arbitral award shall be executed voluntarily in the manner and time frame established in this decision, and if terms are not established, it shall be subject to immediate execution.

10.54. If the award of the arbitral tribunal has not been executed voluntarily by the due date, its enforcement could be carried out according to the rules of enforcement proceedings, applicable at the time of the execution of the arbitral award, based on a writ of execution issued by the competent court to enforce the award.

10.55. The application for issuance of a writ of execution should be submitted by the party in whose favour the judgment was rendered. Such an application usually includes: 1) the original or a copy of the arbitral award, certified by the chairman of the arbitral tribunal or a notary; 2) the original or a certified copy of the arbitration agreement; 3) a document confirming payment of the state fee.

---

[34] See, for example, Article 17J of UNCITRAL Model Law.

10.56. Determination of the competent state court to issue an enforcement order shall take effect immediately, although it may be appealed in the manner prescribed by the procedural legislation.

10.57. The grounds for refusal of a competent state court to recognize and enforce an arbitral award are exhaustively listed in the applicable law.

10.58. Respectively, all grounds for refusal can be divided into two categories. The first are those which are to be proven by an interested person or party (lack of capacity to conclude an arbitration agreement or its invalidity, violation of the arbitral formation or inability of a party to present its case and other similar grounds according to numerous clauses of grounds set by law). The second category includes grounds due to state court' own initiative (non-arbitrability or a violation of public policy).[35]

10.59. The enforcement grounds, described above, are generally the same as the grounds for setting aside the arbitral award (see above)[36]. This can be explained by the strict boundaries of state control which can be exercised towards such an autonomous form of jurisdiction as arbitration.

10.60. Notwithstanding that the grounds for setting aside an award are almost identical to those for refusing recognition or enforcement of the arbitral award, there is a difference worth mentioning. Usually, an application for setting aside an award may be made only to that state court of the country where the award was rendered, whereas an application for recognition and enforcement might be made in a state court in any country. Because of that, the grounds relating to public policy and non-arbitrability may vary in substance with the law applied by the state court such as in the case of setting aside or in the case of recognition and enforcement.

IV. Instead of a Conclusion: The Peaceful Coexisting of Arbitration and State Courts as a Recognized Way of Interaction

10.61. The comparison of the legal and court practice approach to arbitration and its proceedings can be stated as follows. The so-called contract or non-judicial theory of the legal nature of arbitration as a tool in the pre-

---

[35] See Article 35, 36 of UNCITRAL Model Law, which is similar to Article V of V of the Convention on the Recognition and Enforcement of Foreign Arbitral Awards (adopted 10 June 1958, entered into force 7 June 1959).

[36] Because of this, all our comments on setting aside procedure, except where stated otherwise, are applicable to our review of the recognition and enforcement procedure.

trial settlement of disputes is left in the past. Arbitration, which appeared at the dawn of statehood, is now accepted worldwide as a form of alternative dispute resolution. This means that arbitration, though with the inherent character of private law, still has an autonomous jurisdictional nature. That explains why the arbitral award as a result of a settlement in a civil dispute is binding and final.

10.62. Because of this, all forms of state court intervention in arbitration should be strictly bound by law. For example, as Article 5 of the UNCITRAL Model Law states, 'in matters governed by the law on arbitration, no state court shall intervene except where so provided by a specific law'.[37] This kind of approach corresponds to the autonomous jurisdictional nature of arbitration and flows from it.

10.63. Thus, at present modern legislation reflects a kind of worldwide consensus. This consensus emerged to meet the important needs of arbitral proceedings in conjunction with the recognition of the autonomous jurisdictional nature of arbitration. Mandatory provisions of law are aimed to make reasonable boundaries to reduce any inadequate interference of state courts, on behalf of the state itself, to the field of arbitration jurisdiction.

10.64. Restrictions found in legislation are expected and only support the effectiveness of arbitration justice. Examples include the procedure for setting aside awards, the denial of recognition and enforcement of interim measures or arbitral award, etc.

10.65. All of this should encourage parties to submit disputes to arbitration, based on contract autonomy, and including selecting the arbitrators and the rules for conducting the procedure with no more state court involvement than is appropriate and necessary.

| | |

Summaries

DEU [*Wechselspiel von Schiedsverfahren und staatlichen Gerichten: wachsende Konfrontation oder friedliche Koexistenz?*]

Der Beitrag befasst sich mit dem Wechselspiel zwischen Schiedsverfahren und staatlichen Gerichten aus bilateraler Sicht. Man analysiert, inwieweit der Staat das jurisdiktionelle Fundament des Schiedsverfahrens einerseits anerkennt, und inwieweit andererseits die Formen der Interaktion zwischen Schiedsverfahren und staatlichen Gerichten der Bedeutung des Schiedsverfahrens gerecht werden. Die von

---

[37] For example, Article 5 of UNCITRAL Mode Law establish as a general rule restriction for any state court' intervention to arbitration affairs, unless otherwise provided by certain law.

den Autoren gezogenen Schlüsse zeigen, dass eine Abkehr von der Vertrags- bzw. nichtjurisdiktionellen Theorie des juristischen Wesens des Schiedsverfahrens als bloßes vorprozessuales Instrument stattfindet. Das Schiedsverfahren ist weltweit als alternative Form der Entscheidung von Streitigkeiten anerkannt. Das Prinzip, wonach "allein die Gerichte Recht sprechen", schließt für sich genommen noch nicht aus, dass Gerechtigkeit auch über Schiedsrichter erlangt werden kann. Hier sind klar Prinzipien abzugrenzen wie der vom Staat erbrachte Schutz von Rechten einerseits und dem Rechtsschutz als solchem andererseits, wobei die vom Staat wahrgenommene (gerichtliche) Schutzfunktion als Teilbereich des Schutzes von Rechten zu verstehen ist. Die Behauptung, einzig und allein die Justiz vermöge es, die staatliche Aufgabe zu formen und durchzusetzen, steht nicht recht im Einklang mit den verfassungsrechtlichen Prinzipien, die an die Rolle des Rechts angelegt werden. Neben den allgemein anerkannten Rechtsmitteln zur Lösung privatrechtlicher Streitigkeiten stellt das Schiedsverfahren in der modernen Gesellschaft eine abdingbare Grundlage für privatrechtliche Prozessbeziehungen dar, die sich aus der Vertrags- und Willensfreiheit der an Geschäftsbeziehungen und am Wirtschaftsleben Beteiligten ergeben. Vor diesem Hintergrund geht das Wesen der Interaktion zwischen staatlichen Gerichten und dem Schiedsverfahren aus einem Konsensus hervor, wonach die Gerichte die notwendige Unterstützung erbringen und die Vollstreckbarkeit von Schiedssprüchen gewährleisten. Freilich erfährt diese Kontrollfunktion bezüglich des Schiedsverfahrens eine ganze Reihe von Einschränkungen. Die allgemeine Prämisse hinsichtlich der Funktion, welche die Gerichte dem Schiedsverfahren gegenüber einnehmen, wird im Wege der Kontrolle verschiedener Aspekte eingelöst, was die Organisation und den Fortgang eines Schiedsverfahrens anbelangt (also konkret die Ernennung der Schiedsrichter, Einreden gegen selbige, Niederlegung bzw. Entzug des Schiedsrichteramts, die Zuständigkeit von Schiedsgerichten und die Aufhebung von Schiedssprüchen), sowie im Wege einer Kontrolle derjenigen Aspekte, die die effektive Wahrnehmung der strittigen Parteieninteressen betreffen. Die grundlegenden Elemente der Tätigkeit, welche von Gerichten in Bezug auf das Schiedsverfahrens ausgeübt wird, bestehen in der gerichtlichen Hilfestellung bei der Beweisaufnahme, der Kompatibilität von gerichtlich erlassenen einstweiligen Verfügungen mit der Schiedsklausel, der Anerkennung und Vollstreckung von einstweiligen Verfügungen und schließlich der Anerkennung und Vollstreckung der Schiedssprüche.

CZE [*Interakce rozhodčího řízení a státních soudů: Sílící konfrontace nebo pokojná koexistence?*]

Článek se se zabývá interakcí mezi rozhodčím řízením a státními soudy z bilaterálního hlediska. Analyzujeme, zda stát uznává jurisdikční podstatu rozhodčího řízení na straně jedné a zda způsoby interakce mezi rozhodčím řízením a státními soudy odpovídají významu rozhodčího řízení na druhé straně. Závěry autorů ukazují, že dochází k opouštění smluvní, resp. nejurisdikční teorie právní podstaty rozhodčího řízení jako pouhého předprocesního nástroje. Rozhodčí řízení je celosvětově uznáváno jako alternativní forma rozhodování sporů. Princip, že „spravedlnost vykonávají pouze soudy" sám o sobě nevylučuje to, že spravedlnost lze realizovat i prostřednictvím rozhodců. Je zapotřebí jasně rozlišovat takové principy, jako státem realizovaná ochrana práv na jedné straně a na druhé straně právní ochrana, přičemž státem realizovanou (soudní) ochranu je nutno chápat jako podskupinu ochrany práv. Tvrzení, že pouze soudnictví tvoří a dává průchod úloze státu, není zcela v souladu s ústavními principy úlohy práva. Vedle obecně uznávaných právních prostředků pro řešení soukromoprávních sporů reprezentuje rozhodčí řízení v moderní společnosti existenci dispozitivního základu pro soukromoprávní procesní vztahy, vyplývající ze smluvní svobody a z autonomie vůle účastníků obchodních vztahů a hospodářské činnosti. Vzhledem k tomu je podstata interakce mezi státními soudy a rozhodčím řízením výsledkem konsenzu, v němž soudy poskytují nezbytnou podporu a zajišťují vykonatelnost rozhodčích nálezů. Kontrolní funkce ve vztahu k rozhodčímu řízení má ovšem řadu omezení. Obecná premisa ohledně funkce soudů vůči rozhodčímu řízení je realizována kontrolou různých aspektů organizace a postupů rozhodčího řízení (konkrétně jmenování rozhodců, námitky proti rozhodcům a ukončování funkce rozhodce, pravomoc rozhodčího soudu a rušení rozhodčího nálezu), jakož i kontrolou aspektů týkajících se efektivní implementace sporných zájmů stran. Zásadní elementy činnosti soudů ve vztahu k rozhodčímu řízení představuje soudní podpora při dokazování, kompatibilita předběžných opatření vydávaných soudem s rozhodčí smlouvou, uznávání a výkon předběžných opatření a uznávání a výkon rozhodčích nálezů.

||||

POL [*Interakcja między postępowaniem arbitrażowym i sądami krajowymi: narastająca konfrontacja czy pokojowe współistnienie?*]

Niniejszy artykuł został poświęcony interakcjom między postępowaniem arbitrażowym i sądami krajowymi z perspektywy bilateralnej. Autorzy przede wszystkim badają z jednej strony, czy sąd uznaje podstawę jurysdykcyjną postępowania arbitrażowego, a z drugiej strony, czy sposoby interakcji między postępowaniem arbitrażowym a sądami krajowymi odpowiadają znaczeniu postępowania arbitrażowego. Wnioski autorów pokazują, że następuje odchodzenie od umownej, czy też niejurysdykcyjnej teorii podstawy prawnej postępowania arbitrażowego jako wyłącznie instrumentu przedprocesowego. Postępowanie arbitrażowe uznawane jest na całym świecie jako alternatywna forma rozstrzygania sporów. Podstawa interakcji między sądami krajowymi i postępowaniem arbitrażowym jest wynikiem konsensusu, w którym sądy świadczą niezbędne wsparcie i gwarantują wykonywanie orzeczeń arbitrażowych. Jednakże funkcja kontrolna w odniesieniu do postępowania arbitrażowego obarczona jest szeregiem ograniczeń.

FRA [***Les interactions entre l'arbitrage et les tribunaux nationaux : une confrontation ou une coexistence pacifique ?***]

Le présent article se penche sur les interactions entre l'arbitrage et les tribunaux nationaux. Nous examinerons si les tribunaux reconnaissent la nature juridictionnelle de l'arbitrage, d'une part, et si les moyens d'interaction entre l'arbitrage et les tribunaux nationaux rendent compte de l'importance de l'arbitrage, d'autre part. Nos conclusions montrent un abandon de la théorie non juridictionnelle ou contractuelle de la nature juridique de l'arbitrage comme simple outil préjudiciel. L'arbitrage est mondialement reconnu comme une forme alternative de résolution des litiges. La nature des interactions entre l'arbitrage et les tribunaux nationaux est le résultat d'un consensus, dans lequel les tribunaux apportent un soutien utile et garantissent l'exécutabilité des sentences arbitrales. Sa fonction de contrôle dans sa relation à l'arbitrage est cependant fortement limitée.

RUS [*Взаимодействие третейских и государственных судов: растущее противостояние или мирное сосуществование?*]

В статье вопрос о взаимодействии арбитражных и государственных судов рассматривается в двустороннем аспекте: признает ли государство за арбитражем юрисдикционный характер, с одной стороны, и соответствуют ли сформировавшиеся формы взаимодействия арбитражей и государственных судов природе арбитражного разбирательства, с другой стороны. В процессе анализа демонстрируется вывод о том, что договорная (неюрисдикционная) теория правовой природы арбитража как досудебного инструмента урегулирования осталась в прошлом. Арбитражное разбирательство общепризнано альтернативной формой разрешения споров, поэтому характер взаимодействия с государственными судами является результатом такого консенсуса, в рамках которого государственный суд оказывает необходимую поддержку, обеспечивающую исполнимость арбитражных решений, а возможности контроля строго ограничены законом.

ESP   [*Interacción entre el arbitraje y el proceso: ¿Creciente confrontación o coexistencia pacífica?*]

El artículo se refiere a la interacción entre el arbitraje y el proceso ante una autoridad jurisdiccional desde una perspectiva bilateral. Los autores, por un lado, investigan si el tribunal reconoce la naturaleza jurisdiccional del arbitraje y, por otro, si los métodos de interacción entre el arbitraje y los tribunales nacionales corresponden a la importancia del arbitraje. Las conclusiones de los autores muestran que hay un abandono de la teoría contractual, es decir, no jurisdiccional de la naturaleza jurídica del arbitraje como una simple herramienta ante-procesal. El procedimiento de arbitraje es reconocido mundialmente como una forma alternativa de la solución de controversias. La naturaleza de la interacción entre el proceso y el arbitraje es el resultado de un consenso, en el cual los tribunales proporcionan el apoyo necesario para garantizar el cumplimiento de los laudos arbitrales. Sin embargo, la función de control en relación con el arbitraje tiene una serie de limitaciones.

| | |

Martin Svatoš

The Mediator-Judge Interaction: Does the Win-Win Approach Apply?

Key words:
Mediation | confidentiality | judicial settlement | judicial mediation | court referral to mediation | enforcement of mediated agreement | settlement | right to be heard

Abstract | This article focuses on the interaction between judges and mediators. It follows the chronological order of the mediation procedure in order to show the relevant relations that occur between these two rather dissimilar systems of dispute resolution.

First, it addresses the pre-mediation phase, where judges can recruit suitable cases to be resolved in mediation by judicial referral or by less formal advice or recommendation to attend ADR. Second, it describes the relationship between judges and mediation during the mediation procedure itself. Finally, it concentrates on the post-mediation phase where judges can either increase the weight of mediated agreements by making them enforceable or reviewable if the mediated agreement was produced by undue influence, misrepresentation or lack of will. When studying these positions, this contribution will focus not only on theoretical knowledge but also on relevant Czech mediation legislation and experiences.

Dr. Martin Svatoš is a mediator and arbitrator focusing on both international and domestic commercial disputes. He is a lecturer at Charles University in Prague, at the Seminar of European and Comparative Law in Urbino, at the Faculté Libre de Droit Institut Catholique de Toulouse and at the Université des Antilles et de la Guyane in Guadeloupe. He is a visiting lecturer at the Comenius University in Bratislava (Slovakia) and at the Shanghai University of Political Science and Law (China). He gained his experience around the globe having studied at the University of Sorbonne in Paris (FR), at Charles University in Prague (CZ) and at Cornell University (USA) and having worked at the International Court of Arbitration of the ICC in Paris and at the Chamber of Arbitration of Milan (Italy).
e-mail: svatosmartin@forarb.com

| | |

I. Introduction

11.01. The ancient Roman writer Terence stated that when two are doing the same thing, it is not the same.[1] This ancient proverb also applies to the judges' and mediators' missions. Although, both are charged with helping the disputing parties overcome their dispute, their roles, tools and goals are completely different.

11.02. The divergence between them clear: On the one hand, a judge is 'a public official appointed or elected to hear and decide legal matters in court,'[2] while on the other hand, a mediator is 'a neutral person who tries to help disputing parties reach an agreement.'[3]

11.03. Thus the first one is characterized as an official that is publicly appointed or perhaps elected. The other one is a neutral private[4] person, usually chosen by the parties or by an Alternative Dispute Resolution (ADR) institution. The role of the first one consists of hearing and deciding the merit on the legal and factual basis, while the later one is asked to *try* to facilitate the negotiation procedure between the disputing parties. While the outcome of the first one's work is adjudicatory, final and binding decision, the goal of the second one is to find a solution based on the parties' consent.

11.04. Differences can be found also in the position of the procedures both are involved in. Whereas litigation is regarded as the standard or presumed[5] way to resolve disputes, mediation is still considered 'merely' as an alternative. In other words, it would be almost impossible to find more distant and different actors of dispute resolution than a judge and mediator.

11.05. Yet, a more detailed look reveals that there are some connections, or more specifically, interactions between these two. Judges make a referral to mediation and they try to help the parties settle their disputes and provide the mediated agreement with enforceability. Are these relationships exceptions or proofs of hidden connections and

---

[1] P. TERENTIUS AFER (TERENCE), Adelphi: The Brothers, Ter. Ad. 5 In Latin: 'DUO CUM FACIUNT IDEM, NON EST IDEM.'

[2] BLACK'S LAW DICTIONARY, St. Paul: West - A Thomas Reuters business 916 (Bryan A. Garner ed., 9th ed. 2009).

[3] Ibid, at 1071.

[4] In the sense that he or she comes from outside the official system of dispute resolution.

[5] Despite this fact, there are some types of disputes that have to be submitted to resolution through the ADR because the law says so. The collective disputes resolution regulated by the Czech Collective Negotiation Act (Act No. 2/1991 Coll. on the Collective Negotiation) is an example.

cooperation? Can both sides profit from this cooperation or is there only one party winning? Finally, does this interaction work primarily in favour of the disputing parties?

11.06. In order to give answers to these questions, this paper focuses on the three main chronological stages of the mediation procedure: the pre-mediation stage, the mediation stage and the post-mediation stage. As the mediation procedure goes on it comes across different and various kinds of meeting points where the judges encounter mediators or at least mediation. When studying these positions, this contribution will focus not only on theoretical knowledge but also on relevant Czech mediation legislation and experiences.

11.07. The aim of this paper is not to provide the reader with an exhaustive description of all relevant mediator-judge interactions but rather with a brief list of these specific and miscellaneous relations that appear between judge and mediator before, during and after mediation takes place.

II. The Pre-mediation Stage

11.08. The pre-mediation stage can be defined as the time period between the conflict arising and the commencing of the mediation procedure. Sometimes it is also described as a phase of getting the parties to the table. Despite the fact that it can cause some surprises, the most intensive and important interactions between the judge and the mediator take place in this phase.

11.09. Before the parties even meet in the mediation room, they have to be told about the possibility to resolve their dispute out of court. Indeed, the main information burden should be carried by the mediator and parties' legal representatives or in-house lawyers. Yet especially in the countries where mediation does not have a very long tradition, the courts can be very helpful. There are two basic ways how they can help. The courts can issue a so-called 'court referral' by which they order the parties to attend mediation, or through an 'unbinding recommendation' by which judges informally and non-bindingly advise parties to go to mediation.

II.1. Court Referral

11.10. Court Referral could be described as 'any process by which disputants are directed to mediation[6] by a court or tribunal.'[7] Basically, the referral

---

[6] Because of its page-limitation, this article cannot focus on other court referred ADR. Yet, this can be of particular interest. As stated by some authors, mediation can be fitting

is regarded as a compulsory order given by the judge. It consists of an obligation to attempt to settle the dispute through mediation or at least an obligation to attend a meeting with a mediator. The difference between this and the 'recommendation to mediate' is that the latter is not obligatory.

11.11. In the following subchapter, this paper firstly explores the decision making process of ordering the court referral. Secondly, it reflects on the motivation of judges ordering mediation. Finally it uses Czech mediation law to illustrate such a referral.

II.1.1. General comments on Referral

11.12. In studying the court referral, one cannot avoid discussion of many interesting issues, three of which are the most important: The criteria of judges' decision whether to refer or not, the authority to validly refer to mediation and finally the remedies of the parties having been referred to mediation. These three topics are briefly addressed here.

a) Criteria of discretion

11.13. With the court referral, the judge orders the parties to attend mediation or an informative pre-mediation session. In this relation, a question arises of what the judges should take into consideration when so deciding.

11.14. Usually, their discretion to mandate mediation does not depend on any objective criteria. The usual condition as stated by statutory provision would be: 'When it deems appropriate...' without giving to the decision makers any directions. It is up to them to decide upon their preferences.

11.15. In these cases, the referral depends purely on the discretion of the judge, who is usually not obliged to examine the will of the parties.[8]

---

for some of the cases, but rather unfitting or less fitting for the others, where the other ADR procedures can be of some help. In this regard, so called 'multi-door courthouses' (MDC) are worth mentioning. According to this concept, a MDC is a multifaceted dispute resolution centre attached to the national courts. It enables the parties not only to enter one door to the court room, but also other doors to mediation, arbitration and other ADR if it seems appropriate. Compare Ericka B. Gray, *Approach to Diagnostic Assessment of Civil Cases: The Individual Case-Screening Conference.* 7(3) THE COURT MANAGER 21, 21 (1992).

[7] See NADJA ALEXANDER, INTERNATIONAL AND COMPARATIVE MEDIATION – LEGAL PERSPECTIVES, Alphen aan Rijn: Kluwer Law International 148 (2009).

[8] For an opposite example, see French Code of Civil Procedure, Art. 131-1: 'A judge seized of litigation may, after having obtained the consent of the parties, appoint a third person who will hear them and confront their points of view to help them resolve the dispute dividing them.'

Despite that fact, one would expect that the judge should at least take into consideration whether the parties are likely to participate in good faith and whether there is an actual chance to settle.

11.16. This approach is sometimes described as 'rational cost-benefit analysis'[9] and an example of its elaboration appeared in *Oriental Carpet Department Store Pty Ltd* v *Supacenta Pty Ltd.* In this case, when examining the will of the parties the New South Wales Supreme Court stated that 'there are circumstances where mediation may be worthwhile despite the statement of the parties that mediation may be unlikely to resolve the dispute or matter.'[10] This idea was further developed in *McDonald's Properties (Australia) Pty Limited* v *Challenger Property Nominees Pty Limited* where the judge explained that 'experience shows that, notwithstanding in certain circumstances the most stringent opposition to being involved in a compulsory mediation, it is sometimes seen to be successful...'[11]

11.17. Finally, in *Atl. Pipe Corp.*,[12] the US First Circuit Court of Appeals held that a court may refer the parties to mediation

> pursuant to its inherent authority to manage and control dockets; but, absent an explicit statutory provision or local rule authorizing mediation, the court must first determine that a case is appropriate for mediation and then affirmatively set appropriate procedural safeguards to ensure fairness to all parties involved.[13]

b) Authority to validly refer

11.18. Another important issue in relation to the court referral is the court's authority to validly order mediation. This question was also addressed by courts several times. For instance, in *African-American Slave Descendants Litigation*,[14] the US judge held that absent the consent of each party, the court can require mediation only when local rules,

---

[9]   Compare NADJA ALEXANDER, *supra* note 7, at 161.

[10]   Similarly, in *Higgins* v *Higgins* (2002) NSWSC 455, McDonald's Australia Limited (For more details see Andrew Tuch, *Dispute resolution update*, 6(10) ADR BULLETIN 204, 204 (2004).

[11]   See *McDonald's Properties (Australia) Pty Limited* v *Challenger Property Nominees Pty Limited* (2003) NSWSC 963.

[12]   Compare *Pipe Corp.*, 304 F.3d 135 (1st Cir. 2002).

[13]   James Richard Coben; Peter N. Thompson, *Disputing Irony: A Systematic Look at Litigation about Mediation*, 11 (Spring) HARVARD NEGOTIATION LAW REVIEW 43,105 (2006).

[14]   Compare 22 III.272 F. Supp. 2d 755 (N.D. Ill. 2003).

statutes, the Federal Rules of Civil Procedure or the court's inherent powers provide the necessary authority.

11.19. In another US case *LLH* v *SCH*,[15] it was emphasized that the court does not overstep its authority by modifying the parties' agreement and ignoring a mandatory mediation provision. This was because the facts of the case as recorded in the files shows that the parties cannot truly use mediation because of the intensity of their conflict.[16]

11.20. Sometimes, the discussion extends to the scope of the referred mediation. The question here is whether the parties have to follow the scope of the litigation case or whether they can also discuss further matters. The usual approach is to let the parties freely manage the issues in mediation.[17] Still, there are some exceptions as in the case of French Civil Procedure Code which states that 'The mediation may concern the whole or a part of the litigation'.[18]

c) Parties' remedies

11.21. The other issue one should take into consideration when discussing the judicial referral to mediation is the judicial remedies of the parties having been ordered to mediation. In other words, what are the admissible steps to be taken in order to correct or supervise the free discretion of the judge? While this question is interesting, it really belongs in the realm of theory since the challenges to judicially compelled mediation are rare and successful appeals are even rarer. The legal quality of judicial orders mandating mediation can be offered as an explanation for this situation. They are deemed to be interlocutory and un-appealable.[19]

11.22. Some of the legislative provisions explicitly regulate this characteristic. The Czech legislation could serve as an example of that approach.[20]

---

[15] Compare *LLH* v *SCH*, No. S-10174, 2002 WL 1943659 (Alaska Aug. 21, 2002).

[16] James Richard Coben and Peter N. Thompson, *supra* note 13, at 106.

[17] In the author's praxis, the referred cases rarely stick with the initial problem having been the object of litigation.

[18] Compare Art. 131-2 of French Civil Procedure Code.

[19] As the examples, the following cases are mentioned: *Tutu Park, Ltd.* v *O'Brien Plumbing Co.*, 180 F. Supp. 2d 673 (D. V.I. 2002) and *Thomas H.*, No. A100644, 2003 WL 21481113 (Cal. Ct. App. June 27, 2003). Compare James Richard Coben and Peter N. Thompson, *supra* note 13, at 106.

[20] Czech Code of Civil Procedure states in its Section 202 as follows: 'The appeal is not admissible against an order by which (...) the first meeting with the Mediators was ordered (...)'.

II.1.2. Motivation of judges to refer

11.23. As illustrated above, the success and efficiency of court referral depends on the judges' consideration. But what should serve as their motivation? Explanations may seem a bit paradoxical: Referred mediation is a way to promote the fundamental right of access to justice.[21]

11.24. Today's court systems struggle with enormous caseloads and if part of their agenda is settled through mediation, there will be more resources for focusing on the rest. This may shorten the average litigation duration and consequently make 'access to justice' easier. Thus the motivation of sharing the case load is one of the most important engines that is pushing on the mediation in countries including the Czech Republic. On the other hand, one cannot withhold the criticism of mandatory mediation. According to some scholars, it denies the right of access to the courts for the parties who have been ordered to go in front of the mediator.[22] Given the fact that mandatory mediation is more a condition to access than a ban, this opinion seems to be unjustified.[23] This also leaves aside the fact that access to justice is characterized as a combination of cost, delay, judicial economy and proportionality. Ergo, mediation seems to be even more fitting to these prerequisites than litigation.[24] Moreover, mediation is considered a way to protect and save public resources from the perspective of a public budget.

11.25. Thus forward-thinking judges seek to use mediation in order to support the principle of distributive justice, proportionality and effectiveness.[25] On the other hand, there are some types of cases in which the even normally ADR friendly judges seem to be reluctant to order mediation. These are especially when public policy, constitutional or principal rights are involved.

---

[21] This is also one of the reasons of adopting the EU Mediation Directive.

[22] Dorcas Quek, *Mandatory Mediation: An Oxymoron? Examining The Feasibility of Implementing a Court-Mandated Mediation Program*, 11 (spring) CARDOZA JOURNAL OF CONFLICT RESOLUTION, 479, 479 (2010).

[23] Compare Martin Svatoš, *Mandatory mediation strikes back*, available at: http://www.mediate.com/articles/SvatosM1.cfm, (accessed on 25 May 2014).

[24] Warren K. Winkler, *Access to Justice, Mediation: Panacea or Pariah?*, 16(1) CANADIAN ARBITRATION AND MEDIATION JOURNAL 5, 9 (2007).

[25] Compare NADJA ALEXANDER, *supra* note 7, at 165.

III.1.3. The Czech example of Mediation Referral

11.26. The Czech Code of Civil Procedure[26] regulates court referral in its Section 100:

> (3) If this is fitting and appropriate, the chairman of the panel may order the participants of the proceedings the first meeting with a registered Mediator (hereinafter the "Mediator") for 3 hours and interrupt proceedings, however for no more than a period of 3 months. If the participants shall not agree over the person of the Mediator immediately, the chairman of the panel shall select a Mediator from the Register kept by the Ministry. The court shall continue proceedings upon expiry of the 3 months (...).

11.27. In the Czech Republic, the judge cannot order mediation but only the so-called first meeting with the registered mediator. The purpose of this meeting should be an explanation of mediation's advantages, principles and its possible application on the present case. In fact, this step is left out in the majority of cases and mediation is started directly in order not to lose time.[27]

II.2. Recommendation to Attend Mediation

11.28. Apart from the obligatory order, judges can informally advise the parties to go to mediation. This can be done both in the jurisdictions where the statutory provisions do not provide the authorization to order mediation as well as in the jurisdictions that include the possibility of court referral. In the latter case, recommendation can be used prior to referral in order to ensure the maximum autonomy of the free will of the parties or in the cases when the referral demands some specific conditions that are not met.

11.29. Recommendation to attend mediation is usually informal advice, although some of the regulations have specific provisions regarding it. The Czech Code of Civil Procedure provides one such example.[28]

---

[26] Act No. 99/1963 Coll., the Civil Procedure Code.

[27] Compare Martin Svatoš, *Mýty a fakta o prvním setkání s mediátorem, aneb všechno, co jste o mediaci chtěli vědět, ale báli jste se zeptat*, (11) BULLETIN ADVOKACIE 48, 48 (2013).

[28] See Section 114a of the Czech Code of Civil Procedure: 'If this is appropriate in view of the nature of the case, the chairman of the panel (...) shall also inform the participants of the possibility of using mediation under the Mediation Act or social advice under the Social Services Act.' And similarly elsewhere in the Code of Civil Procedure is stated, that the judge when preparing the first hearing inform the parties 'of the possibility of the use of mediation under the Mediation Act or social advice under the Social Service Act, if this is appropriate.' Compare Section 114a of the Czech Code of Civil Procedure.

III. The Mediation Stage

11.30. Despite some expectations, there are relatively few interactions between the mediator and the judge in the stage of the mediation procedures. When it comes to interaction between the judges and the mediation procedure itself, one has to address the question of judges acting as mediators.

III.1. Interaction between the Judge and Mediator during the Mediation

11.31. The issue of interaction between the judge and the mediator during the mediation procedure is rather limited. It is caused by two reasons. Firstly, the mediation procedure is rather short and thus there are not a lot of opportunities that would require some kind of action on the judges' part. Secondly and more importantly, mediators lack jurisdiction[29] in the sense arbitrators have it. Consequently, there are no interim measures and similar institutions in mediation because the mediator does not exercise such power over the parties.

11.32. Yet there is an issue that raises questions especially when the parties were referred to mediation by the court. It concerns confidentiality and the right of the judge to be informed on the mediation once they had ordered it.

11.33. In the Czech law, a mediator is bound by confidentiality:

> The Mediator shall maintain confidentiality of all the facts he has learned in connection with the preparation and performance of mediation even after being struck off the Register. This shall also apply if no mediation contract is concluded.[30]

11.34. Since there is an exception to every rule, the exception to the mediator's privilege can be found in the following provisions of Mediation Act. Firstly, a mediator is not bound by confidentiality once being exempted by the all the parties of the dispute.[31] Moreover, the mediator

> is not bound by the obligation of confidentiality to the extent necessary for proceedings before a court or other relevant authority if the subject of the proceedings is a dispute arising from the activities performed by the Mediator between him

---

[29] Jurisdiction is described as 'power to decide a case' which is obviously lacking in mediation. Compare BLACK'S LAW DICTIONARY, *supra* note 2, at 927.

[30] Compare Section 9 (1) of the Mediation Act (Act No. 202/212 Coll. On Mediation).

[31] Compare Section 9 (2) of the Mediation Act (Act No. 202/212 Coll. On Mediation).

and the Party of the Conflict or its legal representative and also to the extent necessary for his protection as part of the performance of supervision over the Mediator's activities or in disciplinary proceedings.[32]

11.35. But this is all. There are no further provisions and so, although the interest of judges once having ordered mediation would be well based there are no provisions in Czech law that address any further contact. Strictly speaking, a mediator is not allowed to reveal to a judge whether the mediation took place or even whether it is still continuing. In a similar situation, the only possible solution is that the judge should refer to the parties who are not bound by a confidentiality obligation under the Czech mediation law.

11.36. Despite this fact, Czech judges sometimes inquire[33] about the stage of the proceeding mediation or about whether the mediation has started or ended. Saving the situation where the parties have expressly waived their privilege, the only correct response from the mediator's side should be a negative reply to such a demand.[34]

III.2. Judges Acting as Mediators[35]

11.37. The other interaction between judges and mediators are related to the situation when the person of judge and mediator blends. Although not universally accepted,[36] the tradition of mediating judges is very long and rich across different legal systems.[37] Scholars have described different judicial dispute resolutions but for the purposes of this paper, only two main forms[38] will be addressed. These are 'judicial settlement' and

---

[32] Compare Section 9 (3) of the Mediation Act (Act No. 202/212 Coll. On Mediation).

[33] This knowledge comes from author's praxis, as well as from author's colleagues' praxis.

[34] One way to handle this question is in the agreement to mediate. Once the parties will agree with the right of the mediator to inform the judge who ordered mediation, similar problem would be prevented.

[35] The author would like to thank Ms. Šárka Hájková, an honourable judge of the Regional court in Prague for her help and counselling in regard to this chapter.

[36] For many any use of mediation and a judge in the same sentence is an oxymoron. For example, as Spencer says: 'Judges are supposed to judge (not mediate), to apply law (not interests), to evaluate (not facilitate), to order (not accommodate) and to decide (not settle).' Compare David Spencer, *Judicial mediators: are they constitutionally valid?*, 9(4) ADR BULLETIN 1, 1 (2006).

[37] Compare in this sense NADJA ALEXANDER, *supra* note 7, at 127.

[38] Others as addressed by Alexander are judicial moderation and facilitative judging, compare NADJA ALEXANDER, *supra* note 7, at 130.

'judicial mediation'. Since the boundary between these procedures is sometimes quite unclear, there are some procedures regarded as 'mixed'.

III.2.1. Judicial settlement

11.38. The distinction between the judicial settlement and judicial mediation could be defined with two characteristics. The first is timing. In judicial settlement, the litigation comes first and the attempt to amicably resolve is included in it, or in other words, starts *a posterior.*[39] The second characteristic is that the same judge who is going to hear and decide the matter is conducting the settlement procedure. Thus one judge plays both the determinative and consensus searching role. Although there are some minor voices criticizing the settlement procedure especially because of the lack of justice,[40] the majority of opinions appreciate judicial settlement.

11.39. The criticisms of judicial settlement are that it is directive, legalistic and short lasting.[41] Furthermore, there can be a peril of losing impartiality and independence when conducting a mediation-like procedure. In this regard, a judge can come close to the well known dilemma from the 'med-arb' and 'arb-med' procedures.[42]

11.40. Despite said characteristics, there is a requirement of a settlement attempt in many civil law jurisdictions.[43] Therefore we can speak of a specific legal tradition in these countries. In contrast, the common law jurisdictions regard the judicial settlement as rather part of the broader concept of procedure reform and thus the judges are usually not required to do so by law.[44]

11.41. According to the Czech procedural law, there are two types of 'judicial settlement' procedures. The first one stands on the edges of judicial

---

[39]   However, there can be the so-called pre-hearing conference that foregoes the main hearing. Yet, it is regarded as a part of the litigation procedure despite its initial stage.

[40]   Compare STEPHEN B. GOLDBERG; FRANK E.A. SANDER; NANCY H. ROGERS; SARAH R. COLE, DISPUTE RESOLUTION: NEGOTIATION, MEDIATION AND OTHER PROCESSES, New York: Wolters Kluwer 390 (2007).

[41]   Compare Compare NADJA ALEXANDER, *supra* note 7, at 130.

[42]   In this regard compare Martin Svatoš, *Independence and Impartiality of Arbitrators and Mediators – The Castor and Pollux of the ADR World?, in* YEARBOOK OF ARBITRATION, VOLUME IV, 2014, INDEPENDENCE AND IMPARTIALITY OF ARBITRATORS, New York: Juris Publishing Int. 229, 229 (Bělohlávek, A. J., Rozehnalová, N. & Černý, F. eds., 2014).

[43]   Compare the Section 114c (2) of the Czech Code of Civil Procedure: '(3) During the preparatory stage, the President of the Tribunal especially (...) c) attempts to amicably settle the matter (§ 99),'

[44]   Compare Compare NADJA ALEXANDER, *supra* note 7, at 134.

mediation and judicial settlement and thus it will be analyzed later. The second one is regulated by Section 99 of the Czech Civil Procedure Code and can be regarded as a pure 'judicial settlement'.[45] In this procedure, there is an attempt to resolve a dispute that was brought in court by the assistance of the same judge that would eventually decide once the attempt has failed.

11.42. Generally speaking, in order to distinguish the different characteristics of relevant procedures, it is not considered as important whether the relevant method is titled or labelled as mediation. The more important characteristic to be taken in consideration is the real role of the judge. This was confirmed by the decision of the Indiana Court of Appeals in the case *Estate of Skalka* v *Skalka*. In this particular affair, the judge tried to resolve the dispute of the parties in the pre-trial stage and later stated:

> You know, we sat in my chambers, people, and you walked out of my office in agreement. Alright. I did as much as I could possibly do to resolve the conflict. But if you people want to continue fighting, I'm no longer going to be the mediator here, I'm going to be a judge. You are going to go through the cost of this thing. It's going to be financially draining and I can tell you you're going to wind up losing the property.[46]

11.43. One of the parties reproached the judge for acting improperly when carrying out the function of mediator. The appealing judge denied such an argument when stressing:

---

[45] Compare Section 99 of the Czech Code of Civil Procedure: '(1) If it accepts the nature of the case, the parties may terminate the proceedings judicial settlement. Court seeks conciliation between the parties, in an attempt at conciliation President of the Chamber especially with the participants discuss the matter, notifies them of the rules and the opinions of the Supreme Court and the decision published in the Collection of judgments and opinions concerning the case and the circumstances of the case they recommend possibilities of an amicable solution dispute. If the nature of things appropriate, notify the presiding judge participants also the possibility of using mediation under the Act on social mediation or counselling under the Act on Social Services.

(2) The court shall decide on whether to approve a settlement, approve it if it is in conflict with the law. In this case, the court after the final resolution to continue with the procedure.

(3) The approved settlement has the effect of a final judgment. Judgment, however, the court may set aside the order approving the settlement, if the settlement under substantive law invalid. Proposal can be filed within three years of the resolution approving the settlement.'

[46] Compare Court of Appeals of Indiana. *The ESTATE OF John SKALKA, Deceased, John Skalka, Joseph Skalka and Laura Ostergren, Appellants-Plaintiffs,* v *Mark SKALKA, Appellee-Defendant.* No. 46A03-0009-CV-327.

— July 10, 2001.

However, we find that this statement merely indicates the trial judge was attempting, in his role as judge, to assist the parties in reaching a settlement of their disputes, not that he was seeking to act as a mediator in a mediation governed by the Alternative Discipline Resolution (ADR) rules. Mark's brief contains an especially apt description of the trial court's actions: 'the trial judge was simply' 'entertaining settlement discussion at a pretrial conference.' (Br. of Appellee at 19.) Generally, the purpose of a pretrial conference is to narrow the issues for trial; in this case, all the issues were resolved at the pretrial conference. As this was a pretrial conference and not a mediation, the judge did not act improperly.

III.2.2. Judicial Mediation

11.44. In the case of judicial mediation, there are two separate but closely related procedures. However, the judge who is mediating the dispute is, excluded from deciding the matter once the mediation is unsuccessful and the litigation eventually continues in front of a different judge. Thus, contrary to judicial settlement, judicial mediation is based on the concept of separation of the judges' roles.[47]

11.45. However, this model can vary with the quality of the judge performing mediation. In one situation, the judicial mediators are appointed judges of the respective court only assigned with the task of mediating disputes, as opposed to their colleagues who are in charge of case adjudication.[48] The other possibility is that they are sitting judges acting as mediators in addition to the adjudicative activity that constitutes their main occupation.[49] Nevertheless in both cases, the judge deciding the merits is different from the judge mediating the dispute.[50]

---

[47] Compare the distinction included in the European Directive on Mediation: 'This Directive should apply to cases where a court refers parties to mediation or in which national law prescribes mediation. Furthermore, in so far as a judge may act as a mediator under national law, this Directive should also apply to mediation conducted by a judge who is not responsible for any judicial proceedings relating to the matter or matters in dispute.' Compare article 12 of the Preamble of the *Directive 2008/52/EC of the European Parliament and of the Council of 21 May 2008 on certain aspects of mediation in civil and commercial matters.*

[48] DAVID SPENCER, *supra* note 36, at 61.

[49] Louise Otis; Eric H. Reiter, *Mediation by Judges: A New Phenomenon in the Transformation of Justice,* 6 (3) PEPP. DISP. RESOL. L.J. 351, 352 (2006).

[50] A regular mediation that is performed by a former judge as a mediator cannot be described as judicial mediation. This quite common praxis, where a retired judge becomes involved in ADR, cannot be regarded as a specific type of mediation although the approach towards mediation is very specific.

11.46. Judicial mediation raises a lot of controversial issues. According to many scholars, judicial mediators overstep the line of the courts' role as being purely adjudicating neutral persons.[51] It is regarded as a kind of disruption of the separation of powers doctrine that is a very basic principle on which western democracies are built.[52] On the other hand, it has proved a great method for amicably settling parties' conflicts and saving time and public resources. Thus the usage of judicial mediations is increasing.[53]

II.2.3. Mixed procedures

11.47. Some of the procedures cannot be purely distinguished and sorted because of their intermingled nature. One of these *mixed procedures* can be found in Czech procedural law, more specifically in Section 67 of the Czech Code of Civil Procedure. It can be regarded as a particular procedure based upon a request of the parties through which an attempt is made by a judge to help the parties to reach a settlement of their dispute. If this process is successful, the judge approves the parties' agreement.[54]

11.48. However, this process *sui generis* crosses the thin limits of pure judicial mediation as defined above. Although it starts before the same dispute related litigation has started or might have begun, the judge performing the mediation does not have to be different from the judge who may decide the case once the attempt to settle fails. In other words, the judge that is appointed to perform the 'judicial settlement' procedure according to Section 67 of the Czech Code of Civil Procedure may also be appointed to hear the merits of the dispute if the attempt has failed and the parties decide to start an ordinary litigation procedure.[55]

---

[51] Compare LOUISE OTIS & ERIC H. REITER, *supra* note 49, at 352.

[52] The separation doctrine describes a model of three powers, namely legislative, executive and judicial. These are distinct and mutually controlled in order to prevent the concentration of power to the hands of one institution or individual. This concept dates back to the French political philosopher Montesquieu. For further study of the constitutionality of judicial mediation see DAVID SPENCER, *supra* note 36, at 62.

[53] Compare LOUISE OTIS & ERIC H. REITER, *supra* note 49, at 352.

[54] However, in this very same procedure, there can be a previously reached agreement (for instance a mediated agreement) that is only approved or declined by the judge based on its alignment with the law. In this case, the role of the judge is limited to pure examination of the agreement in relation to its accordance with the provisions of law. Consequently, such a process should be regarded as belonging to the post-mediation stage.

[55] The likelihood of the same judge deciding the same case or not depends not only on the parties, who are not forced to continue by litigation once the settlement effort has

11.49. Does it mean that an impartial judge may proceed with the litigation once having been involved in judicial mediation? To answer this question, one has to turn to the provision of Section 14 of the Czech Code of Civil Procedure: 'Judges shall be excluded from hearing and deciding a case where there is a doubt as to their impartiality on account of their personal relationship to the case, parties to the proceedings, or their representatives.' Still this has to be regarded only as an individual exclusion that requires particular circumstances. It cannot be applied in general and thus the general principle of judicial mediation is not met.

IV. The Post-mediation Stage

11.50. A Judge's relationship to mediation does not end with the signature of a mediated agreement. In the post-mediation stage, there is also a significant role for judges that can be considered as a kind of interaction with mediation. This is closely related to the question of the enforcement and review of mediated agreements. Apart from these relations, some examples exist of what is called the '*mediation* paradox'. This is the situation when a mediator appears in front of judge as a party of the dispute between that mediator and one or both parties.

IV.1. Judges and the Mediated Agreement

11.51. Judges also interact with mediation after the signature of mediated agreement signals the end of the mediation procedure. It is the mediation outcome which the judge's activity focuses on in this phase. It can be either improved by an enforceability granting or decreased by a set-aside procedure, upon review and at the request of one party.

IV.1.1. Enforcement of the mediated agreement

11.52. There are several ways to enforce mediated agreements such as deeds of settlement, pure contracts or even arbitral awards.[56] One of the most used tools to make a mediated outcome enforceable is the form of a court order. In this way, judges improve the efficiency of mediation in a significant way.

---

failed, but also on the judge's schedule. Furthermore, the respective court that is going to perform this judicial settlement procedure shall be the same as the court that has jurisdiction to hear the case in ordinary litigation. Compare Section 67 of the Czech Code of Civil Procedure. The only exception is if a Regional court has jurisdiction over the merits, in which case any of the District courts could be appointed.

[56] Compare NADJA ALEXANDER, *supra* note 7, at, p. 301.

11.53. Generally speaking, mediated agreements are not directly enforceable. This is regarded as one of the biggest weaknesses of mediation in general. Thus there is a need for an effective and fast tool that enables making this outcome enforceable, and .this is where the courts come into play. They can quickly and efficiently enforce the agreement while also granting a certain 'judgment' quality to the agreement.

11.54. So for instance the French, Czech and many other legal systems envisage that under certain conditions a mediated agreement can be enforceable after being ratified by the court. In the first case, the compromise[57] referred by way of a petition can be conferred as a writ of execution by the president of the High Court.[58] In the latter case a court shall 'decide on whether to approve a mediation agreement reached pursuant to the mediation within 30 days.'[59] The only criterion to be taken into consideration by the judge is whether the agreement is in accordance with the law.

11.55. It should be added that the other advantage of a mediated agreement approved by the court inside of the European Union is the fact that under certain conditions it can benefit from the provisions of *Brussels I. Regulation*.[60]

IV.1.2. Review

11.56. But it is not only the improvement of the quality of a mediated agreement that can be granted by the courts in the post-mediation stage. The other judge-mediation interaction in this phase is the review mechanism of a mediated agreement by a judge upon the request of one of the parties'. The motivation raised by the parties can vary – from negative consequences of a settlement realized *a posterior,* to the alleged absence of the consent in the agreed-upon agreement. In this

---

[57]   Compare article 2044 of French Code civil.

[58]   Compare article 1441-4 of the French New Code of Civil Procedure. Compare also article 131-12 of the same law that applies to the pre-litigation mediation: 'Upon the request of the parties, the judge will homologate the agreement that they submit to him. The homologation will appertain to non-contentious matters.'

[59]   Compare Section 67 of the Czech Code of Civil Procedure.

[60]   Compare Chapter IV. of said Regulation *Authentic Instruments and Court Settlements* and especially its Article 57: 'A settlement which has been approved by a court in the course of proceedings and is enforceable in the Member State in which it was concluded shall be enforceable in the State addressed under the same conditions as authentic instruments. The court or competent authority of a Member State where a court settlement was approved shall issue, at the request of any interested party, a certificate using the standard form in Annex V to this Regulation.'

sense, the parties seek either to challenge the existence of an agreement or to set it aside.

11.57. Usually the parties rely on traditional contract principles when challenging the mediated agreement and they usually combine this with alternative reasoning. In this sense, the following main arguments are frequently raised by the party looking for review of a mediated agreement:[61]

a) No Meeting of the Minds
b) Misrepresentation
c) Duress
d) Undue Influence
e) Mistake
f) Unconscionability
g) Technical Defenses
h) Other Defenses
i) There have been examples of the disregarding of mediated agreements by judges in the Czech Republic.[62]

IV.2. The Mediation Paradox

11.58. The last kind of interaction between the mediator and judges include cases when a mediator is a party in a litigation procedure that is related to a previous mediation.

11.59. These examples are sometimes called the 'mediation paradox' or 'disputing irony',[63] since the most important aim of mediation is to keep the parties out of the court room. In these cases, even the mediator has to go in front of the judge.

11.60. For example, parties might have problems regarding the mediator's conduct, and this is used as a defense to enforcement claims or it concerns the mediator's ethics or malpractice. The other important group of proceedings concerns fees and costs of mediation. Given the space limitation of this article, these issues cannot be discussed here in further detail, but suffice it to say, an exhaustive scholarship exists on this issue.[64]

---

[61] Compare James Richard Coben; Peter N. Thompson, *supra* note 13, at 77.

[62] In this case, one of the parties sought the dismissal of a mediated agreement on the basis of alleged undue influence. The judge of the first instance complied with it without any investigation. The other party appealed but a decision from the second instance has not been rendered at the time of submission of this paper.

[63] James Richard Coben; Peter N. Thompson, *supra* note 13.

[64] Ibid.

V. Conclusion

11.61. This article sought to answer whether there is some kind of interaction between judges on the one hand, and mediators and mediation on the other. After answering all the above questions we can summarize that there are several relations that usually improve the position and efficiency of mediation.

11.62. In the first stage called pre-mediation, even before the mediation takes place, judges can recruit the suitable cases to be resolved in mediation by judicial referral or at least by informal advice or recommendation.

11.63. Later on, once the mediation procedure has started, quite surprisingly, judges still have a certain influence on mediation. In the case of standard mediation, one can see a dilemma of confidentiality, once the judges demand to know whether there is an ongoing mediation or not. In the case of judicial dispute resolution, one can see a direct involvement of judges in an amicable dispute resolution. This is true whether it is a 'judicial settlement' as an inherent part of litigation or 'judicial mediation' as a separate and relatively independent mediation performed by judges.

11.64. Finally, in the post-mediation phase, judges can improve a mediated agreement by making it enforceable and, at the same time, they can grant an ultimate remedy in the case where the mediated agreement was produced by an error, as in the case of undue influence, misrepresentation or lack of will.

11.65. What does this all mean? Is there any profit regarding the parties in involving judges and mediators in a dispute or is this merely an academic issue? There are certainly several examples of judicial-mediation interaction that are in favour of parties. As illustrated in the example of distributive justice and free access to justice, a judge-mediator interaction can also serve the public interest. In this sense, mediation and judicial structures working together creates a win-win situation, and the ultimate beneficiaries are the parties.

| | |

Summaries

FRA   *[L'approche gagnant-gagnant s'applique-t-elle aux interactions entre le médiateur et le juge ?]*
       Le présent article se consacre aux interactions entre les activités des juges et des médiateurs, en suivant chronologiquement les étapes de la procédure de médiation, et en illustrant dans ses différentes phases les

relations éventuelles entre ces acteurs, fondamentalement très éloignés et très différents, des procédures de résolution des litiges.

Nous nous pencherons d'abord sur la phase précédant la médiation, durant laquelle le juge peut accroître le recours à la médiation par une ordonnance, ou par une instruction moins formelle. Nous examinerons ensuite les interactions entre le médiateur et le juge au cours de la médiation même. Nous terminerons notre tour d'horizon par la phase finale, celle qui succède à la médiation. Le tribunal peut alors soutenir l'accord de médiation, le rendant directement exécutable – en lui donnant son approbation sous la forme d'une conciliation de justice – ou tout au contraire l'annuler pour un quelconque vice matériel ou de forme.

CZE   *[Interakce mezi mediátorem a soudcem: Uplatní se WIN-WIN přístup?]*

Tento článek se věnuje interakci mezi činností soudců a mediátorů, přičemž sleduje chronologický postup mediačního řízení a v jednotlivých fázích ilustruje eventuální vztahy mezi těmito v podstatě velmi vzdálenými a odlišnými aktéry řešícími spory.

Nejprve se zaměřuje na předmediační fázi, během které může soudce zvýšit využívání mediace, a to buď jejím nařízením, nebo méně formálním poučením. Dále tento příspěvek zkoumá interakci mezi soudci a mediátory během samotné mediaci, aby se nakonec věnoval fázi finální, která přichází po ukončení mediace. Tehdy může soud buď podpořit mediační dohodu tím, že ji schválením formou soudního smíru učiní přímo vykonatelnou, nebo ji naopak zruší pro některou formální či materiální vadu.

| | |

POL   *[Interakcja między mediatorem i sędzią: czy znajdzie tu zastosowanie podejście WIN-WIN?]*

Niniejszy artykuł dotyczy interakcji między działalnością sędziów i mediatorów, przy czym bada chronologicznie rozwój postępowania mediacyjnego, ilustrując w poszczególnych fazach ewentualne relacje między tymi, w zasadzie bardzo od siebie odległymi, aktorami rozstrzygającymi spory. Stopniowo analizuje również mediacje orzekane przez sąd, interwencje sędziów w samo postępowanie mediacyjne, badanie porozumień mediacyjnych i ich zatwierdzanie w trybie ugody sądowej.

DEU [*Wechselwirkung zwischen Mediator und Richter: ein Positivsummenspiel?*]

Dieser Beitrag widmet sich dem Wechselspiel zwischen der Tätigkeit von Richtern und Mediatoren, indem er den Ablauf von Mediationsverfahren chronologisch nachzeichnet und in jeder einzelnen Phase die etwaigen Beziehungen zwischen diesen im Grunde sehr disparaten Streitschlichtern erhellt. Der Beitrag konzentriert sich von daher auf die Abfolge der folgenden Schritte: gerichtliche Anordnung der Mediation, gerichtliche Eingriffe ins Mediationsverfahren selbst, Prüfung von Mediationsvereinbarungen sowie deren abschließende Absegnung in Form eines gerichtlichen Vergleichs.

RUS [*Взаимодействие между медиатором и судьей: Будет ли применяться подход WIN-WIN?*]

Данная статья рассматривает взаимодействие между деятельностью судей и медиаторов, причем рассматривает хронологический порядок процедуры медиации, а на отдельных этапах наглядно показывает возможные связи между этими, в принципе, весьма разными актантами, разрешающими споры. Постепенно она переходит к назначению медиации по решению суда, вмешательствам судей непосредственно в процесс медиации, пересмотр соглашений о медиации и их утверждение в виде судебного мирового соглашения.

ESP [*La interacción entre el mediador y el juez: ¿Se aplicará el enfoque WIN-WIN?*]

Este artículo está dedicado a la interacción entre el oficio de los jueces y los mediadores y realiza un seguimiento del orden cronológico del proceso de mediación, ilustrando en cada una de las etapas las relaciones posibles entre estos distanciados actores que resuelven litigios. Sucesivamente se centra en la regulación sobre mediación por el tribunal, las intervenciones de los jueces en el propio procedimiento de mediación, la revisión de los acuerdos de mediación y su aprobación en forma de transacción judicial.

| | |

Ewelina Wyraz

Res Judicata: Differences between International Arbitration and Litigation

Key words:
res judicata | litigation | arbitral award | third-party effect | parallel proceedings

Abstract | *There is no doubt that the principle of res judicata has been recognized and accepted as the 'general principle of international law'. It prevents a party from defending itself twice for the same action. However, certain requirements must be fulfilled before the doctrine of res judicata can be applied. The main aim of this article is to explore the effects of this principle in international arbitration in comparison to litigation, specifically in the case of parallel proceedings. Are there any differences between res judicata in international arbitration and litigation and what kind of legal effects does this principle have for the parties? Moreover, a larger problem arises when an arbitration clause is extended onto third-parties. The third-party effect of an arbitral award has a different scope from that of the res judicata effect. The last section, therefore, contains reflections on third-party effects in international arbitration and litigation in terms of application of the res judicata effect.*

Ewelina Wyraz –
Polish Master's Degree in Law, Ph.D. candidate at the Faculty of Law, University of Silesia in Katowice, Intern at the Notarial Office of Jacek Wieczorek in Tarnowskie Gory, participant of the Willem C. Vis International Commercial Arbitration Moot. She is interested in the international law of succession, particularly in a new European Certificate of Succession.
E-mail address: ewelinawyraz @gmail.com

| | |

'Res judicata changes white to black and black to white,
it makes the crooked straight and the straight crooked'[1]

I. Introduction

12.01. International commercial arbitration is one of the fastest developing branches of law and one of the quickest ways to resolve a conflict between parties. International commercial arbitration did not replace international litigation. It functions beside it as one form of alternative dispute resolution. Arbitration is an 'exceptional service'[2] which serves a different function: as an administration of justice.

12.02. It is clear that the foundations have been laid for a universal culture of arbitration procedure.[3] It recalls a unique relationship of compromise between the tradition of civil law jurisdiction and a typical procedure within the common law systems. However, in the process of the creation of the international model of arbitration, national legal rules that concern this procedure seem to provide an entirely ancillary meaning. Instead, they serve as the source of inspiration from which arbitration draws practical solutions in a free and creative way. Universal principles of arbitration are not a hybrid of international procedures but a unique creation with a different nature.

12.03. One of the most common rules, both in civil law and common law systems, is the principle of *res judicata*, which has been the subject of many interpretations within both the doctrine of procedural law[4] and jurisprudence. The main goal of this general principle is to prevent a different evaluation and different judgment according to the same legal relationship, given the same set of facts and between the same parties.

12.04. Given the paramount significance of this principle in litigation, the question arises whether it is also important in international arbitration and whether all of the assumptions of *res judicata* should apply? Unfortunately, for a few reasons, it cannot simply be an import from litigation.

---

[1] Yuval Sinai, *Reconsidering Res Judicata: A Comparative Perspective*, 21 DUKE JOURNAL OF COMPARATIVE & INTERNATIONAL LAW 353 (2011).

[2] Tomasz Wardyński, *Kilka uwag o istocie arbitrażu, in* KSIĘGA PAMIĄTKOWA 60-LECIA SĄDU ARBITRAŻOWEGO PRZY KRAJOWEJ IZBIE GOSPODARCZEJ W WARSZAWIE, Warszawa: Sąd Arbitrażowy przy Krajowej Izbie Gospodarczej w Warszawie 102, 106 (2010).

[3] Ibid, at 106.

[4] See BIN CHENG, GENERAL PRINCIPLES OF LAW AS APPLIED BY INTERNATIONAL COURTS AND TRIBUNALS, Cambridge: CUP 336 (1953), HERSCH LAUTERPACHT, THE DEVELOPMENT OF INTERNATIONAL LAW BY THE INTERNATIONAL COURT, Cambridge: CUP 19, 325–326 (1958).

12.05. The fundamental objective of international arbitration is 'to provide a final binding resolution of the parties' dispute'[5] and that one manner to achieve such goal is the preclusive effect of the arbitral award. However, in international arbitration *res judicata* displays certain specific features which differ from litigation.

12.06. In discussing the differences between international arbitration and litigation it is crucial to present a general overview of the *res judicata* rule, not only in the systems of common and civil law but also from an international point of view. With this foundation, it should be possible to answer the basic question: What are the policy considerations that underpin the *res judicata* principle in international arbitration, especially in the collision of divergent legally binding arbitral awards?

II. An Overview of the Characteristics of the *Res Judicata* Principle and the Necessary Conditions Which Must Be Fulfilled before Its Application

12.07. The re*s judicata* principle originates from Roman law, especially in its assumption of legal security and the finality of decisions. It is one of the most important principles of judicial economy.[6] Contrary to *litis pendence*, which provides a preventative means of protection of judicial rulings, *res judicata* should be seen as a repressive means of protection of formal legal binding.[7]

12.08. There is a general agreement concerning the basic concepts of preclusion. However, the differences emerge from the details of what this principle provides, especially between civil law and common law systems.

12.09. Generally, *res judicata* causes the positive and negative effects. The positive effect of *res judicata* is that a judgment or award is final and binding between parties and that it should be implemented. The negative effect is that the subject matter of a judgment or award cannot be re-litigated for a second time.

12.10. In common law jurisdictions rules of preclusion are based upon juridical authority, as opposed to the civil law systems where this principle is codified.

---

[5]   II GARY B. BORN, INTERNATIONAL COMMERCIAL ARBITRATION, Austin: Wolters Kluwer 2879, 2880 (2009).

[6]   August Reinisch, *The use and limits of res judicata and lis pendens as procedural tools to avoid conflicting dispute settlement outcomes*, 3(1) THE LAW AND PRACTICE OF INTERNATIONAL COURTS AND TRIBUNALS 37, 43 (2004).

[7]   ANDRZEJ JAKUBECKI, KOMENTARZ DO KODEKSU POSTĘPOWANIA CYWILNEGO, Warszawa: Wolters Kluwer (2012).

12.11. There are specific issues that arise regarding the application of this principle in civil law and common law systems, and these will discussed in the following section. Once this framework has been established, all of the prerequisites can be evaluated with respect to the international forum.[8]

II.1. Civil Law Systems

12.12. The Civil Law doctrine is more restricted than the Common Law in its perspective on *res judicata*. In many countries this principle is codified.[9] Civil Law jurisdictions thus have a broader notion of *res judicata* than common law systems. It expresses the binding nature of a judgment on the parties and mirrors the image of the prohibition upon re-litigating claims which have already been decided. Therefore, all of the effects (positive and negative) of *res judicata* arise.

12.13. Before an action is precluded by a prior judgment, the 'triple identity' requirement must be satisfied. This requirement consists of the judgment involving the same matter and the same issues, and that it relates to the same parties. Two of these provisions constitute objective limits of *res judicata*, while the same parties requirement constitutes a subjective limit of *res judicata*.

II.1.1. The identity of the same matter

12.14. The matter of a litigation is a given section of reality, a set of facts and events. These must confirm the authenticity of claimants` statements and the reality of the maintained law or legal relations, both of which form the claimant`s demand. If this reaching law exists, then the matter of proceedings is this objectively existing law.[10]

12.15. Therefore, the confines of legal procedure and the matter of litigation are determined by acts of claimants' knowledge and will. However, such a solution gives a party an opportunity to modify its demands and the general background of a case during the proceedings. Therefore, 'the thing claimed' should not be interpreted only narrowly[11] but also, and more importantly, 'the matter of a proceeding' should be estimated at the

---

[8] Randy D. Gordon, *Only one kick at the cat: a contextual rubric for evaluating res judicata and collateral estoppel in international commercial arbitration*, 18(2) FLORIDA JOURNAL OF INTERNATIONAL LAW 550 (2006).

[9] See Article 366 of Polish Code of Civil Procedure, §1055 ZPO, Article 480 NCPC, Article 395(5) of Italian Code of Civil Procedure.

[10] ZBIGNIEW RESICH, RES JUDICATA, Warszawa: Wydawn. Prawnicze 50, 54 (1978).

[11] Randy D. Gordon, *supra* note 8, at 555.

moment of judgment, since this moment is crucial for the shape of 'the matter' and only from this moment does it have a *res judicata* effect.[12]

II.1.2. The identity of the same issues

12.16. The identity of *causa petendi* requires that the legal basis for the claim be identical. Therefore, the application of the *res judicata* principle requires the separation of the issue and the matter of such a proceeding. While a set of facts and events of a case decide 'the matter', 'the issue' during the proceedings is a result of perfective, factual arrangements which consist of facts or its units, subsumed by proper regulation.[13]

12.17. Therefore, 'the issue' is a set of facts which characterizes legal relationships between parties and their form, which allows the claimant to formulate the claims against the defendant. However, according to the hypothesis of a regulation, only these facts justify the application of its instruction.

12.18. For 'the matter' the identity of factual and legal basis is required, under the power of the regulation which forms this claim. Otherwise multiple claims exist which depend on multiple regulations.

II.1.3. The identity of the parties

12.19. The subjective limits of *res judicata* relate only to the parties of specific proceedings. However, the legal successors of the original party, as well as a purchaser of a subject of the proceedings, fall within the definition of a 'party'.

12.20. Consequently, we are dealing with the identity of the parties when in both cases the same parties or theirs successors participate, despite a reverse legal role.

12.21. However, it should be emphasized that *res judicata* doesn't exist between the legal persons which participate on the same side.[14]

II.2. Common Law Systems

12.22. Generally, common law systems use two basic preclusion devices: *res judicata* and collateral estoppel.

---

[12] Polish Supreme Court 10 November 1937 I C 482/37.

[13] IV TADEUSZ ŻYZNOWSKI, KODEKS POSTEPOWANIA CYWILNEGO. KOMENTARZ, Warszawa: Wolters Kluwer (2011).

[14] Polish Supreme Court 21 April 1965, I PZ 26/65.

12.23. 'In common law jurisdictions, the doctrine of *res judicata* provides that a judicial judgment accepting or rejecting a particular 'claim' is binding upon the parties to the proceeding that produced the judgment'[15] Whereas, collateral estoppel 'prevents a party from re-litigating, against a counter-party, an issue of fact or law, that was previously contested and decided in a litigation between the same parties'.[16] The main distinction between those two devices amount to their differing emphasis.

12.24. '*Res judicata* acts like a bludgeon, indiscriminately smashing all efforts of a party to re-litigate events that have already been litigated and decided in a prior suit. Collateral estoppel, by contrast, operates like a scalpel, dissecting a lawsuit into its various issues and surgically removing from reconsideration any that have been properly decided in a prior action'.[17]

12.25. For applications of preclusion devices, common law countries require the same parties, cause of action and relief. Common law systems, therefore, introduce one more prerequisite which is needed in the application of the *res judicata* principle – relief.

12.26. Relief is combined with the doctrine of former recovery, which prevents a party 'in whose favor relief was granted from reasserting the same claim in order to obtain further relief, based on the same cause of action'.

12.27. In contrast to civil law systems in common law countries, especially in the English common law system, there are more developed tools for researching the same identity of parties which are based upon the rules of privity and mutuality. The rule of privity stipulates that the parties to the proceedings from which the judgment is derived are the only ones who can take advantage of the preclusive effects, while the rule of mutuality stipulates that the estoppel must be mutual.[18]

II.3. *Res Judicata* in International Law

12.28. In examining the application of *res judicata* it is also necessary to present some conclusions regarding this principle against an international backdrop. This is crucial because international law has some unique features and analytical paradigms devised for use under

---

[15]   GARY B. BORN, *supra* note 5, at 2882.

[16]   Ibid, at 2883.

[17]   JOSEPH W. GLANNON, CIVIL PROCEDURE: EXAMPLES AND EXPLANATIONS, New York: Aspen Law & Business 485 (4th ed. 2001).

[18]   However the rule of mutuality however was rejected in the United States and Ireland, but is still required in Australia and Canada.

domestic litigation that cannot be simply transformed to international application.

12.29. While *res judicata* is uncontroversial as a principle of international law,[19] in comparison with the domestic regulations, one more precondition must be fulfilled before it can be applied. Specifically, a proceeding must be conducted before courts in the international order.

12.30. This means that rules of international *res judicata* relate only to the effect of a judgment of one international tribunal to another international tribunal. Therefore there is no effect of *res judicata* from the decision of a national court as far as the international jurisdiction is concerned.[20] Such an approach follows from the fact that international courts or tribunals are often called upon for the proof of international legality of national courts' rulings.

12.31. As to the remaining conditions,[21] their general assumptions are similar. However as A. Renisch emphasizes 'res judicata [...] usefulness in avoiding the multiplication of international proceedings will [...] depend mainly one the way the identity requirements for their operation are interpreted and applied by international courts and tribunals'.[22]

III. *Res Judicata* in International Arbitration

12.32. One general assumption has to be made when considering the particular differences between international arbitration and litigation. Specifically, arbitration is not tantamount to litigation. Although it is

---

[19]   The existence of *res judicata* rule on international grounds confirm such a judgments e.g. *Pious Fund of the Californias (U.S. v Mex.)*, *Chorzów Factory Case*, *Waste Management v Mexico*, the *UN Administartive Tribunal Case*, *South West Africa Case*, *Cameroon and Nigeria*, *Boundary Dispute between Qatar and Bahrain Case*.

[20]   See e.g. IAN BROWNLIE, PRINCIPLES OF PUBLIC INTERNATIONAL LAW, Oxford: Clarendon Press 50 (6th ed. 2003), also cited in August Reinisch, *supra* note 6, at 58. Such an approach also confirms the ICJ in *Boundary Dispute between Qatar and Bahrain* case, where it is stated 'res judicata is precisely a notion of procedural law intrinsically linked to the form adopted by the procedure and decision concerned and the jurisdictional character of the organ adopting it [...] independently of the name given to it [...]' and *Amco v Indonesia* where it is stated that 'an international tribunal is not bound to follow the result of a national court'.

[21]   There is no doubt that the rest of prerequisites (the same object, grounds and parties) are applicable in the principle of international *res judicata*. This was confirmed e.g. in dissenting opinion of Judge Anzilotti in *Chorzów Factory case*, where he spoke about 'three traditional elements for identification, persona, petitum, causa petendi'. Furthermore in *Polish Postal Service in Danzig case* the PCIJ stated that: 'the doctrine of res judicata [applies when] not only the parties but also the matter of a dispute [are] the same'.

[22]   August Reinisch, *supra* note 6, at 54.

not very apparent, it determines all further considerations. The arbitral proceeding is the result of a contract between the parties and is limited to an arbitral agreement. Its existence depends on it. Parties agree on arbitration not only to avoid the costs and delay of formal court proceedings but sometimes also to avoid winner-take-all awards. As R. Gordon notices, the above 'leads to a system that is at once broader and narrower than litigation'.[23] It is broader because the success of arbitration depends on the satisfaction of the parties with an arbitral award. It is narrower because the scope of the arbitral proceeding is controlled by the agreement. More importantly, the arbitration clause placed in the contract calls for the submission of all disputes between contractual parties that can arise out of or in relation to said contract or its breach. This leads to the conclusion that arbitration is a private institution sustained by the contract, wherein the most important goal is to resolve a dispute between the parties.

12.33. On the contrary, litigation and court judgments provide reliable evidence of interpretation of the rights of citizens under given law, which frequently results in the declaration of rules and principles for future cases. A final and binding conclusion of a given litigation leads to the conversion of a present procedural relationship into a new one, which is based on the respect of the national authorities. This constitutes a strong bond between the parties and national authority which has an obligation to remain alerted to the stability of its own rulings and the stability of the legal situation created as the result of such a judgment. Therefore, the final and binding nature of judgments derives their power from substantial law, or even further, from the abstract regulation which a judgment specifies.[24]

12.34. These two points raise some basic questions, namely: Is *res judicata* needed in international arbitration? And, if the answer is 'yes', then what are the policies of its application?

12.35. If res judicata did not apply to arbitration, parties could safely ignore demands to arbitrate knowing that a default judgment against them would not prejudice their case in a later lawsuit. Losing parties in arbitration could re-litigate their claims in court, and winning parties could attempt to supplement their victories with additional claims and damage theories arising from the same transaction addressed by the arbitrators.[25]

---

[23] Randy D. Gordon, *supra* note 8, at 559.

[24] For further explanation see August Reinisch, *supra* note 6, at 51.

[25] G. Richard Shell, *Res judicata and collateral estoppel effects of commercial arbitration*, 35(623) UCLA LAW REVIEW 664 (1988).

12.36. The above clearly shows that the existence of preclusion devices in arbitration, especially the *res judicata* principle, is crucial for the proper operation of the entire system of international arbitration.

12.37. The answer to the second question seems to be rooted in the issue of procedural economics and the 'economic approach' in starting an arbitration rather than a litigation between the parties.[26] According to the *Miller Brewing Co.* v *Fort Worth Distib. Co. Inc.* case 'Arbitration is ordinarily preferable to litigation, but to allow arbitration on top of the protracted litigation it [...] would be to add insult to injury. The doctrine of res judicata ...[has] probably done more to prevent useless and wasteful litigations than arbitration ever could'.[27]

12.38. Therefore, the necessity of applying the *res judicata* principle to arbitral awards seems to be unchallengeable.[28]

12.39. As it was stated, arbitration – in comparison to litigation – is a unique creation with a different nature. Therefore, the necessary conditions which must be fulfilled before the application of *res judicata* recognized by the common law and civil law systems fall within the characteristic adjustment to international arbitration. However, the recent decision of the British Columbia Supreme Court in *Boxer Capital Corp.* v *JEL Investments Ltd.* held that *res judicata* applies with all its force and effect to arbitration.[29]

III.1. The Identity of the Same Matter

12.40. The requirement of the identity of the same matter is uncontroversial. It relates to the type of relief requested by the claimant. It is directly connected to the grounds of a case, while only the same object based

---

[26] See August Reinisch, *supra* note 6, at 57. An economic approach also confirms an ICC arbitral award from 1982 'The decisions of tribunals progressively create a case law which should be taken into account, because it draws conclusions from economic reality and conforms to the needs of international commerce, to which rules specific to international arbitration, themselves successively elaborated should respond'.

[27] *Miller Brewing Co.* v *Fort Worth Distib. Co. Inc.*, Justicia US Law (Collection of US judgments) http://law.justia.com/cases/federal/appellate-courts/F2/781/494/416126/ (accessed on 28 May 2014).

[28] The application of the *res judicata* principle is prescribed by following international rules e.g.: article 34(6) of the ICC rules – 'Every Award shall be binding on the parties[...]', article 35(1) of UNCITRAL Model Law – 'An arbitral award, irrespective of the county in which it was made, shall be recognized as binding [...]', Article III of New York Convention: 'Each Contracting State shall recognize arbitral award as binding[...].

[29] *Boxer Capital Corp.* v *JEL Investments Ltd.*, What is the effect of res judicata on arbitration? (Article) available at http://www.heintzmanadr.com/arbitaral-award/what-is-the-effect-of-res-judicata-on-arbitration/ (accessed on 28 May 2014).

exactly on the same arguments bares the *res judicata* effect. This approach is the same both in litigation and the arbitration. The most important thing, equally for litigation and arbitration, is the proper determination of the moment from which the rule of *res judicata* takes effect. While in litigation the answer to the above issue is simple, in the arbitration determining the accurate moment is not so easy. Thus, two points become crucial: the moment of publication of an arbitral award and the moment of recognition of an arbitral award by a court.

12.41. As far as the matter under consideration is concerned, with international arbitration the moment crucial for the *res judicata* effect is the moment of the publication of an arbitral award and a formal conclusion of an arbitral proceeding. Therefore, as in litigation, the moment according to which the matter of a proceeding will be defined is the moment of publication of an arbitral award. Such a solution prevents a party from the introduction of slight modifications either in the requested relief or in legal arguments and from seeking their relief on such 'new' basis.

12.42. As A. Reinisch notes while discussing the grounds of establishing the identity of the matter in order to avoid the *res judicata* effect, parties may engage in 'claim splitting'.[30] Such situation may be avoided if the moment of issue of a final and binding arbitral award is defined as tantamount to the moment of its publication.

III.2. The Identity of the Same Issue

12.43. The general assumptions with respect to the identity of the issue of a case are the same as in civil and common law systems. In substance *causa petendi* is related to the legal basis of arbitral proceedings. 'It seeks to ensure that a party cannot have a claim retried once it has been determined, but without precluding the party from advancing a legally distinct cause of action arising from the same set of facts'.[31] Contrary to litigation, however, the problems start with the procedure of making a contract. This is especially true with the choice of jurisdiction proper for the arbitral proceedings, particularly in terms of breaching a contract. The possibility of the choice of jurisdiction for the arbitration is offered to the parties in order to achieve the basic aim of arbitration, namely, the fulfillment of all the interest of the parties. What is more,

---

[30]   August Reinisch, *supra* note 6, at 62. 'Claim splitting' is a situation when a party first sought restitution and in a later litigation it changes and from then on was seeking compensation.

[31]   Vaughan Lowe, *Res judicata and the rule of law in international arbitration*, 8 AFR. J. INT'L & COMP. L. 38 (1996).

jurisdiction, as chosen by the parties embraces all of the disputes which could arise out of a contract. There is no doubt that one of the parties will always be dissatisfied with the governing law in its case.

12.44. Therefore, it is unavoidable for the losing party to seek relief on two or more competitive legal grounds, e.g. one in the international law and another one in BIT.

12.45. The classical examples of such a situation, cited many times in the literature, are the *CME* cases,[32] where the claimant reaches his claims on the basis of different treaties and where different arbitral tribunals handed down two contradictory arbitral awards.

12.46. The above leads to the conclusion that if the request of a party is based on formally different legal grounds (e.g. BIT's, international law, multilateral agreements) it is crucial to examine how far the particular rules are substantively identical. Therefore, searching for the same identity of the grounds in arbitration, a wider approach than in litigation should be applied. However, it cannot limit the parties in reaching their relief.[33]

III.3. The Identity of the Same Parties

12.47. This prerequisite directly links to the arbitral agreement, which identifies the parties to the arbitral proceeding. However, this condition seems to raise difficult questions and in domestic litigations developed some properly functioning tools have been developed which are useful in recognition of the same identity of the parties. Nevertheless, they cannot be simply transposed onto the international arbitration ground. This is because of crucial differences between either common and civil law systems and international law. The differences chiefly manifest in the use of the privity and mutuality assumptions in examination of the same parties to proceedings in common law systems, the rule of universal succession in civil law systems and an 'economic approach'[34] in international law.

---

[32] *CME v. Czech Republic* and *Lauder* v *Czech Republic*, see August Reinisch, *supra* note 6, see also Norah Gallagher *Parallel Proceedings, Res judicata, Lis pendence: Problems and possible solutions*, *in* PERVASIVE PROBLEMS IN INTERNATIONAL ARBITRATION, The Hague: Kluwer Law International 329, 334, 335 (Loukas A. Mistelis, Julian D.M. Lew eds., 2006).

[33] According to the *MOX Plant Case (Ireland* v *United Kingdom)* 'The application of international rules on interpretation of treaties to identical or similar provisions of different treaties may not yield the same results, having regard to, inter alia, differences in the respective contexts, objects and purposes, subsequent practice of parties and travaux préparatoires'.

[34] August Reinisch, *supra* note 6, at 57.

12.48. The search for the same identity of the parties in arbitration requires, therefore, some hybrid solution, which combines all of the above-mentioned methods.

12.49. In 2006, the International Law Association adapted various recommendations related to the application of the *res judicata* rule in international arbitration. Unfortunately, the association refrained from formulating rules regarding the requirement of the identity of parties.[35] They limited their assumptions only to an indication that the applicable law decides the methods of identifying the parties.[36]

12.50. Such a solution cannot be criticized, as the methods of identification in fact depend on the applicable law. However, it seems that in terms of international arbitration, searching for the identity of parties should commence with an 'economic approach', since in most prevalent cases the parties will be connected to one another by some kind of economic bond. How far should the arbitral tribunal examine this relationship? The answer to that question requires some realistic approach, since if the researches were to deepen its cause in situations, the *res judicata* effect will always apply in situations with even a minimum convergence of the parties. Such a situation cannot be accepted because it could lead to the blocking of the whole international arbitration system.

IV. *Res Judicata* Principle and the Third-Party Effect of an Arbitral Award

12.51. The issue of extended effectiveness of an arbitral award is a significant problem, not only on account of the character of an arbitral award but also in its source.

12.52. According to S. Brekoulakis, the current arbitration rules only suggest a legal framework regarding the conclusive effects of the arbitral awards and the third party effect of an arbitral award which 'is refereed to [...] domestic legislation on res judicata.'[37]

12.53. It seems possible to evaluate the extended effectiveness of an arbitral award only in the situation when an arbitration agreement is extended to non-signatories. If it is not, an arbitral award can only affect the parties to the arbitral proceedings. Such a solution, therefore,

---

[35] International Law Association, Toronto Conference International Commercial Arbitration (2006), *Final Report on Lis Pendence and Arbitration*, 34, available at: http://www.ila-hq.org/en/committees/index.cfm/cid/19 (accessed on 28 May 2014).

[36] August Reinisch, *supra* note 6, at 57.

[37] STAVROS L. BREKOULAKIS, THIRD PARTIES IN INTERNATIONAL COMMERCIAL ARBITRATION, Oxford University Press 237, 240 (2010).

corresponds to the rules established in litigation. Thus, the judgment affects only the parties of that specific proceeding. Of course, every rule has its exceptions. Both in common law and civil law systems the *res judicata* effect can be extended to third parties, although such a possibility concerns only limited types of persons, e.g. successors, assignees or privies to one of the parties in action. It all comes to the test of 'community of interests' between parties to the proceedings and third parties. If they are identical, the *res judicata* effect will be extended.

12.54. Such an exception should also apply to international arbitration, while there is a group of crucial third parties that have to remain within the reach of an arbitral tribunal.[38] However, as rightly noticed by S. Brekoulakis, the *res judicata* effect and a third- party effect of an arbitral award should be 'clearly distinguished'[39] as they have a different scope. Thus, *res judicata* covers *petitum* and *causa petendi* of an arbitration, while the third-party effect can only be limited to *petitum*. Therefore, the idea of creating the third-party effect in international arbitration is justified, even though it does not eradicate all difficulties in application. Firstly, according to the nature of arbitral proceedings, third parties, towards whom the binding effect of an arbitral award will apply, should be informed about the proceedings and consent thereto. Secondly, there has to be a source of a third-party effect, which cannot be seen in extended interpretation of an arbitral agreement.

V. Conclusion

12.55. The preceding considerations show that the doctrine of *res judicata* is one of the basic principles of litigation, and more importantly, the importance of their application internationally. Although particular functions differ, the main functions remain the same: to provide a final and binding judgment for a party. As litigation and arbitration are not enemies, they both should gain mutual benefits from its proceedings. There is no doubt that all of the prerequisites which have to be fulfilled before the application of *res judicata* are also crucial for the arbitration. Although they have partially different scope and methods which determine searching for the identity of the matter, issue and parties and depends on the applicable law. Therefore, the application of *res judicata* is one of the most effective tools in the prevention of the existence of parallel proceedings. However, on the grounds of

---

[38] Such persons are e.g. guarantor, surety, subcontractor, architect, engineer (see further Ibid, at 242, 243).

[39] Ibid, at 252.

international law, *res judicata* should be taken into consideration *ex officio*, not only on charge of parties in action.

12.56. Further, in an arbitral proceeding, as it is in litigation, *res judicata* should concern the matter of a case from the moment of the publishing the arbitral award. Thus, not all the issues which arose during a proceeding will bear on the *res judicata* effect. Nevertheless, the above cannot be effective in 'claim splitting'. Therefore, it is important to emphasize that *res judicata* should apply only to the dispositive part of an arbitral award and not to the reasoning which underlies the established solution.

12.57. Moreover, as arbitration constitutes a sign of the parties` autonomy, which gives them competence in determining the rules of a proceeding, in the situation when they refrained from the use of exercising their rights, the general provisions of law should apply. This leads to the conclusion that arbitral institutions should draft more detailed provisions within their procedural rules related to the finality and effectiveness of an arbitral award.

12.58. Finally, there undoubtedly exists a great need to define the arbitral award which qualifies for the *res judicata* effect. Therefore, with the acceptance of the procedural nature of an arbitral award, the *res judicata* effect would dictate that arbitral awards containing final determinations as to the matter of an arbitral proceeding, in an unambiguous manner determined on the legal basis of proceedings and by using all of the methods provided by applicable law, would apply to the parties in the action.

| | |

Summaries

DEU [*Res Judicata: Die Unterschiede zwischen internationalen Schiedsverfahren und Gerichtsverfahren*]
Der Grundsatz der Res Judicata wird zweifelsohne als "allgemeines Prinzip des internationalen Rechts" anerkannt und akzeptiert. Er schützt Parteien davor, sich zweimal gegen dieselbe Klage wehren zu müssen. Freilich geht der Anwendung der Doktrin der Res Judicata die Erfüllung bestimmter Bedingungen voraus. Hauptziel des vorliegenden Beitrags ist es, die Wirkungen dieses Prinzips im internationalen Schiedsverfahren zu analysieren, und zwar im Vergleich zum Gerichtsverfahren, insbesondere in Fällen einer parallelen Verfahrensführung. Gibt es Unterschiede zwischen der rechtskräftigen Entscheidung im internationalen Schiedsverfahren und im Verfahren vor Gerichten? Welche Auswirkungen hat in diesen Fällen die

Anwendung des genannten Prinzips auf die Parteien? Darüber hinaus tun sich erhebliche Probleme dort auf, wo die Wirkungen der Schiedsklausel auf Dritte ausgeweitet wurden: der Umfang, zu dem sich ein Schiedsspruch auf Dritte auswirkt, weicht von den Auswirkungen der Anwendung des Res Judicata-Prinzips ab. Von daher enthält der abschließende Abschnitt dieses Beitrags eine Erwägung hinsichtlich der Auswirkungen der Anwendung des Res Judicata-Prinzips auf Dritte im internationalen Schiedsverfahren bzw. im Verfahren vor den Gerichten.

CZE   [***Res judicata: Rozdíly mezi mezinárodním rozhodčím řízením a řízením před soudy***]

Není pochyb o tom, že zásada res judicata je uznávána a přijímána jako "obecný princip mezinárodního práva". Tento princip chrání stranu před tím, aby se musela dvakrát bránit proti stejné žalobě. Nicméně pro aplikaci doktríny res judicata je nutné naplnit určité podmínky. Hlavním cílem tohoto článku je rozbor účinků tohoto principu v mezinárodním rozhodčím řízení ve srovnání s řízením před soudy, zvláště pak v případech paralelních řízení. Existují rozdíly mezi res judicata v mezinárodním rozhodčím řízení a řízení před soudy? Jaký druh účinků má v těchto případech aplikace daného principu na strany? Velké problémy nadto vznikají v situacích, kdy jsou účinky rozhodčí doložky rozšířeny i na třetí stranu. Rozsah účinků rozhodčího nálezu vůči třetí straně je odlišný od účinků, které má aplikace principu res judicata. Poslední část příspěvku proto obsahuje úvahu ohledně účinků na třetí stranu v mezinárodním rozhodčím řízení a v řízení před soudy ve smyslu aplikace zásady res judicata.

| | |

POL   [***Res judicata: Różnice między postępowaniem sądowym a międzynarodowym postępowaniem arbitrażowym***]

Niniejszy artykuł prezentuje rozważania na temat zagadnienia powagi rzeczy osądzonej w międzynarodowym postępowaniu arbitrażowym. Jego głównym celem jest ukazanie różnic, jakie występują pomiędzy arbitrażem, a postępowaniem sądowym w zakresie zastosowania zasady powagi rzeczy osądzonej.

FRA   [***Res judicata : les différences entre une procédure d'arbitrage international et une procédure judiciaire***]

Le présent article compare les effets de la res judicata dans un arbitrage international et dans une procédure judiciaire, de manière générale puis de manière concrète, en mettant en parallèle des procédures. Son objectif est d'analyser les différences entre la res judicata dans un arbitrage international et dans une procédure judiciaire.

RUS [*Res judicata: Различия между международным арбитражем и судебным процессом*]

В статье анализируются действия принципа res judicata в международном арбитраже по сравнению с судебным процессом, в частности, в параллельных разбирательствах. Основная цель данной статьи заключается в анализе различий между res judicata в международном арбитраже и судебном процессе.

ESP [*Cosa juzgada: las diferencias entre el procedimiento de arbitraje internacional y el proceso ante los tribunales*]

El artículo evalúa los efectos del principio de la cosa juzgada en el arbitraje internacional en comparación con los procesos ante los tribunales, específicamente, los procesos paralelos. El objetivo principal de este artículo es analizar las diferencias entre la cosa juzgada del arbitraje internacional y el proceso ante los tribunales.

| | |

Márton Leó Zaccaria

Equal Employment Disputes: ADR and the Role of the Equal Treatment Authority

Key words:
due process | conflicts of interests | discrimination | employment law | enforcement | EU law | equal treatment | Equal Treatment Authority | Court of Justice of the European Union | fundamental human rights | independence | judicial review | labour court | labour law | settlement

Abstract | *The settlement of employment disputes is a recurring problem in labour law. Such disputes tend to be either debates on collective interests which do not reach the level of litigations or litigations forming the base of judicial proceedings. It is almost impossible to find a 'correct' or at least an appropriate legal solution. The subject of this paper is one of the most problematic fields of this sphere of cases, namely, the employee's fundamental right to equality. To explore this subject, I will analyze legal disputes which originated from employment discrimination. In connection with discrimination cases it also is necessary to address the Equal Treatment Authority, a Hungarian independent administrative body, since it has a special role in this system. This role exists because the Equal Treatment Authority is not a court, nor is it the venue of alternative methods of dispute resolutions. Rather it is an independent administrative body whose exclusive scope is to judge employees' discrimination claims. This study examines the main questions of discrimination cases by interpreting concrete cases and comparing them with the effectiveness of the courts' method. In this comparison, there is an emphasis on the most typical cases as well as the cases which are the most difficult to resolve. Finally, I try to answer the question of whether this independent authority can be the real and effective venue of resolving employment legal disputes, instead of or alongside the judicial enforcement of claims.*

Dr. Márton Leó Zaccaria (Assistant Lecturer, University of Debrecen, Faculty of Law, Department of Agricultural Law, Environmental Law and Labour Law) graduated from the University of Debrecen Faculty of Law in 2010 as a jurist. After his studies he immediately started work at the Faculty of Law in Debrecen as a full-time PhD student in the field of labour law. He has already published several independent publications in Hungarian and in English mostly in connection with equal employment but in connection with other topics as well. Since 1st September he has worked as an assistant lecturer. He became a member of the Hungarian EU OSH (occupational safety and workplace health) research group this April, and he is also member of the Hungarian Labour Law Association.
e-mail: zaccaria.marton @law.unideb.hu

Czech (& Central European) Yearbook of Arbitration

| | |

I. Introduction

13.01. In the world of labour law every day conflicts, conflicts of interests, and disputes are taken into consideration. The objects and settlements of the disputes may be of different kinds, but in their essence they are typical in connection with employment relationships. The ways of settling disputes are different in their effectiveness, outcomes and rules of procedure, but the conduct of the parties decisively influences their outcomes. In the structure of individual and collective labour, conflicts of interests are frequent, and within these main fields any important point of the rules may be the subject of a labour law dispute. Hungarian law specifies the main forms and interoperability of dispute settlement, but more generally in the legal world, judicial proceedings and judicial review are the most common forms.[1]

13.02. In employment relationships the problem of disputes and their settlement are rather dangerous and sensitive.[2] There are several reasons for this, which are the consequences of the special legal nature of the employment relationship and the attitude of labour law. Basically, there is a private law-like legal relationship based on a private law-like contract between the employer and the employee. Because of the legal cogencies and the parties' opposite status one cannot say that there is a clear private law legal relationship between them. Furthermore, the parties' legal relationship is established for long term and continuous fulfilment, consisting of work and paying wages as remuneration. This leads the employee into a state of dependence and this structure forms the basis of the opposite legal positions, mentioned above. Such relationships should be based on trust in the other party regarding the personal character of the performance of work. However, in practice the type of employment relationships often forms an 'inescapable path'; since it is not clear that the parties' trust in each other is appropriate even if the parties' personal trust is taken into consideration by several aspects of labour law regulation.

13.03. Diverging conflicts and methods of dispute resolution are typical of the world of collective labour law and industrial relations, but altogether these attributes can be traceable to the special structure of the employment relationship. In connection with employment relationships we can speak about interest debates, confrontation of interests, rather than about concrete legal disputes. However, it is not

---

[1] See for typical forms: Act III of 1952 on civil procedure, Act I of 2012 on the Labour Code.

[2] Furthermore, the great quantity of latency of employment conflicts causes further problems, because the employees often are afraid to enforce their claims in any way, leaving aside the problem that they are not necessarily aware of their rights and possibilities.

exclusively true that within the frames of these special relations it is the labour court that finally makes the decision on important issues.

13.04. The subject of the present study is the effectiveness of the dispute resolution method, independent from the court, and typical in the special field of labour law. In discrimination cases the employees can turn to the Equal Treatment Authority (the 'Authority' or 'EBH'), rather than having to turn exclusively to the court. The Authority is an independent administrative body with an administrative procedure and its competence is judging cases of discrimination. This process can be regarded as a unique form of dispute settlement because the Authority's procedure can be pending independently of the court's procedure. This is true even if in many cases the joint application of the two procedures is recommended because of the difference in the applicable legal consequences. In what follows, I focus on the main cases resolved by the Authority, emphasizing their effectiveness and correctness in the legal sense. When necessary I refer to the deviations from the courts' procedure, emphasizing the negative and positive points of the method of the Authority's dispute settlements in discrimination cases. For reasons of space constraints, my study focuses on the specific issues related to the principle of equal pay for equal work, and establishing and terminating an employment relationship, as these types of disputes are complex and occur with great frequency.[3]

II. The Role of the Equal Treatment Authority in the Field of the Enforcement of Employee Law

13.05. The Equal Treatment Authority was established in Hungary in order to supply an easier legal remedy for the general public.[4] Although it is not a judicial forum, it can provide a real legal remedy to the complainants in several types of cases. This possibility itself does not result in the real termination of the injurious situation or in the prevention of future discrimination. However, the dispute settlement can be more effective because cases may be processed to the Authority parallel with court

---

[3]   Of course, similar attention should be paid to the distinction between direct and indirect discrimination, and to the conclusion of fact of harassment and victimization, but these could each be the subject of another study entirely. Consequently this study deals with interpreting the most important questions from the standpoint of labour law.

[4]   This principle was emphasized in the first directives, which were born in the middle of the 1970s, mainly because the employment policy of the European Union needed a comprehensive reform. See regarding the regulative aspect of this question: József Hajdú, *A szociális dimenzió fogalma és normatív szabályozásának fejlődése az Európai Unióban*, 1(3) EURÓPAI JOG 17, 17–22 (2001).

procedures but the Authority cures the legal problems only in the administrative way. The history of the Authority shows that due process is easier and less expensive, and since it is an easier way, persons who have suffered discrimination and of course employees as well, prefer to turn to the Authority even if labour law infringements cannot be remedied by the Authority's resolutions. Considering that this is a special, delicate situation of the law generally and labour law specifically, it is perhaps understandable that since the Equal Treatment Authority started operation, it has attracted such cases from the courts[5]. One of the reasons why the authority has managed to build an undoubtedly more effective system of legal remedy than the courts is that it must supply appropriate legal remedy to the complainants according to its function. Its status as a quasi-legitimate organization also contributes to this effectiveness. Taking into consideration the norms of EU law more definitely in order to build a legal protective system in Hungary as effectively as possible is traceable to this circumstance.

III. Enforcing the Principle of Equal Pay for Equal Work

13.06. In one case[6] regarding wages, the Authority resolved that the basis of a company's new benchmarking system was that the performance requirements could be fulfilled to 100% only if at least 85% was the presence of the given employees in the actual period.[7] So leaving aside paid annual leave or holiday and other justified absences, any kind of absences could have the result that the employee was not able to fulfil the modified requirement set even if they otherwise performed over the required maximum. This way the employees lost additional remuneration that they could not receive any other way, so they lost the possibility of performance at 100%. According to the employers, they were trying to select and sanction the lazy employees not those who were absent legally and were not avoiding work. But the real content of this measure affected the complainant employees extremely negatively.[8] Such a measure discriminates against those whose absence

---

[5] From 2006 the number of judgments made by the Curia of Hungary (formerly Hungarian Supreme Court) in cases in connection with the principle of equal treatment is below 100, while the amount of resolutions of the Authority is over 200.

[6] Resolution No. 700/2007. (EBH).

[7] So they had to be at work 85% of the prescribed time.

[8] In practice it is rather difficult to examine the realization of indirect discrimination regarding remuneration, mainly because rates often are difficult to be measured. See: Sandra Fredman, *Reforming Equal Pay Laws*, 37(3) INDUSTRIAL L.J. 193, 202–204. (2008).

occurred because of their state of health, family situation or because of their children. The complainant was put into this situation as a consequence of the rule modification. The employer cited economic reasons for this modification according to which both the employee's and the employer's performance may increase with less absence. But the Authority stated that the economic reason cited by the employer was not justified and could not be the base of discrimination, as it is beyond doubt that it affects only certain groups. If someone is absent from work with the real intention of skipping work, the employer can sanction individually at their own discretion, even terminating the employment relationship in justified cases. Regarding performance pay, the requirement of equal treatment must be fulfilled if the reason for differentiation between employees is a personal circumstance which has nothing to do with the employee's work performance. It must be added that it is clear that the employer basically introduced new requirements with the aim of sanction. It is useless for the employer to argue that they would decrease future absences, since on the one hand this means it is not appropriate for this purpose, and on the other hand it is prohibited to connect the feasibility of performance to personal circumstances so openly and directly. It is also the moral of this case that the fulfilment of the requirement of equal pay is really difficult from the employer's view, and because of the special guarantee rules of performance pay, special attention should be paid to this field as well.

13.07. The principle of equal pay for equal work was likewise not infringed in another case put before the Authority.[9] As a consequence of the employer's annual wage increase, the complainant employee received a significantly smaller increase than the others in a comparable situation. This employee was both a mother and a trade union functionary. However, the cause of the difference could not be traced to her protected attributes but rather to the announced aspects of pay increase. In the case in question the employer defined a variety of factors that would impact a wage increase including work performance before the current year, the number of absences, number of disciplinary warnings or sanctions, or any violation of obligations in connection with working activity. On this basis it was deemed justified that the complainant received a lower increase, since she was absent more and received several disciplinary sanctions. According to the complainant the cause of the difference arose exclusively from her position in the Trade Union and her absences were related to her motherhood. The Authority declared that there was no connection between the trade

---

9   Resolution No. 100/2011. (EBH).

union position and the measure of pay increase since the employer could justify it statistically. Indeed, they determined that the complainant had committed several breaches of duty so serious that they could have been cause for dismissal according to the collective agreement in force. It was clear that there was no connection between the lack of pay increase and the employee's position or family situation. Practically, she got less pay for equal work, but it was justified and proportionately differentiated on the basis of the special circumstances, mainly the quality of work.[10] In connection with her motherhood and absences she could have referred to it as cause of indirect discrimination more successfully regarding the resolution No. 700/2007 interpreted above. However, the complainant did not sustain that her motherhood was in connection with the disadvantage caused by the lower pay rise – in contrast to the resolution of No. 700/2007. The measure of absences was not the exclusive cause of the salary increase, so to treat it as quasi-evidence could have been a mistake. But the complainant did not mention this connection.

13.08. In summary regarding the effectiveness of resolutions on employees' complaints due to supposed or real infringement of the principle of equal pay for equal work or work of equal value it is clear that the Authority's resolution is correct in most of these types of disputes and that the Authority intends to apply the relevant rules broadening. All of this results in more effective dispute settlement. However, the great disadvantage of these procedures when comparing them with labour courts is that the Authority cannot adjudicate the unequal pay or its difference, since it is beyond its competence. This is the case even if the Authority agrees with the employee who suffered discrimination. Of course, the courts are entitled to adjudicate, but their resolutions in cases of the same content are not always identical with the above introduced resolutions. At the same time, the sanctions[11] that can be

---

[10] The legal situation could have been different if the complainant referred to other employees having committed the same number of serious infringements, and their wages remained unchanged or had risen at a greater extent. However, this would have been baseless in this situation, because the employee's pay rise among those who committed serious infringement was even larger than the average. There was only one employee in a similar situation who got significantly higher pay, but their work position was modified in the reference period, which caused a wage increase over the annual pay raise.

[11] According to Article 16. § paragraph (1) of Act CXXV of 2003 on equal treatment and the promotion of equal opportunities, sanctions can consist of the following: an order that the situation constituting a violation of law be eliminated, a prohibition on the further continuation of the conduct constituting a violation of law, a publication of the EBH's decision establishing the violation of law, the imposition of a fine, or the application of a legal consequence determined in a special act.

applied by the Authority may force the employers to take the Authority's resolutions seriously, but this is a problem beyond the issue of the Authority's legal interpretation. The system of legal protection for employees could be more effective if the courts would take on the most important elements of the Authority's legal interpretation, combining the necessary professional resolutions on cases and applying the effective legal consequences.

IV. Possible Change of Social Attitude in Connection with Cases of Establishing an Employment Relationship

13.09. The EBH also typically hears discrimination cases in connection with the establishment of an employment relationship and the preceding procedures such as job advertisements and interviews.[12] In most of these cases discrimination does not appear independently, based on a concrete attribute, but rather appears as humiliating or inappropriate treatment, and the employer's attitude forms the basis of discrimination. Seemingly, the employer's procedures are not against the law. Often the employer does not even know that there are legally forbidden questions or how employers should correspond to the requirements of equal treatment during such a procedure.[13] A dispute settlement in connection with this cannot be effective enough, since cases of discrimination rarely get to the procedure phase. Likewise, the legal consequences applied during the given procedure such as a grievance fee or a fine cannot be a real legal remedy, since the Authority or the court cannot force the employer to establish an employment relationship.

13.10. In resolution No. 219/2012. the Authority made important statements involving all of these significant questions in connection with the case and its argument seems to be correct. The Authority declared that an agency – dealing with manpower-lease[14] – committed age

---

[12] Concerning the interpretation of these aspects of labour law see: Tamás Gyulavári, *Egyenlők és egyenlőbbek*, 6(2) HUMÁN SZALDÓ 34, 34–38 (2009).

[13] Júlia Koltai, *A munkáltatók kiválasztással kapcsolatos szempontjai, in* A MUNKÁLTATÓK MUNKAVÁLLALÓI KIVÁLASZTÁSI GYAKORLATA A DISZKRIMINÁCIÓ TÜKRÉBEN, Budapest: Egyenlő Bánádmód Hatásóság 20–28 (Ágó Anna; Fris E. Kata (eds), 2013), available at: http://www.egyenlobanasmod.hu/tamop/data/2.2_kivalgyak_majus18.pdf (accessed on 27 November 2014).

[14] Manpower-lease means agency work at all but agency work is a broader concept and manpower-lease captures the essence of the attributes of this form of atypical employment relationship between the lender, the borrower and the employee.

discrimination, because they refused to interview based on merit and to consider the application of the applicant/complainant[15] . This was in spite of the fact that the complainant complied with the only real requirement, which was knowledge of the English language. The applicant was informed by the agency that they were refused because of age and would not be accepted for any of the jobs, even though the condition of age was not marked in connection with the jobs, and the only reason of refusal was the applicant's age. The Authority emphasized that this agency had to pay special attention when examining the applicants' and consider the potential employees' suitability and ability The court further suggested that it would be useful to interview them personally – even if the applicant was really incompetent to fill a position because of their age or any other circumstances. When the possibility of filling a position has emerged in connection with a different position, the employer cannot say if someone is unsuitable for that second position, as it is uncertain that they will be incompetent for all other jobs.[16]

13.11. It is interesting that the employer did not deny that the action was discriminatory. The employer referred to the foreign partner-employer's requirements as cause of indirect justification since they set the conditions of application. The Authority could not accept these arguments as legal cause of justification, but at the same time the Authority examined whether the directives themselves (age as a condition of a position) defined by the foreign partner could be legal in the given case. The agency referred to the belief that in general, applicants under 35 were more suitable for the job[17] than those over 35. The main reason was the continuous physical and mental exertion required for the position. The employer, in emphasizing general experiences in connection with the criterion did not intend to discriminate against applicants over 35, but intended to prevent them from failure, being overburden, and unsuccessful. The employer tried to justify this with statistical data, but ultimately it was unsuccessful. It should be added that the petitioner applicant had foreign work experience and therefore it would be justified to examine their

---

[15]   To be more precise: to outsource the applicant.

[16]   Special requirements for job suitability were not published. See: points 32–33 of the CJEU Judgment of 19 April 2012, C-415/10, *Galina Mesiter* v *Speech Design Carrier Systems GmbH* [2012] not yet published. If someone states authentically that they fulfil the requirements of the job and the employer does not have any other reason not to accept the application of this applicant, it is a case of discrimination.

[17]   This job was as a server on a cruise ship.

competence. It is clear that the Authority did not accept this as legal justification. Even if it had been justified that younger people were more suitable for the actual position, they could not refuse older applicants without an aptitude test, mainly because with knowledge of foreign languages and work experiences, the applicant could certainly have been competent for the job.[18]

13.12. One conclusion of the above analyzed example case is that it is not necessarily the Authority's fault if the employment discrimination suffered by the employee during the establishment of an employment relationship is not remedied and remains without real legal consequences. The courts cannot help the Authority in this question because the sphere of applicable legal consequences is rather narrow. At the same time it is positive that employees' interests are in the centre of the dispute settlement arranged by the Authority in most cases, since discrimination suffered in connection with a job advertisement or a job interview can only be remedied with difficulty or not at all.[19] Furthermore, the Equal Treatment Advisory Body made a commitment[20] to address this problem,[21] but unfortunately this promise[22] has not been fulfilled in practice. At the same time in the respect of dispute settlements and prevention of disputes, the Authority's procedure is very important because creating and publishing resolutions are of high importance. They can shape social attitudes, since this kind of legal dispute arise every day. Although publishing texts is not enough, the situation would be more extreme if the Authority would not pay special attention to such cases.[23]

---

[18] The Authority made similar legal consequences in the following cases: Resolutions No. 79/2013., 176/2012., 71/2012., 123/2011., 1087/2011., 281/2010., 160/2010., 69/2010., 1144/2010., 819/2008., 43/2009., 1023/2009, 419/2008., 94/2008., 595/2008., 819/2008., 271/2007., 310/2007., 569/2006., 704/2007., 1/2007., 310/2007., 564/2006., 180/2006., 314/2006., 295/2006. (EBH).

[19] In connection with the effectiveness of enforcement in discrimination cases, ee: Tamás Gyulavári, *Egy próbaper története*, 2(4) FUNDAMENTUM 155, 155–158 (1998) and Tamás Gyulavári, *Próbaper a diszkriminatív álláshirdetések ellen*, 42(4) MUNKAÜGYI SZEMLE 17, 17–19 (1998). The situation is not much better since the establishment of the new regulation.

[20] Commitment is a stance with legal content of the Equal Treatment Advisory Body.

[21] Commitment No. 1/2007. TT. of the Equal Treatment Advisory Body on the possible questions allowed during a job-interview.

[22] For example, guidelines prohibit illegal and discriminative questions mandate the correct behaviour of the employer, the notification of the use of sensitive personal data etc.

[23] In my opinion, issues of a job advertisement, job or carrier tender are more prominent and attract more attention than issues surrounding unequal pay. No one is interested in

V. The Most Dangerous Field – Termination of the Employment Relationship

13.13. From time to time, labour law disputes emerge where employment was terminated by the employer only because of the employee's age[24] while their working activity or attitude was not criticized at all. Similar cases emerge where the legal relationship was not even established because of the employee's age.[25] It is an existing phenomenon in Hungarian law as well, but a unified practice for addressing it does not exist at either the administrative or the court level.[26] However, in the case-law of the Court of Justice of the European Union (CJEU) several such cases have already emerged. These cases typically refer to Council Directive 2000/78/EC, regarding discrimination based on age in connection with employment, interpreting prohibitions and exceptions based on it.

13.14. One noteworthy case involved the employer giving notice to the employee because of the employee being a representative and the employee expressed an opposite opinion to the employer's and this led to discrimination.[27] What is more the employee did it in their function for the other employees' sake, after the employer created impossible working conditions and tried to influence the workplace atmosphere at the employee's expense. Finally, the employer gave notice to the employee and the Authority stated that the employer infringed the requirement of equal treatment. In most cases where termination of the legal employment relationship based on opinion, conviction is typical, but it is clear from several of the Authority's resolutions that in this case it cannot be a one-time, occasional opinion, but settled belief or conviction. It is not enough if this opinion only differs from others, or perhaps from the employer's opinion. It would result in a rather narrow interpretation if termination based only on opinions indirectly connected with the employment relationship would be discriminatory. However, the Authority intends to keep the labour law resolutions of this kind of cases within sensible and definite frames. There are several cases in which the Equal Treatment Authority determined that

such a problem beyond the employment organization, and sometimes even the involved person does not know that they have been discriminated against by their employer referring to any of their protected attributes.

[24] In connection with this phenomenon see: Dagmar Schiek, *Age Discrimination Before the ECJ – Conceptual and Theoretical Issues*, 48(3) COMMON MARKET LAW REVIEW 777, 777–799 (2011).

[25] Resolution No. 219/2012. (EBH).

[26] This is in spite of the fact that the number of cases of such a subject is rather high.

[27] Resolution No. 197/2012. (EBH).

discrimination occurred on the basis that the employer baselessly infringed the employee's human dignity[28] by typically humiliating disciplinary or other sanctions, and then finally gave notice to the employee. In such cases because of the special labour law quantity of the sanctions it is worth examining the procedure of the court and the Authority.[29] The negative outcome of such cases is heightened by the fact that an injury of human dignity means the infringement of fundamental human rights on the employee's side.

13.15. In another case[30] the employer exposed the requirement of equal treatment to danger while practising the right to notice regarding a 'secondary' or 'hidden' cause of the circumstance by which the employer commits discrimination as a result of dismissal. The employee breached their obligation since they did not fulfil certain educational requirements and by exhibiting behavioural problems which can be the cause of dismissal. Namely, the employee used inappropriate tone, had several debates with colleagues, and once fell asleep on duty. However, the complainant was of Romani origin and taking into consideration all circumstances of the case it was assumed that the latter was the real cause of termination. Termination on the basis of breaching obligations may be discriminatory if among employees in a comparable situation only one of the employees is given notice as a sanction for the same or similarly serious infringement. In this case the requirement of equal treatment was not violated but this example shows clearly that special attention should be paid to prohibition of discrimination in the case of several possible causes of termination, even if the employee refers to it lacking any legal ground in a given case. Consequently, in connection with termination of the employment relationship the employer can commit discrimination in several ways, and without consequence in the legal practice it is difficult to prevent this kind of arbitrary employer behaviour. According to the Authority, termination of the legal relationship had an objective legal cause which had a connection with the employment relationship. In other words, the employer did not act with discrimination or with harassment. The issue of harassment is not so clear.[31] Furthermore, I would like to point out two interesting

---

[28] Resolution No. 1/2008. (EBH).

[29] Resolution No. 245/2012. (EBH).

[30] Resolution No. 719/2007. (EBH).

[31] Probably the causes were the employee's ethnic origin. However, another issue was that the complainant recognized a crime committed by the manager and the manager knew about it, so the employee was subject to harassment. However the EBH ultimately

circumstances. The complainant did not have the necessary qualification for the work position in the first place, and because of their repeated breaches of obligation the superior essentially told the employee that they would either give notice freely or would be dismissed. It is clear that several circumstances have emerged in the case from which basis discrimination cannot be excluded, but is is also clear that between these circumstances and the suffered disadvantage – termination – there is no cause and effect relationship.[32]

13.16. The Authority also did not judge the employer's procedure discriminative in a case[33] where the employer did not extend a disabled employee's fixed term employment contract. The employee did not fulfil an obligation to cooperate, and was definitely applied as a substitute, so in the employer's opinion the employee did not have the right to extend the legal relationship or to be put into another position. In this context the complainant argued that the employment relationship was not extended because of their disability, but the employer indicated at the hearing that they did not even know about the disability. The moral of this case is clear: if the employee's employment relationship terminates because of the expiration of definite time spelled out in the contract, and the legal relationship is not extended it is not discriminatory if the cause of future non-application is not the employee's protected attribute.

13.17. It is probable that the effectiveness of dispute resolution is smallest in this field, since the legal disputes on unfair dismissal of the employment relationship are difficult to judge. In Hungarian law there are specially named criteria requiring that the employer's dismissal comply with the requirements of equal treatment,[34] but it seems that the employees' interests do not receive enough emphasis from the point of view of the application of possible legal consequences.

---

judged the harassment established because of the opposite statements.

[32] Similarly to the above interpreted three cases, the Authority has declared that the dismissal was discriminatory in the following resolutions: 447/2013., 135/2013., 543/2010., 43/2012., 464/2012., 245/2012., 353/2011., 95/2011., 151/2011., 122/2010., 303/2009., 694/2009., 1068/2009., 1260/2008., 1201/2008., 1/2008., 516/2007., 142/2007., 307/2006., 404/2006., and one more resolution of 2005 which was published without an official number.

[33] Resolution No. 78/2007. (EBH).

[34] Labour Commitment No. 95 of Curia of Hungary (MK 95.).

VI. The Experiences of Equality Bodies in Europe – Equal Pay and Its Difficulties in Dispute Resolution[35]

13.18. The oft-cited field of the principle of equal treatment[36] that of judging equal pay for equal work or work of equal value is a good example of the kind of difficulties the authorities that enforce the principle of equal treatment have during dispute settlements. After the above description and interpretation of the Hungarian situation, I now turn to the European practice and exercise to make clear the difficulties of judging such cases.

13.19. Basically, the principle of equal pay should be interpreted as a means to prohibit gender discrimination. The differences between the different genders' wages are extremely high in Europe[37] and they do not show any descending trends. At the same time, as it was interpreted in section III., discrimination as consequence of the violation of the principle of equal pay does not only encumber female employees, so this field is a good example for the origins of principle of equal treatment regarding gender discrimination.

13.20. In general it is a problematic case where the employee's equality of pay is injured, and differentiated by the employer referring to several protected attributes at the same time, for example gender and disability.[38] To make a correct judgment is rather difficult, because the proceeding authority has to pay attention to all protected attributes. They have to examine whether discrimination occurred, and if so, on which protected attributes it was based. It is not enough to examine whether discrimination occurred referring to one protected attribute, because any of them – or more than one – may be the basis of discrimination.

13.21. Generally, it may cause difficulty that the proceeding authority explores the real cause of discrimination even if it would be important to settle the legal dispute effectively permanently.[39] According to the Equality Authority of Ireland stereotypes focusing on differences between

---

[35] The basis of this section is information and researches on the website equinet.europa.org. From this website, the activity of all European organizations which enforce the equal treatment can be overviewed.

[36] *Equal Pay for Equal Work and Work of Equal Value: The Experience of Equality Bodies* (an Equinet report on gender equality), available at: http://www.equineteurope.org/Equal-Pay-the-experience-of (accessed on 9 July 2014), 8.

[37] Ibid, at 8–10.

[38] Ibid, at 7.

[39] Let us think of the parties' later deteriorated relationship.

genders result in women's discrimination that makes their situation in the labour market difficult. They can easily get into disadvantageous situations even if there are possibilities for them to engage in work.[40] The employers already have an aspect which results in discrimination and it is built into their personnel policy either in the field of conditions of employment or payment. It is a very serious problem and may weaken the efficiency of settlement of discrimination disputes. What is more, it is such a typical problem, which means it is not clear that it can be solved by law.

13.22. It seems that these disputes often could be prevented if the same job and working conditions would be ensured for the groups with protected attributes (in this case for women).[41] Law and economic-social circumstances should establish such a frame, pushing the labour market into the direction free from discrimination. Instead of settling disputes it would be better to prevent them.[42]

13.23. A precondition for both prevention and effective interference is that parties have information, and materials (mainly on the employees' side) describing the principle of equal treatment and the requirement of equal pay.[43] This is important so that employees can realize when infringements occur and can take a stand against them, and so that employers would know their conditions and limits. In most of the cases these deficiencies can be observed. The Austrian and the Portuguese solutions of widely disseminating information by authorities seem to be correct, but for changing the employers' attitude these actions do not seem to be enough.[44]

13.24. In most cases – and there are Hungarian examples of this as well – the uncertainty of concepts results in a dispute. The French and Portuguese authorities have an interesting solution in the form of a method of job-evaluation, which applies an objective system to questions of equal work or work of equal value. This decreases the number of discrimination cases and turns attention to the fact that the employers often use discriminatory solutions involuntarily.[45] It could be effective alternative dispute settlement if the employer would keep

---

[40] *Supra* note 36, at 7.

[41] Ibid, at 8.

[42] In a given debate or problem, it is also worth thinking about that whether it would be possible to leave out the legal or at least the judicial way. The Authority's procedure, which is the object of this study, seems to be an obvious solution in spite of its difficulties and controversies.

[43] *Supra* note 36, at 18.

[44] Ibid, at 23–25.

[45] Ibid, at 18 and 25–27.

these aspects in mind and would consult with the employees or their representatives about them. This would be a typical case of dispute prevention, but I think it could also be used after the discrimination occurred. The Application of different monitoring and examination methods could also be an effective solution. Essentially, it would provide indirect help to enforce the principle for employees (German Federal Anti Discrimination Agency or FADA).[46]

13.25. Because of the above mentioned informational asymmetry, the Hungarian Authority's dispute settlement is not effective enough as could be seen in the Hungarian cases. Even if the authorities decide carefully, they cannot examine enough cases because the employees cannot or do not dare to enforce their claims. From this point of view the courts' procedure does not necessarily seem more effective. This is true for all complaints concerning discrimination, not only for cases of infringement of the principle of equal pay for equal work. Furthermore, there are clearly some special difficulties in procedures and the division of competences in connection with authorities' independence or lack of it.[47] Both the legislator and the judicature should pay more attention to these special forms of procedure and method, since if they could operate effectively, they could reach the same level of importance as judicial proceedings. This could be a profound change in how legal systems are approached. In terms of the applied legal consequences, the judicial procedure has more advantages for the employees from many points of view. In order to prevent conflicts and to settle them in a humane way, it would be the best for both the employee and the employer if these discrimination cases would not occur at all. If they do occur, it would be best if they could be resolved in-house, or with the help of an authority, but not by long, expensive, often humiliating judicial proceedings.

VII. Conclusion

13.26. To sum up, it is appropriate that the Equal Treatment Authority – or other European authorities with similar competences – serve as a scene of dispute settlements based on employment discrimination. Procedures before these institutions offer a simple, quick, obvious possibility on the employees' side and, importantly, in its resolutions the Authority often espouses the protection of employees' interests and rights. Both the Equal Treatment Authority and the courts should not

---

[46] Ibid, at 31–32.
[47] Ibid, at 20.

only interpret and apply but develop the content and procedural methods of Hungarian equality law. Of course, to abolish discrimination from societies is not the Authorities' or courts' task, but they have an important role. Because of the employees' vulnerability, in the world of work, this form of dispute settlement is often more effective than the courts' procedure and must be taken seriously.

| | |

Summaries

DEU [*Streitigkeiten wg. der Gleichbehandlung im Beruf: alternative Streitschlichtung und die Aufgabe der Schlichtungsorgane hinsichtlich der Gleichbehandlung*]

Die Entscheidung arbeitsrechtlicher Streitigkeiten ist im Arbeitsrecht ein Evergreen. Diese Streitigkeiten tendieren entweder dazu, eine Sache von allgemeinem Interesse zu behandeln, die nicht an das Niveau gängiger zivilrechtlicher Streitigkeiten heranreicht, oder als zivilrechtliche Streitigkeiten in den Zuständigkeitsbereich der allgemeinen Gerichte zu fallen. Es ist praktisch unmöglich, die "richtige" oder doch wenigstens eine angemessene juristische Lösung zu finden. Gegenstand des vorliegenden Artikels ist eine der problematischsten Fragen in diesem Bereich der Streitschlichtung überhaupt, nämlich das Grundrecht von Arbeitnehmern auf Gleichbehandlung. Um diesen Themenkreis aufzuarbeiten, analysiert man rechtliche Streitigkeiten, die aus einer behaupteten Diskriminierung am Arbeitsplatz herrühren. In Verbindung mit diesen Diskriminierungsfällen muss die Gleichberechtigungsstelle in Ungarn angesprochen werden: eine unabhängige Verwaltungsbehörde, die innerhalb des ungarischen Systems eine Sonderrolle spielt - dies im Zusammenhang damit, dass es sich nicht um ein Gericht, aber eben auch nicht um eine Stelle zur außergerichtlichen Streitbeilegung handelt. Vielmehr handelt es sich um eine unabhängige Verwaltungsbehörde, die ausschließlich damit befasst ist, Ansprüche wg. einer behaupteten Arbeitnehmerdiskriminierung zu prüfen. Die vorliegende Studie analysiert die wichtigsten Fragen im Zusammenhang mit Diskriminierungsfällen, indem sie konkrete Fälle seziert und mit der Effektivität von Gerichtsverfahren vergleicht. Im Rahmen dieses Vergleichs hebt man sowohl die typischsten Fälle hervor als auch Fälle, in denen sich die Entscheidung überaus kompliziert gestaltete. Abschließend unternimmt man den Versuch die Frage zu beantworten, ob diese unabhängige Stelle wirklich als vollwertiges und effektives Forum für die Entscheidung arbeitsrechtlicher Streitigkeiten fungieren kann, welches die rechtliche Streitbeilegung zu ersetzen bzw. eine Alternative zu selbiger darzustellen in der Lage ist.

CZE   **[*Spory ohledně rovného zacházení v zaměstnání: ADR a úloha orgánu rozhodujícího spory ohledně rovného zacházení*]**
Rozhodování pracovněprávních sporů je opakujícím se problémem pracovního práva. Tyto spory tendují buď k tomu, že jde o věc obecného zájmu, který nedosahuje úroveň běžných civilněprávních sporů, nebo jde o civilněprávní spory spadající do pravomoci soudů. Je téměř nemožné nalézt „správné" nebo alespoň vhodné právní řešení. Předmětem tohoto článku je jedna z nejproblematičtějších otázek v této oblasti sporů, totiž základní právo zaměstnanců na rovné zacházení. Za účelem rozboru této problematiky budu analyzovat právní spory vyplývající z diskriminace v zaměstnání. Ve spojení s případy diskriminace je zapotřebí zmínit orgán zabývající se rovným zacházením, kterým je v Maďarsku nezávislý správní orgán; tento hraje v daném systému zvláštní roli. Tato jeho postavení souvisí s tím, že orgán zabývající se rovným zacházením není soudem, není ovšem ani místem pro alternativní způsoby řešení sporů. Jde spíše o nezávislý správní orgán, jehož výlučným předmětem je posuzování nároků vyplývajících z diskriminace zaměstnanců. Tato studie rozebírá hlavní otázky případů diskriminace tak, že rozebírá konkrétní případy a srovnává je s efektivitou postupů v soudním řízení. V rámci tohoto srovnání zdůrazňuji nejtypičtější případy, jakož i případy, jejichž rozhodnutí bylo nejvíce složité. Konečně se pokusím podat odpověď na otázku, zda tento nezávislý orgán může být skutečným a efektivním místem pro rozhodování pracovněprávních sporů, který je schopen nahradit nebo představovat alternativu k soudnímu řešení sporů.

| | |

POL   **[*Spory w zakresie równego traktowania w pracy: ADR i rola organu rozstrzygającego spory w zakresie równego traktowania*]**
Przedmiotem niniejszego artykułu jest naruszanie podstawowego prawa pracowników do równego traktowania. Jest to jeden z najbardziej problematycznych obszarów rozstrzygania sporów z zakresu prawa pracy. Dlatego autor analizuje spory prawne wynikające z dyskryminacji w miejscu pracy. Próbuje znaleźć odpowiedź na pytanie, czy specjalny organ, zajmującym się równym traktowaniem może być realnym i efektywnym forum do rozstrzygania sporów z zakresu prawa pracy, zdolnym zastąpić lub występować jako alternatywa do sądowego rozstrzygania sporów.

FRA [*Les litiges portant sur des inégalités de traitement en matière d'emploi et de travail : les MARL et le rôle de l'organisme de résolution des litiges relativement à l'égalité de traitement*]

Le présent article se penche sur la violation du droit fondamental des salariés à une égalité de traitement. Il s'agit d'un des domaines les plus problématiques de résolution des litiges en matière de droit du travail. Nous examinerons par conséquent des litiges juridiques portant sur des discriminations au travail. Nous tenterons d'établir si l'organisme garant de l'égalité de traitement peut-être le lieu d'une résolution efficace et réelle des litiges en matière de droit du travail, s'il est en mesure de suppléer ou de proposer une alternative à un tribunal.

RUS [*Споры относительно равного обращения в сфере занятости: ADR и роль органа, разрешающего споры относительно равного обращения*]

Данная статья посвящена нарушениям основного права трудящихся на равное обращение. Это одна из самых сложных областей урегулирования трудовых споров, и поэтому я анализирую правовые споры, возникшие в связи с дискриминацией в сфере занятости. В настоящей статье я попытаюсь ответить на вопрос, может ли особый орган, деятельность которого связана с рассмотрением равного обращения, быть реальным и эффективным местом для урегулирования трудовых споров, способным заменить или предложить альтернативу урегулированию споров в суде.

ESP [*Litigios en materia de igualdad de trato en el empleo: ADR y el papel de la autoridad que resuelve las controversias en materia de igualdad de trato*]

El tema de este artículo es la violación del derecho básico de los trabajadores sobre igualdad de trato, una de las cuestiones de solución más problemática en los conflictos laborales. Habida cuenta de ello, analizamos los litigios legales derivados de la discriminación en el empleo. Procuramos responder a la pregunta de si es posible que la autoridad especial que se ocupa del tema de la igualdad de trato sea un lugar adecuado y efectivo para tomar decisiones en los conflictos laborales, y si puede reemplazar o representar una alternativa a la resolución judicial de controversias.

| | |

Czech (& Central European) Yearbook of Arbitration

Jozef Zámožík

Judicial Review of Arbitration Awards in the Slovak Republic: Searching for a New Balance between Arbitration and Courts

Key words:
arbitration proceedings |
arbitration | Slovak
Republic | permanent
arbitration court |
arbitrability |
jurisdictional autonomy |
review of an arbitral
award | setting aside an
arbitral award

Abstract | *Slovak arbitral proceedings are mainly regulated by Act No. 244/2002 Coll., on Arbitration. Twelve years of validity of this act has indicated the necessity for its modification and amendment. In the Slovak Republic there are many issues concerning arbitration resulting from legal regulations. This paper focuses on the description and analysis of current legal issues connected with the review competence of courts in arbitration. These issues result from legal regulation allowing intervention in the jurisdictional autonomy of arbitration courts either on the grounds of petitions to set aside an arbitral award or only during enforcement proceedings. The paper deals also with the current case law of the Constitutional Court of the Slovak Republic leading to further disruption of jurisdictional immunity. Legal uncertainty and instability caused by this activity of the courts would suggest a diminishing use of arbitration.*

Jozef Zámožík is a senior lecturer at Trnava University in Trnava, Faculty of Law. He teaches Civil Procedural Law and Arbitration Law. In his research, he primarily focuses on domestic and international arbitration, European and international procedural law and theory of law of civil procedure. He also practices civil and commercial law as an attorney at law in Trnava and Bratislava. e-mail: jozef.zamozik@ gmail.com

| | |

I. Introduction

14.01. Arbitration as a means of dispute resolution was regulated in the legal system valid on the territory of today's Slovak Republic during the entire 20th century. Legal regulations of arbitration date back before 1911 when Act No. I/1911, the Civil Dispute Code regulating arbitration proceedings in Section XVII was adopted. Arbitration was later regulated by the Civil Procedure Code of 1950,[1] then the Act on Arbitral Proceedings in International Commercial Relations and on the Enforcement of Arbitral Awards,[2] and from 1996, by the Act on Arbitration.[3]

14.02. Despite a long continuing tradition of legal regulations of arbitration proceedings in the Slovak Republic, at the beginning of the 21st century only 'a small number of arbitration disputes'[4] – whether national or international commercial disputes – were carried out in arbitration proceedings. Legal regulations of arbitration suffered from many other weaknesses observed by the legislature, including:

- a limited scope of arbitrable matters;
- insufficient freedom of the parties when choosing the structure of arbitration;
- failure to set standard rules for dealing with inactivity;
- absence of a regulation on the choice of substantive law.[5]

14.03. Therefore in 2002 a new act regulating arbitration, Act No. 244/2002 Coll. on Arbitration (Arbitration Act), was adopted.[6] The Arbitration Act was subsequently amended twice, in 2005[7] and 2009.[8] Despite a

---

[1] Zákon NS RČS č. 142/1950 Zb. o konaní v občianskych právnych veciach (občiansky súdny poriadok) [Act No. 142/1950 Coll. on civil proceedings (the 'Civil Procedural Code')].

[2] Zákon NZ ČSSR č. 98/1963 Zb. o rozhodcovskom konaní v medzinárodnom obchodnom styku a o výkone rozhodcovských nálezov [Act No. 98/1963 Coll. on Arbitral Proceedings in International Commercial Relations and on the Enforcement of Arbitral Awards].

[3] Zákon NR SR č. 218/1996 Z. z. o rozhodcovskom konaní [Act No. 218/1996 Coll. on Arbitration].

[4] Dôvodová správa k návrhu zákona č. 448/2001 Z. z. [Explanatory statement to the Act No. 448/2001 Coll.].

[5] Dôvodová správa k návrhu zákona o rozhodcovskom konaní [Explanatory statement to the Arbitration Act].

[6] In Slovak: Zákon č. 244/2002 Z. z. o rozhodcovskom konaní.

[7] Zákon č. 521/2005 Z.z., ktorým sa mení a dopĺňa zákon č. 244/2002 Z. z. o rozhodcovskom konaní a o zmene zákona Slovenskej národnej rady č. 323/1992 Zb. o notároch a notárskej činnosti (Notársky poriadok) v znení neskorších predpisov, [Act No. 521/2005 Coll. on Amendment of the Act No. 244/2002 Coll. on Arbitration and Amendment of the Act No. 323/1992 Coll. on Notaries and their Work Activities (Notarial Procedures)], effective since January 1, 2006.

long tradition of legal regulations of arbitration and more than twelve years of validity of the Arbitration Act, the legal regulations and legal practice related thereto reveal many issues concerning arbitration.[9]

II. Inflation of Arbitral Institutions

14.04. The Arbitration Act was originally prepared as a relatively liberal legal act. Among other things, its aim (according to the explanatory statement to the act) was to increase the number of matters to be resolved in arbitration[10] by liberalisation of the establishment of permanent arbitration courts. The liberalisation was effected by the legislature using a simplified procedure for the establishment of permanent arbitration courts, reduction of the costs of establishment of permanent arbitration courts[11] and by allowing virtually any legal entity to establish permanent arbitration courts without any significant statutory restrictions.[12]

14.05. As a result of such liberal legal regulations, after the inactment of the Arbitration Act in the Slovak Republic, 144 permanent arbitration courts were registered on the list of permanent arbitration courts, of which only 8 were cancelled.[13] For comparison, the judicial system of

---

[8]   Zákon č. 71/2009 Z.z., ktorým sa mení a dopĺňa zákon č. 244/2002 Z. z. o rozhodcovskom konaní v znení zákona č. 521/2005 Z. z. a o zmene a doplnení zákona Slovenskej národnej rady č. 71/1992 Zb. o súdnych poplatkoch a poplatku za výpis z registra trestov v znení neskorších predpisov [Act No. 71/2009 Coll. on Amendment of the Act No. 244/2002 Coll. on Arbitration and Amendment of the Act No. 71/1992 Coll. on Court Fees], effective since July 1, 2009.

[9]   PETR DOBIÁŠ, RECENTNÍ ASPEKTY VNITROSTÁTNÍ A MEZINÁRODNÍ ARBITRÁŽE, Plzeň : Aleš Čeněk (2012).

[10]   Cf. Dôvodová správa k návrhu zákona o rozhodcovskom konaní [Explanatory statement to the Arbitration Act].

[11]   For example, minimum costs for establishing a permanent arbitration court are EUR 252. Out of this amount EUR 66 is a minimum fee for registration of a legal entity (e.g. civic association – item 34 (a) (2) of the tariff of administrative fees of Act of the National Council of the Slovak Republic No. 145/1995 Coll., on Administrative Fees, as amended) in connection with which the permanent arbitration court will be established. EUR 20 is an administration fee for publishing information on the establishment of the permanent arbitration court and its branches in ˙ the Commercial Bulletin. EUR 166 is an administrative fee for publishing a list of arbitrators of the permanent arbitration court, the statute and procedural rules of the permanent arbitration court (item 149a (d) (1) and (2) of the tariff of administrative fees).

[12]   Section 12 of the Arbitration Act.

[13]   Zoznam stálych rozhodcovských súdov SR. [List of Slovak permanent arbitration courts]. Available at: http://www.justice.gov.sk/Stranky/Registre/Dalsie-uzitocne-

the Slovak Republic consists of 54 district courts, 8 regional courts and the Supreme Court of the Slovak Republic.[14] Despite a large number of arbitration courts, many of them have resolved no dispute so far and have been established only formally.

14.06. Although the existence of a large number of arbitration courts cannot be explicitly evaluated in a negative way, it may give rise to a certain degree of mistrust to permanent arbitration courts and arbitration generally. Mistrust in arbitration may be caused by the fact that arbitration courts are often established by commercial companies rather than by civic or interest associations, societies, etc... Independence and impartiality in decision making in the latter might be primarily presumed.

14.07. Due to fragmentation of arbitration among a large number of arbitration courts, selection of several reputable arbitration courts, which could be chosen by parties for their credibility, has not taken place. On the contrary, the reasons behind the choice of a certain arbitration court by the parties to arbitration agreements remain unknown. It cannot be ruled out that the jurisdiction of the arbitration court is thus chosen based on one party's relation to a permanent arbitration court what may raise doubts about their impartiality.

14.08. In the Slovak legal environment where arbitration was used only to a small extent before the adoption of the Arbitration Act and a long tradition of arbitration legal practice is missing, there were and still are cases in which a relationship between an arbitration court and a party to the dispute can be found *prima facie*.[15] The uncertainty is also caused by numerous publicized cases of abuse of the arbitral proceedings in so-called consumer arbitration.[16]

---

zoznamy-a-registre/Rozhodcovske-sudy/Zoznam-rozhodcovskych-sudov.aspx (accessed on 3 November 2014).

[14] Zákon č. 371/2004 Z.z. o sídlach a obvodoch súdov Slovenskej republiky a o zmene zákona č. 99/1963 Zb. Občiansky súdny poriadok v znení neskorších predpisov [Act No. 371/2004 Coll. on Court Seats and Circuits in the Slovak Republic].

[15] For example, there was a case when a permanent arbitration court had several tariffs of fees for arbitration proceedings. One of them was generally to be used for all disputes and the other one was related to a particular legal entity only. Cf. Sadzobník poplatkov [List of Arbitration Fees]. Available at: http://www.rozhodcovskysud.org/poplatky.html (accessed on 3 November 2014)..

[16] E.g. Harabin: Rozhodcovské konania poškodzujú spotrebiteľov. Available at: http://www.sme.sk/c/3993283/harabin-rozhodcovske-konania-poskodzuju-spotrebitelov.html (accessed on 3 November 2014). Rozhodcovské súdy by už nemali zriaďovať obchodné spoločnosti. Available at: http://openiazoch.zoznam.sk/cl/142863/Rozhodcovske-sudy-by-uz-nemali-zriadovat-obchodne-spolocnosti (accessed on 3 November 2014).

III. Jurisdictional Autonomy of Arbitration Courts

14.09. One of the main principles applied in arbitration proceedings is the principle of jurisdictional autonomy or jurisdictional immunity of arbitration courts. The principle reflects the requirement for preventing changes to an arbitral award by a local court or another state body. An arbitral award always becomes valid and enforceable directly *ex lege* and local courts do not have jurisdiction to review such an arbitral award. Thus the state under the rule of law recognizes jurisdiction of the arbitration court to resolve a dispute. Therefore the arbitration court has autonomous jurisdiction to resolve the dispute which in principle cannot be interfered with by local courts. Such a principle is also referred to as the principle of jurisdictional immunity.

14.10. However, the jurisdictional autonomy of arbitration courts is not unlimited. Legal systems maintain a certain possibility of interference by local courts in decision making in the arbitration proceedings. The reasons for interference include breach of the principle of equality of the parties to the arbitration, the guarantee of a fair trial or right to judicial protection or protection of the weaker party in arbitration, to name a few examples. Two types of interference of local courts in arbitration proceedings can be distinguished in terms of time:
- interference before issuing a decision in the matter itself;
- interference after issuing a meritory decision.

14.11. Before issuing an arbitral award, courts can interfere in arbitration proceedings in various ways. Thus, they are performing either their controlling or supporting roles in the arbitration proceedings. These include appointing arbitrators, deciding on challenges to arbitrators on the grounds of impartiality and deciding on jurisdiction of arbitration courts for example. At this stage the supporting roles of courts prevail. However, apart from some exceptions, courts do not have the power to review arbitral awards.

14.12. Once an arbitral award is issued, intervention of local courts is limited only to the review of arbitral awards (and the previous proceedings) and the controlling role of local courts now prevails. These are the important powers of the court which, after issuing an arbitral award, has the power to either set aside the award or not to recognize and not to enforce the arbitral award.

14.13. The legal regulation of arbitration in the Slovak Republic was originally based on the principle of jurisdictional autonomy of arbitration courts. The legal regulation was construed by the legislature liberally and was partially inspired by the UNCITRAL Model Law on International Commercial Arbitration (Model Law), as stated in the Explanatory Statement to the Arbitration Act. The model was adopted for the whole legal regulation of arbitration, which is the same both for national and international arbitration. The legal regulation does not distinguish commercial arbitration and consumer arbitration.

14.14. Based on the Model Law and previous legal regulations of arbitration, the Arbitration Act provided courts with the powers to review arbitral awards in two ways, in proceedings for annulment of the arbitral award and in enforcement proceedings. On the basis of the decision making practice of the Constitutional Court of the Slovak Republic, another possibility of correction of the arbitral award was added to these two possibilities, namely in proceedings before the Constitutional Court of the Slovak Republic.

IV. Setting Aside an Arbitral Award by the Court

14.15. One of the most important competences of local courts in relation to the review of arbitral awards is the competence of the general court to set aside an arbitral award. The competence of the local court to set aside an arbitral award is granted by legal systems of many countries, such as the Czech Republic,[17] and countries which adopted the Model Law.[18] In proceedings on setting aside an arbitral award, the court mostly reviews several procedural aspects of the arbitration proceedings which are of importance for issuing arbitral awards. In exceptional cases some legal systems provide the possibility of reviewing the arbitral award itself. The extent of competence of local courts to set aside the arbitral award is important for the determination of jurisdictional autonomy of arbitration courts in different countries.

14.16. In the Slovak Republic such competence does not apply to all arbitral decisions but only to arbitral awards. In these proceedings the court reviews several procedural aspects and in some cases it also reviews substantive aspects of the arbitration proceedings which were of importance for issuing the arbitral award.

IV.1. Reasons for Setting Aside a National Arbitral Award

14.17. General courts rule on setting aside an arbitral award only for the reasons stipulated in Section 40 (1) of the Arbitration Act, provided that a respective international treaty such as the European Convention on International Commercial Arbitration of 1961 does not stipulate otherwise. The reasons set in the Arbitration Act relate solely to setting

---

[17] Section 31 of Act No. 216/1994 Coll. on Arbitration Proceeding and Enforcement of Arbitral Awards.

[18] Cf. Article 34 of the Model Law.

aside a national arbitral award.[19] National arbitral awards are all arbitral awards in which arbitration proceedings were held in the Slovak Republic.[20] If the arbitration proceedings were conducted outside the Slovak Republic, the setting aside of a foreign arbitral award by the court is regulated by international treaty. In case of absence of an international treaty, the arbitral award cannot be set aside.

14.18. Pursuant to Section 40 (1) of the Arbitration Act, a party to the arbitration may seek setting aside an arbitral award only in the following cases:

- The arbitral award was issued in a case in which the subject matter cannot be settled by arbitration (objective non-arbitrable matter).
- The arbitral award was issued in a case which has already been decided with a final decision by the court, or it has already been decided with a final decision in another arbitral proceeding (restriction of *rei iudicatae*).
- One of the parties to the arbitration challenges the validity of the arbitration agreement.
- The subject matter, on which a decision was made, goes beyond the scope of the arbitration agreement and the party to the arbitration argued this during the arbitration proceedings.
- The party to the arbitration which needs to be represented by a statutory representative was not represented or was represented by a person without the proper mandate and their actions were not subsequently approved.
- An arbitrator who was excluded from the arbitration proceedings for partiality by a decision or an arbitrator whose exclusion for partiality the party to the arbitration could not reach for reasons not related to the party to the arbitration participated in the issue of the arbitral award.
- The principle of equal treatment of the parties to the arbitration was infringed.
- There are reasons for request of a retrial under the Civil Procedure Code.[21]
- An arbitral award was influenced by a criminal offence of the arbitrator, party to the arbitration or expert for which they were lawfully convicted.
- The generally binding legal regulations on consumer protection were breached during the decision making.

---

[19] Section 34(3) of the Arbitration Act.

[20] Section 44(1) of the Arbitration Act.

[21] Zákon č. 99/1963 Zb., Občiansky súdny poriadok v znení neskorších predpisov [Act No. 99/1963 Coll., Civil Procedure Code, as amended (the 'Civil Procedure Code')].

14.19. Most of the reasons for setting aside an arbitral award are standard and although their wording is a little bit different they can also be found in the Model Law.[22] However, the specialties of the Arbitration Act are the reasons for setting aside an arbitral award stipulated in Section 40 (1) (h), (i) and (j) of the Arbitration Act. Similar provisions cannot be found in the Model Law. Thus the court may set aside an arbitral award, if

(h) there are reasons for request of a retrial under the Civil Procedural Code, or

(i) an arbitral award was influenced by a criminal offence of the arbiter, party to the proceedings or expert, for which they were lawfully convicted, or

(j) the generally binding legal regulations on consumer protection were breached during the decision making.[23]

14.20. The reason specified under (h) seems to be the most problematic one. It limits jurisdictional autonomy of arbitration courts significantly, because a petition for setting aside an arbitral award can be submitted if there are reasons for retrial, and these are construed rather boradly. The reasons for retrial are as follows:

a) There are facts, decisions or evidence that the party [to the arbitration] could not apply, without any fault of the party, in the original proceedings if they can bring a decision in the matter that is more favorable for the party,

b) It is possible to advance evidence that could not be advanced in the original proceedings if they can result in a more favorable decision for the party,

c) It has been decided against the party as a result of a criminal offence of the judge;

d) The European Court of Human Rights has decided or come to the conclusion in its judgment that the fundamental human rights or freedoms of the party to the proceedings had been breached by [arbitral award] or proceedings that had preceded that decision and serious consequences of such breaching were not removed by the subsequently awarded reasonable financial compensation;

e) [The arbitral award] is in conflict with the decision of the Court of Justice of the European Communities or any other body of the European Communities;

f) A possibility of its review arises from a special regulation in connection with the recognition or enforcement of a decision of a Slovak [arbitration] court in another Member State of the European Union.[24]

---

[22] Cf. 34 of the Model Law.

[23] Section 40 (1) (h), (i) and (j) of the Arbitration Act.

Czech (& Central European) Yearbook of Arbitration

14.21. Some of the reasons for the retrial envisage review of the merit of the arbitral award by the local court mainly the review of whether it is possible under new facts, decisions or evidence to come to a more favorable decision in the case. A petition for setting aside an arbitral award for retrial can be submitted only in an objective period of three years which starts on the date of the delivery of the arbitral award.[25] This competence of local courts to review the arbitral award creates a long-term legal uncertainty for the parties to the arbitration, during which the bindingness of the arbitral award can be violated. Although only an occasional use of these reasons for setting aside the arbitral award is anticipated, it is a very long period in comparison to a similar period set by the Model Law which is three months[26] or with other reasons set by the Arbitration Act where the period is 30 days.[27] However, parties to the arbitration may avoid such a long-term legal uncertainty as the Arbitration Act stipulates this regulation as an opt-out provision. Thus the parties to the arbitration agreement can exclude such a reason for setting aside an arbitral award by mutual agreement.[28] A more appropriate approach seems to be to leave out the reason from the Arbitration Act or to make it a reason for review of the arbitral award by another arbitrator instead of by a local court.

V. Setting Aside an Arbitral Award by the Constitutional Court of the Slovak Republic

14.22. In accordance with Article 127(1) of the Constitution of the Slovak Republic:

> The Constitutional Court decides on complaints of natural persons or legal entities objecting to violation of their fundamental rights and freedoms, or the fundamental rights and freedoms resulting from an international treaty ratified by the Slovak Republic and declared in a manner laid down by law, unless another court decides on the protection of such rights and freedoms.[29]

---

[24] Section 228(1) of the Civil Procedure Code.

[25] This period is limited by a so-called subjective period, since a petition cannot be filed later then '30 days from the day a party to the arbitration proceeding which is filing a petition learnt of a reason for retrial, or from the day when a party could have make use of it for the first time.' Section 41 (2) of the Arbitration Act.

[26] Article 34(3) of the Model Law.

[27] Section 41(1) of the Arbitration Act.

[28] Section 42 of the Arbitration Act.

[29] The Constitution of the Slovak Republic, No. 460/1992 Coll., as amended.

14.23. Consequently Article 127(2) of the Constitution of the Slovak Republic provides that in case the Constitutional Court accepts a complaint, it declares in its decision that the rights or freedoms of the claimant were infringed by a final decision of a non-appealable nature and it sets aside such a decision while it can return the matter for further proceedings.[30]

14.24. Until 2011 the Constitutional Court of the Slovak Republic did not address in its decisions whether it is entitled also to decide about complaints against decisions of arbitration courts within Article 127 of the Constitution. However, on 31 May 2011, the Constitutional Court issued a judgment in which it, inter alia, states:

1. The special act on arbitration created the legal admissibility of the court governance over the arbitral awards by general courts in the cases listed exhaustively. However, if after the one instance proceedings in front of an arbitration court are closed and no remedy is available through the general courts it is appropriate that the Constitutional Court actively intervenes.

2. According to the Constitutional Court the requirements resulting from the right to judicial and other protection under Article 46(1) of the Constitution and also from the right to fair trial under Article 6(1) of the Treaty apply to an arbitral award as well. It means that such decision also needs to have a legal ground (Article 2(2) of the Constitution) and cannot be a manifestation of arbitrariness (Article 1(1) of the Constitution).

   The arbitration court is not a public authority but the Constitutional Court is of the opinion that the Section 6(1) of the Treaty shall apply to the reasoning of its decision accordingly because it partially performs the function of a general (civil or commercial) court.

3. Because the contested arbitral award violated the identified fundamental rights of the claimant (Point 1 a 2 of the verdict of this judgment), in connection with it the Constitutional Court set aside the contested arbitral award of the arbitration court, File No. VK 507/2010 of November 2, 2010 and returned the case for further proceedings (Point 3 of the verdict of this judgment).[31]

14.25. This striking judgment of the Constitutional Court of the Slovak Republic shows that under Slovak laws the list of reasons for setting

---

[30] Article 127(2) of the Constitution of the Slovak Republic.

[31] Cf. Rozsudok Ústavného súdu Slovenskej republiky sp. zn. III. ÚS 162/2011 z 31. mája 2011 [Judgement of the Constitutional Court of the Slovak Republic of 31 May 2011, Case III. ÚS 162/2011].

aside an arbitral award stipulated by the Arbitration Act is not final. Besides the petition under Arbitration Act, either party to the arbitration has the option to protect themselves against the arbitral award by also submitting a constitutional complaint to the Constitutional Court of the Slovak Republic under conditions set by this judgment. In case the so-called constitutional complaint is accepted, the Constitutional Court of the Slovak Republic may set aside the arbitral award and return the case for further proceedings.

14.26. Although the case-law does not provide specific conditions limiting this jurisdiction of the Constitutional Court of the Slovak Republic, its outlines are visible in this judgment. A violation of the right to a fair trial, mainly under Section 6(1) of the Convention for the Protection of Human Rights and Fundamental Freedoms and the right to a judicial and similar protection under Article 46(1) of the Constitution of the Slovak Republic are the basic conditions for the competence of the Constitutional Court of the Slovak Republic to review an arbitral award. First and foremost the Constitutional Court of the Slovak Republic ruled here on its right to assess the reasoning of arbitral awards within the scope of these regulations.

14.27. As a result of this decision of the Constitutional Court of the Slovak Republic, the legal force of arbitral awards was weakened and further disruption of the jurisdictional autonomy of arbitration courts followed. In addition, because of the amount of unanswered legal questions regarding the review of jurisdiction of the Constitutional Court of the Slovak Republic, on which so far no ruling has been given, the activity of the Constitutional Court of the Slovak Republic led to further undermining of legal certainty and bindingness of arbitral awards.

VI. Reviewing the Arbitral Award in Proceedings for Recognition and Enforcement

14.28. The Slovak legal regulation of the Arbitration Act is specific as the review of an arbitral award might take place in proceedings for recognition and enforcement of arbitral awards. The Arbitration Act recognizes two regimes of recognition (and enforcement) of arbitral awards. The first one is for national arbitral awards[32] and the second one is for foreign arbitral awards.

14.29. The legal regime of the Arbitration Act on recognition and enforcement of foreign arbitral awards is only used exceptionally.

---

[32]   The legal regime of recognition of national arbitral awards is completely absent in the Arbitration Act.

Bilateral and multilateral international treaties which are binding for the Slovak Republic have precedence over Arbitration Act. For instance, the Convention on the recognition and enforcement of foreign arbitral awards (the New York Convention) is considered to have such precedence. Even if the regime for recognition and enforcement of foreign arbitral awards under the Arbitration Act is used, its conditions for the recognition and enforcement and conditions for refusal of recognition and enforcement are identical to the conditions set in the New York Convention.[33]

14.30. A different situation occurs in the legal regime of enforcement of national (not foreign) arbitral awards. Arbitral awards are enforced in enforcement proceedings (in Slovak *exekučné konanie*) in accordance with Act No. 233/1995 Coll., on court officers and distraint activities (the Execution Procedure Act) and on amendments to certain laws, as amended.[34]

14.31. The intent of the legislature was to set the enforcement of arbitral awards in the Arbitration Act in a liberal way.[35] A national arbitral award should be considered to be an enforcement title equivalent to an enforceable court judgment.[36] In principle, this meant that the local court was not entitled to review the arbitral award in the enforcement proceedings.

14.32. However, because of the specific nature of the arbitral award, the legislature provided execution courts with the possibility of suspending the enforcement proceedings in exceptional cases for three reasons:[37]

a) A reason exists for suspending the enforcement under the Execution Procedure Act.[38]

b) The arbitral award was awarded in a matter which cannot be the subject of arbitration, or the arbitral award was awarded in a matter which has been already decided by a court or in another arbitration (restriction of *rei iudicatae*).

---

[33] A significant difference can be found in relation to reasons stipulated in Article V(2) of the New York Convention. In accordance with the New York Convention these are the reasons under which the 'recognition and enforcement of an arbitral award may be refused', while in accordance with the Arbitration Act these are the reasons under which the court "shall refuse the recognition and enforcement".

[34] In Slovak: Zákon č. 233/1995 o súdnych exekútoroch a exekučnej činnosti (Exekučný poriadok) a o zmene a doplnení ďalších zákonov.

[35] Cf. Dôvodová správa k návrhu Zákona o rozhodcovskom konaní [Explanatory statement to the Arbitration Act].

[36] Section 35 of the Arbitration Act.

[37] Section 45(1) of the Arbitration Act.

[38] Section 57(1) of the Execution Procedure Act.

c) The arbitral award obliges the party to arbitration to fulfill an obligation which is objectively impossible, prohibited by law or in contrary to good morals.

14.33. The first reason for setting aside the arbitral award is logical. However, it involves reasons for suspending the enforcement on the grounds of any enforcement title, not only the arbitral award. It is not clear why the legislature duplicated the legal regulation here. The reasons for suspending the enforcement do not apply to the review of an enforcement title but only to the review of conditions of the enforcement proceedings. Therefore these reasons do not intervene with the jurisdictional autonomy of the arbitration courts.

14.34. On the other hand, the second reason for setting the arbitral award aside does intervene with the jurisdictional autonomy of the arbitration courts. It provides the right of the execution court to investigate whether the arbitral award does not derive from the arbitrarity. This concerns whether the subject matter decided in the arbitration proceeding is capable of being the subject matter of settlement by arbitration or whether a restriction of *rei iudicatae* applies. These reasons interlock with the reasons for setting aside the arbitral award.[39] However, the legislature considered them to represent such substantial shortcomings of the arbitral award that it provided the execution court with the right to investigate such shortcomings *ex officio*[40] during the enforcement proceedings. No explanation was provided on why such reasons should be considered in proceedings for setting aside the arbitral award only upon an objection raised and not ex officio.

14.35. The third reason for setting aside the arbitral award concerns the fulfillment itself which the legislature unsystematically inserted into the Arbitration Act. The lack of system can be seen in the lack of arguments justifying the approach in the text of the Act. The legislature provided the execution courts with the right to suspend enforcement proceedings on the grounds of a national arbitral award even without a proposal to do so 'if it binds the participant to fulfillment of obligation which is objectively impossible, prohibited by law or in contrary to good morals.'[41] However, the court is not entitled to set aside an arbitral award upon a claim for these same reasons. Ironically, a situation may occur where an arbitral award obliges the party to fulfil an obligation in contrary to good morals, but where the court rejects

---

[39]   Section 40(1)(a) and (b) of the Arbitration Act.

[40]   Section 45(2) of the Arbitration Act.

[41]   Section 45(1)(c) of the Arbitration Act.

the petition for setting aside the arbitral award for this reason. Following the rejection of the petition and submission of the proposal for enforcement, the execution court suspends the enforcement proceedings for this reason and the arbitral award becomes an unenforceable enforcement title.

14.36. Pursuant to the wording of Section 45(1)(c) of the Arbitration Act, the third reason for setting aside the arbitral award concerns the fulfillment of obligation to which the arbitration court obliges the obliged person and which shall be enforced in enforcement proceedings. The interpretation should be preferred that this reason shall be reviewed by the court in a restrictive manner and that the delivered arbitral award has the same effects as a final court judgment.[42] The third reason should therefore enable the execution court to review the merits of the case and the arbitration proceedings which preceded the awarding of the arbitral award. In the enforcement proceedings, the court shall focus solely on the obligation to be fulfilled.

14.37. The reasons for suspension of enforcement proceedings set by the Arbitration Act represent an exhaustive list. The execution court shall not arbitrarily expand the list by other reasons for suspension of enforcement proceedings. In enforcement proceedings the invalidity or non-existence of an arbitration agreement shall not be addressed. Nevertheless, under the case-law of the European Court of Justice, namely the judgment in the case of Asturcom Telecomunicaciones SL c/a. Cristina Rodríguez Nogueira,[43] the Slovak courts expanded the reasons for suspension.

14.38. The courts encounter cases where arbitral awards were awarded on the basis of an arbitration agreement which the court finds invalid due to the arbitration clause being agreed as an unfair contractual term in a consumer contract. They consider these to fall under the reason that the 'arbitral award obliges the party to fulfill an obligation which is contrary to good morals'.[44] Subsequently the decision making activity of execution courts generalized such an approach and suspended all enforcement proceedings in consumer arbitration cases without reviewing individual arbitration clauses.[45] In many cases they did so

---

[42] Section 35 of the Arbitration Act.

[43] Judgment of the Court (First Chamber) of 6 October 2009, *Asturcom Telecomunicaciones SL* v *Cristina Rodríguez Nogueira*, Case C-40/08.

[44] E.g. Uznesenie Okresného súdu Kežmarok z 24.10.2011 sp. zn. 8 Er 1139/2010 [Decision of the Distric Court in Kežmarok of 24 October 2011, Case 8 Er 1139/2010].

[45] Cf. Nález Ústavného súdu Slovenskej republiky zo dňa 10.7.2013 sp. zn. II. ÚS 499/2012 [Award of the Constitutional Court of the Slovak Republic of 10 July 2013, Case

without giving the opportunity to the entitled party to provide explanation in the enforcement proceedings.[46]

14.39. Such an approach by the court was intended solely for the consumer arbitration. However, it led to several cases where the execution courts started reviewing the competence of the arbitration courts, arbitration agreements, compliance of the arbitral awards with law, etc... in non-consumer arbitrations including commercial arbitration.[47]

14.40. The legal uncertainty in enforcement proceedings based on arbitral awards was also increased by the amending of the Execution Procedure Act by Act No. 144/2010 Coll.[48], effective since 1 June 2010. Until the passage of the amendment, the execution court decided on the application of the bailiff based on the enforcement title (including arbitral awards) within 15 days from delivery of the application. However, after the adoption of the amendment this period was no longer limited by law. In comparison to other execution titles, such as a court judgment, the arbitral award may be enforced much later. During this period the execution court might review the arbitral award which would lead to further prolongations.

14.41. On top of all that, the Slovak courts also passed unpredictable decisions in cases of the enforcement of foreign arbitral awards. For instance, they decided that the regulation on suspension of enforcement proceedings (which under Arbitration Act shall apply solely to national arbitral awards) will also apply to foreign arbitral awards, notwithstanding the relevant international treaties.[49]

14.42. There is no unified case-law or approach by the courts with respect to the scope of the court review of arbitral awards. Therefore the decisions of execution courts are hard to predict. Because such decision

---

II. ÚS 499/2012].

[46] E.g. Uznesenie Najvyššieho súdu Slovenskej republiky z 27. novembra 2012 sp. zn. 7 Cdo 57/2012 [Decision of the Supreme Court of the Slovak Republic of 27 November 2012, Case 7 Cdo 57/2012].

[47] E.g. Rozhodnutia v konaní vedenom na Okresnom súde Liptovský Mikuláš, sp. zn. 5Er/1316/2013 [Decisions of the Distric Court in Liptovský Mikuláš, Case 5Er/1316/2013].

[48] Zákon č. 144/2010 Z.z., ktorým sa mení a dopĺňa zákon č. 8/2009 Z. z. o cestnej premávke a o zmene a doplnení niektorých zákonov v znení neskorších predpisov a o zmene a doplnení niektorých zákonov [Act No. 144/2010 Coll. on Amendment of the Act No. 8/2009 Coll. on Road Traffic an Amendment of Additional Acts].

[49] Uznesenie Okresného súdu Skalica z 19.9.2011 sp. zn. 3Er/327/2011 [Decision of the Distric Court in Skalica of 19 September 2011, Case 3Er/327/2011]. Uznesenie Krajského súdu v Trnave zo dňa 5.12.2013 sp. zn. 11CoE/638/2011 [Decision of the Regional Court in Trnava of 5 December 2013, Case 11CoE/638/2011].

making of execution courts has an impact on the bindingness of arbitral awards and the jurisdictional autonomy of arbitration courts, the logical consequence seems to be the reluctance of parties to choose arbitration as a means of resolving their disputes despite many advantages connected with it.

VII. Conclusions

14.43. The use of arbitrations in the Slovak legal environment is growing, along with the number of arbitration courts, despite a lack of a long-term continuous legal tradition of arbitration. Naturally a number of negative phenomena have occurred, with individuals and groups making use of the rather liberal regulation of arbitration to their advantage. Therefore changes in the legal regulation of arbitration seemed to be necessary. However, instead of changes, an intervention in juridical autonomy and a challenge of the formal and material bindingness of arbitral awards followed as a result of the investigatory activity of the courts. Legal uncertainty and instability caused by this investigatory activity of the courts would suggest a diminishing use of arbitration.

14.44. The imbalance results partially from imperfections in the legal regulation and partially from arbitration activity. It should be tilted in such a way as to arrange for arbitration to fulfill its set purpose without causing legal uncertainty.

14.45. An appropriate measure would be a change in legal regulation to consistently distinguish between consumer and non-consumer arbitration. The legislature should therefore stay out of the unified legal regulation of the arbitration of all civil law and commercial law disputes. A unified legal regulation of arbitration of consumer disputes and commercial disputes is possible. However, such unification seems redundant due to the conflict of interests of the legislature in the protection of the weaker party in consumer agreements on the one hand, and on the other a liberal approach to national and international commercial arbitration. In addition to the possible ambiguity in relation to used terms, it might result either in inadequate protection of consumers in arbitration or in low flexibility and strict restrictions of the arbitration of another matter.

14.46. At the same time the legal regulation of arbitration should be liberalized for the needs of civil and commercial relationships where no protection of a weaker party is necessary, as suggested by the Model Law. In this respect, legislative proposals have already been presented which should lead to an extensive amendment of the

Arbitration Act and separation of consumer arbitration as a separate type governed by a separate law.[50] However, the change of laws itself will not help to strike a balance between arbitration courts and local courts. This can be restored only by the adoption of a constitutional act precluding the Constitutional Court from reviewing arbitral awards and creating a new stable and constant case-law on arbitration.

| | |

Summaries

FRA   [*Le contrôle judiciaire des sentences arbitrales en Slovaquie : la recherche d'un nouvel équilibre entre les cours d'arbitrage et les tribunaux.*]

L'arbitrage est réglementé principalement en Slovaquie par la loi NR SR n° 244/2002 Z.z. o rozhodcovskom konaní (loi sur l'arbitrage). Après 12 années d'application et d'effet de cette loi, on ressent le besoin de la modifier ou de l'amender. On rencontre en effet en Slovaquie un grand nombre de problèmes liés à l'arbitrage dus aux insuffisances de la réglementation. Le présent article décrit et analyse les problèmes juridiques rencontrés actuellement, liés aux activités de contrôle des tribunaux dans la procédure d'arbitrage qui résultent d'une réglementation permettant une ingérence dans l'autonomie juridictionnelle des cours d'arbitrage, sur la base d'une demande d'annulation d'une sentence arbitrale ou bien même au cours de la procédure d'exécution. Nous nous pencherons également sur la jurisprudence actuelle de la Cour constitutionnelle slovaque, dans ses conséquences conduisant à d'autres violations de l'immunité juridictionnelle. Nous ne nous préoccuperons pas ici – à moins de ne pouvoir l'éviter – de la problématique de l'arbitrage en matière de consommation et des questions qui s'y rapportent.

---

[50]   Návrh zákona o spotrebiteľskom rozhodcovskom konaní a o zmene a doplnení niektorých zákonov [Proposal for an Act on Consumer Arbitration]. Available at: https://lt.justice.gov.sk/Material/MaterialDocuments.aspx?instEID=-1&matEID=6931&lang EID=1&tStamp=20140124001534990 (accessed on 3 November 2014). Návrh zákona, ktorým sa mení a dopĺňa zákon č. 244/2002 Z. z. o rozhodcovskom konaní v znení neskorších predpisov a ktorým sa mení a dopĺňa zákon č. 99/1963 Zb. Občiansky súdny poriadok v znení neskorších predpisov [Proposal for an Act on Amendment of the Act No. 244/2002 Coll. on Arbitration and Amendment of the Act No. 99/1963 Coll., Civil Procedure Act]. In: https://lt.justice.gov.sk/Material/Material Workflow.aspx?instEID=-1&matEID=6930&langEID=1.

CZE [*Soudní přezkoumání rozhodčích nálezů ve Slovenské republice: hledání nové rovnováhy mezi rozhodčími a státními soudy.*]
Slovenská právní úprava rozhodčího řízení se nachází především v Zákoně NR SR č. 244/2002 Z.z. o rozhodcovskom konaní. 12 let platnosti a účinnosti tohoto zákona ukazuje potřebu po jeho změně anebo novelizaci. V SR tak existuje množství problémů týkajících se rozhodčího řízení způsobených nedostatečnou právní úpravou. Tento článek opisuje a analyzuje aktuální právní problémy, které jsou spojené s přezkumní činností soudů v rozhodčím řízení, která vyplývá z právní úpravy umožňující zásahy do jurisdikční autonomie rozhodčích soudů buď na základě žalob o zrušení rozhodčích rozsudků nebo až v průběhu exekučního řízení. Článek se zabývá též aktuální judikaturou Ústavního soudu Slovenské republiky v důsledku, které přichází k dalšímu narušení jurisdikční imunity. Až na některé nevyhnutné souvislosti, článek se nezabývá problematikou spotřebitelské arbitráže a s ní související problémy.

| | |

POL [*Badanie orzeczeń arbitrażowych przez sądy na Słowacji: w poszukiwaniu nowej równowagi między sądami arbitrażowymi i krajowymi.*]
12 lat obowiązywania ustawy Rady Narodowej Republiki Słowackiej nr 244/2002 Dz.U. w sprawie postępowania arbitrażowego sugeruje konieczność jej zmiany lub nowelizacji. Niniejszy artykuł opisuje i analizuje aktualną problematykę prawną, związaną z działalnością kontrolną sądów w postępowaniu arbitrażowym, wynikającą z regulacji prawnych, umożliwiających ingerencję w autonomię jurysdykcyjną sądów arbitrażowych albo na podstawie wniosku o uchylenie orzeczenia arbitrażowego, albo już w trakcie postępowania egzekucyjnego.

DEU [*Gerichtliche Prüfung von Schiedssprüchen in der Slowakischen Republik: Auf der Suche nach einem neuen Gleichgewicht zwischen Schiedsgerichten und staatlichen Gerichten.*]
Die zwölf Jahre, während der das Gesetz über Schiedsverfahren (Gesetz des Slowakischen Nationalrats Nr. 244/2002 Slg.) in Kraft ist, verweisen auf die Notwendigkeit einer Änderung bzw. Neufassung. Der Beitrag beschreibt und analysiert die aktuellen juristischen Probleme, die mit dem Engagement der allgemeinen Gerichte in Sachen Überprüfung im Schiedsverfahren einhergehen und die sich aus der

Czech (& Central European) Yearbook of Arbitration

Rechtslage ergeben, die Eingriffe in die Autonomie der Rechtsprechung auf Seiten der Schiedsgerichtsbarkeit erlaubt, entweder auf der Basis von Aufhebungsklagen oder erst im Laufe des Vollstreckungsverfahrens.

RUS [*Пересмотр арбитражных решений в суде в Словацкой Республике: поиск нового равновесия между арбитражами и государственными судами*]

Действие Закона НС СР № 244/2002 Св. «Об арбитраже» в течение 12 лет свидетельствует о необходимости внесения в него изменений или поправок. В данной статье описываются и анализируются актуальные правовые проблемы, связанные с деятельностью судов в области пересмотра арбитражных решений, вытекающей из правового регулирования, позволяющего вмешательство в юрисдикционную автономию арбитражных судов либо на основе ходатайств об отмене арбитражных решений, либо в ходе исполнительного производства.

ESP [*Revisión judicial de los laudos arbitrales en la República Eslovaca: búsqueda de un nuevo equilibrio entre los tribunales de arbitraje y los tribunales nacionales*]

El periodo de 12 años de vigencia de la Ley NR SR N° 244/2002 sobre la ejecución arbitral demuestra la necesidad de cambio o actualización. Este artículo describe y analiza los problemas legales actuales, que están asociados a las revisiones de los tribunales de arbitraje que se desprenden de la legislación y por la que se permiten intervenciones en la autonomía jurisdiccional de los tribunales de arbitraje, ya sea sobre la base de demandas de anulación de las sentencias arbitrales o posteriormente en el curso de procedimientos de ejecución.

| | |

Elena Zucconi Galli Fonseca | Carlo Rasia
Arbitrator versus Judge

Key words:
domestic jurisdiction |
foreign arbitration |
Kompetenz-Kompetenz
principle | state judge |
judicial authority |
translatio iudicii | exceptio
compromissi | lis pendence
| review of the award |
objection to the judge's
jurisdiction | invalidity of
the arbitration agreement |
review of the state
judgment | European
Regulation n° 1215 of 2012

Abstract | The relationship between arbitrator and judge in the Italian system is a relationship of jurisdiction. This is what emerged from the reform of 2006 and from the recent decisions of the Constitutional Court and the Supreme Court in 2013. Moreover, these rules sometimes approach, and sometimes diverge from rules that are common to the courts.

As an example consider the rules related to the different appeal of the judgment and of the award that has decided about the validity of the clause, or consider the lack of binding nature of the decision when the case is transferred between arbitrator and judge (or vice versa).

The equalization of the relationship between arbitrators and judges must be seen, inside Italian system, as a particular relationship of jurisdiction. Moreover, despite the encouraging decisions of the Supreme Court, it cannot be said that there is a total equalization with the relationship between judges and arbitrators.

||||

Elena Zucconi Galli Fonseca is a full professor of Civil Procedural Law. She teaches Civil Procedural Law and International and Domestic Arbitration Law at the Alma Mater Studiorum-University of Bologna, School of Law. She has written more than seventy books, articles and essays. Her research interests include arbitration, with particular reference to the arbitral convention, arbitration and company law, arbitral award; res iudicata, objective and subjective limits, connections between rights and collateral estoppel. Among her books are *La convenzione arbitrale rituale nei confronti dei terzi* (Arbitral convention and third person) Milan, 2006 and

---

*   Sections I, II, and III were authored by Elena Zucconi Galli Fonseca while sections IV, V, VI and VII were authored by Carlo Rasia.

I. Introduction to the Interaction between Judge and Arbitrator in the Italian System

15.01. The relationship between the judge and arbitrator can be examined from two different perspectives.

a) The first concerns the role of the court in the arbitral proceedings. The Italian system includes a series of cases in which the court intervened to overcome any *impasse* in the designation of the arbitrators, during the arbitral proceedings, at the enforcement and the appeal of the arbitration award.

b) The second concerns the impact of the choice of arbitration on the jurisdiction of the State. What happens if a party files an application before the court despite the existence of an arbitration agreement, or if two actions, concerning the same dispute or related disputes, are pending before the judge and the arbitrator?

15.02. This article only deals with the second perspective. After a brief description of the rules of law, some specific aspects of this perspective will be discussed. First, we will examine the discipline of the *exceptio compromissi* before the Italian judge, with respect to *arbitrato rituale*. This is arbitration governed by Articles 806 ff. of the Italian Code of Civil Procedure (with the exception of Article 808-*ter*).[1] Particular attention will be paid to foreign arbitration. Further, we will examine an issue regarding two contemporaries' proceedings before the arbitrator and the judge, on the same dispute, or on related disputes. In particular, we will

Pregiudizialità e rinvio. Contributo allo studio dei limiti soggettivi dell'accertamento (Contribute to doctrine of res judicata and third person), Bologna, 2011. She is a member of the Italian Association of Civil Procedure Law, and of the International Association of Procedural Law. She also practices civil and commercial law in Bologna. Her address is the: Università di Bologna, Scuola di giurisprudenza, via Zamboni n. 22, Bologna, Italy.
e-mail:
elena.zucconigallifonse
ca@unibo.it

Carlo Rasia is a researcher of Civil Procedural Law and a professor of European Procedural Law at the School of Law of the Alma Mater Studiorum-University of Bologna, where he also teaches Domestic and International Arbitration Law. His main research areas are focused on European Procedural Law and on National and International Arbitration. Among his works is the book *Tutela giudiziale europea e arbitrato* (European judicial

---

[1] One of the particularities of Italian arbitration law is that two forms of domestic arbitration are regulated. Arbitration may be qualified as either *rituale* or *irrituale*. The former is treated as a functional equivalent of judicial adjudication of a dispute (see Article 824-*bis* of Code of civil procedure), while the latter is defined as a contractual determination of the parties' dispute.

question whether a *translatio iudicii* between judge and arbitrator and vice versa is possible, in order to maintain continuity in the action, and despite the lack of jurisdiction of the judge. Some brief conclusions will follow.

15.03. The amendments to the Italian arbitration law, which took place in 2006, encoded a suitably detailed regulation of the interaction between jurisdiction and the choice of arbitration.[2]

15.04. Article 817 of Code of Civil Procedure concerns the situation in which the arbitrator's jurisdiction is contested on the grounds of the arbitration agreement, fixing the *Kompetenz-Kompetenz* principle. The rule establishes that if the interested party does not object in the first statement of defense subsequent to the arbitrators' acceptance that they lack jurisdiction because of invalidity/ineffectiveness of the agreement, then the party may not challenge the award on this ground (except in case of a non-arbitrable dispute).

15.05. Especially significant, for the purposes of this article, is Article 819-*ter* of Code of Civil Procedure.[3]

protection and arbitration), Bologna, 2010. He has participated in national and international research projects, such as the European Commission project 'European civil procedure and e-Justice implementation within the European Union' (2010-2011). He is a member of the Italian Association of Civil Procedure Law. Since 2004 he has also practiced civil and commercial law in Bologna. His address is: Università di Bologna, Scuola di giurisprudenza, via Zamboni n. 22, Bologna, Italy. e-mail address: carlo.rasia@unibo.it

---

[2] More recent contributions to the discussion include: Salvatore Boccagna, *Sub art. 817 e 819-ter c.p.c.*, in COMMENTARIO BREVE AL DIRITTO DELL'ARBITRATO NAZIONALE ED INTERNAZIONALE, Padova: Cedam 255 and 276 (M.Benedettelli, C.Consolo, L.Radicati di Brozolo eds., 2010); Modestino Acone, *Arbitrato e translatio iudicii: un parere eretico?*, in STUDI OFFERTI A GIOVANNI VERDE, Napoli: Jovene 1 (2010); Claudio Consolo, *Brussels I Regulation, Arbitration and parallel proceedings: a discussion of the Heidelberg proposal (in the light of West Tankers and Endesa)*, in STUDI OFFERTI A GIOVANNI VERDE, Napoli: Jovene, 245 (2010); Carlo Rasia, *Sub.Art. 819-ter c.p.c.*, in COMMENTARIO BREVE AL CODICE DI PROCEDURA CIVILE, Padova: Cedam 2804-2807 (F.Carpi, M.Taruffo eds., 7th ed., 2012); Mauro Bove, Antonio Briguglio, Sergio Menchini & Bruno Sassani, *Commenti*, RIVISTA DELL'ARBITRATO 81, 88 (2014); Elena Zucconi Galli Fonseca, *Giudice italiano ed exceptio compromissi per arbitrato estero*, RIVISTA TRIMESTRALE DI DIRITTO E PROCEDURA CIVILE 741 (2014).

[3] Art. 819-*ter* (*Relations between arbitrators and judicial authority*) – (1) The arbitrators' jurisdiction shall not be excluded by the pendency of the same dispute before the judge or by the connection between the dispute referred to the arbitrators and a dispute pending before the judge. The judgment by which the judge upholds or denies his or her own jurisdiction with regard to an arbitration agreement may be challenged according to Articles 42 and 43. The objection to the judge's jurisdiction by reason of the

15.06. The rule provides that if a plea of lack of jurisdiction based on the grounds of an arbitral agreement (or *exceptio compromissi*) is not raised in the statement of defense, the court will have jurisdiction on the merits of the dispute. It also determines how to appeal the judicial decision, which affirms or denies jurisdiction based on the arbitration agreement. The Italian system thus recognizes the power of the court to give a ruling on the existence or the validity of the arbitral agreement, refusing the priority principle.

II. *Exceptio Compromissi* in Italian Arbitration

15.07. Doctrine and case law have traditionally addressed the problem of the *exceptio compromissi* before the Italian court from the perspective of the nature of arbitration. In other words, in order to know how the judge should behave in front of an objection on the grounds of an arbitral agreement, it is essential to start from the theoretical relationship between arbitration and state jurisdiction. In the latter regard, two opposing visions have been offered (with an additional intermediate thesis, which for reasons of space, it is not possible to give account of here).

a) In the first vision, arbitration belongs to the jurisdiction of the State; it is an expression of judicial power, with its own peculiarities.[4] It thus becomes natural to compare the relationship between judge and arbitrator to the one between judges belonging to the same judicial order, in terms of jurisdiction. The question of validity of the arbitral agreement, then, concerns the process and not the merits of the dispute.

b) In the second perspective, arbitration belongs to the private sphere and lies outside of the state jurisdiction[5]. It is something other than the exercise of a judicial function, in that it gives a 'private' definition to the dispute. Thus with the choice of arbitration, the

---

arbitration agreement must be raised, under sanction of lapse, in the statement in reply. If such objection is not raised, arbitral jurisdiction shall be excluded in respect of the dispute decided in that proceeding. (2) The provisions corresponding to Articles 44, 45, 48, 50 and 295 shall not be applicable to the relations between arbitration and judicial proceedings. (3) Pending the arbitral proceedings, no requests may be submitted to the judicial

[4]   *Ex multis* Edoardo F. Ricci, *Commentario alla legge 9 febbraio 1983, n. 28, modificazioni alla disciplina dell'arbitrato*, NUOVE LEGGI CIVILI COMMENTATE 736 (1983); Edoardo F. Ricci, *La funzione giudicante degli arbitri e l'efficacia del lodo (un* grand arrêt *della Corte costituzionale)*, RIVISTA DI DIRITTO PROCESSUALE 354 (2002).

[5]   *Ex multis* Carmine Punzi, *La riforma dell'arbitrato*, Rivista di diritto civile 78 (1983); CARMINE PUNZI, DISEGNO SISTEMATICO DELL'ARBITRATO, Padova: Cedam 83 (2nd ed. 2012).

party waives its right of action before the court, as well as its right to judicial protection of substantial rights.

15.08. According to this approach, the objection on the grounds of the arbitral agreement would concern the merits.

15.09. The Supreme Court has assumed conflicting positions. Initially the judges spoke in terms of jurisdiction. Nevertheless, after 2000, they changed their mind, leaning in favor of the private perspective.[6] But then in 2013, they have again returned to the old idea.[7]

15.10. At first sight, the Italian legislature of 2006 seems to favor the judicial nature of arbitration, but, upon a closer look, it has not opted for a clear choice.

15.11. In fact, on the one hand, the legislature frames the relationships between judges and arbitrators in terms of jurisdiction. On the other hand, it does not draw all the necessary consequences.

15.12. For example, the arbitration award on the jurisdiction of the arbitral tribunal is not subjected to the typical appeal of decisions of this type, the *regolamento di competenza* (see *infra* paragraph IV). Besides, the arbitrator is not bound to the decision of the court on the validity of the arbitral agreement – thus creating the risk of contradictory judgments.

15.13. Therefore, the problem is not solved and in our opinion, a proper approach must leave aside the dispute on the nature of arbitration.

15.14. There is no doubt that arbitration, unlike state jurisdiction, is an expression of the parties choice. At the same time, the arbitral solution of the dispute operates on a strictly procedural basis. These features make arbitration unique, an alternative to state jurisdiction.

15.15. However, when dealing with the relationship between arbitrator and judge, these assumptions are not essential. Rather, the arbitration result (the award) is 'economically fungible' with the judicial function. We need specify 'economically' because, arbitrators, like judges, *ius dicunt*, ensure the substantial rights of the parties. On the other hand, the award is not strictly a state judgment, but it has the same effects.

15.16. This means that with the arbitration agreement, the parties mutually constitute a 'right of arbitral action', alternative to the right to seize the state courts.

15.17. Thus, a valid arbitration agreement prevents the application to the court and the judge seized on the merits must decide with a judgment

---

[6]   Cass., sez. un., August 3, 2000 n° 527, Foro Italiano, I, 839 (2001), that it rejected the jurisdictional character of arbitration and it has strongly abolished the distinction between contractual arbitration and *arbitrato rituale* .

[7]   Cass., (ord.), October 25, 2013 n° 24153, Corriere giuridico 91 (2014), note Giovanni Verde.

of *absolutio ab instantia*, according to Article 819-*ter* of Code of Civil Procedure, without entering into the merits of the dispute. In other words, the validity of the arbitration agreement regards only the question of jurisdiction.[8]

15.18. The rules of the Italian system specifically address the jurisdictional question.

a) First, should the party raise an objection after the time limit, the court will have jurisdiction on the dispute, but this does not mean that the arbitration agreement is expired for future disputes. In this case, it must be concluded that the arbitral tribunal is bound to the judgment ruling on its merits.

b) Should the party raise an objection within the time limit (see, *infra* paragraph IV) the statement on the jurisdiction may be challenged with a special appeal. This is known as the *regolamento di competenza* and is directed to the Supreme Court, but this does not prevent the parties from filing an application to the arbitrators.

c) Thus, even if the court has denied its jurisdiction, the arbitrators, seized with the same dispute, could in turn refuse their *potestas iudicandi* (the power of delivering a decision) if they consider that the arbitration agreement is invalid. It is the price one has to pay to ensure mutual independence between arbitrators and courts. However, some commentators have sought alternative solutions.[9]

d) A mitigation of that risk may arise from the time limit imposed on the party who is interested in raising the plea of lack of jurisdiction before the arbitrators (see paragraph I). If the plea is not raised in due time, the arbitral jurisdiction will be confirmed (Article 817 of Code of Civil Procedure).

15.19. Finally, if the Supreme Court rules on jurisdiction in favor of the arbitral tribunal, the parties can file an application, within a fixed time limit, to the arbitrators, in order to preserve the effect of the original action to the courts lack of jurisdiction (interruption of the prescription period, time-bars, etc.).[10]

---

[8]   It is a peculiar jurisdiction. Despite the principle of the *perpetuatio iurisdictionis*, an arbitral agreement is valid and prevents the judge from deciding on the merits, when it is also concluded *lite pendente*.

[9]   Consolo, *Soprassalti delle s.u. intorno all'eccezione di arbitrato estero e alla convenzione di n.y. quanto all'ordine delle questioni di rito e di doppio merito e riflessioni sull'art. 4 l. n. 218/1995*, CORRIERE GIURIDICO 925 (2004); in favour of an action to the court, in order to control the validity of the arbitral agreement, with binding effects in future arbitral or judicial proceedings, 5 LUISO, DIRITTO PROCESSUALE CIVILE, V, Milano: Giuffré 159 (7th ed. 2013).

[10]   Corte costituzionale, July 19, 2013 n° 223, CORRIERE GIURIDICO 1107 (2013), note CLAUDIO CONSOLO; See also Carlo Rasia, *La parziale incostituzionalità dell'art. 819-ter,*

III. Exception of Foreign Arbitration in the Italian Courts

15.20. When a plea on the grounds of an arbitral agreement for foreign arbitration is raised before Italian courts, the same applies. Beyond simply focusing on the nature of the arbitration, it must be examined whether Italian law contains specific rules on that subject matter.

15.21. The New York Convention is the main and prevalent source. Article II, paragraph 3, requires that the court "refer the parties to arbitration" upon request, unless the arbitration agreement is invalid.

15.22. Within Europe, the Geneva Convention of 1961 (spec. Article VI) and, more recently, the European Regulation n° 1215 of 2012 (on jurisdiction and the recognition and enforcement of judgments in civil and commercial matters) should also be taken into account.

15.23. The latter deals for the first time with arbitration. While reaffirming that the rules do not apply to arbitration, it expressly mentions the New York Convention of 1958, 'transforming' it to a European source and dedicates a long 'Whereas' (n. 12) on the interaction between arbitration and the national courts.

15.24. Finally, Law n° 218 of 31 May 1995[11] is the general and residual source. Article 4, paragraphs 2 and 11 apply the same law ruling conflict of jurisdiction as to a foreign court[12] to arbitration.

15.25. The combined effect of the above mentioned rules give rise to the following circumstances. The plea to lack of jurisdiction before the court can only be raised on request of the party, pursuant to Article 11, Law n° 218 of 1995, in compliance with Article II of New York Convention.[13]

15.26. Once the party has raised the plea, Law n° 218 of 1995 allows a preventive ruling for jurisdiction by the Supreme Court (*regolamento di giurisdizione*).[14] It is a good remedy, because it is not necessary to wait

---

comma 2, c.p.c.: una decisione attesa, RIVISTA TRIMESTRALE DIRITTO E PROCEDURA CIVILE 291 (2014).

[11] The 1995 Act, strongly influenced by the spirit of the Brussels Convention of 1968, has completely reformed the Italian system of private and procedural international law. The provisions of Law n° 218 of 1995 will only be applied if no European or conventional rules are applicable.

[12] Sergio La China, *L'arbitrato e la riforma del sistema italiano di diritto internazionale privato*, RIVISTA DELL'ARBITRATO 629 (1995); Antonio Briguglio, *L'accordo compromissorio e il lodo estero fra la convenzione di New York e le recenti novità legislative italiane*, GIUSTIZIA CIVILE, II, 467 (1997).

[13] Except the cases mentioned in Article 11.

[14] As a 'fast track' on the jurisdiction, Claudio Consolo, *L'arbitrato con sede estera, la natura della relativa eccezione e l'essenziale compito che rimane affidato al regolamento*

for the judgment on the jurisdiction of the court seized on the merits. It is reasonable to assume that the judgment of the Supreme Court will only bind the Italian court. Therefore, the risk remains of a negative effect of conflict of jurisdiction. The European Regulation n° 1215 of 2012 follows the same line.

15.27. A detailed analysis of the rules is not possible here.[15] It is sufficient to note that despite a certain lack of clarity in the above-mentioned 'Whereas', a ruling given by the court as to whether or not an arbitration agreement is valid cannot be recognized under the Regulation, 'regardless of whether the court decided on this as a principal issue or as an incidental question'.[16] However, where the court, exercising jurisdiction under the Regulation or national law, has decided on the merits, determining that the arbitral agreement is void, the judgment is automatically recognized in all Europe. This is true even when the arbitration has non-European nationality.[17]

15.28. In practice, the Regulation fills the space left empty by the New York Convention, which does not provide rules on the effects of the judgment declaring the invalidity of the arbitration agreement. Therefore, the ruling on the invalidity of the arbitration agreement should no longer be questioned, for example, in a naked action on the same issue in another state.[18]

15.29. However, because of the prevalence of the New York Convention, any judicial recognition of the judgment on the merits in another state cannot 'affect the jurisdiction of the courts of the Member States to decide on recognition and enforcement of arbitral awards'.[19]

15.30. The judge seized with an *exequatur* of the award will therefore not be bound to the judgment on the same dispute, as to the invalidity of the

---

transnazionale della giurisdizione italiana, in 2 STUDI IN ONORE DI CARMINE PUNZI, Torino: Giappichelli 407 (2008).

[15] See Carlo Rasia, *Il nuovo regolamento Ue n. 1251 del 2012 e l'arbitrato: a storm in a tea cup*, RIVISTA TRIMESTRALE DIRITTO E PROCEDURA CIVILE 193 (2014). Before, about the Green Paper and the Commission proposal, see CARLO RASIA, TUTELA GIUDIZIALE EUROPEA E ARBITRATO, Bologna: Bononia University Press 306 (2010).

[16] From the current Whereas clause n. 12 of European Regulation n° 1215 of 2012.

[17] Carlo Rasia, *Il nuovo regolamento, supra* note 15, at 204; Francesco Salerno, *Il coordinamento tra arbitrato e giustizia civile nel regolamento (Ue) n. 1215/2012*, RIVISTA DI DIRITTO INTERNAZIONALE 1169 (2013).

[18] *Court of appeal*, 17 dicembre 2009, *EWCA Civ.*, 1937 (2009), *National Navigation Co v. Endesa Generacion SA*. In the same meaning of the text, Alexis Mourre-Marie Nioche, *Le règlement Bruxelles I « refondu » évite le risque d'une régionalisation de l'arbitrage*, CAHIERS DE L'ARBITRAGE / PARIS JOURNAL OF INT'L ARB. 567 (2013).

[19] From the current Whereas clause n. 12 of European Regulation n° 1215 of 2012.

arbitration agreement. The above-mentioned restriction is thus greatly diminished.

15.31. The risk remains of conflicting judgments, circulating in different European countries.[20] When the arbitrators deny the jurisdiction already declined by the Italian court, the only way to solve the conflict would be as outlined by Article 4, paragraph 3, Law n° 218 of 1995: the court recovers her *potestas iudicandi* on the merits. Nevertheless, this solution is not fully satisfactory, as it does not preserve all the effect of the original application.

IV. The Review of the Award and of the State Judgment

15.32. As mentioned in the previous paragraphs, the Italian legislature of 2006 does not make a clear choice, although at first sight it seems to opt for the judicial nature of arbitration. On the one hand, it frames the relationships between judges and arbitrators in terms of jurisdiction. On the other hand, it does not draw all the necessary conclusions that the law assigns to the rules about jurisdiction. This difference is evident in the matter of the review of the award and of the state judgment, on which we must reflect further.

15.33. In the Italian system, the arbitrator's decision affirming or denying its own jurisdiction (by virtue of the positive effect of the *Kompetenz-Kompetenz* principle) may be challenged only through the recourse for nullity under Article 829, paragraph 1, n° 10 of the Code of Civil Procedure.[21]

15.34. However, in the opposite case when it is the state court who affirms or denies its jurisdiction in relation to an arbitration agreement, Article

---

[20] Catherine Kessedjian, *Le Règlement 'Bruxelles I revisé': Much ado about...what?*, 23 EUROPE, 5 (2013). If, at the time of recognition of the judgment on the merits, an arbitral award on the same dispute has already been enforced, Article 45, par. 1, lett. c), will apply (Giorgio Gaja, *Arbitrato e procedimento giudiziario in Stati diversi dopo la sentenza della Corte di giustizia nella causa* Marc Rich c. Italimpianti, RIVISTA DELL'ARBITRATO 417, 420 (1995); Hans Van Houtte, *May Court Judgments that Disregard Arbitration Clauses and Awards be Enforced under the Brussels and Lugano Convention?*, ARBITRATION INTERNATIONAL 85 (1997)).

[21] That method avoided the possibility that, after several years, the judge could declare its lack of jurisdiction, with as consequence the need of starting again the proceeding. In literature, Giuseppe Ruffini, *Sub. Art. 819-ter, in* LA NUOVA DISCIPLINA DELL'ARBITRATO, Padova: Cedam 364, 381 (S. Menchini ed., 2010). Recently, Laura Salvaneschi, *Il rapporto tra arbitro e giudice dopo la decisione della consulta*, RIVISTA DI DIRITTO PROCESSUALE 384, 386-387 at note 7 (2014).

819-*ter* of the Code of Civil Procedure recognizes the admissibility of a jurisdictional challenge under Articles 42 and 43 (*regolamento di competenza*). The consequence is allowing the unsuccessful part a direct application to the Supreme Court for a decision on jurisdiction, bypassing the second instance. In this way, it is possible to quickly identify who is the competent judge to decide. The further effect is that the decision of the Supreme Court shall be binding on both the judge and the arbitrator, and it will no longer be questioned at any further stage of the proceeding.

15.35. The relationship between arbitrator and ordinary court is different from the relationship that there is between arbitrator and administrative or tax judge. In fact, the latter courts are 'special judge' in the Italian system. They are judges who carry out specific competences by law and therefore belong to a different and distinct order from the ordinary courts.

15.36. In this context, considering that no ordinary judge or arbitrator has the power to decide in the Italian system,[22] the relationship between the arbitrator and the specialized judge can be decided before any other matter. All that is needed is a request for a preliminary ruling on jurisdiction according to Article 41 of the Code of Civil Procedure, known as *regolamento di giurisdizione*.[23]

15.37. This tool allows each party to request that the Supreme Court give a preventive ruling on the issue of jurisdiction until dispute has been decided on its merits during the first instance. In particular, the ruling will decide the issue in joint divisions by identifying if the judge or arbitrator has jurisdiction and the power to decide the dispute. The practical advantage of this procedure is that the judgment given by the Supreme Court, in its most 'authoritative' composition (i.e. the *Sezioni Unite*), is final and immediately binding on any other court, and not subject to appeal.

15.38. The relationship between judge and a foreign arbitrator is resolved in the same way as the relationship between 'special judge' and arbitrator. The aforementioned judgment n. 24153/2013 solves this report in a relationship between the two different jurisdictions.[24]

15.39. Therefore regarding the validity and the effectiveness of a foreign arbitration clause, the question of whether the dispute is remittable to

---

[22] Recently Cass., February 3, 2014 n° 2323, DE JURE DVD.

[23] Unlike the 'regolamento di competenza', this is not a form of appeal, but rather an incident in the procedure, to definitively solve the jurisdiction issue at the very beginning of the dispute.

[24] This is Cass., (ord.), October 25, 2013 n° 24153, *supra* note 7.

the arbitrators will have to be framed as a matter of jurisdiction and not on merits[25] as it was in the past. If the defendant believes that the foreign arbitration clause should be respected, there is still the opportunity within the state proceeding to request a preliminary ruling on jurisdiction according to Article 41 of the Code of Civil Procedure. The aim is to immediately receive a final decision from the Supreme Court about the validity or invalidity of the arbitration clause for a foreign arbitration.

V. The *Lis Pendens* between Arbitrator and Judge

15.40. The Italian legislature allows the simultaneous pendency of the same or a related dispute both in front of the state court and in front of an arbitrator. This is possible thanks to the mechanism whereby the jurisdiction of the arbitrators is not precluded by the prior submission of the request in the ordinary place (see the first part of paragraph 1 of the Article 819-*ter* of the Code of Civil Procedure).[26] However, in the case of parallel pendency of the same case before the state court and the arbitrator, in the Italian system has not introduced any preventive remedy to prevent possible conflicts between the two decisions.[27] In this respect, the discipline of *lis pendens* between arbitrator and judge contains neither the principle of prevention (it is irrelevant which judgment was first established), or the power to examine *ex officio* (by the court or arbitrator) the contemporary pendency of the judgments. The Italian choice was 'dual input', in the sense of the so-called principle of parallel pathways, where one can follow the path of

---

[25] For case law, Cass., sez. un., (ord.), July 22, 2002 n° 10723, REPERTORIO FORO ITALIANO, voce Arbitrato, I, 1832 (2003); Cass., sez. un., (ord.), April 18, 2003 n° 6349, FORO ITALIANO, I, 1241 (2004); Cass., sez. un., (ord.), January 5, 2007, n° 35, FORO ITALIANO, I, 2173 (2007). See comments of Eduardo F. Ricci, *La cassazione di pronuncia ancora sulla 'natura' della convenzione di arbitrato rituale: tra l'attaccamento a vecchi schemi e qualche incertezza concettuale,* RIVISTA DI DIRITTO PROCESSUALE 1293 (2007).

[26] 'The arbitrators' jurisdiction shall not be excluded by the pendency of the same dispute before the judge or by the connection between the dispute referred to them and a dispute pending before the judge (...)'.

[27] Without an express rule, it is not possible to apply the Italian Code of Civil Procedure, Art. 39, concerning *lis pendens* between two state judgments. In this last case, if actions involving the same parties and having the same object are pending before different judges, the judge before whom the action was later filed issues an order stating the *lis alibi pendens* and orders the striking of the case from the General Register of Proceedings. This can occur at any state and instance of the proceeding, even on the court's own motion.

arbitration or the ordinary judgment, when there is a claim of invalidity or ineffectiveness of the arbitration agreement.

15.41. There is no priority in favor of the arbitrator: the two proceedings – arbitral and court proceedings – can progress in parallel.[28] The model of parallel pathways is characterized by the following elements:

a) there is no priority of one way over the other;

b) the pendency of the dispute in a place does not preclude the submission of the request in the other;

c) The connection between the two pathways comes through their judgments.[29]

15.42. The only corrective to the mutual independence of the two judgments is the case where one of the parties starts the arbitration proceedings and after this, the other party starts the proceeding to the state court asking for the simple declaration of invalidity/ineffectiveness of the arbitration agreement. In this case, paragraph 3 of the Article 819-*ter* of the Code of Civil Procedure prescribes that 'pending the arbitral proceeding, no requests may be submitted to the judicial authorities regarding the invalidity or lack of efficacy of the arbitration agreement'. Therefore the defendant in front of a state court (who is the plaintiff in the arbitration proceeding) could ask the court to stay the second proceeding, promptly joining the proceeding and demonstrating the pendency of the arbitration.

15.43. Apart from this extreme case, it is always sufficient that the defendant in arbitration starts a proceeding in front of the state court proposing the same merits question proposed before the arbitrators. In this way, the defendant can validly start the same proceeding even before the state court. The defendant in the state court – the plaintiff in arbitration – will then have the duty to promptly file a defense referred to as 'the objection to the judge's jurisdiction by reason of the arbitration agreement must be raised' as required by paragraph 1 of the Article 819-*ter* of the Code of Civil Procedure. The choice of such a

---

[28] The Italian legal system does not recognize the negative effect of the *Kompetenz-Kompetenz* principle, which must be kept distinct from the so-called positive effect as regards arbitrators. The question is whether a court seized by a party with the merits of a dispute and whose jurisdiction is challenged on the basis of an arbitration agreement should confine itself to a *prima facie* control that a valid arbitration agreement exists, and refer the parties to arbitration if so satisfied. Among national laws, the French Code of Civil Procedure clearly recognizes the negative effect. The new Article 1884 of the Code (into force on 1 May 2011) allowed courts to examine only whether the arbitration agreement is *manifestement nulle* and whether it is *manifestement inapplicable*.

[29] Likewise Francesco P. Luiso, *Rapporti fra arbitro e giudice*, RIVISTA DELL'ARBITRATO 773, 788 (2005).

solution, which may facilitate the choice to the deemed competent authority at the beginning, has the main effect of causing two decisions (the state's and the arbitration court's) that conflict with each other.

15.44. Now that we have seen that there is not a preventative measure in case of *lis pendence* between arbitrator and judge, we can turn to an analysis of the issue of remedies following the judgment/award rendered in one of the two parallel proceedings. We have to distinguish the situation where (a) the judgment is rendered before the award from (b) where the award is rendered before the judgment.[30]

15.45. a) In the situation (in practice, uncommon) in which the state court renders a decision on the same case pending in arbitration:

1) If the authority of the judgment is invoked and produced before the arbitrators (i.e. the text of the judgment is admitted during the arbitration), the arbitral proceedings shall be stayed according to the Articles 819-*bis*, paragraph 2, and 337, paragraph 2, of the Code of Civil Procedure.[31]

2) If the judgment invoked and produced in arbitration with the *res judicata* effect, the award that is contrary to the court judgment can be set aside in front of the Court of Appeal according to Article 829, paragraph 1, n. 8, of the Code of Civil Procedure because the arbitrators did not consider it.[32]

3) If the judgment has not been invoked or produced in arbitration we will have two valid decisions (the state judgment and the award), but the decision which has become final first will prevail.

15.46. b) Alternatively, in the situation where the arbitrator renders the award before the judge on the same case pending in front of a court:

1) If the award invoked in the state trial is not challengeable, the judgment invoked and produced in the arbitral proceeding in contradiction with the award, may be set aside in the appeal or with the *regolamento di competenza*.[33]

---

[30] See also Mario Olivieri, Giulio Verrina, *Le questioni pregiudiziali di merito e i rapporti tra arbitri e giudice, in* ARBITRATO, Milano: Ipsoa, 143, 156 (2012).

[31] Art. 819-*bis*, paragraph 2 (stay of the arbitral proceedings): 'Should the authority of a judgment be relied upon in the arbitral proceedings and such judgment be challenged, Article 337, paragraph 2, shall be applicable'. According to Art. 337, a special petition has to be filed to obtain the so-called *sospensiva* (stay) of the provisional enforcing authority of the decision.

[32] Art. 829, paragraph 1, n.8 allows the setting aside of an award if it is contradictory to a prior judgment or award, and not to a subsequent judgment, being *res iudicata*.

[33] The *regolamento di competenza* is a special appeal that is brought directly to the Supreme Court, bypassing the second instance appeal judge. The choice between the appeal and the *regolamento di competenza* depends on the decision. If the decision speaks

2) If the award invoked in the state trial has been appealed, the state proceedings can be stayed according to Article 337, paragraph 2, and 824-*bis* of the Code of Civil Procedure.[34]

3) If the award is no longer open to challenge and it was not invoked in the state trial, the judgment that is contrary to the award may be revoked according to Article 395, n. 5 of the Code of Civil Procedure.[35]

15.47. If we want to consider the simultaneous pendency between arbitration and state proceedings in an international context, we can point out three scenarios: (i) competition between state proceedings in Italy and arbitration whose seat was located abroad; (ii) competition between arbitration proceedings in Italy and state proceedings abroad; (iii) competition between arbitration based in Italy and arbitration based abroad.

15.48. i) The parallel pendency of a state proceeding in Italy and a foreign arbitration is not ruled by a specific article of the New York Convention of 1958 (of which Italy is a member). Instead, it is covered under the Geneva Convention of 1961. In Article 6, paragraph 3, it provides that judges 'shall stay their ruling on the arbitrator's jurisdiction until the arbitral award is made, unless they have good and substantial reasons to the contrary'. Certain Italian authors interpret this rule as a case of staying of the proceeding.[36] Outside the scope of the Geneva Convention, it raises the question of how the *lis pendens* between arbitrator and judge should be governed, because we cannot appeal to European Regulation n° 1215 of 2012, nor to the Lugano Convention of 2007.[37] The Italian doctrine questioned about the possibility of applying Article 7, paragraph 1, of the Law n° 218 of 31 May 1995, which governs the *lis pendens*

---

only about the issue of jurisdiction, the decision may be appealed only through the *regolamento*. If the decision speaks about both issues of jurisdiction and other procedural or substantive matters, there is a choice between an ordinary appeal to the Court of Appeal and the *regolamento* to the Supreme Court. However, it will only be for the issue of jurisdiction.

[34] Art. 824-*bis* provides that the award shall have the same effect as a judgment rendered by a judicial authority.

[35] According to Art. 395, n° 5, when there are two conflicting judgments rendered between the same parties on the same subject-matter, the second must give way to the first, in compliance with the *ne bis in idem* principle.

[36] Elisa Picozza, *L'accordo compromissorio per arbitrato commerciale internazionale straniero davanti al giudice italiano*, RIVISTA DELL'ARBITRATO 282 (2004).

[37] See, in literature, *amplius*, Carlo Rasia, *Arbitrato e regolamento Ce n. 44 del 2001: permane l'esclusione dal campo di applicazione?*, GIUSTIZIA SENZA CONFINI. STUDI OFFERTI A FEDERICO CARPI, Bologna: Bononia University Press, 391, 408 (2012).

between Italian and foreign state court. This is because of the same authority and effects between an (*ritual*) award and a judicial decision.[38]

15.49. ii) Concerning the parallel pendency of an arbitration proceeding in Italy and a foreign state proceeding already rooted abroad, it is necessary to refer to Article 819-*ter* of the Code of Civil Procedure. Pursuant to this code, the jurisdiction of the arbitrators is not excluded from the pendency of the same proceeding in front of the Italian judge. This rule will then have to be applied by analogy to pending proceedings abroad.[39]

15.50. iii) Concerning the parallel pendency of an arbitral proceeding in Italy and a foreign arbitral proceeding, the Italian system does not recognize the *lis pendens* between two foreign arbitrators.

VI. The *Translatio Iudicii* between Arbitrator and Judge

15.51. There is a need to have a mechanism for the preservation of the substantive and procedural effects of the claim instituting the proceeding in the relationship between (ritual) arbitration and the state judge. This has long been one of the most difficult points to deal with in the domain of Italian civil procedure.

15.52. The problem rests in the fact that the mistake made by the plaintiff in identifying the state court provided of *potestas decidendi* (the power of delivering a decision) rather than the arbitrator and vice versa should not harm its chances of getting a decision on the merits of the dispute from the organ that had the correct jurisdiction. This happened because foreclosures and forfeitures provided by law had accrued in the meantime. By virtue of the imperfect analogy on the level of jurisdiction among judges and arbitrators, the Italian legislature of 2006 decided that the judgment/award rendered by the judge or by the

---

[38] Also agrees with the use of this rule even in the case where the foreign arbitration was started first, ROBERTO MARENGO, LA LITISPENDENZA INTERNAZIONALE, Torino: Giappichelli, 211 (2000), Carlo Rasia, *Il conflitto transnazionale tra giurisdizione ordinaria e arbitrato sulla medesima lite. Spunti su un principio di lis alibi pendens nell'arbitrato internazionale*, RIVISTA TRIMESTRALE DI DIRITTO E PROCEDURA CIVILE 1071 (2004). Art. 7 of Law n° 218 of 1995, inspired by Art. 21 of the Brussels Convention of 1968, states that the jurisdiction of the Italian court is denied if previous proceedings between the same parties on the same subject-matter are pending abroad, and the Italian Judge comes to the conclusion that the foreign judgment is likely to be recognized in Italy. If this is the case, Italian proceedings are not dismissed but stayed, so that, should the foreign court decline its jurisdiction or the foreign proceedings be discontinued or a decision on the merits of the claim not be rendered, the original stay can be lifted and the case adjudicated upon.

[39] This sentence is confirmed by Cass. (ord.), October 8, 2013 n° 24153, *supra* note 7.

arbitrator concerning its lack of jurisdiction had no binding force for the new judge/arbitrator.

15.53. In fact, Article 819-*ter* excludes Article 50 of the Code of Civil Procedure, which creates the possibility of continuing the dispute in front of the *ad quem* judge after that the former judge has declined jurisdiction.

15.54. This legislative choice had received criticism from scholars of Italian legal doctrine.[40] A recent intervention of the Italian Constitutional Court in 2013 has finally declared the salvation of the substantive and procedural effects of the claim that institutes the proceeding in the relationships between arbitrators. It also spoke about the preservation of the activities carried forward by the wrong authority.[41]

15.55. In framing the relationship between judge and ritual arbitrator under the framework of the jurisdiction, the judges allow the workability of Article 50 of the Code of Civil Procedure with the mechanism of the *translatio iudicii*.[42]

15.56. However, it should be added that, the passage of the case from the arbitrators to judges and vice versa is not complete, but it remains an option and not a mandatory duty for the party who was unsuccessful to the declaration of jurisdiction.

15.57. In fact, the Court leaves the foreclosure by Article 819-*ter* of the Code of Civil Procedure of Article 44 of the Code of Civil Procedure intact. It does not solve the problem of the binding effectiveness of the decision of lack of jurisdiction of the former judge to the second court.

15.58. In this context, the decision of the court or of the arbitrator does not compromise the decision of the second authority, even a negative decision. In a system such as the Italian one, shaped around the principle of the 'parallel pathways' and then around the surrender, a decision does not need to have a preventive coordination mechanism between state and arbitration proceedings. It is clear that the statement of the Constitutional Court does not solve the positive conflict. Above all, it does not solve the negative conflict of the decisions of the arbitrator and the judge. The effect is that the problem of potential double denial of justice remains structural within the current system.

---

[40] Salvatore Boccagna, *Appunti sulla nuova disciplina dei rapporti tra arbitrato e giurisdizione*, in 3 STUDI IN ONORE DI CARMINE PUNZI, Torino: Giappichelli 330 (2008).

[41] This is the decision of Corte costituzionale, July 19, 2013 n° 223, *supra* note 10.

[42] After the first decision has become *res judicata*, and within three months, the parties may bring the case before the court indicated in that decision. At this point, the dispute will continue before the new judge, preserving the substantial and procedural effects of the original claim. The lawmaker has expressly acknowledged the unity of the jurisdictional system of Italian courts, establishing a mechanism for ordinary, administrative, tax and special court to communicate with each other and preserve the parties' rights.

VII. Concluding Remarks

15.59. The relationship between arbitrator and judge in the Italian system is a relationship of jurisdiction. This is what emerges from the reform of 2006 and from the recent decisions of the Constitutional Court and the Supreme Court, examined above.

15.60. However, as we have said, this institution does not, in its entirety, use the typical rules of the system to regulate the jurisdiction between judges. In fact, there are a number of special rules set out in Title VIII of the Code of Civil Procedure that make specific rules for those links. Moreover, these rules sometimes are close to, and sometimes diverge from those rules that are common to the courts.

15.61. Consider, for example, those related to the different appeal of the judgment and of the award that has decided about the validity of the clause. Or consider the lack of binding nature of the decision when the case is transferred between arbitrator and judge or vice versa.

15.62. We therefore believe that the equalization of the relationship between arbitrators and judges must be seen, inside our system, as a *sui generis* relationship of jurisdiction. Moreover, despite the encouraging decisions of the Supreme Court, it cannot be said that there is a total equalization with the relationship between judges and arbitrators. It is not possible to reach different conclusions even after the proposal of reform of the Code of Civil Procedure. In this reform, the Italian legislature gets stronger the will of not solving the entire relationship judge-arbitrator in a matter of jurisdiction *tout court*, as it would be between ordinary judges.[43] Nevertheless, there has been a slow and gradual movement towards the modernization of arbitration as a form comparable to the jurisdiction. The closing of this gap cannot come from the activity of jurisprudence. The intervention of the legislature is necessary. The situation is quite different when the relationship is between the judge and the foreign arbitration clause. Here the connection has to be framed, as when it happens with a foreign court, within a matter of jurisdiction. Therefore, the battle between arbitrator and judge is only at its beginning and there is still much to be written and told.

| | |

---

[43] V. Carlo Rasia, *Le proposte di modifica in materia di arbitrato*, RIVISTA TRIMESTRALE DI DIRITTO E PROCEDURA CIVILE, 417, 418 (2014), who comments on the text of the ministerial committee, chaired by prof. Romano Vaccarella, named to make proposals in civil procedure and mediation matters (the draft was filed at the Ministry of Justice on the 3rd of December of 2013).

Summaries

FRA *[Le juge arbitre par opposition au juge]*

La relation entre le juge et le juge arbitre est dans le droit italien un rapport de compétences. Cela résulte de la réforme adoptée en 2006 et des décisions rendues en 2013 par la Cour constitutionnelle et la Cour suprême. La réglementation de l'arbitrage procède pour certaines questions de la réglementation applicable à une procédure judiciaire, et s'en écarte pour d'autres questions.

Un exemple est donné par la réglementation des recours, qui se différencie du mécanisme de l'examen de la sentence arbitrale, pour lequel on a décidé de la validité des clauses compromissoires. D'autres divergences sont constatées, par exemple en ce qui concerne le caractère contraignant des décisions, dans les cas où il y a un transfert de compétences du juge arbitre vers le juge (ou inversement).

Il est nécessaire d'évaluer la relation existante entre le juge et le juge arbitre - au moins en ce qui concerne le droit italien - comme un rapport d'une compétence particulière avec une compétence générale. Il faut également souligner, qu'en dépit des décisions rendues par la Cour suprême, il semble impossible de considérer que le juge arbitre puisse avoir une position égale à celle du juge.

CZE *[Rozhodce versus soudce]*

Vztah mezi rozhodcem a soudcem je v italském právním řádu vztahem pravomocí. Vyplývá to z reformy provedené v roce 2006 a z nejnovějších rozhodnutí Ústavního soudu a Nejvyššího soudu vydaných v roce 2013. Právní úprava rozhodčího řízení v některých otázkách vychází z úpravy použitelné na řízení před soudem, jindy se od ní odchyluje.

Příkladem je úprava odvolání proti rozsudku, která se liší od mechanismu přezkumu rozhodčího nálezu, v němž bylo rozhodnuto o platnosti rozhodčí doložky. Další odchylky se týkají například závaznosti rozhodnutí v případech, kdy dochází k přenesení z pravomoci rozhodce k soudci (nebo naopak).

Vztah mezi rozhodcem a soudcem je zapotřebí posuzovat, alespoň pokud jde o italský právní řád, jako vztah zvláštní pravomoci k pravomoci obecné. Navíc je nutno zdůraznit, že navzdory rozhodnutím Nejvyššího soudu podporujícím rozhodčí řízení nelze konstatovat, že by bylo možnost rozhodce považovat za osobu rovnou postavení soudce.

||||

POL [*Arbiter versus sędzia*]
Relacja między arbitrem i sędzią we włoskim systemie prawa to relacja uprawnień. Wynika to z reformy przeprowadzonej w 2006 roku oraz z najnowszych orzeczeń Sądu Konstytucyjnego i Sądu Najwyższego, wydanych w 2013 roku. Regulacje prawne w zakresie postępowania arbitrażowego w niektórych kwestiach opierają się na regulacjach mających zastosowanie do postępowania przed sądem, w innych punktach od nich odchodzą. Relacja między arbitrem a sędzią musi być rozpatrywana, przynajmniej w świetle włoskiego porządku prawnego, jako relacja uprawnień szczególnych względem uprawnień ogólnych, stąd aktualnie nie można stwierdzić, czy arbitra można byłoby uznać za osobą równą względem sędziego.

DEU [*Schiedsrichter versus Richter*]
Die Beziehung zwischen Schiedsrichter und Richter ist im italienischen Recht eine durch Zuständigkeiten abgegrenzte Beziehung. Dies ergibt sich aus der im Jahre 2006 umgesetzten Reform und den jüngsten Entscheidungen des Verfassungsgerichts und des Obersten Gerichtshofs aus dem Jahre 2013. In manchen Bereichen hat sich der rechtliche Rahmen des Schiedsverfahrens von der auf gerichtliche Verfahren anwendbaren Regelung inspirieren lassen, anderswo wiederum weicht er von dieser ab. Zumindest insoweit als von der italienischen Rechtsordnung die Rede ist, muss die Beziehung zwischen Schiedsrichter und Richter als Beziehung zwischen spezieller und allgemeiner Zuständigkeit beurteilt werden; momentan lässt sich nicht sagen, dass der Schiedsrichter als dem Richter gleichgestellt betrachtet werden könnte.

RUS [*Арбитр против судьи*]
Отношения между арбитром и судьей в итальянской правовой системе представляют собой отношения, связанные с компетенциями. Это вытекает из реформы 2006 года, а также из недавних решений Конституционного суда и Верховного суда, опубликованных в 2013 году. Правовое регулирование арбитража в некоторых вопросах исходит из регулирования, применимого к судебным разбирательствам, а иногда от него отклоняется. Отношения между арбитром и судьей следует рассмотреть, по крайней мере, если речь идет об итальянской правовой системе, как отношение особой компетенции к общей компетенции, и в настоящее время нельзя утверждать, что арбитра можно считать лицом, равным судье.

ESP   [*Árbitro contra juez*]

En el ordenamiento jurídico italiano, la relación entre el árbitro y el juez se entiende como una relación de jurisdicción. Se desprende de las reformas realizadas en 2006, así como de las recientes decisiones del Tribunal Constitucional y la Corte Suprema dictadas en 2013. Hay algunas cuestiones en las que la legislación de arbitraje parte de la regulación aplicable a los procedimientos ante el tribunal, no obstante, a veces se desvía. La relación entre el árbitro y el juez debe considerarse, al menos en cuanto al ordenamiento jurídico italiano, una relación de jurisdicción especial ante la jurisdicción general, y actualmente es difícil constatar que el árbitro se considere una persona con una posición equivalente a la de juez.

| | |

Case Law

I. Czech Republic – Case Law of Czech Courts on Arbitration

Alexander J. Bělohlávek

CONTENTS

LIST OF ABBREVIATIONS

AC	Arbitration Court at the Economic Chamber of the Czech Republic and Agricultural Chamber of the Czech Republic
ArbAct	Act of the Czech Republic No. 216/1994 Coll., on Arbitration and the Enforcement of Arbitral Awards, as amended
CC	Act of the Czech Republic No. 89/2012 Coll., the Civil Code
CCP	Act of the Czech Republic No. 99/1963 Coll., the Code of Civil Procedure, as amended
Charter	Resolution of the Presidium of the Czech National Council No. 2/1993 Coll., on the promulgation of the Charter of Fundamental Rights and Freedoms as part of the constitutional order of the Czech Republic, as amended
CivC	Act of the Czech Republic No. 40/1964 Coll., the Civil Code, as amended
CJA	Act of the Czech Republic No. 6/2002 Coll., on Courts and Judges, as amended
CJEU	Court of Justice of the European Union
ComC	Act of the Czech Republic No. 513/1991 Coll., the Commercial Code, in effect until December 31, 2013
ConCourt	Constitutional Court of the Czech Republic
CR	Czech Republic
ECtHR	European Court of Human Rights
EU	European Union
ExecC	Act of the Czech Republic No. 120/2001 Coll., on Execution Agents and Execution, as amended
InsAct	Act of the Czech Republic No. 182/2006 Coll., the Insolvency Act, as amended
New York Convention (1958)	New York Convention on the Recognition and Enforcement of Foreign Arbitral Awards (1958)
SC	Supreme Court of the Czech Republic

1. Judgment of Supreme Court of May 29, 2013 in Case No. 23 Cdo 3396/2012: (i) Possibility to Assert Grounds for Annulment of Arbitral Award after Deadline Stipulated in Section 32(1) of ArbAct; (ii) Prohibition of *Revision au Fond*

Abbreviations Used:

ArbAct	Act of the Czech Republic No. 216/1994 Coll., on Arbitration and the Enforcement of Arbitral Awards, as amended[1]
CCP	Act of the Czech Republic No. 99/1963 Coll., the Code of Civil Procedure, as amended
CivC	Act of the Czech Republic No. 40/1964 Coll., the Civil Code, as amended[2]
SC	Supreme Court of the Czech Republic

Key Words:
annulment (setting aside) of arbitral award | appellate proceedings | arbitral award | arbitration clause | concentration of proceedings | grounds for annulment of arbitral award | impossible performance | issue of principal legal significance | limited possibility to assert grounds for annulment | material review | prohibition of revision au fond | revision au fond | time period for filing motion to annul arbitral award | unlawful performance |

---

[1] The decision of the SC in this case is based on the ArbAct in effect until March 31, 2012, but no subsequent changes have any bearing on the conclusions of the SC and their applicability; this particular case does not involve a consumer contract or, as applicable, a dispute arising from a consumer contract, and the rules introduced in the ArbAct by the Consumer Amendment, i.e. Act No. 19/2012 Coll., would not affect the case at hand. Generally, however, it is necessary to point out that the conclusions reached by the court shall not apply to disputes arising from consumer contracts after the passage of Act No. 19/2012 Coll. (or rather, the amendment codified the enhanced consumer protection, but the SC already mentioned the specific aspects of consumer protection in the annotated decision and inferred that the SC would apply these aspects to a consumer dispute).

[2] This Act has been replaced by Act No. 89/2012 Coll., the "new Civil Code" (abbreviated as the "CC" in this annotation), with effect since January 1, 2014. However, legal relationships established before January 1, 2014 shall be governed (save for certain exceptions) by the previous law, i.e. Act No. 40/1964 Coll., the Civil Code, as amended (abbreviated as the "CivC" in this annotation).

Laws and Regulations Applied in Decision:
ArbAct: Section 31,[3] Section 32[4]

---

[3]   ArbAct, Section 31 (cit.):

ArbAct in effect until March 31, 2012 (the law applicable to the given case, cit.): *"At the request of any party the court annuls the arbitral award if: (a) it was made in a case which cannot be submitted to arbitration (cannot be the subject of a valid arbitration agreement), (b) the arbitration agreement is invalid for other reasons or the agreement was cancelled or it does not apply to the agreed case, (c) the arbitrator(s) who took part in the proceedings was/were not authorized to make decisions in the case, whether under the arbitration agreement or otherwise, or lacked the capacity to act as arbitrator(s), (d) the arbitral award was not adopted by the majority of the arbitrators, (e) a party was denied the opportunity to plead his or her case in the arbitral proceedings, (f) the arbitral award orders a party to provide performance which was not requested by the obligee or to provide performance which is impossible or illegal under domestic law, (g) it transpires that there are reasons which would otherwise justify the reopening of civil proceedings in court."*

ArbAct in effect since April 1, 2012 (cit.): *"At the request of any party the court annuls the arbitral award if: (a) it was made in a case which cannot be submitted to arbitration (cannot be the subject of a valid arbitration agreement), (b) the arbitration agreement is invalid for other reasons or the agreement was cancelled or it does not apply to the agreed case, (c) the arbitrator(s) who took part in the proceedings was/were not authorized to make decisions in the case, whether under the arbitration agreement or otherwise, or lacked the capacity to act as arbitrator(s), (d) the arbitral award was not adopted by the majority of the arbitrators, (e) a party was denied the opportunity to plead his or her case in the arbitral proceedings, (f) the arbitral award orders a party to provide performance which was not requested by the creditor or to provide performance which is impossible or illegal under domestic law, (g) the arbitrator or the permanent arbitral institution resolved a dispute arising from a consumer contract contrary to consumer protection laws, or clearly in violation of good morals, or contrary to public policy, (h) an arbitration agreement relating to disputes arising from consumer contracts lacks the information required under Section 3(5) or such information is intentionally or to a non-negligible extent incomplete, inaccurate, or false, or (i) it transpires that there are reasons which would otherwise justify the reopening of civil proceedings in court."*

[4]   ArbAct, Section 32 (cit.):

ArbAct in effect until March 31, 2012 (the law applicable to the given case, cit.): *"(1) The motion to annul an arbitral award must be lodged with the court within three months following the receipt of the arbitral award by the party requesting the annulment of the award, unless this Act stipulates otherwise. (2) The motion pursuant to subsection (1) does not suspend the enforceability of the arbitral award. If requested by the obligor, however, the court may suspend the enforceability of the arbitral award in case an immediate enforcement of the arbitral award could cause serious harm."*

ArbAct in effect since April 1, 2012 (cit.): *"(1) The motion to annul an arbitral award must be lodged with the court within three months following the receipt of the arbitral award by the party requesting the annulment of the award, unless this Act stipulates otherwise. If the arbitral award was made in a dispute arising from a consumer contract and the motion to*

The Supreme Court of the Czech Republic arrived at the following principal conclusions:

(1) The interpretation of Section 32(1) of the ArbAct[5] and Section 31 of the ArbAct[6] requires the analogous application of the Code of Civil Procedure as concerns the possibility of asserting further grounds for the annulment of the arbitral award in proceedings initiated within the period of three months after the arbitral award is served on the party who demands the annulment of the arbitral award. Section 32 of the ArbAct[7] (as applicable before the amendment implemented by Act No. 19/2012 Coll.) is only important from the perspective of determining whether the motion itself to annul the arbitral award was lodged in time. The provision cannot be interpreted as a limitation of the claimant's procedural rights to adduce in the course of the proceedings any relevant circumstances that contain further grounds for the annulment of the arbitral award under Section 31 of the ArbAct. The right to supplement relevant circumstances can only be limited by statutory procedural limits under the Code of Civil Procedure (such as the concentration of proceedings). In other words, the party may assert (further) grounds for the annulment of the arbitral award under Section 31 of the ArbAct in proceedings for the annulment of the arbitral award that were commenced before the expiration of the time period under Section 32 of the ArbAct,[8] even after the time period expires.[9]

(2) "Unlawful" performance as one of the grounds for the annulment of an arbitral award can be interpreted as meaning any performance that is not approved by national (domestic) law. This will apply to

---

annul was lodged by the consumer, the court always examines whether there are grounds to annul the arbitral award pursuant to Section 31(a) through (d) or (h). (2) The motion pursuant to subsection (1) does not suspend the enforceability of the arbitral award. If requested by the obligor, however, the court may suspend the enforceability of the arbitral award in case an immediate enforcement of the arbitral award could cause serious harm or in case the motion to annul the arbitral award justifies the conclusion that the motion is legitimate. (3) If the motion to annul an arbitral award is lodged by the consumer, the court shall establish whether there are grounds to suspend the enforceability of the arbitral award pursuant to subsection (2) without the consumer's request. The court shall rule on the suspension of enforceability within 7 days of receiving the motion; the arbitral award cannot be enforced within said time limit."

5 This provision is quoted in the opening part of the annotation of this SC decision.
6 This provision is quoted in the opening part of the annotation of this SC decision.
7 This provision is quoted in the opening part of the annotation of this SC decision.
8 This provision is quoted in the opening part of the annotation of this SC decision.
9 This provision is quoted in the opening part of the annotation of this SC decision.

performance that is reserved for certain entities only, primarily the state, or that is subject to state supervision or state license (such as explosives, firearms, narcotics, mineral resources, parts of the human body, etc.), dispositions with which can be restricted or proscribed. Considering the nature of arbitration, the purpose of which inheres in the fact that the hearing and resolution of particular types of disputes is transferred from courts to arbitrators, and with respect to the grounds for which an arbitral award can be annulled, we may conclude that the legislator intended to exclude judicial review of the material correctness of the arbitral award, i.e. the accuracy of the findings of fact and legal assessment of the case (prohibition of *revision au fond*). If the court in the proceedings for the annulment of arbitral award were to review the award's material correctness, the legal rules regulating arbitral awards would become pointless.

[*From Facts of Case and Procedure*]:

16.01. In its Judgment of July 5, 2009 in Case No. 26 Cm 197/2009-70, as amended by the Corrective Resolution of November 15, 2011 in Case No. 26 Cm 197/2009-99, the Municipal Court in Prague dismissed the motion to annul the arbitral award rendered by arbitrator YY on August 27, 2009 (*ad hoc* arbitration).

16.02. The court of first instance was called upon to decide whether the respective arbitral award ought to be annulled under Section 31(f) of the ArbAct, because, **as alleged by the claimant, the arbitral award ordered unlawful and impossible performance.**[10] The court of first instance held that the relevant issue in the case inhered in the fact that the respective arbitral award had ordered the claimant to pay the stipulated pecuniary amount to the respondent by the stipulated deadline, as well as reimburse the respondent for the costs of the arbitration by the stipulated deadline, i.e. pay the stipulated pecuniary amount of the costs. The court of first instance ruled that such obligations imposed by the arbitral award were by no means unlawful or impossible under Czech law in terms of the abovementioned provision of the ArbAct. The claimant (respondent in the arbitral proceedings) asserted new grounds for the annulment of the arbitral award in her appeal, namely the invalidity of the arbitration agreement pursuant to Section 31(b) of the ArbAct.[11]

16.03. The Prague High Court, as the appellate court, upheld the decision of the court of first instance and concluded that any and all grounds for

---

[10]   This provision is quoted in the opening part of the annotation of this SC decision.

[11]   This provision is quoted in the opening part of the annotation of this SC decision.

the annulment of an arbitral award must be asserted within the prescriptive three-month period stipulated in Section 32(1) of the ArbAct,[12] and any grounds asserted after the expiration of the said period must be disregarded by the court that is seized with the motion to annul the arbitral award. The appellate court stated that the rule also applied to the given case, even though the arbitration clause on the basis of which the arbitration had been held was invalid (null and void) under Section 39 of the CivC,[13] because the claimant's right to assert those grounds for the annulment of the arbitral award was extinguished upon expiration of the period stipulated in Section 32(1) of the ArbAct.[14] The Prague High Court also agreed with the conclusion reached by the court of first instance in that the grounds for the annulment of the arbitral award under Section 31(f) of the ArbAct[15] were not fulfilled. The performance that the claimant was ordered to provide under the arbitral award (payment of a pecuniary amount with interest and other associated dues) does not represent any impossible or unlawful performance under Section 31(f) of the ArbAct.[16]

16.04. The claimant (respondent in the arbitral proceedings) challenged the judgment of the appellate court by its extraordinary appeal, in which the claimant argued that the case law was not consistent with respect to the issue of whether or not the grounds for the annulment of the arbitral award could be supplemented after the expiration of the time period stipulated in Section 32(1) of the ArbAct;[17] in the given case, the appellate court's decision on the said issue was erroneous. The claimant primarily argued that it is irrelevant whether the claimant pleaded the invalidity of the arbitration clause if the invalidity is classified as invalidity under Section 39 of the CivC,[18] i.e. as nullity. The claimant maintained that the claimant's timely plea of the lack of the arbitrator's jurisdiction raised in the arbitral proceedings and the claimant's timely motion to annul the arbitral award sufficed. The claimant (appellant in the SC proceedings) also challenged the obligation imposed by the arbitral award, which the claimant considered to constitute impossible and unlawful performance. The claimant argued that the conclusion

---

[12] This provision is quoted in the opening part of the annotation of this SC decision.

[13] CivC, Section 39 (cit.): *"A juridical act is invalid if the content or the purpose thereof violates or evades the law or is contra bonos mores."*

[14] This provision is quoted in the opening part of the annotation of this SC decision.

[15] This provision is quoted in the opening part of the annotation of this SC decision.

[16] This provision is quoted in the opening part of the annotation of this SC decision.

[17] This provision is quoted in the opening part of the annotation of this SC decision.

[18] This provision is quoted in the opening part of the annotation of this SC decision.

reached by both courts was wrong, i.e. that the performance is possible and lawful because it orders a cash payment. Considering the above outlined reasons, the claimant maintained that the decision of the appellate court was based on an erroneous legal assessment of the case, and demanded that the Supreme Court vacate the judgments of both courts and remand the case to the court of first instance for further hearing. The respondent did not reply to the claimant's extraordinary appeal.

[*From Conclusions Reached by Supreme Court, and Notes Concerning Decision*]:

16.05. The Supreme Court of the Czech Republic (SC) concluded that the extraordinary appeal in the given case was admissible, because the appellate court made an assessment that is contrary to the case law of the SC[19] with respect to the issue of whether the grounds for the annulment of an arbitral award can be asserted after the expiration of the time period stipulated in Section 32(1) of the ArbAct;[20] consequently, the contested decision of the appellate court had principal legal significance.[21]

---

[19] See also Judgment of the SC of May 9, 2012 in Case No. 23 Cdo 3728/2011.

[20] This provision is quoted in the opening part of the annotation of this SC decision.

[21] CCP, Section 239 (cit.)

CCP in effect until December 31, 2012 (the law applicable to the given case, cit.): *"(1) Extraordinary appeal is admissible against any judgment of the appellate court and any resolution of the appellate court (a) that reversed the decision of the court of first instance on the merits, (b) that upheld the decision of the court of first instance, in which the court of first instance ruled on the merits and which differed from its prior judgment (resolution), because the court of first instance was bound by the legal opinion of the appellate court, which had vacated the prior decision, or (c) that upheld the decision of the court of first instance if the extraordinary appeal is not admissible under Paragraph (b) and the Supreme Court concludes that the merits of the contested decision have principal legal significance. (2) The extraordinary appeal under Subsection (1) is not admissible (a) in any matters where the subject matter of the operative part (order) of the decision that has been challenged by the extraordinary appeal consists of pecuniary performance not exceeding CZK 50,000, or CZK 100,000 in commercial matters, disregarding interest and any other associated dues of the claim, (b) in matters regulated by the Family Act, with the exception of judgments that deprive a person of, or limit, their parental responsibility, or suspend the exercise thereof, judgments whereby parenthood is declared (denied) or judgments regarding irrevocable adoption, or (c) in matters concerning international child abduction pursuant to an international treaty that is incorporated in the legal system[62g] or pursuant to a directly applicable law of the European Communities.[62h] (3) A decision of the appellate court has principal legal significance [Subsection (1)(c)] especially if it resolves a legal issue that has not yet been resolved in the case law of the Supreme Court, or which is not being adjudged consistently by courts, or if the Supreme Court should assess the resolved legal issue*

16.06. In compliance with its prior rulings, the Supreme Court of the Czech Republic (SC) summarized that the interpretation of Section 32(1) of the ArbAct[22] and Section 31 of the ArbAct[23] requires the analogous application of the Code of Civil Procedure as concerns the possibility of asserting further grounds for the annulment of the arbitral award in proceedings that were initiated within the period of three months after the arbitral award was served. **The reason is that Section 32 of the ArbAct** (as applicable before the amendment implemented by Act No. 19/2012 Coll.)[24] **is only important from the perspective of determining whether the motion itself to annul the arbitral award was lodged in time. Hence, the provision cannot be interpreted as a limitation of the claimant's procedural rights to adduce in the course of the proceedings any relevant circumstances that contain further grounds for the annulment of the arbitral award under Section 31 of the ArbAct.**[25] **The right to supplement relevant circumstances can only be limited by statutory procedural limits under the Code of Civil Procedure (such as the concentration of proceedings). In other words, the party may assert (further) grounds for the annulment of the arbitral award under Section 31 of the ArbAct in proceedings for the annulment of the arbitral award that were commenced before the expiration of the time period under Section 32 of the ArbAct**[26] **even after the time period expires.**[27]

16.07. The author of this annotation disagrees with the conclusion, because, in the author's opinion, the proceedings for the annulment of an arbitral award are primarily proceedings under the ArbAct, and only subsidiarily under the CCP. The proceedings are governed by special

---

differently; circumstances asserted under the grounds for extraordinary appeal under Section 241a(2)(a) and Section 241a(3) shall be disregarded."

CCP in effect since January 1, 2013 (cit.): *"Unless stipulated otherwise, an extraordinary appeal is admissible against any decision of the appellate court that terminates the appellate proceedings if the contested decision depends on the resolution of an issue of substantive or procedural law and the appellate court has departed from the consistent case law of the Supreme Court when resolving the issue, or which has not yet been resolved in the case law of the Supreme Court, or which is not being adjudged consistently by the Supreme Court, or if the Supreme Court should assess the resolved legal issue differently."*

[22] This provision is quoted in the opening part of the annotation of this SC decision.

[23] This provision is quoted in the opening part of the annotation of this SC decision.

[24] This provision is quoted in the opening part of the annotation of this SC decision.

[25] This provision is quoted in the opening part of the annotation of this SC decision.

[26] This provision is quoted in the opening part of the annotation of this SC decision.

[27] This provision is quoted in the opening part of the annotation of this SC decision.

law. The crucial issue in the case therefore represents a fundamental issue discussed in Czech arbitration practice with respect to arbitration, i.e. the relationship between the ArbAct and the CCP. However, the author is aware of the fact that the possibility of supplementing grounds for the annulment of an arbitral award in court proceedings has been the subject matter of several recent SC rulings.

16.08. Contrary to the previous case law of the SC,[28] the relevant grounds for annulment were in this particular case asserted as late as in the appellate proceedings, which were instituted to review the decision of the court of first instance on the motion to annul the arbitral award. The conclusion reached by the SC can probably be questioned in this regard. The interpretation of the time period for asserting the grounds for annulment is relatively benign in this case. But if we consider the issue from another perspective, the claimant is not expanding its petition (the claimant still requests that the arbitral award be annulled) and does not necessarily allege new facts or new evidence; the case could only involve a new legal assessment of the case. The reason is that the case law of the Supreme Court of the Czech Republic (SC) indicates that, similarly to other adversarial proceedings, a party may continuously change their legal assessment of the case, even when filing the party's remedial measures. Unfortunately, the author of the annotation did not have at his disposal the decisions of the court of first instance and of the appellate court (the annotation is based solely on the summary of the decisions in the SC decision annotated in this publication). Consequently, the author could not assess the extent to which the claimant fulfilled its duty to state the relevant facts and meet the burden of proof in the proceedings at the court of first instance with respect to the grounds for the invalidity of the arbitration clause. The SC itself stated that, in the Court's opinion, the right (possibility) to supplement the grounds for the annulment of the arbitral award could be limited in the given case by the statutory procedural limits under the CCP (such as the concentration of proceedings). However, the appellate court has not yet assessed the claimant's objection from the perspective of these limits. Considering the fact that the decision of the appellate court was vacated and the case was remanded to the court for further proceedings, the appellate court might hold the supplemented grounds for the annulment of the arbitral award to be inadmissible due to the concentration of the proceedings, i.e. because

---

[28] See also Judgment of the SC of May 9, 2012 in Case No. 23 Cdo 3728/2011, and (ii) Resolution of the Prague Municipal Court of November 8, 2007 in Case No. 20 Co 313/2007-69.

the party will not be allowed to adduce facts and propose evidence that were not adduced or asserted at the court of first instance.[29]

16.09. The appellant argued in its extraordinary appeal that the performance imposed by the contested arbitral award was unlawful or impossible; the SC held the objection groundless. In this connection, the court invoked its prior rulings[30] and held that the performance imposed on the claimant could not be considered impossible or unlawful in the given case (the reasoning regarding this issue was incorporated in the *ratio decidendi* provided in the annotation of this decision).

16.10. The Supreme Court of the Czech Republic (SC) vacated the decision of the appellate court in this case and remanded the case for a new hearing.[31]

| | |

2. Judgment of Supreme Court of Czech Republic of June 24, 2013 in Case No. 23 Cdo 2166/2012: (i) Providing Possibility to State One's Case before Arbitrator; (ii) Inadmissibility of Bill of Exchange/Promissory Note Arbitral Award

Abbreviations Used:

ArbAct	Act of the Czech Republic No. 216/1994 Coll., on Arbitration and the Enforcement of Arbitral Awards, as amended[32]
CCP	Act of the Czech Republic No. 99/1963 Coll., the Code of Civil Procedure, as amended
SC	Supreme Court of the Czech Republic

---

[29] Information regarding further developments in the case following the decision of the SC is not available yet.

[30] See also Judgment of the SC of October 30, 2009 in Case No. 33 Cdo 2675/2007.

[31] Information regarding further developments in the case following the decision of the SC is not available yet.

[32] The decision of the SC in this case is based on the ArbAct in effect until March 31, 2012, but no subsequent changes have any bearing on the conclusions of the SC and their applicability; this particular case does not involve a consumer contract or, as applicable, a dispute arising from a consumer contract, and the rules introduced in the ArbAct by the Consumer Amendment, i.e. Act No. 19/2012 Coll., would not affect the case at hand. Generally, however, it is necessary to point out that the conclusions reached by the court shall not apply to disputes arising from consumer contracts after the passage of Act No. 19/2012 Coll. (or rather, the amendment codified the enhanced consumer protection, but the SC already mentioned the specific aspects of consumer protection in the annotated decision and inferred that the SC would apply these aspects to a consumer dispute).

Key Words:

annulment (setting aside) of arbitral award | arbitral award | arbitration (arbitral proceedings) | arbitration agreement | arbitration clause | arbitrator | bill of exchange/promissory note | bill of exchange/promissory note arbitral award | bill of exchange/promissory note payment order | case management of arbitral proceedings | concentration of proceedings | grounds for annulment of arbitral award | issue of principal legal significance | motion to annul arbitral award | permanent arbitral institution | providing possibility to state one's case before arbitrator | reasonable application of CCP | right to be heard |

Laws and Regulations Applied in Decision:
CCP: Section 175,[33] Section 237[34]

---

[33]   CCP, Section 175 (cit.):

CCP in effect until December 31, 2012 (the law discussed in the given case, cit.): *"(1) If the claimant presents the original of a bill of exchange/promissory note or a check and the court has no reason to doubt its genuineness, and if the claimant also presents other documents necessary to assert their right, the court shall render a bill of exchange/promissory note (check) payment order upon the claimant's motion, in which the respondent will be ordered to pay the requested amount and the costs of proceedings within three days, or to lodge objections within the same time period, in which the respondent must state all their objections against the payment order. The bill of exchange/promissory note (check) payment order must be served on the respondent personally. If the motion for the payment order cannot be granted, the court shall schedule a hearing. (2) Section 174(4) shall apply by analogy. (3) If the respondent fails to lodge timely objections or withdraws the objections, the bill of exchange/promissory note (check) payment order has the effects of a final and conclusive judgment. The court shall reject any belated objections or any objections that are not supported by reasons. The court shall also reject the objections if they were lodged by a person who is not authorized to do so. (4) If the respondent lodges timely objections, the court shall schedule a hearing where the objections shall be discussed; any objections raised at any later stage of the proceedings must be disregarded. The court shall pronounce in its judgment whether the bill of exchange/promissory note (check) payment order remains valid, or whether it is set aside and to what extent. (5) If the respondent withdraws the objections, the court shall terminate the proceedings regarding the objections by resolution; the court is not obliged to schedule a hearing. (6) If a party only wishes to challenge the court's order on the costs of proceedings, the party shall do so by appeal."*

CCP in effect since January 1, 2014 (cit.): *"(1) If the claimant presents the original of a bill of exchange/promissory note or a check and the court has no reason to doubt its genuineness, and if the claimant also presents other documents necessary to assert their right, the court shall render a bill of exchange/promissory note (check) payment order upon the claimant's motion, in which the respondent will be ordered to pay the requested amount and the costs of proceedings within 15 days, or to lodge objections within the same time period, in which the respondent must state all their objections against the payment order.*

The bill of exchange/promissory note (check) payment order must be served on the respondent personally, with substitute service excluded. If the motion for the payment order cannot be granted, the court shall schedule a hearing. (2) Section 174(4) shall apply by analogy. (3) If the respondent fails to lodge timely objections or withdraws the objections, the bill of exchange/promissory note (check) payment order has the effects of a final and conclusive judgment. The court shall reject any belated objections or any objections that are not supported by reasons. The court shall also reject the objections if they were lodged by a person who is not authorized to do so. (4) If the respondent lodges timely objections, the court shall schedule a hearing where the objections shall be discussed; any objections raised at any later stage of the proceedings must be disregarded. The court shall pronounce in its judgment whether the bill of exchange/promissory note (check) payment order remains valid, or whether it is set aside and to what extent. (5) If the respondent withdraws the objections, the court shall terminate the proceedings regarding the objections by resolution; the court is not obliged to schedule a hearing. (6) If a party only wishes to challenge the court's order on the costs of proceedings, the party shall do so by appeal."

[34]   Section 237 of the CCP (cit.)

CCP in effect until December 31, 2012 (the law applicable to the given case, cit.): *"(1) Extraordinary appeal is admissible against any judgment of the appellate court and any resolution of the appellate court (a) that reversed the decision of the court of first instance on the merits, (b) that upheld the decision of the court of first instance, in which the court of first instance ruled on the merits and which differed from its prior judgment (resolution), because the court of first instance was bound by the legal opinion of the appellate court, which had vacated the prior decision, or (c) that upheld the decision of the court of first instance, if the extraordinary appeal is not admissible under Paragraph (b) and the Supreme Court concludes that the merits of the contested decision have principal legal significance. (2) The extraordinary appeal under Subsection (1) is not admissible (a) in any matters where the subject matter of the operative part (order) of the decision that has been challenged by the extraordinary appeal consists of pecuniary performance not exceeding CZK 50,000, or CZK 100,000 in commercial matters, disregarding interest and any other associated dues of the claim, (b) in matters regulated by the Family Act, with the exception of judgments that deprive a person of, or limit, their parental responsibility, or suspend the exercise thereof, judgments whereby parenthood is declared (denied), or judgments regarding irrevocable adoption, or (c) in matters concerning international child abduction pursuant to an international treaty that is incorporated in the legal system[62g] or pursuant to a directly applicable law of the European Communities.[62h] (3) A decision of the appellate court has principal legal significance [Subsection (1)(c)] especially if it resolves a legal issue that has not yet been resolved in the case law of the Supreme Court, or that is not being adjudged consistently by the courts, or if the Supreme Court should assess the resolved legal issue differently; circumstances asserted under the grounds for extraordinary appeal under Section 241a(2)(a) and Section 241a(3) shall be disregarded."*

CCP in effect since January 1, 2013 (cit.): *"Unless stipulated otherwise, an extraordinary appeal is admissible against any decision of the appellate court that terminates the appellate proceedings if the contested decision depends on the resolution of an issue of substantive or procedural law and the appellate court has departed from the consistent case law of the Supreme Court when resolving the issue, or which has not yet been resolved in the*

Czech (& Central European) Yearbook of Arbitration

ArbAct: Section 18,[35] Section 30,[36] Section 31,[37] Section 32,[38] Section 33[39]

---

case law of the Supreme Court, or which is not being adjudged consistently by the Supreme Court, or if the Supreme Court should assess the resolved legal issue differently."

[35] ArbAct, Section 18 (cit.): *"The parties have an equal standing in the arbitral proceedings and must be provided with a full opportunity to assert their rights."*

[36] ArbAct, Section 30 (cit.): *"Application of the Code of Civil Procedure - Unless the Act stipulates otherwise, the arbitral proceedings shall be reasonably governed by the provisions of the Code of Civil Procedure."*

[37] ArbAct, Section 31 (cit.):

ArbAct in effect until March 31, 2012 (the law applicable to the given case, cit.): *"At the request of any party the court annuls the arbitral award if: (a) it was made in a case which cannot be submitted to arbitration (cannot be the subject of a valid arbitration agreement), (b) the arbitration agreement is invalid for other reasons or the agreement was cancelled or it does not apply to the agreed case, (c) the arbitrator(s) who took part in the proceedings was/were not authorized to make decisions in the case, whether under the arbitration agreement or otherwise, or lacked the capacity to act as arbitrator(s), (d) the arbitral award was not adopted by the majority of the arbitrators, (e) a party was denied the opportunity to plead his or her case in the arbitral proceedings, (f) the arbitral award orders a party to provide performance which was not requested by the obligee or to provide performance which is impossible or illegal under domestic law, (g) it transpires that there are reasons which would otherwise justify the reopening of civil proceedings in court."*

ArbAct in effect since 1 April 2012: *"At the request of any party the court annuls the arbitral award if: (a) it was made in a case which cannot be submitted to arbitration (cannot be the subject of a valid arbitration agreement), (b) the arbitration agreement is invalid for other reasons or the agreement was cancelled or it does not apply to the agreed case, (c) the arbitrator(s) who took part in the proceedings was/were not authorized to make decisions in the case, whether under the arbitration agreement or otherwise, or lacked the capacity to act as arbitrator(s), (d) the arbitral award was not adopted by the majority of the arbitrators, (e) a party was denied the opportunity to plead his or her case in the arbitral proceedings, (f) the arbitral award orders a party to provide performance which was not requested by the creditor or to provide performance which is impossible or illegal under domestic law, (g) the arbitrator or the permanent arbitral institution resolved a dispute arising from a consumer contract contrary to consumer protection laws, or clearly in violation of good morals, or contrary to public policy, (h) an arbitration agreement relating to disputes arising from consumer contracts lacks the information required under Section 3(5) or such information is intentionally or to a non-negligible extent incomplete, inaccurate, or false, or (i) it transpires that there are reasons which would otherwise justify the reopening of civil proceedings in court."*

[38] ArbAct, Section 32 (cit.):

ArbAct in effect until March 31, 2012 (the law applicable to the given case, cit.): *(1) The motion to annul an arbitral award must be lodged with the court within three months following the receipt of the arbitral award by the party requesting the annulment of the award, unless this Act stipulates otherwise. (2) The motion pursuant to subsection (1) does not suspend the enforceability of the arbitral award. If requested by the obligor, however, the*

The Supreme Court of the Czech Republic reached the following conclusions:

(1) A bill of exchange/promissory note arbitral award exhibits features identical to a bill of exchange/promissory note payment order provided for under Section 175 of the CCP, which, however, may only be rendered by a court.

(2) The reasonable application of the CCP cannot be interpreted as meaning that the arbitrator would be authorized to render decisions that are reserved exclusively for litigation, such as the decision under Section 175(1) of the CCP, whereby the court decides on the exercise of rights relating to a presented original of a bill of exchange/promissory note.

(3) Consequently, if the current case law of the SC prohibits the arbitrator from making decisions in the form of a bill of exchange/promissory note payment order, the arbitrator is also prohibited by the law from

court may suspend the enforceability of the arbitral award in case an immediate enforcement of the arbitral award could cause serious harm."

ArbAct in effect since April 1, 2012: "(1) The motion to annul an arbitral award must be lodged with the court within three months following the receipt of the arbitral award by the party requesting the annulment of the award, unless this Act stipulates otherwise. If the arbitral award was made in a dispute arising from a consumer contract and the motion to annul was lodged by the consumer, the court always examines whether there are grounds to annul the arbitral award pursuant to Section 31(a) through (d) or (h). (2) The motion pursuant to subsection (1) does not suspend the enforceability of the arbitral award. If requested by the obligor, however, the court may suspend the enforceability of the arbitral award in case an immediate enforcement of the arbitral award could cause serious harm or in case the motion to annul the arbitral award justifies the conclusion that the motion is legitimate. (3) If the motion to annul an arbitral award is lodged by the consumer, the court shall establish whether there are grounds to suspend the enforceability of the arbitral award pursuant to subsection (2) without the consumer's request. The court shall rule on the suspension of enforceability within 7 days of receiving the motion; the arbitral award cannot be enforced within said time limit."

[39]   ArbAct, Section 33 (cit.):

ArbAct in effect until March 31, 2012 (the law applicable to the given case, cit.): "The court shall dismiss a motion to annul an arbitral award which is based on the grounds specified in Section 31(b) or (c) if the party requesting the annulment failed to raise the corresponding objection in the arbitral proceedings before the party's first act in the merits of the case, despite having an opportunity to do so."

ArbAct in effect since January 1, 2014: "The court shall dismiss a motion to annul an arbitral award which is based on the grounds specified in Section 31(b) or (c) if the party requesting the annulment failed to raise the corresponding objection in the arbitral proceedings before the party's first act in the merits of the case, despite having an opportunity to do so. This does not apply to disputes arising from consumer contracts."

rendering bill of exchange/promissory note arbitral awards; Section 30 of the ArbAct does not make such decisions lawful.

(4) **The law of civil procedure is public law, not private law; consequently, the interpretation and application of the law of civil procedure is not automatically governed by the principle that "everything is allowed which is not prohibited". This means, inter alia, that we cannot conclude that arbitrator(s) may render decisions in summary proceedings because it is not explicitly prohibited under any laws or regulations; conversely, it is necessary to consider the wording of the procedural laws and subsequently conclude, on the basis of the individual provisions incorporated in the applicable regulations, which authorities are entitled to resolve specific types of disputes in summary proceedings.**

[*From Facts of Case and Procedure*]:

16.11. In its Judgment of November 9, 2011 in Case No. 14 Cmo 133/2011-309, the Olomouc High Court upheld as materially correct the Judgment of the Regional Court in Brno (court of first instance) of May 18, 2011 in Case No. 20 Cm 7/2008-245, which had **annulled a bill of exchange/promissory note arbitral award** rendered on December 19, 2007 by arbitrator XX in Case No. 02/XI/2007/Mat. Both courts found that the parties to the arbitration had agreed in their bill of exchange/promissory note agreement of July 19, 2007 that all disputes arising from and in connection with the bill of exchange/promissory note and the agreement, as well as issues regarding their (in)validity or their formation and termination, would be resolved with final force and effect by arbitrator XX entered on the List of *Ad Hoc* Arbitrators administered by the company AA *ad hoc*; the parties had also agreed that the arbitral proceedings would be conducted strictly on the basis of and pursuant to the Rules on *Ad Hoc* Arbitration Issued by AA *ad hoc*, and would be conducted only in writing. The claimant received on December 28, 2007 a bill of exchange/promissory note arbitral award, whereby the claimant was ordered to pay CZK 3,000,000 to the respondent, plus the bill of exchange/promissory note interest and the costs of the arbitral proceedings. The arbitral award was served on the claimant together with the request for arbitration. Article XI(2) of the *Rules on Ad Hoc Arbitration* stipulates that if the arbitrator believes that the request for arbitration can be subject to proceedings pursuant to the Rules on Arbitration and can be heard in the arbitration, and if the claimant submits their request for arbitration together with the original of the bill of exchange/promissory note or check, the arbitrator shall render a bill of exchange/promissory note (check) arbitral award and send it to the parties; the respondent shall also be served with a notice that a bill of exchange/promissory note (check) request for arbitration has been lodged and with one original of the request for arbitration, plus copies of the submitted documentary evidence. Unless the respondent lodges timely objections, the arbitral award will have the effects of a final and conclusive judicial decision. The claimant (as the respondent in the arbitral proceedings) did not lodge any objections against the bill of exchange/promissory note arbitral award by the stipulated deadline.

16.12. The appellate court and the court of first instance concluded that the motion to annul the arbitral award had been lodged within the time period stipulated in Section 32(1) of the ArbAct,[40] that the *case is arbitrable*, and consequently, that the grounds for the annulment of the arbitral award under Section 31(a) of the ArbAct[41] could not apply. Considering the fact that the claimant had failed to assert the grounds for the annulment of the arbitral award under Section 31(b) and (c) of the ArbAct[42] during the arbitral proceedings in terms of Section 33 of the ArbAct,[43] the arbitral award could not be annulled for the alleged grounds. However, the appellate court agreed with the conclusion reached by the court of first instance, namely that the claimant had legitimately demanded the annulment of the arbitral award under Section 31(e) of the ArbAct,[44] i.e. that the claimant had been deprived of the opportunity to state their case before the arbitrator if the claimant had only learned of the commenced arbitration from the issued bill of exchange/promissory note award, without having had any opportunity to plead their case before the bill of exchange/promissory note arbitral award was rendered. The appellate court therefore held that the claimant had not had an opportunity to effectively oppose the request for arbitration by adducing the relevant facts of the case and identifying the relevant evidence. In this connection, the Olomouc High Court invoked the decision of the SC of April 28, 2011 in Case No. 23 Cdo 3744/2009 and the decision of the SC of May 26, 2010 in Case No. 23 Cdo 3749/2008, in which the SC repeatedly articulated and substantiated its conclusion that a party is typically deprived of their opportunity to state their case before the arbitrators if the party cannot sufficiently plead their case and is not allowed to comment on all

---

[40] The provision is quoted above in the opening part of this annotation.

[41] The provision is quoted above in the opening part of this annotation.

[42] The provision is quoted above in the opening part of this annotation.

[43] The provision is quoted above in the opening part of this annotation.

[44] The provision is quoted above in the opening part of this annotation.

relevant circumstances. The appellate court also invoked Judgment of the SC of May 31, 2011 in Case No. 29 Cdo 1130/2011, in which the SC, inter alia, articulated and substantiated its conclusion that arbitrators are not entitled to make decisions in the form of bill of exchange/promissory note payment orders. The Olomouc High Court held that the bill of exchange/promissory note arbitral award challenged by the claimant's motion exhibited features identical to a bill of exchange/promissory note payment order provided for under Section 175 of the CCP,[45] which, however, may only be rendered by a court. The appellate court dismissed the respondent's objection that the arbitrator could render such a decision in the said proceedings pursuant to Section 30 of the ArbAct,[46] i.e. based on the reasonable application of the CCP. Invoking the case law of the SC,[47] the appellate court held that the reasonable application of the CCP could not be interpreted as meaning that the arbitrator is allowed to make decisions reserved exclusively for litigation. The Olomouc High Court pointed out that the provision in the *Rules on Ad Hoc Arbitration* was unlawful that set forth rules regulating summary bill of exchange/promissory note proceedings and the arbitrator's possibility to render a bill of exchange/promissory note arbitral award; the reason is that entities other than permanent arbitral institutions are not allowed to adopt their own rules regulating case management of the proceedings.[48]

16.13. The respondent lodged an extraordinary appeal against the judgment of the appellate court; the respondent argued that the extraordinary appeal was admissible, because the decision of the appellate court had principal legal significance. The respondent insisted that the contested decision had principal legal significance with respect to the resolution of the issue of whether the arbitrator could make a decision in the form of a bill of exchange/promissory note arbitral award, or whether such procedure is contrary to the law. The respondent also designated as an issue of principal legal significance the question of whether the summary arbitral proceedings, subject to the analogous application of the CCP, represent proceedings that deprive the parties of the opportunity to state their case before the arbitrator to a sufficient and reasonable extent. The appellant (in the SC proceedings) proposed that the SC vacate the judgments of the appellate court and of the court of

---

[45] The provision is quoted above in the opening part of this annotation.

[46] The provision is quoted above in the opening part of this annotation.

[47] See also Judgment of the SC of May 26, 2010 in Case No. 23 Cdo 3749/2008.

[48] The court based its conclusion on Resolution of the SC of May 11, 2011 in Case No. 31 Cdo 1945/2010.

first instance and remand the case to the court of first instance for further proceedings. In its reply to the extraordinary appeal, the claimant proposed that the extraordinary appeal be dismissed as inadmissible; the claimant argued that the issues designated as issues of principal legal significance by the appellant had already been adjudicated by courts, and the lower courts had had regard to those rulings in their decisions.

[*From Conclusions Reached by Supreme Court, and Notes Concerning Decision*]:

16.14. The Supreme Court of the Czech Republic (SC) concluded that the judgment of the appellate court was lawful and complied with the SC case law from the perspective of the objections raised in the extraordinary appeal, and consequently, did not represent a decision on any issue of principal legal significance in terms of Section 237(3) of the CCP[49] that could be challenged by an extraordinary appeal. As a result thereof, the Supreme Court of the Czech Republic (SC) dismissed the extraordinary appeal, primarily arguing as follows:

16.15. The necessary prerequisite for the conclusion that a decision of the appellate court has principal legal significance is that the resolution of the legal issue was decisive for the decision in the case, i.e. that the relevant legal issue is not an incidental issue on which the judgment of the appellate court was not based from the perspective of the legal assessment of the case. It needs to be pointed out that an extraordinary appeal in terms of Section 237(1)(c) of the CCP[50] is not admissible just because the appellant claims that the merits of the contested decision of the appellate court have principal legal significance. An extraordinary appeal is admissible if the Supreme Court applies the criteria included on the indicative list of Section 237(3) of the CCP[51] and concludes that the contested decision of the appellate court indeed exhibits principal legal significance as to the merits of the case. The conclusion as to whether or not the judgment of the appellate court contested by the extraordinary appeal has principal legal significance is a preliminary conclusion made by the Supreme Court; no special decision is issued in this regard. Only if the Supreme Court finds the extraordinary appeal admissible due to principal legal significance of the contested judgment may the Court address the asserted grounds for the extraordinary appeal.

---

[49] The provision is quoted above in the opening part of this annotation.
[50] The provision is quoted above in the opening part of this annotation.
[51] The provision is quoted above in the opening part of this annotation.

16.16. The Supreme Court of the Czech Republic (SC) concluded that the respondent's extraordinary appeal is not admissible under Section 237(1)(c) of the CCP,[52] because the issues posed by the respondent cannot meet the prerequisite of principal legal significance in terms of Section 237(3) of the CCP.[53] The issue of depriving a party of the opportunity to state their case before the arbitrators has already been analyzed in the SC case law in great detail.[54] The same holds true for the issue of procedures adopted by private legal entities other than permanent arbitral institutions.[55],[56] Similarly, the SC has already ruled on the issue of the arbitrators' decisions made in the form of bill of exchange/promissory note arbitral awards, even though the prior rulings concerned the entitlement of the arbitrator to render a bill of exchange/promissory note payment order;[57] nonetheless, a bill of exchange/promissory note arbitral award (rendered in the given case) exhibits features identical to a bill of exchange/promissory note payment order provided for under Section 175 of the CCP,[58] which may only be rendered by a court. The decision-making of the arbitrator pursuant to Section 30 of the ArbAct,[59] i.e. with the reasonable application of the CCP, has also been the subject of extensive case law of the SC;[60] the reasonable application of the CCP does not entail the arbitrator's entitlement to render decisions reserved exclusively for litigation, such as decisions under Section 175(1) of the CCP.[61]

16.17. The author of this annotation agrees with the conclusions reached by the SC, which in this case essentially just referred to its prior rulings. **The author is of the opinion that the principal asset of the analyzed decision of the SC consists of the SC's emphatic opposition to the various forms of *"summary arbitral proceedings"*; the SC held such methods of case management of the arbitral proceedings to be unlawful,** because they deprive the parties to arbitration of the opportunity to duly state their case before the arbitrators, or rather

---

[52] The provision is quoted above in the opening part of this annotation.

[53] The provision is quoted above in the opening part of this annotation.

[54] See also (i) Judgment of the SC of April 28, 2011 in Case No. 23 Cdo 3744/2009, and (ii) Judgment of the SC of May 26, 2010 in Case No. 23 Cdo 3749/2008.

[55] I.e. a permanent arbitral institution in terms of Section 15 of the ArbAct.

[56] See (i) Judgment of the SC of May 11, 2011 in Case No. 31 Cdo 1945/2010, and (ii) Resolution of the SC of October 30, 2012 in Case No. 23 Cdo 1198/2012.

[57] Judgment of the SC of May 31, 2011 in Case No. 29 Cdo 1130/2011.

[58] The provision is quoted above in the opening part of this annotation.

[59] The provision is quoted above in the opening part of this annotation.

[60] Judgment of the SC of May 26, 2010 in Case No. 23 Cdo 3749/2008.

[61] The provision is quoted above in the opening part of this annotation.

they do not provide the parties to arbitration with the unrestricted opportunity to exercise their (procedural) rights and do not correspond to the specific nature of arbitration. It is also necessary to appreciate that the Supreme Court has addressed the issue of the reasonable application of the CCP in arbitration pursuant to Section 30 of the ArbAct.[62] In this regard, the author of this annotation has been witnessing an increasing tendency to subject arbitration to the standards of classical litigation under the CCP, which is not always for the benefit of effective and informal arbitration. However, as concerns this particular case, the author of the annotation fully agrees with the conclusions reached by the SC, i.e. that summary proceedings are not an admissible method of case management in arbitration. because the reasonable application of the provisions incorporated in the CCP to arbitration under Section 30 of the ArbAct[63] must not result in the application of legal rules that conflict with the fundamental principles[64] and the purpose of arbitration.

| | |

3. Judgment of Supreme Court of Czech Republic of June 25, 2013 in Case No. 23 Cdo 3285/2012: (i) Plea of Set-Off; (ii) Counterclaim; (iii) Jurisdiction; (iv) Equality of Parties; (v) Fair Trial[65]

Abbreviations Used:

AC   Arbitration Court at the Economic Chamber of the Czech Republic and Agricultural Chamber of the Czech Republic[66]

ArbAct   Act of the Czech Republic No. 216/1994 Coll., on Arbitration and the Enforcement of Arbitral Awards, as amended[67]

---

[62] The provision is quoted above in the opening part of this annotation.

[63] The provision is quoted above in the opening part of this annotation.

[64] Section 18 of the ArbAct: *"The parties have an equal standing in the arbitral proceedings and must be provided with a full opportunity to assert their rights."*

[65] The decision is available on the SC website at http://www.nsoud.cz/Judikatura/ judikatura_ns.nsf/WebSearch/068F4FF6824D22B0C1257BC90051FB00?openDocument& Highlight=0,rozhod%C4%8D%C3%AD,%C5%99%C3%ADzen%C3%AD [last accessed on August 28, 2014].

[66] Further information about this permanent arbitral institution is available at www.soud.cz in multiple language versions.

[67] The decision of the SC in this case is based on the ArbAct in effect until March 31, 2012, but no subsequent changes have any bearing on the conclusions of the SC and their

Czech (& Central European) Yearbook of Arbitration

CCP	Act of the Czech Republic No. 99/1963 Coll., the Code of Civil Procedure, as amended
ConCourt	Constitutional Court of the Czech Republic
ECtHR	European Court of Human Rights
SC	Supreme Court of the Czech Republic

Key Words:

allowing evidence | annulment (setting aside) of arbitral award | counterclaim[68] *| counterclaim*[69] *| equality | equality of arms | evidence/proof | extinguishment of claim | fair trial | fundamental procedural right | grounds for annulment of arbitral award | motion to annul arbitral award | mutual claim*[70] *| opportunity to state (plead) one's case | plea of compensation*[71] *| plea of set-off*[72] *| powers (jurisdiction) of arbitrator | procedural defense | procedural right | providing possibility to state (plead) one's case before arbitrator | right to a fair trial | right to be heard | set-off (offset) | statement (allegation) | taking of evidence*

Laws and Regulations Applied in Decision:

CCP: Section 97,[73] Section 98,[74] and Section 237[75]

---

applicability; this particular case does not involve a consumer contract or, as applicable, a dispute arising from a consumer contract, and the rules introduced in the ArbAct by the Consumer Amendment, i.e. Act No. 19/2012 Coll., would not affect the case at hand.

[68] See also "mutual claim" or "counterclaim".

[69] See also "counterclaim" or "mutual claim".

[70] See also "counterclaim".

[71] See also "plea of set-off".

[72] See also "plea of compensation".

[73] CCP, Section 97 (cit.) *"(1) The respondent may also assert their rights against the claimant in the proceedings by means of a mutual claim. (2) The court may exclude the mutual claim to separate proceedings if the conditions for joining the cases are not fulfilled. (3) The mutual claim shall be reasonably governed by the provisions regulating the motion to commence proceedings, amendments and the withdrawal of the motion."*

[74] CCP, Section 98 of the CCP (cit.): *"A mutual claim is defined as the respondent's pleading, whereby the respondent asserts their claim against the claimant for set-off, but only if the respondent proposes that the respondent be awarded more than the claimant has claimed. Otherwise, the pleading shall be regarded by the court as a mere defense against the claimant's claim."*

[75] CCP, Section 237 (cit.): CCP in effect until December 31, 2012 (the law applicable to the given case): *"(1) Extraordinary appeal is admissible against any judgment of the appellate court and any resolution of the appellate court (a) that reversed the decision of the court of first instance on the merits, (b) that upheld the decision of the court of first instance, in which the court of first instance ruled on the merits and which differed from its prior judgment (resolution), because the court of first instance was bound by the legal opinion of*

ArbAct: Section 15,[76] Section 18,[77] Section 30,[78] and Section 31[79]

the appellate court, which had vacated the prior decision, (c) that upheld the decision of the court of first instance if the extraordinary appeal is not admissible under Paragraph (b) and the Supreme Court concludes that the merits of the contested decision have principal legal significance. (2) The extraordinary appeal under Subsection (1) is not admissible (a) in any matters in which the subject matter of the operative part (order) of the decision that has been challenged by the extraordinary appeal consists of pecuniary performance not exceeding CZK 50,000, or CZK 100,000 in commercial matters, excluding interest and any other associated dues of the claim, (b) in matters regulated by the Family Act, with the exception of judgments that deprive a person of, or limit, their parental responsibility, or suspend the exercise thereof, judgments whereby parenthood is declared (denied) or judgments regarding irrevocable adoption, (c) in matters concerning international child abduction pursuant to an international treaty that is incorporated in the legal system[62g] or pursuant to a directly applicable law of the European Communities.[62h] (3) The decision of the appellate court has principal legal significance [Subsection (1)(c)] especially if it resolves a legal issue that has not yet been resolved in the case law of the Supreme Court, or which is not being adjudged consistently by courts, or if the Supreme Court should assess the resolved legal issue differently; circumstances asserted under the grounds for extraordinary appeal under Section 241a(2)(a) and Section 241a(3) shall be disregarded."

CCP in effect since January 1, 2013 (cit.): *"Unless stipulated otherwise, an extraordinary appeal is admissible against any decision of the appellate court that terminates the appellate proceedings, if the contested decision depends on the resolution of an issue of substantive or procedural law and the appellate court has departed from the consistent case law of the Supreme Court when resolving the issue, or which has not yet been resolved in the case law of the Supreme Court, or which is not being adjudged consistently by the Supreme Court, or if the Supreme Court should assess the resolved legal issue differently."*

[76] ArbAct, Section 15 (cit.):

ArbAct in effect until March 31, 2012 (the law applicable to the given case, cit.): *"(1) Arbitrators are entitled to examine their jurisdiction. If they conclude that the arbitration agreement presented to them does not give them jurisdiction to resolve the dispute, they render a corresponding resolution. (2) The plea of lack of jurisdiction, based on the non-existence, invalidity, or expiration of the arbitration agreement, can be raised by a party only before or together with the first act in the proceedings which concerns the merits of the case, unless the invalidity is caused by the fact that no arbitration agreement could have been concluded with respect to the case."*

ArbAct in effect since April 1, 2012: *"(1) Arbitrators are entitled to examine their jurisdiction. If they conclude that the arbitration agreement presented to them does not give them jurisdiction to resolve the dispute, they render a corresponding resolution. (2) The plea of lack of jurisdiction, based on the non-existence, invalidity, or expiration of the arbitration agreement, can be raised by a party only before or together with the first act in the proceedings which concerns the merits of the case, unless the invalidity is caused by the fact that no arbitration agreement could have been concluded with respect to the case. This does not apply to disputes arising from consumer contracts."*

[77] ArbAct, Section 18 (cit.): *"The parties have an equal standing in the arbitral*

The Supreme Court of the Czech Republic arrived at the following principal conclusions:

(1) The ground for the annulment of an arbitral award pursuant to Section 31(e) of the ArbAct[80] is targeted primarily at protecting the observance of the fundamental procedural rights and obligations of the parties with respect to the principle of the equality of the parties to arbitration expressed in Section 18 of the ArbAct. The parties must be provided with a full opportunity to assert their rights.

---

proceedings and must be provided with a full opportunity to assert their rights."

[78] ArbAct, Section 30 (cit.): *"Application of the Code of Civil Procedure - Unless the Act stipulates otherwise, the arbitral proceedings shall be reasonably governed by the provisions of the Code of Civil Procedure."*

[79] ArbAct, Section 31 (cit.):

ArbAct in effect until March 31, 2012 (the law applicable to the given case, cit.): *"At the request of any party the court annuls the arbitral award if: (a) it was made in a case which cannot be submitted to arbitration (cannot be the subject of a valid arbitration agreement), (b) the arbitration agreement is invalid for other reasons or the agreement was cancelled or it does not apply to the agreed case, (c) the arbitrator(s) who took part in the proceedings was/were not authorized to make decisions in the case, whether under the arbitration agreement or otherwise, or lacked the capacity to act as arbitrator(s), (d) the arbitral award was not adopted by the majority of the arbitrators, (e) a party was denied the opportunity to plead his or her case in the arbitral proceedings, (f) the arbitral award orders a party to provide performance which was not requested by the obligee or to provide performance which is impossible or illegal under domestic law, (g) it transpires that there are reasons which would otherwise justify the reopening of civil proceedings in court."*

ArbAct in effect since April 1, 2012: *"At the request of any party the court annuls the arbitral award if: (a) it was made in a case which cannot be submitted to arbitration (cannot be the subject of a valid arbitration agreement), (b) the arbitration agreement is invalid for other reasons or the agreement was cancelled or it does not apply to the agreed case, (c) the arbitrator(s) who took part in the proceedings was/were not authorized to make decisions in the case, whether under the arbitration agreement or otherwise, or lacked the capacity to act as arbitrator(s), (d) the arbitral award was not adopted by the majority of the arbitrators, (e) a party was denied the opportunity to plead his or her case in the arbitral proceedings, (f) the arbitral award orders a party to provide performance which was not requested by the creditor or to provide performance which is impossible or illegal under domestic law, (g) the arbitrator or the permanent arbitral institution resolved a dispute arising from a consumer contract contrary to consumer protection laws, or clearly in violation of good morals, or contrary to public policy, (h) an arbitration agreement relating to disputes arising from consumer contracts lacks the information required under Section 3(5) or such information is intentionally or to a non-negligible extent incomplete, inaccurate, or false, or (i) it transpires that there are reasons which would otherwise justify the reopening of civil proceedings in court."*

[80] The provision is quoted above in the opening part of this annotation.

(2) The evidence proposed by the parties must be addressed by the arbitral tribunal – either the evidence will be examined (read or heard), or the evidence will not be admitted, which will be properly justified by the arbitral tribunal; it is necessary to insist that this principle also applies in arbitration.

(3) All objections targeted at the annulment of an arbitral award under Section 31(e) of the ArbAct[81] must, by necessity, be procedural objections. In other words, they must concern the procedure adopted by the arbitral tribunal in the hearing of the dispute, not the correctness of the factual or legal findings made by the arbitral tribunal.

(4) Considering the principle of the equality of arms between the parties, which also applies in arbitration, both parties must be provided with the opportunity to make statements (pleadings) in the arbitral proceedings, prove their own statements, and contest the statements of the counterparty. The parties also have the right to demand that the arbitral tribunal address the merits of their pleas (objections).

(5) If a claim has been made in arbitration, the respondent must have a right to raise in the arbitral proceedings any and all objections against the claim that could influence the decision in the case. If the party pleads set-off in the proceedings properly, the decision-making authority could conclude that the claimant's claim was extinguished by set-off. In such case, the request for arbitration (statement of claim) would have to be dismissed. Consequently, the respondent cannot be denied the opportunity to assert their claim for set-off against the claimant's claim.

(6) The arbitrator must assess the merits of the respondent's defense, whereby they assert their claim for set-off against the claimant's claim, i.e. determine whether the act resulted in the extinguishment (partial or total) of the claimant's claim. The arbitrator is not allowed to refuse such material assessment, arguing that the arbitrator does not have jurisdiction to do so, because the claim was not the subject matter of the parties' arbitration agreement; otherwise, the arbitrator would be denying the party the opportunity to state (plead) their case before the arbitrators.

(7) The claimant asserted no claim in the arbitration that would offset the claim asserted by the respondent, but only pleaded the non-existence of the claim asserted by the respondent, arguing that the respondent's claim had been extinguished by offset against the claimant's claim; in such case, the claimant only exercised a procedural defense, and

---

[81] The provision is quoted above in the opening part of this annotation.

consequently, the arbitration did not have to be terminated for a lack of jurisdiction on the part of the arbitral tribunal pursuant to Section 15(1) of the ArbAct.

[*From Facts of Case and Procedure*]:

16.18. The Prague Municipal Court, as the court of first instance, rendered its Judgment on October 6 2011 in Case No. 5 Cm 176/2010-79, whereby the motion was dismissed to annul the arbitral award made by the AC under Case No. Rsp 743/10 on July 30, 2010. The court held that the conditions for the annulment of the arbitral award under Section 31(e) of the ArbAct[82] were not fulfilled.

16.19. The claimant (respondent in the arbitral proceedings) maintained that the claimant was denied the opportunity to state (plead) their case before the arbitrator, because the arbitrator refused to address the claimant's plea of the non-existence of the claim resulting from the preceding set-off; the plea was asserted as the claimant's defense against the claim asserted by the respondent in the arbitral proceedings. The court of first instance held that the arbitrator had addressed the plea of the extinguishment of the claim based on the alleged unilateral set-off of the claim; specifically, the arbitrator instructed the claimant that the AC did not have jurisdiction to hear the claimant's procedural defense. The arbitrator duly supported his legal conclusion by reasons, and instructed the claimant about the claimant's opportunity to assert their claim against the respondent (claimant in the arbitral proceedings) by a lawsuit lodged with a court. The arbitrator ruled on the lack of jurisdiction pursuant to Section 15(1) of the ArbAct[83] with reference to the decision of the SC of the Czech Republic in Case No. 29 Cdo 1899/2008, which stipulates that a decision on the lack of jurisdiction of the arbitral tribunal pursuant to Section 15(1) of the ArbAct[84] is procedurally binding on the court, i.e. whether the plea of the set-off could have been made in the arbitration.

16.20. The claimant lodged an appeal with the Prague High Court, which reversed the judgment of the court of first instance by its Judgment of May 14, 2012 in Case No. 8 Cmo 148/2012-106, whereby the arbitral award was annulled. The appellate court based its decision on the finding that, in any of its pleadings submitted to the AC or at any of the

---

[82] The provision is quoted above in the opening part of this annotation.

[83] The provision is quoted above in the opening part of this annotation.

[84] The provision is quoted above in the opening part of this annotation.

two hearings at the AC, the claimant made (i) no plea of compensation (plea of set-off) under Section 98 of the CCP,[85] and (ii) no claim against the respondent (under Section 97 of the CCP[86]). During the arbitral proceedings, the claimant denied the legitimacy of the request for arbitration (statement of claim) by referring to the extinguishment of the respondent's claim before the arbitration commenced, namely extinguishment by an offset, which the respondent itself submitted in the arbitration (as evidence that, in the respondent's opinion, no valid set-off could have been validly and effectively performed, and consequently, the respondent's claim had not ceased to exist). The appellate court held that if the claimant had not made any claim at the AC against the respondent in terms of Section 97 of the CCP,[87] the proceedings regarding the claim should not have been terminated for a lack of jurisdiction on the part of the AC under Section 15(1) of the ArbAct.[88] The court was therefore not bound by that conclusion. As concerns the plea of set-off, the appellate court ruled that the claimant had raised the relevant defense in the arbitral proceedings, which should have been addressed by the arbitral tribunal; it is irrelevant in the given case whether the arbitral tribunal would have had jurisdiction to make decisions regarding the claim "used" by the claimant for the alleged set-off, because the subject matter of the proceedings had only been the claim against which the set-off was asserted.

16.21. Considering the above said, the appellate court concluded that it was necessary to proceed pursuant to Section 31(e) of the ArbAct,[89] because the procedural principles had been fundamentally violated with respect to the principle of equality of the parties expressed in Section 18 of the ArbAct.[90] The reason is that the parties' statements must be heard and assessed based on evidence; this rule also applies in arbitration. The appellate court held that if the arbitral tribunal had examined the proposed evidence (set-off), but refused to assess the evidence in consequence of its wrongful conclusion regarding the lack of jurisdiction on the part of the AC, the arbitral tribunal had not provided the claimant with a full opportunity to state their case before the arbitrator.

---

[85] The provision is quoted above in the opening part of this annotation.
[86] The provision is quoted above in the opening part of this annotation.
[87] The provision is quoted above in the opening part of this annotation.
[88] The provision is quoted above in the opening part of this annotation.
[89] The provision is quoted above in the opening part of this annotation.
[90] The provision is quoted above in the opening part of this annotation.

16.22. The respondent lodged an extraordinary appeal against the judgment of the appellate court. The appellant (in the SC proceedings) argued that the decision of the court of first instance was materially correct. The appellant also insisted that the appellate court in the reasons for its decision had not properly addressed the reference made by the court of first instance to the Judgment of the SC of May 28, 2009 in Case No. 23 Cdo 2570/2007, according to which courts are not entitled to review the merits of the contested decision, i.e. review the correctness of the tribunal's assessment of the examined evidence, and the correctness of the findings of fact and of the subsequent legal assessment of the case. A motion to annul an arbitral award cannot be used as a remedy against arbitral awards. The appellant maintained that the claimant had not presented evidence that would prove that the grounds under Section 31(e) of the ArbAct were fulfilled.[91] Considering the above reasons, the claimant (appellant) proposed that the SC suspend the enforceability of the contested judgment, vacate the judgment of the appellate court and remand the case to the appellate court for further proceedings.

[From Conclusions of SC and Comments Concerning Annotated Decision of SC]:

16.23. The Supreme Court of the Czech Republic (SC) concluded that the extraordinary appeal was admissible in the given case under Section 237(1) of the CCP,[92] because the appellate court reversed the decision of the court of first instance on the merits. Consequently, the Supreme Court of the Czech Republic (SC) reviewed the judgment of the appellate court. Considering the fact that the SC did not find the appellant's petition presented in the SC proceedings, or any part thereof, to be justified, the SC dismissed the extraordinary appeal.

16.24. The Supreme Court of the Czech Republic (SC) already ruled in its preceding decision[93] that the ground for the annulment of arbitral award under Section 31(e) of the ArbAct[94] also covers a situation in which the arbitrator in the arbitral proceedings did not address the merits of a respondent's plea that the claimant's claim asserted in the arbitration had been extinguished by set-off. The author of this annotation also deems it appropriate to add that the SC also analyzed these issues in its Judgment of May 28, 2009 in Case No. 23 Cdo 2570/2007, and came to analogous conclusions. In its decision, the

---

[91] The provision is quoted above in the opening part of this annotation.

[92] The provision is quoted above in the opening part of this annotation.

[93] Judgment of the SC of February 27, 2013 in Case No. 23 Cdo 2016/2011.

[94] The provision is quoted above in the opening part of this annotation.

court of first instance merely referred to part of that SC decision and, unfortunately, failed to have regard to the crucial conclusions articulated in the decision, which indicate that if a party to arbitration is denied a full opportunity to exercise their rights as a result of wrongful procedure adopted by the arbitrators (groundless failure to address a plea of set-off in the said case), the party was denied the opportunity to state (plead) their case before the arbitrators[95] in terms of Section 31(e) of the ArbAct[96] (and consequently, the objection raised by the appellant in the SC proceedings – that the appellate court failed to address the conclusions of the judgment – can be considered to be principally inappropriate and purely artificial).

16.25. The reason is that the ground for the annulment of an arbitral award pursuant to Section 31(e) of the ArbAct[97] is targeted primarily at protecting the observance of the fundamental procedural rights and obligations of the parties to arbitration with respect to the principle of the equality of the parties expressed in Section 18 of the ArbAct.[98] The parties must be provided with a full opportunity to assert their rights. According to the consistent case law of the ECtHR, the principle of the *equality of arms*, as an element of the broader concept of fair trial, requires that every party to civil proceedings should have a reasonable opportunity to present their case to the court in circumstances that do not place them at a substantial disadvantage vis-à-vis the opposing party.[99] The evidence proposed by the parties must be addressed by the arbitral tribunal – either the evidence will be examined (read or heard), or the evidence will not be

---

[95] See Judgment of the SC of May 28, 2009 in Case No. 23 Cdo 2570/2007 (cit.): *"Hence, the arbitral tribunal did not conclude that the respondent (claimant in this litigation) had failed to meet the burden of proof with respect to those claims, or did not assess the examined evidence to the disadvantage of the present claimant, as applicable. The arbitral tribunal refused to examine those claims invoking the lack of the arbitral tribunal's capacity. Given these circumstances, it is necessary to agree with the appellate court that the claimant had not been provided with a full opportunity in the arbitral proceedings to exercise their rights, and consequently, the claimant had been denied the opportunity to state (plead) their case before the arbitrators in terms of Section 31(e) of the ArbAct."*

[96] The provision is quoted above in the opening part of this annotation.

[97] The provision is quoted above in the opening part of this annotation.

[98] The provision is quoted above in the opening part of this annotation.

[99] See (i) Judgment of the ECtHR, Application No. 14448/88, of October 27, 1993 (*Dombo Beheer B. V.* v *The Netherlands*); (ii) Judgment of the ECtHR, Application No. 17748/91, of October 23, 1996 (*Ankerl* v *Switzerland*); (iii) Judgment of the ECtHR, Application No. 53364/07, of June 18, 2013 (*Komanický* v *Slovakia*).

admitted, which will be properly justified by the arbitral tribunal; it is necessary to insist that this principle also applies in arbitration. All objections targeted at the annulment of an arbitral award under Section 31(e) of the ArbAct[100] must, by necessity, be procedural objections. In other words, they must concern the procedure adopted by the arbitral tribunal in the hearing of the dispute, not the correctness of the factual or legal findings made by the arbitral tribunal. Considering the principle of the equality of arms between the parties, which also applies in arbitration, both parties must be provided with the opportunity to make statements (pleadings) in the arbitral proceedings, prove their own statements, and contest the statements of the counterparty. The parties also have the right to demand that the arbitrators address the merits of their pleas (objections).

16.26. If a claim has been made in arbitration, the respondent must have the right to raise in the arbitral proceedings any and all objections against the claim that could influence the decision on the merits. If the party pleads set-off in the proceedings properly, the arbitrators could conclude that the claimant's claim was extinguished by set-off. In such case, the request for arbitration (statement of claim) would have to be dismissed. Consequently, the respondent in the arbitral proceedings cannot be denied the opportunity to assert their claim for set-off against the claimant's claim, or tender evidence proving that the claim made against the respondent had been extinguished on the basis of a prior set-off. The above indicates that the arbitrator must assess the merits of the respondent's defense in arbitration, whereby they assert their claim for set-off against the claimant's claim, or plead the extinguishment of the claimant's claim based on a prior set-off, i.e. determine whether the act resulted in the extinguishment (partial or total) of the claimant's claim. The arbitrator is not allowed to refuse such material assessment, arguing that the arbitrator allegedly does not have jurisdiction to do so, because the claim was not the subject matter of the parties' arbitration agreement. If the arbitrator refuses such assessment, they deny the party the opportunity to state (plead) their case before the arbitrators, because a procedural defense is not a separate claim or subject matter of arbitration, as applicable, and there is thus no reason to terminate the arbitral proceedings for a lack of jurisdiction on the part of the arbitral tribunal under Section 15(1) of the ArbAct.[101]

---

[100] The provision is quoted above in the opening part of this annotation.

[101] The provision is quoted above in the opening part of this annotation.

16.27. The author of the annotation agrees with the SC's conclusions; the author primarily believes that arbitrators are not entitled to claim a lack of jurisdiction in order to reject a plea of the non-existence of the claimant's claim resulting from an offset if the arbitrators concluded that they do have jurisdiction to make decisions with respect to the claim, the non-existence of which is pleaded. The plea of the non-existence of the claim does not change the subject matter of the arbitration in any manner. This situation must be distinguished from the case in which a claim is made against the claimant in arbitral proceedings based on a mutual claim in terms of Section 97 of the CCP;[102] the reason is that the respondent's claim in the latter case is asserted as a separate claim against the claimant, and consequently, the claim could be the subject matter of separate proceedings. When making a decision regarding such a claim, the arbitrators may conclude that they lack jurisdiction to make decisions regarding the claim. A plea of compensation is a special case, because it constitutes a procedural defense under Section 98 of the CCP.[103] The plea does not change the subject matter of the proceedings either, but if the decision-making authority finds both claims justified (i.e. the claimant's claim, as well as the claim asserted for set-off), the operative part of the judgment will always refer only to the claimant's claim (or that part of the claimant's claim that was not extinguished as a result of the compensation). The decision-making authority shall incorporate its conclusions regarding the legitimacy of the claim asserted for set-off against the claimant's claim, and of the set-off itself, in the reasoning for its decision.[104] We may therefore conclude that the arbitrators may only terminate the proceedings for a lack of jurisdiction with respect to a counterclaim (mutual claim), not with respect to a plea of the non-existence of the claimant's claim as a result of a set-off, or the plea of compensation asserted as a procedural defense under Section 98 of the CCP,[105] where the set-off is performed in the course of the proceedings; the reason is that the two pleas do not change the original subject matter of the proceedings.

| | |

---

[102] The provision is quoted above in the opening part of this annotation.

[103] The provision is quoted above in the opening part of this annotation.

[104] See the conclusions reached by the SC in its Resolution of April 29, 2004 in Case No. 20 Cdo 1329/2003.

[105] The provision is quoted above in the opening part of this annotation.

4. Resolution of Supreme Court of Czech Republic of July 10, 2013 in Case No. 31 Cdo 958/2012:[106] (i) Review of Arbitral Award during Execution, (ii) Power of Execution Court to Examine Validity of Arbitration Clause, (iii) Power of Arbitrator to Render Arbitral Award on Basis of Invalid Arbitration Agreement, (iv) Terminating Enforcement of Decision/Enforcement of Arbitral Award Rendered by Arbitrator on Basis of Invalid Arbitration Agreement, i.e. by Arbitrator Who Lacked Jurisdiction to Render Arbitral Award

Abbreviations Used:

SC	Supreme Court of the Czech Republic
CCP	Act of the Czech Republic No. 99/1963 Coll., the Code of Civil Procedure, as amended
ArbAct	Act of the Czech Republic No. 216/1994 Coll., on Arbitration and the Enforcement of Arbitral Awards, as amended[107]
CivC	Act No. 40/1964 Coll., the Civil Code, as amended[108]
CC	Act of the Czech Republic No. 89/2012 Coll., the Civil Code[109]
Charter	Resolution of the Presidium of the Czech National Council No. 2/1993 Coll., on the promulgation of the Charter of Fundamental Rights and Freedoms as part of the constitutional order of the Czech Republic, as amended

---

[106] This decision is available online on the website of the SC at http://www.nsoud.cz/ Judikatura/judikatura_ns.nsf/WebSearch/8394D2A5DD17E388C1257BAC002E4DBB?ope nDocument&Highlight=0 [last accessed on November 8, 2014].

[107] The decision of the SC is based on the ArbAct in effect until March 31, 2012, but no subsequent changes have any bearing on the conclusions of the SC and their applicability in this particular case; generally, however, the protection of consumers has been enhanced, also in relation to enforcement proceedings.

[108] This Act (CivC) has been replaced by Act No. 89/2012 Coll. (the "new Civil Code", abbreviated as the "CC" in the text of this annotation), with effect since January 1, 2014. Legal relationships established before the effective date of the CC, i.e. before January 1, 2014, shall be governed by the provisions of the CivC (with exceptions).

[109] This Act (CC) has replaced Act No. 40/1964 Coll., as amended (the "old Civil Code", abbreviated as the "CivC" in the text of this annotation), with effect since January 1, 2014. Legal relationships established before the effective date of the CC, i.e. before January 1, 2014, shall be governed by the provisions of the CivC (with exceptions).

ExecC   Act of the Czech Republic No. 120/2001 Coll., on Execution Agents and Execution, as amended

ConCourt Constitutional Court of the Czech Republic

Key Words:

Arbitration Rules | B2C dispute | consumer credit | execution (enforcement proceedings) | lex specialis derogat legi generali | permanent arbitral institution | powers (jurisdiction) of arbitrator | review of an arbitral award | selection/appointment of arbitrator | termination of enforcement (proceedings) | title of execution | validity of an arbitration agreement[110] | validity of an arbitration clause[111]

Applicable Laws and Regulations:

ExecC: Section 40(1)(c)[112]

Charter: Article 36,[113] Article 38[114]

---

[110] Depending on the context, "arbitration clause" and "arbitration agreement" may also be interpreted as synonymous, or rather the arbitration clause is a form of the arbitration agreement according to Section 2 of the ArbAct.

[111] Depending on the context, "arbitration clause" and "arbitration agreement" may also be interpreted as synonymous, or rather the arbitration clause is a form of arbitration agreement according to Section 2 of the ArbAct.

[112] ExecC, Section 40(1)(c) (cit.): *An enforceable arbitral award is a title of execution.* Note: This version of the law applied to the respective proceedings, but it has not been subject to any modifications in the meantime and therefore continues to apply.

[113] Charter, Article 36 (cit.): *(1) Everyone may assert, through the legally prescribed procedure, their rights before an independent and impartial court, or in specified cases, before a different authority. (2) Unless the law provides otherwise, a person who claims that their rights were curtailed by a decision of a public administrative authority may turn to a court for review of the legality of that decision. However, judicial review of decisions affecting the fundamental rights and basic freedoms listed in this Charter may not be removed from the jurisdiction of courts. (3) Everyone is entitled to compensation for damage sustained by them as a result of an unlawful decision of a court, another state authority, or a public administrative authority, or as a result of an improper official procedure. (4) Conditions and detailed provisions are laid down by statute.* Note: This version of the law applied to the respective proceedings, but it has not been subject to any modifications in the meantime and therefore continues to apply.

[114] Charter, Article 38 (cit.): *(1) No one may be removed from the jurisdiction of their lawful judge. The jurisdiction of courts and the competence of judges shall be provided for by law. (2) Everyone has the right to have their case debated in public, without unnecessary delays, and in their presence, as well as to express their opinion on all examined evidence. The public may only be excluded in cases specified by law.* Note: This version of the law applied to the respective proceedings, but it has not been subject to any modifications in the meantime and therefore continues to apply.

ArbAct: Section 13,[115] Section 15,[116] Section 31,[117] Section 32,[118] Section 35[119]

---

[115] ArbAct, Section 13 (cit.): *(1) Permanent arbitral institutions can be established only under the law. (2) Permanent arbitral institutions can issue their own statutes and rules which must be published in the Business Journal* [Government Regulation No. 63/1992 Coll.]; *these statutes and rules may determine the method of appointment and the number of arbitrators and may stipulate that the arbitrators shall be selected from a list administered by the permanent arbitral institution. The statutes and rules may also determine how the arbitrators shall conduct the proceedings and render their decisions, as well as resolve other issues connected with the activities of the permanent arbitral institution and the arbitrators, including rules regulating the costs of proceedings and fees for the arbitrators. (3) If the parties agreed on the jurisdiction of a particular permanent arbitral institution and failed to agree otherwise in the arbitration agreement, they shall be deemed to have submitted to the regulations specified in subsection (2), as applicable on the day of commencement of the proceedings in the permanent arbitral institution.* Note: This version of the provision applied to the respective proceedings; the currently applicable version reads as follows (cit.): *(1) Permanent arbitral institutions may only be established by another law or only if another law expressly allows their establishment. (2) Permanent arbitral institutions can issue their own statutes and rules which must be published in the Business Journal* [Government Regulation No. 63/1992 Coll.]; *these statutes and rules may determine the method of appointment and the number of arbitrators and may stipulate that the arbitrators shall be selected from a list administered by the permanent arbitral institution. The statutes and rules may also determine how the arbitrators shall conduct the proceedings and render their decisions, as well as resolve other issues connected with the activities of the permanent arbitral institution and the arbitrators, including rules regulating the costs of proceedings and fees for the arbitrators. (3) If the parties agreed on the jurisdiction of a particular permanent arbitral institution and failed to agree otherwise in the arbitration agreement, they shall be deemed to have submitted to the regulations specified in subsection (2), as applicable on the day of commencement of the proceedings in the permanent arbitral institution. (4) No entity may carry out its activities using a name which evokes a misleading impression that the entity is a permanent arbitral institution under this law unless a different law or regulation or an international agreement integrated in the legal system authorizes the entity to use the name.* Note: The amendments have no bearing on the dispute in question, because there is no doubt that the entity in whose name the arbitral award was rendered, and whose Rules are referred to, is not a permanent arbitral institution within the meaning of the law; the solution therefore resolved the consequences resulting therefrom. For the sake of completeness, the reference in the original version of the ArbAct to the law regulating the Business Journal was also incorrect: the law applicable from January 1, 2001 was Regulation of the Government of the Czech Republic No. 503/2000 Coll., while the law applicable since January 1, 2014 is Regulation of the Government of the Czech Republic No. 351/2013 Coll.

[116] ArbAct, Section 15 (cit.): *(1) Arbitrators are entitled to examine their jurisdiction. If they conclude that the arbitration agreement presented to them does not give them jurisdiction to resolve the dispute, they render a corresponding resolution. (2) The plea of lack of jurisdiction, based on the non-existence, invalidity, or expiration of the arbitration agreement, can be raised*

by a party only before or together with the first act in the proceedings which concerns the merits of the case, unless the invalidity is caused by the fact that no arbitration agreement could have been concluded with respect to the case. Note: This version of the provision applied to the respective proceedings; the currently applicable version reads as follows (cit.): *(1) Arbitrators are entitled to examine their jurisdiction. If they conclude that the arbitration agreement presented to them does not give them jurisdiction to resolve the dispute, they render a corresponding resolution. (2) The plea of lack of jurisdiction, based on the non-existence, invalidity, or expiration of the arbitration agreement, can be raised by a party only before or together with the first act in the proceedings which concerns the merits of the case, unless the invalidity is caused by the fact that no arbitration agreement could have been concluded with respect to the case. This does not apply to disputes arising from consumer contracts.* Note: The SC ruled on the issue of whether the plea of invalidity of the arbitration clause should have been raised in the arbitral proceedings, but the amendment implemented by Act No. 19/2012 Coll. has no bearing on the conclusions reached by the SC, because they are not based on the application of Section 15 of the ArbAct, but on the definition of circumstances that should be reviewed in enforcement proceedings/that should be considered.

[117] ArbAct, Section 31 (cit.): (cit.): *At the request of any party the court annuls the arbitral award if: (a) it was made in a case which cannot be submitted to arbitration (cannot be the subject of a valid arbitration agreement), (b) the arbitration agreement is invalid for other reasons or the agreement was cancelled or it does not apply to the agreed case, (c) the arbitrator(s) who took part in the proceedings was/were not authorized to make decisions in the case, whether under the arbitration agreement or otherwise, or lacked the capacity to act as arbitrator(s), (d) the arbitral award was not adopted by the majority of the arbitrators, (e) a party was denied the opportunity to plead his or her case in the arbitral proceedings, (f) the arbitral award orders a party to provide performance which was not requested by the obligee or to provide performance which is impossible or illegal under domestic law, (g) it transpires that there are reasons which would otherwise justify the reopening of civil proceedings in court.* [Section 228(1)(a) and (b) of the CCP]. Note: This version of the provision applied to the respective proceedings; the currently applicable version reads as follows (cit.): *At the request of any party the court annuls the arbitral award if: (a) it was made in a case which cannot be submitted to arbitration (cannot be the subject of a valid arbitration agreement), (b) the arbitration agreement is invalid for other reasons or the agreement was cancelled or it does not apply to the agreed case, (c) the arbitrator(s) who took part in the proceedings was/were not authorized to make decisions in the case, whether under the arbitration agreement or otherwise, or lacked the capacity to act as arbitrator(s), (d) the arbitral award was not adopted by the majority of the arbitrators, (e) a party was denied the opportunity to plead his or her case in the arbitral proceedings, (f) the arbitral award orders a party to provide performance which was not requested by the creditor or to provide performance which is impossible or illegal under domestic law, (g) the arbitrator or the permanent arbitral institution resolved a dispute arising from a consumer contract contrary to consumer protection laws, or clearly in violation of good morals, or contrary to public policy, (h) an arbitration agreement relating to disputes arising from consumer contracts lacks the information required under Section 3(5) or such information is intentionally or to a non-negligible extent incomplete, inaccurate, or false, or (i) it transpires*

that there are reasons which would otherwise justify the reopening of civil proceedings in court. [Section 228(1)(a) and (b) of the CCP]. Note: The court in the given case concentrated on the issue of whether the grounds for which the execution should have been terminated should have been/had to be asserted following the procedure specified in Sections 31 and 32 of the ArbAct, and consequently, the amendments had no bearing on the decision.

[118] ArbAct, Section 32 (cit.): *(1) The motion to annul an arbitral award must be lodged with the court within three months following the receipt of the arbitral award by the party requesting the annulment of the award, unless this Act stipulates otherwise. (2) The motion pursuant to subsection (1) does not suspend the enforceability of the arbitral award. If requested by the obligor, however, the court may suspend the enforceability of the arbitral award in case an immediate enforcement of the arbitral award could cause serious harm.* Note: This version of the provision applied to the respective proceedings; the currently applicable version reads as follows (cit.): *(1) The motion to annul an arbitral award must be lodged with the court within three months following the receipt of the arbitral award by the party requesting the annulment of the award, unless this Act stipulates otherwise. If the arbitral award was made in a dispute arising from a consumer contract and the motion to annul was lodged by the consumer, the court always examines whether there are grounds to annul the arbitral award pursuant to Section 31(a) through (d) or (h). (2) The motion pursuant to subsection (1) does not suspend the enforceability of the arbitral award. If requested by the obligor, however, the court may suspend the enforceability of the arbitral award in case an immediate enforcement of the arbitral award could cause serious harm or in case the motion to annul the arbitral award justifies the conclusion that the motion is legitimate. (3) If the motion to annul an arbitral award is lodged by the consumer, the court shall establish whether there are grounds to suspend the enforceability of the arbitral award pursuant to subsection (2) without the consumer's request. The court shall rule on the suspension of enforceability within 7 days of receiving the motion; the arbitral award cannot be enforced within said time limit.* Note: The court in the given case concentrated on the issue of whether the grounds for which the execution should have been terminated should have been/had to be asserted following the procedure specified in Sections 31 and 32 of the ArbAct, and consequently, the amendments had no bearing on the decision.

[119] ArbAct, Section 35 (cit.): *(1) Even if the party against whom the enforcement of the arbitral award is sought failed to lodge a motion to annul the arbitral award by the court, the party may still request termination of the pending enforcement proceedings both on the grounds listed in special laws [Section 268 of the CCP] and if: (a) the arbitral award suffers from any of the defects listed in Section 31(a), (d), or (f), (b) the party who must have a statutory representative was not represented by such a representative in the proceedings and the party's acts were not subsequently approved, (c) the person who acted in the arbitral proceedings on behalf of the party or the party's statutory representative lacked an authorization to do so and the person's acts were not subsequently approved. (2) If a motion is lodged pursuant to subsection (1), the court conducting the enforcement of the arbitral award suspends the enforcement proceedings and orders the obligor to lodge a motion to annul the arbitral award with the competent court within 30 days. Unless the motion is lodged within this time limit, the court continues the proceedings on enforcement of the arbitral award. (3) If the arbitral award is annulled, the parties may subsequently proceed*

CivC: Section 39,[120] Section 55(1),[121] Section 56(1)[122]
CCP: Section 268,[123] Section 269(1),[124] Section 274(1)(i)[125]

similarly to Section 34. Note: This version of the provision applied to the respective proceedings; the currently applicable version reads as follows (cit.): *(1) Even if the party against whom the enforcement of the arbitral award is sought failed to lodge a motion to annul the arbitral award by the court, the party may still, irrespective of the time limit stipulated in Section 32(1), request termination of the pending enforcement proceedings both on the grounds listed in special laws [Section 268 of the CCP] and if: (a) the arbitral award suffers from any of the defects listed in Section 31(a), (d), or (f), (b) there are grounds for annulment of the arbitral award issued in a dispute arising from a consumer contract pursuant to Section 31(a) through (f), (h), or there are grounds under Section 31(g) and the arbitral award lacks the information on the right to lodge a motion to annul the arbitral award in court, (c) the party who must have a statutory representative was not represented by such a representative in the proceedings and the party's acts were not subsequently approved, (d) the person who acted in the arbitral proceedings on behalf of the party or the party's statutory representative lacked an authorization to do so and the person's acts were not subsequently approved. (2) If a motion is lodged pursuant to subsection (1), the court conducting the enforcement of the arbitral award suspends the enforcement proceedings and orders the obligor to lodge a motion to annul the arbitral award with the competent court within 30 days. Unless the motion is lodged within this time limit, the court continues the proceedings on enforcement of the arbitral award. (3) If the arbitral award is annulled, the parties may subsequently proceed similarly to Section 34.* Note: The amendments implemented in Section 35 of the ArbAct have no direct influence on the conclusions at which the SC arrived in the respective case; in the said case, the enforcement proceedings were terminated pursuant to the general grounds incorporated in Section 268 of the CCP, not on the basis of the special provision of Section 35 of the ArbAct.

[120] CivC, Section 39 (cit.): *A juridical act is invalid if the content or the purpose thereof violates or evades the law or is contra bonos mores.* Note: This is the version of the law applicable to the respective proceedings. January 1, 2014 is the effective date of the CC, which regulates the said issues in Sections 547 and 588 (both provisions are quoted below in the footnotes to this annotation).

[121] CivC, Section 55(1) (cit.): *Contractual terms in consumer contracts may not depart from the law to the detriment of the consumer. In particular, the consumer may not waive the rights guaranteed to them by the law or impair their contractual position in any other manner.* Note: This is the version of the law applicable to the respective proceedings. January 1, 2014 is the effective date of the CC, which regulates the said issues in Section 1812(2) (the provision is quoted below in the opening part of this annotation).

[122] CivC, Section 56(1) (cit.): *Consumer contracts may not contain terms that, contrary to the requirement of good faith, cause a significant imbalance in the parties' rights and obligations to the detriment of the consumer.* Note: This is the version of the law applicable to the respective proceedings. January 1, 2014 is the effective date of the CC, which regulates the said issues in Section 1813 (the provision is quoted below in the opening part of this annotation).

[123] CCP, Section 268 (cit.): *(1) Enforcement proceedings shall be terminated if (a) the enforcement was ordered despite the fact that the decision has not yet become enforceable; (b) the title of execution (enforcement) has been vacated or has become ineffective after the*

CC: Section 547,[126] Section 588,[127] Section 1812(2),[128] Section 1813[129]

enforcement was ordered; (c) the termination of the enforcement proceedings was proposed by the party that lodged the motion for enforcement; (d) the enforcement proceedings affect property that is excluded from enforcement under Sections 321 and 322; (e) the progress of the enforcement proceedings indicates that the proceeds to be generated by the enforcement will not even suffice to cover the costs thereof; (f) a final and conclusive decision has been rendered that has ruled that the enforcement proceedings affect property to which a person has rights that prohibit enforcement (Section 267); (g) after the decision was rendered, the right awarded thereunder was extinguished, unless the enforcement has already been completed; if the right was awarded by a default judgment, the enforcement proceedings will be terminated even if the right had been extinguished before the judgment was rendered; (h) the enforcement is inadmissible for any other grounds prohibiting enforcement of the decision. (2) Enforcement proceedings shall also be terminated if the obligor has made a deduction prescribed by special laws from the obligee's pecuniary claim subject to enforcement [(i) Section 83 of Act No. 337/1992 Coll., on Taxes and Fees Administration, as amended - Note: This original reference remained in the current version, but the Act has been replaced by Act No. 280/2009 Coll., the Tax Code, as amended, in effect since January 1, 2011, (ii) Section 8 et seq. of Act No. 589/1992 Coll., on Insurance Premiums on Social Security and Contribution to State Employment Policy, as amended, (iii) Section 5 et seq. of Act No. 592/1992 Coll., on Insurance Premiums on General Health Insurance, as amended] *and paid the deduction to the competent authority, to the extent to which the obligor was obliged to make the deduction. (3) Enforcement by sale of collateral shall also be terminated if the security interest was extinguished. (4) If any of the grounds for termination applies only partially to the pending enforcement proceedings, or if the enforcement has been ordered to an extent exceeding the extent that suffices to satisfy the obligee, the enforcement proceedings shall be terminated in part.* Note: This version of the law applied to the respective proceedings, but it has not been subject to any modifications in the meantime and therefore continues to apply.

[124]   CCP, Section 269(1) (cit.): *Pending enforcement proceedings will be terminated by court with or without a motion.* Note: This version of the law applied to the respective proceedings, but it has not been subject to any modifications in the meantime and therefore continues to apply.

[125]   CCP, Section 274(1)(i) (cit.): *Sections 251 through 271, with the exception of Section 261a(2) and (3), shall also apply to the enforcement of other enforceable decisions, approved settlements, and documents the judicial enforcement of which is allowed by law.* Note: The rule is now incorporated in Section 274(1)(h) of the CCP, which reads as follows (cit.): *Sections 251 through 271, with the exception of Section 261a(2) and (3), shall also apply to the enforcement of other enforceable decisions, approved settlements, and documents the judicial enforcement of which is allowed by law; this shall not apply to any title that is subject to enforcement in administrative or tax proceedings.*

[126]   CC, Section 547 (cit.): *The contents and purpose of juridical actions must comply with good morals and the statute.*

[127]   CC, Section 588 (cit.): *The court shall, with or without a motion, have regard to the invalidity of a juridical action that is prima facie contra bonos mores or that is in conflict*

The Supreme Court of the Czech Republic reached the following principal conclusions:

(1) If the arbitrator was appointed by reference to "Rules of Arbitration" issued by a legal entity other than a permanent arbitral institution established by law (statute),[130] the arbitral award is not an eligible title of execution in terms of Section 40(1)(c) of the Execution Code that could be the basis for a decision ordering execution; the reason is that the arbitrator appointed under a null and void arbitration clause (Section 39 of the CivC) lacked jurisdiction to render the arbitral award under the Arbitration Act. If, despite that, the execution was nonetheless ordered in such case, and if the lack of jurisdiction on the part of the authority that rendered the title of execution is (subsequently) established by court, the execution must be terminated at each and every stage for inadmissibility under Section 268(1)(h) of the CCP.[131]

(2) The Arbitration Act (ArbAct) does not exclude the possibility of examining the issue of (a lack of) jurisdiction on the part of the arbitrator in the execution proceedings, including the proceedings initiated by the obligor's motion to terminate the execution for inadmissibility under Section 268(1)(h) of the CCP, if the arbitrator was not appointed in compliance with any transparent rules or, as applicable, if the arbitrator was selected by a legal entity other than a permanent arbitral institution established by law.

(3) Section 15(2) of the ArbAct[132] shall not apply in proceedings for terminating the execution.

---

with the statute and obviously violates public policy. This also applies if the juridical action creates an obligation to provide performance that is impossible ab initio.

[128] CC, Section 1812(2) (cit.): An agreement shall be disregarded if it departs from statutory provisions that provide for consumer protection. This also applies if the consumer waives any special right afforded to them by statute.

[129] CC, Section 1813 (cit.): An agreement is deemed prohibited if, contrary to the requirement of reasonableness, it causes a significant imbalance in the parties' rights or obligations to the detriment of the consumer. This shall not apply to agreements regarding the subject matter of the performance or the price if they are provided to the consumer in plain intelligible language.

[130] In other words, if the entity is a legal entity that does not meet the requirements of Section 13 of the ArbAct (this provision is quoted above in the footnotes in the opening part of this annotation).

[131] This part of the summary of the SC's legal opinion (ratio decidendi) was adopted from the SC website.

[132] This provision is quoted above in a footnote in the opening part of this annotation.

[From Facts of Case]:

16.28. The obligor,[133] against whom the enforcement proceedings were ordered, had on May 25, 2005 entered into Consumer Credit Contract No. 91004277 and the Credit Facility and Credit Card Contract of [...] with the obligee; the Credit Facility and Credit Card Contract were issued by the obligee and are related to the Consumer Credit Contract. The business terms and conditions, which are an integral part of Consumer Credit Contract No. 91004277, contain an arbitration clause, which states that property disputes that arise from or in connection with the Contract shall be submitted to arbitration and resolved by a single arbitrator appointed by the Administrator of the Register of Arbitrators administered by [...][134] according to the Arbitration Rules, that the parties have declared that they understand and agree with the contents of the Arbitration Rules, Rules on the Costs of Arbitration, Tariff of Arbitrator Fees, Organization Rules and Office Rules,[135] that the arbitral proceedings shall be conducted with the exclusion of the public, and that, unless the arbitrator deems it necessary, the dispute will be resolved without an oral hearing, based on the submitted written materials. The arbitral award was rendered on July 29, 2009 under the Case No. E/2009/02118 (the arbitral proceedings were conducted on the basis of the above-described arbitration clause), whereby the obligee was awarded the claim that was the subject matter of the respective proceedings. The obligor failed to meet its obligation in a due and timely manner, and consequently, the obligee lodged a motion for enforcement. Execution was ordered by the Resolution of the District Court in Sokolov rendered on April 12, 2010 in Case No. 28 EXE 1485/2010 – 12. The decision became final and conclusive on October 7, 2010. The obligor lodged a motion for termination pursuant to Section 268(1)(h) of the CCP,[136] in which the obligor reasoned that the respective arbitration clause was invalid, because it provided for a method of the appointment of the arbitrator that referred to the Rules of a private arbitral company, which is prohibited and contrary to the conclusions reached by the High Court

---

[133] A natural person, although it is not explicitly mentioned in the annotated decision; we can infer that the person is a citizen of the Czech Republic and has their address/place of residence in the territory of the Czech Republic. The obligee is a legal entity formed and existing under the laws of the Czech Republic in the form of a limited liability company.

[134] Private arbitral company, a legal entity formed and existing under the laws of the Czech Republic in the form of a joint stock company.

[135] All of them are documents of the abovementioned arbitral company.

[136] The provision is quoted above in the opening part of this annotation.

in Prague in its decision of May 28, 2009 in Case No. 12 Cmo 496/2008.[137]

[*Procedure of Case*]:

16.29. The District Court in Sokolov, as the court of first instance, rendered on June 15, 2011 its Resolution in Case No. 28 EXE 1485/2010 – 43, whereby the enforcement proceedings were terminated. The court of first instance held that the respective arbitral award was, generally, an eligible title of execution under Section 274(1)(i) of the CCP,[138] but it was also necessary to examine whether the dispute arising from a B2C relationship could be resolved by an arbitrator. The court referred to Resolution of the SC of October 3, 2001 in Case No. 21 Cdo 1012/2000.[139] The court invoked Article 1(q) of the Annex to Council

---

[137] This decision is available online at http://pravo4u.cz/judikatura/vrchni-soud-v-praze/12-cmo-496-2008/; in this decision, the court ruled as follows (cit.): *If the arbitration agreement lacks any direct identification of an ad hoc arbitrator, or a specific description of the method of their appointment, and merely stipulates that the arbitrator will be appointed by one of the contracting parties from a list of arbitrators administered by a legal entity other than a permanent arbitral institution established in terms of Section 13 of Act No. 216/1994 Coll., as amended, and that the arbitration will be conducted pursuant to the rules issued by the legal entity, the arbitration agreement is invalid for evading (circumventing) the law.* Note: This is a landmark decision relating to the jurisdiction of private arbitral companies and marks a turning point in the courts' approach to the assessment of arbitration conducted in the name of such companies.

[138] The provision is quoted above in the opening part of this annotation.

[139] This decision is available online on the SC website at http://www.nsoud.cz/Judikatura/judikatura_ns.nsf/WebSearch/3FC7A541E22BFCC8C1257A4E0069264A?openDocument&Highlight=0; in this decision, the court ruled as follows (cit.): *The courts have also ruled that an agreement between the obligee and the obligor that is incorporated in a notarial record containing a consent with enforceability is not a substantive-law agreement. It is one of the obligatory requirements of a notarial record containing a consent with enforceability; the absence thereof renders the record unenforceable from the material perspective in terms of Section 274(e) of the CCP. Consequently, the agreement itself between the obligee and the obligor does not result in the creation, modification or expiration of any rights or obligations of the parties to the legal relationship. A notarial record containing a consent with enforceability does not include (because it is not one of the essentials of the record) any substantive-law act, whether unilateral, bilateral or multilateral, irrespective of whether it concerns the creation or modification of a legal relationship or, as applicable, the acknowledgment of debt, the fulfillment of which is the subject matter of record. Naturally, the above said does not mean that a notarial record concerning such a substantive-law act could not be incorporated in one and the same document with the notarial record containing the consent with enforceability; however, both these records must be scrupulously distinguished and must not be confused. Even if the notarial record containing the consent with enforceability is a title for judicial enforcement, it is not – according to Section 274(e)*

Directive 93/13/EEC of April 5, 1993, on unfair terms in consumer contracts,[140] and Section 56(1) of the CivC,[141] from which the court concluded that arbitration clauses are prohibited in consumer contracts, and that a similar conclusion can also be inferred from Section 55(1) of the CivC.[142] The court concluded that if the arbitrator had lacked jurisdiction, the arbitral award was a null and void act and did not constitute an eligible title of execution; consequently, the court

---

of the CCP – a decision and does not have the effects that the law attributes to decisions. It has the nature of a public deed [cf. Section 6 of Act No. 358/1992 Coll., on Notaries and Their Activities (Notary Act), as amended] and is not endowed with the effects of finality and binding force with respect to the parties and all authorities, as opposed to judicial decisions issued in civil court proceedings (cf. Section 159 of the CCP). The fact that the obligor undertook to provide the obligee with the stipulated performance and that the agreement to this end was incorporated in the notarial record containing a consent with enforceability does not constitute an obstacle that would prevent the hearing of the dispute concerning the same performance before the authority that has the jurisdiction to hear and resolve such dispute. The above indicates that a notarial record containing a consent with enforceability is only a formal document, because it contains the requirements necessary for the record to be enforceable as a title for judicial enforcement; the notary public shall draw up the record on the basis of the agreement between the obligee and the obligor without having the power to examine its foundation in substantive law, and on the basis of the obligor's declaration, whereby the obligor agrees with the enforceability of the record. The notarial record containing a consent with enforceability does not eo ipso constitute an autonomous obligation and does not establish a presumption that the debt existed when the notarial record was drawn up. The court in enforcement proceedings must have regard to the fact that a notarial record containing a consent with enforceability is a title of enforcement that does not eo ipso establish, for the benefit of the obligee, any legal grounds for receiving the enforced performance. But the fact does not prevent the court from ordering the enforcement of the notarial record containing the consent with enforceability. If the obligee is not entitled under substantive law to the performance that is the subject of the enforcement proceedings, the enforcement cannot be deemed admissible, and that fact constitutes grounds for termination of the enforcement pursuant to Section 268(1)(h) of the CCP (cf. Judgment of the Supreme Court of October 10, 2000 in Case No. 21 Cdo 267/2000, published under no. 15 in Soudní judikatura [Court Reports], Vol. 2001).

[140] The law is available at http://eur-lex.europa.eu/legal-content/CS/TXT/?qid=1415527445781&uri=CELEX:31993L0013 (cit.): *Terms that have the object or effect of excluding or hindering the consumer's right to take legal action or exercise any other legal remedy, particularly by requiring the consumer to take disputes exclusively to arbitration not covered by legal provisions, unduly restricting the evidence available to them or imposing on them a burden of proof that, according to the applicable law, should lie with another party to the contract.* Note: It is a list of unfair terms within the meaning of Article 3(3) of the Directive.

[141] The provision is quoted above in the opening part of this annotation.

[142] The provision is quoted above in the opening part of this annotation.

terminated the enforcement proceedings pursuant to Section 268(1)(h).[143]

16.30. The Regional Court in Plzeň, as the appellate court, upheld the abovementioned Resolution of the District Court in Sokolov.[144] The appellate court agreed that the conditions were fulfilled for terminating the execution pursuant to Section 268(1)(h) of the CCP,[145] because the respective arbitration clause was invalid; the appellate court, however, held the arbitration clause invalid for reasons other than those articulated by the court of first instance. The appellate court invoked the case law laying down the requirements for the method of appointing the arbitrator, especially the conclusions according to which an arbitration clause is contrary to the law (i.e. Section 39 of the CivC[146]) if the method of appointing the arbitrator according to the clause consists of a reference to Rules of Arbitration issued by a private arbitral company. The appellate court also concluded that the arbitration clause was in such case also contrary to Article 36 of the Charter.[147] The court invoked the following decisions: **(i)** Resolution of the SC of August 10, 2011 in Case No. 32 Cdo 2123/2011,[148] **(ii)** Resolution of the Grand Panel of the Civil and Commercial Division of the Supreme Court of May 11, 2011 in Case No. 31 Cdo 1945/2010,[149] and **(iii)** Judgment of the ConCourt of November 1, 2011 in Case No.

---

[143] The provision is quoted above in the opening part of this annotation.

[144] By Resolution of December 12, 2011 in Case No. 10 Co 312/2011 - 66.

[145] The provision is quoted above in the opening part of this annotation.

[146] The provision is quoted above in the opening part of this annotation.

[147] The provision is quoted above in the opening part of this annotation.

[148] This decision is available online on the SC website at http://www.nsoud.cz/Judikatura/ judikatura_ns.nsf/WebSearch/49F3964D02285FC3C1257A4E0064EEF2?openDocument&Hi ghlight=0; in this decision, the court ruled as follows (cit.): *If the arbitration agreement lacks any direct identification of an ad hoc arbitrator, or a specific description of the method of their appointment, and refers to "Rules of Arbitration" issued by a legal entity (corporation) other than a permanent arbitral institution established under the law, the arbitration agreement is contrary to law and therefore invalid pursuant to Section 39 of the Civil Code.*

[149] This decision is available online on the SC website at http://www.nsoud.cz/Judikatura/ judikatura_ns.nsf/WebSearch/87312C808746B5D2C1257A4E006568D2?openDocument& Highlight=0; in this decision, the court ruled as follows (cit.): *If the arbitration agreement lacks any direct identification of an ad hoc arbitrator, or a specific description of the method of their appointment, and refers to "Rules of Arbitration" issued by a legal entity (corporation) other than a permanent arbitral institution established under the law, the arbitration agreement is invalid pursuant to Section 39 of the Civil Code.* Note: The summary of the SC's legal opinion (*ratio decidendi*) was adopted from the SC website.

II. ÚS 2164/10.[150] At the same time, the appellate court rejected as inapplicable the objection that the invalidity of the arbitration clause should have been pleaded in the arbitral proceedings pursuant to Section 15 of the ArbAct;[151] the reason is that this case involves an obstacle to execution that renders enforcement of the decision inadmissible, and the defects cannot be cured, not even by the final and conclusive decision ordering the execution; see Resolution of the SC of July 28, 2011 in Case No. 20 Cdo 2227/2011.[152] In this connection, the

---

[150] This decision is available online on the ConCourt website at http://nalus.usoud.cz/ Search/ResultDetail.aspx?id=71879&pos=1&cnt=1&typ=result; in this decision, the court ruled as follows (cit.): *An arbitration clause in consumer contracts is validly agreed if the rules regulating the appointment of the arbitrator are transparent and clear. If the arbitration clause is incorporated in a consumer contract, the arbitration must generally guarantee such procedural rights that are comparable to proceedings that would apply if the consumer had not agreed to the clause in the consumer contract (oral and direct hearing, appeal, absence of any other obstacles preventing the exercise of the consumer's right). The Constitutional Court has therefore concluded that the arbitration clauses agreed in the given case are inadmissible, because if the arbitrator was not appointed in a transparent manner and should make their decision only following the principles of equity, and if, at the same time, the consumer is deprived of their right to lodge a petition (lawsuit) with a civil court, the situation ultimately results in a violation of the right to a fair trial in terms of Article 36(1) of the Charter. The reason is that even if the substantive rules regulating consumer protection afford sound protection to the consumers, the protection cannot be implemented if the consumers cannot effectively avail themselves of this protection. If the arbitration clauses have the result of the parties to a private-law relationship waiving the right to judicial protection guaranteed by the state, it does not mean that they make space for arbitrariness. An arbitral award is an enforceable decision; consequently, state power applies to arbitration as well, and can only be exercised in the situations within the limits and in the manner stipulated by law, honoring fundamental rights and freedoms. We can therefore conclude that an agreement on an arbitration clause in a consumer contract is only constitutionally acceptable if the conditions for the appointment of the arbitrator and the agreed procedural conditions guarantee equal treatment to the parties (meaning increased protection of the weaker party, i.e. the consumer, in the B2C relationship), and if the agreed procedural rules guarantee a fair trial, including the possibility of having the arbitral award reviewed by different arbitrators, as allowed under the valid Arbitration Act.*

[151] The provision is quoted above in the opening part of this annotation.

[152] This decision is available online on the SC website at http://www.nsoud.cz/Judikatura/ judikatura_ns.nsf/WebSearch/64861BDB436E5058C1257A4E006AA0EF?openDocument &Highlight=0; in this decision, the court ruled as follows (cit.): *The court shall always terminate pending enforcement proceedings (execution), with or without a motion, if there is a relevant circumstance that renders the enforcement inadmissible. Defects preventing the enforcement of a decision that already exist at the moment the decision is made cannot be remedied, not even by the legal force and effect of the resolution ordering the enforcement*

court concluded that the requirement under Section 15 of the ArbAct[153] could not be insisted on in execution.

16.31. The resolution of the appellate court was challenged by the obligee in an extraordinary appeal; the obligee argued that the courts acted *ultra vires* (i) in their assessment of the invalidity of the arbitration clause and the arbitral award as an enforceable title, and (ii) in the unlawful termination of the enforcement proceedings pursuant to the CCP. The obligee argued that the courts have de facto challenged the correctness of the arbitral award, which they are not allowed to do in enforcement proceedings. The obligee argued that the obligor should have lodged a motion to annul the arbitral award under Section 31 of the ArbAct[154] by the deadline stipulated in Section 32 of the ArbAct,[155] and should have pleaded the invalidity of the arbitration agreement together with their first act in the case in compliance with Section 15 of the ArbAct.[156] The obligee argued that if the obligor failed to take these steps, the execution court does not have the power to examine the validity of the arbitration clause. The obligee believes that the possibility of such material review is also not enshrined in the case law concerning Council Directive 93/13/EEC of April 5, 1993, on unfair terms in consumer contracts. The obligor would only not be bound by the arbitral award if no arbitration agreement had been entered into at all, and at the same time, the obligor had been entirely passive during the arbitration. From this perspective, the obligee argued that the reasons do not apply that have been articulated in Resolution of the SC of July 28, 2011 in Case No. 20 Cdo 2227/2011[157] – the decision addresses the issue of the non-existence, not the invalidity, of an arbitration clause. The case was first examined by SC Panel No. 20, which held that its opinion differed from the opinions voiced in Resolution of the SC of

---

proceedings. Consequently, pending execution may also be terminated if the court (ex post) discovers that the authority that made the title of execution lacked the necessary jurisdiction (no arbitration agreement was concluded). If the title of execution is an arbitral award, the execution may be terminated both on the special grounds for terminating execution and on the reasons specified in Section 268 of the CCP. Where no arbitration agreement has been concluded, the issued arbitral award is not an eligible title of execution, irrespective of the fact that the obligor in the arbitral proceedings failed to plead the non-existence of the arbitration agreement. Section 15(2) of Act No. 216/1994 Coll. does not apply in the proceedings for terminating pending execution.

153 The provision is quoted above in the opening part of this annotation.
154 The provision is quoted above in the opening part of this annotation.
155 The provision is quoted above in the opening part of this annotation.
156 The provision is quoted above in the opening part of this annotation.
157 The decision is quoted above in this annotation.

October 30, 2008 in Case No. 20 Cdo 2857/2006,[158] and in Resolution of the SC of August 31, 2010 in Case No. 20 Cdo 3284/2008,[159] as concerns the issue of the arbitrator's jurisdiction to render an arbitral award on the basis of an arbitration agreement that is invalid under Section 39 of the CivC;[160] the SC held in the abovementioned Resolutions that the arbitrator had jurisdiction in such case, and the respective party should have defended themselves by means of a motion to annul the arbitral award pursuant to Section 31 of the ArbAct.[161] Considering the above said, SC Panel No. 20 forwarded the case for resolution, in compliance with the applicable procedural rules, to the Grand Panel of the Civil and Commercial Division, which heard the case and rendered the annotated decision.

---

[158] This decision is available online on the SC website at http://www.nsoud.cz/ Judikatura/judikatura_ns.nsf/WebSearch/3C5BBC6777E7E38BC1257A4E006ACEEC?ope nDocument&Highlight=0; in this decision, the court ruled as follows (cit.): *1. The court examines (inter alia) whether the decision proposed for involuntary enforcement was rendered by an authority that possessed the necessary jurisdiction; such examination is already made at the stage of ordering the enforcement (execution). If the court finds that the decision was rendered by an authority that lacked the jurisdiction necessary to resolve an issue incorporated in the decision, the motion to order enforcement of the decision will be dismissed. 2. A property dispute between the parties can be removed from the jurisdiction of courts and submitted to arbitration if an arbitration agreement exists. If no arbitration agreement exists, the arbitrator does not have jurisdiction to resolve the property dispute. It is irrelevant that the obligor remained entirely passive in the arbitral proceedings, did not attend hearings, did not plead the non-existence of the arbitration agreement, and the arbitral award was served on them. 3. Act No. 216/1994 Coll. does not indicate that passivity and inaction on the part of the respondent in arbitration would result in submission to the arbitrator's jurisdiction; this consequence could only be associated with the behavior of a respondent who was active in the hearing of the dispute without pleading the non-existence of the arbitration agreement before or together with their first act on the merits. A different situation would occur if the arbitration agreement were concluded, albeit an invalid one. In such case, the arbitrator would have jurisdiction to render the arbitral award; the respondent's defense would consist of a motion to annul the arbitral award. 4. Where no arbitration agreement exists, the motion to order execution based on an arbitral award must be dismissed.*

[159] This decision is available online on the SC website at http://www.nsoud.cz/Judikatura/ judikatura_ns.nsf/WebSearch/2E49414B7658E266C1257A4E0065B928?openDocument& Highlight=0; in this decision, the court ruled as follows (cit.): *Where no arbitration agreement has been concluded, the issued arbitral award is not an eligible title of execution, irrespective of the fact that the obligor in the arbitral proceedings failed to plead the non-existence of the arbitration agreement.* Note: The summary of the SC's legal opinion (*ratio decidendi*) was adopted from the SC website.

[160] The provision is quoted above in the opening part of this annotation.

[161] The provision is quoted above in the opening part of this annotation.

16.32. The SC confirmed the conclusions that the court arrived at in its case law, according to which an arbitration clause is null and void as contrary to the law (statute) under Section 39 of the CivC[162] if the clause does not contain any direct determination of the arbitrator or method of their appointment, and refers, in this connection, to the rules of a private arbitral company. The court had no doubt that the institution in the given case was not a permanent institution in terms of Section 13 of the ArbAct.[163] The SC therefore ruled that the issue to be resolved was whether an arbitral award rendered on the basis of such an invalid arbitration agreement was a title of execution under Section 40(1)(c) of the ExecC,[164] or whether the enforcement proceedings must be terminated in such case pursuant to Section 268(1)(h) of the CCP.[165] In this connection, the SC identified with the conclusion that the material correctness of the title of execution cannot be reviewed in enforcement proceedings. The SC also accepted the conclusions that the court shall terminate any pending enforcement proceedings with or without a motion pursuant to Section 269(1) of the CCP,[166] if there is any relevant circumstance that prohibits the enforcement, because defects prohibiting enforcement of a decision that already existed at the time when the decision was rendered cannot be cured, not even by the final and conclusive resolution whereby the enforcement was ordered. Consequently, pending execution may also be terminated if the court discovers that the authority that rendered the title of execution lacked the necessary jurisdiction. This case concerned situations where no arbitration agreement was entered into. In such case, the court shall apply the general grounds for terminating enforcement proceedings, namely Section 268(1)(h) of the CCP,[167] not the special provision of Section 35 of the ArbAct.[168] Where such circumstances are involved, the party is also not obliged to plead the non-existence of the arbitration clause during the arbitral proceedings pursuant to Section 15 of the ArbAct.[169] In the following examination of the case, the court also invoked the opinions of the ConCourt regarding the degree to which courts are entitled to have regard, during the enforcement

---

[162] The provision is quoted above in the opening part of this annotation.
[163] The provision is quoted above in the opening part of this annotation.
[164] The provision is quoted above in the opening part of this annotation.
[165] The provision is quoted above in the opening part of this annotation.
[166] The provision is quoted above in the opening part of this annotation.
[167] The provision is quoted above in the opening part of this annotation.
[168] The provision is quoted above in the opening part of this annotation.
[169] The provision is quoted above in the opening part of this annotation.

proceedings, to the issue of the validity of the arbitration agreement/jurisdiction of the arbitrator to render the decision. The court referred to **(i)** Judgment of the ConCourt of September 27, 2012 in Case No. III. ÚS 1624/12,[170] **(ii)** Judgment of the Constitutional Court of April 3, 2012 in Case No. IV. ÚS 2735/11,[171] **(iii)** Judgment of the ConCourt of November 1, 2011 in Case No. II. ÚS 2164/10,[172]

---

[170] This decision is available online on the ConCourt website at http://nalus.usoud.cz/Search/ResultDetail.aspx?id=76218&pos=1&cnt=1&typ=result; in this decision, the court ruled as follows (cit.): *Act No. 216/1994 Coll., on Arbitration and the Enforcement of Arbitral Awards, does not exclude the possibility that the issue of the arbitrator's jurisdiction (or lack thereof) will also be examined in execution. If the court fails to address the party's objections, pleading a lack of jurisdiction on the part of the arbitrator, the court proceeds contrary to Article 36(1) of the Charter of Fundamental Rights and Freedoms. The rule is that if the dispute is not resolved by an arbitrator who was appointed (selected) according to transparent rules, the outcome of such decision-making cannot be acceptable either.*

[171] This decision is available online on the ConCourt website at http://nalus.usoud.cz/Search/ResultDetail.aspx?id=73906&pos=1&cnt=1&typ=result; in this decision, the court ruled as follows (cit.): *Act No. 216/1994 Coll., on Arbitration and the Enforcement of Arbitral Awards, does not exclude the possibility that the issue of the arbitrator's jurisdiction (or lack thereof) will also be examined in execution. The right to one's lawful judge guaranteed under Article 38(1) of the Charter of Fundamental Rights and Freedoms can also be reasonably applied to arbitration. The Constitutional Court emphasizes the requirement of a specific and individual choice of arbitrator, because arbitration represents a "departure" from traditional litigation, the results of which can only be subject to court review under very limited circumstances. Consequently, if the decision is not rendered by an arbitrator who was appointed (selected) according to transparent rules, the outcome of such decision-making cannot be acceptable either.*

[172] This decision is available online on the ConCourt website at http://nalus.usoud.cz/Search/ResultDetail.aspx?id=71879&pos=1&cnt=1&typ=result; in this decision, the court ruled as follows (cit.): *An arbitration clause in consumer contracts is validly agreed if the rules regulating the appointment of the arbitrator are transparent and clear. If the arbitration clause is incorporated in a consumer contract, the arbitration must generally guarantee such procedural rights that are comparable to proceedings that would apply if the consumer had not agreed to the clause in the consumer contract (oral and direct hearing, appeal, absence of any other obstacles preventing the exercise of the consumer's right). The Constitutional Court has therefore concluded that the arbitration clauses agreed in the given case are inadmissible, because if the arbitrator was not appointed in a transparent manner and should make their decision only following the principles of equity, and if, at the same time, the consumer is deprived of their right to lodge a petition (lawsuit) with a civil court, the situation ultimately results in a violation of the right to a fair trial in terms of Article 36(1) of the Charter. The reason is that even if the substantive rules regulating consumer protection afford sound protection to the consumers, the protection cannot be implemented if the consumers cannot effectively avail themselves of this protection. If the arbitration clauses have the result of the parties to a private-law*

(iv) Judgment of the ConCourt of January 17, 2012 in Case No. I. ÚS 871/11,[173] and **(v)** Judgment of the ConCourt of January 26, 2012 in Case No. I. ÚS 199/11.[174] The SC held that the contested decision of the appellate court was based solely on the application of Czech law, and consequently, the obligee's objection could not be accepted that the rulings that concern the application of Council Directive 93/13/EEC of April 5, 1993, on unfair terms in consumer contracts, do not bestow such powers on the courts. Considering the above said, the SC concluded that if the arbitral award was not rendered by an arbitrator appointed according to transparent rules or, as applicable, if the arbitrator was appointed by a legal entity other than a permanent arbitral institution established by law, and if the result of the arbitrator's decision-making cannot be acceptable either, the arbitral award is not an eligible title of

---

relationship waiving the right to judicial protection guaranteed by the state, it does not mean that they make space for arbitrariness. An arbitral award is an enforceable decision; consequently, state power applies to arbitration as well, and can only be exercised in the situations within the limits and in the manner stipulated by law, honoring fundamental rights and freedoms. We can therefore conclude that an agreement on an arbitration clause in a consumer contract is only constitutionally acceptable if the conditions for the appointment of the arbitrator and the agreed procedural conditions guarantee equal treatment to the parties (meaning increased protection of the weaker party, i.e. the consumer, in the B2C relationship), and if the agreed procedural rules guarantee a fair trial, including the possibility of having the arbitral award reviewed by different arbitrators, as allowed under the valid Arbitration Act.

[173] This decision is available online on the ConCourt website at http://nalus.usoud.cz/Search/ResultDetail.aspx?id=72998&pos=1&cnt=1&typ=result; in this decision, the court ruled as follows (cit.): *Section 15(2) of the Arbitration Act stipulates that the plea of lack of jurisdiction, based on the non-existence, invalidity, or expiration of the arbitration agreement, can be raised by a party only before or together with the first act in the proceedings which concerns the merits of the case, unless the invalidity is caused by the fact that the case is not arbitrable (no arbitration agreement could have been concluded with respect to the case). But the said provision by no means indicates that the issue of jurisdiction can no longer be examined in execution. A party to the arbitral proceedings must not be adversely affected by an arbitral award with the issue of which he or she did not agree in advance in the form of an arbitration agreement or clause; this applies even if the party was passive during the arbitral proceedings and failed to plea a lack of jurisdiction on the part of the arbitrator.*

[174] This decision is available online on the ConCourt website at http://nalus.usoud.cz/Search/ResultDetail.aspx?id=72996&pos=1&cnt=1&typ=result; in this decision, the court ruled as follows (cit.): *A party to the arbitral proceedings must not be adversely affected by an arbitral award with the issue of which they did not agree in advance in the form of an arbitration agreement or clause; this applies even if the party was passive during the arbitral proceedings and failed to plea a lack of jurisdiction on the part of the arbitrator.*

execution in terms of Section 40(1)(c) of the ExecC,[175] which could serve as the basis for execution, because the arbitrator appointed on the basis of an arbitration clause that is null and void pursuant to Section 39 of the CivC[176] lacked the jurisdiction necessary for making the arbitral award under the Arbitration Act. If, despite that, the execution was nonetheless ordered in such case or, as applicable, if the lack of jurisdiction on the part of the authority which rendered the title of execution was (subsequently) established by court, the execution must be terminated at each and every stage for inadmissibility under Section 268(1)(h) of the CCP.[177] Where such circumstances are involved, it is also not possible to insist that a party already plead the non-existence of the arbitration clause in the arbitral proceedings pursuant to Section 15 of the ArbAct,[178] or rather the enforcement proceedings must be terminated even if no such plea was raised.

16.33. For this reason, the SC no longer approved of the opinion which was, at the general level and without any connection to the issue of non-existence of the arbitration clause, articulated in Resolution of the SC of October 30, 2008 in Case No. 20 Cdo 2857/2006,[179] and in Resolution of the SC of August 31, 2010 in Case No. 20 Cdo 3284/2008,[180] in which the SC held that the conclusions articulated in the said decision would not apply and a different situation would occur if the arbitration agreement had been entered into, albeit an invalid one, and that in such case the respondent's defense would consist of a motion to annul the arbitral award.

16.34. The SC therefore held that the objections were groundless, according to which the invalidity of an arbitration agreement may only be asserted in the form of a motion to annul the arbitral award under Section 31 of the ArbAct[181] lodged by the deadline stipulated in Section 32 of the ArbAct;[182] the SC invoked the abovementioned case law, which indicates that execution courts have the power (jurisdiction) to examine the validity of the arbitration agreement. Considering the conclusion that the termination of the enforcement proceedings pursuant to Section 268(1)(h) of the CCP[183] shall apply to those cases in

---

[175] The provision is quoted above in the opening part of this annotation.
[176] The provision is quoted above in the opening part of this annotation.
[177] The provision is quoted above in the opening part of this annotation.
[178] The provision is quoted above in the opening part of this annotation.
[179] The decision is quoted above in this annotation.
[180] The decision is quoted above in this annotation.
[181] The provision is quoted above in the opening part of this annotation.
[182] The provision is quoted above in the opening part of this annotation.
[183] The provision is quoted above in the opening part of this annotation.

which a party pleads the non-existence of the arbitration agreement, as well as those cases in which the arbitration agreement is invalid, the SC also did not agreed with the argument that the conclusions reached by the SC in its Resolution of July 28, 2011 in Case No. 20 Cdo 2227/2011[184] do not apply to the case at hand.

[*Arguments Presented by SC*]:

16.35.   The SC first addressed the issue of the extent of the powers enjoyed by execution courts; the SC concluded that execution courts may examine whether the title of execution was rendered by an authority that had the necessary jurisdiction (power), whether the title is enforceable from the formal and material perspective, whether the obligee and the obligor have standing, whether the execution is proposed to an extent that suffices to satisfy the obligee, and whether the right subject to enforcement has not been extinguished. Conversely, the execution court is not allowed to review the material aspects of the title of execution. The SC has based its reasoning on the previous conclusions articulated by the SC in (i) Resolution of the SC of April 14, 1999 in Case No. 21 Cdo 2020/98,[185] (ii) Resolution of the SC of October 25, 2002 in Case No. 20 Cdo 554/2002,[186] (iii) Resolution of the SC of

---

[184]   The decision is quoted above in this annotation.

[185]   This decision is available online on the SC website at http://www.nsoud.cz/Judikatura/ judikatura_ns.nsf/WebSearch/5B5F947857E603ECC1257BD6003A2CE5?openDocument &Highlight=0; in this decision, the court ruled as follows (cit.): *Section 274(e) of the CCP stipulates that a notarial record represents a title for judicial enforcement if it meets the formal requirements applicable to the drafting of notarial records regarding juridical acts, which requirements are listed primarily in Section 62 et seq. of Act No. 358/1992 Coll., on Notaries and Their Activities (Notary Act), as amended by Act No. 82/1998 Coll., if (i) the notarial record contains an agreement of the obligee with the obligor that accurately individualizes the obligee and the obligor and identifies the legal grounds for the performance, the subject of the performance (precise contents and scope of the performance) and the time of the performance (precisely and accurately determined deadline by which the obligor undertakes to provide the subject of performance to the obligee), and if (ii) the obligor gave their consent with enforceability in the notarial record. The requirement that the agreement between the obligee and the obligor must be incorporated in the notarial record containing a consent with enforceability (Section 274(e) of the CCP) can be fulfilled by any of the following alternatives: (i) the obligee and obligor will be parties to a single record (drafted in the presence of both of them, or in the form of a continuation of a notarial record), or (ii) the expression of will incorporated in a notarial record drawn up with one of the parties will be acceded to by the other party in the form of a separate record.* Note: The summary of the SC's legal opinion (*ratio decidendi*) was adopted from the SC website.

[186]   This decision is available online on the SC website at http://www.nsoud.cz/Judikatura/ judikatura_ns.nsf/WebSearch/DCD18F8CCCF07E4FC1257A4E006762A5?openDocument& Highlight=0; in this decision, the court ruled as follows (cit.): *The court in enforcement*

December 16, 2004 in Case No. 20 Cdo 1570/2003,[187] **(iv)** Resolution of the SC of July 21, 2008 in Case No. 20 Cdo 2273/2008,[188] and **(v)** Resolution of the SC of August 5, 2008 in Case No. 20 Cdo 4548/2007.[189] It is possible to conclude that the issue addressed in the given case was limited to the court's power to examine in execution the arbitrators' jurisdiction from the perspective of the validity of the

---

proceedings is not allowed to address the objection, whereby a party argues that the court in the proceedings in which the title of enforcement was rendered appointed a guardian for a party pursuant to Section 29(3) of the CCP, whose place of residence was not established until the termination of the proceedings, despite incomplete investigation of the party's residence. Note: The summary of the SC's legal opinion (*ratio decidendi*) was adopted from the SC website.

[187] This decision is available online on the SC website at http://www.nsoud.cz/Judikatura/judikatura_ns.nsf/WebSearch/53CA3D11B0BB5DE5C1257A4E00653136?openDocument &Highlight=0; in this decision, the court ruled as follows (cit.): *The conditions are not met for the termination of the enforcement proceedings pursuant to Section 268(1)(h) of the CCP if an expression of will had been made before the decision submitted for enforcement was issued, where the object of the expression of will was an offset of claims and the claims met.* The summary of the SC's legal opinion (*ratio decidendi*) was adopted from the SC website.

[188] This decision is available online on the SC website at http://www.nsoud.cz/Judikatura/judikatura_ns.nsf/WebSearch/3CF07FDD6B3C6C1EC1257A4E006A9EA0?openDocument& Highlight=0; in this decision, the court ruled as follows (cit.): *1. Material assessment of the motion to order execution only entails the following considerations: (i) whether the title of execution was made by a competent authority (an authority that had the necessary jurisdiction), (ii) whether it is enforceable from the formal and material perspective, (iii) whether the obligee and the obligor have standing, (iv) whether the enforcement is proposed to an extent that will suffice to satisfy the obligee's claim, (v) whether or not an enforcement that would be ordered or proposed in a different manner would suffice to enforce a pecuniary receivable, and (vi) whether the right has not expired (extinctive prescription). Conversely, the execution court is not allowed to examine the material correctness of the underlying decision; the court is bound by the contents thereof and is obliged to accept it as the basis for ordering the execution. 2. Deficiencies in the identification of the parties in the title of execution shall not prejudice the enforceability of the decision if it is possible to infer from the decision without any doubt to whom the right was awarded or on whom the obligation was imposed.*

[189] This decision is available online on the SC website at http://www.nsoud.cz/Judikatura/judikatura_ns.nsf/WebSearch/2526F36211029AC8C1257A4E00656CB7?openDocument& Highlight=0; in this decision, the court ruled as follows (cit.): *The execution court is not allowed to examine the material correctness of the underlying decision; the court is bound by the contents thereof and is obliged to accept it as the basis for its decision. Similarly, the court does not examine at the moment of ordering the enforcement whether or not the obligor fulfilled the imposed obligation; in this regard, the court accepts the obligee's statement. If the obligor fulfilled the imposed obligation, their defense merely consists of a motion to terminate the enforcement proceedings. If the motion for enforcement was groundless, the obligor may claim against the obligee compensation for damage and losses incurred by the obligor as a result of the groundless penalty imposed on the obligor.*

arbitration agreement; at the general level, and in connection with those situations in which the arbitration agreement was held non-existent (null), not invalid, the jurisdiction of execution courts and their power to terminate enforcement of the arbitral award pursuant to Section 268(1)(h) of the CCP[190] were confirmed, even in those cases in which the non-existence of the arbitration agreement was not pleaded in arbitration by the deadline stipulated in Section 15 of the ArbAct.[191] The SC therefore merely referred to the detailed conclusions reached by the SC in its prior rulings, and held that there is no reason to depart from these conclusions. The court invoked the following decisions: (i) Resolution of the SC of August 31, 2010 in Case No. 20 Cdo 3284/2008,[192] (ii) Resolution of the SC of October 30, 2008 in Case No. 20 Cdo 2857/2008,[193] (iii) Resolution of the SC of September 22, 2005 in Case No. 20 Cdo 168/2005,[194] and (iv) Resolution of the SC of July 27, 2011 in Case No. 20 Cdo 2209/2011.[195] As mentioned above, the

---

[190] The provision is quoted above in the opening part of this annotation.

[191] The provision is quoted above in the opening part of this annotation.

[192] The decision is quoted above in this annotation.

[193] The decision is quoted above in this annotation.

[194] This decision is available online on the SC website at http://www.nsoud.cz/Judikatura/ judikatura_ns.nsf/WebSearch/7733CBD4B7A2A592C1257A4E0067A34A?openDocument &Highlight=0; in this decision, the court ruled as follows (cit.): *Neither Act No. 216/1994 Coll., nor any other generally binding law or regulation contain any provision that would prohibit resolving the issue of incidental performance (other than on the merits), such as the obligation of the obligor to pay the arbitrator's fee, by an arbitral award or resolution (in the given case, a resolution to terminate the arbitral proceedings, whereby the said obligation was imposed on the obligor); the reason is that an arbitration agreement or any special agreement, as applicable, may contain a provision, whereby the parties agree on the management of the proceedings (see Section 19(1) of the abovementioned Act), but also provisions regulating other issues, e.g. the amount and the manner of determining the fee (remuneration) and the costs of arbitration. When ordering execution (enforcement), the court is not allowed to review the material correctness of the title submitted for enforcement; this includes the issue of whether or not the imposed obligation to pay the fees is lawful, the basis of which is incorporated in the parties' agreement.*

[195] This decision is available online on the SC website at http://www.nsoud.cz/ Judikatura/judikatura_ns.nsf/WebSearch/8EA48722870F62CCC1257A4E006ACA81?open Document&Highlight=0; in this decision, the court ruled as follows (cit.): *Firstly, the Supreme Court invokes its rulings that address similar issues raised by the same obligee (see Resolution of June 30, 2011 in Case No. 20 Cdo 1828/2011, or Resolution of the same day in Case No. 20 Cdo 1923/2011), in which the Supreme Court provided reasons for its conclusion, which is also shared by academic literature (cf. JUDr. Vladimír Kurka, JUDr. Ljubomír Drápal, Výkon rozhodnutí v soudním řízení [Title in Translation – Enforcement of Decisions in Court Proceedings], Linde Praha a.s., Prague – Právnické a ekonomické*

issue addressed by the SC was limited to whether and to what extent these conclusions are applicable.

16.36. The SC therefore concluded that the decision of the appellate court was correct. The claimant did not succeed in undermining the decision of the appellate court, and consequently, the SC dismissed the extraordinary appeal.

[*Further Conclusions and Comments Concerning Annotated Resolution of SC*]:

16.37. The annotated decision addressed the issue of the limits applicable to the review of an arbitral award in execution, which is an issue that has always drawn much attention from legal professionals and academics. On top of that, the provisions of the ArbAct were, for a certain period of time, rather fragmentary and suffered from a legislative deficiency – before the amendment implemented by Act No. 19/2012, Section 35 of the ArbAct[196] had no connection to the deadline under Section 32 of the ArbAct[197] for filing the motion to annul the arbitral award in terms of Section 31 of the ArbAct.[198] The abovementioned amendment has clarified that there are no temporal limitations restricting the right to petition for cancellation of the enforcement proceedings based on the

---

nakladatelství a knihkupectví Bohumily Hořínkové a Jana Tuláčka, Praha [Prague, Czech Republic], *2004, pp. 350, 351), i.e. that the court shall always terminate pending enforcement proceedings (execution), with or without a motion (Section 269(1) of the CCP), if there is a relevant circumstance that renders the enforcement inadmissible. Defects preventing the enforcement of a decision that already exist at the moment the decision is made cannot be remedied, not even by the legal force and effect of the resolution ordering the enforcement proceedings. Consequently, pending execution may also be terminated if the court (ex post) discovers that the authority that rendered the title of execution lacked the necessary jurisdiction (no arbitration agreement was concluded). The Supreme Court has also accepted the conclusion that if the title of execution is an arbitral award, the execution may be terminated both on the special grounds for terminating execution (Section 35(1) of Act No. 216/1994 Coll.), and on the reasons specified in Section 268* [of the CCP]. *The court has also previously ruled that where no arbitration agreement is concluded, the issued arbitral award is not an eligible title of execution, irrespective of the fact that the obligor in the arbitral proceedings failed to plead the non-existence of the arbitration agreement. The Supreme Court has also concluded that Section 15(2) of Act No. 216/1994 Coll. does not apply in proceedings for terminating pending execution (cf. Resolution of August 31, 2010 in Case No. 20 Cdo 3284/2008, published under no. 83/2011 in Sbírka soudních rozhodnutí a stanovisek [Reports of Court Decisions and Opinions], Resolutions of October 30, 2008 in Case No. 20 Cdo 2857/2006, and of September 22, 2005 in Case No. 20 Cdo 168/2005).*

[196] The provision is quoted above in the opening part of this annotation.

[197] The provision is quoted above in the opening part of this annotation.

[198] The provision is quoted above in the opening part of this annotation.

special grounds listed in Section 35 of the ArbAct,[199] which expand the general grounds for terminating the proceedings pursuant to Section 268 of the CCP,[200] i.e. the petition can be lodged whether or not the time period has expired for filing the motion to annul the arbitral award. Apart from the above said, courts had to address the issue of the parallel regimes of terminating the enforcement proceedings provided for under the CCP and under the ArbAct. Over the course of time, however, the interpretation has settled and the courts have consistently held that termination of the enforcement of an arbitral award can be requested both under the general provisions of the CCP and (if the given plea cannot be subsumed under any of the grounds contained therein) on the basis of the special grounds listed in Section 35 of the ArbAct.[201]

16.38. When analyzing the decision, we need to realize that the law governing the case is the law preceding the effective date of the Consumer Amendment represented by Act No. 19/2012 Coll., despite the fact that the subject of the case was a claim arising from a B2C dispute. At that time, Section 35 of the ArbAct[202] did not assert the breach of consumer status as a weaker party as grounds for termination of the enforcement proceedings the circumstances that constituted grounds for a motion to annul the arbitral award under Section 31(b) and (c) of the ArbAct.[203] The Consumer Amendment has supplemented these grounds, and consequently, Section 35(1)(b) of the ArbAct,[204] which contains special rules for B2C disputes, could be applied to the given case now. However, this gives rise to an interesting paradox: reasoning to the contrary, we could interpret the ArbAct in such manner as to conclude that the grounds cannot be applied in the case of arbitral awards that were not rendered in connection with B2C disputes. But the existing case law has already arrived at the conclusion that the enforcement proceedings could be terminated pursuant to Section 268(1)(h) of the CCP[205] based on factual circumstances that could be subsumed under the grounds for annulment of arbitral award listed in Section 31(c) of the ArbAct.[206] These decisions were correct at the time, when there was no other possibility of applying those grounds; it is also necessary to

---

[199] The provision is quoted above in the opening part of this annotation.
[200] The provision is quoted above in the opening part of this annotation.
[201] The provision is quoted above in the opening part of this annotation.
[202] The provision is quoted above in the opening part of this annotation.
[203] The provision is quoted above in the opening part of this annotation.
[204] The provision is quoted above in the opening part of this annotation.
[205] The provision is quoted above in the opening part of this annotation.
[206] The provision is quoted above in the opening part of this annotation.

point out that the respective decisions concerned situations in which a party pleaded the non-existence of the arbitration agreement.

16.39. The SC extended this possibility in the annotated decision to cover the grounds concerning the validity of the arbitration agreement, i.e. the grounds that fall within Section 31(b) of the ArbAct.[207] At the same time, it is clear that the conclusions articulated in the respective decision are not, and will not be limited to B2C disputes, but that they are generally applicable,[208] which renders the Consumer Amendment rather pointless in this regard. Or rather, the courts will terminate the enforcement proceedings in commercial cases with reference to Section 268(1)(h) of the CCP,[209] in compliance with the annotated decision, whereas the principle of *lex specialis derogat legi generali* should apply in B2C disputes, and the courts should proceed pursuant to Section 35(1)(b) of the ArbAct.[210] Consequently, it is to be expected that future rulings of the SC will focus on the delimitation of the mutual relationship between these two provisions.

| | |

5. Judgment of Supreme Court of Czech Republic of July 24, 2013 in Case No. 23 Cdo 2251/2011: (i) Providing Possibility to State One's Case before Arbitrator, (ii) Obligation of Arbitrator to Give Instructions[211]

Abbreviations Used:

AC   Arbitration Court at the Economic Chamber of the Czech Republic and Agricultural Chamber of the Czech Republic[212]

---

[207] The provision is quoted above in the opening part of this annotation.

[208] The requirements for the method of appointing the arbitrator that were articulated in Resolution of the Grand Panel of the Civil and Commercial Division of the Supreme Court of May 11, 2011 in Case No. 31 Cdo 1945/2010 are not limited to B2C disputes, and the parties may also invoke these requirements in commercial matters.

[209] The provision is quoted above in the opening part of this annotation.

[210] The provision is quoted above in the opening part of this annotation.

[211] The Judgment is available is available on the SC website at http://www.nsoud.cz/Judikatura/judikatura_ns.nsf/WebSearch/7F77770220A2CBDEC1257BC1002E30E6?openDocument&Highlight=0,rozhod%C4%8D%C3%AD,%C5%99%C3%ADzen%C3%AD [last accessed on August 28, 2014].

[212] Information about this permanent arbitral institution is available at www.soud.cz in

ArbAct	Act of the Czech Republic No. 216/1994 Coll., on Arbitration and the Enforcement of Arbitral Awards, as amended
CCP	Act of the Czech Republic No. 99/1963 Coll., the Code of Civil Procedure, as amended
Charter	Resolution of the Presidium of the Czech National Council No. 2/1993 Coll., on the promulgation of the Charter of Fundamental Rights and Freedoms as a part of the constitutional order of the Czech Republic, as amended
CivC	Act of the Czech Republic No. 40/1964 Coll., the Civil Code, in effect until December 31, 2013[213]
CJA	Act of the Czech Republic No. 6/2002 Coll., on Courts and Judges, as amended
ComC	Act of the Czech Republic No. 513/1991 Coll., the Commercial Code, in effect until December 31, 2013[214]
ConCourt	Constitutional Court of the Czech Republic
SC	Supreme Court of the Czech Republic

Laws and Regulations Applied in Decision:

Charter: Article 38[215]

CivC: Section 37[216]

ComC: Section 68(6),[217] Section 344,[218] Section 345,[219] Section 346,[220] Section 348,[221] Section 351,[222] and Section 352[223]

---

multiple language versions.

[213] This Act has been replaced with Act of the Czech Republic No. 89/2012 Coll., the Civil Code, as well as Act No. 90/2012 Coll., the Business Corporations Act, in connection with the recodification of civil law and with effect since January 1, 2014.

[214] This Act has been replaced with Act of the Czech Republic No. 89/2012 Coll., the Civil Code, as well as Act No. 90/2012 Coll., Business Corporations Act, in connection with the recodification of civil law and with effect since January 1, 2014.

[215] Charter, Article 38 (cit.): *"(1) No one may be removed from the jurisdiction of their lawful judge. The jurisdiction of courts and the competence of judges shall be provided for by law. (2) Everyone has the right to have their case debated in public, without unnecessary delays, and in their presence, as well as to express their opinion on all evidence examined. The public may only be excluded in cases specified by law."*

[216] CivC, Section 37 (cit.): *"(1) A juridical act must be performed freely and seriously, in a clear and intelligible manner, on pain of invalidity. (2) If the subject matter of the juridical act is impossible performance, the juridical act is invalid. (3) A juridical act is not invalid for any mistakes in writing or arithmetic, provided that the meaning is unambiguous."*

[217] ComC, Section 68(6) (cit.): *Upon a motion lodged by a state authority or a person who evidences their legal interest, the court may render a decision on winding up and liquidating a company if: (a) no General Meeting has been held in the past two years or no*

bodies (officers) of the company have been elected in the past year, if their term of office, or the term of office of all members of the bodies, expired more than a year ago, unless this Act stipulates otherwise, or the company has not been conducting any activity for more than two years, (b) the company loses its business license, (c) the company no longer meets the requirements prescribed by the law for the formation of the company, or the company is unable to conduct its activity due to insurmountable conflicts among shareholders, (d) the company is in breach of the duty to create a reserve fund, (e) the company is in breach of Section 56(3), (f) the company is in breach of the obligation to sell part of its enterprise or the obligation to divide itself imposed by a decision of the Office for the Protection of Competition under special laws.

[218] ComC, Section 344 (cit.): *"A contract can only be rescinded in cases stipulated by contract or this Act."*

[219] ComC, Section 345 (cit.): *"(1) If the debtor's (Section 365) or the creditor's (Section 370) default constitutes a fundamental breach of their contractual obligation, the other (non-defaulting) party has the right to rescind the contract, provided that the non-defaulting party notifies the defaulting party thereof without undue delay after the non-defaulting party has learned of the breach. (2) For the purposes of this Act, a breach of contract is fundamental if the defaulting party knew at the time of executing the contract or if it was reasonable to assume at that time considering the object of the contract discernible from its contents or the circumstances attending the execution of the contract, that the non-defaulting party will not be interested in the fulfillment of obligations if such a breach of contract occurs. If in doubt, the breach of the contract is deemed non-fundamental. (3) If the party entitled to demand fulfillment of the other party's contractual obligation (the non-defaulting party) notifies the other party that they insist on the fulfillment of the obligation or if the non-defaulting party fails to exercise their right to rescind the contract under Subsection (1) in time, the non-defaulting party is only entitled to rescind the contract in the manner stipulated for a non-fundamental breach of the contractual obligation; if the non-defaulting party stipulates any deadline for additional performance of the obligation, the non-defaulting party becomes entitled to rescind the contract after expiration of the deadline."*

[220] ComC, Section 346 (cit.): *"(1) If the debtor's or the creditor's default constitutes a non-fundamental breach of their contractual obligation, the non-defaulting party may rescind the contract if the default continues despite an additional reasonable period for remedy provided to the defaulting party and the defaulting party fails to meet their obligation within the said period for remedy. (2) However, if the defaulting party declares that they will not meet their obligation, the non-defaulting party may rescind the contract without providing, or before the expiration of, any additional reasonable period for remedy."*

[221] ComC, Section 348 (cit.): *"(1) A party may rescind the contract with respect to an obligation that is to be performed by the other party in the future if the behavior of the obligor or any other circumstances undoubtedly indicate, even before the time stipulated for performance of the contractual obligation, that the obligation will be fundamentally breached, and the obligor does not provide sufficient security without undue delay following the obligee's request.*

(2) The contract may also be rescinded with respect to an obligation that is to be performed in the future if the obligor declares that they will default on their obligation."

[222] ComC, Section 351 (cit.): *"(1) Rescission of contract extinguishes any and all rights and*

ArbAct: Section 13,[224] Section 15,[225] Section 18,[226] Section 30,[227] Section 31,[228] and Section 33[229]

---

obligations of the parties from the contract. However, rescission of the contract is without prejudice to a claim for compensation for damage or losses sustained as a result of the breach of contract, or to contractual provisions concerning choice of law or choice of this Act under Section 262, resolution of disputes between the contracting parties, and any other provisions that ought to survive the termination of the contract in compliance with the expressed will of the parties or with respect to the nature of the provisions. (2) If a party received performance from the other party before the rescission of the contract, the receiving party shall return the performance; a pecuniary debt shall be returned with interest agreed in the contract for such case, or in the absence of such agreement, with interest determined pursuant to Section 502. If the party returning the performance is the party who rescinded the contract, the party is entitled to reimbursement of the costs associated therewith."

[223] ComC, Section 352 (cit.): *"(1) An obligation shall also be deemed capable of performance if it can be performed using the services of another person.*

(2) An obligation also becomes incapable of performance if any laws or regulations that have been passed after execution of the contract and whose effectiveness is not subject to any temporal limitations prohibit the conduct to which the debtor is bound, or require any official permit that has not been granted to the debtor, despite their proper effort to obtain such permit.

(3) The creditor may rescind the contract with respect to the part of the performance that has not become impossible if, considering the nature of the performance or the object of the contract discernible from the contents of the contract or known to the other party at the time of executing the contract, that part has no economic meaning for the creditor without the provision of the performance that has become impossible. The same applies to partial performance.

(4) Impossibility of performance must be proven by the debtor."

[224] ArbAct, Section 13 (cit.): ArbAct in effect until March 31, 2012 (the law applicable to the given case, cit.): *"(1) Permanent arbitral institutions can be established only under the law. (2) Permanent arbitral institutions can issue their own statutes and rules which must be published in the Business Journal;3) these statutes and rules may determine the method of appointment and the number of arbitrators and may stipulate that the arbitrators shall be selected from a list administered by the permanent arbitral institution. The statutes and rules may also determine how the arbitrators shall conduct the proceedings and render their decisions, as well as resolve other issues connected with the activities of the permanent arbitral institution and the arbitrators, including rules regulating the costs of proceedings and fees for the arbitrators. (3) If the parties agreed on the jurisdiction of a particular permanent arbitral institution and failed to agree otherwise in the arbitration agreement, they shall be deemed to have submitted to the regulations specified in subsection (2), as applicable on the day the request for arbitration is filed with the permanent arbitral institution."*

ArbAct in effect since April 1, 2012 (cit.): *"(1) Permanent arbitral institutions may only be established by another law or only if another law expressly allows their establishment.*

(2) Permanent arbitral institutions can issue their own statutes and rules which must be published in the Business Journal;3) these statutes and rules may determine the method of

appointment and the number of arbitrators and may stipulate that the arbitrators shall be selected from a list administered by the permanent arbitral institution. The statutes and rules may also determine how the arbitrators shall conduct the proceedings and render their decisions, as well as resolve other issues connected with the activities of the permanent arbitral institution and the arbitrators, including rules regulating the costs of proceedings and fees for the arbitrators.

(3) If the parties agreed on the jurisdiction of a particular permanent arbitral institution and failed to agree otherwise in the arbitration agreement, they shall be deemed to have submitted to the regulations specified in subsection (2), as applicable on the day of commencement of the proceedings in the permanent arbitral institution.

(4) No entity may carry out its activities using a name which evokes a misleading impression that the entity is a permanent arbitral institution under this law unless a different law or regulation or an international agreement integrated in the legal system authorizes the entity to use the name."

[225] ArbAct, Section 15 (cit.):
ArbAct in effect until March 31, 2012 (the law applicable to the given case, cit.): *"(1) Arbitrators are entitled to examine their jurisdiction. If they conclude that the arbitration agreement presented to them does not give them jurisdiction to resolve the dispute, they render a corresponding resolution. (2) The plea of lack of jurisdiction, based on the non-existence, invalidity, or expiration of the arbitration agreement, can be raised by a party only before or together with the first act in the proceedings which concerns the merits of the case, unless the invalidity is caused by the fact that no arbitration agreement could have been concluded with respect to the case."*

ArbAct in effect since April 1, 2012 (cit.): *"(1) Arbitrators are entitled to examine their jurisdiction. If they conclude that the arbitration agreement presented to them does not give them jurisdiction to resolve the dispute, they render a corresponding resolution. (2) The plea of lack of jurisdiction, based on the non-existence, invalidity, or expiration of the arbitration agreement, can be raised by a party only before or together with the first act in the proceedings which concerns the merits of the case, unless the invalidity is caused by the fact that no arbitration agreement could have been concluded with respect to the case. This does not apply to disputes arising from consumer contracts."*

[226] ArbAct, Section 18 (cit.): *"The parties have an equal standing in the arbitral proceedings and must be provided with a full opportunity to assert their rights."*

[227] ArbAct, Section 30 (cit.): *"Application of the Code of Civil Procedure - Unless the Act stipulates otherwise, the arbitral proceedings shall be reasonably governed by the provisions of the Code of Civil Procedure."*

[228] ArbAct, Section 31 (cit.): ArbAct in effect until March 31, 2012 (the law applicable to the given case, cit.):

"At the request of any party the court annuls the arbitral award if: (a) it was made in a case which cannot be submitted to arbitration (cannot be the subject of a valid arbitration agreement), (b) the arbitration agreement is invalid for other reasons or the agreement was cancelled or it does not apply to the agreed case, (c) the arbitrator(s) who took part in the proceedings was/were not authorized to make decisions in the case, whether under the arbitration agreement or otherwise, or lacked the capacity to act as arbitrator(s), (d) the

CCP: Section 118a,[230] Section 213b,[231] Section 219a,[232] Section 237,[233] and Section 241a[234]

---

arbitral award was not adopted by the majority of the arbitrators, (e) a party was denied the opportunity to plead his or her case in the arbitral proceedings, (f) the arbitral award orders a party to provide performance which was not requested by the obligee or to provide performance which is impossible or illegal under domestic law, (g) it transpires that there are reasons which would otherwise justify the reopening of civil proceedings in court."

ArbAct in effect since April 1, 2012: *"At the request of any party the court annuls the arbitral award if: (a) it was made in a case which cannot be submitted to arbitration (cannot be the subject of a valid arbitration agreement), (b) the arbitration agreement is invalid for other reasons or the agreement was cancelled or it does not apply to the agreed case, (c) the arbitrator(s) who took part in the proceedings was/were not authorized to make decisions in the case, whether under the arbitration agreement or otherwise, or lacked the capacity to act as arbitrator(s), (d) the arbitral award was not adopted by the majority of the arbitrators, (e) a party was denied the opportunity to plead his or her case in the arbitral proceedings, (f) the arbitral award orders a party to provide performance which was not requested by the creditor or to provide performance which is impossible or illegal under domestic law, (g) the arbitrator or the permanent arbitral institution resolved a dispute arising from a consumer contract contrary to consumer protection laws, or clearly in violation of good morals, or contrary to public policy, (h) an arbitration agreement relating to disputes arising from consumer contracts lacks the information required under Section 3(5) or such information is intentionally or to a non-negligible extent incomplete, inaccurate, or false, or (i) it transpires that there are reasons which would otherwise justify the reopening of civil proceedings in court."*

[229] ArbAct, Section 33 (cit.): ArbAct in effect until March 31, 2012 (the law applicable to the given case, cit.):

The court shall dismiss a motion to annul an arbitral award which is based on the grounds specified in Section 31(b) or (c) if the party requesting the annulment failed to raise the corresponding objection in the arbitral proceedings before the party's first act in the merits of the case, despite having an opportunity to do so.

ArbAct in effect since April 1, 2012: *The court shall dismiss a motion to annul an arbitral award which is based on the grounds specified in Section 31(b) or (c) if the party requesting the annulment failed to raise the corresponding objection in the arbitral proceedings before the party's first act in the merits of the case, despite having an opportunity to do so. This does not apply to disputes arising from consumer contracts.*

[230] CCP, Section 118a (cit.): *"(1) If it transpires during the hearing that a party has not yet presented all relevant statements of fact or has presented them only insufficiently, the chairman of the panel invites the party to supplement their statements and gives them instructions as to the subject matter of the statements that are to be supplemented and the potential consequences of noncompliance. (2) If the chairman of the panel opines that the court's legal opinion of the case could differ from the party's legal opinion, the chairman invites the party to supplement the description of the relevant facts to the necessary extent; the chairman shall proceed similarly to Subsection (1). (3) If the chairman of the panel discovers during the hearing that a party has not yet proposed evidence necessary to prove*

all of their contested statements, the chairman invites the party to identify such evidence without undue delay and gives them instructions regarding the consequences of noncompliance. (4) During the hearings, the chairman of the panel also gives to the parties instructions regarding other procedural rights and duties of the parties; this does not apply if the party is represented by an attorney or a notary public to the extent of the notary's authorization under special laws."

[231] CCP, Section 213b (cit.): "(1) The appellate court proceeds pursuant to Section 118a; however, such procedure must not result in the party asserting new facts or evidence contrary to Sections 205a or 211a, or exercising any procedural rights that are prohibited in the appellate proceedings. (2) Breach of Section 118a(1) to (3) by the court of first instance only renders the proceedings defective if the need to adduce further statements or evidence is the consequence of a different legal opinion maintained by the appellate court."

[232] CCP, Section 219a (cit.): "(1) The appellate court vacates the decision if: (a) the proceedings suffer from such defects that the proceedings should not have taken place for a lack of procedural requirements, or the decision was rendered by a court that did not have the required subject-matter jurisdiction or by a disqualified judge, or the composition of the court was not correct, unless a decision was rendered by a panel of judges instead of a single judge, or if the proceedings suffer from any other defects that could have resulted in an incorrect decision in the case and the defects could not be remedied in the appellate proceedings, (b) the decision is incapable of review for being incomprehensible or for lacking sufficient reasons, (c) the court failed to make sure that an individual or entity joined the proceedings if the individual or entity should have been a party to the proceedings, or (d) the court did not continue the proceedings with the procedural successor to a party that was disqualified from the proceedings after the commencement thereof. (2) The appellate court shall also vacate the judgment or resolution on the merits if the determination of the facts of the case requires the examination of further evidence proposed by the parties, which cannot be examined in the appellate proceedings (Section 213(3) and (4)), without prejudice to Section 213(5)."

[233] CCP, Section 237 (cit.): CCP in effect until December 31, 2012 (the law applicable to the given case): "(1) Extraordinary appeal is admissible against any judgment of the appellate court and any resolution of the appellate court (a) that reversed the decision of the court of first instance in the merits, (b) that upheld the decision of the court of first instance in which the court of first instance ruled on the merits and which differed from its prior judgment (resolution), because the court of first instance was bound by the legal opinion of the appellate court, which had vacated the prior decision, (c) that upheld the decision of the court of first instance if the extraordinary appeal is not admissible under Paragraph (b) and the Supreme Court concludes that the merits of the contested decision have principal legal significance. (2) The extraordinary appeal under Subsection (1) is not admissible (a) in any matters where the subject matter of the operative part (order) of the decision that has been challenged by the extraordinary appeal consists of pecuniary performance not exceeding CZK 50,000, or CZK 100,000 in commercial matters, disregarding interest and any other associated dues of the claim, (b) in matters regulated by the Family Act, with the exception of judgments that deprive a person of, or limit, their parental responsibility, or suspend the exercise thereof, judgments whereby parenthood is declared (denied) or judgments regarding irrevocable adoption, (c) in matters concerning international child abduction pursuant to

an international treaty that is incorporated into the legal system[62g] or pursuant to a directly applicable law of the European Communities.[62h] (3) Decision of the appellate court has principal legal significance [Subsection (1)(c)] especially if it resolves a legal issue that has not yet been resolved in the case law of the Supreme Court, or which is not being adjudged consistently by the courts, or if the Supreme Court should assess the resolved legal issue differently; circumstances asserted under the grounds for extraordinary appeal under Section 241a(2)(a) and Section 241a(3) shall be disregarded."

CCP in effect since January 1, 2013: *"Unless stipulated otherwise, an extraordinary appeal is admissible against any decision of the appellate court that terminates the appellate proceedings, if the contested decision depends on the resolution of an issue of substantive or procedural law and the appellate court has departed from the consistent case law of the Supreme Court when resolving the issue, or which has not yet been resolved in the case law of the Supreme Court, or which is not being adjudged consistently by the Supreme Court, or if the Supreme Court should assess the resolved legal issue differently."*

[234] CCP, Section 241a (cit.):

CCP in effect until December 31, 2012 (the law applicable to the given case): *"(1) The extraordinary appeal must contain the general requirements (Section 42(4)), identify the contested decision, including the extent of the decision challenged by the extraordinary appeal and the grounds for challenging the decision, identify any evidence (if any) that should be examined in order to prove the grounds for the extraordinary appeal, and specify the remedy requested by the appellant (petition of the extraordinary appeal). (2) Extraordinary appeal can be lodged exclusively on the following grounds: (a) the proceedings suffer from a defect that could have resulted in an erroneous decision in the case, or (b) the decision is based on an erroneous legal assessment of the case. (3) If the extraordinary appeal is admissible under Section 237(1)(a) and (b), or under an analogous application of the said provisions (Sections 238 and 238a), the grounds for filing the extraordinary appeal may also consist of the fact that the decision is based on findings of fact that, according to the contents of the dossier, are not to a substantial extent supported by the evidence examined in the case. (4) It is not permitted to assert in the extraordinary appeal any new facts or evidence on the merits."*

CCP in effect since January 1, 2013: *"(1) The grounds for extraordinary appeal may only consist of the fact that the decision of the appellate court is based on an erroneous legal assessment of the case. (2) The extraordinary appeal must contain the general requirements (Section 42(4)), identify the contested decision, including the extent of the decision challenged by the extraordinary appeal and the grounds for challenging the decision, identify the grounds for the extraordinary appeal, describe why the appellant believes the requirements of admissibility of the extraordinary appeal were fulfilled (Sections 237 to 238a), and specify the remedy requested by the appellant (petition of the extraordinary appeal). (3) The grounds for the extraordinary appeal shall be described as follows: the appellant shall identify the legal assessment of the case that they consider erroneous and explain why the appellant considers such legal assessment erroneous. (4) In their extraordinary appeal, the appellant may not refer to any pleadings made in the proceedings at the court of first instance or in the appellate proceedings. (5) The contents of the pleading shall be disregarded in which the appellant stated the extent to which the decision of the*

CJA: Section 14[235]

The Supreme Court of the Czech Republic arrived at the following principal conclusions:

(1) If the proposal for evidence presented by any of the parties to the arbitral proceedings was not accepted, the arbitrators must consider the proposal for evidence and sufficiently justify why the proposed evidence was not examined. The court's decision on the motion to annul the arbitral award must clearly indicate which of the proposed evidence was examined by the arbitral tribunal, and which was not, as well as whether the evidence that was not examined represents evidence proposed to prove any important circumstances.

(2) The conclusion of the arbitral tribunal that the only factor important for the assessment of the case is the assessment of the validity of the rescission of the contract is a question of the legal assessment of the case by the arbitral tribunal, and such legal assessment cannot be subject to a judicial review of the decision rendered by the arbitrator (permanent arbitral institution).

(3) The supervisory function of the courts does not comprise the review of the material correctness of the arbitral award (conflict with substantive law), because the proceedings for the annulment of the arbitral award would thereby become *quasi-appellate proceedings*. The court's supervision may therefore only focus on the assessment of crucial procedural issues. Objections targeted at factual and legal findings contained in the arbitral award are irrelevant for the decision on the

---

appellate court is contested, or in which the appellant identified the grounds for the extraordinary appeal, unless the requirement under Section 241 was fulfilled. (6) It is not permitted to assert in the extraordinary appeal any new facts or evidence."

[235] CJA, Section 14 (cit.): *"(1) The Supreme Court, as the supreme judicial authority in matters falling within the jurisdiction of courts in civil court proceedings and in criminal proceedings, safeguards the unity and lawfulness of the judicial decision-making by (a) making decisions on extraordinary remedial measures in cases stipulated by laws regulating court proceedings, (b) making decisions in other cases stipulated by a special law or a promulgated international treaty that has been approved by the Parliament and that is binding on the Czech Republic. (2) The Supreme Court also makes decisions (a) on the recognition and enforceability of decisions made by foreign courts, if required by a special law or a promulgated international treaty that has been approved by the Parliament and that is binding on the Czech Republic, (b) in other cases stipulated by a special law or a promulgated international treaty that has been approved by the Parliament and which is binding on the Czech Republic. (3) The Supreme Court monitors and evaluates final and conclusive decisions of courts in civil court proceedings and in criminal proceedings, and adopts opinions on the rulings of courts in matters of a particular kind based on the said decisions and in the interest of consistent case law."*

annulment of the arbitral award pursuant to Section 31(e) of the ArbAct.[236]

(4) The purpose of the instructions given to the parties under Section 118a(1) through (3) of the CCP, which must also apply to arbitration, is to make sure that the parties have the opportunity to state the relevant circumstances (meet the duty of stating the relevant facts) and to identify evidence capable of proving the statements (meet the duty of proposing relevant evidence). The objective of the duty to give instructions is to (i) prevent the possibility that the party only finds out from a decision of the court that is adverse to the party (i.e. unforeseeable) that, in the court's assessment, the party did not meet the duty to state the relevant facts or to meet the burden of proof, and to (ii) make sure that the party has an opportunity to supplement their insufficient statements or propose additional evidence. However, if the motion was dismissed (or the defense against the motion was unsuccessful) based on the facts of the case as established by the court, not because the parties failed to meet the burden of proof, there was no reason for the court to proceed according to Section 118a of the CCP. Section 118a(2) of the CCP is specifically targeted at situations in which a party failed to state all facts relevant for the legal assessment of the case because they did not consider them legally significant from the perspective of their legal assessment, being different from the legal assessment of the case adopted by the court. But if the already-presented statements (and proposed evidence) also suffice for clarification of the facts of the case that are decisive from the perspective of the hypothesis of the legal rule envisaged by the court, no instructions pursuant to Section 118a(2) of the CCP are necessary.

(5) A decision is also considered unforeseeable (unpredictable) according to the consistent case law of courts if, viewed from the perspective of the preceding procedure, the decision provides an original assessment of the case at hand, and the adoption of the decision deprives a party to the proceedings of the possibility to make statements of fact and law.

(6) The appellate court's decision can be challenged by an extraordinary remedial measure if it meets the requirement of principal legal significance. The objection that the arbitral panel did not allow an employee of a party to attend a hearing, despite the fact that the person presented a power of attorney granted by the Chairman of the Board of Directors, does not meet the said requirement. Even if the arbitral panel's approach to the issue were wrong, it would not have the result of depriving the claimant of the possibility to state its case before the

---

[236] The provision is quoted above in the opening part of this annotation.

arbitrator, because the hearing was also attended by the claimant's legal counsel, and two more hearings followed, at which the claimant could have asserted its claims.

(7) **The claimant is not deprived of the opportunity to state their case before the arbitrator if the arbitral panel de facto prolonged the respondent's deadline for filing their statement.**

[*From Facts of Case and Procedure*]:

16.40. The Prague Municipal Court, as the court of first instance, dismissed the motion to annul the arbitral award, which had dismissed the claimant's request for arbitration (petition for the provision of performance). The reasons articulated in the arbitral award indicated that the claimant's rescission of the contract for work, which had been entered into by and between the claimant and the respondent, was invalid, because the grounds for rescission of the contract under Section 344 et seq. of the ComC[237] had not been fulfilled in the given case, even though invoked by the claimant. The arbitral tribunal also stated in its award that, considering the validity of the contract for work and the invalidity of the claimant's rescission of the contract, the arbitral panel had not addressed the request for arbitration as concerns the amount of the asserted claim, which, as the claimant had alleged, was the result of the alleged invalidity of the contract, or of the rescission of the contract, as applicable. The arbitration clause was incorporated in the said contract for work. The court of first instance also found that the contract had been signed on behalf of the respondent by Ing. R. Š., who was in the relevant period entered in the Companies Register as a member of the respondent's executive body. In this connection, the Prague High Court rendered a resolution, whereby the court upheld the decision of the court of first instance that dismissed the claimant's motion to wind-up the respondent; the claimant had filed the motion because the respondent, allegedly, did not have a properly appointed executive body. The minutes of the hearing at the AC held on October 3, 2007 indicate that the arbitral panel allowed the claimant to amend its request for arbitration (amendment of February 2, 2007), and that the arbitral panel provided the parties with the period of one month to supplement their pleadings and informed the legal counsel for the claimant that, having studied the dossier, the arbitral panel had concluded that proper case management of the proceedings required that the panel focus on fundamental issues, i.e. statements of fact regarding the invalidity (the arbitrators probably

---

[237] The provisions are quoted above in the opening part of this annotation.

meant the issue of the invalidity of the respective contract for work), or the rescission of the contract, as applicable, and the corresponding documentary or other evidence. The minutes further indicate that the arbitral panel did not allow the claimant's representative, Mgr. P., to attend the hearing; the panel pointed out that the hearing was confidential (with the exclusion of the public), and was attended by the claimant's legal counsel. The arbitral panel also stated that the hearing could be attended by legal counsel to the parties or members of their executive bodies. According to the minutes of the hearing held on February 6, 2008, the arbitral panel rejected the claimant's motion to supplement evidence in the case by interrogating the proposed witnesses and the party to the arbitration. At the same hearing, the parties were also provided with a time period to submit their final proposals by February 11, 2008.

16.41. In the proceedings at the court of first instance, the claimant asserted the grounds for the annulment of the arbitral award under Section 31(b) and (e) of the ArbAct.[238] The court of first instance held that the grounds for the annulment of the arbitral award under Section 31(b) of the ArbAct did not apply in the given case. In this connection, the court invoked Section 33 of the ArbAct,[239] which orders the court to dismiss a motion to annul an arbitral award under Section 31(b) or (c) if the party requesting the annulment failed to assert the grounds for the annulment of the arbitral award under Section 31(b) or (c) in the arbitral proceedings before the party's first act on the merits of the case, despite having had an opportunity to do so. The court of first instance also did not conclude that the grounds for the annulment of the arbitral award under Section 31(e) of the ArbAct would apply to the given case. The court held that a refusal or failure to examine evidence with respect to a requirement for performance does not *eo ipso* constitute grounds for the annulment of the arbitral award. The reason is that the arbitral award addressed the issue of the invalidity of the rescission of the contract for work, as a preliminary issue, and the subsequent assessment of the issue was the reason why the proposal lodged in the arbitral proceedings was rejected. The court of first instance also found that although the arbitral panel had not given any explicit instructions to the parties under Section 118a(3) of the CCP,[240] the panel had clarified (according to the court of first instance) the reasons for the procedure adopted in the records of the hearings of

---

[238] The provisions are quoted above in the opening part of this annotation.
[239] The provision is quoted above in the opening part of this annotation.
[240] The provision is quoted above in the opening part of this annotation.

June 5, 2007 and February 6, 2008; the panel's duty to give instructions to the parties had thereby been fulfilled. The court of first instance also mentioned in the reasoning for its decision that the provision of another deadline to the respondent for filing its statement did not violate the principle of equality of the parties, and the principle was also not violated by the fact that the claimant's employee, Mgr. P., was disallowed from attending the hearing that took place on June 5, 2007. Mgr. P. was neither the claimant's legal counsel nor executive body. The panel reasoned that arbitration was confidential (with the exclusion of the public), and could only be attended by legal counsel to the parties, or members of their executive bodies, as applicable, and the claimant was represented by legal counsel in the arbitration.

16.42. The Prague High Court, as the appellate court, upheld the decision of the court of first instance. The Prague High Court primarily emphasized that it was not allowed to examine (inter alia) whether the material aspects of the award were correct or whether the arbitration suffered from any defects under Section 219a of the CCP,[241] because the court could only annul the arbitral award on grounds on the exhaustive list provided in Section 31 of the ArbAct. As concerns the grounds for the annulment of the arbitral award pursuant to Section 31(b) of the ArbAct,[242] the appellate court upheld the conclusion of the court of first instance, because (as the appellate court concluded) the claimant had only pleaded the invalidity of the contract for work, which also included the assessed arbitration clause, in the claimant's belated submission of July 2, 2007, lodged in the arbitral proceedings, whereas the arbitration had been initiated by the claimant's request for arbitration, followed by the amendment of the claimant's request for arbitration of February 2, 2007. The appellate court held that there were also material reasons why the grounds for the annulment of the arbitral award under Section 31(b) of the ArbAct did not apply – the Prague High Court concluded that the executive body of the respondent had had the power to sign the contract for work at the relevant moment. The court further examined the grounds for the annulment of the arbitral award asserted by the claimant under Section 31(e) of the ArbAct (the alleged failure to provide the claimant with the opportunity to state its case in the arbitral proceedings). The appellate court based its findings on the materials in the dossier of the arbitral tribunal and concluded that three hearings had taken place before the competent tribunal, and the hearings had been attended by the

---

[241] The provision is quoted above in the opening part of this annotation.
[242] The provision is quoted above in the opening part of this annotation.

procedural agents for both parties. Both parties also had the opportunity to provide their written statements to the debated issues. These facts alone refute, in the opinion of the Prague High Court , any suspicions that the claimant was not provided with the opportunity to state their case before the arbitrators, despite the fact that the arbitral panel had not examined all of the evidence proposed by the claimant. The failure to give instructions under Section 118a of the CCP is classified in civil court proceedings as a defect of the proceedings at the court of first instance; see also the explicit provision of Section 213b(2) of the CCP.[243] The Prague High Court therefore concluded that the problem did not inhere in depriving a party of the opportunity to state their case in court; the problem consisted of something else, and consequently, the defects of the arbitral proceedings could not, in the appellate court's opinion, constitute grounds approved by the law for the annulment of the arbitral award. The appellate court also pointed out[244] Section 13(2) and (3) of the ArbAct, pursuant to which the parties had submitted to the Rules of the AC Governing Domestic Disputes; the respective provisions of the Rules which determine the method of case management of the arbitral proceedings do not stipulate that Section 118a of the CCP must be applied in arbitration. But the arbitrators should proceed in such manner as to establish the facts of the case necessary for resolving the dispute. In this connection, the appellate court also invoked Section 30 of the ArbAct, which stipulates that the provisions of the CCP only apply to arbitration reasonably, and only if the ArbAct does not stipulate otherwise. The appellate court did not accept the claimant's reference to the Judgment of the SC of April 25, 2007 in Case No. 32 Odo 1528/2005; the appellate court insisted that each decision resolved a different specific case, and was only binding on the parties to the proceedings, and no "precedential law" was part of the domestic legal system.[245] Considering all of the above reasons, the appellate court arrived at the same conclusion as the court of first instance, i.e. the grounds for the annulment of the arbitral award under Section 31(e) of the ArbAct, as asserted by the claimant, do not apply.

16.43. The claimant lodged an extraordinary appeal against the judgment of the appellate court. The claimant argued that the extraordinary appeal

---

[243] The provision is quoted above in the opening part of this annotation.

[244] Wrongly, in the opinion maintained by the author of this annotation.

[245] The author of this annotation believes that the presented reasoning, in such a rigorous form, is hardly acceptable, which has also been pointed out by the SC (see below).

was admissible under Section 237(1)(c) of the CCP;[246] as regards the grounds for the extraordinary appeal, the claimant invoked the grounds set forth in Section 241a(2)(b) of the CCP,[247] i.e. the decision of the appellate court was allegedly based on an erroneous legal assessment of the case. The appellant (in the SC proceedings) argued that the principal legal significance of the contested decision consisted of the resolution of three legal issues. The first legally important issue invoked by the appellant was whether the plea of the invalidity of the arbitration clause constituted an implicit assertion of the said grounds before the appellant started to act on the merits of the case; the invalidity of the arbitration clause was asserted by the appellant as part of the alleged invalidity of the contract for work (in which the arbitration clause was incorporated) in its pleading of February 2, 2007. The second issue concerned the interpretation of the grounds for the annulment of the arbitral award pursuant to Section 31(e) of the ArbAct.[248] The appellant raised the question of whether hearing (debating) a dispute at the AC means any hearing, without debating the entire scope of the request for arbitration, and whether the principle also applies to arbitration, which stipulates that the court is not bound by the legal classification of the claims and is obliged to discuss the merits of the dispute in their entirety. The appellant also raised the question of whether the requirement of the due hearing of the dispute in arbitration was fulfilled by the very fact that three hearings had been held in the case and the parties had had the opportunity to submit their written pleadings, without, however, evidence being taken by reading the proposed documents and hearing the proposed witnesses, and without the arbitral panel making any decision regarding such evidence, without hearing the merits of the case in their entirety, and without reasonably applying the relevant provisions of the Code of Civil Procedure. The third legally important issue, according to the appellant, was the fact that she had not been given any instructions in the course of the arbitral proceedings pursuant to Section 118a of the CCP,[249] primarily in terms of Subsection (2) of the said provision; in the appellant's opinion, such procedure violated the principle of equality of the parties and the principle of predictable court decisions.

---

[246] The provision is quoted above in the opening part of this annotation.

[247] The provision is quoted above in the opening part of this annotation.

[248] The provision is quoted above in the opening part of this annotation.

[249] The provision is quoted above in the opening part of this annotation.

16.44. The appellant (in the SC proceedings) insisted that the conditions set down in Section 31(e) of the ArbAct[250] had been fulfilled, because she allegedly had not been provided with the opportunity to properly state her case before the arbitrators, i.e. her right had been violated to have the entire scope of the dispute discussed, including the examination of the evidence proposed by the appellant, together with her right to a fair trial in terms of Article 38(2) of the Charter.[251] The reason is, according to the appellant, that the arbitral panel failed to make any decision regarding the evidence and failed to justify why the evidence was not examined. Despite the fact that the arbitral panel principally only resolved the preliminary issue of the validity of the rescission of the contract, the appellant believed that it was clear that even that particular issue had not been the subject of any proper taking of evidence, and the arbitral panel had arbitrarily failed to hear or read, respectively, the proposed evidence, whereby the arbitral panel had prevented the appellant from duly stating her case, i.e. fully and to the entire extent of the request for arbitration. The appellant argued that the court of first instance had entirely failed to properly address and assess the issue, and the appellate court had entirely disregarded it. The principle of equality of the parties and full opportunity to exercise their rights in terms of Sections 18 and 19(2) of the ArbAct[252] were also fundamentally breached, in the appellant's opinion, at the hearing before the AC on February 6, 2008, primarily because the chairman of the panel merely asked at that hearing whether the parties proposed to supplement any evidence regarding the issue of the validity of the rescission of the contract, but then the arbitral panel rendered a resolution, whereby the taking of evidence in the dispute was terminated to the full extent, and the panel ordered the parties to draw up their final proposals. The problem is that the taking of evidence was terminated with respect to the entire dispute discussed in the arbitration, without the parties having been warned of such procedure by the panel and without having been provided with an opportunity to propose additional evidence (if any) other than evidence regarding the preliminary issue of the rescission of the contract for work. The appellant further argued that another breach of the equality of the parties in arbitration occurred at the hearing held on June 5, 2007, namely because Mgr. K. P., the appellant's employee, was not admitted to the hearing, despite a duly granted power of attorney presented to

---

[250] The provision is quoted above in the opening part of this annotation.
[251] The provision is quoted above in the opening part of this annotation.
[252] The provisions are quoted above in the opening part of this annotation.

the arbitral panel. The appellant insisted that the procedure adopted by the arbitral panel had also breached the equality of the parties at the hearing held on June 5, 2007 – the arbitral panel provided both parties with the period of 1 month to supplement their pleadings, which the appellant observed; but the respondent asked the AC for the prolongation of the period to September 30, 2007, and the AC de facto granted the request. Another mistake made by the appellate court, in the appellant's opinion, consisted of the appellate court's erroneous legal assessment of the case from the perspective of the application of Section 118a of the CCP in arbitration – the appellant insisted that the provision applied in arbitration based on Section 30 of the ArbAct. The appellant argued, in that connection, that she should have been given instructions in the respective arbitration pursuant to Section 118a of the CCP.

16.45. In its reply to the extraordinary appeal, the respondent stated that the resolution of the legal issues raised by the appellant (in the SC proceedings) had no decisive importance for the decision in the case. The respondent identified with the conclusions made by the appellate court, which based its decision on the exhaustive list of grounds for the annulment of the arbitral award under Section 31 of the ArbAct.[253] The respondent argued that the plea of invalidity of the arbitration agreement had been made too late and was groundless from the material perspective. In the respondent's opinion, the claimant could not be surprised at the legal opinion of the arbitral panel and had not been prevented from stating any circumstances important from the perspective of the arbitrators' legal opinion. The respondent emphasized that the appellant's disagreement with the AC's assessment of the examined evidence and its subsequent legal assessment of the case did not, and could not, constitute any relevant grounds for the annulment of the arbitral award. Given the above reasons, the respondent proposed that the SC dismiss the extraordinary appeal.

[*From Conclusions Reached by Supreme Court, and Notes and Comments Concerning Decision*]:

16.46. The Supreme Court CR (SC) concluded that the extraordinary appeal was not admissible in the given case under Section 237 of the CCP,[254] because, in the SC's opinion, the decision of the appellate court did not have principal legal significance. The SC therefore dismissed the extraordinary appeal.

---

[253] The provision is quoted above in the opening part of this annotation.

[254] The provision is quoted above in the opening part of this annotation.

16.47. The first objection of the appellant (in the SC proceedings) was targeted at the appellate court's conclusion that the appellant's plea of invalidity of the arbitration agreement was raised too late. Invoking Section 33 of the ArbAct,[255] the Supreme Court (SC) did not find the plea justified, because it was raised too late – according to the findings of fact made by the lower courts. The Supreme Court CR (SC) also upheld the decision of the appellate court in its finding that the plea was unjustified from the material perspective.

16.48. The author of the annotation agrees with the conclusions of the SC in this regard, but needs to point out that the request for arbitration itself is the first act on the merits of the case, because it describes the claimant's claim and the legal grounds, on the basis of which the claimant demands the requested claim, as opposed to, for instance, a statement of a party to the arbitral proceedings regarding the appointment of arbitrator.

16.49. The Supreme Court CR (SC) also held that the appellant's objection does not endow the appellate court's decision with the quality of principal legal significance if the appellant contests the appellate court's assessment of the appellant's allegation that the appellant had not been provided with the opportunity to state its case before the arbitrators because the arbitral panel had failed to examine the evidence proposed by the appellant without having any relevant grounds to do so. The SC held that it is necessary to agree with the appellant that if the proposal for evidence presented by any of the parties was dismissed, the arbitrators must consider the proposal for evidence and sufficiently justify why the proposed evidence was not examined.[256] The Supreme Court CR (SC) first summarized the findings of fact established by the court of first instance and by the appellate court,[257] then **concluded that the findings of fact do not indicate which of the proposed evidence was examined by the arbitral tribunal, and which was not, and whether the evidence that was not examined represents evidence proposed to prove any circumstances important from the perspective of assessing the validity of the claimant's juridical act (rescission of the contract). The SC ruled that, given these facts of the case, it is not possible to conclude that the decision of the appellate court has principal legal significance from this perspective.** The SC did not assess the conclusion reached by the

---

[255] The provision is quoted above in the opening part of this annotation.

[256] The SC invoked the conclusions articulated in its Judgment of May 26, 2010 in Case No. 23 Cdo 3749/2008.

[257] The findings of fact are summarized above in the preceding chapter.

arbitral panel that the assessment of the case only depends on the assessment of the issue of the validity of the rescission of the contract; the reason is that courts should only exercise their review competency within the framework of the grounds for annulment under Section 31 of the ArbAct.[258] The Supreme Court CR (SC) noted in this connection that the supervisory function of the courts does not comprise the review of the material correctness of the arbitral award (conflict with substantive law), because the proceedings for the annulment of the arbitral award would thereby become quasi-appellate proceedings. The court's supervision may therefore only focus on the assessment of crucial procedural issues.[259] Hence, the SC held that the claimant's objections targeted at the factual and legal findings contained in the arbitral award are irrelevant for the decision on the annulment of the arbitral award pursuant to Section 31(e) of the ArbAct.

16.50. According to the SC, the principal legal significance of the judgment rendered by the appellate court was also not established by the appellant's objection that the AC had not addressed the fact that the claimant had broadened the claimant's final proposal and made an *in eventum* claim under Section 351(2) of the ComC.[260] The *in eventum* claim consisted of a claim for a return of the performance provided, which allegedly came into existence as a result of the fact that the performance subsequently (ex post) became impossible, because the respondent had unlawfully ousted the claimant from the construction and then had the finishing works performed by third parties. The reason for the SC's conclusion is that in reviewing the admissibility of the extraordinary appeal under Section 237(1)(c) of the CCP,[261] the SC could only base its conclusions on the facts of the case established by the lower courts, and the judgments rendered by the court of first instance and by the appellate court did not contain such findings of fact. Hence, the SC could not have regard to the facts.

16.51. The author of the annotation believes that the conclusions reached by the SC are correct, because the SC was only authorized in the given case to review the legal assessment of the case (current Czech law, as

---

[258] The provision is quoted above in the opening part of this annotation.

[259] In this connection, the SC invoked the Judgment of the ConCourt of March 8, 2011 in Case No. I. ÚS 3227/07. The author of this annotation believes that this Judgment must be perceived as a landmark decision, which departs from the contractual interpretation of the essence of arbitration and embraces the jurisdictional theory, or at least the modified jurisdictional theory.

[260] The provision is quoted above in the opening part of this annotation.

[261] The provision is quoted above in the opening part of this annotation.

opposed to the previous law, no longer permits challenging the decisions of the lower courts for any other reasons);[262] in compliance with the SC's prior consistent case law, the SC was not allowed to review the findings of fact made by the lower courts[263] and allow the parties to plead facts and evidence that had not been pleaded in the proceedings at the court of first instance and the appellate court.[264]

16.52. The SC also held that the principal legal significance of the contested decision of the appellate court was also not established by the method criticized in the extraordinary appeal, whereby the appellate court addressed the appellant's objection that she **had not been provided with the opportunity to state her case before the arbitrators,** because the arbitral panel had not given the appellant instructions pursuant to Section 118a of the CCP,[265] especially instructions according to Subsection (2) of the said provision.[266] **The Supreme Court CR (SC) emphasized that the Court adheres to its conclusion expressed in its Judgment of April 25, 2007 in Case No. 32 Odo 1528/2005, i.e. that Section 118a of the CCP shall reasonably apply to arbitration. The SC placed great emphasis on its conclusion that the Prague High Court (as the appellate court) was wrong in holding that the failure to give instructions pursuant to the reasonable application of Section 118a of the CCP does not mean that the party was deprived of the opportunity to state their case before the arbitrator and that no such defects of the arbitral proceedings could constitute grounds approved by the law for the annulment of the arbitral award.** Nonetheless, the findings of fact made by the court of first instance or the appellate court, as applicable, did not suggest (in the SC's opinion) that the arbitral panel had proceeded in the respective case contrary to the said provision. The Supreme Court CR (SC) explained in its decisions that the purpose of

---

[262] Here according to Section 241a(3) of the CCP, as amended and in effect until December 31, 2012. This provision is interpreted in the Judgment of the SC of April 3, 2009 in Case No. 28 Cdo 1071/2008.

[263] See also: (i) Judgment of the SC of January 25, 2012 in Case No. 23 Cdo 3885/2011, (ii) Judgment of the SC of June 27, 2012 in Case No. 32 Cdo 2808/2010, and (iii) Judgment of the SC of May 28, 2009 in Case No. 33 Cdo 3692/2007.

[264] Judgment of the SC of May 28, 2009 in Case No. 33 Cdo 3692/2007.

[265] The provision is quoted above in the opening part of this annotation.

[266] It has to be emphasized that the issue of the courts' duty to give instructions under the CCP, which the case law perceives as a fundamental procedural principle and a component of the procedural public policy that helps to prevent any unforeseeable decisions, has been broadly discussed in the Czech Republic. It was the case law of the courts that extended the duty to give instructions to arbitrators (arbitration).

the instructions pursuant to Section 118a(1) to (3) of the CCP is to allow the parties to state the relevant facts (meet the obligation to state the relevant facts) and identify evidence capable of proving their statements (meet the burden of proof). The objective of the duty to give instructions is to (i) prevent the possibility that the party only finds out from a decision of the court that is adverse to the party (*i.e. unforeseeable*) that, in the court's assessment, the party did not meet the duty to state the relevant facts, or meet the burden of proof, and to (ii) make sure that the party has an opportunity to supplement their insufficient statements or propose additional evidence. However, if the motion was dismissed (or the defense against the motion was unsuccessful) based on the facts of the case as established by the court, not because the parties failed to meet the burden of proof, there was no reason for the court to proceed according to Section 118a of the CCP. Section 118a of the CCP can only be applied if the statements made by the parties and the proposed evidence (and, as applicable, any evidence that has not been proposed but has been examined) do not suffice to clarify the facts of the case.[267] Section 118a(2) of the CCP is specifically targeted at situations where a party failed to state all facts relevant for the legal assessment of the case, because they did not consider them legally significant from the perspective of their legal assessment, being different from the legal assessment of the case adopted by the court. But if the already presented statements (and proposed evidence) also suffice for clarification of the facts of the case that are decisive from the perspective of the hypothesis of the legal rule envisaged by the court, no instructions pursuant to Section 118a(2) of the CCP are necessary.[268] **A decision is also considered *unforeseeable* (*unpredictable*) according to the consistent case law of the courts if, from the perspective of the preceding procedure, the decision provides an original assessment of the case at hand, and the adoption of the decision deprives a party to the proceedings of the possibility to make statements of fact and law.**[269] However, no such procedural

---

[267] In this connection, the SC invoked, inter alia: (i) Resolution of the SC of June 27, 2003 in Case No. 21 Cdo 121/2003, and (ii) Resolution of May 25, 2006 in Case No. 22 Cdo 2335/2005.

[268] Cf. the quoted Resolution of the SC in Case No. 21 Cdo 121/2003 and also Judgment of the SC of March 15, 2007 in Case No. 21 Cdo 194/2006, available on the SC website.

[269] Cf. also (i) Judgment of the ConCourt of June 12, 2001 in Case No. III. ÚS 729/2000, and (ii) Judgment of the ConCourt of June 11, 2007 in Case No. IV. ÚS 321/2007, both available on the ConCourt website at www.usoud.cz. Cf. also (iii) Judgment of the SC of September 4, 2007 in Case No. 22 Cdo 2125/2006, available on the SC website and annotated in: Právní rozhledy, 2007, No. 24, and (iv) Judgment of the SC of March 18,

situation occurred in the respective arbitration (according to the SC). The appellant argued that the AC had based its conclusions on reasons other than those asserted in the request for arbitration, as concerns the invalidity of the appellant's rescission of the contract for work and the allegation that the appellant had not accrued the claim for the part of the price that the appellant requested in the arbitration; the SC cannot accept such an allegation. Similarly, the appellant could not have been surprised at the decision of the arbitral tribunal, also with respect to the fact that the arbitral tribunal informed the legal counsel for the claimant at the hearing on June 5, 2007 that, having studied the dossier, the arbitral panel had concluded that systematic case management required that the panel focus on fundamental issues, i.e. statements of fact regarding the invalidity or rescission of the contract, and the corresponding documentary or other evidence. In this connection, the author of this annotation identifies with the conclusions of the SC, because the arbitral panel in the given case subsumed the case under a legal rule analogous to the rule proposed by the claimant. But having applied the rule to the established facts of the case, the arbitral panel arrived at a different legal conclusion than the claimant. Moreover, the arbitral panel repeatedly informed the claimant (appellant in the SC proceedings) of the legal issues that were decisive from the perspective of the panel's considerations. Besides, the claimant's request for arbitration was not dismissed for the party's failure to meet the duty to state the relevant facts or to meet the burden of proof. Consequently, it was not necessary to apply Section 118a in the given case. The reason is that the case law of the SC indicates that if the lower court, within the framework of its legal assessment of the case, considered the same legal classification of the act as the appellant, it is not possible to conclude that the lower court breached the duty to give instructions (incorporated in Section 118a and in Section 213b(1) of the CCP (the part of the sentence preceding the semicolon)[270]), and that its decision was unpredictable or unforeseeable for the appellants (i.e. that the appellants could have been surprised at the court's legal assessment of the case).[271] However, the appellant correctly pointed out the erroneous conclusion drawn by the appellate court as concerns the consequences of the failure to apply Section 118a in arbitration, which conclusion was contrary to the case law of the SC,[272] and moreover, contrary to the

---

2010 in Case No. 32 Cdo 1019/2009, available on the SC website and annotated in: Soudní rozhledy, 2010, No. 9.

[270] The provision is quoted above in the opening part of this annotation.

[271] Judgment of the SC, Case No. 32 Cdo 2808/2010 of 27 June 2012.

[272] Judgment of the SC of December 21, 2000 in Case No. 30 Cdo 4696/2009.

principle that the SC consolidates the case law of courts, and as a result thereof, the interpretation of legal rules by lower courts.[273]

16.53. The appellant also argued that the AC had not allowed the appellant's employee to attend the hearing at the arbitral tribunal, despite the fact that the employee presented a power of attorney granted by the Chairman of the appellant's Board of Directors; the SC held that that objection also did not endow the decision of the appellate court with the quality of principal legal significance. Even if the arbitral panel's approach to the issue were incorrect, it would not (in the opinion of the SC) have the result of depriving the claimant of the possibility to state their case before the arbitrator; the reason is that the hearing was also attended by the claimant's legal counsel, and two more hearings followed, at which the claimant could have asserted her claims. The author of this annotation believes that it is always necessary to ascertain within the whole context of the proceedings whether the right to state one's case before the arbitrators was breached, i.e. from the perspective of the entire course of the proceedings. Based on a purely formalistic interpretation, we could, for instance, argue in an individual case that a party was partially denied the possibility to state their case, but we cannot *eo ipso* conclude that the mistake was sufficiently grave as to fulfill the grounds for the annulment of the arbitral award under Section 31(e) of the ArbAct in the respective case. The author is not familiar with any details regarding the facts of the case other than those that are explicitly stated in the reasoning for the annotated decision; nonetheless, the author agrees with the conclusion drawn by the SC, i.e. that the assessment of the grounds for the annulment of the arbitral award under Section 31(e) of the ArbAct always requires due consideration of the consequences in which the breach of the party's right or any other defects of the proceedings resulted (in the given case).

16.54. The SC does not agree that the claimant was deprived of the opportunity to state their case before the arbitrator because of the fact that the arbitral panel, according to the appellant's allegation, de facto prolonged the respondent's deadline for filing their statement until September 30, 2007. In such case, the *"equality of arms"* premise must also be interpreted within the entire context of the proceedings, and we must keep in mind that, in this respect, and in compliance with the applicable laws and regulations, arbitration is less formal than litigation.

| | |

---

[273] See Section 14(3) of the CJA.

6. Judgment of Supreme Court of Czech Republic of July 29, 2013 in Case No. 23 Cdo 1369/2012:[274] (i) Time Period for Lodging Motion to Annul Arbitral Award, (ii) Possibility of Asserting Further Grounds for Annulment of Arbitral Award in Pending Proceedings, (iii) Prohibition of *Revision au Fond*

Abbreviations Used:

ArbAct	Act of the Czech Republic No. 216/1994 Coll., on Arbitration and the Enforcement of Arbitral Awards, as amended[275]
CCP	Act of the Czech Republic No. 99/1963 Coll., the Code of Civil Procedure, as amended
CJEU	Court of Justice of the European Union
ConCourt	Constitutional Court of the Czech Republic
SC	Supreme Court of the Czech Republic

Key Words

annulment (setting aside) of arbitral award | commencement of hearing of case | consumer | continued arbitration | Court of Justice of the European Union (CJEU) | EU law | European Court of Justice | financial lease | further grounds | grounds for annulment of arbitral award | lease agreement | limitation of actions | limitation of procedural rights | opportunity to state (plead) one's case | powers (jurisdiction) of arbitrator | procedural limits | procedural rights | prohibition of material review | remedial measure | revision au fond | right to state (plead) one's case | time period for lodging motion to annul |

Applicable Laws and Regulations:

ArbAct: Section 15,[276] Section 16,[277] Section 31,[278] Section 32,[279] Section 33,[280] Section 44[281]

---

[274] This decision is available online on the website of the SC at http://www.nsoud.cz/Judikatura/judikatura_ns.nsf/WebSearch/E9B7414622ABD81EC1257BDC0030672B?openDocument&Highlight=0 [last accessed November 4, 2014].

[275] This particular decision of the SC is based on the version of the ArbAct effective until March 31, 2012; no subsequent changes have any bearing on the conclusions of the SC and their applicability.

[276] ArbAct, Section 15 (cit.): *(1) Arbitrators are entitled to examine their jurisdiction. If they conclude that the arbitration agreement presented to them does not give them jurisdiction to resolve the dispute, they render a corresponding resolution. (2) The plea of*

lack of jurisdiction, based on the non-existence, invalidity, or expiration of the arbitration agreement, can be raised by a party only before or together with the first act in the proceedings which concerns the merits of the case, unless the invalidity is caused by the fact that no arbitration agreement could have been concluded with respect to the case. Note: this version of the provision applied to the respective proceedings; the currently applicable version reads as follows (cit.): *(1) Arbitrators are entitled to examine their jurisdiction. If they conclude that the arbitration agreement presented to them does not give them jurisdiction to resolve the dispute, they render a corresponding resolution. (2) The plea of lack of jurisdiction, based on the non-existence, invalidity, or expiration of the arbitration agreement, can be raised by a party only before or together with the first act in the proceedings which concerns the merits of the case, unless the invalidity is caused by the fact that no arbitration agreement could have been concluded with respect to the case. This does not apply to disputes arising from consumer contracts.* Note: The SC has not addressed in the respective proceedings the issue of whether the lack of the arbitrators' jurisdiction to hear and resolve the case was pleaded in time; in other words, even if the claimant were a consumer, the amendment implemented by Act No. 19/2012 Coll. would have no bearing on the conclusions reached by the SC.

[277] ArbAct, Section 16 (cit.): *If the party files its claim with the arbitrators before the expiration of the period of limitation or the prescription period and if the arbitrators decide that they lack jurisdiction in the case, or if the arbitral award was annulled and the party again lodges a lawsuit or a motion to continue the proceedings with the court or another competent authority within 30 days of receipt of the decision on lack of jurisdiction or annulment of arbitral award, the effects of the lodged request for arbitration (statement of claim) are preserved.* Note: this version of the provision applied to the respective proceedings; the currently applicable version reads as follows (cit.): *(1) If the party files its claim with the arbitrators before the expiration of the period of limitation or the prescription period and if the arbitrators decide that they lack jurisdiction in the case and the party again lodges a lawsuit / request for arbitration (statement of claim) with the court, or the competent arbitrators or permanent arbitral institution, or with another competent authority within 30 days of receipt of the decision on lack of jurisdiction, the effects of the lodged request for arbitration (statement of claim) are preserved. (2) The effects of the lodged request for arbitration (statement of claim) are also preserved if the arbitral award was annulled and the party lodged a lawsuit/request for arbitration or a motion to continue the proceedings with the competent arbitrators or permanent arbitral institution, or with any other competent authority within 30 days after the court decision became final and conclusive which annulled the arbitral award.* Note: Again, the implemented amendments (which, moreover, instead focus on the formulations and the technique of the legislative drafting) have no consequences for the conclusions reached by the SC. The reason is that whether or not the motion to continue the proceedings was lodged in time, in the said dispute, it was subject to the court's decision-making only as to whether the issue itself, or the assessment of the issue, as applicable, falls within the jurisdiction of courts, or whether it is a matter of the material review of an arbitral award, which the courts are not entitled to do.

[278] ArbAct, Section 31 (cit.): (cit.): *At the request of any party the court annuls the arbitral award if: (a) it was made in a case which cannot be submitted to arbitration (cannot be the*

subject of a valid arbitration agreement), (b) the arbitration agreement is invalid for other reasons or the agreement was cancelled or it does not apply to the agreed case, (c) the arbitrator(s) who took part in the proceedings was/were not authorized to make decisions in the case, whether under the arbitration agreement or otherwise, or lacked the capacity to act as arbitrator(s), (d) the arbitral award was not adopted by the majority of the arbitrators, (e) a party was denied the opportunity to plead his or her case in the arbitral proceedings, (f) the arbitral award orders a party to provide performance which was not requested by the obligee or to provide performance which is impossible or illegal under domestic law, (g) it transpires that there are reasons which would otherwise justify the reopening of civil proceedings in court [Section 228(1)(a) and (b) of the CCP]. Note: This version of the provision applied to the respective proceedings; the currently applicable version reads as follows (cit.): *At the request of any party the court annuls the arbitral award if: (a) it was made in a case which cannot be submitted to arbitration (cannot be the subject of a valid arbitration agreement), (b) the arbitration agreement is invalid for other reasons or the agreement was cancelled or it does not apply to the agreed case, (c) the arbitrator(s) who took part in the proceedings was/were not authorized to make decisions in the case, whether under the arbitration agreement or otherwise, or lacked the capacity to act as arbitrator(s), (d) the arbitral award was not adopted by the majority of the arbitrators, (e) a party was denied the opportunity to plead his or her case in the arbitral proceedings, (f) the arbitral award orders a party to provide performance which was not requested by the creditor or to provide performance which is impossible or illegal under domestic law, (g) the arbitrator or the permanent arbitral institution resolved a dispute arising from a consumer contract contrary to consumer protection laws, or clearly in violation of good morals, or contrary to public policy, (h) an arbitration agreement relating to disputes arising from consumer contracts lacks the information required under Section 3(5) or such information is intentionally or to a non-negligible extent incomplete, inaccurate, or false, or (i) it transpires that there are reasons which would otherwise justify the reopening of civil proceedings in court* [Section 228(1)(a) and (b) of the CCP].

[279] ArbAct, Section 32 (cit.): *(1) The motion to annul an arbitral award must be lodged with the court within three months following the receipt of the arbitral award by the party requesting the annulment of the award, unless this Act stipulates otherwise. (2) The motion pursuant to subsection (1) does not suspend the enforceability of the arbitral award. If requested by the obligor, however, the court may suspend the enforceability of the arbitral award in case an immediate enforcement of the arbitral award could cause serious harm.* Note: this version of the provision applied to the respective proceedings; the currently applicable version reads as follows (cit.): *(1) The motion to annul an arbitral award must be lodged with the court within three months following the receipt of the arbitral award by the party requesting the annulment of the award, unless this Act stipulates otherwise. If the arbitral award was made in a dispute arising from a consumer contract and the motion to annul was lodged by the consumer, the court always examines whether there are grounds to annul the arbitral award pursuant to Section 31(a) through (d) or (h). (2) The motion pursuant to subsection (1) does not suspend the enforceability of the arbitral award. If requested by the obligor, however, the court may suspend the enforceability of the arbitral award in case an immediate enforcement of the arbitral award could cause serious harm or*

CCP: Section 79(1)[282]

in case the motion to annul the arbitral award justifies the conclusion that the motion is legitimate. (3) If the motion to annul an arbitral award is lodged by the consumer, the court shall establish whether there are grounds to suspend the enforceability of the arbitral award pursuant to subsection (2) without the consumer's request. The court shall rule on the suspension of enforceability within 7 days of receiving the motion; the arbitral award cannot be enforced within said time limit. Note: The changes implemented in Section 32 of the ArbAct have no direct influence on the conclusions reached by the SC in this particular case, but they ultimately indicate that consumers, in certain cases, will no longer have to explicitly invoke the grounds for the annulment of the arbitral award, because the courts are now obliged to examine the existence of selected grounds for the annulment of the arbitral award of their own motion.

[280] ArbAct, Section 33 (cit.): *The court shall dismiss a motion to annul an arbitral award which is based on the grounds specified in Section 31(b) or (c) if the party requesting the annulment failed to raise the corresponding objection in the arbitral proceedings before the party's first act in the merits of the case, despite having an opportunity to do so.* Note: this version of the provision applied to the respective proceedings; the currently applicable version reads as follows (cit.): *The court shall dismiss a motion to annul an arbitral award which is based on the grounds specified in Section 31(b) or (c) if the party requesting the annulment failed to raise the corresponding objection in the arbitral proceedings before the party's first act in the merits of the case, despite having an opportunity to do so. This does not apply to disputes arising from consumer contracts.* Note: In the respective proceedings, the SC did not address the issue of whether the lack of the arbitrators' jurisdiction to hear and resolve the case was pleaded in time; in other words, even if the claimant were a consumer, the amendment implemented by Act No. 19/2012 Coll. would have no bearing on the conclusions reached by the SC.

[281] ArbAct, Section 44 (cit.): *Unless this Act stipulates otherwise, the proceedings in court according to this Act shall be governed by the provisions of the Code of Civil Procedure by analogy.* Note: This version of the law applied to the respective proceedings, but it has not been subject to any modifications in the meantime and therefore continues to apply.

[282] CCP, Section 79(1) (cit.): *The proceedings are initiated by motion. The motion must contain the general essentials (Section 42(4)), and the name, surname, place of residence or, as applicable, birth registration numbers of the parties (company name or name and registered office of a legal entity, designation of a state and the competent organization unit of the state that acts for and on behalf of the state in court), and of the parties' representatives (if applicable), the description of the relevant circumstances, and the identification of evidence invoked by the entity filing the motion; the motion must also stipulate the relief sought by the entity filing the motion. If the case is based on a commercial relationship, the motion must also contain the identification number of the legal entity, identification number of a natural person – entrepreneur, and other data necessary to identify the parties to the proceedings, if applicable. The motion is called a "petition" (lawsuit) if it concerns bilateral legal relations between a claimant and a respondent (Section 90).* Note: This version of the provision applied to the respective proceedings; the currently applicable version reads as follows (cit.): *The proceedings are*

The Supreme Court of the Czech Republic reached the following principal conclusions:

(1) **When making a decision on the annulment of an arbitral award, the court is not entitled to review the merits of the contested decision, i.e. to review the decision from the perspective of the correctness of the assessment of the evidence examined in the proceedings, the correctness of the factual findings, and the ensuing legal assessment of the case (prohibition of** *revision au fond***). A motion to annul an arbitral award cannot be used as a remedy against arbitral awards.**[283]

---

initiated by motion. The motion must contain the general essentials (Section 42(4)), and name, surname, place of residence or, as applicable, birth registration numbers or identification numbers of the parties (company name or name and registered office of a legal entity, identification number, designation of a state and the competent organization unit of the state that acts for and on behalf of the state in court), and of the parties' representatives (if applicable), a description of the relevant circumstances, and the identification of evidence invoked by the entity filing the motion; the motion must also stipulate the relief sought by the entity filing the motion. If the case involves a trustee as a party to the proceedings, the motion must also specify that the respective person is the trustee and identify the trust fund. The motion is called a "petition" (lawsuit) if it concerns bilateral legal relations between a claimant and a respondent (Section 90). Note: Again, the amendments have no consequences for the conclusions reached by the SC.

[283] In this connection, the SC invoked its prior case law, namely its Judgment of May 28, 2009 in Case No. 23 Cdo 2570/2007, which is available online on the SC website at http://www.nsoud.cz/Judikatura/judikatura_ns.nsf/WebSearch/4A42E4DF19BD26F3C125 7A4E0065E608?openDocument&Highlight=0, in which the Court held (cit.): *When making a decision on the annulment of an arbitral award, the court is not entitled to review the merits of the contested decision, i.e. to review the decision from the perspective of the correctness of the assessment of the evidence examined in the proceedings, the correctness of the factual findings and of the ensuing legal assessment of the case. The motion to annul an arbitral award cannot be used as a remedy against arbitral awards. When addressing the issue of whether the party to arbitration was, in the particular case, provided with the opportunity to plead their case before the arbitrators, the court must ascertain whether the party to the arbitral proceedings was, considering all of the circumstances of the case, provided with a sufficient opportunity to exercise their procedural rights in the arbitral proceedings, and whether or not the procedure adopted by the arbitral tribunal disturbed the equality between the parties.* The SC also invoked the Judgment of the ConCourt of March 8, 2011 in Case No. I. ÚS 3227/07, available online on the website of the ConCourt at http://nalus.usoud.cz/Search/ResultDetail.aspx?id=69584&pos=1&cnt=1&typ=result, in which the Court held (cit.): *I. Hearing a case in arbitration does not entail the waiver of legal protection; it indicates the transfer of legal protection to another decision-making authority, which determines the law. II. The arbitrator cannot merely play the role of a passive element; they must conduct the proceedings in such manner that their decision is not a surprise to the parties. To that end, civil court proceedings prescribe that courts must*

(2) **Section 32 of the ArbAct is important only from the perspective of determining whether the motion itself to annul the arbitral award was lodged in time. The provision cannot be interpreted as a limitation of the claimant's procedural rights to adduce in the course of the proceedings any relevant circumstances that contain further grounds for the annulment of the arbitral award under Section 31 of the ArbAct. The right to supplement such grounds can only be limited by statutory procedural limits under the Code of Civil Procedure (such as the concentration of proceedings). In other words, parties may assert (further) grounds for the annulment of the arbitral award under Section 31 of the ArbAct in proceedings for the annulment of the arbitral award commenced before the expiration of the time period under Section 32 of the ArbAct even after the time period expires.[284]**

> *give instructions to the parties; there is no reason to absolve the arbitrator of that obligation in arbitral proceedings, considering the fact that in such proceedings the arbitrator acts as the decision-making authority in place of the court. The ArbAct does not provide for the arbitrator's obligation to give instructions; it is therefore legitimate to reasonably apply the Code of Civil Procedure (Section 30 of the ArbAct). III. The extent of the supervisory function of the courts vis-à-vis arbitration must be carefully balanced – the rule stipulating that arbitration must also guarantee legal protection must not be eliminated, but on the other hand, the advantages of arbitration and its practical applicability must not be entirely wiped out. Consequently, proceedings for the annulment of an arbitral award by a court can never be structured along the lines of remedial civil court proceedings, let alone regular appellate proceedings. The supervisory function of the courts does not comprise the review of the material correctness of the arbitral award (conflict with substantive law), because the proceedings for the annulment of arbitral award would thereby become quasi-appellate proceedings. The supervision may therefore only concentrate on examining the crucial procedural issues, e.g. whether the arbitration could actually have been conducted, whether any important procedural rights were denied to the parties, or whether the arbitral award itself is free of procedural flaws.*

[284] In this connection, the SC invoked its prior case law, namely Judgment of May 9, 2012 in Case No. 23 Cdo 3728/2011, available online on the SC website at http://www.nsoud.cz/Judikatura/judikatura_ns.nsf/WebSearch/639E8E2B6E41525DC1257A4E00678F93?openDocument&Highlight=0, in which the court ruled as follows (cit.): *Section 32 of Act No. 216/1994 Coll., as applicable before the amendment implemented by Act No. 19/2012 Coll., is important only from the perspective of determining whether the motion itself to annul the arbitral award was lodged in time. The provision cannot be interpreted as a limitation of the claimant's procedural rights to adduce in the course of the proceedings any relevant circumstances that contain further grounds for the annulment of the arbitral award under Section 31 of the said Act. The right to supplement relevant circumstances can only be limited by statutory procedural limits under the Code of Civil Procedure (such as the concentration of proceedings).* Note: The summary of the SC's legal opinion (*ratio decidendi*) was adopted from the SC website.

[From Facts of Case]:

16.55. The dispute between the parties is apparently rather old, and the facts of the case as described in the annotated decision only indicate that the arbitral award, which was the result of the first arbitration, was annulled pursuant to Section 31 of the ArbAct.[285] Then a motion to continue the arbitration was lodged in terms of Section 16 of the ArbAct.[286] On May 27, 2010, an arbitral award was rendered in the said arbitral proceedings under Case No. 2587/2009;[287] the arbitral award was subsequently challenged by the claimant,[288] who demanded the annulment of the arbitral award on the grounds stipulated under Section 31(b)[289] of the ArbAct. The claimant argued that the arbitration clause agreed in the General Business Terms and Conditions for Financial Lease, which were enclosed with and formed an integral part of Lease Agreement No. 13001631, entered into by and between the claimant and the legal predecessor of the respondent, was extinguished by notice terminating the Lease Agreement. The claimant subsequently asserted another ground for the annulment of the arbitral award, namely the ground under Section 31(e) of the ArbAct,[290] arguing that the claimant had not been provided with the opportunity to duly state (plead) their case before the arbitrators; the additional ground for annulment was asserted only **in the course of the hearing at the court of first instance.** Last, but not least, the claimant also pleaded the limitation of actions (as mentioned above, it was a second request for arbitration in the case), arguing that the motion to continue the arbitration after the first arbitral award had been annulled was lodged after the expiration of the time period stipulated in Section 16 of the

---

[285] The provision is quoted above in the opening part of this annotation.

[286] The provision is quoted above in the opening part of this annotation.

[287] The forum is unclear at which the arbitration was conducted; it was probably *ad hoc* arbitration.

[288] A natural person; although it is not explicitly mentioned in the annotated decision, we can infer that the person is a citizen of the Czech Republic and has his address/place of residence in the territory of the Czech Republic. Considering the fact that the claimant, as a party to the proceedings, is also identified by his [trade] identification number, we can assume that he is an entrepreneur doing business under a trade license. The respondent is a legal entity formed and existing under the laws of the Czech Republic in the form of a joint stock company.

[289] The provision is quoted above in the opening part of this annotation.

[290] The provision is quoted above in the opening part of this annotation.

ArbAct,[291] and consequently, the effects of the original request for arbitration could not survive.

[*Procedure of Case*]:

16.56. On April 13, 2011, the Prague Municipal Court, as the court of first instance, rendered its Judgment in Case No. 28 Cm 88/2010-25, whereby the claimant's motion was granted and the arbitral award was annulled. The court agreed with the claimant's reasoning as regards the lack of the arbitrators' jurisdiction to hear and resolve the dispute (Section 31(b) of the ArbAct[292]). The court held that the notice of termination extinguished (cancelled) the entire Lease Agreement, and decisions regarding the claim that was the subject matter of the parties' dispute no longer fell within the scope of the arbitration clause. The court also held that the plea had been raised in time within the time period under Section 15 of the ArbAct[293] (upon the first act/the hearing held in the arbitral proceedings on March 4, 2010, together with the plea of the limitation of actions. As concerns the plea of the limitation of actions, the court agreed with the claimant's opinion that, considering Section 16 of the ArbAct,[294] the effects of the original request for arbitration could not have survived). Conversely, as concerns the additionally asserted ground for the annulment of the arbitral award under Section 31(e) of the ArbAct,[295] the court of first instance held that: (i) it was groundless, and (ii) it was raised too late; the court invoked Section 32(1) of the ArbAct.[296]

16.57. The Prague High Court, as the appellate court, reversed the above judgment of the Prague Municipal Court (as the court of first instance) by dismissing the motion to annul the arbitral award.[297] The appellate court held that the motion to annul the arbitral award on the grounds specified in Section 31(e) of the ArbAct[298] had been lodged after the expiration of the time period stipulated in Section 32(1) of the ArbAct.[299, 300] The appellate court disagreed with the court of first instance as concerns the issue of the lack of jurisdiction. The appellate court ruled that the plea of the lack of the arbitrators' jurisdiction to

---

[291] The provision is quoted above in the opening part of this annotation.
[292] The provision is quoted above in the opening part of this annotation.
[293] The provision is quoted above in the opening part of this annotation.
[294] The provision is quoted above in the opening part of this annotation.
[295] The provision is quoted above in the opening part of this annotation.
[296] The provision is quoted above in the opening part of this annotation.
[297] Namely, by Judgment of November 16, 2011 in Case No. 2 Cmo 205/2011 – 50.
[298] The provision is quoted above in the opening part of this annotation.
[299] The provision is quoted above in the opening part of this annotation.
[300] Which should comply with the conclusions reached by the court of first instance.

hear the case was only raised after the hearing of the case commenced (specifically, in the answer to the request for arbitration); the plea had not been raised in the statement (pleading) lodged before the hearing of the case commenced. Invoking Section 33 of the ArbAct,[301] the appellate court therefore concluded that the arbitral award could not be annulled under Section 31(b) of the ArbAct.[302]

16.58. The claimant challenged the judgment of the appellate court by an extraordinary appeal lodged with the SC; the claimant maintained that the issue of fundamental legal significance consisted of the interpretation of Section 32(1) of the ArbAct, because the three-month period only applied to the motion itself to annul the arbitral award, not to supplementing the reasons for the motion.[303] The extraordinary appeal also posed the following questions: (i) referring to Section 16 of the ArbAct, whether the plea of the limitation of actions can be subsumed (as grounds for the annulment of the arbitral award) under Section 31(e) of the ArbAct if the plea in the respective case did not challenge the lack of jurisdiction based on the non-existence, invalidity or expiration of an arbitration agreement, (ii) whether the court is entitled to review, in the proceedings for the annulment of the arbitral award, the arbitrator's conclusion that the plea of the limitation of actions was groundless, and (iii) whether the fact that the arbitral panel entirely disregarded the plea of the limitation of actions in terms of Section 16 of the ArbAct constitutes grounds for the annulment of the arbitral award.[304]

16.59. The SC held that there are grounds for vacating the contested decision of the appellate court, because the court wrongly interpreted and applied Section 32(1) of the ArbAct;[305] the SC maintains that further

---

[301] The provision is quoted above in the opening part of this annotation.

[302] The provision is quoted above in the opening part of this annotation.

[303] The question is whether the court is entitled to dismiss a timely motion to annul an arbitral award if the petition (lawsuit) is supplemented with other provable circumstances after the expiration of the time period for filing the motion, which circumstances constitute grounds for the annulment of the award.

[304] However, the SC did not address these issues. As concerns the issue under Paragraph (ii), the SC concluded that the issue concerns the material review of the arbitral award, which the courts are not entitled to undertake – see the reference to Judgment of the SC of May 28, 2009 in Case No. 23 Cdo 2570/2007, and Judgment of the ConCourt of March 8, 2011 in Case No. I. ÚS 3227/07, as these decisions are quoted above; the SC did not deem it necessary to address the issues under Paragraphs (i) and (iii), because the SC determined that there are grounds for vacating the decision of the appellate court due to the erroneous interpretation of Section 32(1) of the ArbAct.

[305] The provision is quoted above in the opening part of this annotation.

grounds for the annulment of an arbitral award can be asserted even after the time period expires for filing the motion to annul the arbitral award (provided that the proceedings were duly commenced).

[*Arguments Presented by SC*]:

16.60. The Supreme Court CR (SC) primarily focused on the interpretation of Section 32(1) of the ArbAct,[306] because the application thereof by the appellate court could have been based on an erroneous legal assessment of the case. The SC based its decision on the already adjudicated interpretation of that provision, which is based on the presumption that the interpretation of Sections 32(1) and 31 of the ArbAct[307,308] requires the analogous application of the CCP as concerns the possibilities of asserting further grounds for the annulment of the arbitral award in proceedings initiated within the period of three months after the arbitral award is served on the party who demands the annulment of the arbitral award. This conclusion is based on Section 44 of the ArbAct,[309] which stipulates that proceedings at civil courts conducted pursuant to the ArbAct shall be governed by the provisions of the CCP applicable by analogy.

16.61. In this connection, the Supreme Court CR (SC) fully refers to Judgment of the SC of May 9, 2012 in Case No. 23 Cdo 3728/2011.[310] The SC concluded in the said ruling that the interpretation of Sections 32(1) and Section 31 of the ArbAct also requires the analogous application of the CCP as concerns the possibilities for asserting further grounds for the annulment of the arbitral award in proceedings initiated within the period of three months after the arbitral award is served on the party who demands the annulment of the arbitral award. The SC maintains that if the provisions of the CCP are analogously applied to the proceedings for the annulment of arbitral award, the motion to annul the arbitral award must be assessed pursuant to the provisions of the CCP that regulate motions whereby proceedings are commenced. Section 79(1) of the CCP[311] indicates that a motion to annul an arbitral award must also contain a description of the relevant circumstances. The description of the relevant circumstances must clearly indicate what happened, i.e. the act on the basis of which the party asserts their right (to annul the arbitral award); the act must be described to an

---

[306] The provision is quoted above in the opening part of this annotation.
[307] The provision is quoted above in the opening part of this annotation.
[308] The provision is quoted above in the opening part of this annotation.
[309] The provision is quoted above in the opening part of this annotation.
[310] The decision is quoted above in this annotation.
[311] The provision is quoted above in the opening part of this annotation.

extent that allows the unambiguous individualization thereof (excludes the possibility of confusing the act with any other one). The party is not obliged to include in their motion the legal classification of the described facts of the case (which means that the party is also not obliged to specify the alleged grounds for the annulment of the arbitral award, the legal classification of which is found in Section 31 of the ArbAct0;[312]) if the party does include such legal classification, the court is not bound by it. This also applies to the relevant circumstances supplemented by the party during the proceedings. The right to supplement the circumstances during the proceedings is limited only by the procedural limits incorporated in the CCP. The court subsequently subsumes the findings of fact ascertained from the evidence examined in the case under the statutory definitions in the relevant legal rules, and thereby determines which of the grounds for the annulment of the arbitral award under Section 31 of the ArbAct[313] are fulfilled (if any). This interpretation also corresponds to the case law adopted by the SC in relation to proceedings for the declaration of the invalidity of an involuntary public auction, i.e. a party may assert further grounds for the annulment of the arbitral award in the course of the proceedings by supplementing the relevant circumstances.[314]

16.62. Consequently, the SC vacated the decision of the appellate court and remanded the case for further hearing and a new decision. Considering the decision that it adopted, the SC did not deem it necessary or

---

[312] The provision is quoted above in the opening part of this annotation.

[313] The provision is quoted above in the opening part of this annotation.

[314] Judgment of the SC of May 9, 2012 in Case No. 23 Cdo 3728/2011 (as the decision is quoted above), which the annotated decision invokes, refers in this connection to Judgment of the SC of April 11, 2006 in Case No. 21 Cdo 1679/2005, available online on the SC website at http://www.nsoud.cz/Judikatura/judikatura_ns.nsf/WebSearch/D4E8597 BA5DB5D64C1257A4E0068D817?openDocument&Highlight=0, in which the court has ruled as follows (cit.): *I. If the proceedings for the declaration (determination) of the invalidity of an involuntary public auction were commenced within the time period stipulated in Section 48(3) or (4) of Act No. 26/2000 Coll., as amended, the claimant may identify (assert) the grounds on which the claimant considers the auction invalid, not only in their lawsuit or before the expiration of the time periods stipulated in the said provisions, but at any time during the proceedings (unless the claimant is prevented from doing so by the concentration of proceedings or the system of partial appeal in appellate proceedings), and the court may declare (determine) the involuntary public auction invalid on those grounds asserted during the proceedings, as well as those grounds that otherwise transpired during the proceedings, even if they were not identified by any of the parties. II. If the auctioneer failed to publish the auction decree at the central address no later than 60 days before opening the auction only because the central address was not in operation, the involuntary public auction is not invalid in consequence of this reason only.*

possible, as applicable, to address the other grounds for the appeal invoked by the appellant.

[Further Conclusions and Comments Concerning Annotated Resolution of SC]:

16.63. The decision cannot be perceived as surprising or introducing any new interpretation of the said rules, i.e. a decision that would shift the existing doctrinal interpretation. To quite the contrary, it is strictly based on the consistent case law dealing with the issue of the application of the CCP in civil proceedings commenced on the basis of the ArbAct. It is necessary to point out that the conclusions consistently repeated in the SC case law are not affected by the amendments to the ArbAct implemented by the Consumer Amendment, i.e. Act No. 19/2012 Coll. The enhancement of the consumer's position is evidenced by the fact that the consumer will not be obliged, in certain cases, to rely on the above interpretation of Section 32(1) of the ArbAct[315] and on the possibility of supplementing the relevant facts and evidence on the basis of which the award should be annulled during pending proceedings for the annulment of the arbitral award; the reason is that the court is now obliged to examine some of the grounds of its own motion (*ex officio*). This obligation specifically concerns the grounds for the annulment of arbitral award specified in Section 31(a) through (d) or (h).[316] The Explanatory Memorandum to Act No. 19/2012 Coll. states that this amendment is in response to the case law of the CJ EU. In its rulings concerning the Directive on Unfair Terms in Consumer Contracts, the CJ EU has held that the courts must assess, with or without a motion, whether the arbitration clause conflicts with binding national rules, even after a motion for involuntary enforcement of a final and conclusive arbitral award is lodged; the court is obliged to perform the review of its own motion.[317] However, the above said should in no case be interpreted as

---

[315] The provision is quoted above in the opening part of this annotation.

[316] The provision is quoted above in the opening part of this annotation.

[317] Cf. the decision of the Court of Justice (First Chamber) of October 26, 2006 in Case C–168/05 (Elisa María Mostaza Claro ca. Centro Móvil Milenium SL), available at http://curia.europa.eu/juris/document/document.jsf;jsessionid=9ea7d2dc30d58aa531680e 0a45838240f9ba2d85d487.e34KaxiLc3qMb40Rch0SaxuObN50?text=&docid=63926&page Index=0&doclang=cs&mode=lst&dir=&occ=first&part=1&cid=463888, in which the Court held as follows (cit.): *Council Directive 93/13/EEC of April 5, 1993, on unfair terms in consumer contracts, must be interpreted as meaning that a national court seized of an action for the annulment of an arbitration award must determine whether the arbitration agreement is void, and annul that award where that agreement contains an unfair term, even though the consumer has not pleaded such invalidity in the course of the arbitration proceedings, but only in that of the action for annulment.*

inducing the consumers to forego a most accurate and precise specification of the grounds for the annulment of the arbitral award; the reason is that the court seized with the motion to annul the arbitral award only has at its disposal the materials in the dossier, which might not include all relevant nuances. Moreover, the law by no means limits the consumer's possibility to supplement the grounds for the annulment of the arbitral award during the proceedings. The consumer may naturally do so even with respect to those circumstances that the court should examine of its own motion, and thereby increase their chances of success in the dispute.

| | |

7. Judgment of Supreme Court of Czech Republic of July 31, 2013 in Case No. 29 Cdo 392/2011:[318] (i) Review of Arbitral Award during Insolvency Proceedings, (ii) Rebuttal of Arbitral Award as Enforceable Instrument by Insolvency Trustee, (iii) *Different Legal Assessment of Case* Where Arbitral Award Is Rendered Following Principles of Equity

Abbreviations Used:

ArbAct	Act of the Czech Republic No. 216/1994 Coll., on Arbitration and the Enforcement of Arbitral Awards, as amended[319]
CCP	Act of the Czech Republic No. 99/1963 Coll., the Code of Civil Procedure, as amended
ExecC	Act of the Czech Republic No. 120/2001 Coll., on Execution Agents and Execution, as amended
InsAct	Act No. 182/2006 Coll., on Insolvency and Methods of Resolving Insolvency (Insolvency Act), as amended
SC	Supreme Court of the Czech Republic

---

[318] This decision is available online on the website of the SC at http://www.nsoud.cz/ Judikatura/judikatura_ns.nsf/WebSearch/5CE8CB8FA6E8D569C1257C6A0052F3D3?ope nDocument&Highlight=0, [last accessed on November 7, 2014].

[319] The decision of the SC is based on the ArbAct in effect until December 31, 2007, but no subsequent changes have any bearing on the conclusions of the SC and their applicability in this particular case. The subject of the proceedings consisted of the issue of whether or not a claim can be rebutted in the insolvency proceedings that arises from an arbitral award; the primary issue was not arbitration, as such, and the making of arbitral awards.

Key Words:

shares | execution (enforcement proceedings) | insolvency proceedings | common management | rebuttal of a claim | legal force and effect (finality) | transfer of securities | scope of review of arbitral award | confessed judgment | settlement | hearing | enforcement of arbitral award | enforceability | enforceable claim | principles of equity | annulment (setting aside) of arbitral award |

Applicable Laws and Regulations:

ArbAct: Section 24,[320] Section 25,[321] Section 27,[322] Section 28,[323] Section 30,[324] Section 31,[325] Section 32[326]

---

[320] ArbAct, Section 24 (cit.): *(1) Arbitrators shall try to persuade the parties to agree on an amicable settlement of the dispute in the course of the arbitral proceedings. (2) If requested by the parties, the settlement may be concluded in the form of an arbitral award.* Note: This version was applicable to the respective proceedings, but the wording of this particular provision has not been subject to any modifications in the meantime.

[321] ArbAct, Section 25 (cit.): *(1) The arbitral award must be adopted by the majority of the arbitrators, must be made in writing and signed by at least the majority of the arbitrators. The operative part of the arbitral award must be clear and unambiguous. (2) The arbitral award must contain reasons unless the parties have agreed to dispense with reasons; this also applies to any arbitral award rendered pursuant to Section 24(2).* Note: This is the version applicable to the respective proceedings; the current version of this provision of the ArbAct reads as follows (cit.): *(1) The arbitral award must be adopted by the majority of the arbitrators, must be made in writing and signed by at least the majority of the arbitrators. The operative part of the arbitral award must be clear and unambiguous. (2) The arbitral award must contain reasons unless the parties have agreed to dispense with reasons; this also applies to any arbitral award rendered pursuant to Section 24(2).An arbitral award rendered in a dispute arising from a consumer contract must always contain reasons and instructions regarding the right to file a motion with the court to annul the award. (3) When making the award, the arbitrators apply the substantive law applicable to the dispute; they may, however, resolve the dispute according to the rules of equity but only if the parties have explicitly authorized them to do so. In disputes arising from consumer contracts, the arbitrators shall always abide by consumer protection laws and regulations.* Note: The above modifications may only have a general influence on the conclusions of the SC. Firstly, it is unclear whether a securities transfer contract (which is the basis of any and all of the subsequent obligations and contested issues) is a consumer contract under the currently applicable criteria. Secondly, the SC did not base its decision on the fact that the arbitration agreement authorized the arbitrator to make a decision following the principles of equity (the court concluded that even though the arbitrators had that possibility, they de facto rendered a default judgment under the CCP).

[322] ArbAct, Section 27 (cit.): *The parties are free to agree in their arbitration agreement that the arbitral award may be subject to review by other arbitrators at the request of either party or both parties. Unless the arbitration agreement stipulates otherwise, the motion for*

review must be sent to the other party no later than 30 days of receipt of the arbitral award *by the party requesting the review. Review of the arbitral award constitutes part of the* *arbitral proceedings and is subject to the provisions of this Act.* Note: This version of the law applied to the respective proceedings, but it has not been subject to any modifications in the meantime and therefore continues to apply.

[323] ArbAct, Section 28 (cit.): *(1) The arbitral award executed in writing must be served on* *the parties and, having been duly served, stamped with the confirmation of legal force and* *effect. (2) If the arbitral award cannot be subject to review pursuant to Section 27 or if the* *time limit for filing the motion for review pursuant to Section 27 has expired without the* *motion having been lodged, the award has the effects of a final and conclusive court* *judgment and is enforceable by courts upon receipt.* Note: This version of the law applied to the respective proceedings, but it has not been subject to any modifications in the meantime and therefore continues to apply.

[324] ArbAct, Section 30 (cit.): *Unless the Act stipulates otherwise, the arbitral proceedings* *shall be reasonably governed by the provisions of the Code of Civil Procedure.* Note: This version of the law applied to the respective proceedings, but it has not been subject to any modifications in the meantime and therefore continues to apply.

[325] ArbAct, Section 31 (cit.): (cit.): *At the request of any party the court annuls the arbitral* *award if: (a) it was made in a case which cannot be submitted to arbitration (cannot be the* *subject of a valid arbitration agreement), (b) the arbitration agreement is invalid for other* *reasons or the agreement was cancelled or it does not apply to the agreed case, (c) the* *arbitrator(s) who took part in the proceedings was/were not authorized to make decisions in* *the case, whether under the arbitration agreement or otherwise, or lacked the capacity to act* *as arbitrator(s), (d) the arbitral award was not adopted by the majority of the arbitrators,* *(e) a party was denied the opportunity to plead his or her case in the arbitral proceedings, (f)* *the arbitral award orders a party to provide performance which was not requested by the* *obligee or to provide performance which is impossible or illegal under domestic law, (g) it* *transpires that there are reasons which would otherwise justify the reopening of civil* *proceedings in court.* [Section 228(1)(a) and (b) of the CCP]. Note: This version of the provision applied to the respective proceedings; the currently applicable version reads as follows (cit.): *At the request of any party the court annuls the arbitral award if: (a) it was* *made in a case which cannot be submitted to arbitration (cannot be the subject of a valid* *arbitration agreement), (b) the arbitration agreement is invalid for other reasons or the* *agreement was cancelled or it does not apply to the agreed case, (c) the arbitrator(s) who* *took part in the proceedings was/were not authorized to make decisions in the case, whether* *under the arbitration agreement or otherwise, or lacked the capacity to act as arbitrator(s),* *(d) the arbitral award was not adopted by the majority of the arbitrators, (e) a party was* *denied the opportunity to plead his or her case in the arbitral proceedings, (f) the arbitral* *award orders a party to provide performance which was not requested by the creditor or to* *provide performance which is impossible or illegal under domestic law, (g) the arbitrator or* *the permanent arbitral institution resolved a dispute arising from a consumer contract* *contrary to consumer protection laws, or clearly in violation of good morals, or contrary to* *public policy, (h) an arbitration agreement relating to disputes arising from consumer* *contracts lacks the information required under Section 3(5) or such information is*

407

CCP: Section 99(2),[327] Section 114b,[328] Section 153a,[329] Section 157(3)[330]

intentionally or to a non-negligible extent incomplete, inaccurate, or false, or (i) it transpires that there are reasons which would otherwise justify the reopening of civil proceedings in court. [Section 228(1)(a) and (b) of the CCP]. Note: Subsequent modifications of the Act have no bearing on the applicability of this judgment in the given case. The reason is that the crucial issue in the proceedings was not any specific grounds for annulment of the arbitral award (as mentioned above, it is also unclear whether a securities transfer contract, which is the basis of any and all of the subsequent obligations and contested issues, is a consumer contract under the currently applicable criteria); the court in this particular case examined the issue of the extent to which an insolvency trustee may review an arbitral award.

[326] ArbAct, Section 32 (cit.): *(1) The motion to annul an arbitral award must be lodged with the court within three months following the receipt of the arbitral award by the party requesting the annulment of the award, unless this Act stipulates otherwise. (2) The motion pursuant to subsection (1) does not suspend the enforceability of the arbitral award. If requested by the obligor, however, the court may suspend the enforceability of the arbitral award in case an immediate enforcement of the arbitral award could cause serious harm.* Note: This version of the provision applied to the respective proceedings; the currently applicable version reads as follows (cit.): *(1) The motion to annul an arbitral award must be lodged with the court within three months following the receipt of the arbitral award by the party requesting the annulment of the award, unless this Act stipulates otherwise. If the arbitral award was made in a dispute arising from a consumer contract and the motion to annul was lodged by the consumer, the court always examines whether there are grounds to annul the arbitral award pursuant to Section 31(a) through (d) or (h). (2) The motion pursuant to subsection (1) does not suspend the enforceability of the arbitral award. If requested by the obligor, however, the court may suspend the enforceability of the arbitral award in case an immediate enforcement of the arbitral award could cause serious harm or in case the motion to annul the arbitral award justifies the conclusion that the motion is legitimate. (3) If the motion to annul an arbitral award is lodged by the consumer, the court shall establish whether there are grounds to suspend the enforceability of the arbitral award pursuant to subsection (2) without the consumer's request. The court shall rule on the suspension of enforceability within 7 days of receiving the motion; the arbitral award cannot be enforced within said time limit.* Note: Again, the modifications implemented in Section 32 of the ArbAct have no bearing on the assessment of the case by the court (see the reasons specified above), because the SC only examined the issue of whether the only defense against an arbitral award is a motion to annul the award lodged by the deadline stipulated in Section 32 of the ArbAct, or whether the arbitral award can be rebutted by the insolvency trustee.

[327] CCP, Section 99(2) (cit.): *The court shall decide whether it approves the settlement; the court shall not do so if the settlement is contrary to the law. In such case, the court shall continue the proceedings after the resolution becomes final and conclusive.* Note: This version of the law applied to the respective proceedings, but it has not been subject to any modifications in the meantime and therefore continues to apply. The SC has probably invoked this provision because, in their call for statements, the arbitrators also requested

that the parties present their proposals (if any) for an amicable resolution of the dispute, despite the fact that they subsequently rendered a *default judgment*. In such case, however, the reference to the said provision is irrelevant, because the implicit prerequisite of compliance with the law relates to the contents of the settlement, as such, not to the call addressed to the parties to state whether and under what conditions they are willing to consider an amicable resolution. A contrary interpretation would result in an absurd conclusion that any call of the arbitrators for an amicable resolution of the dispute (which, as a matter of fact, the arbitrators are bound to make) must be interpreted in terms of a prejudicial opinion of the arbitrators that the claimant's claim is legitimate.

[328] CCP, Section 114b (cit.): *(1) If required by the nature of the matter or the circumstances of the case, the Chairman of the panel may replace the request under Section 114a(2)(a) with a resolution ordering the respondent to provide a written statement in the case, and if the respondent does not fully acknowledge the claim asserted in the statement of claim, to describe the relevant circumstances in the respondent's statement on which their defense is based, and to enclose any documentary evidence with the statement which the respondent invokes, or identify evidence to prove the respondent's allegations; the resolution may also be issued if the request under Section 114a(2) has not been complied with in a due and timely manner; the procedure according to this subsection is not applicable in cases where settlement cannot be entered into and approved (Section 99(1 and (2)) and in matters specified in Section 118b and Section 120(2). The Chairman shall determine a time period for filing the statement, which must not be shorter than 30 days after the resolution is served. (2) The resolution under subsection (1) can be issued even if the court rendered a payment order in the case. In such case, the time period for filing the statement determined by the court shall start to run after the respondent lodges their appeal against the payment order. (3) The resolution under subsection (1) cannot be issued or served after the first hearing in the case. (4) The resolution under subsections (1) and (2) must be served on the respondent personally; substitute service is excluded. The resolution must not be served on the respondent before they are served with the claimant's petition (lawsuit). (5) If the respondent fails to lodge their statement at the court's request under subsection (1) without having any serious reason to do so, and fails to inform the court, within the stipulated time period, of the serious reason preventing them from filing the statement, the claim asserted against the respondent by the claimant's petition is deemed acknowledged by the respondent; the respondent must be warned of these consequences (Section 153a(3)).* Note: This version of the provision applied to the respective proceedings; the currently applicable version reads as follows (cit.): *(1) If required by the nature of the matter or the circumstances of the case, or if the court rendered a payment order, electronic payment order or European payment order in the case, the Chairman of the panel may replace the request under Section 114a(2)(a) with a resolution ordering the respondent to provide a written statement in the case, and if the respondent does not fully acknowledge the claim asserted in the statement of claim, to describe the relevant circumstances in the respondent's statement on which their defense is based, and to enclose any documentary evidence with the statement which the respondent invokes, or identify evidence to prove the respondent's allegations; the resolution may also be issued if the request under Section 114a(2) has not been complied with in a due and timely manner; this shall not apply in cases where*

settlement cannot be entered into and approved ((Section 99(1) and (2)). (2) The Chairman shall determine a time period for filing the statement under subsection (1), which must not be shorter than 30 days after the resolution is served. If the court rendered a payment order, electronic payment order or European payment order in the case, the court shall determine the time period in such manner that it starts to run from the expiration of the time period for filing an appeal against the payment order, electronic payment order or European payment order. (3) The resolution under subsection (1) cannot be issued or served after the preparatory hearing under Section 114c or after the first hearing in the case. (4) The resolution under subsection (1) must be served on the respondent personally. Substitute service is excluded; this shall not apply if the resolution is being delivered to a data mailbox using the public data network. The resolution must not be served on the respondent before they are served with the claimant's petition (lawsuit). (5) If the respondent fails to lodge their statement at the court's request under subsection (1) without having any serious reason to do so and fails to inform the court, within the stipulated time period, of the serious reason preventing them from filing the statement, the claim asserted against the respondent by the claimant's petition is deemed acknowledged by the respondent; the respondent must be warned of these consequences (Section 153a(3)). This shall not apply if the requirements are fulfilled for terminating the proceedings or striking out the petition. Note: However, the applicable version is not decisive from the perspective of the dispute in question, because the objection is based on the very fact that the arbitrators applied this provision by analogy, not whether or not they applied the provision properly.

[329] CCP, Section 153a (cit.): *(1) If the respondent acknowledges in the course of the judicial proceedings the claim or the basis of the claim asserted against the respondent by the claimant's petition, the court shall render a judgment according to the acknowledgment. If the respondent acknowledges only part of the claim asserted against the respondent by the claimant's petition, the court shall only render a judgment according to the acknowledgment if such procedure is proposed by the claimant. (2) A confessed judgment cannot be rendered in cases where settlement cannot be entered into and approved (Section 99(1) and (2)). (3) The court shall also render a confessed judgment if the respondent is deemed to have acknowledged the claim asserted against the respondent by the claimant's petition (Section 114b(5)). (4) The court is not obliged to summon a hearing for the sole purpose of rendering a confessed judgment.* Note: This version of the provision applied to the respective proceedings; the currently applicable version reads as follows (cit.): *(1) If the respondent acknowledges in the course of the judicial proceedings the claim or the basis of the claim asserted against the respondent by the claimant's petition, the court shall render a judgment according to the acknowledgment. If the respondent acknowledges only part of the claim asserted against the respondent by the claimant's petition, the court shall only render a judgment according to the acknowledgment if such procedure is proposed by the claimant. (2) A confessed judgment cannot be rendered in cases where settlement cannot be entered into and approved (Section 99(1) and (2)). (3) The court shall also render a confessed judgment if the respondent is deemed to have acknowledged the claim asserted against the respondent by the claimant's petition (Section 114b(5) and Section 114c(6)). (4) The court is not obliged to summon a hearing for the sole purpose of rendering a confessed judgment.*

[330] CCP, Section 157(3) (cit.): *The court shall limit the reasoning in a confessed judgment*

ExecC: Section 44(7)[331]
InsAct: Section 193,[332] Section 199,[333] Section 231[334]

or a default judgment to the subject matter of the proceedings and a brief explication of the reasons why the court rendered the confessed judgment or the default judgment. Note: This version of the law applied to the respective proceedings, but it has not been subject to any modifications in the meantime and therefore continues to apply.

[331] ExecC, Section 44(7) (cit.): *After the resolution ordering the execution is served, the obligor is prohibited from making any dispositions with their assets, including real property and assets included in the joint property of spouses; this shall not apply to common business activities, meeting the obligor's fundamental needs, maintenance and management of assets. A juridical act whereby the obligor breached this obligation is invalid. The first and second sentence shall not apply if the respondent is a state.* Note: This version of the quoted provision of the Execution Code, applicable to the case, was in effect until October 31, 2009. Analogous rules are now incorporated in Section 47(5) of the ExecC (cit.): *The obligor is prohibited from transferring to a third person, encumbering or making any other dispositions with the assets to which the execution order applies. Juridical action whereby the obligor breached this obligation is invalid.*

[332] InsAct, Section 193 (cit.): *Rebuttal of the existence of a claim means raising an objection that the claim has not come into existence or is already fully extinguished, or that the whole claim is statute-barred.* Note: This version of the law applied to the respective proceedings, but it has not been subject to any modifications in the meantime and therefore continues to apply.

[333] InsAct, Section 199 (cit.): *(1) The insolvency trustee who rebutted an enforceable claim shall file a lawsuit with the insolvency court within 30 days of the review hearing, whereby the rebuttal will be claimed against the creditor who had entered the enforceable claim. The time period shall not expire if the lawsuit is received by the court on or before the last day of the time period. (2) The grounds for rebutting the existence or the amount of an enforceable claim awarded by a final and conclusive decision of the competent authority may only consist of facts that were not asserted by the debtor in the proceedings preceding the issue of the decision; however, the rebuttal may not be based on a different legal assessment of the case. (3) In their lawsuit under subsection (1), the claimant may only invoke such circumstances against the rebutted claim for which the claim was rebutted by the claimant.* Note: This version of the law applied to the respective proceedings, but it has not been subject to any modifications in the meantime and therefore continues to apply.

[334] InsAct, Section 231 (cit.): *(1) The insolvency court is not bound by a decision of another court or another authority that has found a juridical act concerning the assets or liabilities of the debtor invalid in the course of the insolvency proceedings, or by any other manner of the finding. (2) The invalidity of the juridical act shall be assessed in the course of the insolvency proceedings only by the insolvency court, either as a preliminary issue or in an incidental dispute regarding the issue. A petition in this dispute may be lodged by the parties to the insolvency proceedings, except the debtor (unless the debtor is entitled to make dispositions), by the insolvency trustee and by the public prosecution service. The insolvency trustee must always be the claimant or the respondent. (3) If the invalidity of the juridical act requires that invalidity be invoked by the person affected by the act, invalidity may also*

The Supreme Court of the Czech Republic reached the following principal conclusions:

(1) An enforceable claim awarded by a final and conclusive arbitral award is also subject to the regime of reviewing enforceable claims awarded by final and conclusive decisions of "competent authorities". A contrary opinion would result in absurd consequences: an enforceable claim awarded to the creditor against the debtor by a final and conclusive judicial decision would be reviewable, whereas an identical claim awarded to the creditor against the debtor by a final and conclusive arbitral award would not. Section 28(2) of the ArbAct stipulates that an arbitral award that cannot be subject to review pursuant to Section 27 of the ArbAct or an award with respect to which the time limit for filing the motion for review pursuant to Section 27 of the ArbAct has expired without the motion having been lodged has the effects of a final and conclusive judicial decision, and is enforceable by courts at the moment it has been served. If the arbitral award takes the "effects of a final and conclusive judicial decision" then, logically, this is another reason why the award is reviewable in insolvency proceedings in the same way as the "final and conclusive judicial decision" itself.

(2) Legal assessment of the case is not excluded as grounds for rebutting the existence or the amount of an enforceable claim entered in the creditor's application if no legal assessment of the case is contained in the final and conclusive decision of the competent authority that awarded the claim. [335]

---

be invoked by the insolvency trustee. Note: This version of the provision applied to the respective proceedings; the currently applicable version reads as follows (cit.): *(1) The insolvency court is not bound by a decision of another court or another authority that has found a juridical act concerning the assets or liabilities of the debtor invalid in the course of the insolvency proceedings, or by any other manner of the finding. (2) The invalidity of the juridical act shall be assessed in the course of the insolvency proceedings only by the insolvency court. (3) If the invalidity of the juridical act requires that invalidity be invoked by the person affected by the act, invalidity may also be invoked by the insolvency trustee.* Note: The modification has de facto no bearing on the conclusions of the court; the explanatory memorandum to the respective amendment (i.e. Act No. 294/2013 Coll.) indicates that the amendment was not intended to introduce any material changes, only to eliminate interpretation problems and clarify that the petition is not any specific kind of petition, but that the objective of the provision is to reserve the resolution of such disputes for insolvency courts.

[335] In this connection, the SC invoked the conclusions articulated in a similar case in its prior rulings, namely Judgment Case No. 29 ICdo 7/2013 of July 18, 2013, which is available online on the SC website at http://www.nsoud.cz/Judikatura/judikatura_ns.nsf/WebSearch/5DE494179FCB3712C1257BBF0040E8C2?openDocument&Highlight=0; the

(3) The conclusion that the claim asserted by the creditor can also be the subject of a confessed judgment implies an assessment that the awarded claim is not contrary to any laws or regulations (Section 153a(2), the first sentence of Section 99(2) of the CCP, part of the sentence following the semicolon).[336] At the same time, such assessment suffices for the conclusion that the confessed judgment contains the legal assessment of the case with respect to the awarded claim.

(4) It is possible to rebut an enforceable claim awarded by a final and conclusive arbitral award, despite the fact that (if) the parties explicitly

court reached the following conclusions in the case (cit.): *The grounds for rebutting the existence or the amount of an enforceable claim entered by a creditor that had been awarded by a final and conclusive decision of the competent authority may only consist of factual objections, namely of facts that were not asserted by the debtor in the proceedings preceding the issue of the decision (Section 199(2) of the Insolvency Act). It is irrelevant whether it was the debtor's own fault that they failed to assert such circumstances, for instance, because the debtor entirely resigned on their procedural defense in the respective proceedings, and in consequence thereof, a title of execution was issued that consists of a decision that does not contain any reasons (such as a payment order or a bill of exchange/promissory note payment order), or a decision that contains only minimal reasons (such as a confessed judgment or a default judgment). The legal assessment of a case is not excluded as grounds for rebutting the existence or the amount of an enforceable claim entered in the creditor's application if no legal assessment of the case is contained in the final and conclusive decision of the competent authority that awarded the claim. If the competent authority awards to the creditor against the debtor any interest or dues associated with the claim other than the interest or dues prescribed by statute as a result of the authority's error in the determination of the law that stipulates which type of interest/dues is associated with the claim (the authority awards default charges instead of default interest), any criticism of such a decision constitutes criticism of the correctness of the legal assessment of the case. As concerns confessed judgments and default judgments, the legal assessment of the case (at the level of examining the requirements for rendering such decisions) is reflected in the pre-defined type of reasoning limited by the law (Section 157(3) of the CCP). As concerns a payment order, including an electronic payment order, and as concerns a bill of exchange/promissory note payment order or a check payment order, the legal assessment of the case (at the level of examining the requirements for rendering such decisions) is reflected in the fact that the court rendered such decisions (which contain no reasoning). Where the court concludes that the interest/dues associated with a claim that are claimed by the claimant may also be the subject of a confessed judgment, the conclusion implies an assessment that the awarded interest/dues associated with the claim are not contrary to any laws or regulations (Section 153a(2), the first sentence of Section 99(2) of the CCP, part of the sentence following the semicolon). At the same time, such a consideration suffices for the conclusion that the confessed judgment contains a legal assessment of the case with respect to the awarded interest/dues associated with the claim.*

[336] These provisions are quoted in the footnotes above.

authorize the arbitrator to resolve the dispute following the principles of equity (Section 25(3) of the ArbAct).[337] Besides, the conclusion on whether the arbitral award contains the "legal assessment of the case" is not contingent on how the arbitrator "could have justified" the decision (i.e. that the arbitrator could have invoked the principles of equity), but how the arbitrator "actually justified" the decision.

(5) Section 231 of the InsAct[338] does not address the issue of the validity of juridical acts assessed during the review of claims, the existence, amount or place in the hierarchy of claims of which was rebutted in the insolvency proceedings (whether the claims are enforceable or not); i.e. Section 231 of the InsAct does not limit such review in any manner. The only objective of the provision is to make sure that the issue of the validity of the juridical act, which determines whether the debtor's assets fall within their estate and which is also crucial for the identification of the debtor's liabilities, is not fraudulently forced outside (by motions for declaratory judgments under Section 80(c) of the CCP[339] lodged with courts) the scope of the procedures that are specifically prescribed by the Insolvency Act for the resolution of such issues.

[*From Facts of Case*]:

16.64. The creditor entered a claim in the insolvency proceedings against the assets of the debtor (insolvent);[340] the claim was established by the Securities Transfer Contract – a contract for the transfer of 100 shares in company [x]. The contract was entered into on November 5, 2007 by and between [y], as the transferor, and the debtor, as the transferee. In

---

[337] This provision is quoted in a footnote above.

[338] This provision is quoted in a footnote above.

[339] This provision is quoted in a footnote above.

[340] A legal entity formed and existing under the laws of the Czech Republic in the form of a joint stock company. As concerns the other persons involved, it is clear that their nature is irrelevant for the case itself. The obligation (relationship) that gave rise to the contested claim was entered into by the debtor and a natural person (although it is not explicitly mentioned in the annotated decision, we can deduce that he was a national of the Czech Republic with his place of residence in the Czech Republic). The respective claim was originally entered in the insolvency proceedings by a legal person formed and existing under the laws of the Czech Republic in the form of a limited liability company (hence, the claim had apparently been assigned), and the respondent in the respective proceedings is a different legal entity (also formed and existing under the laws of the Czech Republic in the form of a limited liability company) – the change in the person of the creditor was the subject of Resolution of the Regional Court in Prague (as the insolvency court) of February 4, 2009 in Case No. KSPL 27 INS 4239/2008-P1.

order to secure payment of the purchase price and the agreed penalties, the parties entered into a real property lien agreement; property owned by the debtor as a joint owner served as collateral under the agreement. The parties agreed on an arbitration clause for the resolution of disputes, and the arbitrator was endowed with the power to decide the disputes following the principles of equity; the parties have also agreed that they did not insist on an oral hearing and that the arbitrator need not provide any reasons for their arbitral award. The above contracts were entered into, despite the fact that on October 19, 2007 (i.e. before the signing of the respective contract) the debtor had received Resolution of July 9, 2007 in Case No. 17 Nc 6479/2007-7, whereby the District Court in Sokolov (Czech Republic) ordered execution against the debtor's assets. It was also established that on August 13, 2007[341] (i.e. also before the signing of the contract), proceedings were opened for recording a note in the Land Register, and the debtor's share in the real property was sealed, both on the basis of the Resolution issued by the execution court and the ensuing execution order.

16.65. The debtor failed to pay the agreed purchase price, and consequently, an ad hoc arbitration was commenced (with a sole arbitrator as the decision-making authority), which was terminated by an arbitral award rendered on December 20, 2007, Case No. Rc 169/2007. The claim arising from the Securities Transfer Contract, including the agreed penalties, was recognized as legitimate by the arbitrator. As the arbitral award indicates, the arbitrator issued on December 4, 2007 Resolution Rc 169/2007-01, in which the arbitrator requested that the debtor reply to the request for arbitration (statement of claim), specify any and all circumstances that the debtor asserts in his defense and support his statements by specific documentary evidence, all within 15 days of receiving the Resolution. The debtor was also requested to propose in his reply the terms of a potential amicable resolution of the dispute (if the debtor were interested in such procedure). As the arbitral award indicates, the debtor did not respond to the Resolution at all. The arbitrator therefore ruled that if the debtor failed to provide any reply to the request in time without having any serious reason for such default, and did not inform the arbitrator by the stipulated deadline of any serious reasons preventing the debtor from filing the reply, the claim asserted against the debtor by the request for arbitration (statement of claim) was deemed acknowledged by the debtor. It is also pointed out that the debtor was duly warned of those potential

---

[341] The judgment contains an obvious typographical error, because elsewhere it refers to August 9, 2007.

ramifications in the above-specified procedural resolution. The arbitrator held that such procedure complied with Article 15(4) to (5) of the Rules of Arbitration,[342] and that the procedure also allegedly complied with Section 114b(1) of the CCP,[343] which was applied reasonably based on Section 30 of the ArbAct.[344] The arbitral award became final and conclusive on January 18, 2008.

16.66. On December 29, 2008, the Regional Court in Plzeň, as the insolvency court, rendered Resolution Case No. KSPL 27 INS 4239/2008, whereby the debtor was found insolvent. Considering the existence of the abovementioned final and conclusive arbitral award (whose existence and contents were uncontested), the claim awarded by the award against the debtor was entered in the insolvency proceedings as an enforceable claim. The insolvency trustee rebutted this enforceable claim at the review hearing held in the case on February 10, 2009, as regards its existence, amount and place in the hierarchy of claims. In his incidental petition lodged on March 9, 2009, the insolvency trustee demanded a declaration against the creditor who had filed his application containing the contested claim on grounds that the creditor did not have the said claim against the debtor. It was argued that the Securities Transfer Contract was invalid ab initio due to Section 44(7) of the ExecC,[345] because the debtor was prohibited from making dispositions with his assets when the Contract was signed, including the real property that served as the collateral securing the payment of the purchase price. The insolvency trustee also argued that the other contracting party and the arbitrator must have been aware thereof when signing the contract/during the arbitral proceedings, respectively, because information concerning the execution was available from public sources (Land Register), and both the other contracting party and the arbitrator should and could have discovered the fact.

[*Procedure of Case*]:

16.67. The Regional Court in Plzeň, as the court of first instance, rendered on August 13, 2009 its Judgment in Case No. 122 Cm 4/2009-50, whereby the court ruled that the respective claim did not exist and the insolvency trustee's rebuttal was justified and lawful. The court accepted the reasoning presented in the petition and concluded that after the Resolution of the execution court was served (October 19,

---

[342] As mentioned above, the case involved ad hoc arbitration and it can be presumed that the invoked procedural rules are the Rules of a private arbitral company.

[343] The provision is quoted above in the opening part of this annotation.

[344] The provision is quoted above in the opening part of this annotation.

[345] The provision is quoted above in the opening part of this annotation.

2007), the debtor was not entitled to perform acts that evidently exceeded the scope of the common management of the debtor's assets. Execution of (entering into) the respective contracts, including the lien over the real property, was assessed as falling within that category, and consequently, the claim arising from them could not exist. The court of first instance also held that the existence of the arbitral award had no bearing on the conclusion, because the award could not cure the invalidity of the Securities Transfer Contract, which was subject to Section 44(7) of the ExecC;[346] hence, the act was invalid under the law.

16.68. The High Court in Prague, as the appellate court, upheld the material aspects of the above-mentioned Judgment of the Regional Court in Plzeň.[347] The appellate court dismissed as irrelevant the objection that the court in the incidental proceedings (opened by the insolvency trustee's petition) did not have the power to make a preliminary assessment of the (in)validity of the Securities Transfer Contract entered into by the debtor, which had been the underlying legal instrument for the issued arbitral award, if no motion to declare the invalidity of the contract was lodged; to quite the contrary, the court's power to assess such circumstances is set forth in Section 231(1) of the InsAct.[348] The court also did agreed that it was not possible to undermine and examine in an incidental dispute the materials that had served as the basis for the arbitrator's arbitral award, i.e. that the Securities Transfer Contract and its validity could not be subject to material review. The court noted that the arbitral award itself was not set aside by the decision of the court in the incidental proceedings - the court's decision was a declaratory decision that only served the purposes of the insolvency proceedings, and its objective was to determine the extent to which the claims entered by the debtor's creditors would be satisfied in the insolvency proceedings. The possibility of rebutting enforceable claims is typically available where the debtor's own passivity, willful or negligent, gives rise to the creditor's claim, and the purpose is to give the creditor an advantage over the other creditors. The court was of the opinion that this was indeed the case, because the debtor had not availed itself of the opportunity to make any defense against the claim submitted to arbitration, had not pleaded the invalidity of the Securities Transfer Contract, and had not even availed itself of the possibility open to the

---

[346] The provision is quoted above in the opening part of this annotation.
[347] Namely by Judgment of February 18, 2010 in Case No. 15 Cmo 250/2009-100.
[348] The provision is quoted above in the opening part of this annotation.

debtor under Section 31 of the ArbAct,[349] and had not lodged a motion to annul the arbitral award by the deadline stipulated in Section 32 of the ArbAct.[350] The insolvency trustee could not avail himself of the procedure outlined above due to the expiration of the time limit under Section 32 of the ArbAct;[351] consequently, the trustee was entitled to rebut the enforceable claim entered by the creditor pursuant to Section 199 of the InsAct.[352] The appellate court concluded that the conditions for rebutting an enforceable claim were fulfilled, because the rebuttal of the claim was based on a fact that the debtor had failed to assert in the arbitral proceedings, and at the same time, the insolvency trustee did not petition for a different legal assessment of the case in his motion, because the arbitrator did not examine the validity of the Securities Transfer Contract in the arbitration (the court apparently based its conclusion on the fact that the arbitrator had assumed that the debtor had resigned on any procedural defense and thereby acknowledged the claimant's claim, and consequently, the merits of the case had not been discussed in the arbitration. The court also held as irrelevant that the debtor himself had caused the invalidity of the contract, because the debtor must have been aware of the limitation imposed on his right to make dispositions with his assets; even if the other party had entered into the contract and accrued the claim in good faith, the fact could not curtail the rights of the insolvency trustee (insolvency administrator).

16.69. The judgment of the appellate court was challenged by an extraordinary appeal lodged by the creditor/the entity which entered the contested claim in the insolvency proceedings. The creditor argued that the courts had not addressed all of the creditor's objections, primarily the issue of whether a decision rendered in arbitration can be reviewed in standard judicial proceedings if the arbitrator was authorized to make decisions following the principles of equity, and if, as is the case, the principles of equity do not apply in judicial proceedings; it is necessary to point out that the arbitrator also applied the principles of equity to the assessment of the validity of the Securities Transfer Contract. The creditor argued that the arbitrator was also bound by the duty to assess the validity of juridical acts as a preliminary issue, and the arbitrator had fulfilled that duty following the principles of equity; the creditor thus argued that the conclusion could not stand, according to which the validity of the Securities

---

[349] The provision is quoted above in the opening part of this annotation.
[350] The provision is quoted above in the opening part of this annotation.
[351] The provision is quoted above in the opening part of this annotation.
[352] The provision is quoted above in the opening part of this annotation.

Transfer Contract had not been assessed in the arbitration. Consequently, the issued arbitral award is the outcome of a legal and factual assessment of the case. Considering the fact that the award was made following the principles of equity, the creditor is of the opinion that the arbitrator acted in compliance with the ArbAct if he arrived at a conclusion that differs from mandatory provisions of the law, namely Section 44(7) of the ExecC in this particular case.[353] The creditor also argued that the issue of the validity of the relevant contracts was a question of legal assessment, not a factual circumstance that the debtor had failed to assert; consequently, the insolvency trustee was not entitled to invoke these grounds for rebutting the claim – see Section 199(2) of the InsAct.[354] The creditor thus concluded that the arbitrator had examined the issue of the validity of the contract, and that the only reason underlying the rebuttal of the claim was a different legal assessment of the case (validity of the contract), which is prohibited under the InsAct. The creditor also did not agree with the conclusion that the outcome of the incidental dispute merely related to the insolvency proceedings, because the arbitral award, as a title of execution, survived unchallenged and served as the basis of execution; as a result of the above said, it is necessary to determine for certain the nature of the arbitral award in relation to the court judgment, whereby the claim was declared nonexistent (because there will in fact exist two parallel mutually inconsistent decisions addressing the same issue). The creditor also maintained that Section 231 of the InsAct[355] was interpreted too broadly. The creditor is of the opinion that the court is only entitled to review the invalidity of a juridical act if the decision on invalidity of the juridical act relating to the debtor's assets was rendered in the course of the insolvency proceedings. The intervenor also provided its comments to the extraordinary appeal;[356] as opposed to the creditor, the intervenor identified with the contested decision and pleaded as follows:

- Decision-making following the principles of equity must not result in any evasion of the law and transgression of the framework of rules, the observance of which must be insisted on,[357] and this is

---

[353] The provision is quoted above in the opening part of this annotation.

[354] The provision is quoted above in the opening part of this annotation.

[355] The provision is quoted above in the opening part of this annotation.

[356] A legal entity formed and existing under the laws of the Czech Republic in the form of a limited liability company. Its connection to the respective claim and its interest in the outcome of the incidental dispute is not further clarified in the decision.

[357] In this connection, the judgment refers to the following publication: Alexander J. Bělohlávek: Zákon o rozhodčím řízení a o výkonu rozhodčích nálezů. Komentář. [Title in Translation: Act on Arbitration and Enforcement of Arbitral Awards. Commentary].

exactly what would happen if a decision was made contrary to Section 44(7) of the ExecC.[358] Moreover, the creditor's statements made in the course of the proceedings are allegedly inconsistent as concerns the issue of whether or not the issue of validity of the contract was examined in the arbitration.

- The validity of contracts may be examined within the framework of an incidental dispute. The reason is that Section 199 of the InsAct[359] allows rebuttal of an enforceable claim, and the assessment of existence of the claim necessitates an examination of whether the claim entered by the creditor has come into existence; this necessarily implies the examination of whether the contract was validly executed, from which the creditor derives their claim.

- The insolvency court in proceedings regarding an incidental dispute has the power to review the existence of the claim that was awarded by an arbitral award. A contrary approach would disrupt the equality of arbitral awards and judicial decisions, because decisions rendered by a court with the subject-matter and territorial jurisdiction would be subject to review by the insolvency court, whereas arbitral awards would not.

16.70. The Supreme Court of the Czech Republic based its decision on the above-described facts of the case and invoked the applicable laws and regulations, primarily Section 199 of the InsAct[360] (as concerns the power of the insolvency trustee to rebut enforceable claims), Section 44(7) of the ExecC[361] (as the asserted grounds for rebutting the claim), and Section 25 of the ArbAct,[362] which stipulates the essential requirements of an arbitral award. As concerns the first issue, the SC came to the unequivocal conclusion that the regime for reviewing an enforceable claim awarded by a final and conclusive decision of the *competent authority* also applies to an enforceable claim awarded by a final and conclusive arbitral award rendered by an arbitrator or an arbitral tribunal. The SC also confirmed that it is not possible to invoke the inconsistency between the titles (decisions) as a factor that prohibits the review of the claim, because the relationship between the

---

1st edition. Praha [Prague / Czech Republic]: C. H. Beck, 2004 p. 206. A second edition of the book was published in Czech in 2012 by the same publishing house, while an English version corresponding to the second Czech edition was also published by JurisNet LLC, Huntington, New York, 2013.

[358] The provision is quoted above in the opening part of this annotation.

[359] The provision is quoted above in the opening part of this annotation.

[360] The provision is quoted above in the opening part of this annotation.

[361] The provision is quoted above in the opening part of this annotation.

[362] The provision is quoted above in the opening part of this annotation.

creditor and the debtor remains subject to the final and conclusive decision of the competent authority in other than insolvency relations, and the outcome of the incidental dispute has no bearing on the above said, and its conclusions only have effects within the insolvency proceedings. The review of the claim is also not prevented by the fact that the arbitration clause enabled the arbitrator to resolve the dispute following the principles of equity. In this connection, however, the SC expressed its unequivocal conclusion that the decisive factor in any individual case is the basis on which the arbitrator actually made their decision, not the wording of the arbitration clause, i.e. how the arbitrator could have made their decision. Similarly, the crucial issue according to the SC is what reasons were actually invoked in support of the arbitral award, not what reasons could or should have been invoked (it is not a material review of the arbitral award). In compliance with the Judgment of the SC of July 18, 2013 in Case No. 29 ICdo 7/2013,[363] the SC concluded that if the case is resolved by a confessed judgment, the decision implies a conclusion that the awarded claim is not contrary to any laws or regulations, which necessarily implies that the confessed judgment contains a legal assessment of the case regarding the awarded claim. Considering the above said, the SC held that the appellate court erred in its conclusion that the insolvency trustee was not demanding a different legal assessment of the case because the arbitrator had not examined the validity of the Securities Transfer Contract in the arbitral proceedings. Given these circumstances, the SC examined the issue of whether the grounds for the rebuttal of the claim represent a different legal assessment of the case, or whether they are factual objections that the debtor had failed to assert in the arbitration. The SC concluded that the validity of a written juridical act is not always contingent only on the circumstances ascertainable from the written document in which the juridical act is incorporated; the grounds for invalidity may result from a number of circumstances that (unless they were asserted by the debtor in the proceedings that preceded the issue of the decision that has established the enforceable claim) may constitute grounds for rebutting the existence or the amount of the enforceable claim. The SC held that such circumstances may also consist of the service (delivery) of the decision ordering the execution, as a result of which the debtor was deprived of their right to make dispositions with their assets under Section 44(7) of the ExecC;[364] in the opinion of the SC, the insolvency trustee therefore invoked

---

[363] The decision is quoted above in this annotation.

[364] The provision is quoted above in the opening part of this annotation.

factual grounds for rebutting the claim in the respective case, which the insolvency trustee was entitled to do. At the same time, however, the SC invoked the principle that stipulates that a breach of the prohibition under Section 44(7) of the ExecC[365] need not always render the juridical act invalid; if the obligor made dispositions with their assets contrary to the prohibition under Section 44(7) of the ExecC,[366] the assets were not affected by the execution and the execution was terminated, the obligor's acts are deemed valid, whereby they made dispositions with the assets during the execution. The SC held that the court entirely disregarded the issue and similarly ignored the issue of why the finding of the invalidity of the Securities Transfer Contract did not result in the assessment of whether the creditor had a claim against the debtor based on any other legal grounds, and to what extent, such as unjust enrichment gained by the debtor when the debtor accepted performance based on an invalid juridical act. Considering the absence of any debate regarding these issues, the SC vacated the contested decision and remanded the case for further proceedings. Last, but not least, and in connection with Section 231 of the InsAct,[367] the SC concluded that the provision by no means limits the possibility of assessing the validity of juridical acts (on which the claims entered by the creditors are based) during the review of such claims, because the sole purpose of the provision is to establish the jurisdiction of the insolvency courts to assess these issues.

[*Arguments Presented by SC*]:

16.71. The SC identified with the existing doctrinal interpretations regarding the review powers enjoyed by the insolvency courts in relation to enforceable claims. In this connection, the SC invoked its Judgment of July 18, 2013 in Case No. 29 ICdo 7/2013.[368] At the same time, the SC

---

[365] The provision is quoted above in the opening part of this annotation.

[366] The provision is quoted above in the opening part of this annotation.

[367] The provision is quoted above in the opening part of this annotation.

[368] This decision is quoted above in this annotation; the court primarily invoked the following conclusions (cit.): *The objective of the rule incorporated in Section 199(2) of the Insolvency Act can be easily discerned from the Special Part of the Explanatory Memorandum to the Government Proposal for the Insolvency Act, debated under No. 1120 by the Chamber of Deputies of the Czech Parliament in its 4th Election Term 2002 – 2006. The rule incorporated in Section 199(2) of the Insolvency Act (in the applicable version) was incorporated in Section 199(3) of the draft. According to the Special Part of the Explanatory Memorandum (relating to Sections 198 and 199 of the draft): "Section 199 of the draft significantly curtails the right of the trustee or the creditors to rebut enforceable claims. An enforceable claim may be created (including a fraudulently "fabricated" claim) without any (judicial or other) proceedings (for instance, by a notarial or executorial record containing a*

consent with enforceability) that would be completed by a decision regarding the claim; an enforceable decision may also be adopted without any preceding examination of evidence that would justify the conclusion that the claim exists and its amount is correctly determined (such as a payment order, a default judgment or a confessed judgment). This is one reason why the right to rebut the claim should be preserved. (...) Save for the cases covered by this provision (to wit, Section 199(2) of the draft, which was not included in the Insolvency Act in the end), the grounds for rebutting an enforceable claim established by a decision (pursuant to Section 199(3)) may only consist of those circumstances that the debtor failed to assert in the proceedings preceding the enforceable decision; at the same time, it is not allowed to rebut the claim merely on grounds of a different legal assessment of the case performed by the person rebutting the claim (in this connection, the draft is based on the premise that errors in the legal assessment of a case can never be fully avoided)". Consequently, the general rule is (in accordance with the wording of Section 199(2) of the Insolvency Act) that the grounds for rebutting the existence or the amount of an enforceable claim entered by a creditor that had been awarded by a final and conclusive decision of the competent authority (meaning courts, but also public administration authorities, arbitrators or arbitral tribunals) may only consist of facts that were not asserted by the debtor in the proceedings preceding the issue of the decision. It is irrelevant whether it was the debtor's own fault that they failed to assert such circumstances, for instance, because the debtor entirely resigned on their procedural defense in the respective proceedings, as a result of which the title of execution came into existence that consists of a decision that does not contain any reasons (such as a payment order or a bill of exchange/promissory note payment order), or a decision that contains only minimal reasons (such as a confessed judgment or a default judgment). Whether the rebuttal will be successful or not will, conversely, depend on whether the circumstances that had not been previously asserted by the debtor are capable of changing the outcome of the "dispute over the claim" (the circumstances themselves constitute grounds in the outcome of a different legal assessment of the case). In other words, compared to the facts that the debtor had asserted before, the facts that had not been asserted before are the decisive cause for the determination that the creditor who lodged their application in the insolvency proceedings and who is being sued (by the insolvency trustee) does not have the respective enforceable claim against the debtor (dispute over the existence of the claim), or for the determination that the creditor who lodged their application in the insolvency proceedings and who is being sued (by the insolvency trustee) has the respective enforceable claim against the debtor in a particular amount (determined in the operative part of the decision and lower than the amount of the enforceable claim entered by the creditor in the insolvency proceedings) [dispute over the amount of the claim]. The rule that stipulates that the grounds for rebutting the existence or the amount of an enforceable claim entered in the insolvency proceedings that had been awarded by a final and conclusive decision of the competent authority may not be based on a "different legal assessment of the case" (Section 199(2) of the Insolvency Act, part of the sentence following the semicolon) typically applies to situations where the factual basis of the case is not contested (i.e. the rebuttal of the existence or the amount of the enforceable claim is not based on any circumstances that the debtor failed to assert in the proceedings that preceded the issue of the decision, or such circumstances had been asserted, but did not

also held that the conclusions apply in relation to arbitral awards, which, pursuant to Section 28(2) of the ArbAct,[369] if they cannot be subject to review pursuant to Section 27 of the ArbAct[370] or with respect to which the time limit for filing the motion for review has expired, the awards have the effects of a final and conclusive judicial decision and are enforceable by courts as soon as they are served, and consequently, can be reviewed in the insolvency proceedings analogously to the review of a final and conclusive judicial decisions. Generally speaking, the decisions cannot become mutually inconsistent, because Section 201 of the InsAct explicitly stipulates that decisions of the insolvency court regarding the existence, amount or place of the claims in the hierarchy of claims have effects vis-à-vis all procedural subjects, and have no external effects. The other creditors of the debtor are thereby afforded the opportunity to avoid the possibility that a claim will also be proportionately satisfied in the insolvency proceedings, to the detriment of the creditors, which came into existence only because the debtor failed to protect their rights dutifully (or entirely) in the respective proceedings, or the claim was fraudulently fabricated in cooperation with the debtor. The court also argued that the assessment of whether the examined decision contains legal conclusions does not turn on whether the arbitrator made

---

result in any modification of the factual conclusions compared to the previous decision), and the established facts of the case should have resulted in a different legal assessment of the case than the assessment made by the competent authority in the proceedings preceding the issue of the decision. This occurs, for instance, if the competent authority awarded the claim to the creditor against the debtor as performance under a contract, but the performance should have been awarded as damages or unjust enrichment, or if the competent authority correctly identified (named) the legal rule that should have been applied to the established facts of the case, but the authority's interpretation of the rule or application of the rule to the given facts of the case was erroneous (as concerns the expression "legal assessment of the case", cf. also the definition mentioned above in connection with the grounds for filing an extraordinary appeal pursuant to Section 241a(2)(b) of the CCP). And, at the same time, it is clear that the erroneous legal assessment of the case by the competent authority could have resulted in awarding a claim to the creditor against the debtor where a "different" (correct) legal assessment of the case would have resulted in a conclusion that the claim was not legitimate or should not be awarded to the full extent claimed by the creditor. The legal assessment of the case is not excluded as grounds for rebutting the existence or the amount of an enforceable claim entered in the creditor's application if no legal assessment of the case is contained in the final and conclusive decision of the competent authority that awarded the claim.

[369] The provision is quoted above in the opening part of this annotation.
[370] The provision is quoted above in the opening part of this annotation.

decisions following the principles of equity, or whether the arbitration clause entitled the arbitrator to do so, but which circumstances the arbitrator actually used as the basis for their decision. Having made this finding, the SC concluded in the annotated decision that the respective arbitral award was not issued following the principles of equity, but the arbitrator ruled that the fiction of acknowledgment of claim applied in terms of Section 114b of the CCP,[371] i.e. the case could have been resolved according to the acknowledgment. The SC held that the concept of the arbitral award and the contents of the reasons specified in the award corresponded to a confessed judgment under the CCP and the reasons for such a judgment in terms of Section 157(3) of the CCP.[372]

16.72. As concerns the issue of whether and to what extent a confessed judgment contains legal assessment of the case, the SC has invoked its conclusions reached in Judgment of the SC of July 18, 2013 in Case No. 29 ICdo 7/2013.[373] The said decision also served as inspiration with respect to the issue of the extent to which the validity of a written juridical act results directly from the respective written document, and of the extent to which the validity may result from other (factual circumstances). In this connection, the SC also invoked its Judgment of 29 October 2008 in Case No. 21 Cdo 4841/2007.[374] As concerns the issue of whether the general inhibitorium (prohibition) in terms of Section 44(7) of the ExecC[375] automatically renders the juridical act invalid, or whether the issue requires further assessment, the SC referred to Judgment of the Grand Panel of the Civil and Commercial Division of the Supreme Court of March 9, 2011 in Case No. 31 Cdo

---

[371] The provision is quoted above in the opening part of this annotation.

[372] The provision is quoted above in the opening part of this annotation.

[373] The decision is quoted above in this annotation.

[374] This decision is available online on the SC website at http://www.nsoud.cz/Judikatura/ judikatura_ns.nsf/WebSearch/D9B4163A5C3DA5B0C1257A4E006522CF?openDocument &Highlight=0; in this decision, the court ruled as follows (cit.): *Hence, the court, of its own motion, is not allowed to introduce any circumstances in the proceedings that are not supported by the contents of the file and by the outcome of the proceedings that have been conducted so far (the investigatory principle does not apply). This holds true irrespective of the fact that the new circumstance should consist of a fact that could render the juridical act invalid. The court has regard to the invalidity of the act of its own motion (the appellant is correct on this point), but only if the court learns of the grounds for the invalidity in a procedurally proper manner. Unless specific grounds for invalidity are alleged or otherwise arise during the proceedings, there is no reason for the court to search for such facts of its own motion and thus substitute for the parties' activity presumed by the law with respect to litigation.*

[375] The provision is quoted above in the opening part of this annotation.

4545/2008.[376] The SC also criticized the appellate court for neglecting the issue of whether the claim entered by the creditor could actually exist based on different legal grounds (despite the fact that the SC noted that if the claim had arisen from unjust enrichment, the creditor – logically – could not be granted the agreed contractual sanctions, i.e. contractual default interest and contractual penalty). As regards the identification of the claims entered by the creditors, the SC invoked Judgment of the SC of January 30, 2003 in Case No. 29 Cdo 1089/2000,[377] Judgment of the SC of July 15, 2008 in Case No. 29 Odo 742/2006,[378] and Judgment of the SC of December 22, 2009 in Case No.

---

[376] This decision is available online on the SC website at http://www.nsoud.cz/Judikatura/judikatura_ns.nsf/WebSearch/D5046A62AB37D41BC1257A4E00696B45?openDocument& Highlight=0; in this decision, the court ruled as follows (cit.): *If the obligor made dispositions with their assets contrary to the general inhibitorium (prohibition) in terms of Section 44(7) of Act No. 120/2001 Coll., as amended and in effect until October 31, 2009, but the assets were not affected by the execution and the execution was terminated, the obligor's acts are deemed valid, whereby they made dispositions with the assets during the execution.* Note: The summary of the SC's legal opinion (*ratio decidendi*) was adopted from the SC website.

[377] This decision is available online on the SC website at http://www.nsoud.cz/Judikatura/judikatura_ns.nsf/WebSearch/B0E173A4DF28DA57C1257A4E0066B6E5?openDocument &Highlight=0; in this decision, the court ruled as follows (cit.): *I. If the application whereby a claim is entered in the bankruptcy proceedings contains data that unmistakably identify the act (factual circumstances), on the basis of which the creditor enters their (pecuniary) claim in the bankruptcy proceedings, but the bankruptcy creditor (applicant) failed to describe at or before the end of the review hearing any and all circumstances important for the assessment of whether the claim exists, and whether the amount of the claim and its place in the hierarchy of claims asserted by the creditor are correct, such a situation constitutes grounds for rebutting the claim, not grounds for remedying the defects of the application. II. If the bankruptcy trustee or any of the bankruptcy creditors rebut an unenforceable claim of the bankruptcy creditor (applicant) and the creditor lodges a timely motion to declare the existence or amount of their unenforceable claim or its place in the hierarchy of claims and describes in the motion (or at any later stage of the proceedings initiated by the motion) the relevant circumstances that were already contained in the creditor's application and includes any other necessary statements relevant under the substantive law for the creditor's success in the incidental dispute (for evidencing that the claim exists, that its amount as entered by the creditor in the bankruptcy proceedings was correct or that the alleged place of the claim in the hierarchy of claims is correct), the creditor does not exceed the limits imposed on allegations contained in their motion by the first sentence of Section 23(2) of Act No. 328/1991 Coll., as amended. III. The description of the relevant circumstances can – indirectly – originate from a reference to a document enclosed by the claimant with their motion.*

[378] This decision is available online on the SC website at http://www.nsoud.cz/Judikatura/judikatura_ns.nsf/WebSearch/5ABA070698021B19C1257A4E006601DA?openDocument

29 Cdo 506/2007.[379] All of the above rulings were rendered under the previous law, but continue to apply under the regime of the InsAct.

&Highlight=0; in this decision, the court ruled as follows (cit.): *The conclusion that the description of the relevant circumstances can indirectly originate from a reference to a document enclosed by the claimant (as evidence) with their motion, to which the claimant explicitly refers in the text of their, is an exception to the principle that the description of the decisive facts of the case should be incorporated in the motion itself (Section 79(1) of the CCP), and as such, it should be applied restrictively. Apart from the requirement that the reference in the motion must clearly indicate that the attached documentary evidence is a document that describes the facts underlying the claim, only the said conclusion should apply, unless the necessary description of the relevant circumstances is contained in the motion itself. If the relevant fact is described in the motion, the fact that the documentary evidence enclosed with the motion does not support the statements (allegations) in the motion does not render the motion defective, but can result in a conclusion that the claimant has failed to prove the alleged fact by such evidence.* Note: The summary of the SC's legal opinion (*ratio decidendi*) was adopted from the SC website.

[379] This decision is available online on the SC website at http://www.nsoud.cz/Judikatura/ judikatura_ns.nsf/WebSearch/2A904812EB9C0E1CC1257A4E00691593?openDocument& Highlight=0; in this decision, the court ruled as follows (cit.): *In its Judgment of January 30, 2003 in Case No. 29 Cdo 1089/2000 published in Soudní judikatura [Court Reports] No. 2, 2003 ed., No. 35, the Supreme Court has also explained that the creditor's application in bankruptcy proceedings is a pleading that has the nature of a motion (lawsuit), and if the application whereby the creditor's claim is entered in the bankruptcy proceedings contains data that unmistakably identify the act (factual circumstances), on the basis of which the creditor enters their (pecuniary) claim in the bankruptcy proceedings, but the bankruptcy creditor (applicant) failed to describe at or before the end of the review hearing any and all circumstances important for the assessment of whether the claim exists, and whether the amount of the claim and its place in the hierarchy of claims are correct, such a situation constitutes grounds for rebutting the claim, not grounds for remedying the defects of the application. If the bankruptcy trustee or any of the bankruptcy creditors rebut an unenforceable claim of the bankruptcy creditor (applicant) and the creditor lodges a timely motion to declare the existence or amount of their unenforceable claim or its place in the hierarchy of claims and describes in the motion (or at any later stage of the proceedings initiated by the motion) the relevant circumstances that were already contained in the creditor's application, and includes any other necessary statements relevant under the substantive law for the creditor's success in the incidental dispute (for evidencing that the claim exists, that its amount as entered by the creditor in the bankruptcy proceedings was correct or that the alleged place of the claim in the hierarchy of claims is correct), the creditor does not exceed the limits imposed on allegations contained in their motion by the first sentence of Section 23(2) of the BCA. From this perspective, it is legally irrelevant that the bankruptcy creditor enters their claim as a claim arising from a contract, not a claim arising from unjust enrichment. The rule that applies to common disputes also applies to the review of claims in an incidental dispute within the framework of bankruptcy proceedings, i.e. if the court concludes that the contract is invalid, on which the claim*

16.73. The SC therefore concluded that the decision of the appellate court was not correct. Consequently, the SC vacated the decision of the appellate court and remanded the case for further hearing and a new decision.

[Further Conclusions and Comments Concerning Annotated Judgment of SC]:

16.74. It may prima facie appear that the decision only has a marginal connection to arbitration, and rather contains general conclusions concerning insolvency proceedings, as such; this is not entirely true, though. This decision attempts to define the limits of review of enforceable claims by the insolvency trustee and within the framework of incidental disputes. In this respect, the articulated rules will apply generally, and will also be applicable to the decisions of lower courts. Nonetheless, we may still make some comments in relation to arbitration. Firstly, there should be no further doubt that, as concerns the filing of applications, whereby creditors enter their claims, arbitral awards must be on par with judgments of courts, and consequently, claims arising from arbitral awards can be entered as enforceable claims and should be treated as such in the course of insolvency proceedings. However automatic this conclusion might seem, it is not the case, because we have witnessed situations in practice where the insolvency courts refused to recognize claims as enforceable, while referring to the second sentence of Section 177 of the InsAct, which stipulates that the enforceability of a claim must be attested to by a public deed. The courts often invoked Section 134 of the CCP[380] in the past, and argued that an arbitral award (despite the fact that it is otherwise enforceable, just like a judicial decision) did not have the quality of a public deed, because it was not explicitly designated as such by the legislator. The rules incorporated in Act No. 89/2012 Coll., the new Civil Code, do not clarify this issue either; Section 567 defines a

---

entered by the creditor is based, or that the contract never existed, the court must consider whether the identification of the act in the application and in the motion initiating the incidental proceedings allows the court to conclude that the claim entered by the creditor is justified under any other legal grounds (such as unjust enrichment or damages). A different legal classification of the same act does not change the legal grounds underlying the claim entered by the creditor, and the appellant (in the SC proceedings) errs if he advocates the contrary conclusion in the given case (cf. also Judgment of the Supreme Court of December 18, 2008 in Case No. 29 Odo 729/2006, published in Soudní judikatura [Court Reports] No. 6, 2009 ed., No. 90).

[380] *(Cit.): Documents issued by courts of the Czech Republic or any other state authorities intra vires, as well as documents declared public by any special laws or regulations, confirm that the regulation or declaration was made by the authority which issued the document and, unless proven otherwise, that the facts attested to or confirmed in the document are truthful.*

public deed as a document issued by a public authority *intra vires,* or a document that is designated as a public deed by statute. This does not apply if the document exhibits defects that result in the document not being considered a public deed. Consequently, there should be no further doubt as to how the arbitral award should be handled in insolvency proceedings. Indeed, a contrary interpretation would be absurd, because if the debtor were found insolvent, the creditor would be in the same situation as if no arbitration had ever taken place, and would be facing the obligation to prove the existence of the claim anew. Section 28(2) of the ArbAct[381] explicitly stipulates that as soon as the arbitral award is served, it has the effects of a final and conclusive court decision, and is enforceable by court (unless the award can be reviewed following the procedure under Section 27 of the ArbAct,[382] or unless a motion to annul the award was lodged pursuant to Section 31 of the ArbAct[383] and the court suspended its enforceability). It would be paradoxical if the effects and the enforceability of an arbitral award depended solely on the debtor's financial situation and whether or not the debtor's assets will be subject to the insolvency proceedings, especially if we consider the fact that the creditor can by no means influence such circumstances, and would have significantly worse standing than the standing enjoyed in the insolvency proceedings by creditors who asserted their claims in civil proceedings.

16.75. The second comment does not focus so much on the general conclusions reached by the SC, which can be considered correct, as on their application to this particular case. The decision of the SC, without addressing this issue in any manner, has opened the issue of the nature of the decision-making following the principles of equity in terms of Section 25 of the ArbAct.[384] Lawyers have extensively discussed this topic, especially as concerns the question of whether and to what extent the arbitrators are, in such case, bound by statutes. If we base our considerations on the premise that making decisions following the principles of equity does not mean absolute freedom of the arbitrators to make any decision whatsoever (without the arbitrator being obliged in such case to support their decision with any reasons), it can be expected that the arbitrators will base their assessment regarding the equitable arrangement of the parties' obligation (relationship) on the otherwise applicable laws and regulations, at least with regard to the

---

[381] The provision is quoted above in the opening part of this annotation.

[382] The provision is quoted above in the opening part of this annotation.

[383] The provision is quoted above in the opening part of this annotation.

[384] The provision is quoted above in the opening part of this annotation.

principle of legal certainty and the legitimate expectations of the parties (it is hardly conceivable that a particular arrangement of the parties' rights and obligations will be found equitable if the parties could not have, considering all of the circumstances of the case, envisaged such an arrangement, not even as a hypothetical possibility). In this regard, decision-making following the principles of equity can be perceived as the possibility to opt for a different solution, where the application of laws and regulations would for some reason appear inappropriate, whether or not the respective provisions are binding (a different situation would probably occur if the provisions were imperative rules or rules on which public policy is based).[385] The SC ruled in the annotated decision that the assessment of whether or not the given decision contains any legal assessment of the case cannot be based on the agreement incorporated in the arbitration clause (i.e. it is not possible to conclude that the arbitral award lacks a legal assessment of the case if the arbitration clause empowers the arbitrator to make decisions following the principles of equity), but on the actual procedure adopted by the arbitrators. However logical this conclusion appears at first glance, it does not take account of the specific features of the decision-making following the principles of equity. The reason is that the arbitrators are entirely free to conclude that the most equitable solution appears to be resolving the dispute in compliance with, or otherwise having regard to, the applicable laws and regulations. A literal interpretation of the SC decision would entail that the insolvency trustee would in such case enjoy a significantly limited possibility of rebutting an enforceable claim that was created as mentioned above, because any and all of the trustee's objections would be perceived as a different legal assessment of the case, which, however, the trustee is not entitled to plead under Section 199 of the InsAct.[386] But this conclusion is rather questionable – the respective decision is made because the arbitrator considers the arrangement enshrined in the legal rule as more equitable, not because they assess the legal aspects of the case and apply the corresponding rule. However, this is not a legal assessment of

---

[385] However, it is not the purpose of this note to define the limits of the decision-making following the principles of equity. The issue has been extensively discussed by legal professionals and academics, and many have argued that when making decisions following the principles of equity, the arbitrators are not bound by anything, and it is at their unlimited discretion which approach they opt for, and they cannot be expected to take into account the applicable laws. Our main aim is to prove that the instances will not be isolated in which this method of decision-making will involve due regard for the applicable laws and regulations.

[386] The provision is quoted above in the opening part of this annotation.

the case, because the arbitrator is not bound to apply the legal rule and could have opted for a different solution based on the same factual circumstances.

16.76. Last, but not least, the conclusion of the court is rather controversial as concerns its finding that the respective case involved a confessed judgment in terms of Section 114b of the CCP,[387] or that this was the legal assessment applied to the case, including the conclusion regarding the validity of the contract or, as the case may be, its compliance with laws and regulations in terms of Section 153a(2) of the CCP[388] in conjunction with Section 99(2) of the CCP.[389] The reason is that the decision refers to the reasonable application of the CCP based on Section 30 of the ArbAct,[390] but also on the application of the Rules issued by a private arbitral company. It is unclear which circumstances have contributed to the SC's conclusion that the decision in the form of a default judgment implied the assessment of whether or not the asserted claim was legitimate (see Section 99(2) of the CCP[391]), because the arbitral award[392] refers exclusively to Section 114b of the CCP.[393] If the arbitrator was entitled to make decisions following the principles of equity, and especially if the arbitrator had such powers, it was at the arbitrator's discretion which criteria they would choose for issuing the confessed judgment, and we cannot automatically presume that the decision was made after the arbitrator had concluded that the asserted claim was not contrary to law, including the conclusion regarding the validity of the respective contract.[394] It is similarly questionable to infer any legal assessment of the case from the arbitrators' call for settlement, especially (though not exclusively) considering the increased obligation of the arbitrators to induce the parties to reach a settlement (see Section 24(1) of the ArbAct). The assessment of the

---

[387] The provision is quoted above in the opening part of this annotation.

[388] The provision is quoted above in the opening part of this annotation.

[389] The provision is quoted above in the opening part of this annotation.

[390] The provision is quoted above in the opening part of this annotation.

[391] The provision is quoted above in the opening part of this annotation.

[392] As quoted in the annotated decision.

[393] The provision is quoted above in the opening part of this annotation.

[394] The author intentionally refrains from opening the debate regarding another aspect, namely the excesses of private arbitral companies, which have issued Rules that often contained provisions allowing the arbitrators to render a confessed judgment or a default judgment, whether or not the claimant's claim was legitimate. It was argued that it was an issue falling within the management of the proceedings, which the parties are free to agree on in terms of Section 19 of the ArbAct, and their agreement may also contain a submission to the Rules of a private arbitral company.

claim (whether it is legitimate) is based on the factual contents of the claim, and the mere question asked by the arbitrators and addressed to the parties regarding a potential settlement cannot be deemed to imply any preliminary assessment of the merits of the dispute with a conclusion that the asserted claim is legitimate. Besides, the fact that the settlement is legitimate does not necessarily imply that the asserted claim is also legitimate. For instance, the parties are free to agree that the claimant will drop their claim and withdraw their request for arbitration (if the claimant acknowledges that they did not have the claim), and the other party will simultaneously waive their claim for reimbursement of the already incurred costs associated with the dispute, which the party could otherwise claim. Moreover, if the arbitration clause empowered the arbitrator to resolve the dispute following the principles of equity, the terms of the settlement could in such case have been agreed by the parties as they saw fit. Again, the conclusion is not justified that the settlement would require the fulfillment of all conditions posed by the CCP.

| | |

8. Judgment of Supreme Court CR of August 30, 2013 in Case No. 30 Cdo 2011/2013:[395] (i) Negotiating Arbitration Clause, (ii) Separability of Arbitration Clause from Main Agreement, (iii) Termination of Court Proceedings If Party Pleads Existence of Arbitration Clause

Abbreviations Used:

AC   Arbitration Court at the Economic Chamber of the Czech Republic and Agricultural Chamber of the Czech Republic[396]

---

[395] This decision is available online on the website of the SC at http://www.nsoud.cz/ Judikatura/judikatura_ns.nsf/WebSearch/54F633D4912F8F5AC1257BE20033698D?open Document&Highlight=0, [last accessed on November 5, 2014]. The annotated decision of the SC was subsequently vacated by Judgment of the ConCourt Case No. IV. ÚS 3402/13 but as we have mentioned in the closing notes and comments in the final part of this annotation, it is reasonable to assume, considering the reasons for the decision of the ConCourt, that the conclusions articulated by the SC have not been undermined by the ConCourt (for the purposes of this annotation). This is the reason why the SC decision was also chosen for annotation despite the fact that the decision itself was vacated and the developments in the dispute after the ConCourt decision are unknown.

[396] For more information regarding this permanent arbitral institution, see www.soud.cz.

ArbAct	Act of the Czech Republic No. 216/1994 Coll., on Arbitration and the Enforcement of Arbitral Awards, as amended[397]
CC	Act of the Czech Republic No. 89/2012 Coll., the Civil Code[398]
CCP	Act of the Czech Republic No. 99/1963 Coll., the Code of Civil Procedure, as amended
CivC	Act of the Czech Republic No. 40/1964 Coll., the Civil Code, as amended[399]
CJEU	Court of Justice of the European Union
ConCourt	Constitutional Court of the Czech Republic
SC	Supreme Court of the Czech Republic

Key Words:

(doing) business | arbitration agreement[400] | arbitration clause[401] | B2C dispute | consumer | consumer protection | Court of Justice of the European Union (CJEU) | EU law | European Court of Justice | financial distress | future business | good faith | jurisdiction of court | loan | main agreement/contract | mental disorder | powers (jurisdiction) of arbitrator | procedural law | real property | security transfer of rights |

---

[397] The decision of the SC in this case is based on the ArbAct in effect until March 31, 2012, but no subsequent changes have any bearing on the conclusions of the SC and their applicability; this particular case does not involve a consumer contract or, as applicable, a dispute arising from a consumer contract, and the rules introduced in the ArbAct by the Consumer Amendment, i.e. Act No. 19/2012 Coll., would not affect the case at hand. Generally, however, it is necessary to point out that the conclusions made by the court shall not apply to disputes arising from consumer contracts after the passing of Act No. 19/2012 Coll. (or rather the amendment codified the enhanced consumer protection but the SC already mentioned the specific aspects of consumer protection in the annotated decision and inferred that the SC would apply these aspects to a consumer dispute).

[398] This Act has replaced Act No. 40/1964 Coll., the "old Civil Code" (abbreviated as the "CivC" in this annotation), with effect since January 1, 2014. However, legal relationships established before January 1, 2014 shall be governed (save for certain exceptions) by the previous law, i.e. the "CivC".

[399] This Act has been replaced by Act No. 89/2012 Coll., "new Civil Code" (abbreviated as "CC" in this annotation), with effect since 1 January 2014. However, legal relationships established before 1 January 2014 shall be governed (save for certain exceptions) by the previous law, i.e. Act No. 40/1964 Coll., Civil Code, as subsequently amended (abbreviated as "CivC" in this annotation).

[400] Depending on the context, "arbitration clause" and "arbitration agreement" may also be interpreted as synonyms, or rather the arbitration clause is a form of arbitration agreement according to Section 2 of the ArbAct.

[401] Depending on the context, "arbitration clause" and "arbitration agreement" may also be interpreted as synonyms, or rather the arbitration clause is a form of arbitration agreement according to Section 2 of the ArbAct.

separability of arbitration clause | substantive law | termination of proceedings | validity of a juridical act | validity of an arbitration agreement[402] | validity of an arbitration clause[403] |

Applicable Laws and Regulations:
ArbAct: Section 2(4),[404] Section 3,[405] Section 7[406]

---

[402] Depending on the context, "arbitration clause" and "arbitration agreement" may also be interpreted as synonyms, or rather the arbitration clause is a form of arbitration agreement according to Section 2 of the ArbAct.

[403] Depending on the context, "arbitration clause" and "arbitration agreement" may also be interpreted as synonyms, or rather the arbitration clause is a form of the arbitration agreement according to Section 2 of the ArbAct.

[404] ArbAct, Section 2(4) (cit.): *Unless the arbitration agreement stipulates otherwise, it governs both the rights directly arising from the legal relationships and the issue of legal validity of these legal relationships, as well as any rights associated with the aforementioned rights.* Note: This version of the law applied to the respective proceedings, but it has not been subject to any modifications in the meantime and therefore continues to apply.

[405] ArbAct, Section 3 (cit.): *(1) The arbitration agreement must be executed in writing; otherwise it is invalid. The arbitration agreement is also considered executed in writing if it is negotiated by telegraph, fax or any electronic means which provide a record of the terms of the agreement and the identification of the individuals or entities who concluded the arbitration agreement. (2) However, if the arbitration clause is incorporated in the terms and conditions governing the main contract to which the arbitration clause applies, the arbitration clause is also considered validly negotiated if a written offer of the main contract with the arbitration clause was accepted by the other party in any manner clearly indicating the latter party's consent with the terms of the arbitration agreement.* Note: This version of the provision applied to the respective proceedings; the currently applicable version reads as follows (cit.): *(1) The arbitration agreement must be executed in writing; otherwise it is invalid. The arbitration agreement is also considered executed in writing if it is negotiated by telegraph, fax or any electronic means which provide a record of the terms of the agreement and the identification of the individuals or entities who concluded the arbitration agreement. (2) However, if the arbitration clause is incorporated in the terms and conditions governing the main contract to which the arbitration clause applies, the arbitration clause is also considered validly negotiated if a written offer of the main contract with the arbitration clause was accepted by the other party in any manner clearly indicating the latter party's consent with the terms of the arbitration agreement. (3) An arbitration agreement for the resolution of disputes arising from consumer contracts must be negotiated separately, not integrated in the terms and conditions governing the main contract; otherwise the arbitration agreement is invalid. (4) The professional shall provide the consumer with a proper explanation reasonably preceding the conclusion of the arbitration clause so that the consumer can assess the potential consequences of the conclusion of the arbitration clause for the consumer. Proper explanation shall be interpreted as meaning the explication of all consequences of the arbitration clause. (5) The arbitration clause concluded pursuant to subsection (3) must also contain truthful,*

CCP: Section 104,[407] Section 106[408]

---

accurate and complete information on: (a) the arbitrator or the fact that the arbitral award will be delivered by a permanent arbitral institution, (b) the manner in which the arbitral proceedings are to be commenced and conducted, (c) the fee paid to the arbitrator and the anticipated types of costs the consumer may incur in the arbitral proceedings, and the rules for successfully claiming compensation for such costs, (d) the seat of arbitration, (e) the method of service of the arbitral award on the consumer, and (f) the fact that a final and conclusive arbitral award is enforceable. (6) If the arbitration clause vests the jurisdiction to resolve the dispute in a permanent arbitral institution, the requirement under subsection (5) is also fulfilled by a reference to the statutes and rules of permanent arbitral institutions issued under Section 13. Note: The modifications introduced by Act No. 19/2012 Coll. have no bearing on the case at hand, because the SC reached an unequivocal conclusion that the given case did not involve a dispute arising from a consumer contract and Section 3 et seq. would therefore not apply to the respective relationship. Besides, it is necessary to point out that even if it were a dispute arising from a consumer contract, the changes would not apply to this particular case. The reason is that the transitional provisions of Act No. 19/2012 Coll. (Article II(2)) stipulate that the validity of the arbitration agreement is governed by the ArbAct in effect on the day on which the arbitration agreement was concluded (entered into).

[406] ArbAct, Section 7 (cit.): *(1) The arbitration agreement should, as a rule, determine the number of arbitrators and their identity, or stipulate the method whereby the number and the identity of the arbitrators shall be determined. The final number of arbitrators must always be odd. (2) If the arbitration agreement lacks the determination pursuant to subsection (1), each party shall appoint one arbitrator and these arbitrators shall elect the chairman of the panel.* Note: This version of the provision applied to the respective proceedings; the currently applicable version reads as follows (cit.): *(1) The arbitration agreement should, as a rule, determine the number of arbitrators and their identity, or stipulate the method whereby the number and the identity of the arbitrators shall be determined. The arbitrator may also be selected by a person agreed upon by the parties or following a method of appointment specified in the rules on arbitration pursuant to Section 19(4).The final number of arbitrators must always be odd. (2) If the arbitration agreement lacks the determination pursuant to subsection (1), each party shall appoint one arbitrator and these arbitrators shall elect the chairman of the panel.* Note: It is true that the SC in the respective proceedings examined the terms of the arbitration clause, including the method of appointing the arbitrator, but the Court reached the unequivocal conclusion that the ad hoc arbitrator was directly identified in the arbitration clause and the requirements of the law, as currently applicable, would therefore be fulfilled.

[407] CCP, Section 104 (cit.): *(1) If a procedural requirement is not fulfilled and the deficiency cannot be remedied, the court terminates the proceedings. If the courts lack jurisdiction over the case or if different proceedings must precede court proceedings, the court forwards the case, after the resolution on termination of the proceedings becomes final and conclusive, to the competent authority, without prejudice to the legal effects associated with the filing of the lawsuit (motion to commence the proceedings). (2) If a procedural requirement is not fulfilled and the deficiency can be remedied, the court adopts suitable measures. The court can usually continue the proceedings, but may not decide on the merits. If the court fails to remedy the*

deficiency in the procedural requirements, the court terminates the proceedings. Note: This version of the law applied to the respective proceedings, but it has not been subject to any modifications in the meantime and therefore continues to apply.

[408] CCP, Section 106 (cit.): *(1) As soon as the court discovers, on the respondent's objection lodged together with or before the first act of the respondent on the merits, that the agreement of the parties requires that the case be submitted to arbitrators, the court must desist from further examination of the case and terminate the proceedings; the court, however, hears the case if the parties declare that they waive the agreement. The court also hears the case if the court determines that the matter is not arbitrable under the laws of the Czech Republic, or that the arbitration agreement is invalid or non-existent, or that examining the agreement in arbitration exceeds the scope of jurisdiction vested in the arbitrators by the agreement, or that the arbitral tribunal refused to hear the case. (2) If the court proceedings under Subsection (1) were terminated and the same case was submitted to arbitrators, the original motion to commence the proceedings retains its legal effects, provided that the motion to commence the arbitral proceedings is lodged no later than within 30 days of receipt of the court's resolution terminating the proceedings. (3) If the arbitral proceedings were opened before the court proceedings, the court stays the proceedings on the non-existence, invalidity or expiration/termination of the agreement until the arbitrator(s) decide on their jurisdiction over the case or on the merits.* Note: This version of the provision applied to the respective proceedings; the currently applicable version reads as follows (cit.): *(1) As soon as the court discovers, on the respondent's objection lodged together with or before the first act of the respondent on the merits, that the agreement of the parties requires that the case be submitted to arbitrators or to an arbitral committee of an association, the court must desist from further examination of the case and terminate the proceedings; the court, however, hears the case if the parties declare that they waive the agreement or that they do not insist on having the case heard by the arbitral committee of the association. The court also hears the case if the court determines that the matter is not arbitrable under the laws of the Czech Republic, or that the arbitration agreement is invalid or non-existent, or that examining the agreement in arbitration exceeds the scope of jurisdiction vested in the arbitrators by the agreement, or that the arbitral tribunal refused to hear the case. (2) If the court proceedings under Subsection (1) were terminated and the same case was submitted to arbitrators or to the arbitral committee of the association, the original motion to commence the proceedings retains its legal effects, provided that the motion to commence the proceedings before the arbitrators or the arbitral committee of the association is lodged no later than within 30 days of receipt of the court's resolution terminating the proceedings. (3) If the arbitral proceedings were opened before the court proceedings, the court stays the proceedings on the non-existence, invalidity or expiration/termination of the agreement until the arbitrator(s) decide on their jurisdiction over the case or on the merits.* Note: The new law has only re-formulated the provisions in connection with the new possibility to submit one's disputes to an arbitral committee of associations (although it is necessary to point out that the implementation of the changes is not consistent). The procedure adopted by the court if a party pleads the existence of an arbitration agreement after the commencement of the proceedings is the same, and consequently, the implemented changes have no bearing on the SC's conclusion.

CivC: Section 38(2),[409] Section 52,[410] Section 57(2) and (3)[411]
CC: Section 419,[412] Section 581,[413] Section 1810,[414] Section 1820(1)(f),[415] Section 1829(2)[416]

---

[409] CivC, Section 38(2) (cit.): *A juridical act is also invalid if it is performed by a person acting under the influence of a mental disorder that renders the person incapable of the juridical act.* Note: This is the version of the law applicable to the respective proceedings. January 1, 2014 is the effective date of the CC, which regulates the said issue in Section 581 (the provision is quoted below in the opening part of this annotation).

[410] CivC, Section 52 (cit.): *(1) Consumer contracts include purchase contracts, contracts for work, or any other contracts in which one of the parties to the contract is a consumer and the other party is a supplier. (2) A supplier means a person who, in executing and performing the contract, is acting within the framework of their trade or any other business activity. (3) A consumer is a natural person who, in executing and performing the contract, acts outside their trade or any other business capacity, or outside their profession.* Note: This is the version of the law applicable to the respective proceedings. January 1, 2014 is the effective date of the CC, which regulates the said issues in Sections 419 and 1810 (both provisions are quoted below in the opening part of this annotation).

[411] CivC, Section 57(2) and (3) (cit.): *(2) The supplier must inform the consumer in writing and at or before the execution of the contract of the consumer's right to rescind the contract; the written information must also identify the individual or entity with whom the right must be exercised, including the place of residence or registered office of the individual or entity. (3) If the obligation stipulated in the preceding paragraph is breached, the consumer has the right to rescind the contract within 1 year of the execution thereof.* Note: This is the version of the law applicable to the respective proceedings. January 1, 2014 is the effective date of the CC, which has no particular equivalent provision, because it contains no separate special rules regulating the rescission of consumer contracts entered into outside the premises commonly used for the supplier's business. Consequently, we must apply rules that cover these cases, as well as distance contracts executed by means of communication – Section 1820(1)(f) of the CC in conjunction with Section 1829(2) of the CC (these provisions are quoted below in the opening part of this annotation). However, these provisions are not relevant for the assessment of the case itself, because the SC has arrived at the unambiguous conclusion that this is not a relationship that would involve a consumer.

[412] CC, Section 419 (cit.): *A consumer is a man or a woman who enters into a contract or deals with a professional outside their trade or profession.*

[413] CC, Section 581 (cit.): *If a person does not have full legal capacity, juridical actions of which they are incapable are invalid. Juridical action is also invalid if it is performed by a person acting under the influence of a mental disorder that renders the person incapable of the juridical action.*

[414] CC, Section 1810 (cit.): *The provisions of this Part shall apply to contracts entered into by and between a consumer and a professional ("consumer contracts") and to any obligations arising from such contracts.*

[415] CC, Section 1820(1)(f) (cit.): *If the parties negotiate with the aim of entering into a contract, and if the professional, in negotiating the contract, uses exclusively one or more means of communication that enable the execution of the contract without the simultaneous*

The Supreme Court of the Czech Republic reached the following principal conclusions:

(1) The determination of whether a party is a consumer or not depends on the actual purpose of the acts performed by the parties, not only on their formal status. A consumer is primarily defined as a person acting outside their profession or business. Consequently, a person is a consumer if they act for their private needs, meaning consumption, primarily their own; but by necessity, it also covers the consumption of other individuals, such as the consumer's children, spouse and family. The fact itself that a natural person is not a professional (entrepreneur) does not entail that they must be protected as a consumer.[417]

(2) Section 2(4) of the ArbAct[418] provides that unless the arbitration agreement stipulates otherwise, it governs both the rights directly arising from the legal relationships [juridical acts] and the issue of the legal validity of these legal relationships [juridical acts], as well as any rights associated with the aforementioned rights.[419]

---

physical presence of the parties ("means of distance communication"), or if such negotiation is aimed at executing the contract outside the premises commonly used by the professional for their business, the professional shall also inform the consumer with sufficient advance notice preceding the execution of the contract or the consumer's binding offer of the conditions, time period and procedures for exercising the right to rescind the contract (if the consumer has the right to rescind the contract), as well as the form for rescinding the contract, the essential terms of which are stipulated by implementing legislation.

[416] CC, Section 1829(2) (cit.): *Unless the consumer was informed about their right to rescind the contract in compliance with Section 1820(1)(f), the consumer may rescind the contract within one year and fourteen days of the day on which the time period for rescission started to run pursuant to Subsection (1). However, if the consumer was informed of their right to rescind the contract within the above time period, the fourteen-day time period for rescission starts to run from the day on which the consumer received the information.*

[417] In connection with these conclusions, the SC invokes the case law of the CJEU, specifically the decision of the Court of Justice (Sixth Chamber) of July 3, 1997 in Case C-269/95, **Francesco Benincasa v Dentalkit Srl.**, available at http://eur-lex.europa.eu/legal-content/EN/TXT/?uri=CELEX:61995CJ0269, in which the CJ reached the following conclusion (cit.): *Consequently, only contracts concluded for the purpose of satisfying an individual's own needs in terms of private consumption come under the provisions designed to protect the consumer as the party deemed to be the weaker party economically. The specific protection sought to be afforded by those provisions is unwarranted in the case of contracts for the purpose of trade or professional activity, even if that activity is only planned for the future, since the fact that an activity is in the nature of a future activity does not divest it in any way of its trade or professional character.*

[418] This provision is quoted in the opening part of the annotation of this SC decision.

[419] In connection with these conclusions, the SC referred to its previous case law, namely its judgment of December 19 2007 in Case No. 29 Odo 1222/2005, available on the website

(3) **The jurisdiction on the part of the court is one of the procedural requirements, the absence of which results in termination of the proceedings pursuant to Section 104(1) of the CCP.[420]/[421] The court lacks the jurisdiction to hear a particular case if the case is excluded by law from the jurisdiction of courts until other proceedings before a different authority[422] are completed, or if the case is to be submitted to arbitration according to the agreement of the parties, subject to the conditions stipulated in Section 106(1) of the CCP.[423] Section 106(1) of the CCP[424] principally differs from the general provisions regulating the non-fulfillment of procedural requirements under Section 104 of the CCP[425] only in that the court does not examine the absence of the procedural requirement by its own motion, but only following an objection raised by the respondent in a timely manner, whereby the respondent properly pleaded the absence of the court's jurisdiction.**

[*From Facts of Case*]:

16.77. On September 14, 2009, the parties entered into a loan agreement and an agreement on the security transfer of rights to real property; the latter agreement served as security for the former. The parties agreed in the said agreements that any and all property disputes between the parties shall be resolved in ad hoc arbitration; at the same time, the parties made a direct determination of the single arbitrator. As regards case management (procedure), the parties referred to the AC Rules.[426]

---

of the SC at http://www.nsoud.cz/Judikatura/judikatura_ns.nsf/WebSearch/4C94F8F661E 38E71C1257A4E0066A146?openDocument&Highlight=0, in which the SC held as follows (cit.): *Unless the cause of invalidity applies to the arbitration clause covering the disputes under that contract, the invalidity of the contract does not affect the validity of the arbitration clause. If the arbitration clause (agreement) concerns all future disputes arising from a particular legal relationship (contract), it also covers a dispute over the determination of the invalidity of a rescission (cancellation) of the contract.* Note: The summary of the SC's legal opinion (*ratio decidendi*) was adopted from the SC website.

[420] This provision is quoted in the opening part of the annotation of this SC decision.

[421] It is necessary to point out that the doctrine applied in continental law and in principally all countries of Central and Eastern Europe classifies the issue of jurisdiction as the subject matter of procedural law, not the subject matter of substantive law.

[422] The term "different authority" must also be interpreted as meaning an arbitral tribunal.

[423] This provision is quoted in the opening part of the annotation of this SC decision.

[424] This provision is quoted in the opening part of the annotation of this SC decision.

[425] This provision is quoted in the opening part of the annotation of this SC decision.

[426] The description of the facts of the case contained in the annotated decision suggests that the proceedings were not conducted at the AC, but the parties merely agreed to use the

The claimant[427] subsequently rescinded the abovementioned agreements; the other party disagreed. The claimant pleaded the invalidity (nullity) of the agreements and commenced civil court proceedings for the declaration of invalidity of the agreements or, as applicable and in consequence of the invalidity of the agreements, for the determination of the (ownership) title to the real property securing the loan. The claimant argued in her motion that consumer protection law was violated, namely Section 57(3) of the CivC[428] (the claimant invoked the said grounds as reasons for her rescission of the agreements). However, the respondent invoked the above-described arbitration clause, pleaded a lack of jurisdiction on the part of the court and thereby demanded that the court proceed pursuant to Section 106 of the CCP.[429]

[*Procedure of Case*]:

16.78. The Prague 5 District Court, as the court of first instance, rendered a Resolution of October 20, 2011 in Case No. 6 C 605/2009-236, whereby the court terminated the proceedings initiated by the motion to declare the (ownership) title to the respective real property. The court applied Section 106 of the CCP[430] and concluded that the plea of the lack of jurisdiction was legitimate, because the agreements entered into by the parties on September 14, 2009, i.e. the loan agreement and the agreement for the security transfer of rights, contain an arbitration clause; the clause was found intelligible and serious-minded by the court of first instance (and it was therefore found valid).[431]

16.79. The Prague Municipal Court, as the appellate court, upheld the abovementioned Resolution of the Prague 5 District Court.[432] The court

---

procedural regulations of this permanent arbitral institution. Consequently, the agreement must be interpreted as the parties' agreement on case management in terms Section 19(1) of the ArbAct, not as a reference to the applicable Rules of the permanent arbitral institution.

[427] A natural person, although it is not explicitly mentioned in the annotated decision; we can infer that the person is a citizen of the Czech Republic and has her address/place of residence in the territory of the Czech Republic. The respondent is a legal entity formed and existing under the laws of the Czech Republic in the form of a common-interest association of legal entities.

[428] The provision is quoted above in the opening part of this annotation.

[429] The provision is quoted above in the opening part of this annotation.

[430] The provision is quoted above in the opening part of this annotation.

[431] The validity of a juridical act requires that the juridical act be intelligible and serious, as well as unambiguous. It should be noted that, with effect since the January 1, 2014, the CC introduced in Czech civil law less rigorous criteria for the assessment of the "unambiguousness" of a juridical act; juridical acts are traditionally assessed more rigidly under the laws of the countries of Central and Eastern Europe.

[432] Namely by the resolution of October 31, 2012 in Case No. 72 Co 130/2012-293.

agreed with the legal assessment articulated by the court of first instance, and also approved of the lower court's findings of fact. The courts based their decisions on the finding that by signing the request for the loan and during the negotiations between the parties preceding the signing of the agreements, the claimant had repeatedly demonstrated towards the respondent her clear intention to spend the finances drawn under the loan agreement solely for the purpose of her intended business; consequently, the agreement cannot fall within the category of consumer contracts in terms of Section 52(1) of the CivC.[433] Considering the above conclusion, the court held that Section 57(3) of the CivC,[434] invoked in the rescission of the agreements, could not be applied to the given case. The court also referred to the autonomous nature of arbitration clauses, which has the result that the asserted grounds evidencing the invalidity of the main agreements cannot entail the invalidity of the arbitration clauses incorporated therein. Last, but not least, the appellate court answered the objection that the agreements had been executed at a moment when the claimant suffered from a mental disorder, which would have rendered the agreements invalid under Section 38(2) of the CivC.[435] The court held that the conditions for applying that provision had not been fulfilled, which are stipulated in the SC Judgment of May 19, 2011 in Case No. 30 Cdo 5226/2009[436] and in the SC Judgment of February 15, 2012 in Case No.

---

[433] The provision is quoted above in the opening part of this annotation.

[434] The provision is quoted above in the opening part of this annotation.

[435] The provision is quoted above in the opening part of this annotation.

[436] Available online on the website of the SC at http://www.nsoud.cz/Judikatura/judikatura_ns.nsf/WebSearch/9434841F005F66FBC1257A4E00679DC2?openDocument&Highlight=0; the court reached the following conclusion (cit.): *I. The determination of whether the person performed the respective juridical act under the influence of a mental disorder is contingent on the assessment of circumstances that require expert knowledge in terms of Section 127(1) of the CCP. The court is obliged to enable the experts (psychiatrists, psychologists) in these cases to confront the results of their expert examination with the other findings made on the basis of evidence taken in the case, and to draw a reliable conclusion on the basis of the confrontation with respect to the degree to which the manifestations of the mental illness require that the person be deprived of their legal capacity or that the person's legal capacity be limited. To this end, the court is obliged to secure complete and reliable findings regarding the personal affairs of the examinee; a lack of such factual findings cannot be replaced by the experts' appraisal. Special emphasis must be placed on the requirement of collecting information about the examinee's behavior in everyday life, how the examinee takes care of their needs and the needs of their family, how they manage their finances, their behavior in the workplace, in various life situations, etc. The court does not proceed in compliance with the above requirements if the expert is*

30 Cdo 1560/2011,[437] because it was not possible to reach an unequivocal conclusion regarding the mental disorder, free from any considerations regarding the probability of the disorder.

16.80. The claimant appealed the Resolution of the appellate court; in her extraordinary appeal, the claimant argued that the arbitration clauses were invalid as a result of the invalidity of the main agreements on the

---

appointed and the expert appraisal requested at the very beginning of the proceedings, sometimes even during preparations for a hearing, before the court has collected the other materials necessary for its decision. If a person is to be deprived of their legal capacity, or if their legal capacity is to be limited, the court is primarily obliged to hear and read such evidence before the expert evidence is examined, which would clarify the behavior and the conduct in everyday situations of the person who is to be deprived of their legal capacity or their entire legal capacity is to be limited. This is the only approach that will guarantee that the expert will have a sufficiently broad and reliable factual basis for their expert assessment. II. Invalidity of a juridical act under Section 38(2) of the CivC requires a reliable finding that the party to the juridical act is unable to assess the consequences of, or control, their acts. It is therefore impossible to reach any conclusions regarding acts performed under the influence of a mental disorder on the basis of probability or given such factual circumstances that, despite the evidentiary verification by the court in terms of Section 132 of the CCP, do not allow any unambiguous factual finding in the said regard that could be subject to the application of Section 38(2) of the CivC. An expert appraisal from the relevant field or branch is essential material in the proceedings, in which the court has to make an assessment of whether or not the respective juridical action of the natural person was performed under the influence of a mental disorder. Nonetheless, this does not absolve the court of the obligation to examine whether the report is complete and convincing when assessing the evidence in terms of Section 132 of the CCP, and to evaluate this particular piece of evidence – in the manner envisaged in Section 132 of the CCP – together with other pieces of evidence, and to have due regard for any and all circumstances that transpired during the proceedings, including the statements of the parties.

[437] This decision is available online on the website of the SC at http://www.nsoud.cz/ Judikatura/judikatura_ns.nsf/WebSearch/1084A121E2D676EBC1257A4E006713E7?open Document&Highlight=0; the court reached the following conclusion (cit.): *The court does not proceed properly if the court draws the conclusion of the invalidity of a juridical act of a deceased person based on the reason that the person performed the juridical act while suffering from a mental disorder that rendered the person incapable of the juridical act, on the basis of probability. The result of the evidentiary verification of all conceivable legally relevant means of evidence or, as applicable, the evidence proposed in the proceedings or the evidence that is necessary to establish the facts of the case and follows from the contents of the dossier (Section 120(3) of the CCP), must not, from the perspective of the fulfillment of the conditions for the application of Section 38(2) of the Civil Code, represent any potential or probable facts of the case, but must safely represent the established facts of the case, without any hint of probability, which facts of the case will be subsumable (for the identity of the established facts, on one hand, and the facts envisaged in the hypothesis of Section 38(2) of the Civil Code, on the other) under the said substantive-law rule.*

following grounds: (i) they had been entered into contrary to the statutory provisions regulating consumer contracts, (ii) the claimant had entered into the agreements/clauses acting under a false impression regarding their contents and significance originating from a deceit practiced by the respondent and the respondent's erroneous interpretation of their contents, (iii) they were *contra bonos mores,* because they fulfilled the criteria of usury, (iv) the claimant had entered into the agreements under the influence of a mental disorder, which is another reason why the arbitration clauses could not have been validly agreed, and (v) it was not established whether the agreements were signed by a person acting on behalf of the respondent who was properly authorized to do so. Conversely, the respondent argued that the grounds invoked by the claimant for the purpose of supporting her plea of invalidity of the main agreements should not apply in relation to the validity of the arbitration clauses. The SC held that the respective arbitration clauses were duly negotiated (executed) and are valid, including the appointment of the arbitrator. The SC also voiced an unequivocal conclusion that the respective case does not represent a B2C dispute, because the claimant intended to enter into the agreements as a future professional. As concerns the scope of application of the arbitration clause, the court concluded that unless the parties agree otherwise in their arbitration agreement, the arbitration clause applies in compliance with Section 2(4) of the ArbAct[438] to the rights directly arising from the respective legal relationships (mentioned in the arbitration clause), as well as to the issue of the legal validity of these legal relationships and the rights associated with the aforementioned rights. Considering the above said, the SC approved the procedure adopted by the appellate court and the application of Section 106 of the CCP.[439]

[*Arguments Presented by SC*]:

16.81. In its decision, the SC focused on three separate groups of issues; firstly, the validity and the scope of the arbitration clauses (i.e. whether the arbitration clauses also apply to the issue of the validity of the main agreements in which the clauses are incorporated). In this connection, the SC drew its conclusions directly from the rule enshrined in Section 2(4) of the ArbAct,[440] which provides a clear answer to the question (the law explicitly stipulates that unless the parties agree otherwise, the arbitration clause governs both the legal relationships directly arising

---

[438] The provision is quoted above in the opening part of this annotation.

[439] The provision is quoted above in the opening part of this annotation.

[440] The provision is quoted above in the opening part of this annotation.

from the respective agreements and the validity of these legal relationships, as well as any and all associated rights). The SC similarly referred to the case law that confirms these conclusions, namely Judgment of the SC of December 19, 2007 in Case No. 29 Odo 1222/2005.[441] The Supreme Court of the Czech Republic (SC) held that the proceedings themselves did not reveal anything that would suggest that the parties had limited the applicability of the arbitration clauses to any particular disputes; hence, there was no reason for the court to depart from the above-outlined conclusions. Another issue that was examined with respect to the arbitration clauses was the method of appointing the arbitrator, because the proceedings were *ad hoc* arbitration proceedings. The SC concluded that this aspect of the arbitration clause also complied with the principles incorporated in the decision of the Grand Panel of the SC of May 11, 2011 in Case No. 31 Cdo 1945/2010[442] – the arbitrator was directly identified in the arbitration clauses. The Supreme Court of the Czech Republic (SC) thereby upheld the existing case law, according to which the applicability of the conclusions articulated in the said decision is not limited to B2C disputes, but also applies to obligations (relationships) between professionals.

16.82. The Supreme Court of the Czech Republic (SC) also focused on the issue of whether the given case required the application of enhanced consumer protection with respect to the claimant. The reason is that the claimant argued throughout the proceedings that the given case involved a consumer relationship, and she had in fact invoked the provisions regulating consumer protection (see Section 57(3) of the CivC[443]) as grounds for her acts, primarily the rescission of the respective agreements. The Supreme Court of the Czech Republic (SC) held that the assessment of whether a particular contracting party is a consumer cannot be made on the basis of their formal status; it is necessary to have regard to the actual purpose of their acts, i.e. whether they meet their private needs/consumption in the given case, which can

---

[441] The decision is quoted above in the opening part of this annotation.

[442] This decision is available online on the website of the SC at http://www.nsoud.cz/ Judikatura/judikatura_ns.nsf/WebSearch/87312C808746B5D2C1257A4E006568D2?open Document&Highlight=0; the court reached the following conclusion (cit.): *If the arbitration agreement lacks any direct identification of an ad hoc arbitrator, or a specific description of the method of their appointment, and refers to "Rules on Arbitration" issued by a legal entity other than a permanent arbitral institution established under the law, the arbitration agreement is invalid pursuant to Section 39 of the Civil Code.* Note: The summary of the SC's legal opinion (*ratio decidendi*) was adopted from the SC website.

[443] The provision is quoted above in the opening part of this annotation.

be perceived as acts outside the individual's profession or business. In this connection, the Supreme Court of the Czech Republic (SC) invoked the decision of the European Court of Justice[444] (Sixth Chamber) of July 3, 1997 in Case C-269/95 (*Francesco Benincasa* v. *Dentalkit Srl.*).[445] Unlawful business activities are a typical example of a situation in which the individual's formal status (the person is not a professional in terms of the applicable laws and regulations) should give way to the actual purpose of the individual's acts. If the individual's acts feature the elements of doing business in the given case, the person cannot be perceived as a consumer, despite the fact that they do not have a license to conduct business. Protection is afforded to the good faith of the other party. If the other party acts in good faith that their contracting partner is not a consumer, because, for instance, they use business documents, the other party cannot avail themselves of the status of a consumer.[446] The second example is a situation in which the acts are performed by an individual, who has not yet become a professional, but who is getting ready to start their business. Acts of an individual (natural person) performed for the purpose of an already running business, but also acts performed for the purpose of a business that should be launched by the person in the future, do not fall within the category of consumer acts. In this connection, the Supreme Court of the Czech Republic (SC) has again invoked the decision of the European Court of Justice[447] (Sixth Chamber) of July 3, 1997 in Case C-

---

[444] Predecessor to the CJEU.

[445] The decision is quoted above in this annotation.

[446] In connection with these conclusions, the SC invoked the case law of the CJEU, specifically the decision of the European Court of Justice (Second Chamber) of January 20, 2005 in **C-464/01** (*Johann Gruber* v *Bay Wa AG*), available at http://curia.europa.eu/juris/celex.jsf?celex=62001CJ0464&lang1=sk&lang2=CS&type=TXT&ancre=, in which the CJEU reached the following conclusion (cit.): *(i) a person who concludes a contract for goods intended for purposes that are in part within and in part outside their trade or profession may not rely on the special rules of jurisdiction laid down in Articles 13 to 15 of the Convention, unless the trade or professional purpose is so limited as to be negligible in the overall context of the supply, the fact that the private element is predominant being irrelevant in that respect; (ii) it is for the court seized to decide whether the contract at issue was concluded in order to satisfy, to a non-negligible extent, the needs of the business of the person concerned, or whether, on the contrary, the trade or professional purpose was negligible; (iii) to that end, that court must take account of all the relevant factual evidence objectively contained in the file. On the other hand, it must not take account of facts or circumstances of which the other party to the contract may have been aware when the contract was concluded, unless the person who claims to have the capacity of consumer behaved in such a way as to give the other party to the contract the legitimate impression that they were acting for the purposes of their business.*

[447] Predecessor to the CJEU.

269/95 (*Francesco Benincasa* v. *Dentalkit Srl.*).[448] In this regard, the Supreme Court of the Czech Republic (SC) concluded that this was indeed the situation in the given case, and agreed with the factual conclusions made in this connection by the appellate court, which proved that the claimant had entered into the respective agreements while preparing for her future business.

16.83. The SC also approved the application of Section 106 of the CCP;[449] the SC held that if the case presented to the court was to be submitted to arbitration, it means that an essential procedural requirement was absent necessitating the termination of the proceedings. The SC also ruled that Section 106 of the CCP[450] represents a special rule vis-à-vis the general rules of Section 104 of the CCP;[451] the only difference inheres in the fact that (contrary to the abovementioned general rule) the court is not obliged to examine the procedural obstacle, i.e. the existence of a valid arbitration clause, by its own motion, but exclusively upon a plea duly raised by the affected party.

16.84. The SC therefore concluded that the decision of the appellate court was correct. The claimant did not succeed in undermining the decision of the appellate court, and the proceedings at the appellate court were not found defective (the appellate court already addressed in its decision any and all objections that were subsequently raised in the extraordinary appeal; the appellate court also properly established the facts of the case and assessed them in compliance with the applicable laws and regulations, as well as the consistent case law). The SC therefore dismissed the extraordinary appeal.

[*Further Conclusions and Comments Concerning Annotated Resolution of SC*]:

16.85. Generally speaking, this decision certainly cannot be deemed surprising or as introducing any new interpretation of the said rules, i.e. a decision that would shift the existing doctrinal interpretation. Conversely, it is based strictly on the wording of the applicable laws and regulations, their accepted interpretation, and consistent case law. In this particular case, the Supreme Court of the Czech Republic (SC) approved the procedural solution adopted by the lower courts, because it is undisputable that an executed arbitration clause represents an obstacle to court proceedings that requires the application of Section 106 of the CCP.[452]

---

[448] The decision is quoted above in this annotation.
[449] The provision is quoted above in the opening part of this annotation.
[450] The provision is quoted above in the opening part of this annotation.
[451] The provision is quoted above in the opening part of this annotation.
[452] The provision is quoted above in the opening part of this annotation.

16.86. The conclusions regarding the status of the claimant and the validity of the arbitration clause come as no surprise either. The Supreme Court of the Czech Republic (SC) based its decision on the fundamental principle of the separability of the arbitration clause and arrived at the conclusion (which has indeed been accepted in the Czech Republic for some time now) that the (alleged) invalidity of the main agreements does not *eo ipso* undermine the validity of the arbitration clause (unless the grounds for the invalidity of the main agreement also apply to the arbitration clause itself).

16.87. Similarly, the determination of whether the claimant is a consumer was performed in compliance with the consistent doctrinal approach and case law; in this regard, the SC extensively analyzed and considered the situation in the Czech Republic, as well as the rulings of the CJEU. The latter fully complies with the Czech approach – the CivC defines the supplier as a person who, in executing and performing the contract, is acting within the framework of their trade or any other business activity.[453] The definition of a consumer is the antithesis of the concept of supplier. Hence, a consumer is a natural person who, in executing and performing the contract, *is not acting within the framework of their trade or any other business activity, or within the framework of their profession.* Consequently, the fundamental evaluating criterion is the purpose of the specific acts in question, not the formal status of the parties (despite the fact that the formal status frequently corresponds to the actual cause of the given/assessed act). Hence, the decisive criterion is whether or not the respective acts concern the person's trade or any other business activity.

16.88. The text of the annotated decision does not indicate that the SC departed from the accepted doctrinal conclusions. Nonetheless, it is not possible to overlook the fact that the claimant contested the conclusions of the SC by her constitutional complaint lodged on November 11, 2013 and registered with the ConCourt under Case No. IV. ÚS 3402/13.[454] In her complaint, the claimant basically reiterated the same grounds for the invalidity of the arbitration clause already invoked in the SC proceedings. The Constitutional Court of the Czech Republic (ConCourt) resolved the case by its Judgment of June 4, 2014, whereby the annotated decision was vacated. However, we may postulate that the legal conclusions and opinions formulated by the SC

---

[453] See Section 52(2) of the CivC – the provision is quoted above in the opening part of this annotation.

[454] This decision is available online on the website of the ConCourt at http://nalus.usoud.cz/Search/ResultDetail.aspx?id=84519&pos=1&cnt=1&typ=result.

and outlined in the opening part of this annotation continue to apply, because they were by no means undermined by the ConCourt in the reasoning for its Judgment, and conversely, the Judgment of the ConCourt points out that the lower courts had addressed in great detail all objections raised by the applicant regarding the invalidity of the arbitration clause. The Constitutional Court of the Czech Republic (ConCourt) even concluded that if we applied a strictly legal assessment, the clause could be formally valid, even if the agreement were classified as a consumer contract under Section 52(1) of the CivC,[455] and in theory, the clause would not necessarily result in any serious limitation disrupting the balance between the rights of the contracting parties to the detriment of the applicant.

16.89. However, the ConCourt concluded that it is not always possible to base one's decision on a formal application of the relevant laws and regulations, without proper consideration for any and all specific circumstances of the particular case. The ConCourt held that each case must be examined individually and with respect to the particular circumstances of the case, and above all, in the context of all of the circumstances that indicate that the respondent is executing a number of legally perfect juridical acts (from the formal perspective), which, however, given their mutual interconnection and succession, de facto result in an impairment or even denial of the other contracting party's (in this case the claimant's) right to proper and effective judicial protection. In this context, the ConCourt ruled that law must primarily serve as an instrument of justice, not an instrument that could be misused to attain advantages by mechanical application of the law, disregarding the purpose and object of the particular interest protected by the respective rule.

16.90. As concerns the fact that the claimant had stated that she would use the loan for her future business, the ConCourt has criticized the lower courts for their failure to assess whether the claimant's approach could have been meant seriously (in terms of the claimant's ability to realize the difference between a contract concluded by a consumer and a contract concluded by a professional), and whether the respondent could have in good faith believed that the claimant was not a consumer. When entering into the agreements, the claimant was employed as a shop assistant, she was in financial distress, and the respondent (in the ConCourt's opinion) must have had knowledge of the claimant's insolvency, and could not have presumed that the claimant would be able to pay in excess of CZK 2,000,000 within a short period of time,

---

[455] The provision is quoted above in the opening part of this annotation.

allegedly provided for the claimant's business, if she was not able to pay a debt of CZK 250,000. The Constitutional Court of the Czech Republic (ConCourt) held that the Court has no objections to the SC's finding that the claimant did not perform the act under the influence of any mental disorder and that Section 38(2) of the CivC should have been applied (indeed, the ConCourt could not have raised any such objections, because the issue does not fall within its review powers).[456] However, the Supreme Court of the Czech Republic (SC) should also have had regard to the findings that suggested that the claimant's acts were influenced by her reduced resistance to stress and ability to think through the consequences of the documents she was signing, also with respect to the tense personal situation she was in when she was executing the agreements, despite the fact that if considered alone, the findings could not result in an unequivocal conclusion concerning the claimant's mental disorder.

16.91. The ConCourt concluded, based on the above said, that the respective arbitral clauses were invalid, and vacated the decision of the SC. But the ConCourt pointed out that the decision was made exclusively with regard to the specific factual circumstances of the given case, and consequently, it is not possible to draw any general conclusions regarding the execution and validity of arbitration clauses.

16.92. Naturally, it has to be noted that the criteria for entering into arbitration agreements with consumers have been further tightened by the amendment to the ArbAct implemented by Act No. 19/2012 Coll., which now affords increased protection to consumers in compliance with Section 2(3) et seq. of the ArbAct.[457] Nevertheless, it is necessary to point out, and criticize, that the Czech case law – often guided by political impacts, rather than exclusively legal reasons – as well as the approach of the European Union is most protective towards the consumers. But the protection is provided only after the dispute arises, frequently even after a decision is already made in arbitration. The author of this annotation does not argue that the weaker contracting party deserves a certain measure of increased protection, which, however, cannot be unlimited. But we must realize that there are situations in which prevention should replace prosecution of the consequences that the violations of these consumer rights have, where such prosecution often occurs at the procedural stage, or even the post-procedural stage. Numerous practices continue almost unnoticed, such as those of the banks and financial institutions, which abuse the weaker position of the consumer by their

---

[456] The provision is quoted above in the opening part of this annotation.

[457] The provision is quoted above in the opening part of this annotation.

"you can make it with us" advertising. To quite the contrary, the state (the law and the rulings of courts in the exercise of their supervisory powers vis-à-vis arbitration) intervenes wherever it is simpler and politically less delicate and less confrontational. But this is a very misguided perception of the role of the state and the law.

| | |

9. Judgment of the Supreme Court CR of September 4, 2013 in Case No. 23 Cdo 3896/2012:[458] (i) Pleading Invalidity of Arbitration Agreement/ Arbitration Clause and Timely Plea, (ii) Obligation of Court, by Its Own Motion, to Examine Validity of Arbitration Agreement/ Arbitration Clause in proceedings for Annulment of Arbitral Award

Abbreviations Used:

ArbAct   Act of the Czech Republic No. 216/1994 Coll., on Arbitration and the Enforcement of Arbitral Awards, as amended[459]

CC   Act of the Czech Republic No. 89/2012 Coll., the Civil Code[460]

CCP   Act of the Czech Republic No. 99/1963 Coll., the Code of Civil Procedure, as amended

---

[458] This decision is available online on the website of the SC at http://www.nsoud.cz/ Judikatura/judikatura_ns.nsf/WebSearch/8ACFA10085E243FAC1257BEA003748C5?open Document&Highlight=0, [last accessed on November 5, 2014]

[459] The decision of the SC in this case is based on the ArbAct in effect until March 31, 2012, but no subsequent changes have any bearing on the conclusions of the SC and their applicability; this particular case does not involve a consumer contract or, as applicable, a dispute arising from a consumer contract, and the rules introduced in the ArbAct by the Consumer Amendment, i.e. Act No. 19/2012 Coll., would not affect the case at hand. Generally, however, it is necessary to point out that the conclusions reached by the court shall not apply to disputes arising from consumer contracts after the passage of Act No. 19/2012 Coll. (or rather, the amendment codified the enhanced consumer protection, but the SC already mentioned the specific aspects of consumer protection in the annotated decision and inferred that the SC would apply these aspects to a consumer dispute).

[460] This Act has replaced Act No. 40/1964 Coll., the "old Civil Code" (abbreviated as the "CivC" in this annotation), with effect since January 1, 2014. However, legal relationships established before January 1, 2014 shall be governed (save for certain exceptions) by the previous law, i.e. the "CivC".

CivC	Act of the Czech Republic No. 40/1964 Coll., the Civil Code, as amended[461]
CJEU	Court of Justice of the European Union
SC	Supreme Court of the Czech Republic

Key Words:
European Court of Justice | appointment of arbitrator | purchase price | pleading invalidity of an arbitration clause | pleading invalidity of an arbitration agreement | separability of arbitration clause | consumer protection | validity of a juridical act | validity of an arbitration clause[462] | validity of an arbitration agreement[463] | professional | (doing) business | EU law | arbitration clause[464] | arbitration agreement[465] | ad hoc arbitrator | ad hoc arbitration | contractual penalty | Court of Justice of the European Union (CJEU) | consumer | B2C dispute | permanent arbitral institution | default interest | by own motion (ex officio) | timely plea | annulment (setting aside) of arbitral award |

Applicable Laws and Regulations:
ArbAct: Section 7,[466] Section 15,[467] Section 31,[468] Section 32,[469] Section 33[470]

---

[461] This Act has been replaced by Act No. 89/2012 Coll., the "new Civil Code" (abbreviated as the "CC" in this annotation), with effect since January 1, 2014. However, legal relationships established before January 1, 2014 shall be governed (save for certain exceptions) by the previous law, i.e. Act No. 40/1964 Coll., the Civil Code, as amended (abbreviated as the "CivC" in this annotation).

[462] Depending on the context, "arbitration clause" and "arbitration agreement" may also be interpreted as synonyms, or rather the arbitration clause is a form of arbitration agreement according to Section 2 of the ArbAct.

[463] Depending on the context, "arbitration clause" and "arbitration agreement" may also be interpreted as synonyms, or rather the arbitration clause is a form of the arbitration agreement according to Section 2 of the ArbAct.

[464] Depending on the context, "arbitration clause" and "arbitration agreement" may also be interpreted as synonyms, or rather the arbitration clause is a form of arbitration agreement according to Section 2 of the ArbAct.

[465] Depending on the context, "arbitration clause" and "arbitration agreement" may also be interpreted as synonyms, or rather the arbitration clause is a form of arbitration agreement according to Section 2 of the ArbAct.

[466] ArbAct, Section 7 (cit.): *(1) The arbitration agreement should, as a rule, determine the number of arbitrators and their identity, or stipulate the method whereby the number and the identity of the arbitrators shall be determined. The final number of arbitrators must always be odd. (2) If the arbitration agreement lacks the determination pursuant to subsection (1), each party shall appoint one arbitrator and these arbitrators shall elect the chairman of the panel.* Note: this version of the provision applied to the respective proceedings; the currently applicable version reads as follows (cit.): *(1) The arbitration agreement should, as a rule, determine the number of arbitrators and their identity, or*

stipulate the method whereby the number and the identity of the arbitrators shall be determined. The arbitrator may also be selected by a person agreed upon by the parties or following a method of appointment specified in the rules on arbitration pursuant to Section 19(4).The final number of arbitrators must always be odd. (2) If the arbitration agreement lacks the determination pursuant to subsection (1), each party shall appoint one arbitrator and these arbitrators shall elect the chairman of the panel. Note: It has been argued in the respective proceedings (as grounds for annulment of the arbitral award) that the method of appointing the arbitrators was not in compliance with the provisions of the ArbAct. However, this issue was not the subject of the proceedings at the SC. The SC focused on the issue of whether the courts in the proceedings for the annulment of the arbitral award are obliged to examine the validity of the arbitration agreement/clause by their own motion, i.e. even if the respective party to the arbitral proceedings failed to plead the invalidity in time.

[467] ArbAct, Section 15 (cit.): *(1) Arbitrators are entitled to examine their jurisdiction. If they conclude that the arbitration agreement presented to them does not give them jurisdiction to resolve the dispute, they render a corresponding resolution. (2) The plea of lack of jurisdiction, based on the non-existence, invalidity, or expiration of the arbitration agreement, can be raised by a party only before or together with the first act in the proceedings which concerns the merits of the case, unless the invalidity is caused by the fact that no arbitration agreement could have been concluded with respect to the case.* Note: This version of the provision applied to the respective proceedings; the currently applicable version reads as follows (cit.): *(1) Arbitrators are entitled to examine their jurisdiction. If they conclude that the arbitration agreement presented to them does not give them jurisdiction to resolve the dispute, they render a corresponding resolution. (2) The plea of lack of jurisdiction, based on the non-existence, invalidity, or expiration of the arbitration agreement, can be raised by a party only before or together with the first act in the proceedings which concerns the merits of the case, unless the invalidity is caused by the fact that no arbitration agreement could have been concluded with respect to the case. This does not apply to disputes arising from consumer contracts.* Note: Although the SC has addressed the issue of whether the lack jurisdiction on the part of the arbitrators to hear and resolve the case was pleaded in time, the amendment implemented by Act No. 19/2012 Coll. has no bearing on the conclusions reached by the SC, because the claimant was not a consumer and the rules therefore do not apply.

[468] ArbAct, Section 31 (cit.): (cit.): *At the request of any party the court annuls the arbitral award if: (a) it was made in a case which cannot be submitted to arbitration (cannot be the subject of a valid arbitration agreement), (b) the arbitration agreement is invalid for other reasons or the agreement was cancelled or it does not apply to the agreed case, (c) the arbitrator(s) who took part in the proceedings was/were not authorized to make decisions in the case, whether under the arbitration agreement or otherwise, or lacked the capacity to act as arbitrator(s), (d) the arbitral award was not adopted by the majority of the arbitrators, (e) a party was denied the opportunity to plead his or her case in the arbitral proceedings, (f) the arbitral award orders a party to provide performance which was not requested by the obligee or to provide performance which is impossible or illegal under domestic law, (g) it transpires that there are reasons which would otherwise justify the reopening of civil proceedings in court.* [Section 228(1)(a) and (b) of the CCP]. Note: This version of the provision applied to the

respective proceedings; the currently applicable version reads as follows (cit.): *At the request of any party the court annuls the arbitral award if: (a) it was made in a case which cannot be submitted to arbitration (cannot be the subject of a valid arbitration agreement), (b) the arbitration agreement is invalid for other reasons or the agreement was cancelled or it does not apply to the agreed case, (c) the arbitrator(s) who took part in the proceedings was/were not authorized to make decisions in the case, whether under the arbitration agreement or otherwise, or lacked the capacity to act as arbitrator(s), (d) the arbitral award was not adopted by the majority of the arbitrators, (e) a party was denied the opportunity to plead his or her case in the arbitral proceedings, (f) the arbitral award orders a party to provide performance which was not requested by the creditor or to provide performance which is impossible or illegal under domestic law, (g) the arbitrator or the permanent arbitral institution resolved a dispute arising from a consumer contract contrary to consumer protection laws, or clearly in violation of good morals, or contrary to public policy, (h) an arbitration agreement relating to disputes arising from consumer contracts lacks the information required under Section 3(5) or such information is intentionally or to a non-negligible extent incomplete, inaccurate, or false, or (i) it transpires that there are reasons which would otherwise justify the reopening of civil proceedings in court.* [Section 228(1)(a) and (b) of the CCP]

[469] ArbAct, Section 32 (cit.): *(1) The motion to annul an arbitral award must be lodged with the court within three months following the receipt of the arbitral award by the party requesting the annulment of the award, unless this Act stipulates otherwise. (2) The motion pursuant to subsection (1) does not suspend the enforceability of the arbitral award. If requested by the obligor, however, the court may suspend the enforceability of the arbitral award in case an immediate enforcement of the arbitral award could cause serious harm.* Note: This version of the provision applied to the respective proceedings; the currently applicable version reads as follows (cit.): *(1) The motion to annul an arbitral award must be lodged with the court within three months following the receipt of the arbitral award by the party requesting the annulment of the award, unless this Act stipulates otherwise. If the arbitral award was made in a dispute arising from a consumer contract and the motion to annul was lodged by the consumer, the court always examines whether there are grounds to annul the arbitral award pursuant to Section 31(a) through (d) or (h). (2) The motion pursuant to subsection (1) does not suspend the enforceability of the arbitral award. If requested by the obligor, however, the court may suspend the enforceability of the arbitral award in case an immediate enforcement of the arbitral award could cause serious harm or in case the motion to annul the arbitral award justifies the conclusion that the motion is legitimate. (3) If the motion to annul an arbitral award is lodged by the consumer, the court shall establish whether there are grounds to suspend the enforceability of the arbitral award pursuant to subsection (2) without the consumer's request. The court shall rule on the suspension of enforceability within 7 days of receiving the motion; the arbitral award cannot be enforced within said time limit.* Note: The changes implemented in Section 32 of the ArbAct have no direct influence on the conclusions reached by the SC in this particular case, but they ultimately change the position of consumers – consumers will no longer, in certain cases, have to explicitly invoke the grounds for the annulment of the arbitral award, because the courts are now obliged to examine the existence of selected grounds for the annulment of the arbitral award by their own motion.

CCP: Section 133,[471] Section 134,[472] Section 135[473]
CivC: Section 39[474]
CC: Section 547,[475] Section 588[476]

---

[470] ArbAct, Section 33 (cit.): *The court shall dismiss a motion to annul an arbitral award which is based on the grounds specified in Section 31(b) or (c) if the party requesting the annulment failed to raise the corresponding objection in the arbitral proceedings before the party's first act in the merits of the case, despite having an opportunity to do so.* Note: This version of the provision applied to the respective proceedings; the currently applicable version reads as follows (cit.): *The court shall dismiss a motion to annul an arbitral award which is based on the grounds specified in Section 31(b) or (c) if the party requesting the annulment failed to raise the corresponding objection in the arbitral proceedings before the party's first act in the merits of the case, despite having an opportunity to do so. This does not apply to disputes arising from consumer contracts.* Note: Although the SC has addressed the issue of whether the lack of jurisdiction on the part of the arbitrators to hear and resolve the case was pleaded in time, the amendment implemented by Act No. 19/2012 Coll. has no bearing on the conclusions reached by the SC, because the claimant was not a consumer and the rules therefore do not apply.

[471] CCP, Section 133 (cit.): *Any factual circumstance presumed under the law, where such presumption is rebuttable, is accepted by the court as proven, unless anything to the contrary transpired during the proceedings.* Note: This version of the law applied to the respective proceedings, but it has not been subject to any modifications in the meantime and therefore continues to apply.

[472] CCP, Section 134 (cit.): *Documents issued by courts of the Czech Republic or any other state authorities intra vires, as well as documents declared public by any special laws or regulations, confirm that the regulation or declaration was made by the authority that issued the document, and unless proven otherwise, that the facts attested to or confirmed in the document are truthful.* Note: This version of the law applied to the respective proceedings, but it has not been subject to any modifications in the meantime and therefore continues to apply.

[473] CCP, Section 135 (cit.): *(1) The court is bound by a decision of the competent authorities that declares that a criminal offence, minor offence or any other administrative offence punishable under special laws has been committed, and which identifies the perpetrator of the offence, as well as a decision regarding an individual's personal status; however, the court is not bound by decisions rendered in the ticket procedure. (2) The court may itself assess any other matters that fall within the jurisdiction of other authorities. But if the competent authority has made a decision regarding the issue, the court shall use it as the basis for its decision.* Note: This version of the law applied to the respective proceedings, but it has not been subject to any modifications in the meantime and therefore continues to apply.

[474] CivC, Section 39 (cit.): *A juridical act is invalid if the content or the purpose thereof violates or evades the law or is contra bonos mores.* Note: This is the version of the law applicable to the respective proceedings. January 1, 2014 is the effective date of the CC, which regulates the said issues in Sections 547 and 588 (both provisions are quoted below in the opening part of this annotation).

Czech (& Central European) Yearbook of Arbitration

The Supreme Court of the Czech Republic reached the following principal conclusions:

(1) The appellate court erred in its conclusion that the invalidity of an arbitration agreement should always be assessed by the court's own motion, even if the invalidity of the arbitration agreement was not properly pleaded in the arbitration in terms of Section 31(b) of the ArbAct. The appellate court could only reach this conclusion if the relationship were a B2C relationship (between a professional and a consumer). The respective case, however, is a commercial legal relationship between professionals, and the appellate court's conclusion is in stark contrast to Section 33 of the ArbAct.

(2) The decision of the Grand Panel of the SC of May 11, 2011 in Case No. 31 Cdo 1945/2010,[477] which concerns the invalidity of arbitration clauses, is also applicable to commercial legal relationships between professionals, but the conclusions reached by the Grand Panel of the SC may only be applied to relationships between professionals if the party entitled to plead invalidity in terms of Section 33 of the ArbAct properly pleads the invalidity of the arbitration agreement in the course of the arbitral proceedings.[478]

---

[475] CC, Section 547 (cit.): *The contents and purpose of juridical actions must comply with good morals and the law (statute).*

[476] CC, Section 588 (cit.): *The court shall, with or without a motion, have regard to the invalidity of a juridical action that is obviously contra bonos mores, or that conflicts with the law (statute) and obviously violates public policy. This also applies if the juridical action creates an obligation to provide performance that is impossible ab initio.*

[477] The quoted decision of the Grand Panel of the SC is available online on the website of the SC at http://www.nsoud.cz/Judikatura/judikatura_ns.nsf/WebSearch/87312C808746B5D2C1257A4E006568D2?openDocument&Highlight=0; the court reached the following conclusion (cit.): *If the arbitration agreement lacks any direct identification of an ad hoc arbitrator, or a specific description of the method of their appointment, and refers to "Rules on Arbitration" issued by a legal entity other than a permanent arbitral institution established under the law, the arbitration agreement is invalid pursuant to Section 39 of the CivC.* Note: The summary of the SC's legal opinion (*ratio decidendi*) was adopted from the SC website.

[478] In connection with these conclusions, the SC referred to its previous case law, namely Resolution of February 28, 2013 in Case No. 23 Cdo 2919/2011, available on the website of the SC at http://www.nsoud.cz/Judikatura/judikatura_ns.nsf/WebSearch/09DE58D01FABF969C1257B2B002E823E?openDocument&Highlight=0, in which the SC held as follows (cit.): *Given the facts of the case, the court should have held, in compliance with Section 2(1) and Section 13 of the ArbAct, that the arbitration clause incorporated in the respondent's order was invalid for evading the law pursuant to Section 39 of the Civil Code (the "CivC"), because the clause lacks any direct identification of the ad hoc arbitrator or a specific description of the method of their appointment, as applicable, and regulates the issues of the selection of the arbitrator and the determination of the arbitration rules simply*

[*From Facts of Case*]:

16.93. On November 19, 2010, an arbitral award was rendered in *ad hoc* arbitration conducted under Case No. 6570/2010; the arbitral award was subsequently challenged by the claimant,[479] who demanded the annulment of the arbitral award on the grounds stipulated under Section 31(b) of the ArbAct[480] (inter alia).[481] The claimant's motion rested primarily on the fact that the parties' agreement in the arbitration clause regarding the method of appointing arbitrators was invalid, because the arbitration clause stipulated that disputes shall be resolved by (an) arbitrator(s) who will be principally appointed by

---

by reference to a legal entity that, according to the appellate court's finding, is a limited liability company, not a permanent arbitral institution. In this connection, it is necessary to invoke the decision of the Supreme Court of May 11, 2011 in Case No. 31 Cdo 1945/2010, in which the Supreme Court held that if the arbitration agreement lacks any direct identification of an ad hoc arbitrator, or a specific description of the method of their appointment, and refers to "Rules on Arbitration" issued by a legal entity other than a permanent arbitral institution established under the law, the arbitration agreement is invalid pursuant to Section 39 of the CivC. In the said decision, the Supreme Court held that if an entity other than a permanent arbitral institution established under a special law carries out activities that, according to the Arbitration Act, are reserved for permanent arbitral institutions, the entity has a clear and logically deducible intention that is in conflict with the law and raises reasonable doubts from the perspective of the independent and impartial resolution of disputes. Within the framework of the Court's duty to consolidate case law, the Supreme Court agrees with the conclusion that in the case of an arbitration clause that is, contrary to the law, clearly aimed at causing detriment to the "weaker" contracting party, the principle of party autonomy must not be (mis)used to negate the protection of that party. In the said decision, the Supreme Court also held that a democratic country honoring the principle of the rule of law must not give up on the protection of rights and legitimate interests that could be jeopardized in alternative proceedings conducted instead of litigation. The conclusions pronounced in this decision of the Grand Panel of the Supreme Court are fully applicable to the case at hand, in which the facts of the case indicate that the arbitration was to be conducted according to the Arbitration Rules of a company other than a permanent arbitral institution, and at the same time, the ad hoc arbitrator was not directly identified and no specific method of their appointment was determined. It is irrelevant that the respective case concerns a commercial legal relationship between professionals.

[479] A legal person formed and existing under the laws of the Czech Republic as a limited liability company; the respondent is also a legal person formed and existing under the laws of the Czech Republic, specifically as a joint stock company.

[480] The provision is quoted above in the opening part of this annotation.

[481] The other grounds for the annulment of the arbitral award were not relevant in the proceedings at the SC; consequently, they are not analyzed in any great detail in this annotation.

company [xxx][482] and selected from the list of arbitrators administered by the said company. The parties have also agreed that the procedural rules governing the arbitration, taking of evidence, form of the decision and costs of the arbitral proceedings are governed by the Arbitration Rules issued by the said company. However, the claimant failed to plead invalidity in compliance with Section 15 of the ArbAct,[483] as the invalidity was only pleaded in the proceedings in which the claimant requested the annulment of the said arbitral award. Consequently, it was necessary to examine whether the requirements of Section 33 of the ArbAct[484] were fulfilled, or, as applicable, whether the court should/could assess the validity of the arbitration agreement/clause by a motion of its own accord if the respondent failed to meet the said requirements.

[*Procedure of Case*]:

16.94. On February 15, 2012, the Regional Court in Ostrava (Olomouc Branch), as the court of first instance, rendered its Judgment in Case No. 19 Cm 106/2011-139, whereby the motion to annul the arbitral award was dismissed. The court held that the arbitral award could not be annulled on the grounds falling within Section 31(b) and (c) of the ArbAct if the party had failed to assert the grounds in the arbitration itself. The court of first instance therefore proceeded in compliance with Section 33 of the ArbAct.[485] The court of first instance also held that the grounds for the annulment of the arbitral award under Section 31(d) of the ArbAct[486] did not apply either, because the case had been resolved by a single arbitrator. Given the fact that the claimant had the opportunity to raise the relevant defense in the arbitral proceedings, the court of first instance concluded that the grounds for the annulment of the arbitral award under Section 31(e) of the ArbAct[487] did not apply either. Finally, the court held that the subject matter of the arbitration was the parties' performance under a bilateral contractual relationship, namely payment of the purchase price, default interest and contractual penalty, i.e. claims acceptable under the domestic (Czech)

---

[482] It is a legal person formed and existing under the laws of the Czech Republic as a limited liability company, i.e. an entity classified as a private arbitral company/institution (as opposed to permanent arbitral institutions); the SC analyzed the limits of their activities in great detail in the past.

[483] The provision is quoted above in the opening part of this annotation.

[484] The provision is quoted above in the opening part of this annotation.

[485] The provision is quoted above in the opening part of this annotation.

[486] The provision is quoted above in the opening part of this annotation.

[487] The provision is quoted above in the opening part of this annotation.

legal system; hence, the arbitral award could not be annulled on the grounds specified in Section 31(f) of the ArbAct either.[488]

16.95. The High Court in Olomouc, as the appellate court, reversed[489] the abovementioned Judgment of the Regional Court in Ostrava (Olomouc Branch) and annulled the arbitral award. The court held that the crucial issue in the case was the assessment of the validity of the arbitration clause agreed between the parties.[490] The appellate court admitted that the invalidity of the arbitration agreement under Section 31(b) of the ArbAct was not pleaded in the arbitration from the perspective of the principles stipulated in Section 33 of the ArbAct, despite the party's opportunity to do so. Nevertheless, the court concluded that courts were obliged to have regard to the invalidity (nullity) of the arbitration agreement by their own motion. The appellate court invoked the decision of the Grand Panel of the SC of May 11, 2011 in Case No. 31 Cdo 1945/2010,[491] and concluded that the respective arbitration agreement was invalid (void) for being contrary to the law, i.e. pursuant to Section 39 of the CivC.[492] The court based its ruling on the premise that the said grounds for invalidity apply to cases where the arbitration agreement lacks any direct identification of an *ad hoc* arbitrator, or a specific description of the method of their appointment, and refers to *Rules on Arbitration* issued by a legal entity other than a permanent arbitral institution established under the law.[493]

16.96. The respondent challenged the Judgment of the appellate court by means of an extraordinary appeal. The respondent argued that the respondent disagrees with the legal interpretation presented by the appellate court, namely that the invalidity (nullity) of an arbitration agreement must be considered by the court by its own motion, i.e. even if the invalidity of the arbitration agreement under Section 31(b) of the ArbAct was not pleaded in the arbitral proceedings from the perspective of the principles set down in Section 33 of the ArbAct. The respondent maintains that this option is reserved for B2C disputes

---

[488] The provision is quoted above in the opening part of this annotation.

[489] Namely by Judgment of July 19, 2012 in Case No. 1 Cmo 103/2012 – 174.

[490] As described above in this annotation.

[491] The decision is quoted above in this annotation.

[492] The provision is quoted above in the opening part of this annotation.

[493] See Section 15 of the ArbAct quoted in the opening part of this annotation, which sets forth the requirements for setting up permanent arbitral institutions. Permanent arbitral institutions are also private-law entities, but the fundamental conditions imposed on their formation and activities are stipulated by the ArbAct.

only, which is clear from the case law of the CJEU[494] and from the case law of the SC itself.[495] The respondent also argued that the appellate court's interpretation of the respective clause was wrong. In the respondent's opinion, the clause does not constitute a reference to a document issued by a private arbitral company, as envisaged in the decision of the Grand Panel of the SC of May 11, 2011 in Case No. 31 Cdo 1945/2010,[496] but the determination of the *appointing authority*, which complies with Section 7 of the ArbAct;[497] the said provision does not prohibit the possibility that the arbitrator will be appointed from a pre-defined group of individuals listed in a particular register, provided that the register is publicly known. Moreover, the Arbitration Rules issued by the respective private arbitral company do not regulate the issue of the appointment of arbitrators at all (they focus merely on the

---

[494] Decision of the Court of Justice (First Chamber) of October 26, 2006 in Case C–168/05 (*Elisa María Mostaza Claro* v. *Centro Móvil Milenium SL*), available at http://curia.europa.eu/juris/document/document.jsf;jsessionid=9ea7d2dc30d58aa531680e 0a45838240f9ba2d85d487.e34KaxiLc3qMb40Rch0SaxuObN50?text=&docid=63926&page Index=0&doclang=cs&mode=lst&dir=&occ=first&part=1&cid=463888, in which the Court held as follows (cit.): *Council Directive 93/13/EEC of April 5, 1993, on unfair terms in consumer contracts, must be interpreted as meaning that a national court seized of an action for the annulment of an arbitration award must determine whether the arbitration agreement is void, and annul that award where that agreement contains an unfair term, even though the consumer has not pleaded such invalidity in the course of the arbitration proceedings, but only in that of the action for annulment.*

[495] The court refers to Judgment of the SC of March 28, 2012 in Case No. 33 Cdo 3121/2010, available online on the website of the SC at http://www.nsoud.cz/Judikatura/judikatura_ns.nsf/WebSearch/B1A0C165129C9261C1257A4E0068D632?open Document, in which the court held as follows (cit.): *An arbitration clause in a consumer contract is only acceptable if the conditions for the appointment of arbitrator and the agreed procedural conditions guarantee fair proceedings (fair trial) and equal treatment to the parties (which means, in a consumer-professional relationship, increased protection of the weaker party, i.e. the consumer). If the arbitration clause lacks any direct identification of an ad hoc arbitrator, or a specific description of the method of their appointment, and refers to "Rules on Arbitration" issued by a legal entity other than a permanent arbitral institution established under the law, the arbitration agreement is contrary to the law and is therefore invalid pursuant to Section 39 of the CivC. Invalidity (nullity) of a juridical act also fulfills the public (general) interest, and consequently, it has effects directly by operation of law (ex lege) and from the beginning (ex tunc), whether or not it has been invoked by any party. The court shall have regard to the invalidity (nullity) of a juridical act with or without a motion, i.e. by a motion of its own accord (ex officio), provided the circumstances associated with the invalidity (nullity) transpire during the proceedings.*

[496] The decision is quoted above in this annotation.

[497] The provision is quoted above in the opening part of this annotation.

issues of case management), and consequently, the existence of the Rules could not have caused any damage or losses to the claimant. The respondent also argued that a substantial part of the factual finding underlying the contested decision has no support in the examined evidence. However, in its reply to that objection, the SC held that the respondent failed to substantiate such grounds for appeal, and that the SC itself did not discover anything in the course of the proceedings that would support such grounds for appeal. Consequently, the SC focused exclusively on the issue of the erroneous legal assessment of the case. The SC agreed with the respondent that if the invalidity of the arbitration agreement was not pleaded in the arbitration and the requirements of Section 33 of the ArbAct were not fulfilled as a result thereof, the motion to annul the arbitral award must be dismissed, because the court is not allowed to have regard to such invalidity by its own motion. The SC ruled that a contrary conclusion could only be drawn in the case of a dispute arising from a consumer contract.

[*Arguments Presented by SC*]:

16.97. The SC based its decision on the applicable laws and regulations, primarily Section 33 of the ArbAct.[498] The SC invoked the principle that stipulates that the invalidity of an arbitration agreement/lack of jurisdiction on the part of the arbitrators to hear and resolve the dispute must be pleaded in the course of the arbitration, specifically at or before the moment the arbitrator(s) commence debating the merits of the case. The SC therefore concluded that the decision of the appellate court was in marked conflict with the wording of the law. The court would only be obliged to examine the validity of the arbitration agreement by its own motion if the dispute arose from a consumer contract.

16.98. The SC is of the opinion that the above mentioned conclusion is without prejudice to the applicability of the decision rendered by the Grand Panel of the SC, Case No. 31 Cdo 1945/2010 of 11 May 2011,[499] to obligations (relationships) established between businesspeople (professionals) but only if the lack of jurisdiction on the part of the arbitrators/invalidity of the arbitration agreement is properly pleaded in the arbitration and the requirements of Section 33 of the ArbAct are thereby observed.[500]

16.99. The SC therefore concluded that the decision of the appellate court was not correct. Consequently, the SC vacated the decision of the appellate court and remanded the case for further hearing and a new decision. Considering the decision that it rendered, the SC did not find it

---

[498] The provision is quoted above in the opening part of this annotation.

[499] The decision is quoted above in this annotation.

[500] The provision is quoted above in the opening part of this annotation.

necessary or possible, as applicable, to address the material grounds for the annulment of the arbitral award as asserted in the proceedings (i.e. whether the method of appointing arbitrators that was agreed in this particular case is contrary to the interpretation of Section 7 of the ArbAct[501] adopted by the case law of the SC).

[*Further Conclusions and Comments Concerning Annotated Resolution of SC*]:

16.100. The decision addressed the issue of determining the scope of review of the arbitral award to be performed by the court in proceedings for the annulment of the arbitral award; this generally denotes the limits of the powers and supervisory functions exercised by the state and by state authorities vis-à-vis arbitration. The parties are responsible for pleading, properly and in a timely fashion, the lack of the arbitrators' jurisdiction to hear and resolve the case; this is, indeed, one of the fundamental pillars of arbitration, reflected in Section 15 of the ArbAct[502] and Section 33 of the ArbAct.[503] This does not imply, though, that there is any clear consensus regarding the possibility of demanding the annulment of the arbitral award on the grounds specified in Section 31(b) and (c) of the ArbAct.[504] Legal professionals and academics have discussed whether the courts are bound to examine, by their own motion, the issue of subjective arbitrability if the motion to annul the arbitral award is lodged in a due and timely manner, i.e. by the deadline specified in Section 32(1) of the ArbAct.[505] Some have argued that the courts should indeed do so.

16.101. The main argument against this conclusion is the already settled practice, also supported by the case law of the SC, which suggests that a proactive approach to the proceedings and the hearing on the merits may remedy the deficiencies of the arbitration agreement. It has been argued that the party that adopts this approach, i.e. participates in the proceedings and defends their rights, implicitly expresses their will to waive the possibility of judicial protection and the hearing of the dispute in civil proceedings, and agrees with submitting to the jurisdiction of the arbitrators.[506] The courts were allowed to make the

---

[501]   The provision is quoted above in the opening part of this annotation.

[502]   The provision is quoted above in the opening part of this annotation.

[503]   The provision is quoted above in the opening part of this annotation.

[504]   The provision is quoted above in the opening part of this annotation.

[505]   The provision is quoted above in the opening part of this annotation.

[506]   Cf. Resolution of the SC of October 30, 2008 in Case No. 20 Cdo 2857/2006, available online on the website of the SC at http://www.nsoud.cz/Judikatura/judikatura_ns.nsf/WebSearch/3C5BBC6777E7E38BC1257A4E006ACEEC?openDocument&Highlight=0, in which the court held as follows (cit.): *Act No. 216/1994 Coll. does not indicate that passivity and inactivity on the part of the respondent in arbitration would result in*

finding of the non-existence of the arbitration agreement (whether due to total absence or total invalidity of the agreement) by their own motion, even if the respective party failed to plead the lack of jurisdiction on the part of the arbitrators, but only provided that the party did not proactively participate in the arbitration.

16.102. The issue was possibly clarified by the Consumer Amendment to the ArbAct, i.e. Act No. 19/2012 Coll., which clearly stipulated in Section 32(1) of the ArbAct[507] that the courts are obliged to examine by their own motion certain grounds that may serve as the basis for the motion to annul an arbitral award rendered with respect to a consumer contract (this also applies, inter alia, to the relevant provisions of Section 31(b) and (c) of the ArbAct[508]). Similarly, Section 33 of the ArbAct[509] no longer requires, with respect to disputes arising from consumer contracts, that the respective party raise the respective objection (plea) already in the course of the arbitral proceedings. Reasoning to the contrary, we may therefore conclude that the respective rules do not apply to disputes that cannot be classified as B2C disputes, and consequently, the court is not allowed to examine by its own motion these grounds for the annulment of the arbitral award, and conversely, must insist on the due fulfillment of the requirements stipulated in Section 33 of the ArbAct.[510]

16.103. However, the interesting aspect of the annotated decision is that the above-outlined conclusions were articulated by the court in a situation in which the respective proceedings were governed by the version of the ArbAct preceding the amendment implemented by Act No. 19/2012 Coll.

|||

---

submission to the arbitrator's jurisdiction; this consequence could only be associated with the behavior of a respondent who was active in the hearing of the dispute without pleading the non-existence of the arbitration agreement before or together with their first act on the merits. A different situation would occur if the arbitration agreement were concluded, albeit an invalid one. In such case, the arbitrator would have jurisdiction to render the arbitral award; the respondent's defense would consist of a motion to annul the arbitral award. The conclusions were also reiterated in Resolution of the SC of August 31, 2010 in Case No. 20 Cdo 3284/2008, which is available on the website of the SC at http://www.nsoud.cz/ Judikatura/judikatura_ns.nsf/WebSearch/2E49414B7658E266C1257A4E0065B928?openD ocument&Highlight=0,

[507] The provision is quoted above in the opening part of this annotation.
[508] The provision is quoted above in the opening part of this annotation.
[509] The provision is quoted above in the opening part of this annotation.
[510] The provision is quoted above in the opening part of this annotation.

10. Judgment of Supreme Court CR, Case No. 23 Cdo 3116/2012, of September 19, 2013:[511] (i) Allowing Party to State (Plead) Their Case, (ii) Annulment of Arbitral Award for Failure to Meet Such Obligation under Section 31(e) of the ArbAct, and (iii) Duty to Appoint Interpreter for Party When Such Need Arises in Course of Proceedings

Abbreviations Used:

AC Rules	AC Rules[512]
AC	Arbitration Court at the Economic Chamber of the Czech Republic and Agricultural Chamber of the Czech Republic[513]
ArbAct	Act of the Czech Republic No. 216/1994 Coll., on Arbitration and the Enforcement of Arbitral Awards, as amended[514]
CCP	Act of the Czech Republic No. 99/1963 Coll., the Code of Civil Procedure, as amended
Charter	Resolution of the Presidium of the Czech National Council No. 2/1993 Coll., on the promulgation of the Charter of Fundamental Rights and Freedoms as part of the constitutional order of the Czech Republic, as amended
ConCourt	Constitutional Court of the Czech Republic
Constitution	Act of the Czech Republic No. 1/1993 Coll., the Constitution of the Czech Republic, as amended
SC	Supreme Court of the Czech Republic

---

[511] This decision is available online on the website of the SC at: http://www.nsoud.cz/Judikatura/judikatura_ns.nsf/WebSearch/6784E63DEF7F5231C1257BFA005251A1?openDocument&Highlight=0,rozhod%C4%8D%C3%AD,%C5%99%C3%ADzen%C3%AD [last accessed on October 30, 2014].

[512] The applicable regulation is the Rules of the AC governing Domestic Disputes, effective June 30, 2012 (available on the AC website at: http://www.soud.cz/rady/rad-pro-vnitrostatni-spory-2011, i.e. the Rules as applicable on February 1, 2007). This annotation has also had regard to the new AC Rules 2012, effective July 1, 2012 (also available online on the AC website at: http://www.soud.cz/rady/rad-rozhodciho-soudu-01-07-2012).

[513] For more information regarding this permanent arbitral institution, see www.soud.cz.

[514] This particular decision of the SC is based on the ArbAct effective until March 31, 2012; no subsequent changes have any bearing on the conclusions of the SC and their applicability.

Key Words:
annulment (setting aside) of arbitral award | equal opportunity to assert one's rights | equality of the parties | exercise of procedural rights | interpreter | language of the proceedings | opportunity to state (plead) one's case | violation of procedural rights |

Applicable Laws and Regulations:
CCP: Section 18, primarily Section 18(2)[515]
ArbAct: Sections 18,[516] 30,[517] 31(e)[518]

---

[515]   CCP, Section 18(2) (cit.): *"The court shall appoint an interpreter for a party whose native language is different from the Czech language as soon as the need to do so arises in the course of the proceedings. The same applies to the appointment of an interpreter for a party the communication with whom is only possible when using any of the communication systems for deaf and deaf-blind individuals."* Note: In connection with deaf and deaf-blind people, the law refers to Act No. 155/1998 Coll., on Communication Systems for Deaf and Deaf-Blind People (the text of the Act erroneously refers to the original title of the Act – Act on Sign Language and Amending Other Statutes). The quoted sentences represent the current version of the law; the version applicable on the day on which the arbitral award was rendered (no other temporal data can be extracted from the annotated decision/is available) exhibits only minor modifications to the formulation – the obligation to appoint an interpreter already existed when the respective arbitration was pending – cit.: *"The court shall appoint an interpreter for a party whose native language is different from the Czech language as soon as the need to do so transpires in the proceedings. The same applies to the appointment of interpreter for a party the communication with whom is possible only when using sign language."* Subsection (1) of the quoted provision has not been subject to any modifications at all, and the following text is therefore the version effective both now and at the moment at which the arbitral award was rendered (cit.): *"The parties have equal standing in civil court proceedings. They have the right to appear and state their case in court in their native language. The court is obliged to secure equal opportunities for the parties to assert their rights."*

[516]   ArbAct, Section 18 (cit.): *"The parties have an equal standing in the arbitral proceedings and must be provided with a full opportunity to assert their rights."* Note: This version of the law was applicable on the day on which the arbitral award was rendered, but has not been subject to any modifications in the meantime and therefore continues to apply.

[517]   ArbAct, Section 30 (cit.): *"Unless the Act stipulates otherwise, the arbitral proceedings shall be reasonably governed by the provisions of the Code of Civil Procedure."* Note: This version of the law was applicable on the day on which the arbitral award was rendered, but has not been subject to any modifications in the meantime and therefore continues to apply.

[518]   ArbAct, Section 31(e) (cit.): *"At the request of any party the court annuls the arbitral award if a party was denied the opportunity to plead his or her case in the arbitral proceedings."* Note: This version of the law was applicable on the day on which the arbitral award was rendered, but has not been subject to any modifications in the meantime and therefore continues to apply.

Constitution: Article 96(1)[519]

Charter: Articles 37(3) and 4[520]

The Supreme Court of the Czech Republic reached the following principal conclusions:

(1) If it was necessary to appoint an interpreter for a person in the appellate proceedings, then the need for the interpreter had already existed in the proceedings at the court of first instance and in the preceding arbitration, unless any circumstances had changed in the meantime.[521]

(2) The fact that the party has counsel in the proceedings appointed under a power of attorney shall not release the court from the obligation to appoint an interpreter for the party if the need to do so arises in the course of the proceedings; this applies especially if the party requests an interpreter.[522]

(3) One of the fundamental principles governing civil court proceedings is the principle of the equality of the parties, which requires that the parties must have equal standing before the court, without one or the other party enjoying any procedural benefits. In order to implement this principle, the court is obliged to provide all parties to the dispute with the same opportunity to assert their rights.[523]

[From Facts of Case]:

16.104. On October 10, 2008, the AC rendered an arbitral award in arbitral proceedings, Case No. Rsp 732/08; the arbitral award was subsequently challenged by the respondent (claimant in the court proceedings),[524]

---

[519]   Constitution, Article 96(1) (cit.): *"All parties to the proceedings have equal rights in court."* Note: This version of the law was applicable on the day on which the arbitral award was rendered, but has not been subject to any modifications in the meantime and therefore continues to apply.

[520]   Charter, Article 37(3) and (4) (cit.): *"(3) All parties to the proceedings are equal. (4) Anyone who declares that they do not speak the language in which the proceedings are conducted has the right to an interpreter."* Note: This version of the law was applicable on the day on which the arbitral award was rendered, but has not been subject to any modifications in the meantime and therefore continues to apply.

[521]   The summary of the SC's legal opinion *(ratio decidendi)* was adopted from the SC website.

[522]   The SC invokes its former case law, namely Resolution Case No. 20 Cdo 1540/2006 of August 8, 2006 available online on the SC website at:

[523]   In this connection, the SC invokes the decisions of the ConCourt, namely its Judgment of November 13, 2003, Case No. III. ÚS 202/03, available online on the ConCourt website at: http://nalus.usoud.cz/Search/ResultDetail.aspx?id=44986&pos=1&cnt=1&typ=result.

[524]   A legal person formed and existing under the laws of the Czech Republic as a limited liability company; the respondent is also a legal person formed and existing under the laws of the Czech Republic as a limited liability company.

who demanded the annulment of the arbitral award on the grounds stipulated under Section 31(a),[525] (b),[526] (e),[527] (f)[528] and (g)[529] of the ArbAct. The claimant's motion was based primarily on the fact that the claimant had not been allowed to sufficiently prove her allegations, because the arbitral tribunal had not heard/read the evidence proposed by the claimant and had only examined the evidence proposed by the other party to the proceedings. The claimant's legal counsel also pleaded that the claimant had not been instructed about the possibility of conducting the arbitral proceedings in a different language, or the possibility of having an interpreter, considering the fact that the claimant's Executive Officer did not speak Czech well (however, this objection was raised as late as in the proceedings on appeal against the decision, whereby the motion for the annulment of the arbitral award was dismissed).[530]

[*Procedure of Case*]:

16.105. On November 25, 2010, the Regional Court in Ostrava, as the court of first instance, rendered its Judgment in Case No. 41 Cm 227/2008-225, whereby the motion for the annulment of the arbitral award was dismissed. The court held that there were no grounds that would justify the annulment of the arbitral award.[531]

---

[525]　ArbAct, Section 31(a) (cit.): "*At the request of any party the court annuls the arbitral award if it was made in a case which cannot be submitted to arbitration (cannot be the subject of a valid arbitration agreement).*"

[526]　ArbAct, Section 31(b) (cit.): "*At the request of any party the court annuls the arbitral award if the arbitration agreement is invalid for other reasons or the agreement was cancelled or it does not apply to the agreed case.*"

[527]　The provision is quoted above in the opening part of this annotation.

[528]　ArbAct, Section 31(f) (cit.): "*At the request of any party the court annuls the arbitral award if the arbitral award orders a party to provide performance which was not requested by the obligee or to provide performance which is impossible or illegal under domestic law.*"

[529]　ArbAct, Section 31(f) (cit.): "*At the request of any party the court annuls the arbitral award if it transpires that there are reasons which would otherwise justify the reopening of civil proceedings in court.*" [Section 228(1)(a) and (b) of the CCP]. **NOTE:** Currently Section 31(i) of the ArbAct.

[530]　The claimant argues in its extraordinary appeal that its Executive Officer started to learn Czech in the course of the arbitral proceedings, and that even at the time when the extraordinary appeal was lodged, he was only able to understand some commonly spoken words.

[531]　The SC has ruled that, considering the conclusions that the court has made in relation to the plea of insufficient access to the proceedings due to the unfamiliarity with the Czech language, it was unnecessary to examine the other objections raised by the claimant/appellant in the proceedings at the SC – such as the examination of the evidence

16.106. The High Court in Olomouc, as the appellate court, upheld the abovementioned Judgment of the Regional Court in Ostrava.[532] The Executive Officer of the claimant declared before the first hearing at the appellate court that he wished to attend the hearing, but did not have sufficient command of the Czech language. The court therefore appointed an interpreter at the Executive Officer's request. However, the appellate court held that the right of the claimant (the claimant's Executive Officer) to state his case in his native language had not been breached in the preceding stages of the proceedings (including the arbitral proceedings), because the need for an interpreter only arose in the course of the proceedings at the High Court in Olomouc, as the appellate court in the proceedings for the annulment of the arbitral award. The court especially pointed out that the Executive Officer of the claimant had explicitly declared at the first hearing before the court of first instance that he understood Czech. The court also had regard to the fact that the claimant was represented by an attorney both throughout the arbitral proceedings and in the subsequent proceedings for the annulment of arbitral award. Consequently, the claimant could not sustain any damage or losses; this holds true even if the Executive Officer had not fully understood any expert (legal) expressions.

16.107. The claimant contested the judgment of the appellate court by an extraordinary appeal; the claimant argued that the case involved an issue of fundamental legal importance, namely whether the failure to appoint an interpreter to a person who does not speak Czech has disrupted the equality of the parties to the proceedings. The claimant alleged the violation of Article 37(4) of the Charter,[533] as well as Section 18(2) of the CCP.[534] The claimant further argued that the issue of the need for an interpreter was also erroneously assessed by the court of first instance, because if the conditions for appointing an interpreter had not been fulfilled, the appellate court would not have been free to make such an appointment. The claimant argues, *a maiore ad minus*, that if the need to appoint an interpreter was found to exist in the appellate proceedings, the need must have already existed in the preceding stages of the proceedings, namely in the proceedings at the court of first instance and in the arbitral proceedings. In its extraordinary appeal, the claimant also insisted on other grounds for

---

proposed by the claimant (lack thereof); consequently, these objections are not analyzed and discussed in the annotated decision in any great detail.

[532] Namely Judgment Case No. 5 Cmo 169/2011 – 321 of March 15, 2012.

[533] The provision is quoted above in the opening part of this annotation.

[534] The provision is quoted above in the opening part of this annotation.

the annulment of the arbitral award, which the claimant invoked earlier; however, these grounds were not examined by the SC, and consequently, they will not be analyzed in any greater detail.

[Arguments Presented by SC]:

16.108. The SC based its decision on the applicable laws and regulations, namely the obligation to allow the parties the unfettered opportunity to state their case before the arbitrators (i.e. in the arbitral proceedings); any breach of this obligation is penalized by the possibility of the annulment of the arbitral award (Section 31(e) of the ArbAct[535]). The basic premise employed by the SC is that the opportunity to duly state one's case and to the full extent comprises the appointment of an interpreter for a person who is not a native Czech speaker if the need to do so arises at any time in the course of the proceedings. The SC concluded that if the appellate court established the need to appoint an interpreter, the need indeed existed with respect to the Executive Officer of the claimant within the meaning of Section 18(2) of the CCP.[536]

16.109. The SC acceded to the opinion of the claimant, who has argued that if the need to appoint an interpreter is established at a particular stage of the proceedings, the finding gives rise to the presumption that the need already existed at the preceding stages of the proceedings, whether or not the respective party had previously requested the appointment of an interpreter. According to the SC, the appellate court erred if the court held that the absence of an interpreter in the preceding stages of the proceedings could not result in any violation of the party's procedural rights.

16.110. The SC also argued that the error could not have been cured by the attendance of legal counsel (who could speak the language of the proceedings). In this connection, the SC has invoked its consistent case law, namely Resolution of the SC, Case No. 20 Cdo 1540/2006, of August 8, 2006.[537] The SC also invoked the arguments voiced in the said decision: if the party represented by counsel cannot fully participate in the hearing because they do not speak the language, the party cannot avail themselves of the opportunity to state their case in the proceedings, and consequently, cannot adequately exercise their procedural rights and obligations; a contrary interpretation would render the party's right to attend the court hearing in person procedurally meaningless. In this connection, the SC invoked the

---

[535] The provision is quoted above in the opening part of this annotation.
[536] The provision is quoted above in the opening part of this annotation.
[537] The decision is quoted above in the opening part of this annotation.

principle of the equality of the parties, which can only be fulfilled if the courts ensure that all parties have the same opportunity to assert their rights. The SC again referred to the existing consistent case law (specifically Judgment of the ConCourt, Case No. III. ÚS 202/03, of November 13, 2003).[538]

16.111. The SC concluded that the said right is implemented (inter alia) through the medium of Section 18 of the CCP,[539] which orders the court to secure equal opportunity for the parties in the proceedings to exercise their rights and meet their obligations (commitments) at the level of both substantive and procedural law. Considering the above-said, the SC opined that the claimant's motion should be granted, applying Section 30 of the ArbAct,[540] Section 18(2) of the CCP[541] and Section 31(e)

---

[538] (Cit.): *"One of the fundamental principles governing court proceedings is the principle of equality of the parties which requires that the participants (parties) to the proceedings have equal standing before the court, without one or the other party enjoying any procedural benefits. In order to implement this principle, the court is obliged to provide both parties to the dispute with the same possibility to assert their rights. The principle of equality of the parties is interpreted similarly by the European Court of Human Rights which employs the words "equality of arms" in this connection. According to the consistent case law of the ECtHR, the principle of equality of arms, as an element of the broader concept of fair trial, requires that every party to civil proceedings should have a reasonable opportunity to present his case to the court in circumstances which do not place him or her at a substantial disadvantage vis-à-vis the opposing party (see also Dombo Beheer B. V. versus the Netherlands, 1993, Ankerl versus Switzerland, 1996, Komanický versus Slovakia, 2002). If the lower court failed to serve the applicant with the claimant's appeal, prevented the applicant from pleading his case and made the decision on the costs of proceedings merely on the basis of the lodged appeal, the court curtailed the applicant's procedural rights and thereby violated the equality of the parties protected by the Constitution (Article 96(1) of the Constitution of the Czech Republic, Article 37(3) of the Charter of Fundamental Rights and Freedoms, Section 18(1) of the CCP). The reason is that the objective of court proceedings is an equitable protection of rights and rightful interests of the parties to the proceedings (Section 1 of the CCP). The court proceedings were conducted in the absence of full intervention of both procedural parties because the applicant did not have an opportunity to study the contents of the appeal, as a result of which he could not provide his reply to the appeal. Section 214(2)(e) and Section 210(1) of the CCP must be interpreted both in compliance with the objective of court proceedings, as interpreted above, and in compliance with the requirements imposed on court proceedings by constitutional procedural laws, especially considering the fact that according to Section 214(2)(e) of the CCP the case was debated without an oral hearing and the appellate court's decision on the costs of proceedings differed from the decision of the court of first instance."*

[539] The provision is quoted above in the opening part of this annotation.

[540] The provision is quoted above in the opening part of this annotation.

[541] The provision is quoted above in the opening part of this annotation.

of the ArbAct,[542] if no interpreter was appointed for the claimant from the very beginning, despite the fact that the need to do so arose in the course of the proceedings. The SC believed that these circumstances constitute grounds for the annulment of the arbitral award.

16.112. The SC therefore concluded that the decision of the appellate court was incorrect; the grounds on which the SC's decision were based also applied to the decision of the court of first instance. Consequently, the SC vacated the decisions of the appellate court and of the court of first instance and remanded the case for further hearing and a new decision.

[*Further Conclusions*]:

16.113. Despite appearances, the decision may have more significant ramifications than the mere assessment of a particular situation in an individual case. The decision can be classified in the broad category of decisions that address the scope and the limits of application of the CCP in arbitration based on Section 30 of the ArbAct,[543] which has been an issue that has been discussed extensively among legal academics and practitioners. The general rule is that arbitrators are only allowed to have regard, by analogy, to potential suitable instruments under the CCP in those matters where the arbitrators consider such analogical approach appropriate; they do not proceed according to the CCP automatically and under all circumstances. In connection with the issues analyzed, see also (i) Resolution of the SC, Case No. 32 Cdo 3299/2009, of April 28, 2011,[544] (ii) Judgment of the SC, Case No. 32 Cdo 1201/2007, of June 11, 2008,[545] or (iii) Judgment of

---

[542] The provision is quoted above in the opening part of this annotation.

[543] The provision is quoted above in the opening part of this annotation.

[544] (Cit.): "*The word "reasonably" used in Section 30 of the ArbAct with respect to the application of the Code of Civil Procedure indicates that arbitration is not directly subject to the Code of Civil Procedure and its individual provisions cannot be applied mechanically in arbitration. The word "reasonably" primarily requires that the tribunal has regard to the general principles underlying Czech arbitration, i.e. the rules of the Code of Civil Procedure must be applied within the general framework of the principles of Czech arbitration. The Arbitration Act does not elaborate on the principle of equality of the parties by stipulating any specific rights and obligations of the parties and its fulfillment requires, pursuant to Section 30 of the ArbAct, reasonable application of the relevant provisions of the Code of Civil Procedure. The principle of equality of the parties is fulfilled if the parties to the arbitral proceedings have the opportunity to state their case before the arbitrators or, as applicable, if they have been duly provided with a sufficient opportunity to assert their procedural rights. These requirements must be examined from two perspectives: (i) whether the procedures were formally observed and (ii) whether both parties had an equal and sufficient opportunity to assert or raise their allegations, objections, proposals for evidence, etc.*"

[545] (Cit.): "*The Arbitration Act does not elaborate on the principle of equality of the parties by stipulating any specific rights and obligations of the parties and its fulfillment*

the SC, Case No. 23 Cdo 3749/2008, of May 26, 2010.[546] The abovementioned decisions are notable for the general definition of the relationship between the ArbAct and the CCP, as well as for the more detailed definition of the principle of equality of the parties (which is articulated in general terms in Section 18 of the ArbAct).[547] Conversely, the annotated decision has already progressed and focuses on the issue of applying a specific provision of the CCP in arbitration (just like another, previous decision of the SC, which concerned the obligation to provide instructions under Section 118a[548] of the CCP).

---

requires, pursuant to Section 30 of the Arbitration Act, reasonable application of the relevant provisions of the Code of Civil Procedure. The principle of equality of arms, as an element of the broader concept of fair trial, requires that every party to the proceedings should have a reasonable opportunity to present his case to the court in circumstances which do not place him or her at a substantial disadvantage vis-à-vis the opposing party."

[546]   (Cit.): *"1. The relationship between both statutes is regulated under Section 30 of the Arbitration Act which stipulates that unless the Act stipulates otherwise, the arbitral proceedings shall be reasonably governed by the provisions of the Code of Civil Procedure. The word "reasonably" indicates that arbitration is not directly subject to the Code of Civil Procedure and its individual provisions cannot be applied mechanically in arbitration. The word "reasonably" primarily requires that the tribunal has regard to the general principles underlying Czech arbitration, i.e. the rules of the Code of Civil Procedure must be applied within the general framework of the principles of Czech arbitration. The Arbitration Act does not elaborate on the principle of equality of the parties by stipulating any specific rights and obligations of the parties and its fulfillment requires, pursuant to Section 30 of the Arbitration Act, reasonable application of the relevant provisions of the Code of Civil Procedure. 2. The parties are most typically deprived of the opportunity to state their case in arbitration if they have not been provided with a sufficient opportunity to plead their case and if they have not had the chance to comment on all relevant circumstances. It will usually be necessary to provide the parties with the opportunity to comment on the allegations made by the other party, also in writing, i.e. the respondent must have the right to file his or her statement of defense, the claimant must have the right to comment on the counterclaim or any counter-arguments presented in the statement of defense. As concerns the individual above-mentioned statements, it is reasonable to demand that the parties be provided with the opportunity to make the statements and that the provided opportunity be sufficient, considering all relevant circumstances of the case. Another necessary prerequisite is that the parties are provided not only with the opportunity to propose evidence proving their allegations, but also with the opportunity to hear or read the evidence (unless the evidence is obviously irrelevant for the given proceedings). If the proposal for evidence presented by any of the parties was dismissed, the arbitrators must consider the proposal for evidence and sufficiently justify why the proposed evidence was not examined."*

[547]   The provision is quoted above in the opening part of this annotation.

[548]   (Cit.): *"(1) If it transpires during the hearing that a party has not yet presented all relevant statements of fact or has presented them only insufficiently, the chairman of the panel invites the party to supplement his or her statements and gives him or her instructions*

Czech (& Central European) Yearbook of Arbitration

16.114. The reference to Section 30 of the ArbAct[549] indicates that the SC did not find a violation of the principle of equality of the parties in the particular proceedings in the annotated decision, but the court's conclusions can give rise to a general obligation of the arbitrators to apply in arbitral proceedings those rules incorporated in the CCP that concern the appointment of an interpreter to individuals who do not have a proper command of the language of the proceedings. This interpretation does not attract too much attention at first glance, because the arbitrators have commonly adopted such procedure where necessary. However, they have always done so with due respect for other principles governing arbitration, such as a more flexible and less formal procedure, and primarily, the autonomy of the parties as regards the possibility to manage the progress of/developments in the proceedings. In this case, the autonomy of the parties would also be breached, because the person (Executive Officer of a party) who did not speak Czech, as the language of the proceedings, apparently did not insist on or did not request the appointment of an interpreter in the arbitral proceedings. The wording of the SC decision suggests that the obligation to appoint an interpreter is based on an objective principle, and consequently, the arbitrators will be obliged to do so whether or not the respective party requests the interpreter, and indeed even if the party explicitly waived the right to an interpreter.

16.115. At the same time, the court failed to take account of the fact that, in civil court proceedings, the parties (logically) do not have the possibility to influence the language of the proceedings, and consequently, they

---

as to which statements are to be supplemented and what the consequences of noncompliance are. (2) If the chairman of the panel opines that the court's legal opinion of the case could differ from the party's legal opinion, the chairman invites the party to supplement the relevant statements of fact to the necessary extent; the chairman shall proceed similarly to subsection (1). (3) If the chairman of the panel discovers during the hearing that a party has not yet proposed evidence necessary to prove all of his or her contested statements, the chairman invites the party to identify such evidence without undue delay and gives him or her instructions regarding the consequences of noncompliance. (4) During the hearings, the chairman of the panel also gives to the parties instructions regarding other procedural rights and duties of the parties; this does not apply if the party is represented by an attorney or a notary public to the extent of the notary's authorization under special laws. [Section 3 of Act No. 358/1992 Coll. on Notaries and Their Activities (Notary Act)], as regards the application of the provision in arbitration cf. also Judgment of the SC of 25 April 2007, Case No. 32 Odo 1528/2005 (cit.). *Section 118a of the CCP shall also reasonably apply in arbitration conducted pursuant to Act No. 216/1994 Coll."*

[549] The provision is quoted above in the opening part of this annotation.

enjoy increased protection, on the basis of which they may appear in court and state their case in their native language, and the court is obliged to arrange for the corresponding interpreting. Whereas the language of the proceedings in arbitration is typically an issue falling within the framework of the parties' autonomy, this is indeed reflected in the corresponding procedural rules of the AC – namely Section 7[550] and Section 8(2)[551] of the AC Rules.[552] Hence, it is unclear whether the obligation to appoint an interpreter should also cover those cases in which the language of the proceedings is the outcome of the voluntary agreement of the parties. If this were the case, then a party could in theory demand the annulment of an arbitral award, because the

---

[550] (Cit.): *"The proceedings shall be conducted in the Czech language unless the parties agree otherwise in writing. However, if such agreement is made after the proceedings have been commenced, it shall not be binding on the arbitrators."*

[551] (Cit.): *"The pleadings of the parties shall be submitted in the language in which the proceedings are conducted. Written evidence shall be produced in the language in which it is drawn up. If written evidence is produced in a language other than the language of the proceedings, on request of the arbitral tribunal or on request of a party with consent of the arbitral tribunal, the evidence must be translated and produced in the language in which the proceedings are conducted."*

[552] The following rules applied at the time when the arbitral award was rendered, which was the subject matter of the annotated decision:

For domestic disputes: Section 6(2) of the Rules – *"Except for written evidence, communications shall be made in Czech (or Slovak). If the written evidence is produced in a foreign language, translations thereof into the Czech (or Slovak) shall also be produced at the request of the Arbitral Tribunal, or upon request of the party and with the consent of the Arbitral Tribunal thereto. Section 7 - Oral hearings shall be held, and decisions shall be made, in the Czech (or in the Slovak) language. The oral hearings may be held in a language other than Czech (or Slovak) under the terms and conditions set forth by the Principles governing the costs of arbitral proceedings (Section 41) upon an agreement of the parties and with the consent of the Arbitral Tribunal given thereto."*

For international disputes: Section 6(2) of the Rules – *"Save for written evidence, communications shall be produced in the Czech (or in Slovak) language or in the language of the contract, or in the language used in the correspondence between the parties, as the case may be. If the Arbitration Court thinks it fit, or upon request of a party, the Arbitration Court may direct the party having produced the document to have it translated into Czech (or into Slovak), or may arrange for such a translation at the expense of such party. Section 7 – (1) Oral hearings shall be held, and decisions shall be made, in the Czech (or in Slovak) language; upon request of a party, the hearings and decisions will be translated into another language. Upon such request by a party and at the party's expense, the Arbitration Court will arrange for an interpreter, or for the translation of the decisions or other writings, as the case may be. (2) If necessary, the arbitral tribunal may, provided that both parties agree, hold hearings and, as the case may be, pronounce the decision directly in another language."*

proceedings were conducted in a language the use of which was explicitly approved by the respective party. Naturally, it is possible to envisage a situation in which even such procedure will be logical and justifiable, for instance, if the language of the proceedings is selected with regard to the governing law and/or the anticipated legal counsels. In a number of other cases, however, the parties will be provided with an opportunity to obstruct and hinder the proceedings, which may ultimately frustrate the advantages of arbitration, primarily its expeditiousness and less formal demands compared to civil court proceedings.

16.116. The tendency of the SC to introduce the obligation to appoint an interpreter on an absolute basis may turn out to be a more serious problem, because the court held that the equality of the parties was breached in the given case, even though the Executive Officer of the claimant had explicitly stated that his language skills were sufficient (as stated above) and did not request the appointment of interpreter. While this occurred in the court of first instance, the description of the facts of the case does not clearly indicate how the issue was resolved in the arbitration itself, i.e. whether the arbitral panel entirely dismissed the issue, or whether the Executive Officer of the claimant explicitly waived the possibility of having an interpreter (the text of the decision would lean toward the former). This means a de facto derogation of the parties' autonomy with respect to those issues connected with the practical organization of the proceedings from the linguistic point of view. In light of the annotated decision, the arbitrators should appoint an interpreter whenever the native language of the party to the proceedings is different from the language of the proceedings. The reason is that the other party could hardly argue that the conditions for the appointment of an interpreter were not fulfilled in the subsequent proceedings for the annulment of the arbitral award if the respective party can communicate in the language of the proceedings. The SC has rejected the argument that this common level of communication is sufficient, and that the appointment of legal counsel renders it unnecessary for the party to accurately understand the expert/legal terms; the respective party will always be free to make this objection, and it will be difficult to refute such objection.

16.117. We may conclude that the main reason why the respective decision appears controversial is not the fact that the court assessed the specific situation that arose in the given proceedings as a violation of the party's right to state one's case, but the fact that the court articulated a universal rule and expanded the limits of the application of Section 30 of the ArbAct.[553] None of the above-described practical problems would have arisen if the court had held that the decision was justified due to an individual breach of Section 18 of the ArbAct.[554]

| | |

11. Resolution of Supreme Court of Czech Republic of September 30, 2013 in Case No. 23 Cdo 1034/2012:[555] (i) Place of Arbitration, (ii) Foreign Arbitral Award, (iii) Jurisdiction of Czech Courts to Annul Arbitral Award If Parties Have Agreed on Place of Arbitration Abroad, (iv) International Court of Arbitration Attached to International Chamber of Commerce (ICC ARBCOURT)

Abbreviations Used:

New York Convention (1958)	New York Convention on the Recognition and Enforcement of Foreign Arbitral Awards (1958)[556]
SC	Supreme Court of the Czech Republic
ArbAct	Act No. 216/1994 Coll., on Arbitration and the Enforcement of Arbitral Awards, as amended[557]
ICC	International Chamber of Commerce
ICC ArbCourt	International Court of Arbitration attached to the International Chamber of Commerce (ICC)[558]

---

[553] The provision is quoted above in the opening part of this annotation.

[554] The provision is quoted above in the opening part of this annotation.

[555] This decision is available online on the website of the SC at http://www.nsoud.cz/ Judikatura/judikatura_ns.nsf/WebSearch/742E9D4886B46267C1257C2000426CDE?open Document&Highlight=0 [last accessed on November 3, 2014].

[556] Convention of June 10, 1958. See Decree of the Ministry of Foreign Affairs of the Czechoslovak Republic No. 74/1959 Coll. (http://www.uncitral.org/uncitral/en/uncitral_ texts/arbitration/NYConvention.html).

[557] The SC does not explicitly identify the version of the ArbAct applied in the given case, because the relevant provisions have not been subject to any amendments that could influence the conclusions of the SC and their applicability. The only change that will be elaborated on below in this annotation has been introduced with effect since January 1, 2014, i.e. after the respective decision was made. But the change does not have any influence to the case annotated.

[558] For more information regarding this arbitral tribunal, see http://www.ICC ArbCourtwbo.org/products-and-services/arbitration-and-adr/arbitration/ and http://www.ICC

ICC Rules	Rules of Arbitration of the International Chamber of Commerce (ICC)[559]
ConCourt	Constitutional Court of the Czech Republic
CCP	Act No. 99/1963 Coll., the Code of Civil Procedure, as amended
AC	Arbitration Court at the Economic Chamber of the Czech Republic and Agricultural Chamber of the Czech Republic[560]
PILA	Act No. 91/2012 Coll., on Private International Law[561]

Key Words

annulment (setting aside) of arbitral award | applicable law | autonomy[562] | auxiliary function of court | domestic arbitral award | domestic dispute | domiciliation of dispute | enforcement of arbitral award | fictitious place of arbitration | fictitious seat of arbitration | foreign arbitral award | freedom of contract[563] | hearing dispute | international dimension | international dispute | interpretation of juridical act | jurisdiction of Czech courts | jurisdiction to annul arbitral award | language of arbitration | legal domiciliation of dispute | legitimate interest of parties | lex arbitri | nationality of arbitrator | New York Convention (1958)[564] | ordre public[565] | place of arbitration | place of residence of party | place where arbitral award is made | place where arbitral award is made | preliminary issue/reference for preliminary

---

ArbCourtwbo.org/about-ICCArbCourt/organization/dispute-resolution-services/ICCArb Court-international-court-of-arbitration/.

[559] The applicable Rules are the ICC Rules, as amended, and applicable in 1998, i.e. in effect until December 31, 2011 (available on Internet in the original English language at http://www.ICC ArbCourt.se/skiljedom/rules_arb_english.pdf; we have also considered, for the purposes of this annotation, the New ICC Rules, i.e. arbitration rules in effect since January 1, 2012 (also available online on the ICC website at http://www.ICC ArbCourtwbo.org/products-and-services/arbitration-and-adr/arbitration/ICC-rules-of-arbitration/).

[560] See also the AC website at www.soud.cz in multiple language mutations.

[561] This Act is one of the statutes adopted within the framework of the recodification of Czech civil law; it has replaced Act No. 97/1963 Coll., as amended, on Private International Law and Procedure, with effect since January 1, 2014.

[562] See also freedom of contract.

[563] See also autonomy.

[564] Convention of June 10, 1958. See Decree of the Ministry of Foreign Affairs of the Czechoslovak Republic No. 74/1959 Coll. (http://www.uncitral.org/uncitral/en/uncitral_texts/arbitration/NYConvention.html).

[565] See also public policy.

ruling | public policy[566] | recognition of arbitral award | refusal to enforce arbitral award | refusal to recognize arbitral award | registered office of party | seat of arbitration | subjective internationalization of dispute | supervisory function of court | Terms of Reference | validity of arbitration agreement[567] | validity of arbitration clause[568] |

Applicable Laws and Regulations:
New York Convention (1958)[569]
ArbAct: Section 17,[570] Section 38[571]
PILA: Section 120,[572] Section 122(2)[573]
ICC Rules: Article 14[574]

---

[566] See also ordre public.

[567] Depending on the context, "arbitration clause" and "arbitration agreement" may also be interpreted as synonyms, or rather the arbitration clause is a form of arbitration agreement according to Section 2 of the ArbAct.

[568] Depending on the context, "arbitration clause" and "arbitration agreement" may also be interpreted as synonyms, or rather the arbitration clause is a form of arbitration agreement according to Section 2 of the ArbAct.

[569] See Decree of the Ministry of Foreign Affairs of the Czechoslovak Republic No. 74/1959 Coll. (http://www.uncitral.org/uncitral/en/uncitral_texts/arbitration/NYConvention.html).

[570] ArbAct, Section 17 (cit.): *The arbitration is held in the place agreed by the parties. In the absence of such determination, the arbitration is held in a place determined by the arbitrators having regard to the legitimate interests of the parties.* Note: This version of the law was applicable on the day when the arbitral award was rendered, but has not been subject to any modifications in the meantime and therefore continues to apply.

[571] ArbAct, Section 38 (cit.): *Arbitral awards made abroad shall be recognized and enforced in the Czech Republic like Czech arbitral awards, on condition of reciprocity. The requirement of reciprocity shall also be considered fulfilled if the foreign country generally declares foreign arbitral awards enforceable on condition of reciprocity. However, the decision on enforcement of a foreign arbitral award must always be reasoned.* Note: This version of the law was applicable on the day when the arbitral award was rendered, but it was not subject to any modifications in the meantime, i.e. until the moment of the annotated decision of the SC. January 1, 2014 is the effective date of the PILA, which regulates the said issues in Sections 120 and 122 (both provisions are quoted below in the opening part of this annotation).

[572] PILA, Section 120 (cit.): *Arbitral awards made abroad shall be recognized and enforced in the Czech Republic like Czech arbitral awards, on condition of reciprocity. The requirement of reciprocity shall also be considered fulfilled if the foreign country generally declares foreign arbitral awards enforceable on condition of reciprocity.*

[573] PILA, Section 122(2) (cit.): *Enforcement of a foreign arbitral award shall be ordered by a reasoned decision of a Czech court.*

[574] ICC Rules, Article 14 – (cit.): **(1)** The place of arbitration shall be fixed by the Court, unless agreed upon by the parties. (2) The Arbitral Tribunal may, after consultation with

The Supreme Court of the Czech Republic reached the following principal conclusions:

(1) The Act on Arbitration and Enforcement of Arbitral Awards (ArbAct) does not prohibit entities with their place of residence or registered office in the Czech Republic from internationalizing their dispute [subjective internationalization of the dispute] by creating an international procedural dimension and agreeing that their dispute will be resolved by a foreign arbitral tribunal, with the place of arbitration being abroad.

(2) Section 17 of the ArbAct stipulates that arbitration will be held in the place [seat of arbitration] agreed by the parties. In the absence of such determination, arbitration is held in a place determined by the arbitrators having regard to the legitimate interests of the parties. The "place where arbitration is held" pursuant to Section 17 of the ArbAct must be interpreted as referring to the legal domiciliation of the dispute [place of arbitration, meaning seat of arbitration], not as the place where the dispute is heard. The place of arbitration, in the legal sense, which determines the domicile of a particular arbitration, must be distinguished from the place where the case is heard (place of hearing the case), i.e. the place where the individual stages of the arbitral proceedings actually take place.

(3) If any entities that have their registered office in the Czech Republic have agreed that their dispute (if any) will be resolved by the International Court of Arbitration attached to the International Chamber of Commerce in Paris and the place of arbitration will be in *Vienna* (Austria), the arbitral award rendered in such arbitration is not a domestic arbitral award, and consequently, Czech courts do not have jurisdiction to conduct proceedings for the annulment of the award pursuant to Act of the Czech Republic No. 216/1994 Coll., on Arbitration and the Enforcement of Arbitral Awards (ArbAct). The fact that the hearing organized within the framework of such arbitration was held in Prague, as agreed by the parties, has no bearing on the said conclusion.[575]

---

the parties, conduct hearings and meetings at any location it considers appropriate, unless agreed otherwise by the parties. (3) The Arbitral Tribunal may deliberate at any location it considers appropriate.

The New ICC Rules in effect since January 1, 2012 have not introduced any changes to the contents of the provision, and the text therefore remains the same. However, some of the provisions were renumbered, and the text is now included in Article 18.

[575] The summary of the SC's legal opinion (*ratio decidendi*) was adopted from the SC website.

(4) Arbitral awards rendered abroad (the place where the arbitral award is made is outside the Czech Republic) can be recognized and enforced in the Czech Republic following the procedure under Section 38 of the ArbAct, or subject to the conditions prescribed by the New York Convention on the Recognition and Enforcement of Foreign Arbitral Awards (1958), as applicable; the New York Convention also stipulates the conditions under which the recognition and enforcement of the arbitral award can be refused. The court of the state in which both parties have their registered office/place of residence, but in which the arbitration was not held based on the parties' agreement, has the right to express its reservations (if any) with respect to the arbitral award in the proceedings for recognition/enforcement, if these reservations constitute circumstances that justify a refusal to recognize/enforce the arbitral award.

[*From Facts of Case*]:

16.118. On July 26, 2010, an arbitral award was rendered in arbitration conducted at the International Court of Arbitration attached to the International Chamber of Commerce (ICC) [ICC ArbCourt] in Case ICC 12190/TE/MW/AVH/JHN/GZ; the award was subsequently challenged by the claimant,[576] who demanded the annulment of the award. Considering the fact that the subject matter of the proceedings at the SC was limited to the issue of the jurisdiction of Czech courts to hear and resolve the motion to annul the said arbitral award, the particular grounds were not specified on which the claimant demanded the annulment of the arbitral award. According to Article 20 of the Enterprise Sale Contract of June 19, 2000 entered into by and between IPB, a. s., as the seller, and ČSOB, a. s., as the buyer, the parties agreed to submit their disputes for resolution to the ICC ArbCourt; the parties also agreed that the place of arbitration would be *Vienna* (Austria). However, all other circumstances of the case exhibited an exclusive connection to the Czech Republic – (i) the original parties to the dispute were Czech entities, (ii) the description of the contested issues as the basic framework document concerning the agreement on arbitration (*Terms of Reference*) was signed on April 18, 2003 in Prague, (iii) all arbitrators were Czech nationals, (iv) the proceedings were

---

[576] A legal entity formed and existing under the laws of the Slovak Republic in the form of a joint stock company (although the annotated decision indicates that the original party to the respective obligation was a Czech entity/Czech legal entity); the respondent is a legal entity formed and existing under the laws of the Czech Republic in the form of a joint stock company.

conducted in the Czech language, (v) the hearing was held in Prague,[577] (vi) the arbitration clause was drawn up in Czech, (vii) the Enterprise Sale Contract was entered into in Prague, and (viii) Czech law was the applicable law.

[*Procedure of Case*]:

16.119. The Prague Municipal Court, as the court of first instance, rendered its Resolution of January 13, 2011 in Case No. 14 Cm 180/2010-218, whereby the proceedings for the annulment of the arbitral award were terminated for a lack of jurisdiction. The court based its decision on the finding that the place of arbitration, and at the same time, the place where the arbitral award was made,[578] was *Vienna* (Austria). Based on the said facts, the court arrived at the conclusion that the arbitral award was not a domestic arbitral award, and consequently, the court did not have jurisdiction to hear the motion to annul the award under the ArbAct. Hence, the court applied the first sentence of Section 104(1) of the CCP.[579]

16.120. The Prague High Court, as the appellate court, upheld the abovementioned Resolution of the Municipal Court in Prague.[580] The appellate court based its decision on the finding made by the court of first instance as concerns the place [seat] of arbitration/place where the arbitral award was made. The appellate court also referred to the ICC Rules of Arbitration (ICC Rules), specifically Article 14 of the ICC Rules.[581] The appellate court also invoked the list of contested issues

---

[577] The claimant argued that the parties had agreed to change the place of arbitration; the claimant deduced this conclusion from the fact that Prague was explicitly fixed as the place of the hearing in the procedural resolution of September 22, 2009.

[578] The arbitral award indicates that the place of arbitration should be and is deemed identical to the place where the arbitral award was made.

[579] CCP, Section 104 (cit.): *(1) If a procedural requirement is not fulfilled and the deficiency cannot be remedied, the court terminates the proceedings. If the courts lack jurisdiction over the case or if different proceedings must precede court proceedings, the court forwards the case, after the resolution on termination of the proceedings becomes final and conclusive, to the competent authority, without prejudice to the legal effects associated with the filing of the lawsuit (motion for the commencement of the proceedings). (2) If a procedural requirement is not fulfilled and the deficiency can be remedied, the court adopts suitable measures. The court can usually continue the proceedings, but may not decide on the merits. If the court fails to remedy the deficiency in the procedural requirements, the court terminates the proceedings.* Note: This version of the law applied to the proceedings at the court of first instance, but it has not been subject to any modifications in the meantime and therefore continues to apply.

[580] Namely, by Resolution of September 30, 2011 in Case No. 8 Cmo 62/2011 – 306.

[581] The provision is quoted above in the opening part of this annotation.

(*Terms of Reference*) of April 18, 2003, which explicitly referred to the arbitration agreement that included the agreement of the parties on the place [seat] of arbitration, and that also stipulated that if any procedural issue cannot be resolved by reference to the *Terms of Reference* or the ICC Rules, the issue shall be resolved by the arbitral panel, unless the parties agree otherwise. It was also pointed out that the arbitral panel could have held the hearing in Prague, or in any other place that the panel deemed reasonable, unless one or both of the parties disagreed. Following the request/agreement of the parties, the hearing was held in Prague (namely the building of the AC).[582] The court agreed with the conclusion reached by the Prague Municipal Court that the possibility to annul the arbitral award in terms of Section 31 of the ArbAct[583] applies exclusively to domestic arbitral awards, which must be

---

[582]   The AC merely provided premises where the dispute could be heard.

[583]   (cit.): *At the request of any party, the court annuls the arbitral award if: (a) it was made in a case that cannot be submitted to arbitration (cannot be the subject of a valid arbitration agreement), (b) the arbitration agreement is invalid for other reasons, or the agreement was cancelled or it does not apply to the agreed case, (c) the arbitrator(s) who took part in the proceedings was/were not authorized to make decisions in the case, whether under the arbitration agreement or otherwise, or lacked the capacity to act as arbitrator(s), (d) the arbitral award was not adopted by the majority of arbitrators, (e) a party was denied the opportunity to plead their case in the arbitral proceedings, (f) the arbitral award orders a party to provide performance that was not requested by the obligee or to provide performance that is impossible or illegal under domestic law, (g) it transpires that there are reasons that would otherwise justify the reopening of civil proceedings in court* [Section 228(1)(a) and (b) of the CCP]. The current version of the provision reads as follows: *At the request of any party, the court annuls the arbitral award if: (a) it was made in a case that cannot be submitted to arbitration (cannot be the subject of a valid arbitration agreement), (b) the arbitration agreement is invalid for other reasons, or the agreement was cancelled or it does not apply to the agreed case, (c) the arbitrator(s) who took part in the proceedings was/were not authorized to make decisions in the case, whether under the arbitration agreement or otherwise, or lacked the capacity to act as arbitrator(s), (d) the arbitral award was not adopted by the majority of arbitrators, (e) a party was denied the opportunity to plead their case in the arbitral proceedings, (f) the arbitral award orders a party to provide performance that was not requested by the creditor or to provide performance that is impossible or illegal under domestic law, (g) the arbitrator or the permanent arbitral institution resolved a dispute arising from a consumer contract contrary to consumer protection laws, or clearly in violation of good morals, or contrary to public policy, (h) an arbitration agreement relating to disputes arising from consumer contracts lacks the information required under Section 3(5), or such information is intentionally or to a non-negligible extent incomplete, inaccurate, or false, or (i) it transpires that there are reasons that would otherwise justify the reopening of civil proceedings in court* [Section 228(1)(a) and (b) of the CCP].

interpreted as meaning arbitral awards rendered in the territory of the Czech Republic. In this connection, the appellate court pointed out the place of arbitration/place where the award was made, and noted that the court had not discovered anything that would suggest that the parties' agreement on the said place had changed, as the agreement was incorporated in the arbitration agreement. The appellate court held that the fact alone that the hearing was held in Prague, i.e. in a place different from the agreed place of arbitration, was not contrary to Article 14 of the ICC Rules,[584] and at the same time, had no bearing on the jurisdiction to make a decision on the annulment of the arbitral award (which does not extend to arbitral awards rendered abroad).

16.121. The judgment of the appellate court was challenged an extraordinary appeal filed by the claimant. The claimant argued that the appellate court had wrongly assessed the issue of the jurisdiction of Czech courts to make a decision on the annulment of the arbitral award, because the respective arbitration had, in legal terms, the closest connection with the territory of the Czech Republic and its legal system.[585] It was also argued that the reference to *Vienna* as the place where the arbitral award would be made was contrary to the agreement of the parties affirmed by the arbitral panel[586] and the determination of the forum in the legal sense of the word. The claimant maintained that the arbitral award was a domestic award, because it was not, and could not have become, a foreign arbitral award merely by the subjective and speculative effort of the parties to designate a fictitious place [seat] of arbitration abroad. The claimant argued that arbitration was fully governed by Czech procedural legal rules and subject to the supervisory and auxiliary functions of Czech courts. The claimant therefore concluded that Czech courts had jurisdiction to assess and annul (if applicable) the arbitral award, because all factual and legal circumstances of the proceedings had a connection to the Czech Republic, i.e. there was no relevant international dimension that would connect the respective proceedings to any other legal system. In its extraordinary appeal, the claimant also analyzed the (alleged) procedural errors made by the appellate court, as a result of which the claimant had been allegedly denied the opportunity to duly state their

---

[584] The provision is quoted above in the opening part of this annotation.

[585] As the particular factual circumstances were described above in this annotation.

[586] However, the decision that was referred to as the affirmation of the arbitral panel is the procedural resolution of September 22, 2009, which determined the place where the hearing would be held.

case;[587] the claimant also challenged the panel of the appellate court for their alleged bias. However, considering the fact that these circumstances (although addressed by the SC) had no influence on the decision on the merits of the case, the corresponding arguments are not elaborated on in this annotation.

16.122. We should add, for the sake of completeness, that the annotated decision of the SC was contested by a constitutional complaint,[588] which was heard by the ConCourt under Case No. II. ÚS 105/14. However, the constitutional complaint was rejected as obviously groundless by Resolution of the ConCourt of February 19, 2014.[589, 590]

[*Arguments Presented by SC*]:

16.123. The SC based its decision on the general differentiation between domestic and foreign arbitral awards, and on the principle that stipulates that foreign arbitral awards must be submitted to recognition before they can be enforced in the state where enforcement is sought, as opposed to domestic arbitral awards, which do not require any recognition before the enforcement itself. It is therefore inferred that the jurisdiction of Czech courts is limited to the annulment of domestic

---

[587] It is an issue of the improper service of documents.

[588] Specifically, on January 9, 2014.

[589] This decision is available online on the website of the ConCourt at http://nalus.usoud.cz/Search/ResultDetail.aspx?id=82567&pos=1&cnt=1&typ=result.

[590] The ConCourt has concluded that (cit.): *It is not possible to conclude in the given case that the lower courts had entirely ignored the objections raised by the applicant. It was especially the High Court whose response to the applicant's appellate objections was sufficiently adequate, quoting relevant professional literature (pp. 4-5). Similarly, the Supreme Court has also clarified why the court has held the applicant's arguments groundless (cf. p. 5). In this connection, the objection is also unacceptable which relates to the alleged incapability of review of the contested judicial decisions. If the decisions were indeed unreviewable, the applicant would be unable to make any material objections to the courts' conclusions. But the applicant has articulated very extensive and specific objections to the individual aspects of the legal conclusion pronounced – at whichever level – by the lower courts.* Note: In this connection, the ConCourt also did not agree that the interpretation adopted by the SC was excessively formalistic. The ConCourt also rejected the argument that the decision of the SC is contrary to the existing case law of the lower courts (specifically, the Olomouc High Court). It is the duty of the Supreme Court to unify the case law of the lower courts in extraordinary appeal proceedings in the interests of their uniform decision-making; having heard the appeal, the SC fulfilled the duty. Last, but not least, the ConCourt also rejected the argument that the decision is inconsistent with European standards. The ConCourt agreed with the constitutional complaint that the Supreme Court should have addressed the competing case law (of the High Courts), but nonetheless concluded that failure to do so does not *eo ipso* render the decision of the Supreme Court unconstitutional.

(Czech) arbitral awards. The SC also applied the applicable laws, namely the provisions of Section 38 of the ArbAct,[591] as well as the applicable rules of the New York Convention (1958).[592] Consequently, the assessment of the jurisdiction of Czech courts is contingent on whether or not the respective award is a domestic arbitral award. The Supreme Court of the Czech Republic (SC) based its decision on the fact that foreign arbitral awards are defined by the quoted legal rules as awards that were made in a foreign state. The SC held that this conclusion does not prevent entities with their place of residence or registered office in the Czech Republic from making an agreement that the place of arbitration will be situated in a state different from their place of residence (registered office), and thereby internationalizing their dispute, despite the fact that the dispute did not exhibit any objective international dimension.[593] Consequently, the court allowed the unlimited autonomy (freedom of contract) of the parties. Referring to Section 17 of the ArbAct,[594] the SC held that the place where the arbitral award is made must be considered identical to the place of arbitration.[595] The SC based this conclusion on the premise that the place [seat] of arbitration/place where the arbitral award is made must be perceived in the legal sense of the word, and must be distinguished from the place(s) where the individual stages of the arbitral proceedings are actually taking place.

16.124. The Supreme Court of the Czech Republic (SC) agreed that the parties exercised their autonomy and determined *Vienna* (Austria) as the place of arbitration, even though the dispute involved two domestic/Czech entities. The SC pointed out that the fact that the hearing took place elsewhere, namely in Prague (Czech Republic), has no bearing on the

---

[591] The provision is quoted above in the opening part of this annotation.

[592] See Article 1(1) of the Convention (cit.): *This Convention shall apply to the recognition and enforcement of arbitral awards made in the territory of a State other than the State where the recognition and enforcement of such awards are sought, and arising out of differences between persons, whether physical or legal. It shall also apply to arbitral awards not considered as domestic awards in the State where their recognition and enforcement are sought.*

[593] The SC refers to the following publication: Alexander Bělohlávek. Zákon o rozhodčím řízení a výkonu rozhodčích nálezů. Komentář [Title in Translation: Act on Arbitration and Enforcement of Arbitral Awards. Commentary], 2nd edition, Praha [Prague, Czech Republic]: C. H. Beck 2012, p. 622.

[594] The provision is quoted above in the opening part of this annotation.

[595] The SC refers to the following publication: Alexander Bělohlávek. Zákon o rozhodčím řízení a výkonu rozhodčích nálezů. Komentář [Title in Translation: Act on Arbitration and Enforcement of Arbitral Awards. Commentary], 2nd edition, Praha [Prague, Czech Republic]: C. H. Beck 2012, p. 1356.

agreement of the parties. Considering the above said, the SC held the objection groundless that the place of arbitration should be interpreted as the place with the closest connection to the arbitration, instead of the agreed place [seat] of arbitration. The SC maintained that if the parties agree on the place of arbitration, the arbitral award rendered in such proceedings cannot be deemed a domestic award, and Czech courts do not have jurisdiction to annul the award. However, such arbitral awards are subject to recognition and enforcement pursuant to Section 38 of the ArbAct,[596] or the procedure envisaged under the New York Convention, as applicable; the parties are free to plead any objections in the relevant proceedings, on the basis of which the enforcement and recognition of the award can be refused.[597, 598]

---

[596] The provision is quoted above in the opening part of this annotation.

[597] The SC refers to the following publication: Alexander Bělohlávek. Zákon o rozhodčím řízení a výkonu rozhodčích nálezů. Komentář [Title in Translation: Act on Arbitration and Enforcement of Arbitral Awards. Commentary], 2nd edition, Praha [Prague, Czech Republic]: C. H. Beck 2012, p. 623.

[598] See Section 39 of the ArbAct (as applicable in the course of the proceedings, i.e. until December 31, 2013) – cit.: *Recognition or enforcement of a foreign arbitral award shall be refused if: (a) the arbitral award is not final and conclusive or enforceable according to the law of the state where it was made, (b) the arbitral award suffers from any of the defects listed in Section 31, (c) the arbitral award is contrary to public policy.*

The corresponding provisions are currently incorporated in Section 121 of the PILA (cit.): *Recognition or enforcement of a foreign arbitral award shall be refused if the foreign arbitral award: (a) is not final and conclusive or enforceable according to the law of the state in which it was made, (b) was annulled in the state in which, or according to the law of which, it was made, (c) suffers from a defect that constitutes grounds for the annulment of a Czech arbitral award by the court, or (d) is contrary to public policy.*

As concerns arbitral awards to which the New York Convention (1958) applies, the grounds for the refusal to recognize and enforce an award are stipulated in Article V thereof (cit.): *1. Recognition and enforcement of the award may be refused, at the request of the party against whom it is invoked, only if that party furnishes the competent authority where the recognition and enforcement is sought with proof that: (a) The parties to the agreement referred to in Article II were, under the law applicable to them, under some incapacity, or the said agreement is not valid under the law to which the parties have subjected it or, failing any indication thereon, under the law of the country in which the award was made; or (b) The party against whom the award is invoked was not given proper notice of the appointment of the arbitrator or of the arbitration proceedings, or was otherwise unable to present their case; or (c) The award deals with a dispute not contemplated by or not falling within the terms of the submission to arbitration, or it contains decisions on matters beyond the scope of the submission to arbitration, provided that, if the decisions on matters submitted to arbitration can be separated from those not so submitted, such part of the award that contains decisions on matters submitted to*

16.125. The SC therefore concluded that the decision of the appellate court was correct. The claimant did not succeed in undermining the decision of the appellate court, and consequently, the SC dismissed the extraordinary appeal.

[*Further Conclusions and Comments Concerning Annotated Resolution of SC*]:

16.126. The decision focused on the definition of foreign arbitral awards and the jurisdiction of Czech courts with respect to such awards. The annotated decision can be perceived as the first decision rendered in this connection, and it has become the basis for subsequent rulings on the said issue.[599] The decision has attracted a good deal of attention in the legal community, because it de facto confirmed the possibility of internationalizing otherwise purely domestic disputes, which could be expected to be governed by the ArbAct. Opinions regarding the possibility of internationalization have varied; some have argued that the international dimension must objectively exist, because leaving its existence at the will of the parties (i.e. the existence of international dimension of subjective nature) could ultimately result in evading the supervisory function of the state.[600] Considering the broad procedural autonomy with which the ArbAct affords the parties, we may conclude that such approach is principally possible, especially if we also have regard to the fact that this potential internationalization of the dispute by the parties has purely procedural, not substantive, consequences (i.e. it does not affect the subject matter of the dispute). We could argue

---

arbitration may be recognized and enforced; or (d) The composition of the arbitral authority or the arbitral procedure was not in accordance with the agreement of the parties, or failing such agreement, was not in accordance with the law of the country in which the arbitration took place; or (e) The award has not yet become binding on the parties, or has been set aside or suspended by a competent authority of the country in which, or under the law of which, that award was made. 2. Recognition and enforcement of an arbitral award may also be refused if the competent authority in the country in which recognition and enforcement is sought finds that: (a) The subject matter of the dispute is not capable of settlement by arbitration under the law of that country; or (b) The recognition or enforcement of the award would be contrary to the public policy of that country.

[599] Cf. also Judgment of the SC of November 2013 in Case No. 23 Cdo 2542/2011, which deals with a similar issue.

[600] Cf. Naděžda Rozehnalová. Rozhodčí řízení v mezinárodním a vnitrostátním styku [Title in Translation: Arbitration in International and Domestic Transactions]; 2nd edition, Praha [Prague, Czech Republic] ASPI/Wolters Kluwer, 2008, p. 45. The author arrived at the conclusion that such a choice of the parties could only be allowed under the contractual theory of arbitration (if at all), not if the applicable theory is the jurisdictional or a hybrid theory.

that the parties' freedom of contract (contractual autonomy) should be limited if the parties' agreement clearly and unambiguously targeted the evasion of the provisions of the otherwise applicable *lex arbitri* (here the ArbAct), from which the parties were otherwise prohibited from departing, i.e. provisions that could be classified as mandatory provisions from the conflict-of-laws perspective, or which would even be a component of public policy (*ordre public*).

16.127. As a matter of fact, such a choice of the place [seat] of arbitration was at least implicitly envisaged by the applicable procedural rules of Czech permanent arbitral institutions; this could be illustrated by the example of the most famous of these institutions, the AC – compare the definitions of the domestic and international disputes in Section 1(3) of the AC Rules Governing Domestic Disputes in effect until June 30, 2012;[601] the definition was for some time (apart from other criteria) connected to the place of arbitration (which falls within the autonomy of the parties).[602] Naturally, the division had no effects under

---

[601] The Rules in effect until January 31, 2007 (cit.): *"Domestic dispute" in the sense of these Rules means any dispute in which all parties (participants) have their seats (domicile) within the territory of the Czech Republic, or any dispute in which organizational parts (branches) of foreign persons according to Section 21 of the Commercial Code and/or organizational parts (branches) exercising activities in accordance with a specific Act (e.g. Act No 21/1992, Coll., on Banks) have their seats (domicile) within the territory of the Czech Republic and are entered in the Commercial Register. Further conditions for arbitrating the dispute as domestic are the application of Czech law to the dispute, written statements and pleadings of the parties in the Czech (Slovak) language, the venue of the proceedings in the territory of the Czech Republic, and the decision issued in the Czech (Slovak) language.*

The Rules in effect from February 1, 2007 no longer contained this criterion, and Section 1(3) reads as follows (cit.): *"Domestic dispute" in the sense of these Rules means any dispute in which all parties (participants) have their seats (domicile) within the territory of the Czech Republic, or any dispute in which organizational parts (branches) of foreign persons according to Section 21 of the Commercial Code and/or organizational parts (branches) exercising activities in accordance with a specific Act (e.g. Act No 21/1992, Coll., on Banks) have their seats (domicile) within the territory of the Czech Republic and are entered in the Commercial Register, provided that the law applicable to the dispute is Czech substantive law, and provided that all written statements and pleadings of the parties are in the Czech (Slovak) language, and the arbitration proceedings are held and the decision is made in the Czech (Slovak) language.*

[602] The law applicable to disputes classified as domestic reads as follows:

Section 5 of the Rules in effect until January 31 2007 reads as follows (cit.): *Normally, hearings in pending disputes shall be held at the seat of the Arbitration Court in Prague. Upon suggestion of the Secretary or at the initiative of the Arbitral Tribunal or under an agreement of the parties to the dispute, the hearings may be held at other places within the Czech Republic.*

substantive law, i.e. the differentiation between international and domestic disputes in light of the procedural rules of the AC cannot be deemed identical to the differentiation between domestic and foreign arbitral awards under Section 38 of the ArbAct;[603] but it can be perceived as evidence that the autonomy of the parties was an applicable criterion with respect to those issues.[604] The currently applicable Rules make no distinction between domestic and international disputes, and consequently, the provisions have no equivalent.

Section 5 of the Rules in effect from February 1, 2007 reads as follows (cit.): *Normally, hearings in pending disputes shall be held at the seat of the Arbitration Court in Prague. At the initiative of the Arbitral Tribunal, or under an agreement of the parties to the dispute, and with the consent of the Secretary of the Arbitration Court, the hearings may be held at other places within the Czech Republic.*

International disputes were governed by the following rules:

Section 5 of the Rules in effect until January 31, 2007 reads as follows (cit.): *(1) Normally, hearings in pending disputes shall be held in the seat of the Arbitration Court in Prague. At the initiative of the arbitral tribunal or under an agreement of the parties to the dispute and with consent of the Secretary of the Arbitration Court, the hearings may be held at other places within the Czech Republic or abroad. (2) The arbitral tribunal shall give a notice to the board of hearings to be held abroad. If such hearings are to be held abroad at the initiative of arbitrators, the parties have to agree thereto.*

Section 5 of the Rules in effect from February 1, 2007 reads as follows (cit.): *(1) Normally, hearings in pending disputes shall be held in the seat of the Arbitration Court in Prague. At the suggestion of the Secretary, or at the initiative of the arbitral tribunal, or under an agreement of the parties to the dispute, the hearings may be held at other places within the Czech Republic or abroad. (2) The arbitral tribunal shall give notice to the board of hearings to be held abroad. If such hearings are to be held abroad at the initiative of arbitrators, the parties have to agree thereto.*

The currently applicable provision is Section 5 of the AC Rules in effect since July 1, 2012, which reads as follows (cit.): *(1) Oral hearings shall normally be held at the seat of the Arbitration Court. The seat of the Arbitration Court is Prague. With the consent of the Secretary granted on the basis of the agreement of the parties, or at the initiative of the arbitral tribunal, if the parties have not agreed on the place of the oral hearing, the arbitral tribunal may decide that the oral hearing shall be held at some other place in the Czech Republic or abroad. The consent of the Secretary and the decision of the arbitral tribunal are not required if the proceedings are to be held at a permanent place of arbitration of the Arbitration Court. (2) If proceedings are to be conducted abroad, the place of arbitration shall be the country where the proceedings are conducted.*

[603] The provision is quoted above in the opening part of this annotation.

[604] We must also have regard to the fact that the AC Rules regulate the issue of the place where hearings are held; again, this place cannot be deemed identical to the place of arbitration, as such, and the respective comparison is only illustrative.

16.128. Section 38 of the ArbAct[605] indicates that an arbitral award will be designated as foreign based on the place where the arbitral award is made, not the place of arbitration. To some extent, these 2 criteria merge (or rather, the place of arbitration is usually considered to be the place where the arbitral award is made), but they cannot automatically be deemed identical, because the ArbAct does not set forth any such explicit presumption. We cannot exclude the possibility that the parties will choose the place of arbitration abroad, but simultaneously determine that the arbitral award will be rendered in the Czech Republic. But it is indeed a rather theoretical construct, unsupported by any actual reason why the parties should do so. Should the parties have any practical interests in having the case actually heard outside the territory of the Czech Republic, they do not need to transfer the place of arbitration abroad, since it would fully suffice if the parties made an agreement in such case that would merely regulate the place where the hearing(s) will be held.

16.129. A different situation will occur if the parties directly agree that the arbitral award will be rendered abroad, or if they agree on the place of arbitration (which will be located outside the territory of the Czech Republic), and make no agreement regarding the arbitral award. It is principally inferred in such case that the arbitral award was rendered in the place of arbitration (i.e. abroad). Given these circumstances, it will be necessary to conclude that the arbitral award was rendered outside the territory of the Czech Republic, and consequently, must be perceived as a foreign arbitral award.

16.130. From this perspective, the annotated decision complies with the applicable law, as well as the existing doctrinal principles. From the practical perspective, the decision should induce the parties to give more thought to the consequences of the agreements that they make in connection with the place of arbitration and the place where the arbitral award is made. They must be aware of the fact that they thereby also waive the jurisdiction of Czech courts. However small the risk is in practice, the parties may subsequently encounter a situation in which, given the above circumstances, Czech courts will not have jurisdiction, and at the same time, the courts in the place of arbitration will also deny their jurisdiction, arguing that the case does not have a sufficiently strong connection to the said state.[606] We must also

---

[605] The provision is quoted above in the opening part of this annotation.

[606] In a case in which the place of arbitration will be the only indicator connecting the proceedings to a state other than the Czech Republic.

mention the current AC rules, i.e. Section 5[607] of the AC Rules, which stipulates that if arbitration is held abroad, the state where the arbitration is held is the state where the tribunal makes its decision. The respective provision therefore introduces a presumption that the arbitral award is made abroad, even in those cases where the parties might be entirely unaware of such consequences. Nonetheless, it is necessary to welcome any decisions of the SC (as well as other authorities) that could enhance the parties' knowledge and expertise.

| | |

12. Judgment of Supreme Court of Czech Republic of November 27, 2013 in Case No. 23 Cdo 3365/2011:[608] (i) Reasonable Application of CCP in Arbitration, (ii) Duty to Apply Section 118a of CCP in Arbitration, (iii) Annulment of Arbitral Award If Arbitrators Failed to Instruct Party in Terms of Section 118a of CCP

Abbreviations Used:

AC	Arbitration Court at the Economic Chamber of the Czech Republic and Agricultural Chamber of the Czech Republic
ArbAct	Act No. 216/1994 Coll., on Arbitration and the Enforcement of Arbitral Awards, as amended[609]
CCP	Act No. 99/1963 Coll., the Code of Civil Procedure, as amended
SC	Supreme Court of the Czech Republic

Key Words:
annulment (setting aside) of arbitral award | burden of proof | cooperation agreement | duty to give instructions | duty to state relevant facts | enforcement of claims | equality of parties | evidence/proof | facts of case | form of instructions | grounds for annulment | insufficient evidence | insufficient statements of fact | legal representation (counsel) |

---

[607] The provision is quoted above in this annotation.

[608] This decision is available online on the website of the SC at http://www.nsoud.cz/ Judikatura/judikatura_ns.nsf/WebSearch/71DEF9E1AE69D822C1257C3F004D43EC?open Document&Highlight=0 [last accessed on November 13, 2014].

[609] The SC does not explicitly identify the version of the ArbAct applied in the given case; in this connection, the relevant provisions have not been subject to any amendments that could influence the conclusions of the SC and their applicability.

ordre public[610] | *procedural ordre public*[611] | *procedural public policy*[612] | *procedural rights* | *proposed evidence* | *public policy*[613] | *reasonable application of CCP* | *transfer of equity interest* |

Applicable Laws and Regulations:
ArbAct: Section 18,[614] Section 19,[615] Section 30,[616] Section 31[617]

---

[610] See also "public policy".

[611] See also "procedural public policy".

[612] See also "procedural *ordre public*".

[613] See also "*ordre public*".

[614] ArbAct, Section 18 (cit.): *The parties have an equal standing in the arbitral proceedings and must be provided with a full opportunity to assert their rights.* Note: this version of the law applied to the respective proceedings but it has not been subject to any modifications in the meantime and therefore continues to apply.

[615] ArbAct, Section 19 (cit.): *(1) The parties are free to agree on the procedure to be followed by the arbitrators in conducting the proceedings. Matters regarding the conduct of the proceedings may be resolved by the chairman of the panel providing he or she was authorized to do so by the parties or by all arbitrators. (2) In the absence of an agreement pursuant to subsection (1), the arbitrators shall conduct the proceedings in such manner as they consider appropriate. They conduct the arbitral proceedings in such manner that the facts of the case necessary for the resolution of the dispute are sufficiently ascertained, without any unnecessary formalities and while giving all parties equal opportunity to plead their case. (3) Unless the parties agree otherwise, the arbitral proceedings shall be oral. The proceedings are always conducted with the exclusion of the public.* Note: this version of the provision applied to the respective proceedings; the currently applicable version reads as follows (cit.): *(1) The parties are free to agree on the procedure to be followed by the arbitrators in conducting the proceedings. Matters regarding the conduct of the proceedings may be resolved by the chairman of the panel providing he or she was authorized to do so by the parties or by all arbitrators. (2) In the absence of an agreement pursuant to subsection (1) or in the absence of a determination of the procedure pursuant to subsection (4), the arbitrators shall conduct the proceedings in such manner as they consider appropriate. They conduct the arbitral proceedings in such manner that the facts of the case necessary for the resolution of the dispute are sufficiently ascertained, without any unnecessary formalities and while giving all parties equal opportunity to plead their case. (3) Unless the parties agree otherwise, the arbitral proceedings shall be oral. The proceedings are always conducted with the exclusion of the public. (4) The parties may also determine the procedure to be followed in the rules on arbitration, providing the rules are enclosed with the arbitration agreement. This provision shall not prejudice the application of rules adopted by a permanent arbitral institution.* Note: The implemented amendments have no bearing on the case at hand and the conclusions articulated by the SC, because they concern the parties' agreements on procedure, whereas the annotated decision deals with the procedure applied by the arbitrators and the duties of the reasonable application of the CCP.

[616] ArbAct, Section 30 (cit.): *Unless the Act stipulates otherwise, the arbitral proceedings shall be reasonably governed by the provisions of the Code of Civil Procedure.* Note: This

CCP: Section 118a[618]

version of the law applied to the respective proceedings, but it has not been subject to any modifications in the meantime and therefore continues to apply.

[617] ArbAct, Section 31 (cit.): *At the request of any party the court annuls the arbitral award if: (a) it was made in a case which cannot be submitted to arbitration (cannot be the subject of a valid arbitration agreement), (b) the arbitration agreement is invalid for other reasons or the agreement was cancelled or it does not apply to the agreed case, (c) the arbitrator(s) who took part in the proceedings was/were not authorized to make decisions in the case, whether under the arbitration agreement or otherwise, or lacked the capacity to act as arbitrator(s), (d) the arbitral award was not adopted by the majority of the arbitrators, (e) a party was denied the opportunity to plead his or her case in the arbitral proceedings, (f) the arbitral award orders a party to provide performance which was not requested by the obligee or to provide performance which is impossible or illegal under domestic law, (g) it transpires that there are reasons which would otherwise justify the reopening of civil proceedings in court.* [Section 228(1)(a) and (b) of the CCP]. Note: this version of the provision applied to the respective proceedings; the currently applicable version reads as follows (cit.): *At the request of any party the court annuls the arbitral award if: (a) it was made in a case which cannot be submitted to arbitration (cannot be the subject of a valid arbitration agreement), (b) the arbitration agreement is invalid for other reasons or the agreement was cancelled or it does not apply to the agreed case, (c) the arbitrator(s) who took part in the proceedings was/were not authorized to make decisions in the case, whether under the arbitration agreement or otherwise, or lacked the capacity to act as arbitrator(s), (d) the arbitral award was not adopted by the majority of the arbitrators, (e) a party was denied the opportunity to plead his or her case in the arbitral proceedings, (f) the arbitral award orders a party to provide performance which was not requested by the creditor or to provide performance which is impossible or illegal under domestic law, (g) the arbitrator or the permanent arbitral institution resolved a dispute arising from a consumer contract contrary to consumer protection laws, or clearly in violation of good morals, or contrary to public policy, (h) an arbitration agreement relating to disputes arising from consumer contracts lacks the information required under Section 3(5) or such information is intentionally or to a non-negligible extent incomplete, inaccurate, or false, or (i) it transpires that there are reasons which would otherwise justify the reopening of civil proceedings in court.* [Section 228(1)(a) and (b) of the CCP]. Note: The implemented amendments and the additional grounds for the annulment of an arbitral award in B2C disputes do not influence the case at hand and the conclusions reached by the SC, because there are no indications that the case involved a B2C dispute, and at the same time, the respective grounds for the annulment of the arbitral award existed and applied even before the amendment implemented by Act No. 19/2012 Coll.

[618] CCP, Section 118a (cit.): *(1) If it transpires during the hearing that a party has not yet presented all relevant statements of fact or has presented them only insufficiently, the chairman of the panel invites the party to supplement their statements and gives them instructions as to which statements are to be supplemented and what the consequences of noncompliance are. (2) If the chairman of the panel opines that the court's legal opinion of the case could differ from the party's legal opinion, the chairman invites the party to*

The Supreme Court of the Czech Republic reached the following principal conclusions:

(1) Section 30 of the ArbAct requires the reasonable application of the relevant provision of the Code of Civil Procedure where the ArbAct lacks any detailed regulation; this also applies to Section 118a of the CCP, regulating the duty to give instructions.[619]

---

supplement the description of the relevant facts to the necessary extent; the chairman shall proceed similarly to Subsection (1). (3) If the chairman of the panel discovers during the hearing that a party has not yet proposed evidence necessary to prove all of their contested statements, the chairman invites the party to identify such evidence without undue delay and gives them instructions regarding the consequences of noncompliance. (4) During the hearings, the chairman of the panel also gives the parties instructions regarding other procedural rights and duties of the parties; this does not apply if the party is represented by an attorney or a notary public to the extent of the notary's authorization under special laws [Section 3 of Act No. 358/1992 Coll.]. Note: This version of the law applied to the respective proceedings, but it has not been subject to any modifications in the meantime and therefore continues to apply.

[619] In connection with its conclusions, the SC refers to its previous case law, namely **(i)** Judgment of April 25, 2007 in Case No. 32 Odo 1528/2005, available online on the website of the SC at http://www.nsoud.cz/Judikatura/judikatura_ns.nsf/WebSearch/5CA9EB98 F734DAD3C1257A4E0068C30A?openDocument&Highlight=0, in which the SC held as follows (cit.): *I. The court does not make a decision ultra petita in terms of Section 153(2) of the CCP if the court's legal assessment of the facts of the case (which are the subject matter of the proceedings) differs from the claimant's assessment and if the court awards the requested performance to the claimant on the basis of the court's legal assessment. II. When evaluating the case, the court is not bound by the claimant's legal opinion. III. Section 118a [of the CCP] shall also reasonably apply in arbitration conducted pursuant to Act No. 216/1994 Coll. [...] The relationship between the two statutes is regulated under Section 30 of the Arbitration Act, which stipulates that the arbitral proceedings shall be reasonably governed by the provisions of the Code of Civil Procedure, unless the law stipulates otherwise. The word "reasonably" indicates that arbitration is not directly subject to the Code of Civil Procedure, and its individual provisions cannot be applied mechanically in arbitration. The "reasonable" application means that the forum shall primarily have regard to the general principles underlying Czech arbitration, i.e. the provisions incorporated in the CCP shall be applied subject to the general framework of the principles of Czech arbitration (for instance, the ArbAct does not prescribe the requirements for an arbitral award, and it is therefore necessary to reasonably apply Section 157 [of the CCP]; similarly, it is also conceivable that the arbitral tribunal might issue an interim or a partial arbitral award). The case at hand concerns one of the principles of arbitration that also applies in civil court proceedings, namely the principle of the equality of the parties. This principle is incorporated in Section 19(2) of the Arbitration Act, which stipulates that the arbitrators conduct the arbitral proceedings in such manner that the facts of the case necessary for the resolution of the dispute are sufficiently ascertained, without any unnecessary formalities, and while giving all parties equal opportunity to exercise their rights. Due to the fact that*

the Arbitration Act does not elaborate on this principle by specifying any particular rights enjoyed by the parties to the arbitral proceedings that must not be violated if the principle is to be duly honored, Section 30 of the [ArbAct] requires the reasonable application of the relevant provisions of the Code of Civil Procedure. The abovementioned equality of the parties is realized, inter alia, by insisting on the principle of the predictability of court decisions under the Code of Civil Procedure, the fulfillment of which is also attained by implementing the court's duty to provide instructions pursuant to Section 118a [of the CCP]. Subsection (2) of the said provision stipulates that if the chairman of the panel opines that the court's legal opinion of the case could differ from the party's legal opinion, the chairman invites the party to supplement the description of the relevant facts to the necessary extent. Consequently, the differing legal opinion of the court cannot come as a surprise to the party to the proceedings, nor can they be deemed to have been prevented from adducing facts that are important from the perspective of the court's legal opinion or from offering evidence to prove such facts. Only specific instructions at the level of the duty to adduce the relevant facts and evidence are capable of making the differing legal opinion accessible to the parties. If the arbitral tribunal assessed the claim of the respondent (claimant in the arbitration) as performance under the settlement agreement entered into by and between the respondent and a legal entity different from the claimant, as the claim was asserted in the request for arbitration, and only subsequently asserted in its decision the tribunal's legal opinion that the respondent had a claim for compensation for damage and losses incurred as a result of the invalidity of the settlement agreement, the latter claim constitutes a claim completely different from performance under a contract, i.e. a claim that was neither asserted, nor supported by evidence in the arbitral proceedings. Hence, the arbitral tribunal apparently ruled on a claim that was neither alleged, nor proven in the proceedings. In the opinion of the Supreme Court, the appellate court therefore did not err if the appellate court found grounds for the annulment of the award rendered by the arbitral tribunal stipulated in Section 31(e) and (f) [of the ArbAct]; and **(ii)** Resolution of July 24, 2010 in Case No. 23 Cdo 2251/2011, which is available online on the website of the SC at http://www.nsoud.cz/Judikatura/judikatura_ns.nsf/WebSearch/7F77770220A2CBDEC125 7BC1002E30E6?openDocument&Highlight=0, in which the SC ruled as follows (cit.): *The principal legal significance of the contested decision was neither established by the method criticized in the extraordinary appeal, whereby the appellate court addressed the appellant's objection that they had not been provided with the opportunity to state their case before the arbitrators, because the arbitral panel had not given them instructions pursuant to Section 118a [of the CCP], especially instructions according to Subsection (2) of the said provision. The Supreme Court emphasized that the Court adhered to its conclusion expressed in its Judgment of April 25, 2007 in Case No. 32 Odo 1528/2005, i.e. that Section 118a of the CCP shall reasonably apply to arbitration. The SC placed great emphasis on its conclusion that the appellate court was wrong in holding that the failure to give instructions pursuant to the reasonable application of Section 118a [of the CCP] does not mean that the party was denied the opportunity to state their case before the arbitrator, and that no such defects of the arbitral proceedings could constitute grounds supported by the law for the annulment of the arbitral award. Nonetheless, the findings of fact made by the court of first instance or the appellate court, as applicable, did not suggest that the arbitral panel had*

(2) The purpose of Section 118a(1) and (3) of the CCP is to induce the parties to state the relevant facts and identify evidence proving the alleged facts. The objective is to make sure that (i) the party does not find out as late as from the court's decision that the party failed to meet the duty to adduce the relevant facts or meet the burden of proof, and that (ii) the party is thereby provided with the opportunity to supplement (propose) the lacking statements of fact or evidence in the proceedings. Consequently, the procedure pursuant to Section 118a of the CCP is only available if the statements of fact adduced or the evidence proposed by the parties do not suffice to ascertain the facts of the case.

(3) Whether or not the party is represented by legal counsel has no bearing on the court's duty to give instructions pursuant to Section 118a(1) through (3) of the CCP. Such representation is important, and

proceeded in the respective case contrary to the said provision. The Supreme Court explained in its decisions that the purpose of the instructions pursuant to Section 118a(1) to (3) [of the CCP] is to allow the parties to state the relevant facts (meet the obligation to state the relevant facts) and identify evidence capable of proving their statements (meet the burden of proof). The objective of the duty to give instructions is to (i) prevent the possibility that the party only finds out from a decision of the court that is adverse to the party (i.e. surprising) that, according to the court's assessment, the party did not meet the duty to state the relevant facts or the burden of proof, and to (ii) make sure that the party has an opportunity to supplement their insufficient statements or propose additional evidence. However, if the lawsuit was dismissed (or the defense against the lawsuit was unsuccessful) based on the facts of the case as established by the court, not because the parties failed to meet the burden of proof, there was no reason for the court to proceed according to Section 118a [of the CCP]. Section 118a [of the CCP] can only be applied if the statements made by the parties and the proposed evidence (and, as applicable, any evidence that has not been proposed, but has been examined) do not suffice to clarify the facts of the case (cf. also Resolution of June 27, 2003 in Case No. 21 Cdo 121/2003, in www.nsoud.cz, or Resolution of May 25, 2006 in Case No. 22 Cdo 2335/2005, published under No. C 4255 in Soubor civilních rozhodnutí Nejvyššího soudu [Reports of Supreme Court Civil Decisions], C. H. Beck, Volume CD-4, which was contested by a constitutional complaint that was subsequently dismissed by Resolution of the Constitutional Court of November 1 in Case No. II ÚS 532/06). Section 118a(2) [of the CCP] is specifically targeted at situations in which a party failed to state all facts relevant for the legal assessment of the case, because they did not consider them legally significant from the perspective of their legal assessment, different from the legal assessment of the case adopted by the court. But if the already presented statements (and proposed evidence) also suffice for clarification of the facts of the case that are decisive from the perspective of the hypothesis of the legal rule envisaged by the court, no instructions pursuant to Section 118a(2) [of the CCP] are necessary (cf. the quoted Resolution in Case No. 21 Cdo 121/2003, as well as Judgment of the Supreme Court of March 15, 2007 in Case No. 21 Cdo 194/2006, in www.nsoud.cz).

the court is only not obliged to give instructions with respect to instructions regarding other procedural rights and obligations of the parties under Section 118a(4) of the CCP.

[*From Facts of Case*]:

16.131. The description of the facts of the case in the annotated decision of the SC is quite fragmentary, and thus the detailed factual circumstances of the case are unclear. We can presume that on March 11, 2004, the parties[620] entered into a Cooperation Agreement in the Enforcement of Claims. In order to fulfill the object of the Agreement, it was necessary to achieve the target status, which was precisely specified in the Agreement and consisted, inter alia, of the transfer of the debtor's[621] equity interest in company [x],[622] which required the respondent's consent. Despite the fact that it is not explicitly mentioned in the annotated decision, it is clear that the parties agreed on the jurisdiction of the AC to hear and resolve disputes arising from the said Agreement. The annotated decision does not indicate that the arbitration clause was contested. The respondent argued that the target status envisaged under the Agreement had not been attained, which constituted grounds for the rescission of the Cooperation Agreement. The respondent subsequently made a request in the arbitral proceedings, whereby the respondent demanded the return of the performance provided] (in consequence of the rescission of the Agreement). The claimant's defense[623] consisted of its statement that the target status had been achieved, i.e. the equity interest of the debtor in company [x] had been transferred to a person with whom the respondent had agreed; or rather, the claimant inferred that *the fact that the consent was given had not been refuted*. Without inviting the claimant to prove or supply materials proving the existence of the consent,[624] the

---

[620] Natural person; although it is not explicitly mentioned in the annotated decision, we can infer that the person is a citizen of the Czech Republic and has their address/place of residence in the territory of the Czech Republic. The respondent is a legal entity formed and existing under the laws of the Czech Republic in the form of a joint stock company.

[621] Natural person; although it is not explicitly mentioned in the annotated decision, we can infer that the person is a citizen of the Czech Republic and has their address/place of residence in the territory of the Czech Republic. The person is probably independent of the parties to the contract.

[622] Legal entity formed and existing under the laws of the Czech Republic in the form of a limited liability company.

[623] This party was apparently the respondent in the arbitral proceedings.

[624] This conclusion is made with reference to the record of the hearing held at the AC on January 24, 2008.

arbitrators concluded that if the prior consent with the transfer of the equity interest to the third party had not been pleaded, and if no mention had been made in the arbitral proceedings regarding the existence of any such evidence proving the said fact, the target status provided for in the respective Agreement had not been attained, which constituted grounds for the rescission of the Agreement and the granting of the request for arbitration (statement of claim). Consequently, an arbitral award was rendered on January 30, 2008 in Case No. Rsp. 953/07, which granted the respondent's request for arbitration (statement of claim). The claimant subsequently[625] lodged a motion to annul the arbitral award, in which the claimant argued, inter alia, that the claimant had not been provided with the opportunity to duly state their case in terms of Section 31(e) of the ArbAct,[626] because the arbitrators had failed to invite the claimant to supplement and prove the claimant's statements with respect to the fact that the debtor's equity interest in company [x] had, in compliance with the Agreement, been duly transferred to a person who the respondent had approved.

[*Procedure of Case*]:

16.132. On December 2, 2009, the Prague 1 District Court, as the court of first instance, rendered its Judgment in Case No. 21 C 115/2008-44, whereby the motion to annul the arbitral award was dismissed.[627]

16.133. The Prague Municipal Court, as the appellate court, reversed the abovementioned Judgment of the Prague 1 District Court by setting aside the arbitral award.[628] The appellate court based its decision on the conclusions articulated in the existing case law, which indicate that Section 118a of the CCP[629] is also applicable to arbitration in terms of Section 30 of the ArbAct.[630, 631] The appellate court concluded that,

---

[625] This party was apparently the respondent in the arbitral proceedings.

[626] The provision is quoted above in the opening part of this annotation.

[627] The annotated decision does not mention any other circumstances of the proceedings at the court of first instance.

[628] Namely by Judgment of February 7, 2011 in Case No. 39 Co 277/2010-96.

[629] The provision is quoted above in the opening part of this annotation.

[630] The provision is quoted above in the opening part of this annotation.

[631] In its conclusions, the appellate court specifically invokes Judgment of the SC of May 26, 2010 in Case No. 23 Cdo 3749/2008 (the said decision is identified in the annotated decision only by the wrong case number, 23 Cdo 3749/2005, but the court doubtlessly intended to refer to that particular decision); the decision is available online on the website of the SC at http://www.nsoud.cz/Judikatura/judikatura_ns.nsf/WebSearch/039ACB5A0 B0D5616C1257A4E0069A698?openDocument&Highlight=0, and the court held as follows (cit.): *1. The relationship between the two statutes is regulated under Section 30* [of the ArbAct], *which stipulates that the arbitral proceedings shall be reasonably governed by the*

considering the above, i.e. the claimant invoking fulfillment of the contract of cooperation and the respondent claiming the opposite, the arbitrators should have invited the claimant, pursuant to Section 118a(1) of the CCP,[632] to state the relevant circumstances evidencing the transfer of the equity interest and the respondent's prior consent, or the arbitrators should have invited the claimant under Section 118a(3) of the CCP[633] to identify evidence, as applicable. The appellate court held that if the arbitrators had failed to do so, they had denied the

---

provisions of the Code of Civil Procedure, unless the law stipulates otherwise. The word "reasonably" indicates that arbitration is not directly subject to the Code of Civil Procedure, and its individual provisions cannot be applied mechanically in arbitration. The word "reasonably" primarily requires that the tribunal has regard to the general principles underlying Czech arbitration, i.e. the rules of the Code of Civil Procedure must be applied within the general framework of the principles of Czech arbitration. [The ArbAct] does not elaborate on the principle of equality of the parties by stipulating any specific rights and obligations of the parties, and its fulfillment requires, pursuant to Section 30 [of the ArbAct], the reasonable application of the relevant provisions of the Code of Civil Procedure 2. The parties are most typically denied the opportunity to state their case in arbitration if they have not been provided with a sufficient opportunity to plead their case, and if they have not had the chance to comment on all relevant circumstances. It will usually be necessary to provide the parties with the opportunity to comment on the allegations made by the other party, also in writing, i.e. the respondent must have the right to file their statement of defense, and the claimant must have the right to comment on the counterclaim or any counter-arguments presented in the statement of defense. As concerns the individual abovementioned statements, it is reasonable to demand that the parties be provided with the opportunity to make the statements, and that the provided opportunity be sufficient, considering all relevant circumstances of the case. Another necessary prerequisite is that the parties are provided not only with the opportunity to propose evidence proving their allegations, but also with the opportunity to hear or read the evidence (unless the evidence is obviously irrelevant for the given proceedings). If the proposal for evidence presented by any of the parties was dismissed, the arbitrators must consider the proposal for evidence and sufficiently justify why the proposed evidence was not examined. [...] If the Arbitration Court dismissed as superfluous a motion to examine evidence necessary to prove the claimant's statements, and subsequently dismissed the request for arbitration, stating that the claimant had failed to submit the evidence to the Arbitration Court, the Supreme Court believes that the tribunal failed to provide the claimant with an opportunity to prove their statements. It is necessary to point out that the arbitral panel erred if it failed to invite the claimant, in terms of Section 118a(3) or Section 119a(1) [of the CCP], as applicable, to propose, without undue delay, evidence necessary to prove all of the claimant's contested allegations when the court discovered that the claimant had not yet identified such evidence, as in the present case.

[632]   The provision is quoted above in the opening part of this annotation.

[633]   The provision is quoted above in the opening part of this annotation.

claimant the opportunity to duly state their case in the arbitral proceedings, whereby the grounds for the annulment of an arbitral award under Section 31(e) of the ArbAct were fulfilled.[634]

16.134. The Judgment of the appellate court was challenged by the respondent's extraordinary appeal (dated April 6, 2011 and delivered on April 24, 2011). The respondent maintained that the issue of principal legal significance consisted of the following question: if Section 118a(1) and (3) of the CCP[635] is applicable to arbitration in compliance with Section 30 of the ArbAct,[636] which method or form, as applicable, of the instructions given to the parties to the arbitration in terms of Section 118a(1) and (3) of the CCP[637] complies with the requirements of the reasonable application of Section 118a(1) and (3) of the CCP[638] in arbitration, and does the fulfillment of the requirement of the reasonable application of Section 118a(1) and (3) of the ArbAct[639] in arbitration require an explicit reference to the quoted provisions in the record of the hearing? The respondent maintained that the appellate court had erred if the court had applied Section 118a(1) and (3) of the CCP[640] to arbitration, despite the conclusion articulated in the Judgment of the SC of April 25, 2007 in Case No. 32 Odo 1528/2005,[641] and such erroneous application had resulted in the wrong conclusion that the claimant had not been provided with the opportunity to state their case, which constituted grounds for the annulment of the arbitral award under Section 31(e) of the ArbAct.[642] The respondent argued that the application of Section 118a of the CCP[643] was not reasonable in terms of Section 30 of the ArbAct,[644] but formalistic and mechanical, and the arbitral tribunal ignored the specific features of arbitration. Last, but not least, the respondent maintained that the grounds for the annulment of an arbitral award under Section 31(e) of the ArbAct[645] had not been fulfilled, because the claimant and the respondent had been provided with an identical and sufficient opportunity to exercise

---

[634] The provision is quoted above in the opening part of this annotation.
[635] The provision is quoted above in the opening part of this annotation.
[636] The provision is quoted above in the opening part of this annotation.
[637] The provision is quoted above in the opening part of this annotation.
[638] The provision is quoted above in the opening part of this annotation.
[639] The provision is quoted above in the opening part of this annotation.
[640] The provision is quoted above in the opening part of this annotation.
[641] The decision is quoted above in this annotation.
[642] The provision is quoted above in the opening part of this annotation.
[643] The provision is quoted above in the opening part of this annotation.
[644] The provision is quoted above in the opening part of this annotation.
[645] The provision is quoted above in the opening part of this annotation.

their procedural rights and obligations, and it was not possible to argue that the arbitrators had not examined the evidence proposed by the claimant, because the arbitrators had duly substantiated their decision whereby the evidence was disallowed.

16.135. The Supreme Court of the Czech Republic (SC) held that the extraordinary appeal concerned the issue of the applicability of Section 118a of the CCP[646] in arbitration. The SC ruled in this connection that the SC has no reason to depart from its previous conclusions concerning the said issues, which clearly resolve the issues with a positive outcome. The SC concluded that the rules must also apply to the given case; the SC therefore agreed with the conclusion reached by the appellate court: if, given the circumstances described above, the arbitrators failed to invite the claimant to supplement their statements or propose evidence regarding the fact that the debtor's equity interest in company [x] had been duly transferred and that the respondent had given their prior consent with the transfer, the arbitrators denied the claimant the opportunity to duly plead their case in the arbitral proceedings, which constitutes grounds for the annulment of the arbitral award under Section 31(e) of the ArbAct.[647] The Supreme Court of the Czech Republic (SC) based its decision on the premise that the proper analysis of this particular fact was decisive for the conclusion as to whether or not the rescission of the Cooperation Agreement in the Enforcement of Claims was valid, and whether or not the claims asserted in the request for arbitration (statement of claim) were lawful. The SC also refused the respondent's argument that no instructions were necessary, because the claimant was represented by legal counsel. The SC did not address the specific questions posed by the respondent, arguing that these questions were not relevant for the SC's conclusions, and moreover, that these questions entailed the assessment of particular circumstances of the given case, i.e. the form and method of the instructions, and that they did not involve any legal issue.

[*Arguments Presented by SC*]:

16.136. The SC's decision is based solely on its previous rulings; the SC specifically reiterated the conclusions contained in the Judgment of the SC of April 25, 2007 in Case No. 32 Odo 1528/2005[648] and in the Resolution of the SC of July 24, 2010 in Case No. 23 Cdo 2251/2011.[649]

---

[646] The provision is quoted above in the opening part of this annotation.

[647] The provision is quoted above in the opening part of this annotation.

[648] The decision is quoted above in this annotation.

[649] The decision is quoted above in this annotation.

The SC held that the purpose of Section 118a(1) and (3) of the CCP[650] is to induce the parties to state the relevant facts and identify evidence proving the alleged facts. The objective of these measures is to make sure that (i) the party does not find out as late as from the court's decision that the party failed to meet the duty to adduce the relevant facts or meet the burden of proof, and that (ii) the party is provided with the opportunity to supplement the lacking statements of fact or evidence in the proceedings, or propose that they be supplemented, as applicable. The Supreme Court of the Czech Republic (SC) thus concluded that the procedure pursuant to Section 118a of the CCP[651] is only available if the statements of fact adduced or the evidence proposed by the parties do not suffice to ascertain the facts of the case. As concerns the fact that the party was represented by legal counsel and whether the said fact had any influence on the extent of the duty to give instructions, the SC held that this fact has no bearing on the duty, and referred to the text of the respective provision, which indicates that an exception is only applicable under Section 118a(4) of the CCP,[652] i.e. with respect to instructions on other procedural rights (other than the duty to state the relevant facts and the duty to meet the burden of proof; the duty to give instructions also fully applies, whether or not the party is represented by legal counsel, if the decision-making authority gives instructions pursuant to Section 118a(2) of the CCP[653] with respect to a different legal assessment).

16.137. The SC therefore concluded that the decision of the appellate court was correct. The respondent did not succeed in undermining the decision of the appellate court, and consequently, the SC dismissed the extraordinary appeal.

[*Further Conclusions and Comments Concerning Annotated Resolution of SC*]:

16.138. The decision cannot be perceived as surprising or introducing any new interpretation of the said rules, i.e. a decision that would shift the existing doctrinal interpretation. To quite the contrary, it was strictly based on the consistent case law dealing with the issue of the application of the CCP in civil proceedings commenced on the basis of the ArbAct. The SC already deduced the need to apply Section 118a of the CCP[654] in arbitration in its prior rulings, and the decision at hand did not depart from the SC's conclusions.

---

[650] The provision is quoted above in the opening part of this annotation.

[651] The provision is quoted above in the opening part of this annotation.

[652] The provision is quoted above in the opening part of this annotation.

[653] The provision is quoted above in the opening part of this annotation.

[654] The provision is quoted above in the opening part of this annotation.

16.139. We can generally conclude that the annotated decision did not depart from the general interpretation of Section 30 of the ArbAct,[655] i.e. the unequivocal rule is that arbitrators are not obliged to apply the CCP by analogy and under any circumstances, but only in those cases where such application is found appropriate and serves as the basis for the arbitrators' decisions on further procedure in terms of Section 19 of the ArbAct.[656] Hence, the broad autonomy of the parties, represented by Section 19 of the ArbAct, is preserved.[657] Similarly, the conclusions reached by the SC cannot be interpreted as denoting any derogation of the parties' procedural rights arising from the fundamental principles of arbitration contained in Sections 18[658] and 19(2)[659] of the ArbAct. The duty to give instructions may serve as an example of measures adopted in order to make sure that the decision incorporated in the arbitral award will comply with the legitimate expectations of the parties and will be predictable. From this perspective, the duty can be perceived as a procedure that enables the arbitrators to meet their obligations imposed by Sections 18[660] and 19(2)[661] of the ArbAct.

16.140. This also allows for the due application of the specific features of arbitration, and indeed the parties themselves may demonstrate by their own acts how intensive the reasonable application of the CCP should be (they may, for instance, choose foreign arbitrators). Moreover, it is also necessary to point out that the SC correctly refused to delve into the formal delimitation of the method by which the duty should be fulfilled, as the respondent requested (or indeed, the respondent hoped for a conclusion in which the SC would state that the formal requirements imposed on the form of such instructions in the arbitral proceedings are less rigorous). As a matter of fact, even such procedure could not be fundamentally opposed; the point is that this area falls within the powers of the arbitrators to make decisions regarding the procedure to be applied in the arbitration. From this perspective, the arguments presented by the respondent were not entirely misguided, and were probably intended to argue that the (non)fulfillment of the duty to give instructions should be ascertained

---

[655] The provision is quoted above in the opening part of this annotation.
[656] The provision is quoted above in the opening part of this annotation.
[657] The provision is quoted above in the opening part of this annotation.
[658] The provision is quoted above in the opening part of this annotation.
[659] The provision is quoted above in the opening part of this annotation.
[660] The provision is quoted above in the opening part of this annotation.
[661] The provision is quoted above in the opening part of this annotation.

on the basis of objective circumstances, and a negative conclusion should not be based on formal criteria only, such as the conclusion that the instructions should be explicitly included in the record of the hearing, as was proposed in this particular case. Naturally, we cannot exclude the possibility that instructions will be given to the party in a different suitable form if the arbitrators opt for such procedure. But they should always keep in mind that if a motion to annul the arbitral award is lodged pursuant to Section 31 of the ArbAct,[662] the court in civil proceedings will examine the existence of the instructions, and should the arbitrators choose a procedure so informal that no objective evidence will prove that the instructions were given, the arbitrators (*and*, or rather *especially*, the parties) will run the risk of the annulment of the arbitral award.

16.141. But the case also involves another issue that ought to be subject to critical analysis, namely the automatic application of the CCP to arbitration advocated by the SC in those matters that are not explicitly set forth in the ArbAct. This problem has already been resolved in Czech law in connection with those matters that must be classified as procedural public policy (procedural *ordre public*); for instance, the duty to give instructions has already been classified as procedural public policy under Czech case law. Nonetheless, the SC sometimes forgets in its rulings that the application should be *reasonable*, not automatic. The annotated decision is an example of the SC's efforts, which run counter to that principle and which fundamentally collide with international procedures and approaches, or with the doctrine applied in most countries, as the case may be. Even those countries whose *lex arbitri* is incorporated in codes of civil procedure consider the parts regulating arbitration usually as fully autonomous, and refuse to otherwise apply the codes of civil procedure envisaged for litigation to arbitration.

| | |

---

[662] The provision is quoted above in the opening part of this annotation.

13. Judgment of Supreme Court of Czech Republic of 27 November 2013 in Case No. 23 Cdo 2542/2011:[663] (i) Place of Arbitration, (ii) Foreign Arbitral Award, (iii) Jurisdiction of Czech Courts to Annul Arbitral Award If Parties Have Agreed on Place of Arbitration Abroad, (iv) Possibility of Subjective Internationalization of Domestic Disputes in Consequence of Parties' Autonomy

Abbreviations Used:

AC Rules	AC Rules[664]
AC	Arbitration Court at the Economic Chamber of the Czech Republic and Agricultural Chamber of the Czech Republic[665]
ArbAct	Act No. 216/1994 Coll., on Arbitration and the Enforcement of Arbitral Awards, as amended[666]
Brussels I	Council Regulation (EC) No. 44/2001 of December 22, 2000 on jurisdiction and the recognition and enforcement of judgments in civil and commercial matters
CC	Act No. 89/2012 Coll., the Civil Code
CivC	Act of the Czech Republic No. 40/1964 Coll., the Civil Code, as amended[667]

---

[663] This decision is available online on the website of the SC at http://www.nsoud.cz/J udikatura/judikatura_ns.nsf/WebSearch/6E3A7F5D1E64EFB8C1257C40004EC2D9?open Document&Highlight=0 [last accessed on November 3, 2014].

[664] The applicable regulation is the AC Rules for International Disputes in effect until January 31, 2007 (available on the AC website at http://www.soud.cz/rady/rad-pro-mezinarodni-spory-2007, i.e. the Rules in effect since May 1, 2002, as amended by Amendment of June 5, 2003). This annotation has also had regard to the new AC Rules in effect since July 1, 2012 (also available online on the AC website at http://www.soud.cz/rady/rad-rozhodciho-soudu-01-07-2012).

[665] For more information regarding this permanent arbitral institution, see www.soud.cz.

[666] The SC does not explicitly identify the version of the ArbAct applied in the given case, because the relevant provisions have not been subject to any amendments that could influence the conclusions of the SC and their applicability. The only change that will be elaborated on below in this annotation has been introduced with effect since January 1, 2014, i.e. after the respective decision was made. But the change does not have any any influcence to the case annotated.

[667] This Act has been replaced by Act No. 89/2012 Coll., the "new Civil Code" (abbreviated as the "CC" in this annotation), with effect since January 1, 2014. However, legal relationships established before January 1, 2014 shall be governed (save for certain exceptions) by the previous law, i.e. Act No. 40/1964 Coll., the Civil Code, as amended (abbreviated as the "CivC" in this annotation).

CJEU	Court of Justice of the European Union
ComC	Act of the Czech Republic No. 513/1991 Coll., the
	Commercial Code, in effect until December 31, 2013[668]
New York	New York Convention on the Recognition and Enforcement
Convention	of Foreign Arbitral Awards (1958)[669]
(1958)	
PILA	Act No. 91/2012 Coll., on Private International Law[670]
SC	Supreme Court of the Czech Republic

Key Words:
ambiguity | autonomy[671] | auxiliary function of court | Brussels I | domestic arbitral award | domestic dispute | enforcement of arbitral award | error in writing | foreign arbitral award | freedom of contract[672] | international dimension | international dispute | interpretation of juridical act | jurisdiction of Czech courts | jurisdiction to annul arbitral award | New York Convention (1958)[673] | ordre public[674] | place of arbitration | place of residence of party | place where the arbitral award is made | preliminary issue/reference for preliminary ruling | public policy[675] | recognition of arbitral award | registered office of party | seat of arbitration | subjective internationalization of dispute | supervisory function of court | validity of arbitration agreement[676] | validity of arbitration clause[677] |

---

[668] This Act has been replaced by Act of the Czech Republic No. 89/2012 Coll., the Civil Code, as well as Act No. 90/2012 Coll., the Business Corporations Act, in connection with the recodification of civil law and with effect since January 1, 2014.

[669] Convention of June 10, 1958. See Decree of the Ministry of Foreign Affairs of the Czechoslovak Republic No. 74/1959 Coll. (http://www.uncitral.org/uncitral/en/uncitral_texts/arbitration/NYConvention.html).

[670] This Act is one of the statutes adopted within the framework of the recodification of Czech civil law; it has replaced Act No. 97/1963 Coll., as amended, on Private International Law and Procedure, with effect since January 1, 2014.

[671] See also freedom of contract.

[672] See also autonomy.

[673] See Decree of the Ministry of Foreign Affairs of the Czechoslovak Republic No. 74/1959 Coll. (http://www.uncitral.org/uncitral/en/uncitral_texts/arbitration/NYConvention.html).

[674] See also public policy.

[675] See also ordre public.

[676] Depending on the context, "arbitration clause" and "arbitration agreement" may also be interpreted as synonyms, or rather the arbitration clause is a form of arbitration agreement according to Section 2 of the ArbAct.

[677] Depending on the context, "arbitration clause" and "arbitration agreement" may also be interpreted as synonyms, or rather the arbitration clause is a form of arbitration agreement according to Section 2 of the ArbAct.

Applicable Laws and Regulations:
New York Convention (1958)[678]
ArbAct: Section 17,[679] Section 38[680]
PILA: Section 120,[681] Section 122(2)[682]
Brussels I: Article 1(2)(d)[683]
CivC: Section 35(2)[684]
ComC: Section 266[685]

---

[678] Convention of June 10, 1958. See Decree of the Ministry of Foreign Affairs of the Czechoslovak Republic No. 74/1959 Coll. (http://www.uncitral.org/uncitral/en/uncitral _texts/arbitration/NYConvention.html).

[679] ArbAct, Section 17 (cit.): *The arbitration is held in the place agreed by the parties. In the absence of such determination, the arbitration is held in a place determined by the arbitrators having regard to the legitimate interests of the parties.* Note: This version of the law was applicable on the day when the arbitral award was rendered, but has not been subject to any modifications in the meantime and therefore continues to apply.

[680] ArbAct, Section 38 (cit.): *Arbitral awards made abroad shall be recognized and enforced in the Czech Republic like Czech arbitral awards, on condition of reciprocity. The requirement of reciprocity shall also be considered fulfilled if the foreign country generally declares foreign arbitral awards enforceable on condition of reciprocity. However, the decision on enforcement of a foreign arbitral award must always be reasoned.* Note: This version of the law was applicable on the day when the arbitral award was rendered, but it was not subject to any modifications in the meantime, i.e. until the moment of the annotated decision of the SC. January 1, 2014 is the effective date of the PILA, which regulates the said issues in Sections 120 and 122 (both provisions are quoted below in the opening part of this annotation).

[681] PILA, Section 120 (cit.): *Arbitral awards made abroad shall be recognized and enforced in the Czech Republic like Czech arbitral awards, on condition of reciprocity. The requirement of reciprocity shall also be considered fulfilled if the foreign country generally declares foreign arbitral awards enforceable on condition of reciprocity.*

[682] PILA, Section 122(2) (cit.): *Enforcement of a foreign arbitral award shall be ordered by a reasoned decision of a Czech court.*

[683] Brussels I, Article 1(2)(d) – (cit.): **The Regulation shall not apply to arbitration.**

[684] CivC, Section 35(2) (cit.): *Juridical acts expressed in words must be interpreted not only according to their linguistic expression, but primarily also according to the will of the party who performed the juridical act, unless the will conflicts with the linguistic expression.* Note: This version of the law was applicable on the day when the arbitral award was rendered, but it was not subject to any modifications in the meantime, i.e. until the moment of the annotated decision of the SC. January 1, 2014 is the effective date of the CC, which regulates the said issues in Sections 556 and 557 (both provisions are quoted below in the opening part of this annotation).

[685] ComC, Section 266 (cit.): *(1) An expression of will shall be interpreted according to the intention of the acting party, if the intention was known or must have been known to the intended recipient of the expression of will. (2) If the expression of will cannot be interpreted pursuant to Subsection (1), the expression of will shall be interpreted according to the*

CC: Section 556,[686] Section 557[687]

The Supreme Court of the Czech Republic reached the following principal conclusions:

(1) Foreign arbitral awards are defined as arbitral awards that were made in a foreign state. The Act on Arbitration and the Enforcement of Arbitral Awards (ArbAct) does not prohibit entities with their place of residence or registered office in the Czech Republic from agreeing on a place [seat] of arbitration in a country different from their place of residence (registered office), even if they choose a domestic arbitral tribunal, or the law of the state where they have their place of residence/registered office.[688]

---

meaning that would normally be attributed to the expression of will by a person in the position of the intended recipient of the expression of will. Terms used in commercial transactions shall be interpreted according to the meaning that is normally attributed to them in such transactions. (3) The interpretation of will pursuant to Subsections (1) and (2) shall have due regard for all circumstances relating to the expression of will, including contract negotiations and the practice established between the parties, as well as the parties' subsequent behavior, if allowed by the nature of the case. (4) If in doubt, an expression of will that contains a term allowing for varying interpretations must be interpreted to the disadvantage of the party who was the first to use the term in the negotiations. (5) If the decisive criterion under this Part of the Act is the contracting party's registered office, place of business, place of enterprise or premises, or place of residence, the decisive place is the place specified in the contract, until the other party is notified of a change thereof. Note: This version of the law was applicable on the day when the arbitral award was rendered, but it was not subject to any modifications in the meantime, i.e. until the moment of the annotated decision of the SC. January 1, 2014 is the effective date of the CC, which regulates the said issues in Sections 556 and 557 (both provisions are quoted below in the opening part of this annotation).

[686] CC, Section 556 (cit.): *(1) What is expressed in words or otherwise shall be construed according to the intention of the acting party, provided that the intention was or must have been known to the other party. If the acting party' intention cannot be ascertained, the expression of will shall be attributed the meaning that would normally be attributed to it by a person in the position of the intended recipient of the expression of will. (2) The expression of will shall be interpreted with due regard for the practice established between the parties in their legal transactions and the events preceding the juridical action, as well as with due regard for how the parties subsequently indicated what contents and meaning they attribute to the juridical action.*

[687] CC, Section 557 (cit.): *If in doubt, a term used by a party that allows varying interpretations shall be interpreted to the disadvantage of the party who was the first to use the term.*

[688] The summary of the SC's legal opinion (*ratio decidendi*) was adopted from the SC website.

(2) Section 17 of the ArbAct stipulates that the arbitration will be held in a place agreed by the parties. The place where the arbitral award is made must be deemed identical to the place [seat] of arbitration, as the concept of the ArbAct indicates.

(3) A foreign arbitral award can therefore be recognized and enforced in the Czech Republic pursuant to Section 38 of the ArbAct, and consequently, Czech courts cannot have jurisdiction to annul the foreign arbitral award. The courts are only vested with such jurisdiction with respect to domestic arbitral awards.[689]

[From Facts of Case]:

16.142. On May 29, 2006, the AC rendered an arbitral award in arbitral proceedings in Case No. Rsp 797/05; the arbitral award was subsequently challenged by the claimant,[690] who demanded the annulment of the arbitral award on the grounds stipulated under Section 31(b)[691] of the ArbAct. The motion was primarily based on the fact that the respective arbitration clause was (allegedly) ambiguous, and therefore invalid, despite the application of the rules for interpretation contained in the Czech legal system. However, instead of the material aspects of the case, the decision-making of the courts concentrated on the issue of whether Czech courts have jurisdiction to make a decision on the motion to annul the arbitral award, considering the fact that the parties had agreed on Vienna as the place of arbitration, the entire arbitral proceedings were held in Vienna, and the arbitral award was made in Vienna. At the same point, however, the proceedings involved two Czech entities, and the parties have otherwise agreed on Czech arbitrators and on the application of Czech laws and regulations, including procedural regulations.[692]

---

[689] In this connection, the SC invoked the conclusions articulated in a similar case in its prior rulings, namely its Resolution of September 30, 2013 in Case No. 23 Cdo 1034/2012, available online on the website of the SC at http://www.nsoud.cz/Judikatura/judikatura_ns.nsf/WebSearch/742E9D4886B46267C1257C2000426CDE?openDocument&Highlight=0 [last accessed on November 3, 2014].

[690] A natural person; although it is not explicitly mentioned in the annotated decision, we can infer that the person is a citizen of the Czech Republic and has her address/place of residence in the territory of the Czech Republic. The respondent is a legal entity formed and existing under the laws of the Czech Republic in the form of a limited liability company.

[691] ArbAct, Section 31(b) (cit.): "*At the request of any party the court annuls the arbitral award if the arbitration agreement is invalid for other reasons or the agreement was cancelled or it does not apply to the agreed case.*"

[692] Considering the SC's conclusion that Czech courts lacked jurisdiction to hear the motion to annul the arbitral award, it was unnecessary to address the potential issue of *res*

[*Procedure of Case*]:

16.143. The Ostrava Regional Court, as the court of first instance, rendered a Resolution of July 12, 2009[693] in Case No. 4 Cm 83/2006-70, whereby the proceedings were terminated for a lack of jurisdiction.

16.144. The decision of the court of first instance was reversed by the Olomouc High Court, as the appellate court, by its Resolution of January 16, 2008 in Case No. 5 Cmo 367/2007-93;[694] the court ruled that the proceedings were not terminated.

16.145. Subsequently, the court of first instance dismissed the motion to annul the arbitral award by its Judgment of November 3, 2005[695] in Case No. 4 Cm 83/2006-119.

16.146. The Judgment was vacated by the Olomouc High Court (again the appellate court) by its Resolution of April 2, 2009[696] in Case No. 4 Cmo 85/2009-158, because the appellate court did not approve of the lower court's assessment of the grounds for the annulment of the arbitral award under Section 31(b) of the ArbAct.[697]/[698]

16.147. The court of first instance subsequently rendered its Judgment of April 12, 2010 in Case No. 4 Cm 80/2006-197, whereby the arbitral award was annulled. The court applied the rules for interpretation specified in Section 35(2) of the CivC[699] and in Section 266 of the ComC,[700] and

---

judicata – decisions in the case were apparently also made by the courts of the Republic of Austria; the case specifically refers to the decision of the Commercial Court in Vienna of June 19, 2008 in Case No. 35 Cg 103/06 W.

[693] The date of the decision is obviously incorrect; it is clearly a typing error, because decisions with an earlier date are referred to as subsequent decisions.

[694] This is probably another typing error, because the date does not correspond to the described sequence of events in the proceedings.

[695] This is probably another typing error, because the date does not correspond to the described sequence of events in the proceedings.

[696] This is probably another typing mistake because the date does not correspond to the described sequence of events in the proceedings.

[697] The provision is quoted above in the opening part of this annotation.

[698] The case concerned the assessment of an error in writing that was made in the respective arbitration clause, on the basis of which the arbitration was held. The proposed basis for the annulment of the arbitral award was the fact that the arbitration clause incorporated in Article 10.3 of the Services Agreement of January 9, 2001 was ambiguous, and therefore invalid, because it erroneously stipulated that any disputes, inconsistencies, claims, etc. from that "Credit Agreement" would be resolved, unless settled amicably, through the medium of the AC, by arbitrators of the AC, and the arbitral proceedings would be held in Vienna. The respondent argued that the words *Credit Agreement* used in the arbitration clause were an error in writing, and the meaning of the juridical act was indubitable.

[699] The provision is quoted above in the opening part of this annotation.

concluded that the mistake in the arbitration clause was not a simple error in writing, but that the clause was ambiguous and therefore invalid.

16.148. The Olomouc High Court , as the appellate court, upheld the abovementioned Judgment of the Ostrava Regional Court.[701] The court agreed with the conclusion made by the Ostrava Regional Court that the arbitration agreement was ambiguous and, consequently, invalid. The appellate court also held the objection groundless, whereby the respondent claimed a lack of jurisdiction on the part of the Czech courts; the court held that the parties' agreement on *Vienna* as the place of arbitration only had geographical importance, without any consequences for the legal assessment of jurisdiction. The appellate court ruled that the parties (as mentioned above) had otherwise agreed on Czech arbitrators, as well as the application of Czech laws and regulations, including procedural laws. Last, but not least, the motion was rejected and referred to the CJ EU for a preliminary ruling for the purpose of interpreting Brussels I Regulation;[702] the appellate court reached the unequivocal conclusion that the Regulation did not apply to arbitration, including any intervention in the arbitral proceedings by the courts of the EU Member States (auxiliary and supervisory function of courts regarding arbitration.

16.149. The judgment of the appellate court was contested by the respondent; in its extraordinary appeal, the respondent argued that the issue of principal legal significance consisted of the assessment of whether Czech courts have jurisdiction to annul a foreign arbitral award, and whether an error in writing could render a juridical act invalid (render an arbitration clause invalid). The respondent invoked the violation of Article 37 of the Charter, as well as Section 18(2) of the CCP. The respondent also argued that the choice of the place [seat] of arbitration and of the place where the arbitral award should be made did not have merely geographical importance, but was connected with the application of international treaties, court intervention in arbitration, etc. Considering the above, the respective arbitral award is therefore a foreign arbitral award in terms of Section 38 of the ArbAct,[703] and as such, can only be annulled by the competent court of the Republic of

---

[700] The provision is quoted above in the opening part of this annotation.

[701] Namely by Judgment of February 3, 2011 in Case No. 4 Cmo 278/2010 – 331.

[702] The reference should have been made in connection with the abovementioned objection of *res judicata* consisting of the fact that the case was heard by the Commercial Court in Vienna, which rendered its decision on June 19, 2008 in Case No. 35 Cg 103/06 W.

[703] The provision is quoted above in the opening part of this annotation.

Austria. In this connection, the respondent argued that the New York Convention on the Recognition and Enforcement of Foreign Arbitral Awards (1958)[704] also does not indicate that it would establish the right of the parties to lodge a motion to annul a foreign arbitral award; the Convention only concerns the recognition and enforcement of arbitral awards made in the territory of a state different from the state in which recognition and/or enforcement is sought. Considering the above, the respondent concluded that the claimant should have raised its material objections in the relevant proceedings for the enforcement/recognition of arbitral award. In its extraordinary appeal, the respondent also analyzed in great detail the issue of the rules applicable to the interpretation of juridical acts and the associated issue of the (in)validity of the respective arbitration clause. However, these issues were not examined by the SC, and the corresponding arguments are therefore not elaborated on in this annotation.

[*Arguments Presented by SC*]:

16.150. The SC based its decision on the applicable laws and regulations, primarily Section 38 of the ArbAct.[705] The Supreme Court of the Czech Republic (SC) based its decision on the fact that foreign arbitral awards are defined by the quoted legal rules as awards that were made in a foreign state. Naturally, the SC's conclusion does not prohibit entities with their place of residence or registered office in the Czech Republic from agreeing on a place of arbitration in a country different from their place of residence (registered office), even if they choose a domestic arbitral tribunal or the law of the state where they have their place of residence/registered office. Referring to Section 17 of the ArbAct,[706] the SC held that the place where the arbitral award is made must be considered identical to the place of arbitration.[707] The SC therefore rejected the argument that the place of arbitration has merely geographical importance. Considering the fact that the respective arbitration was held and the arbitral award was made in *Vienna*, the SC classified the arbitral award as a foreign arbitral award.

---

[704] Convention on the Recognition and Enforcement of Foreign Arbitral Awards of June 10, 1958.

[705] The provision is quoted above in the opening part of this annotation.

[706] The provision is quoted above in the opening part of this annotation.

[707] The SC refers to the following publication: Alexander Bělohlávek. Zákon o rozhodčím řízení a výkonu rozhodčích nálezů. Komentář [Title in Translation: Act on Arbitration and Enforcement of Arbitral Awards. Commentary], 2nd edition, Praha [Prague, Czech Republic]: C. H. Beck 2012, p. 1356.

16.151. The SC agreed with the respondent's opinion that the foreign arbitral award can in such case be recognized and enforced in terms of Section 38 of the ArbAct,[708] but Czech courts cannot have jurisdiction to annul the foreign arbitral award, because they are only vested with such jurisdiction with respect to domestic arbitral awards.[709]

16.152. The SC therefore concluded that the decision of the appellate court was not correct. Consequently, the SC vacated the decision of the appellate court and remanded the case for further hearing and a new decision. Considering the decision that it adopted, the SC did not deem it necessary or possible, as applicable, to address the material grounds for the annulment of the arbitral award invoked by the appellant.

[Further Conclusions and Comments Concerning Annotated Resolution of SC]:

16.153. The decision focused on the definition of a foreign arbitral award. The decision has gotten a good deal of attention in the legal community (together with Resolution of the SC of September 30, 2013 in Case No. 23 Cdo 1034/2012), because it de facto confirmed the possibility of internationalizing (subjective internationalization) otherwise purely domestic disputes, i.e. disputes lacking any objective international dimension, which could be expected to be governed by the ArbAct. Opinions regarding the possibility of internationalization have varied; some have argued that the international dimension must objectively exist, because leaving its existence at the will of the parties (i.e. the existence of an international dimension of a subjective nature) could ultimately result in evading the supervisory function of the state.[710] Considering the broad procedural autonomy with which the parties are afforded by the ArbAct, we may conclude that such approach is principally possible, especially if we also have regard to the fact that this potential internationalization of the dispute by the parties has purely procedural, not substantive, consequences (i.e. it does not affect the subject matter of the dispute). We could argue that the parties' freedom of contract (autonomy) should be limited, where the parties' agreement clearly and unambiguously targeted the evasion of the provisions of the otherwise applicable *lex arbitri* (here the ArbAct), from which the parties

---

[708] The provision is quoted above in the opening part of this annotation.

[709] The SC invoked an analogous decision of the SC – Resolution of September 30, 2013 in Case No. 23 Cdo 1034/2012.

[710] Cf. Naděžda Rozehnalová. Rozhodčí řízení v mezinárodním a vnitrostátním styku [Title in Translation: Arbitration in International and Domestic Transactions], 2nd edition; Praha [Prague, Czech Republic] ASPI/Wolters Kluwer, 2008, p. 45. The author arrived at the conclusion that such a choice of the parties could only be allowed under the contractual theory of arbitration (if at all), not if the applicable theory is the jurisdictional or a hybrid theory.

were otherwise prohibited from departing, i.e. provisions that could be classified as mandatory provisions from the conflict-of-laws perspective, or that would even be a component of public policy (*ordre public*).

16.154. As a matter of fact, such a choice was at least implicitly envisaged by the applicable procedural rules of the AC – compare the definitions of domestic and international disputes in Section 1(3) of the AC Rules Governing Domestic Disputes, as applicable to the respective arbitration.[711] The definition was (apart from other criteria) connected to the place [seat] of arbitration (which falls within the autonomy of the parties).[712] Naturally, the division had no effects under substantive law,

---

[711] (cit.): *"Domestic dispute" in the sense of these Rules means any dispute in which all parties (participants) have their seats (domicile) within the territory of the Czech Republic, or any dispute in which organizational parts (branches) of foreign persons according to Section 21 of the Commercial Code and/or organizational parts (branches) exercising activities in accordance with a specific Act (e.g. Act No 21/1992, Coll., on Banks) have their seats (domicile) within the territory of the Czech Republic and are entered in the Commercial Register. Further conditions for arbitrating the dispute as domestic are the application of Czech law to the dispute, written statements and pleadings of the parties in the Czech (Slovak) language, the venue of the proceedings in the territory of the Czech Republic, and the decision issued in the Czech (Slovak) language.*

The Rules in effect from February 1, 2007 no longer contained this criterion, and Section 1(3) read as follows (cit.): *"Domestic dispute" in the sense of these Rules means any dispute in which all parties (participants) have their seats (domicile) within the territory of the Czech Republic, or any dispute in which organizational parts (branches) of foreign persons according to Section 21 of the Commercial Code and/or organizational parts (branches) exercising activities in accordance with a specific Act (e.g. Act No 21/1992, Coll., on Banks) have their seats (domicile) within the territory of the Czech Republic and are entered in the Commercial Register, provided that the law applicable to the dispute is Czech substantive law, and provided that all written statements and pleadings of the parties are in the Czech (Slovak) language, and the arbitration proceedings are held and the decision is made in the Czech (Slovak) language.*

[712] The law applicable to disputes classified as domestic read as follows:

Section 5 of the Rules (cit.): *Normally, hearings in pending disputes shall be held at the seat of the Arbitration Court in Prague. At the suggestion of the Secretary, or at the initiative of the Arbitral Tribunal, or under an agreement of the parties to the dispute, the hearings may be held at other places within the Czech Republic.*

Section 5 of the Rules in effect from February 1, 2007 read as follows (cit.): *Normally, hearings in pending disputes shall be held at the seat of the Arbitration Court in Prague. At the initiative of the Arbitral Tribunal or under an agreement of the parties to the dispute, and with the consent of the Secretary of the Arbitration Court, the hearings may be held at other places within the Czech Republic.*

International disputes were governed by the following rules

Section 5 of the Rules (cit.): *(1) Normally, hearings in pending disputes shall be held in the seat of the Arbitration Court in Prague. At the initiative of the arbitral tribunal, or under an agreement of the parties to the dispute, and with the consent of the Secretary of the*

i.e. the differentiation between international and domestic disputes in light of the procedural rules of the AC cannot be deemed identical to the differentiation between domestic and foreign arbitral awards under Section 38 of the ArbAct;[713] but it can be perceived as evidence that the autonomy of the parties was an applicable criterion with respect to those issues.[714] The currently applicable Rules make no distinction between domestic and international disputes, and consequently, the provisions have no equivalent.

16.155. Section 38 of the ArbAct[715] indicates that an arbitral award will be designated as foreign based on the place where the arbitral award is made, not the place of arbitration. To some extent, these 2 criteria merge (or rather, the place of arbitration is usually considered to be the place where the arbitral award is made), but they cannot be automatically deemed identical, because the ArbAct does not set forth any such explicit presumption. We cannot exclude the possibility that the parties will choose the place of arbitration abroad, but simultaneously determine that the arbitral award will be rendered in

---

Arbitration Court, the hearings may be held at other places within the Czech Republic or abroad. (2) The arbitral tribunal shall give notice to the board of hearings to be held abroad. If such hearings are to be held abroad at the initiative of the arbitrators, the parties have to agree thereto.

Section 5 of the Rules in effect from February 1, 2007 read as follows (cit.): *(1) Normally, hearings in pending disputes shall be held in the seat of the Arbitration Court in Prague. At the suggestion of the Secretary, or at the initiative of the arbitral tribunal, or under an agreement of the parties to the dispute, the hearings may be held at other places within the Czech Republic or abroad. (2) The arbitral tribunal shall give notice to the board of hearings to be held abroad. If such hearings are to be held abroad at the initiative of the arbitrators, the parties have to agree thereto.*

The currently applicable provision is Section 5 of the AC Rules in effect since July 1, 2012 (cit.): *(1) Oral hearings shall regularly be held at the seat of the Arbitration Court. The seat of the Arbitration Court is Prague. With the consent of the Secretary granted on the basis of the agreement of the parties, or at the initiative of the arbitral tribunal, if the parties have not agreed on the place of the oral hearing, the arbitral tribunal may decide that the oral hearing shall be held at some other place in the Czech Republic or abroad. The consent of the Secretary and the decision of the arbitral tribunal are not required if the proceedings are to be held at a permanent place of arbitration of the Arbitration Court. (2) If proceedings are to be conducted abroad, the place of arbitration shall be the country where the proceedings are conducted.*

[713] The provision is quoted above in the opening part of this annotation.

[714] We must also have regard to the fact that the AC Rules regulate the issue of the place where hearings are held; again, this place cannot be deemed identical to the place of arbitration, as such, and the respective comparison is only illustrative.

[715] The provision is quoted above in the opening part of this annotation.

the Czech Republic. But it is indeed a rather theoretical construct, unsupported by any actual reason why the parties should do so. Should the parties have any practical interests in having the case actually heard outside the territory of the Czech Republic, they do not need to transfer the place of arbitration abroad, since it would fully suffice if the parties made an agreement in such case that would merely regulate the place where hearing(s) will be held.

16.156. A different situation will occur if the parties directly agree that the arbitral award will be rendered abroad, or if they agree on the place of arbitration (which will be located outside the territory of the Czech Republic), and make no agreement regarding the arbitral award. It is principally inferred in such case that the arbitral award was rendered in the place of arbitration (i.e. abroad). Given these circumstances, it will be necessary to conclude that the arbitral award was rendered outside the territory of the Czech Republic, and consequently, must be perceived as a foreign arbitral award.

16.157. From this perspective, the annotated decision complies with the applicable law, as well as the existing doctrinal principles. From the practical perspective, the decision should induce the parties to give more thought to the consequences of the agreements they make in connection with the place of arbitration and the place where the arbitral award is made. They must be aware of the fact that they thereby also waive the jurisdiction of Czech courts. However small the risk is in practice, the parties may subsequently encounter a situation in which, given the above circumstances, Czech courts will not have jurisdiction, and at the same time, the courts in the place of arbitration will also deny their jurisdiction, arguing that the case does not have a sufficiently strong connection to the said state.[716] We must also mention the current AC rules, i.e. Section 5[717]of the AC Rules, which stipulates that if arbitration is held abroad, the state where the arbitration is held is the state where the tribunal makes its decision. The respective provision therefore introduces a presumption that the arbitral award is made abroad even in those cases where the parties might be entirely unaware of such consequences. Nonetheless, it is necessary to welcome any decisions of the SC (as well as other authorities) that could enhance the parties' knowledge and expertise.

| | |

---

[716] In a case in which the place of arbitration will be the only indicator connecting the proceedings to a state other than the Czech Republic.

[717] The provision is quoted above in this annotation.

14. Judgment of Supreme Court CR of November 27, 2013 in Case No. 23 Cdo 3705/2011:[718] (i) Factual Delimitation of Grounds for Annulment of Arbitral Award, (ii) Supplementing Grounds for Annulment of Arbitral Award During Proceedings

Abbreviations Used:

ArbAct	Act of the Czech Republic No. 216/1994 Coll., on Arbitration and the Enforcement of Arbitral Awards, as amended[719]
CC	Act of the Czech Republic No. 89/2012 Coll., the Civil Code
CCP	Act of the Czech Republic No. 99/1963 Coll., the Code of Civil Procedure, as amended
CivC	Act of the Czech Republic No. 40/1964 Coll., the Civil Code, as amended[720]
CJEU	Court of Justice of the European Union
SC	Supreme Court of the Czech Republic

Key Words:
annulment (setting aside) of arbitral award | CJEU | concentration of proceedings | consumer contract | Council Directive 93/13/EEC | European Court of Justice | grounds for annulment of arbitral award | invalidity of arbitration agreement | limitation of procedural rights | procedural rights | time period for lodging motion to annul | timeliness | timely plea | unfair terms |

---

[718] This decision is available online on the website of the SC at http://www.nsoud.cz/Judikatura/judikatura_ns.nsf/WebSearch/426A9D1BD02439ECC1257C3F004D1A8D?openDocument&Highlight=0 [last accessed on November 10, 2014].

[719] This decision of the SC is based on the ArbAct in effect until March 31, 2012, but no subsequent changes have any bearing on the conclusions of the SC and their applicability in this particular case (the case concerned the issue of the specification of the grounds for which the annulment of the arbitral award is sought); generally, however, the protection of consumers has also been enhanced in relation to enforcement proceedings.

[720] This Act (CivC) has been replaced by Act No. 89/2012 Coll. (the "new Civil Code", abbreviated as the "CC" in the text of this annotation) with effect since January 1, 2014. Legal relationships established before the effective date of the CC, i.e. before January 1, 2014, shall be governed by the provisions of the CivC (with exceptions).

Applicable Laws and Regulations:
ArbAct: Section 31,[721] Section 32,[722] Section 33[723]

---

[721] ArbAct, Section 31 (cit.): (cit.): *At the request of any party the court annuls the arbitral award if: (a) it was made in a case which cannot be submitted to arbitration (cannot be the subject of a valid arbitration agreement), (b) the arbitration agreement is invalid for other reasons or the agreement was cancelled or it does not apply to the agreed case, (c) the arbitrator(s) who took part in the proceedings was/were not authorized to make decisions in the case, whether under the arbitration agreement or otherwise, or lacked the capacity to act as arbitrator(s), (d) the arbitral award was not adopted by the majority of the arbitrators, (e) a party was denied the opportunity to plead his or her case in the arbitral proceedings, (f) the arbitral award orders a party to provide performance which was not requested by the obligee or to provide performance which is impossible or illegal under domestic law, (g) it transpires that there are reasons which would otherwise justify the reopening of civil proceedings in court.* [Section 228(1)(a) and (b) of the CCP]. Note: This version of the provision applied to the respective proceedings; the currently applicable version reads as follows (cit.): *At the request of any party the court annuls the arbitral award if: (a) it was made in a case which cannot be submitted to arbitration (cannot be the subject of a valid arbitration agreement), (b) the arbitration agreement is invalid for other reasons or the agreement was cancelled or it does not apply to the agreed case, (c) the arbitrator(s) who took part in the proceedings was/were not authorized to make decisions in the case, whether under the arbitration agreement or otherwise, or lacked the capacity to act as arbitrator(s), (d) the arbitral award was not adopted by the majority of the arbitrators, (e) a party was denied the opportunity to plead his or her case in the arbitral proceedings, (f) the arbitral award orders a party to provide performance which was not requested by the creditor or to provide performance which is impossible or illegal under domestic law, (g) the arbitrator or the permanent arbitral institution resolved a dispute arising from a consumer contract contrary to consumer protection laws, or clearly in violation of good morals, or contrary to public policy, (h) an arbitration agreement relating to disputes arising from consumer contracts lacks the information required under Section 3(5) or such information is intentionally or to a non-negligible extent incomplete, inaccurate, or false, or (i) it transpires that there are reasons which would otherwise justify the reopening of civil proceedings in court.* [Section 228(1)(a) and (b) of the CCP]. Note: The subject matter of the case was the issue of the factual delimitation of the grounds for the annulment of the arbitral award. Consequently, the extension of the grounds on the basis of which consumers are entitled to lodge a motion to annul an arbitral award had no bearing on the respective case; moreover, the court concluded that the respective obligation could not be classified as a B2C relationship.

[722] ArbAct, Section 32 (cit.): *(1) The motion to annul an arbitral award must be lodged with the court within three months following the receipt of the arbitral award by the party requesting the annulment of the award, unless this Act stipulates otherwise. (2) The motion pursuant to subsection (1) does not suspend the enforceability of the arbitral award. If requested by the obligor, however, the court may suspend the enforceability of the arbitral award in case an immediate enforcement of the arbitral award could cause serious harm.* Note: This version of the provision applied to the respective proceedings; the currently

CivC: Section 39[724]
CC: Section 547,[725] Section 588[726]

applicable version reads as follows (cit.): *(1) The motion to annul an arbitral award must be lodged with the court within three months following the receipt of the arbitral award by the party requesting the annulment of the award, unless this Act stipulates otherwise. If the arbitral award was made in a dispute arising from a consumer contract and the motion to annul was lodged by the consumer, the court always examines whether there are grounds to annul the arbitral award pursuant to Section 31(a) through (d) or (h). (2) The motion pursuant to subsection (1) does not suspend the enforceability of the arbitral award. If requested by the obligor, however, the court may suspend the enforceability of the arbitral award in case an immediate enforcement of the arbitral award could cause serious harm or in case the motion to annul the arbitral award justifies the conclusion that the motion is legitimate. (3) If the motion to annul an arbitral award is lodged by the consumer, the court shall establish whether there are grounds to suspend the enforceability of the arbitral award pursuant to subsection (2) without the consumer's request. The court shall rule on the suspension of enforceability within 7 days of receiving the motion; the arbitral award cannot be enforced within said time limit.* Note: The subject matter of the case was the possibility of supplementing the grounds for the annulment of an arbitral award after expiration of the time period stipulated for filing the motion to annul; consequently, the implemented changes had no bearing on the respective case. Moreover, the court concluded that the respective obligation could not be classified as a B2C relationship.

[723] ArbAct, Section 33 (cit.): *The court shall dismiss a motion to annul an arbitral award which is based on the grounds specified in Section 31(b) or (c) if the party requesting the annulment failed to raise the corresponding objection in the arbitral proceedings before the party's first act in the merits of the case, despite having an opportunity to do so.* Note: This version of the provision applied to the respective proceedings; the currently applicable version reads as follows (cit.): *The court shall dismiss a motion to annul an arbitral award which is based on the grounds specified in Section 31(b) or (c) if the party requesting the annulment failed to raise the corresponding objection in the arbitral proceedings before the party's first act in the merits of the case, despite having an opportunity to do so. This does not apply to disputes arising from consumer contracts.* Note: Although the SC addressed the issue of whether the lack of the arbitrators' jurisdiction to hear and resolve the case was pleaded in time, the amendment implemented by Act No. 19/2012 Coll. has no bearing on the conclusions reached by the SC, because the claimant was not a consumer and the rules therefore do not apply. Considering the other conclusions reached in the annotated decision, the SC also ruled that (cit.): *[...] it is also irrelevant that the grounds for the annulment of the arbitral award were not asserted already during the arbitral proceedings [...].*

[724] CivC, Section 39 (cit.): *A juridical act is invalid if the contents or the purpose thereof violates or evades the law or is contra bonos mores.* Note: This is the version of the law applicable to the respective proceedings. January 1, 2014 is the effective date of the CC, which regulates the said issues in Sections 547 and 588 (both provisions are quoted below in the opening part of this annotation).

[725] CC, Section 547 (cit.): *The contents and purpose of juridical actions must comply with good morals and the law (statute).*

Council Directive 93/13/EEC of April 5, 1993 on unfair terms in consumer contracts

The Supreme Court of the Czech Republic reached the following principal conclusions:

(1) **The interpretation of Sections 31 and 32(1) of the ArbAct requires the analogous application of the Code of Civil Procedure (CCP) as concerns the possibilities of asserting further grounds for the annulment of an arbitral award in proceedings initiated within the period of three months after the arbitral award is served on the party seeking annulment of the arbitral award.**

(2) **Section 32 of the ArbAct is only important from the perspective of determining whether the motion itself to annul the arbitral award was lodged in time. The provision cannot be interpreted as a limitation of the claimant's procedural rights to adduce in the course of the proceedings any relevant circumstances that contain further grounds for the annulment of the arbitral award under Section 31 of the said Act.**

(3) **The right to supplement grounds for the annulment of an arbitral award can only be limited by statutory procedural limits under the CCP (such as the concentration of proceedings). In other words, parties may assert (further) grounds for the annulment of the arbitral award under Section 31 of the ArbAct in proceedings for the annulment of the arbitral award commenced before the expiration of the time period under Section 32 of the ArbAct, even after the time period expires.**[727]

---

[726] CC, Section 588 (cit.): *The court shall, with or without a motion, have regard to the invalidity of a juridical action that is obviously contra bonos mores, or that is in conflict with the law (statute) and obviously violates public policy. This also applies if the juridical action creates an obligation to provide performance that is impossible ab initio.*

[727] In its conclusions, the SC invoked its prior case law, namely Judgment of May 9, 2012 in Case No. 23 Cdo 3728/2011; the decision is available online on the SC website at http://www.nsoud.cz/Judikatura/judikatura_ns.nsf/WebSearch/639E8E2B6E41525DC125 7A4E00678F93?openDocument&Highlight=0; the court ruled as follows (cit.): *If the provisions of the Code of Civil Procedure are applied by analogy to the proceedings for the annulment of an arbitral award, the motion to annul the arbitral award must be assessed pursuant to the provisions of the Code of Civil Procedure that regulate motions whereby proceedings are commenced. Section 79(1)* [of the CCP] *indicates that a motion to annul an arbitral award must also contain a description of the relevant circumstances. The description of the relevant circumstances must clearly indicate what happened, i.e. the act on the basis of which the party asserts their right (to annul the arbitral award); the act must be described to an extent that allows the unambiguous individualization thereof (excludes the possibility of confusing the act with any other one). The party is not obliged to include in their motion the legal classification of the described facts of the case (which means that the*

[*From Facts of Case*]:

16.158. The claimants and the respondent[728] entered into a contract (which was not identified in any greater detail); the parties *apparently*[729] agreed that disputes arising from the obligation would be submitted to arbitration. Such arbitration was indeed commenced some time later, and an arbitral award was rendered on October 24, 2008 in *ad hoc* arbitration in Case No. R 033/2008-151. The case was resolved by a single arbitrator. The claimants lodged a motion to annul the arbitral award on the grounds specified in Section 31(b), (e) and (f) of the ArbAct.[730]

[*Procedure of Case*]:

16.159. The Hradec Králové Regional Court (Pardubice Branch), as the court of first instance, annulled the arbitral award.[731] No further details and

---

party is neither obliged to specify the alleged grounds for the annulment of the arbitral award which are legally classified in Section 31 [of the ArbAct]; if the party includes their legal classification, the court is not bound by it. This also applies to the relevant circumstances supplemented by the party during the proceedings. The right to supplement the circumstances during the proceedings is limited only by the procedural limits incorporated in the Code of Civil Procedure. The court subsequently subsumes the findings of fact ascertained from the evidence examined in the case under the statutory definitions in the relevant legal rules and thereby determines which of the grounds for the annulment of the arbitral award under Section 31 [of the ArbAct] are fulfilled (if any). Section 32 [of the ArbAct] (as applicable before the amendment implemented by Act No. 19/2012 Coll.), is important only from the perspective of determining whether the motion itself to annul the arbitral award was lodged in time. The provision cannot be interpreted as a limitation of the claimant's procedural rights to adduce in the course of the proceedings any relevant circumstances that contain further grounds for the annulment of the arbitral award under Section 31 [of the ArbAct]. The right to supplement relevant circumstances can only be limited by statutory procedural limits under the Code of Civil Procedure (such as the concentration of proceedings). Note: A part of this summary of the SC's legal opinion (*ratio decidendi*) was adopted from the SC website.

[728] The claimants were natural persons; although it is not explicitly mentioned in the annotated decision, we can infer that they are citizens of the Czech Republic and have their address/place of residence in the territory of the Czech Republic. The respondent is also a natural person; although it is not explicitly mentioned in the annotated decision, we can infer that they are a citizen of the Czech Republic and have their address/place of residence in the territory of the Czech Republic.

[729] We could only use the information summarized in the annotated decision of the SC.

[730] The provision is quoted above in the opening part of this annotation.

[731] The respective decision is not specified in the annotated judgment of the SC; the only available information is that the case was heard at the Hradec Králové Regional Court (Pardubice Branch) under Case No. 36 Cm 18/2009; the website of the Ministry of Justice of the Czech Republic (http://infosoud.justice.cz/InfoSoud/public/list.do?druhVec=CM &rocnik=2009&cisloSenatu=36&bcVec=18&kraj=KSVYCHK&org=KSVYCHK&poradiUd

information regarding the proceedings at the court of first instance are provided in the annotated decision of the SC. The conclusions that were subsequently reached by the appellate court only indicate that the claimants invoked in their motion the grounds for the annulment of the arbitral award under Section 31(b), (e) and (f) of the ArbAct.[732] But the text of the motion itself (as regards the facts of the case) contained no mention of the arbitration agreement being invalid, and no mention of the grounds that allegedly render the agreement invalid according to the claimants. Consequently, it was not possible to ascertain from the motion which particular ground for the annulment of the arbitral award listed in Section 31(b) of the ArbAct[733] should apply in the given case. The claimants described several acts in their motion, but none of the circumstances allegedly concerned any of the grounds specified in Section 31(b) of the ArbAct.[734] The claimants' motion of September 15, 2009 did not contain any such information either. The claimants only pleaded the invalidity of the arbitration clause in their final proposals presented at the hearing before the court of first instance, which took place on October 8, 2010; in this connection, the claimants referred to the decision of the Prague High Court of May 28, 2009 in Case No. 12 Cmo 496/2008.[735]

16.160. The Prague High Court, as the appellate court, reversed the abovementioned Judgment of the Hradec Králové Regional Court (Pardubice Branch) by dismissing the motion to annul the arbitral award.[736] The appellate court held that it was not sufficient to define the

---

alosti=5&cisloSenatuLabel=36&typSoudu=os&agendaNc=CIVIL&druhUdalosti=VYD_R OZH&idUdalosti=null&druhVecId=CM&rocnikId=2009&cisloSenatuId=36&bcVecId=18 &orgId=KSVYCHK) indicated that the judgment was rendered on October 13, 2010.

[732] The provision is quoted above in the opening part of this annotation.

[733] The provision is quoted above in the opening part of this annotation.

[734] The provision is quoted above in the opening part of this annotation.

[735] This decision is available online at http://pravo4u.cz/judikatura/vrchni-soud-v-praze/12-cmo-496-2008/; in this decision, the court ruled as follows (cit.): *If the arbitration agreement lacks any direct identification of an ad hoc arbitrator, or a specific description of the method of their appointment, and merely stipulates that the arbitrator will be appointed by one of the contracting parties from a list of arbitrators administered by a legal entity other than a permanent arbitral institution established in terms of Section 13 of Act No. 216/1994 Coll., as amended, and that the arbitration will be conducted pursuant to the rules issued by the legal entity, the arbitration agreement is invalid for evading (circumventing) the law.* Note: This is a landmark decision relating to the jurisdiction of private arbitral companies, which marks a turning point in the courts' approach to the assessment of arbitration conducted in the name of such companies.

[736] Namely by Judgment of May 7, 2011 in Case No. 5 Cmo 63/2011-96.

grounds for the annulment of the arbitral award in quantitative terms/provide the legal classification of the grounds; it was also necessary to at least provide a general description of the facts underlying the asserted claim. Following this principle, the appellate court held that it was not possible to make a proper claim for the annulment of an arbitral award without specifying any facts in the motion on which the claimant relies. The appellate court concluded that that was exactly the situation in the said case, because the materials in the dossier of the court of first instance, and especially the record of the hearing that took place at the court of first instance on October 8, 2010, did not contain any description of facts that would indicate that the arbitration agreement was invalid; a declaration that the case is similar to another case resolved by the Prague High Court does not constitute a description of the factual relationships between the parties to the proceedings. Considering the above said, the appellate court concluded that the conditions for the annulment of the arbitral award under Section 31(b) of the ArbAct were not fulfilled.[737] The appellate court also reached an identical conclusion with respect to the proposal to annul the arbitral award under Section 31(e) of the ArbAct;[738] the appellate court reasoned that the information in the motion to annul the award, i.e. that the arbitral award was also contested with reference to Section 31(b), (e) and (f) of the ArbAct,[739] could not be deemed, in the absence of any description of the factual basis for the said ground, as a proposal to annul the arbitral award on the said ground. The appellate court also held that the motion to annul an arbitral award had to be lodged within the time period stipulated in Section 32 of the ArbAct,[740] which indicated that the motion to annul the arbitral award could not be supplemented with new acts, the acts could not be changed, etc., and the arbitral award could therefore only be annulled and exclusively on the basis of the acts that were asserted in time as grounds for the annulment of the award. Considering the above conclusions, the appellate court did not consider it necessary to examine whether the requirement under Section 33 of the ArbAct[741] was fulfilled, i.e. whether the claimants had raised the plea of the invalidity of the arbitration clause together with or before their first act in the case performed in the arbitral proceedings. In this connection,

---

[737] The provision is quoted above in the opening part of this annotation.
[738] The provision is quoted above in the opening part of this annotation.
[739] The provision is quoted above in the opening part of this annotation.
[740] The provision is quoted above in the opening part of this annotation.
[741] The provision is quoted above in the opening part of this annotation.

the appellate court held that the plea of the invalidity of the arbitration agreement could only be raised as late as in the proceedings for the annulment of the arbitral award, without being raised previously during the arbitration itself, if the case involved a B2C relationship, i.e. a relationship to which the court was obliged to apply Council Directive 93/13/EEC of April 5, 1993 on Unfair Terms in Consumer Contracts. But the given case does not, in the appellate court's opinion, involve a B2C relationship. In this connection, the appellate court invokes the case law of the CJEU (or rather the ECJ (European Court of Justice) at the time when the quoted decision was adopted).[742]

16.161. The judgment of the appellate court was contested by the claimants by means of an extraordinary appeal of August 12, 2011; the claimants disagreed with the conclusions reached by the court with respect to their alleged failure to meet the duty to describe the relevant circumstances for asserting the grounds for the annulment of the arbitral award under Section 31(b) and (e) of the ArbAct.[743] The claimants argued that the invalidity of the arbitration clause under Section 39 of the CivC[744] (for being contrary to the law) had been clearly pleaded from the beginning of the proceedings, and the plea had been raised in time within the time period stipulated in Section 33 of the ArbAct.[745] As concerns the application of Section 31(b) of the ArbAct,[746] the claimants maintained that it was irrelevant that the plea had not been supported by statements of fact, which the claimants supplemented after the judgment of the Prague High Court of May 28, 2009 in Case No. 12 Cmo 496/2008 was published.[747] The claimants also did not agree with the finding that they did not properly specify

---

[742] Decision of the European Court of Justice (First Chamber) of October 26, 2006 in Case C–168/05 (*Elisa María Mostaza Claro* v. *Centro Móvil Milenium SL*) available at http://curia.europa.eu/juris/document/document.jsf;jsessionid=9ea7d2dc30d58aa531680e 0a45838240f9ba2d85d487.e34KaxiLc3qMb40Rch0SaxuObN50?text=&docid=63926&page Index=0&doclang=cs&mode=lst&dir=&occ=first&part=1&cid=463888, in which the Court held as follows (cit.): *Council Directive 93/13/EEC of 5 April 1993 on unfair terms in consumer contracts must be interpreted as meaning that a national court seised of an action for annulment of an arbitration award must determine whether the arbitration agreement is void and annul that award where that agreement contains an unfair term, even though the consumer has not pleaded that invalidity in the course of the arbitration proceedings, but only in that of the action for annulment.*

[743] The provision is quoted above in the opening part of this annotation.

[744] The provision is quoted above in the opening part of this annotation.

[745] The provision is quoted above in the opening part of this annotation.

[746] The provision is quoted above in the opening part of this annotation.

[747] The decision is quoted above in this annotation.

the grounds for the annulment of the arbitral award pursuant to Section 31(e) of the ArbAct.[748] According to the claimants, the denial of the opportunity to state (plead) one's case consists of the fact that no hearing was summoned after the objections on the merits had been lodged, the arbitrator did not examine the proposed evidence, and on top of that, provided no reasons for the arbitrator's decision, whereby the evidence was disallowed. The claimants believe that they had already properly asserted the grounds for the annulment of the arbitral award on September 19 and 22, 2008.[749]

16.162. The SC held that the arguments presented by the appellate court are misguided, including the argument concerning the time period for filing the motion to annul the arbitral award under Section 32of the ArbAct. The appellate court's arguments were based on the assertion that it was impossible to establish from the motion what specific grounds for the invalidity of the arbitration clause/grounds for the annulment of the arbitral award under Section 31(b) of the ArbAct[750] should apply in the given case.[751] The SC therefore held that we cannot conclude that the claimants sufficiently delimited the grounds under Section 31(b) of the ArbAct,[752] which the claimants invoked as the grounds for the annulment of the arbitral award, if the claimants only invoked the Judgment of the Prague High Court of May 28, 2009 in Case No. 12 Cmo 496/2008[753] at the hearing at the court of first instance, arguing that the arbitration clause underlying the respective arbitral award was identical to the case resolved in the abovementioned decision. The Supreme Court of the Czech Republic (SC) invoked its consistent interpretation of the nature of the time period for filing the motion to annul an arbitral award stipulated in Section 32 of the ArbAct,[754] and concluded that it is fully sufficient if a motion to annul an arbitral award is duly lodged within the said time period, while specific grounds justifying the motion can be supplemented during the proceedings. The SC ruled that it is therefore irrelevant, from this perspective, whether or not any particular grounds were already described in the respective motion. In this regard, the SC considered

---

[748] The provision is quoted above in the opening part of this annotation.

[749] Meaning still during the arbitral proceedings, because the annotated decision indicates that the arbitral award was rendered on October 24, 2008.

[750] The provision is quoted above in the opening part of this annotation.

[751] The provision is quoted above in the opening part of this annotation.

[752] The provision is quoted above in the opening part of this annotation.

[753] The decision is quoted above in this annotation.

[754] The provision is quoted above in the opening part of this annotation.

the legal assessment performed by the appellate court to be erroneous. The SC held that it was irrelevant, considering the given circumstances, that the grounds for the annulment of the arbitral award were not already asserted during the arbitral proceedings, as required under Section 33 of the ArbAct.[755] This is apparently the reason why the SC did not further examine the claimants' objections that they specified the grounds for the annulment of the arbitral award duly and in time.

[*Arguments Presented by SC*]:

16.163. The Supreme Court of the Czech Republic (SC) based its decision on the conclusions articulated in its prior rulings, namely its Judgment (SC) of May 9, 2012 in Case No. 23 Cdo 3728/2011.[756] The Supreme Court of the Czech Republic (SC) did not find any reason to depart from its prior case law. The SC therefore based its decision on the premise that the interpretation of Section 31 of the ArbAct[757] or, as applicable, the determination of the nature of the time period for commencing the proceedings for the annulment of an arbitral award, as stipulated in Section 32 of the ArbAct,[758] requires the analogous application of the CCP.[759] The time period is significant exclusively from the perspective of assessing the timeliness of the motion itself, but it cannot be interpreted as a limitation of the claimants' procedural rights, primarily the right to supplement, in the course of the proceedings, any relevant circumstances that contain further grounds for the annulment of the arbitral award under Section 31 of the ArbAct.[760] Such limitations would only be permissible on the basis of the procedural limits under the CCP, typically the concentration of proceedings.

---

[755] The provision is quoted above in the opening part of this annotation.

[756] The decision is quoted above in this annotation.

[757] The provision is quoted above in the opening part of this annotation.

[758] The provision is quoted above in the opening part of this annotation.

[759] The SC specifically refers to Section 79 of the CCP (cit): *The proceedings are initiated by a motion. The motion must contain the general essentials (Section 42(4)) and name, surname, place of residence or, as applicable, birth registration numbers or identification numbers of the parties (company name or name and registered office of a legal entity, identification number, designation of the state and the competent organization unit of the state that acts for and on behalf of the state in court), and of the parties' representatives (if applicable), a description of the relevant circumstances, and the identification of evidence invoked by the party filing the motion; the motion must also stipulate the relief sought by the party filing the motion. If the case involves a trustee as a party to the proceedings, the motion must also specify that the respective person is the trustee and identify the trust fund. The motion is called a "petition" (lawsuit) if it concerns bilateral legal relations between a claimant and a respondent (Section 90).*

[760] The provision is quoted above in the opening part of this annotation.

16.164. The SC therefore concluded that the decision of the appellate court was not correct. Consequently, the SC vacated the decision of the appellate court and remanded the case for further hearing and a new decision.
[Further Conclusions and Comments Concerning Annotated Decision of SC]:

16.165. The decision cannot be perceived as surprising or introducing any new interpretation of the said rules, i.e. a decision that would shift the existing doctrinal interpretation. To quite the contrary, it is strictly based on the consistent case law dealing with the issue of application of the CCP in civil proceedings commenced on the basis of the ArbAct. It is necessary to point out that the conclusions consistently repeated in the SC case law are also not affected by the amendments to the ArbAct implemented by the Consumer Amendment, i.e. Act No. 19/2012 Coll. The enhancement of the consumer's position is evidenced by the fact that the consumer will not be obliged, in certain cases, to rely on the above interpretation of Section 32(1) of the ArbAct[761] and on the possibility of supplementing the relevant facts and evidence, on the basis of which the award should be annulled, during pending proceedings for the annulment of the arbitral award; the reason is that the court is now obliged to examine certain grounds of its own motion (*ex officio*). This obligation specifically concerns the grounds for the annulment of arbitral award specified in Section 31(a) through (d) or (h).[762] The Explanatory Memorandum to Act No. 19/2012 Coll., which amended the ArbAct with effect since April 1, 2012, states that this amendment is in response to the case law of the CJ EU. In its rulings concerning the Directive on Unfair Terms in Consumer Contracts, the CJ EU held that the courts must assess, with or without a motion, whether the arbitration clause is in conflict with binding national rules, even after a motion for involuntary enforcement of a final and conclusive arbitral award is lodged; the court is obliged to perform the review of its own motion.[763] However, the above said should in no case be interpreted as inducing consumers to forgo a most accurate and precise specification of the grounds for the annulment of the arbitral award; the reason is that the court seized with the motion to annul the arbitral award only has at its disposal the materials in the dossier, which might not include all relevant nuances. Moreover, the law by no

---

[761] The provision is quoted above in the opening part of this annotation.

[762] The provision is quoted above in the opening part of this annotation.

[763] Cf. decision of the European Court of Justice (First Chamber) of October 26, 2006 in Case C–168/05 (*Elisa María Mostaza Claro* v. *Centro Móvil Milenium SL*). The decision is quoted above in this annotation.

means limits the consumer's possibility to supplement the grounds for the annulment of the arbitral award during the proceedings. The consumer may naturally do so even with respect to those circumstances that the court should examine of its own motion, and thereby increase their chances of success in the dispute.

16.166. But the SC's conclusion is rather controversial, in which the SC claims that the possibility to supplement the grounds for the annulment of an arbitral award during the proceedings means that it is not necessary to examine whether the requirement under Section 33 of the ArbAct was fulfilled.[764] The Supreme Court of the Czech Republic (SC) correctly pointed out in the annotated decision that the possibility to propose the annulment of arbitral awards can generally be limited by special laws; despite the fact that the SC referred to procedural rules in this connection (namely, the concentration of proceedings), it is also necessary to have regard to the substantive conditions for the annulment of the arbitral award represented by a timely plea of the invalidity of the arbitration agreement in the arbitral proceedings. Consequently, the above principles must be interpreted as meaning that the claimants were not obliged to describe specific grounds for the annulment of the arbitral award under Section 31(b) of the ArbAct[765] in the motion to annul the award, but the court will not be allowed to annul the arbitral award on the basis of subsequently raised grounds if, following a hearing of the case, the court determines a breach of Section 33 of the ArbAct.[766] Any other interpretation would result in a de facto derogation of Section 33 of the ArbAct.[767] Naturally, proceedings governed by the version of the ArbAct as amended by the Consumer Amendment of the ArbAct will be subject to the exception stipulated for B2C disputes (which *eo ipso* confirms that the due fulfillment of the requirements under Section 33 of the ArbAct[768] must be insisted on in any other cases).

| | |

---

[764] The provision is quoted above in the opening part of this annotation.

[765] The provision is quoted above in the opening part of this annotation.

[766] The provision is quoted above in the opening part of this annotation.

[767] The provision is quoted above in the opening part of this annotation.

[768] The provision is quoted above in the opening part of this annotation.

15. Judgment of Supreme Court of Czech Republic of November 27, 2013 in Case No. 33 Cdo 725/2011:[769] (i) Factual Delimitation of Grounds for Annulment of Arbitral Award, (ii) Fulfillment of Condition under Section 33 of ArbAct If Invalidity of Arbitration Clause Is Pleaded Together with First Act in Case on Grounds Different from Grounds Subsequently Asserted in Proceedings for Annulment of Arbitral Award

Abbreviations Used:

ArbAct	Act of the Czech Republic No. 216/1994 Coll., on Arbitration and the Enforcement of Arbitral Awards, as amended[770]
CC	Act of the Czech Republic No. 89/2012 Coll., the Civil Code
CCP	Act of the Czech Republic No. 99/1963 Coll., the Code of Civil Procedure, as amended
CivC	Act of the Czech Republic No. 40/1964 Coll., the Civil Code, as amended[771]
ConCourt	Constitutional Court of the Czech Republic
SC	Supreme Court of the Czech Republic

Key Words:

ad hoc arbitration | annulment (setting aside) of arbitral award | arbitrability | binding (mandatory) rule | CJEU | commissive act | Council Directive 93/13/EEC | delays in proceedings | enforcement of arbitral award | essentialia of arbitration agreement | essentialia of arbitration clause | final and conclusive arbitral award | invalidity of

---

[769] This decision is available online on the website of the SC at http://www.nsoud.cz/Judikatura/judikatura_ns.nsf/WebSearch/426A9D1BD02439ECC1257C3F004D1A8D?openDocument&Highlight=0 [last accessed on November 11, 2014].

[770] This decision of the SC is based on the ArbAct in effect until March 31, 2012, but no subsequent changes have any bearing on the conclusions of the SC and their applicability in this particular case (the case concerned the issue of the specification of the grounds for which the annulment of the arbitral award was sought); generally, however, the protection of consumers has been enhanced, in consequence of which the court now has regard to selected grounds for the annulment of the arbitral award of its own motion (*ex officio*) .

[771] This Act (CivC) has been replaced by Act No. 89/2012 Coll. (the "new Civil Code", abbreviated as "CC" in the text of this annotation) with effect since January 1, 2014. Legal relationships established before the effective date of the CC, i.e. before January 1, 2014, shall be governed by the provisions of the CivC (with exceptions).

arbitration agreement | jurisdiction | lease | objective arbitrability | of own motion (ex officio) | permanent arbitral institution | pleading invalidity | purchase contract | real property | review proceedings |

Applicable Laws and Regulations:
ArbAct: Section 13,[772] Section 31,[773] Section 33[774]

---

[772] ArbAct, Section 13 (cit.): *(1) Permanent arbitral institutions can be established only under the law. (2) Permanent arbitral institutions can issue their own statutes and rules which must be published in the Business Journal* [Government Regulation No. 63/1992 Coll.]; *these statutes and rules may determine the method of appointment and the number of arbitrators and may stipulate that the arbitrators shall be selected from a list administered by the permanent arbitral institution. The statutes and rules may also determine how the arbitrators shall conduct the proceedings and render their decisions, as well as resolve other issues connected with the activities of the permanent arbitral institution and the arbitrators, including rules regulating the costs of proceedings and fees for the arbitrators. (3) If the parties agreed on the jurisdiction of a particular permanent arbitral institution and failed to agree otherwise in the arbitration agreement, they shall be deemed to have submitted to the regulations specified in subsection (2), as applicable on the day of commencement of the proceedings in the permanent arbitral institution.* Note: This version of the provision applied to the respective proceedings; the currently applicable version reads as follows (cit.): *(1) Permanent arbitral institutions may only be established by another law or only if another law expressly allows their establishment. (2) Permanent arbitral institutions can issue their own statutes and rules which must be published in the Business Journal* [Government Regulation No. 63/1992 Coll.]; *these statutes and rules may determine the method of appointment and the number of arbitrators and may stipulate that the arbitrators shall be selected from a list administered by the permanent arbitral institution. The statutes and rules may also determine how the arbitrators shall conduct the proceedings and render their decisions, as well as resolve other issues connected with the activities of the permanent arbitral institution and the arbitrators, including rules regulating the costs of proceedings and fees for the arbitrators. (3) If the parties agreed on the jurisdiction of a particular permanent arbitral institution and failed to agree otherwise in the arbitration agreement, they shall be deemed to have submitted to the regulations specified in subsection (2), as applicable on the day of commencement of the proceedings in the permanent arbitral institution. (4) No entity may carry out its activities using a name which evokes a misleading impression that the entity is a permanent arbitral institution under this law unless a different law or regulation or an international agreement integrated in the legal system authorizes the entity to use the name.* Note: The amendments have no bearing on the dispute in question, because there is no doubt that the entity in whose name the arbitral award was rendered and whose Rules are referred to is not a permanent arbitral institution within the meaning of the law; the solution therefore resolved the consequences resulting therefrom. For the sake of completeness, we need to add that the reference in the original version of the ArbAct to the law regulating the Business Journal was also incorrect: the law applicable from January 1, 2001 was Government Regulation No. 503/2000 Coll., and the law applicable since January 1, 2014 is Government Regulation No. 351/2013 Coll.

| 529

[773] ArbAct, Section 31 (cit.): *At the request of any party the court annuls the arbitral award if: (a) it was made in a case which cannot be submitted to arbitration (cannot be the subject of a valid arbitration agreement), (b) the arbitration agreement is invalid for other reasons or the agreement was cancelled or it does not apply to the agreed case, (c) the arbitrator(s) who took part in the proceedings was/were not authorized to make decisions in the case, whether under the arbitration agreement or otherwise, or lacked the capacity to act as arbitrator(s), (d) the arbitral award was not adopted by the majority of the arbitrators, (e) a party was denied the opportunity to plead his or her case in the arbitral proceedings, (f) the arbitral award orders a party to provide performance which was not requested by the obligee or to provide performance which is impossible or illegal under domestic law, (g) it transpires that there are reasons which would otherwise justify the reopening of civil proceedings in court.* [Section 228(1)(a) and (b) of the CCP]. Note: This version of the provision applied to the respective proceedings; the currently applicable version reads as follows (cit.): *At the request of any party the court annuls the arbitral award if: (a) it was made in a case which cannot be submitted to arbitration (cannot be the subject of a valid arbitration agreement), (b) the arbitration agreement is invalid for other reasons or the agreement was cancelled or it does not apply to the agreed case, (c) the arbitrator(s) who took part in the proceedings was/were not authorized to make decisions in the case, whether under the arbitration agreement or otherwise, or lacked the capacity to act as arbitrator(s), (d) the arbitral award was not adopted by the majority of the arbitrators, (e) a party was denied the opportunity to plead his or her case in the arbitral proceedings, (f) the arbitral award orders a party to provide performance which was not requested by the creditor or to provide performance which is impossible or illegal under domestic law, (g) the arbitrator or the permanent arbitral institution resolved a dispute arising from a consumer contract contrary to consumer protection laws, or clearly in violation of good morals, or contrary to public policy, (h) an arbitration agreement relating to disputes arising from consumer contracts lacks the information required under Section 3(5) or such information is intentionally or to a non-negligible extent incomplete, inaccurate, or false, or (i) it transpires that there are reasons which would otherwise justify the reopening of civil proceedings in court.* [Section 228(1)(a) and (b) of the CCP]. Note: The subject matter of the case was the issue of the factual delimitation of the grounds for the annulment of the arbitral award. Consequently, the extension of the grounds on the basis of which consumers are entitled to lodge a motion to annul an arbitral award had no bearing on the respective case; moreover, there is no evidence suggesting that the respective obligation is a B2C relationship.

[774] ArbAct, Section 33 (cit.): *The court shall dismiss a motion to annul an arbitral award which is based on the grounds specified in Section 31(b) or (c) if the party requesting the annulment failed to raise the corresponding objection in the arbitral proceedings before the party's first act in the merits of the case, despite having an opportunity to do so.* Note: this version of the provision applied to the respective proceedings; the currently applicable version reads as follows (cit.): *The court shall dismiss a motion to annul an arbitral award which is based on the grounds specified in Section 31(b) or (c) if the party requesting the annulment failed to raise the corresponding objection in the arbitral proceedings before the party's first act in the merits of the case, despite having an opportunity to do so. This does not apply to disputes arising from consumer contracts.* Note: Although the SC addressed

CivC: Section 39[775]
CC: Section 547,[776] Section 588[777]
Council Directive 93/13/EEC on unfair terms in consumer contracts
The Supreme Court of the Czech Republic reached the following principal conclusions:
(1) **If the arbitration clause lacks any direct identification of an *ad hoc* arbitrator and only refers to "Rules on Arbitration" issued by a legal entity other than a permanent arbitral institution established under the law, the arbitration clause is contrary to the law and therefore invalid (as a whole) pursuant to Section 39 of the CivC. Irrespective of the particular wording of the arbitration clause, these conclusions apply whenever the parties fail to agree in their arbitration agreement that their potential dispute will be resolved by an *ad hoc* arbitrator (no arbitrator is specifically identified in the arbitration agreement), and the appointment of arbitrator is not agreed in a manner that would comply with the law.[778]**

---

the issue of whether the lack of the arbitrators' jurisdiction to hear and resolve the case was pleaded in time, the modification implemented by the amendment represented by Act No. 19/2012 Coll. has no bearing on the conclusions reached by the SC, because there is no evidence suggesting that the respective obligation was a B2C relationship.

[775] CivC, Section 39 (cit.): *A juridical act is invalid if the contents or purpose thereof violates or evades the law or is contra bonos mores.* Note: This is the version of the law applicable to the respective proceedings. January 1, 2014 is the effective date of the CC, which regulates the said issues in Sections 547 and 588 (both provisions are quoted below in the opening part of this annotation).

[776] CC, Section 547 (cit.): *The contents and purpose of juridical actions must comply with good morals and the law (statute).*

[777] CC, Section 588 (cit.): *The court shall, with or without a motion, have regard to the invalidity of a juridical action that is obviously contra bonos mores, or that is in conflict with the law (statute) and obviously violates public policy. This also applies if the juridical action creates an obligation to provide performance that is impossible ab initio.*

[778] In connection with its conclusions, the SC refers to its previous case law, namely, Resolution of the Grand Panel of the Civil and Commercial Division of the SC of May 11, 2011 in Case No. 31 Cdo 1945/2010, available online on the website of the SC at http://www.nsoud.cz/Judikatura/judikatura_ns.nsf/WebSearch/87312C808746B5D2C125 7A4E006568D2?openDocument&Highlight=0, in which the SC held as follows (cit.): *If the arbitration agreement lacks any direct identification of an ad hoc arbitrator, or a specific description of the method of their appointment, and refers to "Rules on Arbitration" issued by a legal entity (corporation) other than a permanent arbitral institution established under the law, the arbitration agreement is invalid pursuant to Section 39 of the CivC.* Note: The summary of the SC's legal opinion (*ratio decidendi*) was adopted from the SC website. The decision also invokes Resolution of the Prague High Court of May 28, 2009 in Case No. 12 Cmo 496/2008; the decision is available online at http://pravo4u.cz/

(2) **A timely plea of the invalidity of an arbitration agreement made in the arbitral proceedings has the result that, from the perspective of Section 33 of the ArbAct, the plea also covers grounds for the invalidity of the arbitration agreement other than those that might have been described in the plea by factual circumstances.**[779]

judikatura/vrchni-soud-v-praze/12-cmo-496-2008/; the High Court held as follows (cit.): *If the arbitration agreement lacks any direct identification of an ad hoc arbitrator, or a specific description of the method of their appointment, and merely stipulates that the arbitrator will be appointed by one of the contracting parties from a list of arbitrators administered by a legal entity other than a permanent arbitral institution established in terms of Section 13 of Act No. 216/1994 Coll., as amended, and that the arbitration will be conducted pursuant to the rules issued by the legal entity, the arbitration agreement is invalid for evading (circumventing) the law.* Note: This is a landmark decision relating to the jurisdiction of private arbitral companies, which marks a turning point in the courts' approach to the assessment of arbitration conducted in the name of such companies.

[779] In its conclusions, the SC invoked its prior case law, namely, Judgment of March 27, 2013 in Case No. 23 Cdo 2406/2011; the decision is available online on the website of the SC at http://www.nsoud.cz/Judikatura/judikatura_ns.nsf/WebSearch/EC9B2E7BB51B5137 C1257B6300358E45?openDocument&Highlight=0; the Court held as follows (cit.): *A timely plea of the invalidity of an arbitration agreement made in the arbitral proceedings has the result that, from the perspective of Section 33* [of the ArbAct]*, the plea also covers grounds for the invalidity of the arbitration agreement other than those that might have been described in the plea by factual circumstances.* Note: The summary of this part of the SC's legal opinion (*ratio decidendi*) was adopted from the SC website. *Section 33* [of the ArbAct] *orders the court to dismiss a motion to annul an arbitral award that is based on the grounds specified in Section 31(b) or (c) of the Arbitration Act, if the party seeking the annulment failed to raise the corresponding objection in the arbitral proceedings before the party's first act on the merits, despite having had an opportunity to do so. According to Section 31(b) of the Arbitration Act, the party may plead that the arbitration agreement is invalid based on reasons other than the ground specified in Section 31(a) of the Arbitration Act, or that the arbitration agreement was cancelled, or that it does not apply to the agreed case. Section 31(c)* [of the ArbAct] *stipulates that there are grounds for the annulment of an arbitral award if the arbitrator(s) who took part in the proceedings was/were not authorized to make decisions in the case, whether under the arbitration agreement or otherwise, or lacked the capacity to act as arbitrator(s). Consequently, Section 31(b) and (c)* [of the ArbAct] *applies to cases in which the parties entered into an invalid arbitration agreement [unless the arbitration agreement is invalid under Section 31(a)* [of the ArbAct] *on grounds of a lack of arbitrability, which did not occur in the respective case], and to cases in which no arbitration agreement was executed at all. Hence, the claimant was obliged in the given case to raise the objection that the claimant had not signed the arbitration agreement in the arbitral proceedings before the claimant's first act on the merits. The party seeking the annulment of an arbitral award must assert the grounds under Section 31(b) or (c)* [of the ArbAct] *in the arbitral proceedings before the party's first act on the merits; the fulfillment of this obligation is a prerequisite for the court proceeding pursuant to Section 31(b) and (c)*

(3) Section 31(b) and (c) of the ArbAct applies to cases in which the parties entered into an invalid arbitration agreement [unless the arbitration agreement is invalid under Section 31(a) on grounds of a lack of objective arbitrability], as well as cases in which no arbitration agreement was executed at all. The party seeking the annulment of the arbitral award must assert the grounds under Section 31(b) or (c) of the ArbAct in the arbitral proceedings before the party's first act on the merits; the fulfillment of this obligation is a prerequisite for the court proceeding pursuant to Section 31(b) and (c) of the ArbAct, and is primarily intended to prevent any delays in the subsequent proceedings.[780]

[*From Facts of Case*]:

16.167. On June 29, 2007, the claimant[781] and the respondent[782] entered into a purchase contract, whereby the claimant sold to the respondent the

[of the ArbAct], *and is primarily intended to prevent any delays in the subsequent proceedings. Section 33 of the Arbitration Act imposes an obligation on parties to arbitration to assert the grounds under Section 31(b) and (c)* [of the ArbAct] *before their first act on the merits, not before the first act in the case or before the arbitrator's first act on the merits. "Merits" have been uniformly interpreted by legal theory and judicial practice as the matter for which the proceedings are conducted. Resolving issues of a procedural nature cannot be interpreted as "acts on the merits". The court has made the following findings: At the beginning of the hearing, the chairman of the arbitral panel informed the parties of the composition of the arbitral panel, and the attending counsel for the parties stated they had no objections to the jurisdiction of the tribunal. Next, when asked by the chairman of the arbitral panel, the claimant (respondent in the present proceedings) declared that they insisted on their request for arbitration (statement of claim). Next, the counsel for the third respondent (claimant in the present proceedings) pleaded that the arbitral tribunal did not have jurisdiction to resolve such dispute due to a conflict between Articles 3 and 10 of the bill of exchange agreement, which authorized the bank to claim the bill of exchange in court. The counsel for the claimant had raised the plea before they made any material comments on the essence of the dispute. The findings of fact clearly indicate that the claimant had pleaded the invalidity of the arbitration agreement due to the conflict between the said Articles of the bill of exchange agreement before the claimant's first act on the merits, i.e. before any statements were presented concerning the merits of the case. In other words, the plea was made in time from the perspective of Section 33* [of the ArbAct].

[780] In its conclusions, the SC invokes its prior case law, namely, Judgment of the SC of March 27, 2013 in Case No. 23 Cdo 2406/2011, as the decision is quoted above in this annotation.

[781] Natural person; although it is not explicitly mentioned in the annotated decision, we can infer that they are a citizen of the Czech Republic and have their address/place of residence in the territory of the Czech Republic.

[782] Natural person; although it is not explicitly mentioned in the annotated decision, we can infer that they are a citizen of the Czech Republic and have their address/place of residence in the territory of the Czech Republic.

real property specified in the contract. On the same day, the claimant (as the lessee) and the respondent (as the lessor) also entered into Finance Lease Agreement No. 0707, which provided for permanent occupancy for consideration of real property owned by the lessor (the real property specified in the abovementioned Purchase Contract). Both contracts contained an arbitration clause, in which the parties agreed that any and all potential disputes that arise from or in connection with the contracts (including potential disputes regarding the validity of the contracts or the validity of the arbitration clause) will be submitted to and resolved in arbitration pursuant to the ArbAct, by a single arbitrator appointed by the claimant (claimant in arbitration) from a list of arbitrators administered by a private company [X], a company specializing in organizing arbitration, but which is not a permanent arbitral institution. The parties also agreed that the arbitration would be conducted in compliance with the Rules issued by the private arbitral company. If the private arbitral company were dissolved in the meantime without any legal successor, the parties agreed that the single arbitrator would in such case be selected by the claimant (claimant in arbitration) from a "substitute list of arbitrators" incorporated in Substitute Rules for Dispute Resolution if the Arbitral Center Ceased to Exist, which were enclosed with Real Property Finance Lease Agreement No. 0707 of June 29, 2007. Last, but not least, the parties also explicitly stipulated that the rescission of the contracts by any of the contracting parties would not prejudice the validity of the agreed arbitration clause. Arbitration was indeed commenced some time later, in which the claimant (in its first statement in the case) informed the arbitrator that the claimant had lodged with the competent court a lawsuit for the determination of the claimant's (ownership) title to the contested real property; in that lawsuit, the claimant pleaded the invalidity of the Purchase Contract and the expiration of the Lease Agreement, arguing that the arbitration clause had been cancelled (at least with respect to the Purchase Contract) pursuant to Section 31(b) of the ArbAct,[783] and consequently, the arbitrator lacked jurisdiction to resolve the dispute. Hence, the claimant thereby pleaded a lack jurisdiction on the part of the arbitrator to make decisions on the request for arbitration (statement of claim). The single arbitrator issued his award in the case on April 28, 2008, under Case No. R 002/2008-110.[784] The arbitral award was contested by the claimant following the procedure under Section 31 of the ArbAct;[785] the claimant sought the annulment of the award.

---

[783] The provision is quoted above in the opening part of this annotation.

[784] The annotated decision makes no further comments on the developments in the civil proceedings commenced by the claimant.

[785] The provision is quoted above in the opening part of this annotation.

[*Procedure of Case*]:

16.168. On March 24, 2011, the Prague 3 District Court, as the court of first instance, rendered its Judgment in Case No. 9 C 141/2008-79, whereby the motion to annul the arbitral award was dismissed. The court held that the factual delimitation of the ground invoked by the claimant in the proceedings for the annulment of the arbitral award under Section 31 of the ArbAct[786] did not comply with the plea of a lack of jurisdiction on the part of the arbitrator to hear and resolve the case, as the plea had been made in the arbitral proceedings (as described above) in the pleading delivered to the court on March 29, 2010. The claimant argued that the arbitration clause was invalid, because it lacked any direct identification of an *ad hoc* arbitrator, or a specific description of the method of their appointment, and merely referred, as concerns the selection of the arbitrator and the determination of the rules of arbitration, to a legal entity other than a permanent arbitral institution in terms of the ArbAct, and to the statutes and rules adopted by that corporation. The court of first instance found that the claimant had not pleaded those grounds for invalidity at the beginning of the arbitration, as envisaged by the ArbAct. The court of first instance inferred that if the claimant had failed to raise the plea of the invalidity of the arbitration clause (supported by the reasons specified above) before its first act on the merits, the court had no option but to dismiss the motion under Section 33 of the ArbAct.[787]

16.169. The Prague Municipal Court, as the appellate court, upheld the operative part of the above Judgment of the Prague 3 District Court, whereby the motion to annul the arbitral award was dismissed.[788] The appellate court agreed with the conclusions reached by the court of first instance with respect to the court's holding that the plea of the invalidity of the arbitration clause had been raised late. In this regard, the appellate court invoked **(i)** Judgment of the SC of December 19, 2007 in Case No. 29 Odo 1222/2005,[789] **(ii)** Resolution of the SC of

---

[786] The provision is quoted above in the opening part of this annotation.

[787] The provision is quoted above in the opening part of this annotation.

[788] Namely, by Judgment of February 1 2012 in Case No. 62 Co 327/2011-102.

[789] This decision is available online on the SC website at http://www.nsoud.cz/Judikatura/ judikatura_ns.nsf/WebSearch/4C94F8F661E38E71C1257A4E0066A146?openDocument& Highlight=0; in this decision, the Court ruled as follows (cit.): *Unless the cause of invalidity applies to the arbitration clause covering the disputes under that contract, the invalidity of the contract does not affect the validity of the arbitration clause. If the arbitration clause (agreement) concerns all future disputes arising from a particular legal relationship (contract), it also covers a dispute over the determination of the invalidity of the rescission (cancellation) of the contract.* Note: The summary of the SC's legal opinion (*ratio*

April 28, 2011 in Case No. 32 Cdo 3299/2009,[790] (iii) Judgment of the SC of June 29, 2010 in Case No. 32 Cdo 953/2009,[791] (iv) Judgment of

decidendi) was adopted from the SC website. However, there are other parts of the reasoning that refer to the need to specify the grounds for the annulment of the arbitral award, which are more interesting from the perspective of the present case (cit.): *If the claimant was – judging from the operative part of the appellate court's decision – successful, because their motion to annul the arbitral award was granted, the resolution of the issue of the subjective admissibility of the extraordinary appeal depends on the assessment of whether the claimant's position could have been improved, from the procedural perspective, if the court had found grounds for the annulment of the arbitral award not only pursuant to Section 31(c)* [of the ArbAct], *but also pursuant to Section 31(a) or (b)* [of the ArbAct]. *In this connection, the Supreme Court emphasizes that the grounds for which the arbitral award was annulled [which determine whether the court will continue hearing the merits of the case and resolve the case upon a motion by any of the parties (Section 34(1)* [of the ArbAct]*), or whether the case will involve the situation envisaged under Section 34(2)* [of the ArbAct]*], are undoubtedly significant from the perspective of the parties' legal certainty as regards the jurisdiction of the arbitrators (or the court) to hear and resolve the case after the decision on the annulment of the arbitral award becomes final and conclusive. Although neither the Code of Civil Procedure, nor the Act stipulate that the grounds for which the arbitral award was annulled would have to be explicitly mentioned in the operative part of the court decision on the motion to annul the arbitral award, it is appropriate and desirable, from the perspective of further proceedings anticipated under Section 34 of the Act, and in order to eliminate potential doubts, that the operative part of the court decision on the annulment of the arbitral award also contain information as to whether the court will continue hearing the merits and make a decision upon a motion by any of the parties, or whether the arbitration agreement survives. The absence thereof in the operative part does not eo ipso render the court decision wrongful, but it has the result that the objections raised in the extraordinary appeal, in which the appellant claims that the arbitral award should also have been annulled on the grounds specified in Section 31(a) or (b) of the Act, are not targeted at the reasons for the decision, but at the merits of the case.* Note: Reference to this decision does not appear suitable, because the decision is focused more on the differentiation between general grounds for the annulment of an arbitral award, as defined in Section 31 of the ArbAct, not on the delimitation of particular factual circumstances on the basis of which the party seeks the annulment of the arbitral award.

[790] This decision is available online on the SC website at http://www.nsoud.cz/Judikatura/judikatura_ns.nsf/WebSearch/BB34890939CC8FFCC1257A4E00659A9A?openDocument&Highlight=0; in this decision, the Court ruled as follows (cit.): *The word "reasonably" used in Section 30 of the ArbAct with respect to the application of the Code of Civil Procedure indicates that arbitration is not directly subject to the Code of Civil Procedure, and its individual provisions cannot be applied mechanically in arbitration. The word "reasonably" primarily requires the tribunal to have regard to the general principles underlying Czech arbitration, i.e. the rules of the Code of Civil Procedure must be applied within the general framework of the principles of Czech arbitration. The Arbitration Act*

does not elaborate on the principle of the equality of the parties by stipulating any specific rights and obligations of the parties, and its fulfillment requires, pursuant to Section 30 [of the ArbAct], the reasonable application of the relevant provisions of the Code of Civil Procedure. The principle of the equality of the parties is fulfilled if the parties to the arbitral proceedings have the opportunity to state their case before the arbitrators or, as applicable, if they have been duly provided with a sufficient opportunity to assert their procedural rights. These requirements must be examined from two perspectives: (i) whether the procedures were formally observed, and (ii) whether both parties had an equal and sufficient opportunity to assert or raise their allegations, objections, proposals for evidence, etc. Note: The appellate court made an apparent typing error in the identification of the Resolution invoked by the appellate court (as provided in the annotated decision), as the court referred to the year "0009"; it is highly likely that it was this particular decision, but its relationship to the issues discussed in the present case is unclear.

791   This decision is available online on the SC website at http://www.nsoud.cz/Judikatura/judikatura_ns.nsf/WebSearch/8D870BDC4F731FC8C1257A4E0065D0F2?openDocument &Highlight=0; in this decision, the Court ruled as follows (cit.): *The reasonable application of Section 30 of the ArbAct does not indicate that if the parties agreed that their disputes would be resolved by an arbitrator "with a hearing according to written materials and following the principles of equity", the parties excluded the principle of oral hearings as envisaged under Section 19(3) of the ArbAct. The word "hearing" used by the parties attests to the contrary, i.e. the principle of oral hearings is preserved. If the arbitration was conducted without a hearing as envisaged under the ArbAct, the parties were not provided with the opportunity to plead their case before the arbitrator, which constitutes grounds for the annulment of the arbitral award under Section 31(e) of the ArbAct. The Supreme Court has repeatedly addressed the issue of depriving a party of the opportunity to plead their case before the arbitrators (cf. decision of May 28, 2009 in Case No. 23 Cdo 2570/2007, or decision of June 11, 2008 in Case No. 32 Cdo 1201/2007). The ground for the annulment of an arbitral award by a court specified in Section 31(e) of the ArbAct is targeted primarily at protecting the observance of the fundamental procedural rights and obligations of the parties to arbitration with respect to the principle of the equality of the parties expressed in Section 18 of the ArbAct. The parties must be provided with a full opportunity to assert their rights. All objections targeted at the annulment of an arbitral award pursuant to Section 31(e) of the ArbAct must, by necessity, be procedural objections; in other words, they must concern the procedure adopted by the arbitral tribunal in the hearing of the dispute, not the correctness of the factual or legal findings made by the arbitral tribunal. The motion to annul an arbitral award cannot be used as a remedy against arbitral awards. When addressing the issue of whether the party to arbitration was, in the particular case, provided with the opportunity to state (plead) their case before the arbitrators, the court must ascertain whether the party to the arbitral proceedings was, considering all circumstances of the case, provided with a sufficient opportunity to exercise their procedural rights in the arbitral proceedings, and whether or not the procedure adopted by the arbitral tribunal disturbed the equality between the parties. In its Judgment of November 13, 2003 in Case No. III. ÚS 202/03, published in Sbírka nálezů a usnesení Ústavního soudu [Reports of Judgments and Resolutions of the Constitutional Court], No. 134/2003, the Constitutional*

the SC of April 28, 2011 in Case No. 23 Cdo 3744/2009,[792] **(v)** Resolution of the SC of May 27, 2009 in Case No. 23 Cdo 2273/2007,[793] and

---

Court articulated and substantiated its conclusion that one of the fundamental principles governing court proceedings is the principle of the equality of the parties, which requires that the participants (parties) to the proceedings have equal standing before the court, without one or the other party enjoying any procedural benefits or being discriminated against. In order to implement this principle, the court is obliged to provide both parties to the dispute with the same possibility to assert their rights. The principle of the equality of the parties is interpreted similarly by the European Court of Human Rights, which employs the words "equality of arms" in this connection. According to the consistent case law of the ECtHR, the principle of the equality of arms, as an element of the broader concept of fair trial, requires that every party to civil proceedings should have a reasonable opportunity to present their case to the court in circumstances that do not place them at a substantial disadvantage vis-à-vis the opposing party (see also Dombo Beheer B. V. versus the Netherlands, 1993, Ankerl versus Switzerland, 1996, Komanický versus Slovakia, 2002). Considering the above said, the reasonable application of the Code of Civil Procedure (Section 30 [of the ArbAct]) also permits the application of this conclusion to arbitration in terms of Act No. 216/1994 Coll.

[792] This decision is available online on the SC website at http://www.nsoud.cz/Judikatura/judikatura_ns.nsf/WebSearch/7E2782089C0E013EC1257A4E0065F4DA?openDocument&Highlight=0; in this decision, the Court ruled as follows (cit.): *The parties are typically denied the opportunity to plead their case in arbitration if, inter alia, they have not been provided with a sufficient opportunity to state their case, and if they have not had the chance to comment on all relevant circumstances. It will usually be necessary to provide the parties with the opportunity to comment on the allegations made by the other party, also in writing, i.e. the respondent must have the right to file their statement of defense, and the claimant must have the right to comment on the counterclaim or any counter-arguments presented in the statement of defense. As concerns the individual abovementioned statements, it is reasonable to demand that the parties be provided with the opportunity to make the statements and that the provided opportunity be sufficient, considering all relevant circumstances of the case. The above indicates that the proceedings suffer from a defect that could have resulted in a wrongful decision in the case and which must be considered by the Supreme Court of its own motion (Section 242(3) [of the CCP]). In the reasoning for their judgment, the courts do not set forth, as mentioned above, any findings of fact, except that "the courts have established that the arbitrators heard the case pursuant to the UNCITRAL Rules"; at the same time, the courts' legal assessment of the case is not based on any uncontested statements (if any) made by the parties or any circumstances known to the courts (Section 121 [of the CCP]). A decision is unreviewable and should be vacated in the appellate proceedings if it does not clearly indicate how the court arrived at its factual findings (in the present case, the factual findings that would allow the legal conclusion that the grounds for the annulment of the arbitral award specified in Section 31(e) [of the ArbAct] are not fulfilled). If the appellate court failed to do so, wrongly assuming that "it is not appropriate to take evidence with respect to all of these objections as to whether the allegation is correct regarding the particular procedures adopted by the arbitrators, because even if the arbitrators proceeded as alleged by the claimant, they would not have fulfilled*

(vi) Judgment of the SC of October 30, 2009 in Case No. 33 Cdo 2675/2007.[794] The appellate court also held that the proceedings for the

---

the grounds for the annulment of the arbitral award in terms of Section 31(e) [of the ArbAct]", the appellate proceedings also suffer from a defect that could have resulted in a wrongful decision in the case (cf. also the reasoning for the Judgment of the Supreme Court published under No. 40/2002 of Sbírka soudních rozhodnutí a stanovisek [Reports of Court Decisions and Opinions]).

[793] This decision is available online on the SC website at http://www.nsoud.cz/Judikatura/ judikatura_ns.nsf/WebSearch/84C15F29BBF9CE68C1257A4E0065CF79?openDocument &Highlight=0; in this decision, the Court ruled as follows (cit.): *The ground for the annulment of an arbitral award by a court specified in Section 31(e) of the ArbAct is targeted primarily at protecting the observance of the fundamental procedural rights and obligations of the parties to arbitration with respect to the principle of the equality of the parties expressed in Section 18 of the ArbAct. The evidence proposed by the parties must be addressed by the arbitral tribunal – either the evidence will be examined (read or heard), or the evidence will not be admitted, which will be properly justified by the arbitral tribunal; it is necessary to insist that this principle also applies in arbitration. All objections targeted at the annulment of an arbitral award pursuant to Section 31(e) of the ArbAct must, by necessity, be procedural objections; in other words, they must concern the procedure adopted by the arbitral tribunal in the hearing of the dispute, not the correctness of the factual or legal findings made by the arbitral tribunal. When making a decision on the annulment of an arbitral award, the court is not entitled to review the merits of the contested decision, i.e. to review the decision from the perspective of the correctness of the assessment of evidence examined in the proceedings, or the correctness of the factual findings and of the ensuing legal assessment of the case.*

[794] This decision is available online on the SC website at http://www.nsoud.cz/Judikatura/ judikatura_ns.nsf/WebSearch/DA6CE5C7ECEA2F0AC1257A4E0068F06D?openDocumen t&Highlight=0; in this decision, the Court ruled as follows (cit.): *It is not possible to annul an arbitral award pursuant to Section 31(f)* [of the ArbAct] *because it orders performance that is contra bonos mores.* Note: The summary of this part of the SC's legal opinion (*ratio decidendi*) was adopted from the SC website. *It is necessary to keep in mind that the annulment of an arbitral award under Section 31* [of the ArbAct] *does not represent any regular or extraordinary remedy against the arbitral award (cf. Bělohlávek, A., Zákon o rozhodčím řízení a o výkonu rozhodčích nálezů. Komentář [Title in Translation: Act on Arbitration and Enforcement of Arbitral Awards. Commentary], C. H. BECK, 2004, p. 231); the only remedial measure against an arbitral award that allows the review of both the procedural and the material correctness of the arbitral award is the review by other arbitrators pursuant to Section 27* [of the ArbAct]. *"The purpose of the annulment of an arbitral award by a court is to allow the court to check, in other than enforcement proceedings, whether the basic conditions were met for the hearing and resolution of the case in arbitration, i.e. the basic requirements for suspending the parties' constitutional right to assert their rights in an independent and impartial court in terms of Article 36(1) of the Charter of Fundamental Rights and Freedoms (the "Charter"), in conjunction (inter alia) with the constitutional right under the last sentence of Article 38(2) of the Charter. The Act*

annulment of the arbitral award were not review proceedings; consequently, the court was not entitled to review the material correctness of the award. Despite the fact that this conclusion follows from and is articulated in the abovementioned decisions (as the primary *ratio decidendi*), the appellate court also referred to further case law on this point, namely Judgment of the SC of May 28, 2009 in Case No. 23 Cdo 2570/2007,[795] and Judgment of the ConCourt of March 8, 2011 in Case No. I. ÚS 3227/07.[796]

---

allows judicial supervision primarily by allowing the parties to plead the existence of defects that would affect ad hoc arbitration, as well as arbitration before a permanent arbitral institution, or the arbitral award, where such defects run counter to the fundamental principles underlying arbitration and decision-making, as such [see Hlavsa, P., Poznámky k rozhodčímu řízení (část II) [Title in Translation: Comments on Arbitration (Part II)], Právní praxe v podnikání 6/1995, p. 4, and similarly Macur, J., Rozhodčí řízení a výkon rozhodčích nálezů [Title in Translation: Arbitration and Enforcement of Arbitral Awards], Právo a podnikání 5/1995, p. 6]. Considering the nature of arbitration, the purpose of which inheres in the fact that the hearing and resolution of a particular type of disputes is transferred from courts to arbitrators, and with respect to the grounds for which an arbitral award can be annulled, we may conclude that the legislator intended to exclude the judicial review of the material correctness of the arbitral award, i.e. the accuracy of the findings of fact and legal assessment of the case. If the court were entitled to review the material correctness of the arbitral award in the proceedings for the annulment of the award, the arbitration law would become meaningless. The grounds specified in Section 31(a) – (e) and (g) [of the ArbAct] may undoubtedly be used to challenge the arbitral award for defects of the arbitration agreement (clause) and of the arbitration itself. What remains is the ground specified in Section 31(f) [of the ArbAct]; but even that particular ground cannot be invoked as justification for reviewing the factual or legal conclusions incorporated in the arbitral award (which could also include the conclusion regarding the exercise of a right to performance that is contra bonos mores). Considering the above said, it is not possible to annul an arbitral award with reference to Section 3(1) [of the CivC], holding that the exercise of the right to the performance awarded by the award is contra bonos mores (considering the particular circumstances of the case), and consequently, prohibited under Czech law. Considering the above said, the Supreme Court held that the appellate court wrongly assessed the issue of whether there were grounds for the annulment of the arbitral award rendered by the arbitrator P.P. on April 12, 2006 in Case No. 3/05 in terms of Section 31(f) [of the ArbAct].

[795] This decision is available online on the SC website at http://www.nsoud.cz/Judikatura/judikatura_ns.nsf/WebSearch/4A42E4DF19BD26F3C1257A4E0065E608?openDocument&Highlight=0; in this decision, the Court ruled as follows (cit.): *When making a decision on the annulment of an arbitral award, the court is not entitled to review the merits of the contested decision, i.e. to review the decision from the perspective of the correctness of the assessment of the evidence examined in the proceedings, or the correctness of the factual findings and of the ensuing legal assessment of the case. A motion to annul an arbitral award cannot be used as a remedy against arbitral awards. When addressing the issue of*

16.170. The claimant lodged an extraordinary appeal against the Judgment of the appellate court; the claimant disagreed with the legal assessment of the case by the lower courts and insisted on the claimant's conclusion that the respective arbitration clauses were invalid. The claimant based its conclusion on Judgment of the Prague High Court of May 28, 2009 in Case No. 12 Cmo 496/2008, [797]Resolution of the Grand Panel of the Civil and Commercial Division of the SC of May 11, 2011 in Case No. 31 Cdo 1945/2010, [798]and Resolution of the SC of November 29, 2011 in Case No. 32 Cdo 1824/2011.[799] The claimant also pointed out that the

---

whether the party to arbitration was, in the particular case, provided with the opportunity to state (plead) their case before the arbitrators, the court must ascertain whether the party to the arbitral proceedings was, considering all of the circumstances of the case, provided with a sufficient opportunity to exercise their procedural rights in the arbitral proceedings, and whether or not the procedure adopted by the arbitral tribunal disturbed the equality between the parties.

[796] This decision is available online on the ConCourt website at http://nalus.usoud.cz/Search/ResultDetail.aspx?id=69584&pos=1&cnt=1&typ=result; in this decision, the Court ruled as follows (cit.): *I. Hearing a case in arbitration does not entail the waiver of legal protection; it denotes the transfer of legal protection to another decision-making authority, which finds the law. II. The arbitrator cannot play the role of a merely passive element; they must conduct the proceedings in such manner that their decision is not a surprise to the parties. To that end, civil court proceedings prescribe that courts must give instructions to the parties; there is no reason to absolve the arbitrator of that obligation in arbitral proceedings, considering the fact that in such proceedings the arbitrator acts as the decision-making authority in place of the court. The ArbAct does not provide for the arbitrator's obligation to give instructions; it is therefore legitimate to reasonably apply the Code of Civil Procedure (Section 30 [of the ArbAct]). III. The extent of the supervisory function of the courts vis-à-vis arbitration must be carefully balanced – the rule stipulating that arbitration must also guarantee legal protection must not be eliminated, but on the other hand, the advantages of arbitration and its practical applicability must not be entirely wiped out. Consequently, proceedings for the annulment of an arbitral award by a court can never be structured along the lines of remedial civil court proceedings, let alone regular appellate proceedings. The supervisory function of the courts does not comprise the review of the material correctness of the arbitral award (conflict with substantive law), because the proceedings for the annulment of the arbitral award would thereby become quasi-appellate proceedings. The supervision may therefore only concentrate on examining the crucial procedural issues, e.g. whether the arbitration could actually have been conducted, whether any important procedural rights were denied to the parties, or whether the arbitral award itself is free of procedural flaws.*

[797] The decision is quoted above in this annotation.

[798] The decision is quoted above in this annotation.

[799] This decision is available online on the SC website at http://www.nsoud.cz/Judikatura/judikatura_ns.nsf/WebSearch/FC3450EB66A1874DC1257A4E006A5970?openDocument

claimant had already pleaded a lack of jurisdiction on the part of the arbitrator in the arbitral proceedings, when the claimant objected that the arbitration clause was invalid. Consequently, the claimant insisted that the annulment of the arbitral award was justified under the ground for annulment specified in Section 31(b) of the ArbAct.[800]

16.171. The Supreme Court of the Czech Republic (SC) found the objections raised by the claimant to be legitimate, and agreed that the absence of essential elements of an arbitration clause with respect to the identification or the method of appointment of arbitrators renders the clause invalid. In this connection, the SC invoked Judgment of the Prague High Court of May 28, 2009 in Case No. 12 Cmo 496/2008[801] and Resolution of the Grand Panel of the Civil and Commercial Division of the SC of May 11, 2011 in Case No. 31 Cdo 1945/2010.[802] The Supreme Court of the Czech Republic (SC) inferred that the conclusions articulated in the said decisions also applied to the present case. The SC also referred to Judgment of the SC of March 27, 2013 in Case No. 23 Cdo 2406/2011[803] and ruled that if the invalidity of the arbitration clause was pleaded in time in the arbitral proceedings pursuant to Section 33 of the ArbAct,[804] the plea also covers grounds for the invalidity of the arbitration clause other than those that might have been described in the plea by factual circumstances. The SC therefore ruled that the conditions for the annulment of the arbitral award were fulfilled.

&Highlight=0; in this decision, the Court ruled as follows (cit.): *I. If the arbitration agreement lacks any direct identification of an ad hoc arbitrator, or a specific description of the method of their appointment, and refers to "Rules on Arbitration" issued by a legal entity (corporation) other than a permanent arbitral institution established under the law, the arbitration agreement is contrary to the law and therefore invalid pursuant to Section 39* [of the CivC]. *An entity other than a permanent arbitral institution established under a special statute is not, as opposed to the latter, entitled to issue statutes and rules that would regulate the case management of arbitration and define the method of appointing arbitrators. If the entity performs activities that are reserved for permanent arbitral institutions, the fact itself suggests that the entity's intentions are contrary to the law, and the conditions set by the entity raise legitimate doubts from the perspective of the independent and impartial resolution of disputes. II. Laws and regulations do not allow defects of null and void juridical acts to be cured retrospectively, i.e. they cannot be validated ex post.*

[800] The provision is quoted above in the opening part of this annotation.
[801] The decision is quoted above in this annotation.
[802] The decision is quoted above in this annotation.
[803] The decision is quoted above in this annotation.
[804] The provision is quoted above in the opening part of this annotation.

[Arguments Presented by SC]:

16.172. The SC based its decision on the conclusions already articulated in the preceding rulings of the SC. As concerns the specific issue of the invalidity of an arbitration clause under Section 39 of the CivC,[805] the SC held that this issue must always be examined individually. Consequently, the contested arbitration clause does not have to be identical to the clauses involved in the cases invoked by the SC. Conflict with the law and the invalidity of the clause as the necessary consequence thereof can be inferred whenever the parties fail to agree that their dispute will be resolved by an ad hoc arbitrator, or fail to specifically appoint this arbitrator, as applicable, and at the same time, the arbitration clause lacks any agreement on the method of appointing the arbitrator that would comply with the ArbAct. As concerns the timeliness of the plea under Section 33 of the ArbAct,[806] the SC held that this obligation must be interpreted within the meaning of the general assertion of pleas in arbitration pursuant to Section 31(b) and (c) of the ArbAct.[807] However, the said provisions contain multiple specific statutory definitions, and consequently, if the plea is raised pursuant to Section 31(b) and (c) of the ArbAct,[808] it is generally possible to hear the said grounds for the annulment of the arbitral award in the proceedings commenced in terms of Section 31 of the ArbAct.[809]

16.173. The SC therefore concluded that the decision of the appellate court was incorrect; the grounds on which the SC's decision was based also apply to the decision of the court of first instance. Consequently, the SC vacated the decisions of the appellate court and of the court of first instance and remanded the case for further hearing and a new decision.

[Further Conclusions and Comments Concerning Annotated Decision of SC]:

16.174. The decision cannot be perceived as surprising or introducing any new interpretation of the said rules, i.e. a decision that would shift the existing doctrinal interpretation. On the contrary, it is based strictly on the case law, which can be deemed consistent. A motion under Section 31 of the ArbAct[810] undoubtedly requires that the party had performed a commissive act in the arbitral proceedings, whereby the

---

[805] The provision is quoted above in the opening part of this annotation.

[806] The provision is quoted above in the opening part of this annotation.

[807] The provision is quoted above in the opening part of this annotation.

[808] The provision is quoted above in the opening part of this annotation.

[809] The provision is quoted above in the opening part of this annotation.

[810] The provision is quoted above in the opening part of this annotation.

party defended its rights. Although the conclusions reached by the Court appear straightforward, the issue has multiple implications. Moreover, the SC only provides a very brief description of the facts of the said case, and it is obvious that certain principal circumstances have been neglected. Despite the fact that the description might create a contrary impression, the case is not one in which the claimant pleaded in the arbitral proceedings certain specific grounds for invalidity, which they subsequently entirely ignored in their motion pursuant to Section 31 of the ArbAct[811] and invoked brand new arguments. The arbitral award was rendered on April 28, 2008, and the objection that the arbitration clause is contrary to the law, because it did not properly specify the method of appointment of the arbitrator, was included in the pleading dated March 29, 2010. We can therefore assume that the claimant asserted the same grounds in its motion that had already been previously asserted in the arbitral proceedings (although the annotated decision does not indicate how the court handled the said grounds). Indeed, the database administered by the Ministry of Justice of the Czech Republic[812] also allows such conclusions. The additional question is whether the party in the given case can be required to raise a specific plea based on the courts' legal assessment in a case in which the decisions invoked by the party were issued only after the arbitration had been terminated, and on top of that, the decisions represented a radical break from the preceding case law.

16.175. Moreover, many cases will require an analysis of the contents of the objections, irrespective of their legal classification; the timeliness and the scope of the submitted objections will also have to be assessed from that perspective. Similarly, it will always be necessary to assess the differences between the objections raised in the arbitration and those raised in the proceedings for the annulment of the arbitral award. If, for instance, a party pleads the invalidity of the arbitration agreement in general, it appears too harsh to prevent the party in the court proceedings pursuant to Section 31 of the ArbAct[813] from supplementing or elaborating on the party's arguments that the party had adduced in the arbitration. Firstly, court proceedings would in such case become substantially redundant, because the party would be

---

[811] The provision is quoted above in the opening part of this annotation.

[812] See http://infosoud.justice.cz/InfoSoud/public/search.do?type=spzn&typSoudu=os&krajOrg=VSECHNY_KRAJE&org=OSPHA03&cisloSenatu=9&druhVec=C&bcVec=141&rocnik=2008&spamQuestion=23&agendaNc=CIVIL&backPage=..%2Fpublic%2Fsearch.jsp.

[813] The provision is quoted above in the opening part of this annotation.

limited to the formulations used in the arbitration, and it would be sufficient to refer to the materials included in the dossier. Besides, it is necessary to bear in mind that no such limitations apply to the opposing party, who is entitled to supplement, expand or modify their arguments against the annulment of the arbitral award during the court proceedings, and is not limited to the defense employed in the arbitration. The equality between the parties would be disturbed (if the party seeking the annulment of the arbitral award were strictly bound by the party's submissions in the arbitral proceedings). Besides, we must not overlook the practical implications – such a rigorous interpretation of Section 33 of the ArbAct[814] would result in the parties overburdening the arbitrators with an excessive volume of objections and arguments that could theoretically be perceivable, only to make sure that the party could, if necessary, employ such objections or arguments in the proceedings pursuant to Section 31 of the ArbAct.[815]

16.176. However, the opposite approach, which is, to all appearances, currently maintained by the SC, is not ideal either, i.e. that the parties are bound by no limits at all in raising their objections and pleas. Consequently, a party may in theory challenge the scope of the arbitration agreement in arbitration without raising any objections to its validity. From the perspective of Section 31(b) of the ArbAct,[816] the situation would fall under the ground specified as the inapplicability of the arbitration agreement to the given case. But the party would plead the invalidity of the arbitration agreement as grounds for the annulment of the arbitral award. In such case, the interpretation stating that a timely plea under Section 33 of the ArbAct[817] implies any other pleas that the party could make under Section 31(b) or (c) of the ArbAct[818] (depending on the classification of the original plea) would exceed the scope of the CCP, and be in conflict with the object of Section 33 of the ArbAct.[819]

16.177. The conclusions consistently repeated in the SC case law are not affected by the amendments to the ArbAct implemented under the Consumer Amendment, i.e. Act No. 19/2012 Coll., which has

---

[814] The provision is quoted above in the opening part of this annotation.
[815] The provision is quoted above in the opening part of this annotation.
[816] The provision is quoted above in the opening part of this annotation.
[817] The provision is quoted above in the opening part of this annotation.
[818] The provision is quoted above in the opening part of this annotation.
[819] The provision is quoted above in the opening part of this annotation.

amended the ArbAct with effect since April 1, 2012 The enhancement of the consumer's position is evidenced by the fact that the consumer will no longer be obliged, in certain cases, to rely on the above interpretation of Section 33 of the ArbAct,[820] because the court is now obliged to examine certain grounds for the annulment of the arbitral award of its own motion (*ex officio*). This obligation specifically concerns the grounds for the annulment of arbitral award specified in Section 31(a) through (d) or (h).[821] The Explanatory Memorandum to Act No. 19/2012 Coll. states that this amendment is in response to the case law of the CJ EU. In its rulings concerning Council Directive 93/13/EEC on Unfair Terms in Consumer Contracts, the CJ EU held that the courts must assess, with or without a motion, whether the arbitration clause is in conflict with binding national rules, even after a motion for the involuntary enforcement of a final and conclusive arbitral award is lodged; the court is obliged to perform the review of its own motion.[822] However, the above said should in no case be interpreted as inducing consumers to forgo a most accurate and precise specification of the grounds for the annulment of the arbitral award; the reason is that the court seized with the motion to annul the arbitral award has at its disposal only the materials in the dossier, which might not include all relevant nuances.

|||

---

[820] The provision is quoted above in the opening part of this annotation.

[821] The provision is quoted above in the opening part of this annotation.

[822] Cf. decision of the European Court of Justice (First Chamber) in Case C–168/05 of October 26, 2006 (*Elisa María Mostaza Claro* v. *Centro Móvil Milenium SL*).

Czech (& Central European) Yearbook of Arbitration

16. Judgment of Supreme Court of Czech Republic of November 27, 2013 in Case No. 23 Cdo 1521/2013:[823] (i) Pleading Invalidity of Arbitration Clause and Annulment of Arbitral Award, (ii) Exercising Right to Fully State (Plead) One's Case before Arbitrators, (iii) Reasons for Arbitral Award

Abbreviations Used:

AC Rules	AC Rules[824]
AC	Arbitration Court at the Economic Chamber of the Czech Republic and Agricultural Chamber of the Czech Republic[825]
ArbAct	Act No. 216/1994 Coll., on Arbitration and the Enforcement of Arbitral Awards, as amended[826]
ConCourt	Constitutional Court of the Czech Republic
SC	Supreme Court of the Czech Republic

Key Words:

annulment (setting aside) of arbitral award | changing motion (proposal)[827] | changing request for arbitration (statement of claim)[828] | concentration of proceedings | contract for work | equality | exercising procedural rights | extension of claim | invalidity of arbitration agreement[829] | invalidity of arbitration clause[830] | jurisdiction | pleading

---

[823] This decision is available online on the website of the SC at http://www.nsoud.cz/ Judikatura/judikatura_ns.nsf/WebSearch/E2C0BAA2CE6BD71EC1257C5A004520DC?op enDocument&Highlight=0 [last accessed on November 14, 2014].

[824] The applicable regulation is the Rules of the AC governing Domestic Disputes in effect until June 30, 2012 (available on the AC website at http://www.soud.cz/rady/rad-pro-vnitrostatni-spory-2007, i.e. the Rules as applicable on February 1, 2007). This annotation has also had regard to the new AC Rules in effect since July 1, 2012 (also available online on the AC website at http://www.soud.cz/rady/rad-rozhodciho-soudu-01-07-2012).

[825] For more information regarding this permanent arbitral institution, see www.soud.cz.

[826] The SC does not explicitly identify the version of the ArbAct applied in the given case; the relevant provisions have not been subject to any amendments that could influence the conclusions of the SC and their applicability. The reason is that the case did not involve a B2C dispute, and at the same time, the grounds for the annulment of the arbitral award that were asserted in the case did not fall within the category of grounds, the assertion of which would depend on the status of the party.

[827] See also "changing a request for arbitration (statement of claim)".

[828] See also "changing a motion (proposal)".

[829] See also "invalidity of an arbitration clause".

invalidity | pleading one's case/hearing a case | procedural rights | reasons for arbitral award |

Applicable Laws and Regulations:

ArbAct: Section 6,[831] Section 18,[832] Section 25,[833] Section 30,[834] Section 31,[835] Section 33[836]

---

[830] See also "invalidity of an arbitration agreement".

[831] ArbAct, Section 6 (cit.): *(1) Arbitrators are bound to maintain the confidentiality of any circumstances they have learnt of in connection with their office of arbitrator, unless they are released from the duty of confidentiality. (2) Arbitrators may be released from confidentiality by the parties. If the parties do not release the arbitrator from confidentiality, the decision on the release for serious reasons shall be made by the Chairman of the District Court with jurisdiction over the district in which the arbitrator has his or her residence. If the arbitrator does not have his or her residence in the territory of the Czech Republic, the decision shall be made by the Chairman of the District Court for Prague 1.* Note: this version of the provision applied to the respective proceedings; the currently applicable version reads as follows (cit.): *(1) Arbitrators are bound to maintain the confidentiality of any circumstances they have learnt of in connection with their office of arbitrator, unless they are released from the duty of confidentiality. (2) Arbitrators may be released from confidentiality by the parties. If the parties do not release the arbitrator from confidentiality, the decision on the release for serious reasons shall be made by the Chairman of the District Court with jurisdiction over the district in which the arbitrator has his or her permanent residence. If the arbitrator does not have his or her permanent residence in the territory of the Czech Republic or if the arbitrator's residence cannot be established, the decision on the release from confidentiality shall be made by the Chairman of the District Court with jurisdiction over the district in which the arbitral award was made. If the place where the arbitral award was made cannot be established or if the award was not made in the Czech Republic, the decision shall be made by the Chairman of the District Court for Prague 1.* Note: The amendments implemented in the respective provision have no bearing on the case and the conclusions reached by the SC; the objection raised in the proceedings alleged that the arbitrators had breached the duty of confidentiality. This is not an issue of the court's jurisdiction to absolve the arbitrators of the duty of confidentiality, which was the subject matter of the amendments.

[832] ArbAct, Section 18 (cit.): *The parties have an equal standing in the arbitral proceedings and must be provided with a full opportunity to assert their rights.* Note: This version of the law applied to the respective proceedings, but it has not been subject to any modifications in the meantime and therefore continues to apply.

[833] ArbAct, Section 25 (cit.): *(1) The arbitral award must be adopted by the majority of the arbitrators, must be made in writing and signed by at least the majority of the arbitrators. The operative part of the arbitral award must be clear and unambiguous. (2) The arbitral award must contain reasons unless the parties have agreed to dispense with reasons; this also applies to any arbitral award rendered pursuant to Section 24(2).(3) When making the award, the arbitrators apply the substantive law applicable to the dispute; they may, however, resolve the dispute according to the rules of equity but only if the parties have*

explicitly authorized them to do so. Note: this version of the provision applied to the respective proceedings; the currently applicable version reads as follows (cit.): *(1) The arbitral award must be adopted by the majority of the arbitrators, must be made in writing and signed by at least the majority of the arbitrators. The operative part of the arbitral award must be clear and unambiguous. (2) The arbitral award must contain reasons unless the parties have agreed to dispense with reasons; this also applies to any arbitral award rendered pursuant to Section 24(2).An arbitral award rendered in a dispute arising from a consumer contract must always contain reasons and instructions regarding the right to file a motion with the court to annul the award. (3) When making the award, the arbitrators apply the substantive law applicable to the dispute; they may, however, resolve the dispute according to the rules of equity but only if the parties have explicitly authorized them to do so. In disputes arising from consumer contracts, the arbitrators shall always abide by consumer protection laws and regulations.* Note: The implemented amendments do not influence the case at hand and the conclusions reached by the SC, because the case did not involve a B2C dispute.

[834] ArbAct, Section 30 (cit.): *Unless the Act stipulates otherwise, the arbitral proceedings shall be reasonably governed by the provisions of the Code of Civil Procedure.* Note: This version of the law applied to the respective proceedings, but it has not been subject to any modifications in the meantime and therefore continues to apply.

[835] ArbAct, Section 31 (cit.): *At the request of any party the court annuls the arbitral award if: (a) it was made in a case which cannot be submitted to arbitration (cannot be the subject of a valid arbitration agreement), (b) the arbitration agreement is invalid for other reasons or the agreement was cancelled or it does not apply to the agreed case, (c) the arbitrator(s) who took part in the proceedings was/were not authorized to make decisions in the case, whether under the arbitration agreement or otherwise, or lacked the capacity to act as arbitrator(s), (d) the arbitral award was not adopted by the majority of the arbitrators, (e) a party was denied the opportunity to plead his or her case in the arbitral proceedings, (f) the arbitral award orders a party to provide performance which was not requested by the obligee or to provide performance which is impossible or illegal under domestic law, (g) it transpires that there are reasons which would otherwise justify the reopening of civil proceedings in court.* [Section 228(1)(a) and (b) of the CCP]. Note: this version of the provision applied to the respective proceedings; the currently applicable version reads as follows (cit.): *At the request of any party the court annuls the arbitral award if: (a) it was made in a case which cannot be submitted to arbitration (cannot be the subject of a valid arbitration agreement), (b) the arbitration agreement is invalid for other reasons or the agreement was cancelled or it does not apply to the agreed case, (c) the arbitrator(s) who took part in the proceedings was/were not authorized to make decisions in the case, whether under the arbitration agreement or otherwise, or lacked the capacity to act as arbitrator(s), (d) the arbitral award was not adopted by the majority of the arbitrators, (e) a party was denied the opportunity to plead his or her case in the arbitral proceedings, (f) the arbitral award orders a party to provide performance which was not requested by the creditor or to provide performance which is impossible or illegal under domestic law, (g) the arbitrator or the permanent arbitral institution resolved a dispute arising from a consumer contract contrary to consumer protection laws, or clearly in violation of good morals, or contrary to*

The Supreme Court of the Czech Republic reached the following principal conclusions:

(1) When addressing the issue of whether the party to arbitration in the particular case was provided with the opportunity to state (plead) their case before the arbitrators, the court must ascertain whether the party to the arbitral proceedings was, considering all of the circumstances of the case, provided with a sufficient opportunity to exercise their procedural rights in the arbitral proceedings, and whether or not the procedure adopted by the arbitral tribunal disturbed the equality of the parties.[837]

---

public policy, (h) an arbitration agreement relating to disputes arising from consumer contracts lacks the information required under Section 3(5) or such information is intentionally or to a non-negligible extent incomplete, inaccurate, or false, or (i) it transpires that there are reasons which would otherwise justify the reopening of civil proceedings in court. [Section 228(1)(a) and (b) of the CCP]. Note: The implemented amendments and the additional grounds for the annulment of an arbitral award in B2C disputes do not influence the case at hand and the conclusions reached by the SC, because the case did not involve a B2C dispute, and at the same time, the respective grounds for the annulment of the arbitral award existed and applied even before the amendment implemented by Act No. 19/2012 Coll.

[836] ArbAct, Section 33 (cit.): *The court shall dismiss a motion to annul an arbitral award which is based on the grounds specified in Section 31(b) or (c) if the party requesting the annulment failed to raise the corresponding objection in the arbitral proceedings before the party's first act in the merits of the case, despite having an opportunity to do so.* Note: this version of the provision applied to the respective proceedings; the currently applicable version reads as follows (cit.): *The court shall dismiss a motion to annul an arbitral award which is based on the grounds specified in Section 31(b) or (c) if the party requesting the annulment failed to raise the corresponding objection in the arbitral proceedings before the party's first act in the merits of the case, despite having an opportunity to do so. This does not apply to disputes arising from consumer contracts.* Note: The implemented amendments do not influence the case at hand and the conclusions reached by the SC, because the case did not involve a B2C dispute.

[837] In its conclusions, the SC invokes its prior case law, namely its Judgment of June 11, 2008 in Case No. 32 Cdo 1201/2007; the decision is available online on the website of the SC at http://www.nsoud.cz/Judikatura/judikatura_ns.nsf/WebSearch/3EEA49C0B9EAD7 61C1257A4E0067D074?openDocument&Highlight=0; the court held as follows (cit.): *The parties are most typically denied the opportunity to state their case in arbitration if they have not been provided with a sufficient opportunity to plead their case, and if they have not had the chance to comment on all relevant circumstances. It will usually be necessary to provide the parties with the opportunity to comment on the allegations made by the other party, also in writing, i.e. the respondent must have the right to file their statement of defense and the claimant must have the right to comment on the counterclaim or any counter-arguments presented in the statement of defense. As concerns the individual*

abovementioned statements, it is reasonable to demand that the parties be provided with the opportunity to make the statements and that the so-provided opportunity be sufficient, considering all of the relevant circumstances of the case (cf. also Bohuslav Klein, Rozhodčí řízení [Title in Translation: Arbitration], ASPI 2007, p. 193). Another necessary prerequisite is that the parties are provided not only with the opportunity to propose evidence proving their allegations, but also with the opportunity to hear or read the evidence (unless the evidence is obviously irrelevant for the given proceedings). If the proposal for evidence presented by any of the parties was dismissed, the arbitrators must consider the proposal for evidence and sufficiently justify why the proposed evidence was not examined (cf. ibid). If the request for arbitration (statement of claim) was extended by a further CZK 195,844,748, and the claimant (respondent in the arbitration) was only allowed to submit their final statement after the hearing of the dispute was declared closed, it is necessary to conclude that the claimant was not provided with a sufficient opportunity to plead their case. This conclusion stands despite the fact that the parties to the dispute had agreed, pursuant to Section 27 of the Rules of the Permanent Arbitration Court attached to the Economic Chamber of the Czech Republic and Agrarian Chamber of the Czech Republic, that the arbitral panel should resolve the dispute without a hearing, only on the basis of written documents. Such procedure means that the parties only waived the (oral) hearing(s), but it cannot mean that the parties could limit their procedural rights in terms of disallowing further proposals for evidence, or requirements for the taking of evidence. A contrary approach would violate the right to a fair trial in terms of Section 38(2) of the Charter of Fundamental Rights and Freedoms. Legal literature (cf. also Prof. dr. Alexander J. Bělohlávek, Komentář: Zákon o rozhodčím řízení a o výkonu rozhodčích nálezů [Title in Translation: Commentary: Act on Arbitration and Enforcement of Arbitral Awards], C. H. Beck 2004, 1st edition, p. 241) also maintains that the annulment of an arbitral award pursuant to Section 31(e) [of the ArbAct] for a reason consisting of the fact that the arbitrators did not hear or read the evidence proposed by the parties is principally only possible if the arbitrators refused to address the proposal or addressed it only insufficiently. The court is not entitled to assess this proposal for evidence from the perspective of its potential influence on the result of the arbitration (as is the case, for instance, in appellate proceedings). Consequently, this is another reason why the arbitrators should address, both during the proceedings and in the reasons for their written award, all evidence proposed and examined in the proceedings and all evidence the examination of which they refused, and provide reasons for such refusal. In its Judgment of November 13, 2003 in Case No. III. ÚS 202/03, published in Sbírka nálezů a usnesení Ústavního soudu [Reports of Judgments and Resolutions of the Constitutional Court], No. 134/2003 USn., the Constitutional Court articulated and substantiated its conclusion that one of the fundamental principles governing court proceedings is the principle of the equality of the parties, which requires that the participants (parties) to the proceedings have equal standing before the court, without one or the other party enjoying any procedural benefits or being discriminated against. In order to implement this principle, the court is obliged to provide both parties to the dispute with the same possibility to assert their rights. The principle of the equality of the parties is interpreted similarly by the European Court of Human Rights, which employs the words "equality of arms" in this connection. According to the consistent case law of the ECtHR, the principle of the equality of arms, as an element of the broader concept of fair trial, requires that every party to civil proceedings should have a reasonable opportunity to present their case to the court in circumstances that do not place them at a substantial disadvantage vis-à-vis the opposing party (see also Dombo Beheer B. V. versus the Netherlands, 1993, Ankerl versus Switzerland, 1996, and Komanický versus Slovakia, 2002). Considering the above, the reasonable application of the Code of Civil Procedure also permits the application of this conclusion to arbitration in terms of [the ArbAct]. Hence, if the respondent (claimant in the arbitration) extended their statement of claim by another CZK 195,844,748 after the examination of evidence was finished, and after the parties to the arbitration had agreed to continue the dispute on the basis of written documents, and the claimant (respondent in the arbitration) only had the opportunity to plead their case in the form of a final proposal, the parties to the arbitration clearly did not enjoy an equal opportunity to assert their rights in the arbitral proceedings. The appellant (in the SC proceedings) is right that if the party has at their disposal no remedial measure, the arbitral tribunal should have provided the respondent (claimant in the court proceedings) with any and all statutory procedural measures to protect the respondent's legitimate interests, and should have enabled the respondent to present sufficient defense against the claims that were only raised after the examination of evidence was closed, so that the equal standing of the parties to the arbitral proceedings is not prejudiced. The appellant is also correct in arguing that the arbitral panel considered the claimant's final proposal of July 1, 2004 as a motion to open the examination of evidence (see also the arbitral panel's Resolution of July 16, 2004). But the panel failed to properly handle the motion; the examination of evidence was not allowed, but the procedural decision was not justified by any specific reasons. The arbitral panel merely held that "in the arbitrators' opinion, it is not necessary to reopen the examination of evidence with respect to the modification of the request for arbitration (statement of claim), because the results of the evidence examined so far can serve as the basis for hearing and making a decision on the modified claim in terms of Section 95(2) [of the CCP]". However, in Paragraph 1.51 of the arbitral award in Case No. Rsp 447/03, the arbitral panel stated that the respondent (claimant in the court proceedings) had not made a motion to reopen the examination of evidence in their last pleading, and had not proposed the examination of any specific evidence. The arbitrators held that the evidence examined in the arbitral proceedings was sufficient and enabled the arbitrators to make a decision on all claims asserted by the parties in the proceedings, i.e. including the claims relating to the extension of the request for arbitration (statement of claim). The above indicates that when addressing the issue of whether the party to arbitration was, in the particular case, provided with the opportunity to state (plead) their case before the arbitrators, the court must ascertain whether the party to the arbitral proceedings was, considering all of the circumstances of the case, provided with a sufficient opportunity to exercise their procedural rights in the arbitral proceedings, and whether or not the procedure adopted by the arbitral tribunal disturbed the equality of the parties. The fact that the modified (extended) claim has its basis in evidence that was already examined may constitute grounds for accepting the modification (extension) of the claim; but this may not be used as a justification for not hearing the claim. The fact that the parties consented to the resolution of the dispute on the basis of written documents cannot be invoked if the motion (request for arbitration) was

(2) The fact that a modified (extended) claim is based on evidence already examined may constitute grounds for accepting the modification (extension) of the claim; while this may not be used as a justification for not hearing the claim. The fact that the parties consented to the resolution of the dispute on the basis of written documents cannot be invoked if the motion (request for arbitration) was only modified after the parties had given their consent.[838]

(3) The grounds for the annulment of an arbitral award defined under Section 31(b) of the ArbAct cannot be applied on the basis of Section 33 of the ArbAct if the party did not plead the invalidity of the arbitration agreement in the pleading that represented the party's first act on the merits, but only during the arbitral proceedings.

(4) With the reasonable application of Section 30 of the ArbAct, we can infer that an arbitral tribunal is also bound by the obligation to state in its decision why the tribunal did not examine the other evidence proposed by the parties.[839]

---

only modified after the parties had given their consent. Consequently, the appellant is also correct that the claim representing the extension of the request for arbitration (statement of claim) was not properly heard before the arbitral tribunal.

[838] The SC again invoked its Judgment of June 11, 2008 in Case No. 32 Cdo 1201/2007, as quoted above in this annotation.

[839] In its conclusions, the SC invoked its prior case law, namely its Judgment of January 25, 2012 in Case No. 23 Cdo 4386/2011; the decision is available online on the website of the SC at http://www.nsoud.cz/Judikatura/judikatura_ns.nsf/WebSearch/CE00FA44886 16504C1257A4E006904BD?openDocument&Highlight=0; the court held as follows (cit.): *All objections targeted at the annulment of an arbitral award must, by necessity, be procedural objections; in other words, they must concern the procedure adopted by the arbitral tribunal in the hearing of the dispute, not the correctness of the factual or legal findings made by the arbitral tribunal. The motion to annul an arbitral award cannot be used as a remedy against arbitral awards. When addressing the issue of whether the party to arbitration in the particular case was provided with the opportunity to state (plead) their case before the arbitrators, the court must ascertain whether the party to the arbitral proceedings was, considering all of the circumstances of the case, provided with a sufficient opportunity to exercise their procedural rights in the arbitral proceedings, and whether or not the procedure adopted by the arbitral tribunal disturbed the equality of the parties. [...] In its Judgment of April 25, 2007 in Case No. 32 Odo 1528/2005, the Supreme Court addressed the relationship between [the ArbAct] and [the CCP]; the SC arrived at the conclusion that the relationship between the two laws is regulated by Section 30 [of the ArbAct], which stipulates that arbitration shall be reasonably governed by the provisions of the Code of Civil Procedure, unless the law stipulates otherwise. The word "reasonably" indicates that arbitration is not directly subject to the Code of Civil Procedure, and its individual provisions cannot be applied mechanically in arbitration. The word "reasonably" primarily requires that the tribunal has regard to the general principles*

underlying Czech arbitration, i.e. the rules of the Code of Civil Procedure must be applied within the general framework of the principles of arbitration. Section 157(2) of the Code of Civil Procedure requires, inter alia, that the court provide a brief and clear summary of the findings that the court has made regarding the individual circumstances, on the basis of what evidence, how the evidence has been assessed, and why the other evidence was not examined. The court is obliged to explain why the other evidence was not examined. The court is not bound to examine every piece of evidence proposed by the parties, but it is obliged to address their proposals for evidence. We may infer, following a reasonable application of Section 30 [of the ArbAct], *that an arbitral tribunal is also bound by the obligation to state in its decision why the tribunal did not examine the other evidence proposed by the parties (for an identical conclusion, cf. also Judgment of the Supreme Court of May 26, 2010 in Case No. 23 Cdo 3749/2008). If the arbitral tribunal did not order the supplementation of the expert appraisal proposed by the claimant and failed to address this proposal for evidence (failed to explain why the evidence was not examined), the parties (or rather the claimant) were denied the opportunity to state their case before the arbitrators, and there are grounds for the annulment of the arbitral award under Section 31(e)* [of the ArbAct]. For similar conclusions, see also Judgment of the SC of May 26, 2010 in Case No. 23 Cdo 3749/2008; the decision is available online on the SC website at http://www.nsoud.cz/Judikatura/judikatura_ns.nsf/WebSearch/039ACB5A0B0D5616C12 57A4E0069A698?openDocument&Highlight=0; in this decision, the court ruled as follows (cit.): *1. The relationship between the two statutes is regulated under Section 30* [of the ArbAct], *which stipulates that the arbitral proceedings shall be reasonably governed by the provisions of the Code of Civil Procedure, unless the law stipulates otherwise. The word "reasonably" indicates that arbitration is not directly subject to the Code of Civil Procedure, and its individual provisions cannot be applied mechanically in arbitration. The word "reasonably" primarily requires that the tribunal has regard to the general principles underlying Czech arbitration, i.e. the rules of the Code of Civil Procedure must be applied within the general framework of the principles of Czech arbitration. The Arbitration Act does not elaborate on the principle of equality of the parties by stipulating any specific rights and obligations of the parties, and its fulfillment requires, pursuant to Section 30 of the Arbitration Act, the reasonable application of the relevant provisions of the Code of Civil Procedure. 2. The parties are most typically denied the opportunity to state their case in arbitration if they have not been provided with a sufficient opportunity to plead their case, and if they have not had the chance to comment on all relevant circumstances. It will usually be necessary to provide the parties with the opportunity to comment on the allegations made by the other party, also in writing, i.e. the respondent must have the right to file their statement of defense, and the claimant must have the right to comment on the counterclaim or any counter-arguments presented in the statement of defense. As concerns the individual abovementioned statements, it is reasonable to demand that the parties be provided with the opportunity to make the statements, and that the so-provided opportunity be sufficient, considering all of the relevant circumstances of the case. Another necessary prerequisite is that the parties are provided not only with the opportunity to propose evidence proving their allegations, but also with the opportunity to hear or read the evidence (unless the evidence is obviously irrelevant for the given proceedings). If the*

[*From Facts of Case*]:

16.178. The description of the facts of the case is quite fragmentary, and thus the detailed factual circumstances of the case are unclear. We can consider it established that the parties[840] entered into a contract for work that included an arbitration clause referring to the AC (namely, in Article XXIV(2) of the contract). Afterwards, on April 16, 2010, the parties agreed on a new arbitration agreement. The annotated decision does not indicate why the parties decided to replace the arbitration agreement, nor what the scope of the new arbitration agreement was. We can only assume that the original arbitration clause was (for unspecified reasons) defective, and the claimant (or both parties) considers the clause non-existent. The parties' dispute resulted in arbitration before the AC, which was conducted as accelerated arbitration in terms of Section 27a of the AC Rules.[841] Consequently, an

---

proposal for evidence presented by any of the parties was dismissed, the arbitrators must consider the proposal for evidence and sufficiently justify why the proposed evidence was not examined.

[840] Both the claimant and the respondent are legal entities formed and existing under the laws of the Czech Republic in the form of limited liability companies.

[841] Cit.: *(1) Accelerated proceedings terminated by an arbitral award, or by a ruling (an order) of discontinuance in accordance with Section 40, Paragraph 2 of the Rules a) until one month from payment of the increased arbitration fee shall be held on the basis of a written agreement among the parties submitted to the Arbitration Court, upon application of any party that paid the increased arbitration fee; or b) until three months from payment of the increased arbitration fee shall be held upon application of any party that paid the increased arbitration fee. (2) In the accelerated proceedings the deadlines stipulated by these Rules are shortened to one-third in the case of accelerated proceedings in accordance with Paragraph 1, Letter a), and to one-half in the case of accelerated proceedings in accordance with Paragraph 1, Letter b), with the exception of the deadline for delivery of the Claim and the deadline stipulated by Section 26, Paragraph 6 of the Rules, which remains unaltered. (3) Other conditions of the accelerated proceedings, especially the increased arbitration fee, are provided for in Section 3 of the Principles Governing the Costs of Arbitral Proceedings in Domestic Disputes (Section 41 of the Rules).*

As concerns international arbitration, analogous rules were incorporated in the Rules governing International Disputes (available on the AC website at http://www.soud.cz/rady/rad-pro-mezinarodni-spory-2007), also in Article 27a (cit.): *(1) Accelerated proceedings terminated by an arbitral award, or by a ruling (an order) of discontinuance in accordance with Section 40, Paragraph 2 of the Rules a) until one month from payment of the increased arbitration fee shall be held on the basis of a written agreement among the parties submitted to the Arbitration Court, upon application of any party that paid the increased arbitration fee; or b) until four months from payment of the increased arbitration fee shall be held upon application of any party that paid the increased arbitration fee. (2) In the accelerated proceedings, the deadlines stipulated by these Rules are shortened to one-*

arbitral award was rendered on November 18, 2010 under the Case No. Rsp. 1216/10, which granted the respondent's request for arbitration (statement of claim). The claimant subsequently lodged a motion to annul the arbitral award, substantiated (inter alia) by the claimant's allegation that the claimant was denied the opportunity to duly state (plead) their case in terms of Section 31(e) of the ArbAct.[842] The claimant also invoked the invalidity of the arbitration agreement and the resultant lack of jurisdiction on the part of the AC to hear and resolve the case (or rather, the description in the annotated decision allows the conclusion that the claimant's plea targeted the fact that the arbitrators based their jurisdiction on the – allegedly defective/ extinguished – arbitration agreement incorporated in the contract for work, not the arbitration agreement of April 16, 2010, which according to the claimant, is not mentioned anywhere in the arbitral award). The claimant therefore asserted the grounds for the annulment of an arbitral award under Section 31(b) of the ArbAct.[843] The claimant probably also asserted the grounds for the annulment of an arbitral award under Section 31(g) of the ArbAct,[844] but these grounds are not specified anywhere in the annotated decision.

---

third in the case of accelerated proceedings in accordance with Paragraph 1, Letter a), and to one-half in the case of accelerated proceedings in accordance with Paragraph 1, Letter b), with the exception of the deadline for delivery of the Claim and the deadline stipulated by Section 26, Paragraph 6 of the Rules, which remains unaltered. (3) Other conditions of the accelerated proceedings, especially the increased arbitration fee, are provided for in Section 6 of the Principles Governing the Costs of Arbitral Proceedings.

The rules are now incorporated in Article 30 of the current Rules (cit.): *(1) Expedited proceedings where the arbitral award or a ruling on discontinuing the proceedings is rendered a) within two months of payment of the increased Arbitration Fee shall be conducted on the basis of a written agreement of the parties and based on the application of any party that has paid the increased Arbitration Fee, or b) within four months of payment of the increased Arbitration Fee shall be conducted upon the application of any party that has paid the increased Arbitration Fee, unless the above periods of time have been extended upon request or with the consent of the party that paid the increased Arbitration Fee. (2) The periods of time stipulated by these Rules shall be reduced in expedited proceedings a) pursuant to Paragraph 1 (a) above to one-third; and b) pursuant to Paragraph 1 (b) above to one-half, except for the deadlines pursuant to Section 22 (2) and Section 28 (6). (3) Other conditions of expedited proceedings, particularly the amount of the increased Arbitration Fee, are stipulated in Section 49.*

[842] The provision is quoted above in the opening part of this annotation.

[843] The provision is quoted above in the opening part of this annotation.

[844] The provision is quoted above in the opening part of this annotation.

[*Procedure of Case*]:

16.179. The Brno Regional Court, as the court of first instance, rendered its Judgment of May 21, 2012 in Case No. 49 Cm 2/2011-73, whereby the arbitral award of November 18, 2010 in Case No. Rsp. 1216/10 was annulled.[845]

16.180. The Olomouc High Court, as the appellate court, reversed the above judgment of the Brno Regional Court by dismissing the motion to annul the arbitral award.[846] The appellate court based its decision on the fact that the grounds for the annulment of an arbitral award pursuant to Section 31(e) of the ArbAct[847] apply to violations of fundamental procedural rights of the parties to arbitration. The appellate court therefore held that the objections must be procedural objections, i.e. the grounds for the annulment of an arbitral award must only concern the procedure of the arbitral tribunal adopted when hearing the dispute, not the correctness of its factual or legal conclusions. In this connection, the appellate court held that the claimant had provided extensive comments on the dispute debated in the arbitral proceedings, namely in the claimant's pleadings on the merits of the case dated July 19, 2010, July 30, 2010 and August 24, 2010. On August 30, 2010, the claimant's legal counsel personally attended the hearing called by the AC, and on September 21, 2010, the claimant presented their final written proposal in the case. The appellate court deduced from the above said that the claimant had performed a number of procedural acts during the proceedings, in which the claimant had commented on the merits of the case and presented the claimant's statements to the arbitrators. The appellate court therefore concluded that the claimant had been provided with a sufficient opportunity to state (plead) their case, and the grounds for the annulment of an arbitral award under Section 31(e) of the ArbAct[848] did not apply. As concerns the application of the grounds for the annulment of an arbitral award under Section 31(b) of the ArbAct,[849] the appellate court concluded that the conditions for applying those grounds were not fulfilled either. The claimant had pleaded the invalidity of the arbitration agreement in the arbitral proceedings, but had not done so in its pleading of July 19, 2010,

---

[845] The annotated decision does not mention any other circumstances of the proceedings at the court of first instance.

[846] Namely, by Judgment of February 12, 2013 in Case No. 7 Cmo 294/2012-99.

[847] The provision is quoted above in the opening part of this annotation.

[848] The provision is quoted above in the opening part of this annotation.

[849] The provision is quoted above in the opening part of this annotation.

which the appellate court assessed as its first act on the merits; the claimant only pleaded invalidity in the proceedings that followed. Hence, the condition under Section 33 of the ArbAct was not fulfilled.[850]

16.181. The claimant contested the judgment of the appellate court by its extraordinary appeal, in which the claimant argued that the appellate court's decision conflicted with the existing case law of the SC and of the ConCourt. The claimant specifically refers to **(i)** Judgment of the SC of June 11, 2008 in Case No. 32 Cdo 1201/2007,[851] **(ii)** Judgment of the SC of January 25, 2012 in Case No. 23 Cdo 4386/2011,[852] and **(iii)** Judgment of the ConCourt of March 8, 2011 in Case No. I. ÚS 3227/07.[853] The claimant invoked the breach of Section 6 of the ArbAct[854] (arbitrators allegedly provided information concerning the arbitration to a third party), Section 18 of the ArbAct[855] (the claimant

---

[850] The provision is quoted above in the opening part of this annotation.

[851] The decision is quoted above in this annotation.

[852] The decision is quoted above in this annotation.

[853] This decision is available online on the ConCourt website at http://nalus.usoud.cz/Search/ResultDetail.aspx?id=69584&pos=1&cnt=1&typ=result; in this decision, the court ruled as follows (cit.): *I. Hearing a case in arbitration does not entail the waiver of legal protection; it denotes the transfer of legal protection to another decision-making authority, which finds the law. II. The arbitrator cannot play the role of a merely passive element; they must conduct the proceedings in such manner that their decision is not a surprise to the parties. To that end, civil court proceedings prescribe that courts must give instructions to the parties; there is no reason to absolve the arbitrator of that obligation in arbitral proceedings, considering the fact that in such proceedings the arbitrator acts as the decision-making authority in place of the court. [The ArbAct] does not provide for the arbitrator's obligation to give instructions; it is therefore legitimate to reasonably apply the Code of Civil Procedure (Section 30 [of the ArbAct]). III. The extent of the supervisory function of the courts vis-à-vis arbitration must be carefully balanced – the rule stipulating that arbitration must also guarantee legal protection must not be eliminated, but on the other hand, the advantages of arbitration and its practical applicability must not be entirely wiped out. Consequently, proceedings for the annulment of an arbitral award by a court can never be structured along the lines of remedial civil court proceedings, let alone regular appellate proceedings. The supervisory function of the courts does not comprise the review of the material correctness of the arbitral award (conflict with substantive law), because the proceedings for the annulment of an arbitral award would thereby become quasi-appellate proceedings. The supervision may therefore only concentrate on examining the crucial procedural issues, e.g. whether the arbitration could actually have been conducted, whether any important procedural rights were denied to the parties, or whether the arbitral award itself is free of procedural flaws.*

[854] The provision is quoted above in the opening part of this annotation.

[855] The provision is quoted above in the opening part of this annotation.

was denied the opportunity to duly state their case), and Section 25(3) of the ArbAct[856] (the arbitrators provided insufficient reasons for the award or, as applicable, insufficient references to the applicable provisions of substantive law, which means, according to the claimant, that the arbitrators made their decision in a manner corresponding to decision-making following the principles of equity, despite the fact that the parties had not agreed on such possibility). The claimant therefore maintained that the annulment of the award was justified under the grounds for the annulment of an arbitral award incorporated in Section 31(b), (e) and (g)[857] of the ArbAct.[858] The claimant argued that the arbitrators had limited their reasoning in the arbitral award to a verbatim transcript of the parties' submissions, without providing any explanations as to the statements and the evidence on the basis of which they had reached their conclusion, and that they had entirely failed to assess and address the statements and evidence presented by the claimant. Also (as mentioned above), the arbitral award did not specify any provisions of the applicable substantive laws and regulations on the basis of which the arbitrators made their decision, even though the parties had not agreed that the dispute would be resolved following the principles of equity pursuant to Section 25(3) of the ArbAct.[859] The claimant also argued that the arbitrators had not properly addressed the extension of the request for arbitration (statement of claim). The claimant also argued that if the arbitrators stipulated a three-day period at the hearing held on August 30, 2010 (with respect to Section 27a of the AC Rules[860]), in which the parties were to present any further statements and additional pleadings that they wished to make, the arbitrators could not and should not have had regard to any subsequent statements and evidence (analogy with the concentration of civil proceedings). As concerns the plea of the lack of jurisdiction or, as applicable, the invalidity of the arbitration clause in terms of Section 31(b) of the ArbAct,[861] the claimant contested the opinion of the appellate court that it was possible to infer the continual replacement of the arbitration clause incorporated in the contract for

---

[856] The provision is quoted above in the opening part of this annotation.

[857] As mentioned above, it has not been explained what this ground for the annulment of the arbitral award was based on.

[858] The provision is quoted above in the opening part of this annotation.

[859] The provision is quoted above in the opening part of this annotation.

[860] The provision is quoted above in the opening part of this annotation.

[861] The provision is quoted above in the opening part of this annotation.

work with the arbitration agreement of April 16, 2010. In this connection, the claimant argued that the arbitrators had only referred in their arbitral award to the defective and extinguished arbitration clause from the contract for work and derived their jurisdiction from the said clause, without making a single reference to the arbitration agreement of April 16, 2010 in the entire text of the award.

16.182. The SC concluded that the extraordinary appeal was not admissible, because it failed to meet the necessary essential requirements as to the contents thereof, namely the specification of the allegedly erroneous legal assessment of the case. The SC pointed out in this connection that a reference to existing case law that allegedly conflicts with the contested decision does not give rise to grounds for which the appellate court's decision should be vacated in extraordinary appeal proceedings, or, as applicable, it is not possible to base the extraordinary appeal on this fact alone. Despite the above said, the SC at least briefly commented on the claimant's objections. The conclusions reached by the SC in this connection can be briefly summarized as follows: the claimant's references to case law were assessed as misguided and having no basis in the facts of the said case; moreover, the findings of fact made by the lower courts did not indicate that the objection would be justified by the facts of the case.

[*Arguments Presented by SC*]:

16.183. The SC based its decision exclusively on its preceding rulings. Referring to the Judgment of the SC of January 25, 2012 in Case No. 23 Cdo 4386/2011[862], as well as the Judgment of the SC of May 26, 2010 in Case No. 23 Cdo 3749/2008,[863] the SC confirmed that the arbitral tribunal was also bound by the obligation to state in its decision why the tribunal did not examine other evidence proposed by the parties. However, this was not the situation that occurred in the said proceedings – it was not established that the claimant alleged or proved that the claimant had presented any proposal for supplementing evidence that would have been ignored by the AC, or that the AC would have failed to provide reasons for not examining the evidence. The SC therefore concluded that the annulment of the arbitral award under the grounds for the annulment of an arbitral award incorporated in Section 31(e) of the ArbAct[864] was not justified. In this regard, the SC assessed the objections raised by the claimant in the sense that the arbitrators did not identify with the evidence

---

[862] The decision is quoted above in this annotation.

[863] The decision is quoted above in this annotation.

[864] The provision is quoted above in the opening part of this annotation.

proposed by the claimant. Invoking the Judgment of the SC of June 11, 2008 in Case No. 32 Cdo 1201/2007,[865] the SC held that an assessment of whether or not a party was provided with a due opportunity to state (plead) their case in the proceedings and whether or not the equality of the parties was disturbed must always be made with due regard for all circumstances of the case. In this connection, the SC referred to the abovementioned list of the claimant's pleadings presented to the arbitrators, and pointed out the hearing attended by the claimant, and subsequently concluded that there were no indications supporting the conclusion that the claimant was deprived in arbitration of the opportunity to respond to any change (if any) of a motion. As concerns the objection that the arbitrators based their decision on the respondent's statements and evidence presented after the stipulated deadline, the SC held that there were no materials in the dossier that would support this conclusion. Last, but not least, the SC addressed the plea of the invalidity of the arbitration clause (which was allegedly cancelled). However, the SC concluded, in line with the appellate court, that the grounds for the annulment of an arbitral award under Section 31(b) of the ArbAct[866] could not be applied, because the claimant did not plead the invalidity of the arbitration agreement in its pleading of June 19, 2010 (which was the claimant's first act on the merits), but only during the arbitral proceedings. Hence, the condition under Section 33 of the ArbAct was not fulfilled.[867]

16.184. The SC held the extraordinary appeal to be inadmissible, and as such, the extraordinary appeal was dismissed in compliance with the applicable procedural laws.

[*Further Conclusions and Comments Concerning Annotated Resolution of SC*]:

16.185. The decision cannot be perceived as surprising or introducing any new interpretation of the said rules, i.e. a decision that would shift the existing doctrinal interpretation. On the contrary, it was based strictly on the consistent case law. Moreover, the particular rules were applied to specific facts of the case and the assessment did not focus on legal principles, as such, but on the determination of which principles and to what extent they applied to the given facts of the case. The SC correctly pointed out that the grounds for the annulment of an arbitral award

---

[865] The decision is quoted above in this annotation.

[866] The provision is quoted above in the opening part of this annotation.

[867] The provision is quoted above in the opening part of this annotation.

incorporated in Section 31(e) of the ArbAct[868] have clearly defined limits and cannot be used in a situation where a party disagrees with the factual or legal conclusions reached by the arbitrators. Hence, the grounds do not allow a review of whether, for instance, the arbitrators should or should not have examined a particular piece of evidence submitted by a party, provided that the decision on the (non)examination of the evidence is properly substantiated. Parties to arbitration are not automatically entitled to have the arbitrators deal with each and every piece of evidence that they propose, if the arbitrators opine that the evidence does not relate to the merits of the case and is not necessary for the factual and legal assessment of the case. Similarly, the parties cannot expect to have an *unlimited* opportunity to present their statements; the party's entitlement to state (plead) their case and make statements in the case is always limited by the arbitrators' decision on the procedure followed in the case (provided that the principle of equality of the parties is observed in terms of Section 18 of the ArbAct[869]).

16.186. The SC also concluded, in line with Section 33 of the ArbAct[870] and its unequivocal interpretation, that regard could not be had to the objection of the lack of the arbitrators' jurisdiction if it was not raised in time. We may point out, beyond the extent to which the issue was addressed by the SC, that it would be (in any case) necessary to address the issue of the existence of the arbitration agreement of April 16, 2010. Its existence is an objective fact, and consequently, even if the arbitrators did not explicitly refer to the agreement, we cannot conclude that it would be impossible to prove the arbitrators' jurisdiction on the basis thereof.

| | |

---

[868] The provision is quoted above in the opening part of this annotation.
[869] The provision is quoted above in the opening part of this annotation.
[870] The provision is quoted above in the opening part of this annotation.

17. Judgment of Supreme Court of Czech Republic of December 17, 2013 in Case No. 23 Cdo 3895/2011:[871] (i) Executing Arbitration Clause, (ii) Arbitration Clause in Form of Public Offer (Proposal), (iii) Possibility to Submit Domain Name Disputes Concerning ".cz" Domain to Arbitration

Abbreviations Used:

AC Rules	AC Rules[872]
AC	Arbitration Court at the Economic Chamber of the Czech Republic and Agricultural Chamber of the Czech Republic[873]
ArbAct	Act of the Czech Republic No. 216/1994 Coll., on Arbitration and the Enforcement of Arbitral Awards, as amended[874]
CC	Act of the Czech Republic No. 89/2012 Coll., the Civil Code

---

[871] This decision is available online on the website of the SC at http://www.nsoud.cz/ Judikatura/judikatura_ns.nsf/WebSearch/3B223B1337699200C1257C7E003D58A4?open Document&Highlight=0 [last accessed on November 14, 2014].

[872] The applicable regulation is the Rules of the AC governing Domestic Disputes in effect until June 30, 2012 (available on the AC website at http://www.soud.cz/rady/rad-pro-vnitrostatni-spory-2007, i.e. the Rules as applicable on February 1, 2007). This annotation has also had regard to the Rules for .cz Domain Name Dispute Resolution (".cz Rules") – also available online on the AC website at http://www.soud.cz/rady/rad-pro-reseni-sporu-o-domeny-cz-2010)

[873] For more information regarding this permanent arbitral institution, see www.soud.cz.

[874] The decision of the SC in this case is based on the ArbAct in effect until December 31, 2007 (although it is not stated explicitly), but no subsequent changes have any bearing on the conclusions of the SC and their applicability. The SC's conclusions in the said case were reached irrespective of whether or not the case involved a B2C dispute, and the SC focused on the general possibility of executing an arbitration agreement in the form of a proposal of arbitration. Naturally, the amendments implemented by Act No. 19/2012 Coll. and the requirements imposed on the essential elements of an arbitration agreement automatically exclude any public proposal of arbitration in those cases. From the practical perspective, however, such a situation should not occur in a dispute between a domain name holder and a third party (a dispute that concerns a breach of rights excludes, by definition, the application of law applicable to consumer contracts); we could theoretically envisage disputes between natural persons who register domain names and the CZ.NIC Association.

Charter	Resolution of the Presidium of the Czech National Council No. 2/1993 Coll., on the promulgation of the Charter of Fundamental Rights and Freedoms as part of the constitutional order of the Czech Republic, as amended
CivC	Act of the Czech Republic No. 40/1964 Coll., the Civil Code, as amended
ComC	Act of the Czech Republic No. 513/1991 Coll., the Commercial Code, as amended
ConCourt	Constitutional Court of the Czech Republic
CZ.NIC Rules	Rules of Domain Name Registration under the ".cz" ccTLD, issued by the CZ.NIC Association
SC	Supreme Court of the Czech Republic

Key Words:

".cz" domain | domain name | domain name disputes | executing arbitration agreement | executing arbitration clause | jurisdiction | national domain | public proposal of arbitration | Uniform Domain Name Dispute Resolution | will directed at specific recipient |

Applicable Laws and Regulations:
ArbAct: Section 2,[875] Section 3,[876] Section 31(b)[877]

---

[875] ArbAct, Section 2 (cit.): *(1) The parties are free to agree that their property disputes, except disputes arising from the enforcement of decisions and except disputes generated by bankruptcy or composition proceedings, the hearing and resolution of which would otherwise fall within the jurisdiction of the courts, shall be decided by one or more arbitrators or by a permanent arbitral institution (arbitration agreement). (2) The arbitration agreement will be valid if the law allows the parties to resolve the subject matter of their dispute by settlement [Section 99 of the CCP]. (3) The arbitration agreement may apply to (a) an individual dispute which has already arisen (post-dispute arbitration agreement), or (b) all disputes which would arise in the future under a defined legal relationship or under a defined category of legal relationships (arbitration clause). (4) Unless the arbitration agreement stipulates otherwise, it governs both the rights directly arising from the legal relationships and the issue of legal validity of these legal relationships, as well as any rights associated with the aforementioned rights. (5) The arbitration agreement is also binding on the legal successors to the parties, unless explicitly excluded by the parties in their agreement.* Note: This version of the provision applied to the respective proceedings; the currently applicable version reads as follows (cit.): *(1) The parties are free to agree that their property disputes, except disputes arising from the enforcement of decisions and except incidental disputes, which would otherwise fall within the jurisdiction of the courts or which are subject to arbitration under special laws, shall be decided by one or more arbitrators or by a permanent arbitral institution (arbitration agreement). (2) The arbitration agreement will be valid if the law allows the parties to resolve the subject matter of their dispute by*

settlement [Section 99 of the CCP]. *(3) The arbitration agreement may apply to (a) an individual dispute which has already arisen (post-dispute arbitration agreement), or (b) all disputes which would arise in the future under a defined legal relationship or under a defined category of legal relationships (arbitration clause). (4) Unless the arbitration agreement stipulates otherwise, it governs both the rights directly arising from the legal relationships and the issue of legal validity of these legal relationships, as well as any rights associated with the aforementioned rights. (5) The arbitration agreement is also binding on the legal successors to the parties, unless explicitly excluded by the parties in their agreement.* Note: The amendments have no bearing on the present case, because they consist exclusively of changes to the formulations made in connection with the adoption of Act No. 182/2006 Coll., on Insolvency and Methods of Resolving Insolvency (Insolvency Act) [InsAct].

[876] ArbAct, Section 3 (cit.): *(1) The arbitration agreement must be executed in writing; otherwise it is invalid. The arbitration agreement is also considered executed in writing if it is negotiated by telegraph, fax or any electronic means which provide a record of the terms of the agreement and the identification of the individuals or entities who concluded the arbitration agreement. (2) However, if the arbitration clause is incorporated in the terms and conditions governing the main contract to which the arbitration clause applies, the arbitration clause is also considered validly negotiated if a written offer of the main contract with the arbitration clause was accepted by the other party in any manner clearly indicating the latter party's consent with the terms of the arbitration agreement.* Note: This version of the provision applied to the respective proceedings; the currently applicable version reads as follows (cit.): *(1) The arbitration agreement must be executed in writing; otherwise it is invalid. The arbitration agreement is also considered executed in writing if it is negotiated by telegraph, fax or any electronic means which provide a record of the terms of the agreement and the identification of the individuals or entities who concluded the arbitration agreement. (2) However, if the arbitration clause is incorporated in the terms and conditions governing the main contract to which the arbitration clause applies, the arbitration clause is also considered validly negotiated if a written offer of the main contract with the arbitration clause was accepted by the other party in any manner clearly indicating the latter party's consent with the terms of the arbitration agreement. (3) An arbitration agreement for the resolution of disputes arising from consumer contracts must be negotiated separately, not integrated in the terms and conditions governing the main contract; otherwise the arbitration agreement is invalid. (4) The professional shall provide the consumer with a proper explanation reasonably preceding the conclusion of the arbitration clause so that the consumer can assess the potential consequences of the conclusion of the arbitration clause for the consumer. Proper explanation shall be interpreted as meaning the explication of all consequences of the arbitration clause. (5) The arbitration clause concluded pursuant to subsection (3) must also contain truthful, accurate and complete information on: (a) the arbitrator or the fact that the arbitral award will be delivered by a permanent arbitral institution, (b) the manner in which the arbitral proceedings are to be commenced and conducted, (c) the fee paid to the arbitrator and the anticipated types of costs the consumer may incur in the arbitral proceedings, and the rules for successfully claiming compensation for such costs, (d) the seat of arbitration, (e) the method of service of the arbitral award on the consumer, and (f) the fact that a final and*

ComC: Section 262(1) and (2),[878] Section 269,[879] Section 276,[880] Section 277,[881] Section 278,[882] Section 279[883]

conclusive arbitral award is enforceable. *(6) If the arbitration clause vests the jurisdiction to resolve the dispute in a permanent arbitral institution, the requirement under subsection (5) is also fulfilled by a reference to the statutes and rules of permanent arbitral institutions issued under Section 13.* Note: The amendments implemented by Act No. 19/2012 Coll. only have indirect influence on the case at hand, because the examination of evidence focused on the general possibility to execute an arbitration clause in the form of a public offer (proposal), and consequently, the SC's conclusions apply whether or not the dispute is a B2C dispute.

[877] ArbAct, Section 31(b) (cit.): *At the request of any party the court annuls the arbitral award if the arbitration agreement is invalid for other reasons or the agreement was cancelled or it does not apply to the agreed case.* Note: This version of the law applied to the respective proceedings, but it has not been subject to any modifications in the meantime and therefore continues to apply.

[878] ComC, Section 262(1) and (2) (cit.): *(1) The parties are free to agree that their obligation (relationship), which does not fall within the category of relationships specified in Section 261, shall be governed by this Act. The agreement is invalid if its objective is to worsen the legal position of the contracting party who is not a professional. (2) The agreement under Subsection (1) must be executed in writing.* Note: The dualism and division of obligations (relationships) into civil and commercial ended on January 1, 2014 as a result of recodification; the provision has therefore no equivalent under the new law.

[879] ComC, Section 269 (cit.): *(1) The provisions regulating the individual types of contracts under Chapter II of this Part of the Act shall only apply to contracts the contents of which as agreed by the parties include the essentialia of a contract stipulated in the basic provision for each of these contracts. (2) The parties may also enter into a contract that is not regulated as a type of contract. But if the parties fail to sufficiently define the subject matter of their obligations, the contract is not executed. (3) Agreement on certain parts of the contract may be replaced with an agreement of the parties on the method allowing the subsequent determination of the contents of the obligation, provided that this method does not depend on the will of one party only. If the missing part of the contract is to be determined by a court or by a designated person, the agreement must be executed in writing, and Section 291 applies by analogy.* Note: This is the version of the law applicable to the respective proceedings. January 1, 2014 is the effective date of the CC, which regulates the said issues in Sections 1726 and 1746 (both provisions are quoted below in the opening part of this annotation).

[880] ComC, Section 276 (cit.): *(1) An expression of will whereby the offeror addresses a non-specific group of persons for the purpose of executing a contract is a public offer to enter into the contract ("public offer"), provided that the contents comply with Section 269. (2) An incentive to enter into a contract that lacks the essentialia specified in Subsection (1) shall be deemed merely a call to submit contract offers.* Note: This is the version of the law applicable to the respective proceedings. January 1, 2014 is the effective date of the CC, which regulates the said issue in Section 1780 (the provision is quoted below in the opening part of this annotation).

[881] ComC, Section 277 (cit.): *A public offer can be revoked if the offeror announces the revocation before the public offer is accepted and in the manner in which the public offer*

CivC: Section 39,[884] Section 50[885]
CC: Section 547,[886] Section 588,[887] Section 1726,[888] Section 1746,[889] Section 1767,[890] Section 1768,[891] Section 1780,[892] Section 1781,[893] Section 1782,[894] Section 1783[895]

was publicly announced. Note: This is the version of the law applicable to the respective proceedings. January 1, 2014 is the effective date of the CC, which regulates the said issue in Section 1781 (the provision is quoted below in the opening part of this annotation).

[882] ComC, Section 278 (cit.): *The contract based on the public offer is entered into with the person who is the first to notify the offeror that they accept the offer and to whom the offeror confirms the execution of the contract; the notification shall comply with the contents of the public offer and shall be made by the deadline stipulated therein, or in the absence of any such deadline, within a reasonable period of time. If the public offer is accepted simultaneously by two or more persons, the offeror may choose the accepter to whom the offeror will confirm the execution of the contract.* Note: This is the version of the law applicable to the respective proceedings. January 1, 2014 is the effective date of the CC, which regulates the said issue in Section 1782 (the provision is quoted below in the opening part of this annotation).

[883] ComC, Section 279 (cit.): *(1) The offeror is obliged to confirm the execution of the contract to the accepter without undue delay after the acceptance of the offer was received by the offeror under Section 278. (2) If the offeror confirms the execution of the contract to the accepter later than as stipulated under Subsection (1), the contract is not executed, if the accepter declines the execution of the contract and sends a notification thereof to the offeror without undue delay after the accepter received the offeror's belated confirmation of the execution of the contract.* Note: This is the version of the law applicable to the respective proceedings. January 1, 2014 is the effective date of the CC, which regulates the said issue in Section 1783 (the provision is quoted below in the opening part of this annotation).

[884] CivC, Section 39 (cit.): *A juridical act is invalid if the content or the purpose thereof violates or evades the law or is contra bonos mores.* Note: This is the version of the law applicable to the respective proceedings. January 1, 2014 is the effective date of the CC, which regulates the said issues in Sections 547 and 588 (both provisions are quoted below in the opening part of this annotation).

[885] CivC, Section 50 (cit.): *(1) The parties may also enter into a contract for the benefit of a third party. (2) Unless this Act stipulates or the parties agree otherwise, the third party accrues the rights under the contract as soon as the party has expressed their consent with the contract. The debtor has the same objections against the third party as against the party with whom the debtor executed the contract. If the third party waives their right, the debt is extinguished, unless the parties agreed that the performance shall in such case be provided to the party with whom the debtor executed the contract. (3) Until the third party gives their consent, the contract only applies between the parties who executed the contract; the right to receive the performance accrues to the party who reserves the performance for the benefit of the third party, unless the parties agreed otherwise. The same applies if the third party refused to give their consent.* Note: This is the version of the law applicable to the respective proceedings. January 1, 2014 is the effective date of the CC, which regulates the said issues in Sections 1767 and 1768 (both provisions are quoted below in the opening part of this annotation).

[886] CC, Section 547 (cit.): *The contents and purpose of juridical actions must comply with good morals and the law (statute).*

[887] CC, Section 588 (cit.): *The court shall, with or without a motion, have regard to the invalidity of a juridical action that is obviously contra bonos mores, or that conflicts with the law (statute) and obviously violates public policy. This also applies if the juridical action creates an obligation to provide performance that is impossible ab initio.*

[888] CC, Section 1726 (cit.): *If the parties consider the contract executed, although they in fact failed to agree on a term in the contract on which they should have agreed, the expression of their will is deemed an executed contract, provided that it can be reasonably assumed, especially with respect to their subsequent behavior, that the parties would have executed the contract with or without an agreement on the said term. However, if any of the parties indicated when entering into the contract that an agreement on a particular term is a prerequisite for executing the contract, the contract is deemed not to have been executed; in such case, the agreement on the other terms does not bind the parties, even if they were recorded in the minutes.*

[889] CC, Section 1746 (cit.): *(1) The statutory provisions regulating the individual types of contracts shall be applied to contracts the contents of which include the essentialia of a contract stipulated in the basic provision for each of the contracts. (2) The parties may also enter into a contract that is not separately regulated as a type of contract.*

[890] CC, Section 1767 (cit.): *(1) If the agreement orders the debtor to provide performance to a third party, the creditor may request that the debtor provide the performance to the third party. (2) The contents, nature and object of the contract will determine whether and when the third party also accrued a direct right to request performance. The third party is deemed to have accrued the right if the performance is primarily supposed to benefit the third party. (3) The debtor may raise objections under the contract also vis-à-vis the third party.*

[891] CC, Section 1768 (cit.): *If the third party refuses the right accrued under the contract, the third party is deemed never to have accrued the right to performance. The creditor may request the performance for themselves, unless it is contrary to the contents and object of the contract.*

[892] CC, Section 1780 (cit.): *(1) A public offer is the offeror's expression of will whereby the offeror addresses unspecified offerees with their offer to enter into a contract. (2) An incentive to enter into a contract that does not indicate any intention to enter into a particular contract or that lacks the essentialia specified in Section 1732(1) shall be deemed a call to submit offers.*

[893] CC, Section 1781 (cit.): *A public offer can be revoked if the offeror had publicly announced the revocation before the public offer was accepted, in the manner in which the public offer was publicly announced.*

[894] CC, Section 1782 (cit.): *(1) The contract is executed on the basis of the public offer with the person who is the first to notify the offeror, in time and in compliance with the public offer, that they accept the public offer. If the public offer is accepted by two or more persons simultaneously, the contract is executed with the person chosen by the offeror. (2) Unless the public offer stipulates a time period for acceptance, the time period shall be adequate to the nature of the public offer.*

[895] CC, Section 1783 (cit.): *(1) The offeror shall notify the accepter of the execution of the contract without undue delay after acceptance of the public offer. The others shall be informed by the offeror that they did not succeed. (2) If the offeror confirms the execution of the contract to the accepter later than as stipulated under Subsection (1), the contract is not executed, if the accepter declines the execution of the contract without undue delay after accepter received the offeror's confirmation of the execution of the contract.*

The Supreme Court of the Czech Republic reached the following principal conclusions:

(1) The object of an arbitration agreement, as a bilateral juridical act, is to transfer the jurisdiction to resolve an existing dispute between particular entities to arbitrators in arbitration. Both parties to the dispute, or future dispute, as applicable, must express their consent with arbitration in the arbitration agreement. A public declaration made by a domain name holder in the agreement entered into with the registrar, which is addressed to a non-specific group of third parties and in which the holder declares that they will submit any potential disputes to arbitration, is not an expression of will addressed to a specific person to submit existing disputes to arbitration.

(2) If the domain name holder undertook in the agreement with the registrar that the holder would "irrevocably" and publicly submit to the jurisdiction of the AC in arbitration conducted at that arbitral tribunal if a third party challenges the holder's domain name entered in the electronic database of domain names in the national ".cz" domain, provided that the third party expresses vis-à-vis the holder and in writing their will to submit to the jurisdiction of that arbitral tribunal in the given case and file a request for arbitration with the arbitral tribunal, and the third party has indeed filed their request for arbitration with the arbitral tribunal, the said procedure did not establish any arbitration agreement between the domain name holder and the third party.

(3) A public proposal for arbitration can also not be interpreted as an agreement for the benefit of a third party pursuant to Section 50 of the CivC. The third party does not have to be individually identified in the agreement, but they must be identifiable on the basis of specified objective circumstances. The alleged public proposal to enter into an agreement represents a unilateral juridical act addressed to no person in particular, which does not render a third party objectively identifiable. The fact that any person may feel that their rights have been prejudiced by the recipient of the public proposal, and consequently, and may this lodge a motion with the AC, does not constitute such objective identifiability of the third party. Moreover, the above-described object of arbitration agreements is the contracting parties' submission to the jurisdiction of the AC, i.e. a procedural issue, not a substantive-law commitment of the debtor to the creditor to provide performance benefiting a third party.

(4) The court's conclusions have no impact on the methods of resolving disputes concerning any other domains. Systems for the nongovernmental resolution of domain name disputes concerning

generic domain names have been implemented globally and are known under the title *Uniform Domain Name Dispute Resolution.*

[From Facts of Case]:

16.187. The claimant[896] registered their domain name [x] with a common-interest association of legal entities, CZ.NIC, as the ".cz" domain name administrator, subject to the Rules and Procedures of Domain Name Registration issued by the Association. In consequence thereof, the claimant agreed with the Rules of Alternative Resolution of Disputes that could arise between the claimant, as the domain name holder, and a third party; the CZ.NIC Rules stipulate that a third party who believes that the registration of a particular domain name prejudiced the party's rights may decide to submit the dispute either to a court, or to the AC. The domain name holder is, in the latter case, obliged to submit to arbitration based on the abovementioned public proposal of arbitration,[897] which occurred when the request for arbitration

---

[896] Natural person; although it is not explicitly mentioned in the annotated decision, we can infer that the person is a citizen of the Czech Republic and has their address/place of residence in the territory of the Czech Republic. The respondent is a legal entity formed and existing under the laws of the Czech Republic in the form of a common-interest association of legal entities.

[897] Article 18. 1. of the Rules reads as follows (cit.): *The holder irrevocably and publicly submits to the jurisdiction of the Arbitration Court at the Economic Chamber of the Czech Republic and Agricultural Chamber of the Czech Republic, hereinafter referred to as "Arbitration Court", in arbitration conducted by this Arbitration Court pursuant to the Rules published in the Business Journal, in a property dispute that the parties are free to settle, in which a third party contests the domain name of the Holder registered in the electronic database of domain names in the national ".cz" domain administered by the CZ.NIC Association, if the third party expresses their will vis-à-vis the Holder, in writing, to submit to the jurisdiction of this Arbitration Court in the given case by filing a request for arbitration (statement of claim) with the Arbitration Court.* The above public proposal of arbitration had applied until the CZ.NIC Association drew up and approved CZ.NIC Alternative Dispute Resolution Rules, which entered into force on October 1, 2007. The new public offer of arbitration read as follows (cit.): *The Holder irrevocably and publicly submits to the jurisdiction of the Arbitration Court at the Economic Chamber of the Czech Republic and Agricultural Chamber of the Czech Republic (hereinafter referred to as "Arbitration Court"), in arbitration conducted by this Arbitration Court pursuant to the special amendment to the Rules of the Arbitration Court for On-Line Arbitration published in the Business Journal (hereinafter "On-Line Rules"), in a property dispute that the parties are free to settle, in which a third party contests any Domain Name of the Holder registered in the electronic database of domain names in the national ccTLD .cz domain administered by the CZ.NIC Association, if the third party expresses their will vis-à-vis the Holder, in writing, to submit to the jurisdiction of this Arbitration Court in the given case, especially by*

filing a written request for arbitration (statement of claim) with the Arbitration Court in compliance with the On-Line Rules. The dispute will be resolved by a single arbitrator appointed by the Chairman of the Arbitration Court. The e-mail address of the Holder listed in the registration record of any of the Domain Names that are the subject of the dispute shall serve during the on-line proceedings as the Holder's mailing address. It is necessary to point out, in this connection, that the Rules of Domain Names Registration under the ".cz" ccTLD subsequently omitted the reference to the original public proposal of arbitration and only refer to the CZ.NIC Rules of Alternative Dispute Resolution, as follows (cit.): *The Holder is obliged to make every effort that may reasonably be required from them to achieve an amicable settlement of disputes concerning Domain Names and/or their registration that might arise between the Holder and other persons. If the parties to the dispute do not settle the dispute in an amicable way, they are free to settle their dispute within the scope of valid legal regulations, i.e. through arbitration or litigation. At the request of all parties to the dispute, the CZ.NIC Association will act as mediator of the amicable settlement of their dispute. The Holder hereby makes a public proposal of arbitration in compliance with the Rules of Alternative Dispute Resolution with respect to all domain names of the Holder registered in the electronic database of domain names in ccTLD .cz administered by the CZ.NIC Association".* The currently applicable rules took effect on January 1, 2014; the relevant Articles 23 and 24 read as follows (cit.): *23.1. If the Holder and the CZ.NIC Association are not able to resolve a dispute concerning the Domain Name registered by the Holder and if the Holder files a petition against the CZ.NIC Association at the Arbitration Court attached to the Economic Chamber of the Czech Republic and Agricultural Chamber of the Czech Republic, the CZ.NIC Association will respect the jurisdiction of the arbitration court as long as the arbitration proceedings are conducted by three arbiters in Prague in the Czech language according to the rules of the aforementioned court, and without exclusion of hearings, and as long as the arbitration ruling is final and binding for both parties. 23.2. In other cases, the general courts of the Czech Republic have jurisdiction for resolving disputes between the Holder and the CZ.NIC Association. 24.1. The Holder is obliged to make every effort that may reasonably be required from them to achieve an amicable settlement of disputes concerning Domain Names and/or their registration that might arise between the Holder and other persons. If the litigants do not settle the dispute in an amicable way, they are free to settle their dispute within the scope of valid legal regulations, i.e. through arbitration or municipal courts. 24.2. The Holder hereby makes a public arbitration bid in accordance with the Rules of Alternative Dispute Resolution for all domain names of the Holder listed in the electronic database of the domain names in the .cz ccTLD administered by the CZ.NIC Association.* CZ.NIC Rules of Alternative Dispute Resolution contain the following public proposal of arbitration in Article 2.1 (cit.): *The Holder is irrevocably and publicly subject to the authority of the Arbitration Court attached to the Economic Chamber of the Czech Republic and the Agriculture Chamber of the Czech Republic (hereinafter the "Arbitration Court") in arbitration proceedings before this Arbitration Court pursuant to the Code for the Resolution of Disputes Over .CZ Domains published in the Commercial Bulletin (hereinafter the ".CZ Code"), in property disputes that can be resolved in which a third party challenges any Domain Name of the Holder entered in the electronic database of*

(statement of claim) was delivered to the claimant on June 26, 2007. The claimant responded to the request for arbitration (statement of claim) on July 9, 2007; the AC was served with the pleading on July 11, 2007. The claimant primarily pleaded a lack of jurisdiction on the part of the AC.[898] On November 27, 2007 an arbitral award was rendered under Case No. Rsp 534/07; the arbitral award was subsequently challenged by the claimant (invoking the lack of jurisdiction of the AC), who demanded the annulment of the arbitral award pursuant to the procedure envisaged in the ArbAct.

[*Procedure of Case*]:

16.188. The Prague Municipal Court, as the court of first instance, rendered its Judgment of September 9, 2010 in Case No. 6 Cm 82/2010-68, whereby the motion was granted and the arbitral award rendered by the AC on November 27, 2007 in Case No. Rsp. 534/07 was annulled with reference to Section 31(b) of the ArbAct.[899] The court agreed with the claimant. The court applied Section 276 et seq. of the ComC[900] and concluded that if the domain name holder expressed their will vis-à-vis an unidentified number of persons, namely their will to enter into an arbitration agreement with them for the purpose of resolving disputes that arise from domain name registration, the third party affected by the registration of the domain name that was performed by the holder of the name would have to notify the holder, as offeror, that the third party accepts the public proposal for executing the agreement. Similarly, the offeror would have to confirm acceptance of the proposal. The court of first instance concluded that the execution of an arbitration agreement in the form of a public proposal of arbitration

---

ccTLD .cz domain names maintained by the CZ.NIC Association, or its registration, if the third party expresses its willingness in writing to the Holder to submit to the authority of this Arbitration Court in the given matter by submitting the dispute in writing to the Arbitration Court in accordance with the .CZ Code. The dispute will be decided by a single arbiter named by the President of the Arbitration Court or by three arbiters on the basis of the rules set forth in the .CZ Code. The e-mail address of the Holder listed in the registration record of any of the Domain Names that are the subject of the dispute shall serve during the proceedings for delivering information to the Holder, and the Holder confirms that it is able to communicate using this address in connection with the arbitration proceedings conducted on the basis of these Rules of Alternative Dispute Resolution.

[898] The annotated decision refers to an alleged Resolution of the AC, which indicates that the arbitrators had addressed the issue, but, invoking Article 18.1 of the Rules, concluded that they had jurisdiction to hear the dispute. However, neither the alleged date of the Resolution nor the dossier number correspond to the respective arbitration.

[899] The provision is quoted above in the opening part of this annotation.

[900] The provisions are quoted above in the opening part of this annotation.

could only be accepted if the above conditions were fulfilled. However, the court also held that the third party's notification could not be made in the form of a request for arbitration lodged with the arbitral tribunal, because consensus would be missing in such case (the mutual consensus of will of the offeror and of the accepting offeree).

16.189. The Prague High Court, as the appellate court, reversed the abovementioned Judgment of the Municipal Court in Prague by dismissing the motion to annul the arbitral award.[901] The appellate court invoked Sections 278[902] and 279 of the ComC,[903] and inferred that the provisions must be interpreted as meaning that the offeror's confirmation is not necessary in the given case, because the proposal is addressed to every person who believes that their rights are prejudiced by the domain name registration. The appellate court therefore held that all requirements of Section 276 of the ComC[904] were fulfilled; in the court's opinion, the public proposal can also be made as part of the domain name registration. The appellate court concluded that the method of negotiating the arbitration clause complied in such case with Section 3(2) of the ArbAct.[905] The appellate court simultaneously concluded that the time period for accepting the proposal was observed by the third party filing the request for arbitration (statement of claim), because reasonability must be assessed according to when and under what circumstances the request for arbitration (statement of claim) was lodged; the request for arbitration (statement of claim) itself conforms to the *notification of accepting the proposal* if the request for arbitration is lodged by the *recipient of the proposal (offeree)*, and if it is subsequently delivered to the *offeror*, i.e. the person who makes the public offer (proposal). Alternatively, the appellate court ruled that the public proposal of arbitration could also be considered a contract for the benefit of a third party in terms of Section 50 of the CivC.[906] This idea is, unfortunately, not elaborated on in any greater detail. Finally, the appellate court did not agree with the objection that the acceptance of the Rules (which also entailed the acceptance of the public proposal of arbitration) constituted an enforced, not a voluntary act; the court ruled that each entity was free to decide (also on the basis of the associated rules) whether and under which domain name they would present themselves on internet. The appellate court therefore

---

[901] Namely, by Judgment of April 27, 2010 in Case No. 3 Cmo 367/2010-101.

[902] The provision is quoted above in the opening part of this annotation.

[903] The provision is quoted above in the opening part of this annotation.

[904] The provision is quoted above in the opening part of this annotation.

[905] The provision is quoted above in the opening part of this annotation.

[906] The provision is quoted above in the opening part of this annotation.

concluded that a proper arbitration agreement had been executed pursuant to Sections 2[907] and 3[908] of the ArbAct, and saw no reason to apply Section 31(b) of the ArbAct.[909]

16.190. The judgment of the appellate court was challenged by the claimant by means of an extraordinary appeal, in which the claimant argued that a public proposal of arbitration could not be considered identical to a public offer under Section 276 et seq. of the ComC.[910] The claimant held that the public offer under Section 277 of the ComC[911] was principally revocable, and the absence of revocability renders the offer invalid under Section 39 of the CivC.[912] Similarly, a public offer is characterized by its temporal limitation; unless explicitly stipulated otherwise, a public offer is valid for a reasonable period of time. Consequently, the claimant argued that the acceptance of the offer by filing a request for arbitration (statement of claim) with the AC did not constitute the acceptance of the offer within a reasonable period of time (the claimant also pointed out that the appellate court's conclusion to that extent was unreviewable, because it was not substantiated by any further details). The claimant maintained that the purpose of Section 276 et seq. of the ComC[913] was to enable unilateral juridical acts addressed to no specific person in particular, which are aimed at the execution of contracts that comply with Section 269 of the ComC,[914] not the execution of arbitration agreements, i.e. agreements establishing the jurisdiction of the AC, which is a procedural, not a substantive-law issue. The claimant also did not agree with the interpretation of Section 278 of the ComC[915] as performed by the appellate court; the claimant argued that the rule did not stipulate that the contract would be executed with all persons who accepted the offer (proposal) in time. Conversely, Section 278 of the ComC[916] unambiguously indicates that valid execution of the contract/agreement requires confirmation by the offeror, which did not occur in the present case, and the arbitration agreement could not have been validly executed. The claimant also insisted that one of the *essentialia*

[907] The provision is quoted above in the opening part of this annotation.
[908] The provision is quoted above in the opening part of this annotation.
[909] The provision is quoted above in the opening part of this annotation.
[910] The provisions are quoted above in the opening part of this annotation.
[911] The provision is quoted above in the opening part of this annotation.
[912] The provision is quoted above in the opening part of this annotation.
[913] The provisions are quoted above in the opening part of this annotation.
[914] The provision is quoted above in the opening part of this annotation.
[915] The provision is quoted above in the opening part of this annotation.
[916] The provision is quoted above in the opening part of this annotation.

of a public offer was its public announcement; the absence of that requirement meant that the act had not been and could not be a public offer in terms of Section 276 of the ComC.[917] It was also argued that the ComC could not apply to the given case, because the claimant had registered the domain name as a natural person and was treated as a natural person in the arbitral proceedings. This deficiency could only be remedied by submitting to the ComC under Section 262(1) of the ComC,[918] which, however, did not happen in the said case. The claimant also argued that the act could not constitute a contract for the benefit of a third party under Section 50 of the CivC.[919] Again, the said instrument is a substantive-law instrument and cannot concern the execution of an arbitration agreement, which is procedural in nature. A public proposal of arbitration, incorporated in the Rules, is a unilateral juridical act addressed to no specific person in particular, and it does not have the nature of a contract. Conversely, the essence of a contract for the benefit of a third party is that the debtor assumes an obligation owed to the other party – creditor, who acts in their own name, that the debtor will provide performance to a third party. Moreover, the claimant argued that the third party was not objectively identifiable in the given case, which is a necessary prerequisite of a contract for the benefit of a third party. The claimant also contested the form of the arbitration agreement, because in the claimant's opinion, the requirement of the written form had not been observed, and consequently, the public proposal could not be considered an arbitration agreement under Section 2(3)(b) of the ArbAct;[920] this rendered Section 3(2) of the ArbAct[921] inapplicable, contrary to the opinion of the appellate court. The claimant also repeatedly highlighted the lack of the autonomy of will in accepting the Rules, because each applicant is presented (by the only provider in the Czech Republic) with a standard form contract, which the applicant must accept. The claimant maintained that other domains do not represent a sufficient substitute for the ".cz" domain, and consequently, it is not possible to agree with the appellate court that the applicant is free to choose whether and which domain the applicant registers (and which rules the applicant thereby submits to). The claimant argued that it was unacceptable for entities holding a monopolistic position in the market to force their partners to enter into agreements on transferring the

---

[917] The provision is quoted above in the opening part of this annotation.

[918] The provision is quoted above in the opening part of this annotation.

[919] The provision is quoted above in the opening part of this annotation.

[920] The provision is quoted above in the opening part of this annotation.

[921] The provision is quoted above in the opening part of this annotation.

jurisdiction to resolve disputes to nongovernmental authorities, such as the AC in the present case. Finally, the claimant pointed out that the above-described deficiencies of the public proposal (which does not establish the jurisdiction of the AC as envisaged by the AC) could not be overlooked, because of any long-term trouble-free functioning of the entire system of domain name dispute resolution.

16.191. The SC agreed with the claimant's arguments and arrived at the unequivocal conclusion that *acceptance* of the public proposal of arbitration cannot result in the execution of a proper arbitration agreement; in this connection, the SC held that the legal conclusions reached by the appellate court were erroneous.

[***Arguments Presented by SC***]:

16.192. The SC criticized the appellate court for entirely ignoring the issue of whether or not the respective relationship was governed by the ComC – the appellate court merely held that a public offer under Section 276 et seq. of the ComC[922] is an instrument of commercial law as a result of the method whereby the contract is (exclusively) executed. However, the SC ruled that the arbitration agreement would not have been executed even if the respective relationship had been a commercial relationship. In this connection, the SC invoked Section 2 of the ArbAct[923] and pointed out that the object of an arbitration agreement, as a bilateral juridical act, is to transfer the jurisdiction to resolve an existing dispute between particular entities to arbitrators/arbitration; both parties to the (future) dispute must express their consent with the arbitration in the arbitration agreement. Conversely, a public offer under Section 276 of the ComC[924] is an expression of will whereby the offeror addresses a non-specific group of persons for the purpose of executing an agreement, provided that the contents comply with Section 269 of the ComC.[925] The SC held that a public declaration made by a domain name holder in the agreement entered into with the registrar, which is addressed to a non-specific group of third parties and in which the holder declares that they will submit any potential disputes to arbitration, is not an expression of will addressed to a specific person to submit existing disputes to arbitration, as required under the ArbAct. The SC also agreed and identified with the other objections raised by the claimant, namely that the proposal could only be a public offer if it were revocable (Section 277 of the ComC[926]) and if

---

[922] The provisions are quoted above in the opening part of this annotation.

[923] The provision is quoted above in the opening part of this annotation.

[924] The provision is quoted above in the opening part of this annotation.

[925] The provision is quoted above in the opening part of this annotation.

[926] The provision is quoted above in the opening part of this annotation.

it were properly accepted (Section 278 of the ComC[927]), neither of which happened in the said case (according to the SC).

16.193. The SC also inferred that the act cannot constitute a contract for the benefit of a third party under Section 50 of the CivC.[928] The SC based its conclusion on the fact that the third party does not have to be individually identified in the agreement, but they must be identifiable on the basis of specified objective circumstances. Conversely, the public proposal is a juridical act addressed to no person in particular, which does not render a third party objectively identifiable. The SC concluded that the very fact that any person may feel that their rights have been prejudiced by the recipient of the public proposal and, consequently, may thus lodge a motion with the AC, does not constitute such objective identifiability of the third party. The SC also agreed with the claimant that the object of arbitration agreements is the contracting parties' submission to the jurisdiction of arbitrators, i.e. a procedural issue, not a substantive-law commitment of the debtor to the creditor to provide performance to a third party.

16.194. Last, but not least, the SC explicitly pointed out that its conclusions apply exclusively to the resolution of disputes in terms of the Rules adopted by the CZ.NIC Association; they do not apply to the resolution of disputes arising from any other domains (see generic domains and *Uniform Domain Name Dispute Resolution*). Hence, the SC's conclusions should not be interpreted as the total exclusion of domain name disputes from arbitration, but as reservations (objections) with respect to the method whereby the AC's jurisdiction was established in this particular case.

[*Further Conclusions and Comments Concerning Annotated Resolution of SC*]:

16.195. The SC's decision will undoubtedly influence the resolution of domain name disputes in the Czech Republic, because the public proposal of arbitration has been employed in practice for many years. The conclusions drawn by the SC will continue to apply, because the recodification of Czech private law has not introduced any material changes in the instruments of public offer and contract for the benefit of a third party. Consequently, the objections raised by the SC are still relevant. This primarily applies to the fact that a public offer is, by definition, a revocable act, and logic dictates, in the present case, that the domain name holder was bound by the declaration in which they undertook to resolve disputes in arbitration. It is also necessary, even under the new law, for the party who makes the public offer to properly accept the offer – which is again *ipso facto* excluded. Rules relating to contracts

---

[927] The provision is quoted above in the opening part of this annotation.
[928] The provision is quoted above in the opening part of this annotation.

executed for the benefit of third parties are also inapplicable. The reason is that it will still be impossible to infer the objective identifiability of the third party for whose benefit the agreement is executed.

16.196. We can also not make use of the ArbAct rules, which under certain circumstances (if the party voluntarily participates in the hearing of the case and does not plead a lack of jurisdiction on the part of the arbitrators), allow that the deficiencies of the arbitration agreement be remedied. Or rather, it is perhaps imaginable that arbitrators will have jurisdiction to hear the dispute if the holder of the registered domain name agrees with the submission of the dispute to arbitration. But if the invalidity of the arbitration agreement is pleaded, it will be necessary to grant the objections. It will be interesting to watch whether the arbitrators accept the SC's conclusions, make a decision admitting a lack of jurisdiction based on a proper and timely challenge, and terminate the proceedings – or whether motions for the annulment of arbitral awards will be lodged.

16.197. The only reason that ceased to be relevant after recodification is the differentiation between commercial and civil obligations. Hence, it would no longer be necessary to determine which relationships the rules could theoretically apply to, and which not. We could probably also reconcile the objection that the instruments invoked by the appellate court are purely substantive-law instruments, whereas the arbitration agreement is a strictly procedural act. The nature of arbitration agreements has been extensively discussed, and the conclusion adopted by the SC is definitely not unequivocally accepted.

16.198. The annotated decision resolved the issue of a dispute between a domain name holder and a third party, claiming that their rights had been violated by the domain registration; nonetheless, it should be noted that problems (albeit problems of a different kind) may also arise from disputes between domain name holders and the CZ.NIC Association. If the domain name is registered by a natural person outside their profession or business, the relationship could be a B2C relationship, and the agreement on submitting potential disputes to the jurisdiction of the AC incorporated in the Rules certainly does not comply with the requirements of Section 3(3) et seq. of the ArbAct.[929]

16.199. For the sake of completeness, we must also add that the respondent challenged the Judgment of the SC by a constitutional complaint delivered to the ConCourt on March 21, 2014; the complaint was heard under Case No. III. ÚS 1091/2014. The respondent argued that the decision violated the respondent's right to a fair trial in terms of Article 36(1) of the Charter,[930] the freedom of assembly in terms of Article

---

[929] The provision is quoted above in the opening part of this annotation.

[930] Cit.: *Everyone may assert, through the legally prescribed procedure, their rights before*

20(1) of the Charter,[931] as well as its right to do whatever is not prohibited by law (statute) in terms of Article 2(3) of the Charter,[932] and the right to the free expression of will under Article 1 of the Charter.[933] The ConCourt rejected the constitutional complaint as inadmissible on March 31, 2014; the ConCourt held that the respondent had lodged the constitutional complaint before the respondent availed themselves of all procedural means afforded to the respondent by law to protect their right. Indeed, the respondent themselves admitted that fact, but argued that the appellate court was bound to observe in the next proceedings the legal opinion articulated by the SC, and in consequence thereof, the parties already had a *final* decision at their disposal; the requirement of availing oneself of procedural means available in the proceedings at the appellate court and of the subsequent extraordinary remedial measure lodged with the SC would be a manifestation of legal formalism. The ConCourt disagreed with that conclusion.[934] But we may expect that

---

an independent and impartial court, or in specified cases, before a different authority.

[931] Cit.: *The right of association is guaranteed. Everyone has the right to associate together with others in clubs, societies, and other associations.*

[932] Cit.: *Everyone may do that which is not prohibited by law, and nobody may be compelled to do that which is not imposed upon them by law.*

[933] Cit.: *All people are free and equal in their dignity and rights. Their fundamental rights and freedoms are inherent, inalienable, non-prescriptible, and irrepealable.*

[934] This decision is available online on the ConCourt website at http://nalus. usoud.cz/Search/ResultDetail.aspx?id=83135&pos=1&cnt=1&typ=result; the Court ruled as follows (cit.): *The constitutional complaint is, by definition, a subsidiary procedural instrument. This is formally reflected in the requirement that the applicant must first exhaust all procedural instruments afforded to the applicant by the law to protect their rights (Section 75(1) of the Constitutional Court Act). The above indicates that if a law or regulation stipulates that a particular authority of state power has jurisdiction in a particular procedural situation to make decisions regarding the rights and obligations of natural persons and legal entities, the Constitutional Court may not interfere with the authority's status by delivering its own decision in the case preceding the authority's decision. The principle of the rule of law does not generally allow such parallel decision-making [cf., however, Section 75(2)(b) of the Constitutional Court Act]. The Constitutional Court is not called upon to change or remedy any alleged or actual errors made by the lower courts in pending proceedings; the Constitutional Court is principally called upon to assess, from overall perspectives and after the case is terminated with final force and effect, whether the proceedings as a whole and the results thereof stand the test of constitutionality. The Constitutional Court has already repeated many times that, in the constitutional complaint proceedings, the Court is only entitled to make decisions with respect to final and conclusive decisions, which must be interpreted in the formal sense, but also as "ultimate" decisions. The Constitutional Court has therefore repeatedly rejected as inadmissible constitutional complaints in those cases where a final and conclusive decision was rendered by a court, but*

after the case is heard anew, and after all remedial measures are exhausted, the case will be submitted to the ConCourt again.

| | |

18. Resolution of Supreme Court of CR, Case No. 26 Cdo 282/2014, of March 19, 2014: Electronic Service (Delivery) of Arbitral Award to Data Mailbox

Abbreviations Used:

AC Rules	AC Rules (for the purposes of this annotation, the AC Rules effective since July 1, 2012)
AC	Arbitration Court at the Economic Chamber of the Czech Republic and Agricultural Chamber of the Czech Republic
ArbAct	Act of the Czech Republic No. 216/1994 Coll., on Arbitration and the Enforcement of Arbitral Awards, as amended[935]
CCP	Act of the Czech Republic No. 99/1963 Coll., the Code of Civil Procedure, as amended
CZK	Czech crown, legal tender of the Czech Republic
EAA	Act of the Czech Republic No. 300/2008 Coll., on Electronic Acts and Authorized Conversion of Documents, as amended
SC	Supreme Court of the Czech Republic

Key Words:
autonomy | contractual concept of arbitration | data mailbox | electronic address | electronic message | execution (enforcement proceedings) | finality of arbitral award | nature of arbitration | private

---

the case was not terminated by the said decision, i.e. the case was remanded to a court or any other state authority for further proceedings [cf. also Resolution of March 30, 2006 in Case No. IV. ÚS 125/06 (U 4/40 SbNU 781), Resolution of January 4, 2011 in Case No. IV. ÚS 3256/10, Resolution of February 16, 2011 in Case No. III. ÚS 256/11, and Resolution of May 23, 2013 in Case No. III. ÚS 1492/13 (all available at http://nalus.usoud.cz)]. The consistent case law of the Constitutional Court indicates that the conclusion regarding the inadmissibility of a constitutional complaint also applies if the authority that is called upon to make the new decision in the case is bound by the legal opinion articulated in the contested decision.

[935] The governing law in this case was the ArbAct effective until March 31, 2014.

service (delivery) | public authority | service (delivery) of arbitral award |
service (delivery) to a data mailbox | termination of arbitration |

Applicable Laws and Regulations:
CCP: Section 45[936]
ArbAct: Section 19,[937] Section 19a,[938] Section 23,[939] Section 28[940941]
EEA: Section 1,[942] Section 17,[943] Section 18a[944]

---

[936]   CCP, Section 45 (cit.): "Methods of service of documents – (1) Written documents shall be served by the court during a hearing or any other court act. (2) If the written document was not served pursuant to subsection (1), the court shall deliver the document to a data mailbox using the public data network. If the written document cannot be delivered to a data mailbox using the public data network, the court shall deliver the document to any other address or to an electronic address at the addressee's request. (3) If the written document cannot be served pursuant to subsection (2), the chairman of the panel orders the document to be served (a) by an authority executing service of documents, or (b) by a party to the proceedings or their representative."

[937]   This provision is quoted below.

[938]   This provision is quoted below. The respective provision was incorporated in the ArbAct by amendment implemented by Act No. 303/2013 Coll. effective since January 1, 2014; consequently, it does not apply to the proceedings in which the arbitral award was rendered that is the subject matter of the SC decision annotated in this article. Nonetheless, the provision is referred to at the end of this annotation, in the commentary concerning the application of the respective court decision in the context of the more recent law.

[939]   This provision is quoted below.

[940]   This provision is quoted below.

[941]   The AC Rules are available on the AC website at: www.soud.cz (available in multiple language versions).

[942]   EEA, Section 1 (cit.): "Subject matter of the law – (1) This Act regulates (a) electronic acts performed by state authorities, authorities of self-governing administrative units, state funds, health insurance companies, Czech Radio, Czech Television, self-governing chambers founded by statute, notaries public and execution agents ("public authority") vis-à-vis natural persons and legal entities, electronic acts of natural persons and legal entities vis-à-vis public authorities, and electronic acts between public authorities using data mailboxes, (b) delivery of documents of natural persons, self-employed natural persons (entrepreneurs) and legal entities using data mailboxes, (c) information system of data mailboxes, (d) authorized conversion of documents [Act No. 499/2004 Coll., on Archiving and Records Management and Amending Selected Legislation, as amended] ("Conversion"). (2) This Act shall not apply to documents that contain classified information [Act No. 412/2005 Coll., on the Protection of Classified Information and Security Clearance, as amended.]."

[943]   EEA, Section 17 (cit.): "Delivery of documents by public authorities using data mailboxes – "(1) If the nature of the document permits, the public authority shall deliver the document to another public authority using its data mailbox, unless the document is

delivered on the spot. If the nature of the document permits and if the natural person, self-employed natural person (entrepreneur) or legal entity has their data mailbox activated, the public authority delivers the document to the person or entity using the data mailbox, unless the document is delivered by a public decree or on the spot. If the delivery is executed pursuant to this Act, the provisions of other laws regulating methods of delivery shall not apply. (2) Subsection (1) is without prejudice to the hierarchy of the methods of delivery listed in any other laws, where such laws allow delivery using data mailboxes. (3) A document delivered to a data mailbox is delivered at the moment a person logs into the data mailbox who has access to the delivered document in view of the scope of their authorization. (4) Unless the person under subsection (3) logs into the data mailbox within 10 days after the day on which the document was delivered to the data mailbox, the document is deemed delivered on the last day of this time limit; this shall not apply if any other law excludes substitute delivery.[6] (5) Subject to the conditions stipulated by another law,[7] the person for whom the data mailbox was activated may request that the delivery under subsection (4) be declared ineffective. (6) Delivery of a document pursuant to subsections (3) or (4) has the same legal effects as delivery to the addressee personally. (7) Delivery between public authorities using data mailboxes shall not apply if any other form of electronic communication has been implemented between the authorities for security reasons."

[944] EEA, Section 18a (cit.): "Delivery of documents of natural persons, self-employed natural persons (entrepreneurs) and legal entities – (1) At the request of a natural person, self-employed natural person (entrepreneur) or legal entity, the Ministry shall enable the delivery of documents from the data mailbox of another natural person, self-employed natural person (entrepreneur) or legal entity to the data mailbox of the requesting person/entity. (2) A document delivered pursuant to subsection (1) is delivered at the moment a person logs into the data mailbox who has access to the document in view of the scope of their authorization. (3) The delivery of the document pursuant to subsection (1) is subject to a fee payable to the data mailbox information system operator; the fee shall be calculated according to the applicable price regulations. The fee shall be paid by the natural person, self-employed natural person (entrepreneur) or legal entity from whose data mailbox the document was sent. The said person/entity may also declare that they will pay for the delivery of a reply to the document delivered pursuant to the preceding sentence. The fee under the first sentence may also be paid, instead of by the natural person, self-employed natural person (entrepreneur) or legal entity from whose data mailbox the document was sent, by another natural person, self-employed natural person (entrepreneur) or legal entity if the latter presents the data mailbox information system operator with a written consent with such method of reimbursement of the fee issued by the natural person, self-employed natural person (entrepreneur) or legal entity from whose data mailbox the document was sent, or an output of the consent from the authorized conversion of documents; the person's signature in the written consent must be officially verified. Using the data mailbox information system, the data mailbox information system operator shall report this method of reimbursement to the natural person, self-employed natural person (entrepreneur) or legal entity from whose data mailbox documents ought to be sent, which will be paid for in compliance with the third or fourth sentence."

The Supreme Court of the Czech Republic reached the following principal conclusions:

(1) Arbitrators may serve their arbitral awards rendered in proceedings pursuant to the ArbAct to the data mailboxes of those parties who requested service of documents under Section 18a of the EEA at the Ministry of Interior of the Czech Republic.[945]

(2) The case law of the Constitutional Court of the Czech Republic mandates the application of the jurisdictional approach to the nature of arbitration,[946] although based on the contractual autonomy of will. However, this approach does not entail that arbitrators and permanent arbitral institutions become public authorities. Consequently, Section 17 of the EEA[947] will not apply to the service of arbitral awards (this provision orders public authorities to deliver documents to a data mailbox, unless the document can be served on the spot).

[From Facts of Case]:

16.200. On January 20, 2012, the arbitrator in proceedings at the AC rendered the arbitral award in Case No. Rsp 892/11, which ordered obligor X[948] to pay to obligee Y[949] CZK xxx,xxx.xx, plus the costs of the arbitral proceedings of CZK xx,xxx.xx. The arbitral award was sent to the obligor by post; however, the obligor, as a Czech legal person registered in the Companies Register, has an obligatory data mailbox.

[Procedure of Case]:

16.201. On August 1, 2012, the District Court in Ostrava, as the court of first instance, ordered execution (enforcement proceedings) against the property of the obligor in accordance with the abovementioned arbitral award, together with compensation for the costs of the execution. The court simultaneously appointed an enforcement agent to conduct the execution.

---

[945] The summary of the SC's legal opinion (*ratio decidendi*) was adopted from the SC website. Section 18a of the EEA is quoted above in the opening part of this annotation.

[946] See especially Judgment of the Constitutional Court of the Czech Republic, Case No. I ÚS 3227/07, of March 8, 2011. Cf. also Alexander J. Bělohlávek. Ústavní soud České republiky opustil striktní smluvní výklad koncepce rozhodčího řízení [Title in Translation: The Constitutional Court of the Czech Republic Has Abandoned its Strict Contractual Interpretation of the Concept of Arbitration]. Bulletin advokacie, Praha [Prague, Czech Republic]: Česká advokátní komora [Czech Bar Association], 2011, No. 12, pp. 40-43.

[947] The provision is quoted above in the opening part of this annotation.

[948] A legal entity formed and existing under the laws of the Czech Republic in the form of a limited liability company.

[949] A legal entity formed and existing under the laws of the Czech Republic in the form of a limited liability company.

16.202. The Regional Court in Ostrava, as the appellate court, dismissed the motion for execution. The appellate court held that the underlying decision (arbitral award) was not enforceable, because the service of the arbitral award had not complied with the procedure stipulated under Section 45 of the CCP,[950] i.e. the award had not been delivered to the obligor's data mailbox, and consequently, the arbitral award had not been properly served. The appellate court also invoked the decision of the SC in Case No. 20 Cdo 1592/2006 of April 26, 2007, according to which service of documents is not part of the procedure whereby arbitrators manage the proceedings.

16.203. The obligee lodged an extraordinary appeal against the resolution of the appellate court, arguing that service of documents to a data mailbox was not mandatory in arbitral proceedings, unless the obligor requested such procedure. The obligee also pointed out that the issue of service of documents to a data mailbox by an arbitral tribunal (which is not a public authority) has not yet been addressed and resolved by the SC.

[*Arguments Presented by SC*]:

16.204. In its first premise, the SC reasoned that, according to the consistent case law, the service of arbitral awards or resolutions is governed by the CCP provisions regulating service (delivery) of documents, because the ArbAct does not contain any provisions on the said issue. Similarly to judgments, written arbitral awards are served on the parties personally, and the finality and enforceability of awards is contingent on effective service.

16.205. The available methods of service are hierarchically enumerated in Section 45 of the CCP,[951] which prioritizes service of documents during a hearing or any other act of the court, followed by delivery to a data mailbox, and only then the other methods of service. The chairman of the panel (sole judge), judicial commissioner, or any other court officer is bound by this hierarchy.[952]

16.206. Delivery of documents to a data mailbox is governed by special law, namely the EEA. Section 1(1)(a) of the EEA[953] contains a list of public authorities; the list does not include arbitrators or arbitral tribunals, which complies with the case law of the Constitutional Court of the Czech Republic. Despite the fact that the Constitutional Court of the

---

[950] The provision is quoted above in the opening part of this annotation.

[951] The provision is quoted above in the opening part of this annotation.

[952] See Resolution of the SC, Case No. 21 Cdo 3489/2012, of November 6, 2013. This Resolution was also published in Sbírka soudních rozhodnutí a stanovisek NS [Reports of SC Decisions and Opinions] under No. 37/2014.

[953] The provision is quoted above in the opening part of this annotation.

Czech Republic prefers the jurisdictional concept of arbitration, although based on the contractual autonomy of will, the Court has bestowed the status of public authorities on neither the arbitrators, nor the permanent arbitral institutions.[954] Consequently, Section 17 of the EEA[955] will not apply to the service of arbitral awards (the provision orders the public authorities to deliver documents to a data mailbox, unless the document can be served on the spot).

16.207. The reason is that neither the arbitrators, nor the arbitral tribunals are public authorities; hence, they are not bound by the obligation of prioritizing service of documents to the recipient's data mailbox. Nonetheless, the EEA allows a private-law regime of delivery (i.e. not only between a public authority and a citizen, or between two public authorities). In such case, however, the persons who are interested in service to their data mailboxes must make a corresponding request to the Ministry of Interior of the Czech Republic[956] (see Section 18a of the EEA).[957]

---

[954] It is necessary to point out that permanent arbitral institutions may only be established in the Czech Republic (i.e. within the territorial application of the ArbAct) by another law, or only if another law expressly allows their establishment. The applicable rules are incorporated in Section 13 of the ArbAct (cit.): "Permanent arbitral institutions – (1) Permanent arbitral institutions may only be established by another law or only if another law expressly allows their establishment. (2) Permanent arbitral institutions can issue their own statutes and rules which must be published in the Business Journal [footnote in the text of the Act: Regulation of the Cabinet of the CSFR No. 63/1992 Coll., on Business Journal.]; these statutes and rules may determine the method of appointment and the number of arbitrators and may stipulate that the arbitrators shall be selected from a list administered by the permanent arbitral institution. The statutes and rules may also determine how the arbitrators shall conduct the proceedings and render their decisions, as well as resolve other issues connected with the activities of the permanent arbitral institution and the arbitrators, including rules regulating the costs of proceedings and fees for the arbitrators. (3) If the parties agreed on the jurisdiction of a particular permanent arbitral institution and failed to agree otherwise in the arbitration agreement, they shall be deemed to have submitted to the regulations specified in subsection (2), as applicable on the day of commencement of the proceedings in the permanent arbitral institution. (4) No entity may carry out its activities using a name which evokes a misleading impression that the entity is a permanent arbitral institution under this law unless a different law or regulation or an international agreement integrated in the legal system authorizes the entity to use the name."

[955] The provision is quoted above in the opening part of this annotation.

[956] The Public Administration Website (https://seznam.gov.cz/ovm/welcome.do?ref= podnikani) allows the user to find the data mailbox ID for all persons and entities that have their data mailbox activated, including those persons or entities that activated their data

16.208. The SC therefore concluded that the arbitral tribunal delivers the arbitral award pursuant to Section 45 of the CCP,[958] but it is not a public authority, and consequently, could only serve the arbitral award to the party's data mailbox if the party had requested such delivery. If the party failed to request such delivery, the arbitral tribunal shall serve documents on the said party using the other methods listed in Section 45 of the CCP.[959]

16.209. However, the appellate court entirely dismissed the issue of whether or not the obligor requested delivery to its data mailbox. Consequently, the SC vacated the decision of the appellate court and remanded the case for further hearing and a new decision.

[*Further Conclusions and Notes*]:

16.210. This decision is only significant with respect to those proceedings that were commenced on or after April 1, 2012,[960] because April 1, 2012 is the effective date of the amendment to the ArbAct that postpones the moment of termination of the arbitral proceedings from the moment at which the arbitral award was rendered[961] to the moment at which the arbitral award becomes final and conclusive (see Section 23 of the ArbAct).[962] The arbitral award becomes final and conclusive as soon as

---

mailbox voluntarily, as well as information as to whether or not the person/entity requested the delivery of private-law (postal) data messages.

[957]   The provision is quoted above in the opening part of this annotation.

[958]   The provision is quoted above in the opening part of this annotation.

[959]   The provision is quoted above in the opening part of this annotation.

[960]   See the transitional provisions to Act No. 19/2012 Coll. amending the ArbAct: "Article II – Transitional provisions - 1. Arbitral proceedings commenced before the effective date of this Act, including proceedings regarding disputes from consumer contracts, shall be finished pursuant to the laws and regulations applicable until the effective date of this Act.[...]"

[961]   According to the ArbAct as applicable until March 31, 2014.

[962]   ArbAct in effect until March 31, 2012 (cit.): "Section 23 - The arbitral proceedings are terminated by the issue of: (a) an arbitral award, or (b) a resolution in cases in which no arbitral award is made; the resolution must be signed, must contain reasons, and must be delivered (served) as an arbitral award; if the request for arbitration (statement of claim) lodged with a permanent arbitral institution is withdrawn before the arbitral panel is established or before the arbitrator is appointed, the resolution on termination of the proceedings is made and signed by the chairman of the permanent arbitral institution."

ArbAct in effect since April 1, 2012 (cit): "Section 23 – The arbitral proceedings are terminated – (a) at the moment the arbitral award becomes final and conclusive, or (b) upon the receipt of a resolution in cases in which no arbitral award is made; the resolution must be signed, must contain reasons, and must be delivered (served) as an arbitral award; if the request for arbitration (statement of claim) lodged with a permanent arbitral institution is withdrawn before the arbitral panel is established or before the arbitrator is

it is served (see Section 28 of the ArbAct).[963] Consequently, the amendment to the ArbAct that took effect on April 1, 2012 (Act No. 19/2012 Coll.) prolonged the arbitral proceedings to the moment at which the arbitral award becomes final and conclusive (if an arbitral award is issued), or to the moment at which the resolution terminating the arbitral proceedings is served on the parties; this means that the issue of service of the arbitral award now falls within the sphere of the autonomy of the parties' will.[964] Hence, the parties themselves are free to regulate the issue of service of documents and to have regard to the CCP to whatever extent they see fit (if at all).

16.211. The AC responded to the EEA and to the amendment to the ArbAct effective since April 1, 2012 in the *new* AC Rules effective from July 1, 2012.[965] Section 10[966] of the AC Rules explicitly envisages service of

---

appointed, the resolution on termination of the proceedings is made and signed by the chairman of the permanent arbitral institution."

[963] ArbAct, Section 28 (cit.): "(1) The arbitral award executed in writing must be served on the parties and, having been duly served, stamped with the confirmation of legal force and effect. (2) If the arbitral award cannot be subject to review pursuant to Section 27 or if the time limit for filing the motion for review pursuant to Section 27 has expired without the motion having been lodged, the award has the effects of a final and conclusive court judgment and is enforceable by courts upon receipt."

[964] See the Explanatory Memorandum to the amendment of the ArbAct implemented by Act No. 19/2012 Coll.

See also Jan Kocina. Jan. Vykonatelnost a doručování rozhodčích nálezů. [Title in Translation: Enforceability and Service of Arbitral Awards]. Bulletin advokacie, Praha [Prague, Czech Republic]: Česká advokátní komora [Czech Bar Association], 2012, No. 4.

[965] However, considering the commencement of arbitration in which the arbitral award was rendered which is the subject matter of the above annotated SC Resolution, the AC Rules did not yet apply to the arbitral proceedings, or rather the case was governed by the former AC Rules applicable until June 30, 2012. The *old* AC Rules are also available on the AC website at: www.soud.cz, in multiple language versions.

[966] AC Rules, Section 10 (cit.): "Service of process - (1) Documents intended for the parties shall be sent by the Arbitration Court to the respective addresses specified by the parties or by means of their delivery to the data box if the given party has allowed such delivery (Section 18a(1) of Act No. 300/2008 Coll., on electronic acts and authorized conversion of documents). If a party has not specified any address and delivery to a data box is not possible, documents shall be sent to this party to an address known to the Arbitration Court. If a party has appointed its representative, documents shall be sent to this representative to the address of their registered office or place of residence, or to any other address specified by the party, or by means of delivery to their data box, if possible. (2) Persons authorized by a given party to accept documents, as well as other persons specified as the recipients of documents by the Civil Procedure Code, may also accept documents in their data box, instead of the addressee, with effects of service on the

documents to a electronic data mailbox, if a party requested such procedure and has also allowed private service of documents (service of documents other than those originating from public authorities or, as applicable, persons authorized to exercise selected public-law functions/powers, as anticipated under Section 18a of the EEA).[967] In this connection, service by post to a given address and service to a data mailbox are considered equal under the Rules – as mentioned above, the arbitrators and the permanent arbitral institutions are not public

addressee. (3) Statements of claim, statements of defense, summons, arbitral awards and rulings shall be served on the addressee personally, with confirmation of receipt, or by delivery to the addressee's data box pursuant to special legal regulation (Act No. 300/2008 Coll., on electronic acts and authorized conversion of documents). (4) Other documents shall be sent by registered or regular mail or by means of the public data network to the electronic address of the addressee or by other electronic means, or by delivery of the document to the addressee's data box. A message sent by means of the public data network to the electronic address of the addressee (party) must contain a Recognized Electronic Signature. (5) Any of the documents set out in the preceding paragraphs may also be served in person, with confirmation of receipt. (6) Unless a given document was sent to the addressee's data box, any service of a document by the Arbitration Court shall be valid if made pursuant to paragraphs 1 to 5 above, even if the addressee refused to accept the document or has failed to collect it in spite of a notice made by a postal services operator. A document that the addressee refused to accept is deemed to have been delivered on the date when acceptance was refused. A document intended for personal service (Section 10 (3)) that was not collected by the addressee within 10 days of the notice made by the postal services operator shall be deemed to have been delivered on the last day of this period, even if the addressee was not aware of the fact that the document was to be collected. Other documents that are not collected by the addressee within 5 days of the notice made by the postal services operator shall be deemed to have been delivered on the last day of this period, even if the addressee was not aware of the fact that the document was to be collected. Where documents are served abroad, it is sufficient to serve these documents according to the laws of the country of service. (7) A document that has been sent to a data box is deemed to be delivered at the time when a person who has access to the document being delivered in view of the scope of their authorization logs into the data box. (8) If a party has changed its address after the arbitral proceedings have been commenced without notifying the Arbitration Court of this fact, service is valid if the documents are sent to its last known address. (9) If a document could not be served on a party at its last known address through the procedure pursuant to paragraphs 1 to 8 above, not even through its representative or person authorized by the party to accept documents, the President of the Arbitration Court may appoint a person authorized to accept documents for such party (hereinafter an "Authorized Person"). The date of service on the Authorized Person shall be deemed to be the date of service on the addressee for whom the Authorized Person was appointed. (10) Only a person registered on the list of arbitrators of the Arbitration Court may be appointed as an Authorized Person.

[967] The provision is quoted above in the opening part of this annotation.

authorities, nor are they included on the list of individuals and entities in the EEA who are under the obligation to activate a data mailbox. Similarly, the addressees (parties) are not obliged to have a data mailbox or, as applicable, are not obliged to have permission to receive data messages within the private-law regime.

16.212. Another amendment modified the ArbAct with effect since January 1, 2014;[968] the amendment was synchronized with the effective date of the recodification of private law. Nonetheless, apart from the provisions that reflected the recodification, the amendment also supplemented the ArbAct with a new Section 19a,[969] which concerns service of documents. This provision (effective since January 1, 2014) envisages service to a data mailbox as the primary method of service; other methods in the hierarchy are e-mail (the law, somewhat surprisingly, does not insist on a recognized electronic certificate, i.e. electronic signature), and then service by post. The amendment gives rise to several doubts.

16.213. Firstly, it is unclear what the words *"impossible to deliver to a data mailbox"* mean. Is the condition also fulfilled if the arbitrator or the addressee does not have a data mailbox? It is also necessary to ask whether the addressee (party) is obliged to activate a data mailbox and thereby enable service of documents within the private-law regime, i.e. allow service of private messages through this channel, that is messages other than those originating from public authorities, which category does not include arbitrators (permanent arbitral institutions).

16.214. Another problem arises with respect to the hierarchy of the methods of service under the quoted Section 19a of the ArbAct, as amended, with effect since January 1, 2014. Arbitration is very informal and e-mail communication is common, but it is unclear why the ArbAct prioritizes service of documents through a data mailbox, which can be classified as a special method of service enabling clear identification of the recipient and the sender, if the very next method of service consists of an *ordinary* e-mail message, without the law specifying any other

---

[968]   Act No. 303/2013 Coll.

[969]   ArbAct as amended by Act No. 303/2013 Coll., i.e. with effect since January 1, 2014: Section 19a – (cit.): "Address for service of documents – The arbitrator shall deliver a written document to the data mailbox address; if the written document cannot be delivered to the data mailbox, it shall be delivered to an electronic address notified by the addressee to the arbitrator or designated as their mailing address in the arbitration agreement. If the written document cannot be delivered to the addresses specified above, the arbitrator shall deliver the document to the address notified by the addressee to the arbitrator or to the address specified in the arbitration agreement."

requirements (such as the requirement of an electronic signature or – better still – recognized electronic signature).

16.215. Considering the above controversial issues, the nature of Section 19a of the ArbAct,[970] as amended, with effect since January 1, 2014, remains ambiguous as to whether it is a binding provision of the Act, from which the parties are not free to depart by agreement, or whether it is a non-binding provision allowing a different agreement of the parties. The Explanatory Memorandum to Act No. 303/2013 Coll. (effective January 1, 2014) is silent on this issue, and the legislator's intention therefore remains rather unclear. It is also necessary to point out that this matter was only included when the Act was debated in the Committee for Constitutional Law of the Chamber of Deputies of the Parliament of the Czech Republic.[971] Nevertheless, it appears somewhat illogical for the legislator to prolong the duration of the arbitral proceedings[972] and give the parties the opportunity to regulate themselves the service of documents within the framework of their contractual autonomy, and at the same time adopt a somewhat questionable provision regulating service of documents (Section 19a of the ArbAct[973] within the meaning of Act No. 303/2013 Coll., effective

---

[970] The provision is quoted above.

[971] See Chamber Document 930/2.

[972] This issue has been analyzed above: the amendment to the ArbAct implemented by Act No. 19/2012 Coll. stipulated that the arbitral proceedings are not terminated by the issue of the arbitral award (as was the case under the law effective until March 31, 2014), but only after the arbitral award becomes final and conclusive, i.e. as soon as the arbitral award is served on the parties (see Section 23, in conjunction with Section 28 of the ArbAct, both of which are quoted above). In other words, service of an arbitral award pursuant to the law effective until March 31, 2012, which applied to any proceedings commenced until the said day, was implemented after the termination of the arbitral proceedings, and the SC maintained in its case law that the service of the arbitral award on the parties was no longer subject to the autonomy of the parties with respect to their possibility to agree on the method of service; conversely, service of an arbitral award pursuant to the law effective since April 1, 2014 falls within the autonomy of the parties as concerns their agreements on the management of the proceedings.

[973] ArbAct, Section 19 (cit. here in the current version effective since 1 January 2014): "(1) The parties are free to agree on the procedure to be followed by the arbitrators in conducting the proceedings. Matters regarding the conduct of the proceedings may be resolved by the chairman of the panel providing he or she was authorized to do so by the parties or by all arbitrators. (2) In the absence of an agreement pursuant to subsection (1) or in the absence of a determination of the procedure pursuant to subsection (4), the arbitrators shall conduct the proceedings in such manner as they consider appropriate. They conduct the arbitral proceedings in such manner that the facts of the case necessary for the resolution of the dispute are sufficiently ascertained, without any unnecessary

January 1, 2014). For this reason, we are more inclined to accept the conclusion that Section 19a of the ArbAct,[974] effective since January 1, 2014, is a non-binding provision, from which the parties may depart by agreement, and only the quoted provision applies, unless the parties agree otherwise, or unless the arbitrator(s) regulate(s) the issue of service of documents (see Section 19 of the ArbAct[975] regarding management of the proceedings).

---

formalities and while giving all parties equal opportunity to assert their rights. (3) Unless the parties agree otherwise, the arbitral proceedings shall be oral. The proceedings are always conducted with the exclusion of the public. (4) The parties may also determine the procedure to be followed in the rules on arbitration, provided that the rules are enclosed to the arbitration agreement. This provision shall not prejudice the application of the rules adopted by a permanent arbitral institution."

[974] ArbAct, Section 19 (cit. here in the current version effective since January 1, 2014): "(1) The parties are free to agree on the procedure to be followed by the arbitrators in conducting the proceedings. Matters regarding the conduct of the proceedings may be resolved by the chairman of the panel, provided that they were authorized to do so by the parties or by all arbitrators. (2) In the absence of an agreement pursuant to subsection (1) or in the absence of a determination of the procedure pursuant to subsection (4), the arbitrators shall conduct the proceedings in such manner as they consider appropriate. They conduct the arbitral proceedings in such manner that the facts of the case necessary for the resolution of the dispute are sufficiently ascertained, without any unnecessary formalities and while giving all parties equal opportunity to assert their rights. (3) Unless the parties agree otherwise, the arbitral proceedings shall be oral. The proceedings are always conducted with the exclusion of the public. (4) The parties may also determine the procedure to be followed in the rules on arbitration, providing the rules are enclosed with the arbitration agreement. This provision shall not prejudice the application of rules adopted by a permanent arbitral institution."

[975] ArbAct, Section 19 (cit. here in the current version effective since January 1, 2014): "(1) The parties are free to agree on the procedure to be followed by the arbitrators in conducting the proceedings. Matters regarding the conduct of the proceedings may be resolved by the chairman of the panel, provided that they were authorized to do so by the parties or by all arbitrators. (2) In the absence of an agreement pursuant to subsection (1) or in the absence of a determination of the procedure pursuant to subsection (4), the arbitrators shall conduct the proceedings in such manner as they consider appropriate. They conduct the arbitral proceedings in such manner that the facts of the case necessary for the resolution of the dispute are sufficiently ascertained, without any unnecessary formalities and while giving all parties equal opportunity to assert their rights. (3) Unless the parties agree otherwise, the arbitral proceedings shall be oral. The proceedings are always conducted with the exclusion of the public. (4) The parties may also determine the procedure to be followed in the rules on arbitration, provided that the rules are enclosed to the arbitration agreement. This provision shall not prejudice the application of the rules adopted by a permanent arbitral institution."

16.216. It is most probable, though, that the application of Section 19a of the ArbAct will cause interpretational problems in future.[976] Nonetheless, even if the courts concluded that Section 19a of the ArbAct[977] is binding and the parties are not free to depart therefrom, and consequently, service of documents to a data mailbox is mandatory, it is to be welcomed that improper service of documents can be remedied *ex post facto*. Moreover, the Act contains no provision that would determine the period within which a document must be served *"properly"*; consequently, it is possible to remedy any deficiencies even several years after the service, which could not have the anticipated legal effects due to improper procedure.

| | |

19. Resolution of Supreme Court of CR, Case No. 23 Cdo 3022/2013, of March 24, 2014: Suspension of Enforceability of Arbitral Award[978]

Abbreviations Used:

ArbAct	Act of the Czech Republic No. 216/1994 Coll., on Arbitration and the Enforcement of Arbitral Awards, as amended
ExecC	Act of the Czech Republic No. 120/2001 Coll., on Execution Agents and Execution (Execution Code), as amended
SC	Supreme Court of the Czech Republic

Key Words:
annulment (setting aside) of arbitral award | arbitral award | enforceability of arbitral award | enforcement of arbitral award | sale of enterprise | suspension of execution (enforcement) |

---

[976] The provision is quoted above.

[977] The provision is quoted above.

[978] This decision is available online on the website of the SC at: http://www.nsoud.cz/ Judikatura/judikatura_ns.nsf/WebSearch/9A257AEA1D3F9460C1257CB7002C5208?open Document&Highlight=0,rozhod%C4%8D%C3%AD,%C5%99%C3%ADzen%C3%AD   [last accessed on August 24, 2014].

Applicable Laws and Regulations:

ArbAct: Section 31(b), (c), (e), (i),[979] Section 32(2).[980]

ExecC: Section 54(5),[981] Section 57.[982]

---

[979] ArbAct, Section 31 (approximate translation, cit.):

• Effective until March 31, 2012: "At the request of any party the court annuls the arbitral award if: (a) it was made in a case which cannot be submitted to arbitration (cannot be the subject of a valid arbitration agreement), (b) the arbitration agreement is invalid for other reasons or the agreement was cancelled or it does not apply to the agreed case, (c) the arbitrator(s) who took part in the proceedings was/were not authorized to make decisions in the case, whether under the arbitration agreement or otherwise, or lacked the capacity to act as arbitrator(s), (d) the arbitral award was not adopted by the majority of the arbitrators, (e) a party was denied the opportunity to plead his or her case in the arbitral proceedings, (f) the arbitral award orders a party to provide performance which was not requested by the obligee or to provide performance which is impossible or illegal under domestic law, (g) it transpires that there are reasons which would otherwise justify the reopening of civil proceedings in court."

• Effective since April 1, 2012: "At the request of any party the court annuls the arbitral award if: (a) it was made in a case which cannot be submitted to arbitration (cannot be the subject of a valid arbitration agreement), (b) the arbitration agreement is invalid for other reasons or the agreement was cancelled or it does not apply to the agreed case, (c) the arbitrator(s) who took part in the proceedings was/were not authorized to make decisions in the case, whether under the arbitration agreement or otherwise, or lacked the capacity to act as arbitrator(s), (d) the arbitral award was not adopted by the majority of the arbitrators, (e) a party was denied the opportunity to plead his or her case in the arbitral proceedings, (f) the arbitral award orders a party to provide performance which was not requested by the obligee or to provide performance which is impossible or illegal under domestic law, (g) the arbitrator or the permanent arbitral institution resolved a dispute arising from a consumer contract contrary to consumer protection laws, or clearly in violation of good morals, or contrary to public policy, (h) an arbitration agreement relating to disputes arising from consumer contracts lacks the information required under Section 3(5) or such information is intentionally or to a non-negligible extent incomplete, inaccurate, or false, or (i) it transpires that there are reasons which would otherwise justify the reopening of civil proceedings in court."

[980] ArbAct, Section 32(2) (approximate translation, cit.):

• Effective until 31 March 2012: "(2) The motion pursuant to subsection (1) does not suspend the enforceability of the arbitral award. If requested by the obligor, however, the court may suspend the enforceability of the arbitral award in case an immediate enforcement of the arbitral award could cause serious harm."

• Effective since April 1, 2012: "(2) The motion pursuant to subsection (1) does not suspend the enforceability of the arbitral award. If requested by the obligor, however, the court may suspend the enforceability of the arbitral award in case an immediate enforcement of the arbitral award could cause serious harm or in case the motion to annul the arbitral award justifies the conclusion that the motion is legitimate."

[981] ExecC, Section 54(5) (approximate translation cit.): "(5) If a security deposit is

Czech (& Central European) Yearbook of Arbitration

The Supreme Court of the Czech Republic reached the following principal conclusions:
(1) **The suspension of the enforceability of an arbitral award under Section 32(2) of the ArbAct[983] and the suspension of execution under Section 54(5) of the ExecC[984] are two separate and independent procedural instruments. Consequently, the fulfillment of the conditions for the application of these measures must also be examined separately.**
(2) **The enforcement of an arbitral award by the sale of an enterprise may give rise to serious harm, and as such, may constitute grounds for the suspension of the enforceability of the arbitral award.**

[*From Facts of Case*]:
16.217. On May 15, 2012, the arbitrator[985] rendered an arbitral award in Case No. RŘ 373/2011, which ordered respondent X[986] to pay to claimant Y[987] CZK x,xxx,xxx.xx, plus the costs of the arbitral proceedings of CZK xxx,xxx.xx. This arbitral award served as the basis for the order of June 18, 2012, whereby execution (enforcement proceedings) was declared, to be implemented by the sale of the respondent's enterprise.
[*Procedure of Case*]:
16.218. On May 15, 2012, the respondent lodged a motion with the Municipal Court in Prague for the annulment of the arbitral award on grounds specified in Section 31(b), (c), (e) and (i) of the ArbAct. The respondent

---

deposited with the execution agent in the amount of the receivable subject to execution, the costs incurred by the obligee and the costs of the execution, the execution agent or the execution court suspends the execution, at the obligor's request, until the decision on the motion for termination of execution lodged by the obligor becomes final and conclusive, and rules that the obligor is not bound by the prohibition under Section 44a(1) and Section 47(5) from the day on which the decision on the suspension is rendered. If the execution is not terminated, the security deposit will be distributed in the payment of the receivable subject to execution, the obligee's costs and the costs of the execution; otherwise, it shall be returned to the person who deposited the security deposit."

[982] ExecC, Section 57 (approximate translation cit.): "Execution does not permit restitution to the original condition."

[983] This provision is quoted above.

[984] This provision is quoted above.

[985] The respective arbitration was *ad hoc* arbitration outside the jurisdiction of any permanent arbitral institution.

[986] A legal entity formed and existing under the laws of the Czech Republic in the form of a limited liability company.

[987] A legal entity formed and existing under the laws of the Czech Republic in the form of a joint stock company.

also proposed that the enforceability of the arbitral award be suspended, because the enforcement of the award threatened serious harm to the respondent.

16.219. On August 16, 2012, the Municipal Court in Prague issued a resolution, whereby the court suspended the enforceability of the abovementioned arbitral award under Section 32(2) of the ArbAct until the decision on the motion for the annulment of the arbitral award becomes final and conclusive. The Court reasoned that the sale of the enterprise as a method of execution represents serious harm to the claimant, which, moreover, could not be remedied if the claimant succeeded in the proceedings for the annulment of the arbitral award.

16.220. The obligee appealed the resolution of the Municipal Court in Prague. On February 28, 2013, the High Court in Prague, as the appellate court, rendered a resolution, whereby the court reversed the resolution of the court of first instance by dismissing the motion for the suspension of the enforceability of the arbitral award. In the reasons for its decision, the court stated that two shareholders of the obligor had entered into agreements shortly after the arbitral award had been rendered, whereby they had pledged their shares for the benefit of a third party in order to secure both the existing and any future receivables up to the amount of CZK 30 million (i.e. up to an amount exceeding the sum subject to execution).

16.221. The appellate court also stated that the execution order had been vacated by resolution of the court of first instance, and the execution was suspended until the decision on the claimant's motion for the termination of the execution becomes final and conclusive – the obligor lodged the motion because the obligor deposited a security deposit of CZK 10,200,000 with the execution agent, i.e. an amount that would cover the entire amount subject to execution. Consequently, the court is of the opinion that the claimant (obligor) is not threatened by any harm, and the motion for the suspension of enforceability is groundless. Moreover, the appellate court has also held that it is necessary to have regard to the interests of the obligee, which should not outweigh the interests of the obligor.

16.222. The obligor (i.e. appellant in the SC proceedings) lodged an extraordinary appeal against the resolution, pointing out that the suspension of execution under Section 54(5) of the ExecC and the suspension of the enforceability of an arbitral award under Section 32(2) of the ArbAct are two different instruments. The obligor also argued that, according to the obligor, the suspension of execution only has limited effects, because the execution agent requested an additional amount on top of the security deposit and threatened to cancel the suspension of the execution if the additional amount is not paid. Despite the fact that the appellant (appellant in the SC proceedings) paid the additional amount, the execution agent cancelled the suspension of the execution on April 22, 2013, i.e. after the resolution of the appellate court was rendered, and simultaneously issued several execution orders. Consequently, the suspension of execution is at the arbitrary discretion of the execution agent, and the appellant (appellant in the SC proceedings) has no control over the issue. Hence, the appellant (appellant in the SC proceedings) proposed that the SC examine the issue of whether or not a decision can be made suspending enforceability under Section 32(2) of the ArbAct, and at the same time, another decision suspending execution under Section 54(5) of the ExecC.

16.223. The respondent lodged a reply to the appellant's pleading, in which the respondent argued that execution does not permit restitution to the original condition (see Section 57 of the ExecC), and consequently, no execution would de facto ever be possible, because a serious harm would threaten in each and every case.

16.224. The appellant (appellant in the SC proceedings) filed an additional pleading, in which the appellant argued that the purpose of Section 54(5) of the ExecC (suspension of execution) is to protect the obligee, as well as the obligor. However, the protection of the obligor is, in the appellant's opinion, entirely insufficient, because the amount of the security deposit depends only on the arbitrary discretion of the execution agent. Moreover, the instrument of the security deposit only exists in the ExecC, not in the CCP – hence, the obligee may lodge a motion for court enforcement (of the arbitral award, in this case). This is in fact what the obligee also did in this case, as the obligee petitioned the District Court in Rakovník for the enforcement of the arbitral award by the creation of a judicial pledge over several hundred real estate properties owned by the appellant (appellant in the SC proceedings), and the motion was granted by the District Court in Rakovník. Consequently, the suspension of execution under Section 54(5) of the ExecC does not, in itself, eliminate the threat of serious harm, and it is necessary to complement it with the suspension of the enforceability of the arbitral award.

[*Arguments Presented by SC*]:

16.225. First, the SC held that there are two grounds for suspending the enforceability of the arbitral award under Section 32(2) of the ArbAct: (i) the immediate enforcement of the arbitral award threatens serious harm, and (ii) the motion for the annulment of arbitral award clearly indicates that it is justified. The second reason was supplemented by the amendment of the ArbAct implemented by Act No. 19/2012 Coll. Nonetheless, the relevant date for determination of the applicable version is the day on which arbitration was commenced (see Article II(1) of Act No. 19/2012 Coll., which amended the Arbitration Act with effect since April 1, 2012), which was disregarded by the lower courts.

16.226. The Supreme Court's decision was based on the premise that the suspension of the enforceability of an arbitral award under Section 32(2) of the ArbAct and the suspension of execution under Section 54(5) of the ExecC are two separate and independent procedural instruments. Consequently, the fulfillment of the conditions for the application of these measures must also be examined separately.

16.227. The SC first examined whether the condition under Section 32(2) of the ArbAct was fulfilled, i.e. whether the immediate enforcement of the arbitral award threatened serious harm to the appellant (appellant in the SC proceedings). The SC was of the opinion that the condition was fulfilled; this conclusion is supported by the amount of the sum subject to enforcement and by the fact that the obligee already commenced enforcement of the amount, namely by selling the appellant's enterprise.

16.228. The SC also held that the suspension of enforceability does not entail any disproportionate interference with the obligee's rights - its interests are sufficiently protected by the deposited security deposit.

16.229. Hence, the SC upheld the resolution of the Municipal Court of August 16, 2012 on the suspension of the enforceability of the arbitral award.

[*Further Conclusions*]:

16.230. Although the findings of fact do not clearly indicate whether the applicable law is the ArbAct effective until March 31, 2012 or the version effective since April 1, 2012, the SC's conclusions regarding the differences between the two instruments, i.e. the suspension of the execution and the suspension of the enforceability of the arbitral award, can be applied to both versions – even if there were only one reason for suspending the enforceability of the arbitral award under the ArbAct, as was the case pursuant to the ArbAct effective until March 31, 2012, the two instruments will still be separate and will still target different objectives.

| | |

20. Resolution of Supreme Court CR of April 29, 2014 in Case No. 23 Cdo 2497/2013: Duty to Give Instructions in Arbitration

Abbreviations Used:

AC	Arbitration Court at the Economic Chamber of the Czech Republic and Agricultural Chamber of the Czech Republic
ArbAct	Act of the Czech Republic No. 216/1994 Coll., on Arbitration and the Enforcement of Arbitral Awards, as amended[988]
CCP	Act of the Czech Republic No. 99/1963 Coll., the Code of Civil Procedure, as amended
ConCourt	Constitutional Court of the Czech Republic
ECtHR	European Court of Human Rights
SC	Supreme Court of the Czech Republic

Key Words:

annulment (setting aside) of arbitral award | burden of proof | compensation for damage/losses | duty to give instructions | duty to state relevant facts | ECtHR | equality | equality of arms | surprising decision |

Applicable Laws and Regulations:

ArbAct: Section 30,[989] Section 31(b) and (e)[990]

---

[988] The decision of the SC is based on the ArbAct in effect until March 31, 2012, but no subsequent changes have any bearing on the conclusions of the SC and their applicability in this particular case; generally, however, the protection of consumers has been enhanced, also in relation to enforcement proceedings.

[989] ArbAct, Section 30 (cit.): *"Application of the Code of Civil Procedure - Unless the Act stipulates otherwise, the arbitral proceedings shall be reasonably governed by the provisions of the Code of Civil Procedure."*

[990] ArbAct, Section 31 (cit.):

• ArbAct in effect until March 31, 2012: *"At the request of any party the court annuls the arbitral award if: (a) it was made in a case which cannot be submitted to arbitration (cannot be the subject of a valid arbitration agreement), (b) the arbitration agreement is invalid for other reasons or the agreement was cancelled or it does not apply to the agreed case, (c) the arbitrator(s) who took part in the proceedings was/were not authorized to make decisions in the case, whether under the arbitration agreement or otherwise, or lacked the capacity to act as arbitrator(s), (d) the arbitral award was not adopted by the majority of the arbitrators, (e) a party was denied the opportunity to plead his or her case in the arbitral proceedings, (f) the arbitral award orders a party to provide performance which was not requested by the obligee or to provide performance which is impossible or illegal under domestic law, (g) it transpires that there are reasons which would otherwise justify the reopening of civil proceedings in court."*

CCP[991]: Section 118a[992]

The Supreme Court of the Czech Republic reached the following principal conclusions:

(1) **The duty to give instructions set forth in Section 118a of the CCP, as a manifestation of the equality of arms principle, shall also apply in arbitration; failure to observe the duty is a breach of Section 18 of the ArbAct and could constitute grounds for the annulment of an arbitral award in terms of Section 31(e) of the ArbAct.**

• ArbAct in effect since April 1, 2012: *"At the request of any party the court annuls the arbitral award if: (a) it was made in a case which cannot be submitted to arbitration (cannot be the subject of a valid arbitration agreement), (b) the arbitration agreement is invalid for other reasons or the agreement was cancelled or it does not apply to the agreed case, (c) the arbitrator(s) who took part in the proceedings was/were not authorized to make decisions in the case, whether under the arbitration agreement or otherwise, or lacked the capacity to act as arbitrator(s), (d) the arbitral award was not adopted by the majority of the arbitrators, (e) a party was denied the opportunity to plead his or her case in the arbitral proceedings, (f) the arbitral award orders a party to provide performance which was not requested by the obligee or to provide performance which is impossible or illegal under domestic law, (g) the arbitrator or the permanent arbitral institution resolved a dispute arising from a consumer contract contrary to consumer protection laws, or clearly in violation of good morals, or contrary to public policy, (h) an arbitration agreement relating to disputes arising from consumer contracts lacks the information required under Section 3(5) or such information is intentionally or to a non-negligible extent incomplete, inaccurate, or false, or (i) it transpires that there are reasons which would otherwise justify the reopening of civil proceedings in court."*

[991] CCP in effect until December 31, 2012.

[992] CCP, Section 118a (cit.): *"(1) If it transpires during the hearing that a party has not yet presented all relevant statements of fact or has only presented them insufficiently, the chairman of the panel invites the party to supplement their statements and gives them instructions as to the subject matter of the statements that are to be supplemented and the potential consequences of noncompliance. (2) If the chairman of the panel opines that the court's legal opinion of the case could differ from the party's legal opinion, the chairman invites the party to supplement the description of the relevant facts to the necessary extent; the chairman shall proceed similarly to Subsection (1). (3) If the chairman of the panel discovers during the hearing that a party has not yet proposed evidence necessary to prove all of their contested statements, the chairman invites the party to identify such evidence without undue delay and gives them instructions regarding the consequences of noncompliance. (4) During the hearings, the chairman of the panel also gives the parties instructions regarding the other procedural rights and duties of the parties; this does not apply if the party is represented by an attorney or a notary public to the extent of the notary's authorization under special laws."*

(2) **Arbitrators are not obliged to give instructions to a party in terms of Section 118a of the CCP if the established facts of the case do not permit a positive decision regarding the party's request for arbitration (statement of claim). The duty to give instructions only applies if there is a risk that the party will fail to state the relevant facts or meet the burden of proof.**

[*From Facts of Case*]:

16.231. On December 9, 2011, an arbitrator rendered an arbitral award in arbitration at the AC, Case No. Rsp 1408/08, whereby the arbitrator dismissed the claim for compensation for damage/losses made by claimant X[993] against respondent Y[994].

[*Procedure of Case*]:

16.232. Afterwards, on November 13, 2009, the claimant lodged a motion with the Prague Municipal Court to annul the arbitral award on the grounds specified in Section 31(b) and (e) of the ArbAct; the Prague Municipal Court granted the claimant's motion by its judgment of May 24, 2011.

16.233. The respondent contested the decision of the court of first instance by its appeal to the Prague High Court, which reversed the judgment of the court of first instance on November 23, 2012; the motion to annul the arbitral award was dismissed. The appellate court first examined whether the claimant had been provided with a sufficient opportunity to exercise their procedural rights, and whether or not the equality of the claimant and the respondent had been disturbed.

16.234. In the arbitral proceedings, the claimant claimed compensation for damage/losses that the claimant had allegedly sustained as a result of a breach of obligations by the respondent. The arbitral tribunal made a decision regarding the claim – the tribunal held that the claim did not exist, because, in the opinion of the arbitral tribunal, some of the prerequisites of the respondent's liability for damage/losses had not been fulfilled. The appellate court held that it was not necessary to give instructions pursuant to Section 118a of the CCP.

[*Arguments Presented by SC*]:

16.235. The SC limited its reasoning to the issue of whether the conditions were met for the annulment of the arbitral award under Section 31(e)

---

[993] Legal entity formed and existing under the laws of the Czech Republic in the form of a limited liability company. This party was the claimant both in the arbitral proceedings and in the judicial proceedings for the annulment of the arbitral award.

[994] Legal entity formed and existing under the laws of the Czech Republic in the form of a joint stock company. This party was the respondent both in the arbitral proceedings and in the judicial proceedings for the annulment of the arbitral award.

of the ArbAct, i.e. whether the party was provided with the opportunity to state (plead) their case before the arbitrators. Consistent case law[995] shows that a breach of Section 18 of the ArbAct constitutes grounds for the annulment of the arbitral award under Section 31(e) of the ArbAct.

16.236. The SC held that the court must always examine in such case whether the party was, in the particular case, provided with the opportunity to state (plead) their case before the arbitrators, and whether or not the equality between the parties was disturbed. Indeed, this principle is, according to the ConCourt,[996] one of the fundamental principles governing arbitration. The ECtHR adopted a similar approach to the principle of equality; the ECtHR uses the term *equality of arms,* and requires that each party to the proceedings be afforded a reasonable opportunity to present their case under conditions that do not place them at a substantial disadvantage vis-à-vis the opposing party.[997]

16.237. The SC ruled that this conclusion could be extended to arbitration, because Section 30 of the ArbAct stipulates that the CCP shall reasonably apply to arbitration. The equality of the parties is realized in the CCP primarily in the requirement of predictable judicial decisions, which objective is facilitated by the duty to give instructions under Section 118a of the CCP. The ArbAct does not contain rules regulating the duty to give instructions; hence, Section 118a of the CCP shall also apply in arbitration,[998] but with due regard for the object of the ArbAct.

16.238. The appellant (in the SC proceedings) argued that the appellate court had wrongly interpreted Section 118a of the CCP. Nonetheless, the SC held that the arbitrators had no reason to proceed pursuant to Section 118a of the CCP. The purpose of instructions pursuant to the said provision is to allow the parties to state the relevant facts (meet the obligation to state the relevant facts) and identify evidence capable of proving their statements (meet the burden of proof). The purpose is to prevent the possibility that the party only finds out from a decision of the court that is adverse to the party that the party did not meet the burden of proof or the duty to state the relevant facts.

---

[995] See (i) Judgment of the SC of June 11, 2008 in Case No. 32 Cdo 1201/2007; and (ii) Judgment of the SC of May 26, 2010 in Case No. 23 Cdo 3749/2008.

[996] Judgment of the ConCourt of November 13, 2003 in Case No. III. ÚS 202/03.

[997] See (i) Judgment of the ECtHR, Application No. 14448/88, of October 27, 1993 (*Dombo Beheer B. V.* v. *The Netherlands*); (ii) Judgment of the ECtHR, Application No. 17748/91, of October 23, 1996 (*Ankerl* v. *Switzerland*); and (iii) Judgment of the ECtHR, Application No. 53364/07, of June 18, 2013 (*Komanický* v. *Slovakia*).

[998] See Judgment of the ConCourt of March 8, 2011 in Case No. I. ÚS 3227/07.

16.239. In this case, however, the request for arbitration (statement of claim) was dismissed by the arbitrators, because the established facts of the case did not allow any other option. This does not involve the failure to meet the burden of proof, and consequently, the procedure pursuant to Section 118a of the CCP is not applicable.[999] Section 118a(1) of the CCP shall apply if the proposed evidence does not suffice to prove the facts of the case. Section 118a(2) of the CCP covers those situations in which the court arrives at a legal assessment of the case different from the assessment made by the party, which therefore requires the examination of additional evidence.[1000]

16.240. The Supreme Court of the Czech Republic (SC) also pointed out that, according to the Court's consistent case law, a decision is considered surprising and unpredictable if, viewed from the perspective of the preceding procedure, the decision involves a surprising resolution of the case, and the adoption of the decision deprives a party of the possibility to make statements of fact and law.[1001]

16.241. However, this was not the case here, because the reasons justifying the arbitrators' conclusions do not refer to a failure to meet the duty to state the relevant facts or the burden of proof. Hence, the grounds for the annulment of the arbitral award under Section 31(e) of the ArbAct are not fulfilled.

[**Further Conclusions**]:

16.242. The SC did not specify which version of the ArbAct was applicable to the decision. However, the relevant provisions have not changed, and the issue is therefore moot with respect to the outcome of the dispute.

16.243. This decision complies with the consistent case law and defines in greater detail the unique feature of Czech arbitration, namely the duty of arbitrators to give instructions. Nonetheless, the claimant disagreed with the decision of the SC and therefore lodged a constitutional complaint on August 12, 2014, entered under Reg. No. I. ÚS 2686/2014; the constitutional complaint has not yet been resolved.

| | |

---

[999] See also (i) Resolution of the SC of June 27, 2003 in Case No. 21 Cdo 121/2003; and (ii) Resolution of the SC of May 25, 2006 in Case No. 22 Cdo 2335/2005.

[1000] See also Judgment of the SC of March 15, 2007 in Case No. 21 Cdo 194/2006.

[1001] See also (i) Judgment of the ConCourt of June 12, 2001 in Case No. III. ÚS 729/2000; (ii) Judgment of the ConCourt of June 11, 2007 in Case No. IV. ÚS 321/2007; (iii) Judgment of the SC of September 4, 2007 in Case No. 22 Cdo 2125/2006; and (iv) Judgment of the SC of March 18, 2010 in Case No. 32 Cdo 1019/2009.

21. Resolution of Supreme Court CR of April 29, 2014 in Case No. 23 Cdo 3697/2013: Appointment of Arbitrator/Shareholder and Executive Officer of Private Company Organizing Arbitration Acts as Arbitrator in Particular Dispute

Abbreviations Used:

ArbAct	Act of the Czech Republic No. 216/1994 Coll., on Arbitration and the Enforcement of Arbitral Awards, as amended[1002]
CBA	Czech Bar Association
CCP	Act of the Czech Republic No. 99/1963 Coll., the Code of Civil Procedure, as amended
CivC	Act of the Czech Republic No. 40/1964 Coll., the Civil Code, as amended[1003]
Company	Czech legal entity formed as a limited liability company
SC	Supreme Court of the Czech Republic

Key Words:

ad hoc arbitration | annulment (setting aside) of arbitral award | appointing authority | appointment of arbitrator | Arbitration Rules | attorney | bias | disqualified arbitrator | equality of the parties | evasion of the law | executive body (officer) | fair trial | hearing | impartial process | impartiality | improper procedure of the arbitrator | list of arbitrators | permanent arbitral institution | refusal to interrogate |

[1002] This particular decision of the SC is based on the version of the ArbAct effective until March 31, 2012; no subsequent changes have any bearing on the conclusions of the SC and their applicability.

The SC did not specify which version of the ArbAct is applicable to the decision, but the relevant provisions have not changed and the issue is therefore moot with respect to the outcome of the dispute. Moreover, Article II(1) of Act No. 19/2012 Coll., which amended the Arbitration Act with effect from April 1, 2012, indicates that the applicable version is the law effective until March 31, 2012.

[1003] This Act has been replaced by Act No. 89/2012 Coll., the "new Civil Code" ("CC"), with effect since January 1, 2014. However, legal relationships established before January 1, 2014 shall be governed (save for certain exceptions) by the previous law, i.e. Act No. 40/1964 Coll., the Civil Code, as amended (abbreviated as the "CivC" in this annotation).

transparency | validity of an arbitration agreement[1004] *| validity of an arbitration clause*[1005] *| will of the parties | witness interrogation |*

Applicable Laws and Regulations:
ArbAct: Section 19(3),[1006] Section 30,[1007] Section 31(b) and (e)[1008]
CivC: Section 39[1009]

[1004] Depending on the context, "arbitration clause" and "arbitration agreement" may also be interpreted as synonyms, or rather the arbitration clause is a form of arbitration agreement according to Section 2 of the ArbAct.

[1005] Depending on the context, "arbitration clause" and "arbitration agreement" may also be interpreted as synonyms, or rather the arbitration clause is a form of arbitration agreement according to Section 2 of the ArbAct.

[1006] ArbAct, Section 19 (cit.): *"(1) The parties are free to agree on the procedure to be followed by the arbitrators in conducting the proceedings. Matters regarding the conduct of the proceedings may be resolved by the chairman of the panel providing he or she was authorized to do so by the parties or by all arbitrators. (2) In the absence of an agreement pursuant to subsection (1) or in the absence of a determination of the procedure pursuant to subsection (4), the arbitrators shall conduct the proceedings in such manner as they consider appropriate. They conduct the arbitral proceedings in such manner that the facts of the case necessary for the resolution of the dispute are sufficiently ascertained, without any unnecessary formalities and while giving all parties equal opportunity to plead their case. (3) Unless the parties agree otherwise, the arbitral proceedings shall be oral. The proceedings are always conducted with the exclusion of the public. (4) The parties may also determine the procedure to be followed in the rules on arbitration, providing the rules are enclosed with the arbitration agreement. This provision shall not prejudice the application of rules adopted by a permanent arbitral institution."*

[1007] ArbAct, Section 30 (cit.) *"Application of the Code of Civil Procedure: "Unless the Act stipulates otherwise, the arbitral proceedings shall be reasonably governed by the provisions of the Code of Civil Procedure."*

[1008] ArbAct, Section 31 (cit.): *"At the request of any party the court annuls the arbitral award if: (a) it was made in a case which cannot be submitted to arbitration (cannot be the subject of a valid arbitration agreement), (b) the arbitration agreement is invalid for other reasons or the agreement was cancelled or it does not apply to the agreed case, (c) the arbitrator(s) who took part in the proceedings was/were not authorized to make decisions in the case, whether under the arbitration agreement or otherwise, or lacked the capacity to act as arbitrator(s), (d) the arbitral award was not adopted by the majority of the arbitrators, (e) a party was denied the opportunity to plead his or her case in the arbitral proceedings, (f) the arbitral award orders a party to provide performance which was not requested by the obligee or to provide performance which is impossible or illegal under domestic law, (g) it transpires that there are reasons which would otherwise justify the reopening of civil proceedings in court."*

[1009] CivC, Section 39 (cit.): *"A juridical act is invalid if the content or the purpose thereof violates or evades the law or is contra bonos mores."*

The Supreme Court of the Czech Republic reached the following principal conclusions:

(1) **An arbitration clause is admissible if it stipulates that the arbitrator shall be appointed from the list of attorneys administered by the Czech Bar Association (CBA) by the Executive Officer of a private corporation that organizes arbitration.**[1010]

(2) **If the Executive Officer of a private arbitral company appoints as arbitrator the other Executive Officer of the company, the arbitrator cannot be deemed impartial (unbiased) and the arbitration clause is therefore contrary to the law and invalid under Section 39 of the CivC.**

[From Facts of Case]:

16.244. On December 2, 2009, the parties to the dispute entered into a written contract, which also included an agreement according to which any potential disputes were to be resolved by a single arbitrator appointed by the executive body (officer) of the Company from the list of attorneys administered by the CBA. XX[1011] and YY[1012] are shareholders of the company; they were also Executive Officers of the Company from September 3, 2003 to September 6, 2011. A request for arbitration was lodged with the Company.[1013] YY, as the executive body (officer) of the Company, then appointed Mr XX as arbitrator, i.e. the other shareholder of the Company entered on the list of attorneys administered by the CBA. XX accepted his appointment and

---

[1010] Such companies must be strictly differentiated from "permanent arbitral institutions", which also have the status of private-law entities, but the basic legal framework regulating their formation is contained in Section 15 of the ArbAct. Czech law, similarly to the legal systems of some other countries of Central and Eastern Europe, distinguishes between arbitration conducted by permanent arbitral institutions and arbitration conducted by *ad hoc* arbitrators. There are three permanent arbitral institutions in the Czech Republic, namely: (i) Arbitration Court at the Economic Chamber of the Czech Republic and Agricultural Chamber of the Czech Republic, (ii) Arbitration Court of the Czech Moravian Commodity Exchange, and (iii) Exchange Court of Arbitration at the Prague Stock Exchange. *Ad hoc* arbitration means any arbitration conducted outside the jurisdiction of an entity that meets the requirements of a permanent arbitral institution under Section 15 of the ArbAct. The proceedings in the case analyzed in the annotated court decision were *ad hoc* arbitral proceedings, because the "Company" was not a permanent arbitral institution.

[1011] Natural person.

[1012] Natural person.

[1013] Legal entity formed and existing under the laws of the Czech Republic in the form of a limited liability company.

subsequently rendered an arbitral award in the case on January 21, 2011, and an additional arbitral award on February 15, 2011.

16.245. In its first reply to the request for arbitration, the respondent pleaded the invalidity of the agreed arbitration clause; the respondent also pleaded bias on the part of the appointed arbitrator. The claimant, inter alia, proposed to hear (interrogate) a witness, but the proposal for evidence was not accepted by the arbitrator, who argued that the evidence was unnecessary.

[*Procedure of Case*]:

16.246. The claimant (respondent in the arbitral proceedings) then lodged a motion to annul the arbitral award with the Ostrava Regional Court; the motion lodged by the claimant (respondent in the arbitral proceedings) was granted by the court's judgment of June 12, 2012. The court of first instance invoked the case law of the SC,[1014] and did not find the arbitration clause invalid in terms of Section 31(b) of the ArbAct[1015] (as one of the grounds for the annulment of the arbitral award). Nevertheless, the court held the clause invalid under Section 31(e) of the ArbAct[1016] (the party did not have an opportunity to state their case). The court pointed out that the claimant had proposed to hear a witness, who was to provide testimony regarding the quality of the supplied goods. But the arbitrator did not hear the witness, arguing that the documentary evidence suffices for the decision, and that the witness testimony could not change anything. However, the court of first instance concluded that such an indiscriminate refusal had been insufficient and the position of the claimant (respondent in the arbitral proceedings) had not been equal to the position of the respondent (absence of equality of the parties), because the claimant had been prevented from efficiently protecting its rights. Referring to the case law of the SC,[1017] the court of first instance thus concluded that the claimant had not had the opportunity to state their case before the arbitrator, and annulled both arbitral awards.

16.247. In its decision, the court of first instance did not have regard to the plea raised by the claimant concerning the arbitrator's bias; the court argued

---

[1014] Resolution of the Grand Panel of the Civil and Commercial Division of the SC of May 11, 2011 in Case No. 31 Cdo 1945/2010, which is available on the SC website (www.nsoud.cz), and which was also published in Sbírka soudních rozhodnutí a stanovisek [Reports of Court Decisions and Opinions] under No. 121/2011.

[1015] The provision is quoted above in the opening part of this annotation.

[1016] The provision is quoted above in the opening part of this annotation.

[1017] Decision of the SC, Case No. 23 Cdo 2273/2007 of 27 May 2009, which is available at the SC website (www.nsoud.cz).

that the claimant should have lodged a motion to disqualify the appointed arbitrator. But the claimant had failed to do so, and consequently, she could not request the annulment of the arbitral award on the said grounds.

16.248. The Olomouc High Court , as the appellate court, was seized with the appeal lodged by the respondent (claimant in the arbitral proceedings) and dismissed the motion to annul both arbitral awards. The appellate court agreed with the court of first instance with respect to the conclusions concerning the grounds for annulment under Section 31(b) of the ArbAct,[1018] and with respect to the objection regarding the arbitrator's bias. But the appellate court arrived at a different conclusion as concerns the fulfillment of the grounds for the annulment of the arbitral award pursuant to Section 31(e) of the ArbAct. The appellate court held that the claimant had failed to challenge the improper procedure adopted by the arbitrator; conversely, the appellate court concluded, with respect to the reasonable application of the CCP in terms of Section 30 of the ArbAct,[1019] that if the parties had agreed that the dispute would be resolved without a hearing, the parties had agreed to waive the requirement of an oral hearing in terms of Section 19(3) of the CCP.[1020] The appellate court therefore held that the procedure adopted by the arbitrator complied with the agreement of the parties.

16.249. The claimant (respondent in the arbitral proceedings) challenged the decision of the appellate court and lodged an extraordinary appeal, arguing that if the Company performs activities that the law reserves for a permanent arbitral institution, i.e. appoints arbitrators, administers a list of arbitrators, issues Arbitration Rules, all of which on a long-term basis, the Company (in the claimant's opinion) manifestly evades the law (evades the ArbAct).

[*Arguments Presented by SC*]:

16.250. The SC first invoked its prior rulings,[1021] whereby the SC unified the case law concerning annulment of arbitral awards. The decision of the SC that the Court invoked[1022] stipulates that there are grounds for the invalidity of an arbitration agreement under Section 39 of the CivC if the arbitration agreement lacks any direct method of appointing an *ad hoc* arbitrator (or identification of a particular arbitrator, i.e. a

---

[1018] The provision is quoted above in the opening part of this annotation.

[1019] The provision is quoted above in the opening part of this annotation.

[1020] The provision is quoted above in the opening part of this annotation.

[1021] Decision of the SC of May 11, 2011 in Case No. 31 Cdo 1945/2010.

[1022] Decision of the SC of May 11, 2011 in Case No. 31 Cdo 1945/2010.

particular natural person as an arbitrator), but refers to *"Arbitration Rules"* issued by a legal person other than a permanent arbitral institution.

16.251. The SC also emphasized that the fundamental prerequisite for the validity of an arbitration clause is the determination of transparent and unambiguous rules for the appointment of a particular arbitrator who will make decisions in the arbitral proceedings; the reason is that an arbitrator who guarantees an impartial and fair process is a fundamental prerequisite for the due conduct of the arbitral proceedings.

16.252. The SC therefore concluded that arbitration clauses are especially questionable if they refer to other documents that are not part of the arbitration clause, and the text of which may change, independent of the parties' will. The method of appointing the arbitrator was in this case directly incorporated in the arbitration clause, without any reference to an external document, but the person appointed as arbitrator was a shareholder of the Company, i.e. not an attorney chosen at random from the list of attorneys administered by the CBA. Hence, the arbitrator cannot be considered impartial, and the arbitration clause is *contrary to Section 39 of the CivC* and is therefore invalid.[1023]

[*Further Conclusions and Comments Concerning Annotated Resolution of SC*]:

16.253. The words *"contrary to Section 39 of the CivC"* chosen by the SC are not very fitting.[1024] The Supreme Court CR (SC) was probably referring to the clause being contrary to the ArbAct, namely Section 8(1) of the ArbAct, which concerns potential bias on the part of the arbitrators, which renders the arbitration clause contrary to law, i.e. invalid in terms of Section 39 of the CivC.[1025] We may agree with the SC that impartiality and independence are fundamental prerequisites of arbitration. This is, indeed, emphasized in Section 1(a) of the ArbAct.[1026] If a shareholder of a corporation that specializes in organizing arbitration appoints the other shareholder of the same

---

[1023] The provision is quoted above in the opening part of this annotation.

[1024] The provision is quoted above in the opening part of this annotation.

[1025] The provision is quoted above in the opening part of this annotation.

[1026] ArbAct, Section 1 (cit.): *"This Act sets forth rules regulating (a) resolution of property disputes by independent and impartial arbitrators, (b) resolution by arbitral commissions of associations under the Civil Code of contested matters which fall within the self-government of associations, and c) enforcement of arbitral awards."*

corporation as arbitrator, it is legitimate to question the arbitrator's independence.

16.254. But the author of this annotation must voice certain doubts regarding the conclusion that the appointment of an *"inappropriate"* arbitrator should render the arbitration clause invalid. If the person appointed as arbitrator were a different attorney from the list administered by the CBA who had no relation to the case, to the parties or to the *appointing authority* (in theory, all other attorneys entered on the list of attorneys administered by the CBA, i.e. approx. 13,000 individuals at the moment), the conclusion regarding the invalidity of the arbitration clause would be groundless. The reason is that the arbitration clause entered into between the parties in this particular case provided for a method of appointing arbitrators that was, and continues to be, in compliance with the SC case law. The decision of the SC regarding the invalidity of the arbitration clause is therefore somewhat surprising. The author of this annotation would instead expect the annulment of the arbitral award pursuant to Section 31(c) of the ArbAct,[1027] i.e. because the arbitrator who made decisions in the arbitral proceedings was biased and therefore disqualified from making decisions in the said case. The reasoning of the annotated decision does not clearly indicate whether the claimant had invoked those grounds for the annulment of the arbitral award.

16.255. The question is, naturally, whether such enhanced protection ought to apply to both professionals and consumers, or whether, conversely, protection covering only consumers would suffice. The fact is that a professional should be able to assess for themselves whether an arbitration clause is advantageous for them if it does not identify the arbitrator and does not stipulate any method of their selection, but merely refers to Arbitration Rules, which can be changed at any time, irrespective of the parties' will. Nonetheless, the point is now moot, because the case law of the SC clearly determines that no entities other than permanent arbitral institutions established by law (statute) or on the basis of law (statute) have the right to issue Rules (Arbitration Rules).[1028]

| | |

[1027] The provision is quoted above in the opening part of this annotation.
[1028] See Section 13 of the ArbAct.

Czech (& Central European) Yearbook of Arbitration

22. Resolution of Supreme Court CR of 25 June 2014 in Case No. 23 Cdo 2247/2012: (i) Opportunity to State (Plead) One's Case before Arbitrators; (ii) Equality of Parties[1029]

Abbreviations Used:

AC	Arbitration Court at the Economic Chamber of the Czech Republic and Agricultural Chamber of the Czech Republic[1030]
ArbAct	Act of the Czech Republic No. 216/1994 Coll., on Arbitration and the Enforcement of Arbitral Awards, as amended[1031]
CCP	Act of the Czech Republic No. 99/1963 Coll., the Code of Civil Procedure, as amended
ConCourt	Constitutional Court of the Czech Republic
SC	Supreme Court of the Czech Republic

Key Words:
annulment (setting aside) of arbitral award | equality | interpreter | invalidity of arbitration agreement | language of proceedings | native language | property dispute | settlement |

Applicable Laws and Regulations:
ArbAct: Section 18,[1032] Section 30,[1033] Section 31(a), (b), (e), (f), (g)[1034]

[1029] The decision is available on the SC website at http://www.nsoud.cz/Judikatura/judikatura_ns.nsf/WebSearch/6A5EA0C197FE4DB2C1257D3300345E95?openDocument&Highlight=0,rozhod%C4%8D%C3%AD,%C5%99%C3%ADzen%C3%AD [last accessed on August 28, 2014].

[1030] Detailed information regarding this permanent arbitral institution is available at www.soud.cz in multiple language versions.

[1031] This particular decision of the SC is based on the version of the ArbAct in effect until March 31, 2012; no subsequent changes have any bearing on the conclusions of the SC and their applicability in this particular case.

[1032] ArbAct, Section 18 (cit.): "*The parties have an equal standing in the arbitral proceedings and must be provided with a full opportunity to assert their rights.*"

[1033] ArbAct, Section 30 (cit.): "*Unless the Act stipulates otherwise, the arbitral proceedings shall be reasonably governed by the provisions of the Code of Civil Procedure.*"

[1034] ArbAct, Section 31 (cit.): *At the request of any party the court annuls the arbitral award if: (a) it was made in a case which cannot be submitted to arbitration (cannot be the subject of a valid arbitration agreement), (b) the arbitration agreement is invalid for other reasons or the agreement was cancelled or it does not apply to the agreed case, (c) the*

The Supreme Court of the Czech Republic reached the following principal conclusions:

(1) **The ground for the annulment of an arbitral award by court pursuant to Section 31(e) of the ArbAct is targeted primarily at protecting the observance of the fundamental procedural rights and obligations of the parties to arbitration with respect to the principle of the equality of the parties to the proceedings expressed in Section 18 of the ArbAct.**

(2) **The parties must be provided with a full opportunity to assert their rights; all objections targeted at the annulment of an arbitral award pursuant to Section 31(e) of the ArbAct must, by necessity, be procedural objections.**

[From Facts of Case]:

16.256. On August 20, 2007, the respondent[1035] and the legal predecessor of the claimant[1036] entered into a purchase contract. On November 20, 2007, the parties entered into an amendment to the purchase contract, which contained an arbitration clause, in which the parties agreed that all disputes arising from and in connection with the contract will be resolved at the AC, according to the Rules of the AC and by three arbitrators. In compliance with the agreement, the respondent lodged a request for arbitration with the AC, which resolved the case by an arbitral award on November 7, 2008; the claimant was ordered to pay the stipulated amount to the respondent.

[Procedure Case]:

16.257. The claimant lodged a motion to annul the arbitral award in terms of Section 31(a), (b), (e), (f) and (g) of the ArbAct with the Ostrava Regional Court. The court of first instance dismissed the motion to annul the

---

arbitrator(s) who took part in the proceedings was/were not authorized to make decisions in the case, whether under the arbitration agreement or otherwise, or lacked the capacity to act as arbitrator(s), (d) the arbitral award was not adopted by the majority of the arbitrators, (e) a party was denied the opportunity to plead his or her case in the arbitral proceedings, (f) the arbitral award orders a party to provide performance which was not requested by the obligee or to provide performance which is impossible or illegal under domestic law, (g) it transpires that there are reasons which would otherwise justify the reopening of civil proceedings in court. Note: Section 31 of the ArbAct has been amended with effect since April 1, 2012. However, the amendment is of no importance with respect to the issues analyzed in this case.

[1035] Legal entity formed and existing under the laws of the Czech Republic in the form of a limited liability company. This party was the claimant in the proceedings for the annulment of the arbitral award.

[1036] Legal entity formed and existing under the laws of the Czech Republic in the form of a limited liability company. This party was the respondent in the proceedings for the annulment of the arbitral award.

arbitral award. The court of first instance held that Section 31(a) of the ArbAct did not apply, because the case was a property dispute and was arbitrable (could be the subject of a valid arbitration agreement).[1037]

16.258. As concerns Section 31(b) of the ArbAct, the court of first instance held that the claimant had failed to prove its allegation that the arbitration clause had been antedated and therefore invalid, and failed to present any evidence that would refute the credibility of the other party's statement and the statements provided by witnesses.

16.259. The court further held that the ground for annulment in terms of Section 31(e) of the ArbAct did not apply either, because the claimant had been afforded the opportunity to answer the request for arbitration, and to offer evidence of the claimant in light of the proposed evidence, while the contents of the dossier did not indicate that the arbitral tribunal had violated the principle of the equal treatment of the parties to arbitration.

16.260. The court also dismissed the claimant's arguments concerning the alleged grounds for annulment in terms of Section 31(f) of the ArbAct; the claimant was obliged to make a cash payment in Czech currency, which is undoubtedly permitted, and the performance therefore did not constitute impossible performance.

16.261. The court also stated that the conditions for annulment in terms of Section 31(g) of the ArbAct were not met either.

16.262. The claimant appealed the decision of the court of first instance to the Olomouc High Court; the latter agreed with the conclusions reached by the court of first instance and upheld its decision.

16.263. The claimant lodged an extraordinary appeal against the decision of the appellate court; the claimant argued that it had been deprived of the opportunity to plead its case in its native language (issue of the language of the proceedings), that the appellate court had failed to examine the proposed evidence, and that the arbitral tribunal had refused to examine the proposed evidence, whereby the claimant had been de facto deprived of the possibility of equal standing and the opportunity to exercise its rights.

[*Arguments Presented by SC*]:

16.264. The Supreme Court of the Czech Republic (SC) held that specific objections do not render the extraordinary appeal admissible, but considered the objections as contesting the conclusion that the ground for the annulment of the arbitral award in terms of Section 31(e) of the ArbAct had not been fulfilled.

[1037] It has to be clarified that the ArbAct requires that the dispute be a property dispute and the case – if it submitted to litigation – must be capable of being settled.

16.265. The Supreme Court first invoked its prior case law[1038] and held that the ground for the annulment of an arbitral award by court pursuant to Section 31(e) of the ArbAct is targeted primarily at protecting the observance of the fundamental procedural rights and obligations of the parties to arbitration with respect to the principle of the equality of the parties to the proceedings expressed in Section 18 of the ArbAct. The parties must be provided with a full opportunity to assert their rights. All objections targeted at the annulment of an arbitral award pursuant to Section 31(e) of the ArbAct must, by necessity, be procedural objections; in other words, they must concern the procedure adopted by the arbitral tribunal in the hearing of the dispute, not the correctness of the factual or legal findings made by the arbitral tribunal. When addressing the issue of whether the party to arbitration was, in the particular case, provided with the opportunity to state (plead) their case before the arbitrators, the court must ascertain whether the party to the arbitral proceedings was, considering all circumstances of the case, provided with a sufficient opportunity to exercise their procedural rights in the arbitral proceedings, and whether or not the procedure adopted by the arbitral tribunal disturbed the equality between the parties.

16.266. The Arbitration Act does not elaborate on the principle of equality of the parties by stipulating any specific rights and obligations of the parties, and its fulfillment requires, pursuant to Section 30 of the ArbAct, the reasonable application of the relevant provisions of the Code of Civil Procedure – in this connection, the SC also invoked the Judgment of the ConCourt,[1039] in which the ConCourt held that one of the fundamental principles governing court proceedings is the principle of the equality of the parties, which requires that the participants (parties) to the proceedings must be on par before the court, without one or the other party enjoying any procedural benefits or being discriminated against. In order to implement this principle, the court is obliged to provide both parties to the dispute with the same possibility to assert their rights.

[1038] See:
- Judgment of the SC of April 25, 2007 in Case No. 32 Odo 1528/2005;
- Judgment of the SC of June 11, 2008 in Case No. 32 Cdo 1201/2007;
- Judgment of the SC of May 28, 2009 in Case No. 23 Cdo 2570/2007;
- Judgment of the SC of January 25, 2012 in Case No. 23 Cdo 4386/2011;
- Judgment of the SC of May 28, 2013 in Case No. 33 Cdo 153/2013; and
- Resolution of the SC of April 28, 2011 in Case No. 32 Cdo 3299/2009.

[1039] Judgment of the ConCourt of November 13, 2003 in Case No. III. ÚS 202/03.

16.267. As the SC established, the findings of fact indicated that the claimant had been provided with the opportunity to answer the request for arbitration, had had the opportunity to offer evidence in light of the proposed evidence, and the arbitral tribunal had supplied reasons for its decision not to examine the proposed evidence. The SC therefore held that the conclusions of the lower courts comply with the SC case law. Moreover, the findings of fact did not indicate that the appellant needed an interpreter.

16.268. The SC therefore ruled that the appellant (claimant) had not presented any issue of fundamental legal significance, and dismissed the extraordinary appeal.

[Further Conclusions and Comments Concerning Annotated Resolution of SC]:

16.269. The decision of the SC can be deemed to be in compliance with the current case law.

|||

23. Resolution of Supreme Court of Czech Republic of June 26, 2014 in Case No. 23 Cdo 657/2014: (i) Equal Standing of Parties, (ii) Surprising Decision of Arbitrator[1040]

Abbreviations Used:

ArbAct	Act of the Czech Republic No. 216/1994 Coll., on Arbitration and the Enforcement of Arbitral Awards, as amended[1041]
CCP	Act of the Czech Republic No. 99/1963 Coll., the Code of Civil Procedure, as amended
ConCourt	Constitutional Court of the Czech Republic
SC	Supreme Court of the Czech Republic

[1040] The SC decision is available on the SC website at:http://www.nsoud.cz/Judikatura/judikatura_ns.nsf/WebSearch/621F85ED8231E493C1257D15004B5015?openDocument&Highlight=0,rozhod%C4%8D%C3%AD,%C5%99%C3%ADzen%C3%AD [last accessed on August 28, 2014].

[1041] This particular decision of the SC is based on the version of the ArbAct in effect until March 31, 2012; no subsequent changes have any bearing on the conclusions of the SC and their applicability in this particular case.

Key Words:

annulment (setting aside) of arbitral award | arbitral award without reasons | equality of parties | evidence/proof | expert appraisal | grounds for annulment of arbitral award | reasons/reasoning | supplementing grounds for annulment | surprising decision | time period for lodging motion to annul |

Applicable Laws and Regulations:

ArbAct: Section 18,[1042] Section 31(e) and (g)[1043]

The Supreme Court of the Czech Republic reached the following principal conclusions:

(1) The procedure adopted by the arbitrator does not comply with the requirement of the equal standing of the parties enshrined in the binding provision of Section 18 of the Arbitration Act if the party only learned from the reasoning for the arbitral award that the arbitrator had not examined the evidence proposed by the party, whereby the party to the arbitration was taken by surprise and materially deprived of the opportunity to submit evidence to prove the party's statements.

[From Facts of Case]:

16.270. The claimant[1044] lodged a request for arbitration demanding the payment of CZK 516,776 against the respondent.[1045] The respondent answered the request for arbitration. In answer, the party proposed, inter

---

[1042] ArbAct, Section 18 (cit.): *"The parties have an equal standing in the arbitral proceedings and must be provided with a full opportunity to assert their rights."*

[1043] ArbAct, Section 31 (cit.): *"At the request of any party the court annuls the arbitral award if: (a) it was made in a case which cannot be submitted to arbitration (cannot be the subject of a valid arbitration agreement), (b) the arbitration agreement is invalid for other reasons or the agreement was cancelled or it does not apply to the agreed case, (c) the arbitrator(s) who took part in the proceedings was/were not authorized to make decisions in the case, whether under the arbitration agreement or otherwise, or lacked the capacity to act as arbitrator(s), (d) the arbitral award was not adopted by the majority of the arbitrators, (e) a party was denied the opportunity to plead his or her case in the arbitral proceedings, (f) the arbitral award orders a party to provide performance which was not requested by the obligee or to provide performance which is impossible or illegal under domestic law, (g) it transpires that there are reasons which would otherwise justify the reopening of civil proceedings in court."*

[1044] Legal entity formed and existing under the laws of the Czech Republic in the form of a joint stock company. This party was the respondent in the court proceedings for the annulment of the arbitral award.

[1045] Legal entity formed and existing under the laws of the Czech Republic in the form of a joint stock company. This party was the claimant in the proceedings for the annulment of the arbitral award.

alia, that an expert appraisal be prepared as evidence in the case, which would analyze the issue of the potential defects of the machinery. The arbitrator sent the answer to the claimant with an instruction that if the claimant considers it appropriate, the claimant may lodge a reply. The claimant sent a reply to the respondent's answer in that dispute; the reply did not contain any new facts or any proposals for the examination of new or further evidence. The reply was not forwarded to the claimant. Afterwards, the arbitrator, XY,[1046] rendered an arbitral award on April 14, 2007 granting the claimant's claim (request for arbitration).

16.271. The parties agreed in the given case that the arbitral award would not contain any reasons. The arbitrator nonetheless provided reasons for their arbitral award.[1047] The arbitrator addressed all pieces of evidence proposed by the claimant in the dispute. The arbitrator described in the reasoning for the award which evidence was examined; the arbitrator also explained why any particular piece of evidence was not examined. As concerns the proposed expert appraisal, the arbitrator stated that the claimant had had the possibility to submit the appraisal. But the claimant only learned from the reasoning for the arbitral award that the claimant itself should have procured the expert appraisal and submitted it in the arbitration.

[*Procedure of Case*]:

16.272. The claimant lodged a motion to annul the arbitral award in terms of Section 31(e) and (g) of the ArbAct with the Prague Municipal Court. This was the second occasion on which the Prague Municipal Court was called upon to resolve the case – its first decision dismissed the motion to annul, which was upheld by the Prague High Court, as the appellate court. But the claimant[1048] challenged the decision of the appellate court by means of an extraordinary appeal. The previous decision[1049] of the Supreme Court of the Czech Republic (SC) vacated both decisions of the lower courts and remanded the case to the court

---

[1046] The arbitrator rendered its decision as an *ad hoc* arbitrator, i.e. an arbitrator outside the jurisdiction of any permanent arbitral institution established in terms of Section 15 of the ArbAct.

[1047] The practice has validated the opinion that the arbitrator is entitled, at their discretion, to provide reasons for their arbitral award even if the parties agreed that the arbitral award need not contain any reasons.

[1048] The party is now being referred to as the claimant, whereas they were the respondent in the arbitration summarized above.

[1049] Namely, Judgment of the SC of December 18, 2012 in Case No. 32 Cdo 4968/2010, available on the SC website at:http://www.nsoud.cz/Judikatura/judikatura_ns.nsf/WebSearch/3690ED301945F0A9C1257AED00384400?openDocument&Highlight=0,pdi,a. s. [last access 15 November 2014].

of first instance, with a binding legal opinion that the claimant had not been provided in the arbitral proceedings with a full opportunity to assert their procedural rights if the claimant had only learned from the arbitral award that the claimant's proposal for evidence in the form of the expert appraisal would not be allowed by the arbitrator.

16.273. At the following stage of the proceedings, the court of first instance refused to address the ground for the annulment of the arbitral award in terms of Section 31(g) of the ArbAct, because the claimant asserted the ground after the expiration of the deadline.

16.274. As concerns the ground for the annulment of the arbitral award in terms of Section 31(e) of the ArbAct, the court of first instance referred to the judgment of the SC,[1050] which stipulates that the opportunity to plead one's case before an arbitrator must be interpreted as meaning that the parties are provided with the opportunity to propose evidence to prove their statements, as well as the opportunity to examine the evidence. This conclusion stands, despite the fact that the claimant had voluntarily, by agreement, deprived itself of the opportunity to be informed at a hearing, if necessary, that the claimant should submit the expert appraisal that the claimant proposed.

16.275. However, the court of first instance held that the procedure adopted by the arbitrator did not comply with the requirement stipulated in Section 18 of the ArbAct if the claimant was thereby taken by surprise (surprising decision) and deprived of the opportunity to submit evidence to prove its statements. In such case, the arbitrator should have clearly indicated to the claimant that the proposal to examine the evidence (expert appraisal) would not be allowed, because the appraisal should be procured and presented in the arbitral proceedings by the claimant itself. The claimant could then properly procedurally respond to the arbitrator's standpoint.

16.276. The court of first instance therefore concluded that the arbitral award was not the outcome of proper arbitral proceedings, because the claimant had not been provided with the opportunity to plead their case; hence, the court annulled the arbitral award by the court's judgment of April 11, 2013.

16.277. The decision of the court of first instance was appealed by the respondent to the Prague High Court; the appellate court rendered its judgment on September 3, 2013, in which the court upheld the operative part of the decision made by the court of first instance, arguing that if the arbitrator had decided to reject the proposal for evidence in the form of the expert appraisal and forgo a hearing, the arbitrator should have

---

[1050] Judgment of the Supreme Court of June 11, 2008 in Case No. 32 Cdo 1201/2007.

notified the claimant of the intended procedure, so that the claimant could have responded to the arbitrator's steps before the case was terminated. The arbitrator's procedure breached the equal standing of the parties to the dispute, and the claimant was not afforded a full opportunity to exercise their rights in the arbitral proceedings.

16.278. The respondent lodged an extraordinary appeal against the judgment of the appellate court in which the respondent argued that the arbitrator had proceeded in compliance with the decision of the SC[1051] because the arbitrator had balanced the parties' rights by giving them both a time period for submitting evidence. The fact that the respective evidence was not examined was adequately justified by the arbitrator (in the opinion of the appellant/respondent[1052]).

[*Arguments Presented by SC*]:

16.279. The Supreme Court of the Czech Republic (SC) held the extraordinary appeal to be inadmissible, because the appellate court was bound by the binding legal opinion of the SC, in which the SC held that the procedure adopted by the arbitrator in the said case by no means complied with the requirement enshrined in the binding provision of Section 18 of the Arbitration Act, if the party to the arbitral proceedings was thereby taken by surprise and materially deprived of the opportunity to submit evidence to prove the party's statements. The SC held that this conclusion holds true despite the fact that the arbitrator explained why the evidence was not examined. The SC therefore dismissed the extraordinary appeal.

[*Further Conclusions and Comments Concerning Annotated Resolution of SC*]:

16.280. The decision of the SC can be deemed to be in compliance with the current case law. However, the author of this annotation must point out that the case law of the SC is more than questionable as concerns the issue of the parties' possibility to supplement grounds for the annulment of an arbitral award as late as in the course of the proceedings for the annulment of the arbitral award. The author has already explained his view in other case law annotations that he has written. Nonetheless, the author agrees with the opinion of the SC with respect to the crucial issue of the present case, namely the surprising nature of the decision in relation to the issue of the evidence in the form of the expert appraisal.

| | |

[1051] Decision of the Supreme Court of June 11, 2008 in Case No. 32 Cdo 1201/2007.

[1052] This party was the claimant in the arbitral proceedings.

24. Judgment of High Court in Prague, Case No. 104 VSPH 50/2014-62: Pleading Invalidity of Arbitration Agreement in Insolvency[1053]

Abbreviations Used:

ArbAct	Act of the Czech Republic No. 216/1994 Coll., on Arbitration and the Enforcement of Arbitral Awards, as amended
CC	Act of the Czech Republic No. 89/2012 Coll., the Civil Code, as amended
CivC	Act of the Czech Republic No. 40/1964 Coll., the Civil Code, in effect until December 31, 2013 (in connection with the recodification of civil law and with effect since January 1, 2014, the Act has been replaced by Act No. 89/2012 Coll., the Civil Code /CC/, and Act No. 90/2012 Coll., the Business Corporations Act)
ComC	Act of the Czech Republic No. 513/1991 Coll., the Commercial Code, in effect until December 31, 2013 (in connection with the recodification of civil law and with effect since January 1, 2014, the Act has been replaced by Act No. 89/2012 Coll., Civil Code /CC/, and Act No. 90/2012 Coll., the Business Corporations Act)
ConCourt	Constitutional Court of the Czech Republic
CR	Czech Republic
EU	European Union
InsAct	Act of the Czech Republic No. 182/2006 Coll., the Insolvency Act, as amended
SC	Supreme Court of the Czech Republic

Key Words:

absolute plea (objection) | abusive clause | annulment (setting aside) of arbitral award | arbitral award | arbitration agreement | arbitration clause | burden of proof | consumer | credit card | enforceability of arbitral award | enforcement of arbitral award | EU law | EU-compliant

---

[1053] An annotation of this court decision was also published in: Ladislav Derka. Vrchní soud v Praze: Rozhodčí nález vydaný na základě neplatné rozhodčí doložky [Title in translation: High Court in Prague: Arbitral Award Rendered on the Basis of an Invalid Arbitration Clause]. Právní rozhledy, Praha [Prague / Czech Republic]: C. H. Beck, 2014, Vol. 22, No. 19, pp. 680-684. This annotation is based on the unabridged text of the decision rendered by the High Court in Prague and available in the Insolvency Register.

interpretation | execution proceedings | existence of a claim | final and conclusive judicial decision | good morals (bonos mores) | horizontal effect of EU law | incidental proceedings | indirect effect of EU law | insolvency proceedings | insolvency trustee | invalidity of an arbitration agreement | invalidity of an arbitration clause | legal certainty | legal presumption | legitimate expectations | limitation of actions | limitation of actions with respect to a substantive-law claim | limitation period | motion for annulment of arbitral award | national law | null and void juridical act | principles of a state following the rule of law | relative plea (objection) | Res Judicata | review of a claim | statute-barred claim | substantive law | substantive-law claim | unfair terms | validity of an arbitration agreement | validity of an arbitration clause | vertical effect of EU law | weaker contracting party |

Laws and Regulations Applied in Decision:

InsAct: Section 199(2).[1054]
CivC: Section 39,[1055] Section 55(2),[1056] Section 56,[1057] Section 110(1).[1058]
ComC: Section 403(1).[1059]
ArbAct: Section 15,[1060] Section 16,[1061] Section 31,[1062] Section 34,[1063] Section 35.[1064]

[1054] Section 199 of the InsAct is quoted in the footnotes below.

[1055] Section 39 of the CivC is quoted in the footnotes below.

[1056] Section 55 of the CivC is quoted in the footnotes below.

[1057] Section 56 of the CivC is quoted in the footnotes below.

[1058] Section 110 of the CivC is quoted in the footnotes below.

[1059] ComC, Section 403(1) (cit.): "(1) The limitation period is suspended if the creditor commences arbitration on the basis of a valid arbitration agreement and in the manner stipulated in the arbitration agreement or in the rules governing the arbitration. (2) If the commencement of the arbitration under subsection (1) cannot be established, the arbitration is deemed commenced on the day on which the request for arbitration is delivered to the other party, namely to his or her registered office or place of business or, as applicable, his or her place of residence."

[1060] Section 15 of the ArbAct is quoted in the footnotes below.

[1061] Section 16 of the ArbAct is quoted in the footnotes below.

[1062] ArbAct, Section 31 (cit.):

• Effective until March 31, 2012: "At the request of any party the court annuls the arbitral award if: (a) it was made in a case which cannot be submitted to arbitration (cannot be the subject of a valid arbitration agreement), (b) the arbitration agreement is invalid for other reasons or the agreement was cancelled or it does not apply to the agreed case, (c) the arbitrator(s) who took part in the proceedings was/were not authorized to make decisions in the case, whether under the arbitration agreement or otherwise, or lacked the capacity to act as arbitrator(s), (d) the arbitral award was not adopted by the majority of the arbitrators, (e) a party was denied the opportunity to plead his or her case in the arbitral proceedings, (f) the arbitral award orders a party to provide performance which was not requested by the obligee or to provide performance which is impossible or illegal under domestic law, (g) it transpires that there are reasons which would otherwise justify the reopening of civil proceedings in court."

- Effective since April 1, 2012: "At the request of any party the court annuls the arbitral award if: (a) it was made in a case which cannot be submitted to arbitration (cannot be the subject of a valid arbitration agreement), (b) the arbitration agreement is invalid for other reasons or the agreement was cancelled or it does not apply to the agreed case, (c) the arbitrator(s) who took part in the proceedings was/were not authorized to make decisions in the case, whether under the arbitration agreement or otherwise, or lacked the capacity to act as arbitrator(s), (d) the arbitral award was not adopted by the majority of the arbitrators, (e) a party was denied the opportunity to plead his or her case in the arbitral proceedings, (f) the arbitral award orders a party to provide performance which was not requested by the obligee or to provide performance which is impossible or illegal under domestic law, (g) the arbitrator or the permanent arbitral institution resolved a dispute arising from a consumer contract contrary to consumer protection laws, or clearly in violation of good morals, or contrary to public policy, (h) an arbitration agreement relating to disputes arising from consumer contracts lacks the information required under Section 3(5) or such information is intentionally or to a non-negligible extent incomplete, inaccurate, or false, or (i) it transpires that there are reasons which would otherwise justify the reopening of civil proceedings in court."

[1063] Section 34 of the ArbAct is quoted in the footnotes below.

[1064] ArbAct, Section 35 (cit.):

- Effective until March 31, 2012: "(1) Even if the party against whom the enforcement of the arbitral award is sought failed to lodge a motion to annul the arbitral award by the court, the party may still request termination of the pending enforcement proceedings both on the grounds listed in special laws[5]) and if: (a) the arbitral award suffers from any of the defects listed in Section 31(a), (d), or (f), (b) the party who must have a statutory representative was not represented by such a representative in the proceedings and the party's acts were not subsequently approved, (c) the person who acted in the arbitral proceedings on behalf of the party or the party's statutory representative lacked an authorization to do so and the person's acts were not subsequently approved."

- Effective since April 1, 2012: "(1) Even if the party against whom the enforcement of the arbitral award is sought failed to lodge a motion to annul the arbitral award by the court, the party may still, irrespective of the time limit stipulated in Section 32(1), request termination of the pending enforcement proceedings both on the grounds listed in special laws[5]) and if: (a) the arbitral award suffers from any of the defects listed in Section 31(a), (d), or (f), (b) there are grounds for annulment of the arbitral award issued in a dispute arising from a consumer contract pursuant to Section 31(a) through (f), (h), or there are grounds under Section 31(g) and the arbitral award lacks the information on the right to lodge a motion to annul the arbitral award in court, (c) the party who must have a statutory representative was not represented by such a representative in the proceedings and the party's acts were not subsequently approved, (d) the person who acted in the arbitral proceedings on behalf of the party or the party's statutory representative lacked an authorization to do so and the person's acts were not subsequently approved." (2) If a

Council Directive EC 93/13/EEC of April 5, 1993, on unfair terms in consumer contracts, in order to attain the objective stipulated therein.[1065] The High Court in Prague arrived at the following conclusions:[1066]

(1) If there are grounds for the annulment of an arbitral award (Section 31 of the ArbAct[1067]) on which the enforceability of a claim is based, which was entered by a creditor in their application in insolvency proceedings, then the insolvency trustee must have the opportunity to employ such procedural defense during the review of the claims in the insolvency proceedings that is analogous to the individual defense open to the debtor in execution proceedings under Section 35 of the ArbAct.[1068] Hence, the plea of the invalidity of the arbitration agreement must be allowed in incidental proceedings (considering the principles of the incidental proceedings), despite the fact that no motion for the annulment of the arbitral award has been lodged.

(2) If the arbitral award is rendered on the basis of an invalid arbitration clause in an arbitrable matter, the arbitral award still has the effects of a final and conclusive judicial decision and cannot be deemed a null and void juridical act.

(3) If there are grounds that render an issued arbitral award defective, the award must be cleared off by annulment. If the arbitral award is set aside by annulment, the creditor's substantive-law claim shall not

---

motion is lodged pursuant to subsection (1), the court conducting the enforcement of the arbitral award suspends the enforcement proceedings and orders the obligor to lodge a motion to annul the arbitral award with the competent court within 30 days. Unless the motion is lodged within this time limit, the court continues the proceedings on enforcement of the arbitral award. (3) If the arbitral award is annulled, the parties may subsequently proceed similarly to Section 34."

[1065] The court of first instance undoubtedly misunderstood the doctrine of indirect effect, which concerns the interpretation of national law in compliance with a directive and its objectives (*EU-compliant interpretation*). A directive may only have vertical direct effect (subject to the fulfillment of other conditions, an individual may enforce the provisions of the directive against the state). For more details, see below.

[1066] An annotation of this court decision was also published in: Ladislav Derka. Vrchní soud v Praze: Rozhodčí nález vydaný na základě neplatné rozhodčí doložky [Title in Translation: High Court in Prague: Arbitral Award Rendered on the Basis of an Invalid Arbitration Clause]. Právní rozhledy, Praha [Prague / Czech Republic]: C. H. Beck, 2014, Vol. 22, No. 19, pp. 680-684. The *rationes decidendi* (conclusions of the court) articulated in this annotation are, to some extent, identical to the published annotation and have been partially supplemented according to the abovementioned annotation published in the legal periodical.

[1067] Section 31 of the ArbAct is quoted above in the opening part of the annotation of this decision.

[1068] Section 35 of the ArbAct is quoted in the footnotes below.

become statute-barred if the creditor files a motion for the continuation of the proceedings within a thirty-day period (see Section 16 of the ArbAct[1069] and Section 34(1) of the ArbAct).[1070] If the arbitral

---

[1069] ArbAct, Section 16 (cit.):

• Effective until December 31, 2013: "If the party files its claim with the arbitrators before the expiration of the period of limitation or the prescription period and if the arbitrators decide that they lack jurisdiction in the case, or if the arbitral award was annulled and the party again lodges a lawsuit or a motion to continue the proceedings with the court or another competent authority within 30 days of receipt of the decision on lack of jurisdiction or annulment of arbitral award, the effects of the lodged request for arbitration (statement of claim) are preserved."

• Effective since January 1, 2014: "(1) If the party files its claim with the arbitrators before the lapse of the period of limitation or the prescription period, and if the arbitrators decide that they lack jurisdiction in the case and the party again lodges a lawsuit/request for arbitration (statement of claim) with the court, or the competent arbitrators or permanent arbitral institution, or with another competent authority within 30 days of receipt of the decision on a lack of jurisdiction, the effects of the lodged request for arbitration (statement of claim) are preserved. (2) The effects of the lodged request for arbitration (statement of claim) are also preserved if the arbitral award was annulled and the party lodged a lawsuit/request for arbitration or a motion to continue the proceedings with the competent arbitrators or permanent arbitral institution, or with any other competent authority within 30 days after the court decision became final and conclusive which annulled the arbitral award."

[1070] ArbAct, Section 34 (cit.):

• Effective until March 31, 2012: "(1) If the court annuls the arbitral award on the grounds specified in Section 31(a) and (b), the court proceeds, at the request of any of the parties and after the judgment becomes final and conclusive, to hear the merits and resolves the case. (2) If the court annuls the arbitral award on any grounds other than those specified in subsection (1), the arbitration agreement remains valid. The arbitrators involved in the annulled arbitral award are disqualified from the new hearing and resolution of the case. Unless the parties agree otherwise, new arbitrators will be appointed in the same manner as originally stipulated by the arbitration agreement, or the provisions of this Act shall apply as a subsidiary source of law."

• Effective from April 1, 2012 to December 31, 2013: "(1) If the court annuls the arbitral award on the grounds specified in Section 31(a) and (b), the court proceeds, at the request of any of the parties and after the judgment becomes final and conclusive, to hear the merits and resolves the case. The case can no longer be submitted to arbitration. (2) If the court annuls the arbitral award on any grounds other than those specified in Section 31(a) and (b), the arbitration agreement remains valid. However, unless the parties agree otherwise, the arbitrators involved in the arbitral award annulled on the grounds specified in Section 31(c) are disqualified from the new hearing and resolution of the case. Unless the parties agree otherwise, new arbitrators will be appointed in the same manner as originally stipulated by the arbitration agreement, or the provisions of this Act shall apply as a subsidiary source of law. (3) If the court annuls an arbitral award made in a dispute

| 623

arising from a consumer contract and the arbitral proceedings involved an arbitrator registered in the list of arbitrators administered by the Ministry, the court shall submit a counterpart of the final and conclusive decision to the Ministry."

• Effective since January 1, 2014: "(1) If the court annuls the arbitral award on the grounds specified in Section 31(a) and (b), the court proceeds, at the request of any of the parties and after the judgment becomes final and conclusive, to hear the merits and resolves the case. The case can no longer be submitted to arbitration. If the court annuls the arbitral award on grounds stipulated in Section 31(c) through (f) or (i), the arbitral proceedings shall continue at the request of any of the parties based on the arbitration agreement. However, unless the parties agree otherwise, the arbitrators involved in the arbitral award annulled on the grounds specified in Section 31(c) are disqualified from the new hearing and resolution of the case. Unless the parties agree otherwise, new arbitrators will be appointed in the same manner as originally stipulated by the arbitration agreement, or the provisions of this Act shall apply as a subsidiary source of law."

• Further comments to Section 34 of the ArbAct:

• Act No. 303/2013 Coll., in effect since January 1, 2014, has also amended Section 34 of the ArbAct. The legislator has thereby remedied the obvious legislative mistake that was made in Section 34 of the ArbAct during the passing of the "consumer amendment", i.e. Act No. 19/2012 Coll., which amended the Act on Arbitration and the Enforcement of Arbitral Awards with effect from April 1, 2012; the legislator has also introduced modifications that made the provision and the associated Section 16 of the ArbAct more precise.

• The abovementioned legislative mistake was made during the passing of Act No. 19/2012 Coll., in connection with the submitted proposals for amendments. The problem inheres in a collision between the proposed (and subsequently approved) wording of the first subsection of Section 34 of the ArbAct and the second subsection of the said provision. The provision provides for further procedure to be applied if an arbitral award is annulled by the court based on a motion lodged under Section 31 of the ArbAct. Section 34 of the ArbAct then distinguished, depending on the grounds for the annulment of the arbitral award, whether the arbitration would continue and the case would be heard anew before the arbitrators, or whether the court would continue the proceedings due to a lack of jurisdiction on the part of the arbitrators. Considering the autonomy of the parties, which enables them to subject the resolution of defined disputes to the jurisdiction of arbitrators, the fundamental criterion consists of the determination of whether or not the parties expressed their will in the manner approved by the law, and whether, consequently, the arbitrators have jurisdiction to hear the case. The first subsection of Section 34 contains an exhaustive list of such cases; the second subsection was so far formulated as a residuary clause, i.e. it referred to those grounds for the annulment of an arbitral award that were not included in the first subsection.

• Act No. 19/2012 Coll. inserted into Section 31 of the ArbAct two new grounds for the annulment of arbitral award relating to consumer protection. The first case concerned the failure to meet the requirements imposed on an arbitration agreement entered into with a consumer (see Section 3(3) to (6) of the ArbAct). If the arbitration agreement lacks the necessary requirements, it cannot be deemed properly executed, and the arbitrators lack the jurisdiction to resolve the dispute. Hence, it is only logical that this situation has been included among the other situations in Section 34(1) of the ArbAct, where the arbitral award was set aside due to a lack of jurisdiction on the part of the arbitrators. The second case concerns a situation in which the contested decision was issued contrary to consumer protection laws, or it is prima facie contrary to good morals or public policy (see the separate analysis relating to Section 31(g) of the ArbAct). As mentioned above, the legislator only reflected the said circumstance in the first subsection of Section 34 of the ArbAct; the second subsection, i.e. the list of cases to which the rule would not apply (because the first subsection will apply), only contained reference to Section 31(a) and (b). In other words, the two subsections were mutually inconsistent.

• The amendment has eliminated the deficiency by incorporating in both subsections a positive list of situations to which the two subsections apply. The legislator has also retained the division envisaged from the very beginning, i.e. the court will continue hearing the merits of the case upon a motion of any of the parties, if the proceedings for the annulment of the arbitral award result in the finding that the arbitrators lacked the jurisdiction to hear and resolve the dispute, or that the award exhibits principal material deficiencies (in the case of consumer disputes). According to the former technical solution, Section 34(1) of the ArbAct contained a list of cases to which the rule would apply, and the second subsection was formulated as a residuary clause, i.e. it applied to cases not listed in subsection (1). The current approach is exactly the opposite. Both subsections currently consist of separate lists of situations to which they shall apply.

• Apart from the above said and to avoid any doubts, Section 34(2) of the ArbAct newly explicitly stipulates that Section 16 of the ArbAct also applies to those cases, and the arbitration may therefore only continue upon an express motion lodged by any of the parties. But it is necessary to point out that this amendment is indeed merely a more precise formulation of the already existing rule, not a change in the concept of the provision. The requirement of an expression of will as a prerequisite for continuing the proceedings could have been inferred before, because it is obvious that only the parties may determine whether or not they wish to continue the proceedings after the annulment of the arbitral award. It may happen, in theory, that neither of the parties expresses their will to continue the proceedings or, as applicable, does not take any step to initiate further hearing of the dispute. The motion for the continuation of the proceedings was and continues to be governed, by analogy, by the rules incorporated in Section 14(1) and (2) of the ArbAct, and considering the need to preserve the substantive-law time limits, the motion for continuation of the proceedings must be made within 30 (in words: thirty) days after the decision becomes final and conclusive, whereby the court annulled the arbitral award (see the amended Section 16 of the ArbAct). As concerns Section 16 of the ArbAct before the amendment, the newly appointed arbitrators who should hear the case anew must be interpreted as such "another authority", to which the motion for further hearing of the dispute should have been addressed. Consequently, the law retains the previously applicable rule, i.e. if a party fails to lodge a motion for the continuation of the proceedings in a situation defined in Section 34(2) of the ArbAct, the limitation and prescription periods will continue to run.

• The law also preserves the principle according to which the parties are allowed to agree that further proceedings will be entrusted to those arbitrators who participated in

award is not set aside, it is enforceable, because it has the effects of a final and conclusive judicial decision.

(4) The limitation period was suspended pursuant to Section 403(1) of the ComC even if the creditor commenced arbitration regarding the satisfaction of his property claim on the basis of an invalid (non-existent) arbitration clause.

[From Facts of Case and Procedure]:

16.281. On June 19, 2012, the claimant filed an application in insolvency proceedings against the property of debtor XX, in which the claimant entered its claims nos. P 15/1, P 15/2 and P 15/3 as enforceable claims. The claimant identified the legal title underlying claim no. P 15/1 as the personal credit card contract entered into by and between the claimant and the debtor on May 4, 2007, and argued that the claim had become due and payable on September 19, 2007. The enforceability of the claim was substantiated by the final and conclusive arbitral award in Case No. K/2008/08820 of December 18, 2008, rendered by arbitrator YY.[1071] The claimant identified the legal title underlying claim no. P 15/2 as the credit (loan) agreement entered into by and between the claimant and the debtor on April 19, 2007, and argued that the claim had become due and payable on November 16, 2007. The enforceability of the claim was substantiated by the final and conclusive arbitral award in Case No. K/2008/08844 of December 18, 2008, rendered by arbitrator YY.[1072] The insolvency trustee rebutted all of the abovementioned claims and **found claims nos. P 15/1 and P 15/2 unenforceable**, arguing that the **arbitration clauses were invalid.** The insolvency trustee maintained that both of the abovementioned claims were statute-barred as of the day of filing of the respective application, because claim no. P 15/1 had become due and payable on September 19, 2007 and claim no. P 15/2 had become due and payable on November 16, 2007.

16.282. On July 31, 2012, the creditor filed a motion, whereby the creditor demanded that the rebutted claims nos. P 15/1, P 15/2 and P 15/3 be declared existing. The creditor insisted that claims nos. P 15/1 and P

---

the issue of the contested arbitral award. Hence, the rule continues to apply that the parties must reach an explicit agreement on such possibility. Let us point out, in this connection, that the reverse principle is not uncommon in international practice, i.e. the primary premise is that the case is primarily reheard by the original arbitrators, unless the parties agree otherwise.

[1071] The respective arbitration was *ad hoc* arbitration outside the jurisdiction of any permanent arbitral institution.

[1072] The respective arbitration was *ad hoc* arbitration outside the jurisdiction of any permanent arbitral institution.

15/2 were enforceable claims, because they had been awarded by final and conclusive arbitral awards. The creditor therefore inferred that the respondent (insolvency trustee) had the burden of proof regarding his allegation that the claims did not exist. The creditor emphasized that the bankrupt had acknowledged the claims during the review hearing. The acknowledgment established the legal presumption that the debt existed and, in compliance with Section 110(1) of the CivC,[1073] the acknowledgment thus interrupted the limitation period, which started to run anew. The creditor maintained that claims nos. P 15/1 and P 15/2 entered in the creditor's application were not statute-barred, because the execution courts had found both arbitral awards enforceable when they had ordered execution. Considering the above-said, the creditor believes that holding the claims statute-barred due to the alleged invalidity of the arbitration clauses would seriously violate the principles of the rule of law, primarily the principles of legal certainty and legitimate expectations. The creditor invoked the decision of the SC in Case No. 20 Cdo 1852/2010 of March 26, 2012, in which the SC held that the issue of the validity of an arbitration clause should be the subject matter of the proceedings for the annulment of an arbitral award; according to this decision, execution courts may only examine the existence, not the validity of the arbitration clause. The creditor also referred to Section 31 of the ArbAct in that, after (if) an arbitral award is set aside due to an invalid arbitration agreement, the court shall continue the proceedings on the merits upon a motion lodged by any of the parties, and if the motion is lodged within 30 days,

---

[1073] CivC, Section 110 (cit.): "(1) If the right was awarded by a final and conclusive decision of a court or another authority, it shall become statute-barred ten years after the day on which performance was to be provided according to the decision. If the debtor acknowledged the underlying grounds for and the amount of the right in writing, the right shall become statute-barred ten years after the acknowledgment; however, if the acknowledgment contained a period for performance, the limitation period starts to run after the lapse of the period for performance. (2) The same limitation period also applies to the individual installments into which the performance was divided, which was awarded by the decision or stipulated in the acknowledgment of right; the limitation period applicable to the individual installments starts to run from the day they become due and payable. If a default on any of the installments renders the entire debt due and payable (Section 565), the ten-year limitation period starts to run from the day the unpaid installment becomes due and payable. (3) Interest and repeated performance become statute-barred in three years; however, if the right was awarded by a final and conclusive decision or acknowledged in writing, the three-year limitation period only applies to the interest and repeated performance that has become due and payable after the decision became final and conclusive or after the acknowledgment was executed."

the effects of the motion shall be preserved, i.e. including the effects concerning the running of the limitation period. The claimant therefore concluded that no annulment of an arbitral award could ever deprive a party of the possibility of enforcing their right.

16.283. The respondent (insolvency trustee) proposed that the motion be dismissed. As concerns claims nos. P 15/1 and P 15/2, the respondent stated that the arbitration clauses were invalid under Section 55(2) of the CivC[1074] and Section 56 of the CivC,[1075] because they refer to a sole arbitrator who will be appointed from the list of arbitrators of

---

[1074] CivC, Section 55 (cit.): "(1) Contractual terms in consumer contracts may not depart from the law to the detriment of the consumer. In particular, the consumer may not waive the rights guaranteed to them by the law or impair their contractual position in any other manner. (2) Clauses in consumer contracts specified in Section 56 are invalid. (3) When in doubt as to the meaning of consumer contracts, the interpretation that is more favorable to the consumer shall apply."

[1075] CivC, Section 56 (cit.): "(1) Consumer contracts may not contain terms that, contrary to the requirement of good faith, cause a significant imbalance in the parties' rights and obligations to the detriment of the consumer. (2) Subsection (1) shall not apply to contractual terms that define the subject of the performance under the contract or the price of the performance. (3) Inadmissible contractual terms are, in particular, contractual terms (a) excluding or limiting the legal liability of a supplier in the event of the death of a consumer or personal injury to the latter resulting from an act or omission of that supplier, (b) excluding or limiting the consumer's rights to make claims under liability for defects or liability for damage, (c) stipulating that an agreement is binding on the consumer whereas the supplier's performance is subject to a condition whose realization depends on the supplier's own will alone, (d) permitting the supplier to retain the performance provided by the consumer even if the latter does not conclude a contract with the supplier or cancels the contract, (e) authorizing the supplier to cancel the contract without any contractual or statutory reason where the same facility is not granted to the consumer, (f) enabling the supplier to terminate a contract of indeterminate duration without reasonable notice except where there are serious grounds for doing so, (g) obliging the consumer to fulfill conditions which he or she had no opportunity to get acquainted with prior to the conclusion of the contract, (h) enabling the supplier to alter the terms of the contract unilaterally without a valid reason which is specified in the contract, (i) providing for the price of goods or services to be determined at the time of delivery or allowing a supplier of the goods or services to increase their price without in both cases giving the consumer the corresponding right to cancel the contract if the final price is too high in relation to the price agreed when the contract was concluded, (j) obliging the consumer to fulfill all of their obligations where the supplier does not perform theirs, (k) giving the supplier the possibility of transferring their rights and obligations under the contract, where such transfer jeopardizes the enforceability of the consumer's claim or the guarantees for the consumer, without the latter's agreement."

Společnost pro rozhodčí řízení a.s.[1076] The parties agreed that the arbitrator would be appointed according to the *Rules of Procedure for Arbitration* issued by the said company. In this connection, the respondent invoked the decision of the SC in Case No. 31 Cdo 1945/2010 of May 11, 2011, on the basis of which the respondent reached his conclusions. Considering the invalidity of the arbitration clauses, the respondent maintained that the arbitral awards were null and void, because, in his opinion, the arbitrator had lacked the required jurisdiction. Considering the due dates for the payment of the claims, the respondent maintained that the limitation period applicable to the said claims had already lapsed.

16.284. The Regional Court in Prague, as the court of first instance, rendered its judgment on October 4, 2014; the motion for the declaration of the existence of the claims was dismissed and the claimant was ordered to compensate the costs of the proceedings. In the reasoning for its judgment, the court stated that the evidence heard and read in the case indicated that the debtor, as a consumer, had entered into the personal credit card contract with the claimant on May 4, 2007, which included the *Personal Credit Cards Terms*, and the credit (loan) agreement on April 19, 2007, which included the *Credit Terms for Consumers*. Both Terms included a provision that read as follows: *"property disputes between the debtor and the respondent shall be resolved in arbitral proceedings, by a sole arbitrator appointed by the administrator of the list of arbitrators from the list of arbitrators administered by Společnost pro rozhodčí řízení a.s. ... according to the Rules of Procedure for Arbitration issued by...".* The Regional Court in Prague, as the court of first instance, concluded that both arbitration clauses had been invalid under Section 39 of the CivC,[1077] because Společnost pro rozhodčí řízení a.s. was not a permanent arbitral institution, and consequently, it did not have the authority to issue the *Rules of Procedure, Rules on the Costs of Proceedings* and *Organization and Office Rules*, to which both Terms refer.[1078] In this connection, the court of first instance invoked

[1076] A legal entity formed and existing under the laws of the Czech Republic in the form of a joint stock company. This company organizes arbitration, but does not constitute a "permanent arbitral institution" in terms of Section 13 of the ArbAct. Section 13 of the ArbAct is quoted in the footnotes below.

[1077] CivC, Section 39 (cit.): "A juridical act is invalid if the content or the purpose thereof violates or evades the law or is *contra bonos mores*."

[1078] The reason is that the company is not a permanent arbitral institution. The establishment and status of "permanent arbitral institutions" are governed by Section 13 of the ArbAct (cit.): "Permanent arbitral institutions (1) Permanent arbitral institutions may only be established by another law or only if another law expressly allows their

the decision of the SC in Case No. 31 Cdo 1945/2010 of May 11, 2011 and Resolution of the High Court in Prague in Case No. 12 Cmo 496/2008 of May 28, 2009, on the basis of which the court reached its conclusions. The court therefore concluded that the arbitrator had not had the authority to resolve the arbitral disputes and the asserted claims nos. P 15/1 and P 15/2 were not, in the court's opinion, based on any enforceable instrument. Considering the above-said, the court of first instance held that Section 199(2) of the InsAct[1079] would not apply to the given case, because the plea of invalidity of the arbitration agreement is ultimately, in the court's opinion, a plea of a lack of jurisdiction on the part of the arbitrator. The Regional Court in Prague

---

establishment. (2) Permanent arbitral institutions can issue their own statutes and rules which must be published in the Business Journal[3]); these statutes and rules may determine the method of appointment and the number of arbitrators and may stipulate that the arbitrators shall be selected from a list administered by the permanent arbitral institution. The statutes and rules may also determine how the arbitrators shall conduct the proceedings and render their decisions, as well as resolve other issues connected with the activities of the permanent arbitral institution and the arbitrators, including rules regulating the costs of proceedings and fees for the arbitrators. (3) If the parties agreed on the jurisdiction of a particular permanent arbitral institution and failed to agree otherwise in the arbitration agreement, they shall be deemed to have submitted to the regulations specified in subsection (2), as applicable on the day of commencement of the proceedings in the permanent arbitral institution. (4) No entity may carry out its activities using a name which evokes a misleading impression that the entity is a permanent arbitral institution under this law unless a different law or regulation or an international agreement integrated in the legal system authorizes the entity to use the name."

[1079] The court reached the following conclusion (cit.): *"The grounds for rebutting the existence or the amount of an enforceable claim awarded by a final and conclusive decision of the competent authority may only consist of the facts that were not asserted by the debtor in the proceedings preceding the decision; however, the rebuttal may not be based on a different legal assessment of the case."*

InsAct, Section 199 (cit.): "Rebuttal of an enforceable claim by the insolvency trustee – (1) The insolvency trustee who rebutted an enforceable claim shall file a lawsuit with the insolvency court within 30 days of the review hearing; in the lawsuit, the insolvency trustee will claim the rebuttal against the creditor who had entered the enforceable claim. The time limit shall not lapse if the lawsuit is received by the court on or before the last day of the time limit. (2) The grounds for rebutting the existence or the amount of an enforceable claim awarded by a final and conclusive decision of the competent authority may only consist of the facts that were not asserted by the debtor in the proceedings preceding the issue of the decision; however, the rebuttal may not be based on a different legal assessment of the case. (3) In their lawsuit under subsection (1), the claimant may only invoke such circumstances against the rebutted claim for which the claim was rebutted by the claimant."

held that the case law of the Court of Justice of the EU, primarily the decisions in Cases C-240/98 and C-168/05, **required that, when applying national law, the national courts are obliged to interpret Council Directive** EC 93/13/EEC of April 5, 1993, on unfair terms in consumer contracts, **in such manner as to attain the objective stipulated therein.**[1080] The Regional Court in Prague therefore argued that the case law of the Court of Justice of the EU indicated that an arbitral award from a consumer contract did not have to be *cleared off* in the manner envisaged by national law (Section 31 of the ArbAct[1081] in the Czech Republic), but conversely, the court was obliged to have regard to the nullity of the arbitral award of its own motion.

16.285. The court of first instance concluded that null and void arbitral awards had no effects, and consequently, the limitation period in the given case was not suspended, despite the fact that requests for arbitration had been lodged. In the reasoning for its decision, the court also invoked Section 403(1) of the ComC,[1082] which indicates, according to the court of first instance, that the limitation period is only suspended if arbitration is commenced on the basis of a **valid arbitration agreement.** The application with the claims due and payable in 2007 was delivered to the court on June 19, 2012, i.e. after the lapse of the four-year limitation period (according to the court's opinion). The court also held that the absence of the debtor's rebuttal of the claims at the review hearing could not be deemed an acknowledgment of debt in terms of Section 110(1) of the CC.[1083] Based on the said reasoning, the court of first instance dismissed the motion and ordered the claimant to pay compensation for the costs of the proceedings.

16.286. The claimant appealed the judgment of the court of first instance and proposed that the appellate court reverse the decision and grant the claimant's lawsuit regarding claims nos. P 15/1 and P 15/2. The claimant primarily argued that at the time when the requests for arbitration had been lodged, there had been no doubts about the validity of both arbitration clauses, neither in the case law of the SC, nor in the case law of the ConCourt. The claimant insisted that by filing

---

[1080] The court of first instance undoubtedly misunderstood the doctrine of indirect effect, which concerns the interpretation of national law in compliance with a directive and its objectives (*EU-compliant interpretation*). A directive may only have vertical direct effect (subject to the fulfillment of other conditions, an individual may enforce the provisions of the directive against the state). For more details, see below.

[1081] Section 31 of the ArbAct is quoted in the opening part of this annotation.

[1082] Section 403 of the ComC is quoted in the opening part of this annotation.

[1083] Section 110 of the CivC is quoted above in the footnotes to this annotation.

the requests for arbitration, the claimant had adopted every measure necessary to enforce the claimant's claims, and the lapse of the limitation periods (if such a finding is made) was not the claimant's fault; the claimant had even managed to have the execution declared before the limitation period lapsed. Pleading the limitation of actions would constitute the abuse of the right in compliance with the conclusions made by the SC in its decision in Case No. 33 Cdo 126/2009 of July 29, 2010. The respondent therefore proposed that the appellate court uphold the judgment of the Regional Court in Prague, because the plea of the limitation of actions was not contrary to good morals in the given case - the reason is that the invalid arbitration clauses were drafted by the claimant, and the debtor was in the position of the weaker contracting party.

[From Conclusions of Appellate Court and Notes on Decision]:

16.287. **The appellate court held that the validity of arbitration clauses in consumer contracts can be reviewed in insolvency proceedings, because the Court of Justice of the EU[1084] has ruled that unfair terms in consumer contracts are not binding on the consumer, and the court shall, of its own motion, have regard to the fact that they are not binding.** The appellate court has further examined Czech domestic law on insolvency proceedings. The Insolvency Act contains no provision analogous to Section 35 of the ArbAct, but the review of claims entered by creditors who filed their applications in insolvency proceedings is based on the possibility that these claims can be rebutted by the insolvency trustee, the debtor or any other creditor; the grounds for rebuttal are generally unlimited, save for the limitation of the possibility of rebutting an enforceable claim under Section 199(2) of the InsAct.[1085] The theory and practice[1086] both maintain that as concerns the determination of the existence of a claim arising from a bill of exchange or a promissory note in bankruptcy proceedings, the creditors who rebutted the claim or the trustee have the opportunity in the bankruptcy proceedings to raise any and all absolute and relative pleas (objections) against the bill of exchange or the promissory note during the review of the claims that a party to the relationship established under the bill of exchange/promissory note could raise in

---

[1084] The court explicitly invoked the following decisions:
- decision in Case C-243/08 of June 4, 2009 (*Pannon*);
- decision in Case C-240/98 of June 27, 2000 (*Océano Grupo Editorial*); and
- decision in Case C-168/05 of October 26, 2006 (*Mostazo Claro*).

[1085] Section 199 of the InsAct is quoted above in the footnotes to this annotation.

[1086] The court invoked its own decision 4 Cmo 191/2007 of November 19, 2008.

proceedings for issuing a bill of exchange/promissory note payment order. The High Court in Prague subsequently inferred, based on an analogous deduction, that if there are grounds for the annulment of an arbitral award (Section 31 of the ArbAct[1087]) on which the enforceability of a claim is based, which was entered by a creditor in their application, then the insolvency trustee must have the opportunity to employ such procedural defense during the review of claims in the insolvency proceedings that is analogous to the individual defense open to the debtor in execution proceedings under Section 35 of the ArbAct.[1088] Consequently, if the insolvency trustee supports their rebuttal of an enforceable claim with grounds that could justify the annulment of the arbitral award by the court, the court shall, by analogy and to the extent determined according to Section 35 of the ArbAct,[1089] also review the issue of whether the arbitral award can be applied in the circumstances of the insolvency proceedings, i.e. whether or not the conditions for the annulment of the award are fulfilled under Section 31 of the ArbAct.[1090] The court maintains that such procedure corresponds to the principles of the Insolvency Act, which provides for a review of claims (including enforceable claims) as an instrument for the protection of the rights of creditors against fraudulent juridical acts of the debtor or of the individual creditors which would curtail the other creditors' right to proportionate and maximized satisfaction. The appellate court is therefore of the opinion that when the insolvency court assesses the issue of the enforceability of a claim arising from an arbitral award, the court does not deprive the creditor who has asserted the claim of the opportunity itself to demand satisfaction of the claim in the insolvency proceedings; this only means that the claim asserted by the creditor is deemed unenforceable. If the claim is held well-founded under substantive law, it is irrelevant whether such conclusion was made on the basis of an enforceable or unenforceable claim.

16.288. The appellate court is of the opinion that the rights of the consumer (or the debtor in general) and of the creditors in the insolvency proceedings must be efficiently protected; in order to achieve such aim,

---

[1087] Section 31 of the ArbAct is quoted above in the footnotes in the opening part of this annotation.

[1088] Section 35 of the ArbAct is quoted above in the footnotes in the opening part of this annotation.

[1089] Section 35 of the ArbAct is quoted above in the footnotes in the opening part of this annotation.

[1090] Section 31 of the ArbAct is quoted above in the footnotes in the opening part of this annotation.

the insolvency trustee must have a similar procedural defense available to them which a debtor would have in the case of their individual defense in execution proceedings, if there are grounds for the annulment of the arbitral award on which the enforceability of the asserted claim is based. This holds true despite the fact that Czech insolvency law (here Section 199(2) of the InsAct[1091]) prohibits the rebuttal of an enforceable claim on grounds of a different legal assessment of the case. In this connection, the court has inferred that the creditor's claim awarded by a final and conclusive arbitral award may be held unenforceable by the insolvency trustee, and its existence may be subsequently rebutted, if the insolvency trustee maintains that there are conditions for the annulment of the arbitral award, without the need to first set aside the final arbitral award in the relevant manner or at least lodge a motion for annulment thereof.

16.289. As concerns the argument that Czech domestic law must be interpreted and applied in compliance with EU law, it is necessary to point out that a directive may only have indirect effect as regards its effects on the legal regulation of relationships between individuals (horizontal effect),[1092] which means that if the domestic law of a Member State is susceptible to several interpretations, it is always necessary to prioritize the interpretation that complies with the directive and its objective. In accordance with the decision of the Grand Chamber of the Court of Justice of the EU (formerly the European Court of Justice) in *Pfeiffer*, however, *"even a clear, precise and unconditional provision of a directive seeking to confer rights or impose obligations on individuals cannot of itself apply in proceedings exclusively between private parties."*[1093] Hence, domestic law cannot be interpreted in direct contravention of its literal wording, even on the basis of its potential conflict with a directive or its objectives. The only available remedy is against the Member State that has failed to implement the directive in a due and timely manner, namely the compensation available according to the decision of the European Court of Justice in *Francovich* v. *Italy*[1094] for damage or losses sustained

---

[1091] Section 199 of the InsAct is quoted above in the footnotes to this annotation.

[1092] Opinion of the Civil and Commercial Panel of the SC, Case No. Cpjn 200/2011, of October 9, 2013, published in Sbírka soudních rozhodnutí a stanovisek [Reports of SC Decisions and Opinions] under no. 79/2013.

[1093] Decision of the Grand Chamber of the European Court of Justice in the joined cases C-397/01 to C-403/01 (*Bernhard Pfeiffer et al* v. *Deutsches Rotes Kreuz, Kreisverband Waldshut eV*) of October 5, 2004.

[1094] Decision of the European Court of Justice, Case C-6/90 (*Francovich* v. *Italy*), of November 19, 1991

by individual(s) as a result of the failure to implement the directive;[1095] or the doctrine of vertical direct effect of the directive can serve as the basis for invoking any specific provisions of the directive against the state if the directive was not implemented (or not implemented correctly).[1096]

16.290. In relation to Directive 93/13/EEC, as a whole, the Court of Justice declared that it is a measure that is essential to the accomplishment of the tasks entrusted to the European Community, and in particular, to raising the standard of living and the quality of life throughout the Community; the parties are not free to depart from the provisions of this Directive.[1097] In the *Asturcom* decision, the Court of Justice also addressed the interpretation of the Directive in relation to the proceedings for the enforcement of an arbitral award rendered in the absence of the consumer; the Court held that *a national court or tribunal hearing an action for the enforcement of an arbitration award that has become final and was made in the absence of the consumer is required, where it has available to it the legal and factual elements necessary for that task, to assess of its own motion whether an arbitration clause in a contract concluded between a seller or supplier and a consumer is unfair, insofar as, under national rules of procedure, it can carry out such an assessment in similar actions of a domestic nature. If that is the case (the clause is unfair), it is for that court or tribunal to establish all the consequences thereby arising under national law, in order to ensure that the consumer is not bound by that clause.*

16.291. The examination of the invalidity of an arbitration agreement under Czech law is reserved for proceedings under Section 31 of the ArbAct.[1098] As concerns the issue of allowing a plea of the invalidity of an arbitration clause in incidental proceedings, it is also necessary to bear in mind that the judicial decision made in the incidental proceedings conducted during the insolvency proceedings is a declaratory decision that only serves the needs of the insolvency proceedings. The purpose of the proceedings is to determine the extent to which the claims of the debtor's creditors will be satisfied, which

---

[1095] This is only possible if the directive contains clear, accurate and unconditional provisions that should confer rights or impose obligations on individuals.

[1096] See also Judgment of the European Court of Justice in Case C-41/74 (*Van Duyn*) of December 4, 1974.

[1097] Judgment of the European Court of Justice, Case C-40/08 (*Asturcom Telecomunicaciones SL* v. *Christina Rodriguez Nogueira*), par. 51.

[1098] Section 31 of the ArbAct is quoted above in the footnotes in the opening part of this annotation.

were entered by the creditors in their applications; if the respondent's enforceable claim is held wrongful, the claim will not be satisfied in the insolvency proceedings.[1099] The reason is that insolvency proceedings are considered a specific type of proceedings, which combine the elements of a trial (finding proceedings) and enforcement proceedings, and consequently, there is no need to proceed analogously to Section 35 of the ArbAct[1100] – it is possible to directly determine the (non-) existence and amount of the respective claim in the incidental proceedings. Hence, the invalidity itself of an arbitration clause, free from any other connections, does not give rise to any significant legal consequences in the incidental dispute on the determination of the claim, because the subject matter of the proceedings is merely the assessment of the existence, amount and hierarchy of the claims. The validity or invalidity of an existing arbitration agreement constitutes a legal classification, and consequently, the rebuttal of an enforceable claim on grounds of the invalidity of the arbitration agreement can be held to be unacceptable grounds for rebuttal, despite the fact that this does not constitute an assessment of the case, but an assessment of the juridical act, which is the prerequisite for issuing a decision on the merits in the proceedings regarding the case itself (Section 15 of the ArbAct).[1101] The insolvency trustee should not be entitled to plead the

---

[1099] Judgment of the High Court in Prague, Case No. 45 ICm 57/2011, of November 15, 2012.

[1100] Section 35 of the ArbAct is quoted above in the footnotes in the opening part of this annotation.

[1101] ArbAct, Section 15 (cit.):

• Effective until March 31, 2012: "(1) Arbitrators are entitled to examine their jurisdiction. If they conclude that the arbitration agreement presented to them does not give them jurisdiction to resolve the dispute, they render a corresponding resolution. (2) The plea of lack of jurisdiction, based on the non-existence, invalidity, or expiration of the arbitration agreement, can be raised by a party only before or together with the first act in the proceedings which concerns the merits of the case, unless the invalidity is caused by the fact that no arbitration agreement could have been concluded with respect to the case."

• Effective since April 1, 2012: "(1) Arbitrators are entitled to examine their jurisdiction. If they conclude that the arbitration agreement presented to them does not give them jurisdiction to resolve the dispute, they render a corresponding resolution. (2) The plea of lack of jurisdiction, based on the non-existence, invalidity, or expiration of the arbitration agreement, can be raised by a party only before or together with the first act in the proceedings which concerns the merits of the case, unless the invalidity is caused by the fact that no arbitration agreement could have been concluded with respect to the contract. This does not apply to disputes arising from consumer contracts."

invalidity of the arbitration agreement in the proceedings for the determination of an enforceable claim.[1102]

16.292. Author of this annotation may comment by using analogy with respect to the determination of the existence of the claim arising from a bill of exchange/promissory note in bankruptcy or insolvency proceedings, as applicable, this possibility for the trustee to raise absolute and relative objections that can be raised by a party to the relationship established by the bill of exchange/promissory note in the proceedings for the issue of a bill of exchange/promissory note payment order **has no bearing on the conclusions regarding the enforceability of the claim.** The trustee is only allowed to rebut enforceable claims if the debtor created the creditor's claim by the willful or negligent conduct of the debtor, and thereby favored the creditor to the detriment of the other creditors of the debtor (or, as applicable, disadvantaged the other creditors). Consequently, this does not entail any reversal of the procedural status, where, conversely, the creditor would have to prove that they have a claim against the debtor, or the elimination of the restrictions applicable to the grounds for rebuttal stipulated in Section 199(2) of the InsAct.[1103]

16.293. In accordance with the case law of the SC and the conclusions of legal theory as interpreted by the appellate court in this matter, the rule is that if no arbitration agreement was entered into or if the award was rendered in a matter that is not arbitrable, the issued arbitral award is not an eligible enforceable decision, regardless of whether or not the debtor pleaded the non-existence of the arbitration agreement in arbitration.[1104] These cases must be differentiated from the situation that occurs when an arbitration agreement was entered into, albeit an invalid one.[1105] An arbitral award rendered on the basis of such an arbitration agreement has the effects of a final and conclusive judicial decision and cannot be deemed a null and void juridical act. Until such arbitral award is annulled in the manner envisaged by the ArbAct,[1106]

[1102] Judgment of the High Court in Olomouc, Case No. 2 VSOL 8/2011-64, of December 15, 2011.

[1103] See also:
- Judgment of the Regional Court in Prague, Case No. 37 ICm 1761/2010, of March 9, 2011,
- Judgment of the SC, Case No. 29 ICdo 4/2012, of February 24, 2014.

[1104] Resolution of the SC, Case No. 20 Cdo 3284/2008, of August 31, 2010.

[1105] Resolution of the Grand Panel of the Civil and Commercial Division of the SC, Case No. 31 Cdo 958/2012, of July 10, 2013.

[1106] See the procedure under Section 31 of the ArbAct or Section 31 of the ArbAct et seq., as applicable.

the award is enforceable (provided that it was duly served and the period for voluntary performance has lapsed), because it has the effects of a final and conclusive judicial decision. The *res judicata* principle (obstacle established by an adjudicated case) is also honored by the European Court of Justice,[1107] whose case law does not order the national court to refrain from using national procedural rules that endow a particular decision with the quality of *res judicata*, even if such procedure opened the possibility of remedying a breach of Community law of any kind.[1108]

16.294. The conclusion generally accepted by the practice, in compliance with the conclusions made by the SC in its decision in Case No. 29 NSCR 25/2011 of July 18, 2013, is that the insolvency trustee has the right to reach their conclusion regarding the enforceability of the asserted claim, and this assessment of enforceability of the claim can effectively only be opposed in the incidental proceedings (if any). The incidental proceedings must be initiated by the creditor as the creditor of the unenforceable claim. However, this does not permit any arbitrary and *contra legem* acts of the insolvency trustee when assessing the enforceability of the claim; this procedure only accentuates the specific status of the insolvency trustee, who is a special public authority entrusted with the task of securing the proper conduct of the insolvency proceedings.[1109] Hence, the insolvency trustee is certainly not allowed to arbitrarily hold an enforceable claim unenforceable in order to improve the insolvency trustee's procedural status and evade Section 199 of the InsAct.[1110] Moreover, such a purely fraudulent fabrication would be legally unsustainable, also with respect to the other conclusions of the appellate court[1111] mentioned below. As concerns the limits of rebutting an enforceable claim awarded by an arbitral award, the rule is that the Insolvency Act only allows rebutting enforceable claims if the debtor created the creditor's claim by the debtor's own inaction, whether willful or negligent, and thereby favored the creditor over the other creditors.[1112]

[1107] Judgment of the European Court of Justice, Case C-234/04 (Kapferer), of March 16, 2006, par. 20.

[1108] Judgment of the European Court of Justice, Case C-2/08 (Fallimento Olimpiclub), of September 3, 2009, para. 22.

[1109] See also Judgment of the ConCourt Case No. Pl. ÚS 14/10 of 1 July 2010.

[1110] Section 199 of the InsAct is quoted above in the footnotes to this annotation.

[1111] (Cit.): *"If the arbitral award is rendered on the basis of an invalid arbitration clause in an arbitrable matter, the arbitral award still has the effects of a final and conclusive judicial decision and cannot be deemed a null and void juridical act".*

[1112] Decision of the High Court in Prague, Case No. 45 ICm 57/2011, of November 15,

16.295. Considering the limits of the EU-compliant interpretation, clear rules regulating the possibility of a limited review of enforceable claims, and the relatively significant difference between enforcement proceedings and insolvency proceedings, the author of this annotation is of the opinion that the assessment of the invalidity of the arbitration agreement should not, as a rule, be the domain of incidental proceedings. Contrary to the opinion of the appellate court, the author also believes that the insolvency trustee is not entitled to hold the creditor's claim unenforceable if it was awarded by a final and conclusive arbitral award rendered on the basis of an invalid arbitration clause in an arbitrable matter, because such conclusions are in direct conflict with the literal wording of Czech domestic law.

16.296. The appellate court also analyzed the ramifications that the potential invalidity of the arbitration agreement might have, together with the conclusion that – in the court's opinion – a claim awarded by an arbitral award rendered on the basis of an invalid arbitration agreement is unenforceable. The High Court in Prague concluded that if the arbitral award is rendered on the basis of an invalid (nonexistent) arbitration agreement in an arbitrable matter, the arbitral award still has the effects of a final and conclusive judicial decision, and cannot be deemed a null and void juridical act. In this connection, the court also stated that if there are reasons that render an issued arbitral award defective, the award must be cleared off by annulment. The court held that if the arbitral award is set aside by annulment, the creditor's substantive-law claim should not become statute-barred if the creditor files a motion for the continuation of the proceedings within a thirty-day period (see Section 16[1113] and Section 34(1) of the ArbAct[1114]). If the arbitral award is not set aside, it is enforceable (according to the court), because it has the effects of a final and conclusive judicial decision. The appellate court correctly invoked the internal logic of the ArbAct. This partial conclusion (a correct partial conclusion in the opinion of the author of this annotation) is entirely inconsistent with the conclusion that a claim is unenforceable if it is awarded by a final and conclusive arbitral award rendered on the basis of an invalid (non-existent) arbitration agreement in an arbitrable matter. For this reason, the analyzed decision of the High Court in Prague seems somewhat schizophrenic.

2012.

[1113] Section 16 of the ArbAct is quoted above in the footnotes to this annotation.

[1114] Section 34 of the ArbAct is quoted above in the footnotes to this annotation.

16.297. The appellate court subsequently addressed the issue of the potential limitation of actions with respect to the claim. The appellate court primarily focused on the interpretation of Section 403(1) of the ComC;[1115] the said rule regulating the limitation of actions with respect to commercial obligations was interpreted by the court in compliance with the provisions of the ArbAct. Moreover, the court compared the respective provision with the parallel rule in Section 112 CivC, and had regard to the provisions of Section 648 of the CC[1116] and Section 3017[1117] of the CC (the "CC"). **The appellate court concluded that the limitation period was suspended pursuant to Section 403(1) of the ComC,[1118] even if the creditor commenced arbitration regarding the satisfaction of his property claim on the basis of an invalid (non-existent) arbitration clause.** The appellate court argued that both the ArbAct (which was passed later than the ComC) and the CivC and CC provide for the suspension of the limitation period in the event the creditor files a request for arbitration and continues the duly commenced arbitration, regardless of whether or not the arbitration was initiated on the basis of a valid arbitration agreement. Moreover, an arbitral award that has become final and conclusive (irrespective of the validity or invalidity of the arbitration agreement on the basis of which it was issued) is a *res judicata,* and the creditor cannot successfully assert their claim in court. The High Court in Prague therefore concluded that a literal interpretation of Section 403(1) of the ComC[1119] would de facto constitute a denial of justice, and it is necessary to conclude that the limitation period is suspended even in the event the request for arbitration is lodged and the arbitration proceeds on the basis of an invalid or non-existent arbitration clause. The appellate court also pointed out that even **if the limitation period lapsed in the said case, the plea of the limitation of actions could**

[1115] Section 403 of the ComC is quoted in the footnotes in the opening part of this annotation.

[1116] CC, Section 648 (cit.): "If the creditor asserts his or her right with a public authority before the lapse of the limitation period and duly continues the commenced proceedings, the limitation period does not run. The same applies to an already enforceable right if a motion for the enforcement of the decision or execution has been lodged".

[1117] CC, Section 3017 (cit.): "Provisions of this Act that concern the assertion of a right in court, or judicial proceedings, or judicial decision, shall apply by analogy to the assertion of a right before an arbitrator, to arbitration, or to an arbitral award".

[1118] Section 403 of the ComC is quoted in the footnotes in the opening part of this annotation.

[1119] Section 403 of the ComC is quoted in the footnotes in the opening part of this annotation.

not be granted, because it would, in the said case, be *contra bonos mores* pursuant to Section 3(1) of the CC – the reason is that the lapse of the limitation period was not the creditor's fault, the creditor lodged its request for arbitration in time, and at the same time, did not delay the motion for enforcement, and could by no means anticipate the change in the case law that occurred several years after the creditor entered into the arbitration agreement with the debtor. The author agrees with the said conclusions of the appellate court and believes that a contrary interpretation would constitute tedious formalism and a de facto denial of the principles of legal certainty and legitimate expectations.

16.298. The appellate court made an additional academic comment, namely that after April 1, 2012, courts conducting proceedings for the enforcement of claims arising from consumer contracts may no longer have regard to, without other considerations, **an invalid arbitration agreement** underlying an arbitral award. The above said is a relatively inappropriate choice of words, which allows a twofold interpretation. In accordance with its previous comments, the court concluded that if the consumer fails to exercise their rights under Section 35 of the ArbAct,[1120] the court must not, of its own motion, have regard to the **invalidity of the arbitration agreement** and terminate the enforcement proceedings. The reason is that the amendment of Section 35 of the ArbAct,[1121] which was implemented by Act No. 19/2012 Coll. and took effect on April 1, 2012, allows the consumer not to be bound by an invalid arbitration agreement, even at the stage of enforcement proceedings, because the consumer has the right to initiate finding proceedings during the enforcement proceedings, i.e. file a motion for the annulment of the arbitral award. Hence, the appellate court concluded that the conclusions[1122] reached by the SC in its decision in Case No. 31 Cdo 398/2012 of July 10, 2013 and by the European Court

---

[1120] Section 35 of the ArbAct is quoted in a footnote in the opening part of this annotation.

[1121] Section 35 of the ArbAct is quoted in a footnote in the opening part of this annotation.

[1122] (Cit.): *"Directive 93/13/EEC must be interpreted as meaning that a national court or tribunal hearing an action for enforcement of an arbitration award which has become final and was made in the absence of the consumer is required, where it has available to it the legal and factual elements necessary for that task, to assess of its own motion whether an arbitration clause contained in an agreement concluded between a seller or supplier and a consumer is unfair, in so far as, under national rules of procedure, it can carry out such an assessment in similar actions under national law. If that is the case, it is for that court or tribunal to establish all the consequences thereby arising under national law, in order to ensure that the consumer is not bound by that clause."*

of Justice in its *Asturcom*[1123] judgment are no longer applicable with respect to **unfair terms,** due to the change in procedural law, which provided the consumer with an effective procedural defense mechanism. This conclusion complies with the conclusions reached by the European Court of Justice in its decision in Pfeiffer,[1124] in which the ECJ ruled that an EU-compliant interpretation of a Member State's legal system cannot directly contravene the wording of domestic law. Any interpretation claiming that the court must of its own motion have regard to the **invalidity of the arbitration agreement** in the proceedings for the enforcement of claims arising from consumer contracts and terminate the enforcement proceedings would be in direct conflict with Section 35 of the ArbAct.[1125] The decision of the Court of Justice in *Marleasing*,[1126] which is based on such (*contra legem*) interpretation, has already been superseded by subsequent case law.

|||

[1123] Judgment of the European Court of Justice, Case C-40/08 (*Asturcom Telecomunicaciones SL* v. *Cristina Rodríguez Nogueira*), of May 14, 2009.

[1124] Decision of the Grand Chamber of the European Court of Justice in the joined cases C-397/01 to C-403/01 (*Bernhard Pfeiffer et al* v. *Deutsches Rotes Kreuz, Kreisverband Waldshut eV*), of October 5, 2004.

[1125] Section 35 of the ArbAct is quoted in a footnote in the opening part of this annotation.

[1126] Decision of the European Court of Justice, Case C-106/89 (*Marleasing SA* v. *La Comercial Internationale de Alimentacion SA*), of November 13, 1990.

II. Poland – The Supreme Court Judgments and Decisions of Appellate Courts

Maciej Durbas, associate, Kubas Kos Gałkowski – Adwokaci
e-mail: kamil.zawicki@kkg.pl

Kuba Gąsiorowski, associate, Kubas Kos Gałkowski – Adwokaci
e-mail: maciej.durbas@kkg.pl

Kamil Zawicki, attorney at law, partner, Kubas Kos Gałkowski – Adwokaci (ed.)
e-mail: kuba.gasiorowski@kkg.pl

Abbreviations

k.c. [POL] Kodeks cywilny z dnia 23 kwietnia 1964 r. [*Civil Code*] published in: Dziennik Ustaw [*Journal of Laws*] 1964, No. 15, item 93, as amended;

k.p.c. [POL] Kodeks postępowania cywilnego z dnia 17 listopada 1964 r. [*Code of Civil Procedure of November, 17 1964*], published in: Dziennik Ustaw [*Journal of Laws*] 1964, No. 43, item 296, as amended;

New York Convention New York Convention on the Recognition and Enforcement of Foreign Arbitral Awards of June, 10 1958 [*Konwencja o uznawaniu i wykonywaniu zagranicznych orzeczeń arbitrażowych, sporządzona w Nowym Jorku dnia 10 czerwca 1958 r.*], published in: Dziennik Ustaw [*Journal of Laws*] 1962, No. 9, item 41;[1]

| | |

---

[1] Poland signed the New York Convention on the Recognition and Enforcement of Foreign Arbitral Awards on June 10, 1958; it was ratified by Poland on October 3, 1961 and entered into force in Poland on January 1, 1962. The text of the New York Convention was published in Polish in the Journal of Laws 1962, No. 9, item 41.

1. An arbitration agreement encompasses not only the disputes explicitly mentioned in its substantive scope but also cases relating to these disputes (Appellate Court of Katowice (*Sąd Apelacyjny w Katowicach*) 1st Civil Division, Case No. V ACz 510/14 of June, 2 2014)[2]

Key Words:
domestic arbitration | effect of an arbitration agreement | Polish arbitration law | scope of the arbitration agreement | state courts

States involved:
[POL] – [Poland];

Laws and Regulations Applied in Decision:
Kodeks postępowania cywilnego z dnia 17 listopada 1964 r. [*Code of Civil Procedure of November, 17 1964*] [k.p.c.] [POL], published in: Dziennik Ustaw [*Journal of Laws*] 1964, No. 43, item 296, as amended; Articles: 1165 § 1;[3]

[Rationes Decidendi]:
17.01.   An arbitration agreement encompasses not only the disputes explicitly mentioned in its substantive scope but also cases relating to these disputes. Consequently, the prohibition of hearing the case by the state court is applicable also if the determination of the case presented before the state court and not explicitly covered by an arbitration agreement is impossible without examining a dispute being the subject of such an agreement.

---

[2]   The full text of this Decision is available in Polish on the Appellate Court of Katowice website at: http://orzeczenia.katowice.sa.gov.pl/content/$N/151500000002503_V_ACz_000510_2014_Uz_2014-06-02_001.

[3]   Article 1165 k.p.c. [POL] (unofficial translation): § 1. If a case is brought before a court concerning a dispute covered by an arbitration clause, the court shall reject a statement of claim or a motion to initiate non-contentious proceedings if the defendant or participant to non-contentions proceedings raises the existence of the arbitration clause before entering the merits of the case.

§ 2. The provisions of § 1 shall not apply if an arbitration clause is invalid, ineffective, unenforceable or has expired, and if the arbitration court declines jurisdiction.

§ 3. The fact that an action has been brought before a court does not prevent an arbitration court from hearing the case concerned.

§ 4. The provisions of the preceding paragraphs also apply if the venue of the proceedings before an arbitration court is located outside the borders of the Republic of Poland or is not defined.

[Description of Facts and Legal Issues]:

17.02. On May 27, 2008, A, the claimant and B, a bank, the defendant, entered into a framework agreement for foreign currency options. This agreement contained an arbitration clause submitting all disputes that could have arisen therefrom to arbitration under the auspices of the Arbitration Court at the Polish Bank Association. Subsequently, on August 7, 2009 the parties entered into a credit agreement. The claimant initiated proceedings before a state court relying on the invalidity of the credit agreement which did not contain any arbitration clause. The defendant argued that the case is covered by the arbitration clause from the framework agreement, so the statement of claim should be rejected.

17.03. In the decision of March 21, 2014, the Regional Court of Katowice rejected the statement of claim and acknowledged the jurisdiction of the arbitral tribunal. The court decided that the determination of the case is dependent on the existence of the obligations relating to the foreign currency options stemming from the framework agreement. This is because the alleged invalidity of the credit agreement (providing the basis for the claim) stems from the non-existence of the options obligations arising from the framework agreement, which is covered by the arbitration clause.

17.04. The claimant subsequently filed a complaint to the Appellate Court repeating its argumentation.

[Decision of the Appellate Court]:

17.05. The Appellate Court dismissed the complaint. It reminded that the arbitration agreement entails two kinds of effects. The positive effect pertains to the jurisdiction of the arbitral tribunal to hear the case. The negative effect consists in the prohibition of hearing a case before a state court. This rule is confirmed in Article 1165 § 1 of the Code of Civil Procedure, under which if a case is brought before a court concerning a dispute covered by an arbitration clause, the court shall reject the statement of claim.

17.06. The claimant argued that it paid more than PLN 5 million to the bank without any basis as the credit agreement was null and void. Although the credit agreement contained no arbitration clause, the Appellate Court found that Claimant took credit to pay for the currency options that were organized under the framework agreement that contained such a clause. Consequently, the determination of the case is dependent on finding whether claimant was obligated to pay for the currency options under the framework agreement or not. The aim of the credit agreement was to give the claimant monies to repay its obligations stemming from the framework agreement and not to substitute this agreement. Consequently, the framework agreement and therefore the arbitration clause remained in force.

| 645

Czech (& Central European) Yearbook of Arbitration

| | |

2. While examining the motion to set aside the arbitral award, the state court cannot control the evidential issues of the case; particular, detailed provisions of the Polish Public Procurement Law do not form public policy; if one party does not want to resolve the dispute through the Dispute Adjudication Board, the other party can direct its claim to the arbitral tribunal (Appellate Court of Gdańsk (*Sąd Apelacyjny w Gdańsku*) 1ˢᵗ Civil Division, Case No. I ACa 550/13 of November, 28, 2013)[4]

Key Words:
arbitration award | annulment of the award | dispute resolution clause | domestic arbitration | judicial review | Polish arbitration law | public policy | recourse against the award | review of the arbitral award | state courts

States involved:
[POL] – [Poland];

Laws and Regulations Applied in Decision:
Kodeks postępowania cywilnego z dnia 17 listopada 1964 r. [*Code of Civil Procedure of November, 17 1964*] [k.p.c.] [POL], published in: Dziennik Ustaw [*Journal of Laws*] 1964, No. 43, item 296, as amended; Articles: 1206 § 1;[5]

---

[4] The full text of this Decision is available in Polish on the Ministry of Justice's website at: http://orzeczenia.ms.gov.pl/content/$N/151000000000503_I_ACa_000550_2013_Uz_ 2013-11-28_001. As of October 2014, the case is pending before the Supreme Court of Poland under case No. IV CSK 443/14.

[5] Article 1206 k.p.c. [POL] (unofficial translation): § 1. A party may by petition demand that an arbitral award be set aside if: 1) there was no arbitration agreement, or the arbitration agreement is invalid, ineffective or no longer in force under the provisions of applicable law; 2) the party was not given proper notice of the appointment of an arbitrator or the proceeding before the arbitral tribunal or was otherwise deprived of the ability to defend its rights before the arbitral tribunal; 3) the arbitral award deals with a dispute not covered by the arbitration agreement or exceeds the scope of the arbitration agreement; however, if the decision on matters covered by the arbitration agreement is separable from the decision on matters not covered by the arbitration agreement or exceeding the scope thereof, then the award may be set aside only with regard to the matters

[*Rationes Decidendi*]:

17.07. While examining the motion to set aside the arbitral award, the state cannot control the evidential issues of the case. This is because the recourse proceedings are not the second instance of the same case. Furthermore, particular, detailed provisions of the Polish Public Procurement Law do not form public policy.

[*Description of Facts and Legal Issues*]:

17.08. On October 4, 2006, A, the claimant and B, the defendant, entered into an agreement for building a water supply and sewage network. The FIDIC Conditions of Contract for Construction for Building and Engineering Works Designed by the Employer were applicable. The contract was also entered into as a part of public procurement. In Article 20 of the Conditions, the Parties agreed that B, the contractor would direct its claim to the engineer, then to the Dispute Adjudication Board consisting of one person. The clause stipulated than if the parties did not agree on the composition of the board within 42 days, the Board would be appointed by a third party. Arbitration would be the third level of dispute resolution.

17.09. Within the course of works, B asked A to agree on additional works for the sum of more than EUR 1 million. B proposed a candidate for the Dispute Adjudication Board, but A refused. B did not ask any third party for the appointment and on April 26, 2010, filed a statement of claim to the Arbitration Court at the Polish Chamber of Commerce for the payment of circa EUR 1.5 million in additional works.

17.10. On April 30, 2012, the arbitral tribunal awarded the claim in its totality. The tribunal found that the prearbitral procedure was not obligatory and the lack of the decision of Dispute Adjudication Board is not an obstacle for arbitration.

17.11. On the merits of the case, the tribunal found that B should receive remuneration for additional works as it performed them and duly notified the engineer. This was confirmed by the expert's opinion.

---

not covered by the arbitration agreement or exceeding the scope thereof; exceeding the scope of the arbitration agreement cannot constitute grounds for vacating an award if a party who participated in the proceeding failed to assert a plea against hearing the claims exceeding the scope of the arbitration agreement; 4) the requirements with regard to the composition of the arbitral tribunal or fundamental rules of procedure before such tribunal, arising under statute or specified by the parties, were not observed; 5) the award was obtained by means of an offence or the award was issued on the basis of a forged or altered document; or 6) a legally final court judgment was issued in the same matter between the same parties. § 2. An arbitral award shall also be set aside if the court finds that: 1) in accordance with statute the dispute cannot be resolved by an arbitral tribunal, or 2) the arbitral award is contrary to the fundamental principles of the legal order of the Republic of Poland (public policy clause).

17.12. A filed a recourse against the arbitral award. It argued that the tribunal had exceeded its mandate and its award violated public policy by violating the parties' autonomy, disregarding public procurement law and selective evaluation of evidence. The Regional Court agreed that the arbitral tribunal exceeded the scope of the arbitration agreement. The prearbitral proceedings were obligatory. Under the arbitration agreement, there was only one situation in which the parties could direct their claims to the arbitral tribunal directly and it was when it was impossible to hear the claim before the Dispute Adjudication Board (because its mandate expired or it was impossible to appoint its members). In the case at hand, it was not impossible to appoint the Dispute Adjudication Board as there was a third party designated to act if the parties did not agree.

17.13. Furthermore, the court found that the arbitral award violated the public policy clause as it completely disregarded the Polish Public Procurement Law.

17.14. B challenged the judgment claiming that the Regional Court did not interpret the arbitration agreement properly and violated Article 1206 of the Code of Civil Procedure by finding that there are reasons to set aside the award. A defended its position.

[Decision of the Appellate Court]:

17.15. The Appellate Court changed the judgment of Regional Court and dismissed the motion to set aside the arbitral award. First, as to the argument of the Regional Court that the arbitral tribunal exceeded its mandate, the Appellate Court performed a thorough interpretation of the arbitration agreement. It found that if A, the employer, was not interested in appointing a Dispute Adjudication Board, this body could not resolve the dispute. Consequently, B, in directing the claim to the arbitral tribunal without having the dispute resolved by the Dispute Adjudication Board, did not violate any rules chosen by the parties.

17.16. Furthermore, the court found that the parties to the arbitral proceedings were treated equally and had the proper opportunity to present their case. In examining the motion to set aside the arbitral award the state court cannot control the evidential issues of the case. This is because it does not control the award in its totality, but only certain aspects of the award, arbitration agreement and the proceedings that could be raised in the motion to set aside the award.

17.17. As to violation of the public policy, the Appellate Court explained that such a violation did not take place. Even if it did, the provisions of the Public Procurement Law in question do not constitute Polish public policy.

3. The professional legal counsel representing a party in international arbitration is expected and required to know the legal culture and customs of the place of arbitration and any omissions caused by the lack of this knowledge cannot be cured by the invocation of the public policy clause. (Appellate Court in Gdańsk (*Sąd Apelacyjny w Gdańsku*) First Civil Division, Case No. I ACz 1475/13 of February, 11 2014)[6]

Key Words:
arbitration award | enforcement of the award | international arbitration | public policy

States involved:
[POL] – [Poland];
[CHN] – [China]

Laws and Regulations Applied in Decision:
The New York Convention on the Recognition and Enforcement of Foreign Arbitral Awards of June, 10 1958 [*Konwencja o uznawaniu i wykonywaniu zagranicznych orzeczeń arbitrażowych, sporządzona w Nowym Jorku dnia 10 czerwca 1958 r.*], [New York Convention], published in: Dziennik Ustaw [*Journal of Laws*] 1962, No. 9, item 41;[7] Article V Section 2.[8]

[*Rationes Decidendi*]:
17.18. The professional legal counsel of a party to international arbitration should be expected and required to know not only English, as the

---

[6]   The full text of this Decision is available in Polish on the Appelate Court in Gdańsk's website at: http://orzeczenia.gdansk.sa.gov.pl/content/$N/151000000000503_I_ACz_001 475_2013_Uz_2014-02-11_001.

[7]   Poland signed the New York Convention on the Recognition and Enforcement of Foreign Arbitral Awards on June 10, 1958; it was ratified by Poland on October 3, 1961 and it entered into force in Poland on January 1, 1962. The text of the New York Convention was published in Polish in the Journal of Laws 1962, No. 9, item 41.

[8]   Article V Section 2 of the New York Convention: 2. Recognition and enforcement of an arbitral award may also be refused if the competent authority in the country where recognition and enforcement is sought finds out that: (a) The subject matter of the difference is not capable of settlement by arbitration under the law of that country; or (b) The recognition or enforcement of the award would be contrary to the public policy of that country.

language of arbitration, but also the legal culture and customs of the place of arbitration – any omissions in that respect concerning the lack of challenge of arbitrator in a appropraite time – cannot be later cured by reference to the public policy clause.

17.19. The public policy clause cannot replace the proper challenge of an arbitrator. However, there are situations in which although a party failed to challenge the arbitrator, the arbitral award will not be enforced in the Republic in Poland on the grounds of the public policy under the provisions of the New York Convention.

[*Description of Facts and Legal Issues*]:

17.20. On June 30, 2010 two companies – J, with its registered seat in China, and C, with its registered seat in Poland entered into arbitration before the London Court of International Arbitration ("LCIA") before a sole arbitrator in a case for payment of amounts due to C by J.

17.21. In the course of the proceedings, the sole arbitrator disclosed to the parties on November 25, 2010 that he received an offer to join the same barristers' chamber as counsel of one of the parties. The arbitrator explained that there is no conflict of interest due to the specific nature of the relationships between the members of the barristers' chamber in England. However, at the same time, the arbitrator acknowledged that the parties may be unfamiliar with the organization of the English bar and thus stated that he will resign from his position as an arbitrator if any of the parties requests his resignation within 15 days. No such request was filed. As a result, on December 13, 2010 the sole arbitrator informed that he will proceed with the examination of the case.

17.22. On August 11, 2011 the arbitrator dismissed all of C's claims towards J as to their merits in a first partial award. In a second partial award, delivered on February 1, 2012, the arbitrator decided that C should return the costs of the proceedings to J as it was the losing party.

17.23. By a decision of September 23, 2010 initiated at the motion of J, the Regional Court in Gdańsk decided to enforce the partial award on the costs of the arbitral proceedings of February 1, 2012 against C. This decision was challenged by a complaint of C filed with the Appellate Court in Gdańsk. C claimed, among others, that the arbitral award violated the public policy, as the case was resolved by an arbitrator who was not impartial and independent – namely the sole arbitrator who, in the opinion of C, was "working in the same law firm as the counsel for the petitioner [i.e. Chinese company J] and in a subordinate position".

[*Decision of the Appellate Court*]:

17.24. The Appellate Court dismissed the complaint. Firstly, the Court underlined that C's argument of that the sole arbitrator was working in the same law firm as J's counsel and was subordinate was completely baseless as far the facts of the case were concerned. During the arbitral proceedings the sole arbitrator clearly stated that he does not know the counsel for J. Moreover, the Court stated that the members of a given barristers' chamber run law practices that are independent of each other and are not in any way partners and are not financially connected in any way that would cause a conflict of interest. The Court explained that C was not unfamiliar with international transactions and that it was represented by professional counsel. Thus, even if it had any doubts as to the nature of the relationship between the sole arbitrator and counsel for J, under the English law the arbitrator's brief of November 25, 2010 should be a sufficient indicator to C's counsel that this matter needs further examination. The Court concluded that a professional counsel who represents a party in international arbitrator is expected and required to be familiar with the legal culture and customs of the place of arbitration (in this case England) and cannot invoke the lack of his knowledge in this respect as a legal defense.

17.25. Moreover, the Court stated that the lack of a party's challenge of an arbitrator in a appropriate time in accordance with law and the rules of arbitration cannot be replaced by the invocation of the public policy clause at the stage of proceedings for the enforcement of the arbitral award.

17.26. Notwithstanding the above, the Court reasoned that there are two situations in which a party to arbitration proceedings may successfully invoke the public policy clause in connection with the violation of its right to a fair trial due to the resolution of the dispute by an arbitrator who lacked impartiality and independence.

17.27. The first situation is when an arbitrator violates the *nemo iudex in causa sua* principle which is also covered by the red list of International Bar Associations Guidelines on Conflicts of Interest in International Arbitration. In the opinion of the Court, this principle is covered by the Polish public policy clause in the meaning of Article V section 2 letter b of the New York Convention and should be enforced even if the parties failed to challenge the arbitrator during the arbitral proceedings.

17.28. Secondly, a party may invoke the public policy clause and request the court to refuse to enforce an arbitral award if the arbitrator failed to inform the parties during the arbitration of the circumstances that affect his impartiality and independence that are covered by the red and orange lists of the IBA and deprived the parties of a chance to challenge him on these grounds already in the course of the arbitration.

| | |

4. The Polish public policy includes not only the principles of freedom of contract and *pact sunt servanda* but also rules that limit the freedom of contract – such as principles of contract fairness. In practice, courts more often set aside arbitral awards due to their contradiction with the rules of public policy that limit the principle of freedom of contract than due to the violation of this very principle or the principle of *pacta sunt servanda* (Supreme Court (*Sąd Najwyższy*) Civil Chamber Decision, Case No. V CSK 45/13 of February, 13 2014)[9]

Key Words:
arbitration award | domestic arbitration | public policy | setting aside of an arbitral award

States involved:
[POL] – [Poland];

Laws and Regulations Applied in Decision:
Kodeks postępowania cywilnego z dnia 17 listopada 1964 r. [*Code of Civil Procedure of November, 17 1964*] [k.p.c.] [POL], published in: Dziennik Ustaw [*Journal of Laws*] 1964, No. 43, item 296, as amended; Article 1206 § 2 point 2;[10]

---

[9] The full text of this Decision is available in Polish on the Supreme Court's websiteat: http://www.sn.pl/sites/orzecznictwo/Orzeczenia3/V%20CSK%2045-13-2.pdf.

[10] Article 1206 k.p.c. [POL] (unofficial translation): § 1. A party may by petition demand that an arbitral award be set aside if: 1) there was no arbitration agreement, or the arbitration agreement is invalid, ineffective or no longer in force under the provisions of applicable law; 2) the party was not given proper notice of the appointment of an arbitrator or the proceeding before the arbitral tribunal or was otherwise deprived of the ability to defend its rights before the arbitral tribunal; 3) the arbitral award deals with a dispute not covered by the arbitration agreement or exceeds the scope of the arbitration agreement; however, if the decision on matters covered by the arbitration agreement is separable from the decision on matters not covered by the arbitration agreement or exceeding the scope thereof, then the award may be set aside only with regard to the matters not covered by the arbitration agreement or exceeding the scope thereof; exceeding the scope of the arbitration agreement cannot constitute grounds for vacating an award if a party who participated in the proceeding failed to assert a plea against hearing the claims exceeding the scope of the arbitration agreement; 4) the requirements with regard to the composition of the arbitral tribunal or fundamental rules of procedure

Kodeks cywilny z dnia 23 kwietnia 1964 r. [*Civil Code*] [k.c.] [POL], published in: Dziennik Ustaw [*Journal of Laws*] 1964, No. 15, item 93, as amended; Article 353,[11] Article 484 § 2;[12]

[*Rationes Decidendi*]:

17.29. The Polish public policy includes the principles of parties' autonomy and *pacta sunt servanda*. These rules are, however, not absolute. Under Article 353[1] of of the Civil Code, the parties' autonomy and *pacta sunt servanda* are limited by the nature of the legal relationship, statutory provisions and principles of social coexistence. Therefore, the Polish public policy contains also rules that provide for limits of those two principles.

17.30. Those "limiting principles" include in particular: the principle of freedom of economic activity, the principle of contractual fairness, the principle of compensatory nature of damages.

[*Description of Facts and Legal Issues*]:

17.31. On August 17, 2007, Companies H.P., H. and P, as contractors entered into a contract with Municipality W. as an investor for the expansion of the sewer system at housing complex O. The contractors were also obligated to provide post-construction documentation and file a notification of the handover of the investment for use. The contract provided for contractual penalties if the contractors failed to finish their work on time. H.P., H. and P managed to complete the expansion works on time, but were late with providing of the documentation and filing the notification, which constituted 3% of the value of the contractors' consideration. As a result, Municipality W. requested contractual penalties in the amount of approximately PLN 38 million

---

before such a tribunal, arising under a statute or specified by the parties, were not observed; 5) the award was obtained by means of an offence or the award was issued on the basis of a forged or altered document; or 6) a legally final court judgment was issued in the same matter between the same parties. § 2. An arbitral award shall also be set aside if the court finds that: 1) in accordance with the statute the dispute cannot be resolved by an arbitral tribunal, or 2) the arbitral award is contrary to the fundamental principles of the legal order of the Republic of Poland (public policy clause).

[11] Article 353[1] k.c. [POL] (unoffical translation): Parties making an agreement may arrange their legal relationship as they see it fit as long as its terms or purpose does not contradict the nature of the relationship, the statutory law or principles of social coexistence.

[12] Article 484 § 2 k.c. [POL] (unoffical transaltion): If the obligation was performed in a material part, the debtor may request the reduciton of the contractual penalty; the same applies if the contractual penalty is grossly excessive.

from H.P., H. and P. Subsequently Municipality W. deducted the contractual penalties from the price for the works.

17.32. The contractors initiated arbitration against the Municipality of W. requesting payment of their remuneration. The companies stated that the contractual penalties should be reduced by the arbitral panel under Article 484 Section 2 of the Civil Code as grossly excessive. The arbitral tribunal concurred with their opinion and in the award of April 20, 2011 reduced the contractual penalties to approximately PLN 1.8 million - i.e. declared that it was the amount that the Municipality of W. could deduct from the price for the expansions of the sewer system - and ordered the Municipality of W. to pay the rest of the price.

17.33. The Municipality of W. filed for the setting aside of the arbitral award with the Regional Court. W. stated that the arbitral tribunal, by reducing the contractual penalties which were calculated in full accordance with the provisions of the contract to such a great extent, violated the public policy clause under Article 1206 Section 2 point 2 of k.p.c., namely the principle of parties' autonomy and *pacta sunt servanda*. The Regional Court found this argumentation persuasive and by a judgment set aside the arbitral award. This judgment was later upheld by the court of the second instance. As a result, companies H.P., H. and P filed a cassation complaint with the Supreme Court.

[*Decision of the Supreme Court*]:

17.34. The Supreme Court ruled in favor of H.P., J. and P, set aside the judgment of the Appellate Court and changed the judgment of the Regional Court by dismissing the motion for setting aside of the arbitral award.

17.35. The Supreme Court reasoned that although it is true that the Polish public policy includes principles of freedom of contract and *pacta sunt servanda* they are not absolute and are subject to certain limitations. Those limitations include the principles of a compensatory nature of damages and contract fairness. The "limiting principles" themselves are also the part of the Polish public policy. As a result, the reduction of the contractual penalties by the arbitral tribunal made under Article 484 § 2 k.c. in this case was done in accordance with the law.

| | |

III. Slovak Republic – Current Case Law of the Slovak National Courts regarding Arbitration

Martin Magál, Partner, Allen & Overy Bratislava, s.r.o.
e-mail: Martin.Magal@AllenOvery.com

Martina Kasemová, Lawyer, Allen & Overy Bratislava, s.r.o.
e-mail: Martina.Kasemova@AllenOvery.com

Abbreviations

Arbitration Act	Act No. 244/2002 Coll. on arbitration proceedings, as amended *(Zákon č. 244/2002 Z. z. o rozhodcovskom konini, v znení neskorších predpisov)*
Constitution	Act No. 460/1992 Coll., the Constitution of the Slovak Republic, as amended *(Zákon č. 460/1992 Z. z., Ústava Slovenskej republiky, v znení neskorších predpisov)*
SVK	Slovak Republic

| | |

1. Slovak enforcement courts have a limited right to reject the enforcement of an arbitral award. Ruling of the Constitutional Court of the Slovak Republic [SVK], file No II. US 499/2012-47, dated 10 July 2013

Key Words:
arbitral award | court enforcement proceedings | enforcement of an arbitral award | validity of an arbitration clause | court review | rejection of enforcement

18.01. The case relates to a dispute which arose from an insurance contract entered into between the complainant (insurance company) and its counterparty. The counterparty failed to perform under the insurance contract and, consequently, the complainant sought enforcement on the basis of an arbitral award validly issued by an arbitral tribunal having jurisdiction to hear the case. Following this, the court executor filed a request with the court to grant authorisation to commence enforcement proceedings. Oddly enough, the court requested the submission of additional documents (the insurance contract and terms and conditions of the insurance) and came to the debatable conclusion that the respective arbitration clause was invalid, but without actually examining the issue in detail. The resolution was confirmed by the appellate courts at all instances.

18.02. Based on the evidence, the Constitutional Court concluded that the conduct of the general courts was in conflict with fundamental procedural rights of the complainant, and invalidated the decision of the Supreme Court. In its reasoning, the Constitutional Court drew attention to several important aspects.

18.03. Firstly, conclusions concerning the invalidity of an arbitration clause must be made only after a detailed and thorough examination of facts of a particular case, and the application of legal regulations to those facts. Secondly, before the enforcement stage taking place, the validity of the arbitration clause was already examined and analysed by the arbitral tribunal, which has a statutory authorisation to do so in accordance with the competence-competence principle. Finally, the conclusion regarding the invalidity of an arbitration clause cannot be made during enforcement proceedings without granting the applicant an opportunity to be heard on the issue. As a result of the aforementioned facts, the Constitutional Court concluded that the fundamental rights and freedoms of the complainant were violated, overturned the decision of the Supreme Court and returned it to the Supreme Court for further judicial review.

18.04. The pivotal message of the Constitutional Court's ruling is that an enforcement court cannot deny the enforcement of arbitral awards merely on the basis of a general argument that all arbitration clauses incorporated in consumer contracts are automatically invalid. The court held that such a conclusion can only be made on the basis of examining the specific facts of the case at hand.

18.05. Due to existence of numerous opposing decisions, the issue has been brought before, and subsequently confirmed by, the plenary session of the Constitutional Court consisting of all judges of the Constitutional Court, thus becoming a common unified opinion to be followed by courts.

|||

2. The Constitutional Court indirectly confirmed the admissibility of constitutional complaints against arbitral awards. Ruling of the Constitutional Court of the Slovak Republic [SVK], file No II. US 49/2014-8, dated 29 January 2014

Key Words:
constitutional complaint against arbitral awards | finality of awards

18.06. Under Art. 127 (1) of the Constitution, the Constitutional Court shall have jurisdiction to decide on individual complaints brought by individuals or legal entities objecting to the violation of their fundamental rights and freedoms. Before the 'Big Amendment' to the Constitution in 2001, it was expressly stated that such complaints had to be directed against interference with the fundamental rights and freedoms by public authorities. Although the post-2001 wording does not define the scope of the eligible interfering subjects, legal theory continues to be of the view that it is the public authorities. Technically, arbitral awards are decisions issued by specific bodies empowered by parties to a contract to settle their dispute. Based on this reasoning, it should not be possible to submit a claim against arbitral tribunals as the fact that these do not have the status of "public authorities" is beyond doubt.

18.07. In the given case, the complainant requested the Constitutional Court to set aside the arbitral award on the basis that it allegedly interfered with its fundamental right to judicial protection. According to the Constitutional Court, although arbitral tribunals are not public authorities, the right to judicial protection also applies to arbitration proceedings. The Constitutional Court stated that the purpose of judicial protection of constitutionality is to protect individuals from those interventions to their rights which are constitutionally unjustifiable and unsustainable, rather than to protect individuals from the factual errors of general courts. The Constitutional Court held that arbitral tribunals are also obliged to apply law in such a way that they issue awards which meet the parameters of legality and constitutionality.

18.08. The complaint was however rejected by reference to the principle of subsidiarity. The purpose of the subsidiarity principle is that the system of constitutional protection of fundamental rights and freedoms is divided between general courts and the Constitutional Court whereas the competence of the general courts is primary, while the competence of the Constitutional Court is subsidiary.

18.09. However, what this decision of the Constitutional Court actually means is that constitutional complaints against arbitral awards are in theory possible, despite arbitral tribunals not having the status of public authorities.

| | |

3. The principle of independence and impartiality of arbitrators is essential for due process. Ruling of the Regional Court in Žilina [SVK], file No. 8 Co/ 97/2013, dated 30 August 2013

Key Words:
independence | impartiality | conflict of interest

18.10. This case concerned a dispute between a cooperative society (claimant) and an individual (respondent) regarding the annulment of an arbitral award. Firstly, the court had to decide on its jurisdiction to hear the case. The respondent objected to the Slovak court's jurisdiction on the basis that the place of arbitration was in Bosnia and Herzegovina and, consequently, Slovak courts were not entitled to set aside foreign arbitral awards.

18.11. The respective arbitration clause entered into by the parties provided for arbitration in accordance with the Arbitration Act and under the rules of an arbitral institution with the seat in Žilina, Slovakia (the **Arbitral Institution**), as these were the rules with which the parties were acquainted and to which they submitted. Several months later and after the commencement of the arbitration proceedings, the Arbitral Institution's rules were amended concerning the place of arbitration which was changed to Bijelijna, Bosnia and Herzegovina. The amended rules set out that the amendments were effective as of the date of their publication and also applied to proceedings that had already commenced, if the parties to a dispute did not exclude the effectiveness by a joint submission to the Arbitral Institution.

18.12. The court held that the amendment caused essential substantive-law implications as the originally agreed place of arbitration was changed, which change was not agreed by the parties. The most critical consequence would be the re-characterisation of the arbitral award from domestic to foreign, which would lead to the exclusion of the originally agreed scope for the Slovak court's review. In addition, the Arbitral Institution's rules did not contain any provisions regarding the parties' submission to any future amendments to the rules. The court concluded that the respective provisions of the rules of the Arbitral Institution were in conflict with the law.

18.13. Secondly, the court dealt with the question whether the grounds for annulment were met and ruled that the lack of the arbitrators' impartiality and independence in the case was evident (thus constituting a basis for setting the award aside). Under Section 12 of the Arbitration Act, a legal entity can establish and administer a permanent arbitral institution, subject to other statutory requirements. The lack of independence and impartiality materialised in the fact that the respondent and the director of the Arbitral Institution's founding legal entity were each a shareholder in the same company. In addition, the respondent was an executive of the respective company. Since the arbitral proceedings were expedited, the claimant could not raise an objection of impartiality. Another consideration which led the court to this conclusion was that the director of the Arbitral Institution's founding legal entity had previously been a chairman of the claimant's board of directors, and it was only during that time that the claimant submitted to the Arbitral Institution's rules when contracting.

18.14. Thirdly, since the arbitral award did not contain any reasoning or information about the possibility to file a claim for its annulment, the principle of equality of the parties and the claimant's right to due process were breached, as well as Section 34 of the Arbitration Act, which sets out the formal requirements of arbitral awards.

| | |

Book Reviews

Czech (& Central European) Yearbook of Arbitration

Book Reviews

Gunther J. Horvath and Stephan Wilske, eds.
Guerrilla Tactics in International Arbitration

HORVATH, G. J. and WILSKE, S. (eds.) Guerrilla Tactics in International Arbitration, 2013. Netherlands: Kluwer Law International, 429 P.

International arbitration has recently witnessed an increase in the use of "guerrilla tactics", i.e. attempts by the parties and their legal counsel to unlawfully, or at least unethically, influence the proceedings and the outcome of arbitration. Arbitration is much more vulnerable to such tactics than litigation, due to the private nature of arbitration and the principle of informal procedure and confidentiality applicable in arbitration. At the same time, these methods are often impossible to combat by court intervention, in terms of the auxiliary and supervisory function of courts vis-à-vis arbitration.

The above-mentioned issues are analysed in the publication being reviewed, which has a very apt title, *Guerrilla Tactics in International Arbitration*, issued by Kluwer Law International BV. This book is the 28th volume in the special series *International Arbitration Law Library*. The publication is structured as a compact collection of articles contributed by authors from various countries, with the collection successfully following on discussions among academics and professionals from past years. In this connection, it is important to emphasise that the approach that the editors have adopted is very good with respect to the selection, composition, interconnection and conception of the topics fleshed out in the individual chapters, while it is also necessary to praise their choice of experienced authors for the individual chapters. Publications composed of articles written by different authors often suffer from the incompatibility, but this does not hold true for this book. This can undoubtedly be attributed to the editors, both of whom are experienced experts with both practical and academic knowledge and, first and foremost, extensive knowledge and experience in arbitration, as well as in international legal and commercial transactions, as such.

The first chapter of the book introduces the readers to and explains *guerrilla tactics*. However, it does not stop at the mere definition of the concept, but also describes the essential types of such tactics, distinguishing them from unpleasant and ruthless conduct in arbitration, the latter being in an *ethical grey area* and in compliance with the applicable law. The first chapter also analyses the causes of the increasingly frequent use of guerrilla tactics, and considers potential changes to the rules and standards currently applied in international arbitration that could help to combat such practices more efficiently. The next part of the book focuses on a discussion of who has and who should have the power to impose sanctions on the parties and their legal counsel for using these unfair practices. The publication does not disregard the role of international organisations and permanent arbitral institutions in enforcing *"anti-guerrilla"* changes to the applicable and applied procedural standards. The discussion in this Chapter has neither neglected the issue of the potential creation of uniform, universal and unified rules of conduct in international arbitration,[1] which would prevent the occurrence of the undesirable situation that we are witnessing today, namely that the legal counsel to parties from different states are subject to different rules regulating their conduct as legal counsel, which are incorporated in their home legal systems, and which can differ diametrically from one another. The last part of Chapter One analyses the role of ethics in international arbitration.

Chapter Two, which is more pragmatically oriented, sets forth means by which *guerrilla practices* can successfully be countered. It opens with a detailed analysis of the options that legal counsel have at their disposal at the various stages of the proceedings (including the stage of drafting the arbitration clause). The next sub-chapter deals with the possibilities of combating *guerrilla tactics* offered under the ICC Rules on Arbitration. It also includes paragraphs elaborating on the issue of dealing with *guerrilla tactics* when they are employed by states, state authorities and state institutions. The reason is that hindering and obstructing the enforcement of the law in arbitration is by no

---

[1] In this particular connection, the author of the review mentions the IBA Guidelines on Party Representation in International Arbitration, as adopted by the Resolution of the IBA Council on 25 March 2013, which provide, to a certain extent, a basis for such unification. But it has to be emphasised that, although the IBA standards have major importance, there are many states in which the IBA standards are completely unknown, save to a very small group of experts. Moreover, they certainly do not represent any generally binding standards. Besides, the above-mentioned 2013 IBA Guidelines have not yet been implemented in practice to any major extent, and also lack the quality of enforceable rules from the perspective of potential sanctions.

means limited to private-law individuals and entities – being parties to the arbitral proceedings. On the contrary, states and public-law entities, as parties to a dispute, have substantially greater opportunity to deploy *guerrilla methods* with much more vehemence, relying on their apparatus of power. The fourth sub-chapter deals with sanctions imposed as a penalty for *guerrilla tactics* that the arbitrators have at their disposal. Chapter Two closes with a relatively extensive analysis of the role and potential future role of state courts as concerns their auxiliary function vis-à-vis arbitration, i.e. their assistance to arbitrators in suppressing *guerrilla tactics* and their effects on a particular arbitration.

Chapter Three is the most extensive and by far the most interesting part of the book, dealing with *guerrilla tactics* in national and international arbitration. It opens with a description of the relationship between national laws on the management of arbitration and international arbitration. Chapter Three also analyses the rules regulating the behaviour of the parties and their legal counsel in adversarial proceedings, and the possibility of penalising *guerrilla tactics* in the Anglo-Saxon legal system, in continental legal systems, in post-socialistic legal systems, and in the legal systems of Asian countries (separately for South-Asian countries), African countries and Arab Islamic systems. In connection with the preceding part, Chapter Three analyses corruption and the deployment of *guerrilla tactics* in the countries of Central, Eastern and Southern Europe and in Turkey. This is followed by paragraphs dealing with *guerrilla tactics* before international tribunals and institutions, namely the International Court of Justice (ICJ), the World Trade Organisation (WTO), the International Tribunal for the Law of the Sea, the World Intellectual Property Organisation (WIPO/OMPI), and the Court of Arbitration for Sport (CAS). The authors always concentrate on the specific features of the given institution, then the legal rules regulating proceedings before the institution, and the methods employed by the institution to counter *guerrilla tactics*, including case law, if available. The last sub-chapter analyses the applicability of selected concepts, procedures and solutions incorporated in national laws and the laws of international institutions that concern combating and penalising *guerrilla practices* in international arbitration. Despite the fact that this comparative-analytical part of the publication is relatively brief in the description of the specific features of proceedings in the individual regions, and the individual sections are by no means exhaustive, it still provides a very clear and exceptionally well-founded explanation of the essential common attributes of arbitration laws and the regulation of the conduct and behaviour of legal counsel, and underlines the principal differences between the individual laws. Younger generations and lawyers actively or passively engaged in sports will certainly appreciate the text analysing *guerrilla tactics* at the CAS (Court of Arbitration for Sports), with its sporting flavour and the analysis of proceedings involving well-known sports personalities, comes across as "refreshing" within the context of the book.

The following chapter first deals with the influence of international institutions and bar associations that regulate the rules of conduct applicable to legal counsel. The chapter then proceeds with the issue of potential diplomatic support provided by the state, or the possibilities of diplomatic intermediation by the state, as applicable, in proceedings involving an individual (citizen or resident of the state) against another state, where the latter uses *guerrilla practices* against the individual (counterparty), including the limits of such support, with special emphasis on analysing the possibilities available to diplomatic support in proceedings pursuant to the ICSID Rules.

Chapter Five deals with selected differences in the ethical rules of conduct applicable to legal counsel and incorporated in the national legal systems of their home states (states where they are registered), as well as the difficulties and injustices in international arbitration caused by the absence of any uniform ethical and professional standards applicable to attorneys' behaviour. The Chapter also opens a discussion on the possibility of uniform rules governing the conduct of legal counsel and procedural standards in international arbitration, with the author arguing that uniform rules of conduct applicable to legal counsel and to selected issues of management of the arbitral proceedings (which are subject to different regulation under the individual legal systems) would solve the problem.

The last chapter of the book provides a structured summary of the most important conclusions and recommendations from the preceding chapters. The authors have pinpointed the gravest problem of international arbitration in recent years, namely the increasing endeavours of the parties and their legal counsel to win the dispute or advance their clients' interests at whatever cost, while such approach to arbitral proceedings defeats the original purpose of international arbitration and frustrates the objective thereof, i.e. a fast, confidential, informal and cost-effective means of dispute resolution. I do not fully share some of the authors' opinions concerning restrictions of the arbitrators' confidentiality obligation in relation to *guerrilla practices*, and I am not convinced that any agreement will be reached at the international level with respect to uniform rules of conduct applicable to legal counsel in international arbitration and uniform regulation of the currently controversial aspects of the management of international arbitral proceedings (at least not within any acceptable period, i.e. no time soon), but I am convinced that the editors and authors have managed to define and analyse, in a high-quality, clear and comprehensible manner, one of the most burning issues in international arbitration and to propose well-founded solutions to the problem. Considering the erudition and extensive practical expertise of the authors, and primarily the editors, the book can certainly be highly recommended – despite the fact that it strives to provide a co-authored analysis of a very complicated and extremely broad issue with a number of procedural, substantive, legal-professional, private- and public-law, and numerous other aspects.

The annex to the publication contains a number of existing international standards created on the basis of multiple platforms. These annexes appropriately complement the collection of texts, and allow the readers to delve into a more detailed study of the problem.

The publication being reviewed is a very skilful and comprehensive contribution to the discussion regarding *guerrilla tactics* and the possible restrictions on and combating of these practices, undesirable for international arbitration. It is basically the first comprehensive, but at the same time comparative, publication analysing this topic, with proposals for constructive and suitable solutions that can, indeed, frequently be enforceable in practice. I also appreciate the fact that the book presents potential means of countering such practices that can be used both by legal counsel as well as arbitrators. The quality of the individual contributions is very high, and the editors who compiled this collection of papers have undoubtedly done a very good job. I even dare say that this collection should have a place on the bookshelf of any lawyer who plays an active role in arbitration.

[*Alexander J. Bělohlávek*]

| | |

News & Reports

News & Reports

Forms of Interaction between International Arbitration Courts Created in the Republic of Belarus and Belarusian State Courts

I. General Provisions: Classification of the Forms of Interaction between International Arbitration Courts and Belarusian State Courts

The following two non-state courts in the Republic of Belarus are regulated by two separate legislative acts:

1. arbitration courts that function in accordance with the Act No. 301-Z of the Republic of Belarus dated 18 July 2011 'On arbitration courts' (hereinafter, the 'Arbitration Court Act');
2. international arbitration courts whose creation and functioning comply with the act of the Republic of Belarus 'On international arbitration courts' (hereinafter, the 'International Arbitration Court Act').

In spite of the closely related subject of these two arbitration court types, their legal regulation in the Republic of Belarus has certain distinguishing features that affect the forms of interaction between them and state courts (infra).

Due to the fact that international arbitration courts created in the Republic of Belarus do not administer justice but render binding decisions regarding awards involving conflicting parties, such awards require the enforcement power of the state. Hence there is a need for interaction between arbitration courts and state courts.

Since international arbitration courts must cooperate with state courts by virtue of their existence, it is practically impossible to imagine their normal functioning without such interaction.

In view of the above, the following three forms of interaction can take place between international arbitration courts and state courts:

1. assistance provided by state courts to international arbitration courts including:
   1.1. assistance in identifying the true intention of the disputing parties for resorting to an international arbitration court;
   1.2. assistance in conducting arbitral proceedings;
   1.3. assistance with the future execution of the arbitration award of the international arbitration court;
2. state court control over the compliance of an arbitration award with the requirements of Belarusian legislation;
3. execution of arbitration awards of international arbitration courts:
   3.1. enforcement of international arbitration awards rendered in the Republic of Belarus; and
   3.2. enforcement of international arbitration awards rendered in foreign countries.

Other classifications of interaction between arbitration courts and Belarusian state courts are also mentioned in the doctrine.

For instance, Russian author I. V. Reshetnikov proposes that such forms of interaction be divided into legal procedural forms and legal organizational forms. Appeals of international arbitration awards and the issuance of enforcement court orders, court rulings on interim measures of protection and procedural response measures are considered legal procedural forms.

According to this author, legal organizational forms include the organization of training seminars with participating judges of state courts, cooperative seminars and round table meetings, and providing arbitration courts with compilations of state court case-law.

Other authors, including A. I. Zaitseva and R. N. Gimaov, distinguish between organizational interaction and procedural interaction.

Organizational interaction is performed through the notification of the competent state court of the formation of a permanent arbitration court on its territory.

Procedural interaction comprises court rulings on interim measures of protection during arbitration proceedings, appeals of arbitration court awards and the issuance of enforcement rulings.

When considering state court interaction with international arbitration courts it should be mentioned that the International Arbitration Court Act is based on

UNCITRAL Model Law on International Commercial Arbitration which represents the basis for the continental approach to arbitration courts. The essence of the approach lies in the independence of the composition of the court and the non-appealability of the rendered awards, i.e., a state court may not set aside awards of international arbitration courts regarding infringements of material law.

On the contrary, the common law approach to arbitration courts proceeds from the subordination of international arbitration courts to state courts, which gives the latter the right to review awards of international arbitration courts.

The particular forms (kinds) of interaction between international arbitration courts and Belarusian state courts under Belarusian law will be considered according to these approaches.

||||

II. Assistance in Identifying the True Intention of the Disputing Parties for Resorting to an International Arbitration Court

Pursuant to article 151 of the Code of Commercial Procedure of the Republic of Belarus, a lawsuit may be rejected on the following grounds:

- the parties' agreement to refer a dispute to the arbitration court;
- the defendant's objection to resolving the dispute in Economic Court. The dispute should have been sent to the arbitration court before the trial on merits.

Hence, Belarusian law is based on the concept of the settlement of a dispute with an arbitration agreement by a state court which provides that the state court has the right to adjudicate, even if there is an arbitration agreement, but only in the event that neither party objects.

The plaintiff must directly express the will to resolve a dispute in state court by filing a claim and the other party to the arbitration agreement (the defendant) must not submit a petition to transfer the dispute to the arbitration court.

Thus, Belarusian legislation requires that the parties must have an arbitration agreement and express their will to resolve the dispute in a non-state court at least two times. Otherwise, if neither party has submitted a lawsuit to international arbitration, the dispute will be resolved in a state court. Pursuant to par. 3 of article 151 of the Code of Commercial Procedure of the Republic of Belarus, a Commercial Court shall set aside a lawsuit if the arbitration court is hearing a dispute between the same parties on the same subject and on the same grounds.

Czech (& Central European) Yearbook of Arbitration

According to article 149 of the Code of Commercial Procedure of the Republic of Belarus, one of the grounds for the termination of proceedings by the Commercial Court is the existence of an arbitration award issued by an arbitration court located in the Republic of Belarus in a dispute between the same parties on the same subject and on the same grounds, except when the Commercial Court refuses to grant an order to enforce this award.

The foregoing was confirmed by Resolution № 21 of the Plenum of the Supreme Commercial Court of the Republic of Belarus dated 31 October, 2011, on Issues arising from cases involving foreign parties.

Thus, pursuant to par. 13 of the above Resolution, the existence of an arbitration agreement cannot prevent the other party from filing a lawsuit in a proper Commercial Court.

A Commercial Court has the right to set aside a lawsuit only if the defendant objects to the resolution of the dispute in the Commercial Court. In such case, the defendant should petition to have the dispute transferred to the arbitration court prior to the trial on merits. At the court hearing, the Commercial Court should inform the defendant of his right to object to the proceedings in the Commercial Court.

If the defendant does not submit such petition within the specified period or if its confirms its will to resolve a dispute in Commercial Court in the presentation of a statement of defense or the declaration of procedural petitions, it loses his right to transfer a dispute to the arbitration court.

In other countries, the opposite approach is taken. The basis of this approach is the rejection of state courts in arbitral proceedings under the proper arbitration agreement.

Pursuant to paragraph 13 of resolution № 21 of the Plenum of the Supreme Commercial Court of Belarus on October 31, 2011, on Issues arising from cases involving foreign parties, the Commercial Court resolves on disputes with an arbitration agreement on the merits, regardless of the defendant's request to transfer the dispute to the arbitration court if:

- the arbitration agreement is void; or
- the arbitration award cannot be performed according to point 3, art. II of the New York Convention on the Recognition and Enforcement of Foreign Arbitral Awards.

Herewith, the Commercial Court assesses the validity of the arbitration agreement, especially in terms of:

- its written form;
- the legal capacity and capability of the parties;
- the voluntary will of the parties;

- the existence of an arbitration award involving a dispute between the same parties on the same subject and on the same grounds in the Commercial Court;
- the arbitration body defined for resolving the dispute; and
- the competence of the arbitration court.

Based on the foregoing, the Plenum of the Supreme Commercial Court of Belarus de facto and de jure empowers the Commercial Court to analyze the legal nature and substance of an arbitration agreement (on its own initiative, i.e., without the will of the parties).

Thus, the Commercial Court has the right to resolve a dispute with three independent subjects of a lawsuit:

- the nullity of the arbitration agreement (the first subject);
- the loss of effect of the arbitration agreement (the second subject); and
- the impracticability of the arbitration agreement (the third subject).

In our opinion, this approach does not fully correspond to the nature of the Commercial Court as a body exercising economic justice, which is based on the will of a party to the dispute, not its own initiative.

We do not deny the right of the Commercial Court to annul an arbitration agreement, establish the fact of its loss of effect or void the agreement or its enforceability, especially as a result of the recognition and enforcement of foreign arbitral awards.

Only within the framework of such proceedings can the Commercial Courts establish the foregoing facts and render a judgment.

In our opinion, in the event of the availability of an arbitration agreement and a lawsuit in Commercial Court and the defendant's objections to the resolution of the dispute in Commercial Court, the Commercial Court should not analyze the nullity, loss of effect or impracticability of arbitration agreement. Further, it should disallow a lawsuit. All of the circumstances described above should be the subject of arbitration proceedings.

The exception to this approach is found in the provisions stated in part 2 of article 6 of the European Convention on International Commercial Arbitration, according to which, the courts may refuse to recognize an arbitration agreement if, under the law of their country, the dispute is not capable of being settled by arbitration.

In this case, except for the recognition, enforcement and overturning of an arbitral proceeding of an international arbitration court, we recognize the right of the Commercial Court to assess an arbitration agreement based on the arbitrability of the dispute.

Czech (& Central European) Yearbook of Arbitration

Naturally, if a dispute does not belong to the competence of an international arbitration court, it will belong to the jurisdiction of the state court.

III

III.   Assistance in Conducting Arbitral Proceedings

Assistance with the future execution of the arbitration award of an international arbitration court

Pursuant to article 23 of the International Arbitration Court Act, the composition of the court can render a ruling that will bind a party to impose interim measures of protection it deems appropriate for the matter at hand and force a party to provide proper security due to such measures at the request of any party, unless otherwise agreed by the parties.

Besides that, the court or a party with the consent of the court can petition the state court or the court of a foreign state for the protection of a claim or evidence. Part two of article 23 of the International Arbitration Court Act envisages that the state court fulfills such a petition within its competence and according to procedural legislation.

The provision regarding the ability of a party to petition the state court for the protection of a claim both before and during the trial at an international arbitration court is also contained in article 14 of the International Arbitration Court Act.

Article 12 of the Rules of the International Arbitration Court of the Belarusian Chamber of Commerce and Industry (hereinafter – the IAC of the BelCCI) contains provisions that are much the same as the provisions of articles 12 and 23 of the International Arbitration Court Act.

Par. 2 of article 12 of the Rules of the IAC of the BelCCI envisages that the court or a party with the consent of the court can petition the Belarusian state court or a similar court of a foreign state for the protection of a claim or evidence.

Such consent can be granted by the Chairman of the IAC of the BelCCI prior to the formation of the court.

Thus the matter of the protection of a claim can be considered by both the state court and the IAC of the BelCCI.

The IAC of the BelCCI is entitled to render a ruling that binds a party to take interim measures of protection and:

- petition the Belarusian state court or a similar court of a foreign state for the protection of a claim or evidence;
- give its consent to a party to petition the Belarusian state court or a similar court of a foreign state for the protection of a claim or evidence.

In the practice of the IAC of the BelCCI, the second method is most commonly used.

Thus, on December 11, 2012, the court deciding on a case regarding the invalidity of a contract concluded between Belarusian parties granted the claimant its consent to petition the Minsk Commercial Court for the protection of the claim brought before the IAC of the BelCCI in the form of freezing the monetary asserts of the defendant.

Pursuant to articles 113-116, 118, 119, 212-214 of the Code of Commercial Procedure of the Republic of Belarus and article 23 of the International Arbitration Court Act, the Minsk Commercial Court rendered a ruling on the protection of the claim.

While resolving another dispute that arose from a lease agreement for a vehicle, the claimant (Belarusian party) petitioned the court for its consent to petition the Minsk Commercial Court for interim protective measures.

The claimant asked that the car in the temporary possession and use of the representative office of the respondent in the Republic of Belarus be seized and handed over for the bailment of the claimant and that the respondent be prohibited from concluding certain actions, to be exact, using such car for commercial and other purposes.

After the receiving the proper consent, the claimant petitioned the Minsk Commercial Court with a claim regarding the seizure of the car and the prohibition of its use for commercial and other purposes, which was accepted.

In our opinion, the practice of obtaining the consent to petition the state court with a claim for enforcement measures is extremely useful a number of reasons. Firstly, there are no enforcement measures of an IAC of the BelCCI award to secure a claim.

Secondly, petitioning a state court (usually the state commercial court) requires that the final decision on that issue be made by that court. It's possible that the state court wouldn't agree with the measures to protect the claim or the evidence previously indicated by the IAC of the BelCCI. In that case, it would make sense to obtain the permission of the state court for the proper claim.

The accomplishment of the mentioned claim by the commercial (economic) courts of the Republic of Belarus in accordance with the provisions of the Code of Commercial Procedure of the Republic of Belarus (mainly Chapter 9 on the protection of a claim) correspond to the provisions of article 23 of the International Arbitration Court Act.

According to chapter 9 of the Code of Commercial Procedure of the Republic of Belarus, in order to obtain measures to protect a claim, a written petition should be submitted. The petition must contain:

- the name of the economic court to which the petition is submitted;

- the names, postal addresses and phone and (or) fax numbers, (if they have them) of the claimant and the respondent;
- the circumstances under which the petition for the protection of the claim is based;
- the measure that should be applied;
- if the demands relate to property – the size of the property;
- if the petition relates to the seizure of property – the property and its current location should be mentioned;
- the reasons that led to the need to submit the petition to protect the claim; and
- a list of enclosed documents.

The petition to protect the claim could be used for:

- the seizure of real estate or other property owned by the respondent or garnished by other persons;
- the seizure of financial resources in bank accounts and (or) other non-bank financial organizations;
- the prohibition of the respondent to conclude certain actions;
- the imposition of the respondent to conclude certain actions;
- the prohibition of other persons to conclude certain actions related to the subject of the claim; and
- other measures that do not contradict the legislation.

After a deep analysis of the practice of the use of protective measures, not only by the IAC of the BelICCI, but also other international commercial arbitration courts, and for the purpose of developing this type of resolution of disputes in the Republic of Belarus and attracting foreign subjects (parties) to use this procedure in the Republic of Belarus, we believe that it is rational to make changes to the International Arbitration Court Act. The arbitration court should have the right to declare an interim enforceable award to apply a measure to protect a claim.

When examining cooperation during the application of the measures to protect the claim of state courts with the arbitration courts located in the Republic of Belarus, it should be noted that article 30 of the Arbitration Court Act has only one possible form for applying for measures to protect a claim that is in the process of arbitration. Such provision is completely different to article 23 of the International Arbitration Court Act which offers two possible forms.

According to article 30 of the Arbitration Court Act, a petition for the protection of a claim during arbitration proceedings may only be requested by a party to the claim. This petition is submitted to the state court with jurisdiction over the place of the tribunal proceeding, or over the place where the property (that should be taken under the measures to protect the claim) is located.

In the same way, this Act does not give the party any opportunity to petition the arbitral tribunal for measures to protect a claim. Moreover, this provision can lead to a situation where the arbitration tribunal may not even know about the measures to protect the claim.

This, on our opinion, is absolutely impropriate, but the law does not oblige the parties to the claim to inform the arbitration tribunal of the decision of a state court regarding the measures to protect the claim.

Submitting a petition for measures to protect a claim to the state court during the arbitration proceedings should be carried out under the general rules of jurisdiction stipulated by civil procedure or commercial procedure law. The only difference is that this petition should be submitted with the ruling of the arbitration court about the commencement of proceedings.

When analyzing the form of cooperation between state courts and arbitration courts, it should be noted that article 30 of the Arbitration Court Act stipulates that the submission of a petition for measures to protect a claim and entailing this measure should not be considered as incompatible with the arbitration court's agreement or rejection thereof. Thus, the law stressed that the form of cooperation between state courts and arbitration courts cannot change the will of the parties to solve the dispute by arbitration court only and the denial of the use of the state court.

Article 30 of the Arbitration Court Act emphases that the decision of the state court on measures to protect a claim may only be overturned by the same state court that adjudicated it. The most important cause for the revocation of the measures to protect a claim is the decision of the arbitration court to dismiss the claims.

In conclusion, it should be noted that all of the questions about the measures to protect a claim during arbitration proceedings should be carried out according to the provisions of the civil procedure or commercial procedure law of the Republic of Belarus. Moreover, it depends on the parties to the dispute. In other words, submitting the petition to the state court for measures to protect a claim, submitting the petition for the revocation of such measures, the decision for the entailment of such measures, or the revocation of the petition for the measures to protect the claim should be done in strict accordance with Belarusian law regarding the state courts of the Republic of Belarus. The provisions for arbitration courts do not influence this procedure.

| | |

IV. Control of the State Courts over the Compliance of International Arbitration Court Awards with the Provisions of the Law of the Republic of Belarus

IV.1. General Provisions

As stated previously, one of the main differences and at the same time advantages of the use of international commercial arbitration in the continental law system is the absence of the legal right to revise an award on substance.

According to article 41 of the International Arbitration Court Act, the award of an international arbitration court is final and enters into force immediately.

In both Belarusian national arbitration law and international law, the law of other countries of the continental law system have a specific rule for revising and cancelling arbitration awards. To be specific, these provisions are stipulated in article 34 of the UNCITRAL model laws on international commercial arbitration of 1985, article 34 of the Law of the Russian Federation On international arbitration courts of 1993, article 34 of the Law of Ukraine On international arbitration courts of 1994, and article 34 of the International Arbitration Court Act of 1999.

This type of appeal has some peculiarities:

Firstly, it stipulates compliance with the competent state institution under whose jurisdiction the arbitration award falls.

Secondly, such competent institution is the state court of the country in which the arbitration award was issued.

Third, there are limited grounds for the overturning of an arbitration award and most of them are of a procedural character.

Fourth, the grounds for the overturning of such awards in one country are almost the same as the grounds for the rejection of the recognition and enforcement of such award in other countries. However, if overturning is possible on the grounds of contradiction between the arbitration award and the public order of the country in which it was issued, or under the legislation of which it was issued, the refusal to recognize and enforce such award is possible, specifically if the recognition of the foreign arbitration court award contradicts the public order.

It is worth noting that on the one hand, the procedure for the overturning of an arbitration court award, and, on the other hand, the procedure for its recognition and enforcement have different aims. The first situation is aimed at protecting the interests of the party against whom the award is invoked, while the second is to protect the rights of the party in whose interests the award is invoked.

Fifth, the overturning of an arbitration award in the place where it was issued usually leads to the impossibility of its recognition and enforcement in the countries that are parties to Convention on the Recognition and Enforcement of Foreign Arbitral Awards (New York, 1958) and the European Convention on International Commercial Arbitration (Geneva, 1961). Courts of different countries overturn the enforcement of arbitration awards because if the award is overturned it means that it doesn't exist; consequently, the object of the enforcement does not exist either. In other words, the overturning of an award by state courts of one country renders the award invalid in other countries.

However, there is another point of view that also has a legal basis. According to article 5 of the New York convention, a state court deciding on the recognition and enforcement of a foreign arbitration award may (not 'must') refuse the recognition and enforcement due to the grounds listed in 1) of article 5 (*The award has not yet become binding on the parties, or has been set aside or suspended by a competent authority of the country in which, or under the law of which, that award was made*). Thus, the decision over such issue is made according to the opinion of the competent court. On the other hand, the words 'may refuse' in the official English text of the New York convention are translated as 'must be refused' in the official French version of this document (that has the same legal force as English one) of the New York convention.

Furthermore, since paragraph 1 of article 5 of the New York convention does not include the grounds for the overturning of arbitration awards, this leads to the question of the validity of the usage of such grounds in cases that are not known or accepted by the law of other countries that are parties to the New York convention. This applies to the following examples: when the award is not signed by all of the arbitrators; the interference of the state court in the material content of the award; and the requirements for the gender, religious beliefs, etc. of the arbitrator. There is a rational opinion on this issue; the state court of the other country in which the petition for the recognition and enforcement is submitted should not take into consideration the overturning of the arbitration award on any grounds other than those named in article 34 of the UNCITRAL model laws and article 9 of the European Convention on International Commercial Arbitration. The court of the District of Columbia (U.S.) recognized the enforcement of the arbitration award upon the claim between *Charmalloy Aeroservices* and the *Arabian Republic of Egypt*. The award was previously overturned by the state court of Egypt on the grounds of the incorrect application of the material law. USA arbitration legislation does not have such grounds (the incorrect application of the material law) to dismiss the recognition and enforcement of a foreign arbitration award.

Moreover, article VII (1) of the New York convention entitles any interested party to exercise any available right in an arbitral award in the manner and to the extent allowed by the law or the treaties of the country in which such award is sought to be relied upon. Thus, the Paris city Court of Appeals allowed the petition of the recognition and enforcement of the award in the case *Hilmarton* v *O.T.V.* that was issued in Geneva and overturned by the Swiss court. The court stressed that article 1502 of the Code of Civil Procedure of the Republic of France does not list the refusal of the so-called exequatur as grounds for overturning such award. The Cour de Cassation upheld the decision of the lower court that noted that the decision of the Swiss court was an international decision that wasn't incorporated in the legal system of the other country. And this decision continues to exist, despite the fact that it was overturned by the court of the other country if its recognition does not contradict international public order.

IV.2. Procedure for Overturning Awards of International Arbitration Courts Located in the Republic of Belarus

The procedure for overturning the award of an international arbitration court located in the Republic of Belarus is stipulated in article 43 of the International Arbitration Court Act and article 44 (2) of the Regulations of the IAC of the BelICCI.

Chapter 29 of the Code of Economic Procedure of the Republic of Belarus considers the case of the overturning of an award of an international arbitration court located in the Republic of Belarus and the case for obtaining an execution document as specific types of procedure in a commercial court.

Moreover, other related provisions are mentioned in Resolution № 10 of the Plenum of the Supreme Economic Court of the Republic of Belarus of June 29, 2006 On the case of the issuance of an execution document for the enforcement of an award of an internal international arbitration court.

It is important to note that the award is considered as issued by the international arbitration court located in the Republic of Belarus, regardless of the actual location of the international arbitration court.

This is stipulated in article 10 of the abovementioned Resolution.

The overturning of an award issued by an international arbitration court located in the Republic of Belarus is an exclusive remedy. Such decisions do not undergo substantial revision.

Only an award issued by an international arbitration court located in the Republic of Belarus can be subject to revision. It is not possible to revise other decisions such as the composition of the arbitration tribunal or the presiding arbitrator upon the issues of procedure or the ruling of the Presidium of the permanent arbitration court.

For example, on June 1, of 2012, the IAC of the BelICCI issued a dismissal order on the case before the arbitration tribunal and the ruling of the Presidium of the IAC of the BelICCI on the issues of the competence of the arbitration tribunal were issued. This was due to the fact that the dispute between the parties had a public character.

This dismissal order was submitted to revise the decision of the Supreme Commercial Court of the Republic of Belarus.

In its decision of September 8, 2010, the Supreme Commercial Court of the Republic of Belarus stated that according to the provisions of chapter 29 of the Code of Economic Procedure of the Republic of Belarus (article 255), only awards of an international arbitration court could be revised. Therefore, the Supreme Court dismissed the petition of the party to overturn the order of the IAC of the BelICCI.

Pursuant to the rules stipulated in article 43 (1) of the International Arbitration Court Act and article 252 of the Code of Economic Procedure of the Republic of Belarus, a petition to revise an award of an international arbitration court located in the Republic of Belarus is submitted by a party to the arbitration case. Such petition should be submitted within 3 months from the day on which the submitting party was notified of the award, or on which the decision on the petition for the correction of mistakes in the award was issued (such as lapses, misprints, mathematical mistakes, or other mistakes in the award), or from the day on which the interpretation of a separate part or the award in general was issued. This is provided in article 43 of the International Arbitration Court Act and article 252 of the Code of Economic Procedure of the Republic of Belarus.

Article 43(1) of the International Arbitration Court Act stipulates that the competent institution for such petitions is the Supreme Commercial Court of the Republic of Belarus.

Requirements for the contents of the petition are set out in Article 253 of the Code of Economic Procedure of the Republic of Belarus. The statement must contain:

- copies of such petition according to the number of parties participating in the arbitration proceedings;
- a copy of the award of the international arbitral court certified by the chairman of the court;
- a document confirming the payment of the court fee;
- a document confirming the authorization of the representative of the party to sign the petition.

Pursuant to article 11 of the annex to the Tax Code of the Republic of Belarus, the court fee for the examination of such petition is 10 base units.

Parts 2 and 3 of the International Arbitration Court Act and article 255 of the Code of Economic Procedure of the Republic of Belarus stipulate the grounds for overturning an award of an international arbitration court located in the Republic of Belarus and the burden of proof.

While revising a petition, the Supreme Commercial Court of the Republic of Belarus may issue a decision on the overturning of the award of the international arbitration court or a decision on the denial of the petition. Both decisions can be revised according to the provisions of the Code of Economic Procedure of the Republic of Belarus.

At the moment, such petitions are decided on by the Economic Panel of the Supreme Court of the Republic of Belarus. This is not due to changes in the law, but due to the suspension of the Supreme Commercial Court.

Upon the petition of one of the parties, The Economic Panel of the Supreme Court of the Republic of Belarus may postpone its review of the revision of the overturning of the award of an international arbitration court located in the Republic of Belarus. This decision is made to give the international arbitration court the chance to resume the proceedings or execute other actions that would prevent the existence of grounds for the overturning of the award (article 43 of the International Arbitration Court Act).

IV.3. Grounds for Overturning Awards of International Arbitration Courts Located in the Republic of Belarus

In the process of revising a petition, the Supreme Court of the Republic of Belarus seeks to determine the grounds (named in article 255 of the Code of Economic Procedure of the Republic of Belarus) or the lack thereof for overturning an award of an international arbitration court.

Such grounds are:

- the limited or partial capability of one of the parties at the moment of the conclusion of the arbitration agreement;
- the invalidity of the arbitration agreement according to the law of the country under which that agreement was made, or if there is no indication of such law, the law the Republic of Belarus;
- the failure to properly notify at least one of the parties of the election of an arbitrator or of the arbitration proceedings;
- a valid reason for a party's failure to provide an explanation;
- an award that was issued in a dispute that was not mentioned in the arbitration agreement or its conditions;
- an award that includes issues that are beyond the issues covered in the arbitration agreement (moreover, if some of the provisions can be separated from the ones that are beyond the issues covered in the arbitration agreement, it is possible to overturn only that part of the award of the international arbitration court that is beyond the issues covered in the arbitration agreement); and
- the non-compliance of the panel of arbitrators to the arbitration agreement, if such agreement does not contradict the stipulated law.

In this situation, the question of the burden of proof becomes very important. The existence of the above grounds should be proved by the party that submits the petition for the overturning of the award of the arbitration court.

However, during the process of the revision of such petition, the award may also be overturned by the Supreme Commercial Court of the Republic of Belarus if the subject of the claim may not be subject to arbitration proceedings, according to the law of the Republic of Belarus or if the award of the international arbitration court contradicts the public order of the Republic of Belarus. This does not depend on whether the party has valid grounds for.

It is also worth noting that compared to the European Convention on International Commercial Arbitration (Geneva, 1961), Belarusian law in the field of international arbitration regulations offers two more grounds. The first touches on the violation of the rules of public order of the Republic of Belarus. The second relates to whether the subject of the claim may be subject to arbitration proceedings according to the law of the Republic of Belarus.

Nonetheless, similar to the arbitration law of some other countries, such as Article 34 of the Law of Ukraine On international arbitration courts, and article 34 of the Law of the Russian Federation On international arbitration courts, the list of the grounds, named by the International Arbitration Court Act is close to the list of grounds stipulated in article 34 of the UNCITRAL model laws On international commercial arbitration.

IV.4. The Approach to Deciding on Petitions for the Overturning of Awards of International Arbitration Courts Located in the Republic of Belarus (According to the Example of the Awards of the IAC of the BelICCI)

The approach to deciding on petitions for the overturning of awards of the IAC of the BelICCI shows that usually such petitions are based on the material grounds of the claim.

For example, the respondent (in one of the IAC of the BelICCI) argued that the arbitration panel failed to properly evaluate the written evidence of the case, in addition to its failure to apply the applicable law.

Another petition was grounded on the argument that the arbitration court did not comment on the fact that the claimant had supplied the goods below the contract price concluded by the parties, and, therefore, issued an illegal, unsubstantiated award. In its decision of October 28, 2003, the Supreme Commercial Court of the Republic of Belarus stated that the current law did not permit the revision of an award of the international arbitration court on substance.

In other cases, the Supreme Commercial Court of the Republic of Belarus indicated that it was prohibited from examining the circumstances of a case that were previously established by the arbitration court panel. The same rules should be applied to arguments of the claimant that are not grounds for the overturning of arbitration awards.

In total, the Supreme Commercial Court of the Republic of Belarus upheld 4 petitions for the overturning of the IAC of the BelICCI: 3 on the grounds of the contradiction of the award of the public order of the Republic of Belarus, and one on the grounds that the subject of the claim could not be subject to arbitration proceedings according to the law of the Republic of Belarus.

In two cases, the contradiction of public order was reflected in the fact that the IAC of the BelICCI did not check the legal procedural entitlement of the claimant and the document confirming the authorization of the representative of the claimant before the commencement of the proceedings, and made an award on the substance of the claim. In the third case, the Supreme Commercial Court of the Republic of Belarus came to the conclusion that the award of the IAC of the BelICCI ignored the interests of the Republic of Belarus (about the establishment of the fact of the nullity of the deal that was the subject of the claim of the IAC of the BelICCI)

Parties often cite the breach of public order as the grounds for the overturning of the award of the IAC of the BelICCI.

For example, in one such petition, the respondent, in support of such grounds for the overturning of the award of IAC of the BelICCI, argued that the IAC of the BelICCI violated the principle of the equality of the parties. This was demonstrated by the fact that the court correspondence on the case was addressed to only two representatives, while the third never received a notice regarding the time and place of the proceedings. As a result, such representative could not provide the respondent with legal support and failed to participate in the proceedings. Due to the complexity of the case and the lack of a stated applicable law for the employees of the respondent, the participation of the representative (that was certified by the Ministry of the Justice of the Republic of Belarus) in the process of preparing the objections and the proceeding was compulsory. Furthermore, the interests of the claimant were introduced by a Belarusian attorney.

In addition, according to the applicant, the refusal of the IAC of the BelICCI (during the proceedings) to choose the applicable law represented a breach of public order. In particular, the arbitration court did not apply the provisions of Regulation № 444 of the Cabinet of Ministers of the Republic of Belarus (8 July 1996) on the supply of goods in the Republic of Belarus and Regulation № 1290 of the Council of Ministers on the acceptance of the quality and quantity of the goods (3 September 2008).

The decision of the Supreme Commercial Court of the Republic of Belarus (27 august 2012) states the absence of the grounds for the satisfaction of the petition.

The first argument that was made referred to the contradiction of the public order on the breach of the principle of the equality of the parties.

Pursuant to the International Arbitration Court Act, the IAC of the BelICCI must inform the parties, but not all of the representatives.

The judge of the Supreme Commercial Court of the Republic of Belarus stated in the decision that the documents of the case of the IAC of the BelICCI show the respondent was properly notified. Moreover, two of its representatives participated in the proceedings and did not submit the petition on the necessity of the participation of a third representative.

Speaking on our own capacity, article 20 (1) of the Regulations of the IAC of the BelICCI contains a strict and categorical clause that stipulates that the IAC of the BelICCI must strive to ensure the proper dispatch and serving of the documents of the case to the parties.

Concerning the second argument of the applicant, the Supreme Commercial Court of the Republic of Belarus stated that during proceedings on the scope of the legislative acts, Regulation № 444 of the Cabinet of Ministers of the Republic of Belarus (8 July 1996) on the supply of goods in the Republic of Belarus and Regulation № 1290 of the Council of Ministers on the acceptance of the quality and quantity of the goods (3 September 2008) could not be applied due to the fact that the parties were related parties.

It appears that the petitioner was trying to challenge the use of the material provisions of the law of the Republic of Belarus on the substance of the case.

Determining the validity of the use of the material provisions by the IAC of the BelICCI is beyond the competence of the Supreme Commercial Court of the Republic of Belarus. Thus, it may not revise an award of the IAC of the BelICCI on substance.

Awards of the IAC of the BelICCI are usually overturned if at least one of the parties has not been properly notified of the election of an arbitrator or of the arbitration proceedings, or due to the invalidity or absence of an arbitration clause (to solve disputes in the IAC of the BelICCI).

In one of the petitions, the respondent argued that the arbitration clause in a sales contract between the parties stipulated that the International Arbitration Court of the Belarusian Chamber of Commerce and Industry would solve the dispute; as a result, the IAC of the BelICCI had no jurisdiction.

Moreover, the respondent argued that it wasn't property notified of the arbitration proceedings.

In its decision of November 16, 2010, the Supreme Commercial Court of the Republic of Belarus stated that the arguments were absolutely indefensible.

According to the IAC of the BelICCI, since the respondent hadn't provided the court with evidence that the International Arbitration Court of the Belarusian Chamber of Commerce and Industry existed in Minsk, the inaccurate naming of the arbitration institution didn't create confusion among the parties during the conclusion of the contract. The case materials deny the respondent's claim that it was not properly notified of the arbitration proceedings.

According to the Regulations of the IAC of the BelICCI, the statement of claim with the attached documents, the notification of the IAC of the BelICCI on the initiation on the proceedings, the Regulations of the IAC of the BelICCI and the list of the recommended arbitrators were sent to the respondent by registered mail with the confirmation of delivery to the address listed in the international sales contract between the parties as the location of the respondent.

The authorized representative received such correspondence on October 26, 2010, which is confirmed by the notification.

According to the certificate of state registration provided by the respondent, the location of the respondent changed on December 9, 2009.

In its decision of November 16, 2010, the Supreme Commercial Court of the Republic of Belarus stated that according to article 3-1 of the Regulations of the IAC of the BelICCI, the parties are obliged to notify IAC of the BelICCI of any changes of their mailing addresses during the proceedings. In the absence of such notification, the documents shall be sent to the last known mailing address and shall be considered as delivered, even if the addressee is no longer located on such address.

Considering the fact that the respondent received the notification of the initiation of the proceedings before the change of the location, it was obliged to notify the IAC of the BelICCI about the change of the address.

Since the respondent did not fulfill this obligation, and the IAC of the BelICCI had no information about any other address of the respondent or a change of the address, the delivery of the correspondence to the respondent's last known address was considered as a proper notification.

IV.5. Consequences of the Overturning of Awards of International Arbitration Courts Located in the Republic of Belarus

The overturning of an award of an international arbitration court located in the Republic of Belarus does not prevent any of the parties to appeal again to the previously named arbitration court if the possibility to appeal still exists or to appeal to the commercial (economic) court pursuant to the rules set by the Code of Economic Procedure of the Republic of Belarus.

The relevant rule is stipulated in article 256 of the Code of Economic Procedure of the Republic of Belarus.

The parties to an arbitration process may petition a commercial court to resolve their dispute if, among others, the award of the international arbitration court was overturned due to the invalidity of the arbitration agreement, the award was related to a dispute that was not provided for in the arbitration agreement or its conditions, or the award related to issues not covered by the arbitration agreement.

IV.6. Notable Features of the Overturning of Awards of Domestic Arbitration Courts Located in the Republic of Belarus

The procedure for overturning such an award is similar to the procedure for the overturning of awards of international arbitration courts located in the Republic of Belarus.

Still there are significant differences between the two procedures.

First of all, the award of an international arbitration court may only be overturned by a decision of the Economic Panel of the Supreme Court of the Republic of Belarus.

The overturning of the awards of the arbitration courts created in the Republic of Belarus is governed by the provisions of article 458-1 of the Code of Economic Procedure of the Republic of Belarus. Thus, a petition may be submitted to the regional (municipal) court, of the territory in which the award of the arbitration court was issued. This petition should be submitted within 3 months from the moment in which the appealing party received the notification of the award.

If the parties to the arbitration dispute are companies or private entrepreneurs, the petition on overturning is decided on by the Economic Cases Panel of the Supreme Court of the Republic of Belarus pursuant to the rules of the Code of Economic Procedure of the Republic of Belarus.

The grounds for the overturning of an award of an international arbitration court located in the Republic of Belarus and the grounds for the overturning of an award of an arbitration court created in the Republic of Belarus are not identical. Only the following 4 grounds are almost the same:

- the invalidity of the arbitration agreement according to the law of the country under which, the agreement was made, or if there is no indication of such law, the law the Republic of Belarus (for international arbitration courts located in the Republic of Belarus) and the invalidity of the arbitration agreement according to the Arbitration Courts Act (for arbitration courts created in the Republic of Belarus);

- the failure to properly notify at least one of the parties of the election of an arbitrator or the initiation of arbitration proceedings (for international arbitration courts located in the Republic of Belarus), and the failure to properly notify at least one of the parties of the place and time of the arbitration proceedings or the inability of at least one of the parties to exercise its rights (stipulated in the Arbitration Courts Act) due to valid reasons (for arbitration courts created in the Republic of Belarus);

- the issuance of an award related to a dispute that was not mentioned in the arbitration agreement or its conditions or an award that relates to issues that go beyond the issues covered in the arbitration agreement (for international arbitration courts located in the Republic of Belarus), and the issuance of an award related to a dispute that was not mentioned in the arbitration agreement or that relates to issues that go beyond the issues covered in the arbitration agreement (for arbitration courts created in the Republic of Belarus); and
- the non-compliance of the panel of arbitrators with the arbitration agreement, if such agreement does not contradict the International Arbitration Courts Act (for international arbitration courts located in the Republic of Belarus) and the non-compliance of the panel of the arbitrators due to a violation of the Arbitration Courts Act (for arbitration courts created in the Republic of Belarus).

However, two other grounds (each of them has 6 grounds) for the overturning of the award of an international arbitration court located in the Republic of Belarus, and an arbitration court created in the Republic of Belarus, are completely different. According to the Code of Economic Procedure of the Republic of Belarus, the award of an international arbitration court located in the Republic of Belarus may be overturned on the grounds of the limited or partial capability of one of the parties at the moment of concluding the arbitration agreement or a failure due to a valid excuse of the party to provide an explanation. This last reason is still close to the grounds for overturning an award – the failure of at least one of the parties to use its rights). For the arbitration courts created in the Republic of Belarus there are 2 more grounds for overturning that are based on relevant circumstances:

- the existence of relevant circumstances that were not known by at least one of the parties;
- the court's establishment of the deliberately false testimony of a witness, a deliberately false expert report, a deliberately false translation, or the falsification of documents or material evidence that had led to an illegal and unreasonable award of the arbitration court.

Both of these grounds for the overturning of an award of an arbitration court created in the Republic of Belarus can be characterized as the overturning of a court decision based on newly discovered facts that have significant meaning for the case. The law does not delegate this procedure to the international arbitration court.

Pursuant to article 48 of the Arbitration Courts Act, the overturning of an award does not prevent the possibility of re-appealing to an arbitration court created in the Republic of Belarus to resolve the dispute. However, the overturning of the award of an arbitration court on the grounds of the invalidity of the arbitration agreement or an award that was issued for a dispute that is not mentioned in the arbitration agreement or an award that relates to issues that are beyond the issues covered in the arbitration agreement represents an exception to this rule. Such cases may not be resolved in an arbitration court.

V. Enforcement of Decisions of International Arbitration Courts

V.1. General: Internal and Foreign Arbitration Awards

The law of the Republic of Belarus establishes three legal regimes: the first regulates the order of the execution of internal international arbitration court awards; the second is designed for the recognition and enforcement of foreign arbitral awards; and the third is for the execution of arbitration awards of arbitration courts created in the Republic of Belarus.
Arbitration awards rendered outside the Republic of Belarus are foreign arbitration awards.
Internal arbitration awards are rendered in the Republic of Belarus by international arbitration courts which operate in accordance with the provisions of Act № 279-3 of July 9, 1999 On the International Arbitration Courts. This includes both the Permanent Court of International Arbitration, established in accordance with Chapter 2 of the Act, and the International Arbitration Court for the consideration of a particular dispute which is located in the Republic of Belarus.
Article 44 of the International Arbitration Courts Act provides for the execution of awards of the permanent international arbitral court in the Republic of Belarus constituted in accordance with Chapter 2 of the Act, as well as awards of the international arbitration court in the Republic of Belarus for the consideration of disputes which are resolved in the manner prescribed by the economic procedural law of the Republic of Belarus.

V.2. Regulation of the Enforcement of a Judgment of an International Arbitration Court Located in the Republic of Belarus

The execution of awards of internal international arbitration courts in the Republic of Belarus is a well-oiled procedure.
The execution order of awards of international arbitration courts in the Republic of Belarus is defined in Chapter 29 of the Code of Economic Procedure of the Republic of Belarus and Resolution № 10 of the Plenum of the Supreme Economic Court of the Republic of Belarus of June 29, 2006 (as amended by decision № 19 of the Plenum of December 22, 2006 and decision № 4 of February 8, 2007) on the order of consideration by economic courts of

cases of the recognition and enforcement decisions of foreign courts and foreign arbitration awards, about appealing the awards of international arbitration courts located in the Republic of Belarus, and the issuance of execution documents.

V.3. Applying for an Execution Document Procedure

In order to obtain an execution document to enforce the award of an internal international arbitration court, the party in favor of such arbitral award must do the following.

In accordance with the first paragraph of Article 257 of the Code of Economic Procedure of the Republic of Belarus and paragraph 13 of Resolution № 10 of the Plenum of the Supreme Economic Court of the Republic of Belarus of June 29, 2006, the issuance of an execution document for the enforcement of an award of internal international arbitration court is considered by the economic courts of the regions or Minsk at the place of residence of the debtor – the party to the arbitration or the place of the debtor's property if the debtor's residence is unknown.

Article 257 of the Code of Economic Procedure of the Republic of Belarus contains requirements for the content and form of the above petition; Article 259 of the Code of Economic Procedure of the Republic of Belarus regulates the procedure and terms of this statement and the requirements for the economic court competent for issuing an enforcement document listed in Article 261 of the Code of Economic Procedure of the Republic of Belarus.

Pursuant to the above, the petition for an execution document must contain:

- the name of the economic court to which the petition is submitted;
- the name, location and composition of the international arbitration court that made the award;
- the names of the arbitration parties and their places of places of residence;
- the number, date and place of issuance of the decision of the international arbitration court; and
- the requirement to issue an enforcement document to enforce the award of the international arbitration court.

V.4. Period for the Voluntary Execution of an International Arbitration Court Located in the Republic of Belarus

Pursuant to the fifth paragraph of Article 257 of the Code of Economic Procedure of the Republic of Belarus, the petition for the issuance of an execution document to enforce a judgment of an International Arbitration

Court located in the Republic of Belarus may be filed within six months from the date of expiry of the voluntary execution of the award, and pursuant to the fourth part of the same article, this petition must be accompanied by evidence confirming the other party's failure to carry out the resolutions of the International Arbitration Court within the period specified therein.

In view of the above, pursuant to resolution № 2 of the Presidium of the International Arbitration Court at the BelCCI of December 6, 2004, it was established that the evidence of the beginning of the time allowed for the voluntary compliance of an award should be a certificate which confirms the date of receipt by the defeated party of the notification of its obligation to execute such award.

At the request of the parties, the International Arbitration Court at the BelCCI shall issue such certificates with attachments containing a copy of the e-mail notifications regarding the defeated party's receipt of the notification of its obligation to execute the award.

The deadline for the voluntary execution of an award of the International Arbitration Court at the BelCCI is stated directly in the text of the decision and is usually five days from the moment of receipt of the notification of this award by the defendant (if the award of the International Arbitration Court at the BelCCI is based on an agreement concluded by the parties during the arbitration settlement agreement, the terms for the voluntary execution of such award may be different).

V.5. Formalization of the Authority of the Person Applying for the Enforcement of Decisions of International Arbitration Courts Located in the Republic of Belarus

Point 13 of Resolution № 10 of the Plenum of the Supreme Economic Court of the Republic of Belarus of June 29, 2006 contains a provision stating that a petition for the issuance of an execution document in the manner prescribed by Article 257 of the Code of Economic Procedure of the Republic of Belarus should be regarded as presented by a legal entity or individual entrepreneur in whose favor the decision of the enforcement is rendered, and which, accordingly, should be provided in the authorization of the attorney in the event of such request by the representative.

V.6. Regarding the Proof of the Proper Notification of the Defeated Party in the Arbitration Proceeding

Sometimes in the practice of the International Arbitration Court at the BelCCI there have been cases of appeals by the winning party for an extradition request to prove the proper notification of the respondent about the election of an arbitrator or of the arbitration proceeding, including the time and place of the court hearings.

It appears that the fourth part of Article 257 of the Code of Economic Procedure of the Republic of Belarus stipulates an exhaustive list of documents which must be attached to the petition for the issuance of an executive document to enforce an award of an international arbitration court; however, it does not include proof of the proper notification of the respondent about the election of the arbitrator or arbitration proceedings, including the time and place of the meeting of international arbitration court hearings.

Furthermore, according to Article 260 of the Code of Economic Procedure of the Republic of Belarus, the losing party bears the responsibility for proving that at least one of the parties was not properly notified about the election of an arbitrator or the arbitration proceeding, including the time and place of the meeting of the international arbitration court, or for proving that due to other reasons this party could not present its explanation to the international arbitration court.

V.7. Payment of State Duty and the Consequences of the Violation of Legal Requirements

According to Annex 16 to the Tax Code of the Republic of Belarus, the fee for applying for the issuance of an execution document for the enforcement of an award of an internal international arbitration court is 10 basic units (which is currently about $ 150).

The application will be returned to the applicant if it does not include the document confirming the payment of the court fee, the confirmation of the authority of the person applying for the execution document, or in the event of the failure to provide all of the required information in the application and the accompanying documents.

V.8. Time and Procedure for Considering a Petition for an Execution Document

A petition for the issuance of an execution document for the enforcement of the judgment of internal international arbitration court is considered solely by the judge of the economic court within one month from the date of its receipt by the economic court; this includes the time for preparing the case for proceedings and rendering a court order, according to the rules established by the Code of Economic Procedure of the Republic of Belarus.

Pursuant to Article 261 of the Code of Economic Procedure of the Republic of Belarus, upon the consideration of the above petition, the economic court shall issue a court order which must indicate the issuance of the execution document for enforcement or the refusal to issue an execution document.

(The economic court is not entitled to substantially reconsider an award of an international arbitration court).

V.9. Reasons for the Refusal to Issue an Execution Document

Pursuant to Art. 260 of the Code of Economic Procedure of the Republic of Belarus, the economic court may refuse to issue an execution document for the enforcement of an award of an internal international arbitration court if the losing party in the arbitration proceeding presents evidence that proves that:

- the arbitration agreement was invalid on legal grounds;
- at least one of the parties was not properly notified of the election of an arbitrator or of the arbitration proceedings, including the time and place of the meeting of international arbitration court, or the party could not provide its explanations to the international arbitration court for other valid reasons;
- the award of the international arbitration court was decided in a trial that was not contemplated by the arbitration agreement or that did not fall within the terms of it, or that contains decisions on matters that are beyond the matters covered in the arbitration agreement. (If the decisions on matters submitted to arbitration can be separated from those not so submitted in the decision of the international arbitration court, the economic court may issue an execution document only on the part of the decision of the international arbitration court which contains decisions on matters submitted to arbitration);
- the composition of the international arbitration court or arbitration procedure for the trial did not meet the agreement of the parties or the law; or
- the decision was not yet obligatory for the parties to the arbitration proceedings or was overturned, or its execution was suspended by the economic court.

The economic court shall refuse to issue an execution document for the enforcement of award of internal international arbitration court if it determines that:

- the dispute heard by the international arbitration court is not subject to arbitration in accordance with the laws of the Republic of Belarus; or
- the decision of the international arbitration court violates the fundamental principles of the law of the Republic of Belarus.

It is important to note that if an application for the issuance of an execution document for the enforcement of an award of an internal international arbitration court is refused in whole or in part by the economic court due to the invalidity of the arbitration agreement, or if the decision was made on a dispute not stipulated by the arbitration agreement, or if the award is not subject to the terms of the arbitration agreement, or if the decision contains decrees on matters not covered by the arbitration agreement, the parties to the arbitration may request that the economic court resolve the dispute according to the rules established by the Code of Economic Procedure (Part 4, article 261 of Code of Economic Procedure of the Republic of Belarus).

According to Article 261 of the Code of Economic Procedure of the Republic of Belarus, the refusal to issue an execution document for the enforcement of an award of internal international arbitration court does not prevent the party from appealing to the international arbitration court, if the possibility of such an appeal has not been lost, or to the economic court according to the rules established by this Code.

V.10. Enforcement of Decisions of International Arbitration Courts Located in the Republic of Belarus

Pursuant to Article 328 of the Code of Economic Procedure of the Republic of Belarus, awards of internal international arbitration courts are assigned to court orders that are enforceable in accordance with the Code of Economic Procedure of the Republic of Belarus.

Orders of economic courts issued, in particular, on the basis of awards of international arbitration courts in the Republic of Belarus are executed pursuant to article 329 of the Code of Economic Procedure of the Republic of Belarus.

However, it should be noted that the recovery of monetary funds from the debtor under an execution document should be primarily referred to the funds in the debtor's bank and (or) non-bank financial institution accounts.

Payments by request without approval (an undisputed order for the withdrawal of money) is regulated by Chapter 11 of Resolution № 66 of the National Bank of the Republic of Belarus dated March 29, 2001 on the approval of instructions on bank transfers.

Paragraph 85 of Chapter 11 of the above mentioned Resolution defines the undisputed order for the withdrawal of money from the payer's account without his/her consent, in accordance with the payment instructions on the basis of execution documents in the cases stipulated by the law of the Republic of Belarus.

According to paragraph 87 of Chapter 11 of the same Resolution, in order to withdraw money undisputedly, the collector must arrange for a payment request and send three copies of it to the bank.

In the event of the partial or complete absence of funds in the accounts of the debtor's bank and (or) non-bank financial institution, the collector shall apply to the economic court for the commencement of proceedings.

The requirements for the content of the request for the commencement of proceedings are stipulated in Article 355 of the Code of Economic Procedure of the Republic of Belarus. In particular, the statement must contain:

- the name of the economic court to which the petition is submitted;
- information about the debtor's place of residence or location, current accounts, property, and account number as a payer, if such information is available;
- information about the collector's place of residence or location, current account to which the money should be transferred, and account number as the payer;
- the date of issuance and number of execution documents presented for execution, information about the amount to be recovered by it, the measures taken to protect the claim, if any have been taken at the stage of the economic process by the courts; and
- a list of documents attached to the petition.

V.11. Features of the Execution of Arbitration Decisions Made in the Republic of Belarus

As stated earlier, international arbitration courts and arbitration courts created in the Republic of Belarus operate on the basis of different legal regimes.

As a general rule, Article 49 of the International Arbitration Courts Act states that the arbitration award shall be enforceable. In this case, the original form of this execution is voluntary compliance. The procedure and deadline for the compulsory enforcement of the arbitration award should be set in the decision; however, if the specified deadline is not set in the decision, then by virtue of the above Act the decision must be implemented within 3 days from the date the judgment becomes final.

If the decision is not executed voluntarily, it shall be enforceable according to the rules of execution process provided by the Code of Economic Procedure of the Republic of Belarus or the Code of Civil Procedure of the Republic of Belarus, but on the basis of a specially issued execution document for the enforcement of the judgment by the state.

Due to these circumstances, the interested party must submit a petition for the issuance of an execution document to the state court with jurisdiction over the place of residence of the debtor or the location of its property, if the debtor's location is unknown.

Such petition must be submitted to the state court based on the rules of the jurisdiction of disputes of ordinary courts or economic courts.

The petition for the issuance of an execution document must include:

- the original or a copy of the award of the arbitral court (a copy of the decision of the permanent arbitral court must be certified by the chairman of the court, a copy of the award of the arbitration court to settle a specific dispute must be notarized);
- the original or a copy of the arbitration agreement concluded in accordance with the Arbitration Courts Act;
- the original or a copy of the document confirming the payment of the state fee in the manner and amount established by the legislative acts of the Republic of Belarus;
- evidence supporting the non-execution of the arbitral award within the prescribed period by the other party;
- a document confirming the authority of the representative party applying for the issuance of the execution document, to sign a statement (if the statement is signed by the representative).

Pursuant to Article 50 of the International Arbitration Courts Act, the deadline for submitting a petition for the issuance of an execution document is 6 months from the date of expiry of the voluntary execution of the decision.

However, this period may be extended by the court if the petitioner has a valid reason for its failure to submit the petition on time.

The decision on the petition for the issuance of an execution document for the enforcement of the judgment of arbitration court must be rendered within a month from the date of its receipt at the court solely by a judge and must include a notification of the parties about the time and place of the proceeding. The court may not reconsider the award of the arbitral court.

According to the results of the proceeding, the court may order the issuance of an execution document or to refuse to order the issuance of an execution document. This decision may be appealed.

[*Jan Iosifovich Funk*]
LL.D., Professor, Belarusian State University, Chairman of the International Arbitration at the BelCCI
e-mail: funk25@mail.ru

[*Inna Vladimirovna Pererva*]
Ph.D., Head of Information and Consultation Centre of the International Arbitration Court at the BelCCI
e-mail: iac@cci.by

| | |

New Horizons for Arbitration in Slovakia

The year 2002 was crucial for the Slovak arbitration environment, primarily because of the adoption of Act No. 244/2002 Coll. on arbitration proceedings (the **Slovak Arbitration Act**) on the basis of the 1985 version of the UNCITRAL Model Law (the **Model Law**). This resulted in Slovakia having a solid grounding for the development of arbitration, despite there being several differences and omissions compared to the Model Law's wording.

For more than 12 years, Slovak arbitration has been significantly affected by two issues not governed by the Model Law which, in turn, have had negative practical implications.

The first is arbitrability and the second an excessively liberal framework for institutional arbitration. The latter has resulted in the establishment of approximately 150 domestic arbitral institutions. The quality of many of these institutions has been a cause of concern due to their applying practices that are unacceptable under modern professional and ethical standards of international arbitration. The main problem was the fact that many consumer disputes were administered by these institutions in a manner that blatantly disregarded the consumer protection rules enshrined in EU and Slovak law. This led to a general hostility from Slovak courts to the concept of arbitration, and to their subsequently adopting an extremely narrow view of arbitrability, one which does not take into account the differences between arbitrability in consumer and commercial disputes.

The Slovak arbitration community saw the need for the urgent resolution of these issues. A draft amendment to the Slovak Arbitration Act (the **Amendment**) was therefore prepared by the Ministry of Justice. The draft has since been approved by the Government and is currently pending final adoption by the Parliament. The Amendment's goal is to make Slovakia a true Model Law country (reflecting the 2006 version of the Model Law) and negate the effects of the arbitration-unfriendly approach adopted by some Slovak courts in commercial disputes.

Travaux préparatoires in connection with the Amendment started in August 2012. The first step was the Ministry of Justice creating a commission of experts comprising ministry officials, academic experts, arbitration practitioners and judges. The commission was instructed to draft a proposal to amend Slovak arbitration legislation with the aim of achieving full harmonisation of the commercial arbitration framework with the 2006 version of the Model Law. Another goal was to set clear boundaries between consumer and commercial arbitration, so that regulatory restrictions and stricter court interpretations of the former would not have a negative effect on the latter. The amendment is intended to take effect as of 1 January 2015. From that date, the arbitration of consumer disputes will be excluded from the scope of the Slovak Arbitration

Act and will be governed by a separate act on alternative dispute resolution of consumer-related disputes. This will enable the deletion of certain restrictive provisions from the Slovak Arbitration Act as, from then on, it will apply only to commercial arbitration.

Below we describe some of the most significant proposed changes to the legal regime of commercial arbitration under Slovak law.

I. Arbitrability

Arbitrability will be expanded to cover all disputes that are capable of being settled by agreement of the parties, expressly including disputes regarding the validity of contracts and claims for declaratory relief. The need for such expansion stems from certain recent decisions by some Slovak courts which held that the validity of a legal act can only be determined by a state court and not by an arbitral tribunal.

II. Agreement to Arbitrate

Another novelty is an explicit acknowledgment that arbitration clauses can also be incorporated by reference to documents not directly attached to and not countersigned by the parties, as long as the reference to the document containing the arbitration clause is clear and specific. This change is intended to prevent Slovak courts from declaring invalid arbitration clauses contained in terms and conditions attached to a contract or industry standard that are specifically identified. It will be possible to include arbitration clauses in corporate documents of Slovak companies, which clauses will automatically become binding on new shareholders in the company, without the need for a separate accession or signature. Rules on the use of electronic means for entering into arbitration agreements are going to be simplified and, last but not least, an agreement to arbitrate will also be deemed to exist if the respondent takes part in the arbitration proceedings and does not object to the tribunal's jurisdiction latest by the submission of its memorandum of reply.

III. Interim Measures

The Amendment will introduce the possibility of *ex parte* interim measures being granted by arbitral tribunals, in line with the expanded version of Art. 17 of the Model Law. However, only interim measures granted with prior notice to the other party will be capable of court enforcement in Slovakia. A court review of interim measures granted by arbitral tribunals will also be possible.

In addition, the Amendment will allow for the extended jurisdiction of general courts even after arbitration proceedings have been initiated, but before the arbitral tribunal being constituted. Under the current legal regime, general courts had no jurisdiction to grant interim measures after the commencement of arbitral proceedings, even where the arbitral tribunal has not yet been established. The possibility of allowing the full concurrent jurisdiction of general courts (as contemplated by the Model Law) was rejected due to the anti-arbitration prejudice held by some Slovak courts and the concern that such interim measures could be abused to torpedo arbitral proceedings.

IV. Institutional Arbitration

The Amendment will abolish the practice of permanent arbitration institutions being established by private companies and operated for the founders' profit. Following the Amendment, domestic arbitration institutions will only be able to be established either by a chamber of commerce, a non-profit professional association, and several other entities specified under law. The objective is to significantly reduce the alarming number of arbitration institutions in Slovakia (approximately 150) and give prominence to those that are more reputable, such as the Arbitration Court of the Slovak Chamber of Commerce and Industry, and the Permanent Arbitration Court of the Slovak Banking Association.

V. Recourse against Arbitral Award

The time period for filing a motion to set aside a final award will be extended from 30 to 60 days. The grounds will be fully aligned with the respective Articles of the Model Law and will, compared to the current wording of the law, also include conflict with public policy.

The fact that the current version of the Slovak Arbitration Act does not include public policy as a reason for setting aside an award sometimes led to undesirable outcomes. In one controversial case, one clearly "arbitrary" arbitral award could not have been set aside by the court because it did not fall under the narrow reasons justifying recourse challenge. The award was then challenged by a constitutional complaint. Although such complaint is normally only available against acts by public authorities, and although the Constitutional Court stopped short of describing the tribunal as a public authority, it nonetheless felt compelled to annul the award.[1]

Although some members of the drafting commission argued that the public policy reason may give the courts too much leeway in setting aside an arbitral award, it was concluded that the risk of not having recourse against arbitral

---

[1]   Ruling of the Constitutional Court of the Slovak Republic, file No III. ÚS 162/2011, 31 May 2011.

awards on the basis of public policy ground exceeds the risk of public policy being interpreted too broadly by the courts. The risk of the courts applying a broad domestic concept of public policy is mitigated by specific references to the notion of public policy under the New York Convention.

VI. Recognition and Enforcement of Foreign Awards

The Amendment provides for the possibility of recognising declaratory awards that need not be enforced, with an aim to achieve the effects of *res iudicata* in potential or pending proceedings regarding the same subject matter before the Slovak courts. Furthermore, the grounds for refusing recognition of foreign arbitral awards will be slightly amended to fully align with the provisions of the New York Convention and the Model Law.

VII. Related Changes to the Rules of Civil Procedure

The Amendment requires that certain changes be incorporated in the Slovak Code of Civil Procedure[2], applicable to proceedings before Slovak courts. The principle of the negative effect of competence-competence will be introduced, preventing a general court from having jurisdiction to examine the validity and effectiveness of an arbitration agreement pending an arbitral tribunal making its own decision on jurisdiction. The principle will apply regardless of whether arbitral proceedings have been commenced before or after proceedings before general courts. Furthermore, where an arbitral tribunal has ruled to have jurisdiction in a particular matter, and such ruling has been successfully challenged before a state court, it will be possible for a party to lodge an appeal against such state court decision. This will represent a deviation from the one-instance principle enshrined in Art. 16(3) of the Model Law, but such deviation was felt necessary on the basis of recent negative experiences with certain decisions adopted by courts of lower instance on matters of jurisdiction of an arbitral tribunal.

VIII. Conclusion

More than 12 years after the promulgation of the Slovak Arbitration Act, it can be concluded that the arbitration environment in Slovakia has been fostered by this pro-arbitration piece of legislation based on the Model Law. However, its history also shows that a controversial interpretation (or even misrepresentation) by the courts can hollow out many well-intended provisions in ways that would probably not even have occurred to their drafters.

---

[2] Act No. 991963 Coll, the Civil Procedure Code, as amended.

The intention of the Ministry of Justice, reflected in the Amendment, to fully align Slovak law with the Model Law's 2006 version and to change the way in which Slovak courts have been interpreting some fundamental concepts of arbitration, is praiseworthy and will no doubt be welcomed by the Slovak arbitration community. It remains to be seen whether commercial arbitration, finally separated from its consumer counterpart, will flourish under the new regime.

[*Martin Magál*]
Partner, Allen & Overy Bratislava, s.r.o.
e-mail: Martin.Magal@AllenOvery.com

[*Martina Kasemová*]
Lawyer, Allen & Overy Bratislava, s.r.o.
e-mail: Martina.Kasemova@AllenOvery.com

|||

Is It Moral to Charge VAT on Arbitration?

The assignment of VAT is a difficult issue for many people. Do we have to pay it on all goods and services?

Delivering justice is not an economic activity or a business. If one conceptualizes arbitration as a special type of justice, then it is natural to ask whether it is moral to put a tax on justice. I suggest that the answer is NO.

This question is not merely rhetorical in Poland. For a long time, tax advisors there have been providing contradictory information and interpretations regarding Article 15 par. 3 pt. 3, pt 4)[1] of the Act on Personal Income Tax concerning the remuneration of Polish arbitrators participating in arbitration proceedings with 'foreign partners'. The term 'foreign partner' is not defined in the legislation. Whose partner is he to be? The arbitrator's? Or perhaps the Polish party's? And what if a Pole becomes an arbitrator in a dispute in which neither party is Polish? We would then be dealing with proceedings 'between' foreign partners and not 'with' foreign partners. It is not clear whether 'foreign partner' means 'foreign party'.

This ambiguity could lead to doubts about whether or not an arbitrator's activities are subject to VAT, and if they are then when. These questions could arise in a variety of situations. Consider when:

1. a Polish arbitrator takes part in arbitration proceedings with foreign partners abroad, in an arbitration tribunal at a foreign arbitral institution;
2. a Polish arbitrator takes part in arbitration proceedings with foreign partners abroad in *ad hoc* arbitration;
3. a Polish arbitrator takes part in arbitration proceedings with foreign partners in Poland, on the panel of arbitrators, e.g. in the Court of Arbitration at the Polish Chamber of Commerce, which concludes an agreement with the arbitrator on the terms and conditions of his remuneration and liability;
4. a Polish arbitrator takes part in arbitration proceedings with foreign partners in Poland, e.g. at the Court of Arbitration at the Polish Chamber of Information Technology and Telecommunications, in which the court concludes a fee-for-task agreement with the arbitrator;

---

[1] This regulation is currently worded as follows:

'*The following actions are not regarded as independently performed business activity referred to in par. 1: (...) 4) revenue from the activities of Polish arbitrators taking part in arbitration proceedings with foreign partners; (...)*'.

5. a Polish arbitrator takes part in arbitration proceedings with foreign partners, but the place of arbitration is Poland, although the arbitration is administered by a foreign arbitral institution which has (or has not) concluded an appropriate agreement with the arbitrator;

6. a Polish arbitrator takes part in arbitration proceedings exclusively with Polish partners, although the place of arbitration is abroad, which is possible according to the Code of Civil Procedure, in arbitration administered by a foreign arbitral institution, e.g. the ICC;

7. a Polish arbitrator takes part in arbitration proceedings exclusively with Polish partners (parties), though abroad in *ad hoc* arbitration, on a panel of arbitrators with two foreign arbitrators;

8. a Polish arbitrator takes part in arbitration proceedings with foreign partners (parties) abroad in *ad hoc* arbitration.

Each one of these situations can be complicated further depending on whether a party to the proceedings which has appointed an arbitrator is or is not a Polish entity and VAT payer, or perhaps a foreign entity paying VAT (or not) in another EU state, or in a non-EU state. Finally, what should be done with *ad hoc* arbitration involving a Polish arbitrator in Poland and where the parties are exclusively domestic persons? Now that Poland is in the European Union, an arbitrator should not be given preference depending on the provenance of the parties. Polish regulations, in accordance with Directive 2006/112/EC, specify the place of providing services depending on the status of the acquirer of the services as a VAT payer, or not as the case may be. There is no difference on account of the acquirer's origin. The only difference concerns persons from outside the EU who are not VAT payers – but this is based on Directive 2006/112/EC.

Therefore it could be the case that, soon, tax offices will stop reflecting on the above list of examples of situations and differentiating standpoints with respect to the arbitrator's remuneration depending on whether or not the foreign partner is from an EU member state. In this regard, the VAT Act based on Directive 2006/112/EC applies in Poland. Tax offices do not have much leeway for interpretation here, but nevertheless...

Arbitration is used to resolve more than just commercial cases. Arbitration can be chosen in inheritance or family cases, such as in the partition of joint property. Does the service of amicably resolving how an inheritance is distributed or joint property divided between family members constitute economic activity?

Arbitration is substitute justice. No judge pays VAT on their remuneration. No judge issues an invoice for an award. That would be immoral. Issuing awards is not delivering a service, just as sentencing people to a term of imprisonment cannot be a service. That is the view of legislators and tax authorities in many countries where the tradition and practice of arbitration is old and strong, for example Switzerland, Singapore, Belgium and even Bulgaria.

The acceptance of various regimes for Polish arbitrators, depending on the type of proceedings, the place and the composition of the panel of adjudicators, is immoral and improper. It exposes the best lawyers in Poland to uncertainty. VAT on arbitrators' remuneration should be totally eliminated by law. But at present there is no clear interpretation from the Minister of Finance on this issue. Tax offices apply the interpretation of the Minister of Finance concerning advocates appearing *pro bono* and experts commissioned to work by courts. That is a misunderstanding of concepts and professions. What is more, the Polish Ombudsman (*Rzecznik Praw Obywatelskich)* attacked this interpretation as being wrong, even with regard to advocates acting *pro bono* and court experts.

There should be no VAT on arbitrators' fees. Article 113 of the VAT Act introduces the rule that the sale of services is subject to VAT after the threshold of PLN 150 000 has been crossed in the previous tax year. An arbitrator who exceeds PLN 150 000 must pay VAT on the excess amount of fees paid in new cases received before the end of the year. Their activities before reaching the limit of PLN 150 000 are not subject to VAT.

What about arbitrators who issue an award once in a lifetime? Article 15 par. 2 of the VAT Act defines as economic activity an action performed even once 'in circumstances indicating an intention to perform the action frequently'. The above regulation shows that for taxing an arbitrator's actions, their intention will be of significance. What circumstances and when 'indicate an intention to perform the action frequently', as Article 15 par. 2 requires, and when not? Does an arbitrator whose name is on several lists of arbitrators have an intention to perform arbitration frequently, even if they have received only one case in their lifetime, or one per year, or have never yet received any case? Is another arbitrator, whose name cannot be found anywhere, in a better situation if they have one case but have no intention of taking on any more?

There is no reason why the activity of some arbitrators should be regarded as commercial activity and be made subject to VAT unnecessarily, since the same activity by other arbitrators or those same arbitrators in another case – for example, a family case – is excluded from that category.

Each arbitrator could be criminally and fiscally liable for improperly completing a VAT tax return. All of us run this risk every month if we fail to complete a VAT tax return when we should. Likewise, we run the same risk if we do actually complete a tax return and pay VAT when we should not. Filling out a tax return incorrectly works both ways and is subject to liability, irrespective of the 'direction' of the wrongdoing. Even 'unnecessary' payment of VAT can be prosecuted, e.g. in a situation where a party demands a VAT refund with interest after some time. That party could be a state institution, or even the State Treasury itself.

Being convicted in criminal or fiscal criminal proceedings for a deliberate wrongdoing bars a lawyer from practising the professions of an advocate, legal adviser, notary, judge, public prosecutor, tax advisor, court-receiver, bailiff, academic teacher, politician, police officer, customs officer, insurance agent and even tax officer. As a result, the country's best lawyers are sitting on a powder keg each month, courting disaster, at the mercy of shaky and changeable interpretations by civil servants who typically are not lawyers.

This practice should be ended once and for all, by eliminating VAT from arbitrators' remuneration, in the interests of the entire community and all colleagues. This would have the additional effect of lowering the costs of arbitration proceedings and increasing the prestige of arbitration.

VAT on arbitrators' fees was introduced in Germany and Austria. Ever since, German and Austrian arbitration have become less attractive for foreigners. There has also been a decline in the attractiveness of German and Austrian arbitrators' services because arbitrators there have to add 20 per cent VAT to their fees, where others such as Swiss, Belgian and many other countries do not. VAT was temporarily introduced on arbitrators' fees in Singapore. As a result, arbitrators moved the venue for arbitration proceedings to neighbouring Malaysia with the consent of both parties. Files were packed into taxis and hearings conducted immediately across the Malaysian border. The Singapore authorities quickly realised they were losing more than they were gaining. This was true not only financially, but also in terms of prestige. As a result, VAT was lifted from arbitrators' fees. Singapore has since become a flourishing centre of international arbitration, and Singaporean arbitrators are increasingly in demand.

One of the proposals to change the Polish Law is to introduce arbitration as one of the forms of practising the profession of an advocate. The proposal is an interesting one for advocate circles only. If it is pushed through, it will definitely contribute to popularising arbitration among members of the Bar. It will also enable income from arbitration to be taxed at a flat rate and not with progressive tax, as is the case with income from 'activities performed in person'. However, if arbitration ceases to be regarded as an 'activity performed in person', it will become a commercial activity subject to VAT. Additionally will this be the case only for advocates, and not for other people? If the answer is in the affirmative, the confusion will become even greater.

In Ancient Rome, the Emperor Vespasian introduced charges for using public toilets. His son, outraged by this decision, complained that it was – to put it delicately – not a gentleman's decision, and even shameful. The Emperor Vespasian held a handful of coins to his son's nose and asked whether they had a bad smell. We don't know his son's reply. The phrase *pecunia non olet* (money does not stink), which was attributed to Vespasian, made history. Ever since, every greedy ruler has resorted to this cynical slogan about the 'smell-free' character of money. History has nothing to say about the son's reaction and his subsequent respect for Vespasian, which is a pity. The rule of law is based on justice, and justice is not a provider of services 'just like any other'. Similarly, arbitration is not a business 'just like any other'. Accordingly, it should be protected against the Treasury's greed, even if the fragrance is tempting and their sense of smell leads them astray.

[*Piotr Nowaczyk*]
Advocate (FCIArb), Chartered Arbitrator, partner with DENTONS law firm, member of the International Court of Arbitration of the ICC in Paris, arbitrator and advisor in about 200 arbitration proceedings, former president of the Court of Arbitration at the Polish Chamber of Commerce.
e-mail: piotr.nowaczyk@dentons.com

| | |

A New Belgian Law on Arbitration

I. Aim of the Law

"For arbitration to exist and succeed there must be a regulatory framework which controls the legal status and effectiveness of arbitration in a national and international legal environment."[1]

More and more, we live in an international context. Due to the importance of a national legislation as basis of arbitration, harmonization of these different rules is central. Indeed, this harmonization renders international arbitration more predictable. Fortunately, the UNCITRAL Model Law offers this precious tool for international harmonization.

It is most welcome that the Belgian legislator has decided to align his law with the UNCITRAL Model Law which is one of the most advanced and modern regulations. However, the Belgian law also aims to take into consideration national peculiarities and to provide an adequate basis for international arbitration. The new law tries also to provide more efficient legislation.[2]

Belgium seeks to present itself as a country open to international arbitration and disposing of the most progressive tools to host these arbitration proceedings.[3]

A lot of countries have also adapted their Arbitration law to the UNCITRAL Model Law.[4]

---

* The CYArb® – Czech (& Central European) Yearbook of Arbitration® usually publishes short messages on arbitration practise in the countries of Central and East Europe. Belgian arbitration law and practise however still presents a very important benchmark ("etalon") in international arbitration. Therefore the editorial board decided to publish also a short memo in "News & Reports" particularly regarding Belgium.

[1] See JULIAN D. M. LEW, LOUKAS A. MISTELIS & STEFAN KROLL, COMPARATIVE INTERNATIONAL COMMERCIAL ARBITRATION, Kluwer Law International (2003).

[2] Parliamentary works, Doc 53 2743/ 01 report at the House of Representatives. See on this law, M. Dal, *La nouvelle loi sur l'arbitrage*, 132(6542) JOURNAL DES TRIBUNAUX 785 (2013); Pascal Hollander, *The New Belgian Arbitration Law*, (4) LES CAHIERS DE L'ARBITRAGE 1013 (2013); Guy Keutgen, *La nouvelle loi belge sur l'arbitrage*, REVUE DE DROIT INTERNATIONAL ET DE DROIT COMPARÉ 65 (2014); M. Piers & D. Demeulemeester, *The adoption of the UNCITRAL Model Law encourages arbitration in Belgium*, (2) B-ARBITRA 367 (2013).

[3] Parliamentary works, *supra* note 3, at 1.

[4] Ibid, at 5.

II. Main Characteristics

What are the main characteristics of this reform?

- The new law applies to both national and international arbitration, whereas the UNCITRAL Model Law applies only the international commercial arbitration.[5] It is indeed sometimes very difficult to make a distinction between national and international arbitration[6] and the preparatory work also underlines that there is no reason to render the national arbitration more onerous than international arbitration.[7]
- The new provisions are integrated in the Judicial Code and not in a separate law.

We approve of this choice.

We think that arbitration must be viewed in the framework of the Judicial Code so that, if one of the problems cannot be solved by the provisions specific to arbitration, it must be possible to rely on the provisions of the Judicial Code.

III. Arbitration Agreement

Article 1681 gives the definition of an arbitration agreement.

An arbitration agreement is a convention by which the parties submit to arbitration certain or all of their disputes, which have been raised or which will be raised between themselves on a well determined report of law, contractual or non-contractual.[8] This definition corresponds to the definition given by article 7 of the Model Law.[9]

This definition was not present in the previous version of the law.

In Belgium, a written agreement is not required anymore, as was the case in the former article 1677 of the Judicial Code. The arbitration agreement can also be oral, if the proof can be established, for instance by witnesses.[10] Our law is very flexible.[11]

---

[5] Ibid, at 6.

[6] Ibid.

[7] The distinction between Belgian and foreign arbitral awards only remains relevant with regard to their annulment. Belgian courts are only competent to review Belgian awards.

[8] GUY KEUTGEN & G.A. DAL, L'ARBITRAGE EN DROITS BELGE ET INTERNATIONAL, Tome I, Le droit belge, (2nd ed. 2006).

[9] Preparatory works, at 15.

[10] Preparatory documents 53, 2743-001, at 15.

[11] The preparatory works underline that in certain sectors, (diamond and maritime transport) a written document is not required (see pp. 15 & 16).

The definition of the arbitration agreement is given by article 7 of the Model Law, inspired by the New York Convention of 1958. The Model Law is, we think, more complete than the Belgian law, it mentions that the arbitration agreement can consist of letters, telegrams or other means of telecommunication.

We think that arbitration agreements must be drafted on a very precise and careful basis. Not only the language, the place of arbitration, the number of arbitrators but also the possibility of multiparty arbitration could be taken into consideration in the drafting of the agreement.[12]

IV. Power of the Arbitral Tribunal to Order Provisional and Conservatory Measures

By virtue of article 1691 of the Judicial Code, the Arbitral Tribunal can order provisory measures when asked by one of the parties.[13] This article is inspired by article 17 of the Model Law.[14]

However, the state Court can, before or during the arbitral procedure, also order this measure by virtue of article 1683 of the Judicial Code;[15] this rule can be excluded by the parties.

What are the interim measures which can be ordered? It is not specified by the law, contrary to the Model Law.[16]

The legislator wants to leave the door open for all the possibilities of interim measures.

We think that the legislator is right because experience has shown that new environments and new facts can infer new interim measures. The Arbitral Tribunal will not be entitled, contrary to the state Judge, to issue an injunction towards a third party or a freezing order.

The Arbitral Tribunal cannot order unilateral measures. The Belgian legislator did not follow this faculty left open by article 17B and 17C of the UNCITRAL Model Law.[17] We think personally that, in some very exceptional circumstances,

---

[12] JULIAN D. M. LEW, LOUKAS A. MISTELIS & STEFAN KROLL, *supra* note 2, at 166.

[13] See on the power of the Tribunal in civil and common law, D. Philippe, *Fact-finding in tort law*, 3 INTERNATIONAL JOURNAL OF PROCEDURAL LAW 309 (2013).

[14] Commentary, at 550, Preparatory works, at 23. Article 17 was introduced in the new version of the Model Law of 2006.

[15] See Parliamentary works, *supra* note 3, at 16.

The fact that the Court accepts interim measures does not mean that the Court has the power to declare the compatibility between the resolution a dispute to arbitration and, at the same time, seeking assistance from the Court for interim protection orders. Case No 751, *Swift Fortune Ltd v Magnifica Marine*, Court of Appeal of Singapore, 1st December 2006.

[16] For a statement of these measures, see article 17 of the UNCITRAL Model Law.

[17] See D. De Meulemeester, *Voorlopige of bewarende maatregelen in arbitrage*, in DE NIEUWE ARBITRAGEWET 2013, Antwerpen – Cambridge: Intersentia 66 (M. Piers ed., 2013, 65-82); this article has been introduced in the Model Law in 2006.

unilateral measures can be ordered. We know that the working of unilateral measures has been regulated by the new laws. For instance, article 19JC or article 584JC allows unilateral provisional measures to be submitted in the case of urgent and serious matters.

Articles 1692 to 1695 codify the current state of law. Article 1692 allows the Arbitral Tribunal to modify, suspend or withdraw provisory measures. This can be ordered at the demand of one of the parties but the Tribunal cannot do it on its own initiative contrary to article 17D of the UNCITRAL Model Law. The legislators consider that it infringes the adversarial principle in law. Article 1693 foresees that a security can be demanded to the claimant asking conservatory measure.[18]

Article 1694 foresees that the Tribunal can order the claimant to communicate all changes of circumstances upon which the provisory measure is based.[19] Ordinary measures can be ordered in an award and can also be formalized in a letter.[20]

The party who claimed provisional measures must inform the Arbitral Tribunal about the recognition of the enforcement of this measure.

V. Place of Arbitration (Article 1701 JC)

Once more, the will of the parties should prevail. Failing such an agreement, the Arbitral Tribunal will determine this taking into consideration, following article 1701, paragraph 1 of the Judicial Code, the circumstances of the case and the convenience of the parties.[21]

The reliability of the judicial system will also be taken into consideration.

VI. Competence of the Courts

One important element of the reform is that the litigation related to arbitration is concentrated in the Tribunal where the Court of Appeal has its jurisdiction, in others words, it will be concentrated on the Tribunals of Antwerp, Brussels, Gent, Liège and Mons. Concerning the procedure in annulment or in exequatur, the same rule applies.[22]

---

[18] We can stress that the exception *judicatum solvi* is not applicable within the EU Member States.

[19] Article 17F of the UNCITRAL Model Law.

[20] M. Dal, *supra* note 3, at 785; O. Caprasse & D. De Meulemeester, *De arbitrale uitspraak, in* DE ARBITRALE UITSPRAAK, Brussel: Bruylant 43 (2006).

[21] Commentary, at 592.

[22] See article 1720 § 2 of the Judicial code. See H. VERBIST, "De vordering tot vernietiging van de arbitrale uitspraak na de hervorming van het Belgische arbitragerecht door de wet van 24 juni 2013", in M. Piers, *supra* note 18, at 113.

VII. Appointment of the Arbitrator

As in the Model Law, the Belgian law provides that no person can be precluded from being appointed as arbitrator for reason of nationality. This is based on a non-discrimination principle.[23] This rule is important for international arbitration.

Both Model Law and Belgian law foresee the possibility of derogation. The parties can agree on the procedure of appointment of the arbitrator. The Belgian law adds that the requirement of independence and impartiality in this case must be respected.

The judicial nature of the arbitration process imposes practical limits on the parties' freedom, when choosing the arbitrators. This is because the tribunal exercises judicial functions and it is a war to have the same finality in binding effects as a judgment of a national court. As the State plans its authority for the enforcement of the awards, it requires that the arbitration proceedings as well as the composition of the arbitral tribunal meet certain minimum standards, which are considered to be indispensable characteristics of any fair trial.

The appreciation of impartiality becomes more severe. We think that the fact that the arbitrator has already published a scientific contribution in certain aspects on an abstract basis on legal issues related to the case is, we think, not sufficient to render the arbitrator partial.[24]

Independence means that there should be no relationship between the parties and the arbitrator, which can affect the arbitrators' freedom of judgement; for instance an arbitrator is not independent when he has a financial interest in the outcome of a case. For instance, very acute is the case where one of the partners is an associate of a worldwide law firm, is or has been the counsel of a party involved in the arbitration procedure.[25] It is the reason why the arbitrators have a duty to disclose all relevant information concerning their independence.

In the appointment of the arbitrator, the standards of impartiality and independence are mentioned in article 12 of the Model Law[26] and article 1685, § 2 JC. In the preparatory work of the Model Law, the working group envisages putting a limitation on the freedom of the parties if one of the parties could get a manifestly unfair advantage.[27] Finally, this proposal was rejected because, inter alia, this was too vague.

Impartiality is not a requirement of public policy. The parties can renounce this requirement if they are duly informed beforehand. This obligation to divulge

---

[23]   See for an analysis of this text, article 8 of the Model Law, commentary, at 302.

[24]   See JULIAN D. M. LEW, LOUKAS A. MISTELIS & STEFAN KROLL, *supra* note 2, at 260

[25]   See Ibid, at 263.

[26]   See commentary, at 88.

[27]   Commentary, at 360.

facts and circumstances, which has an influence on this requirement, is of the utmost importance.[28]

The Model Law foresees that a party may challenge an arbitrator appointed by him, the same solution applies also under Belgian law.[29]

VIII. Appointment of the Arbitration Tribunal by the State Court

In the case of an incident in the appointment of the arbitrator, the state Court can assist the parties.

In this case, the President of Tribunal judging like in referee, has the power to appoint or to replace the arbitrator. No recourse is possible against his decision, except when the President considers that there is no need to appoint an arbitrator.[30] This procedure which is already applicable for the appointment and replacement of arbitrators now applies also for challenging the arbitrator.[31]

We have to welcome that the referee Judge can assist the parties in handling the procedure rapidly.

IX. Recourse against the Award

IX.1. Appeal against the Award (Article 1716 JC)

Appeal against an award is not allowed, except if parties have foreseen this faculty in their arbitration agreement.

IX.2. Annulment of the Award (Article 1717 JC)

Article 1717 JC is inspired by article 34 of the Model Law.

First, the demand can only be accepted if the award cannot be challenged before the arbitrators; that means that there is no possibility anymore of rectification, interpretation or additional award.

Paragraph 2 of article 1717 JC foresees that the demand must be introduced by summons before the Tribunal of First Instance. This decision cannot be appealed; only a recourse before the Supreme Court is allowed (see article 609, paragraph 1 JC). It is an important step for the legal predictability of the awards.

---

[28] See M. Dal, *supra* note 3.
[29] Article 12.2.
[30] See Parliamentary works, at 14; article 1460 of the CPC in France.
[31] See Preparatory works, at 14.

IX.3. Contractual Exclusion of the Recourse in Annulment

Article 1718 JC foresees, as in the previous legislation, that the parties can contractually renounce annulment. It is possible to renounce at any moment, even after the notification of the award but this renouncement is only possible for:

- a physical person not having Belgian nationality or not having his domicile or residence in Belgium;
- a legal entity not having his seat of incorporation, his main establishment or branch in Belgium.

The new grounds for annulment of the award are similar to the grounds of the New York Convention which has enhanced the international character of this article.
By limiting the grounds for setting aside the award, predictability and expeditiousness of arbitration were enhanced.[32]
The term "public policy" covers fundamental principles of law in substantive as well as procedural respects. Corruption, bribery and fraud could constitute such grounds.[33,34]
Article 1717, paragraph 3 v) JC is very balanced. First, an annulment will not be possible if the arbitration agreement is contrary to a mandatory provision of the arbitration law; but irregularities, except in the constitution of the Arbitral Tribunal, cannot lead to annulment of the award if it is established that there is no effect or incidence on the award.[35]

IX.4. Remission

It is also very efficient to offer the Judge an option between setting aside the award and suspending his decision, leaving then the time to the arbitrators to rectify the eliminated grounds for annulment. The Court can intervene when it seems appropriate; it is a very broad formula which gives the necessary flexibility for the Judge to intervene.[36]
The article remains very vague on the effect for setting aside the award.[37]
Let us also pay attention to article 1717, paragraph 3, which uses the term "may" for the annulment; that means that the annulment remains at the

---

[32]   See commentary, at 912.
[33]   See commentary, at 914.
[34]   See on fraud and arbitrability, JULIAN D. M. LEW, LOUKAS A. MISTELIS & STEFAN KROLL, *supra* note 2, at 210 and 211.
[35]   See on this text, the commentary, at 916. On the possibility to limit the setting aside to the international public policy, see commentary, at 919.
[36]   See commentary, at 920.
[37]   See commentary, at 921.

appreciation of the Court. For instance, a non-material error can give rights to grounds for setting aside the award but the Judge is not obliged to set it aside when such grounds are present.[38]

An example of fraud leading to annulment is, for instance, an award of agreement between parties just before the bankruptcy between two parties who have no dispute between themselves and which has as sole object, to impose facts to the future receiver of the company.[39] Fraud can also be present if the award has been rendered on the basis of false witness statements or falsified documents.[40]

X. Conclusion

The fact that the Belgian legislator chooses the Model Law as the model for international commercial arbitration shows the will of Belgium to be a centre for international arbitration. We see also that in procedural law, some principles are widely recognised, in Belgian law and in international arbitration for instance, the adequate opportunity to present one's case or the right to equal treatment.[41] This is more than welcome.

However we have seen that the Belgian legislator took also into consideration the peculiarities of Belgian procedural law. We know the benefits that the arbitration world could harvest from the New York Convention. Maybe a Convention applied in the same manner in the countries having ratified this Convention, as is the case for the Vienna Convention on International Sales could further promote arbitration.

[*Denis Philippe*]
Professor at the University of Louvain, Lawyer at the Brussels and Luxemburg Bar (Philippe & Partners)
e-mail: dphilippe@philippelaw.eu

| | |

---

[38] For procedural defects, see commentary, at 922.

See on the very progressive solution of the French law, which introduces a global possibility to renounce globally to the annulment, CHRISTOPHE SERAGLINI, DROIT DE L'ARBITRAGE INTERNE ET INTERNATIONAL, Paris: Montchrestien-Lextenso éd. 858 (2013). See also on the revision of the awards in case of fraud in French law, CHRISTOPHE SERAGLINI, DROIT DE L'ARBITRAGE INTERNE ET INTERNATIONAL, Paris: Montchrestien-Lextenso éd. 863 (2013).

[39] See ibid., at 890, Paris April 9th, 2009, *Cahiers de l'arbitrage*, 2010, p. 889, note E. LOQUIN.

[40] Paris July, 1st, 2009, CHRISTOPHE SERAGLINI, *supra* note 39, note 387.

[41] See EMMANUEL GAILLARD; ANNE VERONIQUE SCHLAEPFER; PHILIPPE PINSOLLE; LOUIS DEGOS, TOWARDS A UNIFORM INTERNATIONAL ARBITRATION LAW? Huntington: N.Y.: Juris Pub. 180 (2005).

Changes to the Arbitration Act in 2013

The most recent changes to Act No. 216/1994 Coll. (the *Arbitration Act*), which became effective on January 1, 2014, were adopted in connection with the recodification of private law in the Czech Republic. The legislature took the opportunity provided by the amendment to correct certain legislative errors encumbering the Arbitration Act. The changes can be divided into two groups, the first comprises technical changes reflecting the new terminology introduced in Act No. 89/2012 Coll., the Civil Code (the *Civil Code*), while the second consists of the legislative and technical clarification of the existing provisions. These changes were implemented by Act No. 303/2013 Coll.[1] (the *amendment*) and took effect at the same time as the new provisions of Czech civil law.

I. General and Terminological Changes

Section 1 of the Arbitration Act, which defines the scope of the law, has been supplemented to reflect the inclusion of the new Part Seven of the Arbitration Act, which regulates proceedings before the arbitration commission of an association. The incorporation of these provisions is explicitly foreseen in Section 267 of the Civil Code. Although the intention of the Civil Code to introduce the possibility of subordinating decision-making on disputes stemming from the administration of an association to an arbitration commission and the fact that a more detailed definition of the rules of such proceedings was to be regulated separately[2] were well known, the Government's draft amendment skirted this issue. The draft provisions inserted into the Arbitration Act as Sections 40e to 40k resulted from a legislative process, specifically, the debate on the amendment by the Constitutional Law Committee of the Czech Parliament's Chamber of Deputies.[3] This effectively gave rise to a situation where the government bill failed to take account of a matter that was fundamental to recodification, despite the fact that the amendment was prepared precisely for this purpose.

---

[1] This law, effective as of September 12, 2013, amended certain laws in connection with the adoption of the recodification of private law. The changes were adopted as part of broader legislative measures amending a large swathe of laws further to the adoption of the Civil Code, and thus necessitating the harmonisation of Czech legislation with the new code of civil law. This fact in itself largely determines the nature of the most recent amendment, which in no way incorporates conceptual changes to arbitration.

[2] See the above-mentioned Section 267 of the Civil Code.

[3] The draft amendment was debated by the committee at its 61st meeting on May 29, 2013. The consequent resolution can be found at http://www.psp.cz/sqw/text/tiskt. sqw?o=6&ct=930&ct1=2 (accessed on 6 December 2014).

II. The Office of Arbitrator

Changes were made to Section 4 of the Arbitration Act which defines the requirements for holding the office of arbitrator. The text was reworded to reflect changes in the terminology in the Civil Code, which now uses the word *svéprávnost* for *legal capacity*, instead of *způsobilost k právním úkonům*. However, in terms of definition, nothing has changed. Another change relates to the enactment of Act No. 91/2012 Coll. on private international law (the *Private International Law Act*), in which arbitration with an international dimension, including the use of arbitrators who are foreign nationals, was incorporated. Therefore, with effect from January 1, 2014, the conditions under which a foreign national is entitled to act as an arbitrator are defined in Section 118 of the Private International Law Act.

The explanatory memorandum to the Private International Law Act and most related commentaries assert that the changes are technical and that the provisions of the Private International Law Act are based on the original Section 4(2) of the Arbitration Act. However, this opinion disregards the fact that the Private International Law Act fails to stipulate the requirements of integrity and the age of majority. The only condition of eligibility for a foreign national interested in serving as an arbitrator is the requirement of full legal capacity, and this is judged according to the personal status of the person in question. Evidently, the legislature's sole intention was to remove provisions on foreign arbitrators from the Arbitration Act and incorporate them, without substantive changes, into the Private International Law Act. However, they failed to reflect the fact that during the approval of the Private International Law Act modifications were made to these provisions. Consequently, the requirements of integrity and the age of majority were deleted.

Having said that, it could be argued that Section 4(1) of the Arbitration Act should be interpreted as a general definition of the prerequisites for serving as an arbitrator that is applicable irrespective of the arbitrator's nationality. As such, this interpretation would apply if the provisions of the Private International Law Act were solely conflict-of-law rules. However, a systematic interpretation of the Private International Law Act indicates that the legislature was trying to define the role of foreign arbitrators comprehensively, and, where the application of the general provisions the Arbitration Act is anticipated, this is expressly noted (see the special requirements imposed on arbitrators for consumer disputes). If Section 4(1) of the Arbitration Act were intended to be applied in the same way, this would have been stated in the Private International Law Act. Moreover, this legislative omission cannot be evaluated negatively, and if the legislature were to decide not to make any further amendments and leave Section 118 of the Private International Law Act unchanged, this would enhance the Czech Republic's attractiveness as a country favourably disposed to arbitration.

III. Preservation of the Effects of a Submitted Application, Procedure for Annulling an Arbitral Award

Other changes are not directly related to recodification. The legislature wanted to correct the legislative error in Section 34 of the Arbitration Act which arose upon the adoption of the change introduced by Act No. 19/2012 Coll., and to formulate this provision and the related Section 16 of the Arbitration Act more precisely. When Act No. 19/2012 Coll. was being adopted, the amendments triggered a contradiction between the wording of the first and second paragraphs of Section 34 of the Arbitration Act regarding further action following a court's annulment of an arbitral award based on an application submitted pursuant to Section 31 of the Arbitration Act. Depending on the reason for annulment, Section 34 the Arbitration Act stipulates whether the matter will be re-heard by arbitrators or whether, as a result of their lack of jurisdiction, a court will take over the proceedings. Bearing in mind the parties' autonomy, an essential criterion is whether the parties have expressed their willingness to submit to the jurisdiction of arbitrators. The first paragraph of Section 34 of the Arbitration Act contains an exhaustive definition of these cases,[4] while the second paragraph has hitherto been conceived as a residual clause referring to the grounds for the annulment of an arbitral award not listed above.

Act No. 19/2012 Coll. inserted two new grounds for the annulment of an arbitral award related to consumer protection into Section 31 the Arbitration Act. The first case involves non-compliance with the requirements of an arbitration agreement concluded with a consumer (Sections 3(3) to (6) of the Arbitration Act). The second case entails situations where a contested decision has been handed down in contravention of consumer protection regulations or where the decision is manifestly contrary to accepted principles of morality or public policy. The legislature took account of the new grounds in the first paragraph of Section 34 of the Arbitration Act, but retained only a reference to Sections 31(a) and (b) of the Arbitration Act in the second paragraph – in the list of cases outside the scope of these provisions. As a result, these two paragraphs contradicted each other. This deficiency has been remedied and now both paragraphs positively stipulate those cases affected by the provisions in question. The rule according to which the court will take over the substantive hearing of a dispute if proceedings on the annulment of an arbitral

---

[4]   Pursuant to the amendment to the Arbitration Act pursuant to Act No. 19/2012 Coll., cases in which proceedings on the annulment of an arbitral award result in the finding that the arbitrators lack jurisdiction were expanded to include situations in which the further hearing of a dispute in arbitration would significantly harm the consumer, thus rendering any decision by arbitrators on the merits undesirable.

award were to result in the finding that the arbitrators lacked jurisdiction, or in fundamental substantive deficiencies of a decision in consumer disputes, continues to apply.

The text of Section 34(2) of the Arbitration Act now explicitly states that these cases are also covered by Section 16 of the Arbitration Act, and therefore it is possible to continue arbitration only at the express request of one of the parties. This constitutes a clarification of the text rather than a conceptual change, as the requirement of an expression of intent to continue proceedings could already be inferred in the past. Applications to continue proceedings are subject to Sections 14(1) and (2) of the Arbitration Act. Pursuant to the text of Section 16 of the Arbitration Act, prior to the amendment, newly appointed arbitrators who were to re-hear a dispute had to be viewed as *another body* to which the petition for the re-hearing of the dispute was to be directed.[5] The Parties may still agree that arbitrators contributing to the issuance of a contested arbitral award will be tasked with further proceedings, but they must expressly agree on this possibility.[6] In international practice, the reverse principle, which works on the assumption that a case is primarily re-heard by the original arbitrators unless the parties agree otherwise, is not uncommon.

These changes in the wording of Section 34(2) of the Arbitration Act follow and reflect the changes in the provisions contained in Section 16 of the Arbitration Act. As such, they definitively establish that Section 16 of the Arbitration Act also needs to be invoked when an arbitral award is annulled in accordance with Section 34(2) of the Arbitration Act.[7] In the text of these provisions, other arbitrators and arbitral tribunals have also been expressly included among entities to which a petition to continue proceedings is submitted. The re-hearing of a case may be sought from them if they retain their jurisdiction.

Section 16 of the Arbitration Act was divided into two separate paragraphs. Provisions were created to cover cases where the arbitrators themselves acknowledge that they lack jurisdiction, as well as cases where, after an arbitral

---

[5]   For the avoidance of doubt, there was a change in the wording, and Section 16 of the Arbitration Act now includes competent arbitrators and permanent arbitration courts among entities to which a petition to continue proceedings is submitted.

[6]   A situation in which the arbitral award is annulled for reasons according to Section 31(c) of the Arbitration Act, i.e., because the hearing of and decision on a case involved an arbitrator who had not been called upon to participate in the decision-making or was not eligible to be an arbitrator, is an exception. Here, arbitrators who participated in the original hearing of the case and in the rendering of the contested arbitration award are excluded from further proceedings, unless the parties agree otherwise. In this case, the agreement could logically relate solely to those arbitrators not covered by grounds for exclusion under Section 31(c) of the Arbitration Act.

[7]   I.e., in cases where an arbitral award is annulled pursuant to Sections 31(c) to (f) and (i) of the Arbitration Act.

award has been handed down, the grounds for annulment under Section 31 of the Arbitration Act are invoked. The list of entities to whom an application for the continuation of proceedings is addressed was therefore extended to include other arbitrators and permanent arbitration courts not only in situations under Section 34(2) of the Arbitration Act, but also in the event that a lack of jurisdiction is established by the original arbitrators. Accordingly, these provisions also apply to situations where a request for arbitration (statement of claim) is lodged with non-competent arbitrators.

There has also been a substantive change. Until now, the thirty-day period within which a party had to submit an application to continue proceedings was calculated from the date on which the corresponding ruling was served on the party. The amendment reflected the fact that the law encompasses two distinct groups of cases. The existing definition of this time limit was preserved for situations where the proceedings were discontinued due to a decision by the arbitrators that they lacked jurisdiction, in which case the reference moment is the day on which the corresponding resolution is served. If an arbitral award is annulled by a court, the provisions of the Code of Civil Procedure, including the possibility of appeal, apply. In these cases, the time limit starts on the date on which the decision to annul the arbitral award becomes final.

IV. New Provisions on Service

The amendment introduced new provisions concerning the service of documents on the parties. This issue was discussed relatively broadly by the professional community, particularly in relation to private arbitration companies. However, it falls under the category of procedure in respect of which the parties are entitled to make an agreement. Moreover, in proceedings before permanent arbitration courts, these court rules, which may also stray from legislation, are applied.[8] The provisions of Section 19(4) of the Arbitration Act, which allow parties to submit the proceedings to rules other than the rules of permanent arbitration courts provided that such rules are attached to the arbitration agreement, cannot be overlooked either. Therefore, the impact of this change will be limited. Furthermore, the new Section 19a of the Arbitration Act was not part of the original draft of the amendment and was not incorporated until the legislative process was in progress. The amendment introduces the priority service of documents in electronic format. Documents should primarily be served on participants by delivery to their data boxes. If this method of service is impossible, the documents must be served by electronic means. If a document cannot be delivered in this way, service by post is used.

---

[8] Cf. Section 13(3) of the Arbitration Act in conjunction with the second sentence of Section 19(4) of the Arbitration Act.

Certain doubts may arise as to the nature of this provision and its practical application. In relation to arbitral awards, the issue of service was debated in the past and depended on the decision-making practices of the courts. The courts based their decisions on Section 23 of the Arbitration Act prior to the changes implemented by Act No. 19/2012 Coll., when the end of arbitration was tied to the rendering of an award. Act No. 19/2012 Coll. introduced a conceptual change that connected the end of arbitration to the finality of an award. Practical reasons apart, this change was motivated by the fact that it was possible to sweep this issue under Section 19 of the Arbitration Act and enable parties to decide on service themselves. As a result, service has become part of the procedural process and thus is an issue governed by the autonomy of the parties. Even now, there is no reason to deviate from these conclusions and withdraw the parties' autonomy to decide on the service method. In this respect, the new provisions can be regarded as optional and the usual hierarchy of procedural rules will be applied to arbitration.

Furthermore, it is unclear how Section 19a of the Arbitration Act should be interpreted in practice, especially as regards the *impossibility* of serving documents in a certain way. Does the concept of *impossibility* apply to the actual impossibility of effecting service, with the arbitrators obliged to attempt service in the prescribed manner, or is it a reference to the broader inability of the parties to effect service in a specific way, e.g., on the grounds that the arbitrator does not have a data box? Practical problems where arbitrators, for the purpose of sending data messages, are defined as public authorities[9] cannot be overlooked either. The service of documents in arbitration proceedings would therefore fall under the procedure stipulated by Section 18a of Act No. 300/2008 Coll., pursuant to which, stakeholders would have to have access to document deliveries between private persons via data box. Unlike communications with public authorities, this is a chargeable service. The second interpretation is not without problems either. If it is possible to waive the obligation to serve documents in a certain way by a declaration that the arbitrator does not have the means for such delivery, the entire provision becomes obsolete. As such, it would be possible to circumvent Section 19a of the Arbitration Act in light of the fact that a document could not be served in the required manner.

V. Obligation to Attach Arbitration Rules to the Arbitration Agreement (Section 19(4) of the Arbitration Act)

The draft amendment contained a provision which was removed during the legislative process. The undesirable situation that arose when Act No. 19/2012

---

9   See Section 1(1)(a) of Act No. 300/2008 Coll.

Coll. amended the Arbitration Act was meant to be fixed. That amendment inserted into Section 19(4) of the Arbitration Act the obligation to attach to the arbitration agreement the rules that were to be applied if they were different from the rules of a permanent arbitration court. A permanent arbitration court should be understood in the sense of Section 13(1) of the Arbitration Act, i.e., as an arbitral tribunal established by or on the basis of another law. This was in response to the practice of *ad hoc* excesses in arbitration when arbitration agreements referenced the rules of private arbitration companies without the other party having the opportunity to become acquainted with them; what is more, the rules often contained conditions restricting the procedural rights of the other party. This made it difficult to identify the version applicable to the proceedings.[10] These provisions also engendered practical problems in relation to international practices, as Section 19(4) of the Arbitration Act applies even in cases in which this obligation was not intended and where, as a result of this administrative burden, the Czech Republic became a less attractive venue for arbitration. Rules were drafted to restrict these provisions to consumer disputes.[11] However, this draft was not accepted due to the fact that when the amendment was being consulted, an amendment proposal was submitted seeking the deletion of this proposal from the amendment. These arguments led to the introduction of the obligation to attach arbitration rules to the arbitration agreement.

VI. Ministry of Justice List of Arbitrators for Consumer Disputes

The legislature remedied the legislative error that arose upon the approval of the Private International Law Act which deleted Part Five of the Arbitration Act. The intention had been to repeal provisions incorporated in the Private International Law Act, i.e., rules concerning relations with other countries, as part of the rectification process. The preparation of changes overlooked the fact that Act No. 19/2012 Coll. had unsystematically included an issue concerning the list of arbitrators authorized to hear consumer disputes in Part Five of the Arbitration Act. As a result, these provisions were accidentally deleted, but have now been restored by the amendment to the Arbitration Act. There were

---

[10] According to Section 13(2) of the Arbitration Act, permanent arbitration courts publish their statutes and rules in the Business Journal (*Obchodní věstník*), which does away with the problem, as parties have access to these documents and have the opportunity to become acquainted with them.

[11] In the explanatory memorandum to the amendment, it was argued that, interpreted strictly, the obligation under Section 19(4) of the Arbitration Act also applied to procedural rules issued by foreign arbitration courts, such as the ICC, and to proceedings held in accordance with UNCITRAL rules.

no substantive changes. The legislature made only minor changes in the wording and modifications to clarify the text.

VII. Proceedings before the Arbitration Commission of an Association

This was a response to new provisions of the Civil Code which introduced the possibility for associations to entrust[12] the hearing of disputes related to the administration of the association to an arbitration commission. It was impossible to automatically apply existing arbitration provisions because proceedings before the arbitration commission of an association include specific factors that need to be taken into account. There is a difference in the defined range of issues on which the arbitration commission has the jurisdiction to decide, as matters related to the administration of an association need not necessarily be of an economic nature. It is also necessary to take into account the nature of the disputes that are to be heard, as relations between an association's members and between an association and its bodies are different in nature from an economic dispute between independent entities.

General rules applicable to arbitration will be applied in all cases, unless otherwise stated. Provisions related to permanent arbitration courts cannot be applied to the arbitration commissions of associations. Conversely, Sections 265 and 266 of the Civil Code should be taken into account. First and foremost, the arbitration commission is entitled to hear disputes to the extent to which such authority is defined in the association's statutes. Alternatively, if the statutes do not specify the scope of the arbitration commission's powers, the commission is empowered to hear disputes related to (i) the payment of membership dues, and (ii) the decision to expel a member from the association.[13]

Section 266 of the Civil Code governs commission membership and the conditions a person must meet in order to become a member. Respecting the freedom of associations to manage their own affairs, the number of commission members is a matter to be stipulated in the statutes. In practice, this could become an important issue with regard to the conditions under which an arbitration commission is able to take decisions, because the different status of arbitrators and arbitration commission members is manifested here. While arbitrators are appointed upon the emergence of a dispute between the parties

---

[12]   Adjudication on disputes deriving from the administration of an association is an option (not an obligation) provided to these legal persons by the legislature. It is up to the founders or the supreme body of the association to set up an arbitration committee. It is also possible to define in the statutes those areas of disputes which the arbitration commission will have the authority to hear.

[13]   See Section 265 of the Civil Code.

and have access to all information in order to consider whether they have sufficient capacity to assume office, the members of an association's arbitration commission are elected without knowing when and to what extent they will be required to act, i.e., when a dispute will arise that they should hear. When deciding on the number of members, it is necessary to take into account the fact that the commission is authorized to carry out its activities if the hearing of a case involves at least a majority of its members, but no fewer than three members.

Section 4(1) of the Arbitration Act is applied analogously to the requirements for becoming a member of the arbitration commission. Persons who are in a relationship with an association, i.e., members of the association's governing body or audit commission, which gives rise to doubts about their ability to take impartial decisions (if the association is a party to a dispute), are not allowed to be members of the arbitration commission. The overlapping of positions is inadmissible here. Foreign nationals also need to prove that they have met the requirements. Section 266(2) of the Civil Code allows for some leeway, stating that if the appointment of a member of the arbitration commission is not contested on the grounds of non-compliance with the condition of integrity, it is assumed that such member is a person of integrity.[14] Commission members must comply with the corresponding conditions for their entire term of office. They may not participate in the hearing of a case where, in light of the circumstances, their impartiality is compromised. This area is regulated both in the Civil Code (Section 266(3)) and in the Arbitration Act.[15] These rules are derived, by analogy, from provisions applicable to arbitrators (see Section 11 of the Arbitration Act). Similar to Section 12(1) of the Arbitration Act, Section 40i of the Arbitration Act states that where grounds for the exclusion of a person become apparent, that person is obliged to suffer the consequences and be excluded from hearing the case in question.[16] The procedure is regulated differently in that, contrary to Section 40i of the Arbitration Act, a commission member is not excluded from hearing a case. In contrast to Section 12(2) of the Arbitration Act, there is no opportunity for parties to agree on the exclusion procedure, because the power to decide on a proposal for exclusion rests directly with the arbitration commission.

Situations where the arbitration commission is unable to reach a decision on the merits of a case are specifically regulated. Since the application of Sections 9

---

[14] It will be interesting to see how this issue is interpreted in practice, as integrity is an objective category and the fulfilment of this condition cannot be replaced fictitiously.

[15] See Section 40i of the Arbitration Act.

[16] Commission membership is not terminated – consider the differences in terminology, with Section 40i of the Arbitration Act referring to *exclusion from hearing a case*, but not to resignation, which is the case with Section 12(1) of the Arbitration Act.

and 10 of the Arbitration Act is excluded, it is impossible for a court to intervene in proceedings and appoint a person authorized to decide on the merits. A commission plainly has the status of a permanent body of an association authorized to resolve disputes according to the statutes. If the commission is unable to reach a decision, it is not possible to add members to achieve the prescribed number or to make substitute appointments of persons called in to decide on the dispute. A commission's powers lapse at this point and the jurisdiction of the court is restored.

The Arbitration Act separately defines the procedure for instituting proceedings before the arbitration commission of an association.[17] Section 14 of the Arbitration Act applies in a supporting role to matters not addressed by Part Seven of the Arbitration Act. It is anticipated that the statutes will specify the addresses to which applications for the initiation of proceedings should be served. Requests to the arbitration commission are only delivered to the association's headquarters in the absence of such information from the statutes. The parties have equal standing in proceedings and must be provided with the opportunity to assert their rights. The principle of the parties' autonomy is preserved in the statutes or other internal regulations (to which the statutes refer), or in a written agreement, in that the steps to be taken in proceedings may be negotiated. These provisions build on Section 19(1) of the Arbitration Act and expand the possibilities for the incorporation of rules on the holding of proceedings. Since members have access to the association's documents, unlike Section 19(4) of the Arbitration Act, there is no requirement for the parties to have the text of the rules demonstrably at their disposal. Compared to *conventional* arbitration, the specification of the period in which the commission is required to reach a decision is different. The law sets a three-month time limit, but allows for a different period to be determined in the same way as the rules of procedure in proceedings. This time limit may be extended to a maximum of nine months. If the arbitration commission fails to reach a decision by the set deadline, the applicant has the right to approach a court with its claim.

In connection with Section 31 of the Arbitration Act, the rules of procedure before the arbitration commission supplement the reasons for which it is possible to petition a court to annul a decision. Similar to consumer disputes, the principle of the prohibition of a substantive review is broken due to the fact that it may be revoked by a court if it is manifestly contrary to accepted principles of morality or public policy. If the subject of proceedings before an arbitration commission is a decision on the expulsion of an association member, irrespective of whether a court is petitioned to annul the arbitration commission's decision, pursuant to Section 40j(1) of the Arbitration Act, the member in question retains the right to seek a court declaration that the

---

[17] See Section 40f(1) of the Arbitration Act.

expulsion decision is null and void by following the procedure stipulated in Section 242 of the Civil Code. The opportunity to discontinue the enforcement of a decision in cases where an application to annul the decision has not been submitted within the time limit stipulated in Section 32(1) of the Arbitration Act is not overlooked either. Increased protection of association members is applied. The adopted rules mirror the rules established for decisions regarding consumer contracts, specifically Section 35(1)(b) of the Arbitration Act. An application to discontinue the enforcement of a decision may be submitted by a party in cases where any of the reasons (except for reasons related to consumer disputes) for the annulment of the decision exists.[18] This process is also possible in a situation where the commission's decision is contrary to accepted principles of morality or public policy if the arbitration commission fails to include advice in the decision that a court may be petitioned to annul it.[19] Section 40j(2) of the Arbitration Act stipulates that decisions of arbitration commissions are covered by Sections 35(1)(c)[20] and (d)[21] and Sections 35(2)[22] and (3)[23] of the Arbitration Act. This procedure applies when the cancellation of enforcement is sought on the grounds that the arbitral award was vitiated, on the basis of which it is possible to seek its annulment in accordance with Sections 31(a) to (f) and Section 40j(1) of the Arbitration Act (i.e., not on general grounds pursuant to Section 268 of the Code of Civil Procedure).

---

[18] I.e., grounds for the annulment of an arbitral award stipulated in Section 31(a) to (f) of the Arbitration Act.

[19] The analogous obligation of the content requirements of awards related to consumer relations (Section 25(2) of the Arbitration Act), which, according to Section 40k of the Arbitration Act, also applies in relation to awards issued by the arbitration commission of an association.

[20] An application to discontinue an ordered enforcement without a party petitioning for the annulment of the decision in accordance with Section 31 of the Arbitration Act, if the party that was required to be represented by a legal representative had no representative and acted alone without such action being subsequently approved.

[21] An application to discontinue ordered enforcement without a party petitioning for the annulment of the decision in accordance with Section 31 of the Arbitration Act, if a third party has acted on behalf of that party or its legal representative without being empowered to do so and the actions of that third person are not approved, even retrospectively.

[22] If, in accordance with the described conditions, an application is submitted to discontinue the enforcement of a decision, enforcement will be suspended and the concerned party will be required to petition for the annulment of the arbitral award within 30 days.

[23] If in proceedings on the annulment of an arbitral award initiated as a result of an application to discontinue enforcement, an award is annulled, the procedure stipulated in Section 34 of the Arbitration Act is followed. Upon the motion of a party, the hearing is continued by a court or arbitration commission (depending on the reason for the annulment of the award).

Rules applicable to consumer disputes are also adopted in Section 40k of the Arbitration Act, according to which the second sentence of Sections 25(2) and 32(3) of the Arbitration Act are applied (if an application for the annulment of an arbitral award is submitted by an association member and not by the association). Awards issued by the arbitration commission will therefore have to include advice on how to submit an application for annulment. Penalties for breaches of this obligation are an extension of the possibility of seeking the discontinuance of enforcement in accordance with Section 40j(2) of the Arbitration Act. Pursuant to Section 32(2) of the Arbitration Act,[24] due to the analogous application of consumer protection, an association member need not request the suspension of enforcement along with the application for the annulment of an arbitral award; the court will be obliged to investigate the existence of statutory reasons for the suspension of enforcement *ex officio*. A court must take a decision on enforceability within seven days, and during this period the decision may not be enforced. Section 32(1) of the Arbitration Act, which requires courts to examine whether there is any reason to annul an award due to the lack of jurisdiction to hear the case in arbitration or due to the fact that an arbitrator was not competent to rule on the case or that the award was not carried by a majority of arbitrators,[25] was not adopted. Association members are not afforded such protection and, unlike consumer disputes in which the facts are reviewed *ex officio*, the circumstances must be claimed and proved by association members.

VIII. Relations with Other Countries

This change became effective on January 1, 2014 and was approved earlier in connection with the adoption of the Private International Law Act. Pursuant to the final provisions of the Private International Law Act, the former Part Five of the Arbitration Act (provisions on relations with other countries) was deleted; those rules are now embodied in Sections 117 and 119 to 122 of the Private International Law Act.[26] An adjustment was made regarding the definition of the law applicable to the assessment of the terms and the conditions for the conclusion of an arbitration agreement. The issue of objective arbitrability and the assessment of whether the parties can submit the subject of a dispute to the authority of arbitrators, imperatively appraised under Czech law, have been

---

[24] That is, assuming that the enforcement of the decision would threaten serious harm or if an application to annul an award contains sufficient evidence for a conclusion on its legitimacy.

[25] I.e., the grounds set out in Section 31(a) to (d) and (h) of the Arbitration Act.

[26] Section 118 of the Private International Law Act has been discussed above in relation to changes adopted by the amendment in relation to Section 4 of the Arbitration Act.

preserved.[27] The second sentence of Section 117(1) of the Private International Law Act introduced a change which could be interpreted as the strengthening of the autonomy of the parties in relation to the place where the proceedings are held/the arbitral award is rendered. The conflict-of-law rules applicable to the determination of the law governing the form of the arbitration agreement remain unchanged.

Where substantive law is designated as the governing law, the Private International Law Act makes changes in wording. Since the issue of arbitration proceedings with a foreign dimension has been shifted from the Arbitration Act to the Private International Law Act, it is no longer possible to interpret provisions in their mutual context or to work on the assumption that general legislation is also automatically applied to arbitration with a foreign dimension.[28] Because this scheme has been disrupted, Section 119 of the Private International Law Act offers the opportunity to delegate an arbitrator to take decisions according to the principles of justice. As already addressed in relation to Section 25(3) of the Arbitration Act, the question arises as to whether the last sentence thereof can be construed as an absolute prohibition of agreeing in consumer disputes on decision-making by the principles of justice, or whether this is permissible; however, arbitrators are obliged to apply legislation protecting the consumer. It is possible to lean towards a conclusion drawn from the explanatory memorandum to Act No. 19/2012 Coll., which allows for arbitrators to be mandated to decide on a dispute in accordance with the principles of justice – taking into account the imperatives of consumer protection law. The same holds true for the new provisions of the Private International Law Act.

The conditions for the enforcement of foreign awards, including the fact that a decision to order enforcement must be justified, remain unchanged. There have only been changes in the wording. From a systematic perspective, the provisions previously contained in Section 38 of the Arbitration Act have been divided into two separate provisions: Sections 120 and 122(2) of the Private International Law Act. The strict approach of Czech law to the possibility of the recognition and enforcement of foreign awards, i.e., the principle according to which an award that has not become final or enforceable under the law of the state in which it was rendered cannot be enforced in the Czech Republic, has

---

[27]   If the place of arbitration is in the Czech Republic and/or the arbitral award is at least to be rendered here. Furthermore, the Private International Law Act no longer refers exclusively to the Arbitration Act, but to the laws of the Czech Republic as a whole.

[28]   E.g. Sections 25 and 37 of the Arbitration Act, where even in proceedings with an international dimension, it was possible to apply Section 25(3) of the Arbitration Act, and thus the parties were able to mandate arbitrators to resolve a dispute in accordance with the principles of justice.

also been maintained. Section 121 of the Private International Law Act extended this principle to include cases where an award has been annulled in the country where it was rendered. There have also been changes in the wording. However, these rules apply only if the Czech Republic is not bound by an international treaty on the recognition and enforcement of foreign awards.[29] Furthermore, substantive changes were not made to the provisions on the recognition of a foreign award. The case remains that no special decision is issued, but the award is taken into account. Aside from whether any of the grounds for annulment exist, the Private International Law Act refers to the need to consider whether reciprocity is guaranteed. This is an addition to the general rules on the recognition of foreign judgments.

[*Tereza Profeldová*]

Mgr. Tereza Profeldová works as a legal trainee in the Law Offices of Bělohlávek, Prague, Czech Republic and is a graduate of the Faculty of Law of Charles University in Prague. Field of Interest: Private international law, arbitration and IP rights.
e-mail: tereza.profeldova@ablegal.cz

| | |

---

[29] E.g. the New York Convention on the Recognition and Enforcement of Foreign Arbitral Awards of 10 June 1958 (the New York Convention) and the European Convention on Commercial Arbitration of 21 April 1961.

The Development of Arbitration Law and Practice in Albania

Arbitration is an important medium of Alternative Dispute Resolution (ADR) which presents similarities to the judicial process by acting within the legal framework of a country, however standing outside of the court system. Alternative dispute resolution does not replace the judicial process *per se*; nonetheless, it offers an opportunity to widen the spectrum of solutions for commercial disputes, thus improving access to justice.

The concept of arbitration is not new to Albanian legislation. However, the legal framework regulating the activity has not been consistent and unified, as a result of the political regimeschanges that Albania has undergone. Despite the ups and downs of arbitration practice in Albania, its history dates back to decades ago. In order to understand the intricacies that explain what makes arbitration a rather old and at the same time a new practice, one must briefly refer to the chronology of political and legal regime changes, rather than expect to unfold a steady consolidation.

The initial legal provisions that regulated arbitration in Albania, as form of alternative dispute resolution were first introduced in 1926 by King Zog, who felt that the laws in force were old, and as such he expressed his concern that they were not fulfilling the needs of the population. Thereby, on 1 April 1929 the second annex to the Code of Civil Procedure, entered into force which provided for both voluntary and obligatory arbitration. These amendments also defined the conditions for the selection of arbiters, the terms of validity of the arbitration agreement, the arbitrations proceedings, the award itself etc. It may be of interest, to point out that the final award was considered equally valid to a final court decision, constituting an already treated case except in those cases when the parties had previously agreed on the possibility of appeal to a higher court.

In 1944, when the communist regime took the lead of the country, it dismissed all legal acts that conflicted with its political principles. In this regard, the second annex of the Code of Civil Procedure was made redundant being substituted by the new concept of 'state arbitration'.[1]

The concept of state arbitration provided solutions to ownership disputes pertaining to contracts or acts undertaken by state enterprises, institutions, agricultural cooperative organizations- independently from the lawsuit (plead) value. As of 1984, upon decree no. 6927 the scope of the law was broadened to also include contractual disputes related to loss or damage of goods during transportation, shortage of supply on export/import goods etc.. Based on the

---

[1] Decree no.5009, date 10.11.1972, as amended by Decree no.6927, dated 14.11.1984

provisions stipulated in the given act, state arbitration was organized as an institution within the Council of Ministers, Ministries and other central institutions, aiming to sanction repeated infringements of state disciplines. These changes, not only implied changes in the legislation, but as one can deduce from the executive nature of the institutions responsible at the time, the procedure became a formality. Arbitration started to be delineated as a political tool enforced by the government, thus drifting away from the judicial nature of the practice as we understand it today.

I. The Climate of Arbitration in Post-communist Albania

Upon the fall of the communist regime, in 1993 upon Decree no.682 a substantial change was made dismissing state arbitration and establishing 'the court' as the competent authority to rule over disputes of every nature. Additionally, the option of voluntary arbitration was introduced in cases when parties agreed on such terms. In 1996, the Albanian Code of Civil Procedure 'CCP' entered into force, providing even to the present day the rules that govern domestic arbitration (Article 400-438).

Despite the early legal regulation of domestic arbitration which coincided with the early days of the establishment of the market economy in Albania, there is still no consolidated practice on these domestic mechanisms. The reasons for the later 'under-development' of the sector were associated with the costs of the procedure, which Albanian entrepreneurs and private companies, coupled with the distrust of the effectiveness of the judicial system, were not willing to embrace. Furthermore, a notable lack of tradition in conjunction with limited access to information, as well as the absence of professional training institutions left domestic arbitration in a barely explored state.

The current provisions of the CCP that regulate the activity of arbitration (Chapter IV) shall be abrogated upon the approval of the new law on arbitration which is yet to come. Until then, the named provisions of CCP on arbitration shall apply accordingly. These provisions set the criteria when domestic arbitration is applied, respectively concerning every dispute which involves a monetary claim that fulfils the following two conditions a) when parties are residents in Albania or have their seat registered in Albania; and b) the seat of the arbitration procedure is within the territory of Albania.

The arbitration agreement may be adopted as a separate agreement between the parties, or the parties may provide in the relevant agreement an arbitration clause. Apart from the written form of the agreement and the fact that such agreement must be signed by the parties, CCP fails to provide explicit elements which must be incorporated in the arbitration agreement. However, such agreement should contain rules on the scope of arbitration, the competent arbitral tribunal, the procedure for the appointment of the arbitrators (number, qualification), as well as rules which sanction the time of the arbitration's commencement, length of procedure, the evidence which will qualify, etc..

The parties are entitled the right of 'choice of law', within the limits determined by the legislation in force. Under consideration of the above, even in cases when the parties have agreed on a governing law different from the Albanian law, the provisions of the Albanian law shall prevail in cases regulated by mandatory provisions of the Albanian legislation.

With regards to jurisdictional issues, when a dispute has been agreed by the parties to be adjudicated in an arbitration court, and a lawsuit is filed with an Albanian court; the latter must declare its lack of jurisdiction, except in instances when the arbitration agreement is invalid (independently if the arbitration proceedings have begun or not). When the rules governing the arbitration procedure are not stipulated in the arbitration agreement or the arbitration clause, the arbitral tribunal may apply the rules of the Albanian CCP or may decide to adopt procedural rules referring to a regulation of an acknowledged arbitration institution. In any case, the arbitration court must adjudicate and rule based on the fulfilment of the principles of the due process of law.

The Albanian CCP provides that notwithstanding the fact that the parties may have agreed on *quitclaim* from appealing the arbitration award, any party may file an appeal in case: (i) the arbitration court was constituted irregularly; (ii) the arbitration court has wrongfully declared the lack of competence/jurisdiction on the adjudication of a case or vice-versa; (iii) the court has ruled on issues surpassing the requests or has not ruled on all of the requests of the claim; (iv) the court did not respect the equality of the parties, or their rights deriving from the contradictory principle; (v) or the court decisions contravenes the public order of the Republic of Albania.

Upon consideration of the above, many law experts consider the current legislation on arbitration as being modern, i.e. guaranteeing the application of the principles of fair trial. However, in practice the private sector has not taken advantage of the above potential benefits offered by the mentioned legal provisions. In an attempt, to institutionalize the practice and 'give life to the only written benefits', on December 2002, with the facilitation of the World Bank, MEDART [The Albanian Centre on Commercial Mediation and Arbitration] was established. MEDART was expected to serve as a private, independent, non-governmental, permanent arbitration forum. The arbitrators were not judges, but acknowledged legal experts such as lawyers, law university professors, etc. Despite the fact that there are no official statistics offered by the centre, based on consultations with professionals involved with the centre, MEDART was able to take over an average of only 20 to 30 cases, over the period between 2002 to 2009, when it ceased to exist.

The issues explaining the limited lifespan of MEDART were substantially linked with the inefficiency of the Albanian judicial system, which even today is characterized by extremely prolonged judicial proceedings, sanctioned even by the ECHR as jeopardizing due process of law. The outstanding prolonged proceedings have at the same time compromised parties' access to justice, as well as implied huge financial costs for both the business operators and the Albanian state. It was precisely, the above explained scenario that made the business community and investors more inclined towards established international arbitration institutions, which were faster and to their perception offered more reliable solutions.

The practice is rather different. It must be noted that after the finalization of the relevant international arbitration procedure, the foreign arbitral award must yet undergo a procedure of recognition at the Tirana Appeal Court. Despite the fact that CCP legal provisions foresee the process to be of a formal nature, it has proven to be a challenging process for the involved parties. The difficulties derive from the national judges' lack of experience and clarity with regard to foreign arbitration procedures, thus providing different standards of the application of law. It is clear that the uniform interpretation of the law and procedures, guiding the courts of lowers instance stands with the Supreme Court of Albania. In this perspective, there is a vast room of contribution that can be expected of the highest judicial instance in Albania.

II. Is the Need for a Dedicated Law on Arbitration Justified?

Despite the benefits or difficulties with the arbitration regulatory framework in Albania, reality has created a dichotomy. While domestic arbitration is well sanctioned and regulated but lacks parties' trust, making thus far the process somehow redundant; international arbitration which enjoys an established reputation (even though it finds reflection at the level of international conventions and bilateral treaties)[2], remains weakly regulated at the domestic level, and as a consequence leads to confusion of both the judiciary and the private sector. Under this light, it has become incumbent to adopt a specific, dedicated law on arbitration that transposes the international prescribed obligations to the level of the national law which is directly applied, while at the same time offering unified guidelines for both domestic and international arbitration.

---

[2] International instruments Albania has adhered in: New York Convention, Washington Convention 1965, Geneva Convention 1927, OSCE Convention on Conciliation and Arbitration, European Convention on International Commercial Arbitration; Albania has entered into bilateral investment treaties with many EU countries, Turkey, China, USA, and it is part of Energy Charter Treaty;

Most of the efforts to draft a cohesive law that would regulate international arbitration within the Albanian legal order were made during the years 2010 to 2011 since even the CCP anticipates that international arbitration in Albania shall be regulated by a dedicated law. The initiative was taken by the Albanian Ministry of Justice, supported even by international partners (GIZ, UNCITRAL, USAID etc.). The draft law aimed at regulating discrepancies in the practice of both domestic and international arbitration, while integrating the rules provided by international treaties, agreements ratified by Albanian Parliament, as well as domestic arbitration procedures. Pursuant to the said draft law, the arbitration procedure would be considered international when: the parties in the arbitration agreement have their seat or residence in different countries; the seat of arbitration procedure as agreed between the parties is outside of the territory of the country, where the parties have their seats or residences; and the parties have agreed that the object of the arbitration agreement extends to more than one country. On the other hand an arbitration process would classify as domestic arbitration when: parties in the arbitration agreement have their seats or residences in Albania; the seat of arbitration procedure as provided by the relevant arbitration agreement is Albania; and the parties are subject to Albanian law;

These efforts found expression even in the National Strategy for the Justice System with a number of dedicated objectives both of a regulatory, as well as of an enforcement and capacity building nature. Nevertheless, despite this ambition from the Albanian government of the time, which was paired even with international assistance, the foreseen measures were never effectuated. The reason for this remain complex, however if trying to offer a balanced opinion which targets only from a technical perspective the formulation of the said strategy; one must say that those objectives remained vague, without enough specific content and with a deadline of achievement which appeared too optimistic.

To the present day, a dedicated law that regulates commercial arbitration within the territory of Albania has not been finalised. Several round tables have been organised, and drafts have been refined a number of times, but the Ministry of Justice has yet to provide an official final draft to be discussed and approved by the Albanian Parliament. The EU Progress Report 2013 has underlined the necessity of the approval of the draft law on arbitration in its Chapter 23. Despite the delay of the said draft law, the expectation of having the law soon seems high. In addition, the review and completion of the draft law on arbitration together with its adoption, are set forth as requests of the EU Commission.

In the light of Albania's hopes to be granted EU candidate status, the Albanian Ministry of Justice which will be assisted by Euralius IV – EU Program for the technical support on Consolidation of Justice System in the frame of EU integration process for Albania[3], will have the finalisation of the law on arbitration as one of the objectives to be fulfilled within this government's term.

III. Conclusion

In recent years, an increased number of commercial disputes that involve foreign parties resulting to international arbitration have been signed. Even though the ratio of these proceedings is not substantial when compared to the number of domestic judicial cases (in any circumstance the investment of a domestic court to recognise and enforce a foreign arbitral award, is requested) it appears that the parties' perception favours international arbitration as more reliable. The parties opt for international arbitration while seeking at least a preliminary guarantee for their claims of infringed rights. For as long as this vivid perception has produced a reality of an increased number of judicial cases coming in front of Albanian courts, further regulatory measures seem necessary.

Hence, based on the above arguments, it appears of paramount importance to unify the Albanian judicial practice with regard to arbitration. The best option to make the latter possible would be through the adoption of comprehensive dedicated legislation, which would regulate both international and domestic arbitration in an integrated manner, leaving little room for equivoques, while guaranteeing efficiency of the proceedings.

Albania is a country that presents an affirmative development potential. Thereby, the improvement of its legal framework offering alternative means and opportunities to improve access to justice, while facilitating procedures of solving commercial disputes, indisputably would incite a better trust amongst foreign investors. As a consequence, these measures would not only provide advantages in terms of the country's consolidation of the rule of law, but will also create a favourable business climate, which will pave the road ahead for greater strategic investments and economic benefits.

[*Antuen Skënderi*]

Currently Chief of Foreign Relations & Research and Analysis Section, at the Supreme Court of Albania. Graduated with distinction from the Diplomatic Academy of London, University of Westminster, London, UK. She is also a Chevening Fellow from the University College London. Holds a BA. Honors degree in International Relations from the University of Malta. Possesses work experience both in the civil society

---

[3] The tender is lately awarded to a consortium headed by Germany, with the participation of Austria.

and the public sector. Coupled with advanced training in the practice of negotiation and mediation. Integrated Degree in Law- in process.
Areas of expertise:
Diplomacy, International law, public policy analysis, comparative policy formulation, strategic planning and structural reform, strategic cooperation and negotiation, EU structures and policies, project management and project cycle development.
e-mail: antuen.skenderi@gmail.com

[*Aulona Hazbiu*]
At present, Legal Advisor at the Supreme Court of Albania. Graduated in law at Albert-Ludwigs Universitaet Freiburg, Germany (First State Exam); Attended Legal Clerkship at Oberlandesgericht (OLG) Duesseldorf (Germany), completed the Second State Exam. Work experience as senior associate at Boga &Associates Law Firm in Albania.
Areas of expertise:
Labor law, arbitration, administrative law, commercial law, concessions, civil procedure, energy law.
e-mail: Aulona.Hazbiu@gmx.de

[*Klotilda Bushka (Ferhati)*]
She graduated in law, at Tirana University in 2001. She has received many qualifications in Albania and abroad in various law fields. Admitted at Albanian Bar Association in 2003. At present, Legal Advisor at the Supreme Court of Albania, 2001–2008 associate and senior lawyer at Tonucci & Partners in Tirana, an international law firm with headquarters in Rome, Italy. She is also a member of the National Council for Gender Equality – a permanent inter-institutional advisory body established by order of the Prime Minister of Albania pursuant to legal provisions on gender equality in Albania.
Areas of expertise:
Commercial law, privatization of state-owned companies operating in strategic sectors; telecommunications, oil and gas, mining, concession procedures and contracts, civil litigation, labor law, family law, administrative law, environmental law, development of the civil society sector.
e-mail: kferhati@hotmail.com

|||

Bibliography, Current Events, CYIL & CYArb® Presentations, Important Web Sites

Bibliography, Current Events, CYIL & CYArb® Presentations, Important Web Sites

I. Select Bibliography for 2014

Opening Remarks:
This overview lists only works published in 2014. The individual chapters into which this overview is divided always cover both substantive and procedural issues.
Titles in translations are indicative.

I.1. [CZE] – [CZECH REPUBLIC] – Titles Published within the Czech Republic

I.1.1. Monographs

Alexander. J. Bělohlávek. Daniela Kovářová (eds.) *Soudní a mimosoudní projednávání sporů (rozhodčí řízení a mediace)* [title in translation – **Litigation and ADR (Arbitration and Mediation)**]. Praha [Prague / Czech Republic]: Havlíček Brain Team, 2014, ISBN: 978-80-87109-52-6.

I.1.2. Periodicals, Collections and Conference Proceedings

Bulletin advokacie [*Bulletin of the Czech Bar*], **Prague: Česká advokátní komora**]*Czech Bar Association*], **2014, ISSN: 1210-6348**[1]

Petr Dobiáš. *Nový rozhodčí řád Mezinárodního rozhodčího soudu v Londýně z roku 2014* [title in translation – *New Arbitration Rules of the*

---

[1]   Papers published in Czech with abstracts in a foreign language. Abstracts in English and in German.

Czech (& Central European) Yearbook of Arbitration

London Court of International Arbitration from 2014]. Published on 1 September 2014 in the electronic version of the periodical.[2]

Obchodněprávní revue [*Commercial Law Review*], **Prague: C. H. Beck, 2014, Vol. 6, ISSN: 1803-6554**[3]

Klára Drličková; Slavomír Halla. *Zmeny v subjektoch hlavnej zmluvy a ich dopad na súvisiacu rozhodcovskú zmluvu.* No. 3, p. 76-82.

Obchodní právo [**Commercial Law**], **Prague: Prospektrum, 2014, Vol. 23, ISSN: 1210-8278**[4]

Petr Dobiáš. *Standardy rozhodčího řízení v nových řádech mezinárodních rozhodčích soudů* [title in translation – *Arbitration Standards in the New Rules of Permanent International Arbitral Institutions*]. No. 12.

Právní rádce [**Title in translation** – *Legal Advisor*], **Prague: Economia, 2014, Vol. 22, ISSN1210-4817**[5]

Zuzana Hušková; Martin Krechler. *Platnost rozhodčích doložek při exekuci z pohledu věřitele* [title in translation – *Validity of Arbitration Clauses in Execution (Enforcement) from the Creditor's Perspective*]

Lenka Mikulcová. *Důsledky neplatné rozhodčí doložky ve spotřebitelských věcech pro exekuci* [title in translation – *Consequences of an Invalid Arbitration Clause in B2C Disputes for Enforcement*]. No. 2, p. 52-58.

Robert Porubský; Ondrej Poništiak. *Proč je důležité místo sudiště v arbitrážním řízení* [title in translation – *Why Is the Seat of Arbitration So Important*]. Právní rádce, 2014, č. 11, s. 54-55

Právní rozhledy [*Law Review*], **Prague: C. H. Beck, 2014, Vol. 22, ISSN: 1210-6410**[6]

Petra Jelínková; *K vybraným problémům nařízeného prvního setkání se zapsaným mediátorem* [title in translation – *Concerning Selected Problems of a Mandatory First Meeting with a Registered Mediator*]. No. 22, p. 790-793.

---

[2]   Available   at   http://www.bulletin-advokacie.cz/novy-rozhodci-rad-mezinarodniho-rozhodciho-soudu-v-londyne-z-roku-2014 [Last visit on 26 November 2014].

[3]   Papers published in Czech. Abstracts in English, sometimes in German.

[4]   Papers published in Czech. Abstracts in English.

[5]   Papers published in Czech, Summary in English.

[6]   Papers published in Czech.

Igor Pařízek. *Postup věřitele po zrušení rozhodčího nálezu pro neplatnou rozhodčí doložku* [title in translation – *Procedure Adopted by the Creditor after the Arbitral Award Is Annulled Due to an Invalid Arbitration Clause*]. No. 20, p. 715-717.

The Lawyer Quarterly, Prague: Ústav státu a práva Akademie věd České republiky [Institute of State and Law of the Academy of Sciences of the Czech Republic], 2014, Vol. IV, ISSN: 0231-6625[7]

Alexander J. Bělohlávek. *Recognition and Enforcement of Foreign Arbitral Awards: The Application of the New York Convention by National Courts – Czech Republic.* No. 2, p. 91-107.[8]

Other Publications

Alexander J. Bělohlávek. *Choice of law in international arbitration (with respect to the corresponding legal regulation in the Czech Republic).* In *Proceedings of the 2nd International Conference on European Integration 2014.* Ostrava: VŠB - Technical University of Ostrava, 2014. ISBN 978-80-248-3388-0.

I.1.3. Books (Monographs) and Articles by Czech Authors and / or on the Topics regarding Arbitration and ADR in the Czech Republic Published outside the Czech Republic

Alexander. J. Bělohlávek. *Substantive Law Applicable to the Merits in Arbitration.* Revista Română de Arbitraj [titel in translation – *Romanian Review of Arbitration*], Bucharest: Arbitration Court attached to the Chamber of Commerce and Industry of Romania, 2014, Vol. 8, Romanian Register of Publications C.N.C.S.I.S., Code 138, reg. No. 9059/5.11.2008. No. 2 30), p. 1-16.

Alexander J. Bělohlávek. *Тенденции в развитии процессуальной оговорки о публичном порядке (ordre public) в европейском контексте с*

---

[7] A subsidiary title to the monthly periodical Právník [in translation – *The Lawyer*] which will be published by the Institute of State and Law of the Academy of Science of the Czech Republic in Czech. Papers published in *The Lawyer Quarterly* are primarily in English, exceptionally in other languages (such as German); abstracts are in English. For papers published in the periodical *"Pravnik"* [in translation – *The Lawyer*], issued monthly, see the separate excerpt from papers listed under the heading of the respective periodical.

[8] National Reports for the Biennial Congress of the International Academy of Comparative Law, Vienna, July 2014. The yearbooks CYIL and CYArb° were partner of the 2014 Congress.

2002 года [transcript of the title: *Tendencii v razvitii processualnoj ogovorki o publichnom porjadke (ordre public) v evropejskom kontekste s 2002 goda,* title in translation – Trends in the Development of the Procedural Reservation of Public Policy (Ordre Public) since 2002] In: S. Ja. Fursa (ed.) *Civilistichna procesualna mysl: Zbirnik naukovich statej,* vypusk III. [title in translation – *Anthology of Civil Proceedings : Collection of Scientific Esseys,* Vol. III]. Kyjev [Kyjiv] [Ukraine]: Kyjivskij nacionalnij universitet imeni Tarasa Chevchenka, Kafedra notarialnovo ta vikonvchovo procesu i advokaturi / Centr pravovich doslidzheny Fursi / Vidavec Palivoda A. V. [Kyjiv National Univerzity Taras Schevchenko, Depart. of Notary and Enforcement Proceedings and Advocacy / Center for Legal Research Fursa / Publisher Palivoda, A., V.], 2014, p. 392-417. ISBN: 978-966-8721-37-3 / ISBN: 978-966-8721-91-7; BBK [Classification of Ukrainian National Library] 67.410ja43 C 57, UDK 347.9(082).[9]

Alexander J. Bělohlávek. *Czech Republic* [Title in translation – *Czech Republic*]. In: Gerhard WEGEN; Stephan WILSKE (eds.) *Arbitration 2014 – Global Arbitration Review – Eddition Getting the Deal Through.* London [United Kingdom]: Law Business Research, 2014. ISSN: 1750-9947, p. 141-148.[10]

Alexander J. Bělohlávek. *Priroda arbitrazha i vzajimodejstvije s zaschitoj osnovnych prav* [title in translation – Nature of Arbitration and Interaction with the Protection of Basic Rights]. In: *Materialy pervych Mezhdunarodnych arbitrazhnych ctenij pamjati akademika Pobirchenko I.G.* [title in translation – Materials of first "International Arbitration Readings in Remembrance of Prof. Pobirchenko"]. Kyjev [Kyjiv] [Ukraine]: MKAS pri TPP Ukrajiny [International Commercial Arbitration Court Attached to the Chamber of Commerce and Industry of Ukraine], 2014, p. 119-140.

I.2. [POL] – [POLAND][11]

Monographs (Incl. Chapters in Monographs) and Collections, Proceedings

Maciej Durbas, Rafał Kos, *The Arbitrators' (Perceived) Power to Revise a Contract vs. the Power of the Public Policy Clause* [in:] Christian Klausegger, Peter Klein, Florian Kremslehner, Alexander Petsche, Nikolaus Pitkowitz,

---

[9] Original language: Russian, Summaries in English, Russian and Ukrainian.

[10] Original language: English

[11] Polish bibliography concerning arbitration and ADR in 2013 was compiled with the kind support provided by Kubas Kos Gałkowski – Adwokaci, Law firm (www.kkg.pl). Kubas Kos Gałkowski specialize (among others) in arbitration and ADR.

Jenny Power, Irene Welser, Gerold Zeiler (eds.), Austrian Yearbook on International Arbitration 2014, Vienna 2014, pp. 135-147.

ADR Arbitraż i Mediacja [*ADR Arbitration And Mediation*], Warszawa: C. H. Beck, 2014, ISSN: 1898-942X[12]

Marcin Orecki, *Jurisdictional Conflicts in Investment Arbitration*, No. 1, pp. 27-38.

Izabela Szmit, *Procedura prejudycjalna a sądownictwo arbitrażowe* [Preliminary Ruling and Arbitration]. No. 1, pp. 39-49.

Maciej Zachariasiewicz, *Kilka refleksji w odniesieniu do możliwości rozwoju postępowań grupowych w arbitrażu w Polsce* [Deliberations on Class Arbitration in Poland]. No. 1, pp. 51-77.

Krzysztof Rokita, *Uzyskanie dokumentów od strony przeciwnej i osoby trzeciej w międzynarodowym arbitrażu handlowym* [Production of Documents by Opposite Party and Third Parties in International Commercial Arbitration]. No. 2, pp. 15-121.

Aleksandra Petrus-Schmidt, Krystian Mularczyk, *Sprawozdanie z konferencji z cyklu Arbitraż i Mediacja w teorii i praktyce pt. „Zastosowanie ADR w wybranych branżach gospodarki" w Nowym Tomyślu (28.3.2014)* [Notes from the Conference "ADR in Certain Branches of Economy" in Nowy Tomyśl on 28.3.2014 (conference series: Arbitration and Mediation in theory and practice)]. No. 2, pp. 141-144.

Michał Pyrz, *Sprawozdanie z ogólnopolskiej konferencji naukowej pt. „Dochodzenie roszczeń przed sądami polubownymi" we Wrocławiu (16.5.2014 r.)* [Notes from the national conference: "Pursuing Claims before Arbitration Courts" in Wrocław]. No. 2, pp. 149-154.

Anna Franusz, *Zdatność arbitrażowa sporów w świetle art. 1157 KPC* [Arbitrability under Article 1157 of the Code of Civil Procedure]. No. 3, pp. 5-16.

Kinga Flaga-Gieruszyńska, *Dochodzenie roszczeń konsumenckich przed sądami polubownymi – wybrane zagadnienia* [Certain Aspects of Pursuing Consumer Claims before Arbitral Tribunals]. No. 3, pp. 15-26.

Piotr Gil, *Współpraca sądów powszechnych i sądów polubownych w zakresie rozstrzygania spraw cywilnych – rola sądów powszechnych w cywilnych postępowaniach pozasądowych; zagadnienia wybrane* [Certain Aspects of Cooperation between State Courts and Arbitral Tribunals in Resolving Civil Disputes – the Role of State Courts in Out-of-the-Court Civil Proceedings]. No. 3, pp. 27-35.

[12] Quarterly. Papers published in Polish.

Bogusław Sołtys, *Koszty postępowania arbitrażowego – wybrane zagadnienia na tle sporów dotyczących kontraktów FIDIC* [Costs of Arbitral Proceedings – Certain Aspects on the Grounds of FIDIC Disputes]. No. 3, pp. 37-45.

Tomasz Strumiłło, *Zabezpieczenie roszczeń dochodzonych przed sądem polubownym – wybrane zagadnienia. Problem równoległych postępowań prowadzonych przed sądem powszechnym oraz sądem polubownym w przedmiocie stosowania tymczasowych środków zabezpieczających* [Securing of Claims before Arbitral Tribunals – Certain Aspects. Problems of Parallel Proceedings for Securing Claims before State Courts and Arbitral Tribunals]. No. 3, pp. 47-60.

Grzegorz Suliński, *Zdatność ugodowa sporów o zaskarżanie uchwał zgromadzeń spółek kapitałowych* [Arbitrability of Disputes on Appealing against the Resolution of Shareholders' or the General Shareholders' Meeting], No. 3, pp. 61-68.

Andrzej Wiśniewski, *Problemy związane z umową pomiędzy arbitrem a instytucją arbitrażową – uwag kilka na tle polskiej praktyki* [Problems Relating to the Contract between an Arbitrator and an Arbitral Institution – Few Practical Remarks]. No. 3, pp. 69-79.

Karol Zawiślak, *"Receptum arbitrii" – uwagi o materialno-prawnym charakterze umowy pomiędzy stronami sporu a Arbitrem* ["Receptum Arbitrii" – Remarks on Substantive Character of a Contract between Parties and an Arbitrator]. No. 3, pp. 81-91.

Biuletyn Arbitrażowy [*Arbitration Bulletin*], Warszawa: Sąd Arbitrażowy przy Krajowej Izbie Gospodarczej, 2014, ISSN: 1896-7124

Marcin Asłanowicz, *Wytyczne IBA dotyczące reprezentacji stron w arbitrażu międzynarodowym – zastosowanie i znaczenie* [IBA Guidelines on party representation in international arbitration – application and meaning]. No. 21, pp. 31-42.

Monika Hartung, *Wytyczne IBA: ciekawa próba ujednolicenia zasad postępowań arbitrażowych* [IBA Guidelines as an interesting attempt to unify arbitral procedural rules]. No. 21, pp. 43-46.

Maciej Jamka, *Wyłączenie pełnomocnika. Kilka uwag na temat rozwoju arbitrażu międzynarodowego na podstawie Wytycznych IBA dotyczących reprezentacji stron w arbitrażu międzynarodowym* [Challenging counsel. Few remarks on the development of International arbitration on the basis of IBA Guidelines on party representation in international arbitration]. No. 21, pp. 47-53.

Bartłomiej Jankowski, *Wytyczne IBA dotyczące reprezentacji stron w arbitrażu międzynarodowym* [IBA Guidelines on party representation in international arbitration]. No 21, pp. 54-59.

Bartosz Krużewski, *Wytyczne IBA dotyczące reprezentacji stron w arbitrażu międzynarodowym – przydatne ujednolicenie standardów czy nadmierna regulacja arbitrażu?* [IBA Guidelines on party representation in international arbitration – useful unification of standards or overregulation of arbitration?]. No 21, pp. 60-65.

Marcin Olechowski, *Nowy wspaniały świat? Kilka dylematów wokół Wytycznych IBA dotyczących reprezentacji stron w arbitrażu międzynarodowym* [Brave new world? Few dilemmas on the IBA Guidelines on party representation in international arbitration]. No. 21, pp. 66-78.

Małgorzata Surdek, *Czy istnieje potrzeba kodyfikowania zasad etyki dotyczących pełnomocników stron w arbitrażu międzynarodowym? Uwagi na kanwie Wytycznych IBA dotyczących reprezentacji stron w arbitrażu międzynarodowym* [Is there a need to prepare codes of conduct for counsels in international arbitration? Remarks on the IBA Guidelines on party representation in international arbitration]. No. 21, pp. 79-84.

Edukacja prawnicza [*Legal education*], Warszawa: C.H. Beck sp. z o.o., 2014, ISSN: ISSN: 1231-0336[13]

Krzysztof Michalak, *Wpływ ogłoszenia upadłości na toczące się postępowanie arbitrażowe – przegląd wybranych zagadnień* [The effect of insolvency on pending arbitral proceedings – certain aspects], No. 5, pp. 15-21.

Glosa – Prawo Gospodarcze w Orzeczeniach i Komentarzach [*The Commentary – Commercial Law in Case Law and Commentaries*] , Warszawa: Wolters Kluwer Polska Sp. z o. o., 2014, ISSN: 1233-4634[14]

Robert Stefanicki, *Klauzula przewidująca wyłączną właściwość sądu polubownego (w świetle art. 3 dyrektywy 93/13/EWG)* [Clause prescribing exclusive competence of arbitral tribunal (in light of Article 3 of the 93/13/EC Directive)]. No. 3, pp. 26-33.

Internetowy Kwartalnik Antymonopolowy i Regulacyjny [*Internet Competition and Regulatory Quarterly*], Warszawa: Centrum Studiów Antymonopolowych i Regulacyjnych, 2014, ISSN: 2299-5749[15]

Mucha Jagna, *Alternatywne metody rozwiązywania sporów konsumenckich w prawie unijnym – nowe rozwiązania prawne (dyrektywa 2013/11/UE w sprawie ADR oraz rozporządzenie nr 524/2013 w sprawie ODR)* [Alternative resolution of consumer disputes in EU law – new rules

---

[13] Monthly. Published in Polish.
[14] Quarterly. Papers published in Polish, summaries in English.
[15] Quarterly. Published in Polish, available at: http://ikar.wz.uw.edu.pl/.

(directive 2013/11/EU on ADR and regulation 524/2014 on ODR)], No. 4, pp. 79-89.

Monitor Prawa Bankowego [_Banking Law Monitor_], Warszawa: Instytut Szkoleń Prawa Bankowego, 2014, ISSN: 2081-9021[16]

Rafał Morek, _Zapis na Sąd Polubowny przy Związku Banków Polskich – glosa do postanowienia Sądu Najwyższego z 19 października 2012 r. (V CSK 503/11)_ [Arbitration agreement selecting the Court of Arbitration at Polish Bank Association – comments to the decision of the Supreme Court of 19 October 2012 (V CSK 503/11)]. No. 1, pp. 54-62.

Nieruchomości [_Real estate_], Warszawa: C.H. Beck sp. z o.o., 2014, ISSN: 1506-2899[17]

Mateusz Gonet, _Arbitraż w sprawach budowlanych – zarys problematyki_ [Construction arbitration – general remarks]. No. 1, pp. 20-22.

Orzecznictwo Sądów Polskich [_Case law of Polish Courts_], Warszawa: Lexis Nexis Polska Sp. z o. o., 2014, ISSN 0867-1850[18]

Alicja Szczęśniak, _Glosa do wyroku Sądu Najwyższego - Izba Cywilna z dnia 13 kwietnia 2012 r., I CSK 416/11_ [Comments to the judgment of the Supreme Court – Civil Chamber of 13 April 2012, I CSK 416/11], No. 1, pp. 11-19.

Palestra [_The Bar_], Warszawa: Naczelna Rada Adwokacka, 2014, ISSN: 0031-0344[19]

Maria Zuchowicz, _Trybunał Arbitrażowy do spraw Sportu_ [Court of Arbitration for Sport]. No 9, pp. 339-342.

e-Przegląd Arbitrażowy [_Arbitration e-Review_], Warszawa: Sąd Arbitrażowy przy Polskiej Konfederacji Pracodawców Prywatnych Lewiatan, 2014, ISSN: 2083-8190[20]

Piotr Golędzinowski, _Skutki uchylenia wyroku sądu polubownego po prawomocnym zakończeniu postępowania o stwierdzenie wykonalności_

---

[16] Monthly. Published in Polish.
[17] Monthly. Published in Polish.
[18] Monthly. Published in Polish.
[19] Monthly. Published in Polish.
[20] Polish and English editions, available at: http://www.sadarbitrazowy.org.pl/pl/eczas opsima-lista and http://www.sadarbitrazowy.org.pl/en/eczasopisma-lista.

[Effects of setting aside of an arbitral award after final and binding decision on enforcement]. No. 1-2, pp. 6-12.

Katarzyna Grabska-Luberadzka, *Skarga o uchylenie wyroku sądu polubownego a praktyka trybunału arbitrażowego ds. sportu przy polskim komitecie olimpijskim* [Motion for setting aside of an arbitral award and practice of Court of Arbitration for Sport at Polish Olympic Comittee]. No. 1-2, pp. 13-24.

Łukasz Gembiś, *Rażące naruszenie prawa jako podstawa do uchylenia krajowego oraz międzynarodowego wyroku arbitrażowego w USA* [Manifest violation of law as a basis for setting aside of national and International arbitral award in USA]. No. 1-2, pp. 25-41.

James Boykin, Jan Dunin-Wąsowicz, *Sądowa kontrola wyroków arbitrażowych w Stanach Zjednoczonych – niepewna przyszłość doktryny „rażącego naruszenia prawa"* [Court control of arbitral awards in USA – uncertainty as to the doctrine of "manifest violation of law"]. No. 1-2, pp. 42-52.

Pietro Balbiano di Colcavagno, *Uchylenie oraz odmowa uznania i stwierdzenia wykonalności wyroku arbitrażowego we Włoszech – przesłanki i kwestie procesowe* [Setting aside and refusal of enforcement and recognition of an arbitral award in Italy – prerequisites and procedural issues]. No. 1-2, pp. 53-64.

Wojciech Bazan, Mykola Zembra, *Skarga o uchylenie wyroku sądu polubownego na Ukrainie* [Motion for setting aside of an arbitral award in Ukraine]. No. 1-2, pp. 65-72.

Katarzyna Skowrońska, *Unieważnienie i rewizja wyroku sądu polubownego w Hiszpanii* [Setting aside and revision of an arbitral award in Spain]. No. 1-2, pp. 73-82.

Lidia Sokołowska, *Zdatność arbitrażowa sporu i jej znaczenie jako przesłanki skargi o uchylenie wyroku arbitrażowego – uwagi prawnoporównawcze w świetle nowelizacji belgijskiego prawa arbitrażowego* [Arbitrability and its significance as a prerequisite for setting aside of an arbitral award – comparative remarks in light of amendment of Belgian arbitral law]. No. 1-2, pp. 83-91.

Marta Cichomska, Ignacy Janas, *Istnienie, ważność i skuteczność zapisu na sąd polubowny zawartego na podstawie INTRA-EU BIT* [Existence, validity and effectivenes of an arbitration clause on the basis of INTRA-EU BIT]. No. 1-2, pp. 92-103.

Przegląd Prawniczy Uniwersytetu Warszawskiego [*Law review of the University of Warsaw*], Warszawa: University of Warsaw, 2014, ISSN: 1644-0242[21]

Krzysztof Wawrzyniak, *Zasada równości stron w postępowaniu przed sądem polubownym w świetle przepisów Kodeksu postępowania cywilnego* [Principle of equality of parties before an arbitral tribunal in light of Code of civil procedure]. No. 2, pp. 13-26.

Polski Proces Cywilny [*Polish Civil Proceedings*], Warszawa: Lexis Nexis Polska Sp. z o. o., Kraków: Towarzystwo Naukowe Procesualistów Cywilnych 2014, ISSN: 2082-1743[22]

Andrzej Olaś, *Potrącenie a zapis na sąd polubowny w prawie polskim – wybrane zagadnienia materialnoprawne i procesowe* [Set off and arbitration agreements – certain procedural and substantive aspects]. No. 1, pp. 61-91.

Stanisław Sołtysik, *Sprawozdanie z konferencji naukowej pt. Wyrok sądu arbitrażowego, Kraków, 8 listopada 2013 r.* [Notes on the conference entitled "Arbitral award", Kraków 8 November 2013]. No. 1, pp. 143-150.

Marcin Orecki, *Polskie przepisy o sądzie polubownym (arbitrażowym) - uwagi de lege ferenda* [Polish regulation on arbitration – *de lege ferenda* remarks]. No 2, pp. 198-237.

Przegląd Prawa Handlowego [*Commercial Law Review*], Warszawa: Wolters Kluwer Polska Sp. z o. o., 2014, ISSN: 1230-2996[23]

Tomasz Szczurowski, *Wprowadzenie klauzuli arbitrażowej do umowy (statutu) spółki handlowej* [Introducing arbitral agreement to the articles of association]. No. 1, pp. 13-18.

Tom Lindstrom, Alex Fawke, *Arbitraż inwestycyjny a kryzys strefy euro* [Investment arbitration and the Eurozone crisis]. No. 1, pp. 39-46.

Stephan Balthasar, *Spory o przyszłość arbitrażu inwestycyjnego w Unii Europejskiej* [Discussions on the future of investment arbitration in EU]. No. 2, pp. 41-44.

Iga Bałos, *O potrzebie utworzenia stałego sądu polubownego do spraw własności przemysłowej* [On the need of creating a permanent court of arbitration for IP issues]. No. 2, pp. 51-54.

---

[21] Journal to our best knowledge is not published on a regular basis.

[22] Quarterly. Papers published in Polish.

[23] Monthly. Papers published in Polish, summaries in English.

Karol Ryszkowski, *Klauzula porządku publicznego jako klauzula generalna w arbitrażu handlowym w prawie polskim* [Public policy as a general clause of commercial arbitration under Polish law]. No. 3, pp. 17-20.

Rafał Kos, *Zdatność arbitrażowa sporów o ważność uchwał spółek kapitałowych* [Arbitrability of disputes on the validity of the resolutions of companies]. No. 3, pp. 28-36.

Wojciech Popiołek, *Skutki zagranicznego orzeczenia arbitrażowego w Polsce* [Effects of foreign arbitral award in Poland]. No 6, pp. 5-10.

Marcin Asłanowicz, *Wyłączenie sędziego a wyłączenie arbitra* [Challenging a judge and challenging an arbitrator]. No. 6, pp. 36-40.

Przegląd Ustawodawstwa Gospodarczego [*Commercial Legislation Review*], Warszawa: Polskie Wydawnictwo Ekonomiczne S.A., 2014, ISSN: 0137-5490[24]

Marcin Asłanowicz, *Arbiter doraźny* [Emergency Arbitrator]. No. 8, s. 18-22.

Tomasz Szczurowski, *Zdatność arbitrażowa sporów ze stosunku spółki* [Arbitralibity qualification of companies disputes]. No. 1.

Marcin Asłanowicz, *Zakres ujawnienia, a bezstronność i niezależność arbitra w postępowaniu arbitrażowym* [Extent of disclosure in the light of an arbitrator's impartiality and independence in arbitration]. No. 4.

I.3. [ROU] – [ROMANIA][25]

Revista Română de Arbitraj [title in translation – *Romanian Review of Arbitration*], Bucharest: Arbitration Court attached to the Chamber of Commerce and Industry of Romania, 2014, Vol. 8, Romanian register of publications C.N.C.S.I.S., Code 138, reg. No. 9059/5.11.2008[26]

Alexander J. Bělohlávek. *Substantive Law Applicable to the Merits in Arbitration*. No. 2 (30), p. 1-16.

Eduard Bertrand. *From A to B: A Step Forward to a Methodology of Amiable Composition*. No. 3 (31), p. 69-73.

---

[24] Monthly. Papers published in Polish, summaries in English.

[25] For further articles on arbitration in Romania see also *Revista Română de Arbitraj* issued by the International Commercial Arbitration attached to the Chamber of Commerce and Industry of Romania (see http://arbitration.ccir.ro/engleza/index.htm). The Romanian bibliography prepared also with the kind support of dr. Alina Cobuz, Managing Partner of Cobuz si Asociatii, the Bucharest based law firm.

[26] Papers published in English, sometimes in French and exceptionally in Romanian. Abstracts in English. Table of Contents in English, French and Romanian. Published quarterly.

Viorel Mihai Ciobanu; Cosmin Vasile. *Considerations on the possibility to enforce a binding but not final DAB decision, through an interim or partial arbitral award, analysed from the perspective of the Romanian law.* No. 3 (31), p. 1-12.

Sandra Dinescu. *Extension of the arbitration agreement: Groups of companies and Groups of contracts.* No. 4 (32), p. 56-61.

Aldo Frignani. *Recognition and enforcement of foreign arbitral awards: the application of the New York Convention by Italian courts.* No 4 (32), p. 9-28.

Ion Gâlea. *The Role of the European Union Policy within the Contemporary Challenges in International Investment Law.* No. 1 (29), p. 1-15.

Duarte G. Henriques. *The New York Convention on the Recognition and Enforcement of Foreign Arbitral Awards of 1958 in the Portuguese Case Law.* No. 4 (32), p. 29-51.

V. Inbavijayan; Kirthi Jayakumar. *The Non-Conveniens of a Forum.* No. 2 (30), p. 24-31.

Florian Nițu; Cristina Alexe. *From Autonomy to Delocalisation in International Commercial Arbitration – the French Experience and the Romanian Echo.* No. 3 (31), p. 13-35.

René Offersen. *Recent Danish Rules on Taking Evidence in Arbitration Proceedings.* No. 2 (30), p. 17-23.

Viorel Mihai Ciobanu; Cosmin Vasile. *Considerations on the possibility to enforce a binding but not final DAB decision, through an interim or partial arbitral award, analysed from the perspective of the Romanian law.* No. 3 (31), p. 1-12.

Vlad Peligrad; Yolanda Ghiță-Blujdescu. *A practical guide on drafting arbitration clauses.* No. 3 (31), p. 46-68.

Luminița Popa. *Investment Treaty Arbitration in Light of the European Union´s Competence over Foreign Direct Investments.* No. 3 (31), p. 36-45.

Cosmin Vasile; Violeta Saranciuc. *Absolute Nullity of Arbitration Agreements without Notary´s Authentication – An Extravagance of the New Civil Procedure Code.* No 4 (32), p. 1-87.

Gerold Zeiler; Michael Nueber. *Arbitration in Austria: Recent Development.* No. 1 (29), p. 27-28.

Tatjana Zoroska-Kamilovska. *Enforcing Arbitral Awards in the Republic of Macedonia.* No. 1 (29), p. 16-26.

| | |

Current Events

II. Current Events

Selected scientific conferences, seminars, academic lectures and other professional events and news in the development of arbitration and ADR in the particular countries[1]

II.1. [CZE] – [CZECH REPUBLIC]

[CZE] **Prague; 14 January 2014**
Conference on **"Arbitration and the New Civil Code"**, organized by the Czech economic journal "Euro".[2]

[CZE] **Prague; 26 August 2014**
Conference on **"The Future of Arbitration and ADR Practice in Central and Eastern European Countries"**, pre-congress seminar organized by the International Association of Young Lawyers".[3]

---

[1]   Contributions mentioned herein represent a selection from papers related to arbitration. CYArb editors hereby apologize to the lecturers for omitting some of them and their topics due to the limited space provided for this section. Editors referred especially to published and other accessible information. Readers are specifically warned that the information about papers presented at the individual conferences and other academic and scientific events is only a selection and definitely does not provide a full report on the entire proceedings and the academic scope of each particular event.

[2]   Further information on http://setkani.euro.cz/arbitr%C3%A1%C5%BEn%C3%AD-%C5%99%C3%ADzen%C3%AD-nov%C3%BD-ob%C4%8Dansk%C3%BD-z%C3%A1kon%C3%ADk [Last visit on 9th January 2014].

[3]   Further information on http://www.aija.org [Last visit on 24th July 2014].

[CZE] **Prague; 17 September 2014**
Seminar on ICC Arbitration organized by the ICC National Committee Czech Republic.

[CZE] **Prague; 08 October 2014**
Seminar on new developments in domestic and international arbitration organized by Law offices Bělohlávek Prague / Czech Republic and by Glatzová & Partners, law offices Prague / Czech Republic. Speakers: Prof. Dr. Alexander J. Bělohlávek & dr.iur. Vít Horáček.

[CZE] **Prague, 21 November 2014**
Conference on **Court Litigation and ADR** under the auspices of the Vice-President of the Supreme Court Czech Republic as well as of the President of the Czech Bar Association, Deputy Mayor of the City of Prague and the CYArb, within the Program "Prague Legal Autumn", Prague [Czech Republic].

II.2. [AUT] – [AUSTRIA]

[AUT] **Vienna, 17 January 2014**
Kolloquium VIAC – CEPANI – YAAP – CEPANI40 VIAC (Vienna International Arbitral Centre). The topic of the seminar was "**Arbitration Landscape in Belgium and in Austria**"; the contributions will be held partly in German and in English.

[ROM] **Bucharest, 23 January 2014**
Presentation of the New Vienna Rules 2013 organized by the Vienna International Arbitral Centre.

[AUT] **Vienna, 28 February – 1 March 2014**
Vienna Arbitration Days 2014 as the leading arbitration conference in Austria. **First panel**: "Substantive issues"(Is there an applicable conflict-of-law system?, Art 28(2) Model Law, Choice of law: party autonomy and its limits, Rome I and Rome II, Iura novit curia, Ex aequo et bono, Lex mercatoria, Ordre public, Request for Preliminary Ruling under Art 267(II) and (III) of the Treaty on the Functioning of the European Union: right or duty of tribunal?; **Second panel**: "Issues of procedure" (Interim Measures, Document Production and Legal Privilege, Soft Laws, Recognition and Enforcement, Prayer for Relief); **Third panel**: "Special Issues" (Set-off claims, Burden of proof, Costs, Arbitration Agreement (extension to third parties).

Czech (& Central European) Yearbook of Arbitration

[AUT] Vienna, 13 March 2014

Seminar on "Pathological Arbitration Clauses at the Institutional Level" by VIAC. The General Secretaries of CAM (Stefano Azzali), DIS (Francesca Mazza), SCC (Annette Magnusson) and VIAC (Manfred Heider) provided insights in the handling of pathological clauses at their institutions. The Seminar has been moderated by Jernej Sekolec.

[SVN] Ljubljana, 20 March 2014

The VIAC presented in Ljubljana in the premises of the Chamber of Commerce and Industry of Ljubljana the New Vienna Rules.

[AUT] Vienna, 25 June 2014

Twin Conference in Vienna organized by ArbAut (Austrian Arbitration Association) and Serbia's Arbitration Association with the support of VIAC (Vienna International Arbitral Centre) and the Belgrade Arbitration Centre.[4]

II.3. [POL] – [POLAND] [5]

[POL] Warszawa [Warsaw], January 2014

The sixth edition of the *Professor Jerzy Jakubowski Competition for the best master's thesis concerning arbitration and mediation issues*, organized by the Court of Arbitration at the Polish Chamber of Commerce (Sąd Arbitrażowy przy Krajowej Izbie Gospodarczej).[6]

[POL] Warszawa [Warsaw], 12 February 2014

Conference held by the Arbitration Court attached to the Polish Chamber of Commerce jointly with the Faculty of Law and Administration of the University of Warsaw on "Directions in Current Changes in Arbitration Law" ("Kierunki zmian w najnowszych regulacjach arbitrażu").[7] Speakers: M. Haładay (Vice-Minister of Economy of Poland), Prof. dr hab. W. Kocot, Prof. dr J. Rajski, dr. Alice Fremuth-Wolf, J.-P. Fierens, J. Kolber, dr. L. Carpentieri, dr.

---

[4] Further information on http://www.arbitration-austria.at/dokumente/int9F16.PDF [Last visit on 3rd June 2014]. See also www.arbitrationassociation.org and www.arbitration-austria.at.

[5] Compiled with the kind support provided by Kubas Kos Gałkowski - Adwokaci, Law firm (www.kkg.pl). Kubas Kos Gałkowski specialize (among others) in arbitration and ADR. Edited by Magdalena Matejczyk, associate, KKG Kubas Kos Gałkowski – Adwokaci. Kamil Zawicki, attorney at law, partner, KKG Kubas Kos Gałkowski- Adwokaci.

[6] Detailed information is available at: https://www.sakig.pl/en/news/competition (in English).

[7] Detailed information available also at: www.sakig.pl. Program available on http://sakig.pl/uploads/upfiles/plakat_pl_12022014.pdf [Last visit on 24 March 2014].

R. B. Bobei, V. Khvalei, O. Perepelynska, dr. M. Hauser-Morel, dr. B Gessel Kalinowska vel Kalisz, dr. L. M. Pair, dr. O. Spiermann, J. Amth Jorgensen, M. Łaszcuk, J. Szpara, dr. M. Asłanowicz, B. Krużewski, J. Palinka, M. Surdek, dr. C. Wisniewski.

The conference entitled *Current Trends in Arbitration Laws and Rules* ' *(Kierunki zmian w najnowszych regulacjach arbitrażu)* organized by the Center of Dispute and Conflict Resolution at the Faculty of Law and Administration of the University of Warsaw (Centrum Rozwiązywania Sporów i Konfliktów przy Wydziale Prawa i Administracji Uniwersytetu Warszawskiego). *Welcome addresses*: Mariusz Haładyj, Wojciech Kocot; *Keynote speech*: Jerzy Rajski. *Panel I: Arbitration Laws of Today and Tomorrow: How Much Does It Take to Be "Arbitration Friendly"?; speakers:* Alice Fremuth-Wolf, Jean-Pierre Fierens, Joanna Kolber, Leonardo Carpentieri, Radu Bogdan Bobel, Vladimir Khvalei, Olena Perepelynska; *panel moderated by:* Rudolf Ostrihansky. *Panel II: Recent Developments in Arbitration Rules: Long-term Trends or Just Passing Fads?; speakers:* Beata Gessel-Kalinowska vel Kalisz, Lara M. Pair, Ole Spiermann, Julie Arnth Jorgensen, Alice Fremuth-Wolf, Maciej Łaszczuk, Justyna Szpara; *panel moderated by:* Marek Wierzbowski and Maria Hauser-Morel. *Panel III: A Way Forward for Regulatory Framework in Poland: Roundtable Discussion; speakers:* Marcin Asłanowicz, Bartosz Krużewski, Józef Palinka, Małgorzata Surdek, Cezary Wiśniewski; *panel moderated by:* Karol Weitz.[8]

[POL] Warszawa [Warsaw], 26 March 2014

Conference entitled *Arbitration, Construction Disputes Resolution (Arbitraż, rozstrzyganie sporów budowlanych)* organized by the Court of Arbitration at the Consulting, Engineers and Experts Association in Warsaw (Sąd Arbitrażowy przy Stowarzyszeniu Inżynierów, Doradców i Rzecznoznawców w Warszawie).[9]

[POL] Warszawa [Warsaw], 27 March 2014

Seminar entitled *Investment Arbitration and Human Rights (Arbitraż inwestycyjny a prawa człowieka)* organized by the Center of Dispute and Conflict Resolution at the Faculty of Law and Administration of the University of Warsaw (Centrum Rozwiązywania Sporów i Konfliktów przy Wydziale Prawa i Administracji Uniwersytetu Warszawskiego) and the Allerhand Institute (Instytut Allerhanda). *Speakers:* Adam Bodnar, Marek Jeżewski,

---

[8]   Detailed information is available at: https://www.sakig.pl/en/news/events/current-trends-in-arbitration-laws-and-rules (in English); https://www.sakig.pl/pl/aktualnosci/lista/kierunki-zmian-w-najnowszych-regulacjach-arbitrazu (in Polish).

[9]   Detailed information is available at: http://www.pssp.org.pl/aktualnosci/konferencja-arbitraz-rozstrzyganie-sporow-budowlanych (in Polish).

Marcin Kałduński, Katarzyna Michałowska, Rafał Morek, Wojciech Sadowski, Rudolf Ostrihansky. *Seminar moderated by:* Łukasz Gorywoda.[10]

[POL] Nowy Tomyśl, 28 March 2014
Conference held by the Arbitration Court attached to the Arbitration Court at Nowy Tomyśl Chamber of Commerce of the series "Arbitration and Mediation in Theory and Practice" entitled: "The Application of ADR in Selected Sectors of the Economy" in the Main Hall of the Old Library Warsaw University.[11]

[POL] Warszawa [Warsaw], March - May 2014
Lewiatan Arbitration Moot Court 2014 (*Konkurs Arbitrażowy Lewiatan 2014*) organized by the Lewiatan Court of Arbitration at the Polish Confederation Lewiatan (Sąd Arbitrażowy przy Polskiej Konfederacji Pracodawców Prywatnych Lewiatan).[12]

[POL] Warszawa [Warsaw], 11 April 2014
Conference entitled *Arbitration as a Legal Institution, Social Phenomenon, Service for Business* (*Arbitraż jako instytucja prawna, zjawisko społeczne, usługa dla biznesu*) organized by the European Center of Arbitration (Europejskie Centrum Arbitrażu). *Inauguration*: Tadeusz Tomaszewski, Krzysztof Rączka, Leszek Balcerowicz, Jerzy Kozdroń, Mariusz Haładyj. *Legal Panel* moderated by: Łukasz Rozdeiczer, *speakers*: Maciej Łaszczuk (*Is Arbitration an Alternative to State Jurisdiction?*), Maciej Jamka (*Can Poland Become the Center of International Arbitration?*), Marcin Asłanowicz (*Do We Need to Change the Principles for Appointing Arbitrators?*), Andrzej Szumański (*Restrictions on the Development of Commercial Arbitration Deriving from Arbitration Law*), Piotr Nowaczyk (*Arbitrator – Position, Mission, Career?*), Tomasz Wardyński (*Effective Proceedings, Effective Arbitration*). *Social Panel* moderated by: Ewa Usowicz, *speakers*: Sylwester Pieckowski (*New Model of Justice Involving Public Arbitration and Mediation Based on Dispute Wise Business Management*), Andrzej Zwara (*Arbitration as a Form of Social Discourse in the Law Application Process*), Jerzy Buzek (*Arbitration as a Sign of Civil Society*), Stanisław Sołtysiński (*Arbitration, Mediation and Negotiation as a Complement to Justice*). *Business Panel* moderated by: Marek Tejchman, *speakers:* Bartosz Krużewski (*Lawyers and Law Firms' Preparation for Providing Services Related to Arbitration Proceedings*), Paweł Pietkiewicz (*Can Every*

---

[10]   Detailed information is available at: http://mediacje.wpia.uw.edu.pl/2014/03/19/otwarta-dyskusja-panelowa-arbitraz-inwestycyjny-a-prawa-czlowieka/ (in Polish).

[11]   Detailed information available at: www.nig.org.pl/sa.

[12]   Detailed information available at: http://www.sadarbitrazowy.org.pl/pl/kal2014 (in Polish).

Commercial Dispute be Subject to Arbitration? Specific Regulations of Dispute Resolution in Specialized Economic Sectors), Piotr Bielarczyk (The *Legal Representative's Role in Arbitration Proceeding)*, Małgorzata Surdek (*When Can Arbitration Become Attractive to Polish Entrepreneurs as an Alternative Method of Commercial Disputes Resolution?)*, Grzegorz Domański (*Polish Law Firms' Experience in Arbitration Proceedings).*[13]

[POL] **Warszawa [Warsaw], 15 April 2014**
Seminar and Round Table held by the Arbitration Court attached to the Polish Chamber of Commerce on **"Application of IBA Guidelines on Party Representation in International Arbitration".** Key note speaker: Mr James Freeman (UK).[14] Speakers: dr Marcin Asłanowicz, r.pr. Monika Hartung, adw. Bartłomiej Jankowski, adw. Bartosz Krużewski, dr Marcin Olechowski, adw. Małgorzat Surdek.

The *IBA Guidelines on Party Representation in International Arbitration* Workshop organized by the Court of Arbitration at the Polish Chamber of Commerce (Sąd Arbitrażowy przy Krajowej Izbie Gospodarczej). *Part I. Guests:* Wojciech Jaworski and James Freeman. *Part II. Panel Discussion*; *speakers*: Marcin Asłanowicz, Monika Hartung, Bartłomiej Jankowski, Bartosz Krużewski, Marcin Olechowski, Małgorzat Surdek. *Workshop moderated by*: Marek Furtek and Maciej Jamka.[15]

[POL] **Warszawa [Warsaw], 25 - 26 April 2014**
The Conference entitled *European ADR – Ethics, Empathy and Exasperation* (*ADR w Europie: Etyka, Empatia, Zniecierpliwienie*) organized by The European branch of the Chartered Institute of Arbitrators. *Day I. Welcome address:* Bennar Balkaya. *Panel I: A Review of Differing Mechanisms for Upholding Arbitration Awards in Europe; panel introduced by:* Beata Gessel-Kalinowska vel Kalisz; *speakers:* Christian Dorda, Dirk de Meulemeester. *Panel II: Exasperation in Investment Arbitration; speakers:* Karen Akinci, Laurence Burger, Matteo Barra; *panel moderated by:* Bernd Ehle. *Panel III: Challenging Ethics in Europe: A Round Table Discussion Looks at Different Approaches to Ethics on Our Continent; speakers:* Bernd Ehle, Susanne Heger, Peter Callans; *panel moderated by:* Laurence Burger. *Keynote address: Do We Need Separate European Regulation*

---

[13] Detailed information is available at: http://forumarbitrazu.pl/wp-content/uploads/2014/03/ECA_PFA_Konferencja_Program1.pdf (in Polish).

[14] Detailed information available at: www.sakig.pl.

[15] Detailed information is available at: https://www.sakig.pl/en/news/events/arbitral-workshops-iba-guidelines-on-party-representation-in-international-arbitration (in English); https://www.sakig.pl/pl/aktualnosci/lista/warsztaty-arbitrazowe-iba-guidelines-on-party-representation-in-international-arbitration (in Polish).

on Arbitration?, speaker: John Gaffney; panel *moderated by:* Tomasz Wardyński. *Gala Dinner, Special guest:* Michael Stephens. *Day II. Panel I: Empathy in ADR: Mock Mediation. Panel II: The Future of the CIArb and Dispute Boards; panel introduced by:* Albert Fortun Costea; *speaker:* Christina Lockwood. *Panel III: The Development of Regional Arbitration Centers in Europe. The View from Spain, Poland and Lithuania; speakers:* Elena Gutierrez, Beata Gessel-Kalinowska vel Kalisz, Vilius Bernatonis. *Conference summary:* Bennar Balkaya.[16]

[POL] Warszawa [Warsaw], April - December 2014
The second edition of the Draft Common Frame of Reference Warsaw International Arbitration Moot, organized by the Court of Arbitration at the Polish Chamber of Commerce (Sąd Arbitrażowy przy Krajowej Izbie Gospodarczej) in cooperation with the European Legal Studies Institute (Europejski Instytut Studiów Prawniczych).[17]

[POL] Warszawa [Warsaw], 14 May 2014
Meeting of *the Arbitrators' Club (Klub Arbitrów)* organized by the Lewiatan Court of Arbitration at the Polish Confederation Lewiatan (Sąd Arbitrażowy przy Polskiej Konfederacji Pracodawców Prywatnych Lewiatan), entitled *Second Instance in Arbitration Proceedings (Druga instancja w postępowaniu arbirażowym).*[18]

[POL] Warszawa [Warsaw], 16 May 2014
National students and PhD candidates conference entitled *Claim before Arbitration Courts (Dochodzenie roszczeń przed sądami polubownymi)* organized by the Center of Mediation and Arbitration (Centrum Mediacji i Arbitrażu), Chamber of Civil Procedure at the Faculty of Law, Administration and Economy of the University of Wrocław (Zakład Postępowania Cywilnego na Wydziale Prawa, Administracji i Ekonomii Uniwersytetu Wrocławskiego) and the Commercial Arbitration Students Scientific Association (Studenckie Koło Naukowe Arbitrażu Handlowego). *Welcome and Opening remarks:* Włodzimierz Gromski, Sławomir Krześ, Agnieszka Templin, *Opening remarks:* Elwira Marszałkowska-Krześ, Łukasz Błaszczak. *Panel I: Competence of Arbitration Courts in Resolving Disputes. Arbitrability; speakers:* Beata Gessel-Kalinowska vel Kalisz, Maciej Zachariasiewicz, Grzegorz Suliński, Anna Franusz, Kinga Flaga-

---

[16] Detailed information is available at: http://www.ciarb.org/conferences/2014/02/10/ Draft%20Warsaw%20Conference%20Programme.pdf (in English); http://www.sadarbitra zowy.org.pl/pl/news;id-137 (in Polish).

[17] Detailed information is available at: https://www.sakig.pl/en/news/2nd-draft-common-frame-of-reference-warsaw-international-arbitration-moot/information-about-moot (in English).

[18] Detailed information is available at: http://www.sadarbitrazowy.org.pl/pl/news;id-143 (in Polish).

Gieruszyńska; *panel moderated by:* Łukasz Błaszczak. *Panel II: Arbitration Proceedings. Arbitrator Status in Arbitration Proceedings; speakers:* Bogusław Sołtys, A. W. Wiśniewski, Joanna Kuźmicka-Sulikowska, Tomasz Sztrumiłło, Marek Zawiślak; *panel moderated by:* Izabela Gil. *Panel III: Arbitral Award. Motion to Set Aside an Arbitration Court Judgment; speakers:* Piotr Gil, Arkadiusz Biliński, Włodzimierz Głodowski, Krystian Markiewicz, *panel moderated by:* Agnieszka Templin. *Panel IV: Students and PhD candidates discussion; speakers:* Anna Banaszewska, Joanna Broniszewska, Agnieszka Regiec, Michał Pyrz.[19]

[POL] Warszawa [Warsaw], 20 May 2014
IInd Polish Congress of Litigation, Mediation and Arbitration 2014. Organised by Instytut Allerhanda.[20] Keynote lectures by Dr. Łukasz Gorywoda, LL.M. and dr. Michelle Glassman Bock.

National conference entitled **Allerhand Arbitration & Dispute Resolution Summit 2014** (*Polski Kongres Sporów Sądowych, Mediacji I Arbitrażu 2014*) organized by the Allerhand Institute (Instytut Allerhanda). *Speakers and topics: Welcome address:* Mariusz Haładyj. *Keynote Lecture:* Michał Romanowski. *Panel I: Does the Dispute Resolution System Keep Up with the Expectations of Business?; speakers:* Małgorzata Surdek, Iwo Gabrysiak, Beata Gessel-Kalinowska vel Kalisz, Zbigniew Milczek; *panel moderated by:* Kamil Zawicki. *Keynote lecture:* Michelle Glassman Bock (*Preparing a Witness to Testify); lecture moderated by:* Łukasz Gorywoda. *Session II: Arbitrability of Company Disputes; speakers:* Andrzej Szumański, Paweł Pietkiewicz, Paweł Lewandowski; *panel moderated by:* Rafał Kos. *Panel III: Adjudication of Corporate Disputes in State Courts; speakers:* Marcin Asłanowicz, Tomasz Szczurowski; *panel moderated by:* Benedykt Fiutowski. *Panel IV: Challenging the Resolutions of Capital Companies by Third Parties; speakers:* Alicja Zielińska, Zbigniew Kruczkowski.[21]

[POL] Warszawa [Warsaw], 17 June 2014
Presentation of the New Rules of the Court of Arbitration at the Polish Chamber of Commerce (*Prezentacja projektu nowego Regulaminu Sądu Arbitrażowego przy Krajowej Izbie Gospodarczej*), organized by the Court of Arbitration at the Polish Chamber of Commerce (Sąd Arbitrażowy przy Krajowej Izbie Gospodarczej). *Part I: Presentation of the New Rules; Welcome remarks:* Marek Furtek; *General introduction:* Maciej Łaszczuk; *speakers:* Andrzej

[19] Detailed information available at: http://www.centrumars.wpia.uj.edu.pl/centrum-ars/aktualnosci/konferencje/-/journal_content/56_INSTANCE_Df4E/31582494/43997821 (in Polish).
[20] Detailed information available at: http://www.kongresy.allerhand.pl/kongresy/arbitraz 2014-ii-polski-kongres-sporow-sadowych-mediacji-i-arbitrazu-2014/ [Last visit 24 March 2014].
[21] Detailed information available at: http://www.allerhand.pl/docs/II_Kongres_Sporow_Sadowych_20_maja_2014_-_podsumowanie.pdf (in Polish).

Szumański, Justyna Szpara, Witold Jurcewicz, Rafał Morek. *Part II: The Subject of Regulation in the Rules of Arbitration Courts; speakers:* Małgorzata Modzelewska de Raad, Bartosz Krużewski, Małgorzata Surdek, Cezary Wiśniewski. *Part III: Discussion. Closing remarks:* Marek Furtek and Maciej Łaszczuk.[22]

[POL] Warszawa [Warsaw], 03 September 2014
Meeting of *the Arbitrators' Club* (*Klub Arbitrów*) organized by the Lewiatan Court of Arbitration at the Polish Confederation Lewiatan (Sąd Arbitrażowy przy Polskiej Konfederacji Pracodawców Prywatnych Lewiatan), entitled *ISAL – Intranet Created by the Lewiatan Court of Arbitration* (*ISAL – Intranet Sądu Arbitrażowego Lewiatan*). *Introduction:* Beata Gessel-Kalinowska vel Kalisz.[23]

[POL] Warszawa [Warsaw], 18 - 19 September 2014
Conference entitled *Diagnosis of Arbitration. The Functioning of Law on Arbitration and Directions of Postulated Changes* (*Diagnoza Arbitrażu. Funkcjonowanie prawa o arbitrażu i kierunki postulowanych zmian*) organized by the Lewiatan Court of Arbitration at the Polish Confederation Lewiatan (Sąd Arbitrażowy przy Polskiej Konfederacji Pracodawców Prywatnych Lewiatan). *Day I. Welcome and Opening remarks:* Beata Gessel-Kalinowska vel Kalisz, Marek Michalski, Maksymilian Pazdan; *Speakers and topics:* Mariusz Haładyj (*Presentation of the Amendments to the Code of Civil Procedure prepared by the Commission at the Minister of Economy*), Agnieszka Rękas (*The Minister of Justice's Stance*), Beata Gessel-Kalinowska vel Kalisz (*Introductory remarks*). *Panel I: General Issues: Abitrability, The Jurisdiction of the Arbitration Court; Introduction:* Rafał Sikorski; *speakers:* Andrzej W. Wiśniewski, Maciej Jamka; *panel moderated by:* Stanisław Sołtysiński. *Panel II: The Arbitration Clause; Introduction:* Grzegorz Żmij; *speakers:* Michał Kocur, Maciej Tomaszewski, Ireneusz Matusiak; *panel moderated by:* Krzysztof Stefanowicz. *Panel III: Composition of the Arbitral Tribunal, Introduction:* Karol Zawiślak; *speakers:* Wojciech Popiołek, Marcin Asłanowicz, Violetta Wysok; *panel moderated by:* Bartłomiej Jankowski. *Panel IV: Arbitration Proceedings. Arbitral Awards; Introduction:* Łukasz Błaszczak; *speakers:* Bartosz Krużewski, Zbigniew Boczek; *panel moderated by:* Tomasz Stawecki. *Panel V: Post-Arbitration Proceedings: Motion to Set Aside a Judgment of an Arbitration Court and the Recognition of an Arbitration Court Judgment; Introduction:* Maciej Zachariasiewicz; *speakers:* Kamil Zawicki, Łukasz Piebiak; *panel moderated by:* Małgorzata Surdek. *Closing remarks of Day I:* Katarzyna Michałowska. *Day II. Individual Panel Discussions: Group I: The Arbitration Clause. Arbitrability. Composition of an*

---

[22] Detailed information is available at: https://www.sakig.pl/pl/aktualnosci/lista/prezentacja-projektu-nowego-regulaminu-sadu-arbitrazowego-przy-kig (in Polish).

[23] Detailed information is available at http://www.sadarbitrazowy.org.pl/pl/news;id-148 (in Polish).

Arbitral Tribunal; Group II: Arbitration Proceedings. Post-Arbitration Proceedings; Meeting of the Arbitration Diagnosis Group.[24]

[POL] Warszawa [Warsaw], 09 October 2014
National conference – *The Inauguration of the Mazovian Center of Arbitration and Mediation (Mazowieckie Centrum Arbitrażui i Mediacji). Opening remarks:* Mariusz Haładyj, Lech Pilawski, Grzegorz Lang, Roman Rewald, Jeremi Mordasewicz. *Panel I: speakers:* Ewa Malinowska, Włodzimierz Chróścik, Paweł Zbigniew Rybiński, Maciej Bobrowicz, Ewa Gmurzyńska. *Panel II: Discussion: Mediation and Arbitration: Opportunites for Coexistence; speakers:* Maciej Bobrowicz, Katarzyna Ciszewska-Przyłuska, Iwo Gabrysiak, Beata Gessel-Kalinowska vel Kalisz, Piotr Jakubik, Piotr Nowaczyk, Sylwester Pieckowski; *panel moderated by:* Roman Rewald.[25]

[POL] Warszawa [Warsaw], 10 October 2014
International seminar – *4th Warsaw Investment Arbitration Debate* organized by the Center of Dispute and Conflict Resolution at the Faculty of Law and Administration of the University of Warsaw (Centrum Rozwiązywania Sporów i Konfliktów przy Wydziale Prawa i Administracji Uniwersytetu Warszawskiego). *Speakers and topic:* Małgorzata Surdek, Wojciech Jaworski, Bartłomiej Niewczas, Bartosz Krużewski *(Costs in Investment Treaty Arbitration: Should the Loser Pay All?). Seminar moderated by:* Rafał Morek.[26]

[POL] Poznan, 21 October 2014
Meeting entitled *Arbitration – Contemporary Alternative to Dispute Resolution in Business (Arbitraż – nowoczesna alternatywa rozwiązywania sporów w biznesie)* organized by the Lewiatan Court of Arbitration at the Polish Confederation Lewiatan (Sąd Arbitrażowy przy Polskiej Konfederacji Pracodawców Prywatnych Lewiatan).[27]

[POL] Łódz, 6 November 2014
Conference on Arbitration held by the Arbitration Court attached to the Polish Chamber of Commerce jointly with the Faculty of Law and Administration of the University of Łódz.

---

[24] Detailed information is available at http://www.sadarbitrazowy.org.pl/pl/diagnoza (in Polish).

[25] Detailed information is available at: http://www.oirpwarszawa.pl/konferencja-inaugurujaca-dzialanosc-mazowieckiego-centrum-arbitrazu-i-mediacji/ (in Polish).

[26] Detailed information is available at: http://www.fdi.wpia.uw.edu.pl/pl/conference (in English); http://mediacje.wpia.uw.edu.pl/2014/10/03/4th-warsaw-investment-arbitration-debate/ (in Polish).

[27] Detailed information is available at http://www.sadarbitrazowy.org.pl/pl/news;id-152 (in Polish).

Czech (& Central European) Yearbook of Arbitration

Conference entitled *Arbitration Proceedings (Postępowanie arbitrażowe)* organized by the Court of Arbitration at the Polish Chamber of Commerce in Warsaw (Sąd Arbitrażowy przy Krajowej Izbie Gospodarczej) and the Chair of Commercial and Business Law at the Faculty of Law and Administration of the University of Łódź (Katedra Prawa Gospodarczego na Wydziale Prawa i Administarcji Uniwersytetu Łódzkiego). *Panel I: Organizing Arbitral Proceedings; speakers:* Krystyna Szczepanowska-Kozłowska, Andrzej Szumański, Łukasz Błaszczak, Marcin Dziurda; *panel moderated by:* Józef Palinka. *Panel II: The Hearing of Witnesses, Experts and Evidence from Documents; speakers:* Bartosz Krużewski, Maciej Jamka, Rafał Morek, Maciej Łaszczuk; *panel moderated by:* **Aleksander Kappes**. *Panel III: Relations between the Arbitration Courts and State Courts; speakers:* Karol Weitz, Paweł Lewandowski, Monika Hartung, Wojciech Popiołek; *panel moderated by:* **Józef Frąckowiak**.[28]

[POL] Warszawa [Warsaw], 02 December 2014
Meeting with Joanna Jemielniak from the University in Copenhagen, organized by the Lewiatan Court of Arbitration at the Polish Confederation Lewiatan (Sąd Arbitrażowy przy Polskiej Konfederacji Pracodawców Prywatnych Lewiatan), entitled *Elaboration on Theses Included in the Legal Interpretation in International Commercial Arbitration* publication *(Omówienie tez zawartych w publikacji: Legal Interpretation in International Commercial Arbitration).*[29]

II.4. [ROM] – [ROMANIA][30]

[ROM] Bucharest, 23 January 2014
Presentation of the New Vienna Rules 2013 organized by the Vienna International Arbitral Centre.

II.5. [RUS] – [RUSSIAN FEDERATION]

[RUS] Moscow; 24 April 2014
International conference "The Future of Arbitration in Russia" [Международная конференция Российской Арбитражной Ассоциации (РАА) «Будущее арбитража в России»] organized by the Russian Arbitration Association.[31]

---

[28] Detailed information is available at: https://www.sakig.pl/en/news/conference-arbitration-proceedings (in English).

[29] Detailed information is available at: http://www.sadarbitrazowy.org.pl/pl/kalendarium (in Polish).

[30] Compiled with the kind support provided by Kubas Kos Gałkowski - Adwokaci, Law firm (www.kkg.pl). Kubas Kos Gałkowski specialize (among others) in arbitration and ADR.

[31] Further informations on http://www.arbitrations.ru/o-konferentsii.php [Last visit 7 February 2014].

[RUS] Moscow; 29 May 2014

Russian Arbitration Day 2014" Annual International Conference organized by the International Commercial Arbitration Court attached to the Chamber of Commerce and Industry of the Russian Federation.[32]

[RUS] Moscow; 19 September 2014

The 6th Annual Conference "International Commercial Dispute Resolution: CIC Countries" [Шестая ежегодная конференция «Разрешение международных коммерческих споров: страны СНГ»]. Organized by the ABA Section of International Law jointly with ICC Russia.[33]

II.6 [SVN] – [SLOVENIA]

[SVN] Ljubljana, 20 March 2014

The VIAC presented in Ljubljana in the premises of the Chamber of Commerce and Industry of Ljubljana the New Vienna Rules.

II.7 [UKR] – [UKRAINE]

[UKR] Kiev / Kyiv, 13 November 2014

"International Arbitration Readings in Memory of Professor Igor Pobirchenko". Organised by the International Commercial Arbitration Court at the Ukrainian Chamber of Commerce and Industry.[34]

| | |

---

[32] Further informations on http://www.arbitrations.ru/files/calendar/uploaded/Russian_Arbitration_Day_2014.pdf [Last visit 15 January 2014].

[33] Further informations on http://www.iccwbo.ru/actions/462/ [Last visit 19 March 2014].

[34] Further information on http://www.ucci.org.ua/arb/icac/ru/icac.html.

Past & Ongoing CYIL/CYArb® Presentations

III. Past & Ongoing CYIL/CYArb® Presentations

III.1. Past Presentations in 2014

- The *Eighth Annual Investment Treaty Arbitration Conference*, Washington D.C. [USA], 28 March 2014

- The *Tenth Annual Leading Arbitrators' Symposium on the Conduct of International Arbitration*, Vienna [Austria], 14 April 2014

- The *XIXth International Congress of Comparative Law*, Vienna [Austria], 20 – 26 July 2014, organized by the International Association of Comparative Law

- The *VIIIth International Conference "Days-of-Law-2014"*, Brno [Czech Republic], 19 - 20 November 2014, organized by the Faculty of Law, Masaryk University.

- University of International and Public Relations, Prague *Conference on Public Administration and Development of Regions* under the auspices of the Minister of Interior Czech Republic, within the program *Prague Legal* Autumn, Prague [CZE], 20 November 2014

- *Conference on* **Court Litigation and ADR** under the auspices of the Vice-President of the Supreme Court Czech Republic as well as President of the Czech Bar Association, within the Program "Prague Legal Autumn", Prague [Czech Republic], 21 November 2014

III.2   Select Ongoing Presentations in 2015

The CYIL and the CYArb® will go for presentations (among other activities) at the following 2015 events:[1]

- The *Ninth Annual Investment Treaty Arbitration Conference*, Washington D.C. [USA], 26 February 2015

- The *Eleventh Annual Leading Arbitrators´Symposium*, Vienna [Austria], 30 March 2015

| | |

[1]   Further events (international conferences and congresses) scheduled.

Important Web Sites

IV. Important Web Sites

http://www.czechyearbook.org.

Czech Yearbook of International Law® and Czech (& Central European) Yearbook of Arbitration®

The web site is currently available in sixteen languages: English, Bulgarian, Czech, Chinese, Japanese, Korean, Hungarian, German, Polish, Romanian, Russian, Portuguese, Slovenian, Spanish, Ukrainian, Vietnamese. This web site allows access to the annotations of all core articles and to information about the authors of these articles as well as to the entire remaining contents (except core articles) of both yearbooks (CYIL and CYArb®).

IV.1.   [CZE] – [CZECH REPUBLIC]

- http://www.cnb.cz.
  Česká národná banka (Czech National Bank as the Central bank of the Czech Republic).[1]

- http://www.compet.cz.
  Office for the protection of competition.[2]

- http://www.concourt.cz.
  The Constitutional Court of the Czech Republic.[3]

- http://www.csesp.cz.
  Czech Society for European and Comparative Law.[4]

- http://www.csmp-csil.org.
  The Czech Society of International Law.[5]

- http://www.czech.cz.
  Portal "Hello Czech Republic". Basic information about the Czech Republic and news interesting for foreigners. Rather a promotional portal.[6]

- http://www.czso.cz.
  Czech Statistical Office.[7]

- http://dtjvcnsp.org.
  Česko-německý spolek právníků. [Czech-German Lawyers Association]. Deutsch-Tschechische Juristenvereinigung e.V.[8]

- http:// ekf.vsb.cz.
  Faculty of Economics, VŠB Technical University of Ostrava.[9]

---

[1]   Web site available in English and Czech.

[2]   Web site available in English and Czech. Basic laws and regulations on the protection of competition in the Czech Republic are also available at the web site, both in Czech and in English (unofficial translation).

[3]   Web site available in English and Czech. Part of the (significant) case law also available in English.

[4]   Web site available in English and Czech.

[5]   Web site available in Czech. In English only a brief summary of the webpages.

[6]   Web site available in English, Czech, French, German, Russian and Spanish.

[7]   Web site available in English and Czech.

[8]   Web site available in German.

- http://ftp.pse.cz/Info.bas/Cz/Predpisy/brs_statut2.pdf.
  Statute of Burzovní rozhodčí soud při Burze cenných papírů Praha, a.s.
  [Exchange Court of Arbitration at the Prague Stock Exchange][10]

- http://www.hrad.cz.[11]
  Web site of the Office of the President of the Czech Republic.

- http://www.icc-cr.cz.
  ICC National Committee Czech Republic

- http://www.iir.cz.
  Institute of International Relations Prague.[12]

- http://www.ilaw.cas.cz.
  Ústav státu a práva Akademie věd ČR, v.v.i. [Institute of State and Law
  of the Academy of Sciences of the Czech Republic][13]

- http://www.jednotaceskychpravniku.cz.
  Jednota českých právníků [Czech Lawyers Union]

- http://www.icc-cr.cz.
  ICC National Committee Czech Republic.

- http://justice.cz.
  Czech justice portal including both courts and the Ministry of Justice,
  prosecution departments, Judicial Academy, Institute of Criminology
  and Social Prevention, as well as the Probation and Mediation Service
  and the Prison Service.[14]

---

[9] Web site available in English and Czech. Some information (regarding post-graduate studies) also available in German. Department of Law see http://en.ekf.vsb.cz/information-about/departments/structure/departments/dept-119 (in English).

[10] The Statute is available in Czech. One of the three permanent arbitration courts established in the Czech Republic by law (statute), in compliance with Section 13 of Act No. 216/1994 Coll., on Arbitration and Enforcement of Arbitral Awards, as subsequently amended.

[11] Web site available in English and Czech. This web site also allows access to the personal webpage of the President of the Czech Republic.

[12] Web site available in English and Czech. This Institute was founded by the Ministry of Foreign Affairs of the Czech Republic.

[13] Web site available in English and Czech.

[14] Web site available in Czech. The individual web sites of the institutions covered by this portal also contain pages or summary information in English.

- http://www.law.muni.cz.
  Faculty of Law, Masaryk University, Brno.[15]

- http://www.mzv.cz.
  Ministry of Foreign Affairs of the Czech Republic.[16]

- http://www.nsoud.cz.
  The Supreme Court of the Czech Republic.[17]

- http://www.nssoud.cz.
  The Supreme Administrative Court of the Czech Republic.[18]

- http://www.ochrance.cz.
  Public Defender of Rights (Ombudsman).[19]

- http://www.ok.cz/iksp/en/aboutus.html.
  Institute of Criminology and Social Prevention.[20]

- http://portal.gov.cz.
  Portal of the Public Administration.[21] This web site allows access to the web sites of most supreme public administration authorities (including ministries).

- http://www.prf.cuni.cz.
  Faculty of Law, Charles University in Prague.[22]

- http://www.psp.cz.
  Parliament of the Czech Republic. Chamber of Deputies.[23]

- http://www.rozhodcisoud.cz.
  The Arbitration Court attached to the Czech-Moravian Commodity Exchange Kladno.[24]

---

[15] Web site available in English and Czech.

[16] Web site available in Czech. Important information from this portal also available in English.

[17] Web site available in Czech. Some basic information also in English and French.

[18] Web site available in English and Czech.

[19] Web site available in English and Czech.

[20] Web site available in English and Czech.

[21] Web site available in English and Czech.

[22] Web site available in Czech. Basic information available in English.

[23] Web site available in English and Czech.

- http://www.senat.cz.
  Parliament of the Czech Republic. Senate.[25]

- http://www.society.cz/wordpress/#awp.
  Common Law Society.[26]

- http://www.soud.cz.
  Arbitration Court attached to the Economic Chamber of the Czech Republic and Agricultural Chamber of the Czech Republic.[27]

- http://www.umpod.cz.
  Office for International Legal Protection of Children.[28]

- http://www.upol.cz/fakulty/pf/.
  Faculty of Law. Palacký University, Olomouc.

- http://www.vse.cz.
  The University of Economics, Prague.[29]

- http://www.zcu.cz/fpr/.
  Faculty of Law, Western Bohemia University in Pilsen.[30]

---

[24] Web site available in English and Czech. Web site of one of the three permanent arbitration courts established in the Czech Republic by law (statute), in compliance with Section 13 of Act No. 216/1994 Coll., on Arbitration and Enforcement of Arbitral Awards, as subsequently amended. This arbitration court was established by Act No. 229/1992 Coll., on Commodity Exchanges, as subsequently amended.

[25] Web site available in English and Czech.

[26] Web site available in Czech.

[27] Web site available in English, Czech, German and Russian. Web site of one of the three permanent arbitration courts established in the Czech Republic by law (statute), in compliance with Section 13 of Act No. 216/1994 Coll., on Arbitration and Enforcement of Arbitral Awards, as subsequently amended. This arbitration court was established by Section 19 of Act No. 301/1992 Coll., on the Economic Chamber of the Czech Republic and the Agricultural Chamber of the Czech Republic, as subsequently amended.

[28] The Office is the Central authority responsible for protection of children in civil matters having cross-border implications. Web site available in English and Czech.

[29] Web site available in English and Czech.

[30] Web site available in Czech.

IV.2. [SVK] – [SLOVAK REPUBLIC]

- http://www.concourt.sk.
  Constitutional Court of the Slovak Republic.[31]
- http://www.flaw.uniba.sk.
  Faculty of Law, Comenius University in Bratislava (SVK).[32]

- http://iuridica.truni.sk.
  Faculty of Law. Trnava University in Trnava (SVK).[33]

- http://www.justice.gov.sk.
  Ministry of Justice of the Slovak Republic.[34]

- http://www.nbs.sk.
  Národná banka Slovenska (National Bank of Slovakia as the Central bank of Slovak Republic).[35]

- http://www.nrsr.sk.
  National Council of the Slovak Republic (*Slovak Parliament*).[36]

- http://www.prf.umb.sk.
  Faculty of Law. Matej Bel University, Banská Bystrica (SVK).

- http://www.prezident.sk.
  President of the Slovak Republic and Office of the President (SVK).[37]

- http://www.test.sopk.sk.
  The Court of Arbitration of the Slovak Chamber of Commerce and Industry in Bratislava.[38]

- http://www.uninova.sk/pf_bvsp/src_angl/index.php.
  Faculty of Law, Pan European University (SVK).[39]

---

[31] Web site available in English and Slovak.
[32] Web site available in English and Slovak.
[33] Web site available in English and Slovak.
[34] Web site available in English and Slovak. This web site also allows access to the following portals: Courts, Slovak Agent before the European Court for Human Rights, Slovak Agent before the Court of Justice of the European Union, The Judicial Academy.
[35] Web site available in English and Slovak.
[36] Web site available in English, French, German and Slovak.
[37] Web site available in English and Slovak.
[38] Web site available in Slovak. Some basic information available in English.

- http://www.upjs.sk/pravnicka-fakulta.
  Faculty of Law, Pavol Jozef Šafárik University in Košice (SVK).[40]

- http://www.usap.sav.sk.
  Institute of State and Law, Slovak Academy of Science.[41]

IV.3 [AUT] – [AUSTRIA]

- http://www.arbitration-austria.at.
  Österreichische Vereinigung für Schiedsgerichtsbarkeit. Austrian Arbitration Association.[42]

- http://www.internationales-schiedsgericht.at/.
  Wiener Internationalen Schiedsgerichts (VIAC). Vienna International Arbitral Centre (VIAC).[43]

IV.4 [BLR] – [BELARUS]

- http://www.cci.by/ArbitrCourt/AboutCourt_en.aspx.
  International Arbitration Court attached to the Belarusian Chamber of Commerce and Industry.[44]

IV.5 [BGR] – [BULGARIA]

- http://www.bcci.bg/arbitration/index.html.
  Arbitration Court at the Bulgarian Chamber of Commerce and Industry.

- http://www.lex.bg.
  Information server on Bulgarian law.

IV.6 [EST] – [ESTONIA]

- http://www.koda.ee.
  Arbitration Court attached to the Estonian Chamber of Commerce and Industry.[45]

---

[39] Web site available in English, German and Slovak.
[40] Web site available in English and Slovak.
[41] Web site available in Slovak.
[42] Web site available in English and German.
[43] Web site available in English, Czech, German and Russian.
[44] Web site available in English and Russian.
[45] Web site available in English, Estonian and Russian.

IV.7 [HRV] – [CROATIA]

- http://www2.hgk.hr/en/about_cce.asp?izbor=pac.
  The Permanent Arbitration Court at the Croatian Chamber of
  Commerce.[46]

IV.8 [HUN] – [HUNGARY]

- http://www.mkik.hu/index.php?id=1406.
  Court of Arbitration attached to the Hungarian Chamber of
  Commerce and Industry.[47]

- http://www.mkik.hu/index.php?id=1409&print=1.
  Act LXXI [Hungary] of 1994 On arbitration. Nonofficial English
  translation published on the portal of the Hungarian Chamber of
  Commerce. [**Law on arbitration**].

IV.9 [LVA] –[LATVIA]

- http://www.chamber.lv.
  The Arbitration Court of the Latvian Chamber of Commerce and
  Industry LCCI.[48]

IV.10 [LTU] – [LITHUANIA]

- http://www3.lrs.lt/pls/inter3/dokpaieska.showdoc_l?p_id=56461.
  Law on Commercial Arbitration of The Republic of Lithuania No I-
  1274 as of 2 April 1996.[49] Official translation by Lietuvos Respulikos
  Seimas (on the portal of the Parliament of the Republic of Lithuania).

- http://www.arbitrazas.lt.
  Vilniaus komercinio arbitražo teismas. Vilnius Court of Commercial
  Arbitration.[50]

---

[46] Web site available in Croatian. Basic information available in English. See the English
presentation of the arbitration court at the web site.

[47] Web site available in Hungarian. Basic information available in English.

[48] Web site available in English, Latvian and Russian.

[49] Published in: Parliamentary record, 1998-04-01, Nr. 4 (*Teisės aktą priėmė - Lietuvos
Respublikos Seimas*).

[50] Web site available in English, Lithuanian and Polish.

IV.11 [MKD] – [MACEDONIA]

• chttp://www.mchamber.org.mk/%28S%28crtmab45gznlucyny
5lvrven%29%29/default.aspx?lId=2&mId=50&smId=0.[51]
The Permanent Court of Arbitration attached to the Economic
Chamber of Macedonia [Стопанската комора на Македонија].

IV.12 [MDA] – [MOLDOVA]

• http://www.arbitraj.chamber.md/index.php?id=93.
Curtea de Arbitraj Comercial International pe linga Camera de
Comert si Industrie a Republicii Moldova. The International
Commercial Arbitration Court of the Chamber of Commerce and
Industry of the Republic of Moldova.[52]

IV.13 [POL] – [POLAND][53]

• http://www.sakig.pl/.
Sąd Arbitrażowy przy Krajowej Izbie Gospodarczej w Warszawie.[54]
Court of Arbitration at the Polish Chamber of Commerce in Warsaw.

• http://www.iccpolska.pl/
Polski Komitet Narodowy Międzynarodowej Izby Handlowej. Polish
ICC National Committee.

• http://oirp.bydgoszcz.pl/index.php?page=statut-2.
Sądu Polubowny przy Okręgowej Izbie Radców Prawnych w
Bydgoszczy. Court of Arbitration attached to the Regional Chamber of
Legal Advisors in Bydgoscz.[55]

• http://www.gca.org.pl/x.php/1,392/Arbitraz.html.
Sąd Arbitrażowy przy Izbie Bawełny w Gdyni. Arbitration Court
attached to the Gdynia Cotton Association.[56]

---

[51] Web site available in English and Macedonian.
[52] Web site available in English, Moldovan and Russian.
[53] Operation and accessibility of all web sites were last checked on 17 November 2010.
[54] Web site available in English, German, French, Polish and Russian.
[55] Web site available in Polish.
[56] Web site available in English and Polish.

- http://oirp.gda.pl/portal-dla-przedsiebiorcow/sad-polubowny.
  Stały Sąd Arbitrażowy przy Okręgowej Izbie Radców Prawnych w Gdańsku. Permanent Court of Arbitration attached to the Regional Chamber of Legal Advisers in Gdańsk.[57]

- http://www.igg.pl/1/node/39.
  Sąd Arbitrażowy przy Izbie Gospodarczej Gazownictwa. Court of Arbitration attached to the Chamber of the Natural Gas Industry.[58]

- http://www.ihk.pl/index.html?id=1635.
  Sąd Arbitrażowy przy Polsko-Niemieckiej Izbie Przemysłowo-Handlowej. Court of Arbitration attached to the Polish – German Chamber of Commerce and Industry.[59]

- http://www.iph.krakow.pl/?a=page&id=31.
  Sąd Polubowny przy Izbie Przemysłowo-Handlowej w Krakowie. Court of Arbitration attached to the Chamber of Industry and Trade in Krakow.[60]

- http://www.iph.torun.pl/index.php?aid=113837484143da38b99fb66.
  Sąd Polubowny przy Izbie Przemysłowo-Handlowej w Toruniu. Court of Arbitration attached to the Chamber of Industry and Trade in Torun.[61]

- http://isap.sejm.gov.pl.
  Legal information (laws and regulations) system on the portal of the Sejm [Parliament] of the Republic of Poland.[62]

- http://www.kigm.pl/index.php?option=com_content&task=view &id=60&Itemid=65&lang=p.
  Międzynarodowy Sąd Arbitrażowy przy Krajowej Izbie Gospodarki Morskiej. International Court of Arbitration attached to the Polish Chamber of Maritime Commerce in Gdynia.[63]

---

[57] Web site available in English and Polish.

[58] Web site available in Polish. Some basic information, especially about the Chamber, also available in English and German.

[59] Web site available in German and Polish.

[60] Web site available in Polish.

[61] Web site available in Polish. The portal also offers English version which, however, was not available during our last visit [17 November 2010] (we cannot rule out technical problems but we could not verify that before handing over this manuscript to CYArb for printing).

[62] Web site available in Polish. See also http://sejm.gov.pl.

- http://www.knf.gov.pl/regulacje/Sad_Polubowny/index.html.
  Sąd Polubowny przy Komisji Nadzoru Finansowego. Court of Arbitration attached to the Polish Financial Supervision Authority.[64]

- http://www.liph.com.pl/index.php?body=7.
  Polubowny Sąd Łódzkiej Izby Przemysłowo-Handlowej. Court of Arbitration attached to the Chamber of Industry and Trade in Łódz.[65]

- http://www.nig.org.pl/sa/pl1.html.
  Sąd Arbitrażowy przy Nowotomyskiej Izbie Gospodarczej w Nowym Tomyślu. Court of Arbitration attached to the Chamber of Economy in Nowym Tomyśl.[66]

- http://www.nsa.gov.pl/.
  Supreme Administrative Court.[67]

- http://oirp.olsztyn.pl/content/blogsection/23/73/.
  Stały Sąd Arbitrażowy przy Okręgowej Izbie Radców Prawnych w Olsztynie. Permanent Court of Arbitration attached to the Regional Chamber of Legal Advisors in Olsztyn.[68]

- http://www.piit.org.pl/piit2/index.jsp?layout=1&news_cat_id=62 &place=Menu01.
  Sąd Polubowny ds. Domen Internetowych przy Polskiej Izbie Informatyki i Telekomunikacji w Warszawie. Arbitration Court for Internet Domains attached to the Polish Chamber of Information Technology and Telecommunications.[69]

- http://www.polubowny.org/index.html.
  Centrum Mediacyjne oraz Stały Sąd Polubowny przy Fundacji Adwokatury Polskiej i Ośrodku Badawczym Adwokatury im. adw. W. Bayera. Mediation Center and Permanent Court of Arbitration attached to the Donation of Polish Bar and Center for Bar Research of W. Bayer.[70]

---

[63]   Web site available in Polish. Some basic information available in English.
[64]   Web site available in English and Polish.
[65]   Web site available in Polish.
[66]   Web site available in Polish.
[67]   Web site available in Polish.
[68]   Web site available in Polish.
[69]   Web site available in English and Polish.
[70]   Web site available in Polish.

- http://www.pssp.org.pl/index.htm.
  Polskie Stowarzyszenie Sądownictva Polubownego – Polish Arbitration Association.

- http://www.riph.com.pl/index.php/Company/sub32.
  Sąd Arbitrażowy przy Regionalnej Izbie Przemysłowo-Handlowej w Gliwicach. The Permanent Court of Arbitration at the Regional Chamber of Commerce & Industry in Gliwice.[71]

- http://www.sadarbitrazowy.org.pl/.
  Sąd Arbitrażowy przy Polskiej Konfederacji Pracodawców Prywatnych Lewiatan. Court of Arbitration at the Polish Confederation of Private Employers Lewiatan.[72]

- http://www.oirpwarszawa.pl/kategoria/pokaz/idk/612/ida/520/strona/.
  Stały Sąd Polubowny przy Okręgowej Izbie Radców Prawnych w Warszawie. Permanent Court of Arbitration attached to the Regional Chamber of Legal Advisers in Warszawa.[73]

- http://www.rig.katowice.pl/default.aspx?docId=30.
  Sąd Arbitrażowy przy Regionalnej Izbie Gospodarczej w Katowicach. Court of Arbitration attached to the Chamber of Economy in Katowice.[74]

- http://www.sa.dig.wroc.pl/sa/index.php?option=com_content&task=view&id=69&Itemid=28.
  Sąd Arbitrażowy przy Dolnośląskiej Izbie Gospodarczej we Wrocławiu. Court of Arbitration attached to the Lower Silesia Chamber of Economy in Wrocław.[75]

- http://www.sejm.gov.pl.
  Sejm Rzeczypospolitej Polskiej. Sejm [Parliament] of the Republic of Poland.[76]/[77]

---

[71] Web site available in Polish. Some basic information also available in English and German.

[72] Web site available in English and Polish.

[73] Web site available in Polish.

[74] Web site available in Polish.

[75] Web site available in Polish. Applicable Rules of proceedings available in English and German.

[76] Web site available in English and Polish.

[77] See also http://isap.sejm.gov.pl – legal information system available through the portal of Sejm.

- http://www.senat.gov.pl.
  Senat Rzeczypospolitej polskiej. The Senate of the Republic of Poland.[78]

- http://www.sn.pl/.
  Supreme Court of the Republic of Poland.[79]

- http://www.ssp.piph.pl/.
  Stały Sąd Polubowny przy Pomorskiej Izbie Przemysłowo-Handlowej w Gdańsku. Permanent Court of Arbitration attached to the See [*Maritime*] Chamber of Industry and Trade in Gdańsk.[80]

- http://www.trybunal.gov.pl.
  Constitutional Court.[81]

- http://www.wib.com.pl/index.php?idkat=11.
  Sąd Arbitrażowy przy Wielkopolskiej Izbie Budownictwa. Court of Arbitration attached to the Wielkopolska Chamber of Construction.[82]

- http://www.wiph.pl/content/view/69/53/.
  Sąd Arbitrażowy Izb i Organizacji Gospodarczych Wielkopolski. Arbitration Court attached to the All Polish Chamber of Industry and Trade.[83]

- http://www.zbp.pl/site.php?s=MGM0YzkzYWY1MTc3Nw.
  Sąd Polubowny przy Związku Banków Polskich. Court of Arbitration attached to the Polish Bank Association (ZBP).[84]

- http://www.ziph.pl/strona,19,polubowny-sad-gospodarczy.
  Polubowny Sąd Gospodarczy przy Zachodniej Izbie Przemysłowo-Handlowej w Gorzowie Wielkopolskim. Court of Arbitration attached to the Western Chamber of Industry and Commerce in Gorzow Wielkopolski.[85]

---

[78] Web site available in English, French, German, Polish and Russian.

[79] Web site available in English and Polish.

[80] Web site available in Polish.

[81] Web site available in English and Polish.

[82] Web site available in Polish. Basic information, especially about the Chamber, available in English.

[83] Web site available in Polish.

[84] Web site available in English and Polish.

[85] Web site available in Polish. Basic information and information about the Chamber also available in English, French, German and Russian.

IV.14 [ROM] – [ROMANIA]

- http://arbitration.ccir.ro.
  The Court of International Commercial Arbitration attached to the
  Chamber of Commerce and Industry of Romania.[86]

IV.15 [RUS] – [RUSSIAN FEDERATION]

- http://www.arbitrations.ru.
  Russian Arbitration Association.[87]

- http://www.iccwbo.ru.
  ICC National Committee Russian Federation

- http://www.spbcci.ru/engarbitaltribunal.
  The Arbitration tribunal at Saint-Petersburg Chamber of Commerce
  and Industry.[88]

IV.16 [SVN] – [SLOVENIA]

- http://www.sloarbitration.org.
  The Permanent Court of Arbitration, although attached to the
  Chamber of Commerce and Industry of Slovenia [CCIS].[89]

- http://www.sloarbitration.org/english/introduction/organization.html.
  Nonofficial English translations of Slovenian law on or related to
  arbitration published on the portal of the Permanent Court of
  Arbitration, although attached to the Chamber of Commerce and
  Industry of Slovenia. (i) Code of Civil Procedure of Slovenia.[90]
  (ii) Private International Law and Procedure Act.[91] [Law on
  arbitration].

---

[86] Web site available in English and Romanian.
[87] Web site available in English and Russian.
[88] Web site available in English and Russian.
[89] Web site available in English and Slovenian.
[90] Published in the: Official Gazette of the Republic of Slovenia, No. 26/99.
[91] Published in the: Official Gazette of the Republic of Slovenia, No. 56/99.

Index

12/57; **14**/9, 10, 13, 15, 20, 27, 33, 34, 42, 43
– of the parties
2/3, 5, 13, 15, 25, 26, 29, 39, 44, 47; **3**/6, 7, 16, 18, 19, 22, 31, 33; **4**/11; **5**/3, 24, 32, 94; 7/1, 15, 17; **10**/15, 19, 34, 65; 11/28; 12/57; **14**/10, 13, 42

C

citation
1/15, 33; **2**/24, 39

challenge
2/17, 26, 37, 41, 43, 44; **3**/1, 2, 3, 7, 9, 10, 12, 13, 14, 17, 19, 21, 23, 29, 31, 33; **4**/12, 14, 15, 16, 28, 33, 36, 38, 39; **5**/2, 8, 11, 16, 73; 7/9, 11, 13, 14, 15, 20, 28; **8**/15, 23, 35, 37, 43; **10**/20, 24, 26, 32, 39; 11/16, 21, 56; **14**/11, 43; **15**/4, 5, 33, 34, 41

choice of seat of arbitration
2/5, 17, 25, 26, 27, 29, 31, 33, 45, 47

comity
4/1, 2, 9, 11, 12, 16, 17, 21, 23, 24, 25, 26, 28, 29, 30, 31, 32, 34, 35, 36, 37, 38, 40, 41

commercial arbitration court
2/2, 5, 20, 32, 39, 42, 43; **3**/1, 15, 17, 22, 25, 26, 27, 28, 34; **4**/1, 12, 18, 30; **5**/26, 31, 46; **6**/4; 7/1, 3; **8**/4, 5, 6, 7, 8, 9, 11, 14, 18, 21, 23, 24, 25, 26, 28, 29, 30, 31, 32, 33, 34, 35, 36, 37, 46, 47; **9**/8, 37; **10**/1, 10, 20, 29; 12/35; **14**/4, 6, 13, 17, 39, 46; **15**/48

confidentiality
3/32, 35; **5**/5, 76; 11/32, 33, 34, 35, 63

conflicts of interests
6/26; **13**/1, 3

constitutional
– court
2/5, 25; **6**/5, 9, 10, 13, 16, 17, 18, 19, 20, 21; 7/13; **8**/1, 2, 3, 4, 5, 6, 7, 8, 9, 10, 11, 14, 15, 20, 23, 24, 25, 26, 27, 28, 29, 30, 31, 33, 34, 35, 36, 37, 38, 39, 40, 41, 42, 44, 45, 46, 47; **10**/8, 14, 16, 17, 19, 27; 11/46; **14**/14, 23, 24, 25, 26, 27, 38, 46; **15**/54, 58, 59
– limits
7/13; **8**/28
– review
6/10; **8**/1, 2, 3, 5, 6, 7, 8, 14, 24, 35, 39, 40, 41, 45; **14**/14, 26, 27, 38, 46

counsels
5/11, 16, 18, 23, 39, 40, 41, 42, 43, 44, 47, 48, 52, 85, 91, 92

court
– interaction
1/15, 33; **3**/25; 7/28; **10**/1, 2, 29, 47; 11/56; **15**/23
– referral to mediation
2/39; **3**/10; **5**/10; **6**/23, 25, 26, 28; 7/1, 17; 11/9, 10, 11, 12, 13, 16, 17, 18, 19, 23, 24, 28, 32, 41, 42, 44, 45, 46, 48, 52, 53, 54, 56, 59; **15**/62

Court of Justice of the European Union
1/5; **9**/1, 2, 3, 4, 5, 6, 8, 9, 12, 13, 15, 17, 18, 19, 20, 21, 27, 28, 32, 33, 35, 36, 37, 38, 40, 41, 42, 43; **13**/10, 13

D

discrimination
8/44; **13**/4, 5, 6, 7, 8, 9, 10, 12, 13, 14, 15, 19, 20, 21, 22, 24, 25, 26

domestic
– jurisdiction
2/2, 13, 25, 43; **4**/12, 20, 32, 34, 35; 7/1; **9**/12; **15**/2

CALL FOR PAPERS FOR VOLUMES 2016/2017

Did you find the articles in the fifth volume of CYArb® interesting?
Would you like to react to a current article
or contribute to future volumes?

We are seeking authors for both
the Czech Yearbook on International Law® and the
Czech (& Central European) Yearbook of Arbitration®.

The general topics for the 2016/2017 volumes are the following:

CYIL 2016
International Dispute Resolution

CYArb® 2016
Rights and Duties of Parties in Arbitration

CYIL 2017
Application and Interpretation of International Treaties

CYArb® 2017
Conduct of Arbitration

More general and contact information available at:

www.czechyearbook.org

CYIL – Czech Yearbook of International Law®, 2016
International Dispute Resolution

Papers published in the previous editions of the CYIL focused primarily on issues of substantive law. The seventh edition aims to concentrate on proceedings with an international dimension and the specific features thereof in terms of private law and public law. Hence, our attention will be devoted to purely private disputes, disputes involving states and state agencies, as well as disputes which are the exclusive domain of public law, primarily public international law. Papers should deal with procedural issues, despite the fact that this edition of our yearbook will not be limited to procedural matters. We therefore aim to focus also on the specifics of the application of substantive law in proceedings with an international dimension, the issue of personal status (personal law), etc. We intend to identify and analyse the specific features of proceedings regarding international disputes as well as the current trends in conflict resolution.

CYArb® – Czech (& Central European) Yearbook of Arbitration®, 2016
Rights and Duties of Parties in Arbitration

The sixth edition of the CYArb® yearbook will concentrate on the status of parties in arbitration, together with the status of other individuals and entities involved in the proceedings (except arbitrators), such as third parties in the proceedings (intervenor, *amicus curiae*). Papers dealing with the special status of expert witnesses and witnesses among others, primarily as regards their connection to the parties and the rights and duties of the parties, will also be appreciated. However, our editorial team is also expecting essays from academicians as well as practitioners regarding parties' counsels, including their special status in arbitration as opposed to litigation (court proceedings) and as opposed to proceedings conducted by other public authorities.

CYIL – Czech Yearbook of International Law®, 2017
Application and Interpretation of International Treaties

The editorial team and the publisher have intentionally opted for a very broad topic. The application and interpretation of international treaties is dealt with in many publications and voluminous international and national case law. Nonetheless, since it continues to generate many controversies, an open discussion is indispensable. Our objective is to analyse the day-to-day application of international treaties from the procedural perspective (in various private- and public-law proceedings), in contractual practice and elsewhere. We also welcome articles focusing on international treaties in connection with the rules applied in regional integration organizations, including the European Union, in connection with the interpretation practice employed by international organizations and others.

CYArb® – Czech (& Central European) Yearbook of Arbitration®, 2017
Conduct of Arbitration
This edition of the CYArb® will be devoted to the methods and procedures of hearing disputes, including the examination of evidence. Our aim is to focus primarily but not exclusively on procedural differences between arbitration and litigation. The nature and, above all, the effects of arbitral awards bring arbitration closer to decisions rendered by courts and other public authorities. However, the contractual autonomy of the parties and arbitrators and the variability of the standards used in arbitration offer a potential which is not always fully exploited. The team of authors therefore wishes to analyse this autonomy and the flexibility of arbitration and include this potential in the broader discussion introduced in the seventh edition of the CYArb®.